Menin Gate North

Menin Gate North

In Memory and In Mourning

Paul Chapman

Pen & Sword
MILITARY

First published in Great Britain in 2016 by
Pen & Sword Military
an imprint of
Pen & Sword Books Ltd
47 Church Street
Barnsley
South Yorkshire
S70 2AS

Copyright © Paul Chapman 2016

ISBN 978 1 47385 091 0

Typeset in Ehrhardt by
Mac Style Ltd, Bridlington, East Yorkshire
Printed and bound in the UK by CPI Group (UK) Ltd,
Croydon, CR0 4YY

Pen & Sword Books Ltd incorporates the imprints of Pen & Sword Archaeology, Atlas,
Aviation, Battleground, Discovery, Family History, History, Maritime, Military, Naval,
Politics, Railways, Select, Transport, True Crime, and Fiction, Frontline Books, Leo
Cooper, Praetorian Press, Seaforth Publishing and Wharncliffe.

For a complete list of Pen & Sword titles please contact
PEN & SWORD BOOKS LIMITED
47 Church Street, Barnsley, South Yorkshire, S70 2AS, England
E-mail: enquiries@pen-and-sword.co.uk
Website: www.pen-and-sword.co.uk

Contents

Author's Note

The role of the historian is to study, draw upon and interpret the narrative for the perception of the future.
Bishop, 1969.

No matter how many times one visits the Western Front of France and Belgium, one cannot fail to be awed by the number of Commonwealth War Graves Commission cemeteries encountered at almost every turn. Some cemeteries are considerably larger than others but they all have one thing in common – the serried ranks of headstones, silently guarding the land in which they stand, paid for in the blood and self-sacrifice of those who lie beneath; their lives given that we might live in freedom. Every headstone and name on a memorial represents a personal tragedy; collectively they represent a lost generation of husbands, fathers, sons and brothers who answered their country's call to duty.

The visitor to these silent cities of the dead (all are easily accessible be it by foot or vehicle) usually falls into one of three categories – they are either personally related in some way to the casualty, historically minded, or casual. The relative, spurred by family connection, might be visiting for the first time. Indeed, it might be the very first time that the casualty has received the comfort of a visit from home. Or the visitor might be returning as part of an annual pilgrimage, paying their respects to someone unknown to them personally yet forever remembered by the family. The historian, documenting his or her findings for personal interest or publication, might be researching a particular individual or action in which a certain division, brigade, regiment or battalion took part. The casual visitor is invariably someone passing through the vicinity, mildly curious, taking a brief break from his or her journey. But, for whatever reason the visit is made – and one can spend hours walking round – those who fail to be touched emotionally are few and far between.

Uniform in size and design, the headstone informs the visitor of the casualty's name, rank, regiment, service number, date of death and (sometimes) age. Poignant epitaphs abound, but few give any insight into the man. The memorials to the thousands of missing record only regiment, rank and name. Examination of the appropriate cemetery or memorial register for further details will, with the exception of Victoria Cross recipients, rarely reveal more than next of kin. Whatever terminology one chooses, without additional information, a list is just a list.

After an association with the Western Front totalling over forty years (in particular, the Ypres Salient), I have frequently asked myself the question – just who were these men? Where did they come from and what happened to them? The answer to these questions can never be fully answered, the detail herein recorded began purely out of personal interest; researching a considerable number of casualties whose graves I had photographed. Initially drawing on the Marquis De Ruvigny's Rolls of Honour, published at the time and shortly thereafter in a series of parts, in time this expanded into page upon page of information bringing a personal aspect to the casualty – explaining and answering much more of the who, what, where and why than the norm.

Almost one hundred years after the Armistice, the death toll of the First World War remains as a roll of honour, commanding as much respect today as it did at the time. Dubbed the Great War for Civilization it was the first total war in British history to affect every aspect of national life, and stands as the supreme icon of the horror and inhumanity of armed conflict. Our picture of the war is still vivid, the poems speak just as freshly to A-Level students today as they did to older generations, and the poignancy of the many photographs and snippets of newsreel footage captured at the time touches us still.

Those smiling, young, unsuspecting faces marching into Flanders; those exhausted, shattered bodies struggling through the mud, the squalor and filth of the trenches where the ever present sense of death and the macabre were just another facet of everyday life – they could be our faces and bodies, or belong to those we know and love.

Throughout Great Britain and the Dominions there were few families who did not know of a husband, father, son, brother or uncle killed or wounded in the conflict. Behind the bald statistics of every account written at the time or years afterwards lie countless stories of individual tragedy. Drawn from a huge variety of sources, the accounts and casualty details herein recorded (many at length), recount the gruesome horror of war in its many facets. Serving as an antidote to the sensationalized adventure stories that pass for tales of war in much of the literature of today, here we have mud, lice, rats, gas and death in every manner imaginable (and unimaginable). The biggest killer – shellfire – often buried men alive, or completely vaporised them, leaving no trace of their existence. Jagged chunks of red hot metal sliced through flesh in an obscene fashion, removing heads and limbs with ease. Snipers, grenades and the scything machine guns, skilfully used by well-trained specialists, all contributed to the horror; all get their due.

How soldiers endured all this is beyond comprehension, any part of the thin veneer of civilisation they had left behind was quickly eroded after a short time at the front. Men became dehumanised by the war, they brutalised and stripped the corpses of their enemies for souvenirs; snipers took special enjoyment in knocking off members of burial parties. But, it was a different matter when it came to their own dead. Under strict orders to ignore wounded comrades in an advance, soldiers repeatedly strove heroically to protect their own. Time and time again they risked their own lives to go out onto the bullet and shell swept battlefield to search for wounded and fallen comrades; bringing in the latter that they might be given 'the dignity of a decent burial' – rites that all too often proved short-lived. Some, hastily buried, re-emerged from the earth during the next rainstorm; countless numbers were exhumed or blown to pieces by bombardments. On reflection the question arises: 'Why bother at all?' In part the answer lies with those of the battalion who, after the fighting, answered the roll-call, heard the repeated silences that followed the reading of the names, only to be informed from higher up the attack had failed due to 'lack of pluck' on their part. When one takes all this into account one realises the importance of remembering the dead; it was often as much an act of tenderness by their comrades as it was an act of defiance.

Within the confines of the Ypres Salient are to be found one hundred and sixty nine Commonwealth War Grave Commission cemeteries and three memorials to the missing, honouring the memory of British and Commonwealth servicemen who gave their lives in the defence of this relatively small yet strategically important region of Belgium. Of the 210,000 casualties buried or commemorated in the Ypres Salient, extended details relating to over 20,000 were drawn upon to compose these books. A small percentage of the total - but details relating to who these men actually were, where they came from and how they died are all as important as the reason why. These men and the actions in which they gave their lives are a part of our history, our heritage; hopefully, by bringing something of the personal about them to the visitor, these books will ensure their memory never fades.

In Memory and In Mourning
Paul Chapman
July 2016

Acknowledgements

First and foremost to my long suffering wife Sandra who, without complaint over the almost thirteen years this work has taken, has not only put up with my spending days on end with my head stuck in one book or another, making copious quantities of notes (and leaving papers all over the house), typing or searching the internet at all hours, but has also endured alone my long periods away from home spent trekking the salient.

Secondly to the staff of the Commonwealth War Graves Commission, Maidenhead and Ypres, the Imperial War Museum, London, and the National Archives, Kew; for their many kindnesses and willing assistance. Also to the Australian War Memorial, Canberra, the Auckland Cenotaph, New Zealand and the Canadian National War Memorial, Ottawa, whose archival material greatly assisted in providing additional detail, clarified numerous points and answered many queries.

Special thanks to Gladys Lunn, MBE, for her continued interest and encouragement, without whose personal influence I would never have made the acquaintance of so many regimental associations: Royal Army Medical Corps; Royal Tank Regt.; Machine Gun Corps; Royal Berkshire, Wiltshire & Gloucestershire Regiments, Major A.R. McKinnell, Black Watch; Capt. A.W. Hughes – Cheshire Regt.; Corpl. Bingley and the late Major Louch – Coldstream Guards; Major T.W. Stipling – Duke of Cornwall's Light Infantry; Major P.R. Walton – King's Liverpool Regt., Manchester Regt.; Major C.M.J. Deedes – King's Own Yorkshire Light Infantry; Lieut.Col. G. Bennett – Lancashire Fusiliers; David Ball and Harry 'Aitch' Hogan – Leinster Regt. Association; Capt. Richard 'Dick' Hennessy-Walsh – The Life Guards; Major

J.C. Rogerson – Middlesex Regt., Queen's Own (Royal West Kent Regt.); The Buffs (East Kent Regt.); George, Bob and J.P. – Northamptonshire Regt.; Leslie Frater – Northumberland Fusiliers; Major S.A. Kennedy – Prince of Wales's Own (West & East Yorkshire) Regt.; Major R.J.R. Campbell – Queen's Own Cameron Highlanders, Seaforth Highlanders; Capt.

W.G. 'Bill' Sutherland – Royal Scots; Major A.W. Russell – Queen's Royal West Surrey Regt.; Major G. Correa – Royal Artillery; Lieut.Col. P.A. Roffey, Royal Army Veterinary Corps; Major R.G. Mills – Royal Warwickshire Regt; Major A. Ellingham – Royal Welch Fusiliers: And, Major John Baines and John Howells – New South Wales Lancers Museum (Australian Light Horse); Capt. Gary 'Poppa Holdfast' Silliker, Royal Canadian Air Force (Engineers); and Alison Taylor, Auckland Museum.

Also a big thank you to the many people whose contributions to this work have in various degrees, enhanced the whole. In particular the members of the internet sites 'The Great War Forum,' 'World War 1 Remembered' and 'The Aerodrome' whose knowledge (and resourcefulness) never ceased to amaze. My friend and work colleague Dick Atkins who, when my computer crashed at 1500 pages and all seemed lost, completely restored everything including my sanity. Steve 'One Shot' Clews for his photographic expertise. Steve 'For Canada' Douglas, The British Grenadier Bookshop, Ypres, for his untiring assistance with queries regarding the C.E.F.; often closing shop to check names and panel numbers on the Menin Gate. Linda 'Linny' Carrier, Sue Cox, Richard 'Daggers' Daglish, Ian 'Scoop' Davies, Derek 'Del' Doune, Pete Folwell, Frank 'The Oracle' Grande, Sandra Hanley, Bryan Harris, Tim Harrison & Anna Parker, Patricia Healey, John & Elizabeth Holbrook, Clive Hughes, Patricia Jackson (Jamaica), Carol Johnson, Ken Jones, the late Dr. John Laffin, Brian Little, Tony 'Squirrel' Nutkins, Dave Pain, Col. Graham Parker, Paul 'Nationwide' Smith, the late Ted Smith and the late Tony Spagnoly, Jennifer Spooner, Sandra Taylor, Colin & Geraldine Ward, Sylvia Watkins, my many colleagues 'in the job' who over the years have supplied copious quantities of notes and peripheral information gleaned from personal research and war memorials throughout the length and breadth of the British Isles, and – too numerous to mention – the many visitors I have had the pleasure to meet who kindly entrusted their stories to me in Flanders Fields.

In the years it took to compile and prepare this work, the like of which has never been attempted before, there were many times when it became necessary to call on local assistance – 'over there.' Particularly deserving of special mention: Dries Chaerle and Jacques Ryckebosch whose combined knowledge of the region, including many obscure and little known details and secrets, is second to none. And 'Brother' Bart Engelen and An 'Girly' Van Der Smissen who, in response to many email (and postal) enquiries, always managed to find time out to visit (sometimes in atrocious weather) various sites, accurately recording and promptly supplying the information required. I'm grateful that they willingly continue to accompany me on my travels.

And finally, a special thank you to Laura Hirst and Jonathan Wright, Pen & Sword, for their support, interest, advice and attention throughout the seemingly unending days of editing, proof-reading, checking and cross-checking, embedding, the bits and pieces here and there that necessitated more than one delay: all this (and more) would have exhausted the patience of a saint. I thank you both.

Every reasonable effort has been made to trace copyright holders, but if there are any errors or omissions, the publishers will be pleased to insert the appropriate acknowledgement in any subsequent printings or editions.

Paul Chapman
July 2016

Menin Gate Memorial, Ypres

Who will Remember, passing through this Gate,
The unheroic dead who fed the guns?
Who shall absolve the foulness of their fate:-
Those doomed, conscripted, unvictorious ones?
Crudely renewed the Salient holds its own.
Paid are its dim defenders by this pomp;
Paid with a pile of peace complacent stone,
The armies who endured that sullen swamp.

Here was the world's worst wound. And here with pride,
'Their name liveth forever', the Gateway claims.
Was ever immolation so belied
As these intolerably nameless names?
Well might the dead who struggled in the slime
Rise and deride this sepulchre of crime.

Siegfried Sassoon

Ypres (now known as Ieper) is one of the oldest towns in Flanders, indeed, eight centuries ago it was the greatest of them. Through changes in trade and industry, political disruptions, sieges and many changes of occupying powers, it decayed and lost importance.

By 1914 Ypres was, comparatively, one of the smaller towns of Belgian West Flanders: linked by canals and railways to the nearby French border and the coast. The town was situated in flat, intensively cultivated country, encircled by a low range of hills running from Kemmel in the southwest to Godewaersvelde and Cassel. To the north and east, a series of ridges later known as the Pilckem, Passchendaele and Bellewaarde/Menin Road Ridges. In 1905 the town was described as dead, a ghost town, a cemetery, deserted by trade and industry; its only purpose to guard its great and grandiose buildings for posterity. The town's defensive ramparts, built by Louis XIV's architect Vauban, were modernised by the Dutch Government prior to Belgian independence in 1830 and, after being almost totally dismantled by the Belgian Government in 1854, remain only as two wide promenades on the eastern and southern sides. There were two main gateways: the Lille Gate (Rijselsepoort) which retains its defensive flanking towers and the Menin Gate (Meensepoort) which was only ever a passage between two wall ends.

Before the Great War was 18 months old Fabian Ware, founder and head of the Forces Graves Registration Unit, later to become the Imperial (now Commonwealth) War Graves Commission (CWGC), foresaw that there would come a time when the need would arise for memorials recording the names of the missing. The Graves Registration Unit saw the daily casualty lists and witnessed first-hand the destruction, by subsequent fighting, of burial sites previously documented.

"I should like us to acquire the whole of the ruins of Ypres .. A more sacred place for the British race does not exist in the world."

Winston Churchill

At the end of the First World War, Winston Churchill proposed the ruins of Ypres be left as a permanent memorial, a kind of Pompeii, in everlasting testimony to the destruction and sacrifice of war; further proposing that if the town were rebuilt it should be sited outside of its then boundaries. It was Churchill's sole decision that the largest 'British Memorial to the Missing' in the Ypres salient be situated where the Hangoart, or Antwerp, Gate had once been. Other sites suggested included Lille Gate and the 'Small Island.'

The Menin Gate set the standard for all other Commission memorials to the missing because at each stage of the planning for the Gate problems arose that rebounded on other Commission plans. The Menin Gate was designed to accommodate up to 60,000 names but, it soon became evident that one memorial would not suffice for the Ypres salient. A second site was chosen at Tyne Cot (the largest CWGC cemetery in the world – 11,908 burials) and, to commemorate the missing of the fighting in the Franco-Belgian border sector, the decision was taken to site a third memorial at Ploegsteert near Armentieres. The reshuffling of plans was due partly to geographical location but mostly to the casualty figures – missing – that arose during the Battle of Messines and Third Ypres (Passchendaele) in 1917.

It should be borne in mind that the Indian Army figures and names recorded on the Menin Gate are not wholly representative, as their army records were inaccurately kept. Moreover, the Indian government, whilst wishing some form of commemoration for missing Indians, such as were known, requested they not be commemorated on a memorial outside of Europe. In the end some 13,500 names were saved for posterity by the construction and engraving of a memorial arch in Delhi, designed by Sir Edwin Lutyens.

The most direct route taken by the British soldier to the front line of the Ypres salient was the Menin Road. For those that knew this route it was both the road to Hell and 'Via Sacra'. Many of those who passed through here would have seen two stone lions flanking either side of the road; these were later donated to Australia in recognition of that young country's part in the defence of Ypres – they now reside in the National War Memorial, Canberra. Therefore, it is quite significant (yet indicative of the British Empire) that a recumbent lion, sculpted by Sir William Reid Dick, is situated atop the Menin Gate gazing serenely out across the salient. Situated on the 'town side' of the Gate – a sculpted, wreathed and flag draped sarcophagus signifying burial 'and to remind the citizens of Ypres of the sacrifices made for them by the British Empire'. Beneath each sculpture a text reads:

TO THE ARMIES OF THE BRITISH EMPIRE
WHO STOOD HERE FROM 1914 TO 1918
AND TO THOSE OF THEIR DEAD
WHO HAVE NO KNOWN GRAVE

The Menin Gate was designed by Sir Reginald Blomfield together with Sir Herbert Baker, Charles Holden and Sir Edwin Lutyens: the four most highly respected British architects of the day. Lutyens, designer of the National War Memorial, the Cenotaph, Whitehall, was at the time heavily involved in the design and construction of the many military cemeteries and the Thiepval Memorial to the Missing of the Somme Battles. Sir Reginald Blomfield, born in London in 1856 to a family of clergy, studied architecture and art at Exeter College, Oxford, during the course of which he made a three month study trip through France and Spain where the Neo Gothic styles he encountered made little impression on him, whereas the linear qualities of Renaissance and classical architecture inspired him to such a degree that he often adopted them in his own works. Publishing a number of architectural books he found employment in London where he designed a number of different buildings; his style noticeable by his propensity for flat roofs, cupolas and red bricks. He designed both the entrance building and Cross of Sacrifice for Lijssenthoek Military Cemetery, Poperinghe. He died in London in 1942.

The construction of the Menin Gate was proposed as early as 1919 for an estimated £150,000.00 and although the British High Command was more than well acquainted with the famous Yperian clay – they had dug out over 5 miles of tunnels in the area for the Messines Offensive alone – local architect Jules Coomans was requested to provide a sample of earth from the proposed construction site. Blomfield described the running sand found when excavations began in 1923, "The worst possible ground for foundations …" At a depth of 3.5 metres, the skeletons of 28 Yprian civilians were discovered. They had taken shelter in a small café, 'De Oude Wacht', when it was hit and destroyed by a shell on 22 April 1915, killing all the occupants. Construction of the memorial was initially projected for 90 weeks to completion but, due mostly to the foundation problems encountered; the contractors D.G. Somerville & Co. almost went bankrupt when the Belgian franc was devalued in 1926, causing a number of the workers to cross the border into France where wages were considerably higher. At this point only the foundations had been laid consisting of 500 concrete pillars set 12 metres deep capped by a 500 ton steel reinforced concrete raft. But, after reconstituting the workforce, construction of the monument continued and was completed using 6,000 tons of bricks, Euville stone, and 11,000 tons of white Portland cement. Each column bearing the Gate itself weighs 4 tons and the fascia stones between 4 and 8 tons apiece. The Portland Stone panels, carved by 120 stonemasons of the firm of Messrs A. Burslem & Sons, of Tunbridge Wells, Kent, number in excess of 1,200, in 30 different sizes. Prior to being shipped to Belgium and placed in-situ (by Ypres stonemasons De Plancke) they were erected, for perspective, on scaffolding at 82, Baker Street, London. Weighing in excess of 20,000 tons the Menin Gate, from ground level to the top of the lion, stands 25 metres high, the arches 9.5 metres wide – 14.8 metres high. The 'Hall of Memory' 36.5 metres long, 20 metres wide, is covered in by a coffered half-elliptical arch in a single span. The overall length of the memorial – 42.5 metres. The internal staircase arches measure 3.5 metres wide – 7 metres high. Above the entrance to the southern staircase is inscribed, 'Here are recorded names of officers and men who fell in Ypres Salient but to whom the fortunes of war denied the known and honoured burial given to their comrades in death'; and 'They shall receive a crown of glory that fadeth not away' above the northern. At each corner two enormous Doric columns atop bloc form footings give access to pedestrian pathways above which, left and right, they are surmounted by entablatures inscribed 'Pro Patria' (For Kingdom) and 'Pro Rege' (For King).

He is not missing. He is here.

Sir Hubert Plumer

The Menin Gate was officially inaugurated on 24 July 1927 in a ceremony led by Sir Hubert Plumer in the presence of King Albert of the Belgians, British Ambassador Sir George Grahame, and M. Albert le Brun, President of France. Approximately 40,000 ex-British and Empire servicemen and women were in attendance including 700 mothers who had travelled courtesy of the St. Barnabas Hostels Association. The Archbishop of Canterbury composed a special prayer for the occasion. The ceremony was broadcast live by a contingent from the BBC. 'Last Post' was sounded by buglers of the Shropshire Light Infantry followed by 'Flowers of the Forest' played by pipers of 1st Bn. Scots Guards.

> *Then came a terrible minute of silence – a silence so absolute that it seemed as if the whole Salient must be standing hushed in prayer … As always, before the long minute was up it grew almost unendurable and the crash of bugles in the Reveille came as an immense relief. The Brabanconne was played, and then came a quite ineffaceable moment when once again the roll of British drums went out from the Menin Gate and the company sang God Save the King. They always make one shudder, those drums. But here, at such a place and in such surroundings, the splendour and the terror of them were beyond words.*

The Times

The memorial lists the names of officers and men, by date of death, regiment and rank of all British Dominion forces who fell in defence of Ypres with the exception of New Zealand whose missing are recorded at other locations. Of the 54,896 (this is the official figure excluding the addenda panels detailing approximately another 1,000) names listed here, there were initially believed to be 96 anomalies: 18 names of men listed or commemorated elsewhere by either burial or memorial (this figure is now known to be considerably higher) and 78 minor spelling mistakes. There was another error – a veteran who visited here after 1927 was surprised to find his name and details recorded – this has since been corrected!

During the First Battle of Ypres, late 1914, the Royal Welch Fusiliers suffered such enormous casualties they, quite literally, almost ceased to exist, and most of their bodies lost due to shell-fire; their names are preserved here for posterity. A unique soldier recorded here – Pte. J. Smith, the Black Watch; his service number – '1'.

Captain Bruce Bairnsfather, officer and cartoonist, of the 6th Battalion Royal Warwickshire Regt. served in the Ypres salient. During his time here he created the famous walrus moustached character 'Old Bill' of 'If you knows of a better 'ole go to it!' fame. The inspiration for 'Old Bill' can be found at the bottom of the Warwicks panel – L/Corpl. Thomas "Pat" H. Rafferty. Other names with a literary connection include the poets Lieut. Walter Scott-Lyon, Royal Scots and Lieut. John Collinson Hobson, MGC.; 2nd Lieut. William 'Billy' Grenfell, Rifle Brigade (brother of poet Julian Grenfell), 2nd Lieut. Arthur O. Hornung, 3rd attd. 2nd Bn. Essex Regiment, 6 July 1915 (son of E.W. Hornung, creator of *Raffles* and nephew of A. Conan-Doyle).

On 4 July 1917 the 7th Bn. King's (Liverpool) Regiment sent out a patrol commanded by Lieut. Aidan Chavasse. Lieut. Chavasse and 8 other ranks were to patrol no man's land and report on the enemy trenches. Nearing the German wire they were fired upon by an enemy patrol, which was also out, and Lieut. Chavasse was wounded. This Lieut. was left in a shell hole covering the withdrawal of his men whilst they returned to their lines to summon assistance. Later a thorough search was made for the Lieut. but no trace of him could be found. Exactly one month to the day later his elder brother, Capt. Noel Chavasse, died and was posthumously awarded a Bar to his Victoria Cross (Noel is buried in nearby Brandhoek New Military Cemetery). Aidan Chavasse's name is near to the top of the panel commemorating the King's (Liverpool) Regiment. Incidentally, Edith Chavasse, their mother, never accepted the fact that Aidan was dead; every year on the anniversary of his being reported 'missing' she heard him, in her sleep, calling to her across no man's land. On the 10th anniversary of his 'disappearance' Aidan called to her for the last time – Edith joined her beloved son.

Seven holders of the Victoria Cross are recorded here:- (Panel 24) L/Corpl. F. Fisher, Quebec Regt.; (Panel 3) Brigdr.Gen. C. Fitzclarence, Irish Guards; (Panel 24) Sergt.Major F.W. Hall, Manitoba Regt.; (Panel 35) 2nd Lieut. D.G.W. Hewitt, Hampshire Regt.; (Panel 35) Capt. J.F. Vallentin, South Staffordshire Regt.; (Panel 33) Pte. E. Warner, Bedfordshire Regt., and (Panel 46) 2nd Lieut. S.C. Woodroffe, Rifle Brigade. And three men who were executed:- Driver T. Moore, 24 Div. Train A.S.C. – shot by firing squad for the capital crime of murder; Corpl. G. Povey, Cheshire Regiment and Pte. W. Scotton, Middlesex Regiment – both shot for desertion.

During the Second World War, Ypres was occupied by the Germans and Adolf Hitler, whilst visiting the sector in which he had served over twenty years previously, passed through the Menin Gate and raised his arm in the characteristic Nazi salute in recognition of the dead recorded here; an act unrepeated anywhere else in occupied Europe. Also during the Second World War a story, albeit unsubstantiated, relates a drunken German soldier, caught while in the act of urinating on the memorial, was promptly arrested by two SS officers who were drinking in a bar opposite, and shortly thereafter found himself on the next transport to the Russian Front. Visiting Ypres on 17 May 1985, during his famous world tour, prior to conducting a mass on the Grote Markt, Pope John Paul II requested his driver stop beneath the Menin Gate. Alighting from the vehicle, His Holiness ascended the steps of the northern portico where he knelt and kissed the floor. An engraving commemorates this act.

> *"What are you guarding, Man-at-Arms?*
> *Why do you watch and wait?"*
> *"I guard the graves," said the Man-at-Arms,*
> *"I guard the graves by Flanders Farms,*
> *Where the dead will rise at my call to arms,*
> *And march to the Menin Gate."*
>
> *"When do they march then, Man-at-Arms?*
> *Cold is the hour and late."*
> *"They march tonight," said the Man-at-Arms,*
> *"With the moon on the Menin Gate.*

They march when the midnight bids them go,
With their rifles slung and their pipes aglow,
Along the roads – the roads they know,
The road to the Menin Gate."

"What are they singing Man-at-Arms
As they march to the Menin Gate?"
"The marching songs," said the Man-at-Arms,
"That let them laugh at Fate;
No more will the night be cold for them,
For the last tattoo has rolled for them;
And their souls will sing as old, for them,
As they march to the Menin Gate."

Anon.

In November 1929 the nightly 'Last Post' ceremony began. Every evening at 20.00hrs 'Last Post' is sounded in commemoration of all who fell in Ypres Salient during the Great War. From its inception it has continued virtually uninterrupted; the exception being during the Second World War when it ceased on the evening of 28 May 1940; beginning anew on 6 September 1944, the day Ypres was liberated by the Polish Army (the tradition was kept at Brookwood Cemetery, near London, during the occupation). The Buglers are mostly members of the local Brandweer (Fire Brigade): their forebears were taught the style in which they play 'Last Post' by the late Dick Collick, a Great War veteran and ex-IWGC gardener. Between *Last Post* and *Reveille* the *Exhortation* (an extract from Laurence Binyon's poem *For The Fallen*) is given and a two minute silence observed.

They shall grow not old, as we that are left grow old:
Age shall not weary them, nor the years condemn.
At the going down of the sun and in the morning
We will remember them.

Every year on Armistice Day, 11 November, there is a 'Poppy Parade' through the town. Beginning in Van de Peerbloomplaats, between St Martin's Cathedral and St. George's Church, it makes its way slowly towards the Menin Gate where all those participating in the Services of Remembrance are allocated places, forming one enormous congregation beneath the great arch of the Gate: which takes on a cathedral-like atmosphere (whether taking part in the ceremonies, or just attending out of respect, this is possibly the most evocative ceremony one will ever witness). Towards the end of the ceremonies the hymns *O Valiant Hearts* and *Abide With Me* are sung during the course of which a million poppy petals, each one symbolising a life given, are released from the roof to float down softly, carpeting the Menin Road blood red.

If I should die, think only this of me:
That there's some corner of a foreign field
That is forever England. There shall be
In that rich earth a richer dust concealed;
A dust whom England bore, shaped, made aware,
Gave, once, her flowers to love, her ways to roam,
A body of England's, breathing English air,
Washed by the rivers, blest by suns of home.

Rupert Brooke

Menin Gate (North)

(Panel 1) Capt. Hugh Clervaux Chaytor, 26th King George's Own Light Cavalry, I.A. attd. 'B' Sqdn., 11th Hussars: 2nd *s.* of the late Clervaux Darley Chaytor, of Spennithorne, co. York: *b.* 28 November 1883: *educ.* Clifton College; Royal Military College, Sandhurst: gazetted 2nd Lieut. Unatt'd. List 21 January 1903: posted Indian Army, 6 April, 1904: promoted Lieut. 21 April 1905; Capt. 21 January 1912: Regimental Adjutant; Commandant, Bodyguard – Governor of Madras, 1913–1914: served with the Expeditionary Force in France and Flanders, attd. 11th Hussars; killed in action at Messines, 31 October 1914. Tpr. B.E. Minton, 11th Hussars wrote, "Our squadron, along with the rest of the 1st Cavalry Brigade were occupying the town of Messines, in Belgium, a strategic point in our line, and had been there for many days. Our horses were some miles in the rear and we were stretched along a line of trenches just outside the town. The town was further defended by barricades etc. in the streets. The 5th Dragoon Guards relieved us every two days to enable us to get a sleep. The town and vicinity were bombarded all day by the heavy howitzers of the Germans, immense damage was done and the town fired in several places. Little damage to us until 2 p.m. on Friday last, when shells started falling all along in front of the trench occupied by our squadron, making the ground rock like an earthquake. At last one fell not five yards from me, but did not hit me, owing to a buttress of the trench being in the way. I crept round into the crater made by the shell and found the officer and men next to me buried alive. Saw a tuft of the man's hair sticking out, and cleared the dirt away from his mouth so that he could get his breath. Dug him out and half dug the officer out, but found he was dead. The man had his leg smashed frightfully. I made a tourniquet of handkerchiefs and bound his leg to a long stick. He has been saved, and my bandages were left on by the doctor, who simply added another splint. Shells fell along the trench, burying the whole of the troop alive…" Age 30. On the date of Capt. Chaytor's death 'B' Sqdn. lost two officers killed (Capt. H.C. Chaytor, Lieut. T.E. Lawson-Smith) and buried. Sqdn. Comdr. Capt. J.A. Halliday, although severely wounded, insisted on reporting back to regimental headquarters before having his wounds attended to. He died two weeks later.

Lieut. Lawson-Smith also has no known grave, he is recorded below; Capt. Halliday is buried in Chicklade (All Saints) Churchyard, Wiltshire (G2.1).

(Panel 1) Capt. Leslie Sedgwick Whitchurch, 21st (Prince Albert Victor's Own) Punjab Cavalry (Daly's Horse) (F.F.), Indian Army attd. 5th Dragoon Guards: 2nd *s.* of the late Rev. Walter Beaumont Gurney Whitchurch, Rector of Spixworth, co. Norfolk, by his wife Margaret Elizabeth, *née* Sedgwick (Old Catton, co. Norfolk): *b.* Lockeridge House, co. Wilts, 6 April 1880: *educ.* Marlborough College; R.M.C., Sandhurst (took Queen's Gold Medal – Military Proficiency, and Sword of Honour, with six other prizes), on passing out, broke the college 'record' – awarded 6 months seniority: gazetted 2nd Lieut. Indian Army (Unatt'd. List), 19 July 1899: entered Indian Staff College, 1 October 1900; promoted Lieut. 19 October 1901: apptd. Squadron Officer, 21st Cavalry, 29 May 1902; promoted Capt. 19 July 1908: served N.W. Frontier of India, Waziristan 1901–02 (Medal with clasp); took part in operations against the Darwesh Khel Waziris, 1902: home on leave when the European War broke out, applied to be attd. British Regt.: trained Reserves (9th Lancers, Tidworth) for a short time: sent to France to join 5th (Princess Charlotte of Wales) Dragoons, 10th Squadron, 16 August; killed in action at Messines, 31 October following, during the First Battle of Ypres. His commanding officer wrote, "He was a most gallant and capable officer, and I was most fortunate to have had him with me. He was killed when most gallantly holding on to an advanced post, which he had occupied with a few men on the edge of the town, when the enemy made a very determined attack on the town we were holding. He held on there though the enemy in force were only a few yards away from him. He was quite dead when I reached him. I grieve to tell you we were unable to bring him back. All I can say is that it was not possible. I reported especially upon his conduct as having been most gallant." Age 34. *unm.*

Messines 1914: '4th Dragoon Guards had been manning the barricade that blocked the way west of Messines, and had lost half a troop before the retirement to Wulverghem. A brave young officer, Lieut. Railston (18th Lancers, I.A.), made a brave effort to save the life of an old woman who had lost her way, and got between the lines. He was killed in the effort. During this day Sergt. Woodland was recommended for a V.C. for his gallant stand with the machine gunners after their officer had been killed. This gun was isolated for twenty-four hours, but he kept it in action, covering the left flank, and maintaining touch with the French where main German attacks were being launched. He received a D.C.M.'

(Panel 1) Lieut. Spencer Julian Wilfred Railston, 18th King George's Own Lancers, Indian Army attd. 4th (Royal Irish) Dragoon Guards (1914): *yr. s.* of Col. Henry Edward Railston, of Stow-on-the-Wold, Gloucestershire, late Cameronians, by his wife Magdalen, *dau.* of Rev. Charles Edward Oakley, Rector of Wickwar, co. Gloucester; subsequently St. Paul's, Covent Garden, by his wife Lady Georgina, *née* Moreton, eldest *dau.* of Henry George Francis, 2nd Earl of Ducie: *b.* Hamilton, co. Lanark, 8 January 1889: *educ.* Radley College (won Champion Cup, Gymnastics; represented the school in the Boxing Competition, Aldershot); passed directly into Royal Military College, Sandhurst (aged 17); passed out tenth (1907): gazetted 2nd Lieut. (Unattd.), Indian Army, 17 August 1907; attd. (for his first year) to his father's regt. 'The Cameronians.' Entered Lightweight Boxing Championship (shortly after joining – India) without training, and won: apptd. 18th K.G.O. Lancers (India), and played in their polo team: promoted Lieut. 15 November 1909, and after going through the cavalry course at Sangor came home on a year's leave, (1914) preparatory (on expiration) to appt. Regtl. Adjt.; played polo through the London season in Count de Madre's team ('The Tigers'): volunteered for Active Service on the outbreak of the European War; immediately apptd. attd. 4th (Royal Irish) Dragoon Guards with whom he went to the Front, 16 August and served with them through the Battle of Mons and all subsequent actions until his death in action at Messines, Belgium, 1 November 1914. The Major-General Commanding 1st Cavalry Division sent the following account of Lieut. Railston's death to his father, "I am deeply grieved at the death of your gallant boy, who on every occasion of this war has so distinguished himself. He is a great loss to his regt. He lost his life by a gallant act. His regt. was holding one-half of the village of Messines, south of Ypres, and the Germans the other half for 24 hours. In front of his troop a poor woman was lying wounded, and your boy left his cover to bring her in. He was struck by many bullets and killed. Had he lived he would certainly have been Mentioned in Despatches." Another officer wrote, "His loss will be felt by the whole Cavalry Brigade, as he has been simply splendid through all these trying times, always cheery, and full of go, and ready to take on anything. Surely, when the war is over, there will be no more gallant act than that to write of, and we are all so proud of him." A keen cricketer he played in the Cricket XI at both his Public School and Sandhurst. He was also a good big game shot and steeplechase rider. When riding a steeplechase at Jubbulpore, a few months before his death, his girths broke after the first fence. Managing to pull the saddle and the weight cloth from under him he rode the remaining two-and-a-half miles bareback, carrying them on his arm and, notwithstanding the horse falling once, finished the course. A memorial tablet was erected to his memory in Tortworth Parish Church, Gloucestershire. Age 25 *unm.*

(Panel 1) Brevet Lieut.Col. Charles Augustus Vivian, 15th (Ludhiana) Sikhs, Indian Army: 3rd & *yst. s.* of the late Col. Aylmer MacIver-Campbell, formerly Vivian, of Asknish, C.B., D.L., J.P., Bengal S.C., by his wife Margaret Agnes (Asknish House, Lochgair, Co. Argyle), elder *dau.* and *co. h.* of Col. James Duff MacIver-Campbell, of Asknish: *b.* Dalhousie, India, 28 July 1874: *educ.* Clifton College; Royal Military College, Sandhurst: gazetted 2nd Lieut.

(Unattd. List) Indian Army, 30 August 1893: attd. Gordon Highlanders for his first year: joined Indian Staff Corps, 27 January 1895; promoted Lieut., 30 November 1895; Capt. 30 August 1892; Major 30 August 1911: served (1) with Chitral Relief Force, 1895 (Medal with clasp): (2) N.W.

Frontier, (India), 1897–98, including operations on the Samana and in the Kurram Valley, August–September 1897; Flying Column (Kurram Valley), under Col. Richardson, 20 August–1 October 1897 (two clasps): (3) Tirah Expedition, 1897–98, including actions of Chagree Kotal and Dargai; capture of the Sampagha and Arghana Passes; reconnaissance of the Saran Sar and action of 9 November 1897; operations of the Waran Valley, action of 16 November 1897 (clasp): (4) with the Expeditionary Force in France and Flanders, October 1914–27 April 1915. Delayed by illness in Egypt, joined his regt. at the Front, October 1914, wounded December following: returned to duty, January 1915: Mentioned in Sir John (now Lord) French's Despatch, 14 January 1915; promoted Brevet Lieut.Col., 18 February following, for service in the field. At the Battle of Neuve Chapelle, where his regt. took a leading part, he was again wounded but refused to leave his men and remained in the trenches under very heavy fire: killed in action nr. St. Julien, during the 2nd Battle of Ypres, 27 April 1915. About 5.30 p.m., under cover of a bombardment of the Sirhind Brigade, the 1st Highland Light Infantry and the 15th Sikhs were ordered to advance, but were met with such a terrific fire that a check ensued. Col. Vivian had to rush with his company over a fire swept zone to join the remainder of his regt. Just as he arrived he was shot through the body. An officer wrote, "I think that Col. Vivian was the bravest man I ever met – he seemed absolutely fearless of bullets, and his patrol work in front of our trenches at night was really wonderful. He inspired all the Sikh officers and men of his company with the greatest confidence, and made them nearly as fearless as himself. Once there was a house 30 yards in front of our trenches and it obscured our field of fire. The regt. who occupied the trenches before we did, said that they had tried to pull down the house, but had had to give up the attempt, because the enemy fired on them. Col. Vivian called for volunteers of his company to assist him to demolish the house. The whole company to a man volunteered – he chose the requisite number and, in two days, the house was flat; although they worked in daylight not a single man was hit. I shall never forget the thrill of admiration I had for him when he volunteered to go behind the German line for two or three nights and reconnoitre the German position at La Bassée, but I was very relieved when the General would not allow him to go. Each time that he was wounded he insisted on going on with his work; any ordinary man would have been very shaken. We have lost a very dear friend, and England one of her bravest soldiers." Col. Abbott, writing to *The Pioneer*, regarding the Tirah Campaign said, "Your report, moreover, makes no mention of the very gallant and prompt manner in which, when Capt. Lewarne's party was rushed from the wood, the next one was brought up to his aid by Lieut. Vivian. The second party also got to close quarters with the enemy and to them must be accredited a large proportion of the Afridi losses on that occasion." Age 41. He *m*. Portsmouth, 30 August 1906; Mary Hastings, eldest *survg. dau.* of the late Joseph Studholme, of Ballyeighan, Kings Co., J.P., and had three children – Margaret Ruth, *b*. 25 June 1907; Aylmer Studholme, *b*. 17 August 1909; John, *b*. 30 August 1913.

In one of the numerous encounters on India's North-West Frontier – about which the British public read little or nothing in the newspapers – a young subaltern and half a company of one of India's 'less martial races,' were pinned down by murderous and accurate fire from Pathans concealed behind the rocks. Ammunition and water were dangerously low, the men were tired, thirsty, hungry and frightened, and the relief force five miles away. The young officer, thinking aloud, said, "Oh, for a hundred Sikhs with fixed bayonets." A plea from the heart. The Sikhs have always ranked high among India's fighting men, ever since the Sikh War of 1845 when they gave the British Army more than enough to worry about. The Sikhs, those fierce and proud bearded warriors with their strange and rigid religious customs – the hair on the head and face must never be cut, they must not smoke, every man wears a steel bracelet on his wrist. A company of Sikhs on parade is a splendid sight; mostly six feet tall, the rows of grave faces from which flash fierce and unfathomable brown eyes from beneath their puggris, creates an impression of disciplined arrogance calculated to warm the heart of any commander. Volatile by nature, in battle they charge with an élan which has struck terror into the British, Germans, Turks, Pathans, and Japanese, and their battle cry *Sat sri kal!* is as frightening a sound as any opposition could ever dread to hear. But, on the Western Front even these brave warriors were daunted. Raw courage of the very highest order was no match for scything machine gun fire and barbed wire. Proof of this was evidenced when on the afternoon of 26 April

1915, the Jullundur Brigade, of which 15th Ludhiana Sikhs formed part, repeated their attack on the Mauser Ridge. Mown down in swathes by machine gun and almost point-blank artillery fire, they lay in ranks where they fell. The following day, despite great gallantry on the part of the Indians, a further attack managed only to swell the already enormous list of casualties. The Ludhiana Sikhs got less than 400 yards from the enemy; some never even got that far, killed as they crested Hill Top Ridge.

(Panel 1) Sepoy 752, Maluk Singh, 15th Ludhiana Sikhs, Indian Army: *s.* of Phuman Singh, of Takhat, Sirsa, Hissar, Punjab. Killed in action, 27 April 1915.

(Panel 1) Capt. George Neville Mackie, 54th Sikhs (Frontier Force): *s.* of the late Lieut.Col. William Mackie, J.P., of Newton Cottage, Privett Road, Alverstoke, co. Hants, and his wife: late *husb.* to Constance Julia Mackie (25, Denmark Villas, Hove, co. Sussex): served in the South African Campaign, and with the Expeditionary Force in France. Killed in action, 26 April 1915; Mauser Ridge, nr. Ypres, Belgium. Age 31. Mentioned in Despatches. See Capt. P.D'A. Banks, Q.V.O. Corps of Guides attd. 57th Wildes Rifles (below).

(Panel 1) Capt. William Finlay Adair, 129th (Duke of Connaught's Own) Baluchis, Indian Army: *yst. s.* of the late Major Wallace Adair, Northumberland Fusiliers ('The Fighting Fifth'): *b.* Mauchline, co. Ayr, 21 September 1877: *educ.* French College, St. Servan, Brittany; and Jersey: gazetted 2nd Lieut. (Unattd. List) 20 January 1897: joined Indian Staff Corps 19 March, 1898: promoted Lieut. 3 July, 1899; Capt. 20 January 1906: served for some years as Adjt., 130th King George's Own Baluchis; transf'd. 129th. on appt. to Double Company Commander, between-time qualified First Class Interpreter (French): served (1) China, 1900 (Medal): (2) East Africa, 1902–04, took part in operations in Somaliland (Medal with clasp): (3) Aden, 1903–04, including operations in the interior: (4) with the Expeditionary Force in France and Flanders, and was killed in action at Hollebeke, Belgium, 30 October 1914, having been, at his own request, left mortally wounded in a trench when his men had to retire. The following account of the circumstances was relayed to his relatives, "On October 30th. 1914, at Hollebeke, Belgium, Capt. Adair had orders from his General to retire, as the Germans were close up; while giving instructions to his men he was shot high up under the arm. The native corporal wished to carry him away, but he refused, fearing to delay them, and so insisted on being left in the trench alone. The Germans came up almost immediately, and nothing further has been heard. The Corporal, who said Captain Adair was mortally wounded and could not have lived long, led the men back to a safe position already prepared, without any loss, and so the sacrifice was not in vain." Mentioned in Despatches, 14 January 1915 (*London Gazette*, 17 February 1915), by F.M. Sir John (now Lord) French, for 'gallant and distinguished service in the field.' He was a member of the Junior Army & Navy Club, and the Bath & County Club, Bath. Age 37. *unm.*

(Panel 1) Capt. Percival Campbell Hampe-Vincent, 129th (Duke of Connaught's Own) Baluchis, Indian Army: 3rd *survg. s.* of the late Robert W.E. Hampe-Vincent, C.I.E., Commissioner of Police, Bombay (ret'd.): *b.* Hyderabad, India, 27 August 1881: *educ.* Bedales, and Northwood Park School: gazetted 2nd Lieut. (Unattd. List) Indian Army, 8 May 1901: posted Indian Army, 6 November 1902; promoted Lieut. 8 August 1903; Capt. 8 May 1910: served in East Africa 1903–1904, as Special Staff Officer; took part in the operations in Somaliland (Medal with clasp): employed with King's African Rifles, 18 September 1905–27 September 1912; during which period he commanded a contingent of Sikhs in Zomba, Nyassaland for two years, and, having been promoted Capt., subsequently commanded a double company of his own regiment at Ferozepore, Punjab: accompanied the Indian Contingent to France; served with the Expeditionary Force there, and was killed in action, 26 October 1914, nr. Ypres – one of the first Indian Army officers to fall – leading his men to attack Prussian cavalry. Age 33. He *m.* Blanche Robinson, *dau.* of Foster (& Mrs) Robinson; she died at Kasauli, India, May 1914, leaving no children.

Engraving:

The 2,384 soldiers of the New Zealand Expeditionary Force who fell in Ypres Salient and have no known graves are commemorated on memorials in Tyne Cot, Passchendaele; The Buttes New British Cemetery, Polygon Wood and Messines Ridge British Cemetery.

(Panel 1A) Major Edward Egerton Barwell, 57th Wilde's Rifles (F.F.), Indian Army: *yst. s.* of the late Gen. Charles Arthur Barwell, C.B. (served throughout the Indian Mutiny): *b.* Harrow, 20 May 1872: *educ.* Harrow (Home Boarder; 1886–1889); Royal Military College, Sandhurst (Queen's India Cadet): gazetted 2nd Lieut. (Unattd. List) 3 September 1892; posted India, there attd. East Lancashire Regt., Lucknow: joined India Staff Corps, 28 December 1893, being attd. 9th Gurkhas for two months, thereafter transf'd. 4th Punjab Infantry, Punjab Frontier Force, now 57th Wilde's Rifles (Frontier Force), December 1895: promoted Lieut. 2 December 1895; Capt. 3 September 1901; Major 3 September 1910: served (1) Waziristan Expedition, 1894–95 (Medal with clasp): (2) North-West Frontier (India), 1897–98, Tochi (Medal with clasp): (3) Boxer Rebellion, China 1900 (Medal): (4) North-West Frontier (India), 1908 (Staff); took part in the operations in Zakka Khel country; operations in Mohmand country, including engagements at Matta and Kharga: apptd. D.A.Q.M.G. Bazar Valley Field Force, 12 February 1908– 2 March following; D.A.Q.M.G. Mohmand Field Force, 12–31 May 1908. Mentioned in Despatches (*London Gazette*, 14 August 1908, Medal with clasp): (5) with the Expeditionary Force in France and Flanders: killed in action, at Messines, on or about 30 October 1914, while leading his men into action. Age 42. He *m.*, 1902; Mary Cicely; eldest *dau.* of H. Tunstill, of Thornton Lodge, Aysgarth, co. York, and had three children – James William, *b.* December 1903; Eric, *b.* June, 1908; Cicely Egerton, *b.* August 1909. (*IWGC record W.E. Barwell, 29 October 1914*)

(Panel 1A) Capt. Percy D'Aguilar Banks, Queen Victoria's Own Corps of Guides, attd. 57th Wildes Rifles (F.F.), Indian Army: only *s.* of Col. Samuel Henry O'Brien Banks, of 9, Eaton Place, Brighton, by his wife Katherine Rosa, *dau.* of the Rev. John Burton D'Aguilar, late Senior Chaplain, H.M. Forces: and *gt.*-nephew of Sir John Banks, Dublin; also cousin to the Hon. Lady S. Henniker-Heaton: *b.* Bath, 9 May, 1885: *educ.* St. Peter's, Weston; Cheltenham College; R.M.C. Sandhurst: gazetted 2nd Lieut. 2nd Wiltshire Regt., 10 October 1903; joined 16 November following, left to join 1st Battn., India, April 1904: apptd. The Guides, Indian Army (1905): promoted Lieut. 10 January 1906; Capt. 10 October 1912: A.D.C. to Hon. A.D. Younghusband, C.S.I., Commissioner (Scinde), during the visit of the King, then Prince of Wales, to India, 1906; thereafter, having passed through the Musketry and Transport courses with distinction, served as Transport Officer, Chitral Relief Force and, in August 1907, performed good work transporting 15,000 mules and stores over the Lowarai Pass at an altitude of 10,600 feet: served with the Expeditionary Force in France and Flanders, from January 1915. Killed, 26 April 1915, during the Second Battle of Ypres, only 50 yards from the German lines. On this day, Wilde's Rifles were in the front line of the Ferozepore Brigade, having been hurried up from Neuve Chapelle to help the Canadians when gas was being used by the enemy for the first time. Capt. Banks' double company guides formed centre, and he, the only English officer, led them. The position to be assaulted was an extremely strong one, and the assaulting force laboured under heavy disadvantages. It had been impossible to reconnoitre the ground in a satisfactory manner, and little was known of the exact position of the German line beyond the fact that it was somewhere on the opposite side of the ridge about 1,500 yards in the distance. The ground was devoid of cover, and rose slightly for the first 500 yards, then dipped and ended in a gradual upward slope towards the German position which commanded the whole line of advance. On crossing the first ridge the regt. came under an absolute tornado of fire of every description – shrapnel, machine-gun, rifle, and, last but not least, high explosive shells filled with asphyxiating gas. From this point onwards the men began to fall rapidly, but still the gallant regt. pushed on. The murderous nature of the fire can be gauged by the fact that when the bottom of the slope was reached, at a point some 200 yards from the start, the Commanding Officer, Major Williams, and four of his colleagues had been severely wounded. Still the attack was pressed to a point about 80 yards from the German trenches. Here Major Duhan, Capt. Mackie, and Capt. Banks were all killed, as were also two of the Indian officers. Capt. Banks' orderly, a Sikh named Bhan Singh, had been severely wounded in the face early in the action. In spite of this he insisted on following Capt. Banks till he was killed, shot through the head. As soon as darkness set in, in the face of the appalling fire, as severely wounded as he was, his one thought was to bring back the body of his officer. Weak as he was from loss of blood, he staggered along carrying the body until he fell from exhaustion. They were both brought in, and Capt. Banks was buried near a farmhouse two miles north-east of Ypres. For this act of devotion and gallantry Bhan Singh received the Indian D.C.M., and later a Russian decoration. Col. Egerton wrote, "We were all very fond of him in the Guides, and he had a great many other friends besides who will feel his loss very keenly I am sure. His men were also very fond of him, and were following him bravely when he fell. His name was, of course, brought to notice by Col. Gray, and I was proud and glad to endorse his mention, and I know that it was passed on by the next higher authority, the Divisional Commander." A brother officer also wrote, "Many of the Eusafzai Pathans who were with him, and actually in the advance in which he was killed, are back here wounded or invalided, and I have spoken to many of them; the Subadar, one Afzal Khan, in particular. The very genuine love they had for him and their admiration for his great personal pluck and power as a leader is apparent in everything they say about him, and the Subadar broke down altogether when telling me of him. He says that not the smallest detail relating to the men's' comfort was overlooked, and that in fact they really had a father to command them. I've never seen any native express such genuine sorrow at the loss of one of their sahibs." A few days before he died he heard he had passed the Staff College Entrance Examination. Mentioned for 'conspicuous bravery' in F.M. Sir John (now Lord) French's Despatch, 30 November 1915 (*London Gazette*, 1 January 1916). He was a good all-round athlete and sportsman. At Cheltenham he won the School Racquets and Fives, and he was in the eleven both there and at Sandhurst. In April 1902 he played in the Public Schools Racquets at Queen's, and in the same year played cricket for Cheltenham *v.* Haileybury at Lord's, making a score of 132 runs for his side. He also played for the Somerset Colts, making 135 runs, and afterwards he played for the Somerset County Eleven. He also played cricket in the Punjab *v.* Frontier Province match, and for the Army against the Rest at Lahore, in 1904. After his appointment to the Guides, 1905, he played polo for them almost from the first, at which game he made a great reputation for himself. He twice, in 1913, led the Guides Infantry to victory, and also the same year took part in a tour in Germany, playing for the Frankfurt team, which won three events – the Challenge Cup, Champion Cup, and the Ladies Cup. An able man, and a most promising officer, Capt. Banks was possessed of an exceptional tact and charm of manner that endeared him to his comrades and friends to a remarkable degree, whilst his native N.C.O.'s and men almost worshipped him. Age 39. *unm.*

Major F.T. Duhan, 19th Punjabis attd. 57th Wildes Rifles, and Capt. G.N. Mackie, 54th Sikhs also have no known grave; they are recorded on Panel 2 & Panel 1 respectively.

(Panel 1A) Capt. Ronald Steuart Gordon, 57th Wilde's Rifles (Frontier Force), Indian Army: 5th *s.* of the late John Lewis Gordon, of Colombo, Ceylon; and West Park, Elgin: *b.* 24 November 1876: *educ.* Trinity College, Glenalmond, co. Perth; Royal Military College, Sandhurst (entered July 1885): gazetted 2nd Lieut. (Unattd. List) 20 January 1897: posted Indian Army, 22 March 1898; serving for a short time with 61st Pioneers, later transf'd. 57th Wilde's Rifles: promoted Lieut. 20 April, 1899; served as Regtl. Adjt.: promoted Capt. 20 January 1906: served (1) Boxer Rebellion, China, 1900 (Medal with clasp): (2) North-West Frontier (India) 1908, taking part in operations in the Mohmand country, and the engagements of Kargha and Matta: Mentioned in Despatches (*London Gazette*, 14 August 1908; Medal with clasp, Durbar Medal): (3) with the Expeditionary Force in France and Flanders, and was killed in action at Messines, 31 October 1914, the following account of the circumstances being received from an officer of a British regiment who was present, "He did the most gallant thing I have ever seen; he took a platoon and went forward to check the advance of the Germans to cover the retirement of the rest of his company, though he must have known it was certain death. While advancing he was shot through the head and died instantaneously." Another officer wrote, "He was the best officer I have ever known. He was extraordinarily popular with the men, and I have never seen them so cut up about anything as they were when they came in." When at Sandhurst he won the bronze medals for cricket and Rugby and Association

Football. A member of the Caledonian Club, London; he was a very fine shot and keen fisherman and, being a good all-round athlete and sportsman he helped to win many cups for polo, football, golf and cricket while in India. He *m.* 6 August 1914, St. Peter's, Melbourne, Australia; Ruby Mary (421, Collins Street, Melbourne), eldest *dau.* of Henry Byron Moore, of Melbourne, and sailed the following day for India to rejoin his regiment. Age 37.

Taking into consideration the statement in the introduction to the Menin Gate regarding the names and figures for the Indian Army recorded hereon as 'being not wholly representative as their records were inaccurately kept,' it is highly probable Jemadar Muhammad Khan is one such example. Recorded here, but thought (despite the slight difference in personal details) to be the same man who is buried in the Indian Plot, Bedford House Cemetery, the I.W.G.C. afforded him two commemorations rather than risk the possibility of omitting one.

(Panel 1A) Jemadar Muhhamad Khan, 57th Wilde's Rifles (Frontier Force), Indian Army: *s.* of Zabardast Khan, of Dhamali, Kahuta, Rawalpindi, Punjab. Missing/believed killed in action at Wytschaete 29–31 October 1914. (*IWGC record 29 October*) See Bedford House Cemetery, Indian Plot (B.5/Enc.No.4).

PANEL 3 BEGINS: BRIG.GEN. FITZCLARENCE, COMMANDS & STAFF

East of Nonne Boschen and Glencorse Wood 1914: here on 12 November 1914 fell he whose valour and leadership in these battles had gained that very distinctive honour, a name given by the troops – Brigadier-General Charles Fitzclarence, V.C., "G.O.C. Menin Road."

In the middle of a night of storm and torrential rain he led a counter-attack to clear the Prussian Guard from the trenches they occupied after their repulse of yesterday. Heading the remnant of 2nd Grenadiers and Irish Guards marching in column of fours, he came, went forward alone to reconnoitre, and was shot down by rifle fire. Thus, after the last critical day of the stupendous battle, went forth for ever a great spirit that had inspired victory.

The 1st (Guards) Brigade that had been Brigadier-General Fitzclarence's command mustered on the 12th November less than the strength of half a battalion. It was made up as follows:-

Battalions	Officers	Other Ranks
1/Coldstream Guards	None	150
1/Scots Guards	1 Captain	69
1/Black Watch	1 Lieutenant	109
1/Cameron Highlanders	1 Lieut.-Colonel	
1/Cameron Highlanders	1 Major, 1 Lieutenant	140
Totals	5	468

(Panel 3) Brigdr.Gen. Charles Fitzclarence, V.C., Comdg. 1st Guards Brigade, Irish Guards: eldest *s.* of the late Hon. George Fitzclarence, Capt. R.N., by his wife Lady Maria Henriette, *née* Scott, eldest *dau.* of John Henry, 3rd Earl of Clonmell, and *gdson.* of George, 1st Earl of Munster (eldest *s.* of King William IV): *b.* Bishops' Court, Co. Kildare, 8 May, 1865: *educ.* Eton, and Wellington College, Crowthorne: gazetted Lieut. Royal Fusiliers from the Militia, 10 November 1886; promoted Capt. 6 April 1898: transf'd. Irish Guards, 6 October 1900: apptd. Brevet Major, 29 November following; confirmed Major, 2 May 1904: promoted Lieut.Col. 14 July 1909; Col. 6 March 1913; Brigdr.Gen. 5 August 1914: served in the South African War 1899–1900: Special Service Officer, Protectorate Regt. 15 July 1899–28 August 1900; Brigade Major (Staff) 29 August 1900–4 February 1901: took part in the defence of Mafeking, twice wounded, Mentioned in Despatches (*London Gazette*, 8 February 1901): apptd. Brevet of Major (Queen's Medal, 3 clasps): decorated with the Victoria Cross for three specific acts of Bravery (*London*

Gazette, 6 July, 1900), *viz.* '…on 16 October 1899, taking with him about 50 unseasoned men of the Protectorate Regt. he went to the relief of an armoured train which was in difficulties. Capt. Fitzclarence advanced his men under a furious fire. At one time the squadron was nearly surrounded but it was saved with few casualties through coolness and clever handling on the part of its leader. About a fortnight later he led a night sortie of 60 men and drove the Boers from their trenches at the point of the bayonet. On that night Capt. Fitzclarence was the first to leap into the trenches sword in hand, and it is said that he himself killed four of the enemy and was wounded. On December 26 he again distinguished himself in the action at Game Tree, where he was shot through the legs.': apptd. Bde. Major, 5th Bde., Aldershot Army Corps 22 April 1903–31 March 1906: Bde. Comdr., 5th London Inf. Bde. and Military Member London Territorial Force Association; Lieut.Col. Comdg. Irish Guards 14 July 1913–August 1914: Officer Comdg. 29th Bde., 10th Divn., The Curragh, 23 August–22 September: went to France, 23 September; assumed command 1st Guards Brigade, 27 September 1914. At 'the most critical moment of the Battles of Ypres, 1914 (31 October), he directed the counter-attack of the 2nd Worcesters in the successful recapture of Gheluvelt.'. Killed in action leading his Brigade in the night attack at Ypres, 11–12 November 1914. Age 49. Specially Mentioned in F.M. Sir John (now Lord) French's Despatch of 20 November (*London Gazette*, 30 November) 1914, wherein Sir John said, "His loss will be severely felt." He *m*. Citadel Church, Cairo, 20 April 1898; Violet (12 Lowndes Street, London, S.W.), 4th & *yst. dau.* of the late Lord Alfred Spencer Churchill, M.P., and *grand-dau.* of John, 6th Duke of Marlborough, and had two children – Edward Charles, *b*. 3 October 1899; Joan Harriet, *b*. 23 December 1901. His twin brother, Edward, Capt. 1st Dorsetshire Regt. attd. Egyptian Army, was killed in action at Abu- Hamed, 7 August 1897; his cousin, Capt. A.A.A. Fitzclarence, was killed in action at Gallipoli, 29 June 1915.

His cousin Augustus also has no known grave; he is commemorated on the Helles Memorial.

(Panel 3) Lieut. John Charles Close-Brooks, 1st Life Guards: Reserve of Officers: eldest *s*. of the late John Brooks Close-Brooks, J.P., of Birtles Hall, Chelford, co. Chester: *b*. 18 June 1876: *educ*. Harrow, and Trinity College, Cambridge: joined the ranks of the Imperial Yeomanry (Cheshire), 1900: served in the South African War, 1900–1902; took part in operations in the Transvaal, west of Pretoria, 1900; operations in Cape Colony, north of the Orange River: granted a commission 2nd Lieut. 5th Dragoon Guards (from the Yeomanry) 23 May 1900; promoted Lieut. February 1901: present at operations in Transvaal and Orange River Colony, November 1900–August 1901, and November 1901–March 1902: served on the Zululand Frontier of Natal, September–October 1902: Queen's Medal, 3 clasps; King's Medal, 2 clasps: subsequently served with his regiment in India, thereafter returned to Bloemfontein, South Africa: resigned his commission, August 1904; afterwards voluntarily joined Reserve of Officers. Attd. 1st Life Guards on the outbreak of war; volunteered for Active Service, proceeded to the Front, 7 October 1914. On the 30th. of that month 1st Life Guards were assisting to hold the line on the right of VIIth Division down to the Wervicq-Ypres Canal. Dismounted and, acting as infantry on that occasion, the regiment bore the brunt of XVth German Army Corps. The attack took the form of a storm of shrapnel and high explosives of so terrific a nature that by 9 a.m. the Household Cavalry had been literally blown to pieces, and the brigade was forced to retire slowly down the hill. The retirement was effected in good order, but 'C' Squadron (to which Lieut. Close-Brooks belonged) did not succeed in withdrawing with the rest of the brigade. It is possible the order to retire did not reach them. Since the fighting at Ypres, in October 1914, no definite word of Lieut. Close-Books was heard until September 1916, when news was received from a trooper of the regiment, then a prisoner of war in Germany, to the effect that on 30 October 1914, at Zandvoorde, he was close to Lieut. Close-Brooks when the bursting of a shell killed him instantaneously. Age 38. A partner in the firm Marsden, Close-Brooks & Robertson, Stockbrokers, Manchester, he was keenly interested in politics – Chairman of the Conservative Party, Macclesfield (from 1901), also County Councillor and Justice of the Peace (Cheshire). He *m*. 1904; leaving a widow, Marie, *dau*. of Major-General Beresford- Lovett, C.B., C.S.I., two sons, and a daughter. (*IWGC record Closebrooks*)

(Panel 3) Lieut. Hugh de Lacy Hulton-Harrop, Reserve of Officers attd. 1st Life Guards: eldest *s*. of the late William Edward Montagu Hulton-Harrop, J.P., D.L., of Lythwood Hall, Shrewsbury (*d*.1916), by his wife Lady Margaret, 3rd *dau*. of the late Col. William Assheton- Cross, J.P., D.L., of Red Scar, co.

Lancaster: *b.* 1880: *educ.* Eton College; Cambridge University: served in the South African Campaign; Tpr., Shropshire Yeomanry; received a commission (*London Gazette*, 25 January 1901) 2nd Lieut./ Temp Lieut. 5th Lancers, 14 March 1901 (twice Mentioned in Despatches): joined 1st Life Guards, Vlamertinghe, nr. Ypres, 11 May 1915; killed by heavy trench-mortar (*minenwerfer*) fire in the trenches nr. Verlorenhoek the following day. Age 35. A Freeman of the Borough of Cambridge; he leaves a wife (*m.*1904), Delitia Mary Hulton-Harrop (29, Hyde Gardens, Eastbourne), *yst. dau.* of the late Rev. William Hulton, Vicar of Watlington, co. Oxford; and *s.* Hugh David Montagu (*b.* 15 April 1905). Remains recovered; unmarked grave (28.I.11.b.5.3) 'Unknown British Lieut. 1/Life Gds.,' exhumed, identified – Officers' Clothing, Badge of Rank, Buttons; reinterred, registered, 10 February 1928. (See 2nd Lieut. Blofeld, below). *Buried in Sanctuary Wood Cemetery (II.B.30).*

The Lord Of Peace Himself Give You Peace Always

(Panel 3) Lieut. the Hon. Gerald Ernest Francis Ward, M.V.O., 1st Life Guards: 6th & *yst. s.* of the late William Ward, 1st Earl of Dudley (*d.*1885), by his wife Countess Dudley, Georgina Elizabeth, *dau.* of Sir Thomas Moncreiffe, 7th Bt.: and brother to Capt. the Hon. R. Ward, D.S.O., formerly Royal Horse Guards (*d.*1904); Capt. the Hon. C.A. Ward, M.V.O., Royal Navy (*d.*1930); W.H. Ward, G.C.V.O., D.L., 2nd Earl of Dudley, former Lord Lieut. Ireland, 1902–03, and Governor-General, C.-in-C. Australia, 1903–11 (*d.*1932); Sir the Hon. J.H. Ward, K.C.V.O., formerly 4th Battn. Worcestershire Regt. and Brevet Major, General List, Equerry to H.M. King Edward VII (1902–10), Extra Equerry to H.M. King George V (1910–36), H.M. King Edward VIII (1936), and H.M. King George VI (1937–38) (*d.*1938); and Lieut. R.A. Ward, O.B.E., formerly Worcestershire Imperial Yeomanry, M.P. (Crewe 1895–1900); served in the Matabeleland Campaign, Boer War, and Great War (*d.*1942): *b.* Witley Court, Stourport, 9 November 1877: *educ.* Eton: served (1) in the South African War (Queen's Medal with clasps): (2) with the Expeditionary Force in France and Flanders from 8 October 1914; reported missing following the fighting at Zandvoorde Ridge and subsequent retirement from that place, 30 October 1914; now believed killed. Age 36. Lieut. Ward *m.* 7 November 1899, Lady Evelyn Selina Louisa Ward (52, Davies Street, London), *dau.* of John Henry Crichton, 4th Earl of Crom Castle, and Lady Florence Mary, *née* Cole; his wife. A talented cricket player whilst at Eton, Lieut. Ward played for the school XI (1896); he also played for Gloucester County and, after joining the Army, played for the Household Brigade XI. His mother, invested as a Dame of Justice, Order of St. John of Jerusalem (D.J.St.J.), served with the British Red Cross Society during the South African Campaign against the Boers and First World War; for her services in the latter she was decorated with the award of Royal Red Cross (R.R.C.).

(Panel 3) Corpl. of Horse, 2350, Herbert William Dawes, 1st Life Guards: *s.* of George Henry Dawes, of 48, Channel View Road, Eastbourne, co. Sussex, by his wife Sarah Jane: and elder brother to Pte. 5315, T.R. Dawes, 3rd Dragoon Guards attd. 2nd Life Guards, killed in action the following day: *b.* Pickney, co. Sussex, 1881: enlisted Eastbourne: served with the Expeditionary Force in France from 16 August 1914; recorded wounded and missing following the action between six and ten o'clock on the morning of 30 October 1914, at Zandvoorde. Age 33.

His brother Thomas also has no known grave; he is recorded on Addenda Panel 58.

(Panel 3) Corpl. 2666, William Flaxman, 'B' Sqdn., 1st Life Guards: eldest *s.* of Arthur Charles Flaxman, Thatcher & Reed Layer; of Burgh Castle, by his wife Eliza, *dau.* of Sergt. John Ellis, 52nd Oxford Light Infantry (served in the Crimean War; lost his right arm in the Indian Mutiny): *b.* Bradwell, co. Suffolk, 26 September 1888: *educ.* there: enlisted 1st Life Guards, 9 March 1908; promoted Corpl. 14 October 1913: went to France, August 1914, and was killed in action at Potijze, Ypres, 13 May 1915, by a shell. His commanding officer wrote, "…he was a real good soldier and a great loss to B Squadron." Age 26. *unm.*

(Panel 3) Tpr. 3054, Maurice Gardner Abrahams, 1st Life Guards: *s.* of the late Herbert Read Abrahams, by his wife Julia (86, Constantine Road, Hampstead, London): *b.* Hornsey, *c.*1890: enlisted London: killed by shellfire (*minenwerfer*) 13 May 1915, in the trenches at Verlorenhoek, Ypres. Age 24. *unm.*

(Panel 3) Tpr. 2770, John Black, 1st Life Guards: *s.* of John (& Mrs) Black, of 2, Reform Street, Montrose, co. Forfar: enlisted Aberdeen: killed in action, 19 September 1914. Age 22. One of two earliest dated casualties recorded on the Menin Gate. See also Gunner A.W. Hall, Royal Field Artillery (Panel 5).

(Panel 3) Tpr. 2922, Thomas Herbert Helliwell, 1st Life Guards: *s.* of Barker (& Frances) Helliwell, of 38, William Street, Newark): *b.* Newark-on-Trent, co. Nottingham: Occupation – Draughtsman: enlisted Newark, October 1912: killed in action, 20 November 1914. (*IWGC record Hellewell*)

(Panel 3) Tpr. 3080, Oscar George Pye, 1st Life Guards: 3rd *s.* of William Pye, Farmer & Landowner; of Jeskyns Court, Cobham, Gravesend, co. Kent, by his wife Mary, *dau.* of the late William Miskin: *b.* Cuxton, Rochester, co. Kent, 12 August 1892: *educ.* Thanet College, Margate: Occupation – Manager of Farms; Cuxton & Cobham: joined 1st Life Guards, 5 September 1914; proceeded to France, 1 November, took part in the fighting during the winter of 1914–15, and was killed in action in the advance trenches at Potijze, nr. Ypres, 13 May, 1915. Buried on the battlefield about 1½ miles from Ypres, on the Ypres-Menin Road. An officer wrote, "Your son was in my troop from the time he came up from the base, and I have never known any man who was more liked and respected by all his comrades, myself included. He was always an example to everybody by his cheerfulness and the way he did his work, and the troop feel his loss very much." And a comrade, "He was an exceedingly brave man, he never showed any sign of fear, and was always one of the first to volunteer for any dangerous or disagreeable job." Age 22. *unm.*

(Panel 3) Capt. Alexander Moore Vandeleur, 2nd Life Guards: only *s.* of the late Hector Stewart Vandeleur, formerly Capt., Rifle Brigade; H.M. Lieut., J.P., High Sheriff (1873), of Kilrush and Cahircon, Co. Clare (*d.*1909), by his wife Charlotte Louise, *dau.* of William Orme Foster, M.P., of Apley Park, co. Salop: and *gd-son* to the late Col. Crofton Moore Vandeleur (*d.*1881), and Lady Grace Graham-Toler (*d.*1872): kinsman to Lieut.Col. C.F.S. Vandeleur, D.S.O., Irish Guards (of Kilrush), who, after being severely wounded at Middlefontein, South Africa, was killed (31 August 1901) when the train on which he was being transported was blown up near Waterval by a force of about 250 Boers; also Capt. W.M.C. Vandeleur, 2nd Essex Regt. (of Moyville), killed in action, September 1914; and Lieut. J.B. Vandeleur (of Ballinacourty), 3rd Leicestershire Regt., killed in action, 7 November 1914, at Ploegsteert Wood: *b.* 25 December 1883. Killed in action, 30 October 1914, at Zandvoorde. Age 30. He *m.*, 3 November 1910; the Hon. Violet Ethel Meysey-Thompson (since remarried, now wife to Major Sir Algar Henry Stafford Howard (Thornbury Castle, co. Gloucester), eldest *dau.* of Henry Meysey Meysey-Thompson, 1st Baron Knaresborough, of 40, Charles Street, Berkley Square, London, and Kirby Hall, co. York, and Baroness Knaresborough, Ethel Adeline Pottinger, his wife. Capt. Vandeleur was father to Giles Alexander Meysey, *b.* 1911; and Pamela Violet, *b.* 1913.

Kinsman William is buried in Esnes Communal Cemetery (1); John has no known grave, he is recorded on Panel 33. Brother-in-law Capt. the Hon. C.H.M. Meysey-Thompson, 3rd Rifle Brigade, died of wounds, 17 June 1915, at Ypres; his body, contrary to instructions, was repatriated to England; he is interred in Little Ouseburn (Holy Trinity) Churchyard.

(Panel 3) Lieut. the Hon. Arthur Edward Bruce O'Neill, 'A' Sqdn., 2nd Life Guards: eldest *survg. s.* of Edward O'Neill, 2nd Baron O'Neill, of Shane's Castle, Co. Antrim, and Lady Louisa Katherine Emma O'Neill, *dau.* of Thomas Barnes Cochrane, 11th Earl of Dundonald, by his wife Louisa Harriet Mackinnon: *b.* 19 September 1876: *educ.* Eton: commissioned 2nd Lieut. 2nd Life Guards, May 1897, from 4th (Militia) Bn. Argyll & Sutherland Highlanders: promoted Lieut. June 1898: served in the South African War, 1899–1902; present at the Relief of Kimberley; took part in operations in Orange Free State, Paardeberg, and Cape Colony, including actions at Driefontein and Colesberg: Queen's Medal, 3 clasps: promoted Capt. 3 January 1902; Adjutant to his regiment from that date to January 1903: seconded January 1910, having been elected M.P. for Midlothian, but rejoined his regiment, August 1914, consequent to the declaration of war with Germany: served with his regiment in France and fell, 6 November 1914, while leading his men in a most gallant attempt to save a situation. He was shot on the Klein Zillebeke Ridge, nr. Ypres, and shouting to his men to line the ridge, was being carried out when he received another wound, and then begged his bearers to leave him and save themselves. He did not know what fear was. He saw his task accomplished. Capt. O'Neill, J.P. and D.L. for Co. Antrim was a member of the Carlton, Ulster and

Bachelors' Clubs; he was also very musical, a good shot, and fond of all sports. He *m*. 1902; Lady Annabel Hungerford Crew-Milnes, since re-married, now Lady Dodds, eldest *dau*. of the 1st Marquis of Crewe, and left five children – Sibyl, *b*. December 1902; Mary Louisa Hermione, *b*. August 1905; Shane Edward Robert, *b*. February 1907; Brian Arthur, *b*. March 1911; Terence Marne, *b*. 10 September 1914. Lieut. O'Neill was the first Member of Parliament to be killed in the Great War. Age 38.

His son Shane, killed in action in Italy, October 1944, is buried in Coriano Ridge War Cemetery (XVII.A.1); Brian, Dunkirk, May 1940, has no known grave; he is commemorated on the Brookwood Memorial (Panel 8). Terence (*d*.1990), a long serving member of the Stormont Parliament was Northern Ireland Prime Minister, 1963–69.

(Panel 3) 2nd Lieut. Frank D'Arcy Blofeld, 2nd Life Guards: late of Staverton, nr. Cheltenham: only *s*. of Frank Blofeld, of Dunster Lodge, Alcombe, West Somerset, by his wife Leslie Blanche, only *dau*. of Major Thomas Perkins, R.H.A., H.A.C., of Doverhay Place, Porlock, co. Somerset: *b*. Dunster Lodge, 21 April 1890: *educ*. St. Michael's (Mr Hawtrey), Westgate-on-Sea; and Eton (Mr E.L.Churchill's House, 1903–1908), where he won the Junior Pulling in his last year: served three years Eton College volunteers, but ill health prevented his going on to R.M.C. Sandhurst, and he spent several years in the Argentine where he became interested in the breeding and schooling of polo ponies: joined Gloucestershire Yeomanry on the outbreak of war: gazetted 3rd Reserve Regt. of Cavalry, 9 September and took his duties at Canterbury: posted Household Cavalry, 24 October; joined 2nd Life Guards, Windsor: went to Flanders, 7 November and served with his regt. in the trenches: granted and came home on 72 hours leave shortly before Christmas. His second experience of the trenches was early in February, after which he obtained a week's leave but, after four days, was recalled and from then until his death, nr. Ypres, on 13 May, he was at the Front. He and four other officers (Lieut. Hulton-Harrop, 1st Life Guards; 2nd Lieuts. A.C. Hobson & S.J. Townsend), were killed instantaneously by the explosion of a *minenwerfer* shell. Fond of all sport, he was a finished horseman and most promising polo player (a member of Cheltenham and West Somerset Polo Clubs); his handicap being 5 goals, Hurlingham, 1914. And, having hunted with the Devon & Somerset Staghounds, and the West Somerset Foxhounds since early boyhood, during the time he was at Staverton he rode with the Cotswold Hunt. 2nd Lieut. Blofeld was a fine example of how relatively easily the discipline required to become a good sportsman can be adopted to become a good soldier. Greatly beloved by all who knew him, he had won the liking of his brother officers and the confidence of his men. His Col. wrote, "As a horsemaster he was invaluable to me, and the fact that he had been chosen for the duty in which he met his death, proves that his Squadron leader relied on him." Age 25. *unm*.

(Panel 3) 2nd Lieut. Alwyne Chadwick Hobson, 2nd Life Guards: *educ*. Eton (Ernest Lee's House); Magdalen College, Oxford University (1911–14): gazetted 2nd Lieut. 26 August 1914: served with the Expeditionary Force in France and Flanders from 8 October 1914: took part in the fighting at Zandvoorde, Zwarteleen (Ypres sector), Battle of Neuve Chapelle (March 1915): Killed in action 2.35 p.m., 13 May 1915, in an advance vicinity Verlorenhoek – Hooge. His last words, as he ordered his men forward, "Fix bayonets and dry your butts!" Dedicated – "Our Dead Through Whom We Live" 2nd Lieut. Hobson is remembered on the Edensor (St. Peter's) Church War Memorial, Derbyshire. (See 2nd Lieut. Blofeld, above)

(Panel 3) 2nd Lieut. Sidney John Townsend, 2nd Life Guards: *s*. of Alfred Markham Townshend, of 29, Palace Gate, Kensington, London, by his wife Mary Alice: and elder brother to W.E. Townsend, wounded at the siege of Peking, died Yokohama, Japan, 23 September 1900: *b*. New York, 19 March 1884. Killed in action, 13 May 1915. Age 31. (See 2nd Lieut. Blofeld, above)

(Panel 3) Corpl. of Horse, 1921, Reginald Joseph Fox Marsh, 2nd Life Guards: late *husb*. to E Marsh: *b*. Barnstaple, co. Devon: enlisted Exeter. Killed in action, 13 May 1915. Remains recovered, unmarked grave 28.I.6.a.05.20; identified – G.S. Uniform, Boots, Titles, Discs, Chevrons; reinterred Cement House Cemetery Extension, 31 December 1939. *Buried in Cement House Cemetery (XVI.C.32)*.

(Panel 3) Tpr. 2633, John Bryce, 'D' Sqdn., 2nd Life Guards: *s*. of the late Mr (& Mrs) Bryce, of Southwick, co. Sunderland: *b*. Durham, 1888: enlisted Pirbright, co. Surrey. Killed in action,. 19 October 1914. Age 26. He leaves a wife, Bertha (88, St. John's Wood Terrace, St. John's Wood, London, N.W.8).

(Panel 3) Tpr. 2803, Thomas Harold Clements, 2nd Life Guards: *s.* of the late Robert Harry Clements, by his wife Harriett (27, St. Mary's Street, Monmouth), *dau.* of Richard Smith: *b.* Monmouth, 17 October 1892: *educ.* Grammar School there (1907–1911), winning several scholarships: enlisted 17 October 1911: served with the Expeditionary Force in France from 15 August 1914. On the night of 12 May 1915, he was in the trenches at Potijze, under very heavy shellfire for three hours. The trenches were blown in, and while returning from the support trenches he was struck by shrapnel and killed instantly. Buried at Potijze, 1 mile north-east of Ypres. Tpr. Clements was an excellent athlete, and one of the finest forwards of the school Rugby football team, his work in the open and at the line-outs being particularly good, besides being a fearless tackler. He also played several times for the Monmouth Rugby Club. While at the school he secured prizes at the sports, and in his last year won the mile in 5 mins. 28 secs., and secured second place in the open hurdles. In 1910 he rowed in the school crew and was also a member of the crew in 1911, which defeated Hereford Cathedral School, at Hereford, by three lengths, this being the first victory for the Monmouth crew for some years. The triumphant crew led from the start. On joining the Guards he immediately interested himself in the regimental athletics and was a member of their team which was defeated in the final Army Cup, 1912–1913, season. A keen church-goer he was for many years a member of the parish church choir, and also a server. Age 22. *unm.*

(Panel 3) Tpr. 2782, Frederick Charles Keene, 2nd Life Guards: 3rd *s.* of Albert Keene, of 94, Faircross Avenue, Barking, co. Essex, Army Pensioner, served 22 years (Rifle Brigade), by his wife Mary Ann, *dau.* of James Bayford, of Billericay, co. Essex: *b.* Cherat, India, 27 June 1894: *educ.* Barking National School, co. Essex: enlisted 1912: went to France with the British Expeditionary Force, 9 August 1914; killed in action at Wytschaete, Flanders, 30 October following. Age 20. *unm.*

(Panel 3) Tpr. 2508, Frank Payne, 2nd Life Guards: *b.* London: enlisted Combermere Barracks, Windsor. Killed in action, 5 June 1915. Remains recovered, unmarked grave 'Small Battle Cemetery, Sanctuary Wood,' 29 February 1928. Identified, reinterred. *Buried in Sanctuary Wood Cemetery (II.D.7).*

(Panel 3) Tpr. 2634, Samuel John Alexander Potts, 2nd Life Guards: *s.* of Samuel John Alexander Potts, of 'Frost Mead,' Hamilton Avenue, Barkingside, Ilford, co. Essex: *b.* London: enlisted Pirbright, co. Surrey. Killed in action, 13 May 1915. Age 29. He was married to Maud Aird, *née* Potts (No.1, Flat, Police Buildings, Bishopsgate, London).

(Panel 3) Tpr. 2674, Harry Arthur Tyler, 2nd Life Guards: brother to F.G. Tyler, Esq., 29, Caroline Street, Reading, co. Berks: *b.* Portsmouth, co. Hants: enlisted Combermere Barracks, Windsor. Killed in action, 4 June 1915. Age 23. Remains recovered, unmarked grave 'Small Battle Cemetery, Sanctuary Wood,' 29 February 1928. Identified, reinterred. *Buried in Sanctuary Wood Cemetery (II.D.6).*

(Panel 3) Capt. Geoffrey Vaux Salvin Bowlby, Comdg. 'A' Sqdn., Royal Horse Guards (The Blues): 6th, but 2nd *survg.,* *s.* of the late Edward Salvin Bowlby, of Gilston Park, Harlow, Essex, and Knoydart, Inverness, J.P., D.L., by his 2nd wife Elizabeth, *dau.* of Robert Vans-Agnew, of Barnbarroch and Sheuchan, co. Wigtown: *b.* London, 1 December 1884: *educ.* Eton, thereafter joining Royal Horse Guards from the Militia (King's Own Scottish Borderers) as 2nd Lieut. 9 March 1904; promoted Lieut. 1 February 1905; Capt. 6 May 1908: went to Ireland (1909) as A.D.C. to Sir Neville Lyttleton, returning to his regt., September 1910, to take over the Adjutancy, which he held until September 1913. On the outbreak of war he was sent to France in advance of the composite regt., as billeting officer to 4th Cavalry Brigade, rejoining his regt. the day before the Battle of Mons. After the fight at Wytschaete, 29 October–1 November 1914, Capt. Bowlby was the senior officer remaining and took over command of the composite regt. for a short time until each squadron went back to its own regt. Killed on the afternoon of 13 May 1915 leading his squadron in a charge across 1,000 yards of open country north of Bellewaarde Farm, during the 2nd Battle of Ypres. Age 30. His commanding officer wrote, "I cannot tell you what a loss he is to the regt.; he was as gallant as he could be and a magnificent soldier. He was so keen and energetic and proud of his squadron, of which he took the greatest care." Capt. Bowlby was a fine polo player, and enjoyed great popularity at the London grounds. In his day there were few to surpass him in skill and dash. For several seasons he was No.1 in the Blues' team, and in two years (1910 and 1912) he helped the side to win the Inter-Regimental Cup at Hurlingham. The other members of those victorious sides were:- Capt. Lord Alastair Innes-Kerr, Capt. H.E. Brassey, Capt. J.F. Harrison. Capt. Bowlby was in the team again in 1913 and 1914, but his regt. was, in both years, beaten by the 1st Life Guards. He *m.* Holy Trinity Church, Sloane Street, 18 October 1911; the Hon. Lettice *née* Annesley, 4th *dau.* of Arthur, 11th Viscount Valentia, C.B., M.V.O., and had two children – Elizabeth Mary, *b.* 3 February 1913; John Edward Richard, *b.* 8 May 1914.

Colwyn Philipps was a born soldier; he never had the slightest doubt as to his true vocation from the moment he decided to join the Army whilst he was at Eton School. Well-aware that the mastery of modern warfare, a science as well as an art, required a highly trained intelligence and a great deal of common sense; he read widely to attain the knowledge that would enable him to become a good officer, taking the greatest pains to master the minutest details of every aspect of all that would be expected of him and more. He taught himself to think and write both accurately and clearly – things he believed every young officer ought to do – understanding that an ill-thought out or inaccurately worded order would almost certainly lead to unnecessary loss of life. Above all he made it his chief priority to get to know his men individually, to earn and keep their confidence, and to consider their comfort and well-being in every possible way. He realised the attitude of cheerfulness in all circumstances as an asset and took great delight in noting some of the humorous sayings of his men, a number of which he related in letters to his mother, among them the following address he overheard given to three new recruits by an N.C.O. who had been told to enforce their *esprit de corps* by anecdotes and references: "'Ave you ever 'eard tell o' the Black Prince? No? – Well, you are ignorant blighters! 'E was a cove what rode about in armour, 'eavy cavalry 'e was, and 'e licked the French. Well, a pal o' 'is was St. George what 'as 'is birthday tomorrow: 'e's the cove as I want to tell yer about. Never 'eard tell o' 'im? Why, look at the back of 'arf a quid. There you see 'im sitting on a nanimal a-fighting of a dragon. You will note as 'is thigh is in the c'rect position – but 'is toe is too depressed – don't forget as the sole of the foot is to be kept parallel to the ground – however, 'e was fighting of a dragon, which accounts for it. Well, this 'ere St. George is the patron Saint of cavalry, and don't yer forget it. What's that? What is a patron saint? Now, none of your back answers 'ere my lad, or you and me will fall out. Carry on!"

(Panel 3) Capt. the Hon. Colwyn Erasmus Arnold Philipps, Royal Horse Guards (The Blues): eldest *s.* of Sir John Wynford Philipps, the Rt. Hon. 1st Viscount St. Davids, P.C., of 3, Richmond Terrace, Whitehall, London, by his 1st wife the late Nora Gerstenberg, Lady Davids (*d.* 30 March 1915): and *gdson.* to the late Rev. Sir James Erasmus Philipps, 12th Bt. of Picton; and brother to Capt. the Hon. R.E. Philipps, M.C., 9th Royal Fusiliers, killed in action, 7 July 1916: *b.* 11 December 1888: *educ.* Farnborough School; Eton; and Royal Military College, Sandhurst, from whence he was commissioned 2nd Lieut., Royal Horse Guards, 7 October 1908; promoted Lieut. 30 July 1909; Lieut. (Temp. Capt.), Scots Guards vice Royal Horse Guards, 15 May 1915: led the Royal Escort from Windsor for the King and Queen's return, following the Coronation, June 1911: served with the Expeditionary Force in France and Flanders from October 1914: took part in the defence of Antwerp and First Battle of Ypres, and was killed in action, 13 May 1915, at the Battle of Frezenberg, nr. Ypres. Brother Officers give a gallant picture regarding the manner of his death in a counter-attack by two cavalry brigades which, in spite of very heavy shrapnel and rifle fire, succeeded in regaining the original line of trenches. "He gave a few view-halloos as the advance was made; a little later he was seen on his knees, facing those following on, waving his cap and shouting 'Come on, boys!' He was the first man into the recovered trenches, and he killed five Germans before being shot at close quarters and killed instantaneously. Thus died the bravest of the brave, a type and exemplar of undying chivalry." He was a keen sportsman and a great lover of animals, particularly horses and dogs. A fearless horseman who could take a toss as well as any man, he had good hands and a fine judgement of pace, and won many regimental steeplechases and point-to-point races in his native Pembrokeshire. Capt. Philipps was also a poet of some note, an anthology of his poems *In Memoriam* was published privately after his death. Age 26. Dedicated – 'Greater Love Hath No Man Than This That A Man Lay Down His Life For His Friends' – Colwyn and Roland are recorded on the Parish War Memorial, Manorbier, Pembroke.

The Barrier

A wall and gulf for ever lie between,
Not all that we may do through love or wit
Can quite avail to pull away the screen,
Nor yet succeed in bridging o'er the pit.
He knows the reason, He that ordered it,
Who bade us love but never understand.
He fixed the barrier as He saw fit,
And bade us yearn and still stretch forth the hand
Across the very sea He'd said should ne'er be spanned.
Be sure this great and aching love of mine,
That ever yearns to know and to be known,
Can tear the veil that sometimes seems so fine
As though 'twere cobweb but the blow
To fall asunder and for ever go.
E'en as I rise to strike, it is too late,
The cobwebs billow, thicken, seem to grow
To a thick wall with buttress tall and great ...
I stand alone, a stranger at a city gate.

C.E.A. Philipps

His brother Roland is buried in Aveluy Communal Cemetery Extension (H.32).

(Panel 3) Lieut. Lord Spencer Douglas Compton, Royal Horse Guards (The Blues): *yst. s.* of the late William George Spencer Scott Compton (*d.* 1913), 5th Marquess of Northampton, by his marriage to the late Hon. Mary Florence Baring (*d.* 1902), *dau.* of William Bingham Baring, 2nd Baron Ashburton, and his wife Louisa Caroline, *née* Mackenzie: *gdson.* to Admiral William Compton, 4th Marquess of Northampton, and Lady Eliza Elliott: *b.* 3 May 1893. Killed in action, 13 May 1915, at Ypres Age 22. *unm.* On the village green opposite the 16th Century 'Falcon Inn,' Castle Ashby, Northamptonshire, stands the local war memorial. Erected by the parishioners of Castle Ashby and inscribed 'To the Glory of England and to Those Men of this Parish who Served their Country in the War 1914–1919,' the memorial records the names of thirty-one men who served (seven wounded) and four – Lieut. Lord Spencer Compton, Pte. B.J. Barcock, Pte. R.M. Lucas, Pte. C. Wooding – who made the supreme sacrifice. Returned to the family seat at Compton Wyniates, co. Warwick after the war; Lieut. Compton's sword and scabbard hangs in the parish church there.

(Panel 3) 2nd Lieut. the Hon. Francis Lambton, Royal Horse Guards (The Blues): 9th *s.* of the late George Frederick D'Arcy Lambton, 2nd Earl of Durham (*d.*1879), and the late Countess, Lady Beatrix Frances Lambton (*d.*1871), *dau.* of James Hamilton, 1st Duke of Abercorn, and Lady Louisa Jane Russell: *b.* 18 January 1871: joined Reserve of Officers, Royal Horse Guards, September 1914: served with the Expeditionary Force in France and Flanders, and was killed in action nr. Ypres, Belgium, between 25 and 31 October 1914. Mr Lambton was a member of the Turf Club. Age 43. A Memorial Plaque to his memory was 'erected by some of those friends who knew and loved him' in St. Agnes' Church, Newmarket.

To Live In Hearts We Leave Behind Is Not To Die

St. Agnes Church

(Panel 3) 2nd Lieut. Guy Harper Pullen, Royal Horse Guards (The Blues): 2nd *s.* of Hugh Charles George Pullen, Merchant; Messrs Davidson, Pullen & Co., Rua de Quintanda, 145, Rio de Janeiro, and *gdson.* to the late Capt. T.C. Pullen, R.N.: *b.* Rio de Janeiro, 26 February 1889: *educ.* Bedford Grammar School; St. Xavier's College, Bruges: afterwards engaged in business in the city of San Paulo, Estado de San Paulo, Brazil, being well-known in the business circles of both Rio de Janeiro and San Paulo as a thorough sportsman, and a member of the big clubs of both cities. On the outbreak of war he returned from Rio to join the Army, and obtained a commission, Royal Horse Guards, 10 November 1914: served with his regt. in France and Flanders, and was killed in action at the Second Battle of Ypres, in the charge of the Royal Blues, at Verlorenhoek, 13 May 1915. Age 26. *unm.*

(Panel 3) Corpl. of Horse, 1385, William Appleyard Wells, Royal Horse Guards (The Blues): *s.* of William Appleyard Wells, Merchant; of Grasmere, Fairbolt Road, Stamford Hill, by his wife Annie Matilda, *dau.* of Henry Scott: *b.* Tottenham, London, N., 21 August 1890: *educ.* Cowper Street School, City Road: enlisted Royal Horse Guards, 30 November 1909: promoted Corpl., September 1914: served with his regt. in France and Flanders; killed in action at Verbrandenmoelen, Flanders, 6 November 1914. Age 24. *unm.*

(Panel 3) Tpr. 1884, Theo Bennett Hallett, Royal Horse Guards (The Blues): *yst. s.* of the late George Henry Hallett, for many years H.B.M. Vice-Consul, Ghent; by his wife Clara, *dau.* of the late John Lewis, of St. Albans: *b.* Ghent, 22 February 1897: *educ.* L'Athenee Royal, Ghent: after the German occupation came to England with his family, 21 August 1914: volunteered and enlisted Royal Horse Guards, October 1914: went to France, April 1915, and was killed in action on the Menin Road, Hooge, nr. Ypres, 13 May 1915, while crossing an open space with his regt. with three machine guns firing on them. Age 18.

(Panel 3) Tpr. 1601, George Neville Forde Hawkes, Royal Horse Guards (The Blues): late of Ryde, Isle of Wight: *b.* Bromyard, co. Hereford: enlisted Southampton: served with the Expeditionary Force in France and Flanders from October 1914; killed in action, 19 November following. Remains (three) recovered, unmarked grave (shell-hole), 22 April 1929. Identified – Clothing, Boots, Disc.; reinterred. Of the three sets of remains recovered only those of Tpr. Hawkes could be identified with any degree of certainty. *Buried in Sanctuary Wood Cemetery (V.H.24).*

(Panel 3) Tpr. 1456, Ernest Percival Munson, 'C' Sqdn., Royal Horse Guards (The Blues): eldest *s.* of William Robert Munson, of 35, London Road, Lexden, Colchester, by his wife Frances Elizabeth: and brother to Pte. 235201, B.R. Munson, 8th Canadian Infantry, died 12 November 1917, of wounds: enlisted Colchester, co. Essex. Killed in action, 13 May 1915, nr. St. Julien. Age 24.

His brother Bertie is buried in Vlamertinghe New Military Cemetery (X.D.7).

(Panel 3) Lieut. Lionel Hope Hawkins, 1st (King's) Dragoon Guards attd. 6th Dragoon Guards (Carabiniers): only *s.* of Isaac Thomas Hawkins, C.E., of 90, Drayton Gardens, London, S.W., late Colonial Civil Service; by his wife Mary Hope, *yst. dau.* of Richard Butterworth, of Lancaster: by the marriage of a great aunt he was related to the Berkley family, and was thus cousin to the late Capt. H. Berkley, Royal Navy, and the late Francis Berkley, Secretary, War Office: *b.* Chichester, 28 July 1886: *educ.* Waynfleet, Winchester; and Royal Military College, Sandhurst: gazetted 2nd Lieut. 1st Dragoon Guards, 2 February 1907; proceeded to India with his regt. November following: promoted Lieut. 18 February 1908. Passed Captains' Examination, October 1912, and did good work with the signalling; having charge of a brigade for two years. Being in England on leave when war broke out, volunteered and was attached 6th Dragoon Guards: proceeded to France, 15 August 1914; served through the retirement from Mons, the Battles of the Marne and the Aisne, and was killed in action on the night of 31 October–1 November, when the Germans broke through our lines between Messines and Wytschaete in the 1st Battle of Ypres. The two forces had got mixed up, and Lieut. Hawkins observing a party approaching the trench, which he held with his troop, got out of the trench and went forward. According to a statement made by a brother officer they shouted, "Don't fire! We are the London Scottish!" and he therefore continued to go forward. He had not gone more than 30 yards when he fell, shot through the right side. Two of his men immediately went out and brought him back to the trench, and he was carried back by his own men and the London Scottish towards Kemmel, but died shortly afterwards. His Adjutant, Capt. P.M.A. Kerans wrote, "Your son, of whom we had all grown very fond, was killed in an attack by the Germans in a line between Messines and Wytschaete, in Southern Belgium, on the night of 31 October and 1 November. It appears that after the enemy had penetrated our line a party was observed by your son approaching the trench, which he held with his troop. He ordered fire to open on them, but they shouted 'Don't fire, we are the Scottish' and he ordered his men to cease fire; himself, bravely, but incautiously got out of his trench and went towards them. He had gone about thirty yards when the Germans – for it was the

Germans and not the London Scottish – opened fire and your son was seen to fall. Two men at once went out and brought him back to the trench. He was seen to be badly wounded in the right side and he was carried back by our men, and the London Scottish, towards Kemmel. On reaching a place of comparative safety two of the men went off to try and find a stretcher, and two of the men remained with your son who died very shortly afterwards. He had been unconscious from a few minutes after he had been hit and passed quietly away. The men were unable to bury him then and were obliged to leave him covered with a blanket at the edge of a wood where, I have no doubt, he has since been buried, but as, unfortunately, the Germans now hold the piece of ground, it has not been possible to do what would otherwise have been done. You have lost a gallant son and we a brave and well-beloved comrade who showed military qualities of high order." And Major S.W. Webster, "The farm we held was rushed by the Germans about midnight on 31 October, I at once went to the trench in which your son was. We retired from there to some reserve trenches about 200 yards in rear. I was there with him for about half an hour. I then left him to go and see a troop who were holding a trench on his right. After I had gone I believe he went forward a little to see if they really were Germans, as he seemed to think they were our own troops – it was pitch dark at the time. He was shot through the body and some of my own men carried him back. He died when they had carried him about a ¼ of a mile to the rear. My man, Pte. Willings, then left the body under a fence. It was impossible to recover the body, or even the wounded, as we had to evacuate the position at dawn. I am perfectly certain, from what the men told me, that your son died within ½ an hour of his wound. It must seem strange to you, that we could not recover the body, but we were fighting for our lives through the night, in the pitch dark, over a front of at least ½ a mile. Three of our own officers, and many men, were left behind, and we do not even know if they are dead or prisoners." Col. I. Annesley also wrote (12 December), "Had your son lived it would not have been long before he earned great distinction, for he was very brave and a fine leader of men. On the night of the poor fellow's death there were so many heroic actions on the part of my officers and men that it was impossible to pick out anyone in particular as being better than his fellows. As I say, had your son lived I should certainly have sent his name in for consideration at a later period for his splendid work as a troop leader from the beginning of hostilities, and I have written to this effect to the Brigadier General Commanding the 4th Cavalry Brigade, as I now hold a Staff appointment." and Brig.-Gen. the Hon. Cecil Bingham, 4th Cavalry Brigade, "I only met your son, Lionel, when he became attached to the 6th Dragoon Guards, but I got to know him pretty well, and my regard for him grew as we got to know each other. During the retirement, and subsequently, he had several difficult patrols to carry out, and he always did his part with conspicuous success. He was a very brave man, and was careful of the lives of his men. On the night of his death, he, in company with many others, performed acts which redounded to their everlasting credit, but you will understand that all cannot be rewarded, the number was limited to two per unit, and a selection made from the reports." The Carabiniers were in such fierce fighting that at one place after a night attack, on 31 October–1 November, the French, when advancing, counted three thousand five hundred dead in front of the trenches of the London Scottish and Carabiniers only. Mrs Hawkins received a telegram and letters of sympathy from the whole of her son's regiment. At school Lieut. Hawkins had received many nicknames indicative of his fleetness of foot and athletic prowess, such as 'Agag' and 'Diabolo.' In the Army he was very popular with his men, and the officers of his regiment wrote, saying, "He is a great loss to us." In India he was known as one of the finest polo players, and was in the winning team of many tournaments, and besides was a good all-round sportsman. He played cricket for his school, won the steeplechase for his House at Winchester, and ran with his troop in the Marathon Race in June, 1908, when they won the Harkness Shield. "An excellent report which reflects great credit on Lieut. Hawkins, the Signalling Officer," was the remark of the G.O.C., Ambala Cavalry Brigade, on Individual Tests, 31 March 1913. He was a member of the Junior Army & Navy, Junior Naval & Military Clubs, and of Hurlingham and Ranelagh. Age 28. *unm.*

(Panel 3) Corpl. 6108, Wallace Walter Rhodes, 1st (King's) Dragoon Guards: *s.* of the late Arthur Rhodes, of Smethwick, Birmingham, and Selina, his wife: enlisted Malvern, co. Worcester. Killed in action, 19 October 1914. Age 28. 1st (King's) Dragoon Guards first active service N.C.O. fatality.

(Panel 3) Pte. 7383, Ernest George Bishop, 1st (King's) Dragoon Guards: *s.* of Henry Bishop, of 'Greenville Boarding House,' West Malvern, co. Worcester, by his wife Elizabeth: *b.* West Malvern, August 1892: *educ.* West Malvern School: Occupation – Farm Labourer: attempted to join Royal Navy, Woolwich, September 1912, but – rejected being one year underage – travelled to Liverpool where, within a few days, he enlisted: posted 5th (Princess Charlotte of Wales') Dragoon Guards; transf'd. 1st King's Dragoons, Curragh, Ireland: Absent Without Leave, 29 December 1912–8 January 1913; Sentenced 28 days detention: went to India with his regiment, November 1913, where it formed part of the Lucknow Cavalry Bde., 1st Indian Cavalry Divn.: departed Bombay for the European War, 16 October 1914: served with the Expeditionary Force in France and Flanders from November following, and was killed in action, 1 June 1915 by the bursting of a shell. Age 22. *unm.*

(Panel 3) Pte. 6282, John Sidney Burrington, 1st (King's) Dragoon Guards: *s.* of the late William George Burrington, and Mary Elizabeth, his wife: *b.* Bampton, Tiverton, co. Devon: enlisted Exeter. Killed in action, 1 November 1914, at Messines. Age 31.

(Panel 3) Pte. 6265, Tom McDonald, 1st (King's) Dragoon Guards: late of Sutton, co. Surrey: *b.* Edinburgh: enlisted London: served in India; France and Flanders, and was killed in action, 6 November 1914, at Ypres.

(Panel 3) Pte. 2561, Ernest Sore, 1st (King's) Dragoon Guards: *s.* of the late Arthur George Sore, by his wife Eliza, *née* Sargeant (82, East Street, Sudbury): and elder brother to Pnr. 528081, H.C. Sore, 54th Divn. Signal Coy., Royal Engineers, who fell in Palestine, 19 April 1917, aged 21 years, 9 months; and cousin to Drmr. 4487, E.T. Sore, 2nd Norfolk Regt., who died, 30 June 1916, in Mesopotamia: *b.* Westgate Street, Long Melford, 21 March 1892: enlisted Sudbury, co. Suffolk. Died of wounds, 3 June 1915. Age 23 years, 2 months. *unm.*

His brother Horace and cousin Ezekiel also have no known grave; they are commemorated on the Jerusalem Memorial (Panel 9) and Basra Memorial (Panel 10) respectively.

(Panel 3) Pte. 6361, Frederick Sylven Tingley, 'D' Sqdn. 1st (King's) Dragoon Guards: *s.* of Thomas Tingley, of 17, Parklands Road, Hassocks, co. Sussex, by his wife Emily: and elder brother to Pte. G/1153, G.A. Tingley, 7th Royal Sussex Regt., killed in action, 7 July 1916: *b.* West Tarring, 1886: enlisted Chichester: served in India, and with the Expeditionary Force in France and Flanders from September 1914, and was killed in action, 6 November 1914 at Ypres. Age 28. *unm.* Recorded on the Ditchling (St. Margaret of Antioch) Parish Church War Memorial.

His brother George is buried in Ovillers Military Cemetery (VII.H.4).

(Panel 3) Pte. 7477, Silas John Whiteman, 'A' Sqdn., 1st (King's) Dragoon Guards: *s.* of Silas Whiteman, of 40, Purley Road, Ashbrooke, Cirencester, co. Gloucester, by his marriage to the late Mary Whiteman: enlisted Cirencester: served with the Expeditionary Force in France and Flanders from 7 November 1914; killed in action, 2 June 1915. Age 24. *unm.* Remains (four) recovered; unmarked grave (collective), 15 January 1929. Identified – Clothing, Discs, Titles; reinterred. Of the four sets of remains recovered only those of Pte. Whiteman could be identified with any degree of certainty. *Buried in Sanctuary Wood Cemetery (V.B.28).*

Rest In Peace

(Panel 3) 2nd Lieut. Gavin Paul, 2nd Dragoon Guards (Queen's Bays): elder *s.* of the late Gavin Paul, Coalmaster; of Edinburgh, by his wife Jane Gill: *b.* Edinburgh, 8 August 1893: *educ.* Bramcote, Scarborough, and Radley College, nr. Oxford: gazetted 2nd Lieut. 2nd Dragoon Guards, 4 March 1914: served with the Expeditionary Force in France and Flanders, from August 1914, and was killed in action at Messines, 31 October following. Age 21. *unm.* (*IWGC record 30 October 1914*)

(Panel 3) Pte. 5204, William James Caine, 2nd Dragoon Guards (Queen's Bays): *s.* of John Caine, of Mount Pleasant, Lindford, Bordon, co. Hants, by his wife Emily: and brother to Pte. PO/12625, J. Caine, Royal Marines, died of wounds, 26 August 1917: *b.* Liphook: enlisted Aldershot. Killed in action, 25 February 1915. Age 30. He was married to Kate King, *née* Caine (92, Rushes Road, Petersfield, co. Hants), and leaves three children.

His brother John is buried in Duisans British Cemetery, Etrun (VI.C.33). After a brief two days' rest at Vlamertinghe where reinforcements, including six young officers, were received from base, Queen's Bays were ordered, on 16 May 1915, back into the line at Hooge; taking up positions slightly below Bellewaarde Lake, left of Hooge Chateau. After five days, described as 'quiet' and sustaining just one casualty, they were relieved by 4th Dragoon Guards on 21 May and returned to Vlamertinghe. Called out again on the 24th by a sudden crisis arising from a German gas attack, which had caused heavy casualties and enabled the enemy to advance on either side of Bellewaarde Lake, the Bays, joined by 2nd Lieuts. R.A. Biddulph, H.F. Etherington and Mitcherin, set out and strengthened the line south of the lake through Zouave and Sanctuary Wood; beating off one attack, losing one killed and three wounded from shell-fire. Relieved during the early morning of the 26th the regiment, totally exhausted, returned once more to Vlamertinghe. Thereafter, at the end of the month, the Bays were moved back to Hardifort, near Cassel, where they remained until the latter end of September 1915; their time spent – awaiting use as cavalry in a breakthrough – in refitting, inspections, and training. During this period of relative inactivity the experience of a man like Sergt. Petty, the Bays one casualty at Hooge, would have been invaluable; no doubt he was sorely missed.

(Panel 3) Sergt. 5120, John William Petty, 2nd Dragoon Guards (Queen's Bays): *s.* of John Petty, of 147, Priestman Street, Manningham, Bradford, co. York, by his wife Jane: *b.* Bradford: enlisted there: served in the South African Campaign. Killed in action, 21 May 1915. Age 36.

Consequent to wounds received in France 2nd Lieut. Biddulph died, 19 November 1916, he is buried in Killoughy Church of Ireland Churchyard; H.F. Etherington, died of wounds, 8 January 1916, is buried in Bethune Town Cemetery (II.M.1).

(Panel 3) Pte. 4058, Ernest Pacey, 2nd Dragoon Guards (Queen's Bays) attd. 2nd Life Guards: *s.* of the late William Pacey, by his wife Maria (8, West View, New Park, Harrogate, co. York): *b.* Bilton, 1890. Killed in action, 6 November 1914. Age 24. *unm.* Remains recovered, unmarked grave; identified – Boots, marked No.4058, 2.D.G.; reinterred, 8 November 1929. *Buried in Kemmel No.1 French Cemetery (I.C.19).*

(Panel 3) Pte. 7967, Arthur Seaby, 'A' Sqdn., 2nd Dragoon Guards (Queen's Bays): *s.* of Arthur Seaby, Street Trader; of 3, Walham Avenue, Fulham, London, by his wife Norah: and brother to Pte. 202629, R. Seaby, 2/4th Leicestershire Regt., killed in action, 4 December 1917: *b.* Fulham: enlisted Kingston-on-Thames. Killed in action, 31 October 1914. Age 20.

His brother Richard also has no known grave; he is commemorated on the Cambrai Memorial (Panel 5).

(Panel 3) Capt. Edgar Ralph Coles, 3rd (Prince of Wales' Own) Dragoon Guards: 2nd *s.* of Ernest Harry Coles, of 'Arnolds,' Holmwood, Dorking, co. Surrey, by his wife Adele Caroline, *dau.* of James Heslop Powell: *b.* Caterham, co. Surrey, 13 May 1889: *educ.* Hazlewood (Limpsfield), Marlborough, and Magdalene College, Cambridge, whence having taken his degree, he entered the Army (University Candidate); gazetted 2nd Lieut. 3rd Dragoon Guards, 23 February 1910; promoted Lieut. 28 March 1911; Capt. 18 November 1914: in Cairo with his regt. for two years, returned to England, summer 1914; went to Aldershot to attend Signalling course. On the outbreak of war he left with his regt. for the Front, served in France and Flanders, and was killed in action in the trenches nr. Hooge, late on the night of 12 May (the eve of his twenty-sixth birthday). Buried at Witte Poort Farm, two miles east of Ypres. Mentioned in F.M. Sir John French's Despatch (14 January 1915) for exceedingly good work in carrying messages and maintaining communication under heavy shell fire at Zillebeke, November 1914. His commanding officer, Major Burt, wrote, "His gallantry had already been recognised by the authorities, and his splendid example and comradeship will be greatly missed by all ranks in the regt." Lieut. Holt, Acting Adjutant, 3rd Dragoon Guards, said, "His gallantry was an inspiration to his men;" and his soldier servant, Pte. Harvey, who had been with him ever since he joined the Army, "He was one of the coolest officers that was ever under fire." Age 25. *unm.*

(Panel 3) Capt. Gerard Gloag Sadler, 3rd (Prince of Wales' Own) Dragoon Guards: *s.* of the late Sir Samuel A. Sadler, of Eaglescliffe, Co. Durham, by his wife Lady Sadler: *b.* Eaglescliffe, 12 January 1881: *educ.* Durham School: joined Durham Light Infantry (Militia) 1899: transf'd. 3rd Dragoon Guards, September 1910: served in the South African War; took part in operations in the Transvaal, Orange

River Colony, and Cape Colony, February 1901–May 1902 (Queen's Medal, five clasps): promoted Capt. April 1910: retired from Active List, February 1911; joined Special Reserve Dragoon Guards: attd. 6th Dragoon Guards (Carabiniers), on the outbreak of war; present at the Battles of Mons, the Marne, the Aisne, and First Ypres. Reported missing after a night attack, nr. Ypres, 1 November 1914; reported (fifteen weeks later) to have died of wounds on that date, and buried at Wytschaete, nr. Messines, Belgium. Age 33. A member of the Junior Naval & Military Club; he *m*. Miss Phoebe Margaret Roche ('Tenter Close,' Husthwaite, co. York), *dau*. of W.M. Roche, of Sunderland, Co. Durham, and leaves a daughter, Elizabeth, *b*. August 1914.

(Panel 3) Corpl. 5821, Ernest Edward Fraser, 'C' Sqdn., 3rd (Prince of Wales' Own) Dragoon Guards attd. 1st Life Guards: late of Clifton, Bristol: *s*. of William (& Mrs) Fraser, of St. John's, Middlesbrough: served in the South African Campaign; and as Sergt.Major, South African Constabulary: *b*. St. John's, 1881: enlisted Newcastle-on-Tyne. Killed in action, 30 October 1914. Age 35. He was married to Ethel Agnes Mary Cockshutt, *née* Fraser ('Hillmead,' 102, Headcorn Road, Thornton Heath, co. Surrey).

(Panel 3) L/Corpl. 4114, Harry Andrews, 3rd (Prince of Wales' Own) Dragoon Guards: *s*. of Sophia Andrews (11, Market Place, Olney): *b*. Olney, co. Buckingham: enlisted Bedford. Killed in action, 1 June 1915. Age 23. *unm*. (*IWGC record 44114*)

(Panel 3) Pte. 5098, Henry William Batchelor, 3rd (Prince of Wales's Own) Dragoon Guards: *s*. of Joseph Batchelor, of 42, Tucker Street, Watford, co. Hertford, by his wife Eliza: and *yr*. brother to Pte. 2484, J. Batchelor, 3rd Dragoon Guards, killed in the same action, 31 October 1914: Age 28. He leaves a wife, Alice Maud Batchelor (46, Tucker Street, Watford).

His brother Joseph also has no known grave; he is recorded below.

(Panel 3) Pte. 2484, Joseph Batchelor, 3rd (Prince of Wales' Own) Dragoon Guards: *s*. of Joseph Batchelor, of 42, Tucker Street, Watford, co. Hertford, by his wife Eliza: and elder brother to Pte. 5098, H.W. Batchelor, 3rd Dragoon Guards, killed in the same action, 31 October 1914. Age 29. He leaves a wife, J. Batchelor (94, Kilravock St., Queen's Park Estate, North Kensington, London).

His brother Henry also has no known grave; he is recorded above.

(Panel 3) Pte. 6566, Frederick Philip Coleman, 3rd (Prince of Wales' Own) Dragoon Guards: *s*. of Frederick Coleman, of 52, Cardigan Street, Dogpool, Birmingham, by his wife Minnie: *b*. Dogpool, *c*.1894: enlisted Birmingham: served with the Expeditionary Force in France and Flanders from November 1914, and was killed in action, 2 June 1915, nr. Hooge, Belgium. Age 21. *unm*. Remains (three) 'Unknown British Soldier. 3rd D.G.,' recovered, unmarked grave (collective), 14 February 1928; identified – Disc, Titles; reinterred. Of the three sets of remains recovered, only those of Pte. Coleman could be identified with any degree of certainty. *Buried in Sanctuary Wood Cemetery (II.C.2).*

A Daily Thought A Silent Tear Keeps His Memory Ever Dear

(Panel 3) Pte. 6595, James Thompson, 3rd (Prince of Wales' Own) Dragoon Guards: *s*. of Elizabeth Thompson (77, Central Street, St. Helen's, co. Lancaster): and brother to Pte. 6535, J. Thompson, 3rd (P.W.O.) Dragoon Guards, died of wounds, 13 November 1914: *b*. St. Mark's, St. Helen's: enlisted Warrington, co. Chester. Killed in action, 13 May 1915. Age 25.

His brother John also has no known grave; he is recorded below.

(Panel 3) Pte. 6535, John Thompson, 3rd (Prince of Wales' Own) Dragoon Guards: *s*. of Elizabeth Thompson (77, Central Street, St. Helen's, co. Lancaster): and brother to Pte. 6595, J. Thompson, 3rd (P.W.O.) Dragoons, killed in action, 13 May 1915: *b*. Toxteth, Liverpool: enlisted Liverpool. Died of wounds, 13 November 1914.

His brother James also has no known grave; he is recorded above.

(Panel 3) Pte. 3653, Henry John Francis White, 3rd Dragoon Guards (Prince of Wales's Own): *s*. of Harry (& Maria) White, of New Kent Road, London, S.E.: late *husb*. to Edith Emily White (47, Ormside Street, Old Kent Road): *b*. Lambeth, co. Surrey: employee London County Council Tramways Dept.: enlisted London. Missing/believed killed, 31 October 1914, nr. Messines. Age 37.

(Panel 3) Lieut. Kenward Wallace Elmslie, 4th (Royal Irish) Dragoon Guards (Special Reserve): 2nd *s.* of Kenward Wallace Elmslie, of May Place, Hampton Wick, co. Middlesex: *educ.* Cambridge, LL.B.: gazetted 2nd Lieut. Special Reserve, May 1909; promoted Lieut., May 1914: served in the European War, and was killed in action, 4 November 1914, while in charge of a machine gun section.

(Panel 3) 2nd Lieut. Harold Osborne Powell, 'C' Sqdn., 4th (Royal Irish) Dragoon Guards: only *s.* of Hubert John Powell, Land Agent; of Hill Lodge, Lewes, co. Sussex, by his wife Mabel, *dau.* of Charles Francis Trower, Barrister-at-Law: *b.* Lewes, 20 August 1888: *educ.* Winchester: Occupation – Land Agent; in his father's office, Lewes: joined Sussex Yeomanry, 1908; Inns of Court, O.T.C., 1912: volunteered for Foreign Service on the outbreak of war; given a commission 2nd Lieut. 15 August 1914; gazetted as attd. 4th Reserve Regt. of Cavalry, on the 22nd.: went to France, 8 October 1914, and was killed in action at Messines, during the First Battle of Ypres, 31 October following. Buried in a cottage garden at Messines. His commanding officer at Tidworth, where he went through his training, wrote, "I considered him one of the smartest and quite the most able of the young officers here, that was the reason why I selected him as the first of his class to go to the Front. He had a charming personality and was always so full of energy." His Commanding Officer at the Front also wrote, "He was fighting in the town of Messines, guarding a barricade, at very close quarters with the enemy. I sent him with a message to the Queen's Bays on my left, and while carrying the message he was shot by a sniper." And the officer commanding his squadron, "I had many opportunities of seeing your son's behaviour under fire – it was in the highest sense praiseworthy. He showed himself in this his first and only action to be a very cool and efficient officer." At Winchester he was a member of the Commoner football XV, 1903–06, and captain of the Commoner VI, 1905–06. Age 26. *unm.*

PANEL 3 ENDS: PTE. E. BARCLAY, 4TH DRAGOON GUARDS

PANEL 5 BEGINS: PTE. W. BOURLET, 4TH DRAGOON GUARDS

(Panel 5) Pte. 6826, Robert Gray, 4th (Royal Irish) Dragoon Guards: *s.* of Joseph (& Mrs M.) Gray, of 7, Bell's Terrace, Attercliffe, Sheffield, co. York: and yr. brother to Sergt. 7137, J. Gray, D.C.M., 2nd York & Lancaster Regt., killed in action, 9 August 1915: *b.* Gainsborough, co. Lincoln: enlisted Sheffield. Killed in action, 14 May 1915. Age 23. He leaves a wife, Frances Gray (2, Ashworth Cottages, Britannia Road, Darnall, Sheffield), to mourn his passing.

His brother Joseph also has no known grave; he is recorded on Panel 55.

(Panel 5) Pte. 5103, Albert Greenwood, 4th (Royal Irish) Dragoon Guards: *s.* of John William Greenwood, of 23, Reynolds Street, Burnley, co. Lancaster, by his wife Susannah: and elder brother to L/Corpl. 51744, E. Greenwood, King's (Liverpool) Regt., killed in action at Passchendaele exactly three years to the day later: *b.* Burnley, *c.*1892: enlisted there. Killed in action, 3 November 1914. Age 22. *unm.*

His brother Ernest also has no known grave; he is commemorated on the Tyne Cot Memorial (Panel 31).

(Panel 5) Sh./S. 5387, William John Warwick, 4th (Royal Irish) Dragoon Guards: late of Radford, Nottingham: *s.* of Arthur Warwick, of 1, Gamble Street, Nottingham, by his wife Sarah Annie. Died, 11 May 1915, of wounds.

(Panel 5) Lieut. Cyril Frederick Wilson, 5th (Princess Charlotte of Wales's) Dragoon Guards: *s.* of the late Frederick T. Wilson, M.F.H., of Stardens, Newent, and Mrs Ernesto Larios (Gibraltar, & Monte de la Torre, Algeciras, Spain): *educ.* Horton School; Eton College; Royal Military College, Sandhurst: passed out July 1914; gazetted 2nd Lieut. 5th Dragoon Guards, August; promoted Lieut. November following. The following account of the young officer appeared in the *Eton Chronicle* (4 June 1915) – "He was a vigorous athlete, and was Captain of Games for his house at Eton, and on the river he became prominent and was just outside the Eight in 1912. He was a very keen sportsman, a fine rider, and a promising polo player." Killed by a high explosive shell, nr. Ypres, 13 May 1915.

(Panel 5) Major Walter Gabriel Home, 6th Dragoon Guards (Carabiniers): *s.* of the late Rev. Robert Home, by his wife Annie, *née* Swinton: *b.* 25 October 1872: received his commission 2nd Lieut.

Carabiniers from the Militia, October 1892: promoted Lieut. May 1897; Capt. July 1900: served on the Staff in the South African War – Brigade Signalling Officer, December 1899–November 1900; Divisional Signalling Officer, December 1901–August 1902; also served as A.D.C. to Officer Comdg. Cavalry Bde.: took part in the relief of Kimberley, and was present at operations in Orange Free State, Paardeberg, the Transvaal (east and west of Pretoria); Cape Colony, including actions at Poplar Grove, Driefontein, Karee Siding, Zand River (nr. Johannesburg), Pretoria, Diamond Hill, Riet Vlei, and Belfast (twice Mentioned in Despatches *London Gazette*, 10 September 1901; 29 July 1902): promoted Brevet-Major 22 August 1902: (Queen's Medal, six clasps; King's Medal, two clasps): obtained his substantive Majority, November 1905. Shortly after the outbreak of the Great War Major Home proceeded to the Continent for Active Service, and was present at much of the fighting during the early stages of the Campaign, including the Battle of the Aisne (Mentioned in Sir John French's Despatch, 8 October 1914), and is believed to have died on 13 November 1914, of wounds received in action nr. Messines, France, on 31 October 1914. Age 41. He was married to Helen Gordon, *née* Davidson, now Mrs Cole ('Avondale,' Chesterfield Road, Eastbourne).

(Panel 5) Major William Ernest Watson, D.S.O., 6th Dragoon Guards (Carabiniers): *s.* of William Watson, of 'Lancelyn,' Bromborough, co. Chester: *b.* 3 September 1876: gazetted 2nd Lieut. 6th Dragoon Guards, from the Militia, May 1897; promoted Lieut. January 1899: served in the South African War – Adjt., 1st Imperial Horse, January 1901–May 1902: took part in the Relief of Kimberley: present at operations in Orange Free State, Paardeberg, and the Transvaal, May–November 1900: Cape Colony, including actions at Poplar Grove, Driefontein, Karee Siding, Zand River, nr. Johannesburg, Pretoria, Diamond Hill, Riet Vlei, Belfast, and Colesberg: (Mentioned in Despatches, *London Gazette*, 10 September 1901; Queen's Medal, six clasps; King's Medal, two clasps): promoted Capt. December 1901; Regtl. Adjt., July 1907–April 1910; obtained his Majority in the latter year. In the Great War he was shown among the casualties included in the Army List, March 1915, as 'missing, believed killed,' 31 October 1914. Age 38. He was married to Florence Daisy (South Hill, Canterbury, co. Kent). (*IWGC record age 37*)

(Panel 5) Lieut. John Arnold 'Jack' St. Clair Anstruther, 6th Dragon Guards (Caribiniers) attd. 2nd Life Guards: only *s.* of the late Col. Charles Frederick Anstruther-Thomson, D.S.O., M.V.O., late Comdg. 2nd Life Guards (*d.* 1925), by his wife Agnes Dorothea (Charleton, Kilconquhar, co. Fife), *dau.* of James Alexander Guthrie, of Craigie, co. Forfar: *b.* 23 February 1888: *educ.* Summerfields (1897–1900); Eton College (Philip Williams' House): obtained his commission on leaving school; subsequently apptd. A.D.C. to Gov. General of Australia, 1914: served with the Expeditionary Force in France and Flanders from 8 October 1914; killed in action, 30 October 1914; Zandvoorde. Sir Morgan Crofton wrote, "Vandeleur, Todd and Jack Anstruther were in a squadron that was in the trenches when they were rushed by the Germans on October 30th. at Zandvoorde. These trenches were perfect death traps, the supports being a mile and a half away, and out of sight behind a hill. Only one man ever returned and his tale was very incoherent. He remembers hearing Anstruther call out 'Good God, they've got round us' and then seeing him rush out with his revolver and fall." Age 25. *unm.*

(Panel 5) Pte. 4164, William Frederick Blowers, 6th Dragoon Guards (Carabiniers): *s.* of Mr (& Mrs) Blowers, of 44, Waveney Road, Ipswich: enlisted Ipswich, co. Suffolk. Killed in action, 26 May 1915. Age 23. *unm.* Remains exhumed 28.H.12.d.9.7.; identified – Burial cross, clothing, 9 May 1924. *Buried in Bedford House Cemetery (IV.A.66/Enc.No.2).*

(Panel 5) Pte. 806, James Illingworth, 6th Dragoon Guards (Carabiniers): served with the Expeditionary Force in France from 8 October 1914; killed in action on the 20th of that month: 20 October 1914. Age 26. He leaves a widow, Effie Letitia (24, Hartington Road, Custom House, London).

(Panel 5) 2nd Lieut. Geoffrey Hamilton Bagshawe (formerly Carver), 5th (Reserve) Regt. of Cavalry attd. 1st (Royal) Dragoons: elder *s.* of Ernest Bagshawe (formerly Carver; took the name Bagshawe by Royal Licence, March 1914), of Poise House, Hazel Grove, co. Chester, by his wife Alice, *dau.* of the late W.H. Greaves-Bagshawe, D.L., of Ford Hall, Chapel-en-le-Frith, co. Derby: *b.* Poynton, co. Chester, 24 June 1889: *educ.* Stone House, Broadstairs; Harrow (The Knoll), and Christ Church, Oxford (1907–11), where he was a member of the O.T.C.; on taking his degree, was nominated a University candidate for the Army: gazetted 1st Dragoons, February 1911; joined his Regiment, South Africa, 1912: left the Army, 1913, to farm in Rhodesia, but on the outbreak of war hurried back to his country: offering his services, was given a temporary commission as 2nd Lieut. 5th (Reserve) Regt. of Cavalry, September 1914, attached to his old regiment for Active Service, and went to Flanders the following month: wounded (shrapnel, leg), 12 November at the First Battle of Ypres: returned to the Front a few weeks later, and was killed in action north of Bellewaarde Lake, nr. Hooge, 13 May 1915. Buried 'in the open near the road (west of Railway Wood), south of Square i.11.b. Map Sheet 28.' Age 25. *unm.* In a letter to his father a senior officer wrote, "In your son we have lost as good a troop leader as there ever was in the Regiment, absolutely cool and undisturbed under the most trying circumstances, knowing not the meaning of the word fear; well-loved and rightly, highly esteemed and deeply regretted by Officers and all ranks of the Regiment. He has died a gallant death, in a good and just cause – and I can only say I most deeply regret him as a friend and as an invaluable officer. We, alas, lost heavily in the Regiment – out of 340 all ranks, there remained this morning, I believe, 180. The General told me tonight they fought right gallantly, and that is the only point we can be thankful for. May we in our turn do as well."

(Panel 5) Sergt. 5336, Robert Henry Vanson, 1st (Royal) Dragoons: *s.* Henry Vanson, of 22, Hope Street, Maidstone, co. Kent, by his wife Frances: and brother to Corpl. 2601, A.J. Vanson, 1st (Royal) Dragoons, killed in the same action, 30 October 1914. Age 28. He was married to Flora Ada Barrett, *née* Vanson (54, Havelock Street, Canterbury).

His brother Archibald also has no known grave; he is recorded below.

(Panel 5) Corpl. 2601, Archibald John Vanson, 1st (Royal) Dragoons: *s.* Henry Vanson, of 22, Hope Street, Maidstone, co. Kent, by his wife Frances: and *yr.* brother to Sergt. 5336, R.H. Vanson, 1st (Royal) Dragoons, killed in the same action, 30 October 1914. Age 26. *unm.*

His brother Robert also has no known grave; he is recorded above.

(Panel 5) L/Corpl. 5733, John Edward Dore, 1st (Royal) Dragoons: *s.* of Bessie Dore (5, Highweek Street, Newton Abbot, co. Devon): and elder brother to Pte. PLY/16932, F.W.H. Dore, Royal Marine Light Infantry killed, 28 May 1915, at Gallipoli: *b.* Torquay, co. Devon, 1892: enlisted Newton Abbot. Killed in action, 13 May 1915. Age 22. *unm.*

His brother is buried in Lancashire Landing Cemetery (C.29).

(Panel 5) Pte. 6703, James Albert Andrews, 1st (Royal) Dragoons: formerly 2nd Dragoons (Royal Scots Greys): eldest *s.* of James Andrews, of 60, Wilcox Road, South Lambeth, London, by his wife Rose Rebecca: *b.* Lambeth, 1892: Occupation – Porter; South West Railways: enlisted London. Killed in action, 12 November 1914. Age 22. *unm.*

(Panel 5) Pte. 943, William Richard Henderson, 1st (Royal) Dragoons: *s.* of R.F. Henderson, of 26, Machett Road, Nunhead, London, S.E.: formerly employee London County Council, Asylums Dept. Missing 30 October 1914; nr. Gheluvelt. Age 27.

(Panel 5) Pte. 4978, Henry May, 1st (Royal) Dragoon Guards: *s.* of John May, of 47, Beauchamp Road, East Molesey, Surrey, by his wife Elizabeth: enlisted London. Killed in action, 13 February 1915. Age 33. Remains recovered, unmarked grave 28.I.29.d.5.6, Unknown Soldier; identified – Clothing, Titles; reinterred, 24 August 1929. *Buried in Kemmel No.1 French Cemetery (I.D.8).*

(Panel 5) Pte. 3448, George McGibbon, 1st (Royal) Dragoons: *s.* of George (& Mrs) McGibbon, of 33A, Gibson Terrace, Edinburgh: and elder brother to Spr. 21178, R. McGibbon, Royal Engineers, killed in action, 9 August 1915: *b.* Coldingham, Roston, co. Berwick: enlisted Edinburgh: served with the Expeditionary Force in France and Flanders from 8 October 1914, and was killed in action, 5 June 1915. Age 26. *unm.*

His brother Robert also has no known grave; he is recorded on Panel 9.

(Panel 5) Sh./S. 280, Thomas Welsh, 1st (Royal) Dragoons: 5th *s.* of James (& G.) Welsh, of Hope Park Lodge, Rattray, Blairgowrie, co. Perth: and brother to Pte. D. Welsh, Black Watch (wounded, surv'd.): *b.* Pitlandie, co. Perth, *c.*1886: joined Royal Scots Greys, 1906; transf'd. 1st Dragoons, 1909 – served 2 yrs. India, 2 yrs. South Africa – thereafter (early 1914) joined Rhodesian Mounted Police: returned to England on the outbreak of war, re-enlisted 1st Dragoons, Blairgowrie: proceeded to France, mid-October. Died 5 November 1914; Cavalry Divn. HQrs, Ypres; 'his death being particularly painful and distressing having been burnt to death by fire.' Buried at Ypres. Age 28. *unm.*

(Panel 5) Pte. 2671, Peter Ramage, 2nd Dragoons (Royal Scots Greys): *b*. Canongate, c.1890: enlisted Edinburgh: served with the Expeditionary Force in France and Flanders from August 1914, and was killed in action, 16 October following. Age 24. *unm.* All correspondence should be addressed c/o his brother, G. Ramage, Esq., 21, Jock's Lodge, Edinburgh, Midlothian.

(Panel 5) 2nd Lieut. Charles Henry Gath, 3rd (King's Own) Hussars: *s*. of the late John Gath, by his wife Emily (44, Airedale Road, Balham, London, S.W.): *b*. London, September 1882: joined ranks 18th Hussars, 1899: served in the South African War 1899–1902 (Queen's & King's Medals with clasps): subsequently transf'd. 3rd Hussars with whom he served in India for four years: returned to Pretoria, South Africa; spending three years there: returned to England, 1911, for a course of instruction at the Cavalry School, Netheravon: went to the Front at the outbreak of war, served with the Expeditionary Force in France and Flanders, being gazetted 2nd Lieut., 1 October 1914, and was killed in action at Klein Zillebeke on the 30th. Age 32. *unm.*

(Panel 5) Sergt. 4750, Walter Grimshaw, 3rd (King's Own) Hussars: late of Great Wakering, co. Essex: a pre-war Regular, mobilised on the outbreak of war, served with the Expeditionary Force in France and Flanders taking part in the Battle of Mons and subsequent retirement, and was killed in action at Klein Zillebeke, 30 October 1914. Buried there. His Commanding Officer said that he was a great loss to the Regiment. 'A very gallant soldier, and as a non-commissioned officer, he was a credit in every way to the 3rd Hussars.'

(Panel 5) Lieut. Alfred Felix Schuster, 4th (Queen's Own) Hussars: *yst. s*. of Dr. Ernest J. Schuster, Barrister-at-Law; of 12, Harrington Gardens, South Kensington, London, S.W., and Mrs Schuster: *b*. Hampstead, 30 July 1883: *educ*. Stoke House, Stoke Poges; Charterhouse (held junior and senior scholarships), and New College, Oxford (Exhibitioner), taking second class in Moderations and Lit. Humanitores: joined Kerry Militia; 2nd Lieut. July 1905; promoted Lieut., August 1908: upon disbandment of the aforesaid Militia, transf'd. 4th Hussars (Special Reserve), July 1910: served with 4th Hussars in France and Flanders from August 1914, and was killed in action, 20 November following, in the most advanced trench at Hooge, nr. Ypres. Lieut. Schuster was called to the Bar in 1906, and joined the publishing firm of Messrs Sidgwick & Jackson, 1913. He was a member of the New University Club, the Cavendish Club, and the Garrick. He hunted with the Quorn, V.W.H. Devon and Somerset Staghounds, and won the Bar Point-to-Point Lightweight Race, 1908. Age 31. *unm.*

(Panel 5) Pte. 10227, Thomas Alfred Ivory, 4th (Queen's Own) Hussars: *s*. of William Ivory, of 11, Windsor Terrace, City Road, London, N.1, by his wife Jane: and brother to L/Corpl. 8468, W. Ivory, Leicestershire Regt., died of wounds, 6 October 1915: *b*. St. Luke's, London, E.C.1: enlisted Stratford. Killed in action, 20 May 1915. Age 21. *unm.*

Buried at the time, the exact whereabouts of his brother William's grave are uncertain; he is commemorated in Manor Park Cemetery (Screen Wall, 128,389).

(Panel 5) Capt. John Lionel Wordsworth, 5th (Royal Irish) Lancers: *yr. s*. of the late John Wordsworth, of Black Gates, co. York: and brother to Capt. W.H.L. Wordsworth, of 'The Glen,' Scalby, co. York: *b*. Wakefield, 21 April 1882: orphaned before aged 5 yrs.: *educ*. Caius College, Cambridge (matriculated 1901): entered Yorkshire Royal Garrison Artillery (Militia), April 1902, becoming Lieut. June 1904: gazetted 2nd Lieut. 5th Lancers from the Militia, 23 May 1906; promoted Lieut. 16 May 1908: A.D.C. to General Officer Commanding in Chief, Northern Command, 1 August 1909–9 November 1911: served with the Expeditionary Force in France and Flanders (from 15 August 1914); killed in action nr. Ypres, 4 November 1914, by shellfire. Age 32. A noted college rower, and dedicated member of the Boat Club; the coach Dr. R.W. Michell also died in the war.

Robert Michell (Capt., R.A.M.C.) is buried in Cambridge (St. Giles & St. Peter) Churchyard, Cambridge.

(Panel 5) Lieut. Edwin Winwood Robinson, "D" Sqdn., 5th (Royal Irish) Lancers: 5th *s.* of the late Herbert J. Robinson, by his wife Agnes E. (Moor Wood, Cirencester): *b.* 25 November 1887: *educ.* Malvern College, Upper IV.A (Lower Shell), and Hertford College, Oxford: joined 5th Lancers from Special Reserve, December 1911: obtained his Lieutenancy, August 1914; went to France with his regiment on the outbreak of war. Accidentally killed in action on the night of 26–27 October 1914, while the regiment was engaged as dismounted infantry. Buried close to the church wall in the north-east corner of the churchyard at Voormezeele, Belgium. The grave is marked with a wooden cross bearing his rank, name, and the Regiment to which he belonged. Lieut. Robinson was fond of hunting, polo, and steeple chasing. Age 26. *unm. Commemorated by a Special Memorial in Voormezeele Churchyard; this was replaced 7 April 1970 by a permanent headstone. (IWGC record 25 October)*

(Panel 5) Capt. Geoffrey Wilmot Herringham, 6th (Inniskilling) Dragoons attd. 5th (Princess Charlotte of Wales's) Dragoon Guards: *s.* of Sir Wilmot Herringham, M.D., by his wife Christina Jane, *dau.* of T.W. Powell: *b.* London, 7 August 1883: *educ.* Eton, and Royal Military Academy, Woolwich: gazetted 2nd Lieut. Royal Artillery, 21 December 1900; promoted Lieut. 21 December 1903: transf'd. 6th Dragoons, 21 November 1906, becoming Capt. 9 March 1910: passed the Staff College 1912: served with the Expeditionary Force in France and Flanders from August 1914; shot and killed in action at Messines, 31 October following, while in command of the machine-gun section of 5th (Princess Charlotte of Wales's) Dragoon Guards, to which regiment he was attached at the time. Age 31. *unm.*

(Panel 5) Pte. 4425, William Bow, 6th (Inniskilling) Dragoons attd. 'C' Sqdn., 1st Life Guards: *s.* of George Bow, of 10, Welch Gate, Bewdley, by his wife Emma: enlisted Kidderminster. Killed in action, 30 October 1914, at Zandvoorde. Age 30. He leaves a wife, Maud A. Bow (20, Pleasant Place, Dog Lane, Bewdley, co. Worcester).

(Panel 5) Pte. 49466, Arthur Thomas Davies, 6th (Inniskilling) Dragoons: eldest *s.* of Thomas Davies, Time Keeper, by his wife Susan Ann: *b.* Bilston, co. Stafford, 29 December 1884: *educ.* Wolverhampton: enlisted 27 August 1902: served in Egypt and Ireland: proceeded to France 3 October 1914; reported wounded and missing after the fighting at Ypres on the 29th of that month, and is now assumed to have been killed in action on that date. Age 29. He *m.* Dublin, 27 August 1905; Bertha (18, Bone Mill Lane, Wolverhampton), *dau.* of Leonard Lester, and had two daughters – Norah Maud, *b.* 18 January 1907; Constance Edith, *b.* 22 February 1913. *(IWGC record 4946, 30 October 1914)*

(Panel 5) Pte. 2520, Cecil Clement Victor Green, 6th (Inniskilling) Dragoons attd. 1st Life Guards: *s.* of the late Clement (& Mrs E.S.A.) Green, of Reformatory Farm, Kingswood, Bristol: *b.* Horsley Stroud, Gloucester: enlisted Bristol. Killed in action, 30 October 1914. Age 26. *unm.*

(Panel 5) Capt. Stanes Geoffrey Bates, 7th Queen's Own Hussars, and Adjutant North Somersetshire Yeomanry: only *s.* of the late Gilbert Thompson Bates, J.P. (*d.* 1915), tenant of Mells Park, Frome, Somerset (2nd *s.* of Sir Edward Bates, 1st Bart., M.P.), by his wife Charlotte Thaxter (Donnington Hall, Ledbury, co. Hereford), *dau.* of George Warren, of Woolton: *b.* London, 2 June 1884: *educ.* Farnborough, Winchester, and R.M.C., Sandhurst: joined 7th Queen's Own Hussars, 22 April 1903: promoted Lieut. 27 April, 1907; Capt., 11 May 1912: spent 2½ years in South Africa and returned with his regt. December 1906, when they were quartered at Norwich, and afterwards at Aldershot: went to Bangalore with the regt. October 1911, where he remained until July 1913, when he returned to England on leave, shortly afterwards (1 November) receiving the Adjutancy, North Somersetshire Yeomanry: went to France with this regt. where he was wounded at Vlamertinghe during the First Battle of Ypres, 16 November 1914, but was able to return to the Front from the Base Hospital after a few days. Killed instantaneously at the Second Battle of Ypres, in the trenches at Hooge, by a shell explosion, 13 May 1915. Buried there the same day, amid a few trees behind the line held by the North Somersets. For their conduct on this occasion the North Somersets were specially Mentioned in Despatches. Much beloved by his men in both regts., his loss is deeply regretted by his Colonel and brother officers of the 7th Hussars. A good all-round sportsman and well known with the Blackmore Vale Hounds. Age 30. *unm.*

It is an interesting fact, illustrating how the same family name recurs in military history, that the first name in 'The Last Post,' a work containing biographies of officers who lost their lives in the South

African War, which commenced fifteen years before the present war, was also that of a cavalry officer named Abadie, *viz.*, Lieut. H.B. Abadie, 11th Hussars. That officer was Major E.H.A. Abadie's eldest brother; and another brother, Capt. G.H.F. Abadie, late 16th Lancers, died of fever in February 1904, at Kam, West Africa, where he had been serving as Resident, after having been awarded the C.M.G. for his services in the Kam- Sohoto Campaign. Major-General Abadie, the late officer's father, also had a most distinguished military career of 46 years. Not surprisingly in the Ypres (Menin Gate) Memorial Register the first name recorded is that of Major E.H.A. Abadie.

(Panel 5) Major Eustace Henry Agremont Abadie, D.S.O., 9th (Queen's Royal) Lancers: elder *survg. s.* of the late Major-General Henry Richard Abadie, C.B., 9th Lancers, whose death occurred after that of his son: *b.* 24 January 1877: joined 9th Lancers August 1897, became Lieut. May 1899: served with distinction in the South African War; took part in the advance on, and relief of, Kimberley, including the actions at Belmont, Enslin and Magersfontein; present at actions in the Orange Free State, and Paardeberg, including actions at Poplar Grove, Driefontein, Karee Siding, Houtnek (Thoba Mountain), Vet River and Zand River, February–May 1900: operations in the Transvaal, East of Pretoria, and in the Cape Colony, November 1900–May 1902: Mentioned in Despatches (*London Gazette*, 10 September 1901), awarded the D.S.O., Queen's Medal, 8 clasps; King's Medal, 2 clasps. It is believed no other officer received more than eight clasps with the Queen's Medal in that campaign. Major Abadie, who was a Staff College Graduate, was promoted Capt. March 1904: Adjutant of his regiment, February 1906–August 1907: received his Majority March 1912. Major Abadie is reported to have been killed in action at Messines in October 1914. He was at first officially reported to be a prisoner of war; as no official confirmation of his death has been received, and as nothing has been heard of or from him since, it must be unhappily assumed that the gallant officer has lost his life. Killed in action, 30 October 1914. Age 37. For his services in the Great War he was Mentioned in Sir John French's Despatch, 14 January 1915.

(Panel 5) Lieut. Frank Lennox Harvey, 9th (Queen's Royal) Lancers: *s.* of the Rev. Edward Douglas Lennox Harvey, of Beedingwood, Horsham, co. Sussex, J.P., D.L., Vice Chairman West Sussex County Council, by his wife Constance Annie: and elder brother to 2nd Lieut. D.L. Harvey, 9th Lancers, killed in action, 3 November 1914, aged 22 years: *b.* 1891: *educ.* Eton: commissioned 2nd Lieut. September 1911; promoted Lieut. October 1913: served with the Expeditionary Force in France and Flanders, including the great charge of the 9th against the Prussian Dragoons at Moncel, 7 September. Reported missing/ presumed killed in action, 30 October 1914, nr. Messines. Age 23. *unm.* His father was awarded the O.B.E. for his services in the Great War. Commemorated on the Regimental Memorial, Canterbury Cathedral, and Colgate (St. Saviour's) Parish War Memorial, Sussex.

His brother Douglas is buried in Dranoutre Churchyard (III.D.1).

(Panel 5) L/Corpl. 5573, Cecil Hawkins,9th (Queen's Royal) Lancers: *b.* Wootton Bassett, co. Wilts: enlisted Devizes: a pre-war Regular; proceeded to France August 1914, took part in the fighting at Mons (and subsequent retirement), Audregnies, the Marne, Aisne, La Bassée, Messines, and was killed in action, 18 October 1914, nr. Ypres. Remains (six, 9.Lancers) recovered – L/Corpl. 5573, C. Hawkins; L/Corpl. 1528, E. Matthews; L/Corpl. 400, T.W. Veness & Pte. 1852, G.F. White; L/Corpl. 5055, R.D. Gingell & Pte. 3877, G.H. Barnett – four unmarked graves, 28.U.27.b.75.20, opposite Convent, Le Gheer, Warneton. 'According to local information these six men were killed 11.10.14, and buried by the British.' Identified – Khaki, Boots & Spurs; reinterred, 7 November 1928. *Buried in Sanctuary Wood Cemetery (III.K.25/27).*

(Panel 5) L/Corpl. 4522, George Hawkins, 9th (Queen's Royal) Lancers: *s.* of Sarah Hawkins (56, Salesbury Road, West Ealing, London): *b.* Acton: enlisted Hounslow. Missing/believed killed, 24 May 1915; Gravenstafel. Age 24. *unm.* Remembered on the Regimental Memorial, Canterbury Cathedral.

(Panel 5) Pte. 4900, Albert Edward Fellingham, 9th (Queen's Royal) Lancers: *s.* of William Fellingham, of 2, Ross' Gardens, Edward Street, Brighton, by his wife Matilda: enlisted Brighton: served with the Expeditionary Force in France from August 1914, and was reported missing believed killed following the fighting near Messines, 30 October 1914. Age 20. *unm.*

(Panel 5) Pte. 1844, Edward Nicholson, 9th (Queen's Royal) Lancers: *s.* of Joseph Nicholson, of Canada, by his wife Elizabeth (8, Archie Street, Harrogate, co. York): *b.* Knaresborough: enlisted York. Killed in action, 13 May 1915; Frezenberg. Age 29. A comrade wrote, "Ed was orderly to General D. Campbell at the time and we were being heavily bombarded in the trenches. We lost nearly all our men; that was in the 2nd Battle for Ypres, and the situation was rather bad. As far as I know the General came up and a big shell wounded the General and those with him and I was told, his orderly was killed."

War Diary: 10th Hussars, 1 November 1914: "The Regiment were in support of the 7th Division, remaining in the woods, west of Hooge until 3.00 pm when they advanced, dismounted to trenches, retiring at dusk. 2 Other ranks killed, Captain Gibbs and six others ranks wounded."

(Panel 5) L/Corpl. 5544, Frederick Louis Hollister, 10th (Prince of Wales's Own Royal) Hussars: *s.* of William Charles Hollister, of 2, Prospect Place, St. John's Road, Newbury, by his wife Mary Ann: *b.* Hungerford, co. Berks, 1884: enlisted Gifford: served with the regiment at Lucknow, India, and in France from 8 October 1914. One of two other ranks killed in action, 1 November 1914. Age 30. Remembered on Hungerford (Bridge Street) War Memorial. Conjecture suggests L/Corpl. Hollister may be one of two unidentified 10th Hussars buried in Larch Wood (Railway Crossing) Cemetery, Zillebeke. See Pte. E. Gomersall, below.

(Panel 5) L/Corpl. 7730, Leonard Pattle, 10th (Prince of Wales's Own Royal) Hussars: *s.* of Lazarus Pattle, of Groton Wood Lane, Boxford, co. Suffolk: and elder brother to Rfn. R/17059, W. Pattle, King's Royal Rifle Corps attd. 6th London Regt. (Rifles), killed in action, 31 August 1918: *b.* Ipswich, *c.*1893: enlisted York. Killed in action, 31 October 1914. Age 23. *unm.*

His brother William also has no known grave; he is commemorated on the Vis-en-Artois Memorial (Panel 9).

(Panel 5) Pte. 2830, George Adams, 10th (Prince of Wales's Own Royal) Hussars. Died of wounds, 14 November 1914, consequent to being severely wounded by a close range sniper two days previously (12 November), nr. Klein Zillebeke

Although Aubrey Bloomer and Patrick Devlin died a few days apart they were buried together and a cross erected over the grave dedicated to their memory. Over the next few years continual shellfire and movement back and forth across the region rendered it totally unrecognisable. Sanctuary Wood existed in name only; its trees and undergrowth were no more than shattered stumps, the region resembled a lunar landscape, a swamp of thick viscous mud and shell-holes brimming with water as far as the eye could see. Remarkably, due in no small part to the diligence of the Graves Registration Units, thirteen years after their death and burial on the battlefield their remains were found, exhumed and laid to their final rest; together once more. Exactly which grave holds Bloomer and which holds Devlin is open to conjecture, but it cannot be denied that their identity 'either or' owes a great deal to those of their comrades who erected the original cross denoting they were buried together and, despite all the odds being against it, remains of it still marking the spot.

(Panel 5) Pte. 5894, Aubrey Rupert Bloomer, 10th (Prince of Wales's Own Royal) Hussars: late of Luton, co. Bedford: *s.* of William Bloomer, by his wife Mary: *b.* Stourbridge, co. Worcester, *c.*1895: enlisted Nottingham. Killed in action, 4 June 1915. Age 20. *unm.* Remains 'Unknown British Soldier' recovered 'Small Battle Cemetery Sanctuary Wood;' joint cross: Pte. Bloomer & Devlin, 10th Hussars (Graves 8 & 9); identified – 10th Hussar button found in pocket, piece of French belt marked No.46767. Reinterred, 29 February 1928. *Buried in Sanctuary Wood Cemetery (II.D.8/9).*

We Shall Never Forget
Mud, Stan And Red

(Panel 5) Pte. 6499, Patrick Devlin, 10th (Prince of Wales's Own Royal) Hussars: *b.* Edinburgh, co. Midlothian: enlisted Beverley, co. York: served with the expeditionary Force in France from October 1914, and was killed in action, 31 May 1915. Remains 'Unknown British Soldier' recovered 'Small Battle Cemetery Sanctuary Wood;' joint cross: Pte. Bloomer & Devlin, 10th Hussars (Graves 8 & 9); identified – 10th Hussar button, Clothing. Reinterred, 29 February 1928. *Buried in Sanctuary Wood Cemetery (II.D.8/9).*

(Panel 5) Pte. 8200, Walter Draper, 10th (Prince of Wales's Own Royal) Hussars: *s.* of the late Thomas Draper, by his wife Maria (Station Road, Radcliffe-on-Trent, co. Nottingham): and brother to Pte. 7888, P. Draper, 1st Lincolnshire Regt., died 22 February 1915, of wounds: *b.* Nottingham: enlisted there. Killed in action, 13 May 1915. Age 20. Dedicated – "In Memory Of The Gallant Men Of Radcliffe-on-Trent Who Fell In The Great War A.D. 1914–1919, Their Name Liveth For Evermore" – the brothers Draper are remembered on the St. Mary's (Parish Church) Roll of Honour.

His brother Percy, whose grave was lost in later fighting, is commemorated in Hooge Crater Cemetery (La Chapelle Farm Sp.Mem.4).

(Panel 5) Pte. 3205, Wilfred Fewster, 'B' Sqdn., 10th (Prince of Wales's Own Royal) Hussars: *s.* of John Fewster, of 3, Severns Street, Acomb, co. York, by his wife Jane: served with the Expeditionary Force in France. Killed in action at Ypres, 13 May 1915. Age 25. *unm.*

(Panel 5) Pte. 958, Edward Gomersall, 10th (Prince of Wales's Own) Hussars: *s.* of the late Joshua Gomersall,of Leeds, by his wife Sarah Ann: killed in action, 1 November 1914. Age 28. *unm.* Conjecture suggests Pte. Gomersall may be one of two unidentified 10th Hussars buried in Larch Wood (Railway Crossing) Cemetery, Zillebeke. See L/Corpl. F.L. Hollister, above.

(Panel 5) Pte. 11658, Thomas George Starkey, 10th (Prince of Wales's Own Royal) Hussars: *b.* Greenwich: enlisted London. One of four other ranks killed in action, 26 October 1914; Capt. Sir F.S.D. Rose and Lieut. C.R. Turnor also fell. See account re. Zandvoorde Churchyard.

(Panel 5) Pte. 8499, James Stephen Wareham, 10th (Prince of Wales's Own Royal) Hussars: *b.* Fenton, co. Stafford: enlisted Stoke-on-Trent. Killed in action, 26 October 1914; L/Corpl. J.H. Waugh, Ptes. R.S. Mackenzie, and T.G. Starkey also fell. See account re. Zandvoorde Churchyard.

(Panel 5) Pte. 11295, Cyril William Worboys, 10th (Prince of Wales's Own Royal) Hussars: *s.* of the late Arthur Worboys, by his marriage to Emily Bray, *née* Worboys (12, Alfred Street, Luton, co. Bedford): *b.* Luton, 1890: enlisted Bedford. Killed in action, 17 October 1914. Age 24. *unm.*

(Panel 5) Lieut. Francis James Gunter, 11th (Prince Albert's Own) Hussars: elder *s.* of the late Major General James (& Mrs) Gunter, of Aldwark Manor, Alne, co York: *b.* Eastcote House, Ruislip, 5 August 1893: *educ.* Eton, and Brasenose College, Oxford: gazetted 2nd Lieut. 11th Hussars, August 1914, attached 12th Reserve Cavalry Regiment for training: promoted Lieut. 11th Hussars, September 1914: went to the Front, 9 December 1914, rapidly gaining the confidence of officers and men. Killed in action nr. Hooge, Flanders, Whit-Monday, 24 May 1915. In the words of his fellow officers he was a most gallant and fearless soldier who could be relied on to do his best. The following is an extract from the *Oxford Magazine*, "F.J. Gunter came up to Brasenose from Eton in October 1912. Quiet, reserved and self-contained, he made in those two years a place of his own in the College life, and the news of his death comes as a great sorrow to those who knew him more intimately. Under a stoical mask of reserve lay hid a deep sense of loyalty and duty; though young he faced the position which lay before him with a sober sense of the responsibilities it involved; to fear God and honour the King he owned, in one of his rare moments of confession, as his ideal for himself and for those among whom he hoped to pass his life; a mysterious Providence has only allowed him to leave to them his example. A brilliant horseman, with no knowledge of what fear meant, he rode, as he lived, his own line quiet and straight. Faithful friend and gallant gentleman, he has died a soldier's death and has left his College and all who knew him yet another example of duty done." Age 21. *unm.*

(Panel 5) Pte. 4986, George Bugler, 11th (Prince Albert's Own) Hussars: *s.* of Samuel Bugler, of Thornford, Sherborne, co. Dorset, by his wife Elizabeth: and elder brother to Pte. 10288, G. Bugler, 18th Hussars, who fell, 6 May 1915, at the Second Battle of Ypres: *b.* Stockford, Yeovil, co. Somerset, 1888: enlisted Sherborne: served with the Expeditionary Force in France and Flanders, and was killed in action, 6 November 1914, at the First Battle of Ypres. Age 26. He was married to Bertha Alice Bugler (1, Finger Lane, Sherborne).

His brother George also has no known grave; he is recorded below.

(Panel 5) Pte. 9591, Harry Cheeseman, 'A' Sqdn., 11th (Prince Albert's Own) Hussars: *s.* of Henry Cheeseman, Watchman, Mersey Chemical Works; of 2, Brownlow Road, New Ferry, by his wife Frances, *dau.* of the late Thomas Howell, of Warrington: *b.* Warrington, co. Lancaster, 26 September 1895: *educ.* Garston Council Schools, and on leaving there was employed in the Toilet Dept.; Messrs Lever Brothers Ltd.: enlisted 11th Hussars, January 1913: held certificates for Third and Second Class of Education from the Inspector of Army Schools, and had intended sitting for the First Class at the next examination, when he hoped to pass for a commission: served with the Expeditionary Force in France and Flanders from September 1914, and was killed in action at Ypres 13 May, 1915. Buried near the farm 500 yards east of Chateau Potijze. Captain A.S. Lawson wrote, "He was bringing up ammunition, and was hit by a shell on the way to the trench. He was killed at once and so suffered no pain; he was buried close to where he fell. I can assure you that I shall miss him very much from my squadron." He was a good shot and won a silver watch and money prize for shooting at the Aldershot Sports, 1914. Age 20. *unm.*

(Panel 5) Pte. 7555, Albert Eaves, 11th (Prince Albert's Own) Hussars: *s.* of the late William Eaves, by his marriage to Mary Elizabeth Keates, *née* Eaves (Kingsbury Road, Minworth, co. Warwick): and brother to Pte. 306753, T. Eaves, 1/8th Royal Warwickshire Regt., killed in action, 27 August 1917: *b.* Birmingham, 1894: served with the Expeditionary Force, and was killed in action, 1 November 1914. One of seven brothers who served. Age 20. *unm.*

His brother Thomas is buried in Tyne Cot Cemetery (X.B.14).

(Panel 5) Pte. 22507, Fred Mills, 11th (Prince Albert's Own) Hussars: *s.* of John Mills, of 11, Wansford, nr. Peterborough, by his wife Elizabeth: and elder brother to Pte. 55477, A. Mills, 17th Royal Welsh Fusiliers, killed in action, 31 July 1917: *b.* Wansford, *afsd.*: enlisted Melton Mowbray, co. Northampton. Killed in action, 24 May 1915. Age 25. *unm.* Commemorated on the Thornhaugh and Sibson-cum-Stibbington War Memorials.

His brother Albert also has no known grave; he is recorded on Panel 22.

(Panel 5) Major Eustace Crawley, XIIth (Prince of Wales's Royal) Lancers: 3rd *s.* of the late Baden Crawley: *b.* 16 April 1868: *educ.* Harrow (1881–86); Trinity College, Cambridge: gazetted 2nd Lieut. 12th Lancers from the Militia, 7 August 1889: promoted Lieut., 7 January 1891; Capt. 17 November 1897; Brevet Major, 29 November 1900; Major, 29 July 1905: A.D.C. (extra) to Lord Lieutenant, Ireland, 19 February 1904–8 July 1905: took part in operations in Sierra Leone, 1898–99 (Medal with clasp): served in West Africa 1898; Officer Commanding Expedition to Bula: Mentioned in Despatches by Gen. Wilcox, December 1899; Officer Commanding Nigeria Company Constabulary from the latter date: served in the South African War, 1899–1902; Special Service Officer, being afterwards employed on the Staff (D.A.A.G. Ridley's Corps of Mounted Infantry), April–December 1900: took part in the advance on Kimberley, including action at Magersfontein, and the Relief of Kimberley: operations in Orange Free State, February–May 1900, including actions at Paardeberg, Poplar Grove, Dreifontein, Houtnek (Thoba Mountain) and Zand River: took part in Gen. (now Sir) Ian Hamilton's march, being present at operations in Transvaal, May–June 1900, including actions nr. Johannesburg and Diamond Hill: operations in Transvaal, west of Pretoria, July–29 November 1900: operations in Orange River Colony, May–29 November 1900, including actions at Lindley, Bethlehem and Wittebergen, and those in Cape Colony, under Gen. (now Lord) French, August 1901–31 May 1902: Intelligence Officer to Capper's Column at the end of 1901, and Staff Officer to Doran's Column, December 1901–May 1902: Mentioned in Despatches (*London Gazette*, 10 September 1901) by Lord Roberts (Brevet of Major; Queen's Medal, four clasps; King's Medal, two clasps). From May to November 1902 was D.A.A.G. on the staff of Col. Hickman, commanding troops at Middleburg, Cape Colony: again served in West Africa (Northern Nigeria) 1902–03: took part in the Kano-Sokoto Campaign (Medal with clasp), and in the operations in the district to the east of Zaria, being in command of a column: commanded Mounted Infantry in India 1903: was officiating Brigade Major, Amballa Cavalry Brigade, and to the Inspector General of Cavalry in India 1906–07: D.A.A.G. India, 17 April 1909–16 April 1913: served with the Expeditionary Force in France and Flanders, and was killed in action by a shell nr. Wytschaete, Ypres, 2 November 1914. Age 46. He *m.* 14 December 1904; Lady Violet Ella (5, Lancaster Gate Terrace, London), elder *dau.* of Major Charles Wightwick Finch, 8th Earl of Aylesford, and Marcella Araminta Victoria, *née* Ross-Finch. A keen cricket player, he played for Herefordshire County Cricket Club, and was a member of White's and I Zingari.

(Panel 5) Capt. Fane Wright Stapleton Murray, XIIth (Prince of Wales's Royal) Lancers: eldest *s.* of the late Col. Charles Edward Gostling Murray, J.P., D.L., of Whitton Park, Hounslow, and 'The Moat,' Charing, Kent, J.P., D.L. (*gdson.* of the Right Rev. Lord George Murray, Bishop of St. David's, 2nd *s.* of John, 3rd Duke of Atholl, K.T.), by his 2nd wife Margaret Frances Elizabeth, only *dau.* of the Rev. John William Conant: and brother to Lieut. C. de Grey Murray, currently serving with the Motor Transport; and Capt. R.A.C. Murray, Seaforth Highlanders, who died at Lillers, 11 March 1915, of wounds received at the Battle of Neuve Chapelle the previous day: *b.* Whitton Park, Hounslow, co. Middlesex, 16 October 1879: *educ.* Eton: gazetted 2nd Lieut. 12th Lancers from the Militia, 20 December 1899; promoted Lieut. 3 October 1900; Capt. 27 November 1907: served in the South African War, 1899–1902, taking part in operations in Transvaal and Cape Colony (Queen's medal, five clasps): and with the Expeditionary Force in France and Flanders 1914. Shot through the heart in the trenches at Wytschaete, between St. Eloi and Messines, 30 October 1914. His body was never recovered for burial as, immediately after he fell, the 12th Lancers were obliged to abandon their trenches. Age 35. *unm.*

His brother Rupert is buried in Lillers Communal Cemetery (II.D.1).

(Panel 5) Lieut. Edward Hubert Leatham, XIIth (Prince of Wales's Royal) Lancers: only *survg. s.* of the late E.E. Leatham, of Wentbridge House, Pontefract, co. York: *b.* Wentbridge, *afsd.*, 20 July 1886: *educ.* Eton; and Royal Military College, Sandhurst: gazetted 2nd Lieut. 12th Lancers, October 1906; promoted Lieut. August 1908: played in his regimental polo team when it won the Inter-regimental Cup 1914, and the Coronation Cup: served with the Expeditionary Force in France and Flanders 1914, and was killed in action nr. Ypres, 31 October 1914, being struck by a shell while returning from helping to get a wounded man back into a trench into which he had safely got the rest of his men. Age 28. *unm.*

(Panel 5) Lieut. Thomas Edward Lawson-Smith, 13th Hussars: *s.* of Edward Maule Lawson-Smith, of Colton Lodge, Tadcaster, co. York, by his wife Ethel Mary, *dau.* of the late Gen. Sir William Davies: *gdson.* to the late Rev. Edward Lawson, of Longhirst: and *yr.* brother to Lieut. J. Lawson-Smith, West Yorkshire Regt., killed in action nr. Bois Grenier, 20 October 1914: *b.* Colton, 14 March 1889: *educ.* Warren Hill, Eastbourne; Stubbington (Foster's); Harrow; Royal Military College, Sandhurst: gazetted 13th Hussars, 15 September 1909; joined his regt. in India, same month: promoted Lieut. 6 December 1913: served with the Expeditionary Force in France and Flanders, attd. 11th Hussars (his own regiment remaining in India), missing, believed killed in the trenches at Ypres, on the night of 31 October–1 November 1914. Age 25. *unm.* The Amble War Memorial, Northumberland stands on land donated by his father. (*IWGC record 1 November*)

His elder brother John also has no known grave; he is commemorated on the Le Touret Memorial.

(Panel 5) L/Corpl. 438, Alfred Charles Grey Peirson, 14th (King's) Hussars attd. Royal Horse Guards (The Blues): late *husb.* to Elizabeth Ada (20, Talbot Terrace, Whitchurch, co. Salop). Killed by shellfire, 13 May 1915.

(Panel 5) L/Corpl. 4143, Samuel Shaw, 14th (King's) Hussars attd. Royal Horse Guards (The Blues): *s.* of Samuel Shaw, of Altrincham, nr. Warrington, co. Chester: *husb.* to Katie Marie (19, Market Street, Altrincham). Killed in action at the Second Battle of Ypres, 13 May 1915. Age 33.

(Panel 5) Pte. 3075, Alfred John Edwards, 14th (King's) Hussars attd. Royal Horse Guards (The Blues). Killed by shellfire, 13 May 1915.

When Alex Patterson left the Army after fourteen years he could never have envisaged his services being needed again ten years later. In the intervening period he had secured a job, got married and had a family; in short, he had settled down to 'civvy life.' Readjusting to Army ways would have been quite a challenge, much had changed in the interim period but, after just a few weeks retraining, he went off to war for the second time in his life. His previous experience of two years fighting the Boers under the hot South African sun was far removed from fighting the Germans in the cold, wet and mud of Flanders. On 13 May 1915, after eight months rotating in and out of the trenches, Alex and five of his comrades were killed by shellfire while taking part in a charge near Bellewaarde.

He went without fears, went gaily, since go he must,
And drilled and sweated and sang, and rode in the heat and dust
Of summer; his fellows were round him, as eager as he,
While over the world the gloomy days of the war dragged heavily.

Ferenc Békassy

(Panel 5) Tpr. 4238, Alexander Patterson, 14th (King's) Hussars attd. Royal Horse Guards (The Blues): eldest *s.* of Alexander Patterson, Tin Plate Worker; of Smawthorne Grove, Castleford, co. York: *b.* Evesham, co. Worcester, 6 September 1876: *educ.* Castleford Council School: enlisted 14th Hussars, October 1900: served in the South African War, 1900–02, under Gen. (now Lord) French (Queen's Medal, 3 clasps): served 14 years with the Colours, thereafter joined the Reserve; employed as a Groom; Selby: mobilised 5 August 1914: went to France, September following attd. Royal Horse Guards, and was killed in action there, 13 May 1915. Age 37. He *m.* Castleford Parish Church, 1906; Sarah Ann (16, Douglas Street, off Brook Street, Selby, co. York), *dau.* of Joseph Clements, and had three children – Joseph, *b.* 12 November 1906; George Alexander, *b.* 21 April 1909; John Stanley, *b.* 29 September 1911.

(Panel 5) Pte. 5461, Charles Smith, 14th (King's) Hussars attd. Royal Horse Guards (The Blues). Killed in action nr. Bellewaarde, Ypres, 13 May 1915.

(Panel 5) Pte. 3070, Maurice Sutton, 14th (King's) Hussars attd. Royal Horse Guards (The Blues). Killed by shellfire, 13 May 1915.

(Panel 5) Capt. Brian Osborne, 15th (The King's) Hussars: *yr. s.* of the late Capt. Frank Osborne, of Harlbury Hall, nr. Leamington, co. Warwick, 13th Hussars, by his wife Helen, *dau.* of Thomas Lever Rushton: *b.* Sydney, New South Wales, Australia, 18 November 1888: *educ.* Harrow; and Royal Military College, Sandhurst: gazetted 2nd Lieut. 15th Hussars, 8 February 1908; promoted Lieut. 22 January 1909; Capt. (posthumously) 15 November 1914: went to France, 23 August 1914, and was killed in action, 11 November 1914, during the assault on the trenches nr. Herenthage Chateau by the Prussian Guard. Age 31. *unm.* Sent with his machine gun to support the Duke of Wellington's Regt.; he was at first reported missing, and it was not until the following March that confirmation of his death was received in a letter from one of his machine gun section, a prisoner of war in Germany. At Harrow he was successful in both cricket and football, and was first strong at racquets: won Sword of Honour, Sandhurst, and, after joining 15th Hussars, 1908, attained a great record of first-spears in pig-sticking when quartered at Muttra. As a polo player he came to the fore with his amazing rapidity, playing for his regimental team and winning the South African Inter-Regimental Tournament, 1911; repeating the event against more powerful opponents in the English Inter-Regimental Tournament at Hurlingham, 1913. As a member of the Cavalry School Team and the Cavalry Club team he lent his aid successfully, and was invited by Lord Ashby St.Leger, now Lord Wimborne, to practise in the international team of 1914, as choice for the American Expedition. He was a fine rider to hounds, and well known throughout Warwickshire. Remains recovered, unmarked grave, 28.J.21.a.40.40; Unknown British Officer, identified – Stars, Badge; reinterred 22 April 1921. Headstone erected A Lieutenant Of The Great War, 15th The King's Hussars: Detail amended headstone replaced, February 1993. *Buried in Bedford House Cemetery (IV.A.1/Enc.No.4). (IWGC record Osbourne)*

(Panel 5) Lieut. David Ronald Cross, M.C., 16th (The Queen's) Lancers: only *s.* of Adam (& Annie) Cross, of Lamport Hall, Lamport, nr. Brixworth, co. Northampton: *b.* Midlothian, 18 October 1889: *educ.* Marlborough College; Christ Church College, Oxford: gazetted 2nd Lieut. 16 August 1911; promoted Lieut. 16 April 1913: served with the Expeditionary Force in France and Flanders from 6 September 1914: wounded at Messines, late October and invalided home. Twice Mentioned in Despatches (29 October 1914; 17 February 1915) by F.M. Sir John (now Lord) French for his services in the Great War. Missing/believed killed in action, 21 February 1915; Shrewsbury Forest. Age 25. *unm.* Major A. Neave, Capt. E.R. Nash, Lieuts. N.W.R. King and R.A.J. Beech also fell; all are buried in Ypres Town Cemetery.

(Panel 5) L/Sergt. 5402, Gilbert Percy Liggins, 16th (The Queen's) Lancers: late of Kenilworth, co. Warwick: enlisted Warwick: proceeded to France with 3rd Cavalry Bde., August 1914; killed in action, 21 February 1915; Shrewsbury Forest, Ypres.

(Panel 5) Corpl. 1017, George Annett, 16th (The Queen's) Lancers: *b.* Southampton, co. Hants: enlisted there: served with the Expeditionary Force in France from August 1914, and was killed in action when, on the night of 21 February 1915, the enemy detonated a mine beneath the Lancers position at Shrewsbury Forest, Ypres.

(Panel 5) A/Corpl. 316, Alfred Jackson, 16th (The Queen's) Lancers: *s.* of Ambrose Jackson, of 11, Devonshire Road, Custom House, London, E.: *b.* Wandsworth, S.W.: enlisted Stratford: proceeded to France with 3rd Cavalry Bde., August 1914, and was killed in action, 21 February 1915, at Shrewsbury Forest. Age 28. *unm.*

(Panel 5) L/Corpl. 3225, Herbert Henry Chapman, D.C.M., 16th (The Queen's) Lancers: *s.* of Walter Chapman, of 82, St. Peter's Road, Great Yarmouth, co. Norfolk, by his wife Sarah Ann: enlisted Norwich. Killed in action, 5 November 1914. Age 24. Remains (three, 16 Lancers) recovered 28.N.36.d.0.3; identified – Disc, Chevron, Clothing; reinterred, 14 December 1927. Of the three sets of remains recovered only those of L/Corpl. Chapman could be identified with any degree of certainty. *Buried in Sanctuary Wood Cemetery (IV.L.21).*

(Panel 5) L/Corpl. 5595, William Futrill, 16th (The Queen's) Lancers: late of Norwich, co. Norfolk: *s.* of George Futrill, of Coventry, co. Warwick, by his wife Fanny: and brother to Pte. 5270, C. Futrill, 1st Coldstream Guards, killed in action, 14 September 1914: *b.* co. Worcester: enlisted Coventry: served with the Expeditionary Force in France from August 1914, and was killed in action, 6 a.m., 21 February 1915, when the enemy detonated three mines beneath the Lancers trench at Shrewsbury Forest.

His brother Charles is buried in Vailly British Cemetery (I.B.21).

(Panel 5) L/Corpl. 5182, Isaac Frederick Welbourn, 16th (The Queen's) Lancers: *s.* of Isaac Wellbourn, of 117, Commercial Road, Spalding, co. Lincoln: and brother to Pte. 27213, J. Welbourn, 2nd Royal Warwickshire Regt., killed in action, 4 May 1917: *b.* Spalding: enlisted Redford: served with the Expeditionary Force in France and Flanders from 18 August 1914: took part in the Retirement from Mons, the fighting at Marne, the Aisne, First Battle of Ypres, and was killed in action, 19 February 1915, by shellfire; Shrewsbury Forest, north of Klein Zillebeke. (*IWGC record Wellbourn*)

His brother Jacob also has no known grave; he is commemorated on the Arras Memorial (Bay 3).

(Panel 5) L/Corpl. 5685, Sydney Leonard White, 16th (The Queen's) Lancers: late of Basingstoke: *b.* Odiham, co. Hants: enlisted Winchester. One of twelve other ranks (16th Lancers) killed in action, 21 February 1915, by the detonation of an enemy mine beneath their position at Shrewsbury Forest.

(Panel 5) Pte. 3838, Frederick Charles Adam, 'A' Sqdn., 16th (The Queen's) Lancers: *s.* of James John Adam, of 18, Norah Street, Bethnal Green Road, Bethnal Green, London, by his wife Catherine Matilda: *b.* Bethnal Green: enlisted London: killed in action, 21 February 1915, by the detonation of a mine beneath the Lancers position at Shrewsbury Forest, 3 miles south-east of Ypres. Age 35.

(Panel 5) Pte. 5714, Charles 'Charlie' Alderson, 16th (The Queen's) Lancers: *s.* of Thomas Alderson, of 76, Beaconsfield Street, Greenbank, Darlington, Co. Durham, by his wife Margaret: *b.* St. John's, Durham: enlisted Newmarket, co. Suffolk. Killed in action on the night of 21 February 1915, at Shrewsbury Forest. Age 23. *unm.*

(Panel 5) Pte. 3270, Walter Oliver Basson, 16th (The Queen's) Lancers: *s.* of William Basson, of 28, Woodstock Road, Shepherd's Bush, London, by his wife Sarah Ann: *b.* Notting Hill, London: enlisted Woking, co. Surrey: killed in action, 21 February 1915, by the detonation of an enemy mine beneath the Lancers position; Shrewsbury Forest. Age 20. *unm.*

(Panel 5) Pte. 1389, George Birmingham, 16th Lancers (The Queen's): *s.* of George William Birmingham, of 'Holmes,' Rowledge, Farnham, co. Surrey, and Jane his wife: *b.* Benstead, Alton, co. Hants, about 1886: enlisted Aldershot: served with the Expeditionary Force in France and Flanders from August 1914: took part in the fighting at Mons and the retirement, the Battle of the Marne, the Aisne, and was killed in action, 5 November 1914, nr. Ypres. Age 28. *unm.* Remains recovered 28.N.36.d.0.3, identified – Damaged Disc, Clothing, Boots, Spurs; reinterred, 9 December 1927. *Buried in Sanctuary Wood Cemetery (IV.L.20).*

(Panel 5) Pte. 6006, Harold Cutfield, 16th (The Queen's) Lancers: late of Ealing, co. Middlesex: *b*. Ross, co. Hertford: enlisted Cambridge. Killed in action on the night of 21 February 1915; Shrewsbury Forest, Ypres.

At 11 a.m., 16 October 1914, 16th Lancers received orders to send one squadron with their machine gun into Warneton at 4 p.m., and to clear out the enemy in order that the Engineers could build a bridge over the river Lys. Arriving in the afternoon, 'D' Squadron (with the machine gun), held the south-west corner of the village, but were unable to make any further progress as the place was well prepared defensively and strongly held. 'C' Squadron was then sent up dismounted, but was held up by a barricade at the cross-roads in the centre of the village. The road down which the attack had to be made curved slightly about 150 yards from the barricade, and this could not be seen until the curve was passed. Eventually, when it got dark, a gun sent up from 'E' Battery was man-handled down to the curve and three troops were formed in column on the road behind it. Everything being ready, the gun was shoved round the curve and had fired six shots at the barricade when, without waiting to see the effect, the storming party rushed forward only to find the barricade still standing and began to pull it down under a heavy fire from the cross-roads and houses. The following account of what followed is taken from the diary of an officer of 'C' Squadron: "As soon as we started pulling it down the Germans opened fire from the houses. We pushed a maxim up into the window of a house, some of us stood in the street and fired, others tried to break into the houses on either side, and the noise and crackling of a burning house was appalling. After about 10 minutes of this the Germans retired round the corner towards the bridge. On looking round the corner we found another barricade about 70 yards away. They opened on us with a maxim and started throwing flares, while our gun began shelling from over our heads." The fighting to take the second barricade, although prolonged, failed in its objective and, at 11.30 p.m., the Lancers were withdrawn.

At this point it was discovered two wounded men (Ptes. Gibbons and Redding) had been left in the square behind the first barricade, and three men volunteered to go back and bring them in, which they managed to do, though the square was swept by fire from the enemy's maxim in addition to rifle fire. In recognition of their gallantry the three volunteers – Farrier Sh./Smith Glasgow, L/Corpls. Boynton and Chapman – each received the D.C.M. Sadly, by the time he was brought in, Pte. Gibbons was dead; Redding died shortly afterwards.

(Panel 5) Pte. 6133, James Patrick Gibbons, 16th (The Queen's) Lancers: *s*. of the late Peter Gibbons, by his wife Ann (29, Barrett Street, Keighley): *b*. Keighley, co. York: enlisted Halifax. Killed in action, 16 October 1914, at Warneton. Age 38.

(Panel 5) Pte. 4937, William Henry Giles, 16th (The Queen's) Lancers: *s*. of John Giles, of Cornworthy, Totnes, co. Devon, by his wife Elizabeth: *b*. Totnes: enlisted there: served with the Expeditionary Force in France and Flanders from August 1914, and was killed in action, 21 February 1915. Age 19.

(Panel 5) Pte. 4529, George Henry Jones, 16th (The Queen's) Lancers: *b*. Wednesford, Walsall, co. Stafford: enlisted Birmingham. Killed in action, 21 February 1915.

(Panel 5) Pte. 5045, Charles Alfred Lindsey, 16th (The Queen's) Lancers: *s*. of the late Charles Lindsey, by his wife Sarah (Wharfe Lane, Tibshelf, Alfreton, co. Derby): *b*. Eastwood, co. Nottingham: enlisted Nottingham. Killed in action, 21 February 1915. Age 20. *unm*.

(Panel 5) Pte. 2809, Christopher Redding, 16th (The Queen's) Lancers. Died of wounds, 16 October 1914, received in action at Warneton. See account re. Pte. Gibbons (above).

(Panel 5) Pte. 6493, Joseph Benjamin Pratt, 'D' Sqdn., 17th (Duke of Cambridge's Own) Lancers attd. 2nd Life Guards: late of Chelmsford, co. Essex: *s*. of Benjamin Pratt of Heale House, Woodford, Salisbury, by his late wife Elizabeth: *b*. Dublin, 1885. Killed in action, 19 October 1914. Age 29.

(Panel 5) Corpl. 2553, Arthur Dunne, 18th (Queen Mary's Own Royal) Hussars: *s*. of Major (& Mrs) F. Dunne, of 3, Alexandra Road, Kingston Hill, co. Surrey: and brother to 2nd Lieut. W.E. Dunne, 2nd Lancashire Fusiliers, died 18 October 1915, aged 35; and Tpr. 3827, A. Dunne, died of wounds, 11 October 1917, aged 17: *b*. Bury, co. Lancaster, *c*.1893: enlisted Dublin: served with the Expeditionary Force in France and Flanders from August 1914, and was killed in action, 13 May 1915. Age 21. *unm*.

His brother Walter is buried in Beauval Communal Cemetery (A.3); Alfred, Mendinghem British Cemetery (VI.E.6)

(Panel 5) Pte. 10288, George Bugler, 18th (Queen Mary's Own Royal) Hussars: *s.* of Samuel Bugler, of Thornford, Sherborne, co. Dorset, by his wife Elizabeth: and *yr.* brother to Pte. 4986, G. Bugler, 11th (Prince Albert's Own) Hussars, who fell, 6 November 1914: *b.* Yeovil, co. Somerset, about 1896: enlisted Dorchester, co. Dorset: served with the Expeditionary Force in France and Flanders, and was killed in action, 6 May 1915, at the Second Battle of Ypres. Age 19.

His brother George also has no known grave, he is recorded above.

(Panel 5) Pte. 12370, Herbert Bernard Cooper, 18th (Queen Mary's Own Royal Hussars): *s.* of George Cooper, of Avon Dassett, co. Warwick, by his wife Emma: *b.* Scarborough, co. York: enlisted Leamington Spa: served with the Expeditionary Force in France and Flanders, and was killed in action, 13 May 1915, at the Second Battle of Ypres. Age 25. One of three men of Avon Dassett parish who gave their lives in the Great War.

(Panel 5) Lieut. William Torquill Macleod Bolitho, 'B' Sqdn., 19th (Queen Alexandra's Own) Royal Hussars: elder & only *survg. s.* of the late Lieut.Col. William Edward Thomas Bolitho, of York House, Trevelloe, Penzance, and Hannaford, Ashburton, D.S.O., and J.P., Banker; by his wife Ethel Grace, 2nd *dau.* of Robert Bruce Aenaeas Macleod, of Cadboll, co. Cromarty, and Invergordon Castle, co. Ross, J.P., D.L., Comm. R.N.: *b.* Pendrea, Penzance, co. Cornwall, 13 November 1892: *educ.* Warren Hill, Eastbourne, and Osborne and Dartmouth Royal Naval Colleges: passed into Osborne College aged 12¾ years, and was given a remove from his own term to a term above, which was only very specially done: continued to be head of his term, and passed out of Osborne and Dartmouth Colleges with top marks: thereafter joined H.M.S. 'Cumberland,' Devonport, January 1909; after a six months' cruise, passed first out of there also, taking three prizes: subsequently appointed midshipman with four months seniority to H.M.S. 'Commonwealth': served aboard H.M.S. *Cochrane* and H.M.S. *Bellerophon* ('Billy Ruffian') thereafter left the Navy of his own accord. As midshipman in the Bellerophon he won the Stoddart Cup for Boat Sailing, presented by Admiral Sir John Jellicoe: joined the Army (Special Reserve), serving four months with 11th Hussars, Aldershot; passing into the Army by examination, Portsmouth, April 1913: gazetted 2nd Lieut. 19th Hussars, 23 May; joined 24 June following: crossed to France with 'B' Squadron, 23 August 1914, and served with that unit throughout the entire winter and spring. Lieut. Bolitho was killed by a shell, nr. Chateau Hooge, 24 May 1915, while gallantly attempting to make his way through a zone of poisonous gas. His Major, writing to his father, said, "Your son is a great loss to us, his name had been sent in for special mention after the operations on 13 May, when he found himself in temporary command of the squadron and made very good use of his opportunity." Age 22. *unm.* His father (a Cadet of Bolitho of Trewidden) raised and served (initially as Major) with 2nd/1st Battn. Royal Devon Yeomanry, Exeter and, until the Armistice, in Ireland where he held the rank of Lieut.Col. Comd'g. Dedicated – *These men of ours, unselfish, unafraid, went to the world wide fight. Forget not how they fought and how we prayed for England and for right. 1914–1918,* Lieut. Bolitho and his father are remembered on Madron War Memorial, Cornwall. Remembered on Penzance War Memorial, Battery Rocks; a stained glass window in St. Paul's Church, Mousehole, dedicated to his memory records, *"And you will speed us onward with a cheer, and wave beyond the stars that all is well."*

Lieut.-Col. W.E.T. Bolitho died, 21 February 1919, at Bath, co. Gloucester, after a long and protracted illness; he lies in the family vault, Gulval Churchyard, Penzance.

(Panel 5) Sqdn.Sergt.Major 4536, Frederick William Barnett, 'C' Sqdn., 19th (Queen Alexandra's Own) Royal Hussars: *s.* of Richard Barnett, and Elizabeth, his spouse: late *husb.* to Ellen Barnett (33, Wilbraham Street, Preston, co. Lancaster): *b.* Bermondsey: enlisted London. Killed in action, 23 May 1915. Age 45. Remains recovered small Battle Cemetery in Sanctuary Wood, Unknown British Sergt. Major, 19th Hussars; identified – Khaki, Badge of Rank, Chevrons, Crown, Titles, Trench Boots (estimated size 9); reinterred, 25 February 1929. *Buried in Sanctuary Wood Cemetery (V.E.10).*

(Panel 5) Pte. 8961, Charles Atherton, 'B' Sqdn., 20th Hussars: late of Vernon Street, Farnsworth: brother to Pte. W.H. Atherton, Loyal North Lancashire Regt. (surv'd); Pte. T. Atherton, 3rd Manchester

Regt. (surv'd), who, at the time of his brother's death, was guarding German prisoners at the concentration camp, Leigh: *b.* Farnsworth: *educ.* St. John's School: Occupation – Stripper and Grinder; Messrs Kearsley Spinning Mill, Stoneclough: enlisted Bury, co. Lancaster, 1913: served with the Expeditionary Force in France and Flanders from August 1914: wounded (spine) at the First Battle of Ypres, 1 November 1914; hospitalised Boulogne: returned to duty March 1915, and died of wounds received in action, 2 May 1915. In a letter to his sister, Miss Atherton (90, Park Street, Farnsworth), Major A.C. Little said that on the night of May 1st. a shell burst in Pte. Atherton's trench, badly wounding him; a doctor who was in attendance could do nothing for him, and he died about an hour later. In his last letter home, written on the eve of his death, he said, "30 April 1915…Just a line to let you know I received your letters and papers this morning. We are in the trenches, so I do not know how long they have been waiting. The Germans have been using poisonous shells on us, and they kill you if the dose is heavy enough. Quite a lot of our infantry were killed like that during this past week. We only had a few on us, but quite enough for they nearly blinded us for an hour or so. I have no time just now to write more. I will let you know how I am getting on by post card if I can't write a letter." A postcard dated 1 May informed he was quite well. Well-known and respected in Farnsworth, he was an excellent swimmer and winner of many prizes and trophies in the town galas and elsewhere. Whilst stationed at Colchester, prior to his departure for France, he won a silver trophy put up to the garrison by Scottish Highlanders. He also earned a rise in his pay for marksmanship. Formerly a member of the Farnsworth Parish Church choir; until shortly before enlistment he was a member of the Men's Institute.

(Panel 5) Lieut. John Herbert Butler Hollings, 21st (Empress of India's) Lancers: *s.* of Herbert John Butler Hollings, D.L., J.P., of 'Watchetts,' Frimley, co. Surrey, by his wife Nina. Killed in action, 30 October 1914. Age 26. Remains recovered, unmarked grave, Unknown British Officer, 21st Lancers, identified – Clothing, Buttons; reinterred, 21 January 1922. Headstone erected; Detail amended, September 1992. *Buried in La Brique Military Cemetery No.2 (I.D.6).*

(Panel 5) Lieut. Philip Francis Payne-Gallwey, 21st (Empress of India's) attd. 9th (Queen's Royal) Lancers: 2nd *s.* of the Rev. Francis Henry Payne-Gallwey, M.A., Rector of Sessay, Thirsk, by his wife Florence Kate, 2nd *dau.* of Col. Arthur Lowry Cole, C.B., 17th Regt. (Earl of Enniskillen coll.,) and *gt-gdson.* of Gen. Sir William Payne-Gallwey, 1st Bart.: *b.* Kirby Knowle Rectory, 7 March 1893: *educ.* West Downes, and Winchester College: gazetted 2nd Lieut. November 1912; promoted Lieut. 5 August 1914; attd. 9th Lancers, 12 August following. Killed in action at Messines, 31 October 1914. Age 21. *unm. Buried in Messines Ridge British Cemetery (II.F.8).*

For King And Country

On the opening day of the Third Battle of Ypres, 31 July 1917, each divisional sector held a squadron of cavalry in reserve who, as soon as the second objective had been attained, were to advance ahead of the forward-most infantry to reconnoitre and possibly exploit any breakthrough made. On XVIII Corps front, following 51st (Highland) Division's capture of their second objective, the signal was given for 1st King Edward's Horse to advance and, whilst in other sectors units had most of their horses killed in gallantly attempting to carry out this order, the King Edward's managed to advance to within 150 yards of the Steenbeek before being forced to dismount and dig in near Ferdinand Farm where they remained until the following morning.

(Panel 5) Capt. William Henry Dillon Bell, 1st King Edward's Horse: late of 47, Molesworth Street, Wellington, New Zealand: *s.* of the Rt. Hon Sir Francis Bell, G.C.M.G., K.C., of Wellington, 20th Prime Minister of New Zealand, and Lady Caroline Bell, *née* Robinson: *b.* 1884: was Member of Parliament (Wellington Suburbs and Country), 1911–14: relinquished his political career to enlist August 1914: appointed no.1/10, Lieut., Headquarters Unit, Samoan Advance Party: departed Wellington, 14 August 1914, aboard HMNZT 1 'Moeraki': served with the Samoa Expeditionary Force (from 28 August 1914) and in France and Flanders, and was shot and killed by a sniper, 31 July 1917, in the vicinity of Ferdinand Farm, before Maison du Rasta. Age 33. Capt. Bell was married to Gladys Bell (c/o Union Bank of Australia Ltd., London, England). He was the first member of the New Zealand Parliament to volunteer and serve on Active Service in the Great War.

(Panel 5) Pte. 1504, Ernest Walter Fearnley, 1st King Edward's Horse: *s.* of R. (& Mrs F.) Fearnley, of 31, James Street, Leeds, co. York: and elder brother to Pte. 1503, W.G. Fearnley, King Edward's Horse, died 26 August 1917, of wounds: *b.* Horwich, co. Lancaster: enlisted Chelsea, London. Killed in action, 31 July 1917, in the advance at St. Julien. Age 26. *unm.*

His brother William is buried in Duhallow A.D.S. Cemetery (I.B.39).

(Panel 5) Pte. 2580, Charles Ellis, (Alexandra, Princess of Wales's Own) Yorkshire Hussars (Yeomanry): late of Ilkley, co. York: *s.* of Mr (& Mrs) Lister-Ellis, of Cragg House Farm, Addingham Moorside, co. York: and elder brother to Pte. 47052, W.J. Ellis, 15th Durham Light Infantry, who died of wounds on the eve of the Armistice, 10 November 1918, aged 22 years: enlisted York: killed in action, 24 May 1915. Age 29.

His brother William is buried in Caudry British Cemetery (I.B.5).

(Panel 5) Pte. 2589, William George Ireland, (Alexandra, Princess of Wales's Own) Yorkshire Hussars (Yeomanry): enlisted York. Killed in action, 25 May 1915.

(Panel 5) Major William Francis Martin, Leicestershire Yeomanry (T.F.): 2nd *s.* of the late Robert Frewen Martin, M.A., J.P., of Anstey, by his wife Henrietta Susan (The Brand, Loughborough, co. Leicester); *dau.* of Rev'd. E.R. Larken, Rector of Burton-by-Lincoln: *b.* February 1876: *educ.* Harrow, and Trinity College, Cambridge: joined Yeomanry (ranker), 1897: gazetted 2nd Lieut. September 1898: served with Imperial Yeomanry, South Africa, 1900–1901: (Queen's Medal, three clasps): appointed Hon. Lieut., Regular Army, July 1901; after cessation of hostilities: became Major, Leicestershire Yeomanry, August 1911: (with the entire Regiment) undertook Imperial Service obligations on the outbreak of the war in Europe: proceeded to France, November 1914, the Leicestershire Yeomanry being brigaded with 1st and 2nd Life Guards: served in the trenches about Ypres, winter/spring 1914–1915. On the night of 12 May 1915, during the 2nd Battle of Ypres, he went up (with 2nd Cavalry Divn.) into the trenches between Zonnebeke Road and Roulers Railway; his squadron occupying part of the front-line trench north of the railway. Heavy shelling on the morning of 13 May drove back the troops on their left, and Major Martin was killed by rifle-fire while assisting in beating off an enemy flank attack from that direction. The Colonel, Leicestershire Yeomanry, with whom he fought in South Africa, wrote, "Having been with him in South Africa, no one knew his worth more than I did, and I was proud to call him a friend. His work with the Yeomanry, before they went out, and since he has been in France, has been the best a man could give." A brother-officer, "He was the finest man I ever met. In the fight he behaved as everyone knew he would. He was like a rock and by his steady courage kept his men together. He was well backed up, which must have made him very happy. You will be very sad, but, when you know exactly how he died, you will be very proud of him." And his Sergt-Major, "In Major W. F. Martin we have lost the best Squadron Leader the Leicestershire Yeomanry has ever known." Mentioned in Sir John (now Lord) French's Despatch, 30 November 1915. Director (& Secretary); Mount Sorrel Granite Co., he took an active part in Leicestershire public life. Major Martin was married (1912) to Violet Anne Philippa (The Holt, Woodhouse Eaves, Loughborough), elder *dau.* of Col. Walter Wynter; and leaves a son and a daughter. He was a member of the Cavalry Club, and was fond of hunting and shooting. Age 39. *Buried in Oostaverne Wood Cemetery (VI.H.23).*

Christ's Faithful Soldier And Servant Unto His Life's End

(Panel 5) Lieut. Thomas Edward Brooks, Leicestershire Yeomanry (T.F.): late of Queniborough Hall, nr. Syston, co. Leicester: sometime served with 11th (P.A.O.) Hussars; also Leicestershire Yeomanry, 1907–08: undertook Overseas Service Obligations, and joined Leicestershire Yeomanry, on the outbreak of war: served with the Expeditionary Force in France and Flanders, and was killed instantly by a sniper, 13 May 1915, at Frezenberg. *Buried in Oosttaverne Wood Cemetery (VI.H.24).*

(Panel 5) Lieut. Samuel Pestell Donald Thomson, 1/1st Leicestershire Yeomanry (Prince Albert's Own): elder *s.* of the late Marshall Thomson, Colliery Proprietor and Landowner, by his wife Edith Mary (Grey Lodge, Groby, co. Leicester): and brother to Lieut. K.C. Thomson, Royal Scots Fusiliers, who fell, 31 December 1914: *b.* Glasgow, 19 October 1888: *educ.* Southcliffe, Filey; 'The Lodge,' Uppingham, and Pembroke College, Cambridge – school Cadet Corps member, and O.T.C., Pembroke (3 years): commissioned 2nd Lieut. Leicestershire Yeomanry, after leaving university: gazetted Lieut. November 1913: served with the Expeditionary Force in France and Flanders from 13 November 1914, and was killed by the bursting of a shell while in his dug-out on the evening of 12 May 1915, on which date the Leicestershire Yeomanry were holding a section of trenches beside the Ypres – Menin road. He was a member of the Bath Club, and his favourite recreations were riding, golf, shooting, and hunting with the Atherstone Hunt, of which he was a member. An enthusiastic supporter of the Unionist Cause, he frequently spoke at political meetings and took a great interest in the Irish question. Age 27. *unm.* His medals – 1914 Star (with Bar), British War, Victory – and a portrait photograph realised £575 at auction by Messrs Christie (1995). (*IWGC record 13 May*) Remains recovered; unmarked grave (28.I.11.b.5.3) 'Unknown British Lieut., Leicester Yeo.,' exhumed, identified – Officers Clothing, Collar Badge (of Rank), reinterred, registered, 14 March 1928. *Buried in Sanctuary Wood Cemetery (II.B.32).*

His brother Kenneth is buried in Merville Communal Cemetery (I.L.1).

(Panel 5) Lieut. Alan Fletcher Turner, 1/1st Leicestershire Yeomanry (Prince Albert's Own): *s.* of the late T.V. (& Mrs) Turner: late *husb.* to R.M. Stella Turner ('Finisterre,' Robin Hood's Bay, co. York): served with 3rd Yorkshire Hussars (in which unit he was commissioned) in the South African War (twice Mentioned in Despatches). Killed in action, 13 May 1915, nr. Verlorenhoek. Age 40. Remains recovered; unmarked grave (28.I.11.b.5.3) 'Unknown British Lieut., Leicester Yeo.,' exhumed, identified – Officers Clothing, Collar Badge (of Rank), reinterred, registered, 14 March 1928. *Buried in Sanctuary Wood Cemetery (II.B.31).*

Served Throughout The Boer War
3rd I.Y. Mentioned In Despatches

(Panel 5) Sergt. 1643, Lionel Sidney Burton, 'B' Sqdn., 1/1st Leicestershire Yeomanry (T.F.): *s.* of H.H. Burton, Jeweller; of 116, Granby Street, Leicester. Killed in action, 13 May 1915, at Frezenberg. Age 26. In a letter to his parents Sergt. Cookson said, "I regret to inform you that your son was killed yesterday (13th inst.) when doing his duty in the trenches. There is a long list of others, and as it may take some time to send information officially, I have thought it best, though it is a painful duty, to inform you privately. I cannot as yet give any details, except death was instantaneous. May I express the sympathy of the whole Squadron – I may, indeed, say the whole of the Regiment – with you and Mrs. Burton, and perhaps especially Leo's young bride." He married, November 1914 (shortly before leaving for France), Lilian Hulls, *née* Burton ('Astley,' The Avenue, Ickenham, Uxbridge). A well-known rugby football forward, he played three seasons for Leicester Rugby Football Club and was the first member of that club to fall in the Great War.

(Panel 5) Pte. 1845, William Moore, Leicestershire Yeomanry (T.F.): *s.* of William Moore, of 44, Loughborough Road, Quorn, Loughborough, co. Leicester, by his wife Ann Mary: and brother to Dvr. L/23568, H.M. Moore, Royal Field Artillery, killed in action, 5 September 1918; and Pte. 1678, D. Moore, Leicestershire Yeomanry, killed in action, 13 May 1915: *b.* Quorn: enlisted Loughborough. Killed in action, 13 May 1915, at Frezenberg. Age 23. *unm. Buried in Oosttaverne Wood Cemetery (VI.H.27).*

In Sure And Certain Hope

His brother Hubert also has no known grave; he is commemorated on the Vis-en-Artois Memorial; Daniel is buried in Bedford House Cemetery (III.C.4/Enc.No.4).

(Panel 5) Pte. 1987, Francis Henry Smith, Leicestershire Yeomanry: *b.* Melton Mowbray, co. Northampton: enlisted there. Killed in action, 13 May 1915, at Frezenberg. In a letter to Mrs Smith, Corpl. F. Usherwood, 3rd Dragoon Guards, wrote, "Dear madam, it is with deep regret I have to inform you of the death of your son. He has indeed answered his Kings and Country's call to the utmost…We had a terrific battle on the 13th, and your son was killed on that day. The following day I was crawling about the ground between our trench and the Germans' line looking for wounded when I came across an empty trench in which the body of your son was. He had been shot through the head, and had fallen in a sitting position in the trench. I can assure you Madame, he died a peaceful and instantaneous death, as his poor face had a happy expression of one who had done his duty. The 13th was a terrible day for all us Cavalry. We, 3rd DG, lost 107 men, and every Regiment that was in action that day lost 100 or more. We were shelled for 18 hours, and all we could do was to crouch in the trench and hope for the best. Our troop officer was in the trench with me, and he said his prayers that day, and I also did, and I think every man did. We were attacked at one o'clock, but we beat them back by sheer bulldog fighting. My God, what a day! We suffered the worst shelling that was ever delivered on the trenches in the whole war. I hope I have not broken it too blunt to you, as possibly you have not been officially notified yet. Please excuse the scribble, as I am writing this on the ground. I have written to your son's fiancée, enclosing her a pocket frame with his photos in and some letters to him. I also send you some papers of his. Please let me know anything more you desire to know, and I will try and tell you all in my power…"

(Panel 5) Capt. Robert Ernest English, North Somerset Yeomanry: 2nd *s.* of the late Robert English, by his wife Mary: *b.* South Africa, 6 November 1883: *educ.* Harrow (North Acre), 1897–1901, and Magdalen College, Oxford: joined North Somerset Yeomanry 1909: promoted Lieut. August 1912; Capt. September 1914: volunteered for Imperial Service on the outbreak of war: served with the Expeditionary Force in France and Flanders from November 1914, and was killed by a shell, 13 May 1915, in a trench near Hooge during a heavy bombardment by the Germans. The President, Magdalen College, wrote, "Robert Ernest English was certainly one of the most pleasant and popular of the many pleasant and popular men Harrow has sent to this College in the last dozen years. Without any special or specialized ability, either in athletics or in the Schools, he soon became a leading man in the College, known and liked by all, and exercising an undemonstrative but valuable influence. His healthy, sensible, pleasant, and very kindly disposition, and unselfish love of his fellows, displayed itself no less when he went down. He devoted himself with much ardour and readiness to the College Mission, and in particular to the Boys Clubs, for which no one ever did more. When the War came he gave up business to join the North Somerset Yeomanry. Every Magdalen man knew what a good officer he would make, but, alas very little scope was given him, for the end came almost directly he had got abroad. Simple, unselfish, good-hearted, no one was ever more ready to sacrifice himself. For none will there be more unqualified regret, among those who knew him here." He was a member of the Bath Club, and devoted to all kinds of shooting and fishing; he went to Nairobi for big-game shooting in 1913. Age 31.

(Panel 5) Tpr. 2263, John Laurence Pumphrey, 'B' Sqdn., Northumberland Hussars, Imperial Yeomanry: *yr. s.* of Joseph Pumphrey, Colliery Owner; of Hindley Hall, Stocksfield-on-Tyne, by his wife Frances, *dau.* of Jonathan Priestman: *b.* Shotley Bridge, Co. Durham, 27 April 1891: *educ.* Sedbergh School, and Trinity College, Oxford (graduated B.A., 1914): volunteered and joined Northumberland Hussars after the outbreak of war in August 1914: went to Belgium with them, in the 7th Division, early October, and died in hospital at Ypres, on the 25th of that month, from wounds received in action during the First Battle of Ypres the previous day. The Hussars were dismounted and advancing to attack when he was shot through the head. Buried in Ypres Cemetery. His Major wrote, "He was one of the best and was enormously liked by officers and men. He always did his bit and a bit extra." While at Sedbergh he was head of the school, and in the O.T.C. both there and at Oxford, where he took a 3rd Class in Moderates, and a 3rd in Greats. He played Rugby for his College and was President of the College Athletics in 1913. Age 23. *unm.*

(Panel 5) Capt. Brian Charles Baskerville Molloy, Oxfordshire Yeomanry (Queen's Own Oxfordshire Hussars) (T.F.): *s.* of James Molloy, of Conolare, Kings Co.: *b.* 1 June 1875: *educ.* Oratory School, Birmingham: entered the Yeomanry May 1901: served in the South African War, in which he was severely wounded: took part in the operations in the Orange River Colony, and Transvaal, 1900–01, including actions at Lindley, Rhenoster River, and Venterskroon: Queen's Medal, four clasps: retired from the Oxfordshire Yeomanry, February 1905, joining the Reserve of that regiment the same year, when he was also promoted Capt.: King's Foreign Service Messenger, 1901–13; Honorary Army Lieut. from May 1910: called up on mobilisation August 1914, and returned to his former rank: served with the Expeditionary Force in France and Flanders, and was killed in action, 1 November 1914. Age 39. He was a member of the St. James's and

Cavalry Clubs. Capt. Molloy was married to May, widow of Major Harry Pakenham, 60th Rifles, *dau.* of Col. Markham, of Becca Hall, co. York, and left a *dau.*, Mary Elizabeth, *b.* January 1912.

Potijze, between Chateau and Verlorenhoek, 1915: on 13th May 1915 the 8th Cavalry Brigade received orders to counter-attack and recapture a front-line trench on Frezenberg Ridge. The Essex Yeomanry had orders to come up on the right of the 10th Hussars in front of Potijze, under command of their C.O., Lieut.-Colonel Shearman. The Essex advanced from their trenches in echelon of squadrons to come alongside the Hussars, ready for the attack. Major Roddick led them out, a pipe between his teeth, his stick in his hand, as they filed from their trenches. The men dashed forward cheering and shouting and reached the Hussars when – at the exact moment of their arrival – a little bunch of Germans bolted from a trench 200 yards ahead, across the open. A wild shout of "Tally-ho! Tally-ho! Yonder they go!" burst from the Essex. Nothing could hold the two regiments, and up the hill, like hounds in full cry, they went. They surged over the crest, and, ahead of time, ran into our bombardment. The trench was captured, the Germans retiring after a final burst of fire at close range, and Major Roddick was killed at the head of his men. This trench was ankle-deep in mud, but the battalions promptly comforted themselves with cigars, cigarettes, and rations left by the enemy. The lull, however, was short, and soon violent and accurate fire began to pour into the trench. The line was a single one and unsupported, and strong parties of the enemy came round threatening the right. Lieut.-Col. Shearman was shot down and killed (Vlamertinghe Military Cemetery). The bombardment grew in intensity, but for two hours the men in the trench endured. Rifles were jamming in the liquid mud, and the position was becoming untenable. 'B' Squadron of the Essex had manned an irregular line of shell-holes, a few men in each, where the O.C., Capt. E.A. Ruggles-Brise, has described the drumming of incessant machine gun fire as reminding him "of the song of a sewing machine." In his shell-hole were seven men, and as the rifles jammed and the magazines would not work, four who were already wounded sat in the slop of the drizzling rain in the bottom and acted as loaders. But though they tried to clean up the rifles as they loaded, only single shots could be fired. Sergeant Deakin was shot through the temple and died as he stood, and in these crowded quarters his body stiffened in the attitude of firing at the enemy. Towards evening the squadron in the forward trench received orders from the 10th Hussars to file out and retire from the line they had captured, and which had now become impossible to hold. Lieut.-Colonel Deacon was never heard of again. Capt. Ruggles-Brise, in too exposed a position to move, hung on till nightfall, when the squadron quietly slipped away. The stand that the 8th Brigade had made "did more than anything else to stop the front here going entirely;" the Germans had been held back long enough to allow of an unbroken line being established during the night.'

(Panel 5) Lieut.Col. Edmund Deacon, Comdg. Essex Yeomanry: formerly 1st (King's) Dragoon Guards: late *husb.* to Sybil Deacon (Sloe House, Halstead, co. Essex). Missing in action near Potijze, during the Second Battle of Ypres, 13 May 1915; a search party sent out on the 17th to look for him and others found no trace and it is now believed he was killed in action on the aforementioned date. Age 43.

(Panel 5) Major Andrew Roddick, Essex Yeomanry: *yst. s.* of the late Andrew Roddick, by his wife Alice (Upshire Hall, Waltham Abbey): *b.* Springfield, High Beech, co. Essex, 13 May 1873: related, on his father's side, to Thomas Carlyle, and on his mother's to Edward Irving: *educ.* City of London School: joined Paget's Horse for service in the South African War: took part with that regiment in the relief of Mafeking, operations in the Transvaal and Cape Colony, and at the actions at Zilikats Nek, Elands River, Venterskroon, Frederickstad, Ruidam and Fabers Put: Queen's Medal, three clasps: afterwards received a commission and became Lieut. Regular Army July 1901: subsequently joined the Essex Yeomanry, becoming Lieut. December 1901; Major, January 1909: served with the Expeditionary Force in France and Flanders from the outbreak of war, and was killed in action, on his 42nd birthday; being shot through the heart while leading a desperate attack near Potijze, Ypres, 13 May 1915. He was in the highest spirits just before he was killed and was gallantly encouraging his men. He was very popular in his regiment.

(Panel 5) Lieut. Geoffrey Stewart Johnston, 1st Essex Yeomanry: *yst. s.* of Reginald Eden Johnston, of 'Terlings,' Gilston, Hereford: *b.* 9 August 1889: *educ.* Eton, and New College, Oxford: after leaving there, joined Essex Yeomanry, becoming Lieut. September 1913, and was killed in the charge of his regiment at the Second Battle of Ypres, 13 May 1915. Age 25. *unm.* (*IWGC record 14 May*)

(Panel 5) 2nd Lieut. Alexander Glen Swire, 1st Essex Yeomanry: *yr. s.* of the late John Swire, by his wife Emily (Hillingdon House, Harlow, co. Essex): *b.* 26 November 1896: *educ.* Horris Hill, Newbury, co. Berks; Eton (R.B.L. Booker's House), where he had his House Football Colours, and was a member of the O.T.C.: was to have entered University College, Oxford, October 1914: received his commission, August 1914, and immediately undertook Imperial Service obligations – as did his entire Regiment. He was killed in action near Ypres, 13 May 1915, being shot during a successful counter-charge on foot by the Blues, 10th Hussars and Essex Yeomanry. The position had to be retaken 'at all costs,' and the casualties were very heavy. He loved his rod and gun, and hunted with the Essex Hounds, of which his father was Master during the seasons 1906–10. At the time of his death he was only 18½ years old.

(Panel 5) Sergt. 1117, Lionel Clarence Deakin, Essex Yeomanry: *s.* of Alexander Deakin, of 'Fern Villa,' Orsett, Grays, co. Essex, by his wife Kate Eliza. Killed in action, 13 May 1915, being shot through the head by a sniper, whilst giving supporting fire from a shell-hole in a forward position near Ypres. Age 22. *(IWGC record 14 May 1915)*

(Panel 5) Sergt. 1093, Stanley Francis Newman, Essex Yeomanry: 3rd *s.* of Francis Newman, of Moor Hall, Thorley, Bishop's Stortford, Farmer, by his wife Emily, *dau.* of Richard Stock: *b.* Moor Hall, Thorley, co. Hertford, 18 July 1885: *educ.* Bishop's Stortford College: served six years Essex Yeomanry, 1906–12, then went to Singapore and later to Australia, where he was farming: returned to England in July 1914, and when war broke out the following month, immediately rejoined his old regt., and volunteered for Foreign Service. Went to France, 28 November 1914, and was killed in action in an attack on the German trenches at Ypres, 13 May 1915. The Capt. commanding 'C' Squadron wrote, "The regt. was sent up to reinforce the infantry at this part of the line about a week ago. On the 13th the Germans succeeded in taking a bit of our line and the regt., together with the two other regts. of our Brigade, was ordered to retake it. They had to advance 500 yards of open ground, most of it going under a very heavy fire from shells, rifle and machine-gun fire. Your son reached the enemy's trenches safely, and helped to recapture them, but a few minutes later he was shot standing near Mr Holt who was also wounded. His death is a great blow to us all, officers and men alike, and leaves a place in the Squadron, which will be hard to fill. Everybody agreed that he was one of the very best N.C.Os. in the regt. and his troop would do anything for him." And Trooper H.J. Tucker, writing to his father, said, "Will you just break the news on my behalf that my two comrades, Sergt. Stanley Newman and Corpl. Frank Bird, have both been killed in action during a great charge which took place two days ago. When there was a roll call the whole regt. had 168 casualties – killed, wounded and missing; amongst them our Colonel and many officers." Age 29. *unm.*

Corpl. Bird also has no known grave; he is recorded below.

(Panel 5) Corpl. 964, Thompson Allen, Essex Yeomanry: *s.* of Edgar Allen, Farmer; of 'The Laurels,' Great Horkesley, Colchester, by his wife Sophia: *b.* Great Horkesley, 5 December 1893: joined Essex Yeomanry, November 1913, and was killed in action nr. Ypres, 13 May 1915, while taking part in what Brigadier-Gen. Johnson described as one of the finest charges he had ever seen. He was buried in a graveyard on the road running from Ypres to Zonnebeke, about a ¼ of a mile beyond the village of Potijze. Lieut. Victor Hinde wrote, "I had a personal pride and a fondness for your son. He has always been my ideal of a soldier. Nothing was too much for him to do, and he always took a pride in himself and his work; in fact, I relied upon him more than I can say." Age 21. *unm.*

(Panel 5) Corpl. 476, Frank Edward Bird, 'C' Sqdn., Essex Yeomanry: eldest *s.* of Frederick Bird, of Hither Farm, Thorley, Bishop's Stortford, co. Hertford, by his wife Fanny Alberta, *dau.* of George Fowler: and brother to Gnr. H.C. Bird, Royal Field Artillery (surv'd.); and Pte. A.W. Bird, 6th The Queen's (surv'd.): *b.* Thorley, 25 March 1893: *educ.* Hockerill Boys' Practising Schools: joined Essex Yeomanry, Trumpeter, November 1909, and having completed his four years' service, re-joined for a further period: served with the Expeditionary Force in France and Flanders from November 1914, and was killed in action near Ypres, 13 May 1915. Age 22. Mentioned in Despatches for 'bravery and coolness under fire,' and Capt. R.G. Proby, commanding the Stortford Troop, writing to his father, said, "He took part with the rest of the Stortford Troop in a very gallant attack on the German lines. The attack succeeded, but unfortunately our losses were heavy – he is among the number. I need hardly say how sorry I am to have to tell you this news. His death will be very greatly felt by the whole squadron, and especially by his friends in the Stortford Troop, with whom he was very popular. It will be some consolation to you to know how bravely he fell." *unm.*

(Panel 5) Pte. 1026, Cecil Hubert Cray Cattell, Machine Gun Section, 'B' Sqdn., Essex Yeomanry: *s.* of Henry Richard Trist Cattell, of 'Shencliffe,' 19, Leighton Avenue, Leigh-on-Sea, by his wife Maude Elsie, *née* Cray: *b.* West Ham, London, E.: *educ.* Southend Boy's High School: enlisted, 4 August 1914 (aged 15 years): trained Melton, co. Suffolk: served with the Expeditionary Force in France and Flanders attd. H.Q. Staff (Veterinary Officer's servant) from 1 December 1914. One of sixteen ORs to join Machine Gun Section, 7 May 1915; reported wounded and missing, 13 May 1915, following the charge east of Potijze, since confirmed killed in action on that date, Capt. E.A. Ruggles-Brise, in reply to a letter from Mr and Mrs Cattell wrote, "I very much regret to have to tell you that I fear there is no doubt whatever that your son was killed on May 13th as I have now ascertained that he was seen to be dead. I had no idea your son was so young but it may be of some consolation to you to know that he died fighting like a man and a soldier. Assuring you of my deepest sympathy in the terribly sad loss you have sustained." Age 16. (*IWGC record 14 May*)

(Panel 5) Pte. 1135, William Ewer Gardiner, Essex Yeomanry: eldest *s.* of William (& Charlotte Mary) Canning Gardiner, of Upper Yeldham Hall, Great Yeldham, co. Essex: served in France from December 1914; killed in action, 13 May 1915, in the front rank of a counter-attack nr. Wieltje, Ypres. Age 32.

(Panel 5) Tpr. 1269, Horatio Andrew David McTurk, Essex Yeomanry: *yst. s.* of Robert McTurk, Farmer; of Frieze Hall, South Weald, Brentwood, co. Essex, by his wife Janet, *dau.* of John Crawford, of Sproulston, co. Renfrew: *b.* Frieze Hall, 12 March 1896: *educ.* High School, Brentwood: enlisted September 1914; went to the Front, December 1914, and was killed in action at Ypres in the famous charge of the 8th Cavalry Brigade, the 10th Hussars, the Blues and the Essex Yeomanry, 13 May 1915. Age 19.

(Panel 5) Pte. 927, Hugh Miller, Essex Yeomanry: late of Epping, co. Essex: *s.* of Hugh Miller, of San Geronimo, La Cumbra, F.C.G., N.A., Cordoba, South America, by his wife Agnes: *b.* Belleville, Argentina, 1889: enlisted Abbey Farm 1913: on the outbreak of war, August 1914, was arranging to return to Argentina but opted to volunteer for Active Service with his regiment and went to France, serving with the Expeditionary Force there from 1 December 1914, and was recorded missing, believed killed by shellfire whilst digging trenches north of Hooge, 13–14 May 1915. Age 24. (*IWGC record age 19*)

(Panel 5) Pte. 989, Ernest John Petchey, Essex Yeomanry: *s.* of the late William J. Petchey, by his wife Laura (8, Princes Street, Maldon, co. Essex): and yr. brother to Pte. G/15658, W.H. Petchey, The Buffs (East Kent Regt.), died 30 September 1917, of wounds: *b.* Maldon: enlisted there. Killed in action, 13 May 1915. Age 17.

His brother William is buried in Dozinghem Military Cemetery (VIII.H.15).

(Panel 5) Pte. 805, William Roberts, 'A' Sqdn., Essex Yeomanry: late of Wickford, co. Essex: enlisted Brentwood: served with the Expeditionary Force in France from 1 December 1914. Killed by shellfire, 8 February 1915, whilst proceeding to Hooge with a party under 2nd Lieut. Buxton for the purpose of fetching ammunition and rations; nine other men were wounded. Essex Yeomanry's first fatality.

(Panel 5) Tpr. 956, Charles Taylor, Essex Yeomanry: *s.* of John Taylor, of Maypole Road, Tiptree, co. Essex, by his wife Maria: *b.* Tiptree, 1891: enlisted Maldon: served with the Expeditionary Force in France and Flanders, and was killed in action, 13–14 May 1915. Age 23. *unm.*

(Panel 5) Tpr. 977, James William Taylor, Essex Yeomanry: *s.* of Charles Taylor, of Bull Corner, Tiptree, co. Essex: *b.* Darcy, co. Essex, 1889: enlisted Maldon: served with the Expeditionary Force in France and Flanders, and was killed in action at Ypres, 13–14 May 1915. Age 25. He leaves a widow, Grace (Brew Office Row, Tiptree): *s.p.*

(Panel 5) Capt. Gerald Gadsden Fitze, 'C' Bty., Royal Horse Artillery: elder *s.* of the late Samuel Fitze, of Trevanion, Eastbourne, East India Merchant, by his wife Ada ('Kiln Meadow,' Kingsley Green, Haslemere, co. Surrey, late of 'Trehayne,' Ashburnham Road, Eastbourne), eldest *dau.* of the late John Stephens: *b.* 56, Kensington Park Road, London, W., 11 January 1886: *educ.* Lambrook, Bracknell; Marlborough, and Royal Military Academy, Woolwich: gazetted 2nd Lieut. R.A. 25 July 1906; promoted

Lieut. 25 July 1909; Capt., 30 October 1914 (gazetted posthumously): joined 31st Battery R.F.A. at Kilkenny, Ireland, January 1907: apptd. 'C' Battery R.H.A., 1912: went to France, 5 October 1914. Reported wounded and missing on, or about, 28 November following, and is now assumed to have been killed in action about that date, while reconnoitring at, or near, Zandvoorde (25 November 1914). Capt. Fitze's favourite recreation was hunting; he was a member of the Junior Army & Navy, and Marlborough Clubs. Age 28. *unm.* (*IWGC record 'Between 28th and 31st October 1914.'*)

(Panel 5) Lieut. Harry Llanover Davies, 'F' Bty., Royal Horse Artillery: *yst. s.* of the late Theophilus Harris Davies, of Craigside, Honolulu, and Tunbridge Wells, co. Kent, by his wife Mary Ellen: *b.* 29 January 1895: gazetted 2nd Lieut. R.H.A., 29 July 1904; promoted Lieut. 29 July 1907: served in the European War, and died, 26 October 1914, from wounds received in action. Age 29. Lieut. Davies leaves a widow, Barbara, *née* Childeroy (Woodmancote Place, Henfield, co. Sussex). (*IWGC record 25 October 1914*)

(Panel 5) Major George Baillie, 46th Bty., 39th Bde., Royal Field Artillery: *s.* of the late Capt. George Baillie, Bengal Artillery, Indian Army, and Mrs Baillie (Meonstoke, nr. Southampton, co. Hants): nephew to Major-General John Baillie, Bengal Staff Corps: *b.* Mhow, Central India, 23 November 1870: *educ.* Cheltenham College, and Royal Military Academy, Woolwich: joined Royal Artillery, 2nd Lieut. 25 July 1890; promoted Lieut. 25 July 1893; Capt. 13 February 1900; Major 15 April 1908: served in the South African War, November 1899–May 1902, firstly with 'P' Battery, Royal Horse Artillery, and then, on promotion to Capt. (1900), in flying columns with Pompom Section F: present at the Relief of Kimberley; took part in operations in Orange Free State, February–May 1900, including actions at Paardeberg (17–26 February) and Driefontein: also present at operations in Transvaal, May–June 1900, including the actions at Johannesburg and Diamond Hill (11–12 June): afterwards took part in further operations in the Transvaal, west of Pretoria, July–29 November 1900, and operations in Orange River Colony (July–29 November 1900), including the action at Wittebergen (1–29 July): present at subsequent operations in the Transvaal and Orange River Colony, 30 November 1900–31 May 1902: Queen's Medal, 6 clasps; King's Medal, 2 clasps: served with the Expeditionary Force in France and Flanders, and was killed in action nr. Ypres, 18 November 1914. Age 43. Of Major Baillie's death Col. Carey, Royal Field Artillery, wrote, "He was a most gallant soldier, and had always set such a good example to those about him for courage, and kindness, and thoughtfulness for others. I saw him only a few minutes before his death. We had been rather heavily shelled in our cottage, and he came down from his battery to see how we were. While we were talking the shelling began again, and we moved our headquarters to a safer place, while he walked away towards his battery, and was killed about 100 yards from the house. I am glad to think that he suffered no pain, as he was killed instantaneously. His death has caused a gap in the 39th Brigade which it will be impossible to fill. All the officers in the Brigade, and the men in his battery were devoted to him, and his loss is very keenly felt by all. He was always thinking of others, and what he could do to make things pleasant for everybody; to soldier with him was a real pleasure." A junior officer wrote, "He was beloved by everyone, Officers and men, and their grief was pitiable to behold when I returned to the battery, as I had been sent away at the time of the sad event." Major Baillie *m.* Louise Isabel (who died in childbirth, 6 December 1904), *dau.* of the late Major Phillipp, of Barham, Suffolk, and left a son, born, 6 December 1904.

(Panel 5) Capt. Sylvester Cecil Rait-Kerr, 22nd Trench Howitzer Battery, Royal Field Artillery: 2nd *s.* of Sylvester Rait-Kerr, of Rathmoyle, Edenderry, King's Co., Ireland, by his wife Mary, *dau.* of the late Major-General Charles Scrope Hutchinson, C.B., R.E.: and brother to Capt. W.C. Rait-Kerr, D.S.O., Royal Field Artillery, killed in action, 10 November 1914, at Veldhoek: *b.* Rathmoyle, 14 October 1887: *educ.* Arnold House, Llandulas, Rugby School, and Royal Military Academy, Woolwich: gazetted 2nd Lieut. R.F.A., 18 December 1907; promoted Lieut. 18 December 1910: went to South Africa, October 1910, with 100th Battery, R.F.A., afterwards proceeding to India: home on leave when war broke out: employed for some weeks training men in various places: promoted Capt. 30 October 1914: left for France with 'G' Battery, R.H.A., 6 November: subsequently transf'd. 41st Battery R.F.A. In April 1915 he was given the command of a Trench Howitzer Battery, with which he went into the trenches near Wieltje, 6 May, and was killed in action on the 13th, being shot through the head by a German sniper whilst carrying bombs to his guns. Buried in the trenches close to the spot where he fell. The General Officer Commanding 11th Infantry Brigade wrote, "I have been informed that you would like a few particulars of the gallant work done by your son and the 22nd Trench Mortar Battery while they were under me in the hard fighting of May 9 to 13, during the 2nd Battle of Ypres. Your son was posted in the trenches to the left of a building, named by the troops, 'Shelltrap Farm,' which was about the hottest part of the line, and his duty was to assist the infantry in keeping back the enemy from sapping up to the farm buildings, and to endeavour to blow in their saps. The enemy's shelling was so intense that time after time the trench mortars were silenced and the crews buried, but they were dug out and started on again, and they refused to be relieved. Cooke, the subaltern, was hit and his shoulder dislocated but he refused to go to hospital, and the whole battery displayed a similar spirit all through the fighting, the severity of which may be judged from the fact that Shelltrap Farm was lost and re-taken with the bayonet three times in twenty-four hours." And the General Officer Commanding the 4th Division, "I remember Rait-Kerr and his 22nd Trench Mortar Battery well. It was the best battery of that sort that we ever had with the 4th Division, and under him it did invaluable service in the front trenches during the fighting from the 6th to the 13th May (1915), which was some of the worst we had in France. I know he was a great loss to the Division and to the service." The officer in charge of the Trench Howitzer School, 2nd Army Corps, wrote, "He had done magnificently with his Trench battery and received the congratulations of the Divisional and Brigade commanders to whom his battery was attached. He was a great friend of mine, and without a doubt the finest officer who had passed through the Trench Howitzer School. There was no officer in the British Army who could have done it better. He was a gallant fellow. He was the ideal British officer, a real tiger with his men, but loved and admired by them. In this Army (the 2nd) he *made* trench howitzers. He was, of course, recommended for a decoration, and he richly deserved it." And the subaltern under him in his battery wrote, "His death was a great blow to all of us in the battery. He was a splendid fellow and did not know what fear was. He was recommended to General Commanding 4th Division for gallantry during the action by Officer Commanding the 2nd Monmouths, who told me he had upheld the best traditions of the Royal Artillery." Age 27. *unm.*

His brother William also has no known grave; he is recorded below.

(Panel 5) Capt. William Charles Rait-Kerr, D.S.O., 57th Howitzer Bty., Royal Field Artillery: eldest *s.* of Sylvester Rait-Kerr, of Rathmoyle, Edenderry, King's Co., Ireland, by his wife Mary, *dau.* of the late Major-General Charles Scrope Hutchinson, C.B., R.E.: and brother to Capt. R.C. Rait-Kerr, Royal Field Artillery, killed in action, 13 May 1915, nr. Shell Trap Farm, Wieltje: *b.* Rathmoyle, 6 August 1886: *educ.* Arnold House, Llandulas, Rugby School, and Royal Military Academy, Woolwich: gazetted 2nd Lieut. R.F.A. 23 July 1907; promoted Lieut. 23 July 1910; Capt. 30 October 1914: went to France, 16 August 1914, with 1st Division, Commanded by Sir Douglas Haig, as Lieut., 57th Howitzer Battery, 43rd Brigade, R.F.A.: took part in the Battle of, and retreat from, Mons, the Battles of the Marne and the Aisne, and the 1st Battle of Ypres, and was killed in action at Veldhoek, near Ypres, 10 November following whilst in charge of an advanced gun 250 yards from the enemy, being shot through the head by a German sniper. The rest of his battery had gone to the rear for rest and refit, having been out since the beginning of the war. Buried at Veldhoek beside the gun 'he had commanded so well.' He was awarded the D.S.O. 'For gallant conduct in bringing up a gun to within 250 yards of the enemy in a wood, and blowing down a house in which the enemy were working a machine-gun.' (*London Gazette*, 1 December 1914), and was Mentioned in F.M. Sir John (now Lord) French's Despatch (14 January 1915). His Colonel wrote, "He was in charge of a gun which had for some days been placed in a forward position for a special purpose, to destroy some houses from which some German snipers were causing heavy losses in our trenches. He had been doing splendid work which had been specially noticed by the General, and only the day before his death the Commander of the French troops on our left had sent a letter of thanks for one particularly useful lot of shooting which he had put in and destroyed some German trenches in front of them. He was a brave and excellent officer and man. He had just appeared in the Gazette as Capt. and was so delighted that I had been able to get him posted to one of my batteries." Another officer wrote, "He was up in the infantry trenches with one gun close behind, in communication by telephone with him. He was there about a fortnight, and in that time did very fine work, knocking houses down with Germans and machine-guns in them, and various other jobs. He was highly praised by all the people up there, and by the General in command of the Infantry Brigade. He had a very rough time from both shell and rifle fire, but had done great execution in spite of it." Age 28. *unm.*

His brother Sylvester also has no known grave; he is recorded above.

(Panel 5) Capt. Aubrey Ulick Marshall O'Brien, 39th Bde., Royal Field Artillery: *s.* of the late Edward William O'Brien, of Cahirmoyle, Ardagh, Co. Limerick, by his 2nd wife, Julia Mary, *née* Marshall: *b.* 7 June 1882: *educ.* Marlborough (Mitre) 1895–99: gazetted Royal Field Artillery from the Militia, December 1903: promoted Lieut. December 1906: passed out of the Royal Military Academy, Woolwich, 1900, for the Royal Engineers, but ill-health prevented him accepting his commission: after recovery, joined Limerick Militia, so as to enter the Army as he intended. One of a large number of Officers, Royal Field Artillery, to be promoted Capt. 30 October 1914, he was killed in action two days later, 1 November 1914. His brother, Mr Dermod O'Brien, is President of the Royal Hibernian Academy, and an honorary member of the Royal Academy. Age 32. *unm.* (*The Times*, 19 November 1914)

(Panel 5) Capt. the Hon. Lyon George Henry Lyon Playfair, 69th Bty., 31st Bde., Royal Field Artillery: only *s.* and heir of Brigdr.Gen. Lord George J. Playfair, of St. Andrews, and Redgrave Hall, co. Suffolk, C.V.O., T.D., 2nd Baron, by his wife Lady Augusta Mary Playfair, *dau.* of H.T. Hickman, Esq., J.P.: *b.* London, 19 October 1888: *educ.* St. Andrews, and Eton, from whence he passed into the Royal Military Academy, Woolwich: received his commission, December 1908, being posted 126th Battery, R.F.A., January 1909: promoted Lieut. December 1911; Capt. December 1914. Capt. Playfair was killed near Ypres, 20 April 1915, while acting as Observation Officer in a trench close the German lines. He was a member of the United Service Club. Age 26. *unm.*

(Panel 5) Capt. Charles Francis Ward, 75th Bty., Royal Field Artillery: only *s.* of Charles Ward, F.R.C.S., of Pietermaritzburg, and Dorothea Agnes, his wife: and *gdson.* of the late Capt. James Charles Yorke (*d.*1867), formerly 5th Dragoon Guards, and Georgina Augusta Yorke, *née* Hawkins (*d.*1886): *b.* 20 January 1884: *educ.* Aysgarth School; Marlborough College, and Royal Military Academy, Woolwich: gazetted 2nd Lieut. Royal Artillery, December 1903; promoted Lieut. December 1906; Capt. October 1914: served in South Africa and India with 85th Bty., and with B.B. Bty., Royal Horse Artillery: present at King Edward VII's Coronation, as a Cadet: King George V's, with B.B. Bty.: on the outbreak of war proceeded to the Continent with 75th Bty. Royal Field Artillery, and, as Advanced Observation Officer, 16 May 1915, he went forward to locate an enemy battery and was killed instantaneously by a sniper. He *m.* Marjorie, *dau.* of Mr (& Mrs) Billson, of Benoni, Transvaal, and left two daughters. He was a good polo player, and also played football. Age 31.

(Panel 5) Capt. Alfred James Woodhouse, 35th Bde. Royal Field Artillery: 2nd *survg. s.* of the late Robert H. Woodhouse, of 1, Hanover Square, London, W., and Mrs Woodhouse ('Ralsbury,' Ealing Common, London, W.): brother to Lieut. R.W. Woodhouse, who was killed in the South African War, and two other brothers who fell in the Great War – 2nd Lieut. G.S. Woodhouse, Royal Field Artillery, died of wounds, 14 October 1915; Pte. 1453, J.A.H. Woodhouse, Honourable Artillery Company, killed in action, 15 February 1915: *b.* 1 August 1886: *educ.* Cheltenham, and Royal Military Academy, Woolwich, where he became Senior Under Officer, and was awarded the Sword of Honour: gazetted 2nd Lieut. 23 July 1907: served two years at Eveshott, from whence he went to India: promoted Lieut. 23 July 1910: served with the Expeditionary Force in France and Flanders: promoted Capt. 30 October 1914, and was killed in action the same day. Age 28. At Cheltenham he was Head Prefect of the school, and captain of the Rifle Corps and Shooting VIII. During the whole of his time in India, outside of his military duties, he spent his time on shooting expeditions in the jungle, and brought home many specimens which sportsmen of longer experience would envy and prize. He *m.*, August 1914, Esther Margaret ('Womborne Cottage,' Speldhurst, co. Kent), *dau.* of Rev. A.C. Woodhouse, Rector of Winterborn, Monckton, co. Dorset. *s.p.*

His brother Gordon is buried in Sailly Labourse Communal Cemetery (L.5); Julian lies in Wytschaete Military Cemetery (II.F.6).

(Panel 5) Lieut. Gerald Henry Broadhurst, 52nd Bty., Royal Field Artillery: 2nd *s.* of Capt. Arthur Brooks Broadhurst, of Waterfoot, Penrith, 14th Hussars, by his wife Blanche, *dau.* of Capt. Robert Hawthorn-Stewart, late 93rd Highlanders & 13th Light Dragoons; Glasserton and Physgill Estates: *b.* The Anchorage, Ayr, 22 March 1892: *educ.* West Downs, Winchester (entered 1901); Winchester College, and Royal Military Academy, Woolwich (where he passed out fifth and won the Tombs Memorial Scholarship): gazetted 2nd Lieut. R.F.A., 23 December 1911 (awarded Aviators Certificate, Brooklands, 29 November 1913); promoted Lieut. March 1915: left for France, 17 August 1914, with 52nd Battery; severely wounded at Le Cateau on the 26th of that month and invalided home; returned to the Front, February 1915, posted to 103rd Battery, 28th Division, and served with this battery until 8 May following when he was reported "missing." His end was of a particularly gallant nature, and showed great devotion and self-sacrifice. He was forward observing officer, and saved many lives that day, but remained at his post too long to be able to save himself. According to a statement made by the German authorities, he fell mortally wounded and died as a prisoner of war in German hands, being buried on the spot. His Commanding Officer wrote, "It must be some consolation that, as his Battery Commander, I can assure you that no more gallant officer has fallen in this war than your son. He was chief support and helper in the most critical times that I have been through since I came out here, and his loss was a very serious one, not only to his battery, but for the whole of the Infantry in the section which we were holding, as it was through his reports and observations, which were maintained longer than any of the other batteries in our section, that we were able to inflict losses on the enemy, advancing in great superiority at this point, and to check them sufficiently long enough to enable reinforcements to come up. I had strongly recommended him for the Military Cross for his conspicuous gallantry and energy, and, indeed, I had told him of this the evening before he went out. Your son went out to observe fire during the engagements of May 8th, and has not been heard of since 11a.m. on that day, when telephonic communication between him and the battery broke. The situation was then very critical, and the enemy occupied the position where he was last seen." He was a good sportsman, and a good shot, but his chief delight was hunting, and he will be remembered both in Kildare and Warwickshire. He won the Kildare Hunt Heavy-weight Point to Point Race in the spring of 1914. Age 23. *unm.*

(Panel 5) Lieut. James Owen Cunninghame Dennis, 12th Bty., 35th Bde., Royal Field Artillery: only *s.* of the late Col. Dennis, 6th (Inniskilling) Dragoon Guards, and Mrs Dennis (Cumberland Mansions, London, W.): *b.* 5 August 1888: *educ.* Malvern College, 1903–07, where he was a school prefect, head of his house, in the Shooting VIII, 1906–07, and the House Football XI: entered Royal Military Academy, Woolwich, London, S.E., July 1909: gazetted 2nd Lieut. R.A. 23 July 1909; promoted Lieut. 23 July 1912: served in the European War, and was killed in action, 24 October 1914. The following account of the circumstances attending his death was published in *The Malvernian*, December 1914 – "Owen Dennis was killed by a shell when he was directing his battery's fire from the infantry trenches. His Major states that he considered him to be the smartest officer. Throughout the time that he was at the front he displayed unflinching bravery. This was quite in accordance with what we noted in him at school." Age 26.

(Panel 5) Lieut. Samuel Sanford Forsyth, 43rd (Trench Howitzer) Bty., Royal Field Artillery: 3rd *s.* of the late Lieut. Col. Frederick Arthur Forsyth; 5th Fusiliers, of 'Netherleigh,' Kenilworth Road, Lillington, by his wife Ellen, *née* Sanford ('Ashley House,' Lillington Avenue, Leamington Spa, co. Warwick): and brother to Lieut. Col. C.G. Forsyth, D.S.O., 2nd Northumberland Fusiliers attd. 6th Yorkshire Regt., killed in action, 14 September 1916; Lieut. (Adjt.) J.C. Forsyth, 23rd Bde. Royal Field Artillery, killed in action, 22 September 1914, at the Aisne; and Capt. (Brevet Major) F.R.G. Forsyth (surv'd.): *b.* Lillington, afsd., 1885. Killed in action, 25 September 1915. Age 30. Mentioned in Despatches for his services in the Great War. Another brother Arthur, Royal Norfolk Regt.; died in Camberwell, 1909.

His brother Cusack is buried in Blighty Valley Cemetery, Authuile Wood (I.F. 13); John is commemorated in Braine Communal Cemetery, Aisne (Sp.Mem.B.8/9).

(Panel 5) 2nd Lieut. James William Brown, 26th Bde., Royal Field Artillery: *b.* Upper Dean, co. Bedford, 26 May 1888: joined 117th Bty., Royal Field Artillery as Gunner 1907: obtained First Class Certificate 1909; passed through School of Gunnery, Shoeburyness, same year: served with the

Expeditionary Force in France and Flanders from 16 August 1914: gazetted 2nd Lieut. 25th Bde., Royal Field Artillery, 1 October 1914, and died in No.5 Field Hospital, 2 November following, from wounds received in action two days previously. Age 26. Lieut. Brown leaves a wife, Hetty M.H. Brown ('Avondale,' 10, St. Matthew's Drive, St. Leonards-on-Sea). (*IWGC record 26th Bde.*) Having previously served as a sergeant with the Royal Horse Artillery, at Poona, India, William Edgington had seen plenty of service prior to the outbreak of war. He had come over to France with the B.E.F., in August 1914, fought at the Battle of Mons and during the Retreat, and taken part in many subsequent actions. He had been twice promoted since First Ypres: Sergeant-Major in December and, moving from the Royal Horse Artillery to the Royal Field Artillery, became 2nd Lieut. in early April 1915. His rise to officer status was destined to be short-lived. On Monday, 1st May, 1915, he hastily wrote the following entry in his diary, "... Battle still going on. Hear all kinds of reports, both good and bad. Talk of falling back. I fully believe we have had a critical time which is not yet ended. The Huns do not appear to be short of Ammo by the way their shells are flying. I took my guns back about 2 miles, just out of Ypres, NE corner. No sleep now. Shells come from all directions, N-S and East, and also from the sky. We are evidently going to fall back after holding this line for 6 months. Hard lines." The following day he noted: "Our casualty list must be growing alarmingly. One continual stream of wounded being carried back along the roads, the dead being buried where they fall. When will it end?" For William it came six days later:-

(Panel 5) 2nd Lieut. William Edgington, 62nd Bty., Royal Field Artillery. Killed in action, 8 May 1915.

(Panel 5) 2nd Lieut. James Douglas Herbert Farmer, 9th Bty., 41st Bde., Royal Field Artillery: 2nd of the five sons of James Herbert Farmer, of 'Fairfield,' Mundesley, co. Norfolk, by his wife Edith Gertrude, *dau.* of the late Alderman Sir George Harris, J.P., L.C.C., and *gdson.* of the late James Farmer, of London and St. Andrew's, J.P.: *b.* 2 December 1892: *educ.* Colet Court; St. Paul's (Mr Cholmeley's House); Army College, Farnham, and Royal Military Academy, Woolwich: gazetted 2nd Lieut. R.F.A. July 1913, being posted 17th Battery, 41st Brigade, Bordon Camp: went to the Front with the Expeditionary Force, August 1914: there transf'd. 9th Battery, and was killed in action, 4 November 1914. Buried in the Chapel grounds at Eksternest (Westhoek), near Ypres. Age 21. *unm.* Keen on all games, he played football for the Aldershot command, and occasionally cricket and football for his School XI and XV. Three of his brothers are on active service – 2nd Lieut. F.S.H. Farmer, 3rd Norfolks; Sub. Lieut. L.G.H. Farmer, R.N.; and 2nd Lieut. C.R.H. Farmer, 18th Hussars.

(Panel 5) 2nd Lieut. Reginald William Fletcher, 118th Bty., 26th Bde., Royal Field Artillery: *yst. s.* of C.R.L. Fletcher, of Norham End, Oxford, by his wife Katherine: *b.* 19 March 1892: *educ.* Eton (scholar), 1905–1910, and Balliol College, Oxford (commoner), 1910–1914: graduated B.A. (member University O.T.C. – Artillery Section); rowed in the Leander IV, Henley Regatta, 1913; Oxford University VIII, 1914; also for some years stroke of his college boat: gazetted 2nd Lieut. Royal Artillery, December 1912: served with the Expeditionary Force in France and Flanders, and was killed in action at the First Battle of Ypres, 31 October 1914. Age 22. *unm.*

(Panel 5) 2nd Lieut. John Lewis Milner, 62nd Bty., 8th Bde. Royal Field Artillery: *s.* of John William Milner, of 'Armadale,' Penkett Road, Wallasey, co. Chester, by his wife Annie. Killed in action, 9 May 1915. Age 23. *unm.* Remains recovered 'Small Battle Cemetery Sanctuary Wood,' unmarked grave 'Unknown British Officer. Artillery;' identified – Officers Clothing, Officers Collar Badge, Button;' reinterred, registered, 1 March 1928. *Buried in Sanctuary Wood Cemetery (II.D.12).*

(Panel 5) 2nd Lieut. John Collett Tyler, 122nd Bty., Royal Field Artillery: *yr. s.* of Col. John Charles Tyler, of 8, Cambridge Road, Colchester, late Royal Engineers, by his wife Florence Mary, only *dau.* of the late General Sir Alexander Robert Badcock, K.C.B., C.S.I., and *gdson.* of the late Sir Henry Whateley Tyler, M.P., and great-*gdson.* of General Sir Charles Pasley, K.C.B., R.E. (the father of Lady Tyler), who founded the School of Military Engineering at Chatham, and who, in early life, was extra A.D.C. to Sir John Moore at the time of his death and burial at Corunna: *b.* Roorkee, India, 9 December 1893: *educ.* Wellington College, Crowthorne, co. Berks, where he was head of the school and captain of football, and the Royal Military Academy, Woolwich, where he was Senior under-officer and obtained the Sword of Honour, July 1914, the Commandant on that occasion observing that he would specially mention Senior under-officer J.C. Tyler who had shown in his present responsible position that he possessed in a high degree those qualities which were looked for in the best type of officer: gazetted 2nd Lieut. R.F.A., 17 July 1914; joined at Woolwich, 9 August 1914, left for Dundalk, Ireland, on the 10th, and embarked for France on the 17th, and was killed in action at Hill 60, 18 April 1915. On 21 April the Major commanding his battery wrote, "There is a big battle going on here now which started at 7 p.m. on the 17th. John and I went forward that day to observe. I had to send John and a signaller on by night to the newly captured trench to let me know if the Germans were counter-attacking and to observe by day. This job he did in his usual gallant way. Three times he came back to me under heavy fire and great difficulties to mend the telephone wires. He was shot at dawn, a rifle bullet clean through the forehead. He died as he lived, doing his duty gallantly and well. Had he lived he would certainly have had the D.S.O. He was killed in the foremost trench captured from the Germans. Just after he was killed the Germans retook the trench and held it for about 12 hours. We then took it back again." And the General Officer Commanding wrote a few days later, "I had already sent in his name for good service. His cheery gallant example was worth everything at these times." Age 21. *unm.* (*IWGC record 12 April 1915*)

(Panel 5) Sergt.Major, W.O.I, 68888, John Lawrence Moloney, 22nd Bde., Royal Field Artillery: *s.* of Michael Moloney, Sergt. Sussex Regt., by his wife Mary: *b.* Chichester, co. Sussex, 17 June 1873: enlisted 24 September 1888: served in the South African War (wounded at Lindley: Queen's Medal, two clasps); and with 7th Division of the Expeditionary Force in France and Flanders from 5 October 1914. Killed in action nr. Gheluvelt, Belgium, 29 October following. An officer wrote, "We were in a position near the village of Gheluvelt and were being heavily shelled. The Brigade Staff horses were in a farm shed behind our position and, as a shell set it on fire, Mr Moloney ordered the horses to be taken out. He saw all safely out and led out the last one himself. Before he was ten yards away from the building, another shell burst near him killing him almost instantly. As you will see from this, he died doing his duty; he is buried near where he fell, and the spot is marked by a cross bearing his name. You have all our sympathy, and his loss was deeply felt by all ranks." Age 41. Sergt.Major Moloney was an all-round sportsman and had won many cups and medals for riding and jumping, tent pegging and shooting. He had the Silver Medal for best Man-at-Arms, Bombay Army, won at Poona, 1903, and was for many years a successful competitor at the London Military Tournament. He had the Good Conduct Medal. He *m.* Wimborne, co. Dorset, 17 January 1905; Janet Christine (14, New Boro', Wimborne), twin *dau.* of Samuel (& Isabella) Foster, of Holmleigh, Wimborne: *s.p.* (*IWGC record Regimental Sergt. Major*)

(Panel 5) Sergt. 41567, Basil Gwynne Griffiths, 56th Bty., Royal Field Artillery: *s.* of Isaac Griffiths, D.C.M., Quartermaster-Sergt. (W.O.), Welsh Regt. (served in the Boer War; South Wales Borderers; Mentioned in Despatches; awarded Distinguished Conduct Medal), by his wife Sarah Ann, *dau.* of Martin Walsh, Farmer; of Kilrane, Co. Wexford: *b.* Aldershot, 16 January 1892: *educ.* Intermediate School, and Christ's College, Brecon: enlisted January 1906 (aged 14 years): promoted Sergt., August 1914: went to France, August 1914, and was killed in the fighting around Hooge, nr. Ypres, 3 November 1914. Major B. Crozier, commanding 56th Battery R.F.A., wrote, "He was killed while in charge of his gun, and was buried by his comrades the same evening at the same spot as three other men of his battery, at the edge of a wood about 800 yards south of the village of Eksternest, Westhoek Ridge. I served with him previously, in the 47th Battery, and had a great regard for him. He did well while out here and will be a great loss to the battery he served so well. He was always so cheery and helped to cheer many when depressed." Sergt. Griffiths was an expert 'Rough-Rider,' swimmer and boxer. Age 22. *unm.* (*IWGC record 4 November 1914*)

(Panel 5) Corpl. 94166, Charles Sheffield, 1st Bty., 45th Bde., Royal Field Artillery: *s.* of George F. Sheffield, of Spring Hill, Enstone, co. Oxford, and his wife Mary E.: and yr. brother to Gnr. 59065, F. Sheffield, 100th Bde., Royal Field Artillery, died 18 September 1915, aged 21 years: *b.* Enstone: enlisted there. Killed in action, 15 August 1917. Age 20. Remembered on Enstone (St. Kenelm) Parish Church Roll of Honour.

His brother Frank also has no known grave; he is commemorated on the Thiepval Memorial, Somme.

(Panel 5) Gnr. 810715, Archibald Adamson, 'B' Bty., 232nd Bde., Royal Field Artillery: *s.* of Robert Adamson, of Garfield, Cardross, co. Dumbarton: and brother to Corpl. S/11312, T. Adamson, 2nd Cameron Highlanders, killed in action, 11 May 1915, at Ypres: *b.* Cardross: enlisted Derby: went to France and was killed in action there, 30 July 1917. The brothers Adamson are remembered on Cardross (Dumbarton; Helensburgh District) War Memorial.

His brother Thomas also has no known grave; he is recorded on Panel 38.

(Panel 5) Gnr. 74210, David John Austin, 51st Bty., Royal Field Artillery: *s.* of G.J.W. Austin, of 103, Old Woolwich Road, Greenwich, London, S.E.10, by his wife Mary Jane: *b.* Greenwich, 1895: enlisted Woolwich, London, S.E.18. Killed in action, 20 November 1914. Age 19. Remains 'Unknown British Soldier' recovered unmarked collective grave (28.J.13.c.5.2); refers GRU Report, Zillebeke 5-52E; identified – Clothing, Pack Strap mkd. 13–123, R.F.A.; reinterred, registered, 28 March 1927. *Buried in Sanctuary Wood Cemetery (III.H.27/34).*

(Panel 5) A/Bmdr. 52519, George Bourne, 367th Bty. Royal Field Artillery: *s.* of Henry Bourne, of Droitwich, co. Worcester: *b.* Droitwich. Killed in action, 2 May 1915. Age 25. *Buried in Roulers Communal Cemetery (II.D.1).*

(Panel 5) Bmdr. 55752, Lawrence Eade, 51st Bty., Royal Field Artillery: *s.* of Alfred Eade, of 'The Home of Rest,' Graffham, nr. Midhurst, co. Sussex, by his wife Georgina: and elder brother to Gnr. 75431, V.C. Eade, 51st Bty., who fell the same day: *b.* Havant, *c.*1890: enlisted Petworth, co. Hants: killed in action, 20 November 1914. Age 24. Bmdr. Eade leaves a widow, Ethel (35, Durdham Street, Benwell, Newcastle-on-Tyne). Remains recovered unmarked collective grave (28.J.13.c.5.2); refers GRU Report, Zillebeke 5-52E; 'These remains were buried in blankets, fastened with puttees, and are evidently men of a gun team;' identified – Clothing, Disc; reinterred, registered, 28 March 1927. *Buried in Sanctuary Wood Cemetery (III.H.27).*

At The Going Down Of The Sun
And In The Morning We Will Remember Them

His brother Victor is recorded below.

(Panel 5) Bmdr. 98677, John McDonald, 'C' Bty., 79th Bde., Royal Field Artillery: *s.* of the late John McDonald, by his wife Elizabeth (16, Mackeson Road, Hampstead, London). Killed in action, 16 November 1915. Age 18. Remains 'Three Unknown British Soldiers' recovered, unmarked collective grave (28.I.3.c.30.65); identified – Clothing, Titles; 'Impossible to separate remains – J. McDonald, RFA; J. Kershaw, RGA; Unknown British Sergt. – which were found together in one small grave.' Reinterred 12 December 1930. *Buried in Strand Military Cemetery (VII.A.35/37).*

(Panel 5) Gnr. 17688, John Edwin Cornish, 51st Bty., Royal Field Artillery: *b.* Birmingham, co. Warwick, 18 November 1884: *educ.* there: served some years with the Colours, thereafter joined the Reserve: called up on the outbreak of war, 4 August 1914: served with the Expeditionary Force in France and Flanders, and was killed in action at Ypres, 18 November 1914; his thirtieth birthday. He was married to Florence (19, Lune Street, Barnsley, co. York), and had three children.

(Panel 5) Gnr. 11053, Harry Dewhirst, 109th Bty., 231st Bde., Royal Field Artillery: *s.* of Albert E. Dewhirst, of 21, Upper Bolton Street, Bradford, co. York, by his wife Ada: enlisted Bradford. Died of wounds, 15 August 1917. Age 23. *unm. Buried in Sanctuary Wood Cemetery (V.F.27).*

(Panel 5) Gnr. 75431, Victor Charles Eade, 51st Bty., Royal Field Artillery: *s.* of Alfred Eade, of 'The Home of Rest,' Graffham, nr. Midhurst, co. Sussex, by his wife Georgina: and *yr.* brother to Bmdr. 55752, L. Eade, 51st Bty., who fell the same day: *b.* Emsworth, *c.*1896: enlisted Petworth, co. Hants: killed in action, 20 November 1914. Age 18. Remains recovered unmarked collective grave (28.J.13.c.5.2); refers GRU Report, Zillebeke 5-52E; 'These remains were buried in blankets, fastened with puttees, and are evidently men of a gun team;' identified – Clothing, Boots mkd.75431; reinterred, registered, 28 March 1927. *Buried in Sanctuary Wood Cemetery (III.H.34).*

God Grant Him Peace And Rest

His brother Lawrence is recorded above.

(Panel 5) Dvr. 72600, Richard Dyet, 30th Bty., Royal Field Artillery: resident with his mother at Corsehill, Kilwinning, co. Ayr: served with the Expeditionary Force. Killed in action, 1 November 1914. Age 19.

(Panel 5) Gnr. 25776, Arthur William Hall, 128th Bty. Royal Field Artillery: *s.* of Mrs W. Corps, *née* Hall ('Ivelle,' Baynards, co. Sussex): late *husb.* to Sarah Honor Wills-Hall (30, Horsford Street, The Nothe, Weymouth): *b.* Petworth, co. Sussex: enlisted Aldershot. Died of wounds, 19 September 1914. Age 30. One of two earliest dated casualties recorded on the Menin Gate. See also Tpr J. Black, 1st Life Guards (Panel 3).

(Panel 5) Gnr. 72304, Arthur George Harding, 51st Bty., Royal Field Artillery: *s.* of Henry James Harding, of 56, Winchester Road, Shirley, Southampton, by his wife Elizabeth Jane: *b.* Cowes, Isle of Wight, 1894: enlisted Southampton. Killed in action, 20 November 1914. Age 20. *unm.* Remains 'Unknown British Soldier' recovered unmarked collective grave (28.J.13.c.5.2); refers GRU Report, Zillebeke 5–52E; identified – Clothing, Boots mkd. x.1914, R.F.A.; reinterred, registered, 28 March 1927. *Buried in Sanctuary Wood Cemetery (III.H.27/34).*

(Panel 5) Sdlr. 38151, James Hawkins, 51st Bty., Royal Field Artillery: late *husb.* to Daisy L. Tustain, *née* Hawkins (12, 'F' Block, Blackdown, co. Hants): *b.* Waltham Abbey, co. Essex, 1887: enlisted London. Killed in action, 20 November 1914. Age 27. Remains recovered unmarked collective grave (28.J.13.c.5.2); refers GRU Report, Zillebeke 5–52E; identified – Clothing, 2 G.C. Badges, Saddler's Badge, Gun Layer's Badge; reinterred, registered, 28 March 1927. *Buried in Sanctuary Wood Cemetery (III.H.27/34).*

(Panel 5) Dvr. 9673, Horace Walter Hogg, 57th Bty., 45th Bde., Royal Field Artillery: *s.* of Charles Nathaniel Hogg, of 16, Crusoe Road, Mitcham, co. Surrey, by his wife Ellen: and elder brother to Pte. 3337, E.F. Hogg, Royal Fusiliers, who fell 10 May 1915, near Rue Petillon: *b.* Battersea, London, S.W., 1891: enlisted Kingston-on-Thames: served with the Expeditionary Force in France and Flanders, and was killed in action, 20 June 1917. Age 26. *unm.*

His brother Ernest also has no known grave; he is recorded on the Ploegsteert Memorial (Panel 10).

(Panel 5) Gnr. 62761, Albion William Newman, 51st Bty., Royal Field Artillery: *s.* of Mrs M.A. Newman (5, Rupert Road, Upper Holloway, London, N.19): *b.* Hoxton, London, N.1, 1892. Killed in action, 20 November 1914. Age 22. *unm.* Remains 'Unknown British Soldier' recovered unmarked collective grave (28.J.13.c.5.2); refers GRU Report, Zillebeke 5–52E; 'These remains were buried in blankets, fastened with puttees, and are evidently men of a gun team;' identified – Clothing, Boots mkd. J.1914; reinterred, registered, 28 March 1927. *Buried in Sanctuary Wood Cemetery (III.H.27/34).*

(Panel 5) Gnr. 110213, Harold Victor Randall, 'B' Bty., 71st Bde., Royal Field Artillery: *s.* of Mrs Blanchard, *née* Randall (52, Allestree Road, Fulham, London): *b.* Fulham: enlisted Battersea. Killed in action, 31 July 1917. Age 20. *unm.* His father and four brothers also served, one of whom fell.

(Panel 5) Dvr. 73164, Albert Woodey, 47th Bty., 44th Bde., Royal Field Artillery: *s.* of John Woodey, of Shortwood Lane, Mangotsfield, Bristol, by his wife Sarah: and yr. brother to L/Stoker SS/111381, F. Woodey, H.M.S. 'Anchusa,' Royal Navy, lost at sea, 16 July 1918, when that ship was sunk off the coast of Ireland by U.54: *b.* Mangotsfield, afsd.: enlisted Bristol. Killed in action, 1 November 1914. Age 18. With no known grave but the sea, his brother Frank is commemorated on the Plymouth Naval Memorial (28).

PANEL 5 ENDS: GNR. C.A. WRIGHT, R.H.A. & R.F.A.

PANEL 7 BEGINS: LT. R.H. NEAVERSON, AUSTRALIAN LIGHT HORSE

Australia Answers

They come from the distant stations, bushmen bold and free,
The silent men of our silent land, knights of the saddle tree.
They come from the rush of the gold mines, steady and strong and true –
Sons of the Southland, one and all, ready to see it through.

They leave the desk in the city, they come from the survey camp,
The pearling boat on the north coast, the garden by the swamp.
From every part of the country, from every sphere of life,
Eager they come to the training camps, longing to join the strife.

Winifred May

(Panel 7) Lieut. Keith Harrison George, 1st Bde. Australian Field Artillery, A.I.F.: *s.* of William Henry Harrison George, Economic Store Proprietor (Wellington & Melbourne); of 'Hillsborough,' Kelburn, Wellington, New Zealand; by his wife Esther Bell George: and brother to Capt. W.S. George, R.A.M.C. (surv'd.); Lieut. D. George, R.F.C. (surv'd): *b.* Bairnsdale, Victoria, 1890: Religion – Baptist: Occupation – Warehouseman: 5'8¼" tall, fresh complexion, blue eyes, brown hair: previously served 3 yrs., N.Z.F.A. (dischgd. on removal to Australia): joined A.I.F., St. Kilda, 15 August 1914; apptd. Sergt., No.1298, 2nd Field Artillery Bde. Ammunition Column, Broadmeadows Camp, 31 August 1914: departed Melbourne, 19 October 1914: joined Mediterranean Expeditionary Force, Gallipoli, 5 April 1915: transf'd. Rest Camp, Embros, 7 July: promoted Bty.Sergt.Major, 5 August 1915: apptd. 2nd Lieut., 16 August (In the Field); transf'd. 1st Bde. 28 August, joined 1st Bty., 9 October: admitted Field Ambulance, Anzac (jaundice), 6 November; transf'd. hospitalised Malta, 12 November; transf'd. All Saints Convalescent Camp, 3 December; promoted Lieut., 8 December; dischgd. to duty/proceeded to Egypt, 30 December 1915: rejoined 1st Bde., Tel-el-Kebir, 6 January 1916: proceeded to join Expeditionary Force, France, 21 March; disembarked Marseilles, 27 March: killed in action at 1st Battery Officers Mess Dugout position, Montauban, in the early morning of 7 November 1916; 1st and 2nd Bty. positions being subject to a rapid German 18 and 10.5 cm. artillery bombardment. Age 26. Mentioned in Sir Douglas Haig's Despatch, 13 November 1916 (*London Gazette*, No.2890, 2 January 1917) for 'distinguished and gallant services and devotion to duty in the field.' Buried Battery Position, East of Flers, Bancourt L'Abbaye Road (57.M.36.b.3.9). His Forms of Commission (2nd Lieut./Lieut.); 1914–1915 Star, British War & Victory medal (Oak Leaf attd.), Memorial Plaque & Scroll, M.i.D. Certificate were received by his father, 9 October 1919–28 December 1922. Booklet *Where The Australians Rest*, forwarded 24 December 1920. *Details re. this casualty dictate commemoration on the Villers-Bretonneux Memorial.*

Lieut. I.C. Bromilow – severely wounded ('leg and arm blown off') by the same shell burst – died shortly thereafter. Buried Bernafay Wood British Cemetery, Montauban (H.37).

(Panel 7) 2nd Lieut. Cyril Linton Verso, 4th Bde., Australian Field Artillery, A.I.F.: only *s.* of the Rev. Canon Jacob Verso, Th.L., of St. Arden's Vicarage, Berrigan, New South Wales, by his wife Florence Hill: *b.* Hillston, New South Wales, 5 July 1890: *educ.* Sydney High School, Ultimo: Occupation – Licensed Surveyor; New South Wales Land Dept.: joined Australian Artillery, August 1915: came to England with a contingent January 1916; served with the Expeditionary Force in France and Flanders from March following, and was killed in action on the Menin Road, 19 September 1917. Buried where he fell. Age 27. He *m.* Christ Church Cathedral, Grafton, New South Wales, 16 September 1915; Myrel Trefusis ('Begelle,' Villier Street, Grafton), *dau.* of Thomas Trefusis Bawden, and had a son, Murray Linton, *b.* 1 October 1916.

(Panel 7) Corpl. 10338, George Finlayson Boyd, 12th Bde., Australian Field Artillery, A.I.F.: *s.* of the late George Gordon Boyd, Shoemaker; of Lochland Street, Arbroath, Scotland, by his wife Helen Lundie (48, Hayburn Street, Partick, Glasgow), *dau.* of the late William Finlayson: *b.* Arbroath, 5 June 1886: *educ.*

Keptle School: went to Australia, 1912, where he was employed by Messrs W.D. Grant & Sons, Engineers, Equitable Place, Collins Street, Melbourne: enlisted 16 July 1915: served with the Expeditionary Force in Egypt (from January 1916); thereafter France and Flanders: wounded and gassed, 3 June 1917; invalided home: returned to France on recovery, rejoined his unit, and was killed in action, 24 September 1917, by a shell whilst asleep in his dug-out. Buried at Dickebusch. A comrade wrote, "Dear old George was killed early on the morning of 24 September by the bursting of an enemy shell while asleep in his dug-out. When the news went round it spread a gloom over the whole battery, as he was a great favourite with the men. All the boys in the battery wish me to convey to you their deepest sympathy in the great loss you have sustained in the death of your noble son and my hero friend." And his Sergt., "I can hardly yet realise that dear old George is gone. He was the life and soul of the Battery, and all the boys join with me in sending deepest sympathy to you in the loss of your noble son and my heroic friend." Age 31. He was married to Helen Carrie (36, John Street, Arbroath)

(Panel 7) Corpl. 11053, Alfred Cecil Dingle, 37th Bty., 10th Bde., Australian Field Artillery, A.I.F.: *s*. of Thomas Dingle, of 201, Albany Street, Gloucester Gate, Regent's Park, London: *b*. Plymouth, co. Devon, England, 1888: Occupation – Ship's Purser: enlisted Holsworthy, New South Wales, 21 September 1915; posted Gnr., 14th Rfts, 3rd Artillery Bde., 9 December: trained Egypt; transf'd. 10th Bde., 5 June. (apptd. Temp. Bmdr.); served in France from the 13th. of that month: apptd. Temp. Corpl., 27 May 1917. Killed in action on the morning of 14 October 1917 when, while taking breakfast in the gun pit, 'a shell came over and blew his left arm off.' Buried beside a pill-box nr. 37th Bty. position, Bellewaarde Ridge, nr. Ypres, Belgium. Age 29. *unm*. On the day prior to his death, Corpl. Dingle remarked to a comrade, "It's a funny thing how all the best men get killed. I suppose it will be my turn next." Recorded as Bmdr. in his service record at the time of his death; 'Acting rank not upheld, proceedings irregular' – posthumously amended (dated 14 October) Temp.Corpl.

On 15 December 1921, Rose Benjamin wrote to the Australian Graves Registration Service requesting details regarding the burial place of Gnr. M.D. Benjamin, her son. She received the following reply – "31 December 1921. Dear Madam, With reference to your letter…I regret to inform you that although a very thorough search of the Zillebeke area has been made by exhumation parties employed by the War Office it has not been possible to find and identify your son's remains. I regret very much that I am unable to offer you any more satisfactory information but the Zillebeke area during September and October 1917 was the scene of very fierce fighting which resulted in the obliteration of a large number of grave markings and even in the destruction of the graves themselves. This would probably account for your having received no burial information in connection with your son…." An interval of twelve years followed before Mrs Benjamin received the information she longed for. Four other families were similarly informed.

(Panel 7) Gnr. 32061, Maurice Duncan Benjamin, 14th Bty., 5th Bde., Australian Field Artillery, A.I.F.: *s*. of David Benjamin, of 'Kalbar,' Windermere Road, Hamilton, Brisbane, by his wife Rose Stanley: *b*. Southport, Queensland, 1886: Occupation – Bank-Teller: enlisted Royal Agricultural Showground, Sydney, 8 October 1916; posted 10th Rfts., 22nd Field Artillery Bde.: departed Australia, RMS 'Osterley,' 8 February 1917: served with the Expeditionary Force in France from 9 August; joined 14th Bty. 18 August, and was killed in action, 26 August 1917. Buried 2½ miles S.E. of Ypres. Age 30. *unm*. His parents received his Memorial Plaque, Scroll, British War and Victory medals June 1921–May 1923. Remains 'Unknown Australian Soldier' (five) recovered (28.I.29.b.20.25) unmarked grave; identified – Australian Clothing, Boots; reinterred, registered, 24 December 1931; family notified, January 1933. *Buried in Sanctuary Wood Cemetery (V.S.1/5)*. See Gnr. N.R. Cox, below.

Spes Tutissima Caelis

(Panel 7) Gnr. 4516, John Maurice Orr Colahan, 14th Bty., 5th Bde., Australian Field Artillery, AI.F.: 2nd *s*. of Surgeon-Major-General John Colahan, of Kangatong, East St. Kilda, Victoria, Australia, by his wife Elizabeth Newton Orr ('Eno'), *dau*. of F. (& Mary) McDowell Orr: *b*. Kenilworth, South Africa, 17 February 1894: *educ*. Christian Brothers' College, St. Kilda, and Melbourne University: Occupation – Law Student: enlisted 29th Battn., 8th Infantry Brigade, Australian Imperial Force, 9 March 1916:

proceeded to England, and passed for a commission, but by his own wish transferred to the Artillery: served with the Expeditionary Force in France and Flanders from May 1917: wounded July following; rejoined his battery September; killed in action at Passchendaele Ridge, 14 October 1917. Buried on the bank of the Hannebeek stream, east of the Westhoek Ridge. Age 23. His Commanding Officer wrote, "A fine gunner, a brave soldier, beloved and mourned by officers and men." He *m.* Mornington, Victoria, 23 March 1916; Martha Eleanor de B. Whitehouse, *née* Colahan ('Telok,' Anson, Perak, Federated Malay States), *yst. dau.* of the late Thomas Fogarty, of Melbourne. *s.p.*

Fifteen and a half years after her husband was killed in action, Violet Michie, *née* Cox received the following letter: "16 January 1933. Dear Madam, with further reference to the regrettable loss of the late No.12366, Gunner N.R. Cox, 5th Field Artillery Brigade. I am now in receipt of advice from the Imperial War Graves Commission that during the course of exhumation work in Belgium a grave containing five unknown Australian soldiers was discovered just north of Hill 60. By means of certain regimental titles and 2nd Australian Divisional signs found at the time, and an examination of the Commission's records, it has been established that the remains in question are those of the above named soldier and four of his comrades of the 14th Battery 5th Field Artillery Brigade, who were reported killed in action in August 1917. In keeping with the usual practice of concentrating all isolated burials in established military cemeteries under British control, the remains of these fallen have since been exhumed and re-interred with every measure of care and reverence in Graves 1–5, Plot 5, Row 'S' of Sanctuary Wood Cemetery, situated near Zillebeke, Belgium where permanent headstones of uniform design will be erected and engraved with their full regimental particulars and date of death, together with any verse or epitaph previously selected in the form of a personal inscription. It is noted that the names of these soldiers were formerly shown among those commemorated on the Memorial to the Missing at Menin Gate, Ypres. Steps will now be taken to add their names to the list of burials in Sanctuary Wood Cemetery for inclusion in the Register proper."

(Panel 7) Gnr. 12366, Norman Ronald Cox, 14th Bty., 5th Bde., Australian Field Artillery, A.I.F.: *s.* of Mrs M. Cox (36, Gerrard Street, Alexandria, New South Wales): *b.* Bury Street, Brisbane, Queensland, 21 February 1892: Occupation – Labourer: previously rejected 'Medically Unfit;' joined A.I.F., Marybyrnong, Victoria, 4 February 1915; posted Tpr.(No.836), 'F' Sqdn., Light Horse, Broadmeadows: transf'd. 2nd Field Artillery Bde., 1 December: departed Australia, 28 January 1916: served with the Expeditionary Force in France from 3 April following: Awarded (24 April) 7 Days, C.B., for (1) Causing a disturbance after lights out, (2) Using obscene language: Tried by F.G.C.M. (16 May 1916), for (1) Absenting himself without leave from billets, Grand-sec-Bois, 14.30–21.00, 4 May. (2) An act prejudicial to good order and military discipline in that he at Grand-sec-Bois, on or about 4 May, was jointly, with Gnr. A.H. Kirk, 2nd D.A.C., wrongly in possession of certain goods, to wit, 1 Blanket, 1 Waterbottle and 1 Haversack, to which he was not entitled. Awarded 90 Days Field Punishment No.1; Forfeiture 103 Day's pay (1 Day A.W.O.L., 90 Days F.P.No.1, 12 Days Awaiting trial): hospitalised Defective Vision, 6 July: returned to duty 18 July; transf'd. 14th Bty., 27 January 1917: hospitalised, sick (P.U.O. – Pyrexia, Unknown Origin – 'Trench-fever') 14 April; discharged to duty 29 June: rejoined 14th Bty., 2 August, and was killed in action, 5 August 1917. He was married to Violet Michie, *née* Cox, *née* Falkingham (19, Nott Street, Port Melbourne, Victoria), and had a son, Jonathan N.R. Cox. Remains recovered 1931; identified, registered, reinterred; next of kin notified, 16 January 1933. *Buried in Sanctuary Wood Cemetery (V.S.1/5).*

(Panel 7) Gnr. 26176, John Leonard Herbert Lamb, 14th Bty., 5th Bde., Australian Field Artillery, A.I.F.: *s.* of John Clark Lamb, of Eastbourne Terrace, Paddington, South Australia, by his wife Mary, *née* George: *b.* Port Adelaide, *c.*1895: enlisted Adelaide, 7 January 1916: departed Melbourne, 1 August: proceeded to France, 25 February 1917: joined 14th Bty. In the Field, 14 March: hospitalised (Debility) 6 July; discharged to duty 14 July: rejoined 14th Bty. on the 29th of the latter month and was killed in action, 5 August 1917. Age 22. *unm.* Buried 2 ½ miles S.E. of Ypres; remains recovered 1931, reinterred; family notified, January 1933. *Buried in Sanctuary Wood Cemetery (V.S.1/5).*

Sacred Heart Of Jesus Have Mercy On His Soul
R.I.P.

(Panel 7) Gnr. 3369, John Patrick O'Neill, M.M., 3rd Bty., 1st Bde., Australian Field Artillery, A.I.F.: *s.* of Charles O'Neill, of 'Bethany,' Sebastopol Street, Marrickville, New South Wales, by his wife Catherine (109, Macaulay Road, Stanmore, Sydney), c/o Post Office, Queanbeyan: and brother to Tpr. 1263, C.B. O'Neill, 1st Australian Light Horse (surv'd.); Dvr. 9957, W.E. O'Neill, 1st Bde., Australian Field Artillery (surv'd.); and Pte. 7367, F.J. O'Neill, 13th Bn. Australian Infantry, who joined up at 16 years of age (surv'd.): *b.* Marrickville, 1894: Religion – Roman Catholic: Occupation – Labourer: 5′3½″ tall, fair complexion, blue eyes, light brown hair: previously rejected by both the Militia and Regular services "too small;" enlisted Holdsworthy, 2 November 1915, posted 7th Rfts., 18th Battn. (22 November): transf'd. 3rd Battn. 14 February 1916 (Egypt): served with the Expeditionary Force in France and Flanders from 28 March 1916: transf'd. 21st Bde. Field Artillery, 26 September 1916: hospitalised (Trench Foot) France (2–20 December 1916), King Edward Hospital, England (21 December–27 January 1917): discharged to leave and, on return (15 February), underwent a course of retraining and instruction, Perham Downs, Wareham, Hurdcott, Larkhill: returned to France, 8 August, transf'd. 1st Bde. one week later, and was killed in action, 16 October 1917. Age 23. *unm.* (Actg./Adjt.) Lieut. C.J. Gates, 1st Bde., wrote, "…killed in action at about 9 pm. on 16.10.17. The 3rd Battery of which he was a member was firing in response to a 'S.O.S.' call when the enemy scored a direct hit on No.2 gun with a 5.9 shell. Gunner O'Neill was hit in two places, head and chest, resulting in his being killed instantly. He was carried out about 200 yards in rear of the battery position (Sheet 28: J.7.c.42.56) 500 yards SW of Westhoek, where he was buried by a party of men from the Battery. His personal effects were handed to his brother Dvr. W.E. O'Neill, 3rd Battery…." Buried Bellewaarde Ridge Military Cemetery, 28NW.J.7.c.6.6. Posthumously awarded the Military Medal *London Gazette*, No.30364, 30 October 1917, for 'conspicuous bravery and devotion to duty;' it was received by his father, 21 June 1918. Gnr. O'Neill's British War Medal (29593), Victory Medal (29411), Memorial Plaque (336043), Scroll, and the booklet *Where The Australians Rest* were returned 'not known at address.' (*IWGC record age 21*).

(Panel 7) Gnr. 7447, George Geoffrey Taylor, 5th Bde., Australian Field Artillery, A.I.F.: *s.* of George Henry Taylor, of Crotonhurst Avenue, Caulfield, Victoria, by his wife Adeline: *b.* Elmore, Victoria, *c.*1894. Killed in action, 26 August 1917. Age 23. *unm.* Remains 'Unknown Australian Soldier' (five) recovered (28NW.I.29.b.20.25) unmarked grave; identified – Australian Clothing, Boots; reinterred, registered 24 December 1931. GRU Report, Zillebeke 5-431E refers – "These five Australian soldiers remains (McNamara, Lamb, Cox, Taylor, Benjamin) were properly buried wrapped in blankets, and the graves equally spaced; probably artillery men as all were dressed like cavalry men." *Buried in Sanctuary Wood Cemetery (V.S.1/5).*

Until The Day Break And The Shadows Flee Away

(Panel 7) Gnr. 26755, Clarence Cecil Whitehead, 14th Bty., 5th Bde., Australian Field Artillery, A.I.F.: *s.* of Mrs J.W.M. Whitehead (Narnar Goon, Victoria), by her marriage to the late Charles Whitehead. Killed in company with Gnr. W.L.J. Lynch (decapitated) by the explosion of a howitzer shell which hit the officer's mess cookhouse – Tokio, nr. Ypres, 30 October 1917. Buried beside Gnr. Lynch. Age 24. *unm.*
    Gnr. Walter McGeehan (served as Lynch) is buried in Hooge Crater Cemetery (XVIII.C.2).

(Panel 7) Lieut. 1572, Hugh Edmund Lyddon, 1st Field Coy., Australian Engineers, A.I.F.: c/o Harbour Trust Office, Circular Quay, Sydney, New South Wales: *s.* of the late William Hookins Lyddon, of Islington, London, England, by his wife Elizabeth: and brother to Herbert H. Lyddon Esq., of 27, Milton Park, Highgate, London, N.: *b.* Islington, 30 November 1881: Occupation – Assistant Engineer, Sydney Harbour Trust: a serving member of the A.I.F., volunteered his services, Sydney, 21 December 1915: gazetted 2nd Lieut. 2nd Field Coy., Engineer Depot, Moore Park, 16 March 1916; departed Australia, 3 May: served with the Expeditionary Force in France and Flanders from 17 October; transf'd. 1st Field Coy., 14 November 1916: promoted Lieut. 22 March 1917. Killed in action, 4 October 1917; Belgium. Age 35. His Capt. wrote, "Lieut. Lyddon was killed in action during the operations in the Ypres Sector 4.10.17. He was Officer in Charge, No.1 Section, and at the time was selecting a suitable position for the construction of a strong-point, in company with Sergt. Austin his section sergeant. They were about thirty yards from the front line at the time when Lieut. Lyddon was sniped through the heart. Death was instantaneous. He was buried by Sergt. Austin in a shell hole as hostile artillery was too active to permit the removal of the body." Memorial cross erected, Belgian Battery Corner Cemetery.

(Panel 7) L/Corpl. 119, William George Pitt, 1st Field Coy., Australian Engineers, A.I.F.: *s.* of Alfred Nathaniel (& Sarah Elizabeth) Pitt, of 95, Elizabeth Street, Paddington, New South Wales: *b.* Paddington, 1895: Occupation – Carpenter: serving member 5th Field Coy., enlisted, 19 August 1914; posted 1st Field Coy., Engineers, 21 September: served with the Mediterranean Expeditionary Force (from 3 March 1915); France and Flanders from 28 March 1916: apptd. L/Corpl. 30 September 1917; reported wounded and missing at Zonnebeke, 4 October 1917, since confirmed by a Court of Enquiry (31 March 1918) died of wounds. Age 22. Pte. 2162, R.J. Denny said, "He was badly wounded in the face, and I saw him being carried back to the Advanced Dressing Station, but I can't say what happened after that." Recommended (3 October 1917) for Military Medal for 'Conspicuous courage, devotion to duty and valuable services as runner (operations nr. Ypres 20–21 September 1917);' declined. L/Corpl. Pitt was Mentioned in Routine Orders (31 October 1917) 'For gallant services rendered during recent operations.' Two brothers also served, both survived.

(Panel 7) Spr. 16527, Stanley James Herbert Cole, 1st Field Coy., Australian Engineers, A.I.F.: *s.* of James David (& Edith Bertha) Cole, of 41A, Rathfern Road, Catford, London, S.E.6, England: *b.* Lee Green, London, S.E., May 1893: Occupation – Clerk: previously rejected 'defective chest measurement;' re-volunteered and enlisted, 16 October 1916: departed Sydney, 2 December: served with the Expeditionary Force in France and Flanders from 18 May 1917; and was killed in action, 10 a.m., 4 October 1917 in company with ten other members of 1st Field Coy., when a shell struck the crater in which they were sheltering mid-way between first and second Australian objectives; Broodseinde. Age 24. Memorial cross erected, Belgian Battery Corner Cemetery.

In June 1922 an enquiry by Ralph Curry, of Strathfield, regarding photographs of his son Frank's grave he had received one year previously elicited the following reply, "Dear Sir, With further reference to the regrettable loss of your son…I am now in receipt of advice from the Overseas Authorities intimating that the photographs which were forwarded to you on 24/5/20 purporting to depict the late soldier's final resting place in Belgian Battery Corner Cemetery were those of a memorial only and not actually marking an individual grave site. This disclosure was made as the result of an enquiry by the Imperial War Graves Commission regarding the reports of burial of other members of this unit in the same cemetery, and an examination of the ground served to assure the authorities that no burials had been effected under the several crosses in question. It was later ascertained that the regimental particulars of these soldiers (including those of your son) were first inscribed on a collective memorial erected in the above named cemetery, and when subsequently it was found necessary to replace this, by some unfortunate mischance, individual crosses erected in such a manner as to imply actual graves were substituted in place – hence the erroneous reports of burial originating. Despite an exhaustive search by the Graves Services no trace of your son's remains can be obtained and, failing their recovery and identification, it is proposed to suitably commemorate his sacrifice by the inclusion of his full regimental description and date of death on one of the memorials to be erected to the missing. Meanwhile, the Memorial Cross depicted by the photographs in your possession will be permitted to remain. Assuring you of the Department's profound regret at the distressing circumstances arising in this connection … Major McClean, Officer I.C. Base Records."

(Panel 7) Spr. 1891, Frank Curry, 1st Field Coy., Australian Engineers, A.I.F.: *s.* of Ralph (& Mrs E.R.) Curry, of 38, The Avenue, Strathfield, New South Wales: and brother to Pte. 6651, W.C. Curry, 19th Bn. A.I.F., who fell three days later: *b.* Balmain, Sydney: Religion – Methodist: Occupation – Engineer's Apprentice, Messrs Vale & Son, Auburn: 5′3″ tall, brown eyes, brown hair: enlisted Liverpool, 4 August 1915; posted 9th Rfts., 1st Field Coy., Moore Park, 12 October: served with the Expeditionary Force in France from April 1916: severely wounded (G.S.W. chest, face), 23 July, and invalided to England; returned to France, 9 October: Charged 'Insolence to a N.C.O. and Breaking away from Work Party, 22 October; Awarded Forfeiture 3 Days pay: Charged 'Attempting to assault a Prisoner of War, In the Field,'

15 July 1917; Awarded 7 Days F.P. No.2. Reported missing in action, 4 October 1917; since confirmed (March 1918) killed. Age 20. Spr. 2155, R.C.W. Brown, 1st Field Coy., reported, "On the morning of 4 October 1917, I was with 1891 Pte. Curry and others taking shelter in a shell crater between the first and second objectives, about 10 a.m. Enemy were shelling heavily. One shell burst in the midst of us. There was about twelve in the party and I was the only one not hit; remainder were all either killed or wounded. Pte. Curry and the men on each side of him were killed. Pte. Curry was blown to pieces, beyond identification. I was talking to him just before the shell burst, I am sure it exploded on him." Lieut. H.E. Lyddon, L/Corpl. W.G. Pitt, Sprs. S.J.H. Cole, J.R. Hollingworth, R. Mair, S.H.G. McKern, C. Smith; L/Corpl. J.C. Nicholls, Sprs. M. Flatley and E.G. Brown were also killed. Memorial crosses to the memory of Spr. Curry and his comrades were erected in Belgian Battery Corner Military Cemetery, 1 mile S.W. of Ypres. Age 20.

His brother William also has no known grave; he is recorded on Panel 23. Similarly, Lieut. Hugh Lyddon, L/Corpl. William Pitt, Sprs. Stanley Cole, Jack Hollingworth, Robert Mair, Stewart McKern and Charles Smith; all are recorded on Panel 7. L/Corpl. James Nicholls is buried in Buttes New British Cemetery (XXVI.C.9); Sprs. Martin Flatley and Edmund Brown, Tyne Cot Cemetery (XXV.F.24, XLI.B.6).

(Panel 7) Spr. 3333, Alfred Henry Darvall, 11th Field Coy., Australian Engineers, A.I.F.: *s.* of Charles George Darvall, by his wife Julia: *b.* Chiltern, Victoria. Killed in action, 4 October 1917. He was married to Lina A.C. Darvall (19, Wilson Street, Long Gully, Victoria). GRU report Memorial Cross – Spr. A.H. Darvall (50.134/C), Pte. J. Bradshaw (50.132/C), Sergt. W. Dalton (50.150/C), and Pte. S.G. Edwards (50.145/C) – erected Perth (China Wall) Military Cemetery. No remains recovered.

Pte. Bradshaw is recorded below, Sergt. Dalton (Panel 23); Pte. Edwards (Addenda Panel 59).

(Panel 7) Spr. 190, Jack Raymond Hollingsworth, 1st Field Coy., Australian Engineers, A.I.F.: *s.* of Mrs A. Hollingworth (345, Glebe Road, Glebe Point, New South Wales): *b.* Moree, January 1895: Religion – Church of England: Occupation – Motor Driver: 5′11″ tall, grey eyes, fair hair: serving member of 6th Field Coy., volunteered and enlisted Paddington Barracks, 5 September 1914; posted Dvr., 1st Field Coy., 21 September: apptd. Spr. 22 April 1917: served with the Mediterranean Expeditionary Force in Egypt; thereafter trained in England, joined Expeditionary Force in France, 17 June 1916: killed approximately 10 a.m., 4 October 1917, in company with several other members of 1st Field Coy. when a large shell landed and exploded in a crater in which they were sheltering. Age 22. *unm.* Memorial cross erected Belgian Battery Corner Cemetery, Plot 1, Row B., 1 mile S.W. of Ypres. No remains recovered.

(Panel 7) Spr. 10936, Robert Mair, 1st Field Coy., Australian Engineers, A.I.F.: late of 'Strathdene', Artarmon, North Sydney: *s.* of George Mair, of by his wife Annie, *née* Taylor: *b.* Ruthven, Buckie, co. Banff, Scotland, June 1887: Religion – Presbyterian: *educ.* Ruthven Public School: Occupation – Stonemason & Builder: 5′9½″ tall, blue eyes, dark hair: previously served 4 years Gordon Highlanders (T.F.); volunteered and enlisted Rosebery Park, Sydney, 3 May 1916; posted Spr., 1st Rfts., 9th Field Coy., 20 May: departed Sydney, 5 July: served with the Expeditionary Force in France from 26 January 1917 (transf'd. 1st Field Coy., 13 February), and was killed in action, 4 October 1917, Zonnebeke – Broodseinde. Age 30. Memorial cross erected, Belgian Battery Corner Cemetery, Plot 1, Row B., 1 mile S.W. of Ypres. No remains recovered. Remembered on Findochty War Memorial.

(Panel 7) Spr. 16217, Stewart Hessel George McKern, M.M., 1st Field Coy., Australian Engineers, A.I.F.: *s.* of James McKern, of 'Murrurundi,' 17, Redan Street, Mosman, New South Wales, and Mary Eldridge, his wife: and yr. brother to Corpl. 454, H.T. McKern, 4th Australian Infantry, died of wounds, 16 August 1915, received in action at Lone Pine, Gallipoli: *b.* Summerhill, 1895: Occupation – Surveyor: enlisted, 1 May 1916; posted 1st Field Coy., 12 June: departed Australia, 11 November 1916: served with the Expeditionary Force in France from 14 April 1917; reported wounded and missing in action, 4 October 1917, since confirmed (31 March 1918) died of wounds. Age 22. Believed to have been sheltering with a number of comrades in a shell hole when a large shell landed and killed the majority outright; Corpl. 2632, T.B. Oakes stated, "I saw Spr. McKern wounded by shellfire near Broodseinde, and being dressed by stretcher-bearers who are unknown to me. We were in 1st Brigade at the time, and about

400 yards in rear of the front line. As my duty necessitated my moving forward I was unable to find out anything more with regard to this soldier." Spr. McKern was awarded the Military Medal (*London Gazette*, 14 December 1917) 'For bravery in the field.' Remembered on Mosman War Memorial.

His brother is buried in Pieta Military Cemetery, Malta (B.VI.5).

(Panel 7) Spr. 6304, Charles Smith, 1st Field Coy., Australian Engineers, A.I.F.: *b*. Bondi, Sydney, June 1882: Religion – Presbyterian: Occupation – Engineer Driver/Fitter; Railway Workshop, Sydney: 5'5¼" tall, blue eyes, brown hair: volunteered and enlisted Moore Park, Engineer Depot., 15 December 1915; posted 15th Rfts., 1st Field Coy., 22 January 1916: served with the Expeditionary Force in France from 29 May 1917, and was killed in action at Passchendaele, Belgium, 4 October following. Age 35. Memorial cross erected Plot 1, Row B, Belgian Battery Corner Cemetery, 1 mile S.W. of Ypres. A widower, in the event of his death Spr. Smith requested all effects and correspondence be received by his sister, Miss Amy Smith (Rivers Street, Bellevue Hill, Sydney); disbursement of his estate as instructed in his will, recorded and held by Messrs Hindeyer & Williams, Solicitors, to be handled by that firm accordingly. His effects, medals, plaque, etc. were all returned, his sister being unknown and untraceable; Messrs Hindeyer & Williams were unable to process any instruction Spr. Smith may have included in his will, they had no knowledge or record of business with him. No remains recovered

(Panel 7) Spr. 5278, Francis Hugh 'Frank' Armstrong, 1st Coy., Australian Tunnelling Corps, A.I.F.: *s*. of Thomas Armstrong, of Luke Street, Charters Towers, Queensland: *b*. Charters Towers, 1890: Occupation – Labourer: joined Mining Corps, 10 April 1916: departed Melbourne, 30 September: served with the Expeditionary Force in France, attd. 1st Anzac Entrenching Battn., from 2 January 1917; transf'd. 1st Tunnelling Coy. 27 January: hospitalised (Hydrocele / Varicosis) 15 February, discharged to duty, 9 September. Reported missing/believed wounded, 1 October 1917; confirmed (Court of Enquiry, 3 April 1918), killed in action. Age 27. *unm*. Corpl. 2342, A. Minton reported, "I am afraid that it is quite impossible that Spr. Armstrong can be a prisoner as he was behind the line when he was missing on October 1st. between Westhoek Ridge and Anzac. I was told by Capt. Clinton that Spr. Armstrong, Spence and another man went out ration carrying and never came back. We all believe they must have been hit by a shell. I think one disc was found…Spr. Winter was out for four or five hours looking for them, but never found them…"

(Panel 7) Spr. 5501, Donald Mitchell Blair, 1st Coy., Australian Tunnelling Corps, A.I.F.: *s*. of the late James Blair, by his wife Eliza ('Nephi,' Rawson Street, Punchbowl, New South Wales): *b*. Moe, Gippsland, Victoria, January 1897: Occupation – Dairyman: enlisted Broadmeadows, 9 May 1916; posted Mining Corps, Seymour, 5 July: departed Melbourne, 25 October: proceeded to France, 28 January 1917; joined 1st Tunnelling Coy. In the Field, 6 February, and was killed in action, 8.23 p.m., 20 April 1917. Buried by enemy mine explosion. Body not yet recovered. Age 20. Memorial Cross erected Aeroplane Military Cemetery, Row A. British War, and Victory Medal, Memorial Plaque and Scroll received by Mrs Blair, April 1921–1923; Death Certificate released, 25 October 1968.

(Panel 7) Spr. 517, William Coleman, 2nd Coy., Australian Tunnelling Corps, A.I.F.: *b*. Boors Plain, South Australia, late 1873: Religion – Presbyterian: Occupation – Labourer: 5'8" tall, brown eyes, dark hair: previously served 18 months Mounted Rifles; enlisted Adelaide, 9 October 1915, posted 'E' Coy., 2nd Depot Mining Corps, Casula, 14 October; transf'd. No.2 Coy., Mining Corps 1 November: departed Sydney, 2 February 1916; joined Expeditionary Force in France 5 May; transf'd. 2nd Tunnelling Corps, 29 December, and was killed in action, 10 July 1917; during the German attack on Nieuport. Age 43. His effects – Testament, Metal Brooch, Letter – Memorial Plaque, Scroll, British War and Victory medals were received by his widow, Emily Francis Coleman ('Acton,' Harriett Street, Croydon Park, South Australia), November 1918–January 1923.

Following the death of Walter Leonard, his mother, anxious for news regarding her son, wrote several letters to the Australian Base Records Office – "7 July 1918 … It is some nine months and as we have not received any further news or belongings, have you not heard from France yet; it seems an anxious time. I would like to know if you have heard anything further as some of my friends have heard of theirs and are even all settled up. Hoping to hear something soon….P.S. I may add we have not heard from any of his officers even to say if he was buried or how it really was. Surely some are left." Spr. 3361, G.A. Rose responded, "He was buried on the field by the side of his pal who fell with him. The grave would not be registered as it is not in a military cemetery, but he had every attention to the very last. As near as I can describe the poor lad, about 5'8", complexion dark with rather large eyes, and a very pleasing countenance, always ready to laugh at the merest trifling joke. I may add that he was a great favourite among the lads and never wavered in performing his duties, no matter how dangerous. He was buried where the Australians took their 1st Objective on 20th September 1917;" And Lieut. J. Whettam, X Corps Burial Officer, "Buried (28.NW.J.10.a.65.80) by his comrades, The Butte, Polygon Wood." On receipt of this information she wrote, "11 February 1919, I have heard through one of his comrades that he was buried with others, but what has become of any of his belongings. It seems hard to think not getting anything, not even his disc, as I hear of several here that have got that if nothing else, and I am quite sure he would have some little belongings. Trusting you will find out and let me know how he came to his end, or is he still living, as I really feel it can't be true until I have some more proof although it's so long ago. Waiting anxiously...." Sadly, a little over one year previously the fortunes of war had decided Walter's mother would be one of many denied the comfort of some small item of personal association. Spr. 263, C.F. Sealfield said, "He, with four others, was buried on the field and not in a military cemetery...his belongings were put in a sandbag with the other dead men's, and they went astray on the way out through the man carrying them being wounded."

(Panel 7) Spr. 5361, Walter William 'Froggie' Leonard, 1st Coy., Australian Tunnelling Corps, A.I.F.: *s.* of Alfred Leonard, of 37, Norma Street, West Adelaide, by his wife Jane Amelia: *b.* Norwood, South Australia, 1890: Religion – Methodist: Occupation – Machinist: 5'3½" tall, brown eyes, dark hair: enlisted Adelaide, 8 February 1916; posted 2nd Depot Battn.: apptd. Spr., Base Engineers, 16 March: departed Melbourne, 30 September: joined the Expeditionary Force in France and Flanders, 2 January 1917, attd. 1st Anzac Entrenching Battn. Rfts. 13 January, transf'd. 1st Tunnelling Coy. 12 March: hospitalised (Diarrhoea) 26 August, discharged to duty, 1 September. Killed in action, 1 October 1917, by a shell fragment through the head. Buried near where he fell. Age 27. *unm.* His friend Miss Lizzie Knott (c/o YWCA, Hindmarsh Square, Adelaide), would appreciate news regarding Spr. Leonard from his comrades. His British War, and Victory Medal, Memorial Plaque and Scroll were received by his mother, 22 April 1921–7 April 1923.

(Panel 7) Spr. 5394, Alfred O'Neill, 1st Coy., Australian Tunnelling Corps, A.I.F.: *s.* of James O'Neill, of 13, Smith Street, Balmain, New South Wales, by his wife Anne: *b.* Launceston, Tasmania, 1895: Religion – Roman Catholic: Occupation – Miner: 5'8½" tall, hazel eyes, brown hair: enlisted Darwin, Northern Territory, 5 April 1916, posted 1st Mining Corps, Seymour, 20 June: departed Melbourne, 30 September: joined the Expeditionary Force in France, 2 January 1917, attd. 1st Anzac Entrenching Battn., transf'd. 1st Tunnelling Coy., 27 January: hospitalised (trench feet) 6–11 April. Killed in action, 1 October 1917. Age 32.

(Panel 7) Spr. 276, James 'Jim' Skillen, M.M., 1st Coy., Australian Tunnelling Corps, A.I.F.: late of Grassbanks Estate, Lower Booval Road, Booval: *s.* of James Skillen, of Amberley, via Ipswich, Queensland; late of Blind Lane, Silkstone, by his wife Isabella Catherine: and brother to Sergt. 275, W. Skillen, 1st Tunnelling Coy. (surv'd.); Pte. 293, A. Skillen, 4th Machine Gun Battn. (surv'd.); and Pte. 294, J. Skillen, 4th M.G. Battn. (surv'd.): *b.* Paisley, Scotland, 1893: Religion – Methodist: Occupation – Miner: 5'4" tall, brown eyes, brown hair: enlisted Ipswich, 28 November 1915, posted 1st Mining Corps, Casula: served in France and Flanders from 5 May 1916. Reported missing, 1 October 1917; confirmed (Court of Enquiry, 3 April 1918), killed in action. Age 24. In response to enquiries Pte. 170, E. Lovett reported, "Skillen, Spence and Armstrong were on a ration party on the Menin Road on the 1st October, and were said to have been blown into a shell hole or something. They were never seen again...The general opinion among the men is that they were blown to pieces." And Lieut. H.S. Vinycombe, 15th Durham Light Infantry, "10 February 1918 ... We dug some trenches near his body on the night of October 2/3rd, and buried him in a shell hole where he lay on October 3rd without a cross, there being no wood available. I sent the approximate map reference, which I am sorry I cannot give now, to the Headquarters A.I.F. we thought, by the look of the body, that it had been lying there for at least a week, but you state that he was missing on October 1st. There was another Australian lying somewhere near him, but owing to the very heavy shelling, we were unable to dispose of the body, and I was wounded myself shortly afterwards. If there was another man known to be with Pte. Skillen and who is also missing I think it will probably be his body we saw lying near. The point was about 150 yards east of Glencorse Wood and about 100 yards north of the track leading from Clapham Junction to the front line, and 30 yards east of a large German M.G. emplacement lying on the north side of the track. Any further information could be best supplied from the A.I.F. Headquarters." His effects – Wallet, Photos, Disc, Postcards, Notebook – retrieved by the Lieutenant, were received by Spr. Skillen's parents, October 1918. He was awarded the Military Medal (*London Gazette*, 6 July 1917) for gallantry in operations 20–25 April. See account re. J.W. Saxton, Railway Dugouts Burial Ground (IV.C.13)

(Panel 7) Spr. 5623, William Joseph 'Bill' Spence, 1st Coy., Australian Tunnelling Corps, A.I.F.: *s.* of Margaret Spence (366, King Street, West Melbourne, Victoria): and brother to Francis Spence Esq., Customs Official, Railway Pier, Melbourne: *b.* Newton, North Auckland, New Zealand, 1880: Religion – Roman Catholic: Occupation – Miner: 5'5" tall, blue eyes, fair hair: enlisted Seymour, Victoria, 13 March 1916; posted Tunnelling Rfts., Guildford, 24 June; transf'd. 1st Mining Corps, 1 July: hospitalised (Venereal) Langwarrin, 4 July–24 August (negative): departed Australia, 25 October 1916: joined 1st Tunnelling Corps, France, 6 February 1917: hospitalised sick (Myalgia/Otitis Media/Rubella/Chronic Rheumatism) 8 March, evacuated to England: rejoined 1st Coy., 20 August. Reported missing, believed wounded, 1 October 1917; confirmed (Court of Enquiry, 3 April 1918), killed in action. Age 36. *unm.* In response to an enquiry made by his brother Spr. 5577, J. Mitchell replied, "During one of the engagements at Ypres in September last, the exact date of which I cannot recollect, Spr. J. Spence, a mate of mine in the same company as myself and a friend in civil life, was detailed with others to carry rations to our men on shift working near the line. We were then stationed at the 'Halfway House' near Hellfire Corner, off the Menin Road, and Spr. Spence did not return, neither did any of this ration party; as nothing was seen or heard of them again during the lapse of three to four days before returning to rest camp. I have since learnt that he has been officially reported as missing."

(Panel 7) Major Philip Llewellyn Howell-Price, D.S.O., M.C., 1st Bn. Australian Infantry, A.I.F.: *s.* of the late Rev. John Howell-Price, by his wife Isabella: and brother to Lieut.Col. O.G. Howell-Price, D.S.O., M.C., Comdg. 3rd Battn., died of wounds, 4 November 1916, received at the Battle of Flers; and 2nd Lieut. R.G. Howell-Price, M.C., who fell on 4 May 1917, at Bullecourt: *b.* Mount Wilson, New South Wales, 1894. Following the death of Major Howell-Price's two brothers, in an endeavour to save his life, General Birdwood appointed him to 1st Anzac Staff, but, on hearing his old battalion was going into action at Broodseinde, requested he be permitted to rejoin and was reported missing believed killed by the intense enemy barrage which immediately preceded zero-hour, 4 October 1917. Age 23. *unm.* See account Reninghelst New Military Cemetery; Capt. J.R. Eddy (IV.C.4).

His brother Owen is buried in Heilly Station Cemetery, Mericourt-L'Abbe (V.A.14); Richmond lies in Vraucourt Copse Cemetery (II.B.7).

(Panel 7) Lieut. Victor Cleveland McKell, 1st Bn. Australian Infantry, A.I.F.: *s.* of the late T.C.K. McKell, State Magistrate, Newcastle, New South Wales, by his wife Isabel ('Mona,' Roberts Street, Artarmon, Sydney): *b.* Cobar, New South Wales, December 1887: Religion – Church of England: a member of School Cadets, 2 years; prior to joining Australian Imperial Force; Pte. (no.119) 17 August 1914, was a Bank Clerk: 5'10½" tall, fair complexion, eyes and hair: posted 23rd Rfts., Randwick, 21 August; 1st Infantry Bde., Kensington, 7 September: served at Gallipoli, 25 April–13 December 1915 (on which latter date he was hospitalised 'eye trouble'): apptd. 2nd Lieut. 6 August 1915; promoted Lieut. 1 December, transf'd. 53rd Battn. (confirmed 14 February 1916): rejoined his unit in Egypt, 8 January 1916, where he was again hospitalised 'Defective Vision;' diagnosed 'Debility – Astigmatism,' 24 January: returned Karoola, Australia, 12 April: departed Australia for the European War, 9 November 1916: served with the Expeditionary Force in France and Flanders from 11 February 1917, and was killed in action, 4 October following when, on approaching its assembly positions for the Battle of Broodseinde, the battalion was severely shelled by the enemy. Age 29. *unm*. L/Corpl. 694, W.S. Gaskell, Stretcher-Bearer, 10th Bn., A.I.F., informed "He was killed at Anzac Ridge, two days after we came back into the line, on October 4th. We were in support and the 1st. Battn. were going up on our left to relieve another battalion. There was a block as they were going up the 'Jabber' track and a single shell wounded six and killed seven together in a shell-hole on the track. I bandaged the six as well as I could, and I buried all the seven together in the one shell-hole. I did not know Mr McKell, but I took off his disc and gave it to a stretcher-bearer of the 1st. Battn., that they called 'Monty,' who was helping with the wounded ... It was the first shell-hole immediately to the left of where the 'Jabber' track crossed the first support trench on 28.9.17; and the reference on the Message Map would be J.4b.4.2, between Polygon Wood and Zonnebeke..."

(Panel 7) 2nd Lieut. Charles Farry, 1st Bn. Australian Infantry, A.I.F.: *b*. Ashfield, New South Wales, 1886: Religion – Church of England: Occupation – Grocer: joined A.I.F., Liverpool, 13 June 1915; Pte. 2835; posted 9th Rfts., 1st Battn. 20 August: joined 1st Bn., Tel-el-Kebir, 6 January 1916: proceeded to France, disembarked Marseilles, 28 March: wounded (GSW buttock) 22 July (promoted Corpl. 9 August) rejoined 1st Bn. 8 November 1916: promoted Sergt. 6 February 1917: joined No.4 Officers' Cadet School, Oxford, England 9 March; appointed 2nd Lieut. 28 June; returned to France, 28 June, rejoined 1st Bn. 28 July. Missing believed killed by the intense enemy barrage which immediately preceded zero-hour, 4 October 1917. Age 31. All correspondence regarding 2nd Lieut. Farry to be addressed c/o his brother Henry Farry, 38, Orpington Street, Ashfield. See account Reninghelst New Military Cemetery; Capt. J.R. Eddy (IV.C.4).

(Panel 7) Siglr. 6112, Reginald Arthur Clarke, Headquarters Staff, 1st Bn. Australian Infantry, 1st Bde. A.I.F.: eldest *s*. of Charles William Clarke, Journalist; of 'Euroma,' Oxford Street, Epping, Sydney, New South Wales, Australia, by his wife Sarah Ingram, *dau*. of John R. McCaw: and brother to Siglr. 6113, W.A.J. Clarke, 1st Bn., A.I.F. (surv'd.): *b*. Rushden, co. Northampton, England, 16 December 1894: *educ*. Technical School, Portsmouth, co. Hants: went to Australia with his family in 1913; there articled as a Lawyer: joined Australian Forces, December 1915: came to England, September 1916: served with the Expeditionary Force in France and Flanders from December following. Hit in the chest by shell fragments, and died within moments, 17 September 1917; Polygon Wood. Age 22. *unm*. Lieut. F.A. Presnell wrote, "Besides being prized for his many qualities, he was the kind of soldier we cannot afford to lose nowadays. Your son was a trained specialist, and the stamp of soldier who is invaluable in a regiment, not only for his skill, but on account of his fine example, which inspired younger and newer men." At the time of Reginald's death his brother William was at his side and caught him as he fell.

The Menin Gate records the names of 6,249 Australian soldiers to whom the fortunes of war denied the known and honoured burial afforded their comrades in death; the earliest of these – Pte. W. Campbell, 2nd Bn. and Pte. G.E. Carter, 4th Bn. – are both dated 12 September 1916.

(Panel 7) Pte. 4159, William Campbell, 2nd Bn. Australian Infantry, A.I.F.: *s*. of John Campbell, of 'Glenrock,' Darby Street, Katoomba, New South Wales, by his wife Isabella: *b*. Red Range, nr. Glen Innes, 1895: Religion – Presbyterian: Occupation – Clerk: 5'9½" tall, fair complexion, blue eyes, light hair: serving member of the Cadet Militia, rank Corpl.; joined A.I.F., Armidale, 7 August 1915: apptd. A/Corpl., posted 13th Rfts., 3rd Battn. 17 December, departed Sydney, 20 December: disembarked Suez, Egypt, 17 January 1916; joined 2nd Battn., Tel-el-Kebir, 14 February: reverted to Pte. (inc. pay) at his own volition (20 February): served with the Expeditionary Force in France from 28 March, and was reported missing believed killed in the vicinity of Zillebeke Bund, 12 September 1916. Age 21. *unm*. His Memorial Scroll, Plaque, War and Victory medals were received by his parents, April 1922–February 1923.

(Panel 7) Pte. 3025, John Bradshaw, 4th Bn. Australian Infantry, A.I.F.: *s*. of the late John (& Ellen) Bradshaw: c/o Mrs M. Surman, Grandmother (69, George Street, Waterloo, New South Wales): *b*. Miller's Point, Sydney, January 1897: Religion – Church of England: Occupation Woolwashing Dryer's Hand: joined A.I.F., Holsworthy, 24 August 1915; apptd. 7th Rfts., 19th Battn., 16 November; transf'd. 4th Battn., Tel-el-Kebir, 4 February 1916: served with the Expeditionary Force in France from 30 March: wounded (GSW Facial), 19 August, hospitalised France, returned to duty, 29 September: hospitalised (Trench Feet), 2 December 1916, hospitalised France, transf'd. England, discharged to furlough, 29

March 1917; returned to training camp, Perham Downs, 6 April: returned to France, 13 September, rejoined 4th Battn. 25 September. Killed in action, 4 October 1917; Operations Passchendaele. Age 20. GRU report Memorial Cross erected – Perth (China Wall) Military Cemetery – re. Pte. J. Bradshaw (50.132/C), Spr. A.H. Darvall (50.134/C), Sergt. W. Dalton (50.150/C), and Pte. S.G. Edwards (50.145/C). No remains recovered.

Spr. Darvall is recorded above; Sergt. Dalton (Panel 23), Pte. Edwards (Addenda Panel 59).

(Panel 7) Pte. 4468, George Edward Carter, 'B' Coy., 4th Bn. Australian Infantry, A.I.F.: *b.* Townsville, Queensland, 1885: Religion – Roman Catholic: Occupation – Labourer: 5'5" tall, dark complexion, hazel eyes, brown hair: joined A.I.F., Town Hall, Casula, 23 November 1915: posted 14th Rfts., 4th Battn., 14 January 1916: departed Sydney, 3 February: disembarked Alexandria, Egypt, 7 March: served with the Expeditionary Force in France from 4 April; joined 4th Battn. In the Field, 4 June: Admonished (5 August) by O.C. 4th Battn., Awarded Forfeiture 4 Days Pay, 'Absent Without Leave, 10a.m. 1 August–4 p.m. 4 August. Killed in action, 12 September 1916, on the morning of which date 'B' Coy. lines were heavily bombarded by *minenwerfers* to such an extent that the trenches were all but obliterated and four men of the company were killed. Age 31. Buried between Ypres and Mount Sorrel, S.E. of Ypres (28.N.W.I.30). Married to Constance Myrtle Lister, *née* Carter (9, Metcalfe Street, North Sydney, New South Wales); she received his Memorial Scroll, Plaque War and Victory medals, but provided no additional information for inclusion in the Memorial Register.

(Panel 7) Pte. 1690C, Gilbert Holt, 5th Bn. Australian Infantry, A.I.F.: c/o Cyril Frederick Holt, Esq., Orbost, Victoria: *s.* of the late Thomas Grosvenor Holt, by his wife Elizabeth E., *née* Mitchell: and brother to Pte. 6863, T.M. Holt, 5th Bn. A.I.F., who fell the same day: *b.* Stratford, Victoria, *c.*1897: Religion – Anglican: Occupation – Butcher: 5'6¾" tall; medium complexion, blue eyes, brown hair: joined A.I.F., 29 January 1916; apptd. 1st Rfts., 37th Battn., Seymour, 18 April: joined Expeditionary Force in France, 1 September; transf'd. 5th Battn., 29 September: hospitalised (Trench Feet), November, hospitalised England: returned to France, 8 February 1917: wounded (S.W. Facial), 23 February, hospitalised France; rejoined battn., 15 March: hospitalised (sick) 16–29 May. Killed in action, 20 September 1917. Age 20. *unm.* Sergt. 3045, J. Bunting reported, "Casualty was in the front-line at Black Watch Corner, Passchendaele, consolidating our position after taking it, when the biggest brother was hit in the thigh by a piece of high explosive shell; the smaller brother volunteered to help carry him out on a stretcher and, while carrying him to the Dressing Station, the enemy opened a barrage and the smaller brother stood by the side of the stretcher and a high- explosive shell landed alongside him and killed them both. Death was instantaneous…" Buried about 300 yards SW of Glencorse Wood.

His brother Thomas also has no known grave; he is recorded below.

(Panel 7) Pte. 6863, Thomas Mitchell Holt, 5th Bn. Australian Infantry, A.I.F.: c/o Cyril Frederick Holt, Esq., Orbost, Victoria: *s.* of the late Thomas Grosvenor Holt, by his wife Elizabeth E., *née* Mitchell: and brother to Pte. 1690C, G. Holt, 5th Bn. A.I.F., who fell the same day: *b.* Stratford, Victoria, *c.*1885: Religion – Anglican: Occupation – Labourer: 5'10½" tall; dark complexion, grey eyes, black hair: joined A.I.F., 6 March. 1916; apptd. 22nd Rfts., 5th Battn., Royal Park, 24 October: departed Melbourne, 25 October: joined Expeditionary Force in France, 29 March 1917. Killed in action, 22 September 1917. Age 22.

His brother Gilbert also has no known grave; he is recorded above.

(Panel 7) 2nd Lieut. Elgar Watts Opie, 'A' Coy., 6th Bn. Australian Infantry, A.I.F.: *s.* of Ernest C.E. Opie, of 3, Laurel Bank Parade, Newtown, Geelong, Victoria, by his wife Alice Estelle: joined 6th Battn. In the Field 29–30 September 1917, and was killed in his first action by a bullet through the stomach in the early hours of 4 October 1917; death was almost instantaneous, being conscious for only a few moments before he passed away. Age 23. *unm.* Buried by Lieut. H. Taverner, 3rd Battn., nr. the Dressing Station, Anzac Ridge. See account Reninghelst New Military Cemetery; Capt. J.R. Eddy (IV.C.4).

(Panel 7) Pte. 7016, Ernest 'Snowy' Victor Hey, 'B' Coy., 6th Bn. Australian Infantry, A.I.F.: *s.* of George Hey, of Best Street, Devonport, Tasmania, by his wife Ann: and brother to Corpl. 2369, C.L.T. Hey, 24th Bn. A.I.F., who fell four days later. Killed in action, 4 October 1917; being shot through the head by a sniper during the advance at Broodseinde. Age 29.

His brother Charles also has no known grave; he is recorded on Panel 23.

(Panel 7) Pte. 3464, Michael 'Twinkle' Francis Starr, 6th Bn. Australian Infantry, A.I.F.: *s.* of the late Michael Starr, by his wife Mary ('Comely Bank,' Healsville, Victoria): and elder brother to Pte. 3465, P.J. Starr, 6th Battn., who fell the same day; and Corpl. 6891, P.H. Starr, 21st Battn. (surv'd.): *b.* Bendigo, Victoria, *c.*1889. Reported wounded and missing 4 October 1917, since confirmed killed in action. Corpl. 1814, W.M. Griffiths said, "On the morning of 4th October we were making an attack on Moorslede Ridge, near Passchendaele. I saw Starr on top of the ridge lying on the road which skirts the top, he had been badly wounded on the head and had been dressed. I helped to improve the dressing and put him in a small hole at the side of the road. When I returned about an hour later he was not there and no shell had burst on the spot; I concluded the stretcher-bearers had taken him away. The Battn. asked me whether I 'considered the wound bad enough to cause his death,' and I replied, 'Yes.'" Age 28. *unm.*

His brother Patrick also has no known grave; he is recorded below.

(Panel 7) Pte. 3465, Patrick 'Paddy' James Starr, 6th Bn. Australian Infantry, A.I.F.: *s.* of the late Michael Starr, by his wife Mary ('Comely Bank,' Healsville, Victoria): and *yr.* brother to Pte. 3464, M.F. Starr, 6th Battn., who fell the same day; and Corpl. 6891, P.H. Starr, 21st Battn. (surv'd.): *b.* Footscray, Victoria, *c.*1895. Killed in action, 4 October 1917, at Broodseinde Ridge; hit in the head by a shell fragment, death being instantaneous. Age 22. *unm.* Buried 600 yards S.E. of Zonnebeke, a few yards E. of debris known as Retaliation Farm, midway between two small woods – Romulus and Remus (28D.28.d.4.7); registered by Lieut. Q.S. Spedding, Corps Burial Officer. On receiving information regarding Patrick's burial his brother Philip wrote to the Missing Inquiries Office, "…I understand his grave has been located. I have however been informed he was buried with two others near a place called Retaliation Farm. The grave was a shell hole and is in front of two concrete pill-boxes, which are close to each other. I received the information from a member of the A.M.C. who assisted in the burial. There are not many other graves in the vicinity. My reason for writing to you is to pass this information on to whatever body is concerned with grave registrations and burial matters, as I am unacquainted with them. The information is meagre but it may coincide with other particulars they may have and thus assist them in locating this grave. It would be much better to have a cross in an appropriate position than none at all; I would also like you to have his name coupled with that of his brother Pte. M.F. Starr, 3464 – reported 'Wounded and Missing' on the same day, and since reported 'Killed in Action,' and of whom no trace can be found. So, if they can locate the grave of the first named, would you ask them to mark it with both their names?"

His brother Michael also has no known grave; he is recorded above.

(Panel 7) Lieut. George Heaton, 7th Bn. Australian Infantry, A.I.F.: *s.* of John William Heaton, by his wife Eliza Bennett: *b.* Derby, England, January 1878: *educ.* Boarding School, England, and Victoria State School: Occupation – Managing Law Clerk: served in the South African Campaign; Tpr., Imperial Light Horse, took part in operations in Transvaal and Orange River Colony, 4 March–26 June 1902; also served Victorian Militia, March 1904–October 1908; Armed Constabulary, Papua, 1909–1911; Senior Cadets, 23 December 1912–30 April 1915, and, at the time of his application (January 1916), was Lieut. 50th Infantry: joined A.I.F. as Lieut., 1 April; posted 17th Rfts., 7th Battn., Broadmeadows Camp: departed Melbourne aboard H.M.A.T. A14 'Euripides,' 4 April 1916: trained Egypt (May 1916); England (June 1916–March 1917): joined 7th Battn., France, 1 April 1917; wounded in action (G.S.W. Right leg) on the 22nd of that month: rejoined his battn. 29 July 1917; reported wounded in action at Broodseinde Ridge, 4 October 1917; since (13 October) confirmed killed. Age 39. Pte. 1349, L. Moore, 7th Battn., reported, "He was my Platoon Officer. On the day in question he was in the next shell hole to me, about ten feet off, when a shell came right into it and exploded. We then got out of ours to go forward, but another man (H. Crute) and I saw it was one of those that scatter fire and several wounded men were shrieking with agony, and I thought of my Lieut. and with the other man went to assist them. The Lieut. was absolutely blown to bits. I had seen him just before so I know he was there, but all we could find of him was his revolver. He was the only man in the pit that had one. No service was held as there was nothing to bury." He leaves a wife Helen Elizabeth Heaton, *née* Carmichael, late of 29, Neptune Street, St. Kilda (c/o Mr P.

Carmichael, Cusack Street, Wangaratta, Victoria), and a son, Owen Carmichael Heaton. See account Reninghelst New Military Cemetery; Capt. J.R. Eddy (IV.C.4).

'Part of him mud, part of him blood, The rest of him – not at all' – Robert Service.

On the night of 3 October 1917, despite the risk of getting too close to the enemy, it was decided the jumping off tapes for 1st Australian Brigade should be positioned in front of a bog of thick black mud which lay before the Brigade's front near Molenaarelsthoek. The task of laying the tapes fell to the Brigade Intelligence Officer, Lieut. J.F. Barnes; with battalion officers Lieut. H.D. Robb (3rd Bn.), Lieut. H.V. Chedgey (1st Bn.) and Lieut. W.A. Tebbutt (4th Bn.) assisting. Having decided on the centre point for the brigade front, Barnes ran his tape directly from it to the rear to serve as the boundary between the left and right battalions, and the battalion officers ran their tapes along the front of their respective units. This was extremely dangerous work. The officer, by means of a compass, would send one of his scouts with the tape as far as he could see him, directing him by means of tugging on the tape – one tug meant 'go right,' two tugs 'go left,' and a long tug 'halt' – the tape being fixed in position by sticks or clods of earth. To tape the entire brigade front required fifty rolls of tape and during the time it took to complete the work the Australians had to keep very low to avoid being sighted by the Molenaarelsthoek pill-boxes where the Germans could be seen moving about by the light of their own flares. In the left sector, that of 2nd Australian Brigade, there was no tape for the left rear battalion, the 7th, the Intelligence Officer, Lieut. Pollock, being killed by a shell while in the process of laying them.

(Panel 7) Lieut. William Grieve Pollock, 7th Bn. Australian Infantry, A.I.F.: 2nd Australian Brigade Intelligence Officer: *s.* of James Pollock, of Clifton House, 50, Park Street West, Brunswick, Victoria, by his wife Margaret: and nephew to Mrs C. Grieve (10, Regent Park Terrace, Strathbungo, Glasgow): *b.* Clifton Hill, Victoria: Religion – Presbyterian: Occupation – Traveller: 5'9½" tall, fresh complexion, blue eyes, fair hair: previously served 6 years, 52nd (Scottish) Regt.; Pte. 931: joined Australian Imperial Force, Melbourne, 22 July 1915; Pte. 2742: posted 6th Rfts., 24th Battn., Broadmeadows, 15 October 1915: transf'd. 7th Battn. 24 February 1916: promoted Corpl. 22 March (Egypt): served with the Expeditionary Force in France from 31 March 1916: promoted Sergt. 21 April: commissioned 2nd Lieut. 13 September 1916, In the Field (Belgium): hospitalised, Amiens, Incised Head Wound (accidental) 21–29 January 1917: promoted Lieut. 31 May: on leave (England) 20 June, rejoined his unit 5 July, and was killed by a shell while in the process of laying his battalion's jumping off tapes between Molenaarelsthoek and Zonnebeke on the night of 3 October 1917. Age 24. *unm.* 2nd Lieut. P.R. Carne wrote, "On the night of 3.10.17, just before our advance on the following morning, Lieut. Pollock with another officer and myself were making preparations for our troops in the front line, when a shell suddenly struck Lieut. Pollock, killing him instantly, he never even groaned so sudden was his death. As I was to advance with our troops I did not deem it wise to collect his papers etc. in case I became a casualty ... His death upset me very much as I had been working with him for some time. He was a fearless officer and died doing his duty. As near as I can remember the time of Lieut. Pollocks death, it was a few minutes before midnight." Pte. 4226, F. Lawrence recalled Lieut. Pollock being hit by a shell which passed clean through his body before exploding behind him, and Lieut. C.P. Clowe said, "...Lieut. Pollock fell at my side and at the time I thought he was only wounded, but I turned him over and found he had received the full burst in the back. He was carrying a water-bottle, haversack, compass and several other things strung over the shoulder and these were all cut off, so you can form some idea of the wounds he received. He never felt any pain whatever, he died on the spot, never even spoke one word to me and we were bosom pals..." Buried where he fell by L/Corpl. 2046, J.T. Walker, 7th Battn.; Garter Point, Anzac Ridge.

(Panel 7) Pte. 6987, Charles Arthur Eacott, 7th Bn. Australian Infantry, A.I.F.: *s.* of the late William James Eacott, by his wife Mary Ellen (Sand Road, Longwarry, Victoria): and brother to Gnr. 20240, J.H. Eacott, A.F.A. (surv'd.): *b.* Daylesford, July 1893: Religion – Church of England: Occupation – Farmer: 5'10" tall, fresh complexion, grey eyes, brown hair: enlisted Warragul, 18 October 1916; apptd. 23rd Rfts., 7th Bn., Royal Park, 14 November: departed Melbourne, A20 'Hororata,' 23 November: trained England (from 29 January 1917): proceeded to France, 14 May; joined 7th Bn. In the Field on the 28th of that month, and was killed in action, 20 September 1917. Age 24. *unm.* In July 1922 the remains of three 7th Bn. A.I.F. soldiers were recovered from an unmarked grave (28NW.J.15.a.9.7). At the time only one of these (Private Grace) could be positively identified with any degree of certainty and, reinterred in Birr Cross Roads Cemetery; the other two were buried beside him. Their headstones recorded 'A Soldier of The Great War 7th Bn. Australian Inf., 20 September 1917. *Known Unto God.*' In March 2015, after an interval of almost one hundred years, extensive research led to one set of these remains being attributed to Private Eacott. His headstone was replaced/re-dedicated in September 2015. *Buried in Birr Cross Roads Cemetery (I.D.19–20).*

(Panel 7) Pte. 5808, Hugh James Prowd, 7th Bn. Australian Infantry, A.I.F.: *s.* of Thomas Prowd, of Lang Lang, Victoria, by his wife Elizabeth: and elder brother to Pte. 2658, R.E. Prowd, 8th Battn., A.I.F. (surv'd), and Dvr. 2423, H.B. Prowd, 2nd Pioneer Battn., A.I.F. (surv'd): *b.* Bonny Doon, Victoria, 1884: Occupation – Blacksmith: enlisted Melbourne, 24 July 1915; posted 18th Rfts., 7th Battn., A.I.F.: departed Australia, 3 July 1916: underwent training, Perham Downs, September 1916–February 1917: served with the Expeditionary Force in France from 4 February 1917, joining his battalion In the Field on the 11th of that month, and was reported missing following the attack on the enemy trenches near Westhoek Ridge on the morning of 4 October 1917; later verified as having been killed instantaneously by a H.E. shell. Buried three days later by members of 26th Battn. A.I.F.. Age 33. He was married to May Prowd (Hunter Street, Euroa, Victoria), to whom all personal belongings and letters should be addressed. Remains recovered unmarked grave, refers GRU Report, Zillebeke 5-10E (28.D.29.a.0.6); identified – Clothing, Disc; reinterred, registered March 1927. *Buried in Sanctuary Wood Cemetery (III.J.12).*

In Memory Of The Dearly Loved Son Of May Prowd
Euroa. Australia

(Panel 7) Pte. 6830, Harry Thomas Travis, 7th Bn. Australian Infantry, A.I.F.: *s.* of Henry Travis, of 214, West Street, Crow's Nest, North Sydney, New South Wales, by his wife Ada: and elder brother to Pte. 5103, F. Travis, 20th Battn, who fell four days later: *b.* Richmond, New South Wales, *c.*1894. Reported missing, since confirmed killed in action, 4 October 1917. Pte. 6810, L.R. Parsonage said on the date of his death Travis was acting as runner to the battalion, which was in action at Passchendaele, and, although he did not see Travis killed, saw his body lying in a shell hole 'evidently having been hit and killed outright by a shell fragment.' Age 21. *unm.*

His brother Fred also has no known grave; he is recorded on Panel 23.

(Panel 7) Pte. 703A, David Weir, 7th Bn. Australian Infantry, A.I.F.: eldest *s.* of Hugh Weir, of Straid, Gracehill, Co. Antrim, by his wife Mary Ellen: and brother to Pte. S/40159, H. Weir, 8th Argyll & Sutherland Highlanders, who fell 21 March 1918, at the Second Battle of the Somme: *b.* Ballymena, Eire, 1889: Occupation – Labourer: enlisted Swan Hill, Victoria, 24 February 1916; posted 'B' Coy., 38th Battn., Bendigo, 27 March; proceeded to France transf'd. 7th Battn. 15 September 1916: joined his battalion In the Field on the 29th of that month. Reported wounded, since confirmed killed in action, 4 October 1917. Age 27. He leaves a widow Sarah Weir (Lisnafillen, Golcorm, Ballymena), and two *daus.* – Mary Sarah, and Edith. David and his brother are commemorated on the Ahoghill Church of Ireland Roll of Honour. (*IWGC record wife, B. Weir*)

His brother Hugh also has no known grave; he is commemorated on the Pozieres Memorial. (Panel 7) Capt. 389, John Robert Davidson, 8th Bn. Australian Infantry, A.I.F.: only *s.* of John Davidson, of Creswick, by his wife Elizabeth: *b.* Creswick, Victoria, December 1894: Religion – Church of England: Occupation – Carpenter; Messrs Deakins & Sons, Warrambool: 5'11¾" tall, grey eyes, fair hair: joined A.I.F., Warrambool, 19 August 1914; posted 'B' Coy. 8th Battn., Broadmeadows, 26 August: departed Australia, H.M.A.T. A24 'Benalla,' 21 October: promoted Sergt., 17 September 1914; Coy.Sergt.Major, 27 December 1915; gazetted 2nd Lieut., 20 February 1916; promoted Lieut. 26 July following; Capt., 20 September 1917: served at Gallipoli; wounded 8 May 1915 (G.S.W. Shoulder) and, after recovery, rejoined his unit on the Peninsula 24 August: hospitalised Mudros (jaundice) 11–31 October 1915: returned to the Peninsula prior to proceeding to France via Egypt: joined the Expeditionary Force in

France, 31 March 1916 and, after a period of leave (May–June) and officer training at the School of Instruction rejoined 8th Battn. In the Field, 29 April 1917. Reported to have died of wounds, 4 October 1917, it has since been confirmed (13 October) by Major R.R. Wallis, 8th Battn., that Capt. Davidson was killed by a shell at the battalion assembly point while waiting for the barrage to open. Age 22. *unm.* Buried where he fell (D.28.c.8.3), approximately 800 yards south of Zonnebeke. All correspondence regarding the late Capt. Davidson should be addressed to his aunt, Mrs Sarah Jane Selby ('Clifton,' nr. Warrambool, Victoria), by whom he was adopted following the death of his parents. See account Reninghelst New Military Cemetery; Capt. J.R. Eddy (IV.C.4).

(Panel 7) Capt. 737, Rudolph Norman Clive Kirsch, 'G' Coy., 8th Bn. Australian Infantry, A.I.F.: *s.* of Simon Kirsch, of 48, Auburn Grove, Auburn, Victoria, by his wife Julia Annie: and brother to Pte. 2347, V.R. Kirsch, 38th Battn. A.I.F., who was killed in action the same day: *b.* Boorandara, Hawthorn, Bourke, 1893: Religion – Roman Catholic: Occupation – Clerk: 5′11″ tall, brown eyes, brown hair: serving member 48th Senior Cadets; joined A.I.F., Victoria, 17 August 1914; posted 'G' Coy., 8th Battn., Broadmeadows, 24 August: promoted Colr.Sergt. 18 September 1914; 2nd Lieut. 29 April 1915; Lieut. 4 August; Temp/ Capt. 19 November 1915; and Capt. 12 March 1916: departed Melbourne aboard H.M.A.T. A24 'Benalla,' 19 November 1914: trained Egypt, thereafter served Gallipoli, April–December 1915 (hospitalised July– August, Myopia); returned Egypt (January–April 1916): joined the Expeditionary Force in France, 30 April 1916, and was severely wounded (shrapnel lacerations, both thighs) when advancing at Pozieres, 5 July 1916; following hospitalisation and convalescence in England, discharged to duty January 1917: returned to France, 20 February 1917; rejoined 8th Battn. In the Field, 1 March, and was killed by a shell at the battalion assembly point while waiting for the barrage to open, 4 October 1917. Age 23. *unm.* Buried where he fell (D.28.c.8.3), approximately 1,000 yards south-east of Zonnebeke. See account Reninghelst New Military Cemetery; Capt. J.R. Eddy (IV.C.4).

His brother Vivian also has no known grave; he is recorded on Panel 25.

PANEL 7 ENDS: LT. G.F. JOHANSEN, 8TH BN. AUSTRALIAN INF.

North Portal

Ad Majorem Dei Gloriam

Here Are Recorded Names
Of Officers And Men Who Fell
In Ypres Salient But To Whom
The Fortune Of War Denied
The Known And Honoured Burial
Given To Their Comrades
In Death

PANEL 9 BEGINS: GNR. W.WYLES, R.H.A. & R.F.A.

Kitchener Wood 1915: 'On the 22nd April 1915 the 2nd London Battery, a heavy battery of Territorial artillery armed with four 7-inch guns which had been placed in action at Kitchener Wood behind the French position, was overrun, but the gunners remained with their guns until the German infantry were close upon them, when they rendered the breech-blocks useless so that the guns could not be fired, and withdrew. Both young officers present, Lieuts. Sandeman and Hamilton Field, died beside their guns, according to the tradition of their regiment.'

(Panel 9) Lieut. Dare Hamilton Field, 2nd (London) Heavy Bty., Royal Garrison Artillery (T.F.): *s.* of the late Henry Kearns Hamilton Field, by his wife Belle ('The Cedars,' Langley, co. Bucks). Killed in action, 22 April 1915. Age 22.

(Panel 9) Lieut. Sidney Robert Sandeman, 2nd (London) Heavy Bty., Royal Garrison Artillery (T.F.). Reported missing, 22 April 1915, subsequently confirmed killed in action on that date.

(Panel 9) Corpl. 25915, Harry Hother, 43rd T.M.Bty., Royal Garrison Artillery: s. of Thomas Hother, of Farm House, Walberton, co. Sussex, by his wife Mary Ann: and brother to Pte. TF/201073, H. Hother, 4th Royal Sussex Regt., killed in action, 26 March 1917, in Egypt: b. Yapton: enlisted Chichester. Killed in action, 25 September 1915. Age 35. He leaves a widow, Florence Alice Hother (5, Arthur Street, Plumstead, London).

His brother Harold also has no known grave; he is commemorated on the Jerusalem Memorial.

(Panel 9) Gnr. 27487, Frederick Blackwell, 35th Heavy Bty., Royal Garrison Artillery: brother to Pte. 12856, F.W. Blackwell, Northamptonshire Regt., killed 27 August 1915; victim to an enemy sniper nr. Vermelles: b. Broughton, nr. Kettering, 1890: enlisted Desborough, co. Northampton. Killed in action, 31 October 1914. Age 24.

His brother Frank is buried in Vermelles British Cemetery (I.B.22).

(Panel 9) Gnr. 115627, Lionel Charles Burnett, 298th Siege Bty., Royal Garrison Artillery: s. of the late Surgeon-General W.F. Burnett, Army Medical Service, and Mrs A.M.A. Burnett (The Vineyard, 24, Marlborough Road, Richmond Hill, co. Surrey): and elder brother to Capt. M. Burnett, R.A.M.C., killed in action, 14 April 1915, at Shaiba, Mesopotamia: b. Dover, co. Kent, about 1886: previously served as Lieut., Royal Navy (ret'd): volunteered and re-enlisted Whitehall, London, W.: served with the Expeditionary Force in France and Flanders, and was killed in action at Ypres, 10 August 1917. Age 31.

His brother Maurice is buried in Basra War Cemetery, Iraq (III.C.1).

(Panel 9) Gnr. 100815, Charles Edward Gerrie, 1st Siege Bty., Royal Garrison Artillery: s. of Hugh Reid Gerrie, of Manor Park, London, E.: b. London, 17 September 1887: educ. Page Green School, Tottenham, London, N.: Occupation – Salesman: enlisted, 1 June 1916: served with the Expeditionary Force in France and Flanders from 13 June 1917, and was killed in action at Zillebeke, 15 August following. Buried there. Age 29. He m. St. John's Church, Tottenham, London, N., 3 August 1913; Ada Ethel (15, Antill Road, South Tottenham, London, N.), dau. of Thomas Hull, and had two children – Edward Hugh Wallace and Ethel.

(Panel 9) Bmdr. 2893, John Kershaw, 123rd Heavy Bty., Royal Garrison Artillery: late of Gomersal, co. York: s. of the late Thomas (& Sarah Ann) Kershaw, of 40, Elsham Terrace, Burley Hill, Leeds: enlisted Leeds. Died of wounds, 8 May 1915. Age 33. Remains 'Three Unknown British Soldiers' recovered, unmarked collective grave (28.I.3.c.30.65); identified – Clothing, Titles; 'Impossible to separate remains – J. McDonald, RFA; J. Kershaw, RGA; Unknown British Sergt. – which were found together in one small grave.' Reinterred, 12 December 1930. *Buried in Strand Military Cemetery (VII.A.35/37).*

(Panel 9) Capt. Frederick Ernest William Hoare, Honourable Artillery Company attd. 11th Bn. Royal Fusiliers: late *husb.* to Lily Ethel Hoare (1, Stradella Road, Herne Hill, London, S.E.4), late of 61, Muncaster Road, Clapham Common, London, S.W. Killed in action, 10 August 1917. Age 32. Remains recovered from an unmarked grave (28NW.J.13.a.8.4); identified – 2 Damaged (Paper-maché) Discs (Lt. F.W.E. HO…), Officers Clothing, Knee Boots, H.A.C. Badge (Capt.), Royal Fusiliers Badge (Capt.); GRU Report, Zillebeke 5-361E – "These particulars possibly refer to Capt. F.W.E. Hoare, H.A.C. attd. 11th Bn. Royal Fusiliers whose particulars appear on the Menin Gate Memorial." Reinterred, registered 10 April 1929. *Buried in Sanctuary Wood Cemetery (V.H.5).*

(Panel 9) 2nd Lieut. William George Hoare, 1st Honourable Artillery Company: s. of A.P. (& J.) Hoare, of Town Farm, Amersham, co. Buckingham: educ. Elstow (Bedford) County School. Killed in action, at Bellewaarde, 16 June 1915. Age 29. See Capt. C. Tatham, Bailleul Communal Cemetery Extension (I.C.136).

(Panel 9) Pte. 2694, Reginald Frederick William Abbott, 1st Bn. Honourable Artillery Company: s. of the late John Octavius Abbott, of The Priory, Breakspears Road, Brockley, London, S.E.4, Architect, A.R.I.B.A., F.S.I., by his wife Mary Jane, dau. of the Rev. Francis Ellis, of Pocklington, co. York: and brother to Pte. G/9221, A.L.V. Abbott, 6th The Buffs, killed in action on the Somme front, 3 July 1916: b. Brockley, 28 May 1882: educ. St. Peter's College there: Occupation – sometime Clerk; London Stock

Exchange; previously served three years, Royal Naval Volunteer Reserve (R.N.V.R.); thereafter engaged for six years, mining in Rhodesia: returned from the latter following the outbreak of war; enlisted H.A.C., Armoury House, Finsbury, 2 December 1914: went to France, February 1915, and was killed in action during the British attack at Hooge, Flanders, 16 June 1915. Age 33. *unm.*

His brother Arthur also has no known grave; he is commemorated on the Thiepval Memorial, Somme (Pier & Face 5.D.).

(Panel 9) Pte. 2336, Sydney Clement Collings, 1st Bn. Honourable Artillery Company (T.F.): 4th *s.* of John R. (& S.A.) Collings, of 36, Goring Road, Bowes Park, Wood Green, London: *b.* Hornsey, co. Middlesex, 8 June 1894: *educ.* Harringay Council School: was employed in a Merchant's Shipping business: joined H.A.C. August 1914, after the outbreak of war: served with the Expeditionary Force in France and Flanders from 28 December following, and was killed in action at Hooge, 30 September 1915. Buried Maple Copse, Hooge. Age 21. *unm.*

(Panel 9) Pte. 2565, Louis Ignatius DeWeck, 1st Bn. Honourable Artillery Company (T.F.): *s.* of Albert Joseph DeWeck, of 61, Melbury Gardens, Wimbledon, London, SW20, by his wife Marguerite Christine Marie: enlisted H.A.C., Armoury House, Finsbury, London, E.C.: served with the Expeditionary Force in France and Flanders from 28 December 1914, and was killed in action, 16 June 1915, at Hooge, nr Ypres. Age 29.

(Panel 9) Pte. 2504, Harry Dukinfield Jones, 1st Bn. Honourable Artillery Company (T.F.): *yst. s.* of Edward Dukinfield Jones, of Castro, Reigate, by his wife Bertha, *dau.* of Holbrook Gaskell: *b.* Sao Paulo, Brazil, 11 April 1880: came to England when 12 years of age: *educ.* Liverpool College Preparatory School, and Lancing College. From an early age he devoted himself to music, and decided to make it his profession, choosing the piano as his instrument. For about four years he worked in the Leschetizky method, under Mr. George Magrath. Early in 1912 he went to Vienna and studied under Frau Bree, with occasional lessons from Leschetizky himself. On his return to England (1913), he continued his studies under Mr. Howard Jones at the R.C.M., taking singing as his second study: joined Honourable Artillery Coy. October 1914, went to the Front with a draft for the 1st Battn. at the end of December; in April was "doing very stiff work" somewhere near Ypres, and was killed in action in the charge of the Honourable Artillery Company; Hooge, 16 June 1915. Age 35. *unm*

(Panel 9) Pte. 2292, Wilfred Alan Granville Southwell, 1st Bn. Honourable Artillery Company: late of Catford, London, S.E.6: *s.* of Mr (& Mrs) Southwell, of 93, Queen Street, Filey, co. York: and brother to Lt. F.E.G. Southwell, East Yorkshire Regt., died 19 August 1916, of wounds: *educ.* Elstow (Bedford) County School: enlisted Armoury House. Killed in action, 16 June 1915. A student from his old school (November 2003) left the following lines:

> *Though in rude lettered, maybe nameless tomb,*
> *Some lie out there 'neath unrecording sod,*
> *Who died for King, Country, School and Home,*
> *Not, unremembered have all met their God.*

His brother Frederick is buried in Duisans British Cemetery, Etrun (II.D.5).

(Panel 9) Pte. 1510, Edward Lawrence Sprunt, 1st Bn. Honourable Artillery Company (T.F.): (Stretcher-bearer section): 3rd *s.* of John Dalziel Sprunt, of 3, East India Avenue, London, E.C., by his wife Jane, *dau.* of John Naismith: yr. brother to 2nd Lieut. A.D. Sprunt, 4th Bedfordshire Regt. attd. 2nd South Staffordshire Regt., died in hospital, Lillers, France, 17 March 1915, from wounds received in action on the 10th, nr. Neuve Chapelle; and Lieut. G.H. Sprunt, 2nd Bedfordshire Regt., died 15 October 1919, consequent to wounds received in action, August 1918, nr. Morlancourt: *b.* Hampstead, London, 28 August 1892: *educ.* Berkhampstead School, and Jesus College, Oxford, at which latter he held an open exhibition. Having served about nine years in the O.T.C., he was offered a commission on the outbreak of war, but being eager to go to the Front as soon as possible, and thinking he would probably be sent for months to a regimental depot to train recruits (as his elder brother was), he enlisted as a Private in the Honourable Artillery Coy., and went to the Front with them and served through the winter of 1914–

15. Later, was again offered a commission and the War Office instructed his Col. to send him home that he might take it up. After getting his discharge he went back to the Col. and said he had heard there was to be a battle next day, and as he did not wish to leave on the eve of it, he asked permission to remain and see his comrades through it. The Col. replied that as he had put it so gallantly he could not refuse his request, and so he might remain. That evening the Battn. went up to the trenches and was under fire about 36 hours, including the fierce fight of 16 June 1915, losing about half its numbers. On 17 June, about 2 a.m., near Chateau Hooge, Belgium, he was helping to carry a wounded comrade on a stretcher, and had got to within 15 yards of the Dressing Station, when a shell came over and exploded underneath the stretcher, killing him and two others, and wounding the remaining two stretcher-bearers. He was buried on the battlefield, near the Ypres-Menin Road. His Commanding Officer wrote,: "Your son had the opportunity of not going up (to the trenches) and of returning home, but refused to leave his comrades at such a time, and so showed a magnificent spirit – worthy of a man in this Regt. He discharged his duties with great valour under great danger. The circumstances were such as to lead me to specially recommend him for gallant conduct and the enclosed card has been received from the General. I have pleasure in sending it to you, while regretting very much the circumstances which have been greatly appreciated by his comrades." The card is of the first class, being printed in gilt letters, the ordinary card being in black letters. It reads – "Third Division, British Expeditionary Force, 1510, Private E.L. Sprunt, Hon. Artillery Coy. Your commanding officer and brigade commander have informed me that you distinguished yourself by your conduct in the field on 16 June 1915. I have read their report with much pleasure, and have brought it to the notice of higher authority." Later the Assistant Military Secretary wrote that he had been Mentioned in a Despatch from Sir John (now Lord) French 'for gallant and distinguished service in the field.' "I am to express to you the King's high appreciation of these services, and to add that His Majesty trusts that their public acknowledgement may be of some consolation in your bereavement." Age 22. *unm*. (*IWGC record 16 June 1915*)

He Saved Others, Himself He Could Not Save

His brother Alexander is buried in Lillers Communal Cemetery (II.D.2); Gerald is commemorated on the Hollybrook Memorial, Southampton.

(Panel 9) **Major Charles Napier North**, Comdg. 5th Field Coy., Royal Engineers: eldest *s*. of the late Col. Roger North, Royal Artillery, and his wife ('Briarwood,' Camberley, co. Surrey): *gt.-gdson* of Capt. Roger North, 50th Regt., who fought in the Peninsula, and died after his retirement from the effect of wounds received in that campaign, and *gdson*. of Col. Charles Napier North (Godson of Sir Charles Napier), 60th Regt. (King's Royal Rifle Corps), which he commanded for some-time; Mentioned in Despatches for his services in the Indian Mutiny; he was also present at the taking of the Taku Forts, China: *b*. Bristol, 16 August 1873: *educ*. Radley, where he held a scholarship; and Royal Military Academy, Woolwich, from which he joined Royal Engineers, 1893: promoted Lieut. February 1896; Capt. 1904: served in the South African War, being present at operations in Orange Free State, the Transvaal, Orange River Colony, and Cape Colony, being afterwards employed on the Staff under the Director of Military Intelligence, South Africa, May–August 1902 (Queen's Medal, three clasps; King's Medal, two clasps): promoted Major, July 1913. When the present war with Germany broke out he was in command of 5th (Field) Company, Royal Engineers, Aldershot: went to France with IInd Division, early August. On 1st November following, he was shot by a sniper while superintending the erection of wire entanglements at Zonnebeke during the First Battle of Ypres. His company suffered terribly, and between August and December lost four officers killed, and two severely wounded, while casualties among the men were very heavy. A high percentage of the latter have received the D.C.M. Major North was Mentioned in Sir John (now Lord) French's Despatch, 14 January 1915, for conspicuous gallantry. Age 41. He *m*., December 1913; Norah ('Westholme,' Horsell, Woking, co. Surrey), *dau*. of the late Col. Gribbon. A daughter was born, after his death, in March 1915.

(Panel 9) **Major John Palgrave Heathcote Ouchterlony**, D.S.O., Royal Engineers: eldest *s*. of Lieut.Col. Thomas Heathcote Ouchterlony, of The Guynd, Arbroath, co. Forfar, late Royal Artillery, by his wife the late Mary Ann Ouchterlony, *née* Wilmot: *b*. Plymouth, co. Devon, 10 June 1884: *educ*. Inverness College, King's College School; and Royal Military Academy, Woolwich, out of which he passed 2nd Lieut. R.E., December 1901; promoted Capt. December 1912; Major December 1916: specially employed in the Ashanti, January 1910: served with the Expeditionary Force in France and Flanders from August 1915, and was killed in action nr. Ypres, 7 June 1917. Buried near Fosse Wood, near Zillebeke. His Commanding Officer wrote, "He was one of the finest officers I have ever known." Twice Mentioned in Despatches (*London Gazette*, 15 June 1916; 18 May 1917) by F.M. Sir Douglas Haig, for 'gallant and distinguished service in the field;' awarded the D.S.O. (*London Gazette*, 4 June 1917), "For gallantry and devotion to duty on several occasions during the period 20 September–2 October 1916, on which he reconnoitred sites for new trenches and posts in front of our first line, going personally over the ground in daylight under considerable shell and rifle fire, and afterwards marking out the lines by daylight under very trying conditions. His example has been freely followed by his men, and has enabled work to be considerably accelerated." Age 33. He *m*. St. Mary's Church, Cadogan Street, London, S.W., 26 September 1908; Constance Kathleen Gaisford, *dau*. of the late W.H. Spackman, of New Zealand, and had a *dau*., Marjorie Mary, *b*. 11 August 1915.

(Panel 9) Major Alfred Herbert Tyler, Comdg. 5th Field Coy., Royal Engineers: *s*. of the late Sir Henry Whatley Tyler, Royal Engineers, M.P., by his wife Margaret, *dau*. of the late General Sir Charles Pasley, K.C.B., Royal Engineers: and uncle to Lieut. A. Tyler, Royal Engineers, killed in action at the same place the following day: *b*. Hampton Court, 27 December 1870: *educ*. Cheltenham College, where he held a scholarship, and Royal Military Academy, Woolwich: gazetted 2nd Lieut. Royal Engineers 25 July 1890;: promoted Lieut. 25 July 1893; Capt. 25 July 1901; Major, 25 July 1910: employed on the Sierra Leone Boundary Commission, December 1895–May 1896: took part in the operations in Sierra Leone 1898–99, with the Karene Expedition, where he was wounded (Medal with clasp): served in the South African War 1900–02, as Special Service Officer, Rhodesian Field Force, March 1900–January 1901: employed as Staff Officer (graded Staff Captain) January–May 1901: took part in operations in Transvaal, June 1901, and October 1901–March 1902; and in Cape Colony, July–September 1901, and April–May 1902, on the Staff (Queen's Medal, four clasps; King's Medal, two clasps): First Assistant Superintendent Building Works, Royal Arsenal, Woolwich, January 1907–25 April 1912: served with the Expeditionary Force in France and Flanders, initially on the lines of communication, afterwards commanding No.5 Field Coy., R.E., 2nd Divn., and was killed in action, 11 November 1914. Age 43. At the time of his death, Major Tyler was advancing along a communication trench between Nonne Boschen and Polygon Wood when, after advising Corpl. Curtis and three sappers to keep their heads down, he neglected to heed his own advice and was shot through the head and killed. His body was carried back along the communication trench by Sappers Farmfield and Kellogg and buried nearby. Major Tyler left a widow and three young boys.

His nephew Albert also has no known grave; he is recorded below.

Arthur Collins entered Clifton College in 1897; the same year as a volume of poetry by Old Cliftonian Sir Henry Newbolt was published.

> There's a breathless hush in the Close tonight
> Ten to make and the match to win
> A bumping pitch and a blinding light, an hour to play and the last man in
> And it's not for the sake of a ribboned coat
> Or the selfish hope of a season's fame
> But his Captain's hand on his shoulder smote
> Play up! Play up! And play the game.

(Panel 9) Capt. Arthur Edward Jeune 'James' Collins, 5th Field Coy., Royal Engineers: eldest *s*. of the late Arthur Herbert Collins, J.P., Indian Civil Service, by his marriage to the late Esther Ida: and brother to Lieut. H.C. Collins, 24th Manchester Regt., died 11 February 1917, of disease; and 2nd Lieut. N.C. Collins, 7th Suffolk Regt., killed in action, 9 August 1916, at the Somme: *b*. Hazaribagh, India, 18 August 1885: *educ*. Clifton College (Clarke's House, entered September 1897) where, in June 1899, aged 13 years, he astonished the cricket world by scoring 628 not out in a Junior House Match between Clarke's House and North Town over four afternoons, carrying his bat through the innings of 836. Hitting his first stroke at 3.30 pm., 23 June, by close of play, at 6 p.m.., he had scored an impressive 200 runs. The following day so brilliant was his play that an Old Cliftonian match nearby lost its spectators interest, and large crowds gathered to watch Collins' phenomenal performance. Despite a dropped catch at 400, by 5.30 p.m.. – only five hours after his start – he surpassed Andrew Stoddart's then world record score of 485, remaining unbeaten at close of play on 509. On Monday, 26 June, when play resumed at 12.30 p.m., escalated media interest had drawn crowds unlike anything ever witnessed at a school sporting event before, or since, and again, by close of play – despite another two dropped catches at 505 and 519 – he had reached 598, but was rapidly growing short of partners. The following day his final partner, Thomas Refern, was caught by Elison Fuller-Eberle at point for 13, with Collins' score on 628. And, when North Town House went in to play, Collins' showed his capabilities as an all-rounder with his right-arm medium pace bowling taking 11 wickets for 63 runs. Later, in Senior School, he moved to North Town House, and was in the 1st Cricket XI, the 1st Football XV, the 1st Racquet Pair with R.P. Keigwin (1902), and represented the school in featherweight boxing at the Public Schools Competition, Aldershot (1901),where he took a bronze medal with E.A. Hughes and H.P. Hewett. He was Head of his House, and at the age of 17 passed into the Royal Military Academy, Woolwich, taking the fourth place in the list of successful candidates: gazetted 2nd Lieut. R.E., 21 December 1904, aged 21 years: went to India, to command 'C' Coy, 2nd Queen Victoria's Own Sappers and Miners, Secunderbad: promoted Lieut. 23 June 1907; Capt. (posthumously) antedated 30 October 1914: went to the Front with No.5 Field Coy., Royal Engineers, August 1914: served with the Expeditionary Force in France and Flanders. On 11th November his Company, of which he was then in command (his Senior Officers, Majors North and Tyler, having been killed 1st and 11th November), was called up to help thrust the enemy back at Polygon Wood, near Ypres. It was whilst signalling for reinforcements during this action that he was killed. Age 29. The Commander, Royal Engineers, 2nd Division, reported, "At about 9.30 a.m., 11 November 1914, 5th (Field) Coy., R.E., were in dug-outs in Polygon Wood and a heavy shell-fire had been going on for some hours. Major Tyler (also killed) was informed by Brigade Headquarters that the Germans had broken through. Some twenty men, under Sergt. Lethbridge, were sent to the south side of Polygon Wood to the trenches there and the rest of the sappers, with all the officers, went south into the open and occupied a disused trench and a short length of hedge on the left rear of it. The latter was under Lieut. Gowlland with Corpl. Curtis and six sappers and a few men of the Connaught Rangers. Some Germans from the wood on the right enfiladed this trench and the right flank was turned back by six or eight men under Corpl. chambers. In signalling up more men to protect this flank Lieut. Collins was killed. Sapper Farmfield, at great risk to himself, lifted Lieut. Collins into the trench." Capt. Collins was Mentioned in Despatches (*London Gazette*, 17 February 1915) by F.M. Sir John (now Lord) French, for 'gallant and distinguished service in the field.' While in India Capt. Collins played polo, racquets and tennis; but on returning to England took up cricket again, having excelled at this sport while at College and played for the R.E. at Aldershot, also at Lord's against the Royal Artillery. He was a member of the Junior Army and Navy Club. He *m.*, April, 1914; Ethel A. (11, Park Mansions, Bath, co. Gloucester), *dau.* of the late Stanley Slater, and *grand-dau.* of the late Col. Slater, 82nd Regt. Capt. Collins, whose parents both died before he began his schooling, was described in a newspaper article as – "…an orphan whose guardians lived in Tavistock, Devon. He was a reserved boy, short and stockily built, fair-haired and pale. He was remembered by his contemporaries as one who led by example, rather than by inspiration, although paradoxically he was regarded as likely to fall short of the highest standards as a cricketer because of his recklessness at the crease." After leaving school, whilst Capt. Collins preferred not to be reminded of his famous innings – testimony to the event being available from the scorebook which still hangs in the pavilion – the ground on which the match was played, Guthrie Road, Bristol, was renamed Collins' Piece.

His brother Herbert is buried in Etaples Military Cemetery (I.A.82), Norman has no known grave, he is commemorated on the Thiepval Memorial; similarly, Majors North and Tyler also have no known grave, both are recorded above.

(Panel 9) Capt. John Aloysius McEnery, 1st Field Coy., Royal Engineers: 4th *s.* of Dr. William McEnery, of Semington House, Sherborne, co. Dorset: *b.* 23 December 1877: Religion – Roman Catholic: *educ.* Sherborne School: entered Royal Engineers, 5 December 1896: promoted Lieut. 5 December 1899: took part in the Tibet Expedition, 1903–04; Assistant Field Engineer, Mentioned in Despatches (*London Gazette*, 13 December 1904), Sapper Farmfield, at great risk to himself, lifted Lieut. December 1905: served with the Expeditionary Force in France and Flanders, and was accidentally killed – shot by a sentry – at Zandvoorde, nr. Ypres, 26 October 1914. Age 36.

(Panel 9) Capt. Andrew Holmes Scott, M.C., Royal Engineers: Brigade Major, General Staff: *s.* of the late Col. Edward Holmes Scott, late Bengal Staff Corps, by his wife Emily Isabella, *née* Seagar (31, St. Cuthbert's Street, Bedford): *b.* Sliema, Malta, 23 November 1888: *educ.* Geneva, Switzerland; Cheltenham College; Royal Military Academy, Woolwich, out of which he passed second, 1908: gazetted 2nd Lieut. 27 July 1908; promoted Lieut. July 1911; Capt. September 1915: represented Royal Engineers in the Army Pageant, Fulham, 1910: served with the Expeditionary Force in France and Flanders July 1915–31 July 1917 (being in command of 15th Divisional Signal Coy., and subsequently employed on the Staff) and was killed in action on the latter date while so employed at the Third Battle of Ypres. Age 28. Awarded the Military Cross (*London Gazette*, 3 June 1916), for 'devotion to duty;' twice Mentioned in Despatches (*London Gazette*, 1 January 1916), by F.M. Sir John (now Lord) French, and Gen. (now F.M.) Sir Douglas Haig (*London Gazette*, 4 January 1917), for 'gallant and distinguished service in the field.' Captain Holmes Scott was one of the first English officers to take up wireless telegraphy, and was an Army Interpreter in five languages. He *m.* Buxton, 21 April 1915; Doris, only *dau.* of the late James Simpson Clayton, V.D., M.B., F.R.C.S., of Accrington, co. Lancaster, and had a *dau.*, Elizabeth Miranda, *b.* (posthumous) 21 August 1917.

(Panel 9) Capt. John Kearsley Dawson-Scott, 5th Field Coy., Royal Engineers: *s.* of General Dawson-Scott, Colonel Commandant Royal Engineers, by his wife Grace, *née* Nicholl-Crane: *gdson.* of Col. Robert Kearsley Dawson, C.B., Royal Engineers: *b.* London, 18 May 1883: *educ.* Tonbridge School; and Royal Military Academy, Woolwich, passed out fourth on the list, entering School of Military Engineering, Chatham, July 1902: subsequently stationed in a Field Company, Aldershot, from thence served five years in Egypt: on return to England apptd. Asst. Instructor (Fortifications), School of Engineering, Chatham: on the outbreak of war with Germany, joined 5th Field Coy., Royal Engineers, leaving England, 15 August 1914: served with the Expeditionary Force in France and Flanders, and was killed, 29 October 1914, by a high-explosive shell while making a reconnaissance in connection with trench fighting at the Battle of Ypres. For his services earlier in the war he had been awarded the Chevalier of Legion of Honour for 'special gallantry between the dates 21–30 August 1914.' Good at all games, he won many cups for rifle shooting, and at the Royal Military Academy had his colours for hockey. He was a good polo player, won cups at the Turf Club, Cairo, and prizes for cricket, tennis, and croquet. He was also very musical, playing the cello, and sketched well. Age 31. *unm.*

The Victoria Cross, the highest award given to British and Commonwealth service personnel for single acts of courage performed above and beyond the call of duty, was instituted by Her Majesty Queen Victoria, 9 January 1856. The Royal Warrant setting out the criteria for the award, in fifteen parts, carries a number of clauses: "VII/I. – When the fleet or army in which such act has been performed, is under the eye and command of an admiral or general officer commanding the forces" – and "VIII – It is ordained where such act shall not have been performed in sight of a commanding officer as aforesaid, then the claimant for the honour shall prove the act to the satisfaction of the captain or officer commanding his ship, or to the officer commanding the regiment to which the claimant belongs, and such captain or such commanding officer shall report the same through the usual channel to the admiral or commodore commanding the force employed on the service, or to the officer commanding the forces in the field, who shall call for such description and attestation of the act as he may think requisite, and on approval shall recommend the grant of the decoration."

The charter also records reasons for not granting the award, sometimes it was rejected because the reviewing body deemed the deed not worthy enough for such high recognition; sometimes the need for witness verification could not be achieved; in many instances – particularly on the Western Front – the 'claimant' was dead. Under the conditions that prevailed in the various theatres of war, the single acts of gallantry and self-sacrifice performed daily by a substantial number of individuals went – for whatever reason – without recognition, among them Capt. R.B.M. Wills – recommended for the Victoria Cross – Recommendation Declined.

(Panel 9) Capt. Robert Bruce Melville Wills, 2nd (Wessex) Field Coy., Royal Engineers (T.F.): Recommended for the Victoria Cross: 2nd *s.* of Walter Melville Wills, Tobacco Manufacturer, Messrs W.D. & H.O. Wills; of Bracken Hill, Leigh Woods, co. Somerset, and Killilan, co. Ross, and Louisa Gertrude, *née* Wilson, his wife: and brother to the late Harold E.M. Wills, killed 11 February 1925, by an avalanche: *b.* Clifton, Bristol, 26 May 1890: *educ.* Charterhouse, and Trinity College, Cambridge (O.T.C. member, 1908–11); Hons. Degree (Mechanical Sciences Tripos): gazetted 2nd Lieut. Royal Engineers (T.F.) June 1911: passed first on the List of his year after the course of instruction at Chatham: promoted Lieut. September 1913; Capt. September 1914: served with the Expeditionary Force in France; killed, at St. Eloi, nr. Ypres, 15 February 1915, while helping to carry out a wounded officer, who lay, the sole occupant, in a trench Capt. Wills and his men had been sent to repair. He *m.* 16 June 1914, and leaves a widow, Beryl Emmeline 'Daisy' (Birdcombe Court, Wraxall, co. Somerset), *dau.* of John Robert (& Mrs) Sutton, of Clifton, Bristol, and a *dau.*, Ione Bruce Melville, *b.* 16 July 1915, after her father's death. His recreations were stalking, shooting, fishing and hunting. Age 24.

(Panel 9) Lieut. Arthur Clunes Hooper Carr, Royal Engineers *yr. s.* of Col. George Anderson Carr, Royal Engineers (ret'd); of 'Nymans,' Midhope Road, Woking, co. Surrey, by his wife Harriet Anna: and *yr.* brother to Capt. W.B.H. Carr, Royal Engineers (surv'd.): *b.* New Brompton, Chatham, co. Kent, 27 April 1893: *educ.* St. Mary's Hill, Horsell, near Woking (Arnold F. Saunders, Esq.); Dover College (St. Martin's House), and the Royal Military Academy, Woolwich, where he passed out with honours, taking the prizes in Artillery and Military Engineering, also the Armstrong Memorial Medal for Science: gazetted 2nd Lieut. Royal Engineers, 20 December 1912; promoted Lieut. 25 October 1914: served with the Expeditionary Force in France and Flanders from August 1914, with 59th Field Coy., Royal Engineers, Vth Division: present at the Battle of Mons, and the fighting in the subsequent retirement, and the Battles of the Marne and Aisne: in October, when the British Expeditionary Force was transferred from the Aisne, he took part in the fighting near La Bassée, being wounded at Lorgies, on the 20th of that month, and invalided home: after recovery, returned to France with XXVIIth Division, 21 December 1914. Lieut. Carr was employed in the neighbourhood of Ypres, and was killed on the occasion of the German (Bavarian) attack on the British position in front of St. Eloi, on the afternoon of Sunday, 14 February 1915; being on duty in the front trenches there at the time of the attack. These trenches fell into the hands of the enemy, and it was not until they were re-taken by a counter-attack on the next day that his body was found, the Official Casualty List recording – 'Died of wounds on active service, 15 February 1915.' Buried where he fell. Age 21. *unm.*

(Panel 9) Lieut. Morys Wynne-Jones, 54th Field Coy., Royal Engineers: only *s.* of the Rev. John William Wynne-Jones, of Trejorwerth, Anglesey, Vicar of Carnarvon, by his wife the Hon. Jessie Frances *née* Bruce, *dau.* of Henry Austin, 1st Baron Aberdare: *b.* Carnarvon, 13 May 1887: *educ.* Fonthill, Charterhouse, and Trinity College, Cambridge, where he rowed in his college boat and won his oar. Graduated B.A. (1909), and after passing his A.M. Inst. C.E. examination, was for nearly two years an Engineer on the Cardiff Railway, under the late Lord Merthyr, being subsequently appointed one of the engineers of the Mexican Eagle Oil Co., at Tampico, Mexico: joined Special Reserve of Officers (Royal Engineers), as 2nd Lieut., 26 June 1912, and on the outbreak of war, without waiting to be summoned, immediately returned to England: promoted Lieut. 4 October 1914: left for France same day with 7th Division, and was killed in action at Zandvoorde, during the 1st Battle of Ypres, on the 29th of the same month. Capt. (now Major) Guy Williams, Comdg. 54th Field Coy., wrote that they were called upon to counter-attack with the Yorkshire Regt. at a point where the Germans had broken through the British firing line. "Lieut. Wynne-Jones was leading his section when the enemy's shrapnel found them, and he was killed instantaneously. The Coy. feel his loss very much. He understood his men and his job. I miss him personally as a most efficient subaltern and as a good friend." Capt. R.M. Burgoyne, 2nd Royal Scots Fusiliers, now a prisoner in Germany, also wrote of two engineer officers, Lieut. Wynne-Jones and Lieut. J.M. Smeathman, who he said, "Did a lot of good work for them, both as engineers and infantry, always being ready to take a rifle and bear a hand. They were two very gallant fellows." Age 27. *unm.* (*IWGC record 36th Coy.*)

(Panel 9) Lieut. Julian Missenden Smeathman, Royal Engineers: 2nd *s.* of Lovel Smeathman, of South Hill, Hemel Hempstead, co. Hertford, by his wife Frances Ann: brother to Lieut. C. Smeathman, Leicestershire Regt., died of wounds at Bailleul: *b.* 24 December 1887: *educ.* Rugby (Steel) from 1900, afterwards entering Royal Military Academy, Woolwich: obtained his commission, and was gazetted 2nd Lieut. July 1910; promoted Lieut. April 1910: served with the Expeditionary Force in France and Flanders and was killed in action, 24 October 1914. Age 26. Lieut. Smeathman married, only a few months before his death, on returning home from Foreign Service. Remembered on Hemel Hempstead War Memorial.

His younger brother Cecil died the same day; he is buried in Bailleul Communal Cemetery (C.7).

(Panel 9) Lieut. Arthur Gilliat-Smith, 26th Field Coy., Royal Engineers: *s.* of Harold Gilliat- Smith, of 37, Kenilworth Street, St. Leonards-on-Sea, by his wife Laura Sybil: *gt.-gdson.* of the late Joseph Smith, formerly of The Oaks, Woodmansterne: related to Sir Edmund Bainbridge, K.C.B.: *b.* Blackheath, London, S.E., 3 July 1888: *educ.* St. Paul's House, St. Leonards-on-Sea; Hillside, Godalming; Rugby, and Royal Military Academy, Woolwich: gazetted 2nd Lieut. Royal Engineers, December 1908: after leaving Chatham joined 26th Field Coy., Bordon Camp, co. Hants, serving there for the duration of his time spent in England: promoted Lieut. February 1911: served with the Expeditionary Force in France and Flanders, and was killed near Ypres, 1 November 1914, when leading his section to reinforce some infantry under a very hot fire. His Commanding Officer wrote, "I have lost a loyal friend, and a most keen and efficient officer." Lieut. Gilliatt-Smith was a cross-country rider, and won several point-to-point races 1913–1914. He was also an expert skier, and always spent part of his winter leave in Norway. Age 26. *unm.*

(Panel 9) Lieut. Albert Tyler, Royal Engineers: only child of Col. (& Mrs) H.E. Tyler, Royal Engineers, Wetherden, Warwick's Bench Road, Guildford, co. Surrey: *gdson.* to Capt. H.W. Tyler, R.E.: and *gt.-gdson* of General C.W. Pasley, K.C.B., R.E.: and nephew to Major A.H. Tyler, R.E., who fell at Ypres, in almost the same place, 11 November 1914: *b.* 1 February 1893: *educ.* Mr Parry's School, Stoke House; and Charterhouse, where he took Junior and Senior Scholarships, and passed fourth for the Royal Military Academy, Woolwich: passed out third; gazetted (*London Gazette*, 9 August. 1912) 2nd Lieut. Royal Engineers 19 July 1912; promoted Lieut. July 1914: on leaving Chatham, posted 11th Field Coy., R.E., Aldershot: served with the Expeditionary Force in France and Flanders from August 1914: fought at Mons, through the retirement at the Aisne, and again at Ypres. The 5th and 11th Field Companies were improving defences by night, and supporting infantry by day throughout the attack by the German Guards, and on 12 November, Lieut. Tyler with two sections of his company, by his prompt action saved the situation when the flank of the Staffordshire's had become exposed, before he was killed by a bullet through his heart. His uncle – Major A.H. Tyler, R.E. – had been killed on similar duty in command of 5th Field Coy., R.E., the day before The Brigadier General in command reported that had Lieut. Tyler lived he would have been recommended for the D.S.O. He was Mentioned in Field Marshal Sir John (now Lord) French's Despatch of 14 January 1915, for 'gallant and distinguished service in the field'. Age 21. *unm.*

His uncle Alfred also has no known grave; he is recorded above.

(Panel 9) 2nd Lieut. Arthur Gordon Haigh, 172nd Coy., Royal Engineers: only child of Arthur Harry Haigh, of St. Catherine's, Ontario, Canada, M.Inst.C.E., by his wife Mary Browne, *dau.* of John Browne Nicholson: *b.* Natal, South Africa, 29 June 1885: *educ.* St. Paul's School; University College School, London, Aberystwyth University College; Christ's College, Cambridge (graduate): Occupation – Civil Engineer; A.M.I.C.E., employed London County Council Sewerage; Bombay, Baroda & Central India Railway Company, Rajputana, and National Transcontinental Railway Construction, Canada: obtained a commission, 12 June 1915: served with the Expeditionary Force in France and Flanders, and was killed in action, in the Ypres salient, 14 February 1916. Buried in Gordon Terrace Military Cemetery, near where he fell. Major G.A. Syme wrote, "On behalf of all the officers of the company, may I ask you to accept our very deepest sympathy … He was always absolutely cool and collected, even in the most trying and dangerous situations that occur in mining from time to time, and for that reason, as well as his technical ability, he is a man we can ill afford to lose." Age 30. *unm.* (*IWGC record 15 February 1916*)

(Panel 9) 2nd Lieut. George Minchin Hume, 2nd (Northumbrian) Field Coy., Royal Engineers (T.F.): *s.* of George Haliburton Hume, of Durham, by his wife Frances Diana, *née* Jackson: *b.* 1897. Killed in action, 12 June 1915. Age 18. GRU Report, Zillebeke 5-326E: Remains 'Unknown British Officer. 2/ Lieut. Royal Engineers' exhumed 3 January 1929 isolated grave (28.I.24.d.15.45); identified – Dark brown hair, approximately 6'5" tall; Officers Khaki Tunic, Breeches, Boots Leggings, Badge & Buttons Royal Engineers, Boots mkd. S & C.W. Dixon Ltd., 36, Northumberland Street, Newcastle-on-Tyne, Badge of Rank 2/Lieut., Skull smashed; reinterred, registered 4 January 1929. Remembered on Broadstone (St. John's) Parish Church War Memorial, Dorset. *Buried in Sanctuary Wood Cemetery (IV.T.10).*

(Panel 9) 2nd Lieut. Henry Frederick Thornton Renny-Tailyour, 5th Field Coy., Royal Engineers: *s.* of Col. Henry Waugh Renny-Tailyour, J.P., late Royal Engineers; of Newmanswalls, Montrose, co. Forfar, and Shrewsbury House, Dublin, by his wife Emily Rose, *dau.* of John Wingfield Stratford, of Addington Park, West Malling, co. Kent: *b.* Hornebush, Sydney, New South Wales, 31 July 1893: *educ.* Arnold House, Llandulas, North Wales; Rugby School, and Royal Military Academy, Woolwich, where he was successful in athletics, winning the mile-race, and running second in the two-mile: gazetted 2nd Lieut., Royal Engineers, 20 December 1912: went to France from School of Military Engineering, Chatham, having been posted 5th Field Coy., forming part of IInd Division, 1st Army Corps, 15 August 1914: went through the retirement from Mons, the advance to the Marne, the Battle of the Aisne, and the Battle of Ypres. On 14 September 1914, at the fighting on the Aisne, he was wounded but remained on duty, and was killed near Ypres, 11 November 1914, while leading his section in a successful counter-attack on a German trench held by the Prussian Guard. Mentioned in Sir John (now Lord) French's Despatch, 14 January 1915, for 'gallant and distinguished service in the field.' Age 21. *unm.*

(Panel 9) 2nd Lieut. Charles George Augustine Sibeth, 12th Field Coy., Royal Engineers: *s.* of Charles (& Monica) Sibeth, of 26, Marsham Street, Westminster, London: Religion – Roman Catholic: Associate Member Institute of Chartered Engineers; on the outbreak of war was engaged in Cairo. Missing/believed killed in France, 9 August 1915. Age 34. In a letter to Mr Sibeth a fellow officer wrote, "Your son and his section were attached to an infantry battalion in an attack on the 9th. inst., and after some of the German trenches had been captured, your son was hit in the open. One of his corporals very gallantly attempted to get him under cover, but was killed in the attempt. One of the sappers then succeeded in getting him into a captured German trench where, with the assistance of the infantry, he managed to bandage his wounds and place him in a German dug-out. Our infantry were then driven back by a counter-attack and could not carry off your son with them. The Colonel of the infantry regiment to which your son was attached spoke most highly of your son's gallantry, and held out some hopes that he had been taken prisoner by the Germans."

(Panel 9) 2nd Lieut. Sydney Vernon Young, 59th Field Coy., Royal Engineers: *s.* of Professor Sydney Young, F.R.S., of 13, Clyde Road, Dublin, and Grace Young, his wife: *b.* 8 January 1897: *educ.* Charterhouse, and Royal Military Academy, Woolwich: apptd. 2nd Lieut., proceeded to France and was killed in action, 25 September 1915, at Hooge. Age 18.

16 June 1915: At 4.15 a.m., after a two hour concentrated bombardment of the German lines at Bellewaarde, an attack by units of 3rd Division began their advance and within a short while had achieved their objective and taken the first line trenches. The supporting troops then advanced – with them 1 and 3 sections 1st (Cheshire) Field Coy. R.E. – who were to help to consolidate the captured positions as quickly as possible; the attack had meanwhile progressed to the German second line and in some places as far as the third line…'A digging party of 150 which was at our disposal had advanced with the attack! The situation appeared uncertain on our left and it was not until 2 p.m. that the officers of 2 and 4 sections were sent for with ref. to CT. An officer went to reconnoiter and found that the sunken road leading forward from our old line to the captured first line was covered from view and rifle fire for anyone

going up. At 3 p.m. a minor assault on the left was contemplated, the question of the CT was therefore left in abeyance, as the sunken road afforded good communication. At dusk the company was relieved by 56 Company and returned to billets. Total casualties for that day – 6 NCOs and 12 Sappers wounded, 2 Sappers killed, 1 NCO and 1 Sapper missing.'

(Panel 9) Corpl. 57, David Jones, 1st /1st (Cheshire) Field Coy., Royal Engineers (T.F.): served with the Expeditionary Force. Missing presumed killed at Bellewaarde, 16 June 1915.

(Panel 9) 2nd Corpl. 19185, Thomas O'Shea, 12th Field Coy., Royal Engineers: *s.* of Richard (& Maria) O'Shea, of Kilmacshane, Instioge, Co. Kilkenny: *b.* Instioge: enlisted Naas, Co. Kildare. Killed in action, 9 August 1915, while attempting to remove his officer (2nd Lieut. Sibeth) to a place of safety, during an attack to recapture some lost trenches at Hooge Crater. Age 29.

2nd Lieut. Sibeth also has no known grave; he is recorded above.

(Panel 9) Corpl. 28519, Ernest Rigby, Royal Engineers Motor Cyclists, 3rd Signal Coy., attd. 15th Hussars: *yr. s.* of John Rigby, Cotton Broker; of Greenheys, Aigburth, Liverpool, by his wife Janie, *dau.* of the late I. Powell, of Liverpool: *b.* Liverpool, 17 November 1888: *educ.* Liverpool College High School: established in business in London as a Merchant; volunteered his services as a Motor Scout and Express Rider, 5 August, the day following the declaration of war: went to France early September: proceeded to the firing line, 15 October, attd. 'A' Squadron, 15th Hussars, and was killed in action at Veldhoek, nr. Ypres, 12 November following, being shot through the heart. Buried there in the garden of the ruined chateau. He wrote only three days before that his commanding officer had offered him a commission. The Sergt.-Major, Squadron, 15th Hussars, who first announced his death, wrote offering the sympathy of the officers, non-commissioned officers, and men, and added, "He had won the esteem of us all by his pluck, unassuming manner, and the happy knack he had of overcoming every hardship with a smile, and he died as he had lived through the campaign, bravely, for whenever or whatever danger threatened he was always a volunteer, and had done splendid work as a cyclist on many an occasion." Age 25. *unm.* (*IWGC record 28159, age 22*)

(Panel 9) L/Corpl. 25312, James Brannan, 9th Field Coy., Royal Engineers: *b.* Old Cuinnock, co. Ayr: enlisted Glasgow, co. Lanark. Killed in action, 4 May 1915. Remains exhumed from a grave marked as belonging to an 'Unknown British Soldier' unmarked grave (28.I.24.d.15.45), 8 January 1929; identified – Khaki, Title, Stripe, 2 Medal Ribbons; reinterred, registered 28 January 1929. *Buried in Sanctuary Wood Cemetery (V.C.34).*

(Panel 9) L/Corpl. 86654, John Henry Davies,171st Tunnelling Coy., Royal Engineers: formerly no.260, York & Lancaster Regt.: eldest *s.* of Charles Davies, by his wife Ellen: *b.* Newcastle-on-Tyne, 1 April 1880: Occupation – Collier: joined 13th (Service) Battn. York & Lancaster Regt., Barnsley, September 1914, after the outbreak of war; subsequently transf'd. Royal Engineers: served with the Expeditionary Force in France and Flanders, and was killed in action at Hill 60, Ypres 20 June 1915. Buried there. Age 35. Sapper E. Roberts wrote, "We have lost one of the finest men who came out of Newhall Camp, Silkstone. There was not a more willing or better lived man in the camp. A man who did his duty thoroughly, and everyone thought the world of him, and all that we can say is that he died a noble death." He *m.* Morcott, nr. Uppingham, co. Rutland, 13 April 1903; Esther Ann (15, Vernon Street North, Barnsley, co. York), and had three sons – John, *b.* 12 July 1904; Charles, *b.* 7 May 1908; George, *b.* 18 September 1910. (*IWGC record Sapper*)

(Panel 9) L/Corpl. 506, Alexander Mitchell, 1st (London) Field Coy., Royal Engineers: *s.* of James Mitchell, of Rhynie, co. Aberdeen, by his wife Williamina: and brother to Pte. 9803, C.A. Mitchell, M.M., 2nd Scots Guards, died 28 March 1918, of wounds: *b.* Aberdeen: enlisted London. Killed in action, 7 August 1915. Age 28. He leaves a wife Jeanette Marie Mitchell (87, Tyndall Road, Leyton, London), to mourn his loss. *Buried in Sanctuary Wood Cemetery (V.Q.11).*

His brother Charles is buried in Doullens Communal Cemetery Extension No.1 (V.D.28).

(Panel 9) Spr. 86649, Thomas Frederick Bell, 171st Mining Coy., Royal Engineers attd. 13th Bn. York & Lancaster Regt.: *s.* of Matthew Bell, of June Street, Barnsley, co. York, by his wife Lilly, *dau.* of Isaac Sykes: and brother to Pte. 32623, J. Bell, 2/8th Sherwood Foresters, who was killed in action (or died of wounds) on, or about, 26 September 1917: *b*. Barnsley, co. York: *educ*. St. Mary's School, there: Occupation – Miner: enlisted September 1914: served with the Expeditionary Force in France and Flanders, from March 1915, and was killed in action at Ypres, 19 December 1915. Buried there. Age 23. He *m*. Barnsley, August 1914; Fanny, *née* Dickson (148, Bridge Street, Barnsley), and had a son – Frederick.

His brother Joseph also has no known grave; he is commemorated on the Tyne Cot Memorial (Panel 100).

(Panel 9) Spr. 18943, Matthew Robertson Brown, 9th Field Coy., Royal Engineers: enlisted Edinburgh. Killed in action, 4 May 1915. Age 27. All correspondence should be addressed c/o his brother J.D. Brown Esq., 7, Church Place, Edinburgh, co. Midlothian. Remains 'Unknown British Soldier. Royal Engineers.' exhumed unmarked grave (28.I.24.d.15.45), 8 January 1929; identified – Khaki, Disc; reinterred, registered 26 January 1929. *Buried in Sanctuary Wood Cemetery (V.C.33).*

(Panel 9) Spr. 442, Percy Richmond Byrne, 1st /1st (Cheshire) Field Coy., Royal Engineers (T.F.): *s*. of Mrs. J. (& late Mr.) Byrne, of Birkenhead, co. Chester. Killed in action at the Battle of Bellewaarde, 16 June 1915. Age 18. See account re. Corpl. D. Jones (above).

(Panel 9) Spr. 82783, Robert Clifford, 171st Tunnelling Coy., Royal Engineers: late of Cheadle, co. Chester: brother to Pte. 1527, J. Clifford, 1/5th Cheshire Regt., killed in action, 1 July 1916, at the Somme: *b*. Marsden: enlisted Manchester. Killed in action, 19 April 1915. Remembered on Cheadle Congregational Church War Memorial.

His brother John also has no known grave; he is commemorated on the Thiepval Memorial.

(Panel 9) Spr. 325, Charles Edmund Hughes, 1st (Cheshire) Field Coy., Royal Engineers (T.F.): *s*. of William Hughes, Property Jobber; of 302, Borough Road, Birkenhead, by his wife Ellen: *b*. Birkenhead, co. Chester, 17 December 1893: *educ*. Woodlands School, and St. John's, Birkenhead: Occupation – Painter: joined 1st Cheshire Coy., R.E., and was called up on mobilisation, 5 August 1914: served with the Expeditionary Force in France and Flanders, and was killed in action at Hooge, 16 June 1915. Buried where he fell. Age 21. *unm*. See account re. Corpl. D. Jones (above).

(Panel 9) Spr. 18688, Charles Hutchison, 9th Field Coy., Royal Engineers: *s*. of Oswald Hutchison, of 12, Meadow Bank Avenue, Edinburgh: *b*. Leith: enlisted Edinburgh. Killed in action, 4 May 1915. Age 32. Remains exhumed from a grave marked as belonging to an 'Unknown British Soldier' unmarked grave (28.I.24.d.15.45), 8 January 1929; identified – Khaki, reinterred, registered 28 January 1929. *Buried in Sanctuary Wood Cemetery (V.C.35).*

(Panel 9) Spr. 21178, Robert McGibbon, 12th Field Coy., Royal Engineers: *s*. of George (& Mrs) McGibbon, of 33A, Gibson Terrace, Edinburgh: and *yr*. brother to Pte. 3448, G. McGibbon, 1st (Royal) Dragoons, killed in action, June 1915: *b*. Edinburgh, 1890. Killed in action, 9 August 1915. Age 25. *unm*.

His brother George also has no known grave; he is recorded on Panel 5

(Panel 9) Spr. 82944, John James Moore, 171st Tunnelling Coy., Royal Engineers: late of South Shields, Co. Durham: *b*. there: Occupation – Mine worker: joined Royal Engineers, London, proceeded to France March 1915, and was killed in action, 4 April 1915, nr. Hill 60. First member of 171 Coy. killed in action. See also account re. Spr. D. Sheldon (died of wounds), Bedford House Cemetery (IV.A.13/Enc.No.2).

(Panel 9) Spr. 18650, Stanley Harold Mullins, 1st Field Sqdn. Royal Engineers: *s*. of James Mullins, of 'Woodside Cottage,' Barming Heath, Maidstone, co. Kent, by his wife Bertha Mary: and yr. brother to Spr. 2816, E.J. Mullins, 15th Field Coy., Royal Engineers, died of wounds, 21 August 1915: *b*. Barming: enlisted Chatham. Killed in action, 24 May 1915. Age 27. *unm*.

His brother Edward is buried in Boulogne Eastern Cemetery (VIII.B.73).

(Panel 9) Spr. 25277, Alfred William George Rittey, 56th Field Coy., Royal Engineers: *s*. of Alfred Rittey, of 4, Roselyn Place Brockhurst, Gosport, co. Hants, by his wife Alice: and elder brother to Pte. 15756, A.C. Rittey, 14th Hampshire Regt., killed in action, 3 September 1916: *b*. Alverstoke: enlisted Gosport. Killed in action, 2 March 1916. Age 20. *unm*.

His brother Arthur also has no known grave; he is commemorated on the Thiepval Memorial, Somme.

(Panel 9) Spr. 388, Walter Smith, 1st /1st (Cheshire) Field Coy., Royal Engineers (T.F.). Missing in action, 16 June 1915, Bellewaarde. See account re. Corpl. D. Jones (above).

(Panel 9) Spr. 966, James Vallely, 1/2nd (Northumbrian) Field Coy., Royal Engineers: *s.* of Sarah Jones, *née* Vallely (9, Havelock Street, Newcastle-on-Tyne). Killed in action, 2 May 1915. Age 19. Remains exhumed from a grave marked as belonging to an 'Unknown British Soldier' (28.I.24.d.15.45); identified – Khaki, Boots size 7; reinterred, registered 3 January 1929. *Buried in Sanctuary Wood Cemetery (IV.U.4).*

(Panel 9) Major Lawrence Robert Vaughan Colby, No.4 Coy., 1st Bn. Grenadier Guards: only *s.* of the late John Vaughan Colby, of Ffynone, co. Pembroke: *b.* 3 April, 1880: *educ.* Eton: gazetted 2nd Lieut. Grenadier Guards, 11 February 1899; promoted Lieut. 1 January 1900; Capt. 30 September 1905; Major September 1914: served in the South African War 1899–1902: took part in the operations in Orange Free State, April–May 1900: operations in Orange River Colony, May–29 November 1900; including actions at Biddulphsberg and Wittenbergen (1–29 July), and those in Orange River Colony, December 1900–31 May 1902 (Queen's Medal, two clasps; King's Medal, two clasps): served with the Expeditionary Force in France and Flanders from 6 October 1914, and was killed in action near Gheluvelt on the 24th of that month, on which day Major Colby's company, No.4, was sent up to restore the line where the enemy were trying to break through between the Grenadiers and the Yorkshire Regt., and in spite of heavy enfilade fire and exceedingly difficult wired ground they succeeded in driving back a much larger body of the enemy with the loss of all but one officer and 45 men. Major Colby was killed while leading his men in the attack. Buried in a soldier's grave on the field of battle, close to where he fell. He was Mentioned in Despatches (*London Gazette*, 17 February 1915) by F.M. Sir John (now Lord) French, for 'gallant and distinguished service in the field.' Major Colby was a member of the Guards' Club. Age 34.

(Panel 9) Lieut. Edmund Antrobus, No.4 Coy., 1st Bn. Grenadier Guards: only *s.* of Col. Sir Edmund Antrobus, 4th Bart., late Grenadier Guards; of Antrobus, co. Chester; Amesbury Abbey, co. Wilts., and Rutherford, co. Roxburgh, by his wife Florence Caroline Mathilde, *dau.* of the late Jules Alexander Sartoris, of Hopsford Hall, co. Warwick: *b.* Eaton Square, London, S.W., 23 December 1886: *educ.* Eton and in France: gazetted 2nd Lieut. Grenadier Guards from the Militia, 27 May 1908; promoted Lieut. 21 November 1908. Killed in action at Ypres, 24 October 1914. At the time 1st Battn. Grenadier Guards formed part of 20th Brigade, VIIth Division, which was in the centre of our line at the First Battle of Ypres. On 24th October the Germans made a determined effort to break through on the left of the Grenadiers, near Kruiseecke, and No.4 Coy., to which Lieut. Antrobus belonged, made a counter-attack, driving back the enemy. He was killed while gallantly fighting with his platoon, only one officer and forty-five men of the Company returning unhurt. Buried in the orchard of a small farmhouse in the village of Keghside. Lieut. Antrobus was reported a very keen and courageous officer, and highly popular. Age 27. *unm.*

End-note: In 1898 Lieut. Antrobus' father offered to sell the ancient site of Stonehenge, which formed part of the Antrobus estate, to the British Government for the sum of £125,000.00; the offer was refused. Thereafter Sir Edmund had the site enclosed and requested visitors pay an admittance fee of 1/-. The controversial nature of this action resulted in a great deal of ill-feeling, protestations and a mass picket of the site. And, some years later a somewhat heated exchange of words between Sir Edmund and the 'Druids' regarding their paying toward the upkeep of the site resulted in the Druids placing a curse on him and his family. Circumstances, fate – whatever one chooses to believe, the fact remains that within twelve months Sir Edmund and his son Edmund were both dead.

(Panel 9) Lieut. Lord Ian Basil Gawen Temple Hamilton-Temple-Blackwood, 2nd Bn. Grenadier Guards: 3rd *s.* of the late Hon. Frederick Temple Hamilton-Temple-Blackwood, 1st Marquis of Dufferin and Ava, K.P., of Clandeboye, Co. Down (*d.* 12 February 1902), Governor General of Canada, Viceroy of India, Ambassador to Russia, Turkey, Italy and France, by his wife the Hon. Lady Hariot Georgina Rowan-Hamilton, *dau.* of Archibald Rowan Rowan-Hamilton, J.P., of Killyleagh Castle, Co. Down, and his wife Catherine Anne, *née* Caldwell: *b.* Clandeboye, 4 November 1870: *educ.* Harrow, and Balliol College, Oxford: was intended for the Bar (to which he was called in 1896) but, a career in the legal profession held no attraction and when war broke out in South Africa he went there, initially as a newspaper correspondent, being present at all the major engagements at the beginning of the conflict, and thereafter as Deputy Judge Advocate to the Forces; joining Judge Milner's Staff, Johannesburg, following the occupation of the

Republics, 1901: Assistant Colonial Secretary, Orange River Colony, 1903–07, during which period he was called upon to act as Colonial Secretary and Acting Governor: transf'd. Colonial Secretary, Barbados 1907: returned London 1909, finding employ on the newly constituted Labour Exchanges; subsequently became Assistant Secretary, Development Commission: served with the Expeditionary Force in France from 6 August 1914, attd. 9th Lancers: severely wounded at Messines, October 1914, and invalided home and, during his convalescence (1915), went to Ireland as Private Secretary to the Lord Lieutenant; remaining in that capacity until the cessation of the Sinn Fein Rebellion 1916: obtained a commission 2nd Lieut. Grenadier Guards early 1916: returned to France October following, and was killed in action, 4 July 1917, during a night raid on the German trenches at Boesinghe. Age 47. *unm.* A brother-officer, 9th Lancers, wrote, "His record is the finest imaginable and ought to be handed down and taught in every school as that of the ideal Englishman. With all his capabilities, age, influence, and record, to join as a Second Lieutenant is in itself a deed of which the country should be proud." And the Adjutant, 2nd Grenadier Guards, "I do not think that a more gallant figure than his can ever have gone to join the great company of fearless men who so gladly gave up everything that was theirs." Lord Blackwood executed the illustrations for Hilaire Belloc's *The Bad Child's Book of Beasts, More Beasts (for Worse Children)*, and *The Modern Traveller*.

(Panel 9) Lieut. the Hon. Alan George Sholto Douglas-Pennant, 1st Bn. Grenadier Guards: eldest *s*. and heir of E. Douglas-Pennant, 3rd Baron Penrhyn, of Llandegai, co. Carnarvon, formerly 1st Life Guards, Major and Hon. Lieut.Col. Buckinghamshire Imperial Yeomanry, J.P., D.L. for County of Carnarvon, by his wife the Hon. Blanche Georgiana Fitzroy, Lady Penrhyn (Wicken Park, Stony Stratford, co. Buckingham), *dau*. of the 3rd Lord Southampton; and cousin to the Hon. C. Douglas-Pennant, Coldstream Guards, who fell at Gheluvelt, the same day: *b*. 11 June 1890: *educ*. Eton: gazetted 2nd Lieut. Grenadier Guards February 1910; promoted Lieut. May 1911: apptd. extra A.D.C. to Lord Carmichael, G.C.I.E., K.C.M.G., Governor of Bengal, April 1914, but rejoined his regiment for Active Service on the declaration of war with Germany: served with the Expeditionary Force in France and Flanders. Unofficially reported wounded and missing, 29 November 1914; since confirmed as killed in action on or about that date. Age 24. *unm*. On his death his brother, 2nd Lieut. the Hon. H.N. Douglas-Pennant, became heir to the barony.

His cousin Charles is buried in Perth Cemetery (China Wall), Zillebeke (X.A.26).

(Panel 9) Lieut. Frederic William Joseph Macdonald Miller, 2nd Bn. Grenadier Guards: eldest *s*. of Sir William Frederic Miller, 5th Bt., of Glenlee, co. Kirkcudbright; and 57, Ennismore Gardens, Prince's Gate, London, by his wife Mary Augusta, *dau*. of Charles J. Manning and Louise Augusta, *née* Henniker, his wife: *b*. 21 December 1891. Killed in action, 23 October 1914. Age 22. *unm*.

(Panel 9) Lieut. Godfrey Vassal George Augustus Webster, 3rd Bn. Grenadier Guards: *s*. of the late Major, Sir Augustus F.W.E. Webster, 8th Bart., of Copthall, co. Essex (*d*.1923), by his wife Lady Mabel Webster, *née* Crossley (Battle Abbey, co. Sussex): *b*. 2 September 1897: *educ*. Eton. Killed in action on the night of 3–4 August 1917, being hit by a shell during the battalion's relief of 1st Scots Guards; vicinity Grand Barriere House. Age 20. Remembered on the Eton School Roll of Honour and the War Memorial situated in the churchyard of St. Mary the Virgin, Battle, co. Sussex.

Kruiseecke area 1914: 'For seven days at the end of October, under heavy shell fire and against constant attacks, the 1/Grenadier Guards held a dangerous salient inclusive of the village of Kruiseecke, and had it not been for two machine guns which remained in position during the whole period, under continuous fire, and fired 56,000 rounds, their losses would have been enormous. It is difficult to make individual distinctions and select any particular company or platoon for special notice when all must have fought so gallantly, but perhaps mention may be made of two platoons that were sent up to hold vacated trenches a mile to the left of the battalion. This particular part of the line proved to be the objective of two German battalions supported by machine guns, but these two platoons succeeded in holding the line, and never gave an inch, although they were nearly all killed, including the two officers, 2nd Lieut. Walter and 2nd Lieut. Somerset.'

(Panel 9) 2nd Lieut. Sydney Walter, 1st Bn. Grenadier Guards: only *s*. of Godfrey Walter, of Malshanger, nr. Basingstoke, co. Hants, by his wife Edith Elizabeth, 5th *dau*. of the late Robert Abel Smith, of Goldings, co. Herts: *b*. 16 March 1893: *educ*. Eton, and Royal Military College, Sandhurst, from which he was gazetted Grenadier Guards, February 1913. His battalion, which formed part of 20th Brigade, VIIth Division, mobilized at Lyndhurst, and, having embarked on 4th October, landed at Zeebrugge on the 7th. Killed at Kruiseecke, Belgium, on the 25th of that month: 25 October 1914. Age 21. *unm.*

Subsequently buried by the Germans, after the war the grave of 2nd Lieut. N.A.H. Somerset could not be found; he is commemorated in Harlebeke New British Cemetery (Kolenberg Forest German Cemetery Sp.Mem.11)

(Panel 9) Coy.Q.M.Sergt. 10217, George Leswell, Richardson, No.2 Coy., 1st Bn. Grenadier Guards: *s.* of the late Col.Sergt.2402, George Richardson, Grenadier Guards (*d.*18 August 1902), by his wife Bridget (Maidstone, co. Kent): and brother to L/Corpl. 15006, H.G. Richardson, No.3 Coy., who fell three days later: *b.* Dublin 1883: Occupation – Labourer: enlisted Maidstone, 11 March 1902: served with the Expeditionary Force in France and Flanders from 4 October 1914; reported missing after the fighting at Kruiseecke on the 29th of that month; since confirmed (16 May 1915) killed in action. Age 31. One of six brothers who served – Corpl. W.G. Richardson, 3rd Grenadier Guards; Dvr. J. Richardson, Army Service Corps; Pte. J. Richardson, 1st Gordon Highlanders; and Tpr. E. Richardson, 11th Hussars all survived. Another brother Charles pledged to enlist just as soon as he was old enough.

His brother Henry also has no known grave; he is recorded below.

(Panel 9) Coy.Q.M.Sergt. 10463, Ernest John Thompson, 1st Bn. Grenadier Guards: *s.* of Bernard George Thompson, of School House, Hall Road, Leckhampton, co. Gloucester, by his wife Susan Isabel: and brother to Sergt.Major 6207, S.B. Thompson, 9th (Queen's Royal) Lancers, killed in action at Neuve Chapelle the previous day (28 October): served with the Expeditionary Force in France from 4 October 1914; reported missing/believed killed at Kruiseecke, 29 October 1914; since confirmed (1915) killed in action. Age 31.

His brother Sidney also has no known grave; he is commemorated on the Le Touret Memorial (Panel 1).

(Panel 9) Corpl. 21384, Albert Munn, M.M., 3rd Bn. Grenadier Guards: *s.* of Samuel Munn, of 7, Ivy Terrace, South Elmsall, nr. Pontefract, by his wife Eliza Jane: *b.* Chartsmoor, co. Stafford: enlisted Pontefract, co. York. Killed in action, 25 July 1917. Age 38. He was married to Amy E. Munn (84, Victor Street, South Elmsall). Five of his brothers also served.

(Panel 9) Corpl. 11880, Alfred Henry Tuttle, 2nd Bn. Grenadier Guards: *s.* of Henry Tuttle of 4, Lambfield Cottages, Theale, co. Berks, by his wife Alice: and elder brother to Pte. 10350, E.J. Tuttle, 2nd Royal Berkshire Regt., killed in action, 31 July 1917, at the Third Battle of Ypres: *b.* Sulhampstone, co. Berks: enlisted Reading. Killed in action, 7 November 1914. Age 29. He leaves a wife, Jane Tuttle (16, Balfern Street, Battersea, London, S.W.11).

His brother Edward also has no known grave; he is recorded on Panel 45.

(Panel 9) L/Corpl. 14488, Bert Richard Clements, 2nd Bn. Grenadier Guards: only *survg. s.* of William Clements, late King's Royal Rifles (served in the Afghan Campaign, *d.* 31 May 1906), by his wife Elizabeth (30, Brook Street, Barry Dock, Cardiff), *dau.* of William Western: *b.* Barry Dock, nr. Cardiff, 20 April 1892: *educ.* Council Schools, Barry Dock: Occupation – (2 years) Telegraph Boy; Barry Dock Post Office: enlisted R.G.A. but, being an only son, was claimed out by his mother: thereafter enlisted Grenadier Guards; Cardiff Barracks, 2 January 1909: served three years with the Colours; thereafter joined Cardiff City Police Force. Recalled on the outbreak of war, returned to the regiment, 5 August 1914: served with the Expeditionary Force in France and Flanders; went through the retreat from Mons, and Battle of the Aisne; killed by shrapnel in action nr. Ypres, 7 November 1914. Buried at Zillebeke. Age 22. *unm.*

(Panel 9) L/Corpl. 15965, Fred Onion, 1st Bn. Grenadier Guards: *s.* of James Onion, of Bishop's Wood, Brewood, Stafford, by his wife Annie: and brother to Pte. 18020, J. Onion, 7th South Staffordshire Regt. attd. Machine Gun Corps, died 14 October 1916, of wounds: enlisted Wolverhampton. Killed in action, 29 October 1914, at Kruiseecke. Age 20. *unm.*

His brother James is buried in Etaples Military Cemetery (VII.F.3).

(Panel 9) L/Corpl. 15006, Henry George Richardson, No.3 Coy., 1st Bn. Grenadier Guards: *s.* of the late Col.Sergt. 2402, George Richardson, Grenadier Guards (*d.*18 August 1902), by his wife Bridget (Maidstone, co. Kent): and yr. brother to Coy.Q.M.Sergt. 10217, G.L. Richardson, No.2 Coy., who fell three days previously: *b.* 1891: Occupation – Labourer: enlisted Maidstone, 17 December 1910: served with the Expeditionary Force in France and Flanders from 4 October 1914, and was killed in action, 1 November following. Age 22. *unm.* One of six brothers who served – Corpl. W.G. Richardson, 3rd Grenadier Guards; Dvr. J. Richardson, Army Service Corps; Pte. J. Richardson, 1st Gordon Highlanders; and Tpr. E. Richardson, 11th Hussars all survived. Another brother Charles pledged to enlist just as soon as he was old enough.

His brother George also has no known grave; he is recorded above.

(Panel 9) Pte. 16125, Ernest William Abbott, 1st Bn. Grenadier Guards: eldest *s.* of William Abbott, of 123, Ranelagh Road, Ipswich. Killed in action at Kruiseecke, France, 26 October 1914. Age 20. *unm.*

(Panel 9) Pte. 14584, Herbert James Button, 2nd Bn. Grenadier Guards: eldest s. of the late James David Button, Carman; of 3 Marriages Square, Chelmsford, co. Essex, and his wife Sarah Jane (74, Rainsford Road, Chelmsford): *b.* Marriages Square, 13 December 1890: *educ.* Chelmsford School; thereafter joined Grenadier Guards: a pre-war Reservist, prior to the outbreak of war was (from January 1913) Police Constable (Dovercourt), Essex County Constabulary: immediately rejoined 2nd Grenadier Guards, London on mobilisation. Shortly before rejoining he greatly distinguished himself by stopping a runaway horse in the main thoroughfare of Dovercourt, being dragged a considerable distance in the process: proceeded to France, 14–17 August: joined B.E.F. on the retirement from Mons (Landrecies, 26 August); took part in the fighting at Villers Cotteret (1 September), and actions in the vicinity of Soupir: took part in the opening stages of the First Battle of Ypres (Zonnebeke – Langemarck road) 21–23 October, and was killed in action, 1 November 1914; Shrewsbury Forest, before Reutel, Belgium. Age 23. *unm.* In a letter to his Inspector, written two weeks before his death, he said, "We are having a lively time; been engaged in a battle here for a month. My first time under fire a poor fellow in front of me got a piece of shell through his stomach that would have had me. We see terrible sights out here, among the maimed and wounded. The German artillery is deadly and does all the damage, and the woods are full of their snipers who pop you off and you can't see them. I hope I may be lucky and come back again. They are fighting hard now, but are a dirty lot. They dress in our uniforms and come right up to our trenches adios the white flag, and when we go to fetch them they open fire. Our battalion have lost heavily; my company alone has lost 150 now." In memory of and in farewell to P.C. Button, his friend P.C. Layton (Harwich) composed:

> Farewell our faithful comrade,
> Admired and loved by all;
> Thou hast responded bravely
> To heed thy country's call.
> Your noble life you've given,
> On the field you took your place,
> To maintain England's honour
> And save it from disgrace.
>
> To you we owe our safety,
> Our freedom and our right;
> For Liberty and Justice,
> You've helped us in the fight.
> To keep back threatening nations
> From off old England's shores,
> That we might still be governed
> With just and righteous laws.

We never shall forget thee,
While we remain on earth;
Your noble courage makes us feel
Proud of a Briton's birth.
And now you've found a hero's grave,
Midst the struggle and the fight;
Let's hope again in God's good time
We shall again unite.

(Panel 9) Pte. 14106, Robert Cameron, 2nd Bn. Grenadier Guards: *s.* of the late Robert Cameron, by his wife Jane (7, Somerset Avenue, Iver, Uxbridge): *b.* Paddington, London, W.2, 1892: enlisted Willesden, London, N.W.10. Killed in action, 26 October 1914. Age 22. *unm. Buried in Tyne Cot Cemetery, Passchendaele (LXV.H.4).*

(Panel 9) Pte. 15228, Charles Thomas Clarke, 2nd Bn. Grenadier Guards: *s.* of George Clarke, of 10, Portland Cottages, Kingsdown, Bristol, by his wife Sarah Ann: served with the Expeditionary Force in France; killed in action nr. Zillebeke, 7 November 1914. Age 21. *unm.* Remains recovered from a grave marked as belonging to an 'Unknown British Soldier' (28.I.29.d.60.20); identified – Clothing, Boots; reinterred, registered 10 April 1929. *Buried in Sanctuary Wood Cemetery (V.H.3)*

(Panel 9) Pte. 22496, Harry Day, 2nd Bn. Grenadier Guards: *s.* of Alfred Day, Plasterer; of 38, Molesworth Street, Lewisham, London, S.E., by his wife Mary: *b.* 14 August 1880: *educ.* Lewisham: enlisted, 26 January 1915: served with the Expeditionary Force in France: reported wounded and missing after the fighting on the River Steenbeke, 31 July 1917; now assumed to have been killed in action on that date. Age 36. *unm.* (*IWGC record age 37*)

(Panel 9) Pte. 14717, James Farrell, 2nd Bn. Grenadier Guards: *s.* of Patrick Farrell, of 4, West Street, Goldenhill, co. Stafford, by his wife Mary: a pre-war Reservist, returned to the Colours on the outbreak of war, August 1914; killed in action, 30 October 1914, nr. Kruiseecke. His close friend Pte. 15122, J.H. Rhodes informed his family that at the time of his death Pte. Farrell was wiring in front of the trenches when the enemy began bombarding the Grenadier's positions and, taking cover in a nearby shell-hole, was killed by a shell which landed directly in it. Age 22. *unm.*

(Panel 9) Pte. 25419, William Hazelby, 2nd Bn. Grenadier Guards: *s.* of the late Isaac Hazelby, by his wife Emma (School Cottage, Stibbington, Wansford, Peterborough): and yr. brother to Pte. 25418, T. Hazelby, 2nd Grenadier Guards, died 29 March 1917: *b.* Wansford: enlisted Huntingdon. Killed in action, 31 July 1917; Canal bank sector, Boesinghe. Age 23. *unm.*

His brother Thomas is buried in Bray Millitary Cemetery (II.F.34).

(Panel 9) Pte. 27042, Frederick Percival Leaman, 3rd Bn. Grenadier Guards: *s.* of James Leaman, of 29, South View Terrace, Heavitree, Exeter, by his wife Susan Ellen: and brother to Sergt. M2/204762, J.B.J. Leaman, M.M., Army Service Corps, died 26 November 1918, of sickness: *b.* Wonford, co. Devon: enlisted Exeter. Killed in action, 31 July 1917, nr. Boesinghe. Age 19.

His brother James is buried in Busigny Communal Cemetery Extension (VIII.B.19).

(Panel 9) Pte. 15268, Amos Paxton, 2nd Bn. Grenadier Guards: *s.* of Amos Paxton, Gardener, of 9, Aston Abbotts, Aylesbury, co. Buckingham, by his wife Harriet, *née* Mansfield; and brother to Corpl. 13592, W. Paxton, 1st Duke of Cornwall's Light Infantry, killed in action, 23 July 1916; and Pte. 80011, E.J. Paxton, 1st Sherwood Foresters, killed in action, 25 August 1918: *b.* October 1892: a pre-war Regular, enlisted Bristol: served with the Expeditionary Force in France and Flanders; took part in the retirement from Mons, and fighting at the Aisne; killed in action, 1 November 1914, at Ypres. Age 22. *unm.* Remembered on Aston Abbotts (St. James) Parish Church War Memorial, Bristol.

His brother Walter also has no known grave, he is commemorated on the Thiepval Memorial, Somme; Edward is buried in La Targette British Cemetery, Neuville-St. Vaast (III.B.12).

(Panel 9) Pte. 16452, Percy James Sargent, No.4 Coy., 1st Bn. Grenadier Guards: *s.* of John (& Charlotte) Sargent, of Park Lane, Turvey, co. Bedford: and cousin to Pte. 18576, H. Sargent, 8th Bedfordshire Regt., killed in action, 20 April 1916; and L/Corpl. 18774, S. Sargent 2nd Bedfordshire Regt., killed in action, 11 July 1916: *b*. Turvey: enlisted Bedford: proceeded to France, 7 October 1914; killed in action eighteen days later, 26 October 1914; Kruiseecke, Belgium. Age 21. Inscribed "Their Name Liveth For Ever More. This cross is erected to the honoured and undying memory of the men of this parish who laid down their lives for King and country in the Great War A.D. 1914–1919," Percy and his cousins are remembered on Turvey War Memorial and on the Roll of Honour situated in the porch of Turvey (All Hallows) Parish Church.

His cousins Horace and Sidney are buried in Essex Farm Cemetery, Ypres (II.Q22); and Bernafay Wood British Cemetery, Somme (G.0), respectively.

(Panel 9) Pte. 12331, Sidney Joseph Smith, No.3 Coy., 2nd Bn. Grenadier Guards: *yr. s.* of Francis Louis Smith, Gardener; of 35, Alfred Street, Neath, by his wife Margaret, *dau.* of Julia O'Leary, of Caerleon, Monmouth: *b*. Newport, co. Monmouth, 6 February 1888: *educ.* Brynock National Schools: enlisted 1 September 1905: went to France with the Expeditionary Force about 12 August 1914: took part in the retreat from Mons, the Battle of the Marne and the advance to the Aisne, and was killed in action at Zillebeke, 7 November 1914. Buried 1½ miles east of Zillebeke, near Ypres. Age 26. His company officer, the late Capt. Alwyn Gosselin, D.S.O., wrote expressing regret at his loss, and added, "Your son was always cheerful under the very trying conditions of the campaign, and he is a great loss to his comrades." He was at one time considered the Army champion in bayonet exercises. He *m.* at St. Joseph R.C. Church, Neath, South Wales, 16 November 1913, Mary Anne (Crythan Road, Neath), *dau.* of John (& Eliza) Singleton.

PANEL 9 ENDS: PTE. G.H. WALL, GRENADIER GUARDS.

PANEL 11 BEGINS: PTE. A. WALLINGTON, GRENADIER GUARDS.

(Panel 11) Major the Hon. Leslie D'Henin Hamilton, M.V.O., 1st Bn. Coldstream Guards: 3rd *s.* of John Glencairn Carter-Hamilton, 1st Lord Hamilton of Dalzell, J.P., D.L., by his wife the Hon. Lady Emily Eleanor Leslie-Melville (4, South Eaton Place, London), *dau.* of David, Earl of Leven and Melville: *b*. 19 December 1873: gazetted 2nd Lieut., Coldstream Guards, 22 March 1893; promoted Lieut. 3 April 1897; Capt. 16 February 1901; Major 29 March 1910: served in the South African War, 1899–1902 (Queen's Medal, 4 clasps); and in the European War. Killed in action, 29 October 1914. Age 40. He *m.* 9 September 1905; Amy Cecile, *dau.* of Col. Horace Ricardo, C.V.O., Grenadier Guards, and had a *s.* John, *b*. 1 May 1911.

(Panel 11) Capt. Henry Robert Augustus Adeane, 4th attd. 1st Bn. Coldstream Guards: only *s.* of Admiral Edward Stanley Adeane, R.N.; C.M.G., by his wife Lady Edith Isabella Dalzell, 2nd *dau.* of Harry Burrard, 14th Earl of Carnwarth: *b*. 28, Eaton Place, London, S.W., 31 July 1882: *educ.* Winchester; Royal Military College, Sandhurst: gazetted 2nd Lieut., Coldstream Guards, 18 January 1902; promoted Capt. 1910 (retired 17 May 1913): rejoined 4th (Special Reserve) Bn. on mobilisation, 5 August 1914: proceeded to France on the 12th.; killed in action nr. Ypres, 2 November following, attd. 1st Battn.. Age 32. He *m.* Chapel Royal, St. James' Palace, 15 September 1909; Victoria Eugenie (1, Dean Trench Street, Westminster, London), *dau.* of Col. Sir Arthur Bigge (Lord Stamfordham), and had a *s.* Michael Edward, *b*. 30 September 1910.

(Panel 11) Lieut. Nigel Walter Henry Legge-Bourke, 2nd Bn. Coldstream Guards: only *s.* of Col. the Hon. Sir Henry Charles Legge, K.C.V.O., late Coldstream Guards, by his wife Amy Gwendoline (Maid of Honour to H.M. Queen Victoria, 1877–84), *dau.* of Gustavus William Lambart, of Hayes, Beau Parc, Co. Meath: *b*. Grosvenor Square, London, S.W., 13 November 1889: *educ.* Evelyns (Mr G.T. Worsley's); Eton; Royal Military College, Sandhurst: Page-of-Honour to H.M. King Edward VII, 1902–06: gazetted 2nd Lieut., Coldstream Guards, 6 February 1909; promoted Lieut. 6 June 1910: served with the Expeditionary Force in France and Flanders from 12 August 1914; killed in action nr. Ypres, 30 October following, while in command of a platoon of No.1 Coy., holding advanced trenches in Reutel Wood. Age

24. He *m.* Guards' Chapel, Wellington Barracks, 3 June 1913; Lady Victoria Alexandrina Carrington, now Lady Victoria Forester (Furze Hill, Broadway, co. Worcester), *dau.* of Charles Robert (Wynn-Carrington), 1st Marquis of Lincolnshire, K.G., P.C., G.C.M.G., and had a *s.* Edward Alexander Henry, *b.* 16 May 1915. Born Nigel Walter Legge, his name was changed by Royal Licence to Legge-Bourke, 26 April 1911.

(Panel 11) Lieut. Geoffrey Arthur Campbell (Temp.Capt./Adjt.), 1st Bn. Coldstream Guards: 4th & *yst. s.* of George Augustus Campbell, Partner, Messrs Cox & Co., Army Bankers (Cadet of Cawdor); of 46, Wilton Crescent, London, S.W.; and Market House, Brackley, co. Northampton, by his wife the Hon. Alice Campbell, *née* Barrington: *b.* Wilton Crescent, London, 8 January 1885: *educ.* Eton: joined 3rd Royal Scots 1904: gazetted 2nd Lieut. 3rd Coldstream Guards, 1 February 1907; promoted Lieut. 1 June 1909: served in Egypt 1908–12: apptd. Adjt., 1st Battn., 15 January 1912: proceeded to France – 1st Army Corps, British Expeditionary Force – 12 August 1914; killed in action nr. Gheluvelt, 29 October following, during the First Battle of Ypres. Mentioned in Sir John (now Lord) French's Despatch, 14 October 1914; promoted Temp. Capt. Mr Campbell was a member of the Guard's Club, and was fond of hunting and polo. Age 29. *unm.*

(Panel 11) Lieut. Charles John Murray, No.2 Coy., 1st Bn. Coldstream Guards: 3rd *s.* of Charles Archibald Murray, of Taymount, Stanley, co. Perth (*gdson.* of David William, 3rd Earl of Mansfield, K.T.), and only *s.* by his second wife Blanche, 5th *dau.* of Sir Thomas Moncreiffe, 7th Bart.: *b.* Taymount, co. Perth, 1 December 1881: *educ.* Haileybury College: joined Black Watch Militia, December 1899: gazetted 2nd Lieut. Coldstream Guards, 4 December 1901; promoted Lieut. 7 September 1904: served in the South African War, 1902: took part in operations in Cape Colony, May 1902 (Queen's Medal, 2 clasps): A.D.C. to Sir Percy Girouard, High Commissioner & Commander-in-Chief, N. Nigeria, 10 March 1907–6 May 1908; and to Governor & Commander-in-Chief, N. Nigeria, 7 May 1908–1909; thereafter to Governor, East African Protectorate, 1909–12, when he resigned his commission to take up farming, and the breeding and training of horses at Invershura, Njoro, British East Africa: returned to England on the outbreak of war with Germany; rejoined Coldstream Guards, Windsor, 19 September 1914: proceeded to France with his regt. 7 October following; killed in action when leading an attack on Poezelhoek, nr. Ypres, 26 October 1914. Lieut. Murray was a member of the Guard's, Bachelor's, and Caledonian Clubs. Age 32. *unm.*

(Panel 11) Lieut. Richard Charles Graves-Sawle, 2nd Bn. Coldstream Guards: only *s.* of Rear- Admiral Sir Charles Graves-Sawle, 4th Bart, of Penrice, co. Cornwall; and Barley, Exeter, by his wife Lady Graves-Sawle (60, Queen's Gate, London, W.): and nephew to Col. Sir Francis Graves-Sawle, Bart., M.V.O., one time Officer Comdg. Coldstream Guards: *b.* 1888: *educ.* Harrow; Royal Military College, Sandhurst, received his commission; gazetted 2nd Lieut., Coldstream Guards 1908; promoted Lieut. 1910: Asst. Adjt., 2nd Battn. from 1913 until the outbreak of war with Germany: served with the Expeditionary Force in France and Flanders from 12 August 1914: fought in the action at Mons, all through the Retirement, and all subsequent actions until his death in action nr. Ypres, 2 November 1914. Age 26. *s.p.* Originally arranged for October 1914, his marriage to Muriel, *dau.* of Lieut.Col. Heaton-Ellis, was, due to the outbreak of war, brought forward to 6 August. A member of the Guards' Club, Lieut. Graves-Sawle was a keen yachtsman, and big-game hunter. His widow has since re-married; now Mrs. A.L.C. Cavendish.

(Panel 11) Lieut. Granville Keith-Falconer Smith, 1st Bn. Coldstream Guards: eldest *s.* of Col. Granville R.F. Smith, C.B., C.V.O., of Daffield, co. Derby, by his wife Lady Blanche: and nephew to the Earl of Kintore: *b.* 26 February 1886: *educ.* Eton: gazetted 2nd Lieut. Coldstream Guards, August 1907; promoted Lieut. December 1909: served with the Expeditionary Force in France and Flanders from 7 October 1914; reported missing in that month, and again in November; has since been unofficially reported killed nr. Gheluvelt, 29 October, during the First Battle of Ypres. The circumstance of his death being – while in command of the battalion machine-gun section, he went forward with a party of volunteers and succeeded in retaking a trench. Immediately thereafter he was shot through the head, dying at once. Age 28. He *m.* March 1910; Lady Kathleen Clements Studd (66, Great Cumberland Place, London), *yst. dau.* of the Earl of Leitrim, and left two *daus.*, aged 3 years and 15 months respectively.

(Panel 11) Lieut. Henry Digby Wallis, Special Reserve attd. 3rd Bn. Coldstream Guards: only *s.* of Aubrey (& H.G.B.) Wallis, of Drisham Castle, Millstreet, Co. Cork: *b.* Auckland, New Zealand, 3 June 1885: *educ.* Wellington College, co. Berks: joined Royal Scots on probation, but resigned and travelled abroad for some time: afterwards joined Special Reserve, Coldstream Guards, 2nd Lieut. March 1912; promoted Lieut. September 1914: served with the Expeditionary Force in France and Flanders, attd. 3rd Coldstream Guards, IInd Division; killed in action at St. Julien, 21 October 1914. A fine horseman, he was a good four-in-hand whip, played polo, rode in many point-to-point races, whipped in the Duhallow Hounds, and in the Four Burrno. Age 29. *unm.* See also Lieut. F.R. Pollock, St. Julien D.S. Cemetery (II.F.13).

(Panel 11) 2nd Lieut. the Hon. Vere Douglas Boscawen, Special Reserve attd. 1st Bn. Coldstream Guards: 3rd *s.* of Sir Evelyn Edward Thomas Boscawen, 7th Viscount Falmouth, K.C.V.O., C.B., by his wife Kathleen, *dau.* of George Sholto Gordon, 2nd Baron Penrhyn: *b.* 3 August 1890: gazetted 2nd Lieut. Special Reserve, Coldstream Guards, 14 March, 1914: served with the Expeditionary Force in France and Flanders, attd. 1st Battn. *The Times,* 21 December 1914, reported 'On 29 October 1914 … four companies of the Coldstream Guards were completely surrounded….and Mr Boscawen, refusing to surrender, fell fighting against overwhelming odds.' His death was notified in the 'Official Monthly List' dated January 1915. Age 24. *unm.*

(Panel 11) Sergt. 7983, William Brown, No.2 Coy., 1st Bn. Coldstream Guards: *s.* of Joseph Brown, of Saltley, Birmingham, by his wife Mary: enlisted Birmingham: served with the Expeditionary Force; killed in action nr. Ypres, 29 October 1914. He held the Order of St. George, 2nd Class (Russia). Age 26. *unm.*

(Panel 11) Sergt. 6856, Walter Charles Farrance, 3rd Bn. Coldstream Guards: served with the Expeditionary Force. Killed in action at St. Julien, 21 October 1914.

(Panel 11) Sergt. 5048, George Johnson, 2nd Bn. Coldstream Guards: *s.* of Henry Johnson, of Stratford-on-Avon, co. Warwick: *b.* Shotterey: enlisted Birmingham: served with the Expeditionary Force in France; killed in action at Reutel, nr. Ypres, 5 November 1914. Remains exhumed from a (collective) grave marked as belonging to an various theatres of war, the single acts of gallantry and self-sacrifice NW.J.10.d.8.3); identified – Clothing, Buttons; reinterred, registered 24 October 1927. *Buried in Sanctuary Wood Cemetery (IV.J.8).*

(Panel 11) Sergt. 6681, Richard Jones, 2nd Bn. Coldstream Guards: served with the Expeditionary Force in France. Killed in action at Reutel, Belgium, 26 October 1914.

(Panel 11) Sergt. 7309, Walter John Jones, 3rd Bn. Coldstream Guards: served with the Expeditionary Force. Killed in action at Reutel, 15 November 1914.

(Panel 11) L/Sergt. 7310, George Edward Newsome, 2nd Bn. Coldstream Guards: only *s.* of Albert Newsome, Colliery Worker; of 135, Falsgrave Road, Scarborough, co. York, by his wife Jane: *b.* Batley Carr, Dewsbury, April 1889: Religion – Church of England: Occupation – Grocer's Assistant: enlisted West Yorkshire Regt., Dewsbury, 20 June 1907; transf'd. Coldstream Guards, July following; apptd. 2nd Battn., 17 August: apptd. L/Corpl., 15 May 1908: Deserted, 16 July 1909; returned voluntarily, 26 August following; Awarded Forfeiture of time served with the Regiment, Reduction to rank Pte., 3 months Detention (returned to duty 28 November): re-apptd. L/Corpl. 14 March 1910; promoted Corpl. August 1914: served with the Expeditionary Force in France from 13 August; apptd. L/Sergt., 3 September: shot and killed by a sniper, 12 November 1914; Reutel Woods. Age 25. Referring to George Newsome's death in a letter to a friend, L/Sergt. Pateman said, "…This is all I can send you, just a card, and it is written in the firing line, too, with bullets flying and shells rushing past. But still I must let you know I am still A1. Had hard lines yesterday, a poor soldier next to me got hit, and also one on the other side, so I shall get back yet. It is lively here I can tell you. Hell is not in it, shooting and killing day and night, so we have to dodge a few…." And in a letter to George's parents, in which he enclosed some postcards and French bank-notes retrieved from George's body, Pateman informed "…death was instantaneous and painless."

(Panel 11) Corpl. 5902, Henry Alderson, 3rd Bn. Coldstream Guards: *s.* of Thomas Alderson, Carpenter; of 33, Martin Street, Sheffield: *b.* Sheffield, 18 November 1885: *educ.* there: enlisted October 1904. Killed in action at St. Julien, 21 October 1914: Age 26. He *m.* St. Andrew's Church, Islington, 24

December 1911; Ethel Francis (75, Copenhagen Street, Islington, London, N.), *dau.* of Thomas Barker, of London, and had a son, Edward Thomas, *b.* 21 July 1913.

(Panel 11) Corpl. 5160, Frank Hill, 3rd Bn. Coldstream Guards: served with the Expeditionary Force. Killed in action at Ypres, 21 October 1914.

(Panel 11) Corpl. 8095, Edwin Cecil Tonkin, 2nd Bn. Coldstream Guards: late of Mountain Ash, co. Glamorgan: *b.* Camelford, co. Cornwall: enlisted Devonport: served with the Expeditionary Force in France. Killed in action, 9 November 1914. Remains exhumed from a (collective) grave marked as belonging to an 'Unknown British Soldier. Coldstream Guards', (28NW.J.10.d.8.3); identified – Clothing; reinterred, registered 26 October 1927. *Buried in Sanctuary Wood Cemetery (IV.J.8).*

(Panel 11) L/Corpl. 4635, Arthur Baxter, 3rd Bn. Coldstream Guards: *s.* of Richard Baxter, of Tamworth, co. Stafford: served with the Expeditionary Force; killed in action at Reutel, 28 October 1914.

(Panel 11) L/Corpl. 2872, William Joseph Biggs, 2nd Bn. Coldstream Guards: served with the Expeditionary Force in France and Belgium; killed in action at Reutel, 26 October 1914.

(Panel 11) L/Corpl. 4943, Albert Victor Brown, D.C.M., No.3 Coy., 2nd Bn. Coldstream Guards: *s.* of Edward Brown, late Col.Sergt. Coldstream Guards, c/o Royal Hospital Chelsea; formerly of 34, Cemetery Road, Forest Gate: *b.* Tower of London: enlisted as a boy soldier, 2 January 1903: became Driver, 5 August 1908; apptd. L/Corpl. 26 May 1914: served with the Expeditionary Force in France and Flanders from 12 August 1914. Awarded Distinguished Conduct Medal (*London Gazette*, 17 December 1914) "for gallantry on 28 September 1914, in assisting to remove into safety the wounded who were lying exposed in the open;" killed in action at Reutel, 5 November following. Mentioned in F.M. Sir John (now Lord) French's Despatch, 8 October (*London Gazette*, 9 December) 1914. Age 26. Remains exhumed from a (collective) grave marked as belonging to an 'Unknown British Soldier. Coldstream Guards', (28NW.J.10.d.8.3); identified – Clothing, Buttons, Keg Tab mkd 'L.D.;' reinterred, registered 21 October 1927. *Buried in Sanctuary Wood Cemetery, Zillebeke, (IV.J.8).*

(Panel 11) L/Corpl. 5899, John Allison Caile, 3rd Bn. Coldstream Guards: enlisted Bishop Auckland, Co. Durham: served with the Expeditionary Force; killed in action at St. Julien, 21 October 1914. *m.*

(Panel 11) L/Corpl. 5460, Ewart Frederick Chapman, 1st Bn. Coldstream Guards: *s.* of Frederick Chapman, of Shepton Mallet: served with the Expeditionary Force; killed in action, 25 October 1914.

(Panel 11) L/Corpl. 8287, William John Cheney, 2nd Bn. Coldstream Guards: late of Littleport, co. Cambridge: enlisted Birmingham: served with the Expeditionary Force in France and Flanders; killed in action at Reutel, Belgium, 14 November. 1914. Remains exhumed from a (collective) grave marked as belonging to an 'Unknown British Soldier, 2/Coldstream Guards', identified – Clothing; reinterred, registered 27 October 1927. GRU Report, Zillebeke 5-160E refers to 'Three skulls and a few small bones recovered from three graves which had apparently been disturbed by shellfire.' *Buried in Sanctuary Wood Cemetery (IV.J.8).*

(Panel 11) L/Corpl. 8004, Wilkinson Bond Cooper, 1st Bn. Coldstream Guards: late of Chester-le-Street, Co. Durham: served with the Expeditionary Force; killed in action at Ypres, 29 October 1914. *m.*

(Panel 11) L/Corpl. 6388, Henry Samuel Foulks, No.4 Coy., 1st Bn. Coldstream Guards: *s.* of the late Henry (& Eliza) Foulks: served with the Expeditionary Force; killed in action at Langemarck, 22 October 1914. Age 26. He leaves a wife, Violet Foulks (The Green, Warborough, Wallingford, co. Berks).

(Panel 11) L/Corpl. 10714, Andrew Joseph Gorman, 1st Bn. Coldstream Guards: eldest *s.* of Thomas Gorman, Labourer; of 95, Spring Street, Hull, co. York, by his wife Margaret: *b.* Hull, 7 November 1894: *educ.* St. Charles' R.C. School, there: enlisted, 29 April 1914: appointed L/Corpl. 24 September following: went to France, 7 October; killed in action at Ypres, 2 November 1914, by a shell. Age 19.

(Panel 11) L/Corpl. 8457, Joshua Thomas Grantham, 2nd Bn. Coldstream Guards: *s.* of Albert Grantham, of West Green, Upper Cottingham, co. York, by his wife Martha: enlisted Hull: served with the Expeditionary Force in France; died No.3 Field Ambulance, 15 November 1914, from wounds received at Ypres. Age 22. *unm.*

(Panel 11) L/Corpl. 9723, James Henry Norman Hill, 1st Bn. Coldstream Guards: *s.* of William James Hill, of 16, Southlawn Terrace, Heavitree, Exeter, by his wife Florence Louisa: and elder brother to L/

Corpl. 11794, A.E. Hill, 2nd Coldstream Guards, died 21 November 1915, of wounds: *b*. Heavitree, co. Devon, *c*.1894: enlisted Taunton, co. Somerset. Killed in action, 19 November 1914, at Ypres. Age 20. *unm*.

His brother Albert is buried in La Gorgue Communal Cemetery (II.C.7).

(Panel 11) L/Corpl. 5829, Alan Huggard, 1st Bn. Coldstream Guards: *b*. Wykeham, co. York: enlisted Birmingham: served with the Expeditionary Force in France; killed in action, 25 October 1914.

(Panel 11) L/Corpl. 7300, Charles Richard Pearson, 2nd Bn. Coldstream Guards: *b*. Owlerton, co. York: enlisted Sheffield. Killed in action nr. Ypres, 11 November 1914. Remains exhumed from a (collective) grave marked as belonging to an 'Unknown British Soldier. Coldstream Guards', (28.J.10.d.8.3); identified – Clothing; reinterred, registered 25 October 1927. *Buried in Sanctuary Wood Cemetery (IV.J.8).*

(Panel 11) Pte. 10349, Francis Henry Adams, 1st Bn. Coldstream Guards: *s*. of Edwin Adams, of New Barn, Stanton Fitzwarren, Highworth, co. Wilts. Reported missing, 29 October–2 November 1914; now assumed to have been killed in action in France between these dates. Age 18. Dedicated – 'To The Brave Lads Of Stanton Fitzwarren Who Gave Themselves To God, King And Country In The Great War Beginning August 1914: On Whom & All Souls Jesu Mercy;' Pte. Adams is one of seven men remembered on the St. Leonard's (Parish Churchyard) War Memorial. (*IWGC record 29 October*)

(Panel 11) Pte. 10447, Sidney Charles Aitken, 2nd Bn. Coldstream Guards: *s*. of Charles William Aitken, of 72, Clinton Lane, Kenilworth, by his wife Harriett Elizabeth: *b*. Warwick. Killed in action on the Western Front, 23 October 1914. Buried 700 yards south of crossroads, north-west of Zonnebeke. Age 19.

(Panel 11) Pte. 7219, William Allen, 3rd Bn. Coldstream Guards: *s*. of John Allen, of 4, Church Lane, Barnsley, co. York (late of 43, Littlefield Terrace, Wombwell), by his wife Eliza: *b*. York, about 1891: served with the Expeditionary Force; killed in action at St. Julien, 21 October 1914. Age 23. *unm*.

(Panel 11) Pte. 5229, Fred Archer, 2nd Bn. Coldstream Guards: *s*. of Charles Archer, of 163, St. Anne's Well Road, Nottingham: *b*. Nottingham: enlisted 24 October 1903: served with the Expeditionary Force in France and Flanders from 12 August 1914; killed in action at Reutel, Belgium, 28 October 1914. Age 31.

(Panel 11) Pte. 5660, Clement Arnell, 1st Bn. Coldstream Guards: *s*. of Edward Arnell, of 482, Wortley Road, Rotherham, co. York: *b*. Northfield, York: enlisted, 15 August 1904: served with the Expeditionary Force in France from 13 August 1914; killed in action at Ypres, 25 October following.

(Panel 11) Pte. 18929, Percy Aspden, 2nd Bn. Coldstream Guards: *s*. of John Aspen, of 11, Ash Grove, Burnley Road, Rawtenstall, co. Lancaster, by his wife Sarah Jane: and yr. brother to Pte. 42835, J.W. Aspden, 3rd Lancashire Fusiliers, died 16 October 1917; and Pte. 26286, W. Aspden, 1st East Lancashire Regt., died of wounds, 1 October 1916: *b*. Haslingden: enlisted Rawtenstall. Killed in action, 1 August 1917. Age 21.

His brother John is buried in Crowhurst (St. George's) Churchyard, Sussex; Willie, Grove Town Cemetery, Meaulte (I.P.2).

(Panel 11) Pte. 9629, Charles James Auton, 1st Bn. Coldstream Guards: *s*. of Edward Auton, of Woodbury, Salterton, co. Devon: served with the Expeditionary Force; killed in action at Ypres, 28 October 1914. *unm*.

(Panel 11) Pte. 9703, Arthur Edward Bailey, 1st Bn. Coldstream Guards: *s*. of William Bailey, Farm Labourer; of Hyam Cottages, Malmesbury, Wilts., by his wife Annie, *dau*. of the late Matthew Clark, of Malmesbury: *b*. Brokenborough, nr. Malmesbury, co. Wilts, 2 August 1890: *educ*. Malmesbury National School: enlisted, 31 July 1912. Killed in the fighting round Ypres, 29 October 1914. Age 24. *unm*.

(Panel 11) Pte. 10761, George Henry Bailey, 1st Bn. Coldstream Guards: served with the Expeditionary Force. Reported missing, 29 October–2 November. 1914; now assumed killed. (*IWGC record 29 October*)

(Panel 11) Pte. 7799, Richard Banks, 2nd Bn. Coldstream Guards: *s*. of Mrs Banks (30, Marlborough Street, Burnley): *b*. Crawshaw, Booth, co. Lancaster, 1882: *educ*. Red Lion Street Day School, from whence he won a scholarship to Burnley Grammar School: Occupation – Book-keeper; Lancashire & Yorkshire Tobacco co., Burnley, and, prior to enlistment (1908), owned a business in Kidderminster: served with the Expeditionary Force in France from 28 August 1914, took part in the fighting at

Mons, the retirement and subsequent engagements, and was killed in action at Reutel, nr. Ypres, 11 November 1914. Age 32. In a letter to his mother written shortly before his death, reflecting on the state of affairs as they appeared to him (he was of the opinion that if the enemy routed it would be as a rush), he said, "I think the Germans have seen the highest point of their progress and from now forward, if we could have a little more weight on our flank, things will move." He leaves a wife (since removed to Sherborne, co. Dorset) and two children. Remains exhumed from a (collective) grave marked as belonging to an 'Unknown British Soldier. Coldstream Guards', (28.J.10.d.8.3); identified – Clothing, Cap Badge; reinterred, registered 20 October 1927. *Buried in Sanctuary Wood Cemetery (IV.J.8).*

(Panel 11) Pte. 4138, Josiah Banner, 3rd Bn. Coldstream Guards: *s.* of William Banner, Wheelwright, of Birmingham, by his wife Elizabeth, *née* Herbert: *b.* Birmingham, 20 October 1879: *educ.* St. Anne's Boys' School, Duddeston, Birmingham: enlisted Coldstream Guards, 12 March 1901: served in Egypt (September 1906–January 1909); and with the Expeditionary Force in France and Flanders 1914. Killed in action nr. St. Julien, 3 November 1914. Believed to be buried in Reutel Woods. Age 35 years, 14 days. He *m.* Birmingham, 24 April 1909; Bertha Elizabeth Charlotte Sophia (4, County Terrace, Pears Road, Hounslow, co. Middlesex), *dau.* of James Kingston Merrick, of Hounslow, and had two sons – Joseph James, *b.* 29 April 1910; William Albert Kingston, *b.* 26 October 1913.

(Panel 11) Pte. 4467, Noah Barker, 3rd Bn. Coldstream Guards: *yst. s.* of the late William Barker, by his wife Elizabeth: *b.* Ketley Sands, Wellington, co. Salop, 22 July 1881: *educ.* Board School, there: enlisted 21 November 1901: served with the Expeditionary Force in France and Flanders from 26 August 1914; died at Reutel, Belgium, 11 November 1914, of wounds received in action. Age 33. He *m.* Denaby, nr. Rotherham, co. Yorks, 12 November 1905; Rose (10, Albert Street, South Kirkby, nr. Wakefield), *dau.* of Samuel Alfred Hodgetts, and had a *dau.* – Edith Florence, *b.* 13 February 1906.

(Panel 11) Pte. 10120, Gilbert Barraclough, 1st Bn. Coldstream Guards: *s.* of Jonathan Barraclough, of Manchester: *b.* York: served with the Expeditionary Force; killed in action at Ypres, 25 October 1914. *unm.*

(Panel 11) Pte. 1977, Richard Henry Barrow, 1st Bn. Coldstream Guards: *b.* Warwick, 1876: enlisted 5 September 1898: served in South Africa, 18 March 1900–20 June 1902: Queen's & King's Medals (5 clasps): served with the Expeditionary Force in France from August 1914; killed in action, 18 November following. Age 38. Pte. Barrow leaves a wife, Rose (254, Bridge Street West, Birmingham). (*IWGC record 18 November 1915*)

(Panel 11) Pte. 10499, James Baynes, 13th Coy., 2nd Bn. Coldstream Guards: 2nd *s.* of Edward Clemminson Baynes, Chauffeur; of 46, Parry Street, Barrow-in-Furness, by his wife Annie, *dau.* of George Dixon, Bootmaker; of Blackburn: *b.* Barrow-in-Furness, 9 July 1894: *educ.* Oxford Street Schools: enlisted November 1913. Killed in action at Zonnebeke, 21 October 1914. Age 20. *unm.*

(Panel 11) Pte. 8251, Frederick James Beer, 2nd Bn. Coldstream Guards: *s.* of James Beer, Granite Quarry Steam Crane Drive; of 18, Kinsman Dale, Moretonhampstead, co. Devon, by his wife Eliza Ann, *dau.* of John Underhill Ford: *b.* Moretonhampstead, 20 June 1890: *educ.* Pound Street Boys' School: enlisted 9 January 1909: served three years with the Colours; passed into the Reserve, joining Tiverton Police Force: recalled to serve the Colours on the declaration of war, 4 August 1914: left Windsor, 26 August, arrived Southampton.3 pm., departed aboard 'Lake Michigan,' sailing 3.30 on the morning of the 27th. Extracts from his diary record, "Arrived at Havre 4 o'clock on the 28th, and went into camp; distance seven miles. Left camp Monday afternoon about 3 o'clock, and embarked on board the Minneapolis, and after a rough voyage arrived at destination and went into camp about three miles west of St. Nazaire, about 18,000 in camp. Left St. Nazaire on 18 September by train, passing through Segre. Took part in the Battle of Chevonne. On 25 September took up our position in trenches. Could hear the band of the Germans playing. 5 October went out sniping, got shelled, and brought in a wounded comrade from a wood to the trenches, a distance of 200 yards. A shell exploded injuring five. On 4 October attacked the Germans to the left of the town of Boeschepe and drove them off. 26 October saw an aeroplane burned at 3 o'clock." He was killed in action at Reutel Woods, Belgium, 5 November 1914. Age 24. *unm.* Remains exhumed from a (collective) grave marked as belonging to an 'Unknown British Soldier. Coldstream

Guards', (28.J.10.d.8.3); identified – Clothing, Buttons; reinterred, registered 20 October 1927. *Buried in Sanctuary Wood Cemetery (IV.J.8).*

(Panel 11) Pte. 5495, George Bell, 1st Bn. Coldstream Guards: *s.* of Mary Smith (Ward Street, Longtown, Carlisle): served with the Expeditionary Force; died No.3 Field Ambulance, 24 October 1914, from wounds.

(Panel 11) Pte. 6968, George Henry Bell, 2nd Bn. Coldstream Guards: served with the Expeditionary Force; killed in action at Reutel, 8 November 1914. *m.*

(Panel 11) Pte. 3574, Frank Benneyworth, 1st Bn. Coldstream Guards: enlisted Hull, co. York: served with the Expeditionary Force; died of wounds received in action, 16 November 1914.

(Panel 11) Pte. 8916, Thomas Sidney Bird, 1st Bn. Coldstream Guards: *s.* of Charles Sidney Bird, of 50, York Road, King's Cross, London, N., by his late wife Bridget: *b.* Westminster, co. Middlesex, 1891: served with the Expeditionary Force; reported missing, 29 October 1914; assumed killed. Age 23. *unm.*

(Panel 11) Pte. 10797, William Platts Bishop, 1st Bn. Coldstream Guards: *s.* of William (& Elizabeth) Bishop, of 43, South Street, Sheffield: served with the Expeditionary Force. Reported missing, 29 October 1914; assumed killed. Age 18.

(Panel 11) Pte. 5023, Henry Bond, 1st Bn. Coldstream Guards: enlisted Taunton, co. Somerset: served with the Expeditionary Force in France. Reported missing between 29 October and 2 November 1914; now assumed killed in action.

(Panel 11) Pte. 8732, John Booker, 1st Bn. Coldstream Guards: *s.* of Richard Booker, of 81, Day Street, Anlaby, Hull, co. York, late of Flinton Street, Hessle: enlisted Hull: served with the Expeditionary Force in France; killed in action there, 25 October 1914.

(Panel 11) Pte. 9686, Fred Box, 2nd Bn. Coldstream Guards: late of Dudley, co. Worcester: enlisted Birmingham, co. Warwick. Killed in action, 6 November 1914, at Reutel. Remains exhumed from a (collective) grave marked as belonging to an 'Unknown British Soldier. Coldstream Guards', (28.J.10.d.8.3); identified – Clothing, Buttons; reinterred, registered 21 October 1927. *Buried in Sanctuary Wood Cemetery (IV.J.8).*

(Panel 11) Pte. 10345, Thomas William Boyle, 1st Bn. Coldstream Guards: only *s.* of William Boyle, Coldstream Guards; by his wife Bridget (102, Marian Street, Gateshead, Co. Durham), *dau.* of Thomas Jackson: *b.* Gateshead, 18 July 1896: enlisted, 4 September 1913. Died of wounds received in action at Ypres, 23 October 1914. Age 18.

(Panel 11) Pte. 9139, George Bracher, 2nd Bn. Coldstream Guards: *s.* of Matthias Bracher, of Gerrard's Farm, Fovant, Salisbury, co. Wilts, by his wife Louisa: *b.* Sutton Mandeville, 1893: enlisted Salisbury. Killed in action, 12 November 1914. Age 21. *unm.* Remains exhumed from a (collective) grave marked as belonging to an 'Unknown British Soldier. Coldstream Guards', (28.J.10.d.8.3); identified – Clothing, Buttons; reinterred, registered 21 October 1927. *Buried in Sanctuary Wood Cemetery (IV.J.8).*

(Panel 11) Pte. 9409, Edward Chapness Bradbury, 2nd Bn. Coldstream Guards. 2nd *s.* of Samuel Bradbury, of 65, Queen Street, Palfrey, Walsall, by his wife Annie, *dau.* of William Baker: *b.* Walsall, 18 December 1893: *educ.* Palfrey School, Walsall: Occupation – Portmanteau Lock Maker; Messrs Neville Bros.: enlisted 18 January 1911, and three months before war was declared was transferred to 2nd Life Guards, but then transferred back to his old regt., and was killed in action by a shell in an attack on a farmhouse, 16 November 1914. Age 20. *unm.*

(Panel 11) Pte. 3245, Albert Henry Britt, 1st Bn. Coldstream Guards: enlisted, 16 January 1900: served in South Africa, 7 November 1901–4 October 1902 (Queen's Medal, 3 clasps), and with the Expeditionary Force in France and Flanders, 11 September–29 October 1914. Reported missing on the latter date; now assumed killed in action between 29 October–2 November 1914. He *m.* Rose (1, The Row, Elmdon Heath, Solihull, Birmingham), and had six children. (*IWGC record 29 October 1914*)

(Panel 11) Pte. 6015, Richard Brotherton, 1st Bn. Coldstream Guards: 1st *s.* of Richard Brotherton, former Engine Driver, Great Northern Railway; of 34, Lindum Avenue, Lincoln, by his wife Betsy, *dau.* of John Graves: *b.* Lincoln, 2 February 1881: *educ.* St. Peter-at-Gowts Public School, there: enlisted 18 January 1905, served three years with the Colours, thereafter joined Huddersfield Borough

Police Force: called up on mobilization, 5 August 1914, went to France with the Expeditionary Force; reported missing after the fighting at Ypres, 29 October 1914; assumed killed on or about that date. Age 33. He *m*. Lincoln, 24 May 1908; Fanny (8, Fairfield St., off Monk's Rd., Lincoln), *yst. dau.* of the late George Brown, of Poolham Hall, Horncastle, and had a *s*. George Richard, *b*. posthumously, 9 (*d*.31) January 1915.

(Panel 11) Pte. 5171, Charles Brown, 2nd Bn. Coldstream Guards: *s*. of John Brown, of Wookey, Wells, Somerset: *b*. co. Somerset: enlisted, 24 August 1903: served with the Expeditionary Force in France and Flanders from 12 August 1914; killed in action at Reutel, 8 November 1914: *unm*. (*IWGC record 5172*)

(Panel 11) Pte. 10127, Herbert Brumby, 1st Bn. Coldstream Guards: *s*. of Fred Brumby, of 1, The Arch, Finkle Street, Cottingham, co. York, by his wife Annie: served with the Expeditionary Force; killed in action at Langemarck, 23 October 1914. Age 20. *unm*. Partial remains (1 of 3) exhumed from a (collective) grave marked as belonging to an 'Unknown British Soldier. 2/Coldstream Guards', (28.J.10.d.8.3).

(Panel 11) Pte. 5860, Thomas John Brumby, 2nd Bn. Coldstream Guards: served with the Expeditionary Force; killed in action at Reutel, 9 November 1914. *m*.

(Panel 11) Pte. 10492, Frederick Burgoyne, 2nd Bn. Coldstream Guards: *s*. of Jane Ann Burgoyne (50, Back Lane, Thurnscoe, Rotherham, co. York): served with the Expeditionary Force; killed in action at Reutel, Belgium 7 November 1914. Age 22. *unm*. Partial remains (1 of 3) 'Unknown British Soldier. 2/Coldstream Guards' exhumed unmarked grave (28.J.10.d.8.3); identified – Clothing; reinterred, registered 27 October 1927. GRU Report, Zillebeke 5-160E refers to 'Three skulls and a few small bones recovered from three graves which had apparently been disturbed by shellfire.' *Buried in Sanctuary Wood Cemetery (IV.J.8)*

(Panel 11) Pte. 8201, William John Burrow, 2nd Bn. Coldstream Guards: *s*. of Frank Burrow, of Lower Street, Chagford, co. Devon, by his wife Susan: served with the Expeditionary Force in France; killed in action at Reutel, Belgium 6 November 1914. Age 26. *unm*. Remains exhumed from a (collective) grave marked as belonging to an 'Unknown British Soldier. Coldstream Guards', (28.J.10.d.8.3); identified – Clothing, Buttons; reinterred, registered 21 October 1927. *Buried in Sanctuary Wood Cemetery (IV.J.8)*

(Panel 11) Pte. 3209, Henry George Burt, 2nd Bn. Coldstream Guards: of Dinton, nr. Salisbury, co. Wilts: served with the Expeditionary Force; killed in action at Reutel, 29 October 1914. *m*.

(Panel 11) Pte. 7898, Archibald Harry Butler, 1st Bn. Coldstream Guards: *s*. of Mr (& Mrs) Butler, of 106, Dudderton Mill Road, Saltley: enlisted Birmingham: served with the Expeditionary Force in France; killed in action at Reutel, 25 October 1914. Age 23. He was married to Kate Elizabeth Hatton, *née* Butler (128, Adderley Road, Saltley).

(Panel 11) Pte. 9468, Valentine Victor Carrier, 1st Bn. Coldstream Guards: *s*. of the late Arthur Carrier, by his wife Sarah Eliza (5, Wellington Place, Albion Road, Great Yarmouth): served with the Expeditionary Force. Reported missing, 29 October 1914; now assumed killed. Age 21. *unm*.

(Panel 11) Pte. 3015, Albert Henry Catling, 1st Bn. Coldstream Guards: *s*. of Jane Catling (120, Pelham Road, Wimbledon, London, S.W.): *b*. Wimbledon, 1879: served in the South African War, and with the Expeditionary Force in France; killed in action at Ypres, 25 October 1914. Age 35.

(Panel 11) Pte. 4333, Charles Chipchase, 2nd Bn. Coldstream Guards: late *husb*. to Elizabeth (7, Poplar Street, Hull, co. York): served with the Expeditionary Force in France; killed in action at Reutel, 5 November 1914. Age 34. Remains exhumed from a (collective) grave marked as belonging to an 'Unknown British Soldier. Coldstream Guards', (28.J.10.d.8.3); identified – Clothing; reinterred, registered 24 October 1927. *Buried in Sanctuary Wood Cemetery (IV.J.8)*.

(Panel 11) Pte. 4969, Charles William Clifford, 1st Bn. Coldstream Guards: late of Hampstead, London, N.W.: served with the Expeditionary Force in France; killed in action at Ypres, 28 October 1914. *m*.

(Panel 11) Pte. 6945, Walter John Clode, 2nd Bn. Coldstream Guards: late of Burlscombe, nr. Wellington, co. Devon: enlisted Taunton, co. Somerset: served with the Expeditionary Force. Killed in action at Zonnebeke, 22 October 1914.

(Panel 11) Pte. 4527, William Coles, 3rd Bn. Coldstream Guards: *s.* of Samuel Coles, of Station Road, Cullompton, co. Devon, by his wife Harriett: and brother to Pte. 406265, A.J. Coles, 58th Canadian Infantry, killed in action, 8 October 1916: *b.* Cullompton: enlisted Taunton: served with the Expeditionary Force. Died of wounds, 13 November 1914, received in action at Reutel. Age 33. He leaves a wife, Florence Coles. Dedicated – 'The Great War 1914–1918. This Memorial Was Raised By The Inhabitants Of Cullompton To The Glory Of God And In Honour Of Those Whose Names Are Hereon Recorded Who, Placing Country Before Comfort And Honour Before Ease, Gave Their Lives For The Cause Of Freedom. Faithful Unto Death" – the brothers Coles are remembered on the Cullompton War Memorial.

His brother Albert has no known grave; he is commemorated on the Canadian National Memorial, Vimy.

(Panel 11) Pte. 10650, John Miles Cooke, 3rd Bn. Coldstream Guards: *s.* of Henry Cooke, of Preston, Brighton, co. Sussex: served with the Expeditionary Force; killed in action at Reutel, 28 October 1914.

(Panel 11) Pte. 3868, James Cox, 1st Bn. Coldstream Guards: *s.* of the late James Cox, by his wife Sarah Ann: *b.* co. York, 1883: enlisted Hull: served with the Expeditionary Force in France; killed in action, 23 October 1914. Age 31. He was married to Emma Jane Sharp, *née* Cox (6, Walters Terrace, Saltcoats Lane, Hull).

(Panel 11) Pte. 5090, John Cunnane, 2nd Bn. Coldstream Guards: *s.* of Patrick Cunnane, of Ballaghadareen, Co. Mayo: enlisted Wigan, co. Lancaster: served with the Expeditionary Force; killed in action at Reutel, Belgium, 1 November 1914.

(Panel 11) Pte. 10686, Reginald Montague Darby, 1st Bn. Coldstream Guards: *s.* of James Darby, of The Star Inn, Bentley, Cosham, co. Hants, by his wife Amelia: served with the Expeditionary Force. Reported missing, 29 October 1914; now assumed killed. Age 20. *unm.*

(Panel 11) Pte. 7742, Thomas Daw, 1st Bn. Coldstream Guards: served with the Expeditionary Force. Reported missing, 29 October 1914; now assumed killed.

(Panel 11) Pte. 10338, John Dawson, 1st Bn. Coldstream Guards: foster *s.* of the late John Greenhalgh, and his wife Elizabeth Jane (16, Booth Lane, Walshaw, co. York): *b.* Tottington, co. Lancaster, 1895: enlisted Bury: served with the Expeditionary Force; reported missing, 29 October 1914; assumed (Court of Enquiry, 1916) killed. Age 19.

(Panel 11) Pte. 10131, Thomas Denniff, 1st Bn. Coldstream Guards: *s.* of Thomas Denniff, of 137, Shoreham Street, Sheffield, co. York, by his wife Mary Ann: served with the Expeditionary Force; reported missing, 29 October 1914; assumed (Court of Enquiry, 1916) killed. Age 20. *unm.*

(Panel 11) Pte. 10582, Lott Ditchburn, 2nd Bn. Coldstream Guards: *s.* of Thomas Ditchburn, of 105, De Walden Place, Pegswood Colliery, Ashington, by his wife Mary Jane: *b.* Flemby, co. Cumberland, *c.*1889: served with the Expeditionary Force; killed in action at Zonnebeke, Flanders, 21 October 1914. Age 25.

(Panel 11) Pte. 4054, William John Dunn, 1st Bn. Coldstream Guards: *s.* of the late John William Dunn: served with the Expeditionary Force; killed in action, 29 October 1914. Age 33.

(Panel 11) Pte. 2182, Ernest Edward Evans, 1st Bn. Coldstream Guards: served with the Expeditionary Force; killed in action, 25 October 1914. *m.*

(Panel 11) Pte. 9482, Cecil Herbert Facey, No.4 Coy., 2nd Bn. Coldstream Guards: *s.* of Herbert Facey, of Station Road, Colyton, nr. Exeter; late of Witheridge, co. Devon; by his wife Betsy Ann: and yr. brother to Pte. 8630, W.R.E. Facey, 1st Coldstream Guards, killed in action, 25 January 1915, aged 21: *b.* Torquay, co. Devon, *c.*1895: enlisted Exeter: served with the Expeditionary Force in France; killed in action at Reutel, Belgium, 6 November 1914. Age 19.

His brother William is buried in Cabaret-Rouge British Cemetery, Souchez (XXV.B.4).

(Panel 11) Pte. 9587, John Albert Fenn, 3rd Bn. Coldstream Guards: *s.* of Harry Fenn, of 36, Leader Road, Hillsborough, Sheffield, co. York, by his wife Phillis: served with the Expeditionary Force; killed in action at Reutel, Belgium, 29 October 1914. Age 19.

(Panel 11) Pte. 6711, Philip John Finch, 2nd Bn. Coldstream Guards: *s.* of the late Henry Finch, by his wife Alice E. (now wife of James Mead, of 68, The Crescent, London, N.), *dau.* of Philip Stone:

b. Fulham, London, S.W., 3 September 1887: *educ.* Castle Wood Road, Stamford Hill, London, N.: Occupation – Conductor; M.E.T. Company: enlisted March 1906: served three years with the Colours; on mobilisation, August 1914, was called up from the Reserve: served with the Expeditionary Force in France and Flanders from that month; killed in action at Ypres, 3 November following. Buried St. Mary's Convent, Ypres. Sergt. S. Watson wrote, "Your son was one of the best; he fought like a man, and died a soldier's death as only a true soldier can. He was brave to the last and respected by all ..." Age 27. He *m.* St. Anne's Road Church, 22 April 1911; Rebecca (45, Dawlish Road, Bruce Grove, South Tottenham, London, N.), *dau.* of John Clements, and had a son, Philip Sidney, *b.* 21 February 1912.

(Panel 11) Pte. 9106, Charles William Fowler, 3rd Bn. Coldstream Guards: *s.* of George Fowler, of 130, Elsley Road, Battersea, London, by his marriage to the late Regenda Fowler: and *yr.* brother to Rfn. 5/5016, G.A. Fowler, King's Royal Rifle Corps, who also fell: *b.* Wandsworth, 1896: enlisted London: served with the Expeditionary Force; killed in action at St. Julien, 21 October 1914. Age 18.

His brother George also has no known grave; he is commemorated on the Tyne Cot Memorial (Panel 117).

(Panel 11) Pte. 3527, Hugh Reginald Fulcher, 1st Bn. Coldstream Guards: *s.* of the late Charles Fulcher, by his wife Sarah Ann ('Hethel,' Atthey, nr. Norwich, co. Norfolk): served with the Expeditionary Force; reported missing after the fighting at Ypres, 29 October 1914; assumed killed. Age 37.

(Panel 11) Pte. 6943, Arthur Funnell, 3rd Bn. Coldstream Guards: *s.* of Stephen Funnell, of 21 Trevor Gardens, Glynde, nr. Lewes, co. Sussex: served with the Expeditionary Force; killed in action at St. Julien, 22 October 1914. Age 29.

(Panel 11) Pte. 5767, William Harold Gabb, 3rd Bn. Coldstream Guards: late *husb.* to Ellen Eliza Brinkley, *née* Gabb (88c, Guinness Buildings, Hammersmith, London): served with the Expeditionary Force. Died 7 November 1914, from wounds received in action at Reutel the same day. Age 34.

(Panel 11) Pte. 1518, Charles William Crowne Gibbons, 1st Bn. Coldstream Guards: eldest *s.* of the late Charles William Gibbons, by his wife Emily Marion (now wife of Charles Emery, of 35, Wandle Road, Wandsworth Common, London, S.W.), *dau.* of William Johnstone Harris: *b.* London, 2 December 1884: *educ.* Tennyson Street Council School, Queen's Road, S.W.: enlisted 2 September 1914: went to France, 7 October 1914, and was reported missing after the fighting at Ypres, 29 October 1914; now assumed to have been killed in action on that day. Age 29. *unm.*

(Panel 11) Pte. 3257, William Goddard, 1st Bn. Coldstream Guards: *s.* of the late Joseph Goddard, of Reading, by his wife Harriet: *b.* Windsor, 3 December 1880: *educ.* Royal Schools there: enlisted 23 January 1900: served in the South African War, 7 November 1901–4 October 1902, obtained his discharge 6 November 1902: re-enlisted 9 September 1914: went to France, 7 October; died on the 29th. of that month of wounds received in action. He was buried in the lawn in front of the Chateau at Gheluvelt, west of the village. Age 35. He *m.* Windsor, 1 June 1905; Mary Ann (3, Waterloo Square, Spital, Windsor), *dau.* of Thomas Redrup, and had three *daus.* – Ena, *b.* 27 August 1906; Laura, *b.* 27 September 1907; Vera, *b.* 27 January 1910.

(Panel 11) Pte. 8558, Ralph Sneath Gray, 2nd Bn. Coldstream Guard: *s.* of Sneath Gray, of Leicester: enlisted Leicester: served with the Expeditionary Force; killed in action nr. Reutel Woods, 6 November 1914. Age 30. Remains exhumed from a (collective) grave marked as belonging to an 'Unknown British Soldier. Coldstream Guards', (28.J.10.d.8.3); identified – Clothing; reinterred, registered 24 October 1927. *Buried in Sanctuary Wood Cemetery (IV.J.8).*

There Is No Service Like His That Serves Because He Loves

(Panel 11) Pte. 19761, Robert Rigby Grimshaw, 1st Bn. Coldstream Guards: *s.* of John Grimshaw, of 1, Victoria Terrace, Wheelton, Chorley, co. Lancaster, by his wife Mary: and brother to Pte. 28457, T. Grimshaw, 8th Border Regt., killed in action, 13 June 1917: *b.* Chorley: enlisted Preston. Killed in action, 31 July 1917, at Boesinghe.

His brother Thomas also has no known grave; he is recorded on Panel 35.

When the First Battle of Ypres began on 19 October 1914, the three battalions of the Coldstream Guards were all with First Corps in front of Ypres; on the road from Bixschoote to Zonnebeke from whence they advanced on the 21st in the direction of Bruges. The Germans, encountered in overwhelming numbers, although staying the Guards advance, failed to cause them to break. On the 22nd the enemy broke through the line held by 1st Coldstream but – managing to rally themselves – they held firm, denying the enemy advance, until they were relieved by some French Territorials on the 24th. During the second stage of the battle the Coldstream were positioned between Zonnebeke and Gheluvelt, strategically the most important part of our line, and on the 29th, 1st Bn. was in the thick of the action. The men were driven from their trenches, four companies were surrounded, but many of them refused to surrender and, as a consequence, died fighting. One of these was the Hon. V.D. Boscawen, son of Lord Falmouth. Two days later the remaining companies, also driven from their trenches, met a still fiercer attack and by the time the day was over the 1st Battalion had ceased to exist as a fighting unit, with no officers and only 80 men remaining at roll call. A terrible price had been paid for the successes of First Ypres. The three battalions had lost over 1,500 men; the majority of them have no known grave:-

(Panel 11) Pte. 10253, Victor Henry Grover, 1st Bn. Coldstream Guards: eldest *s*. of Frederick Grover, Market Gardener; of 10, Downview Terrace, Lancing, co. Sussex, by his wife Ada (formerly of Shambrook, co. Bedford): *b*. Blacksmith House, The Street, North Lancing, 5 May 1886: enlisted Coldstream Guards, Worthing, 24 July 1913, stating his age as 18 years, 2 months: served with the Expeditionary Force in France and Flanders from 14 August 1914: after a few days acclimatisation nr. Boulogne, went to the Front at Binche, nr. Mons, where, on 23 August, he was put to work digging trenches; took part in the following day's fighting and subsequent retirement: took part in the rear-guard action at Landrecies, the Battles of the Marne and the Aisne, the fighting on the road between Bixschoote and Zonnebeke, 21–24 October 1914, at the First Battle of Ypres, and was killed in action nr. Gheluvelt, on the 29th of that month. Age 18.

(Panel 11) Pte. 7540, Walter Hallam, D.C.M., 2nd Bn. Coldstream Guards: *s*. of Samuel Hallam, Private Estate Steward: *b*. Horsham, co. Sussex, 11 May 1886: enlisted, 25 November 1907. Killed in action at Reutel Woods, 11 November 1914. Age 28. The officer to whom he acted as servant wrote, "We were holding the trenches in front of Ypres in a wood just by a place called Reutel. There was a German attack in progress, and they were firing hard at that part of the line. Hallam, with his accustomed fearlessness, was firing, with his head well above the parapet, and was most unfortunately shot right through the head." He was awarded the Distinguished Conduct Medal, the official record (*London Gazette*, 17 December 1914), stating he 'always volunteered and carried out successfully duties of an extraordinary dangerous character, such as sniping and patrol work. Has shown great qualities of nerve and resource in difficult situations.' He *m*. Paddington, 13 December 1913; Harriette Matilda, *dau*. of Henry George Shore, and had a *dau*., Lily Edith Walter Jessie, *b*. 12 August 1914. Remains exhumed from a (collective) grave marked as belonging to an 'Unknown British Soldier. Coldstream Guards', (28.J.10.d.8.3); identified – Clothing; reinterred, registered 24 October 1927. (*Menin Gate records Hallan, D.C.*) *Buried in Sanctuary Wood Cemetery (IV.J.8).*

(Panel 11) Pte. George Harbridge, 2nd Bn. Coldstream Guards: *s*. of James Harbridge, of Bromsgrove, co. Worcester: *b*. Worcester: served with the Expeditionary Force. Killed in action at Reutel, Belgium, 11 November 1914. Buried in Reutel Woods.

(Panel 11) Pte. 9480, Reginald Heseltine, 1st Bn. Coldstream Guards: *s*. of Bernard Heseltine, of Barrowford, Nelson, co. Lancaster: served with the Expeditionary Force; killed in action, 25 October 1914.

(Panel 11) Pte. Walter Hessel, 1st Bn. Coldstream Guards: served with the Expeditionary Force; killed in action at Ypres, 29 October 1914. *m*.

(Panel 11) Pte. 9633, Alfred Higginson, 1st Bn. Coldstream Guards: *s*. of Robert Higginson, of 1, South Street, Kidderminster, co. Worcester: served with the Expeditionary Force; killed in action, 25 October 1914. Age 30.

(Panel 11) Pte. 10502, Alfred Sidney Denman Higginson, 2nd Bn. Coldstream Guards: *s.* of Harry Higginson, of Leicester: served with the Expeditionary Force; killed in action at Reutel, 5 November 1914.

(Panel 11) Pte. 10268, Albert Hindmarsh, 1st Bn. Coldstream Guards: 4th *s.* of the late Charles Hindmarsh, Fireman; of Monkwearmouth Colliery, by his wife Mary (28, Fulwell Road, Sunderland), *dau.* of James Archbald: *b.* Southwick-on-Wear, Co. Durham, 25 October 1893: *educ.* Southwick Board School: Occupation – Miner, Monkwearmouth: enlisted, 7 August 1913: went to France, 10 August 1914; killed in action at Ypres, 29 October 1914. Age 21. *unm.* His four brothers – Pte. 5454, Robert Hindmarsh, 3rd Durham L.I., Pte. William Hindmarsh, 14th Durham L.I., Dvr. 690, John Hindmarsh, R.G.A., and Pte. 15488, Arthur Hindmarsh, 14th Durham L.I. (wounded), are all on active service; and his brother-in-law, Pte. 14373, T. Elliott, 10th West Yorks, was killed in action at the Somme. (*IWGC record Hindmarch*)

Thomas Elliott, killed in action, 1 July 1916, also has no known grave; he is commemorated on the Thiepval Memorial, Somme.

(Panel 11) Pte. 4290, Arthur Hiscox, 1st Bn. Coldstream Guards: late of Stoke St. Michael, co. Somerset: served with the Expeditionary Force. Reported missing, 29 October 1914; now assumed (Court of Enquiry, 1916) killed.

(Panel 11) Pte. 7673, Taylor Holden, 1st Bn. Coldstream Guards: *s.* of Jane (Bury Road, Haslingden, co. Lancaster): served with the Expeditionary Force. Reported missing, 29 October–2 November 1914; assumed killed. Age 30.

(Panel 11) Pte. 10335, Edward George Holland, 3rd Bn. Coldstream Guards: *s.* of Edward Holland, of Bermondsey, London, S.E.: *b.* Walworth, London: served with the Expeditionary Force in France; killed in action at Reutel, 13 November 1914. *unm.* Remains exhumed from an unmarked grave (28.J.10.d.3.9) 31 December 1926; identified – Disc; reinterred, registered 1 January 1927. *Buried in Sanctuary Wood Cemetery (III.B.18).*

(Panel 11) Pte. 5610, George Hughes, 2nd Bn. Coldstream Guards: *s.* of Edward Hughes, of Wolverhampton, co. Stafford, by his wife Mary Ann: served with the Expeditionary Force; killed in action at Zonnebeke, 21 October 1914.

(Panel 11) Pte. 10071, Joseph Jennings, 2nd Bn. Coldstream Guards: *s.* of Joseph Jennings, of 203, Oldbury Road, West Smethwick, co. Stafford: *b.* Oldbury, co. Worcester, 1893: served with the Expeditionary Force. Killed in action at Reutel, 8 November 1914. Age 21. *unm.*

(Panel 11) Pte. 10769, Frederick Charles Jones, 3rd Bn. Coldstream Guards: *s.* of William Robert Jones, of 20, Sandyford Street, Stafford: served with the Expeditionary Force. Killed in action at Reutel, 28 October 1914. Age 19.

(Panel 11) Pte. 6761, Edgar Kallaway, 1st Bn. Coldstream Guards: *yst. s.* of the late James Kallaway, of 46, Grays Road, Taunton, by his wife Jane, *dau.* of John Lewis, of Bridgwater: *b.* West Monkton, Taunton, co. Somerset, 19 September 1886: *educ.* Taunton: enlisted, 2 May 1906: served three years with the Colours, thereafter (1913) removed to Canada, settled Manitoba: recalled on the declaration of war; arrived in England, 7 September 1914; left for France, 7 October following. His last postcard was written on 26 October. In the action at Ypres, on the 29th of that month, 1st Battn. suffered very heavily, and after it Kallaway was reported missing. Assumed (Court of Enquiry, 1916) to have been killed that day: 29 October 1914. Age 28. *unm.*

(Panel 11) Pte. 6508, Alfred Percy Keddie, 'A' Coy., 1st Bn. Coldstream Guards: brother to Jane Alice Keddie (27, Bramwell Street, Hendon, Sunderland): served with the Expeditionary Force. Reported missing, 29 October 1914; assumed killed. Age 26. *unm.*

(Panel 11) Pte. 8644, Ernest Arthur Kirby, 1st Bn. Coldstream Guards: *s.* of the late William Kirby, by his wife Agnes: served with the Expeditionary Force. Reported missing, 29 October 1914; assumed killed. Age 21. *unm.*

(Panel 11) Pte. 8884, James Mather, 2nd Bn. Coldstream Guards: *s.* of James Charles Mather, Labourer; of 25, Fraser Street, Bolton, by his wife Elizabeth, *dau.* of Ralph Hough, Stripper & Grinder: *b.* Halliwell, Bolton, co. Lancaster, 17 November 1890: *educ.* Brownlowfold Council School: enlisted 3 October 1910; killed at Reutel, Belgium, 2 November 1914. Age 23. *unm.*

(Panel 11) Pte. 5533, Charles Henry Matthews, 1st Bn. Coldstream Guards: *s.* of William Henry Matthews, of 42, Butlin Street, Nechells, Birmingham, Millwright, by his wife Frances: *b.* 24 June 1885: *educ.* Cromwell Street Council School: enlisted 30 April 1904: went to France, 17 August 1914; reported missing after the severe fighting, 29 October 1914, on which date the 2nd Coldstreams and the rest of the 1st Division were at one time driven from their trenches near Gheluvelt; assumed killed. Age 29. He *m.* St. Clement's Church, Nechells, 3 October 1909; Charlotte (18, Brighton Grove, Great Francis Street, Birmingham), *dau.* of Samuel Woodin, Painter, and had two children – Edna Frances, *b.* 9 December 1910; Charles Henry, *b.* 9 February 1915.

(Panel 11) Pte. 8829, Charles Naisbitt, 2nd Bn. Coldstream Guards: enlisted Darlington, Co. Durham. Killed in action at Reutel, Belgium, 6 November 1914. Remains exhumed from a (collective) grave marked as belonging to an 'Unknown British Soldier. Coldstream Guards', (28.J.10.d.8.3); identified – Clothing, Buttons; reinterred, registered 25 October 1927. (*Menin Gate records no initial*) Buried in Sanctuary Wood Cemetery *(IV.J.8).*

(Panel 11) Pte. 4986, Richard Naves, 1st Bn. Coldstream Guards: *b.* Purfleet, co. Essex: a pre-war Reservist – Police Constable, No.520, serving the Penge and Camberwell communities – recalled to the Colours on mobilisation; reported Woolwich: served with the Expeditionary Force in France from August 1914; killed in action, 29 October following, nr. Gheluvelt. Age 31. He leaves a wife Lily May Naves, *née* Shephard (6, Stanstead Road, Forest Hill, London), to whom he had been married just over three years. One of sixteen officers who made the supreme sacrifice remembered on the Catford (Police Station) War Memorial.

(Panel 11) Pte. 10347, John Charles Nicholson, 3rd Bn. Coldstream Guards: *s.* of John William Nicholson, of 15, Villa Terrace, Alexandra Street, Hull: *b.* co. York: served with the Expeditionary Force in France and Flanders. Killed in action at Zillebeke, 19 November 1914. Age 19.

(Panel 11) Pte. 107344, William Norris, 1st Bn. Coldstream Guards: *yst. s.* of Joseph Norris, of 35, Albert Road, Tamworth, Warwick, Carpenter (a native of Lancashire), by his wife Elizabeth, *dau.* of David Marney, of Melbourne, Victoria, Australia: *b.* Melbourne, 28 November 1893: came to England with his parents when two years of age: *educ.* Tamworth Council School: Occupation – Platelayer; London & North Western Railway: enlisted May 1914; killed in action at Ypres, 29 October 1914. Age 20. *unm.*

(Panel 11) Pte. 7345, Albert Page, 2nd Bn. Coldstream Guards: *s.* of the late William Page, by his wife Jane (12, Andover Road, Hornsey Road, Holloway), *dau.* of William Finch: and brother to Pte. L/11334, F.J. Page, 2nd Middlesex Regt., killed in action, 10–14 March 1915: *b.* Highgate, 27 November 1887: *educ.* St. Mary's School, there: enlisted 12 July 1907: served three years with the Colours, then passed into the Reserve: Occupation Carman: mobilised, 5 August 1914: served with the Expeditionary Force in France and Flanders; killed in action, 30 October following. Buried in Reutel Woods. Age 28. Two other brothers also served; both survived. *unm.*

His brother Frederick also has no known grave; he is commemorated on the Le Touret Memorial.

(Panel 11) Pte. 4000, John Remnant, 1st Bn. Coldstream Guards: *s.* of the late Charles (& Sarah) Remnant. Killed in action, 25 October 1914. Age 33. He was married to Elsie Remnant (11, St. John Street, Farncombe, co. Surrey). A staff member of Charterhouse School, Pte. Remnant is remembered on the school roll of honour.

(Panel 11) Pte. 2670, Oswald Henry Roberts, 1st Bn. Coldstream Guards: *s.* of James Casimir Roberts, of New Brighton, Wallasey, co. Chester, by his wife Elizabeth: served in the South African War, and with the Expeditionary Force in France and Flanders; killed in action, 29 October 1914; Reutel, Belgium. Age 34.

(Panel 11) Pte. 7900, Wilfrid Slinn, 1st Bn. Coldstream Guards: *s.* of Ephraim Slinn, by his wife Sarah: *b.* Sheffield, co. York, 17 September 1892: *educ.* there: Occupation – Postman (G.P.O. Sheffield): enlisted Coldstream Guards, 4 August 1914: served with the Expeditionary Force in France and Flanders; killed in action, 31 July 1917. Buried where he fell. Age 25. 2nd Lieut. Marrington wrote, "It was very hard luck, after just coming back from leave, but I can assure you he laid down his life very cheerfully, and went into action in the best of spirits. He proved himself a very good soldier, and did his duty for the sake of home and country." He *m.* Sheffield, 1 September 1913; Elizabeth (98, Fowler St., Pitsmoor), *dau.* of Frederick Holmes, and had two sons – Wilfrid, *b.* 13 August 1915; Frederick, *b.* (posthumously) 25 April 1918.

(Panel 11) Pte. 5510, James William Stone, 2nd Bn. Coldstream Guards: *s.* of the late James W. (& Mrs) Stone: *b.* St. Mary's, co. Lincoln: enlisted Gainsborough. Missing/believed killed in action, 12 November 1914. Age 31. He was married to Harriet Stone ("Fernlea," Clifton Grove, Skegness). Remains exhumed from a (collective) grave marked as belonging to an 'Unknown British Soldier. Coldstream Guards', (28.J.10.d.8.3); identified – Clothing; reinterred, registered 25 October 1927. *Buried in Sanctuary Wood Cemetery (IV.J.8).*

He Died For King And Country
From His Wife And Son

(Panel 11) Pte. 8150, Tom Henry Winter Taylor, 2nd Bn. Coldstream Guards: *b.* Eston, co. York: enlisted Redcar. Died 2 November 1914, of wounds. Age 23. He was married to Florence Wheeler, *née* Taylor (7, Widgeon Street, Warrenby, Redcar, co. Yorks). Remains exhumed from a (collective) grave marked as belonging to an 'Unknown British Soldier. Coldstream Guards', (28.J.10.d.8.3); identified – Clothing, Cap Badge; reinterred, registered 25 October 1927. *Buried in Sanctuary Wood Cemetery (IV.J.8).*

Greater Love Hath No Man Than This

(Panel 11) Pte. 8356, Arthur Vernon Tompkins, 2nd Bn. Coldstream Guards: *b.* Birmingham: enlisted there. Killed in action, 5 November 1914, at Reutel. Remains exhumed from a (collective) grave marked as belonging to an 'Unknown British Soldier. Coldstream Guards', (28.J.10.d.8.3); identified – Clothing; reinterred, registered 25 October 1927. *Buried in Sanctuary Wood Cemetery (IV.J.8).*

(Panel 11) Pte. 10497, John Toner, 2nd Bn. Coldstream Guards: *s.* of William Toner, of 18, Regent Road, Stockport, co. Chester, by his wife Bertha: *b.* St. George's, Chester, *c.*1896: enlisted Stockport. Killed in action, 5 November 1914. Age 18. Remains exhumed from a (collective) grave marked as belonging to an 'Unknown British Soldier. Coldstream Guards', (28.J.10.d.8.3); identified – Clothing; reinterred, registered 26 October 1927. *Buried in Sanctuary Wood Cemetery (IV.J.8).*

(Panel 11) Pte. 16673, Frederick Peter Towse, 1st Bn. Coldstream Guards: *s.* of Albert Owen Towse, Gardener; of 1, Hayes Road, Slinfold, by his wife Mary, *dau.* of William Reeves, Farmer: *b.* Five Oaks, nr. Billingshurst, co. Sussex, 1 August 1889: *educ.* Council School, there: enlisted Coldstream Guards, 12 August 1915: served with the Expeditionary Force in France and Flanders from 7 June 1916, and was killed in action near Langemarck on his 28th birthday, 1 August 1917. Buried in the Military Cemetery there. His Officer, 2nd Lieut. A.G.H. Fowler, wrote, "I was very grieved to lose him as his work was always well done, and his cheeriness under all conditions was undoubtedly a great help to his comrades. I fear this letter can hardly console you, but I wished to show you how his work and bearing in all circumstances was generally appreciated by not only me, his Platoon Officer, but by all his friends in my platoon." Age 28. *unm.* (*IWGC record age 27*)

(Panel 11) Pte. 8456, Albert Turner, No.6 Coy., 2nd Bn. Coldstream Guards: *s.* of Mr (& Mrs) Turner, of Chapel House, Ringmer, nr. Lewes, co. Sussex. Missing/believed killed in action, 6 November 1914. Age 24. He was married to Nellie Cuckson, *née* Turner (40, Fernhead Road, Paddington, London). Remains exhumed from a (collective) grave marked as belonging to an 'Unknown British Soldier. Coldstream Guards', (28.J.10.d.8.3); identified – Clothing; reinterred, registered 26 October 1927. *Buried in Sanctuary Wood Cemetery (IV.J.8).*

(Panel 11) Drmr. 8495, Charles Watkins, 2nd Bn. Coldstream Guards: late of Windsor, co. Berks: *s.* of William Henry Watkins, of 10, Union Street, Stourbridge, co. Worcester: *b.* Caterham, co. Surrey: enlisted Oxford. Killed in action, 10 November 1914. Age 21. Remains exhumed from a (collective) grave marked as belonging to an 'Unknown British Soldier. Coldstream Guards', (28.J.10.d.8.3); identified – Clothing; reinterred, registered 26 October 1927. *Buried in Sanctuary Wood Cemetery (IV.J.8).*

(Panel 11) Pte. 9527, Herbert Gideon West, 2nd Bn. Coldstream Guards: 2nd *s.* of John West, Farmer; of Silver Street, Steeple Ashton, nr. Trowbridge, by his wife Annie, *dau.* of John Kingman: *b.* Steeple Ashton, co. Wilts, 18 January 1895: *educ.* National School, there: enlisted Coldstream Guards, 18 March 1912: went to France, 12 August 1914; killed in action at Reutel, 6 November 1914. Buried in Reutel Woods. Age 19. Remains exhumed from a (collective) grave marked as belonging to an 'Unknown British Soldier. Coldstream Guards', (28.J.10.d.8.3); identified – Clothing, Buttons; reinterred, registered 26 October 1927. *Buried in Sanctuary Wood Cemetery (IV.J.8).*

We Loved Him In Life Let Us Not Forget Him In Death

(Panel 11) Pte. 8157, Arthur White, 2nd Bn. Coldstream Guards: *s.* of James Henry White, of Fawcett Street, Sheffield, by his wife Lydia: *b.* 1887: a Pre-War Regular (enlisted Sheffield, 1908), proceeded to France, 12 August 1914. Reported missing, believed killed in action, 5 November 1914, at Reutel. Age 28. He was married (April 1912) to Gertrude Smith, *née* White (66, Wayland Road, Sharrow, Sheffield), *dau.* of Arthur J.C. Simms; Grocer. Remains exhumed from a (collective) grave marked as belonging to an 'Unknown British Soldier. Coldstream Guards', (28.J.10.d.8.3); identified – Clothing, Buttons; reinterred, registered 27 October 1927. *Buried in Sanctuary Wood Cemetery (IV.J.8).*

(Panel 11) Pte. 10577, John Whitehead, 2nd Bn. Coldstream Guards: late of St. Mary's, co. Lincoln: enlisted Spilsby. Killed in action, 6 November 1914. Partial remains exhumed from a grave marked as belonging to an 'Unknown British Soldier. 2/Coldstream Guards', (28.J.10.d.8.3); identified – Clothing; reinterred, registered 27 October 1927. GRU Report, Zillebeke 5-160E refers 'Three skulls and a few small bones recovered from three individual graves which had apparently been disturbed by shellfire.' *Buried in Sanctuary Wood Cemetery (IV.J.8).*

(Panel 11) Pte. 10723, William John Wilkins, 1st Bn. Coldstream Guards: eldest *s.* of George Wilkins, of 59, Waterloo Street, Leamington, by his wife Elizabeth, *dau.* of William Hortin: *b.* Leamington, co. Warwick, 11 September 1894: *educ.* St. Peter's R.C. School: Occupation – Dairyman: joined 7th Warwickshire Territorials, about January 1911: enlisted Coldstream Guards, 2 May 1914, went to France, 6 October 1914; killed in action during the First Battle of Ypres, 29 October 1914. Age 20. *unm.*

(Panel 11) Major the Hon. Hugh Joseph Fraser, M.V.O., 2nd Bn. Scots Guards: 3rd & 2nd *survg. s.* of the late Simon Fraser, 15th Lord Lovat, by his wife Alice Mary (Beaufort Castle, Beauly), *dau.* of Thomas Weld Blundell, of Ince Blundell: *b.* Phoiness, Beauly, co. Inverness, 6 July 1874: *educ.* St. Benedict's Abbey School, Fort Augustus, co. Inverness: gazetted 2nd Lieut. from the Militia to Scots Guards, 12 December 1894; promoted Lieut. 15 November 1897; Capt. 16 March 1901; Major, 12 June 1907: served in the South African War, 1900–02: took part in operations in Orange Free State, May–29 November 1900, including actions at Biddulphsberg and Wittenbergen (1–29 July), also in those there and in the Transvaal, 30 November 1901–31 May 1902; Mentioned in Despatches (*London Gazette*, 10 September 1901), Queen's Medal, 3 clasps; King's Medal, 2 clasps: Adjutant, Lovat's Scouts (Imperial Yeomanry), 1 April 1903–31 July 1907; Aide-de-Camp, Viceroy of India, November 1910–April 1913: went to the Front with 2nd Scots Guards, 7th Division, following the outbreak of war with Germany, and was killed in action at the 1st Battle of Ypres, 27 October 1914. At the time of his death he was Second in Command of his battalion. He was made a M.V.O. (4th Class), 1912. Age 40. *unm.* (*IWGC record 28th October 1914*)

(Panel 11) Capt. Robert Frederick Balfour, 1st Bn. Scots Guards: eldest *s.* of Edward (& Mrs) Balfour, J.P., D.L., of 'Balbirnie,' Markinch, co. Fife: *gdson.* to the late Colonel John Balfour, and Lady Georgina Isabella, 2nd *dau.* of the 1st Earl of Cawdor: and nephew to Brevet-Colonel A.G. Balfour, late of the Highland Light Infantry; served in the Great War as Assistant Embarkation Commandant (apptd. August 1914): *b.* 16 March 1883: gazetted 2nd Lieut. Scots Guards, 24 January 1903; promoted Lieut. 29 June 1904: Battalion Adjt. 1 July 1907–1 August 1910; promoted Capt. 18 January 1913: apptd. A.D.C. to General Officer Commanding (G.O.C.) VIth Division, Irish Command, 1 April 1912–17 January 1913. In the Great War the 1st Battn. Scots Guards formed part of the 1st Infantry Brigade, 1st Division, which was the first portion of the Expeditionary Force to leave Great Britain, being present at the fighting from the very commencement of the war. Capt. Balfour was killed in action at Gheluvelt, nr. Ypres, 28 October

1914. Age 31. Remains exhumed from a grave marked as belonging to an 'Unknown British Capt. Scot Guards', (28.J.22.b.6.1) Gheluvelt Chateau; identified – Clothing, Badge of Rank, Buttons, Silver Watch; reinterred, registered 18 May 1927. *Buried in Sanctuary Wood Cemetery (IV.D.14).*

(Panel 11) Capt. Thomas Henry Rivers Bulkeley, C.M.G., C.V.O., 2nd Bn. Scots Guards: *s.* of Col. C. Rivers Bulkeley, C.B., and the late Constance Clementine, his wife: and brother to Capt. C.I.R. Bulkeley, C.M.G., M.V.O., Scots Guards, killed in action, 16 May 1915: *b.* 23 June 1876: *educ.* Eton: joined Oxfordshire Militia, 1894; became Capt. 1897: transf'd. from Militia to Scots Guards; gazetted 2nd Lieut. 4 January 1899; promoted Lieut. 4 April 1900; Capt. 1 July 1904: served in the South African War, 1899–1902: took part in the advance on Kimberley, including action at Belmont (slightly wounded): operations in Orange Free State, February–May 1900, including operations at Paardeberg (17–26 February): operations at Poplar Grove, Dreifontein, Vet River (5–6 May) and Zand River: operations Transvaal, May–June 1900, including actions nr. Johannesburg, Pretoria and Diamond Hill (11–12 June): operations Transvaal, east of Pretoria, July–29 November 1900, including action at Belfast (26–27 August): operations Transvaal, west of Pretoria, July–29 November 1900: operations Orange River Colony, May–29 November 1900: operations Transvaal, December 1900–July 1901: operations Orange River Colony, July 1901–May 1902, and those in Cape Colony, December 1900 (Mentioned in Despatches; *London Gazette*, 26 January 1900, 10 September 1901, 29 July 1902; Queen's Medal, six clasps; King's Medal, two clasps): Adjutant of his regiment, 20 July 1901–19 July 1904, and, 13 December 1904–17 November 1905, A.D.C. and Comptroller of the Household to Lord Curzon, Viceroy of India, holding the same post under Lord Minto, 18 November 1905–26 September 1907. From 28 September 1907 to 20 December following he was A.D.C. to Field Marshal H.R.H. the Duke of Connaught, Inspector-General of the Forces, High Commissioner in the Mediterranean, and more lately Governor General and Commander-in-Chief in Canada; 31 December 1907–31 July 1909. Apptd. Equerry to H.R.H. The Duke of Connaught, 20 October 1909, and Comptroller of his Household in Canada. Capt. Rivers Bulkeley resigned this appointment on the outbreak of the European War, and rejoined his regiment. Served with the Expeditionary Force in France and Flanders, and was killed in action, 22 October 1914, while commanding the left flank Company of 2nd Battn. Scots Guards, forming part of VIIth Division; he was leading his company to fill a gap in the fighting line. He *m.* 19 April 1913; Annie Evelyn, Lady of Grace of St. John of Jerusalem, formerly Lady-in-Waiting to H.R.H. Duchess of Connaught, *dau.* of Sir Henry Carstairs Pelly, 3rd Bart., J.P., D.L., M.P., and had a *s., b.* January 1914. Capt. Rivers Bulkeley was a member of the Guard's, Carlton, Junior Carlton, and Shrewsbury County Clubs. Age 38.

His brother Charles also has no known grave; he is commemorated on the Le Touret Memorial.

(Panel 11) Capt. Colin Frederick Fitzroy Campbell, 1st Bn. Scots Guards: only *s.* of Major-Gen. Frederick Lorn Campbell, of Highfield House, West Byfleet, co. Surrey, late Scots Guards (of the Melfort family, Argyll), by his wife Caroline, *dau.* of John Alexander Smyth, and *gdson.* of Rear-Admiral Frederick Archibald Campbell: *b.* London, 29 September 1880: *educ.* Stubbington and Haileybury: obtained his first commission in the Cameron Highlanders from the Militia, 5 January 1901; promoted Lieut. 3 August 1904: transf'd. Scots Guards, 29 March 1905: Adjt., Guards Depot, Caterham, September 1911–September 1913; promoted Capt. 29 October 1914, on which day he was killed in action close to the village of Gheluvelt, nr. Ypres. Age 34. He *m.* Guards' Chapel, London, 11 June 1914; Helen Margaret; eldest *dau.* of Charles John Stewart, of 32, Eccleston Square, London, S.W., by his wife Lady Mary Graham, *née* Toler. He was a member of the Guard's and Caledonian Clubs.

(Panel 11) Capt. Charles Edward Mary De La Pasture, 1st Bn. Scots Guards: Count de la Pasture: eldest *s.* of Gerard Gustavus Ducarel, 4th Marquis De La Pasture, Cefn, Usk, co. Monmouth, by his 2nd. wife Georgiana Mary, *dau.* of Robert J. Loughnan, J.P., Indian Civil Service: *b.* Caley Hall, Otley, co. York, 15 September 1879: Religion – Roman Catholic: *educ.* Downside Abbey, Bath: served with the embodied Militia for almost three months, after which he was gazetted to the Derbyshire Regt., 4 April 1900: later in the year, being in South Africa, he joined Plumer's Force as a trooper for the relief of Mafeking, and was also present at operations in Rhodesia, October 1899–May 1900 (Queen's Medal, two clasps): gazetted 2nd Lieut. Scots Guards, 22 September 1900; promoted Lieut. 1 April 1903; Capt.

5 June 1907: A.D.C. to the late General Sir Frederick Forestier Walker, Governor and Commander- in-Chief, Gibraltar, June 1907–August 1910: proceeded with the Expeditionary Force to France early August 1914. Officially reported missing (was commanding Right flank Coy., 1st Scots Guards at the time) 29 October 1914, and has since been unofficially reported killed on this date, although his name has not yet appeared in any official casualty lists. Age 35. Mentioned in Despatches by F.M. Sir John (now Lord) French (*London Gazette*, 17 February 1915) for 'gallant and distinguished service in the field.' Capt. De La Pasture was a member of the Guards' and Travellers' Clubs. He *m.* 20 April 1911, Agatha, 2nd *dau.* of Alexander Moseley, C.M.G., of Gibraltar.

(Panel 11) Capt. William Joseph Wickham, 1st Bn. Scots Guards: eldest *s.* of Capt. Henry Lamplugh Wickham, late Rifle Brigade, of Wooton Hall, co. Warwick, by his marriage to, the Hon. Teresa Mary Josephine (Down Grange, Basingstoke, co. Hants), *dau.* of 11th Baron Arundell, of Wardour, and widow of Sir Alfred Joseph Doughty Tichbourne, Bart.: and elder brother to Capt. C.H. Wickham, 1st Royal Fusiliers, died of wounds, 15 January 1915: *b.* 5 November 1874: Religion – Roman Catholic: *educ.* The Oratory, Edgbaston, and Trinity Hall, Cambridge: gazetted 2nd Lieut. Scots Guards August 1900: served in the South African War: present at operations in Orange River and Cape Colonies (Queen's Medal, three clasps): promoted Lieut. January 1903; Capt. June 1906: held Coronation Medal: served with the Expeditionary Force in France, and was killed in action at the Battle of Ypres, 31 October 1914. Buried at Chateau Gheluvelt. Capt. Wickham was a member of the Guards', Bachelors', Boodle's, Pratt's, and the Army & Navy Clubs. His recreations were shooting, golf, and boating. Age 39.

His brother Cyril is buried in La Chapelle D'Armentieres Communal Cemetery (A.3).

(Panel 11) Lieut. Clement Cottrell-Dormer, 2nd Bn. Scots Guards: elder *s.* of Capt. Charles Walter Cotterell-Dormer, late 13th Hussars, J.P., D.L., of Rousham Hall and Middle Steeple Aston, co. Oxford, and Heath House (and Stapleton Park), co. Gloucester, by his wife Ursula, *yst. dau.* of Thomas Robert Brook Leslie-Melville-Cartwright, of Melville House, co. Fife, J.P., D.L., and Lady Elizabeth, *née* Leslie-Melville, his wife: and brother to Lieut. C.M. Cottrell-Dormer, D.S.O., 3rd Battn. Coldstream Guards, died Bethune Hospital, 8 February 1915, of wounds received in action at La Bassée two days previously: *b.* 6 February 1891: *educ.* Mr Lionel Herbert's Preparatory School, West Downs, Winchester, from 1901; Eton (Mr. J.H.M. Hare's House) from 1905, where he rowed in the Junior House Four, and became a member of the boats, rowing in the 'Alexandra;' joined Eton Volunteer Band and became a member of the Eton Volunteer Corps (also joined Eton Debating Society). After leaving Eton (1910), went for a short time to Mr William Trevor's, Lathbury Park; thereafter entered Royal Military College, Sandhurst: given a commission May 1910, 2nd Lieut. Queen's Own Oxfordshire Hussars (Yeomanry), with whom he served one year; the Duke of Marlborough being his Colonel, and Major the Hon. Eustace Fiennes, Squadron Commander. The latter wrote of him, "Clement is a first-rate officer, and will make an A1 soldier." He was gazetted to the Scots Guards on probation in 1911. His ever bright and cheerful disposition made him the idol of his brother officers and men; and, being a 2nd Lieut., the honour to carry the Colours fell to him in the Coronation Procession, 1911. He was finally gazetted 2nd Lieut. The Scots Guards 1 February 1913. Previous to the outbreak of hostilities he had undertaken a course of signalling, as a help to his future career, and worked hard all day long. He was very keen, and had been promised the post of Assistant-Adjutant at the next vacancy: went to France with the Expeditionary Force in August 1914: promoted to the rank of Lieut. 23 October 1914, and was killed in action three days later at Kruiseecke, nr. Ypres. A member of the regiment wrote that he was defending his trench when struck by a shell and killed, adding, "He was splendid in front of his men." The Commanding Officer of his battalion – now a prisoner-of-war – wrote, "We were captured the same day that your boy was killed whilst gallantly defending his trenches against repeated and most determined attacks in force. He was one of the very best and bravest of regimental officers I have ever seen on active service, besides being most popular with his brother officers. His Captain, C. Fox, could not say enough, he told me, to express his thorough confidence in him in all occasions, which confidence was always justified up to the hilt in everything he most cheerfully did so well. It will, I hope, comfort you a little to know this, and how dreadfully we all deplore his loss." A Brigade Major wrote, "His men loved him; yet he was strict with them, and always upheld discipline before everything. He was just the bravest boy we had; and, though little more than a boy, he set every officer an example of what a soldier should be. He died as he had lived – a soldier and a man." His family had been settled in Oxfordshire for over four centuries, and, through his mother, he was a great-grandson of David, 8th Earl of Leven and 7th Earl of Melville. The first of his name to achieve distinction was Sir Michael Dormer, Lord Mayor of London in 1541. Possibly one of the most famous of the family was James Dormer, *b.* 1679, who served under Marlborough at Blenheim, and was engaged in the sieges of Mons, Liége and Namur. He also commanded a brigade in the ill-starred Jacobite uprising in 1715 Lieut. Cottrell-Dormer, who was devoted to hunting and a very good rider, had hunted all his life with the Bicester and Heythrop Hounds. He was very keen on beagling, and was an expert carpenter. He was a member of White's and the Guards' Clubs: 26 October 1914. Age 23. *unm.*

His brother Charles is buried in Bethune Town Cemetery (II.B.7).

(Panel 11) Lieut. David Robert Drummond, 2nd Bn. Scots Guards: 2nd *s.* of George James Drummond, of Swaylands House, Penshurst: *b.* 14, Belgrave Square, London, W., 30 October 1884: *educ.* Harrow: after leaving joined 3rd Black Watch (Militia), from which he transf'd. Scots Guards 1904: having previously held a commission, voluntarily joined Reserve of Officers, and, in July 1911, Special Reserve – Scots Guards: rejoined 2nd Battn. for Active Service on the outbreak of the European War: served with the Expeditionary Force in France and Flanders, and was killed in action at Ypres, 3 November 1914, having been shot in the head by a German sniper. He *m.* 1907; Hilda Margaret; *dau.* of Alfred Harris, of Donnington, Chichester, and had three daughters – Joan Cecile, *b.* 1909; Violet Hilda, *b.* 1911; Winifred Pansy, *b.* 1914. He was a member of the Carlton, Guard's, and Royal Automobile Clubs, and was fond of cricket and shooting. Age 30. Remembered on Old Bexley War Memorial, Kent.

(Panel 11) Lieut. Reginald Nigel Gipps, 1st Bn. Scots Guards: c/o Evelyn L. Rower (Addington Manor, Thrapston, co. Northampton); sister: *s.* of the late General Sir Reginald Ramsay Gipps, Scots Guards, of Sycamore House, Farnborough, co. Hants, G.C.B., who served in the Crimean War (*d.*1886); and Evelyn Charlotte Wilhemina (*d.*1914), *dau.* of Lieut. Col. Robert Feilden: and brother to George L. Gipps, died at Larkhill, Salisbury Plain, 26 January 1914, in an aircraft training accident: *b.* Sycamores, 22 November 1891: *educ.* Wellington College, Crowthorne, co. Berks, and Royal Military College, Sandhurst: gazetted 2nd Lieut. Scots Guards, 4 February 1911; promoted Lieut. 19 January 1913: served with his battalion later that year in Egypt, accompanying it to France, as part of the Expeditionary Force, August 1914, and was killed in action near Ypres, 7 November following. The Battalion Diarist stated, "The 4th (November 1914) was a comparatively quiet day, on which a *point d'appui* was made at a burnt farm-house near Gheluvelt. In this position the line remained till the 7th, suffering from German artillery fire on each day. On the 4th and 5th, reinforcements of 110 men arrived, and Lieuts. R.N. Gipps and F.A. Monckton were killed on the 7th." Lieut. Gipps was a member of the Guard's, and Boodle's Clubs. In 1913 he played polo for his battalion. Age 22.

(Panel 11) Lieut. Ralph Hamilton Fane Gladwin, Special Reserve, attd. 1st Bn. Scots Guards: *yst. s.* of the late Hamilton Fane Gladwin, of Seven Springs, co. Gloucester, and his wife Sophia, 3rd *dau.* of the late Richard Charles Mellish; Foreign Office: *b.* 4 October 1885: *educ.* Cheltenham College: gazetted 2nd Lieut. Scots Guards, 1 February 1907; promoted Lieut. 18 November 1909: subsequently retired from the Army, but rejoined on the outbreak of the European War, being gazetted to the Special Reserve of the Scots Guards: served with the Expeditionary Force in France and Flanders, attached 1st Battn., and was officially reported as missing in November 1914, but has since been stated to have been killed in action near Ypres, 26 October 1914. Age 29.

(Panel 11) Lieut. William Bernard Webster Lawson, 1st Bn. Scots Guards: *yr. s.* of Col. the Hon. William Webster Lawson, D.S.O., of Barton Court, Kintbury, nr. Newbury, co. Berks: *gdson.* to 1st Baron Burnham: *b.* London, 22 August 1893: *educ.* Eton, and Royal Military College, Sandhurst: apptd. Scots Guards, September 1912; gazetted Lieut. 15 September 1914: served with the Expeditionary Force in France and Flanders, and was killed in action at Boesinghe, 22 October 1914, while showing a French Territorial officer the direction for the advance of his men. He was a good rider to hounds, a promising polo player, and a member of the Royal Automobile Club. Age 21. *unm.*

(Panel 11) Lieut. Francis 'Frank' Algernon Monckton, 1st Bn. Scots Guards: eldest *s.* of Francis Monckton, M.P., of Stretton Hall, Stafford, by his wife Evelyn Mary, *dau.* of Algernon Charles (& Emily) Heber-Percy: *gdson.* to Gen. Henry Monckton, and Anne Smythe, his wife: and brother to Lieut. G.V.F. Monckton, 1st Scots Guards, killed in action, 25 January 1915, at Cuinchy; and cousin to Lieut. C. Monckton, 13th Sqdn. Royal Flying Corps & Royal Irish Fusiliers, killed in action, 1 July 1916: *b.* Granville Place, London, 6 May 1890: *educ.* Wixenford School, Wokingham; Eton; and Christ Church, Oxford. Killed in action, 8 November 1914; Veldhoek, nr. Ypres. Age 24. *unm.*

His brother Geoffrey also has no known grave, he is commemorated on the Le Touret Memorial; cousin Christopher is buried in Mons-En-Chaussee Communal Cemetery (II.1).

(Panel 11) Lieut. Sir Gilchrist Nevill Ogilvy, 1st Bn. Scots Guards: 11th Baronet of Inverquharty: only *s.* of the late Major Angus Howard Reginald Ogilvy, 13th Hussars, D.S.O. (*d.* 4 July 1906), of Baldovan, co. Forfar, by his wife Isabel Louisa, *dau.* of the Hon. Ralph Pelham Nevill, J.P., High Sheriff of Kent: *gdson.* to the late Col. Sir R.H.A. Ogilvy, 10th Bt. and the Hon. Olive Barbara Kinnaird, his wife: *b.* 6 September 1892: *educ.* Eton, and Royal Military College, Sandhurst: gazetted 2nd Lieut. Scots Guards, January 1913; promoted Lieut., September 1914 (notification appearing in the *London Gazette* after his death): served with the Expeditionary Force in France and Flanders; killed in action at Gheluvelt, Belgium, 27 October 1914. Age 22. *unm.* A member of the Guards' and Bath Clubs; his favourite recreations were hunting and shooting. He succeeded his grandfather as 11th Baronet, 12 March 1910. (*IWGC record 29 October*)

(Panel 11) 2nd Lieut. Ronald Charles Melbourne Gibbs, 2nd Bn. Scots Guards: *yr. s.* of the late Hon. Henry Lloyd Gibbs, of 10, Lennox Gardens, London, S.W., partner in the firm of Anthony Gibbs & Sons, of 22, Bishopgate, E.., by his wife Alice Mary (10, Lennox Gardens.), *yst. dau.* of the late Gen. Charles Crutchley, of Sunninghill Park, Ascot, co. Berks, and *gdson.* of Henry Hucks, 1st Baron Aldenham, Aldenham House, Elstree: *b.* 'Salisbury,' South Yarra, Melbourne, Australia, 26 August 1894: *educ.* Wellington House, Westgate-on-Sea (Rev. Herbert Bull), and Eton College (P.L. Broke's House), where he was in the O.T.C. and obtained certificate 'A': received a commission; gazetted 2nd Lieut. Special Reserve of Officers, 27 September 1913: served with 1st Battn. Scots Guards, Aldershot and, on declaration of war, with 3rd Battn.: passed Army Examination, June 1914: joined 3rd Battn. Scots Guards, 5 August 1914: exchanged to 2nd Battn., Lyndhurst 1 September; proceeded with that battalion to the Front, 4 October 1914, and was killed in action at Ypres, 28 October 1914, his battalion forming part of 20th Infantry Bde., VIIth Division. Buried at Chateau Gheluvelt. His Commanding Officer, Lord Esme Gordon Lennox, wrote, "He was a splendid young officer. He had a charming disposition, and showed such keenness and ability as an officer that the blow was all the harder. Liked by everybody he came in contact with, both officers and men, his death has been a great loss to the Regt." 2nd Lieut. Gibbs rowed in the boats at Eton, 4 June 1913, and also rowed when their Majesties King George and Queen Mary visited Eton, 6 June 1913. He was a member of the Guard's Club. Age 21. *unm.*

(Panel 11) 2nd Lieut. James Stirling-Stuart, 1st Bn. Scots Guards: elder *s.* of William Crawford Stirling-Stuart, Solicitor (formerly Capt., Scots Dragoon Guards); Laird of Castlemilk, co. Lanark, and Harriet, *née* Boswell, his wife: *b.* 1891: *educ.* Eton, and Christ Church, Oxford, where he took his degree: gazetted Territorial Force July 1912: gazetted 2nd Lieut. Scots Guards on the outbreak of war; antedated, as a University Candidate, to January 1913: promoted Lieut. 17 September 1914; notification (*London Gazette*, 26 November 1914) posthumously: served with the Expeditionary Force in France and Flanders: wounded at the Battle of the Aisne, 14 September: on recovery rejoined his regiment, and died 9 November 1914; L'Ecole de Bienfaissance, Ypres, of wounds received while leading his platoon in an attack on a machine-gun position at Veldhoek the same day. Buried in the cemetery there. Age 23. He leaves a widow, Valerie (Cowbridge Lodge, Malmesbury, co. Wilts).

(Panel 11) Col.Sergt.Major 2395, William Ross Dilworth, 1st Bn. Scots Guards: served with the Expeditionary Force. Killed in action, 26 October 1914. *m.*

(Panel 11) L/Sergt. 7455, William Albert Cooper, 1st Bn. Scots Guards: *s.* of William Cooper, of Worcester: served with the Expeditionary Force. Killed in action, 12 November 1914.

(Panel 11) L/Sergt. 6551, Arthur Forrest, 1st Bn. Scots Guards: served with the Expeditionary Force. Died 31 October 1914, from wounds. He *m.* in London, 15 April 1913, Emily Elizabeth, *née* Gale, and had a son, Arthur William Robert, *b.* 22 February 1914.

(Panel 11) L/Corpl. 9442, Walter Dennett, 2nd Bn. Scots Guards: served with the Expeditionary Force. Killed in action, 26 October 1914. Age 35. He was married to Bessie (Witchampton, Wimbourne, co. Dorset).

(Panel 11) L/Corpl. 5192, John Howard Frampton, 1st Bn. Scots Guards: *s.* of the late Edmund (& Sarah) Frampton, of Sandown, Isle of Wight: enlisted 14 January 1904: served with the Expeditionary Force in France and Flanders. Killed in action, 21 October 1914. Age 39. He *m.* St. George's, Hanover Square; Clara Alice C., *née* Alp (1, Harefield Villa, High Road, Edgware, co. Middlesex).

(Panel 11) L/Corpl. 8980, William Lindsay Oliver, 'F' Coy., 2nd Bn. Scots Guards: late of Liscard, co. Chester: *s.* of William Lindsay Oliver, of 56, Greenwood Lane, Wallasey, co. Chester, by his marriage to the late Eliza Lily Oliver: *b.* Liverpool, 1888: enlisted 6th (Volunteer) Bn. King's (Liverpool) Regt. 1902 (aged 14) as Bugler, served 6 years; attained rank Sergt.: thereafter served 4 years, Duke of Lancaster's Yeomanry: volunteered for Active Service, joining Scots Guards on the outbreak of war; went to France with his regiment, and was killed in action near Gheluvelt, Ypres 28 October 1914. Age 26.

(Panel 11) Pte. 8494, Lewis Alexander Affleck, 1st Bn. Scots Guards: *s.* of George Affleck, of 74, High Street, Loanhead, Midlothian: *b.* Lesmahagow, co. Lanark. Killed in action on the Western Front, 12 November 1914. Age 20. *unm.*

(Panel 11) Pte. 7853, Harry Alexander, 2nd Bn. Scots Guards: *s.* of Anthony Alexander, of Kirkstall Road, Leeds, co. York: and nephew to Mary Ann Spencer (16, Kepler Grove, Roseville Road, Roundhay Road, Leeds): served with the British Expeditionary Force in France, and died of wounds, 29 October 1914. Age 24. *unm.*

(Panel 11) Pte. 7280, Dan Walter Allison, 1st Bn. Scots Guards: *s.* of William Henry Allison, of Bawburgh, Norfolk, by his wife Maria Keziah: and elder brother to L/Corpl. 16588, A.E. Allison, 7th Norfolk Regt., died of wounds, 13 October 1916; and Corpl. RMA/12886, H.A. Allison, Royal Marine Artillery, HMS 'Africa,' died 14 September 1918, during the sickness epidemic which swept through the colony: *b.* Cossey, nr. Norwich: enlisted Stratford, 27 November 1908: served with the Expeditionary Force in France and Flanders; reported missing after the fighting, 11 November 1914, since confirmed killed in action on that date. Age 26. *unm.*

His brother Alphonso is buried in Heilly Station Cemetery, Mericourt l'Abbé (III.C.38); Horace, Freetown (King Tom) Cemetery (I.C.1).

(Panel 11) Pte. 4337, Henry Backhouse, 1st Bn. Scots Guards: *b.* Inskip, co. Lancaster: enlisted Preston, 21 February 1902: served with the Expeditionary Force. Killed in action, 4–12 November 1914. He leaves a wife and two children. (*IWGC record 12 November*)

(Panel 11) Pte. 7224, William Ball, 2nd Bn. Scots Guards: *s.* of Thomas Ball, Farmer; of St. Anne's-on-Sea, co. Lancaster, by his wife Alice, *dau.* of John Eaton: *b.* St. Anne's-on-Sea, Blackpool, 31 October 1888: *educ.* St. Anne's Parish School: enlisted Preston, co. Lancaster, 7 May 1914: served with the Expeditionary Force in France from 2 September 1914, and was killed in action during the fighting at Ypres, 4–12 November following. Age 26. He *m.* Preston; Annie (13, Rose Cottage, Eastgate Street, Rochdale), *dau.* of Edward (& Hannah) Cole, and had two children – Mary Adelaide, *b.* 8 September 1908; William Edward, *b.* 28 February 1912.

(Panel 11) Pte. 6575, Frederick James Bean, 1st Bn. Scots Guards: *s.* of Alfred Bean, of Station Road, Northam, co. Sussex, by his wife Mary: *b.* co. Sussex, 1889: enlisted 2 July 1906: served with the Expeditionary Force in France and Flanders. Killed in action between 4–12 November 1914. Age 25. *unm.* (*IWGC record 12 November 1914*)

(Panel 11) Pte. 7346, Ernest Beech, 1st Bn. Scots Guards: *s.* of Thomas Beech, of Secombe, co. Chester, by his wife Catherine: *b.* Birkenhead, co. Chester, 24 June 1889: *educ.* Liscard, co. Chester: enlisted 26 January 1909: went to France with the Expeditionary Force 12 August 1914, and was killed in action, nr. Ypres, between 4 and 12 November following. Age 25. He *m.* London, 25 October 1913; Edith

(67, Ardington Wick, Wantage, co. Berks), and had one son, Ernest Frederick, *b.* 11 September 1914. (*IWGC record 12 November 1914*)

(Panel 11) Pte. 6530, James Best, 2nd Bn. Scots Guard: *s.* of John Best, 62, Rumford Street, Glasgow, an old soldier, by his wife Agnes, *dau.* of John Gaw: and elder brother to Pte. 8879, T. Best, who fell 29 April 1915, aged 20 (*IWGC record 29 April 1918*): *b.* Newtownards, Co. Down, 1885: enlisted Glasgow, 24 May 1906: served with the Expeditionary Force in France and Flanders, and was killed in action there, 28 October 1914. Age 29. He *m.* Rutherglen, 31 December 1913; Elizabeth C. (77, Greenhill Road, Rutherglen, Glasgow). *s.p.*

His brother Thomas is buried in Aubers Ridge British Cemetery (V.B.13).

(Panel 11) Pte. 8393, Horace Blackburn, 2nd Bn. Scots Guards: *s.* of Mr (& Mrs) Blackburn, of 5, Sheridan Street, Wakefield Road, Bradford, co. York: *b.* Bradford: enlisted, 31 August 1912, aged 21: served with the Expeditionary Force in France and Flanders. Reported wounded and missing, 20 October 1914. Age 23.

(Panel 11) Pte. 5443, Owen Carty, 1st Bn. Scots Guards: *s.* of Owen Carty, of 3, Peter Street, Ashton-in-Makerfield, nr. Wigan, co. Lancaster: enlisted Warrington, co. Chester: served with the Expeditionary Force. Killed in action, 24 October 1914. Age 30.

(Panel 11) Pte. 8709, James Chrystal, 2nd Bn. Scots Guards: *s.* of W. Chrystal, of Thornton-by-Kirkcaldy, co. Fife: enlisted Edinburgh: served with the Expeditionary Force. Killed in action at Ypres, 20–26 October 1914. (*IWGC record 26 October*)

(Panel 11) Pte. 4690, Horace Chumley, 1st Bn. Scots Guards: *husb.* to the late Sarah Chumley (Swanley, co. Kent): enlisted Sevenoaks: served with the Expeditionary Force in France, and was killed in action, 3 November 1914. Age 30.

(Panel 11) Pte. 5359, Joseph Clancy, 1st Bn. Scots Guards: *s.* of Patrick Clancy, of Glenague, Gurteen, Manor Hamilton, Co. Leitrim, by his wife Catherine: served with the Expeditionary Force. Killed in action, 12 November 1914.

(Panel 11) Pte. 7730, John William Collins, 'C' Coy., 1st Bn. Scots Guards: *s.* of Charles Collins, of Manresa Farm, Roehampton, co. Surrey: served with the Expeditionary Force. Killed in action, 29 October 1914. Age 24. *unm.*

(Panel 11) Pte. 9578, Frank Copeland, 1st Bn. Scots Guards: served with the Expeditionary Force. Killed in action, 12 November 1914. Age 34. He *m.* Paisley, 6 November 1903; Helen (McCormack Copeland, 65, Broomlands, Paisley), and had four children – Mary, *b.* 22 December 1904; Agnes, *b.* 4 October 1905; William, *b.* 16 January 1910; Margaret, *b.* 27 March 1914. (*IWGC record 8 November 1914*)

(Panel 11) Pte. 6755, David Bruce Croll, 1st Bn. Scots Guards: *s.* of the late David Croll, of Brechin, co. Forfar, by his wife Anne: enlisted London: served with the Expeditionary Force, and was killed in action, 12 November 1914. Age 28. He leaves a widow, Florence Helen (14, Basing Road, Notting Hill, London, W.).

(Panel 11) Pte. 9623, William Dick, 1st Bn. Scots Guards: *s.* of William Dick, of 2, Marchall Place, Edinburgh, by his wife Margaret, *née* Lamb: *b.* St. Cuthbert's, *c.*1879: served with the Expeditionary Force. Killed in action, 4–12 November 1914. Age 35. (*IWGC record 11 November*)

(Panel 11) Pte. 8728, Mandy Diver, 1st Bn. Scots Guards: *s.* of Neil Diver, of Maghermagourgan, Carrigart, Co. Donegal, by his wife Katherine, *née* Coyle: *b.* Letterkenny, Co. Donegal, *c.*1894: enlisted Glasgow: served with the Expeditionary Force. Killed in action, 29 October 1914. Age 20. *unm.*

(Panel 11) Pte. 6450, Arthur Donnelly, 1st Bn. Scots Guards: *s.* of the late Arthur Donnelly, of Clough Mills, Co. Antrim: enlisted Middlesbrough: served with the Expeditionary Force. Killed in action, 26 October 1914. Age 36.

(Panel 11) Pte. 8603, Richard Edwardson, 1st Bn. Scots Guards: *s.* of Margaret Jane Edwardson (8, Higher Anstey Street, Accrington, co. Lancaster), and the late Pte. 17480, R.E. Edwardson, 8th East Lancashire Regt., killed at the Battle of the Somme, 15 July 1916: served with the Expeditionary Force. Killed in action, 12 November 1914. Age 21. *unm.*

His father Richard also has no known grave; he is commemorated on the Thiepval Memorial.

(Panel 11) Pte. 6255, Frank William Fay, 1st Bn. Scots Guards: *s.* of George Fay, of Mottisfont, Romsey, co. Hants, by his wife Mary: enlisted Romsey: served with the Expeditionary Force in France and Flanders from 14 August 1914, and was killed in action, 11 November following. Remains recovered from an unmarked grave (28.J.22.b.6.1) Gheluvelt Chateau; identified – Clothing, Damaged Disc; reinterred, registered 19 May 1927. *Buried in Sanctuary Wood Cemetery (IV.D.19).*

(Panel 11) Pte. 8468, Daniel Albert Fellowes, 1st Bn. Scots Guards: *s.* of Anne Fellowes (109, Arkwright Street, Everton, Liverpool): served with the Expeditionary Force. Died a prisoner of war, 2 November 1914. Age 20.

(Panel 11) Pte. 7253, William Fenton, 1st Bn. Scots Guards: *s.* of James Fenton, of Glasgow: served with the Expeditionary Force. Killed in action, 12 November 1914.

(Panel 11) Pte. 6396, James Freemantle, 1st Bn. Scots Guards: brother to Pte. 6268, T. Freemantle, Scots Guards, who fell the same day: *b.* Easton, co. Hants: previously served 7 years with the Colours, Scots Guards, 15 January 1906–14 January 1913: thereafter joined the Reserve, employed as Moulder: joined Surrey Constabulary, Guildford, 15 March 1913, appointment no.1665, P.C. 66, stationed Ripley: recalled on the outbreak of war, and rejoined Scots Guards, Winchester August 1914: served with the Expeditionary Force in France and Flanders, and was killed at the First Battle of Ypres, 11 November 1914. Pte. Freemantle was 5'11" tall, of fresh complexion, brown hair, blue eyes.

His brother Thomas also has no known grave; he is recorded below.

(Panel 11) Pte. 6268, Thomas Freemantle, 1st Bn. Scots Guards: brother to Pte. 6396, J. Freemantle, Scots Guards, who fell the same day: *b.* Easton, co. Hants, 1888: previously served 7 years with the Colours, Scots Guards, 26 October 1905–25 November 1912: thereafter joined the Reserve, employed as Gardener, to Miss Christian: joined Surrey Constabulary, Guildford, 8 December 1913, appt. no.1701, P.C. 150, stationed Horley: recalled on the outbreak of war, and rejoined Scots Guards, Winchester, August 1914: served with the Expeditionary Force in France and Flanders, and was killed at the First Battle of Ypres, 11 November 1914. Age 26. Pte. Freemantle was 5'11½" tall, of fresh complexion; he had brown hair and blue eyes.

His brother James also has no known grave; he is recorded above.

(Panel 11) Pte. 8678, John Friars, 1st Bn. Scots Guards: *s.* of John Friars, of Richmond Terrace, Bo'ness, West Lothian: served with the Expeditionary Force. Killed in action, 26 October 1914. Age 21. *unm.*

(Panel 11) Pte. 10083, Walter Fudge, 2nd Bn. Scots Guards: *s.* of Theophilus Fudge, by his wife Martha: served with the Expeditionary Force. Killed in action, 26 October 1914. Age 36. He leaves a wife, Mildred Lilyian (125, Windham Road, Bournemouth, co. Dorset).

(Panel 11) Pte. 8280, James Gillan, 1st Bn. Scots Guards: *s.* of Frank Gillan: enlisted, 8 May 1912: served with the Expeditionary Force, and was killed in action, 12 November 1914.

(Panel 11) Pte. 9307, John Godfrey, 1st Bn. Scots Guards: *s.* of Alexander (& Mrs) Godfrey, of Crispin Place, Falkirk: enlisted, 12 August 1914: served with the Expeditionary Force in France, and was killed there, 12 November following: 12 November 1914. Age 38.

(Panel 11) Pte. 4579, William Godfrey, 2nd Bn. Scots Guards: *s.* of Robert Godfrey, of 26, Wardlaw Place, Edinburgh, by his wife Annie: enlisted 25 August 1902: served with the Expeditionary Force, and was killed in action, 26 October 1914. Age 31. He was married to Sophia South-Patterson, *née* Godfrey (3, Seafield, Eyemouth, co. Berwick), *dau.* of Mr (& Mrs) Smith, and had three children – Christina, *b.* 18 December 1906; Charles, *b.* 4 May 1908; Edward, *b.* 21 January 1912.

(Panel 11) Pte. 5545, John Goodread, 1st Bn. Scots Guards: enlisted, 19 August 1904: served with the Expeditionary Force, and was killed in action, 2 November 1914. He was married to Elizabeth C. Goodread, *dau.* of Mr (& Mrs) Burkill, and had a *dau.*, Hilda May, *b.* 13 March 1910.

(Panel 11) Pte. 6606, Frank Churchill Goulden, 1st Bn. Scots Guards: *s.* of Henry Charles Goulden, of 68, Bellemoor Road, Southampton, by his wife Fanny Margaret: served with the Expeditionary Force. Killed in action, 12 November 1914.

(Panel 11) Pte. 4963, Robert Graham, 1st Bn. Scots Guards: *s.* of Robert Graham, late of West Calder, co. Midlothian, by his wife Agnes (111A, Mid Street, Pathead, Kirkcaldy, co. Fife): enlisted, 29 July 1903: served almost 12 years with his regiment, and was killed in action at Ypres, 31 October 1914. Age 31.

(Panel 11) Pte. 8795, Thomas Groves, 1st Bn. Scots Guards: *s.* of William Groves, of 14, Warden Road, Bedminster, Bristol, by his wife Henrietta Maria: a pre-war Regular, enlisted Bristol, 3 December 1913: mobilised on the outbreak of war; served with the Expeditionary Force in France and Flanders from August 1914, and was killed in action, 12 November following: 12 November 1914. Age 21.

(Panel 11) Pte. 7918, Walter Haggas, 1st Bn. Scots Guards: *s.* of Charles Haggas, of Clark's Mills, Oneida Co., New York, United States, by his wife Annie: and yr. brother to Spr. 213580, W.G. Haggas, Royal Engineers (Training Centre, Newark), died 11 January 1918: *b.* Sutton, co. York, England: enlisted Keighley: served with the Expeditionary Force in France from August 1914, and was killed in action, 11 November following. Age 21. *unm.*

His brother William is buried in Sutton-in-Craven Baptist Burial Ground (B.101).

(Panel 11) Pte. 7997, Charles Spencer Hampton, 1st Bn. Scots Guards: *b.* Devizes, co. Wilts: enlisted 14 August 1911: served with the Expeditionary Force. Killed in action, 26 October 1914.

(Panel 11) Pte. 6741, Herbert Hanley, 1st Bn. Scots Guards: *b.* Chorley, co. Lancaster: enlisted Preston, 4 May 1907: served with the Expeditionary Force. Died in No.3 Field Ambulance, Ypres, 8–9 November 1914, of wounds. Buried in Staar Welphoos School, Ypres.

(Panel 11) Pte. 6644, Terence Hannaway, 2nd Bn. Scots Guards: *b.* Belfast, Co. Antrim: enlisted 14 November 1906: served with the Expeditionary Force. Killed in action, 20–26 October 1914.

(Panel 11) Pte. 6391, Charles Harding, 1st Bn. Scots Guards: *b.* Adderley, co. Salop: enlisted Market Drayton, 8 January 1906: served with the Expeditionary Force, and was killed in action, 29 October 1914. He *m.* 28 October 1910; Carrie Smith, and had three children – Alexander, *b.* 19 February 1912; Eva, *b.* 16 August 1913; Doris, *b.* 7 January 1915.

(Panel 11) Pte. 2670, John Robert Cameron Harrison, 1st Bn. Scots Guards: *b.* Dundee: served in the South African Campaign, and with the Expeditionary Force in France and Flanders; killed in action, 4 November 1914. Age 34. He leaves a wife, Mary Harrison, and family. (*IWGC record 12 November*)

(Panel 11) Pte. 9581, Edward Hart, 1st Bn. Scots Guards: served with the Expeditionary Force. Killed in action, 4 November 1914. (*IWGC record 12 November*)

(Panel 11) Pte. 5831, Thomas Hart, 1st Bn. Scots Guards: *b.* Wellington, co. Salop: served with the Expeditionary Force; killed in action, 26 October 1914.

(Panel 11) Pte. 7574, Frederick Gilbert Hartwright, 1st Bn. Scots Guards: *s.* of Frederick William Hartwright, of Salisbury, Queensland, Australia (formerly of North Amersham, Fernhurst, co. Sussex), by his first wife Kezia, *née* Slingo (dec'd.): and brother to Rfn. 391903, H.I.V. Hartwright, Queen Victoria's Rifles, who also fell: and uncle to Flying Officer, 44570, V.R. Hartwright, D.F.M., No.7 Sqdn. Royal Air Force, who died a prisoner of war, 30 June 1941: *b.* North Amersham, 22 September 1894: *educ.* The Schools, Fernhurst: enlisted 1910, aged 15 years: served in Egypt, and with the Expeditionary Force in France and Flanders from 13 August 1914. Reported missing, 11 November following; assumed killed. Age 20. *unm.*

His brother Harold is buried in Tyne Cot Cemetery (XII.C.15); his nephew Valentine, Becklingen War Cemetery, Germany (XIII.F.11-14).

(Panel 11) Pte. 3018, William Heather, 2nd Bn. Scots Guards: served with the Expeditionary Force. Died 29 October 1914, from wounds.

(Panel 11) Pte. 8715, Thomas Hetherington, 2nd attd. 1st Bn. Scots Guards: eldest *s.* of John Hetherington, by his wife Helen (20, Orwell Place, Dalry Road, Edinburgh), *dau.* of Andrew Waters: *b.* Edinburgh, 28 July 1894: *educ.* Higher Grade School, Torpichen Street, Borough Muir: Occupation – Clothier's Assistant: enlisted September 1913: went to France, August 1914. Reported missing from 11 November 1914; afterwards presumed to have been killed in action on that date, or to have died soon after. Age 20. *unm.*

(Panel 11) Pte. 8209, Percy Hodge, 1st Bn. Scots Guards: *s.* of Joseph Hodge, of 3, Wheatleigh Terrace, New Cut, Poole, by his wife Elizabeth: *b.* Poole, co. Dorset 1894: enlisted, 27 July 1911: served with the Expeditionary Force. Reported missing, 11 November 1914; now assumed killed. Age 20. *unm.*

(Panel 11) Pte. 8141, John Hubberstey, 2nd Bn. Scots Guards: *s.* of John Hubberstey, of Preston, co. Lancaster: served with the Expeditionary Force. Killed in action, 26 October 1914.

(Panel 11) Pte. 7490, Harold Kennedy, 1st Bn. Scots Guards: *s.* of Donald Kennedy, of Inverness: served with the Expeditionary Force. Killed in action, 26 October 1914.

Wherever Scottish troops have fought, the distinctive sound of the bagpipes has been heard. In the heat of battle, by the lonely grave (where the cry of 'The Lament' over fallen comrades is but a reminder of the undying spirit and sacredness of the cause), and in the long hours of waiting, the pipes stirred the spirit and recalled to memory the proud traditions and heritage of the Scottish race. During the course of the war over 500 pipers were killed, 600 were wounded, and with the ranks of the individual regimental bands thus depleted many of them ceased to exist. By the end of March 1915, 1st and 2nd Scots Guards had lost 7 pipers killed, 17 wounded, 3 taken prisoner and although the bands of both battalions were reconstituted in 1916 both, because of their previous losses, were as far as possible saved from further decimation.

(Panel 11) Pte. Piper 6241, Murdo McKenzie, 1st Bn. Scots Guards: late of Stornoway, co. Ross: enlisted Glasgow, co. Lanark: served with the Expeditionary Force in France and Flanders from August 1914; killed in action at Ypres, 11 November following.

(Panel 11) Pte. 5362, Albert Victor Mehrtens, 'F' Coy. 1st Bn. Scots Guards: *s.* of Frederick William Mehrtens, of 30, Sperling Road, Bruce Grove, Tottenham, London, by his wife Rosa: and elder brother to Sergt. 63335, S.C. Mehrtens, 13th Royal Fusiliers, killed in action, 23 August 1918: *b.* Highbury: enlisted Tottenham. Killed in action, 9 November 1914. Age 27. *unm.*

His brother Stanley is buried in Achiet-le-Grand Communal Cemetery Extension (III.E.1).

(Panel 11) Pte. 8792, Robert Arthur Oliver, 2nd Bn. Scots Guards: *s.* of John Oliver, of Wold View, Spittle, Wilberfoss, co. York, by his wife Martha: and elder brother to Pte. 269073, H. Oliver, Duke of Wellington's (West Riding) Regt., killed in action, 20 September 1917: *b.* Fangfoss, York: enlisted York. Killed in action, 19 April 1916. Age 21. *unm.* The Fangfoss Parish War Memorial – "...Erected By The Parishioners...To The Glory Of God And To Record The Names Of The Men Of This Parish Who Fell In The Great War A.D. 1914–1919. R.I.P" – records six names, the Oliver brothers and Pte. 24677, F.F. Pearson, East Yorkshire Regt. who died September 1919; the remaining three survived.

His brother Harold also has no known grave, he is commemorated on the Tyne Cot Memorial (Panel 84); Francis Pearson is buried in Yapham (St. Martin) Churchyard.

(Panel 11) Pte. 7947, Clifford Porter, 1st Bn. Scots Guards: *s.* of Fred Porter, of 6, Kliffen Place, Coronation Road, Halifax, co. York: *b.* Harrogate, *c.*1890. Died 30 November 1914, at Ypres. Age 24. *unm.* Remains exhumed from Menin Communal Cemetery (German Grave No.13); identified – Burial List, Disc; reinterred, registered 29 May 1928. *Buried in Sanctuary Wood Cemetery (II.K.5).*

In Loving Memory Of A Gallant Son Who Gave His All For His Country

(Panel 11) Pte. 6364, Walter Purver, 1st Bn. Scots Guards: *s.* of Elijah Purver, of New Cottages, Sutton Scotney, co. Hants, and Clara Purver, his spouse: and brother to Pte. 6363, A. Purver, 1st Scots Guards, died in enemy hands, 28 February 1915; and Pte. 10364, E. Purver, 10th Hampshire Regt., killed in action, 10 August 1915, at Gallipoli: enlisted Winchester. Killed in action, 11 November 1914. Age 28. The brothers Purver are remembered on Wonston (Holy Trinity Church) Roll of Honour and Sutton Scotney War Memorial.

His brother Alfred's grave could not be located after the war; he is commemorated in Poznan Old Garrison Cemetery (Pila P.O.W.Cem.Mem.12). Ernest has no known grave; he is commemorated on the Helles Memorial.

(Panel 11) Pte. 7227, George Sherlock, 1st Bn. Scots Guards: *s.* of George Sherlock (late 1st Scots Guards), of 130, Westrigg, Blackridge, co. West Lothian, by his wife Euphemia: *b.* Harthill, co. Lanark:

enlisted Edinburgh, 1909: a pre-war Reservist, employed Blackrigg Colliery; returned to the Colours on mobilisation: served with the Expeditionary Force in France from 2 September 1914: missing believed taken prisoner at Gheluvelt, 11 November 1914. Since confirmed – information having been received via the Red Cross from German authorities – to have died and been buried at Gheluvelt on that date. Age 25.

(Panel 11) Pte. 7594, John Whiteside, 1st Bn. Scots Guards: late of Blackpool, co. Lancaster: *s.* of William Whiteside, by his wife Arabella: and yr. brother to Pte. 26600, W. Whiteside, East Lancashire Regt., who also fell: *b.* Blackburn: enlisted Preston. Killed in action, 12 November 1914. Age 25. *unm.*

His brother William also has no known grave; he is recorded on Panel 34.

(Panel 11) Major Herbert Arthur Herbert-Stepney, 1st Bn. Irish Guards: *s.* of George Herbert-Stepney, whose father Col. Arthur St.George Herbert-Stepney, commanded 2nd Battn. Coldstream Guards: *b.* 10 January 1879: *educ.* Rugby, and Royal Military College, Sandhurst, from which he passed out first: joined Coldstream Guards 1898; promoted Lieut. 1899: transf'd. Irish Guards 1901, soon after their formation: Battn. Adjt., January–December 1902; promoted Capt. September 1904: served in the South African Campaign, 1900–1901; present at operations in the Transvaal, including the action at Belfast (slightly wounded); Queen's Medal, three clasps. On the outbreak of war with Germany he left Wellington Barracks with his battalion for France, as Senior Company Commander, 12 August 1914: following the action at Villers-Cotterêts (1 September 1914) – during which the Commanding Officer Lieut. Col. The Hon. H.G. Morris, and Second-in-Command Major H.F. Crichton were killed, and the Adjutant Capt. Lord D. Fitzgerald wounded – was Officer Comdg. 1st Battn., until after the Battle of Aisne when (18 September) Lieut.Col. Lord Ardee, Grenadier Guards took command: assumed command again 28–31 October, and, in the early morning of 7 November 1914, nr. Klein-Zillebeke, he went out from the support trenches to inspect the battalion's position and was not seen again alive. His body was found between the lines in the late evening. Age 35. Mentioned in Sir John (now Lord) French's Despatch, 14 January 1915 'For his services in the Great War.' An Irishman, his home had always been in that country, he was a good shot, keen fisherman, and fond of all games. Lieut.Col. Morris is buried in Guards Grave, Villers-Cotterêts Forest (II.1); Major Crichton, Montreuil-Aux-Lions British Cemetery (III.E.7).

(Panel 11) Capt. Edward Charles Stafford-King-Harman, No.1 Coy., 1st Irish Guards: eldest *s.* of Sir Thomas Stafford, of Rockingham, Co. Roscommon, 1st Bart., C.B., J.P., D.L., by his wife Francis Agnes, only *survg.* child of the late Col. the Right Hon. Edward Robert King – Harman, of Rockingham, P.C., M.P.: *b.* Belfast, 13 April 1891: *educ.* Eton, and Sandhurst: gazetted 2nd Lieut. Irish Guards, 9 September 1911; promoted Lieut. 11 June 1912; Capt. 15 November 1914: went to France, 20 September 1914, and was killed in action at Klein Zillebeke, 6 November following. Age 23. "He came to Mr Vaughan's House in 1904. Even as a Lower Boy he had a quiet dignity, which made him as much respected as he was liked, and this was always a characteristic which gave him a certain distinction wherever he went. Though he was much hampered by ill health, he gained the House Colours, and many will remember his dashing game. In 1910 he was in the Shooting VIII, and a Colour-Sergt., and brought the Section Cup to his House, in the same year winning the Scott Cup and Bucks County Cup. No boy had ever a higher standard of conduct; devoted to all manly sport (he kept a pack of harriers in Ireland after he left Eton), and full of Irish humour, he had at the same time the refinement of mind of a saint, though few knew the thoughts which underlay his life. Any boy who was weak found in him a protector, and his presence was a silent rebuke to all meanness" (*Eton College Chronicle*). He *m.* Guard's Chapel, Wellington Barracks, 4 July 1914; Olive, only child of Capt. Henry Pakenham-Mahon, of Strokestown Park, Co. Roscommon, Ireland, and had a *dau.* – Lettice Mary, *b.* 10 April 1915.

(Panel 11) Lieut. Langton Sacheverell Coke, 1st Bn. Irish Guards: F.K.G.S., J.P.: eldest *s.* of the late Col. William Langton Coke, of Brookhill Hall, Alfreton, co. Derby, J.P., D.L., 4th Light Dragoons (*d.* 1913), by his wife Ada Caroline Catherine, *dau.* of Christian William Heugh, of Cape of Good Hope: *b.* Brookhill Hall, 25 January 1878: *educ.* France and Germany: served for a time with Royal Warwickshire Regt.: joined Irish Guards 1901, soon after their formation: subsequently served two years with the Egyptian Army on secondment: retired 1908, and joined Special Reserve. Intending to take up a political career, he obtained, in 1913, the appointment of Private Secretary to Mr Hobhouse, Postmaster-General: rejoined his old regiment on the outbreak of the European War: served with the Expeditionary Force in France and Flanders from 11 September 1914, and was killed in action at Klein Zillebeke, nr. Ypres, 31 October following; a critical day on which the enemy, after heavy shelling of our lines, made a counter-attack which, at the cost of considerable casualties, was successfully driven back. Buried in the garden of the farm behind Klein-Zillebeke. Age 36. He was a good big game shot, fisherman, motorist and member of the Traveller's and Guards' Clubs. He *m.*, November 1908, Dorothy Maye (Brookhill Hall, co. Derby), only *dau.* of Capt. George Huntingford, R.N., and had two children – Elizabeth Joan, *b.* August 1909, and Roger Sacheverell, *b.* October 1912. The Brookhill Estate has been the family seat for twenty-three generations, being handed down from father to son; on his father's death Roger Sachervell succeeded to the title. One of Lieut. Coke's ancestors was Sir John Coke, Secretary of State to King Charles the First.

(Panel 11) Lieut. William Edward Hope, 1st Bn. Irish Guards: *s.* of the late William (& Mrs) Hope, M.D., 18, Carlisle Mansions, London, S.W.: *b.* 56, Curzon Street, Mayfair, London, W., 28 February 1887: *educ.* for a short time at Beaumont, Windsor, and subsequently by Army tutors: joined Duke of Cornwall's Light Infantry, age 17; transf'd. Irish Guards 1910: remained with the battalion for three years and, after leaving to go on the Battalion Special Reserve, was appointed A.D.C. to the Lord Lieutenant of Ireland, December 1912: rejoined Irish Guards on the outbreak of the European War, and proceeded with the Expeditionary Force to France, August 1914: present at every battle from Mons up to the action at Klein Zillebeke, where he fell, 6 November 1914. The Major commanding the battalion said that Lieut. Hope made many valuable sketches of the enemy's position under fire. He took a keen interest in all sports, and was a member of the Guards' Club. Age 27. *unm.*

(Panel 11) Lieut. Kenneth Ronald Mathieson, Special Reserve attd. 1st Bn. Irish Guards: elder *s.* of Kenneth Mathieson, of 50, Princes Gate, South Kensington, London, S.W., by his wife Margaret: *b.* 1886: apptd. Lieut. Special Reserve (Irish Guards), 18 August 1914. Killed in action near Ypres, 1 November 1914. Age 28. *unm.* All through 1 July 1916 the British guns bombarded the front chosen for a large scale raid by 2nd Irish Guards scheduled for the following day. The objective of the bombardment was to cut the wire where the raid was to take place, and prepare the way on the right for an attack by 3rd Guards Brigade on a small German salient that needed to be reduced. On the morning of 2 July it was planned that the 18-pounders and 4.5 howitzers, with a couple of trench-mortars, would open heavily at 09.40, followed ten minutes later by Stokes mortars; at 10 am the guns would lift and form a barrage while the Stokes attended to the flanks of the attack. The evening of 1 July was clear and so light that at the last minute the men were told to keep their jackets on lest their shirts should betray them (men later said that it was then that the raid should have been postponed). Everything was quiet, too quiet. Hardly a shot was being fired anywhere and, when the party lined up under Lieut. F.M. Pym, the bombardment opened punctually, but drew no answer from the enemy for ten minutes. Then all of a sudden a barrage came crashing down behind the Guards assembly position, increasing in intensity on Nile Trench and causing a gap in the front line. When the raiders went over the top there was still enough visibility, despite the smoke from the barrage, to give a good view of the German front line parapets from behind which (the second line) several machine-guns opened fire. This did not bode well, because, with the leading raiders out in the open, it would have been murder to have held the rest back, thus they all went forward into the barrage and the machine-gun fire, from which point onwards what actually, or supposedly, happened could only be ascertained from survivors. It appears the attack succeeded in reaching the German wire which was "well cut in places," but then faltered; checked by machine-gun fire (they probably ran up to the muzzles of them) and some bombing to which the Guards replied in kind. Lieut. Pym rushed forward through the leading men, jumped into the trench, landed in an empty German bay, shouting to them to follow, turned left with a few men, reached the door of a machine-gun dug-out with its gun in full blast, broke in, found two men at work, knocked one of them off the gun and, with the help of Pte. Walshe, made him prisoner. Meantime, the Guards bombers spread left and right to hold each end of the captured section of trench, but had also to block a communication trench which entered about the middle, where the enemy was trying to force his way in; whether there was an attack on both flanks as well is uncertain. In the ensuing bomb fight the raiders held up the enemy and attempted to collect prisoners, but the captured section of trench only contained one dead and five living of which one "proved unmanageable and had to be killed," and of the remaining four hurried back under escort, two were killed by their own shell-fire on the road. The attached R.E. officer looked round, as was his duty, to find things to demolish, but the trench was clean and empty. Also attached to the raid were three gas experts, two were wounded on the way forward; the third searched the trench but found no trace of any gas devices. Some papers and documents were snatched from the dug-outs, but he who took them did not live to hand them over. The barrage grew heavier, the machine-gun fire from the enemy second line never ceased; and the raiders could see their own parapet going up in clumps. It was an exquisitely balanced choice of evils when, at about 10.10 am., Lieut. Pym blew his horn for the withdrawal. Within minutes men began returning through the barrage, over the parapet, into the 'safety' of their front line. But, it was here that the bulk of the casualties occurred. The British guns ceased fire at 10.20, but the enemy battered savagely at the Guards front line with heavies and trench-mortars until 11.00. The result was that the front line, never very good, was now a scene of utter chaos. It was both hopeless and pointless to attempt to call the roll there, so what raiders could stand, with the two surviving prisoners, were sent up to Brigade Headquarters while the wounded, after being collected in an undamaged bay, were got across the open to Lancashire Farm and the trolley-line there. Lieut. Pym was nowhere to be found, and though some men said, and honestly believed, that they had seen him re-enter the British lines, he was not of the breed which would have done this till he had seen the last of his command out of the German trenches. He may have got as far as the German wire on his way back and there, or in that neighbourhood, have been killed; but he never returned to the Guards trench after leading forward from it. The raid had been a fair, flat, but heroic failure, due, as most men said, to its being loosed in broad daylight at a fully prepared enemy. Outside the two prisoners, nothing, not even a scrap of paper, was gained except the knowledge that the Battalion could handle such affairs as these in their day's work, put it all equably behind them, and draw fresh lessons for fresh tomorrows. Perhaps the most surprising fact of all is that, despite the confused state of affairs in the Guards front line trench on their return, the subsequent roll-call revealed casualties of 1 Officer, 12 other ranks killed.

(Panel 11) Lieut. Francis Melville Pym, 2nd Bn. Irish Guards: *s.* of Claude George Melville Pym, of Canwick House, Lincoln, by his wife Lucy Victoria Leslie-Pym, *dau.* of Alexander Samuel Melville-Leslie, and the Hon. Albinia Frances Brodrick: and brother to Lieut. C.J. Pym, 2nd Irish Guards, died 26 March 1917, of wounds received in action: *b.* 1894. Missing, believed killed in action, 2 July 1916. Age 22. His grandmother Albinia Brodrick was a direct descendant of William the Conqueror.

His brother Claude is buried in Grove Town Cemetery, Meaulte (III.A.11).

Footnote: "Their brigadier had a little talk with the raiding-party next day on the Canal Bank, when he made much of them, and told them that he was very pleased with "their gallant behaviour under adverse circumstances." It was gratifying, because they had done all that they could. But after every raid, as indeed after every action, there follows interminable discussion from every point of view of every rank, as to the "might-have-beens"—what would have happened had you been there, or they been here, and whether the bay where the raid wrecked itself against the barricade none suspected might have been turned by a dash across the top, in the pauses of the shifting and returning overhead machine-gun fire. The messes discuss it, the estimates where the men talk pick up those verdicts from the mess waiters and go over them again and again; the front line scratches diagrams on the flank of sand-bags with bits of burned stick, and the more they explain, argue, and asseverate, the deeper grows the confusion out of which the historian in due time weaves the accepted version – at which all who were concerned scoff." Or a member of the raiders put it more succinctly: "We lost one dam' good officer, and more good men than was worth a thousand Jerries, but, mark you, we might have lost just that same number any morning in the front line, as we have lost them again and again, under the expenditure of half a dozen, maybe one, shell the devil happened to be riding that time. And them that it took would never have had even the exercise, let alone the glory, of all them great doings of ours. So, ye see, everything in war is good luck or bad."

(Panel 11) Lieut. Neville Leslie Woodroffe, 1st Bn. Irish Guards: *s.* of Allen Woodroffe, of 21, Cornwall Gardens, South Kensington, London, S.W., by his wife Beatrice Ellen: *b.* 1893: *educ.* Eton, and Trinity College, Cambridge: joined Irish Guards, 2nd Lieut. (Probationary) February 1913, being confirmed in rank some months later: served with the Expeditionary Force in France and Flanders; killed in action at Klein Zillebeke, nr. Ypres, in an attack on the German trenches, 6 November 1914. Age 21. *unm.* Gazetted Lieut. Posthumously; rank antedated to 2 November 1914. Mentioned in Sir John (now Lord) French's Despatch, 14 January 1915. Three days before his death (3 November 1914) he wrote, "The last two days have been ghastly. The Germans broke through the line. We have lost ten officers in the last two days and yesterday the battalion was less than 200 men, though I expect some stragglers will turn up. All the officers in my company were lost except myself. We have had no rest at all. Everyone is very shaken. I do hope we are put in reserve to reform for a few days." The following condolence was received by his family, "Lieut. Woodroffe was killed (6 November) leading his men against the German trenches. Of the 35 men that went with him none returned. Only 2 days before he had been specially mentioned for bravery in action. He had held a position long after the rest of the battalion had retired." On the night of 18 June 1916 2nd Irish Guards relieved 1st Coldstream "in an all but obliterated section of what had been the Canadians' second line and was now our first, running from the Culvert, on the Menin road, west of Hooge, through Zouave Wood, and into the north end of Sanctuary Wood. Four to eight hundred yards lay between them and the enemy, who were settling down in the old Canadian front line across the little swampy valley. The left of the Irish Guards' sector was, even after the Coldstream had worked on it for three days, without dug-outs, and blown in in places, but it offered a little cover. Their right line, for nearly half a mile, was absolutely unrecognizable save in a few isolated spots. The shredded ground was full of buried iron and timber which made digging very difficult, and, in spite of a lot of cleaning up by their predecessors, dead Canadians lay in every corner. It ran through what had once been a wood, and was now a dreary collection of charred and splintered stakes, "to the tops of which, blown there by shells, hung tatters of khaki uniform and equipment." There was no trace of any communication-trenches, so companies had to stay where they were as long as the light lasted. Battalion H.Q. was situated in a small room beneath the remains of a brick-kiln, just west of the Zillebeke road, and company commanders walked about in the dark from one inhabited stretch to the next, trusting in Providence. So, too, did the enemy…In truth, neither front line knew exactly where the other lay in that chaos; and, both being intent upon digging themselves in ere the guns should begin again, were glad enough to keep still." Trusting in providence, 'luck' was, under the circumstances, as reasonable as any other attitude to adopt; keeping still sensible. Unfortunately, neither one nor a combination of both was any guarantee of survival; as the saying goes 'If it's got your number on it….' On 20th June 'an unlucky shell' pitched into No. 1 Company, killing three, wounding two, and shocking five men.

(Panel 11) L/Sergt. 6786, Philip Nolan, No.1 Coy. 2nd Bn. Irish Guards: *s.* of the late Philip Nolan, by his wife Julia (Freynestown, Dunlavin, Co. Wicklow): enlisted Dublin. Killed in action, 20 June 1916, by 'an unlucky shell'. Age 28.

(Panel 11) L/Corpl. Peter Byrne, No.1 Coy., 2nd Bn. Irish Guards: *s.* of Peter Byrne, of Ballinacarrig, Co. Wicklow, by his wife Mary: *b.* Wexford: enlisted Dublin. Killed in company with L/Sergt. P. Nolan and Pte. P. Lennon, 20 June 1916. Age 20. See above.

(Panel 11) Pte. 3802, Patrick Birmingham, 1st Bn. Irish Guards: *s.* of John Birmingham, of Drish Bridge, Thurles, Co. Tipperary, by his wife Margaret: *b.* Thurles: enlisted Waterford. Killed in action, 6 November 1914. Age 24. *unm.* Remains recovered from an unmarked grave; identified – Disc; reinterred, registered 9 May 1927. Remembered on the Thurles (St. Mary's Churchyard) Great War Memorial. *Buried in Sanctuary Wood Cemetery (IV.C.38).*

At Rest

(Panel 11) Pte. 3258, William Brennock, 1st Bn. Irish Guards: *s.* of Michael Brennock, of 4, Mill Street, Galway, by his wife Mary, *dau.* of the late James Bolger: and brother to Stoker 1719U, P. Brennock, H.M.S. Europa, died at sea, 26 August 1915, en-route from Gallipoli to England; and Sergt. 20432, T.B. Brennock, 1st Royal Dublin Fusiliers, killed in action, 1 March 1917, at Sailly-Saillise: *b.* Dublin, 25 March 1891: *educ.* there: served with the Expeditionary Force in France and Flanders, and was killed in action at Klein Zillebeke, 6 November 1914. Buried there. Age 23. *unm.*

His brothers also have no known grave, Patrick, buried at sea, is commemorated on the Portsmouth Naval Memorial (10); Thomas, Thiepval Memorial, Somme (Pier & Face 16C).

(Panel 11) Pte. 3103, Andrew Breslin, 1st Bn. Irish Guards: *s.* of Patrick Breslin, Labourer; of Ballyore, nr. Londonderry: *b.* St. Johnston, Co. Donegal, 4 December 1885: enlisted, August 1908: served with the Expeditionary Force in France, and was killed in action during a charge on a strong enemy position, 1 November 1914. Age 28. *unm.*

(Panel 11) Pte. 2742, Thomas Carberry, 1st Bn. Irish Guards: *s.* of the late Edward Carberry, Farmer; by his wife Annie (The Batherees, Athlone): *b.* Athlone, 1877: *educ.* there: called up from the Reserve, August 1914, on the outbreak of war: served with the Expeditionary Force in France and Flanders, and was killed during the fighting at Ypres, 1 November following. Age 37. *unm.* (*IWGC record age 30*)

(Panel 11) Pte 4449, Thomas Carroll, 1st Bn. Irish Guards: *s.* of the late Martin Carroll, of Thurles, by his wife Mary (Stradooner Street, Thurles, Co. Tipperary), *dau.* of Joseph Pollard: *b.* Thurles, 24 August 1892: *educ.* Christian Brothers School, there: enlisted, 30 April 1913: served with the Expeditionary Force in France and Flanders from August 1914: present at the Battles of Mons, the Marne and Aisne, and, after taking part in the First Battle of Ypres, was shot and killed by a sniper, 1 November 1914. Buried in a small wood near that place. Age 22. *unm.*

(Panel 11) Pte. 4990, Thomas Cassidy, 2nd Bn. Irish Guards: *s.* of Thomas Cassidy, of 7, Usher Street, Dublin, by his wife Bridget: *b.* Dublin: enlisted there. Killed in action, 2 July 1916, during a large scale raid made by the battalion in the Canal Bank sector; 1 Officer and 11 other ranks were also killed. Age 22. See Lieut. F.M. Pym, above.

(Panel 11) Pte. 3351, Patrick Curtis, 1st Bn. Irish Guards: *s.* of John Curtis, of Kilcrow, Athy, Co. Kildare, and Margaret Curtis his wife: *b.* Athy, 1886: enlisted Glasgow, co. Lanark. Killed in action, 5 November 1914. Age 28. *unm.* Remains recovered from an unmarked grave refer to a GRU Report, Zillebeke 5-398E; (28.C.23.d.05.85); identified – Clothing, Disc, Titles; reinterred, registered 12 February 1931. *Buried in Sanctuary Wood Cemetery (V.O.12).*

(Panel 11) Pte. 4636, Philip Lennon, No.1 Coy., 2nd Bn. Irish Guards: *b.* Dublin: enlisted there. One of three men of his company killed in action, 20 June 1916, by 'an unlucky shell.' See L/Corpl. P. Byrne, above.

(Panel 11) Pte. 3428, Charles McConnell, 1st Bn. Irish Guards: late of Kilcogy, Co. Longford: *s.* of John McConnell, of 17, Park Place, Island Bridge, Dublin, and Ellen McConnell his wife: and brother to L/Corpl. 6343, W. McConnell, M.M., 1st Irish Guards, died 19 September 1918, of wounds: *b.* Chapelizod, Co. Dublin: enlisted Dublin. Killed in action, 1 November 1914. Age 29. The St. Jude's Church Roll of Honour, Chapelizod, records 25 names; dedicated 'To The Glory Of God And In Proud And Loving Memory Of Those Members Of Our Congregation Who Nobly Gave Their Valued Lives In The Great War 1914–1918' and 'The Strife Is O'er The Battle Won.' The brothers McConnell are remembered thereon.

His brother Walter is buried in Sunken Road Cemetery, Boisleux-St. Marc (II.C.19).

(Panel 11) Pte. 3024, William McVeigh, 1st Bn. Irish Guards: *s.* of the late John McVeigh, by his wife Bridget (95, Lower Gardiner Street, Dublin): and brother to Dvr. 187357, P. McVeigh, Royal Field Artillery, died at home, 29 December 1918; consequent to wounds received in the Great War: *b.* Dublin: enlisted there. Killed in action, 29 October 1914. Age 28.

His brother Patrick is buried in Grangegorman Military Cemetery (RC.642).

(Panel 11) Pte. 13, David George Marcus Anderson, 2nd Section, 4th Machine Gun Guards: *s.* of John Anderson, Postmaster, Horwich, co. Lancaster, by his wife Anna ('Sunnyside,' Papcastle, Cockermouth, Cumberland): *b.* Denny, co. Stirling, 20 May 1895: *educ.* Bede Collegiate School, Sunderland: was employed on the staff of the Marquis of Londonderry's Offices, Seaham Harbour, Durham: enlisted Grenadier Guards, 6 March 1915: served with the Expeditionary Force in France and Flanders from February 1916: took part in the operations at Ypres, and later at the Somme where he was wounded at Ginchy, 11 September following, while carrying a badly wounded comrade to the clearing station, although wounded in the knee himself: sent to England on sick leave, on recovery returned to France with the Machine Gun Guards, and was killed in action at Pilckem Ridge, 6 August 1917. Buried at Captain's

Farm, between Pilckem and Langemarck. His Commanding Officer wrote, "He came unscathed through all the battle of 31 July. A bomb blew up the dug-out just before his section was relieved. All his officers, N.C.O.'s and comrades highly appreciated Pte. Anderson's sterling qualities. Although dying himself, he never complained, his whole solicitude was centred on his wounded comrades by his side – how *they* were – unselfish to the last." Age 22. *unm.*

(Panel 11) Capt. the Hon. Henry Lyndhurst Bruce, 3rd attd. 2nd Bn. (1st Foot) The Royal Scots (Lothian Regt.): eldest *s.* of Henry Campbell Bruce, 2nd Baron Aberdare, of Duffryn, Mountain Ash, co. Glamorgan, by his wife Constance Mary, only *dau.* of the late Hamilton Beckett: *b.* 42, Lowndes Street, London, S.W., 25 May 1881: *educ.* Winchester, and New College, Oxford: gazetted Lieut. 3rd Hampshire Regt. 1903; promoted Capt. 3rd Royal Scots, 19 May 1906: served with the Expeditionary Force in France and Flanders: took part in the fighting at Ypres during the autumn of 1914, and was killed in action near Wyschaete, 14 December following, while leading an attack on the enemy lines across very difficult ground. The first line of trenches had been taken and as he was climbing out of the captured position to lead the assault on the second line of trenches he fell, shot through the head. Buried where he fell. Age 33. Mentioned in Despatches (*London Gazette*, 17 February 1915) by F.M. Sir John (now Lord) French, for 'gallant and distinguished service in the field.' He *m.* 11 October 1906; Camilla Antoinette, *dau.* of the late Reynold Clifton, and had a *dau.* Margaret, *b.* 13 (*d.* 18) August 1909.

(Panel 11) Capt. Gilbert Davidson Pitt Eykyn, The Royal Scots (Lothian Regt.) attd. 4th Bn. Alexandra Princess of Wales's Own (Yorkshire Regt.), (The Green Howards), (T.F.): only *s.* of the late Rev. Pitt Eykyn, sometime Vicar of Magor-cum-Berwick, co. Monmouth, and, at the time of his death, Chaplain of Parel, Bombay, India; by his wife Charlotte Elizabeth (82, Prince of Wales Mansions, Battersea Park, London, S.W.), *dau.* of James Davidson, Bengal Civil Service: *b.* France Lynch Parsonage, co. Gloucester, 22 August 1881: *educ.* Haileybury College; and Clayesmore School: received his first commission 3rd Loyal North Lancashire Regt. 1899; gazetted 2nd Lieut. 4th Manchester Regt. 4 May 1901; promoted Lieut. 24 December 1901: transf'd. Indian Army 12 February 1904: joined Royal Scots, 4 February 1905: appt'd. Adjt. 4th Yorkshire Regt. (T.F.) 13 February 1913; promoted Capt. Royal Scots, 26 June following: served 11 years in India, and in the South African Campaign, taking part in operations in Orange River Colony and the Transvaal, for which latter service he received the Queen's medal with three clasps (Cape Colony, Wittenbergen, Transvaal). Capt. Eykyn fell in the first engagement of the 4th Yorks at the Second Battle of Ypres, after only a few days at the Front, while gallantly leading his regt. into action at the storming of St. Julien, 24 April 1915, and was buried in a wood to the left of the reserve trenches. Age 33. Col. Maurice Bell wrote to his wife, "Remember this, he trained the battn. and the General (Plumer) has personally thanked us for our behaviour at a critical moment. His is the credit." And Corpl. Wearmouth, "It is only natural we looked up to our Adjutant, as he was responsible for all our training whilst at home, and naturally, he having been through the South African Campaign, we followed him. The Adjutant never drew his revolver, all he thought about was the regts' first conduct under fire, and I am glad to say we are Mentioned in the General's Despatches, and it was all due to our Adjutant. The loss is being avenged, as every shot fired by our lads, they say as they pull the trigger 'There's one for the Adjutant.'" The following is an extract from the *Yorkshire Evening Post*, 29 April 1915, "Capt. Eykyn was an ardent worker on behalf of the military forces long before the war broke out, and he addressed public meetings on the advantages of joining the service. He was also an amateur actor of considerable talent, and took part in playlets given on behalf of the National Service League. *The Green Howards Gazette*, for May, 1915, said, "The splendid work that he did as Adjutant has borne fruit in the gallantry displayed by the battn. in action, and the death of this fine young officer is deplored by all." A qualified Instructor in Gymnasia, Capt. Eykyn was a gifted linguist fluent and qualified in French, Hindustani and Russian; he held also a 'D' in Musketry. He *m.* Bombay Cathedral, 28 November 1902; Constance ('Fir Lodge,' South Parade, Northallerton, co. York), late of The Cottage, Northallerton; elder *dau.* of the late Arthur Norton, of Guildford, and had a *s.* Duncan Arthur, *b.* 11 August 1906.

On A Grave In A Trench Inscribed "English Killed for the Patrie"

You fell on Belgian land,
And by a Frenchman's hand
Were Buried. Now your fate
A kinsman doth relate.

Three names meet in this trench:
Belgian, English, French;
Three names, but one the fight
For Freedom, Law and Light.

And you in that crusade
Alive were my comrade
And theirs, the dead whose names
Shine like immortal flames.

And though unnamed you be,
Oh, "Killed for the Patrie",
In honour's lap you lie
Sealed of their company.

Lieut. W.S.S. Lyon

(Panel 11) Lieut. Walter Scott Stuart Lyon, 9th (Highlanders) Bn. The Royal Scots (Lothian Regt.), (T.F.): *s.* of the late Walter Fitzgerald Knox Lyon, by his wife Isabella Romanes (Tantallon Lodge, North Berwick): and brother to Capt. C.J. Lyon, Royal Scots Fusiliers, who fell at Ypres, 14 November 1914, and Lieut. A.P.F. Lyon, Gordon Highlanders, who fell at Bertry, 27 August 1914: *b.* North Berwick, 1 October 1886: *educ.* Haileybury College; Balliol College, Oxford (entered 1905), and Edinburgh University (Law Graduate, 1912): on leaving Edinburgh University became an Advocate: served with the Expeditionary Force in France, and was killed at the Second Battle of Ypres 8 May 1915, during a heavy enemy bombardment of Potijze Wood, south of the Menin Road. One of the War Poets, Lieut. Lyon is commemorated on the Chapel Passage, West Wall War Memorial, Balliol College. Age 28. *unm.*

His brother Charles also has no known grave, he is recorded on Panel 33; Alexander is buried in Bertry Communal Cemetery (BB.1).

(Panel 11) Lieut. Thomas Selby Robson-Scott, 2nd Bn. (1st Foot) The Royal Scots (Lothian Regt.): *s.* of John Alexander Robson-Scott, of Newton, Jedburgh, co. Roxburgh, by his wife Margaret Suter, 2nd *dau.* of William Lang, of Wargram, New South Wales: *b.* 1894. Missing, presumed killed in action during the diversionary attack on Petit Bois, 14 December 1914. Age 20. Remembered on Bedrule Parish (& Church) War Memorial.

(Panel 11) 2nd Lieut. Alastair Hunter MacFarlane, 9th (Highlanders) Bn. The Royal Scots (Lothian Regt.), (T.F.): *s.* of the Hon. Lord Ormidale, Senator of the College of Justice, Scotland, by his wife Lady Ormidale (3, Colme Street, Edinburgh): *b.* 14 June 1894: *educ.* Edinburgh Academy; Balliol College, Oxford, where he had just finished his second year when war broke out: gazetted 2nd Lieut. October 1914: joined 2/9th (Highlanders) Battn. Royal Scots, selected as one of the first draft of officers sent out on 1 May 1915, to join 2nd Battn. Killed in action in the trenches nr. Ypres, 12 May 1915. Sergt. R.W.F. Johnstone recorded, "Very soon after dawn broke, all the soldiers in each fire bay 'stood to', i.e. with rifle in hand and bayonet fixed, standing in the trench ready to jump up to the fire step if the sentry who was watching the front gave any alarm. About half an hour later Mr MacFarlane, who had joined us for 'stand to', took Tam Yates and me along the platoon's front to see what work was required in each section's fire bay. We halted for a moment beside a little stream which flowed through the wood (Sanctuary Wood) across our front. As we stopped the officer was hit in the head and fell dead to the ground at our feet. It was a great shock to see sudden death at first hand and so very early in my war service. The reality of war had become very apparent. We laid the body on the side of the trench, covering the face and hands with sandbags, and proceeded on our way, Tam now as Platoon Commander and I as his Platoon Sergeant. That night we buried our officer in a clearing near Battalion Headquarters." 2nd Lieut. MacFarlane's recreations were shooting, auto-cycling and motoring. Age 20. *unm.*

(Panel 11) 2nd Lieut. Henry Cyril Pecker, 3rd (Reserve) attd. 1st Bn. (1st Foot) The Royal Scots (Lothian Regt.): *s.* of Major George Pecker, 5th Border Regt.: *b.* Shrewsbury, co. Salop, 8 October 1894: *educ.* St. Bees, where he was a member of the O.T.C.: on leaving school entered the service of St. Helen's Colliery Co., with a view to taking up a profession as a Mining Engineer: voluntarily joined Reserve of Officers O.T.C. May 1913: on call up for service was rejected on medical examination, his heart being 'too weak': applied/requested to go before a Medical Board – pronounced fit for Active Service; attd. 3rd Border Regt., August 1914: shortly thereafter took a draft to France: attd. 2nd Battn. for Active Service there: wounded (GSW hand), Wytschaete 14 December 1914; hospitalised and, after a short convalescent leave at home, returned to duty March 1915: gazetted 2nd Lieut. from Reserve of Officers to 3rd Royal Scots, April 1915, attd. 1st Battn. with which he was serving when he was killed by a shell at Hooge, nr. Ypres, 30 April 1915. Age 20. *unm.* A man of fine physique and a popular Rugby football player, he was one of the representatives of the Workington Rugby Club in the season's match 1913–14. 2nd Lieut. Pecker has a brother in the Shropshire Light Infantry, lately invalided home from the front; his father, Major Pecker, is currently serving with 5th Battn. Border Regt. somewhere in France. One of the most deadly concepts of the First World War was the 'diversionary attack.' Every major offensive was habitually preceded by a series of minor actions, carried out some distance from the intended main operation, with the objective of confusing the enemy and thereby tying down their reserves. These actions were carried out with limited objectives, limited resources, and with limited chance of success. An officer of the Royal Warwicks, who was himself to die in an action of this kind at Fromelles in 1916, explained, "There is an urgent need for drastic measures on our front to hold back Hun reinforcements for the south, and to do this certain troops have to be more or less sacrificed ... That is war, of course, and all in a day's work." On 14 December 1914, one of the earliest diversionary attacks took place in the Petit Bois – Maedelstede Farm sector. Designed to support the French offensive in Artois, the attack was carried out by 1st Gordon Highlanders and 2nd Royal Scots. After a derisory 15 minute bombardment that served only to alert the Germans they were coming, the two battalions made a headlong dash across No Mans' Land. After entering the German trenches in front of Maedelstede Farm, a small party of Highlanders were surrounded and killed. The Royal Scots fared a little better, seizing two small stretches of trench near Petit Bois, but the combined casualties of both units had been high – over 200 killed, missing, wounded. The French offensive in Artois gained nothing. That attacks of this kind achieved anything at all, was due to the selfless gallantry of men like William Baird, one of 49 members of 2nd Royal Scots killed, who – knowing their chances of survival were practically nil – followed their orders and did their duty: That is war, of course, and all in a day's work.

(Panel 11) Sergt. 999, William Baird, 2nd Bn. (1st Foot) The Royal Scots (Lothian Regt.): *s.* of the late John Baird, by his wife Frances: late *husb.* to Bridget Byrnes, *née* Baird (5, Holme Terrace, Carlisle): served with the Expeditionary Force. Killed in action at Petit Bois, 14 December 1914. Age 35.

(Panel 11) Sergt. 4258, Richard Ellis Griffiths, 2nd Bn. (1st Foot) The Royal Scots (Lothian Regt.): *s.* of Catherine Jones (157, Vittoria Street, Birkenhead, co. Chester): served with the Expeditionary Force. Killed in action at Petit Bois, nr. Kemmel, Belgium, 14 December 1914. Age 31.

(Panel 11) Sergt. 9784, Shayler Paintin, 1st Bn. (1st Foot) The Royal Scots (Lothian Regt.): *yst. s.* of the late Joseph Paintin, Carpenter; of West End, Witney, by his wife Isabella, *dau.* of J. Mann, of Witney: *b.* Witney, co. Oxon, 5 April 1885: *educ.* Wesleyan Higher Grade School, there: Occupation – Grocer: enlisted Royal Scots, 17 September 1906: went to India with 1st Battn. 1909; served there until the outbreak of war: returned to England, November 1914, proceeded to France the following month, and was killed in action at the Second Battle of Ypres, 12 May 1915. His Coy.Sergt.Major wrote, "He was highly respected by the officers, N.C.Os. and men, and a better soldier never wore the uniform. He died like a good British soldier, in the trench, not far from the machine gun he was in charge of. We buried him in the Bellewaarde Wood, nr. the village of Hooge, about four kilometres from the now ruined city of Ypres." A keen sportsman, and a first-class shot, at the Royal Scots Rifle Meeting, India (1912) Sergt. Paintin won the championship medal; he was also in 'C' Coy. hockey team, which won the Meay Ahmed Hockey Cup, 1911–12, and at the Royal Scots Rifle Meeting (1914), won 3rd prize, aggregate. Age 29. *unm.*

(Panel 11) Sergt. 196, Walter Thomson, 9th (Highlanders) Bn. The Royal Scots (Lothian Regt.), (T.F.). Killed in action, 11 May 1915. Age 34. Remains of an 'Unknown British Soldier.' exhumed 22 January 1929, from an unmarked grave in a small cemetery in Sanctuary Wood (28.I.18.d.65.00); identified – Khaki, Kilt; reinterred, registered 25 February 1929. *Buried in Sanctuary Wood Cemetery (V.E.15).*

(Panel 11) Corpl. 3550, Charles F. Hay, 2nd Bn. (1st Foot) The Royal Scots (Lothian Regt.): enlisted Musselburgh: served with the Expeditionary Force, and was killed in action at Petit Bois, nr. Kemmel, 14 December 1914.

(Panel 11) Corpl. 10515, Andrew Kennedy (served as John Carr), 1st Bn. (1st Foot) The Royal Scots (Lothian Regt.): late of Glasgow, co. Lanark: *s.* of James (& Margaret) McMahon Kennedy: *b.* Dublin, *c.*1887: enlisted Bathgate, co. West Lothian. Killed in action, 12 May 1915. Age 27. Remains recovered from an unmarked grave (28.J.13.c.2.2); identified – Clothing, Damaged Disc; reinterred, registered 4 August 1927. *Buried in Sanctuary Wood Cemetery (IV.F.22).*

(Panel 11) L/Corpl. 15252, William Bolton, 2nd Bn. (1st Foot) The Royal Scots (Lothian Regt.): served with the Expeditionary Force in France and Flanders. Killed in action at Kemmel, 29 May 1915. *m.* (*IWGC record Pte.*)

(Panel 11) L/Corpl. 7111, David Ferguson, 2nd Bn. (1st Foot) The Royal Scots (Lothian Regt.): served with the Expeditionary Force. Killed in action at Petit Bois, 14 December 1914.

(Panel 11) L/Corpl. 10776, James Haggerty, 2nd Bn. (1st Foot) The Royal Scots (Lothian Regt.): served with the Expeditionary Force. Killed in action at Petit Bois, nr. Kemmel, 14 December 1914.

(Panel 11) L/Corpl. 1215, Alexander J. McDougall, 'A' Coy., 9th (Highlanders) Bn. The Royal Scots (Lothian Regt.): *s.* of Peter McDougall, of 21, Eglinton Street, Edinburgh, co. Lothian; and Christina his wife: enlisted East Claremont Street, Edinburgh: served with the Expeditionary Force in France and Flanders from 26 February 1915, and was killed in action at Hooge, 16 May 1915. Age 22. *unm.* Partial remains exhumed from a grave in a small cemetery in Sanctuary Wood, marked as belonging to an 'Unknown British Soldier', 23 January 1929 (28.I.18.d.65.00); identified – Khaki; reinterred, registered 26 February 1929. *Buried in Sanctuary Wood Cemetery (V.E.20).*

(Panel 11) Pte. 33176, John Barr, 13th (Service) Bn. The Royal Scots (Lothian Regt.): late of 34, Glover Street, Leith, co. Midlothian: brother to Pte. 4213, J.C. Barr, 2nd Royal Scots, killed in action, 1 May 1915: enlisted in Leith. Killed in action, 1 August 1917. Age 25. He was married to Elizabeth E.A. Barr (95, Dumbledykes Road, Edinburgh).

His brother James is buried in Kemmel Chateau Military (E.18).

(Panel 11) Pte. 14162, Alexander Bell, 2nd Bn. (1st Foot) The Royal Scots (Lothian Regt.): *s.* of Alexander Bell, of Bridgeton, Glasgow: served with the Expeditionary Force in France and Flanders. Killed in action near Ypres, 25 September 1915.

(Panel 11) Pte. 11113, William Beresford, 1st Bn. (1st Foot) The Royal Scots (Lothian Regt.): served with the Expeditionary Force in France and Flanders. Killed in action at Vierstraat, 17 February 1915.

(Panel 11) Pte. 10674, Thomas Black, 1st Bn. (1st Foot) The Royal Scots (Lothian Regt.) 2nd *s.* of the late Thomas Black, Calendar Worker; (formerly Pte., Black Watch), by his wife Agnes (5, Ramsey Street, Dundee), *dau.* of Jack Fields: *b.* Dundee, 23 September 1892: *educ.* Mitchel Street Public School, there: Occupation – Rope Spinner; Messrs Halket & Adams Rope Works, Dundee: enlisted Royal Scots, 7 June 1910; posted 1st Battn., Allahabad, India: returned to England with his regiment on the outbreak of the European War, proceeded to France, 20 December 1914, and was killed in action, 12 May 1915, at Ypres, Belgium. Age 22. *unm.*

(Panel 11) Pte. 9655, Bertie William Bridger, 1st Bn. (1st Foot) The Royal Scots (Lothian Regt.): *s.* of the late Albert Bridger, of Hackney, London, E., by his wife Hannah: and brother to Pte. 7006,

E.J. Bridger, 2nd Border Regt., who fell at the First Battle of Ypres three months previously: enlisted Stratford, co. Essex: served with the Expeditionary Force, and died, 18 January 1915, while on Active Service at Ypres. Age 26. *unm.*

His brother Ernest also has no known grave; he is recorded on Panel 35.

(Panel 11) Pte. 2524, Bertram Brown, 'A' Coy., 1/9th (Highlanders) Bn. The Royal Scots (Lothian Regt.), (T.F.): *s.* of the late George Brown, by his wife Christina Jane Adie Brown, 15, Warrender Park Terrace, Edinburgh, *dau.* of the late William Mitchell, of Leith: *b.* Leith, 27 September 1892: *educ.* Edinburgh: prior to the outbreak of war was serving as 2nd Engineer on the S.S. 'Glitra,' which was sunk by U.17, being one of the first of our merchant ships to suffer that fate. Brown and his comrades were compelled to row to the Norwegian coast in their boats. A week later (31 October 1914) he enlisted in the "Dandy Ninth," and was shot by a sniper at Ypres, 9 April 1915, when entering the trenches with supplies. Age 22. *unm.*

(Panel 11) Pte. 15258, James Burke, 2nd Bn. (1st Foot) The Royal Scots (Lothian Regt.): *s.* of John Burke, Labourer, of 76, Giles Street, Leith, Edinburgh: *b.* Leith, 23 April 1893: *educ.* St. Mary's R.C. School, there: volunteered and enlisted Leith, August 1914: served with the Expeditionary Force in France; killed in action, 8 April 1915 nr. Kemmel. Age 21. He *m.* at Leith, 29 May 1904, Allison C. (3, Block, Corporation Buildings, Leith), *dau.* of Mr (& Mrs) Hinks, of 8, Wilkie's Place, Leith, and had a *dau.* Mary Hinks, *b.* 16 March 1915. (*IWGC record age 22*)

(Panel 11) Pte. 7761, James Burns, 2nd Bn. (1st Foot) The Royal Scots (Lothian Regt.): enlisted Edinburgh: served with the Expeditionary Force. Killed in action at Petit Bois, nr. Kemmel, 14 December 1914. From their arrival in the Ypres sector in early January 1915 until their departure for the Franco-Belgian frontier region around Armentieres at the end of May, 1st Royal Scots lost 4 officers and 133 other ranks killed; of the latter, 97 are recorded on the Menin Gate. The first two casualties – Ptes. William Forrester and James O'Brien – and the last, incurred on the eve of the battalion's departure:-

(Panel 11) Pte. 8493, Donald Campbell, 'B' Coy., 1st Bn. (1st Foot) The Royal Scots (Lothian Regt.): *s.* of Donald Campbell, of 29A, Madras Street, Inverness, by his wife Annie Macdonald: enlisted Inverness: served in India, and with the Expeditionary Force in France and Flanders. Died 23 May 1915, of wounds received in action the same day. Age 32.

(Panel 11) Pte. 4242, George Charles, 1st Bn. (1st Foot) The Royal Scots (Lothian Regt.): *s.* of the late George Charles, of Leven, co. Fife, by his wife Catherine, *dau.* of the late Alexander Mitchell, of Leven: *b.* Leith, 1871: *educ.* Bonnington Road School there: enlisted November 1914, and was killed in action at Ypres, 4 May 1915. Age 43. He *m.* Leith, 29 July 1894, Catherine (*d.*30 April 1911), *dau.* of James Dalgleish, and had two *s.* George, Pte. 6410, Royal Scots Fusiliers (twice wounded), *b.* 1895; James, Pte. 1942, Canadian Expeditionary Force, *b.* 1897 (both – 1916 – on active service); and four twin *daus.* Barbara & Lizzie, *b.* 9 June 1901 and Kate & Isabella, *b.* 3 October 1907.

(Panel 11) Pte. 16363, Joseph John Cleveland, 1st Bn. (1st Foot) The Royal Scots (Lothian Regt.): *s.* of the late Mr (& Mrs) Cleveland, sometime resident Lowestoft, co. Suffolk: enlisted North Shields: served with the Expeditionary Force; killed in action, 19 May 1915. Age 47. Remains recovered from a grave marked as belonging to an 'Unknown British Soldier. Royal Scots', Sanctuary Wood Old Cemetery (29.I.24.b.90.97), identified – Clothing, Titles; reinterred, registered 11 May 1928. *Buried in Sanctuary Wood Cemetery (II.G.31).*

(Panel 11) Pte. 7031, Henry Collins, 2nd Bn. (1st Foot) The Royal Scots (Lothian Regt.): *s.* of Joshua Collins, of Cowley Road, Littlemore, Oxford, by his wife Elizabeth Ann: served with the Expeditionary Force; killed in action at Petit Bois, nr. Kemmel, 14 December 1914. Age 35.

(Panel 11) Pte. 10371, Herbert James Compton, 1st Bn. (1st Foot) The Royal Scots (Lothian Regt.): *s.* of Emma Compton: served with the Expeditionary Force in France. Killed in action at Voormezeele, 18 February 1915. Age 23.

(Panel 11) Pte. 11523, James Conway, 2nd Bn. (1st Foot) The Royal Scots (Lothian Regt.): *s.* of Arthur Conway, of 17, Stankard Rows, Uphall, co. Linlithgow, by his wife Annie: *b.* Edinburgh: enlisted there: killed in action, 27 March 1916, the battalion being shelled whilst moving up to take over trenches recently captured by 4th Royal Fusiliers; St. Eloi sector. Age 25. Capt. R.R. Davidson, 2nd Lieut. J.W.M. Rainie, Ptes. 8950, R. Laidlaw, 3788, D.H. Rodger, and 3836, J. Stewart were also killed. Capt. Davidson and 2nd Lieut. Rainie are buried in Reninghelst New Military Cemetery (I.C.12 / I.D.12); Ptes. Laidlaw, Rodger and Stewart have no known grave, they are recorded below.

(Panel 11) Pte. 9743, Douglas Cousins, 2nd Bn. (1st Foot) The Royal Scots (Lothian Regt.): *s.* of Joseph Cousins, 16, Marshall Street, Edinburgh, late of 44, Bristo Street: served with the Expeditionary Force. Killed in action at Klein Vierstraat, 28 February 1915. Mentioned in Despatches by F.M. Sir John (now Lord) French, for 'gallant and distinguished service in the field.' Age 25. *unm.*

(Panel 11) Pte. 1832, Louis Victor Cowan, 'C' Coy., 9th (Highlanders) Bn. The Royal Scots (Lothian Regt.), (T.F.): *s.* of William Cowan of 16, Woodburn Terrace, Edinburgh, by his marriage to the late Kate Amelia: *b.* Ipoh, Malay States, *c.*1897: enlisted Edinburgh: served with the Expeditionary Force, and was killed in action, 8 May 1915. Age 18. Remains of an 'Unknown British Soldier. 9/Royal Scots' exhumed 22 January 1929 from an unmarked grave in a small cemetery in Sanctuary Wood (28.I.18.d.65.00); identified – Khaki, Titles, Kilt; reinterred, registered 25 February 1929. *Buried in Sanctuary Wood Cemetery (V.E.12).*

(Panel 11) Pte. 10723, Arthur Edward Crawley, 1st Bn. (1st Foot) The Royal Scots (Lothian Regt.): 4th *s.* of Alfred Thomas Crawley, Printer; of 14 Queen's Road, Peckham, London, by his wife Emma, *dau.* of T. Bennet: *b.* Bloomsbury, London, W.C., 23 March 1891: *educ.* Colls Road L.C.C. School, Peckham: enlisted, 10 August 1910: served in India, 7 October 1911–October 1914, and with the Expeditionary Force in France and Flanders, 19 December 1914–22 January 1915, on which latter date he was killed in action at Vierstraat. Age 24. *unm.*

(Panel 11) Pte. 1523, George Cuthbertson, 2nd Bn. (1st Foot) The Royal Scots (Lothian Regt.): *s.* of John Cuthbertson, of 25, Bridge Street, Leith, by his wife Reubena: served with the Expeditionary Force. Killed in action at Petit Bois, nr. Kemmel, Belgium, 14 December 1914. Age 23. He was married to Winifred, *née* Sproul (2/2, Corporation Buildings, Leith, Edinburgh).

(Panel 11) Pte. 11483, Joseph Duff, 'B' Coy., 2nd Bn. (1st Foot) The Royal Scots (Lothian Regt.): *s.* of James Duff, of 1, Haylynn Street, Whiteinch, Glasgow, by his wife Isabella: *b.* Glasgow, *c.*1895: enlisted Glencorse, co. Midlothian: served with the Expeditionary Force. Killed in action at Petit Bois, nr. Kemmel, 14 December 1914. Age 19.

(Panel 11) Pte. 9859, Richard Early, 1st Bn. (1st Foot) The Royal Scots (Lothian Regt.): late of Southampton: *b.* Dartford, co. Kent: enlisted Stratford. Killed in action, 15 May 1915. Remains recovered from a grave in Sanctuary Wood Old Cemetery, marked as belonging to an 'Unknown British Soldier. Royal Scots' (29.I.24.b.90.97), 'Unknown British Soldier. Royal Scots;' identified – Clothing; reinterred, registered 11 May 1928. *Buried in Sanctuary Wood Cemetery (II.G.30).*

(Panel 11) Pte. 326189, Frank Alfred Richard Elliott, 9th (Highlanders) Bn. The Royal Scots (Lothian Regt.), (T.F.): formerly no.5200, Royal Sussex Regt.: late of 4, Cinque Ports Street, Rye, co. Sussex: *s.* of Frank Elliott, of 2, Seymour Place, Rye, by his wife Louisa: and brother to Pte. G/55331, G.D. Elliott, 10th Royal Fusiliers, died of wounds 9 October 1918: *b.* Rye: enlisted Hastings: served with the Expeditionary Force in France, and was killed in action, 4 August 1917, nr. Ypres, Belgium. Age 21.

His brother George is buried in Beaulencourt British Cemetery, Ligny-Thilloy (I.B.37).

(Panel 11) Pte. 3361, John Ferguson, 2nd Bn. (1st Foot) The Royal Scots (Lothian Regt.): 2nd *s.* of the late Thomas Ferguson, Wool Factory Worker, by his wife Mary (16, Lothian Street, Hawick), *dau.* of John Watts: and brother to Mrs. James Jolly: *b.* Weensland, Hawick, co. Roxburgh, 20 September 1879: *educ.* Trinity School: employee North British Railway: enlisted 10 September 1914; went to the Front in France 10 October, and was killed in action at Petit Bois, Kemmel, Belgium 14 December 1914. Age 34. *unm.*

(Panel 11) Pte. 8353, Robert Christie Finlay, 2nd Bn. (1st Foot) The Royal Scots (Lothian Regt.): 3rd *s.* of Thomas Finlay, of 233, Morningside Road, Edinburgh, by his wife Helen, *dau.* of Peter Heatly: and brother to Lieut. J.H. Finlay, 9th Australian Infantry, 3rd (Australian) Bde. (surv'd.): *b.* Edinburgh, 21 December 1887: *educ.* South Morningside Board School: enlisted 4 December 1902; served three years with the Colours; thereafter joined the Reserve and, at the time of the outbreak of war, was a Bricklayer;

Messrs Colin McAndrew, of Lauriston Gardens: proceeded to the Front, 11 November 1914, and was killed in action in a bayonet charge at Petit Bois, nr. Kemmel 14 December 1914. Age 27. He was a member of St. Matthew's Parish Church, Edinburgh. He *m*. Edinburgh, 18 June 1909; Jane Johnstone (22, Wardlaw Place, Edinburgh), *yst. dau.* of David Purves Hall, and had a *dau.* Margaret Johnstone Hall, *b.* 11 May 1914.

(Panel 11) Pte. 11305, John Fleming, D.C.M., 2nd Bn. (1st Foot) The Royal Scots (Lothian Regt.): eldest *s.* of the late Thomas Fleming, by his wife Henrietta (5, St. Peter's Place, Edinburgh), *dau.* of Thomas Aitchison: *b.* Edinburgh, 19 October 1895: *educ.* there: enlisted Royal Scots July 1911: went to France, August 1914, and was killed in action at the Battle of Hooge, 25 September 1915, and buried in Sanctuary Wood. He was Mentioned in Despatches by F.M. Sir John (now Lord) French, for 'gallant and distinguished service in the field;' awarded the Distinguished Conduct Medal (D.C.M.). Age 19. Remains recovered from an unmarked grave (28.J.13.c.1.4); identified – Disc; reinterred, registered 29 August 1927. (*IWGC omit D.C.M.*) *Buried in Sanctuary Wood Cemetery (IV.F.35).*

(Panel 11) Pte. 10939, William Forrester, 1st Bn. (1st Foot) The Royal Scots (Lothian Regt.): *b.* Leith: enlisted Glencorse, co. Midlothian: served in India, October 1911–October 1914, and with the Expeditionary Force in France and Flanders from 19 December 1914 to 12 January 1915, on which date he was killed at Vierstraat; 1st Battalion's first fatality of the Great War.

(Panel 11) Pte. 2988, Archibald Fraser, 9th (Highlanders) Bn. The Royal Scots (Lothian Regt.), (T.F.): *s.* of William Fraser, by his wife Helena: enlisted Manchester. Killed in action, 10 May 1915. Age 22. *unm.* Remains of an 'Unknown British Soldier. 9/Royal Scots' exhumed 22 January from an unmarked grave in a small cemetery in Sanctuary Wood (28.I.18.d.65.00); identified – Khaki; reinterred, registered 25 February 1929. *Buried in Sanctuary Wood Cemetery (V.E.14).*

(Panel 11) Pte. 3193, Walter Young Gibson, 1st Bn. (1st Foot) The Royal Scots (Lothian Regt.): *b.* Glasgow, co. Lanark, about 1886: enlisted Edinburgh, co. Midlothian: killed in action, 20 May 1915. Age 29. Pte Gibson leaves a widow, Jane (54, South Bridge, Edinburgh). Remains recovered from a grave marked as belonging to an 'Unknown British Soldier. Royal Scots', Sanctuary Wood Old Cemetery (29.I.24.b.90.97), identified – Clothing; reinterred, registered 11 May 1928. *Buried in Sanctuary Wood Cemetery (II.G.32).*

(Panel 11) Pte. 11588, Joseph Gough, 2nd Bn. (1st Foot) The Royal Scots (Lothian Regt.): *s.* of Eliza Gough (104, Wolverhampton Road, Heath Town, Wolverhampton): served with the Expeditionary Force. Killed in action at Petit Bois, nr. Kemmel, 29 December 1914. Age 17.

(Panel 11) Pte. 1871, Thomas Graham, *a.k.a.* Thomas Grimes, 2nd Bn. (1st Foot) The Royal Scots (Lothian Regt.): *b.* Cowdenbeath, co. Dunfermline: served with the Expeditionary Force, and was killed in action at Petit Bois, nr. Kemmel, 14 December 1914.

(Panel 11) Pte. 2319, Gordon Hardie, 'C' Coy., 9th (Highlanders) Bn. The Royal Scots (Lothian Regt.): *s.* of Gordon Hardie, Clerk of Works; of 5, Saville Place, Edinburgh, by his wife Margaret, *dau.* of James Munro: *b.* Edinburgh, 29 January 1896: *educ.* Craiglockhart School, Edinburgh: enlisted Edinburgh, after the outbreak of war, 11 September 1914: went to France, 23 February 1915; killed in action at Ypres, 23 April following. Buried at St. Jean. Age 19.

(Panel 11) Pte. 2887, Robert Dunn Hood, 2nd Bn. (1st Foot) The Royal Scots (Lothian Regt.): *s.* of Janet Grant (138, High Street, Linlithgow, West Lothian): served with the Expeditionary Force. Killed in action at Petit Bois, 14 December 1914. Age 19.

(Panel 11) Pte. 3026, David Hunter, 2nd Bn. (1st Foot) The Royal Scots (Lothian Regt.): served with the Expeditionary Force. Killed in action, 29 December 1914.

(Panel 11) Pte. 2367, Ian Campbell Hutton, 9th (Highlanders) Bn. The Royal Scots (Lothian Regt.) (T.F.): *s.* of William Hutton, of 12, Craiglockhart Terrace, Edinburgh; Chief Engineer, Public Works Dept., Madras: enlisted Edinburgh: served with the Expeditionary Force in France and Flanders from 26 February 1915, and was killed in action at Sanctuary Wood, 16 May following. Age 18. Remains exhumed on 25 January 1929 from a grave marked as belonging to an 'Unknown British Soldier', Sanctuary Wood

(28.I.18.d.65.00); identified – Khaki; reinterred, registered 26 February 1929. *Buried in Sanctuary Wood Cemetery (V.E.21)*.

(Panel 11) Pte. 2092, Frank Caton Jack, 9th (Highlanders) Bn. The Royal Scots (Lothian Regt.): *s.* of Francis Jack, of 15, Tennyson Avenue, Manor Park, co. Essex, by his wife Elizabeth: enlisted Edinburgh. Killed in action, 17 May 1915. Age 21. *unm.* Remains exhumed on 25 January from a grave marked as belonging to an 'Unknown British Soldier', located in a small cemetery in Sanctuary Wood (28.I.18.d.65.00); identified – Khaki; reinterred, registered 26 February 1929. *Buried in Sanctuary Wood Cemetery (V.E.22)*.

(Panel 11) Pte. 3845, Robert Jenkins, 2nd Bn. (1st Foot) The Royal Scots (Lothian Regt.): 3rd *s.* of Robert Jenkins, of Townhead, Glasgow, by his wife Mary Jane (Hamilton): *b.* Glasgow, 27 June 1882: *educ.* Saint Rollox Board School, Glasgow: employee Steel Company of Scotland, Garthamloch Collieries: joined 2nd Royal Scots, 7 September 1914: left for France December following, and was killed in action near Hooge, 25 September 1915. Age 32. He *m.* Glasgow, 31 December 1908; Janet, *dau.* of Arthur Morrow, of Hogganfield, and had a *s.* and a *dau.* – Arthur, *b.* 15 January 1910; Mary Jane, *b.* 8 January 1911.

(Panel 11) Pte. 6619, John Jollie, 2nd Bn. (1st Foot) The Royal Scots (Lothian Regt.): served with the Expeditionary Force. Killed in action nr. Kemmel, 5 December 1914.

(Panel 11) Pte. 3311, John Jones, 2nd Bn. (1st Foot) The Royal Scots (Lothian Regt.): *s.* of the late William (& Mrs) Jones, of Edinburgh: served with the Expeditionary Force. Reported missing, 14 December 1914; now assumed killed. Age 38. *m.*

(Panel 11) Pte. 11564, James Young King, 2nd Bn. (1st Foot) The Royal Scots (Lothian Regt.): *s.* of the late William King, by his wife Euphemia (11, Melbourne Place, Edinburgh): *b.* Edinburgh, 1894: enlisted Glencourse, Midlothian: served with the Expeditionary Force. Killed in action at Petit Bois, Kemmel, 29 December 1914. Age 20. *unm.*

(Panel 11) Pte. 8950, Robert Laidlaw, 2nd Bn. (1st Foot) The Royal Scots (Lothian Regt.): formerly no.6020, Seaforth Highlanders: *s.* of the late Andrew Laidlaw, by his wife Helen (37, Warrender Park Road, Edinburgh). Killed in action, 27 March 1916, the battalion being shelled whilst moving up to take over trenches recently captured by 4th Royal Fusiliers; St. Eloi sector. Age 36. See Pte. J. Conway, above.

(Panel 11) Pte. 13837, William Laidlaw, 2nd Bn. (1st Foot) The Royal Scots (Lothian Regt.): *s.* of William Laidlaw, of 139, Great Junction Street, Leith, and his wife Helen: and brother to Pte. 157479, W.J. Laidlaw, 9th Machine Gun Corps (Inf.), killed in action, 17 October 1918: *b.* Saline, co. Fife: enlisted Leith. Killed in action, 17 June 1915.

His brother Walter is buried in Dadizeele New British Cemetery (I.A.9).

(Panel 11) Pte. 1483, David Lamb, 2nd Bn. (1st Foot) The Royal Scots (Lothian Regt.): *s.* of David (& Mrs) Lamb, of Mill Road, Linlithgow Bridge, West Lothian: served with the Expeditionary Force. Killed in action at Petit Bois, 14 December 1914. Age 27. *unm.*

(Panel 11) Pte. 2155, James Hamilton Maxwell, 'B' Coy., 9th (Highlanders) Bn. The Royal Scots (Lothian Regt.), (T.F.): *s.* of Hamilton Maxwell, of 13, Albert Terrace, Edinburgh, by his wife Catherine, *née* Watson. Killed in action, 22 May 1915. Age 22. Remains of an 'Unknown British Soldier. 9/Royal Scots' exhumed on 26 January 1929 from a grave located in a small cemetery in Sanctuary Wood (28.I.18.d.65.00); identified – Khaki, Titles, Kilt; reinterred, registered 27 February 1929. See account re. Pte. J. Pearson, below. *Buried in Sanctuary Wood Cemetery (V.E.28)*.

(Panel 11) Pte. 1701, Hugh McGilp, 9th (Highlanders) Bn. The Royal Scots (Lothian Regt.), (T.F.): *s.* of Archibald McGilp, of 35, Montpelier Park, Edinburgh, by his wife Allison: *b.* Oban, co. Argyll: enlisted Edinburgh. Killed in action, 14 May 1915. Age 20. Remains of an 'Unknown British Soldier' exhumed on 23 January 1929 from a grave located in a small cemetery in Sanctuary Wood (28.I.18.d.65.00); identified – Khaki, Kilt, Boots size 10; reinterred, registered 26 February 1929. *Buried in Sanctuary Wood Cemetery (V.E.17)*.

(Panel 11) Pte. 30534, James McLeod, 13th (Service) Bn. The Royal Scots (Lothian Regt.): *s.* of D. (&Mrs) McLeod, of 35, Buchanan Street, Leith, co. Midlothian: and brother to Corpl. 66213, D. McLeod, 59th Machine Gun Corps (Inf.), killed in action, 21 March 1918; and Pte. 41764, J. McLeod,

1st Royal Scots Fusiliers, killed in action, 28 June 1918: *b*. South Leith: enlisted Edinburgh. Killed in action, 31 July 1917. Age 19.

His brother Donald also has no known grave, he is commemorated on the Arras Memorial (Bay 10); John is buried in Sandpits British Cemetery, Fouquereuil (H.K.9).

(Panel 11) Pte. 3385, James McNulty, 1st Bn. (1st Foot) The Royal Scots (Lothian Regt.): a native of co. Sligo: enlisted Edinburgh: served with the Expeditionary Force in France and Flanders. Killed in action near Ypres, 15 May 1915. Remains recovered from a grave in Sanctuary Wood Old Cemetery, marked as belonging to an 'Unknown British Soldier' (29.I.24.b.90.97), identified – Clothing; reinterred, registered 11 May 1928. *Buried in Sanctuary Wood Cemetery (II.G.29).*

(Panel 11) Pte. 2586, John F. Meston, 9th (Highlanders) Bn. The Royal Scots (Lothian Regt.), (T.F.): *s*. of the late John Meston, of Edinburgh, by his wife Janet: *b*. Edinburgh, *c*.1895: enlisted there: served with the Expeditionary Force in France and Flanders from 26 February 1915, and was killed in action, 14 May following. Age 19. Remains 'Unknown British Soldier' exhumed 23 January 1929 from an unmarked grave in a small cemetery in Sanctuary Wood (28.I.18.d.65.00); identified – Khaki, Kilt; reinterred, registered 26 February 1929. *Buried in Sanctuary Wood Cemetery (V.E.18).*

(Panel 11) Pte. 9918, William Monaghan, 1st Bn. (1st Foot) The Royal Scots (Lothian Regt.): *s*. of William Monaghan (Clones, co. Monaghan), of 46, Lord Street, Jarrow-on-Tyne, by his late wife Catherine, *née* Casey (Castleshane, co. Monaghan): and elder brother to Pte. 3428, F. Monaghan, 2nd Northumberland Fusiliers, who – prior to the outbreak of war had served as a Leading Seaman aboard H.M.S. 'Monmouth,' which was sunk with the loss of all hands at the Battle of Coronel, 1 November 1914 – fell at La Chapelle Farm, nr. Ypres, 76 days previously: and to Catherine Wadey, *née* Monaghan (46, Lord Street, Jarrow-on-Tyne): *b*. 10, Dunn Street, Jarrow, 29 June 1887: *educ*. Jarrow: enlisted Haddington, co. Lothian, *c*.1912: served with the Expeditionary Force in France and Flanders from 19 December 1914, and was killed in action at Sanctuary Wood during the Second Battle of Ypres, 9 May 1915. Age 27. *unm*. Buried at the time, his brother Frank's grave was lost in later fighting; he is commemorated in Hooge Crater Cemetery (La Chapelle Farm Sp.Mem.13).

(Panel 11) Pte. 20231, Adam Montgomery, 2/5th Bn. The Royal Scots (Lothian Regt.), (T.F.): 3rd *s*. of the late William Montgomery, Road Surfaceman, Glasgow Corporation; of Possilpark, Glasgow, by his wife Margaret (378, Gasscube Road, Glasgow), *dau*. of Gilbert Connell: *b*. Dunoon, co. Argyle, 15 July 1884: *educ*. Dunoon Grammar School: Occupation – Plumber; Messrs R. Munro & Son, Springburn: enlisted 25 January 1915: joined Royal Scots, Glencorse Barracks; Monday 29th: sent to Weymouth the following Wednesday for training: crossed to France, 1 May: wounded in action on the 16th of that month and invalided into hospital: discharged from there on the 21st.; back in the firing line on the 23rd., and was killed in action at Ypres, 26 May 1915. Age 30. *unm*.

(Panel 11) Pte. 1896, David Sydney Moore, 9th (Highlanders) Bn. The Royal Scots (Lothian Regt.), (T.F.): *b*. Belfast: enlisted Edinburgh: served with the Expeditionary Force. Died 9 May 1915, of wounds. Remains of an 'Unknown British Soldier. 9/Royal Scots' exhumed on 22 January 1929 from a grave in a small cemetery located in Sanctuary Wood (28.I.18.d.65.00); identified – Khaki, Titles, Kilt; reinterred, registered 25 February 1929. *Buried in Sanctuary Wood Cemetery (V.E.13).*

(Panel 11) Pte. 1958, James Brown Morgan, 9th (Highlanders) Bn. The Royal Scots (Lothian Regt.), (T.F.): *s*. of James (& Mrs) Morgan, of 104, Causewayside, Newington, Edinburgh: *b*. Glasgow, co. Lanark: enlisted Edinburgh. Died 3 May 1915, of wounds received from shellfire 'while plying his spade most industriously, digging a new line of trenches in Sanctuary Wood.' Age 16.

(Panel 11) Pte. 10589, James O'Brien, 1st Bn. (1st Foot) The Royal Scots (Lothian Regt.): *b*. Ulster, Co. Fermanagh: enlisted Edinburgh, co. Lothian: served in India, October 1911–October 1914, and with the Expeditionary Force in France and Flanders, 19 December 1914–16 January 1915, on which latter, date he was killed in action at Vierstraat; 1st Battalion's second fatality of the Great War.

(Panel 11) Pte. 2309, Francis Alexander Patrick, 'A' Coy., 9th (Highlanders) Bn. The Royal Scots (Lothian Regt.), (T.F.): eldest *s*. of John Bonthron Patrick, Wholesale Merchant; of 1, Morningside Terrace, Edinburgh, Scotland, by his wife Wilhelmina Frances, *dau*. of the late William Goldie:

b. Edinburgh, 6 December 1892: *educ*. George Watson's College, Edinburgh; Edinburgh University; Besancon University, France; Jena University, Thuringia, Germany; Guelph University, Canada: studied for the Indian Police, and passed the examination in 1912, but afterwards took up the study of Indian and Colonial Agriculture, and in the prosecution of his researches studied at Besancon, Jena and Guelph. On the outbreak of war he was studying for his B.Sc. at the Edinburgh University, but relinquished this and joined 9th Royal Scots, September 1914: went to France, February 1915, and was killed in action during the Second Battle of Ypres, 12 April following. Buried at Ypres. Age 23. *unm*. An officer, writing home to a brother, said, "This sad event cast a gloom over the battn., with whom Patrick had been very popular, and I assure you, I feel his loss very keenly, He was a lad I was proud to have in my platoon, a fellow Watsonian, and the first Watsonian to fall in the Dandy 9th." A keen golfer, fisherman, a good horseman, and one of the best shots in the regiment, above all, he was a diligent student. "If you want to find Patrick," wrote one of his comrades at the Front in the few days of rest that fell to them, "go to the roofless library or convent ruins and there you will find him rummaging among the old and shell-torn books, smoking his pipe." His brother, Lieut. John Cairns Patrick, Royal Scots, and ten of his cousins, also served. At 11 p.m., 22nd May, 1915, 9th Battalion Royal Scots were relieved by 1st King's Own Yorkshire Light Infantry after three weeks in the Sanctuary Wood trenches. During this time they had been subjected to continual enemy bombardment, suffering casualties of 2 officers and 15 other ranks killed, 82 other ranks wounded, and one officer, 2/Lt. B.E.Yeats, evacuated to hospital suffering from shell shock. The War Diary for 22nd May, records:- "… Three other ranks killed and four other ranks wounded." Sergeant R.W.F. Johnstone recorded the burial of the three killed:- "One night, just after our relief from the front to the support line, I had to take charge of a burial party for three of the Company who had been killed that day. They included Jimmy Pearson, a famous Watsonian Rugger player with a Scottish cap, who was our Company Runner. At this early stage of the war, we were most meticulous to ensure the correct burial of our comrades. We dug three shallow graves in a plot set aside as a cemetery, near Zouave and Sanctuary Wood, lined the foot with sandbags, placing the bodies on them with their hands crossed in front. More sandbags were placed on the face and hands and knees. Like us, they were all kilted soldiers and I noticed that Jimmy Pearson's leather sporran was still on the body. I removed it and wore it for many months … The Padre read the short service and a piper played *Flowers of the Forest* which was interrupted by a salvo of shells, which caused all present to lie down flat very promptly until the shelling ended. We heard the approach of the ration limbers and saw ourselves surrounded by Verey lights and the fires of Ypres behind us, and set off for our duties with many poignant thoughts …"

(Panel 11) Pte. 2061, James Pearson, 'B' Coy., 9th (Highlanders) Bn. The Royal Scots (Lothian Regt.), (T.F.): enlisted Edinburgh: served with the Expeditionary Force in France from 26 February 1915, and was killed in action, 22 May following. Remains of an 'Unknown British Soldier. 9/Royal Scots.' exhumed on 26 January 1929, from a grave in a small cemetery located in Sanctuary Wood (28.I.18.d.65.00); identified – Khaki, Titles; reinterred, registered 27 February 1929. *Buried in Sanctuary Wood Cemetery (V.E.27).*

(Panel 11) Pte. 25176, John Riddell, 13th Bn. The Royal Scots (Lothian Regt.): late of Station Road, Armadale: *s*. of Alex (& Mrs) Riddell, of South Street, Armadale, co. Linlithgow: and brother to Pte. A. Riddell, Royal Scots (surv'd.): *b*. Armadale: Occupation – Colliery worker; Bathville: served with the Expeditionary Force in France and Flanders from July 1915: took part in the Battle of Loos and many other engagements; served continuously without leave for two years, and was killed in action, 1 August 1917. At some point following the fighting at High Wood, Somme, Pte. Riddell put to verse an outline of the war thus far; it concludes:-

....when the din is over,
And the roar of cannons cease,
May the world know the blessings of
An everlasting peace.

Twelve months and another major offensive later, John was granted his everlasting peace.

(Panel 11) Pte. 3788, Daniel Hood Rodger, 2nd Bn. (1st Foot) The Royal Scots (Lothian Regt.): late of Glasgow: *s*. of William Rodger, by his wife Agnes: *b*. Ladyburn, co. Renfrew: enlisted Bo'ness, co. Linlithgow: served with the Expeditionary Force. Killed in action, 27 March 1916, the battalion being shelled whilst moving up to take over trenches recently captured by 4th Royal Fusiliers; St. Eloi sector. Age 37. See Pte. J. Conway, above.

(Panel 11) Pte. 1665 James Russell, 9th (Highlanders) Bn. The Royal Scots (Lothian Regt.), (T.F.): *s*. of Robert Russell. Killed in action, 9 May 1915. Age 19. Remains of an 'Unknown British Soldier. Royal Scots' exhumed on 21 January 1929 from a grave in a small cemetery located in Sanctuary Wood (28.I.18.d.65.00); identified – Khaki, Kilt; reinterred, registered 5 March 1929. *Buried in Sanctuary Wood Cemetery (V.E.2)*. After being withdrawn from the Loos sector 11th and 12th Royal Scots sampled the miseries of the Salient for three months. The perpetual rain, the leaky shelters, the ubiquitous mud, the unsightly ruins and the general untidiness of the Flemish landscape, even if there had been no shelling, would have predisposed the mind to melancholy. It required an effort to rise above the depression caused by the evidences of decay that seemed to brood over Ypres and its surroundings, and it was possibly a blessing in disguise that the sodden ditches, which passed for trenches, necessitated unflagging labour on the part of the Royal Scots to prevent them from tumbling in. Systematic training was impossible on account of the mud, and the men kept themselves fit by the daily exercise they derived from the wielding of pick and shovel. For many weeks most of the companies were commanded by mere boys, second lieutenants, who balanced their lack of experience by an abundance of enthusiasm. Neither the 11th nor the 12th was engaged in close conflict with the Bosches, but both ever afterwards looked back on the sojourn in the salient as their most unpleasant experience of trench warfare. During the month of November, 12th Battalion lost 12 other ranks killed, 5 died of wounds; 11th Battalion, 10 killed, 2 died of wounds. Among the dead, 16 year old Herbert Sangster, his young life ended during what, had fate decreed differently, he might have acknowledged as his most unpleasant experience of trench warfare; his parents most unpleasant experience would begin in about three or four days with the arrival of the morning's mail.

(Panel 11) Pte. 22982, Herbert Sangster, 11th (Service) Bn. The Royal Scots (Lothian Regt.): brother to Elizabeth Sangster (40, Prior Road, Forfar): *b*. Coupar Angus, co. Forfar, 1899: enlisted Blairgowrie, co. Perth. Killed in action, 14 November 1915. Age 16.

(Panel 11) Pte. 2033, James Smith, 9th (Highlanders) Bn. The Royal Scots (Lothian Regt.), (T.F.): *s*. of the late John Smith, by his wife Helen (28, Melville Terrace, Edinburgh): *b*. Edinburgh, co. Midlothian: enlisted there. Killed in action, 11 May 1915. Age 18. Remains of an 'Unknown British Soldier' exhumed on 23 January 1929 from a grave in a small cemetery located in Sanctuary Wood (28.I.18.d.65.00); identified – Khaki; reinterred, registered 26 February 1929. *Buried in Sanctuary Wood Cemetery (V.E.16)*.

(Panel 11) Pte. 2492, Martin Stark, 1st Bn. (1st Foot) The Royal Scots (Lothian Regt.): *s*. of James Stark, of Loanburn Cottages, Penicuik, co. Midlothian, and Mary his wife: *b*. Penicuik: enlisted Glencorse: served with the Expeditionary Force, and was killed in action at Ypres, 14 May 1915. Age 22. Remains recovered from a grave in Sanctuary Wood Old Cemetery, marked up as belonging to an 'Unknown British Soldier', (29.I.24.b.90.97), identified – Clothing; reinterred, registered 10 May 1928. *Buried in Sanctuary Wood Cemetery (II.G.27)*.

To Memory Ever Dear

(Panel 11) Pte. 3836, James Stewart, 2nd Bn. (1st Foot) The Royal Scots (Lothian Regt.): *b*. Dumfries: enlisted Edinburgh. Killed in action, 27 March 1916, the battalion being shelled whilst moving up to take over trenches recently captured by 4th Royal Fusiliers; St. Eloi sector. See Pte. J. Conway, above.

(Panel 11) Pte. 1679, William J. Whitlie, 'B' Coy., 9th (Highlanders) Bn. The Royal Scots (Lothian Regt.): *s*. of Walter Whitlie, of 106, Raeburn Place, Edinburgh, by his wife Jane. Killed in action, 22 May 1915. Age 20. Remains of an 'Unknown British Soldier' exhumed on 25 January 1929, from a grave in a small cemetery located in Sanctuary Wood (28.I.18.d.65.00); identified – Khaki, Titles; reinterred, registered 26 February 1929. See account re. Pte. J. Pearson, above. *Buried in Sanctuary Wood Cemetery (V.E.23).*

Until The Day Break

(Panel 11) Capt. Eardley Apted, 9th attd 11th Bn. The Queen's (Royal West Surrey Regt.): 2nd *s.* of Oliver Cromwell Apted, Alderman, of Doods Brow, Reigate, co. Surrey, by his wife Prudence: *educ.* Holmesdale School, Cranleigh School, and Gray's Inn (Law Student), from whence, after graduating (1913) he was called to the Bar: joined Inns of Court O.T.C., 1914, and commissioned 2nd Lieut., 9th The Queen's (attd. Training Reserve, Watford): actively supported the Mid-Surrey Recruiting Campaign: subsequently went to France and was reported missing, believed killed, following the fighting at St. Eloi, 1 August 1917. Age 33.

(Panel 11) Lieut. John Greville Hobart Bird, 2nd Bn. (2nd Foot) The Queen's (Royal West Surrey Regt.): only *s.* of William Hobart Bird, M.Inst.C.E., of The Gate House, Coventry: *gdson.* of Alderman Maycock, J.P., former Mayor of Coventry: *b.* Wolverhampton, co. Stafford, 11 November 1888: *educ.* Eversley House, Southwold, and privately: gazetted 2nd Lieut. Royal West Surrey Regt. 24 May 1913; promoted Lieut. (posthumous) *London Gazette*, 22 May 1915, antedated as from 21 October 1914: served with the Expeditionary Force in France and Flanders, and was killed, 24 October 1914, at the First Battle of Ypres. After having been sent with his platoon to defend a trench at a spot where the enemy's fighting was particularly severe, and while directing his men's return fire, he was told one of his best men had been hit and in attempting to go to his aid was instantaneously killed. Age 25 *unm.*

(Panel 11) Lieut. Frank Molyneux Eastwood, 1st Bn. (2nd Foot) The Queen's (Royal West Surrey Regt.): 4th *s.* of John Edmund Eastwood, of 14, Chichester Terrace, Brighton, co. Sussex, formerly of 'Enton,' Witley, by his wife Ethel: *b.* 1 November 1892: *educ.* Mr Arthur Dunn's, Ludgrove; Eton, and Royal Military College, Sandhurst: gazetted 2nd Lieut. Queen's Royal West Surrey Regt. 4 September 1912; promoted Lieut. September 1914: served with the Expeditionary Force in France and Flanders, and died, 30 October 1914, of wounds received nr. Gheluvelt on the evening of the same day. He was a member of the Conservative Club. Age 21. *unm.*

(Panel 11) Lieut. (Adjt.) Charles Roderick Haigh, 2nd Bn. (2nd Foot) The Queen's (Royal West Surrey Regt.): elder *s.* of the late Arthur Elam Haigh, M.A., Fellow and Tutor, Corpus Christi College, Oxford: *b.* 3 September 1888: *educ.* Oxford Preparatory School; Winchester College (Exhibitioner, 1902–07), and Corpus Christi College, Oxford, where he graduated B.A.: gazetted 2nd Lieut. 20 April 1910: promoted Lieut. 18 April 1912: served with the Expeditionary Force in France and Flanders, and was killed in action during an attack on the German position at Klein Zillebeke, near Ypres, 7 November 1914. Age 26. *unm.*

(Panel 11) Lieut. Gerald Sclater Ingram, 2nd Bn. (2nd Foot) The Queen's (Royal West Surrey Regt.): only child of the late William (& Beatrice) Ingram, of 77, Eccleston Square, London, S.W.: *b.* July 1890: *educ.* Horris Hill; Winchester, and Christ Church, Oxford: gazetted 2nd Lieut. The Queen's, 3 September 1912; promoted Lieut. September 1914: served with the Expeditionary Force in France and Flanders, and was killed in action at Zonnebeke near Ypres, 21 October 1914. Age 24. *unm.*

(Panel 11) Lieut. Howard Bertie Strong, 1st Bn. (2nd Foot) The Queen's (Royal West Surrey Regt.): only *s.* of Mr (& Mrs) E. Howard Strong, of 30, Bramham Gardens, South Kensington, London, S.W.: *b.* Sutton, co. Surrey, 15 August 1892: *educ.* The College, Epsom, co. Surrey, where he was in the first Football XI, the Fives team, and the O.T.C.: served for two years in the Special Reserve, The Queen's, prior to becoming 2nd Lieut. 1st Bn. December 1912: served with the Expeditionary Force in France and Flanders from August 1914: promoted Lieut. September following: took part in the Battle of Mons, the Aisne and the Marne, and was killed in action at the First Battle of Ypres, 30 October 1914. At the time of his death he was acting as Capt. of 'C' Company. Lieut. Strong was interested in flying and took his certificate at Brooklands in August 1913. He was a member of the Junior Army and Navy Club. Age 22. *unm.* (*IWGC record 29 October 1914*)

(Panel 11) Lieut. David Rex Wilson, 2nd Bn. (2nd Foot) The Queen's (Royal West Surrey Regt.): *s.* of George David Wilson, C.C., of Darlington: *gdson.* of Alderman Jonathan Angus, of Newcastle-on-Tyne:

b. Pensbury, Darlington, 5 February 1891: *educ.* Aysgarth Preparatory School; Clifton College, and Jesus College, Cambridge: whilst at Clifton he was captain of the Shooting VIII, and of the football team: at Cambridge he was captain of the O.T.C., and thirty-eighth in the King's Hundred at Bisley: joined The Queen's, December 1912: went to Bermuda, March 1913, being promoted Lieut. the same month: thence to South Africa 1914. On the outbreak of war, August 1914, the battalion returned to England, and went to Flanders with 22nd Brigade, VIIth Division, early in October. Lieut. Wilson was killed, 30 October 1914, at Ypres, after having retaken with his platoon some trenches from the enemy. His gallantry on the day he was killed is mentioned in *The First Seven Divisions* by Lord E. Hamilton. The order to retire did not reach him as he was in an advanced position with his platoon; being a marksman he laid himself out to pick off Germans right and left, and appears by his audacity to have rendered splendid service until he was eventually shot through the head and killed. Age 23. *unm.*

(Panel 11) Lieut. Ernest Harold Hamley Woodward, 10th (Service) Bn. The Queen's (Royal West Surrey Regt.): elder *s.* of the Rev. Alfred Ernest Woodward, M.A., Vicar of Ugley, co. Essex, formerly Classical Master, Christ's Hospital; by his wife Alice Harriet, *dau.* of J. Hamley, of Guernsey: *b.* Dulwich, London, S.E., 29 January 1888: *educ.* Shirley House School, Blackheath, London, S.E., and Old Charlton; Christ's Hospital, London, and Horsham – Head of House, Grecian & School Exhibitioner; Hertford College – Senior Classical Scholar (open), graduated B.A. Classical Honours (Second & Third Class); and Grenoble University, France: Occupation – Assistant Classical Master and Football Coach, Oundle School; subsequently Assistant Classical Master, Perse School, Cambridge: volunteered for Active Service on the outbreak of war, refusing a commission, and enlisted as Pte., 18th (Public Schools) Bn. Royal Fusiliers, September 1914: served with the Expeditionary Force in France and Flanders from 1915 to 1916, and when the Public Schools & Universities Battn. was disbanded, he accepted a commission – gazetted 2nd Lieut. 10th Royal West Surrey Regt.: joined his regiment in France, September 1916, taking part in the Somme offensive of that year, having at one time to take command of his company owing to the other officers being wounded. Reported wounded and missing at Vierstraat 24 December following; now known to have been killed in action on that date. His Commanding Officer, Lieut.Col. Talbot Jarvis, wrote, "Lieut. Woodward went out on patrol, as he has done so many times before, and was shot by a German sentry. Your son did so well in the action on the Somme, and has always shown such great personal bravery, that it has endeared him to all ranks," and his Commanding Officer, Major R. Gwynne, "I considered him a very, very noble, gallant officer and gentleman, as brave as a lion, and I know all here had the very, very highest opinion of him and affection for him." The Chaplain also wrote, "Your son wished to crown the night's work with the capture of a German. He therefore, apparently alone, went ahead, and attained the German barbed wire in front of their trenches. A sudden rush, and he might quite well have succeeded in bustling a surprised and terrified sentry, and bringing him into our lines a short distance away. But he had the misfortune, according to the reports of his men, to stumble accidentally against one or more Germans out repairing their wires, and before he had the time to defend himself, was struck down and almost certainly killed. He was therefore reported 'missing believed killed,' and his body would be taken in and buried (I hope with honours as befitted so brave a man)." Lieut. Woodward was famous at Rugby football, having been captain of his School XV., also of the college team, and of the Old Blues' First XV.; he also played in the Surrey County XV., as well as several times for Oxford University, though he just missed his 'Blue.' Age 28. *unm.*

(Panel 11) 2nd Lieut. David Ive, 2nd Bn. (2nd Foot) The Queen's (Royal West Surrey Regt.): *s.* of Ernest (& Mrs) Ive, of 'The Hermitage,' Meadvale, Redhill, co. Surrey, Assoc. M.Inst.C.E.: nephew to Roland Ive, 'The Wallands,' Bedford Grove, Eastbourne: *b.* Kensington, London, W.8., 27 May 1894: *educ.* Reigate Grammar School, joining the O.T.C. from its inauguration, and obtaining the 'A' certificate May 1912: subsequently received tuition from private tutors in Eastbourne and London: gazetted 2nd Lieut. 3rd The Queen's, October 1913: passed the Army entrance examination the following month: received probationary training at Bordon Camp, being transferred to the 2nd Battn. as 2nd Lieut. September 1914: left England with his battalion, as part of VIIth Division, 4 October following: landed at

Zeebrugge and was fatally wounded, being shot in the abdomen, in the fighting before Ypres on the 23rd of that month. Age 20. *unm.*

(Panel 11) Sergt. L/6486, Henry Dawes, 2nd Bn. (2nd Foot) The Queen's (Royal West Surrey Regt.): served with the Expeditionary Force. Killed in action, 21 October 1914.

(Panel 11) Sergt. L/4928, George Pocock Buxton Dean, 1st Bn. (2nd Foot) The Queen's (Royal West Surrey Regt.): served with the Expeditionary Force. Reported missing, 31 October 1914, and now assumed killed. Age 35. He leaves a wife, Ann A. Dean (61, Sherwood Street, Reading, co. Berks).

(Panel 11) Sergt. L/9201, Richard James Dossett, 2nd Bn. (2nd Foot) The Queen's (Royal West Surrey Regt.): *s.* of David Dossett, of 38, Pyrmint Road, Strand-on-the-Green, Chiswick, London, W.: served with the Expeditionary Force in France from 6 October 1914; reported missing, 7 November 1914; now assumed killed. Age 26.

(Panel 11) Sergt. L/7830, Francis Thomas Claude Ilett, 2nd Bn. (2nd Foot) The Queen's (Royal West Surrey Regt.): *s.* of John William Ilett, of 74, Ruskin Buildings, Millbank, London, S.W.1, by his wife Mary Theresa: *b.* Southwark, co. Surrey, 1884: served with the Expeditionary Force. Reported missing at Gheluvelt, 7 November 1914; now assumed killed. Age 30.

(Panel 11) Sergt. L/9095, Joseph Downing Lake, 2nd Bn. The Queen's Royal West Surrey Regt.: *s.* of the late Sergt. J. Lake, by his wife Rosa Alice (27, Albion Road, Folkestone); and elder brother to L/Corpl. L/9878, J. A. Lake, 1st The Buffs (East Kent Regt.), killed in action nr. Armentieres the previous day: *b.* Shorncliffe, co. Kent, 1893: enlisted London: a pre-war Regular, served 7 yrs. with the Colours: proceeded to France, 6 October 1914; killed in action, 21 October 1914. Age 21.

His brother James also has no known grave; he is commemorated on the Ploegsteert Memorial (Panel 2).

(Panel 11) L/Sergt. L/9075, James Willis Diggins, 2nd Bn. (2nd Foot) The Queen's (Royal West Surrey Regt.): *s.* of James Diggins, of Kilburn, London, N.: served with the Expeditionary Force from 6 October 1914; killed in action at Gheluvelt, 7 November 1914.

(Panel 11) L/Sergt. S/7023, Stephen John Alexander Palmer, 7th (Service) Bn. The Queen's (Royal West Surrey Regt.): formerly no.10174, 1st Bn. The Buffs: *s.* of John Alexander Palmer, by his 1st wife Annie (*d.* 1887); stepson to Harriet Palmer (204, Union Road, Buckland, Dover): and brother to Pte. G/5181, G.T. Palmer, 8th The Buffs, who fell, 19 August 1916, at the Somme; Gnr. W. Palmer, Royal Garrison Artillery (surv'd.); and Pte. E.G. Palmer, 1st Buffs (surv'd.): *b.* River, nr. Dover, *c.*1886: enlisted March 1914: served with the Expeditionary Force in France, and was one of three other ranks killed in action, 16 July 1917, at Sanctuary Wood by the explosion of a shell. Age 20. *unm.* Pte. G/1515, C. Humphreys, wounded by the same shell, died of wounds the following day. *Dover Express*, August 1922:-

> *In ever affectionate memory of my two beloved sons…Six years have passed, yet still I miss them.*
> *A silent thought, a secret tear, Keeps their memory very dear.*
> *From their ever loving Mother. R.I.P.*

L/ Sergt Palmer's brother George also has no known grave, he is commemorated on the Thiepval Memorial, Somme; Pte. Humphreys is buried in Lijssenthoek Military Cemetery (XVI.D.1A).

(Panel 11) Corpl. L/9225, Robert Sargent Coomber, 1st Bn. (2nd Foot) The Queen's (Royal West Surrey Regt.): late of East Grinstead, co. Kent: *s.* of Edmund Coomber, of Edenbridge, co. Kent: and brother to Pte. 9836, R.C. Coomber, The Queen's, died of wounds, 27 October 1914: enlisted Tonbridge: served with the Expeditionary Force in France, and was killed in action at Ypres, 31 October 1914.

His brother Richard is buried nearby in Ypres Town Cemetery Extension (II.A.51).

(Panel 11) Corpl. L/8272, William Davies, 1st Bn. (2nd Foot) The Queen's (Royal West Surrey Regt.): *s.* of Thomas Davies, of Shottermill, nr. Haslemere, co. Surrey: served with the Expeditionary Force. Reported missing and wounded, 31 October 1914; now assumed killed.

(Panel 11) Corpl. L/8975, Mark Charles Dowlen, 2nd Bn. (2nd Foot) The Queen's (Royal West Surrey Regt.): *s.* of Mark Dowlen, of 3, Hawthorn Cottages, Hookwood, Horley, co. Surrey, by his wife

Edith: and brother to Pte. L/10791, W. Dowlen, 1st Queen's, who fell on 13 April 1918: served with the Expeditionary Force in France. Killed in action, 6 November 1914. Age 26. *unm.*

His brother William also has no known grave; he is commemorated on the Ploegsteert Memorial (Panel 2).

(Panel 11) Corpl. L/8931, William Henry Kilty, 2nd Bn. (2nd Foot) The Queen's (Royal West Surrey Regt.): *s.* of John Kilty, of 7, St. James Road, Carshalton, co. Surrey, by his wife Harriet Kitty: and brother to AB. 22356, L.J. Kilty, HMS 'Black Prince,' Royal Navy, killed in action/lost at sea when that ship was sunk at the Battle of Jutland, 31 May 1916: served with the Expeditionary Force, and was killed in action, 7 November 1914.

His brother Leonard, having no known grave but the sea, is commemorated on the Portsmouth Naval Memorial (13).

(Panel 11) Corpl. L/9338, Samuel James Terry, 2nd Bn. (2nd Foot) The Queen's (Royal West Surrey Regt.): *s.* of the late Samuel Terry, by his wife Mrs R. Terry (21, Minerva Avenue, Dover): and brother to Pte. P. Terry, The Queen's (surv'd): *b.* Christchurch, *c.*1890: enlisted Dover: served with the Expeditionary Force in France from 7 October 1914, and was killed in action, 7 November 1914, nr. Zillebeke. Age 24. *unm. Dover Express,* In Memoriam, November 1940:-

> *Some may think that we forget him, when at times they see us smile;*
> *They little know the silent heartache that is hidden all the while.*
> *Never forgotten by his Mum, Sister & Brother.*

PANEL 11 ENDS: CPL. S.J. TERRY, THE QUEEN'S (ROYAL WEST SURREY)

PANEL 13 BEGINS: L/CPL. W. ADAMSON, THE QUEEN'S (ROYAL WEST SURREY)

(Panel 13) L/Corpl. G/10431, William Adamson, 'D' Coy., 1st Bn. (2nd Foot) The Queen's (Royal West Surrey Regt.): *s.* of Alfred (& Mrs I.) Adamson, of 1, Prospect Place, Mason's Hill, Bromley, co. Kent: served with the Expeditionary Force. Reported missing, 31 October 1914; assumed (Court of Enquiry, 1916) killed. Age 18.

(Panel 13) L/Corpl. L/8133, George Bishop, 1st Bn. (2nd Foot) The Queen's (Royal West Surrey Regt.): late of Chippenham, co. Wilts: served with the Expeditionary Force, and was killed in action, 31 October 1914. *m.*

(Panel 13) L/Corpl. 10404, Hammond George Walford Brazier, 1st Bn. (2nd Foot) The Queen's (Royal West Surrey Regt.): *b.* Poona, India: served with the Expeditionary Force. Reported missing, 31 October 1914; now assumed killed.

(Panel 13) L/Corpl. 6229, William Obed Clark, 2nd Bn. (2nd Foot) The Queen's (Royal West Surrey Regt.): eldest *s.* of the late William Obed Clark, R.N., by his wife Lydia Maria, *dau.* of William F. Unsworth: *b.* Birmingham, 13 October 1881: *educ.* Southampton Street Board School, Camberwell: enlisted, 3 November 1898: served throughout the South African War, 1899–1902 (Queen's Medal, two clasps; King's Medal, two clasps), thereafter passed into the Army Reserve: Occupation – Packer of essences for export: called up on the outbreak of war, August 1914: served with the Expeditionary Force in France from 11 September. Killed in action at the First Battle of Ypres, 31 October following. Age 33. He *m.* St. George's Church, Camberwell, 25 December 1905; Rosina Eliza (59, Edmund Street, Camberwell, London, S.E.), *dau.* of the late Edwin Sims, and had four children – Ivy Ellen, *b.* 28 November 1907; Lydia Elsie, *b.* 17 January 1909; Emily Alice, *b.* 21 August 1911; Obed Edwin, *b.* 1 July 1913.

(Panel 13) L/Corpl. L/9761, Thomas George Cook, 2nd Bn. (2nd Foot) The Queen's (Royal West Surrey Regt.): *s.* of Thomas Cook, of 4, Victoria Avenue, Hythe, co. Kent, by his wife Amelia: *educ.* St. Leonard's School, Hythe: served with the Expeditionary Force. Killed in action at Gheluvelt, 7 November 1914. Age 20. *unm.*

(Panel 13) L/Corpl. L/10190, Harold George Cooke, 1st Bn. (2nd Foot) The Queen's (Royal West Surrey Regt.): *s.* of Charles Cooke, of 50, Rymer Road, Addiscombe, Croydon, co. Surrey, by his wife Rose: served with the Expeditionary Force. Reported missing, 31 October 1914, and now assumed killed. Age 21. *unm.*

(Panel 13) L/Corpl. L/9652, Albert Charles Gaskin Coomber, 2nd Bn. (2nd Foot) The Queen's (Royal West Surrey Regt.): *s.* of Charles Coomber, of 7, Butts Villas, Woking, co. Surrey, by his wife Hetty: enlisted Guildford: served with the Expeditionary Force. Killed in action, 21 October 1914. Age 24. *unm.*

(Panel 13) L/Corpl. L/9921, Samuel Cooper, 2nd Bn. (2nd Foot) The Queen's (Royal West Surrey Regt.): *s.* of Margaret Cooper (25, Russell Road, Peckham, London, S.E.): served with the Expeditionary Force. Reported missing, 21 October 1914; now assumed killed. Age 22. *unm.*

(Panel 13) L/Corpl. L/9003, Charles Deadman, 2nd Bn. (2nd Foot) The Queen's (Royal West Surrey Regt.): enlisted Guildford, co. Surrey: served with the Expeditionary Force. Killed in action, 31 October 1914.

(Panel 13) L/Corpl. L/7043, John Edmonds, 2nd Bn. (2nd Foot) The Queen's (Royal West Surrey Regt.): served with the Expeditionary Force. Killed in action at Zillebeke, 7 November 1914.

(Panel 13) L/Corpl. L/9959, Edward Goring, 2nd Bn. (2nd Foot) The Queen's (Royal West Surrey Regt.): *s.* of Amos Goring, of 93, Oval Road, East Croydon, co. Surrey, by his wife Esther: served with the Expeditionary Force. Reported missing, 4 November 1914, and now assumed killed. Age 21. *unm.*

(Panel 13) L/Corpl. L/10119, Henry Edward Hopper, 1st Bn. (2nd Foot) The Queen's (Royal West Surrey Regt.): *s.* of William Hopper, of Diamond Cottage, Lower Street, Eastry, Dover, by his wife Eliza: *b.* Dover, 1890: served with the Expeditionary Force. Reported missing, 23 October 1914, and now assumed killed on or about that date. Age 24.

(Panel 13) L/Corpl. L/8965, Albert Victor Hungerford, 2nd Bn. (2nd Foot) The Queen's (Royal West Surrey Regt.): late of Camden Town, London, N.W.: served with the Expeditionary Force in France from 6 October 1914; killed in action, 2 November 1914.

(Panel 13) L/Corpl. L/9689, Frank Charles Ironmonger, 2nd Bn. (2nd Foot) The Queen's (Royal West Surrey Regt.): enlisted Chatham, co. Kent: served with the Expeditionary Force. Reported missing 30 October 1914, and now assumed killed.

(Panel 13) L/Corpl. L/7860, Thomas Kaywood, 1st Bn. (2nd Foot) The Queen's (Royal West Surrey Regt.): served with the Expeditionary Force. Reported missing, 31 October 1914, and now assumed killed. *m.*

(Panel 13) L/Corpl. L/8435, Walter Thomas Keeton, 1st Bn. (2nd Foot) The Queen's (Royal West Surrey Regt.): *s.* of Mr (& Mrs) Keeton, of 17, Blue Anchor Lane, Bermondsey, London, S.E.: served with the Expeditionary Force. Reported missing, 31 October 1914, and now assumed killed. Age 27. He leaves a wife, Florence Ellen (7, Durham Hill, Dover).

(Panel 13) L/Corpl. L/7715, Daniel Reilly, 1st Bn. (2nd Foot) The Queen's (Royal West Surrey Regt.): *s.* of Daniel Reilly, of 10, Queen's Row, Walworth, London, S.E., ex-soldier, by his wife Mary: *b.* Walworth, 14 May 1885: *educ.* Sacred Heart School, Camberwell, London, S.E.: enlisted Royal West Surrey Regt., served seven years with the Colours; joined the Reserve; employee London County Council Tramways Dept.; recalled on mobilisation, 5 August 1914: served with the Expeditionary Force in France and Flanders from 6 October 1914; reported wounded and missing after the fighting at Ypres, 31 October 1914, and is now assumed to have been killed in action on or about that date. Age 29. He *m.* at the Sacred Heart Church, Camberwell, 7 July 1907, Ellen (2, Paradise Lane, Peckham, London, S.E., late of 7, Baring Place, Peckham), *dau.* of James Ermes, and had four children. (*IWGC record Pte., age 30*)

(Panel 13) L/Corpl. G/15538, William Voice, M.M., 8th (Service) Bn. The Queen's (Royal West Surrey Regt.): *s.* of William Voice, of 'Ifield House,' Wood Street, Ash Vale, co. Surrey, and Mary Ann Voice: and brother to Ab/S. J/28250, J.V. Voice, HMS 'Marksman,' R.N., died 25 September 1919: *b.* Horsham, 1886: Occupation – Carpenter: served with the Expeditionary Force in France and Flanders from 1916. Killed in action, 1 August 1917. Age 31. He leaves a widow, Agnes Ethel Voice (Portslade-by-the-Sea, co. Sussex), to whom he had been married for nine years.

His brother James is buried in St. Mary's Churchyard, Stockleigh Pomeroy, Devon.

(Panel 13) Pte. L/7834, George Henry Ainsley, 1st Bn. (2nd Foot) The Queen's (Royal West Surrey Regt.): served with the Expeditionary Force in France and Flanders. Reported missing after the fighting on 31 October 1914, and is now assumed to have been killed in action on that date. He *m*. Susan Ainsley (254, Bensham Road, Thornton Heath).

(Panel 13) Pte. L/7045, James Alexander, 1st Bn. (2nd Foot) The Queen's (Royal West Surrey Regt.): *s*. of Rebecca Alexander (5, Napier Street, Deptford, London, S.E.): served with the Expeditionary Force in France, and was killed in action there, 22 October 1914. Age 34.

(Panel 13) Pte. L/8926, Frank Alford, 'D' Coy., 2nd Bn. (2nd Foot) The Queen's (Royal West Surrey Regt.): *s*. of John Alford, of Cowley Farm, Chertsey, co. Surrey, by his wife Hannah: served with the Expeditionary Force in France. Reported missing, and now assumed to have been killed in action, 31 October 1914. Age 25. *unm.*

(Panel 13) Pte. L/10370, William Francis Allen, 1st Bn. (2nd Foot) The Queen's (Royal West Surrey Regt.): *s*. of William Charles (& E.) Allen, of 37, Croydon Grove, West Croydon, co. Surrey (late of 103, Pendevon Road): enlisted Guildford: served with the Expeditionary Force, and was killed in action on the Western Front, 30 October 1914. Age 18.

(Panel 13) Pte. S/5020, George Ernest Alston, 2nd Bn. (2nd Foot) The Queen's (Royal West Surrey Regt.): *s*. of Albert Henry Alston, of 16, Leven Street, West Ham, co. Essex: served with the Expeditionary Force. Killed in action, 7 November 1914. Age 24. *unm.*

(Panel 13) Pte. L/8743, Frederick Ambler, 1st Bn. (2nd Foot) The Queen's (Royal West Surrey Regt.): served with the Expeditionary Force. Reported missing, 31 October 1914; now assumed killed.

(Panel 13) Pte. L/9193, Walter Ernest Atkins, 2nd Bn. (2nd Foot) The Queen's (Royal West Surrey Regt.): *s*. of William Atkins, of 60, Union Street, Canterbury, co. Kent: enlisted Chatham: served with the Expeditionary Force in France, and was killed in action, 7 November 1914; Zillebeke.

(Panel 13) Pte. 8267, Albert Austin, 1st Bn. (2nd Foot) The Queen's (Royal West Surrey Regt.): late *husb.* to Julia May Calloway, *née* Austin (26, Salisbury Road, Noel Park, Wood Green, London, N): served with the Expeditionary Force. Killed in action, 23 October 1914. Age 27.

(Panel 13) Pte. G/39497, Alfred George Austin, 'D' Coy., 10th (Service) Bn. The Queen's (Royal West Surrey Regt.): *s*. of John T. Austin, of 7, Higham Road, Burton Latimer, co. Northampton, by his wife Alice: and brother to Corpl. 8638, P. Austin, 2nd Northamptonshire Regt., who fell 14 March 1915, at the Battle of Neuve Chapelle; and Pte. 3826, H. Austin, 4th Northamptonshire Regt., killed in action, 22 September 1915, at Hill 60, Gallipoli: *b*. Corby, co. Northampton: enlisted Kettering: served with the Expeditionary Force in France and Flanders, and was killed in action, 4 August 1917, nr. Messines. Age 19. A fourth brother, Thomas, served with 2nd Northamptons from 1914 and survived. (*IWGC record 39397*)

His brother Percy also has no known grave, he is commemorated on the Le Touret Memorial; Harry is buried in 7th Field Ambulance Cemetery (IV.E.10).

(Panel 13) Pte. L/8193, Aubrey John Austin, 1st Bn. (2nd Foot) The Queen's (Royal West Surrey Regt.): eldest *s*. of the late Christopher Austin, Engine Driver, by his wife Amy: *b*. Hampstead, London, N.W., 8 August 1886: *educ*. Fleet Road School, Hampstead: enlisted Guildford, co. Surrey, about 1904: served with the Expeditionary Force in France from 12 August 1914, and was reported missing after the fighting around Ypres, 31 October following, and is now assumed to have been killed in action on that day. He was Mentioned in Despatches by F.M. Sir John (now Lord) French (*London Gazette*, 19 October 1914) for 'gallant and distinguished service in the field.' Age 28. He *m*. at Hampstead, 7 November 1910, Lilian Edith Tripp, of 3, Gilpon Terrace, Rock Estate, Oulton Broad, Lowestoft, (since re-married, now Mrs Fox, of 'Lakeview', Harbour Road, Oulton Broad, co. Suffolk), *dau*. of Henry Tripp, late Regtl.Sergt. Major, R.F.A. (with 31 years service), and had two children; Margaret Edith Amy, *b*. 13 August 1911; Henry Aubrey, *b*. 25 February 1913. (*IWGC record A.J.L. Austin, age 26*)

(Panel 13) Pte. L/6238, Alfred Avery, 1st Bn. (2nd Foot) The Queen's (Royal West Surrey Regt.): formerly no.5502, Duke of Edinburgh's (Wiltshire Regt.): *s*. of G. Avery, of 6, North Street, Kennington

Road, London, S.E.: *b*. Lambeth, co. Surrey: served with the Expeditionary Force. Died on service, 31 October 1914. Age 36.

(Panel 13) Pte. L/9858, Edward Bailey, 2nd Bn. (2nd Foot) The Queen's (Royal West Surrey Regt.): *s*. of William Bailey, of 52, Russell Road, Croydon, co. Surrey: served with the Expeditionary Force. Killed in action at Zonnebeke, 21 October 1914.

(Panel 13) Pte. L/8288, William Joseph Basterfield, 1st Bn. (2nd Foot) The Queen's (Royal West Surrey Regt.): *s*. of Joseph Basterfield, of 22, King's Road, Belmont, co. Surrey: *b*. Greenwich, co. Kent, *c*.1885: employee London County Council Education Dept.: enlisted Guildford: served with the Expeditionary Force; reported missing/assumed killed, 31 October 1914, nr. Gheluvelt. He was married to Ellen Basterfield (51, King's Road, Belmont). Age 29.

(Panel 13) Pte. L/9455, John Henry Beer, 2nd Bn. (2nd Foot) The Queen's (Royal West Surrey Regt.): *s*. of George Beer, of 45, Queen's Road, South Farnborough, co. Hants, by his wife Elizabeth: *b*. Gibraltar, Spain, 1888: enlisted Guildford, co. Surrey: served with the Expeditionary Force. Reported missing, 21 October 1914; now assumed killed. Age 26. *unm*.

(Panel 13) Pte. G/829, William Bellfield, 2nd Bn. (2nd Foot) The Queen's (Royal West Surrey Regt.): enlisted Croydon: served with the Expeditionary Force: killed in action at Zillebeke, 7 November 1914. *m*. (*IWGC record S.829*)

(Panel 13) Pte. G/22862, Joseph Bennett, 7th (Service) Bn. The Queen's (Royal West Surrey Regt.): formerly no.44273, King's Own Yorkshire L.I.: *s*. of James Bennett, of 30, Jodrell Street, New Mills: *b*. New Mills, 1891: enlisted Buxton: served with the Expeditionary Force at Gallipoli, and in France and Flanders; killed in action, 10 August 1917, at Ypres, Belgium. Age 26. A lifelong member of the Newtown Wesleyan Chapel, where up until his departure for the war he taught Sunday School, a memorial service was held in Brookbottom Methodist Chapel. He leaves a widow, Mary Ellen Bennett (7, New Street, Upper End, Peak Dale). See account re. Pte. C. Dingvean, below.

(Panel 13) Pte. L/10397, William Henry Biddlecombe, 1st Bn. (2nd Foot) The Queen's (Royal West Surrey Regt.): late of Walton-on-Thames: served with the Expeditionary Force. Reported missing, 31 October 1914; now assumed killed.

(Panel 13) Pte. L/10388, William Bishop, 2nd Bn. (2nd Foot) The Queen's (Royal West Surrey Regt.): *s*. of William Bishop, of 41, Brook Road, Brentford, by his wife Emma: and brother to L/Corpl. 19862, F.G. Bishop, 10th Hampshire Regt., killed in action, 1 September 1918: b. Brentford: enlisted Kingston-on-Thames: served with the Expeditionary Force. Killed in action, 7 November 1914.

His brother Frederick is buried in Karasouli Military Cemetery (C.650).

(Panel 13) Pte. L/7660, Alfred Blackwell, 1st Bn. (2nd Foot) The Queen's (Royal West Surrey Regt.): *b*. Battersea, London, S.W.: enlisted Guildford, co. Surrey: served with the Expeditionary Force. Reported missing, 23 October 1914; now assumed killed.

(Panel 13) Pte. L/9412, William Blackwell, 2nd Bn. (2nd Foot) The Queen's (Royal West Surrey Regt.): late of Harlesden, co. Middlesex: *b*. Willesden, London, N.W.: served with the Expeditionary Force. Killed in action, 31 October 1914.

(Panel 13) Pte. L/10658, John Robert Blake, 2nd Bn. (2nd Foot) The Queen's (Royal West Surrey Regt.): *b*. Southwark, co. Surrey: served with the Expeditionary Force. Killed in action, 21 October 1914.

(Panel 13) Pte. L/6769, Francis George Blanchard, 1st Bn. (2nd Foot) The Queen's (Royal West Surrey Regt.): late of Camberwell, co. Surrey: *b*. Southwark: served with the Expeditionary Force. Died while on Active Service in France, 31 October 1914. *m*.

(Panel 13) Pte. S/8, Timothy Boyle, 2nd Bn. (2nd Foot) The Queen's (Royal West Surrey Regt.): *b*. South Lambeth: enlisted Battersea, London, S.W.: served with the Expeditionary Force in France. Reported missing, 31 October 1914; now assumed killed.

(Panel 13) Pte. L/7200, James Patrick Brett, 1st Bn. (2nd Foot) The Queen's (Royal West Surrey Regt.): *s*. of James Patrick Brett, of 96, Neptune Street, Rotherhithe, London, S.E., by his marriage to the late Henrietta: served with the Expeditionary Force: Reported missing, 31 October 1914, and now assumed killed. *unm*. (*IWGC record L/7300*)

(Panel 13) Pte. L/5967, Joseph Henry Brewer, 1st Bn. (2nd Foot) The Queen's (Royal West Surrey Regt.): late of Lisson Grove, London, W.: served with the Expeditionary Force. Reported missing, 31 October 1914, and now assumed killed. *m.*

(Panel 13) Pte. L/10137, William Bridges, 2nd Bn. (2nd Foot) The Queen's (Royal West Surrey Regt.): *s.* of James John Bridges, of 72, Ealing Road, Brentford, co. Middlesex, by his wife Rosina: *b.* Brentford, *c.*1892: enlisted Hounslow: served with the Expeditionary Force, and was killed in action, 21 October 1914. Age 22. *unm.*

(Panel 13) Pte. L/9550, Albert Edmund Brockwell, 2nd Bn. (2nd Foot) The Queen's (Royal West Surrey Regt.): *s.* of Albert Brockwell, of Chobham, nr. Woking, co. Surrey: enlisted Guildford: served with the Expeditionary Force in France; reported missing, 24 October 1914, now assumed killed.

(Panel 13) Pte. L/7141, George Frederick Brooks, 1st Bn. (2nd Foot) The Queen's (Royal West Surrey Regt.): of Camberwell, London, S.E.: served with the Expeditionary Force. Reported missing, 31 October 1914; now assumed killed. *m.*

(Panel 13) Pte. L/7006, Arthur Richard Brown, 1st Bn. (2nd Foot) The Queen's (Royal West Surrey Regt.): enlisted Guildford, co. Surrey: served with the Expeditionary Force in France, and was killed in action there, 23 October 1914. *m.*

(Panel 13) Pte. L/6960, Robert Browning, 1st Bn. (2nd Foot) The Queen's (Royal West Surrey Regt.): served with the Expeditionary Force. Reported missing, 23 October 1914; assumed killed.

(Panel 13) Pte. L/9044, Reginald Bryant, 2nd Bn. (2nd Foot) The Queen's (Royal West Surrey Regt.): *s.* of Alfred Bryant, of Keephills, Alberta, Canada, by his wife Alice: *b.* Farnham, co. Surrey, *c.*1890: served with the Expeditionary Force. Reported wounded and missing in action, 7 November 1914; now assumed killed. Age 24. *unm.* His brothers George and Thomas also served; both survived.

(Panel 13) Pte. L/9955, Edgar Buckland, 2nd Bn. (2nd Foot) The Queen's (Royal West Surrey Regt.): *s.* of Arthur Buckland, of Springfield Cottage, Baldwin's Hill, East Grinstead, co. Surrey: served with the Expeditionary Force. Killed in action, 22 October 1914.

(Panel 13) Pte. L/9473, Albert Buckle, 2nd Bn. (2nd Foot) The Queen's (Royal West Surrey Regt.): *s.* of Philip Buckle, of 10, Hounslow Road, Whitton, co. Middlesex, by his wife Mary Ann: served with the Expeditionary Force, and was killed in action at Zonnebeke, Flanders, 21 October 1914. Age 25. *unm.*

(Panel 13) Pte. L/9838, William Bull, 2nd Bn. (2nd Foot) The Queen's (Royal West Surrey Regt.): *s.* of Harry Bull, of 3, Home Cottages, Distillery Lane, Hammersmith, London, W., by his wife Mary: served with the Expeditionary Force. Reported missing, 7 November 1914, and now assumed killed. Age 21. *unm.*

(Panel 13) Pte. S/5657, William Thomas Burkin, 2nd Bn. (2nd Foot) The Queen's (Royal West Surrey Regt.): *s.* of George Burkin, of Walworth, London, S.E.: served with the Expeditionary Force. Reported missing, 21 October 1914; assumed killed.

(Panel 13) Pte. 5912, Frederick William Butler, 1st Bn. (2nd Foot) The Queen's (Royal West Surrey Regt.): *s.* of William Butler, Carpenter; of Bracknell, nr. Ascot, by his wife Elizabeth: *b.* Bracknell, co. Berks, 29 May 1882: *educ.* Bracknell National School: enlisted, 18 February 1899: served (1) in the South African War, 1899–1902 (Queen's & King's Medals), (2) with the Expeditionary Force in France from 6 October 1914, and was killed in action at Ypres, Flanders on the 21st. of that month, and buried at Langemarck: 21 October 1914. Age 32. *unm.*

(Panel 13) Pte. L/6747, Henry James Cahill, 1st Bn. (2nd Foot) The Queen's (Royal West Surrey Regt.): served with the Expeditionary Force in France. Reported missing, 31 October 1914, and now assumed killed. *m.*

(Panel 13) Pte. S/6813, William Robert Cane, 2nd Bn. (2nd Foot) The Queen's (Royal West Surrey Regt.): served with the Expeditionary Force. Killed in action, 3 November 1914. *m.*

(Panel 13) Pte. L/8564, William Canfield, 1st Bn. (2nd Foot) The Queen's (Royal West Surrey Regt.): *s.* of Sarah Ann Wales (Stone Cottage, Old Oxted, co. Surrey): served with the Expeditionary Force. Killed in action, 23 October 1914. Age 30.

(Panel 13) Pte. S/6299, Charles Thomas Cantwell, 2nd Bn. (2nd Foot) The Queen's (Royal West Surrey Regt.): *s.* of the late George Edward Cantwell, Labourer; of 'Sunnydene,' Birdhurst Rise,

Croydon, co. Surrey, by his wife Mary Jane (1, Oakwood Road, West Croydon), *dau.* of Joseph Copeman: *b.* Waddon, co. Surrey, 5 March 1894: *educ.* Boston Road County Council School, Croydon: enlisted 11 November 1913: went to France 5 October 1914, and was killed at the First Battle of Ypres, 7 November following. Age 20. *unm.*

(Panel 13) Pte. L/7174, Arthur William Carman, 1st Bn. (2nd Foot) The Queen's Royal West Surrey Regt.): served with the Expeditionary Force. Died of wounds received in action at Langemarck, 22 October 1914.

(Panel 13) Pte. G/272, George Cawson, 2nd Bn. (2nd Foot) The Queen's (Royal West Surrey Regt.): *s.* of Tom (& Mrs E.T.) Cawson, of Brickfield Cottages, Wanborough, Guildford, co. Surrey: served with the Expeditionary Force. Killed in action, 7 November 191. Age 33.

(Panel 13) Pte. L/7299, Arthur Ernest Chamberlain, 1st Bn. (2nd Foot) The Queen's (Royal West Surrey Regt.): 5th *s.* of William Chamberlain, of 119, S.Block, Fulham Palace Road, London, S.W., by his wife Sophia, *dau.* of Charles Mathews: *b.* Wandsworth, London, S.W., 19 December 1876: *educ.* Wandsworth: served some years with the Colours, thereafter worked as a Storeman: called up from the Reserve on mobilisation, 4 August 1914: served with the Expeditionary Force in France and Flanders, and was reported missing after the fighting, 31 October following, and is now assumed to have been killed in action on that day. Age 37. *unm.*

(Panel 13) Pte. 10599, Francis H. Chambers, 2nd Bn. (2nd Foot) The Queen's (Royal West Surrey Regt.): *s.* of Francis Chambers, of Guildford, co. Surrey: served with the Expeditionary Force. Reported missing, 7 November. 1914; assumed killed.

(Panel 13) Pte. 7812, Frank Cleverley, 1st Bn. (2nd Foot) The Queen's (Royal West Surrey Regt.): only child of the late John Thomas Cleverley, by his wife Eliza (24, Howley Road, Croydon), *dau.* of John Eyles: *b.* London, 4 November 1884: *educ.* London and Croydon: enlisted about 1900: served in India and Bermuda, and with the Expeditionary Force in France from August 1914: slightly wounded, 19 September; and killed in action, 31 October 1914, four days short of his thirtieth year. Age 29. (*IWGC record Cleverly*)

(Panel 13) Pte. L/10279, William Thomas Cocup, 'C' Coy., 1st Bn. (2nd Foot) The Queen's (Royal West Surrey Regt.): *s.* of H.G. (& Mrs) Cocup, of Cherry Tree Cottage, 1, South Street, Dartford, co. Kent: served with the Expeditionary Force. Reported wounded and missing, 31 October 1914; now assumed killed. Age 23. *unm.*

(Panel 13) Pte. L/10624, Cecil Harry Coffin, 2nd Bn. (2nd Foot) The Queen's (Royal West Surrey Regt.): late of Woking, co. Surrey: served with the Expeditionary Force. Killed in action, 7 November 1914.

(Panel 13) Pte. 9054, George Frederick Cole, 2nd Bn. (2nd Foot) The Queen's (Royal West Surrey Regt.): eldest *s.* of the late Fred Cole, of 'Sunnyfield,' Lower Bourne, Surrey, Gardener, by his wife Alice (Middle Bourne, Farnham), *dau.* of George Geoffrey: *b.* Tilford, near Farnham, co. Surrey, 6 October 1890: *educ.* Bourne Council School, Farnham: enlisted April 1907; served with his regiment in Gibraltar, Bermuda and South Africa, from whence he returned to England, and proceeded to France on the outbreak of war, and was killed in action there, 7 November 1914. He was in possession of first class certificates for swimming and shooting. Age 24. (*IWGC record L/9054*)

(Panel 13) Pte. L/9496, Harry Collins, 2nd Bn. (2nd Foot) The Queen's (Royal West Surrey Regt.): served with the Expeditionary Force. Reported missing, 29 October 1914, and now assumed killed.

(Panel 13) Pte. 6118, Richard Collins, 2nd Bn. (2nd Foot) The Queen's (Royal West Surrey Regt.): *s.* of Mrs Southion (16, Godman Road, Rye Lane, Peckham, London, S.E.): served with the Expeditionary Force. Reported missing, 7 November 1914, and now assumed killed. Age 18. (*IWGC record S/6118*)

(Panel 13) Pte. L/8602, Thomas Edward Cook, 1st Bn. (2nd Foot) The Queen's (Royal West Surrey Regt.): *s.* of William John Cook, of 35, Sewardstone Road, Bethnal Green, London, E., by his wife Kate Elizabeth: served with the Expeditionary Force. Reported missing, 31 October 1914, and now assumed killed. Age 26. *unm.* Remembered on St. James the Less Parish Church War Memorial Roll of Honour.

(Panel 13) Pte. S/4403, Albert Cox, 2nd Bn. (2nd Foot) The Queen's (Royal West Surrey Regt.): served with the Expeditionary Force. Reported missing, 7 November 1914; assumed killed.

(Panel 13) Pte. L/10375, Frederick John Cox, 'D' Coy., 1st Bn. (2nd Foot) The Queen's (Royal West Surrey Regt.): *s.* of C.D. Cox, of 4, Pettram Court Cottages, Swanley Junction, co. Kent, by his wife Alice: *b.* Worthing, co. Sussex: served with the Expeditionary Force. Died (believed killed) in action, 31 October 1914. Age 19.

(Panel 13) Pte. S/5131, George Ernest Cox, 2nd Bn. (2nd Foot) The Queen's (Royal West Surrey Regt.): *s.* of William Cox, of Bath Road, Tetbury, co. Gloucester: enlisted Croydon, co. Surrey: served with the Expeditionary Force. Reported missing, 7 November 1914, and now assumed killed. Age 27. *unm.*

(Panel 13) Pte. L/8044, Joseph Robert Cox, 1st Bn. (2nd Foot) The Queen's (Royal West Surrey Regt.): served with the Expeditionary Force. Reported missing, 31 October 1914, assumed (Court of Enquiry, 1916) killed in action on or about that date.

(Panel 13) Pte. G/23107, Charles Richard Crawford, 8th (Service) Bn. The Queen's (Royal West Surrey Regt.): late of Benington, co. Hertford. Killed in action, 30 July 1917. A comrade, in a letter to his mother, wrote, "5 August 1917 … It is with deepest sympathy and regret that I am writing to tell you the painful news of the death in action of your son Richard. I have known your son since he joined the army, as he joined up the same time as I did. He was very popular amongst his chums, and we believe he thought a lot about his home and parents. His loss has cast a feeling of deep regard amongst his pals, and they join me in sending their deepest and heartfelt sympathy. He was shot through the chest on the field on battle. I do not think he suffered much pain. It can truly be said he died a hero fighting for liberty and justice. I believe it will be some consolation to you to know that he fell doing his duty…."

(Panel 13) Pte. S/6545, George Frederick Croft, 2nd Bn. (2nd Foot) The Queen's (Royal West Surrey Regt.): *s.* of Harriet Lucy Young, *née* Croft (83, Victoria Road, Bromley, co. Kent): Reported missing, 21 October 1914; now assumed killed. Age 18.

(Panel 13) Pte. 9170, Thomas Richard Keats Cuff, 2nd Bn. (2nd Foot) The Queen's (Royal West Surrey Regt.): *s.* of Richard 'Dick' Cuff, of 1, Camden Terrace, Heath End, Farnham, co. Surrey, by his wife Harriett Ann: served with the Expeditionary Force. Killed in action, 7 November 1914. Age 25.

(Panel 13) Pte. L/9649, William Alfred Daniels, 1st Bn. (2nd Foot) The Queen's (Royal West Surrey Regt.). Reported missing, 31 October 1914, and now assumed killed. *m.*

(Panel 13) Pte. L/8674, Henry Thomas Davey, 2nd Bn. (2nd Foot) The Queen's (Royal West Surrey Regt.): *s.* of the late Alfred George Davey, by his marriage to Emma Sophia: served with the Expeditionary Force. Died 7 November 1914. Age 34.

(Panel 13) Pte. L/8784, James Davis, 1st Bn. (2nd Foot) The Queen's (Royal West Surrey Regt.): served with the Expeditionary Force. Died 31 October 1914.

(Panel 13) Pte. L/9842, William Davis, 1st Bn. (2nd Foot) The Queen's (Royal West Surrey Regt.): served with the Expeditionary Force. Killed in action, 21 October 1914. *m.*

(Panel 13) Pte. L/8963, James Deeley, 1st Bn. (2nd Foot) The Queen's (Royal West Surrey Regt.): *s.* of W.H. (& Mrs) Deeley, of 4, Haymarket, London, W.: served with the Expeditionary Force in France. Reported missing, 31 October 1914; now assumed killed. Age 23. *unm.*

(Panel 13) Pte. L/6234, George Ernest Dennis, 1st Bn. (2nd Foot) The Queen's (Royal West Surrey Regt.): served with the Expeditionary Force. Reported missing, 31 October 1914; now assumed killed.

(Panel 13) Pte. L/9613, Ernest Frank Dicker, 2nd Bn. (2nd Foot) The Queen's (Royal West Surrey Regt.): *s.* of Elias Dicker, of New Barn Cottage, Nore Lane, Hascombe: *b.* Godalming, co. Surrey, *c.*1891: served with the Expeditionary Force. Killed in action, 31 October 1914. Age 23. *unm.*

(Panel 13) Pte. L/6667, Henry Joseph Dimmock, 1st Bn. (2nd Foot) The Queen's (Royal West Surrey Regt.): served with the Expeditionary Force. Reported missing, 31 October 1914; now assumed killed. *m.* 4 August 1917. After four days heavy and incessant rain, during which period 7th Queen's had received a draft of replacements, the battalion moved up with the West Kents into the old Sanctuary Wood trenches. For the newcomers it was a frightful apprenticeship to Active Service. Nothing went smoothly; it was a pouring wet night; there were casualties on the way, 'C' and 'D' Companies losing heavily; the trenches had been shelled or swilled away, and an adjustment of some 100 yards was needed to put the line where it appeared to be on the official chart. In preparation for an attack planned for August 10th, 7th Queen's were designated assaulting battalion on the right of the Brigade's front. As in so many instances before and after, the enemy not only knew what was coming and when but had put out a fresh line of wired posts very near to the Queen's forming up tapes. Some of the Queen's, stealing forward under cover of darkness, collided noisily with these posts with the result that green flares immediately shot skyward from the German lines, illuminating the hapless Queens as a heavy rifle fire and artillery barrage was unleashed on them. As disorganised gaps appeared in the right company, and two platoons of the left company were also caught, the havoc was accentuated by a second German barrage which fell almost on the stroke of zero hour. Amazingly, the surviving officers and non-commissioned officers managed to form a line from the remaining fragments of the battalion and jumped off at their given signal! One platoon of the right company of the Queen's, on reaching their objective at the south-west corner of Inverness Copse, found it protected by a machine gun post and well guarded tunnel. All but one who reached the wood at this point had become casualties. Further north, high numbers of casualties and lack of support dictated 2nd Lieut. J.H. Wilson (the only unwounded officer by this time) to withdraw to the north-west. Incredibly, despite the lack of numbers he had at his command, Wilson managed to successfully organise an attack on a concrete emplacement and take a party into Jasper Lane trench in the wood where, with the aid of two Vickers guns, he held on until relieved eighteen hours later. The attack on Inverness Copse and Glencorse Wood failed, and, under the circumstances, it is difficult to see how success could have been expected. During this fighting the casualties incurred by the battalion amounted to 10 officers and 272 other ranks killed, wounded and missing.

(Panel 13) Pte. G/5592, Charles Dingvean, 7th (Service) Bn. The Queen's (Royal West Surrey Regt.): late of Tooting, London, S.W.: enlisted Lambeth: served with the Expeditionary Force. Killed in action, 10 August 1917. One of eighty other ranks of his battalion known to have been killed in action that day.

(Panel 13) Pte. L/9560, Alfred Dinnage, 2nd Bn. (2nd Foot) The Queen's (Royal West Surrey Regt.): *s.* of Albert Dinnage, of 16, Queen's Street, Horsham, co. Sussex, by his wife Mary: enlisted Guildford, co. Surrey: served with the Expeditionary Force. Killed in action, 7 November 1914. Age 22. *unm.*

(Panel 13) Pte. L/10516, Frederick 'Fred' Drage, 2nd Bn. (2nd Foot) The Queen's (Royal West Surrey Regt.): *s.* of Eliza Drage (11, Cannon Street, Wisbech, co. Cambridge): served with the Expeditionary Force. Killed in action at Zonnebeke, 21 October 1914. Remembered on Wisbech 1914–18 War Memorial. (*IWGC record L/10518*)

(Panel 13) Pte. L/10464, William Arthur Victor Drake, 2nd Bn. (2nd Foot) The Queen's (Royal West Surrey Regt.): *s.* of Arthur Drake, of Brighton, co. Sussex: served with the Expeditionary Force. Killed in action, 30 October 1914, during the First Battle of Ypres.

(Panel 13) Pte. L/5119, William Draper, 1st Bn. (2nd Foot) The Queen's (Royal West Surrey Regt.): late of Godalming, co. Surrey: enlisted Deepcut, co. Hants: served with the Expeditionary Force. Died 31 October 1914, believed killed nr. Ypres.

(Panel 13) Pte. L/8995, Joseph Driscoll, 2nd Bn. (2nd Foot) The Queen's (Royal West Surrey Regt.): *s.* of Timothy Driscoll, of Whitechapel, London, E.C.: served with the Expeditionary Force, and was killed in action, 29 October 1914.

(Panel 13) Pte. L/10041, Harry Durrant, 2nd Bn. (2nd Foot) The Queen's (Royal West Surrey Regt.): *s.* of Thomas Durrant, of Guildford: served with the Expeditionary Force. Reported missing, 7 November 1914; now assumed killed.

(Panel 13) Pte. L/9214, Sidney Eade, 2nd Bn. (2nd Foot) The Queen's (Royal West Surrey Regt.): *s.* of James Eade, of Upper Bourne, nr. Farnham, co. Surrey: served with the Expeditionary Force. Killed in action at Gheluvelt, 30 October 1914.

(Panel 13) Pte. L/10242, Herbert Eades, 2nd Bn. (2nd Foot) The Queen's (Royal West Surrey Regt.): *s.* of Fanny Eades (Hartford Bridge, Hartley Wintney, co. Hants): enlisted Guildford, co. Surrey: served with the Expeditionary Force. Died 7 November 1914. Age 22. *unm.* The Hartley Wintney War Memorial is dedicated – 'Being Dead They Live, Being Silent They Speak': Pte. Eades is one of 83 villagers remembered thereon (+20 WWII).

(Panel 13) Pte. L/8611, Alfred Ernest Earl, 'C' Coy., 1st Bn. (2nd Foot) The Queen's (Royal West Surrey Regt.): *s.* of Alfred Earl, of Beeley Lodge, nr. Rousley, co. Derby, by his wife Sarah E. (The Green, Matlock): served with the Expeditionary Force. Reported missing, 31 October 1914; (Court of Enquiry, 1916) assumed killed. Age 27. *unm.*

(Panel 13) Pte. L/10192, Albert David Easterbrook, 2nd Bn. (2nd Foot) The Queen's (Royal West Surrey Regt.): *s.* of Albert Easterbrook, of Thornton Heath, co. Surrey: enlisted Croydon: served with the Expeditionary Force. Killed in action at Ypres, 6 November 1914.

(Panel 13) Pte. L/10255, Charles Edward Framfield Eastwood, 'C' Coy., 1st Bn. (2nd Foot) The Queen's (Royal West Surrey Regt.): *s.* of Charles Edmund Eastwood, of Buxted Wood, Buxted, co. Sussex, by his wife Ruth: and elder brother to Boy 2/C, J92268, F. Eastwood, HMS 'Powerful,' R.N., died 28 December 1918, aged 18 years: a pre-war Regular; enlisted Chichester, proceeded to France, 13 August 1914, served with the Expeditionary Force there, and was killed in action, 31 October following, nr. Windmill, Gheluvelt. Age 20. *unm.*His brother Frank is buried in Buxted (St. Mary's) Churchyard.

(Panel 13) Pte. L/8971, Frederick William Howard Eccles, 2nd Bn. (2nd Foot) The Queen's (Royal West Surrey Regt.): only *s.* of the late Thomas (& Fanny) Eccles, of 36, Deerings Road, Reigate, co. Surrey: *b.* Stoughton, co. Surrey: enlisted Hounslow, co. Middlesex, 1906, aged 14 years: served with the Expeditionary Force in France, and was killed in action at Ypres, 31 October 1914. Age 22. *unm.*

(Panel 13) Pte. L/7960, Philip Walter Edges, 1st Bn. (2nd Foot) The Queen's (Royal West Surrey Regt.): *s.* of Philip Edges, of 26, Red Lion Street, Wapping, London, by his wife Dora: served with the Expeditionary Force. Reported missing, 31 October 1914; now assumed killed. Age 26. *unm.*

(Panel 13) Pte. L/9342, James Ediker, 2nd Bn. (2nd Foot) The Queen's (Royal West Surrey Regt.): *s.* of the late James (& Mrs) Ediker, of Battersea, London, S.W.: served with the Expeditionary Force. Died 29 October 1914, believed killed; Ypres, Belgium. Age 36.

(Panel 13) Pte. L/7867, Charles James Edwards, 1st Bn. (2nd Foot) The Queen's (Royal West Surrey Regt.): served with the Expeditionary Force. Reported missing, 31 October 1914; now assumed killed. Pte. Edwards leaves a daughter, Miss M.A. Edwards (184, Leander Road, Brixton Hill, London, S.E.).

(Panel 13) Pte. L/9701, Albert Eldridge, 2nd Bn. (2nd Foot) The Queen's (Royal West Surrey Regt.): *s.* of William Eldridge, of Black Cottage, Grange Farm, Boxley, Maidstone, by his wife Mary Ann: served with the Expeditionary Force. Killed in action, 7 November 1914. Age 25. *unm.*

(Panel 13) Pte. L/9630, Alfred Ellis, 2nd Bn. (2nd Foot) The Queen's (Royal West Surrey Regt.): *s.* of Abel Ellis, by his wife Emily: served with the Expeditionary Force. Reported missing, 7 November 1914, now assumed killed. Age 22. *unm.*

(Panel 13) Pte. G/14931, Fred Etchells, 7th (Service) Bn. The Queen's (Royal West Surrey Regt.): *s.* of Fred Etchells, of Thornton House, Cote Green, Marple Bridge, Stockport, by his wife Fanny. Killed in action, 16 July 1917, at Sanctuary Wood by the explosion of a shell; L/Sergt. S.J.A. Palmer and Pte. G/21195, B. Press were also killed. Age 21. *unm.*

(Panel 13) Pte. S/6552, Walter John Etchells, 2nd Bn. (2nd Foot) The Queen's (Royal West Surrey Regt.): *s.* of George Etchells, of Woolwich, London, S.E.: served with the Expeditionary Force. Reported missing, 7 November 1914, now assumed killed.

(Panel 13) Pte. S/6687, Henry Etherington, 2nd Bn. (2nd Foot) The Queen's (Royal West Surrey Regt.): *s.* of the late J. Etherington, by his wife Ellen (51, Claremont Street, Greenwich, London, S.E.): and brother to Pte. L/9894, G. Etherington, Royal Fusiliers, killed in action, 11 November 1914, and L/Corpl. 11430, C. Etherington, Wiltshire Regt, who also fell: served with the Expeditionary Force. Died 29 October 1914. Age 23. *unm.*

His brother George also has no known grave, he is recorded on Panel 6; Charles is buried in Kemmel Chateau Military Cemetery (M.11).

(Panel 13) Pte. G/6105, Albert Fewster, 1st Bn. (2nd Foot) The Queen's (Royal West Surrey Regt.): late *husb.* to Grace Fewster: served with the Expeditionary Force. Reported missing, 31 October 1914, and now assumed killed. Age 38.

(Panel 13) Pte. L/10078, Edwin Field, 1st Bn. (2nd Foot) The Queen's (Royal West Surrey Regt.): *s.* of Thomas Field, of Uxbridge, co. Middlesex: served with the Expeditionary Force. Killed in action, 23 October 1914.

(Panel 13) Pte. L/6397, George Fisher, 1st Bn. (2nd Foot) The Queen's (Royal West Surrey Regt.): served with the Expeditionary Force. Killed in action, 23 October 1914. *m.*

(Panel 13) Pte. L/9370, Randolph Foote, 2nd Bn. (2nd Foot) The Queen's (Royal West Surrey Regt.): *s.* of George Foote, of Aldershot: served with the Expeditionary Force. Killed in action, 19 October 1914.

(Panel 13) Pte. G/23060, Samuel John Froment, 10th (Service) Bn. The Queen's (Royal West Surrey Regt.): formerly no.125734, Army Service Corps: *yst. s.* of Arthur Froment, of High Street, Swavesey, co. Cambridge: Occupation – Attendant; St.Audrey's Mental Asylum, Melton, nr. Woodbridge, co. Suffolk: enlisted A.S.C., Ipswich, co. Suffolk, as a Baker, 6 August 1915; having for many years been a Baker at Swavesey and, prior to his present position, at Huntingdon: transfd. Infantry Training March 1916, temporarily attd. Border Regt.; proceeded to France, 28 June 1917, served with the Expeditionary Force there and in Flanders until his death in action at Hollebeke, Belgium, 5 August following. His Company Commander wrote to his widow (*m.* 15 September 1915), "It is with extreme sorrow that I have to inform you that your husband, Pte. S.J. Froment, was killed in action on the 5th August while doing his duty. He had not been with the company very long, but it was long enough to prove him a good and willing soldier, and his loss will be felt by all the company. He was killed instantaneously, and was buried within our lines." (*IWGC record 6 August*)

(Panel 13) Pte. L/6526, William John Frost, 1st Bn. (2nd Foot) The Queen's (Royal West Surrey Regt.): *s.* of Elizabeth A. Frost (7, Marlborough Road, Wealdstone, Harrow, co. Middlesex): served in the South African Campaign, and with the Expeditionary Force in France and Flanders. Died 31 October 1914; Ypres. Age 33.

(Panel 13) Pte. L/7936, Frederick James Gearey, 'A' Coy., 1st Bn. (2nd Foot) The Queen's (Royal West Surrey Regt.): *s.* of Charles Gearey, of Lambeth: enlisted Walworth, London, S.E.: served with the Expeditionary Force. Reported missing, 31 October 1914, and now assumed killed. Age 28. He was married to Alice Louise More, *née* Gearey (57, Inville Road, Walworth).

(Panel 13) Pte. G/15325, Joseph James Gerred, 8th (Service) Bn. The Queen's (Royal West Surrey Regt.): formerly no.5435, Royal Fusiliers: *yst. s.* of William John Gerred, of 16, Raynham Terrace, Upper Edmonton, London, N., by his wife Emily Jane, *dau.* of Charles Algar: *b.* 17, Phoenix Street, St. Pancras, London, N., 26 June 1893: *educ.* Raynham Road Board School, Upper Edmonton: Occupation – Munition Worker: enlisted 12th Royal Fusiliers, Tottenham, September 1914: transf'd. Army Cyclist Corps; subsequently Royal West Surrey Regt.: served with the Expeditionary Force in France and Flanders from 1915; killed in action at Passchendaele, 31 July 1917. Buried where he fell. Age 23. *unm.*

(Panel 13) Pte. L/9996, Albert Gibb, 2nd Bn. (2nd Foot) The Queen's (Royal West Surrey Regt.): *s.* of James Gibb, of 82, Quicks Road, South Wimbledon, London, S.W., by his wife Susan: served with the Expeditionary Force. Killed in action, 21 October 1914. Age 25. *unm.*

(Panel 13) Pte. L/8544, Albert Goddard, 1st Bn. (2nd Foot) The Queen's (Royal West Surrey Regt.): of Ash, co. Surrey: served with the Expeditionary Force, and was killed in action, 31 October 1914; Gheluvelt.

(Panel 13) Pte. G/7745, Hubert Arthur Goodwin, 7th (Service) Bn. The Queen's (Royal West Surrey Regt.): late of Broadstairs, co. Kent: *b.* Margate: enlisted Canterbury. Killed in action, 16 July 1917; Sanctuary Wood.

(Panel 13) Pte. L/7676, George William Goulding, 1st Bn. (2nd Foot) The Queen's (Royal West Surrey Regt.): served with the Expeditionary Force. Killed in action at Ypres, 29 October 1914. *m.*

(Panel 13) Pte. L/8040, Charles Grainger, 'A' Coy., 1st Bn. (2nd Foot) The Queen's (Royal West Surrey Regt.): *s.* of the late Samuel Grainger, by his wife Eliza (17, Crimea Road, Aldershot): served with the Expeditionary Force. Reported missing, 31 October 1914; assumed killed. Age 26. *unm.*

(Panel 13) Pte. 8289, Henry John Grainsford, 1st Bn. (2nd Foot) The Queen's (Royal West Surrey Regt.): *s.* of Mrs F.E. Grainsford (Lower Dairy, Okehurst, Billingshurst, co. Sussex): served with the Expeditionary Force. Reported missing, 31 October 1914; assumed killed. Age 29. *unm.*

(Panel 13) Pte. L/6231, Percy Lewis Green, 1st Bn. (2nd Foot) The Queen's (Royal West Surrey Regt.): enlisted Guildford, co. Surrey: served with the Expeditionary Force. Reported missing, 31 October 1914; assumed killed.

(Panel 13) Pte. L/5976, Henry Greenstreet, 1st Bn. (2nd Foot) The Queen's (Royal West Surrey Regt.): served with the Expeditionary Force. Reported missing, 31 October 1914; now assumed killed. He was married to Nellie Hannah Greenstreet (17, Sansom Street, Camberwell, London, S.E.5).

(Panel 13) Pte. L/6196, William Grevitt, 1st Bn. (2nd Foot) The Queen's (Royal West Surrey Regt.): enlisted Guildford, co. Surrey: served with the Expeditionary Force. Killed in action, 31 October 1914.

(Panel 13) Pte. G/9676, William Edward Timothy Guilfoy, 11th (Service) Bn. The Queen's (Royal West Surrey Regt.): *s.* of William Guilfoy, of 22, Corunna Road, New Road, Battersea, London, by his wife Jane: and yr. brother to Rfn. 392195, J. Guilfoy, Queen Victoria's Rifles, killed in action, 16 August 1917: *b.* Battersea: served with the Expeditionary Force. Killed in action, 1 August 1917. Age 21. *unm.*

His brother John also has no known grave; he is recorded on Panel 54.

(Panel 13) Pte. L/10246, Arthur Gunn, 2nd Bn. (2nd Foot) The Queen's (Royal West Surrey Regt.): *b.* Romford, co. Essex: served with the Expeditionary Force. Reported wounded and missing, 30 October 1914; now assumed to have been killed in action on or about that date.

(Panel 13) Pte. L/8268, Harry Charles Haddrill, 1st Bn. (2nd Foot) The Queen's (Royal West Surrey Regt.) *s.* of George Haddrill, by his wife Lucy: served with the Expeditionary Force. Reported missing, 31 October 1914; now assumed killed. Age 29. He leaves a wife, Sophie Nancy (Lower Street, Ninfield, Battle, co. Sussex). On 31 July 1917, 11th Queen's (123rd Bde.) attacked north of the canal and, moving forward with the barrage, 'captured their first objective without any real difficulty.' However, about 300 yards from their final objective the Battalion encountered three strongly defended German blockhouses, upon which the British barrage had 'made little or no impression, and their capture by infantry bordered on the impossible.' Two parties of the Queen's managed to get within 50 yards but, after suffering heavy casualties, were forced to withdraw; by the end of the day the Queen's had incurred over 200 casualties. The following day, August 1st, the battalion were relieved but not before losing another 43 killed:-

(Panel 13) Pte. G/18440, Robert Henry Hall, 11th (Service) Bn. The Queen's (Royal West Surrey Regt.): enlisted Mitcham, co. Surrey. Killed in action, 1 August 1917.

(Panel 13) Pte. L/8872, Thomas Hall, 1st Bn. (2nd Foot) The Queen's (Royal West Surrey Regt.): *s.* of Edward Hall, of 13, Foreign Street, Camberwell, London, S.E.5, by his wife Sarah Ann: served with the Expeditionary Force. Reported missing, 31 October 1914, and now assumed killed. Age 27.

(Panel 13) Pte. L/6209, Henry Hammond, 1st Bn. (2nd Foot) The Queen's (Royal West Surrey Regt.): of Limehouse, co. Middlesex: served with the Expeditionary Force. Reported missing, 31 October 1914; now assumed killed. *m.*

(Panel 13) Pte. L/947, Hugh Frederick George Hancock, 2nd Bn. (2nd Foot) The Queen's (Royal West Surrey Regt.): *s.* of Thomas B.J. Hancock, of 3, St. Margaret's Villas, Elmers End, Beckenham, by his wife Margaret: served with the Expeditionary Force. Killed in action at Gheluvelt, 30 October 1914. Age 29.

(Panel 13) Pte. L/6226, John Harding, 1st Bn. (2nd Foot) The Queen's (Royal West Surrey Regt.): *s.* of Stephen Harding, of Liss, co. Hants: served with the Expeditionary Force. Reported missing, 31 October 1914; now assumed killed. Age 33.

(Panel 13) Pte. G/14837, Leslie Robert Abbot Hasketh, 8th Bn. The Queen's (Royal West Surrey Regt.): formerly G/15226, Royal West Kent Regt.: only *s.* of Robert George Hasketh, of 17A, St. Matthew's Street, Ipswich, co. Suffolk, by his wife Beatrice Mary, *née* Abbot: *b.* Littlehampton, co. Sussex: enlisted Ipswich: served with the Expeditionary Force. Killed in action, 14 June 1917. Age 19. Pte. Hasketh was the last male in the lineage of the ancient Abbot family of Devon.

(Panel 13) Pte. L/6356, Frederick Haver, 1st Bn. (2nd Foot) The Queen's (Royal West Surrey Regt.): served with the Expeditionary Force in France. Reported missing, 31 October 1914, and now assumed killed. Age 34. He leaves a wife Annie Haver (52, Queens Crescent, Kentish Town, London, N.W.5).

(Panel 13) Pte. L/9152, Frederick Frank Hayward, 'D' Coy., 2nd Bn. (2nd Foot) The Queen's (Royal West Surrey Regt.): *s.* of the late Sydney Hayward, and his widow Mercy Leigh, *née* Hayward (5, Mitchell's Cottage, Chilworth, Blackheath): and elder brother to Pte. 2301, H.J. Hayward, 6th Queen's, died of wounds, 24 August 1917: *b*. Chilworth: enlisted Guildford. Killed in action, 7 November 1914. Age 24. *unm*. Recorded on the Wonersh (St. John the Baptist) Parish Church Roll of Honour.

His brother Henry is buried in Monchy British Cemetery (I.K.27).

(Panel 13) Pte. S/6742, Charles Heather, 2nd Bn. (2nd Foot) The Queen's (Royal West Surrey Regt.): *s*. of Eliza Heather (Fleet, co. Hants): enlisted Guildford, co. Surrey: served with the Expeditionary Force. Reported missing, 7 November 1914; now assumed killed. Age 27.

(Panel 13) Pte. L/8980, James William Heather, 2nd Bn. (2nd Foot) The Queen's (Royal West Surrey Regt.): *s*. of James Heather, of Jordon's Crossing, Woking: enlisted Guildford, co. Surrey: served with the Expeditionary Force. Reported missing, 27 October 1914, and now assumed killed. Age 34.

(Panel 13) Pte. L/9587, Herbert Henry Higgins, 2nd Bn. (2nd Foot) The Queen's (Royal West Surrey Regt.): s. of Robert Higgins, of 28, Alwyns Lane, Chertsey, co. Surrey, late of Stevenage, co. Hertford, by his wife Mary: enlisted Guildford, co. Surrey: served with the Expeditionary Force. Killed in action at Ypres, 27 October 1914.

(Panel 13) Pte. L/8419, Henry Hill, 1st Bn. (2nd Foot) The Queen's (Royal West Surrey Regt.): *s*. of the late George Hill, by his wife Sarah (3, Pink Cottages, Mitford, co. Surrey): enlisted Guildford: served with the Expeditionary Force. Reported missing, 21 October 1914, believed killed. Age 26. *unm*.

(Panel 13) Pte. G/7620, William John Hilleard, 11th (Service) Bn. The Queen's (Royal West Surrey Regt.): *s*. of the late William Hilleard, by his wife Charlotte Maria (27, Dean's Buildings, Flint Street, Walworth, London, S.E.): *b*. Bermondsey: enlisted Southwark. Killed in action, 26 July 1917. Age 27. *unm*.

(Panel 13) Pte. L/6705, Arthur Edward Hogan, 2nd Bn. (2nd Foot) The Queen's (Royal West Surrey Regt.): late of Islington, London, N.: served with the Expeditionary Force. Reported missing, 31 October 1914, and now assumed killed.

(Panel 13) Pte. L/9069, Arthur Hoggins, 2nd Bn. (2nd Foot) The Queen's (Royal West Surrey Regt.): *b*. Charlton, co. Northampton: enlisted Guildford, co. Surrey: served with the Expeditionary Force in France, and was killed in action there, 7 November 1914.

(Panel 13) Pte. L/9621, Arthur Hollick, 2nd Bn. (2nd Foot) The Queen's (Royal West Surrey Regt.): *s*. of John Hollick, of Chertsey, co. Surrey: enlisted Guildford, co. Surrey: served with the Expeditionary Force. Reported missing, 7 November 1914; assumed killed.

(Panel 13) Pte. L/9345, Balaam Holmes, 2nd Bn. (2nd Foot) The Queen's (Royal West Surrey Regt.): *s*. of Clare Holmes (3, Unity Cottages, Gardiner Street, Gillingham, co. Kent): served with the Expeditionary Force. Killed in action at Gheluvelt, 30 October 1914. Age 26.

(Panel 13) Pte. L/7007, Stephen John Homewood, 1st Bn. (2nd Foot) The Queen's (Royal West Surrey Regt.): *s*. of Jonathan Homewood, of Mertsham, co. Surrey, by his wife Mary: enlisted Reigate: served with the Expeditionary Force. Reported missing/believed killed in action, 31 October 1914. Age 30.

(Panel 13) Pte. T/207054, Fred Hopwood, 11th (Service) Bn. The Queen's (Royal West Surrey Regt.): formerly no.265976, Suffolk (C.V.C.) Regt.: late of Clare, co. Suffolk: *s*. of Joseph Henry Hopwood, of 6, Church Street, Marple, Stockport, by his wife Eliza: and elder brother to Pte. 203224, W.B. Hopwood, 1/5th Lancashire Fusiliers, died 10 April 1918, of wounds: *b*. Marple, co. Chester: enlisted Sudbury, co. Suffolk: served with the Expeditionary Force in France. Killed in action, 31 July 1917. Age 23.

His brother Walter is buried in Etaples Military Cemetery (XXXIII.F.20).

(Panel 13) Pte. L/6031, Robert House, 1st Bn. (2nd Foot) The Queen's (Royal West Surrey Regt.): late *husb*. to Nellie Margaret House, *née* Hurworth: *s*. of Francis Alfred House, of Plumstead, co. Kent, by his wife Hannah Maria: *b*. Woolwich, co. Kent, 1879: served with the Expeditionary Force. Reported missing, 31 October 1914, and now assumed killed. Age 35.

(Panel 13) Pte. L/9757, Stanley Herbert Howland, 2nd Bn. (2nd Foot) The Queen's (Royal West Surrey Regt.): *s*. of Frederick Howland, of Canterbury, co. Kent: *b*. High Wycombe, co. Buckingham: served with the Expeditionary Force. Killed in action, 2 November 1914.

(Panel 13) Pte. L/9119, Richard Hubbard, 2nd Bn. (2nd Foot) The Queen's (Royal West Surrey Regt.): *s*. of James Hubbard, of Chelsea, London, S.W.3: enlisted South Western Police Court, Wandsworth,

London, S.W.18: served with the Expeditionary Force. Reported missing, 21 October 1914; now assumed killed.

(Panel 13) Pte. L/7177, Frederick Hughes, 1st Bn. (2nd Foot) The Queen's (Royal West Surrey Regt.): served with the Expeditionary Force. Reported missing, 31 October 1914; now assumed killed. *m.*

(Panel 13) Pte. L/7876, Charles Hunt, 1st Bn. (2nd Foot) The Queen's (Royal West Surrey Regt.): *s.* of W. Hunt, of Bermondsey, London, S.E.: served with the Expeditionary Force in France. Reported missing, 31 October 1914, and now assumed killed.

(Panel 13) Pte. L/7238, Richard Francis Ingham, 'C' Coy., 2nd Bn. (2nd Foot) The Queen's (Royal West Surrey Regt.): *s.* of the late Robert Ingham, of Bethnal Green Road, London, E.: served with the Expeditionary Force. Killed in action, 7 November 1914. Age 38.

(Panel 13) L/9817, Alfred Charles Kemp, 2nd Bn. (2nd Foot) The Queen's (Royal West Surrey Regt.): served with the Expeditionary Force. Killed in action at Gheluvelt, 30 October 1914.

(Panel 13) Pte. L/10440, Albert Reginald Kenna, 1st Bn. (2nd Foot) The Queen's (Royal West Surrey Regt.): *s.* of Edward Kenna, of Balham, London, SW12: enlisted Kingston: served with the Expeditionary Force. Killed in action at Gheluvelt, 31 October 1914.

(Panel 13) Pte. L/9733, James Kennard, 'B' Coy., 2nd Bn. (2nd Foot) The Queen's (Royal West Surrey Regt.): *s.* of James Kennard, of 56, Mount Road Terrace, Chatham, co. Kent, by his wife Alice: enlisted Chatham: served with the Expeditionary Force. Killed in action at Zillebeke, nr. Ypres 7 November 1914. Age 24.

(Panel 13) Pte. L/10361, James Richard Kent, 1st Bn. (2nd Foot) The Queen's (Royal West Surrey Regt.): enlisted Guildford: served with the Expeditionary Force in France. Killed in action, 21 October 1914.

(Panel 13) Pte. G/905, George Kibble, 2nd Bn. (2nd Foot) The Queen's (Royal West Surrey Regt.): *s.* of Charles Kibble, of Somersham, co. Hants: enlisted Bermondsey, London, S.E.: served with the Expeditionary Force. Killed in action at Ypres, 29 October 1914.

(Panel 13) Pte. L/1033, Walter Knight, 'B' Coy., 1st Bn. (2nd Foot) The Queen's (Royal West Surrey Regt.): *s.* of Charles J. Knight, of 68, Winterbourne Road, Thornton Heath, co. Surrey, by his wife Martha: served with the Expeditionary Force. Reported missing, 31 October 1914; assumed killed.

(Panel 13) Pte. L/8800, Harry James Kosh, 1st Bn. (2nd Foot) The Queen's (Royal West Surrey Regt.): *s.* of Harry Kosh, of Victoria Park, London, E., and Mrs F.A. Kosh (12, Partrip Street, Homerton, London, E.9): served with the Expeditionary Force. Reported missing, 31 October 1914; now assumed killed. Age 29. *unm.*

(Panel 13) Pte. L/10395, George Lambert, 1st Bn. (2nd Foot) The Queen's (Royal West Surrey Regt.): *s.* of William (& L.M.) Lambert, of Rose Hill, Isfield, Uckfield, co. Sussex: served with the Expeditionary Force. Killed in action at Gheluvelt, 31 October 1914. Age 18.

(Panel 13) Pte. L/6136, John Lang, 1st Bn. (2nd Foot) The Queen's (Royal West Surrey Regt.): *s.* of E. Sullivan, of 5, Currey St., Battersea, London, SW11: and late *husb.* to Gertrude Alice (31, Dornton Road, Balham, London, S.W.12): enlisted South Western Police Court, Clapham, London, S.W.4: served with the Expeditionary Force. Reported missing, 31 October 1914; assumed killed. Age 34.

(Panel 13) Pte. L/9771, Henry Ernest Lawrence, 2nd Bn. (2nd Foot) The Queen's (Royal West Surrey Regt.): *s.* of the late Henry Lawrence, of West Ealing, London, W., by his wife Alice (30, Williams Road, Tooting, London, SW): served with the Expeditionary Force. Killed in action, 28 October 1914. Age 23. *unm.*

(Panel 13) Pte. L/6220, Charles Phillip Libretto, 1st Bn. (2nd Foot) The Queen's (Royal West Surrey Regt.): *s.* of Luigi Libretto, of 14, Hawthorn Grove, Penge, London, S.E., by his wife Polly: and yr. brother to Pte. 202505, J.E. Libretto, 4th Suffolk Regt., who fell at the Third Battle of Ypres, 26 September 1917: *b.* The Minories, London: enlisted Croydon, co. Surrey: killed in action, 31 October 1914, at the First Battle of Ypres. Age 18. (*IWGC record 3 brothers fell*)

His brother James also has no known grave; he is commemorated on the Tyne Cot Memorial (Panel 40).

(Panel 13) Pte. G/37493, James Merricks, 11th (Service) Bn. The Queen's (Royal West Surrey Regt.): late *husb.* to Sarah Merricks (10, Union Road, St. John's, Redhill, co. Surrey): and father to Pte. 10374, J. Merricks, 2nd East Surrey Regt., killed in action, 11 February 1915, aged 18 years: *b.* Westerham, co. Kent: enlisted Redhill: served with the Expeditionary Force. Killed in action at Messines, 7 June 1917. Age 41.

His son James also has no known grave; he is recorded on Panel 34.

(Panel 13) Pte. G/8933, John Merriman, 'C' Coy., 2nd Bn. (2nd Foot) The Queen's (Royal West Surrey Regt.): *s.* of Henry Merriman, of 62, Donald Road, West Croydon, co. Surrey, by his wife Caroline: and elder brother to Pte. 41839, A.P.. Merriman, 16th Manchester Regt., killed in action, 31 July 1917, at the Third Battle of Ypres: *b.* Penge: enlisted Guildford. Killed in action, 21 October 1914, at the First Battle of Ypres. Age 24. *unm.*

His brother Arthur also has no known grave; he is recorded on Panel 55.

(Panel 13) Pte. G/12334, Clarence William Moule, 8th (Service) Bn. The Queen's (Royal West Surrey Regt.): *s.* of William Moule, of Crown Hill, Botesdale, Diss, by his wife Annie Theresa ('La Chaume,' Willow Corner, Wortham, co. Suffolk): and brother to Rfn. 61312, E.R. Moule, 5th King's Royal Rifle Corps, died 6 November 1918: *b.* Wattisfield, co. Suffolk: enlisted Rickinghall. Killed in action, 1 August 1917. Age 22. *unm.*

His brother Edan is buried in Wattisfield Cemetery.

(Panel 13) Pte. L/6685, William John Newson, 2nd Bn. (2nd Foot) The Queen's (Royal West Surrey Regt.): *s.* of William John Newson, of 3, Bridson Street, Tustin Street, Old Kent Road, London, S.E. by his wife Martha: and elder brother to Pte. G/13086, G.A. Newson, 6th The Buffs, killed in action, 3 October 1917: *b.* Camberwell: enlisted Woolwich, London, S.E.: served with the Expeditionary Force, and was killed in action, 7 November 1914. Age 39. He leaves a wife, Bridget Newson (21, Cambrook Street, Tustin Street, Old Kent Road).

His brother George is buried in Windmill British Cemetery, Monchy-le-Preux (I.E.17).

(Panel 13) Pte. L/9498, William Thomas Pilgrim (*a.k.a.* Beams), 2nd Bn. (2nd Foot) The Queen's (Royal West Surrey Regt.): 3rd & *yst. s.* of George Pilgrim, Gardener; of 78, Burlington Road, Thornton Heath, co. Surrey, formerly 17, Moffatt Road, Thornton Heath, by his wife Sarah, *dau.* of Thomas Beams, of Ewell, co. Surrey: *b.* Thornton Heath, 30 August 1887: *educ.* Beulah Road Board School: enlisted 1907: served Gibraltar, Bermuda, South Africa, and with the Expeditionary Force in France and Flanders September–October 1914, during which time the battalion suffered extremely heavy losses; only 200 officers and men being left, and was killed in action at Ypres, 28 October 1914. Buried at Menin. He was a keen cricketer, and was in the Regimental team that won the cup at Gibraltar. Age 26. *unm.* (*IWGC record Beams*)

(Panel 13) Pte. G/18222, Edward Charles Preece, 7th (Service) Bn. The Queen's (Royal West Surrey Regt.): *s.* of Henry Thomas Preece, of 32, Rutland Street, Pimlico, London, S.W.1, by his wife Ellen: and brother to Pte. 53123, H.F. Preece, 15th Durham Light Infantry, killed in action, 10 April 1917; and Pte. 232476, P.G. Preece, 2/2nd London Regt., killed in action, 15 June 1917: *b.* Pimlico: enlisted Kingston-on-Thames. Killed in action, 10 August 1917. Age 34. He was married to Madeline Susan Preece (26, Borneo Street, Putney, London, SW15).

His brother Horace is buried in Cojeul British Cemetery (B.8); Percy has no known grave, he is commemorated on the Arras Memorial (Bay 9).

(Panel 13) Pte. 207025, Arthur Edward Price, 11th Bn. The Queen's (Royal West Surrey Regt.), (T.F.): formerly no.26583, Suffolk Regt.: 3rd *s.* of the late William Joseph Valentine Price, by his wife Alice Louisa, *dau.* of William Wootten: *b.* Croydon, 6 August 1893: *educ.* Oval Road Council School, Croydon, co. Surrey: enlisted Suffolk Regt., November 1916: transf'd. West Surrey Regt. June 1917: served with the Expeditionary Force in France and Flanders from that month, and was killed in action on the Yser Canal, nr. Zandvoorde, 1 August following. Buried in Battle Wood. His Commanding Officer wrote, "He was a good soldier, and was greatly admired by all his comrades, being always cheerful and ready to go where duty called." Age 23. *unm.*

(Panel 13) Pte. G/21195, Bertie Press, 7th (Service) Bn. The Queen's (Royal West Surrey Regt.): formerly no.27596, Middlesex Regt.: *b*. Poringland, co. Norfolk: enlisted Norwich. Killed by the explosion of a shell, 16 July 1917, at Sanctuary Wood. L/Sergt. S/7023, S.J.A. Palmer and Pte. G/14931, F. Etchells were also killed; Pte. G/1515, C. Humphreys, wounded by the same shell, died the following day. L/Sergt. Palmer (Panel 11) and Pte. Etchells (above), also have no known grave; Pte. Humphreys is buried in Lijssenthoek Military Cemetery (XVI.D.1A).

(Panel 13) Pte. T/207028, Frederick Arthur Saunders, 11th (Service) Bn. The Queen's (Royal West Surrey Regt.): formerly no.290281, Suffolk Regt.: 3rd *s*. of the late George Saunders, of Hadlow, by his wife Caroline, *dau*. of Isaac Rossiter: *b*. Hadlow, nr. Tonbridge, co. Kent, 4 January 1883: *educ*. Board School, there: enlisted Suffolk Regt., Tonbridge, 2 June 1916: subsequently transf'd. Royal West Surrey Regt.: served with the Expeditionary Force in France and Flanders, and was killed in action at Ypres, 1 August 1917. Buried where he fell. Age 34. He *m*., Tunbridge Wells, 27 May 1907, Elizabeth (14, Houselands Road, Tonbridge, late of 145, Pembury Road), *dau*. of John Whenday, and leaves two children – Reginald Frederick, *b*. 27 August 1908; Winifred Agnes, *b*. 10 October 1910.

PANEL 13 ENDS: PTE. F.A. SAUNDERS, THE QUEEN'S (ROYAL WEST SURREY)

PANEL 15 BEGINS: SOUTH AFRICAN HEAVY ARTILLERY.

(Panel 15) Corpl. 7699, Robert Sharp, 1st Regt. South African Infantry, S.A.E.F.: only *s*. of James Sharp, of Jamestown, Scotland, by his wife Agnes, *dau*. of James Halliday: *b*. Ayr, 7 November 1895: *educ*. Preston Grammar School, and Harris' Agricultural School: went to South Africa, July 1913: on the outbreak of war, volunteered for Active Service, and joined the Middleburg Mounted Rifles, September 1914: took part in the fighting in German South-West Africa, where he was taken prisoner: on the surrender of the enemy to General Botha, he volunteered for Foreign Service, and returned to England, February 1916: served in France and Flanders from the following August, and was killed in action on the Menin Road, 20 September 1917. Buried where he fell. His Commanding Officer wrote, "Corpl. Sharp was one of my most promising N.C.O.'s, a lad to be proud of; he died as he had lived, gallantly." Age 21. *unm*.

(Panel 15) Pte. 13380, D. Branford, 1st Regt. South African Infantry, S.A.E.F.: *s*. of the late T.H. Branford, and Getrude 'Gertie' Branford, his spouse ('Jupiter,' 67, Perth Road, Westdene, Johannesburg): and yr. brother to Pte. 12721, L.F. Branford, South African Infantry, killed in action, 10 April 1918: served in France and Flanders. Killed in action, 20 September 1917. Age 26.

His brother Laurence also has no known grave, he is recorded below.

(Panel 15) Pte. 12721, Laurence Frederick Branford, 1st Regt. South African Infantry, S.A.E.F.: *s*. of the late T.H. Branford, and Getrude 'Gertie' Branford, his spouse ('Jupiter,' 67, Perth Road, Westdene, Johannesburg): and elder brother to Pte. 13380, D. Branford, South African Infantry, killed in action, 20 September 1917: served in France and Flanders. Killed in action, 10 April 1918. Age 31.

(Panel 15) Lieut. David Elmar Lucas, 2nd Regt. South African Infantry, S.A.E.F.: *s*. of Frederick G.C. (& Maggie Gordon) Lucas, of Durban, Natal: and elder brother to Sergt. 6679, J.G. Lucas, South African Infantry, killed in action, 20 September 1917: served in France and Flanders. Killed in action, 21 September 1917. Age 24.

His brother John also has no known grave; he is recorded below.

(Panel 15) Sergt. 11409, Archie Burgess, 2nd Regt. South African Infantry, S.A.E.F.: *s*. of Harry Burgess, of 14, Sycamore Road, Congella, Durban, Natal, by his wife Laura: and elder brother to Pte. 12866, W. Burgess, South African Infantry, killed in action, 20 September 1917: served in France and Flanders. Killed in action, 20 September 1917. Age 41.

His brother Walter also has no known grave; he is recorded below.

(Panel 15) Sergt. 6679, John Gordon Lucas, 2nd Regt. South African Infantry, S.A.E.F.: *s*. of Frederick G.C. (& Maggie Gordon) Lucas, of Durban, Natal: and yr. brother to Lieut. D.E. Lucas, killed in action, 21 September 1917: served in France and Flanders. Killed in action, 20 September 1917. Age 21.

His brother David also has no known grave; he is recorded above.

(Panel 15) L/Sergt. 10471, John Philips, 2nd Regt. South African Infantry, S.A.E.F.: 2nd *s.* of the late John Philips, of 343, Lansdowne Avenue, Westmount, Montreal, Canada, by his wife Elizabeth, *dau.* of John Ritchie: *b.* Montreal, 26 September 1876: *educ.* Westmount Academy, Canada: served in the South African War 1899–1900, with 1st Canadian Contingent (Queen's Medal with clasps): returned to Canada thence (1902) back to South Africa, where he joined the Natal Border Police, and went through the Natal Native Rebellion, 1906 (Medal & clasp). On the outbreak of the European War he took part in the military operations in German South Africa, and in the Union of South Africa, 1914–15; thereafter volunteered for service abroad and joined South African Infantry: served with the Expeditionary Force in France and Flanders from October 1915; took part in the fighting at Delville Wood, Somme; and was killed in action at the Battle of the Menin Road, 20 September 1917. Age 40 years, 359 days. *unm.*

(Panel 15) L/Corpl. 12950, James Houston Black, 2nd Regt. South African Infantry, S.A.E.F.: eldest *s.* of Peter Black, Town Chamberlain; of 21, Paton Street, Alloa, co. Clackmannan, by his wife Jane, *dau.* of David Houston: *b.* Cupar, co. Fife, 7 August 1875: *educ.* Alloa: went to South Africa, 1896: Occupation – Clerk; Bloemfontein, Orange Free State, subsequently transf'd. Johannesburg, Transvaal: joined an infantry regiment on the outbreak of war, and took an active part in the German South-West Africa Campaign under General Botha and, when hostilities concluded there, was appointed Sergt. in charge of a detachment at Windhuk for the distribution of relief to the civilian population: resigned after 18 months service and returned to Johannesburg, and his former employ as a Clerk. The South African Government subsequently issued an urgent appeal for reinforcements for the South African Infantry in France, so he re-enlisted at Potchefstroom towards the end of 1916; being transported to England shortly afterwards: served with the Expeditionary Force in France and Flanders from 10 July 1917, and was killed in action at Kemmel Hill, 1 April 1918. Age 42. *unm.*

(Panel 15) L/Corpl. 3149, Albert Stretton Symes, 2nd Regt. South African Infantry, S.A.E.F.: *s.* of John Symes, and Sarah Ann, his wife: and yr. brother to Pte. 7218, J.R. Symes, South African Infantry, killed in action, 20 September 1917: served in France and Flanders. Killed in action, 13 October 1917. Age 23.

His brother James also has no known grave; he is recorded below.

(Panel 15) Pte. 12866, Walter Burgess, 2nd Regt. South African Infantry, S.A.E.F.: *s.* of Harry Burgess, of 14, Sycamore Road, Congella, Durban, Natal, by his wife Laura: and yr. brother to Sergt. 11409, A. Burgess, South African Infantry, killed in action, 20 September 1917: served in France and Flanders. Killed in action, 20 September 1917. Age 21.

His brother Archie also has no known grave; he is recorded above.

(Panel 15) Pte. 7663, E. Harney, 2nd Regt. South African Infantry, S.A.E.F.: *s.* of Michael Joseph Harney, of 57, Park Street, East London, Cape Province (sometime resident – Devonshire House, Port Alfred), and Frederika Johanna Harney, his wife: and yr. brother to L/Corpl. 6184, D.J. Harney, 2nd Regt. S.A. Inf., fell in service, 30 August 1916: served in France and Flanders. Killed in action, 21 September 1917. Age 19.

His brother Dennis is buried in Cabaret-Rouge British Cemetery, Souchez (II.B.9).

(Panel 15) Pte. 7218, James Robert Symes, 2nd Regt. South African Infantry, S.A.E.F.: *s.* of John Symes, and Sarah Ann, his wife: and elder brother to L/Corpl. A.S. Symes, South African Infantry, killed in action, 13 October 1917: served in France and Flanders. Killed in action, 20 September 1917. Age 32.

His brother Albert also has no known grave; he is recorded above.

PANEL 15 ENDS: 2ND REGT. SOUTH AFRICAN INFANTRY.

PANEL 15A BEGINS: CPL. F.C. SULLY, BRITISH WEST INDIES REGT.

PANEL 15A ENDS: PTE. C. HOWELL, BRITISH WEST INDIES REGT.

PANEL 17 BEGINS: LT. J.T. MAGUIRE, M.C., 8TH BN. AUSTRALIAN INF.

(Panel 17) Lieut. John Timothy Maguire, M.C., 8th Bn. Australian Infantry, A.I.F.: *s.* of John Maguire, of Bowenvale, Victoria, by his wife Johanna: *b.* Bowenvale, May 1896: Religion – Roman Catholic: Occupation – Postal Official: enlisted Melbourne, 9 August 1915: served in France from 4 May 1917, and was killed in action, 4 October 1917 when, on approaching its starting positions for the Battle of Broodseinde, his battalion was subjected to enemy shellfire. Age 21. Awarded the Military Cross, "For conspicuous gallantry and devotion to duty. He was in command of the right platoon of the division in an attack, and it was largely owing to his splendid coolness under fire and in the face of heavy opposition that direction was maintained. He kept touch with the division on his right, captured two objectives and showed great skill in the consolidation. He set a fine example to his men."

(Panel 17) Pte. 5336, Frederick Betts, Lewis Gun Team, 8th Bn. Australian Infantry, A.I.F.: *s.* of Frederick E. Betts, of Marshalltown, Victoria, by his wife Julia: served with the Expeditionary Force. Killed in action, 4 October 1917; when a H.E. shell landed in his team's Lewis Gun post at Broodseinde. Age 22. *unm.*

(Panel 17) Pte. 4765, William Augustine Curtain, Lewis Gun Team, 8th Bn. Australian Infantry, A.I.F.: *s.* of Michael Curtain, of Mitcham, Victoria, by his wife Mary Ellen. Killed about 09.30 hrs, 4 October 1917, in company with L/Corpl. J.W. Mardling, Ptes. F.G. Mardling, F. Betts and L.J. Lukey. Age 21. *unm.*

(Panel 17) Pte. 6552, Leonard James Lukey, Lewis Gun Team, 8th Bn. Australian Infantry, A.I.F.: *s.* of the late John Lukey, by his wife Annie (46, Rathmine Street, Fairfield, Victoria). Killed by the explosion of a H.E. shell, 4 October 1917; Broodseinde. A comrade – first on the scene – said that the explosion of the shell had virtually blown the four members of the machine gun team to pieces, 'Lukey had face and chest very much injured.' Buried where he fell.

(Panel 17) Pte. 3848, Farnel 'Farn' George Mardling, Lewis Gun Team, 8th Bn. Australian Infantry, A.I.F.: *s.* of the late William Cooke Mardling, Postmaster; Port Fairy, Victoria; by his wife Ellen Isabella Grey Mardling (8, Webb Street, Brighton, Victoria): and elder brother to L/Corpl. 4834, J.W. Mardling, 8th Battn., killed at the same time: *b.* South Yarra, Victoria, October 1886: Religion – Roman Catholic: Occupation – Accountant: 5'8" tall, fresh complexion, brown eyes, dark brown hair: enlisted Melbourne, 16 July 1915; posted 12th Rfts., 8th Battn., Broadmeadows, 4 November following: departed Melbourne, H.M.A.T. A.40 'Ceramic', 23 November: embarked for the European War, Alexandria, Egypt, 29 March 1916: served with the Expeditionary Force in France and Flanders from 4 April 1916: joined 8th Battn. In the Field, 26 May: (slightly) wounded in action (G.S.W. Rt. Leg) 26 July, and removed to 1st Canadian General Hospital, Etaples: rejoined his battalion, 26 August: admitted 8th Field Ambulance (trench foot) 21 April 1917; returned to duty, 27 July following treatment and convalescence: rejoined 8th Battn. 18 August and, after a period of leave (10–23 September), was killed in action about 09.30 hrs, 4 October 1917, at Broodseinde, Passchendaele. Age 31. Pte. A.R. Roberts said he was in the same platoon and advance as 'Farn' at Passchendaele Ridge. And continued, "He was on a machine-gun, and had just reached the first objective when an H.E. shell exploded on the gun, killing 'Farn' instantly, and Ptes. F. Betts, W.A. Curtain and L.J. Lukey. I was 12 yards away at the time the shell exploded, and I saw his body immediately afterwards, but he was beyond all aid…I helped to bury him." And Pte. J.J. Pearce, "Buried on the spot within 20 feet of Lieut. Glanville, with his 4 mates of the platoon."

His brother James is buried in Oxford Road Cemetery (II.F.16); Lieut. R.B. Glanville, Dochy Farm New British Cemetery (III.B.27); Ptes. Betts, Curtain and Lukey have no known grave. They are recorded above.

(Panel 17) Pte. 6831, John 'Jock' Neilson, 'D' Coy., 8th Bn. Australian Infantry, A.I.F.: *s.* of Alexander Neilson, of Seaham No.2 Colliery, West Wallsend, Newcastle-upon-Tyne, and his wife Jessie, *née* Hunter: *b.* Mount Kembla, New South Wales, September 1890: Religion – Presbyterian: Occupation – Engine Driver: volunteered and enlisted A.I.F., 26 October 1916; departed Sydney, 17 November: trained England (from 29 January 1917): proceeded to France, 3 May 1917: joined 8th Bn., Bienvillers, on the 21st. of that month: severely wounded, both legs blown off by a shell when coming out of the line, 10 October 1917. Attended and bandaged by Pte. W.G. Thomson, 'D' Coy., thereafter taken by stretcher-bearers to the Dressing Station, Westhoek Ridge, ¾ mile from where he was hit. Age 27. Buried between road running through D28c and main road through D29 (Sht.28), few hundred yards S.E. of Zonnebeke. Remains recovered 2 July 1919 – Collective grave (28.J.7a.20.20). One cross bearing four details: 'Unknown Australian Soldier, 8/A.I.F., 10.10.17; Bmdr. 44976, A.E. Joyce, R.F.A., 10.10.17; Pte. 3619, J.A. McKenzie, 4/A.I.F., 10.10.17; Pte. 1507, H.W.T. Andrews, 9/A.I.F., 10.10.17.' Buried in Birr Cross Roads Cemetery (IV.E.11). His original headstone recorded 'A Soldier of The Great War 8th Bn. Australian Inf., 10th October 1917. *Known Unto God*'- after extensive research and DNA analysis, Pte. Neilson's remains were positively identified; his headstone replaced/re-dedicated September 2015. Of the four sets of remains recovered, only those of Bmdr. Joyce could be identified with any degree of certainty. Birr Cross Roads Cemetery (IV.E.11).

(Panel 17) Pte. 6948, Albert Fred Hass, 10th Bn. Australian Infantry, A.I.F.: *s.* of Peter Heinrich Hass, of Peterborough, South Australia, by his late wife Lisette, *née* Lohmann: and brother to Corpl. 2517, W.T. Hass, 48th Bn. A.I.F., killed in action, 12 October 1917: *b.* Greenville, Wisconsin, U.S.A., *c.*1893: missing believed taken prisoner of war, 20–21 September 1917; following thorough examination of German records, certified (10 October 1919) as having been killed in action, 20 September 1917. Age 24.

His brother Walter also has no known grave; he is recorded on Panel 27.

(Panel 17) Pte. 28218, Oscar Vincent Vigar, 10th Bn. Australian Infantry, A.I.F.: *s.* of William Vigar, of 32, Hawker's Road, Medindie, South Australia, by his wife Elizabeth: and brother to Pte. 1715/C, N.J. Vigar, 10th Australian Infantry, killed in action, 21 September 1917: *b.* Boothby, South Australia. Killed in action, 9 October 1917. Age 23.

His brother Norman is buried in St. Sever Cemetery Extension, Rouen (P.III.G.2A).

> *They were the boys from the Western State,*
> *Brave Battalion Eleven;*
> *They did not tarry, they did not wait,*
> *When the call was given.*
> *First to respond to their country's need*
> *Nothing they feared, nor death did they heed.*
> *Brave Battalion Eleven.*
>
> S.M. Harris, Kalgoorlie

(Panel 17) Lieut. Willie Irving, 'C' Coy., 11th Bn. Australian Infantry, A.I.F.: *s.* of Arthur Irving, of 55, Mercers Street, Kanowna, Western Australia, and Gertrude his wife: and brother to L/Corpl. 1485, H. Irving, 16th Australian Infantry (surv'd.): *b.* Lucknow, New South Wales, February 1893: Religion – Church of England: Occupation – Grocer: served 3 years Militia; joined 11th A.I.F., Bellevue, 17 August 1914; Pte. 1001: served at Gallipoli, Egypt, and France and Flanders (from 16 May 1916): apptd. L/Corpl. 31 July 1916; promoted Corpl. 20 January 1917: wounded (subsequently diagnosed gonorrhoea), hospitalised Havre, 11 April; discharged to duty, 24 May: rejoined 11th Bn. 2 June: promoted Sergt. 4 June; 2nd Lieut. 23 July. Killed in action shortly after midnight, 2 November 1917, when one of the battalion's posts situated in Decoy Wood was hit by a shell and blown in; 4 O.R. were also killed, 5 wounded. Buried Passchendaele Ridge, nr. Ypres – Menin Railway, Broodseinde. Age 24. On 6 November 1921, Sergt. Henry Black's mother wrote to the Australian Base Records Office, "Dear Sir, I will feel very grateful if you will tell me how I can obtain information of my late son's burial place. It is four years since he was killed and I have not been able to learn where he is buried. I have been reading such dreadful things about the bodies being exhumed and left lying exposed for days before being reburied. Some mothers have received photos of their sons graves. Hoping you will be able to assist me in some way, Yours Sincerely, Janet Black." Due to the circumstances of his death – being hit by a high-explosive shell – the likelihood of finding any part of him was extremely remote and, mangled beyond all recognition, would have been impossible to identify from the similarly ripped and torn body parts of L/Corpl. W. Kennelly, killed by the same shell; Janet received the reply – "Although exhaustive searches and investigations have been made with the object of locating the grave of (Sergt. Black), it has not been possible to locate his actual burial place or obtain any information which might indicate his probable original or present resting place."

(Panel 17) Sergt. 4155, Henry Alexander 'Nigger' Black, D.C.M., M.M., 'C' Coy., 11th Bn. Australian Infantry, A.I.F.: *s.* of Alexander (& Janet) Black, of North Hill, Forbes, New South Wales: *b.* Forbes, February 1879: Religion – Church of England: Occupation – Miner: previously served 1 year, 3rd New South Wales Bushmen; 15 months, Remington Scouts: joined A.I.F., Kalgoorlie, 24 September 1915; apptd. 13th Rfts., 11th Bn., Blackboy Hill, 22 November: served Egypt (from 9 February 1916); France and Flanders (from 5 April): wounded (GSW arm), Pozieres, 22 July: hospitalised Rouen; evacuated England, 25 July from whence, after treatment and convalescent leave (from 25 August), returned to France, 22 September: rejoined 10th Bn. 3 October: apptd. L/Corpl. 11 Decemebr 1916; promoted Corpl. 10 February 1917: hospitalised Rouen (P.U.O.), 21 March–11 April: rejoined battn. 24 April: Awarded Military Medal (*London Gazette*, 11 May 1917) 'For conspicuous services and bravery in the field': promoted Sergt. 12 May: Awarded Distinguished Conduct Medal (*London Gazette*, 14 August 1917) 'For conspicuous gallantry and devotion to duty. He was in charge of a post in the front line, owing to heavy shelling, a number of men became buried. He showed great courage and determination in digging them out, although he himself was buried whilst doing this, he was rescued and continued with his task. He succeeded in rescuing ten men under heavy shell fire.'. Killed in action, 31 October 1917, nr. Zonnebeke. Age 38. Capt. W.C. Belford said, "Besides the ordinary shelling and mustard gas shells, the Germans put over a great deal of blue-cross gas, but there were no casualties from this source. The battalion suffered considerably from high-explosive shell. Among those killed was Sergt. H.A. (Nigger) Black, a very fine soldier, and one who had been the life of 'C' Company. Nigger was killed on patrol duty by a H.E. shell." No burial. Age 38. His effects – Photos, Cards, 4 Medal Ribbons, Pencil – British War & Victory Medals, Memorial Plaque & Scroll, were received by his mother, September 1918–February 1923. (*IWGC record age 35*)

(Panel 17) Sergt. 3362, Alexander Holm, M.M., 'C' Coy., 11th Bn. Australian Infantry, A.I.F.: *s.* of Stewart Holm, of John Street, North Fremantle: and brother to Pte. 2837, R.C. Holm, 44th Australian Infantry (surv'd.): *b.* Auburn, Victoria, August 1894: Religion – Presbyterian: Occupation – Clerk: enlisted A.I.F., Perth, 14 July 1915; apptd. 11th Rfts., 11th Bn., 28 October: joined 11th Bn., Egypt, 2 March 1916: served with the Expeditionary Force in France from 5 April: wounded (GSW Lt. arm / shldr.) 22 July, hospitalised Rouen, transf'd. England; discharged to duty, 16 October, granted leave to 31 October: Awarded 7 Days Confined to Camp 'Absent without leave, 31 October–7 November': hospitalised (V.D.) 1–30 December 1916: returned to France, 24 January: rejoined 11th Bn., 28 January: promoted Corpl. 12 May 1917; Sergt. 8 July: Awarded Military Medal, 31 October (*London Gazette*, 13 December 1917) 'For bravery in the field.' Killed in action, 2 November 1917. Letters of condolence from his comrades said, "He was one of the finest soldiers in the grand old 11th." Age 23.

(Panel 17) L/Corpl. 5356, Lewis John Broad, 11th Bn. Australian Infantry, A.I.F.: *s.* of Edward Broad, of Manarra Station, Mingenew, Western Australia, and Ellen Jane, his wife: *b.* Mingenew, 1894: Occupation – Farmhand: joined A.I.F., 12 January 1916: trained Egypt (from 14 May); England (from 29 July): served with the Expeditionary Force in France and Flanders from 30 August 1916; joined 11th Battn. In the Field, 12 September: apptd. L/Corpl. 6 February 1917: wounded (G.S.W. Rt. knee), 10 April, admitted 3rd Field Amb.; transf'd. 56th C.C.S.; transf'd. 6th Gen. Hospital, France: rejoined battn. 29 May: apptd. Temp. Corpl. 8 July; substantive from 25 July, and was killed in action, 20 September 1917, nr. Ypres. Age 23. *The Western Mail*, 'In Memoriam,' 2 November 1917:

> *Somewhere in France he is lying, He answered his country's call,*
> *He died an Australian hero, Fighting to save us all.*

(Panel 17) L/Corpl. 6069, William Kennelly, 11th Bn. Australian Infantry, A.I.F.: *s.* of Thomas Kennelly, of Cobargo, New South Wales: brother to Q.M.Sergt. 1323, J.D. Kennelly, Australian Army Veterinary

Corps (surv'd.); and *husb.* to Ethel Mary Kennelly (16, Arundel Street, Fremantle, Western Australia): *b.* Bermagui, Cobargo, 1883: Religion – Roman Catholic: Occupation – Commercial Traveller: joined A.I.F., Blackboy Hill, Kalgoorlie, 24 March 1916; apptd. 19th Rfts., 11th Bn., 26 June: departed Fremantle, 9 August 1916: served with the Expeditionary Force in France from 18 December 1916: joined 11th Bn., 17 January 1917: apptd. L/Corpl. 25 July. Killed in action, (Night Patrol) No Man's Land, before Passchendaele, 31 October–1 November 1917; High-Explosive shell. No Burial. Age 34.

(Panel 17) Pte. 1716, Herbert Bradford, 11th Bn. Australian Infantry, A.I.F.: *s.* of Mrs H.B. Bradford (49, Hubble Street, Fremantle): late *husb.* to Florence Bradord (26, St. John's Road, East Ham, London, England): *b.* Melbourne, 1890: Religion – Church of England: Occupation – Labourer: joined A.I.F., Perth, 18 January 1915; apptd. 4th Rfts., 11th Bn., Blackboy Hill, 16 February: served with the Expeditionary Force at Gallipoli; Egypt and, from 1 October 1916, France. Killed in action, 2 November 1917; Decoy Wood. Age 27.

(Panel 17) Pte. 3753, James Carlos, 11th Bn. Australian Infantry, A.I.F.: *s.* of Martin (& Cecilia) Carlos, of 'Carmalasson,' Four Mile House, Lanesborough Street, Roscommon, Ireland: *b.* Roscommon, 1885: Religion – Roman Catholic: Occupation – Labourer: joined A.I.F., Blackboy Hill, 15 September 1915; apptd. 12th Rfts., 11th Bn., 1 November: joined 11th Bn., Habieta, Egypt, 2 March 1916: served with the Expeditionary Force in France from 5 April: wounded (SW Lt. hand), 22 July; hospitalised Rouen, discharged to duty (Etaples), 31 July: rejoined battalion, 18 September, Railway Dugouts, Zillebeke: wounded (SW Rt. knee), 9 November; hospitalised Etretat/Havre, discharged to duty (Etaples), 21 November 1916: attd. 1st Anzac HQrs., 1 January 1917: rejoined battalion, 11 August, Doulieu: On Leave, England, 4–14 September. One of six men of his battalion killed by a single shell, 1 November 1917, before Passchendaele. Buried near where he fell. Age 32. His effects – Disc, Letters, 4 Religious Medallions, Purse, 2 Coins, 3 Rosaries, Pouch, Prayer Book, Wallet – were received by his mother, March 1918. Excluding British, New Zealand and Canadian born servicemen (and women) the largest number of foreign nationals – over one thousand – who served in the A.I.F. were Russian. Besides native Russians their number included persons from a diverse range of ethnic groups – Jews, Georgians, Estonians, Latvians, Lithuanians, Byelorussians, Ukrainians, Poles, Tatars, Ossetia's – as well as Finns, Scandinavians, Germans and other Western European nationals either born in Russia or posing as Russian subjects at the time of enlistment. For the most part, these Russian ANZACs served well, earning 5 Distinguished Conduct Medals, 34 Military Medals, 1 Distinguished Service Order, 1 Croix de Guerre (France), 9 Mentions in Despatches, 2 M.S.M. and an American Distinguished Service Medal among them. However, there were exceptions. By November 1914, the time of Latvian born Rudolf Danberg's enlistment, the war in France was barely three months old; thousands of miles away in Australia the population were reliant on newspapers for information regarding the progress of the war which, due to the distance involved, was old news by the time it reached the reader. Heavily censored and exaggerated reports told of great victories over the enemy but gave little or no mention to the heavy toll in terms of killed and wounded; it would somewhat diminish the term 'victory' and do little to assist in the securing of volunteers. Reading between the lines Danberg's records suggest he may have volunteered after a bout of drinking, certainly not from anything he may have read in a newspaper but, whatever his reason may have been, his record indicates he initially served satisfactorily. His behaviour, however, changed dramatically after being shot through the right shoulder at Gallipoli. Thereafter, throughout an extended period of hospitalisation, transfer to training units, returns to his battalion and service in France his records show almost continuous bouts of hospitalisation and misdemeanours escalating in degrees of seriousness. If Danberg had not been killed at the Battle of the Menin Road, it is quite possible his behaviour would have earned him a dishonourable discharge.

(Panel 17) Pte. 1529, Rudolf Danberg, 11th Bn. Australian Infantry, A.I.F.: late of Helena Vale, Western Australia: *s.* of Fredrika Schultz (Große Lagerstraße 12, Hagensberg, Riga, Latvia): *b.* Latvia, 1881: Religion – Church of England: Occupation – Labourer: 5'8" tall, blue eyes, fair hair: joined A.I.F., Black Boy Camp, 27 November 1914: posted 3rd Rfts., 11th Battn., 18 February 1915: landed at Gallipoli with a draft of 244 reinforcements, 7 May 1915: wounded (GSW Right Shoulder), Leane's Trench, 6 August;

evacuated (via Hospital Ship 'Gloucester Castle') to Egypt (10 August): after treatment at Alexandria, Heliopolis, Helouan, Abbassia (Absent Without Leave, 11 August–16 August, on which latter date he was apprehended; Awarded 7 Days Confinement, 6 Days Forfeiture of Pay), was discharged to duty, 20 August: re-admitted Heliopolis (Facial Wound), 21 August; transf'd. Zeitoun, 26 November; transf'd. Ghezireh, 8 December; discharged to duty Tel-el-Kebir, 28 December 1915: departed Alexandria, 29 March 1916; joined the Expeditionary Force in France, 5 April: hospitalised (Cystitis) 20–25 April; transf'd. Northumberland Hospital, 2 June–18 August 1916: returned to France, 21 August: rejoined his battn. Dominion Camp, nr. Reninghelst, 4 September: hospitalised (Asthma, Pleurisy), 7–15 September: (Absent Without Leave, Etaples, 16–17 September; awarded 3 days Forfeiture of Pay), 18 September: hospitalised (Injured Penis), 9–13 November: hospitalised (Abscesses) 22–25 November: discharged to Base Depot, 29 November: (Drunkenness, 23 December; Awarded 14 days Forfeiture of Pay), 28 December: hospitalised (Haematosis), 29 December 1916–16 January 1917; transf'd. Royal Victoria Hospital, Netley (Mentally Sick), 17 January 1917: granted therapeutic leave, England, 9–14 February: admitted 16th Field Ambulance (N.Y.D), 3 March: returned to Base Depot, Etaples, France, 3 May: (Drunkenness, 8 May; awarded 7 days F.P. No.2); returned to battn. Bapaume, 10 May: confined, 15 June awaiting trial (F.G.C.M. 4 July, charged with 'When on Active Service conduct to the prejudice of good order and military discipline in that he at Ribemont, on 15 June, loaded a rifle in his billet without orders, whilst in a state of intoxication, thereby endangering the lives of his comrades.' Awarded 40 days F.P. No.2): moved up with his battn. in stages (July–September) to vicinity of Ypres, and was killed in action nr. Clapham Junction, Polygon Wood, 20 September 1917. Age 36.

(Panel 17) Pte. 243A, Thomas 'Tom' Glennon, 'B' Coy., 11th Bn. Australian Infantry, A.I.F.: formerly No.1650, 44th Bn.: *s.* of the late John Patrick Glennon, of 168, Harold Street, Highgate Hill, Perth, Western Australia, and his wife Eugenie Mary Caroline Annie Josephine Glennon (9, Byron Street, Leaderville): and brother to Gnr. 26956, J.P. Glennon, Australian Field Artillery (surv'd.): *b.* Kilmore, Victoria, 1890: Religion – Roman Catholic: Occupation – Metal Ceiling Fixer: joined A.I.F., Perth, 24 January 1916, apptd. 1st Rfts., 44th Bn., 14 February, apptd. 'B' Coy., Claremont 3 June; transf'd. (243A) 11th Bn., Perham Downs, 22 September: proceeded to France, 24 September: hospitalised Etaples (strangulated hernia), 28 September; transf'd. Havre 13 October, transf'd. England following day; discharged to duty, 1 November: Awarded Forfeiture 9 Days Pay 'Absent Without Leave, Windmill Hill, 30–31 July 1917': returned to France with draft of reinforcements, 9 October; rejoined 11th Bn., 16 October. Killed in action, 1 November 1917. Buried. Age 27. A comrade said, "It was during the third stunt at Passchendaele, Tom and six others were killed instantaneously by the same shell. I saw it happen; he was next to me at the time. He was buried in a shell-hole near to where he was killed. I saw his grave; a cross with his name, number, etc. had been put up. He was very popular with the boys."

(Panel 17) Pte. 3399, John Alexander Anderson Latto, 11th Bn. Australian Infantry, A.I.F.: *s.* of David Latto, of Henry Street, Midland Junction, Western Australia, and his wife Annie: and brother to Pte. 85, G.S. Latto, 51st Bn. (imprisoned June 1917; 10 yrs., Penal Servitude, Desertion: Suspended October 1918, Discharged.); and Pte. 2354, R. Latto, 51st Bn. (discharged. Med. 1918): *b.* Koroit, Victoria, 1897: Religion – Church of England: Occupation – Apprentice Saddler; Messrs T. McCornish, Perth: served four years in Cadets; six months in Engineers: joined A.I.F., Blackboy Hill, 2 August 1915; apptd. 11th Rfts., 11th Bn., 28 October: joined 11th Bn. Egypt, 2 March 1916: served with the Expeditionary Force in France from 5 April: wounded (GSW Lt. ear) 22 July, hospitalised Rouen; transf'd. England, 9 August; discharged 29 September: returned to France with reinforcement draft, 9 October 1917; joined 11th Bn. 16 October, and was killed in action, 1 November 1917; five other men were also killed by the same shell. No Burial. Age 20.

(Panel 17) Pte. 7368, Sydney Clyde Smith, 11th Bn. Australian Infantry, A.I.F.: *s.* of George Arthur (& Elizabeth Lillas) Smith, of 732 Beaufort Street, Mount Lawley, Perth: *b.* East Perth, July 1898: Religion – Congregationalist: Occupation – Joiner: joined 88th Infantry (Pte. 2680) 29 July 1916; enlisted A.I.F., Perth, 1 August; apptd. 23rd Rfts., 11th Bn., Kalgoorlie, 15 August; transf'd. 24th Rfts., 26 January 1917: departed Fremantle 29 January: trained Durrington, England from 28 March: Reprimanded 'When in camp leaving kit in untidy condition, 10 August': proceeded to France 30 August: joined 11th Bn. 11 September. Reported missing after the fighting at Glencorse Wood, 21 September 1917, subsequently confirmed by a Court of Enquiry (La Kreule, 26 July 1918), killed in action on that date. Age 19. On 23 September, Spr. 3085, J. Carr, 8th Field Coy., Australian Engineers, found the body of Pte. Smith to the right of Glencorse Wood and, after removing his testament and diary from his tunic pocket, forwarded these items to Pte. Smith's parents. His personalised silver wristwatch, engraved S.C. Smith, was among the personal effects forwarded to the widow of Pte. 6725, N.D. Barrett, who died of wounds six weeks later; it is not known if this was returned to Mr & Mrs Smith. Pte. Nathan Barrett is buried in Lijssenthoek Military Cemetery (XXI.HH.20A).

(Panel 17) Pte. 5212, Joseph Patrick Thompson, 'A' Coy., 11th Bn. Australian Infantry, A.I.F.: late of Badger Warren, Bolgart, Western Australia: *s.* of Alfred Charles Thompson, of Wongan Hills, and his wife Johannah Mary: *b.* Mogumber, 1896: Religion – Roman Catholic: Occupation – Farm Hand: joined A.I.F., Kalgoorlie, 11 February 1916; apptd. 16th Rfts., 11th Bn., Bunbury 25 March; departed Fremantle, 31 March: served Egypt; thereafter trained England; proceeded to France with draft of reinforcements, 31 July: joined 11th Bn. 13 August: hospitalised (Foot/ankle injury, serious) France, 26 November; transf'd. England, 14 December 1916: returned to France (following treatment/convalescence/retraining) 10 October 1917: rejoined 11th Bn. 16 October. One of six men killed by the same shell, 1 November 1917, nr. Zonnebeke. No Burial. Age 21.

(Panel 17) Pte. 5500, Maurice Patrick Walther, 12th Bn. Australian Infantry, A.I.F.: brother to Pte. 5495, W.C. Walther, 12th Bn. Australian Infantry, killed in action, 3 June 1918: *b.* Brunswick, Melbourne, Victoria, 1890: Religion – Roman Catholic: Occupation – Labourer: 5'11" tall, grey eyes, brown hair: enlisted Cairns, Queensland, 18 January 1916: departed Sydney, 20 April: joined 12th Battn. in France, 22 September 1916. Killed in action, 31 October 1917. Age 27. *unm.* His effects – Purse, Rosary, Badge, Metal Wrist Watch, Coin – were forwarded (1 March 1918) c/o Mrs Louisa McCarthy (75, Jeffcott Street, West Melbourne). His brother Walter is buried in Borre British Cemetery (II.B.3).

(Panel 17) Sergt. 1094, John 'Jack' Francis Long (*a.k.a* 'Long John Francis'), 'B' Coy., 13th Bn. Australian Infantry, A.I.F.: *s.* of Michael Long, of 'The Cedars,' Gobondery Street, Trundle, New South Wales, and Mary Long his wife: *b.* Gillenbine, nr. Trundle, *c.*1892: Religion – Roman Catholic: *educ.* Trundle Public School: Occupation – Carpenter: 5'9" tall, brown eyes, dark brown hair: enlisted Liverpool, New South Wales, 30 October 1914; apptd. Pte., 'B' Coy., 13th Battn., Broadmeadows Camp, 21 December: departed Melbourne, 22 December: served in Egypt, Gallipoli from 12 April 1915, wounded (GSW Lt. Arm/Shoulder), 30 April; promoted Corpl. 22 August 1915: joined Expeditionary Force in France, 15 October 1916: promoted Temp. Sergt. 10 May 1917; Sergt. 16 July. Killed in action, 27 September 1917. Age 25. Corpl. 1124, R.E. Chapman reported, "He was in the Bn. football team, tall, thin, always smiling...We were at Polygon Wood, digging communication trenches to the new objective following the 3 attacking Bns. It was about 6 am on 27th September. I was digging next to Long, when a dud shell hit him in the chest on the right side and killed him instantly. He uttered no sound and fell dead alongside me. I gave his damaged wallet and pay book to the OC of the Coy. I then helped to bury him 5 yards away in No Man's Land. We made a rough cross and wrote his name and regiment on in pencil." Remembered on the Trundle (War Memorial Hall) Honour Roll, and Avenue of Remembrance, Forbes Street.

(Panel 17) Pte. 1206, James Wesley Cook, 'C' Coy., 13th Bn. Australian Infantry, A.I.F.: *s.* of Peter Cook, of Nambucca River, Macksville, New South Wales, by his wife Margaret: and elder brother to Pte. 1079, P.G. Cook, 36th Battn., killed in action, 7 June 1917: *b.* Stewart's Point, January 1896: joined A.I.F., Broadmeadows, 23 May 1916: departed Sydney, 7 October: trained England, 22 November–3 May 1917: proceeded to France on the latter date, and was killed in action, 16 June 1917; Belgium. Memorial Cross erected Strand Military Cemetery, Ploegsteert Wood. Age 21.

His brother Peter is buried in Strand Military Cemetery (V.A.3).

Often referred to as 'Jacka's Mob,' in the opening stages of 5th Australian Division's part in the fighting for Polygon Wood, 14th Battalion, A.I.F., attacked over ground which was 'in a frightful state, in places knee-deep in mud. There were shell holes every few yards, most of them filled with water. These conditions made the going very arduous' and, 'as the advance progressed the opposition stiffened, and the machine-gun fire of the enemy became greater, causing a fair number of casualties. Several enemy machine-guns and their crews were captured, one machine-gunner captured being chained to his gun. Few of the enemy outside the pill-boxes waited for our barrage, though some did, and occasionally a German would fly skyward as one of our shells lobbed in a hole beside him. The majority, however, either bolted through the barrage, or retired before its advent, forming excellent targets for our men, of which they took full advantage.' By 8 a.m. the battalion had successfully reached their second objective and at their commander's insistence, each company pushed ahead another fifty yards beyond in order to avoid the enemy's counter-attack barrage. A wise precaution but fifty yards too late for Capt. H.B. Wanliss, he was killed by a German machine gun, moments after his company had reached the Second Objective.

(Panel 17) Capt. Harold Boyd Wanliss, D.S.O., 'A' Coy., 14th Bn. Australian Infantry, A.I.F.: *s.* of Newton Wanliss, of 'Rayleigh,' Point Lonsdale, Victoria, by his wife Margaret: *b.* Ballarat, Victoria, 1892. The Australian historian C.E.W. Bean wrote, "This was a grievous loss. By his friends, including General Monash, Colonels Peck and Durant, Chaplain Rolland and men of all ranks, Harold Wanliss had been recognised as a young man possibly destined, had he lived, to lead Australia. Peck, formerly his battalion commander, wrote, 'Many brave men, many good men I have met … but he was the king of them all.' He added that he 'cursed the day' that had deprived him of preserving Wanliss' life. He had studied agriculture, and had taken up land just before the war. His periods of furlough he had devoted to the study of industry new to Australia, which he would endeavour to introduce there after the war." He was awarded the D.S.O. (*London Gazette*, 27 July 1916) for gallantry in leading a raiding party in the Bois Grenier sector: 'He forced the wire which was uncut, entered the trench, inflicted heavy loss on the enemy and supervised the withdrawal. While forcing the wire he was wounded in the face, later he was wounded by a bullet in the neck, and finally when withdrawing he was again wounded and had to be carried in.' Killed in action, 26 September 1917. Lieut. N.C. Aldridge wrote, "14 June 1916. I was with Capt. Wanliss in the attack on September 26th 1917, near Zonnebeke and Polygon Wood. I was his Company Second in Command and was alongside him when he was killed. He was kiled by machine-gun bullets just as we reached the objective – He was shot in the throat, heart and side, and was buried by L/Corpl. 1447, J. Andrews, that same afternoon just where he fell. His death was instantaneous. He was a thorough gentleman and was respected by everyone in the battalion – also he was brave with his other gifts which was proved by his winning the D.S.O. as a 2/Lt. in a raid in June 1916, when the battalion first came to France from Egypt. I gave the map reference where he was buried etc. to his father, whose address is c/o Commercial Bank of Australia, Bishopsgate Street, London…Capt. Wanliss was Adjutant for about 9 months and gave the job up to take charge of A Coy. A couple of weeks before the attack on Zonnebeke and Polygon Wood…" Age 25. *unm.*

(Panel 17) Pte. 6755, Ernest William Hubbard, 14th Bn. Australian Infantry, A.I.F.: *s.* of the late Thomas Tuckwood Hubbard, by his wife Mary (Church Lane, Wymeswold, Loughborough), *dau.* of Joseph Brown, of Broughton: *b.* Wymeswold, co. Leicester, 18 February 1885: *educ.* there: went to Australia, 4 January 1911; settled Uppingham, New South Wales, as a Sheep Farmer: joined Australian Imperial Force 1916: served with the Expeditionary Force in France and Flanders from 1 April 1917, and was killed in action nr. Ypres, 16 October following. Buried where he fell. Major-General E.G. Sinclair MacLagan, C.B., D.S.O., Comdg. 4th Australian Division, wrote congratulating Pte. Hubbard on his courage and untiring energy in saving wounded near Zonnebeke, 26 September 1917. Age 33. *unm.*

(Panel 17) Corpl. 2525A, Frederick Treeby, 'B' Coy., 15th Bn. Australian Infantry, A.I.F.: *s.* of Alice Maud Treeby (Pie Creek, South Side, Gympie, Queensland), and the late Edward Washington Treeby: and brother to Pte. 2211, G.A. Treeby, 4th Australian Pioneers (surv'd.); Sergt. 2226, H.P. Treeby, 2nd Light Horse (surv'd.); Pte. 1986, R. Treeby, 47th Australian Infantry (surv'd.); L/Corpl. 2237, S. Treeby, 2nd Light Horse (surv'd.); and Pte. Q24769, W. Treeby, 3rd Light Horse (surv'd.): *b.* Gympie, 1893: Occupation – Teamster: joined A.I.F., Rifle Range, Queensland, 25 November 1915: posted 5th Rfts., 47th Battn., Enoggera, 2 September 1916; departed Brisbane, A49 'Seang Choon,' on the 19th: joined

12th Training Battn., Codford, England, 9 December: Obtained 1st Class Qualification (3 February 1917), 'having fair knowledge of Lewis Gun, 6th Rifle Course, Tidworth' (3–25 January 1917); promoted Corpl. 24 January: Severely Reprimanded by Major Rowland (11 March); Forfeited 1 Day's Pay 'Failing to obey an order, in that after being duly warned for In Lying Piquet failed to report for same at proper time': proceeded to France, 22 May: transf'd. 15th Battn. 10 June. Killed in action, 27 September 1917. Buried (29 September) nr. Polygon Wood (28.N.E.9.a.3.52). Sergt. 4316, J. Holt recorded, "16 July 1918. Treeby was a clean-shaven jelly man, about 5ft. 8ins. On the night of September 26th, when we were in Polygon Wood, 4 of our men were killed and 2 wounded by a shell which burst in the shell hole where they were. The time would be about 1 a.m. I stayed with them until daylight and then helped to take them in. One of the 4 men killed was Treeby. I did not know this at the time but it was given out next day. The shell hole was about a mile behind the line, and the Pioneers would bury the four men in the same place. The Germans now hold this part of the ground." Age 24. *unm.*

(Panel 17) L/Corpl. 6867, David 'Dave' Alexander Murphy, 'B' Coy., 15th Bn. Australian Infantry, A.I.F.: *s.* of E.H. (& Agnes) Murphy, of George Street, Roma, Queensland: Occupation – Cabinetmaker: joined A.I.F., Roma, 29 May 1916: joined 15th Battn. La Plus Douve Farm, 12 June 1917: apptd. L/Corpl. 19 September; and was killed in action one week later, 26 September 1917, in the vicinity of Gordon House. Buried near where he fell. Pte. 6545, G.E. Pruce recorded, "I saw Murphy shot through the heart. He never moved again as he was killed instantaneously. His face was not touched, and there was no blood and no mutilation. We were in an advance and I was quite near at the time, about 20 yards off…" Age 23. *unm.* See also Pte. N. Crawford, 31st Bn. A.I.F. (Panel 23).

(Panel 17) Pte. 6706, Hugo Edmund Haapaniemi (served as Asplund, H.), 15th Bn. Australian Infantry, A.I.F.: late of South Brisbane, Queensland: *s.* of Josephina Haapaniemi (Makison Soujeluskoti, Merikatu 19–21, Helsingfors, Suomi, Russia): *b.* Wasa, Suomi (Finland), 1887: Religion – Church of England: Occupation – Sailor: 5'3½" tall, blue eyes, dark brown hair: enlisted Adelaide Street, Brisbane, 16 October 1916; posted 22nd Rfts., 15th Battn.: departed Brisbane, HMAT A.55 'Kyarra,' 17 November: admitted ship's hospital, 30 November, N.Y.D., and 1 January 1917, Venereal Disease: disembarked Plymouth, 30 January 1917, proceeded Codford Camp for training: Awarded 168 hours Detention, Codford (16 March 1917) for (1) Drunkenness, (2) Resisting Escort, 15 March: proceeded to France 3 May; joined 15th Battn., Ribemont 8 May. Died of wounds, 15 October 1917, received in action in support line, Zonnebeke. Age 30. *unm.* Battalion War Diary records throughout 15th October the battalion supports were constantly bombarded by the enemy; between 12 midnight and 2 am. (16 October) with gas. 'A good number of men were affected by it, and 12 men had to be evacuated. It was found that it had a delayed action, some men not being affected until 24 hours later. It makes eyes water and causes irritation of the throat.'

(Panel 17) 2nd Lieut. Victor Frederick Doran, 16th Bn. Australian Infantry, A.I.F.: *s.* of Joseph Teran Doran, of 48, North Street, Midland Junction, Western Australia, by his wife Annie May: and brother to Pte. 3101, A.P. Doran, 48th Bn. A.I.F., who fell at Ypres exactly four months and one day later: *b.* Echuca, Victoria, *c.* 1890. Killed in action, 11 June 1917. Age 27. *unm.*

His brother Albert also has no known grave; he is recorded on Panel 27.

(Panel 17) Sergt. 2351, Harold Long, 16th Bn. Australian Infantry, A.I.F.: *s.* of William Long, of High Street, Burham, Rochester, co. Kent, by his wife Rosetta: and elder brother to L/Sergt. 8800, R. Long, 2nd Oxford & Bucks Light Infantry, who fell 21 October 1914, at the First Battle of Ypres: Occupation – Labourer: enlisted Mypolonga, South Australia, 29 December 1914: departed aboard HMAT 'Konowna,' 25 June 1915, with draft of reinforcements to 16th Battn. Killed in action, 25 September 1917. Age 27.

His brother Reginald is buried in Perth Cemetery (China Wall) (XIV.B.21).

(Panel 17) 2nd Lieut. 4792, Alexander Robert McDowell, 17th Bn. Australian Infantry, A.I.F.: late of 'Kelvin,' Cooper Street, Marrickville, New South Wales: *b.* Pyrmont, Sydney, February 1892: Occupation – Clerk: enlisted, 19 January 1916, Royal Agricultural Showgrounds, Sydney: departed Australia, 14 April 1916, proceeded to Egypt, and departed Alexandria, 28 May: on arrival in England, 7 June, underwent a course of instruction Tidworth; returned to his unit, 10 September 1916: apptd. Corpl. January 1917:

joined 17th Battn. France, 19 March 1917: wounded in action (GSW, L. Arm) 3 May, removed to England on the 17th. of that month from whence, after treatment and recuperative leave, he returned to France 17 July: rejoined 17th Battn. 1 August: wounded, 20 September 1917 (remained at duty); promoted 2nd Lieut. on the 29th., and was killed by shell-fire at Passchendaele, 9 October 1917. Age 25. It is believed he was buried where he fell but, owing to casualties in the unit, further particulars are not available. He married three days prior to his departure, Susan *née* Miner (since remarried, now Mrs Smith); it is believed she may sometime have been resident with her late husband's mother, Mabel Ann McDowell, at 56, Goodsell Street, Newtown, Sydney. *The Sydney Morning Herald*, In Memoriam, 9 October 1918:-

> *No shroud, no flowers, adorned his breast,*
> *With his comrades he was laid at rest.*

> Inserted by his father and mother-in-law,
> Mr & Mrs Miner; nieces Doris and Blanche

(Panel 17) 2nd Lieut. Thomas Lloyd Ryan, M.M., 17th Bn. Australian Infantry, A.I.F.: *s.* of Timothy Ryan, of Farley, Wellingrove, New South Wales, by his wife Sarah Ann: and *yr.* brother to 2nd Lieut. C.F. Ryan, 45th Battn. A.I.F., who fell 7 June 1917: *b.* Strathbogie, Glasgow, Victoria, *c.*1892. Killed in action, 20 September 1917, at the Battle of the Menin Road. Age 25. *unm.*

His brother Charles also has no known grave; he is recorded on Panel 27.

(Panel 17) Pte. 6281, William Burkett, 17th Bn. Australian Infantry, A.I.F.: *s.* of William Burkett, by his wife Elizabeth: *b.* Double Bay, Sydney. Reported wounded and missing, 20 September 1917, at the Battle of the Menin Road; confirmed (May 1918) killed in action. Buried by Pte. 4661, W.H. Back, 21st Battn., vicinity Westhoek and Anzac Ridge. Age 26. He leaves a wife, Mrs M.M. Burkett (23, Bank Stret, North Sydney). See Sergt. 3596, S. Oakley, M.M., Buttes New British Cemetery (XXX.B.4).

(Panel 17) Pte. 6346, John Henry McGinley, 17th Bn. Australian Infantry, A.I.F.: Killed in action, 20 September 1917, at the Battle of the Menin Road. Buried by Pte. 4661, W.H. Back, 21st Battn., in the vicinity of Westhoek and Anzac Ridge. See Sergt. 3596, S. Oakley, M.M., Buttes New British Cemetery (XXX.B.4).

(Panel 17) Pte. 5449, Wallace Richard Meller, 17th Bn. Australian Infantry, A.I.F.: *s.* of Herbert William Meller, by his wife Ellen: *b.* St. Leonard's, New South Wales. Reported wounded and missing 20 September 1917; Battle of the Menin Road; confirmed (17 June 1918) killed in action. Age 18. Buried by Pte. 4661, W.H. Back, 21st Battn., Westhoek/Anzac Ridge. See Sergt. 3596, S. Oakley, M.M., Buttes New British Cemetery (XXX.B.4).

(Panel 17) Pte. 2013A, Albert George Ernest Mewburn, 17th Bn. Australian Infantry, A.I.F.: *s.* of the late John Mewburn, by his wife Margaret (Boorowa, New South Wales): and elder brother to Pte. 2693, R.E. Mewburn, 55th Battn., who fell five weeks previously: *b.* Rugby, New South Wales, 1894. Killed in action, 5 November 1917. Age 23. *unm.* C.A. Lloyd, 17th Battn., wrote, "…I beg to inform you that during the execution of my duties as stretcher-bearer, I saw fully the regrettable case of Mewburn. It was about 11 p.m. on the night of November 5th when Mewburn with others were in a dugout, heavily reinforced by heavy wood, when the enemy obtained a direct hit on the dugout with a 5.9 H.E. shell, and a fragment of shell amputated his left leg about 6 inches below the thigh. He also had an artery cut in the right leg, and a great amount of debris on his body. During the time we took to extricate him, in bad weather and darkness, haemorrhage had set in severely. I endeavoured to stop the bleeding, but every effort was in vain, and he was being taken to the doctor when he died and was buried by me at the intersection of the communication sap and the front line of the 17th Battn. on Tokio Ridge. He was unfortunately buried in a shell hole, marked by a rifle. He was not in possession of a pay book, but had an identification disc which I left on him. What private effects he had were handed in…"

His brother Earl also has no known grave; he is recorded on Panel 29.

(Panel 17) Pte. 2173, John Leslie Milthorpe, 'B' Coy., 17th Bn. Australian Infantry, A.I.F.: *s.* of William Lucas Milthorpe, of 42, Kemp Street, Northcote, Victoria, by his wife Mary Ann: *b.* Oaklands, New South Wales. Reported wounded and missing, 20 September 1917, at the Battle of the Menin Road;

confirmed (8 May 1918) killed in action. Age 23. *unm.* Buried by Pte. 4661, W.H. Back, 21st Battn., in the vicinity of Westhoek and Anzac Ridge. See Sergt. 3596, S. Oakley, M.M., Buttes New British Cemetery (XXX.B.4).

(Panel 17) Pte. 6174, George Ross Seabrook, 'C' Coy., 17th Bn. Australian Infantry, A.I.F.: *s.* of William George Seabrook, of Great North Road, Five Dock, Sydney, New South Wales, by his wife Fanny Isabel: and brother to Pte. 6147, T.L. Seabrook, who fell the same day, and 2nd Lieut. W.K. Seabrook, 17th Battn. A.I.F., died of wounds at Poperinghe the following day. Killed (previously reported missing) in action at the Battle of the Menin Road, 20 September 1917. Age 25. *unm.*

His brother Theo also has no known grave, he is recorded below; William is buried in Lijssenthoek Military Cemetery (XXIII.B.5).

(Panel 17) Pte. 6147, Theo Leslie Seabrook, 'C' Coy., 17th Bn. Australian Infantry, A.I.F.: *s.* of William George Seabrook, of Great North Road, Five Dock, Sydney, New South Wales, by his wife Fanny Isabel: and brother to Pte. 6174, G.R. Seabrook, who fell the same day; and 2nd Lieut. W.K. Seabrook, 17th Battn. A.I.F., who died of wounds at Poperinghe the following day. Killed (previously reported missing) in action at the Battle of the Menin Road, 20 September 1917. Age 24. Sergt. C. Troupe, 17th Battn., A.I.F., wrote (4 December 1917), "I knew two brothers called Seabrook, 17th Battn., one of them was killed instantaneously beside me on September 20th in front of Ypres. The 18th Battn. had taken Anzac House, and we were advancing from there. The Germans were putting up a very heavy barrage and we were consolidating our position. Sergt. Eric Powell helped me to lift him up onto the parados. We were relieved the next morning and the trench was deserted altogether. I cannot say whether his initials were G.R. or T.L. The brother I mean was the taller of the two." (Theo was 5'7" tall, George was 5'4"; both brothers were slightly built with fair hair) Pte. 6312, W. Hilder, reported, "I knew Seabrook who was one of three brothers who were killed. This one was in the support trench on the night of September 20th. His brother G.R. Seabrook was with him at the time and as they stood in the trench together a shell landed and killed both of them. With regard to burial, our men had no chance for doing it as we had to clear out for a Canadian Battn. which relieved us and they undertook to bury the dead that we had to leave behind." *unm.*

His brother George also has no known grave, he is recorded above; William is buried in Lijssenthoek Military Cemetery (XXIII.B.5).

(Panel 17) Pte. 6420, Jackson Smith, 17th Bn. Australian Infantry, A.I.F.: Killed in action in the advance from Anzac House, 20 September 1917, at the Battle of the Menin Road. Buried by Pte. 4661, W.H. Back, 21st Battn.; vicinity Westhoek/Anzac Ridge. See Sergt. 3596, S. Oakley, M.M., Buttes New British Cemetery (XXX.B.4).

(Panel 17) Pte. 1062, James Smith, 17th Bn. Australian Infantry, A.I.F.: Killed in action in the advance from Anzac House, 20 September 1917, at the Battle of the Menin Road. Buried by Pte. 4661, W.H. Back, 21st Battn.; Westhoek/Anzac Ridge. See Sergt. 3596, S. Oakley, M.M., Buttes New British Cemetery (XXX.B.4).

(Panel 17) Pte. 6421, Alexander Thompson, 17th Bn. Australian Infantry, A.I.F.: Killed in action in the advance from Anzac House, 20 September 1917, at the Battle of the Menin Road. Buried by Pte. 4661, W.H. Back, 21st Battn., in the vicinity of Westhoek and Anzac Ridge. See Sergt. 3596, S. Oakley, M.M., Buttes New British Cemetery (XXX.B.4).

PANEL 17 ENDS: PTE. W.O. WOMSLEY, 17TH BN. AUSTRALIAN INF.

PANEL 19 BEGINS: CORPL. I. AMBROSE, ROYAL SCOTS FUSILIERS.

(Panel 19) Corpl. 10809, Daniel Clark, 'C' Coy., 2nd Bn. (21st Foot) The Royal Scots Fusiliers: *s.* of Sergt. James Clark, of Inkerman Cottage, Ayr, by his wife Jane: served with the Expeditionary Force. Killed in action near Ypres, 21 October 1914. Age 20. *unm.*

(Panel 19) Corpl. 6594, William Dorans, 1st Bn. (21st Foot) The Royal Scots Fusiliers: served with the Expeditionary Force. Reported missing at Ypres, 13 November 1914; now assumed killed. *m.*

(Panel 19) Corpl. 10507, Bertie E. Johnstone, 2nd Bn. (21st Foot) The Royal Scots Fusiliers: *s.* of C. (& Mrs) Johnstone, of 12, Wharf Terrace, Wantage, co. Berks: served with the Expeditionary Force. Killed in action at Ypres, 2 November 1914. Age 21. *unm.* (*IWGC record Johnson*) Mustering only one piper after the First Battle of Ypres (Pipe Major A. Meikle and all but one of the N.C.O.s. having been either killed, wounded or taken prisoner) 2nd Royal Scots Fusiliers managed to scrape together a small band composed of such acting pipers as could be spared from the trenches until drafts from other battalions arrived to bring the band back up to strength.

(Panel 19) Corpl. Piper 9481, Albert Victor Jennings, 2nd Bn. (21st Foot) The Royal Scots Fusiliers: enlisted Dover, co. Kent: served with the Expeditionary Force in France and Flanders, and was reported missing 31 October 1914; now assumed killed. He leaves a wife, and *dau.* Mary Maud (7, Distillery Lane, Waterside, co. Londonderry). One of three 2nd Battalion Pipers killed at the First Battle of Ypres.

(Panel 19) Corpl. Piper 8799, Walter A. Richardson, 2nd Bn. (21st Foot) The Royal Scots Fusiliers: late of Waterside, Co. Londonderry: *s.* of Pipe Major (& Mrs) Richardson, of 16, Selbourne Terrace, Folkestone Road, Dover: enlisted Dover, co. Kent: served with the Expeditionary Force in France, and died of wounds, 30 October 1914, received at the First Battle of Ypres. One of three 2nd Battalion Pipers to make the supreme sacrifice at the First Battle of Ypres. His Commanding Officer, J.H.W. Pollard, wrote, "26 March 1915…I should like to add that Corporal Richardson was a most promising non-commissioned officer and did well during the present campaign. Prior to the War he had been one of our best pipers, and had been employed as orderly to the Commanding Officer for two years during training and manoeuvres. I am very sorry to have lost him." Should his remains be recovered, his father requested the epitaph:-

A Soldier Born, As A Soldier He Died, Facing The Murderous Hun

(Panel 19) L/Corpl. 9460, Robert Brown, 1st Bn. (21st Foot) The Royal Scots Fusiliers: *s.* of James Tod Brown, of Millfield Cottage, Kettle Road, Freuchie, co. Fife: served with the Expeditionary Force. Killed in action at Ypres, 11 November 1914.

(Panel 19) L/Corpl. 9264, William Clark, 2nd Bn. (21st Foot) The Royal Scots Fusiliers: *s.* of William Clark, of King's Cross, London, N.: served with the Expeditionary Force. Killed in action at Ypres, 24 October 1914.

(Panel 19) L/Corpl. 10048, John Flynn, 1st Bn. (21st Foot) The Royal Scots Fusiliers: served with the Expeditionary Force. Killed in action at Ypres, 11 November 1914. *m.*

(Panel 19) L/Corpl. 10650, Daniel Johnson, 2nd Bn. (21st Foot) The Royal Scots Fusiliers: *s.* of Daniel Johnson, of Great Yarmouth, co. Norfolk: served with the Expeditionary Force. Reported missing 31 October 1914, and now assumed killed.

(Panel 19) L/Corpl. 8456, Leonard Keen, 2nd Bn. (21st Foot) The Royal Scots Fusiliers: served with the Expeditionary Force in France. Killed in action at Ypres, 11 November 1914. He leaves a wife, Daisy Elizabeth Keen (Littleworth Wing, Leighton Buzzard, co. Bedford).

(Panel 19) Pte. 7418, Richard Allen, 1st Bn. (21st Foot) The Royal Scots Fusiliers: served with the Expeditionary Force. Reported missing, 12 November. 1914; now assumed killed.

(Panel 19) Pte. 8778, David Anderson, 2nd Bn. (21st Foot) The Royal Scots Fusiliers: served with the Expeditionary Force. Reported missing, 23 October 1914; now assumed killed.

(Panel 19) Pte. 9889, Robert Graham Wilson Anderson, 2nd Bn. (21st Foot) The Royal Scots Fusiliers: *s.* of Alexander Anderson, of 130, Walker Road, Torry, Aberdeen, by his wife Selina: *b.* Aberdeen, 1890: served with the Expeditionary Force, and died 21 October 1914, of wounds received in action nr. Ypres. Age 24. *unm.*

(Panel 19) Pte. 7937, Peter Andrews, 1st Bn. (21st Foot) The Royal Scots Fusiliers: enlisted Inverkeithing, co. Fife: served with the Expeditionary Force in France, and was killed in action there, 1 January 1915.

(Panel 19) Pte. 10701, Joseph H. Ashcroft, 2nd Bn. (21st Foot) The Royal Scots Fusiliers: *s.* of Abia Ashcroft (14, Eaves Street, North Shore, Blackpool, co. Lancaster): served with the Expeditionary Force. Killed in action nr. Ypres, 21 October 1914. Age 22. *unm.*

(Panel 19) Pte. 6000, Walter Duncan Bain, 2nd Bn. (21st Foot) The Royal Scots Fusiliers: served with the Expeditionary Force. Reported missing, 24 October 1914; now assumed killed.

(Panel 19) Pte. 10075, James Beattie, 2nd Bn. (21st Foot) The Royal Scots Fusiliers: enlisted Ayr: served with the Expeditionary Force. Killed in action nr. Ypres, 4 November 1914.

(Panel 19) Pte. 10816, James Beattie, 2nd Bn. (21st Foot) The Royal Scots Fusiliers: *s.* of J.A. Beattie, of 19, Chronicle Lane, late of 29, Meat Market, Aberdeen: enlisted Aberdeen: served with the Expeditionary Force. Killed in action, 24 October 1914.

(Panel 19) Pte. 10970, David Boland, 1st Bn. (21st Foot) The Royal Scots Fusiliers: *s.* of Martin (& Mrs) Boland, of 1, Wilson Street, Wilson Place, Lochee, Dundee: *b.* Liff, co. Forfar, 1896: enlisted Dundee: served with the Expeditionary Force. Reported wounded and missing, 11 November 1914; assumed killed in action. Age 18.

(Panel 19) Pte. 7855, William Bramwell, 1st Bn. (21st Foot) The Royal Scots Fusiliers: enlisted Preston, co. Lancaster: served with the Expeditionary Force. Killed in action at Ypres, 12 November 1914.

(Panel 19) Pte. 6127, James Taylor Bridges, 2nd Bn. (21st Foot) The Royal Scots Fusiliers: *s.* of Thomas Taylor Bridges, of 60A, Pitt Street, Leith, Edinburgh: *b.* Edinburgh, *c.*1891: served with the Expeditionary Force. Reported missing, 25 October 1914; believed killed. Age 23. *unm.*

(Panel 19) Drmr. (Pte) 10057, Thomas Greenfield Bruce, 2nd Bn. (21st Foot) The Royal Scots Fusiliers: *s.* of William Bruce, of Edinburgh: enlisted Ayr: served with the Expeditionary Force. Killed in action, 24 October 1914.

(Panel 19) Pte. 9646, Charles Butcher, 2nd Bn. (21st Foot) The Royal Scots Fusiliers: *s.* of the late John Butcher, of Bethnal Green, London, N.: and brother to James Butcher, of 155, Quinn's Buildings, Russia Lane, Bethnal Green: served with the Expeditionary Force. Reported wounded and missing, 31 October 1914; assumed killed. Age 29. *unm.*

(Panel 19) Pte. Piper 10397, George Robert Butterworth, 2nd Bn. (21st Foot) The Royal Scots Fusiliers: late of Ashton-under-Lyne: enlisted Manchester: served with the Expeditionary Force in France and Flanders; died of wounds received in action, 28 October 1914. One of three 2nd Battalion Pipers to make the supreme sacrifice at the First Battle of Ypres. See Corpl. 9481, A.V. Jennings and 8799, W.A. Richardson, above.

(Panel 19) Pte. 8788, Harry Benjamin Cyril Byrne, 1st Bn. (21st Foot) The Royal Scots Fusiliers: *s.* of Patrick Byrne, of 29A, Bessborough Gardens, Grosvenor Road, Pimlico, London, by his wife Mary: *b.* Tipperary, *c.*1884: served with the Expeditionary Force, and was killed in action at Ypres, 13 November 1914. Age 30.

(Panel 19) Pte. 6572, Joseph Cairns, 1st Bn. (21st Foot) The Royal Scots Fusiliers: *s.* of the late Joseph (& Agnes) Cairns: foster *s.* to Henry Cairns, of Kilmarnock, and his wife Mary Ann: *b.* Glasgow, *c.*1880: served with the Expeditionary Force. Killed in action at Ypres, 11 November 1914.

(Panel 19) Pte. 7228, Quintin Caldwell, 2nd Bn. (21st Foot) The Royal Scots Fusiliers: served with the Expeditionary Force. Reported wounded and missing, 31 October 1914; assumed killed. Age 40. He was married to Mary, *née* O'Hara (8, Reid's Square, Russell Street, Ayr).

(Panel 19) Pte. 10589, James Campbell, 2nd Bn. (21st Foot) The Royal Scots Fusiliers: late of Garlieston, nr. Newton Stewart, co. Wigtown: served with the Expeditionary Force. Killed in action, 31 October 1914, nr. Ypres. (*IWGC record 10389*)

(Panel 19) Pte. 10068, James Campbell, 2nd Bn. (21st Foot) The Royal Scots Fusiliers: of Crossgates, co. Fife: served with the Expeditionary Force. Reported wounded and missing, 31 October 1914; assumed killed.

(Panel 19) Pte. 10550, Andrew Carey, 2nd Bn. (21st Foot) The Royal Scots Fusiliers: *s.* of James Carey, of 19, Harriet Street, Pollokshaws, Glasgow, by his wife Mary: served with the Expeditionary Force. Reported wounded and missing, 23 October 1914; assumed killed. Age 22. *unm.*

(Panel 19) Pte. 7443, James Cawley, 1st Bn. (21st Foot) The Royal Scots Fusiliers: served with the Expeditionary Force. Died of wounds received in action nr. Ypres, 12 November 1914. *m.*

(Panel 19) Pte., 10266, William Clark, 2nd Bn. (21st Foot) The Royal Scots Fusiliers: *s.* of George Clark, of Arbroath: served with the Expeditionary Force. Killed in action, 30 October 1914.

(Panel 19) Pte. 10725, William Clifford, 1st Bn. (21st Foot) The Royal Scots Fusiliers: served with the Expeditionary Force. Killed in action at Ypres, 11 November 1914.

(Panel 19) Pte. 9721, Frederick Cochrane, 2nd Bn. (21st Foot) The Royal Scots Fusiliers: *s.* of M. Cochrane, of Irvine: served with the Expeditionary Force, and was killed in action nr. Ypres, Belgium 31 October 1914.

(Panel 19) Pte. 9055, Daniel Coll, 2nd Bn. (21st Foot) The Royal Scots Fusiliers: served with the Expeditionary Force, and was killed in action at Ypres, 23 October 1914.

(Panel 19) Pte. 6558, Charles Collins, 2nd Bn. (21st Foot) The Royal Scots Fusiliers: *s.* of Charles Collins, of 104, Reid Street, Bridgeton, Glasgow; late of Church Street, Dumbarton: served with the Expeditionary Force in France, and was killed in action at Ypres, 23 October 1914. Age 25. *unm.*

(Panel 19) Pte. 7419, Luke Connor, 2nd Bn. (21st Foot) The Royal Scots Fusiliers: *s.* of Patrick Connor, of Enniskillen: served with the Expeditionary Force in France. Killed in action nr. Ypres 21 October 1914.

(Panel 19) Pte. 7718, Thomas Connor, 2nd Bn. (21st Foot) The Royal Scots Fusiliers: *s.* of John Connor, of 1, St. John's Street, Edinburgh, by his wife Margaret: served with the Expeditionary Force in France. Reported missing, 31 October 1914; assumed killed. Age 31.

(Panel 19) Pte. 8089, James Cornock, 1st Bn. (21st Foot) The Royal Scots Fusiliers: *s.* of John Cornock, of Kilmarnock: served with the Expeditionary Force. Reported missing, 12 November 1914; now assumed killed. Age 28. He leaves a wife, Agnes McLachlan Cornock (Red Hill, Durban, Natal, South Africa).

(Panel 19) Pte. 9302, Thomas Walter Craggs, 2nd Bn. (21st Foot) The Royal Scots Fusiliers: served with the Expeditionary Force, and was killed in action nr. Ypres, 23 October 1914.

(Panel 19) Pte. 6179, James Craig, 2nd Bn. (21st Foot) The Royal Scots Fusiliers: enlisted Glasgow: served with the Expeditionary Force. Reported missing, 24 October 1914; now assumed killed. *m.*

(Panel 19) Pte. 9433, James Craig, 2nd Bn. (21st Foot) The Royal Scots Fusiliers: late of Coatbridge, co. Lanark: *b.* Maybole, Glasgow: served with the Expeditionary Force in France. Reported missing, 23 October 1914; now assumed killed in action on or about that date.

(Panel 19) Pte. 9275, Charles Crosbie, 1st Bn. (21st Foot) The Royal Scots Fusiliers: *s.* of the late Alexander Crosbie, by his wife Annie (27, Springwell Place, Edinburgh): served with the Expeditionary Force, and was killed in action, 13 November 1914. Age 24.

(Panel 19) Pte. 10644, Frank Cruickshank, 2nd Bn. (21st Foot) The Royal Scots Fusiliers: served with the Expeditionary Force. Reported missing 24 October 1914; assumed killed in action on or about that date.

(Panel 19) Pte. 9368, James Davis, 2nd Bn. (21st Foot) The Royal Scots Fusiliers: served with the Expeditionary Force. Reported wounded and missing, 31 October 1914; now assumed killed.

(Panel 19) Pte. 10956, David Dempsey, 1st Bn. (21st Foot) The Royal Scots Fusiliers: *s.* of Peter Dempsey, of 44, High Street, Ayr, by his wife Jeannie, *née* Marr: served with the Expeditionary Force. Reported missing after the First Battle of Ypres, 11 November 1914; now assumed killed. Age 18.

(Panel 19) Pte. 4376, James Devine, 2nd Bn. (21st Foot) The Royal Scots Fusiliers: *s.* of James Devine, of Glasgow: *b.* Magherafelt, Londonderry: served with the Expeditionary Force, and was killed in action nr. Ypres, 5 November 1914.

(Panel 19) Pte. 6603, William Dillon, 2nd Bn. (21st Foot) The Royal Scots Fusiliers: *b.* Whifflet, co. Lanark: enlisted Glasgow: served with the Expeditionary Force. Reported wounded and missing, 31 October 1914; now assumed killed.

(Panel 19) Pte. 11003, John Mitchell Dingwall, 'A' Coy., 2nd Bn. (21st Foot) The Royal Scots Fusiliers: *yr. s.* of David Mason Dingwall, Schoolmaster; of The Schoolhouse, Flisk, Newburgh, Fife, by his wife Jeannie, *dau.* of John Mitchell, of Fliskmillan, Fife, J.P., Farmer: *b.* Flisk Schoolhouse, co. Fife, 27 October 1895: *educ.* Flisk Public School: Occupation – Apprentice; William Watt, Nurseryman & Seedsman, Cupar-Fife: enlisted, 21 January 1914: served with the Expeditionary Force in France from

6 October following, and was reported missing after the First Battle of Ypres, 31 October 1914; now assumed killed in action on that day. The regiment was surrounded and cut off, and only one officer and about 70 men answered the Roll-call afterwards. Age 19.

(Panel 19) Pte. 10937, Richard Docherty, 2nd Bn. (21st Foot) The Royal Scots Fusiliers: *s.* of Hugh Docherty, of Greenock: served with the Expeditionary Force. Reported wounded and missing, 31 October 1914; now assumed killed.

(Panel 19) Pte. 9534, James Don, 2nd Bn. (21st Foot) The Royal Scots Fusiliers: brother to Robert Don Esq., of 19, Russell Street, Ayr: served with the Expeditionary Force, and was reported wounded and missing, 31 October 1914, now assumed killed. Age 24.

(Panel 19) Pte. 8101, William Donnelly, 1st Bn. (21st Foot) The Royal Scots Fusiliers: *b.* Maybole, co. Ayr, *c.*1884: enlisted Ayr: served with the Expeditionary Force in France and Flanders from 3 December 1914. Reported missing after the fighting, 16 June 1915; Bellewaarde. Age 29–30. His mother, after receiving information regarding her son being reported as missing and no further word or news thereafter, contacted *The Ayr Advertiser* which, on 29 July, carried – "Private William Donnelly (8101), 1st Battalion Royal Scots Fusiliers, who has been officially reported as missing since 16th June, and of whom nothing further has been heard. Private Donnelly is a son of Mrs Donnelly, Kirklands Street, Maybole, and previous to the war was employed in a bakery business in New Zealand. He returned from there after the war broke out, after an absence of about 10 years, and joined the Royal Scots Fusiliers, a regiment with which he had previously served. He left for the front in November, and since that time, up until he was reported as being missing, he had taken part in all the engagements in which his regiment had figured. He is about 30 years of age, and the last word his mother received from him was about six weeks ago, when he stated he was well and expected to get home shortly for a holiday. Naturally his mother and other relatives are much upset at his being missing, and anyone who may know anything of him will be doing a much valued service by informing his mother at the above address."

(Panel 19) Pte. 9708, William Doran, 2nd Bn. (21st Foot) The Royal Scots Fusiliers: served with the Expeditionary Force. Killed in action at Ypres, 23 October 1914.

(Panel 19) Pte. 9679, James Douglas, 2nd Bn. (21st Foot) The Royal Scots Fusiliers: nephew to Joan Shiels Douglas Smith (4, Liberton Dams, Edinburgh): served with the Expeditionary Force. Reported missing, 31 October 1914; now assumed killed. Age 25.

(Panel 19) Pte. 10483, Frederick J. Dovey, 2nd Bn. (21st Foot) The Royal Scots Fusiliers: late of Chelsea, London, S.W.: enlisted Reading, co. Berks: served with the Expeditionary Force, and was reported wounded and missing, 24 October 1914; assumed killed.

(Panel 19) Pte. 10837, Sidney Draper, 2nd Bn. (21st Foot) The Royal Scots Fusiliers: served with the Expeditionary Force. Killed in action, 31 October 1914.

(Panel 19) Pte. 10924, Samuel Drysdale, 2nd Bn. (21st Foot) The Royal Scots Fusiliers: served with the Expeditionary Force. Killed in action, 26 October 1914.

(Panel 19) Pte. 19227, John Duffy, 6/7th (Service) Bn. The Royal Scots Fusiliers: brother to Pte. 260166, A. Duffy, 1/5th Gordon Highlanders, killed in action on the same day: *b.* Anderston, Glasgow, co. Lanark: enlisted Glasgow: served with the Expeditionary Force in France and Flanders, and was killed in action, 31 July 1917. Age 37. He was married to Annie Duffy (9, Cavendish Place, South Side, Glasgow).

His brother Alfred also has no known grave; he is recorded on Addenda Panel 59.

(Panel 19) Pte. 8469, Edward Dyson, 1st Bn. (21st Foot) The Royal Scots Fusiliers: *s.* of Richard Dyson, of 59, Redwald Road, Clapton, London, E., by his wife Jane: served with the Expeditionary Force. Killed in action at Ypres, 13 November 1914. Age 29.

(Panel 19) Pte. 6663, David Espie, 2nd Bn. (21st Foot) The Royal Scots Fusiliers: *s.* of John Espie, of 22, Rowchester Street, Whitevale, Glasgow: served with the Expeditionary Force. Reported missing, 24 October 1914; now assumed killed. Age 17.

(Panel 19) Pte. 11874, James Fleming, 1st Bn. (21st Foot) The Royal Scots Fusiliers: *husb.* to Sarah Fleming, *née* McBride (20, Strathclyde Street, Bridgeton, Glasgow): served with R.S.F. in the South

African Campaign, and the Expeditionary Force in France. Reported missing after the battn. action on the Menin Road, during the First Battle of Ypres, 18 November 1914; now assumed killed. Age 45.

(Panel 19) Pte. 9841, Wallace Denis French, 1st Bn. (21st Foot) The Royal Scots Fusiliers: *s.* of John French, of New Town, Ringmer, Lewes, co. Sussex: served with the Expeditionary Force. Reported wounded and missing after the fighting at Ypres, 11 November 1914; now assumed killed in action on that date. Age 23.

(Panel 19) Pte. 7199, Albert Edward Gillett, 2nd Bn. (21st Foot) The Royal Scots Fusiliers: served with the Expeditionary Force. Killed in action at Ypres, 21 October 1914. *m.*

(Panel 19) Pte. 6247, Thomas Givens, 2nd Bn. (21st Foot) The Royal Scots Fusiliers: served with the Expeditionary Force, and was killed in action at Ypres, 21 October 1914. He leaves a wife, Rosie Givens (135, Bank Street, Coatbridge, co. Lanark).

(Panel 19) Pte. 9789, Peter Graham, 2nd Bn. (21st Foot) The Royal Scots Fusiliers: *s.* of Joseph (& Mrs) Graham, of 17, High Street, Falkirk: served with the Expeditionary Force. Killed in action at Ypres, 24 October 1914. Age 25. *unm.*

(Panel 19) Pte. 10274, Henry Hagan, 2nd Bn. (21st Foot) The Royal Scots Fusiliers: *s.* of the late Henry Hagan, of New Stevenston, by his wife Margaret (Stevenston House, Carfin Road, Holytown, co. Lanark): and brother to Pte. 5117, H. Hagan, Cameron Highlanders, died of wounds, 17 October 1915: served with the Expeditionary Force, and was killed in action at Ypres, 26 October 1914. Age 21.

His brother Hugh is buried in St. Sever Cemetery, Rouen (A.13.5).

(Panel 19) Pte. 4562, James Halliday, 1st Bn. (21st Foot) The Royal Scots Fusiliers: served with the Expeditionary Force. Reported wounded and missing at Ypres, 11 November 1914; now assumed killed.

(Panel 19) Pte. 5240, Thomas Hanratty, 1st Bn. (21st Foot) The Royal Scots Fusiliers: *s.* of Barnard Hanratty, of Silver Bridge, Co. Armagh: enlisted Irvine, co. Ayr: served with the Expeditionary Force. Reported wounded and missing at Ypres, 11 November 1914; now assumed killed.

(Panel 19) Pte. 9418, George Hardie, 2nd Bn. (21st Foot) The Royal Scots Fusiliers: *s.* of E. Hardie (Police Quarters, Portobello, co. Midlothian): served with the Expeditionary Force in France. Reported missing, 31 October 1914; now assumed killed. Age 24. *unm.*

(Panel 19) Pte. 10505, Albert Harris, 2nd Bn. (21st Foot) The Royal Scots Fusiliers: *s.* of Alfred Harris, of 22, William Street, Reading, co. Berks: served with the Expeditionary Force. Killed in action at Ypres, 26 October 1914. Age 20. *unm.*

(Panel 19) Pte. 10300, James Hay, 2nd Bn. (21st Foot) The Royal Scots Fusiliers: *s.* of Jane L. (85, Castle Street, Townhead, Glasgow): *b.* Glasgow, 1889: served with the Expeditionary Force. Reported missing at Ypres, 23 October 1914, and now assumed killed. Age 25. *unm.*

(Panel 19) Pte. 9942, John Hendry, 2nd Bn. (21st Foot) The Royal Scots Fusiliers: late of Rutherglen: enlisted Glasgow, co. Lanark: served with the Expeditionary Force. Killed in action at Ypres, 23 October 1914. Remains 'Unknown British Soldier' recovered unmarked grave (28.J.17.a.9.6); identified – Clothing, Boots mkd. 9942 RSF, Spoon mkd. 8699 RSF; reinterred, registered 28 November 1927. *Buried in Sanctuary Wood Cemetery (IV.K.28).*

(Panel 19) Pte. 9826, Frederick William Higgins, 2nd Bn. (21st Foot) The Royal Scots Fusiliers: *s.* of Alice Fanny Higgins (1, Alma Road, New Town, West Malling, co. Kent): served with the Expeditionary Force. Reported missing, 24 October 1914; now assumed killed. Age 27.

(Panel 19) Pte. 10458, William Hill, 2nd Bn. (21st Foot) The Royal Scots Fusiliers: *s.* of Alex Hill, of Castle Kenny, nr. Stranraer: served with the Expeditionary Force. Reported missing after the fighting at Ypres, 31 October 1914; now assumed killed in action on that date.

(Panel 19) Pte. 9129, Henry James Hughes, 2nd Bn. (21st Foot) The Royal Scots Fusiliers: *s.* of Henry James Hughes, of 17, Southwold Road, Clapton, London, E.5: served with the Expeditionary Force. Killed in action at Ypres, 4 November 1914. Age 27.

(Panel 19) Pte. 10168, Joseph Hughes, 2nd Bn. (21st Foot) The Royal Scots Fusiliers: served with the Expeditionary Force. Killed in action, Ypres 22 October 1914.

(Panel 19) Pte. 10760, Thomas Hughes, 2nd Bn. (21st Foot) The Royal Scots Fusiliers: served with the Expeditionary Force. Killed in action, Ypres 22 October 1914.

(Panel 19) Pte. 5234, John Jack, 1st Bn. (21st Foot) The Royal Scots Fusiliers: *s*. of Thomas Jack, of 70, Mill Street, Ayr: enlisted Irvine, co. Ayr: served with the Expeditionary Force. Killed in action at Ypres, 11 November 1914. Age 24. *unm*.

(Panel 19) Pte. 9808, Robert Jenner, 2nd Bn. (21st Foot) The Royal Scots Fusiliers: served with the Expeditionary Force. Killed in action at Ypres, 31 October 1914.

(Panel 19) Pte. 9276, John William Johnson, 2nd Bn. (21st Foot) The Royal Scots Fusiliers: served with the Expeditionary Force. Killed in action at Ypres, 23 October 1914.

(Panel 19) Pte. 6281, Thomas W. Johnson, 1st Bn. (21st Foot) The Royal Scots Fusiliers: *s*. of the late Frederick Johnson, by his wife Mary: *b*. Bootle, Liverpool, 1881: enlisted Seaforth: served with the Expeditionary Force. Reported missing, 11 November 1914; now assumed killed. Age 33. He leaves a widow, Margery Geraldine Johnson.

(Panel 19) Pte. 10869, Dempter Johnston, 2nd Bn. (21st Foot) The Royal Scots Fusiliers: *s*. of Peter Johnston, of 29, Colebrooke Street, Cambuslang, Glasgow: served with the Expeditionary Force. Reported missing, 24 October 1914; now assumed killed. Age 28. *unm*.

(Panel 19) Pte. 10489, Henry Keatley, 2nd Bn. (21st Foot) The Royal Scots Fusiliers: *s*. of Thomas Keatley, of Glasgow: served with the Expeditionary Force. Killed in action at Ypres, 23 October 1914.

(Panel 19) Pte. 9540, David Kelly, 2nd Bn. (21st Foot) The Royal Scots Fusiliers: served with the Expeditionary Force. Reported missing after the Battle of Ypres, 24 October 1914; now assumed killed.

(Panel 19) Pte. 7136, Patrick Kilcullen, 1st Bn. (21st Foot) The Royal Scots Fusiliers: *b*. Sligo, 1874: served with the Expeditionary Force. Reported missing at Ypres, 12 November 1914. Age 40. He was married to Margaret, *née* Slater (32, Fairfield Street, Govan, co. Lanark).

(Panel 19) Pte. 9446, Thomas King, 2nd Bn. (21st Foot) The Royal Scots Fusiliers: *s*. of Robert King, of Leith: served with the Expeditionary Force in France. Killed in action at Ypres, 26 October 1914.

(Panel 19) Pte. 9861, John Laird, 2nd Bn. (21st Foot) The Royal Scots Fusiliers: *s*. of Archibald Laird, of 20, New Street, Rickarton, Kilmarnock: served with the Expeditionary Force. Killed in action, Ypres, 22 October 1914. Age 24. *unm*.

(Panel 19) Pte. 6931, Walter John Lake, 2nd Bn. (21st Foot) The Royal Scots Fusiliers: served with the Expeditionary Force. Killed in action at Ypres, 28 October 1914. He was married to Mrs M.A. Dowson, *née* Lake (5, Rosedale Street, Newcastle-on-Tyne).

(Panel 19) Pte. 9972, Benjamin Lane, 2nd Bn. (21st Foot) The Royal Scots Fusiliers: *s*. of W. Lane, of Deptford, London, S.E.: *b*. Wood Green, London, N.: served at Gibraltar, and with the Expeditionary Force in France, and was killed in action at Ypres 31 October 1914.

(Panel 19) Pte. 6597, Frederick Law, 2nd Bn. (21st Foot) The Royal Scots Fusiliers: *s*. of William Law, of Liverpool: enlisted Newton Stewart, co. Wigtown: served with the Expeditionary Force in France and Flanders from 6 October 1914. Reported missing after the fighting at Ypres, 31 October 1914, from which date, no word having been received, is now assumed to have been killed in action.

(Panel 19) Pte. 8676, Albert Jesse Lawrence, 2nd Bn. (21st Foot) The Royal Scots Fusiliers: On the outbreak of war was with his battalion at Gibraltar: returned to England in September; proceeded to France, disembarked Zeebrugge, 6 October following, and was killed in action at Ypres, 24 October 1914.

(Panel 19) Pte. 32436, Duncan Murray, 6/7th (Service) Bn. The Royal Scots Fusiliers: late of Kilwinning, co. Ayr: *b*. West Longrig, co. Lanark: enlisted Ardeer. On 31st July 1917, 6/7th R.S.F. and 6th Cameron Highlanders, were designated attack troops 45th Brigade, 15th Divn., with 11th Argyll & Sutherland Highlanders and 13th Royal Scots in support. (45th Brigade was support to 46 and 44 Bdes.) Attacking astride Cambridge Road the Royal Scots Fusiliers objective was the Frezenberg Redoubt. After hard fighting, the Redoubt was finally taken, but a counter-attack from the left flank at 2 p.m. caused heavy casualties; by the end of the day the Division had attained its objectives and that night consolidated its line astride the Frezenberg Ridge. During the course of the day, 6/7th Royal Scots Fusiliers had been reduced to a strength of 150 men. Duncan Murray posted as missing/wounded, was subsequently recorded – Believed Killed.

(Panel 19) Pte. 6093, Michael Rourke (*a.k.a* Groark), 1st Bn. (21st Foot) The Royal Scots Fusiliers: eldest *s*. of Patrick Rourke; Farm Labourer, of Wooller Houses, Batley, co. York, by his wife Bridget: and brother to Pte. 19677, J. Groark, York & Lancaster Regt., killed in action, 12 April 1918; and Pte. 18810, H. Groark, King's Own Yorkshire Light Infantry, died 19 September 1917, of wounds: *b*. Dewsbury, 1878: a pre-war Regular, served in the South African Campaign, and with the Expeditionary Force in France from August 1914, and was killed in action, 16 June 1915. Age 37. He leaves a wife, Margaret Rourke, *née* Haley. (*IWGC record Rourke*) All three brothers are recorded on the Batley and St. Mary's (Roman Catholic) Church War Memorials and, in the name Groark, on individual brass plaques in St. George's Memorial Church, Ypres. A fourth brother, Frederick, served with King's Own (Yorkshire Light Infantry); he survived.

His brother James also has no known grave, he is commemorated on the Ploegsteert Memorial (Panel 8); Henry is buried in Lijssenthoek Military Cemetery (XIX.A.2).

(Panel 19) Pte. 41199, John Scoon, 2nd Bn. (21st Foot) The Royal Scots Fusiliers: *s*. of the late Thomas Scoon, of Stockbridge, Edinburgh, and Ann Lillie, his wife: and elder brother to Pte. 19916, J.R. Scoon, 16th Royal Scots, killed in action, 9 April 1917: enlisted Edinburgh: killed in action, 31 July 1917. Age 29. He leaves a wife, Elizabeth Marshall Scoon (24, Highland Dykes, Bonnybridge, co. Stirling), to mourn his passing. Inscribed – 'In Memory Of Teachers & Scholars Of St. Bernard's Sunday Schools Who Fell In The Great War;' gifted by Miss M.A. and Miss E.S. Shaw 'for many years teachers,' the Scoon brothers are remembered on the Stockbridge (Edinburgh) Parish Church War Memorial.

His brother James also has no known grave; he is commemorated on the Arras (Faubourg d'Amiens) Memorial.

(Panel 19) Pte. 32377, Thomas Stevenson, 6/7th (Service) Bn. The Royal Scots Fusiliers: late of 5, Cross Row, Kilwinning. Thomas was listed as missing presumed killed during the fighting in front of Frezenberg, 31 July 1917. Nine months later, his brother Andrew was listed the same way; his parents would have to wait until the end of the war for news of him – he survived as a PoW.

(Panel 19) Pte. 16933, George Titterington, 1st Bn. (21st Foot) The Royal Scots Fusiliers: late of Mottram-in-Longdendale, co. Chester: *s*. of William Titterington, of 83, Highfield Terrace, Broadbottom, nr. Manchester, by his wife Elizabeth Ann: and yr. brother to L/Corpl. 15182, T. Titterington, 1st Royal Scots Fusiliers; died in the Base Hospital, St. Omer, 6 July 1916, of wounds: enlisted Stalybridge: served with the Expeditionary Force. Killed in action, 27 March 1916. Age 20. *unm*.

His brother Tom is buried in Longuenesse (St. Omer) Souvenir Cemetery (II.C.28).

(Panel 19) Pte. 8350, David Willis, 1st Bn. (21st Foot) The Royal Scots Fusiliers: *s*. of David Willis, of Kilbirnie, Ayrshire: late *husb*. to Margaret Willis (12, Bridgend Lane, Kilwinning): an Army Reservist, employed by Messrs Nobel; Dynamite Manufacturers; volunteered for Active Service on the outbreak of war: served with the Expeditionary Force in France and Flanders, took part in the fighting at Mons, Le Cateau and the Battle of the Aisne, and was killed in action near the Menin Road, during the First Battle of Ypres, 13 November 1914.

(Panel 19) Pte. 15734, Fred Wordsworth, 1st Bn. (21st Foot) The Royal Scots Fusiliers: 3rd *s*. of Mence Wordsworth, Steel Worker; of Upper Middlewood Road, New Houses, Oughtibridge, by his wife Ada, *née* Firth: *b*. Oughtibridge, nr. Sheffield, co. York, 1897: served with the Expeditionary Force. Killed in action, 16 June 1915. Age 18.

(Panel 19) Capt. Charles Raymond Andrews, 2nd Bn. (22nd Foot) The Cheshire Regt.: only *s*. of the late Lieut.Col. Robert Charles Andrews, Indian Army, by his wife Alice Gertrude (6, Ennismore Gardens, Dover, co. Kent), *dau*. of the late Col. C.Y.O. Chambers, Indian Army: *b*. Rangoon, Burma, 1 February 1890: *educ*. Army School, Stratford-on-Avon, co. Warwick: gazetted 2nd Lieut. (Special Reserve) Liverpool Regt. 21 April 1909; subsequently transf'd. 2nd Cheshire Regt.: served with the Expeditionary Force in France and Flanders from 17 January 1915. Reported wounded and missing after the fighting at Bellewaarde Farm, nr. Hooge, 25 May following, and is now assumed to have been killed in action on or about that date. His Brigadier wrote, "Your son was seen by one of my Staff Officers just before the night attack, in which he led his battalion with great gallantry, and, as far as I can gather .. he was first into the German trench, where he was seen to fall or stumble. I think he must have been hit." Capt. Andrews was commanding his battalion at the time, all the senior officers having become casualties. He was Mentioned in Despatches for 'gallant and distinguished service in the field.' Age 25. *unm.*

(Panel 19) Capt. Cyril Robert Wightman Mountain, 13th (Service) Bn. The Cheshire Regt.: *s.* of Frank Wightman Mountain, Partner, Messrs Wightman Mountain & Andrews Ltd., Printers & Stationers, 31, Victoria Street, London, S.W.; and 'Glengariff,' 8, Ravenslea Road, Wandsworth Common, London, and Minnie Clara, his wife: and brother to Lieut. S.W. Mountain, R.A.F. (surv'd.): *educ.* Emmanuel School, Wandsworth Common (1906–10); Dulwich College (1910–15): gazetted 2nd Lieut. 13th Cheshire Regt. April 1915: proceeded to France, 1916: promoted Capt. June 1917. Killed in action, 5 August 1917; vicinity of Chateau Wood, Westhoek, Ypres. Age 21.

(Panel 19) Capt. Charles Wetherell Hayes-Newington, 2nd Bn. (22nd Foot) The Cheshire Regt.: eldest *s.* of Major (& Mrs) C.M. Hayes-Newington, late 22nd Cheshire, and King's (Liverpool) Regt., of Ticehurst, co. Sussex; and 16, Merton Road, Southsea, co. Hants: and brother to 2nd Lieut. H.M. Hayes-Newington, King's (Liverpool) Regt., killed during an advance at Givenchy, 10 March 1915, when his battalion lost many of its officers; and 2nd Lieut. B.Y. Hayes-Newington, 2nd Cheshire Regt., who, whilst in command of a double company on 8 May 1915, was severely wounded and made a prisoner of war: *b.* 17 June 1893: Religion – Roman Catholic: *educ.* St. Cyprian's College, Eastbourne; Dover College, and – as an Honorary King's Cadet – Royal Military College, Sandhurst: gazetted 2nd Lieut. Cheshire Regt. September 1912; promoted Lieut. July 1914; (Temp.) Capt. January 1915 (subsequently confirmed); initially 1st Battn. with which he served in the north of Ireland for over a year, thereafter transf'd. 2nd Battn., Jubbulpore, India: served with the Expeditionary Force in France and Flanders, 84th Bde., 28th Divn., and was killed in action at Hooge, 8 May 1915, while in command of No.1 Double Company of his battalion. He was a good all-round sportsman, a fine shot, keen fisherman, expert swimmer, and diver. He also played cricket for his regiment, a left-hand bowler, and a fine field; while in India he was in charge of the regimental cricket and was very popular, Age 21. *unm.*

His brother Harold is buried in Vielle-Chapelle New Military Cemetery, La Couture (IX.E.14).

(Panel 19) Capt. John Cyril Routh, 2nd Bn. (22nd Foot) The Cheshire Regt.: only *s.* of Cyril E. (& Mrs) Routh, of Newland House, Twickenham, co. Middlesex: and *gdson.* to the Rev. J.W. Routh, late Rector of Tylehurst, co. Berks: *b.* Richmond, co. Surrey, 31 July 1885: *educ.* Bradfield College; Fosters, Fareham, and Royal Military College, Sandhurst: gazetted 2nd Lieut. Cheshire Regt. January 1905; promoted Lieut. April 1906: seconded for employment with West African Frontier Force, April 1912: at the outbreak of the present war with Germany, was heavily engaged in the Cameroons initially, but invalided home after a serious operation: promoted Capt. November 1914: sent to France, to join 2nd Battn. March 1915: served with the Expeditionary Force, and was killed in action nr. Ypres, by a shell, 2.30 a.m., 6 May 1915. Buried at Verlorenhoek. Age 29. *unm.*

(Panel 19) Capt. William Oscar Wilkinson, 7th Bn. The Cheshire Regt. (T.F.): Killed in action, 5 August 1917; Chateau Wood – Menin Road, Ypres. See account re. Chaplain Rev. H.H. East (Panel 56).

(Panel 19) Lieut. Humphrey Marmaduke Chaplin, 3rd (Reserve) attd. 2nd Bn. (22nd Foot) The Cheshire Regt.: 3rd *s.* of the late Marmaduke Kaye Chaplin, of Etwall, co, Derby: *b.* Etwall, 8 January 1892: *educ.* Glyngart School, Cheltenham, and Rossall School, and Balliol College, Oxford, scholar and member of the O.T.C.: received his commission 2nd Lieut. 3rd Cheshire Regt. 15 August 1914: attd. 2nd Bn. on its return from India, January 1915, and left for the Front the same month, being promoted Lieut. February 1915: slightly wounded, 13 March, and rejoined a month later (19 April). The battn. was moved up immediately afterwards to the advanced trenches in the Ypres salient, from which only a few men returned after the termination of the second battle for Ypres. Lieut. Chaplin was posted missing, 11 May 1915, and was afterwards reported as having been killed in action near Ypres, 8–9 May. He was buried by the Germans near St. Julien. Lieut. Chaplin was a Craven scholar, and had gained a first in Moderations, and was a Charles Oldham Prizeman. Age 23. *unm.*

(Panel 19) Lieut. George Bleazard Cowpe, 6th Bn. The Cheshire Regt. (T.F.): eldest *s.* of Alexander Cowpe, of Pendlehurst, Burnley, co. Lancaster, by his wife Annie: *b.* 10 January 1895: *educ.* Burnley Grammar School; Rydal Mount School, Colwyn Bay, and Manchester University School of Technology, where he was a member of the O.T.C.: was preparing to enter his father's business of Cotton Manufacturing: obtained a commission, 2nd Lieut. 27 January 1916; promoted Lieut. 27 July 1917: served with the Expeditionary Force in France and Flanders, and was killed in action at St. Julien, 31 July 1917. Lieut. Col. W.H. Stanway, D.S.O., M.C., wrote, "He was killed while leading his company in the attack in a most gallant manner ... I know what a loss he will be to you, but I can assure you that he will also be a great loss to myself, and the battalion, for he was a very gallant and efficient officer, and was held in high esteem by all ranks. I cannot speak too highly of his conduct during the period under my command." And another officer, "He was chosen to take command of his company in the attack because the Commanding Officer knew his job would be done thoroughly, because the men loved and trusted him; he has proved beyond doubt his excellence as a soldier and a leader of men, and it was with a light heart he laid down his life for his King, Country, and all that was dearest to him ... I have seen the Commanding Officer recently, and he is deeply grieved; his remark was 'One of my very best lads gone.'" Another officer also wrote, "He was one of the bravest men I ever knew – the coolest – in the presence of danger. He was a good, clean lad, with a strong sense of duty that was an example to us all. Everybody loved him, and his loss will be felt most keenly." Age 22. *unm.*

(Panel 19) Lieut. Norman Alexander Newson, 3rd (Reserve) attd. 1st Bn. (22nd Foot) The Cheshire Regt.: *s.* of Arthur Bell Newson, late of Danehurst, Bognor, co. Sussex: *gdson.* to the late Thos. (& Mrs) Newson; Kingston-on-Thames: *b.* Nevern Mansions, Earl's Court, London, S.W., 20 August 1891: *educ.* Middleton School, Bognor; Clifton House School, Eastbourne: gazetted to Cheshire Regt., on probation April 1912: confirmed in rank, December 1912; promoted Lieut. May 1913: served with the Expeditionary Force in France and Flanders from August 1914: fought at the battles of Mons and Le Cateau; wounded during the fighting at Compiegne: after recovery at home, returned to the Front with the Service Battn. January 1915, and was shot in the trenches, 18 February following. Buried some two miles south of Ypres. His parents received appreciative letters from his Commanding Officer and the Captain of his company, saying he was a good and competent officer "who died doing his duty, as he always did." He was a member of the Isthmian Club. Age 23. *unm.*

(Panel 19) 2nd Lieut. Gerard Rupert Laurie Anderson, 3rd (Reserve) attd. 1st Bn. (22nd Foot) The Cheshire Regt.: *s.* of Rev. Prebendary David Anderson, of 20, Chester Street, Belgrave Square, London, S.W., late Rector of St. George's, Hanover Square, and Prebendary of St. Paul's, 1891–1911, by his wife Blanche Alice May, *dau.* of Sir Emilius Laurie, of Maxwelton, Moniaive, co. Dumfries, 3rd Bart.: *educ.* Eton; Trinity College, Oxford (Scholar), where he took a First Class in Mods and Greats: subsequently entered the firm of Messrs Camell Laird; Birkenhead: obtained probationary commission, 3rd Cheshire Regt. 15 August 1914: served with the Expeditionary Force in France and Flanders from 31 September; attd. 1st Battn. for Active Service: twice wounded at La Bassee, but remained at duty, and was killed in action, 8 November following, being shot through the heart while leading a charge against the German trenches. Posthumously Mentioned in Despatches (*London Gazette*, 17 February 1915) by F.M. Sir John (now Lord) French, for his 'gallant and distinguished service in the field.' He was a good all-round sportsman, and while at Eton excelled at Fives and the Field game, winning the School Fives and House Fives each three times, and the Hurdles also thrice. Lieut. Anderson was Captain of the Oppidans, President of the Eton Society, and Keeper of the Field; he was also President of the University Athletic Club, being elected a Fellow of All Souls in 1913. He continued his athletic successes at the Varsity, where he ran in the quarter and the half miles and Hurdles, also competing in 1911 for Oxford and Cambridge against Yale and Harvard; he twice won the English, and once the Scotch Championship over hurdles, and made his final appearance in the athletic field at Stockholm. Age 25.

(Panel 19) 2nd Lieut. John Edward Gresson, 3rd (Reserve) attd. 2nd Bn. (22nd Foot) The Cheshire Regt.: 7th & *yst. s.* of the late Major W.H. Gresson, 27th Royal Inniskilling Fusiliers, and 65th York & Lancaster Regt., by his wife ('Fernleigh,' Cheltenham, co. Gloucester): and brother to Lieut.Col. T.T.

Gresson, D.S.O., York & Lancaster Regt.; Capt. R.H.A. Gresson, Advanced Remount Depot, B.E.F.; Cmdr. A.L. Gresson, Royal Navy, H.M.S. *Impregnable*; and Gnr. George Gresson, Canadian Field Artillery: *b.* Woodville, Birr, King's Co., 3 June 1881: *educ.* Cheltenham College, and Rossall: afterwards went to China, where he was engaged in business with Messrs Jardine, Matheson & Co.: home on leave when war broke out, he immediately volunteered for Active Service: gazetted 2nd Lieut. September 1914, posted 3rd Cheshire Regt, with which he served at Birkenhead, and on Coastal Defence, Scotland: served with the Expeditionary Force in France and Flanders from March 1915, attd. 2nd Battn. for Active Service; and was killed 25 May following, in the general attack on the German trenches at Ypres. Buried in Hooge Wood. He was a very keen horseman, and was known in China for the active interest he took in polo, steeplechasing, and coursing; he was also associated with both the Shanghai and Hong Kong Light Horse. A commemorative plaque dedicated to his memory was erected in St. Stephen's Church, Cheltenham. Age 33.

(Panel 19) 2nd Lieut. Ronald Malcolm McGregor, 3rd (Reserve) attd. 2nd Bn. (22nd Foot) The Cheshire Regt.: *s.* of Josiah McGregor, C.E., of 'Glengyle,' 45, Victoria Road, Upper Norwood, London, S.E., by his wife Fanny: and brother to 2nd Lieut. M. McGregor, attd. 2nd Cheshire Regt., killed in action at the Hohenzollern Redoubt, 2 October 1915, after it had been taken from the Germans at the Battle of Loos: *b.* 'Glenisla,' Vermont Road, Upper Norwood, 2 February 1889: *educ.* Dulwich College, where, for three years, he was a zealous member of the Volunteer Corps and Football Club: after leaving school, went to the Argentine: returned to apply for a commission, December 1914: gazetted 2nd Lieut., Reserve Battn. Cheshire Regt. January 1915: trained Birkenhead; took Sandhurst Course, Freshfield. Highly commended by his Commanding Officer, in May he was sent to France with a draft of 30 men. On arrival he was attached to the 2nd Battn. of his regiment, in which his brother was also serving. Arriving on the 23 May, he intended to go and see his brother (who was on guard duty at Poperinghe), but he and his platoon were called into action near Ypres where the Germans were attacking with gas. The following day he was found in a shell-hole by the doctor of the regiment, slightly gassed, and recommended to return to Headquarters with another officer, who was badly gassed, but he refused to go, and after he felt better took command of his company in the open all that day. He was one of the few of his battalion who came out of the battle untouched. The ground taken was not tenable, and they had to retire into the trenches, where, while serving out the ammunition with another officer the next morning, 25 May, he was shot through the head by a sniper. The verdict of his fellow officers was that, all through the action of the 24th he was "splendid." In two days he had fought his first and last battle! Buried near where he fell, three miles west of Ypres: 25 May 1915. Age 26. *unm.*

His brother Marcus also has no known grave; he is commemorated on the Loos Memorial (Dud Corner).

(Panel 19) 2nd Lieut. Hugh Hathorn Nicholson, 3rd (Reserve) attd. 2nd Bn. (22nd Foot) The Cheshire Regt.: eldest *s.* of Hugh Nicholson, of Sutton Hall, Little Sutton, co. Chester: *b.* Bebbington, co. Chester, 16 July 1883: *educ.* Malvern College: applied for a commission on the outbreak of war with the Central Empires, August 1914: gazetted 2nd Lieut. 3rd Cheshire Regt. October 1914: served with the British Expeditionary Force in France, attd. 2nd Battn. for Active Service, and was killed in action, 25 May 1915, nr. Ypres. Buried where he fell. Age 21. *unm.*

(Panel 19) 2nd Lieut. Geoffrey Christian Lansdale Walsh, 13th (Service) Bn. The Cheshire Regt.: *s.* of J. Leo Walsh, of 'Larchwood,' Chelford, co. Chester, by his wife Frances E. Reported missing after an aborted patrol near Messines, 22 June 1917; despite exhaustive searches made for this officer it is now assumed he was killed in action on that date. Age 20. See also 2nd Lieut. Harrington, St. Quentin Cabaret Military Cemetery (II.H.5).

(Panel 19) Coy.Sergt.Major, 265012, James Finn, 1/6th Bn. The Cheshire Regt. (T.F.): *b.* Edgley, Stockport, co. Chester: enlisted there: served with the Expeditionary Force in France and Flanders from 10 November 1914. Missing/killed in action, 31 July 1917, in the attack at St. Julien, the companies of the battalion being pinned down by heavy artillery and machine-gun fire, Sergt. Major Finn and his officer (Lieut. G.B. Cowpe) proceeded forward to assess the situation. Neither were seen again. Lieut. Cowpe also has no known grave; he is recorded above.

(Panel 19) Sergt. W/1033, William Nicholas Deakin, 13th (Service) Bn. The Cheshire Regt.: only *s.* of John Deakin, Mill Foreman; of 26, Brentwood Street, Seacombe, co. Chester, by his wife Annie, *dau.* of William Crellin: *b.* Poulton, Birkenhead, 26 February 1896: *educ.* Sommerville, Seacombe: Occupation – Apprentice Engineer: enlisted 5 September 1914: served with the Expeditionary Force in France and Flanders from 26 September 1915. Killed in action at the Battle of Messines Ridge, 7 June 1917. Buried to the north of Wulverghem, south of Ypres. Age 21. *unm.*

(Panel 19) L/Sergt. 265675, Walter Depledge, 1/6th Bn. The Cheshire Regt. (T.F.): formerly no.2652: *s.* of Joseph Depledge, of 318, Hempshaw Lane, Stockport, co. Chester, by his wife Mary Ann: *b.* Parish of St. Thomas, Stockport: a pre-war Territorial, enlisted Stockport. Killed in action, 31 July 1917; between St. Julien and the Steenbeek. Age 25. Under cover of darkness in the early hours of 28 January 1915 a German patrol crossed No Man's Land, crept up un-noticed on the front line trenches held by 1st Cheshires near Wulverghem, grabbed a sentry's rifle through a loophole in the parapet, and departed. Within minutes rifle fire was being poured out along the Cheshire's front, and a rumour rapidly circulated to the effect that the enemy were in the British trenches. Corporal Povey and four Privates of his section departed their portion of trench, giving as reason their hearing someone shout, 'Clear out! The Germans are on us! We have no chance!' With the sudden outbreak of firing, taut nerves and the all-prevailing darkness, it was no wonder a certain amount of confused panic ensued. An immediate assessment of the situation by an officer and a sergeant taking control discovered the Cheshires position had not been penetrated and, after order had been restored, Corporal Povey and the four Privates were arrested. At their subsequent Court Martial, the five men were tried together on a charge of leaving their post without orders from their superior officer; the Privates each received ten years penal servitude; Corporal Povey was condemned to death by firing squad.

(Panel 19) Corpl. 10459, George Povey, 1st Bn. (22nd Foot) The Cheshire Regt.: *s.* of Dinah Povey (51, Primrose Street, Connah Quay): Executed – Leaving Post, 11 February 1915. Age 23.

(Panel 19) L/Corpl. 17924, Joshua Makin, 1/6th Bn. The Cheshire Regt. (T.F.): *s.* of Joshua Makin, of 5, Derby Street, Macclesfield, by his wife Sarah, *dau.* of Edward Dale: *b.* Macclesfield, co. Chester, 17 April 1879: *educ.* St. Alban's: Occupation – Harness Maker: enlisted 11th Cheshire Regt. 7 November 1914: served with the Expeditionary Force in France and Flanders from September 1915: invalided home, 6 July 1916; shell-shock and trench fever: transf'd. 6th Battn., May 1917; returned to France on the 16th of that month; reported wounded and missing after the fighting at St. Julien, nr. Ypres, 31 July following; assumed killed in action on or about that date. Age 38. He *m.* Parish Church, Macclesfield, 21 June 1903; Laura (28, Hayes Yard, Macclesfield), eldest *dau.* of Charles Bamford, and had four *daus.* – Lily, *b.* 6 January 1905; Jessie, *b.* 24 December 1905; Rose, *b.* 1 June 1910, and Sarah Ellen, *b.* 8 May 1912. (*IWGC record Pte.*)

(Panel 19) L/Corpl. 10518, Arthur Pearce, 1st Bn. (22nd Foot) The Cheshire Regt.: only *s.* of George Edwin Pearce, of 71, Stovell Avenue, Longsight, Manchester, by his wife Martha: served with the Expeditionary Force, and was killed in action, 29 April 1915. Age 16.

(Panel 19) L/Corpl. 52478, Charles Henry Reeves, 11th (Service) Bn. The Cheshire Regt.: *s.* of Charles Reeves, Railway Wagon Examiner; of 23, Lark Hill Road, Stockport, by his wife Fanny, *dau.* of Edwin Knight: and *yr.* brother to Pte. 277243, H.W. Reeves, Manchester Regt., killed in action nr. Ypres 7 October 1917: *b.* Liverpool, co. Lancaster, 25 August 1897: *educ.* St. Matthew's School, Stockport: Occupation – Clerk; Portwood Spinning Company, Stockport: enlisted Cheshire Regt. 24 September 1914: served with the Expeditionary Force in France and Flanders from 20 January 1916, and was killed in action at Messines Ridge, 7 June 1917. Buried east of Messines. Age 19.

His elder brother Herbert also has no known grave; he is commemorated on the Tyne Cot Memorial (Panel 123).

(Panel 19) L/Corpl. 265400, William Spilsbury, 1/6th Bn. The Cheshire Regt. (T.F.): *s.* of William Spilsbury, of 17, Bamford Street, Stockport, by his wife Mary Elizabeth: and brother to Pte. 265817, S. Spilsbury, Cheshire Regt., killed in the same action: employee to Messrs Robinson, Hat Manufacturers, Reddish: a pre-war Territorial, undertook Active Service obligations on the outbreak of war: proceeded to France, November 1914. Reported missing presumed (since confirmed) killed in action, 31 July 1917, nr. St. Julien, Ypres: Age 19.

His brother Samuel is buried in Tyne Cot Cemetery (VIII.H.9).

(Panel 19) Pte. 9622, David Ainscough, 1st Bn. (22nd Foot) The Cheshire Regt.: *s.* of William Ainscough, Labourer; of 9, George Street, Birkenhead, and Martha Ann, his wife: *b.* Oliver Place, 4 June 1894: *educ.* St. Werbourgh's School: Occupation – sometime Boiler Cleaner; Pacific Steam Navigation Co.: enlisted Cheshire Regt. February 1914: stationed in Ireland on the outbreak of war, proceeded to France, 14 August, served with the Expeditionary Force there from the 16th., and was killed in action, 6 May 1915; Trenches, Larch Wood. Age 19. Two brothers also served, both survived.

(Panel 19) Pte. 12166, Robert Ashton, 1st Bn. (22nd Foot) The Cheshire Regt.: *b.* Marple, co. Derby: enlisted Hyde, co. Chester. Killed in action, 6 March 1915. Remembered on Marple (Cheshire) War Memorial.

(Panel 19) Pte. 50634, Walter Bates, 10th (Service) Bn. The Cheshire Regt.: formerly no.50222, Leicestershire Regt.: *b.* New Mills, *c.*1883. Missing believed killed in action, 1 August 1917. Age 38. An employee of Bate Mill Printworks, on receiving notification of his death the company flag was lowered to half-mast as a mark of respect. He leaves a widow, Edith Bates, *née* Smith (Westfield Terrace, Thornsett). A regular churchgoer, Pte. Bates taught the scriptures at Thornsett Independent Sunday School.

(Panel 19) Pte. 265360, Leonard Blease, 1/6th Bn. The Cheshire Regt. (T.F.): *s.* of the late George Blease, by his wife Mary Florence (20, Petersburg Road, Edgeley, Stockport): and yr. brother to Sergt. 10081, J.D. Blease, 18th Manchester Regt., killed in action, 9 July 1916: *b.* Edgeley: enlisted Stockport, co. Chester. Killed in action, 31 July 1917. Age 21.

His brother John also has no known grave; he is commemorated on the Thiepval Memorial.

(Panel 19) Pte. 18426, Jordan Bradbury, 2nd Bn. (22nd Foot) The Cheshire Regt.: *b.* Glossop, co. Derby: served with the Expeditionary Force in France. Killed in action, 16 May 1915. Age 28. He was married to Eliza J. Bradbury (5, Stanyford Street, Hadfield, Manchester).

(Panel 19) Pte. 13303, Joseph Brady, 11th (Service) Bn. The Cheshire Regt.: 3rd *s.* of Thomas Brady, Docker; of 12, Myrtle Court, Birkenhead, by his wife Mary: *b.* Birkenhead, co. Chester: *educ.* Our Lady's School, there: Occupation – Frame Room, Assistant; Messrs Lever Brothers, Port Sunlight: enlisted Birkenhead, September 1914: served with the Expeditionary Force in France and Flanders from about August 1915, and was reported missing believed killed in action at Messines Ridge, on or about 8 June 1917. *unm.* (*IWGC record 7 June*) When the mines beneath Hill 60 were detonated on 17 April 1915 1st Cheshires were in trenches at Zillebeke and, despite the ensuing fighting to wrest the hill from the Germans being bitter, bloody and costly in terms of sacrifice and loss, the battalion were not called upon to take part. Nonetheless, the following few days saw the Cheshires suffer a steady loss of men, mostly due to enemy shellfire of the approaches and back areas. On 23 April the battalion lost two men, killed when their dug-out was hit by a shell, both came from Stockport, fate decreed they should share the same surname and initial; neither man was related to the other.

(Panel 19) Pte. 11375, James Burns, 1st Bn. (22nd Foot) The Cheshire Regt.: *b.* St. Matthew's, Stockport: enlisted Stockport, co. Chester. Killed in action, 23 April 1915, in the trenches at Zillebeke; the dug-out he was occupying in company with Pte. John Burns being hit by a German shell.

(Panel 19) Pte. 10060, John Burns, 1st Bn. (22nd Foot) The Cheshire Regt.: *b.* Edgeley, co. Chester: enlisted Stockport. Killed in action, 23 April 1915, in the trenches at Zillebeke; the dug-out he was occupying in company with Pte. James Burns being hit by a German shell.

(Panel 19) Pte. 21505, Walter Thomas Edwards, 11th (Service) Bn. The Cheshire Regt.: 2nd *s.* of Edwin Edwards, by his wife Annie, *dau.* of Charles Fuller: *b.* Hove, co. Sussex, 3 April 1895: *educ.* Ellen Street School: Occupation – Errand Boy: enlisted Hove, November 1914: served with the Expeditionary Force in France and Flanders from February 1916, and was killed in action, 7 June 1917. Age 22. *unm.*

(Panel 19) Pte. 49968, Herbert Garside, 13th (Service) Bn. The Cheshire Regt.: *s.* of Sam Garside, of 6, Park Road, Dukinfield, co. Chester, by his wife Alice: served with the Expeditionary Force. Killed in action, 7 June 1917. Age 20.

(Panel 19) Pte. 58275, Frank Grimes, 10th (Service) Bn. The Cheshire Regt.: *s.* of the late Charles Grimes, of Grappenhall, co. Chester, by his marriage to Margaret Broadfield, *née* Grimes, *née* Ryder (1, Cedar Terrace, Thelwall New Road, Latchford Locks, Warrington): and yr. brother to Seaman C.J. Grimes, S.S. 'Hidalgo' (Hull), Merchant Marine, one of 15 crew lost at sea, 28 August 1917, when that ship, en-route from Manchester to Archangel, was torpedoed and sunk by U.28 (*IWGC record 31 August*): *b.* Grappenhall: enlisted Chester. Killed in action, 1 August 1917. Age 19. Remembered on the Grappenhall (St. Wilfred's) Church War Memorial.

Having no known grave but the sea, his brother Charles is commemorated on the Tower Hill Memorial, London.

(Panel 19) Pte. 51000, Ernest Glostilow Halford, 9th (Service) Bn. The Cheshire Regt.: *s.* of Thomas Halford, of Binley, Coventry, by his wife Martha: and brother to Pte. 16433, S.A. Halford, 14th Royal Warwickshire Regt., died 3 September 1916, of wounds: *b.* Wyken: enlisted Coventry: served with the Expeditionary Force, and was killed in action, 7 June 1917.

His brother Sidney also has no known grave; he is commemorated on the Thiepval Memorial, Somme.

PANEL 19 ENDS PTE. L. HANVEY, CHESHIRE REGT.

PANEL 21 BEGINS LIEUT.-COL. H.E.R. BOXER, D.S.O., LINCOLNSHIRE REGT.

Bellewaarde Spur 1915: 'On 16th June 1915 the 1/Lincolnshires took a leading part in the 3rd Division's attack on the Bellewaarde Spur. They advanced at 4.20a.m. with the Liverpool Scots on their left and the 1/Wiltshires on their right. This line passed through the enemy's front trenches which had been captured five minutes previously by the 9th Brigade, and attacked the enemy's second line. The Lincolnshire's bombers drove the enemy at a run down the communication trenches leading back to his second line, and by 4.30a.m. this line, running from Bellewaarde Farm to the corner of a copse in front of Bellewaarde Lake, was captured by the Lincolnshires at the point of the bayonet. The commanding officer, Major H.E.R. Boxer, then led a party of fifty Lincolnshires along a communication trench which led to the enemy's third line on the western border of the lake, and succeeded in bombing their way there when the British artillery recommenced a barrage which cut them off from the remainder of the battalion. Major Boxer then ordered his party to fall back on to the main body of the battalion., but he himself was mortally wounded and remained in the enemy's third line with a small escort, none of whom returned. Major Boxer's name appeared in the Gazette for the D.S.O. on this date.'

(Panel 21) Lieut.Col. Hugh Edward Richard Boxer, D.S.O., 1st Bn. (10th Foot) The Lincolnshire Regt.: 2nd & only *survg. s.* of the late Lieut. Edward William Frederick Boxer, R.N. (who was lost in H.M.S. Captain when she foundered off Cape Finisterre, 7 September 1870); by his wife Edith Graham, of Thorpe Lodge, Sandown, Isle of Wight (who *m.* 2ndly Col. Frederick Swaine Le Grice, Royal Artillery), *dau.* of Coutts Stone: *gdson.* of Major-General Edward Mournier Boxer, R.A., F.R.S., and *gt.-gdson.* of Rear Admiral Sir Edward Boxer, K.C.B.: *b.* Norbiton, co. Surrey, 8 January 1871: *educ.* Royal Naval School, Stubbington; Kelly College, and Royal Military College, Sandhurst (Queen's Cadet): gazetted 2nd Lieut. Lincolnshire Regt. 27 January 1892; promoted Lieut. 14 August 1893; Capt. 7 April 1900; Major, 25 March 1911; Lieut.Col. 27 May 1915: took part in the Nile Expedition, 1898, including Battle of Atabra, where he was severely wounded (Mentioned in Despatches [*London Gazette*, 24 May 1898]: Egyptian Medal and clasp: Medal): Adjutant of Militia Battn. and Special Reserve of his Regt. 1 September 1903–31 August 1908: served in Malta, Egypt, India, Gibraltar and Bermuda: came home with his regiment, September 1914: joined British Expeditionary Force in France, November, and experienced all the hardships of the winter campaign. Though the wound he received at Atabra frequently caused him great pain, he never let it interfere with his duties, and his cheerfulness and courage endeared him, not only to his brother officers, but to every man in his battalion: sometime after going to the Front, transferred 1st Battn. as Second-in-Command in the fighting around Ypres, and was afterwards, March 1915, transferred 2nd Battn.: took part in the engagements at Festubert, and then took over command of 1st Battn. at Hooge, on 27 May, and was killed in action there, 16 June 1915, when his battalion was ordered to attack the German lines near Bellewaarde Farm, Hooge, and Lieut.Col. Boxer ordered the advance, leading the charge himself. They quickly got through four lines of German trenches, but were ordered to retire to the second line trench, and during the retirement Lieut.Col. Boxer was wounded badly in the left shoulder and leg. However, he continued to direct his battalion, refusing any assistance, and cheerfully encouraging his men. When a very heavy German counter-attack was launched against their only half-prepared defences, he again gave the order to advance to meet it, and tried to lead his battalion, but it is supposed he must have become exhausted and dropped, as he was not seen again. After the action he was reported wounded and missing, and it was not until information was received from German sources in January 1916, that it was known he had died from his wounds. The German Red Cross reported that after the action at Hooge that day they had buried an English officer whose field glasses were engraved 'Captain Boxer' – he had never troubled to have the rank altered – and this was afterwards confirmed by the German Government. He was Mentioned in Despatches (*London Gazette*, 22 June 1915) by F.M. Sir John (now Lord) French, for 'gallant and distinguished service in the field,' and was awarded the D.S.O. (*London Gazette*, 23 June 1915). He *m.* at St. Columba, Pont Street, London, S.W., 23 September 1897, Jane 'Jeannie' ('Soraba,' Shanklin, Isle of Wight), *yst. dau.* of Myles Patterson (Conygar, nr. Dorchester, co. Dorset), and had three children – Hugh Myles, 2nd Lieut. Lincolnshire Regt., *b.* 10 July 1898; Charles Ralph, *b.* 8 March 1904; Beryl Alice, *b.* 21 September 1905. He was a member of the Junior United Service Club, and was very keen on hunting and golf, but his wounded leg prevented him from taking part in any other sport. Age 44.

(Panel 21) Capt. John Dobrée Durell Wickham, 1st Bn. (10th Foot) The Lincolnshire Regt.: elder *s.* of Dobrée Charles Wickham, of 'Wynscote,' Crowborough, co. Sussex, by his wife Madelaine A.: *b.* 17 September 1884: *educ.* Brighton College, where he was Capt. of Football for two years, and was in the Cricket XI: apptd. 2nd Lieut. Lincolnshire Regt. from the Militia, May 1905: promoted Lieut. July 1907; Capt. May 1914. After serving in India for five years he was seconded, October 1910, to West African Frontier Force, Southern Nigeria, where he took part in several punitive expeditions. On the outbreak of the Great War he served with Yola Column, British Expeditionary Force, Cameroons, but after five months was invalided home with blackwater fever. Rejoined 1st Battn. Lincolnshire Regt. in Flanders, 1 June 1915, and died of wounds received near Ypres, 24 June 1915. Age 20. *unm.*

(Panel 21) Lieut. Joseph Walter Harris, 3rd (Reserve) attd. 1st Bn. (10th Foot) The Lincolnshire Regt.: *s.* of George Harris, of Swallowbeck, Lincoln, Secretary of the Lincoln Co-operative Society, by his wife Sarah Ann, *dau.* of John Thacker: *b.* Lincoln 19 June 1889: *educ.* Lincoln Grammar School, at which he won a scholarship from the elementary school, and Nottingham University, where he was a member of the O.T.C.: graduated B.Sc. (First-class Hons.), London University, 13 December 1911: devoted himself to chemical research; became F.I.C., 15 May 1914: gazetted 2nd Lieut. 3rd Lincolns, from Nottingham University O.T.C. 15 August 1914; promoted Lieut. 30 January 1915: went to France, 2 December 1914, attd. 1st Battn. of his Regt., and was killed by shell fire at Hooge, 3 June 1915. Age 25. He *m.* Grimsby, 3 October 1914; Mabel (Swallowbeck, Lincoln), *dau.* of Joseph Laughton, of North Somercotes. (*IWGC record 2 June 1915*)

(Panel 21) 2nd Lieut. Eric Barnes, 1st Bn. (10th Foot) The Lincolnshire Regiment: *s.* of John Barnes; Solicitor: *gdson.* of the late John Carter Holding, of Kingsclere and Southsea: *b.* Kingsclere, co. Hants, 26 October 1894: *educ.* King's School, Bruton, 1904–1912, where the Headmaster's report of him was 'an admirable specimen of the best type of all-round usefulness at athletics, and of good intellectual attainments,' and Royal Military College, Sandhurst: gazetted 2nd Lieut. 1st Lincolnshire Regt. 1 February 1914: served with the Expeditionary Force in France and Flanders, in the fighting line from the commencement of the war until he fell on 1 November 1914, while leading his men in an attack to take the village of Wytschaete, nr. Ypres, Belgium, from the enemy. The Commanding Officer of his regiment wrote, "He fell whilst gallantly leading his Company in the attack on a village called Wytschaete which the regiment had been ordered to take. He was struck by a bullet and died immediately. He died, as he lived, upholding the best traditions of the regiment he loved so well, and his loss is deplored by us all." Another brother officer wrote, "Eric was near me in the advance, and when I got up to take a few men forward, he was the next to come, but as he stood up from the ditch where we had been lying, to lead his men under very heavy fire forward, he was shot straight through the head and died immediately. He was so plucky, always eager and active in the firing line." His friends expressed their appreciation of him, "There are some who possess a certain indefinable charm which makes them general favourites, Barnes was one of these. Strangers took a fancy to him and the longer one knew him, the more one liked him. One of the traits which made him such an attractive character was his cheerfulness; he was a born optimist, and genuine optimism is infectious. Another was the frankness so clearly expressed in his features. A third was the keenness he displayed in everything he took up. The fact that he enjoyed life immensely heightens the tragedy of his early death." Age 20. *unm.*

(Panel 21) 2nd Lieut. Alfred John Bush, 'D' Coy., 2nd Bn. (10th Foot) The Lincolnshire Regt.: eldest *s.* of Alfred Walter Bush, of 'Albrian,' View Road, Highgate, London, N., by his wife Alice Maud, *dau.* of George Brinsley, of Norwood: *b.* London, 13 December 1894: *educ.* Broadstairs, and Highgate College: subsequently entered his father's business: unable to join the Army immediately when war broke out owing to a surgical operation, he joined University of London O.T.C. just as soon as he was fit; gazetted 2nd Lieut. Lincolnshire Regt. September 1916: served with the Expeditionary Force in France from the following December, and was killed in action at Westhoek Ridge, 31 July 1917. Buried about two miles east of Ypres. Age 22. *unm.*

(Panel 21) 2nd Lieut. William Francis Wells-Cole, 1st Bn. (10th Foot) The Lincolnshire Regt.: eldest *s.* of William Francis Wells-Cole, of Digby, co. Lincoln, by his wife Ellen Slorey: and cousin to Major N.W. Wells-Cole, Royal Field Artillery, killed by shellfire, 6 January 1918, at Langemarck: *b.* Sedgeford, King's Lynn: *educ.* Dragon's School, Bardwell Road, Oxford; Repton (The Priory), and Royal Military College, Sandhurst (entered 1915): served with the Expeditionary Force, and was killed in action nr. July Farm, Wambeke, Ypres, 31 July 1917, on which date the Lincolns (in company with the Middlesex) after gaining their objective, endured much close fighting. In the face of an overwhelming German counter-attack and with no reinforcements available, the battalion fought where they stood until all were either killed or wounded. Age 19. Inscribed 'To The Glory Of God And In Grateful Remembrance Of Men Of This Parish Who Gave Their Lives For Justice, King And Country In The Great War 1914–1918,' 2nd Lieut. Wells-Cole is one of twenty men commemorated on the Digby (St. Thomas-a-Becket Church) War Memorial.

His cousin Neville is buried in Canada Farm Cemetery (III.G.2).

(Panel 21) 2nd Lieut. Frank Clifford Green, attd. 1st Bn. (10th Foot) The Lincolnshire Regt: 3rd *s.* of John (& Mrs) Green, of 193, Browning Road, Manor Park, co. Essex: *b.* East Ham, co. Essex, 4 May 1890: *educ.* Hartley University College, Southampton, and while there trained in 5th Battn. Hampshire Regiment, T.F., with his College Corps: afterwards became a Teacher under East Ham Education Authority: joined Artists' Rifles, Pte. no.2452, soon after the outbreak of war, August 1914: was for some time stationed at the Tower of London, and afterwards at Watford: went to France in October 1914, where, shortly after its arrival, the Corps was transformed into an O.T.C., and Pte. Green was promoted L/Corpl.: gazetted Temp. 2nd Lieut. attd. 1st Lincolnshire Regt. 23 April 1915, and was killed in action at Hooge, nr. Ypres, 16 June following. A Captain in his battalion, who was with him when he was killed wrote, "Your son was standing with me in a hail of shell and rifle fire, and we decided to jump into a trench captured from the Germans, close by. He jumped in while talking to me, and suddenly said, 'Oh! I'm hit.' After a short pause he added, 'I'm finished.' I cut off his equipment and clothes and did my best to bandage the wound, which went right through the chest, but could not stop the bleeding. I left him in the hands of a stretcher-bearer with instructions to do the best he could. I regret to say your son was unconscious then, and the stretcher-bearer missing." And in a later letter he wrote, "I asked a doctor afterwards if there was anything I could have done to have saved him, and he told me nothing. I made every effort to stop the bleeding, but could not do so. I handed him over to a stretcher-bearer who belonged to another regiment; your son was alive then, but unconscious, and I am afraid very near the end. It was in the Germans second-line trench where your son was hit, and that night we were ordered to evacuate the trench owing to the line not being straight." Mr Green was a member of the Ilford Wanderers' Rugby Club, and was chairman of the Local Teachers' Swimming Club. He was a fine swimmer, and was awarded two medals by the Royal Life Saving (Swimming) Society, one for passing the test, the other for an Honorary Instructorship. Age 25. *unm.*

(Panel 21) Sergt. 1503, Lingard Carr, 1/4th Bn. The Lincolnshire Regt. (T.F.): *s.* of Mrs M.J. Carr (6, Holt Lane, Horncastle, co. Lincoln), and her late husband Jesse Carr: *b.* Hameringham, co. Lincoln, 1887: enlisted Horncastle: served with the Expeditionary Force in France and Flanders from 1 March 1915, and was killed in action, 2 August 1915. Age 28. Remains 'Unknown British Soldier;' recovered unmarked grave (28.J.20.d.8.8), 10 December 1928; identified – Khaki, Titles; reinterred, registered, 12 December 1928. *Buried in Sanctuary Wood Cemetery (IV.P.5).*

(Panel 21) Sergt. 7147, Harry Dungay, 1st Bn. (10th Foot) The Lincolnshire Regt.: *s.* of the late Robert Dungay, by his wife Sarah (Ryston Gate House, Downham Market, co. Norfolk): and brother to L/Corpl. 28991, R. Dungay, 7th Bedfordshire Regt., killed in action, 16 November 1916: *b.* Denver, co. Norfolk, *c.*1887: enlisted Downham Market. Killed in action, 1 November 1914. Age 27. *unm.*

His brother Robert is buried in Regina Trench Cemetery, Grandcourt (I.B.25).

(Panel 21) Sergt. 402, Percy Lilley, 1/5th Bn. The Lincolnshire Regt. (T.F.): *s.* of Charles Lilley, of 8, Kebir Terrace, Gainsborough, co. Lincoln: enlisted Gainsborough: served with the Expeditionary Force in France and Flanders from 1 March 1915, and was one of four men recorded missing, believed killed, 20 May 1915, following the detonation of an enemy mine beneath the trench his company were occupying at the time. See account re. Packhorse Farm Shrine Cemetery, and Ptes. 3217, C. Parrott, 2287, C. Shaw, and 1304, C.W. Stubbins (below).

(Panel 21) Corpl. 1578, Ralph Clark, 1/4th Bn. The Lincolnshire Regt. (T.F.): *s.* of George Henry Clark, of 34, Priory Terrace, St. Leonard's Street, Stamford, co. Lincoln, by his wife Rose Ann: *b.* Huntingdon, *c.*1893: served with the Expeditionary Force in France and Flanders from 1 March 1915, and was killed in action, 28 July 1915. Age 22. *unm.* Remains 'Unknown British Soldier. Lincolns;' recovered from an unmarked grave (28.J.20.d.8.8), 10 December 1928; identified – Khaki, Titles; reinterred, registered 12 December 1928. *Buried in Sanctuary Wood Cemetery (IV.Q.2).*

(Panel 21) L/Corpl. 2640, Samuel 'Sam' Hawley, 'B' Coy., 1/4th Bn. The Lincolnshire Regt. (T.F.): *s.* of Eliza Hawley (Denton, nr. Grantham, co. Lincoln), and her late husband: enlisted Luton, co. Bedford: served with the Expeditionary Force in France and Flanders from 1 March 1915, and was killed in action, 2 August following. Age 29. *unm.* Remains 'Unknown British Soldier;' recovered from an unmarked grave (28.J.20.d.8.8), 10 December 1928; identified – Khaki, Stripe, Titles; reinterred, registered 12 December 1928. *Buried in Sanctuary Wood Cemetery (IV.P.6).*

(Panel 21) Pte. 3180, George Allen, 1/4th Bn. The Lincolnshire Regt. (T.F.): *s.* of Martha Allen (20, Alexandra Terrace, West Parade, Lincoln): enlisted Lincoln: served with the Expeditionary Force in France and Flanders from 1 March 1915, and was killed in action, 15 August following. Age 23. *unm.* Remains recovered from an unmarked grave (28.I.24.d.15.45) 'Unknown British Soldier. 4/Lincoln;' identified – Khaki, Titles; registered, reinterred 30 November 1928. *Buried in Sanctuary Wood Cemetery (II.M.7).* The origin of 'Tommy Atkins' as a sobriquet for the English soldier is highly disputed; the most common belief is that the Duke of Wellington chose the name in 1843, but Lieutenant-General Sir William MacArthur – writing in the *Army Medical Services Magazine* – says the War Office used the name 'Thomas Atkins' as a representative name in the 1815 issue of the *Soldier's Book*, and, as far back as 1743, long before both Wellington and MacArthur were born, a letter from Jamaica referring to a mutiny among hired soldiery there said, "Except for those from N. America, ye Marines and Tommy Atkins behaved splendidly." The Commonwealth War Graves Commission record twelve Great War casualties named T. Atkins – 8 United Kingdom, 2 Australian, 1 Canadian, 1 New Zealand. Of these, five are buried in Commonwealth cemeteries and the remainder recorded on Memorials to the Missing. Only two are to be found within the confines of the Ypres Salient, one in Lijssenthoek Military Cemetery, Poperinghe – the other, the earliest recorded 'Tommy Atkins' killed in the Great War:-

(Panel 21) Pte. 7146, Thomas Henry Atkins, 1st Bn. (10th Foot) The Lincolnshire Regt.: *s.* of William H. Atkins, of 7, Northwick Avenue, Worcester, by his wife Kate H.: served with the Expeditionary Force in France, and was killed in action whilst attacking the village of Wytschaete under heavy enemy fire, 1 November 1914. Age 29.

(Panel 21) Pte. 202085, Cecil Borman, 8th (Service) Bn. The Lincolnshire Regt.: *s.* of Frederick Borman, of 120, Ripon Street, Lincoln, and Martha Borman, his spouse: and yr. brother to R/18142, H.J.W. Borman, HMS *Invincible*, R.N., lost at sea, 31 May 1916, when that ship was sunk at the Battle of Jutland: *b.* Bracebridge, co. Lincoln. Missing/believed killed in action, 31 July 1917. Age 19.

His brother Herbert has no known grave but the sea; he is commemorated on the Portsmouth Naval Memorial (17).

(Panel 21) Pte. 2992, William Bristow, 1/4th Bn. The Lincolnshire Regt. (T.F.): *s.* of Robert Bristow, of Old Quarrington, Sleaford, co. Lincoln: served with the Expeditionary Force in France and Flanders from 1 March 1915, and was killed in action, 31 July following. Age 22. Remains 'Unknown British Soldier. Lincolns,' exhumed from an unmarked grave Sanctuary Wood; identified – Khaki, Titles; reinterred, registered 3 December 1928. *Buried in Sanctuary Wood Cemetery (II.M.16).*

Rest In Peace Till We Meet Again

(Panel 21) Pte. 14545, Frederick William Clarke, 1st Bn. (10th Foot) The Lincolnshire Regt.: *s.* of George Clarke, of Wilsford Heath, Grantham, by his wife Eliza: and elder brother to Pte. 14567, H. Clarke, Lincolnshire Regt., who fell two weeks later: *b.* Canwick, about 1896: enlisted Lincoln: served with the Expeditionary Force, and was killed in action, 2 June 1915. Age 19.

His brother Herbert also has no known grave; he is recorded below.

(Panel 21) Pte. 14567, Herbert Clarke, 1st Bn. (10th Foot) The Lincolnshire Regt.: *s.* of George Clarke, of Wilsford Heath, Grantham, by his wife Eliza: and *yr.* brother to Pte. 14545,

F.W. Clarke, Lincolnshire Regt., who fell two weeks previously: *b.* St. Swithin's, about 1897: enlisted Lincoln: served with the Expeditionary Force, and was killed in action, 16 June 1915. Age 18.

His brother Frederick also has no known grave; he is recorded above.

(Panel 21) Pte. 13979, Stanley Clarke, 1st Bn. (10th Foot) The Lincolnshire Regt.: *s.* of Henry Clarke, Miner; of 11, North Street, Sutton-in-Ashfield, by his wife Elizabeth: *b.* Royston, nr. Barnsley, *c.*1894: enlisted Sutton-in-Ashfield: served with the Expeditionary Force in France from March 1915. Reported missing following the fighting, 16 June 1915; confirmed (April 1916) as having been killed in action on that date. Age 21. *unm.* (*IWGC record Clark*) *The Notts Free Press*, In Memoriam, 16 June 1916:-

> *Home is dark without our loved one,*
> *Bitterly we miss his face;*
> *Sadness lurks where once was sunshine,*
> *None can fill the vacant place.*
>
> Mother, Father, Sisters & Brothers

(Panel 21) Pte. 5246, Arthur Deacle, 1st Bn. (10th Foot) The Lincolnshire Regt.: late of Liverpool: *s.* of William Deacle, of 5, Sunbury Street, Thatto Heath, St. Helens, co. Lancaster, and Rebecca Deacle, his spouse: and brother to Pte. 21753, H. Deacle, 11th South Lancashire Regt., killed in action, 28 March 1918: *b.* Eccleston: enlisted St. Helens: served with the Expeditionary Force in France and Flanders from August 1914; died of wounds, 27 April 1915 received from retaliatory fire following a reconnaissance patrol of the enemy wire during which Sergt.Drmr. W.J. Stevens was killed; 2nd Lieut. L.T. Brook and Lieut. (Q.M.) F.W. Masters, wounded.

His brother Henry also has no known grave, he is commemorated on the Pozieres Memorial; Sergt. Drmr. W.J. Stevens is buried in Dickebusch New Military Cemetery (D.16).

(Panel 21) Pte. 2605, John William Fanthorpe, 1/5th Bn. The Lincolnshire Regt. (T.F.): late of Little Coates, co. Lincoln: enlisted Lincoln: served with the Expeditionary Force in France and Flanders from 1 March 1915, and was killed in action, 13 August following. Remains recovered from an unmarked grave (28.I.24.d.15.45) 'Unknown British Soldier. 4/Lincoln;' identified Khaki, Titles, Pouch Cover, Equipment Scabbard no.7/L.440; registered, reinterred 30 November 1928. *Buried in Sanctuary Wood Cemetery (II.M.13)*.

(Panel 21) Pte. 15991, Joseph Fielding, 6th (Service) Bn. The Lincolnshire Regt.: *s.* of William Fielding, of North Street, Owston Ferry, co. Lincoln, by his wife Eliza: and brother to L/Corpl. 40726, W. Fielding, 1st West Yorkshire Regt., killed in action, 18 April 1917: *b.* Gainsborough, co. Lincoln, *c.*1893: enlisted there. Killed in action, 8 June 1917. Age 24. *unm.* The Owston Ferry War Memorial, unveiled 1922, dedicated – To The Honoured Memory Of Those Who, Leaving Their Homes In This Parish, Gave Their Lives For King And Country In The Great War – records the names of 27 local men (5 WWII) who made the supreme sacrifice; among them the brothers Fielding.

His brother William also has no known grave; he is commemorated on the Loos Memorial.

(Panel 21) Pte. 13505, Fred Fox, 6th (Service) Bn. The Lincolnshire Regt.: *s.* of Robert Fox, of 'The Cottages,' Pullwoods, Ambleside, by his wife Jane, *dau.* of the late, Joseph Lambert, of Leyburn, co. York: *b.* Bowdon, co. Chester, 19 April 1893: *educ.* Bowdon and Ambleside: Occupation – Under Gardener; Croft Bank, Shaw: enlisted Lincolnshire Regt. 7 November 1914: served with the Mediterranean Expeditionary Force at Gallipoli from July 1915; took part in the landing at Suvla Bay, August: proceeded to France in July 1916, and was killed in action at the Battle of Messines, 8 June 1917. Buried where he fell. His officer wrote, "He was one of my best men, always willing to do any work, and whatever he did you could rely on it being done well." Age 24. *unm.*

(Panel 21) Pte. 12109, Ernest Gamwell, 7th (Service) Bn. The Lincolnshire Regt.: late of Blyton, co. Lincoln: *s.* of the late George Richard Gamwell, of High Street, Gainsborough, co. Lincoln, by his wife Harriett (Gilby Cottages, Pilham, Gainsborough): and elder brother to Pte. 1776, W. Gamwell, 1st Lincolnshire Regt., killed in action, 25 September 1916: *b.*

Gringley-on-the-Hill, co. Nottingham: enlisted Gainsborough: served with the Expeditionary Force. Killed in action, 2 March 1916. Age 21.

His brother Walter is buried in Combles Communal Cemetery Extension (I.A.21).

(Panel 21) Pte. 2440, Arthur Goodacre, 1/4th Bn. The Lincolnshire Regt. (T.F.): *s.* of S. (& Mrs M.E.) Goodacre, of 51, Frampton Place, Boston, co. Lincoln: enlisted Luton, co. Bedford: served with the Expeditionary Force, and was killed in action, 31 July 1915. Age 28. *unm.* Remains 'Unknown British Soldier;' recovered from an unmarked grave (28.J.20.d.8.8), 10 December 1928; identified – Khaki, Titles; reinterred, registered 12 December 1928. *Buried in Sanctuary Wood Cemetery (IV.P.2)*.

(Panel 21) Pte. 235246, Samuel Walter Gray, 8th (Service) Bn. The Lincolnshire Regt.: formerly no.269595, Hertfordshire Regt.: late of Kirby Cross, co. Essex: brother to Pte. 260159, F.A. Gray, Worcestershire Regt., killed in action, 27 August 1917: enlisted Colchester. Killed in the vicinity of Rifle Farm; Battle of Pilckem, 31 July 1917. Age 34. He was married to Caroline Susan Farrow, formerly Gray (Kirby Cross, Clacton-on-Sea).

His brother Frederick is buried in Perth Cemetery (China Wall), Zillebeke (VIII.D.13).

(Panel 21) Pte. 12408, George Henry Hannath, 7th (Service) Bn. The Lincolnshire Regt.: *s.* of Harriett Taylor: *b.* Ketsby, co. Lincoln, *c.*1896: volunteered and enlisted Tetford, with his friend Robert Trolley: posted 7th Lincolnshire Regt., 51st Bde., XVIIth (Northern) Divn.: served with the Expeditionary Force in France and Flanders: indoctrinated into trench warfare, 27 July 1915, when his Battalion linked up with the Territorial battalions of his Regiment: took part in the fighting at Hooge, 9 August 1915. Between 14–17 February 1916 his battalion were in the front line at The Bluff, and suffered losses of 1 officer and 20 other ranks killed due to repeated attacks and counter-attacks by the enemy who were determined to recapture ground lost to them in early 1915. He was killed in action, 15 February 1916, aged 19 years; one of 20 men of his battalion to make the supreme sacrifice during those four days, but not the last – two weeks later his friend Pte. R. Trolley was also killed at The Bluff. Robert Trolley also has no known grave; he is recorded below.

(Panel 21) Pte. 10897, James William Hogg, 7th (Service) Bn. The Lincolnshire Regt.: *s.* of C.B. (& Ann) Hogg, Broughton, Brigg, co. Lincoln: and elder brother to Pte. 3349, C. Hogg, 1/5th Lincolnshire

Regt., killed in action, 13 October 1915: *b*. Broughton: enlisted Brigg: served with the Expeditionary Force, and was killed in action, 2 March 1916. Age 23. *unm*.

His brother Charles also has no known grave; he is commemorated on the Loos (Dud Corner) Memorial.

(Panel 21) Pte. 2534, Sidney George Inckle, 1/4th Bn. The Lincolnshire Regt. (T.F.): only *s*. of Henry Inckle, of 11, Sincil Bank, Lincoln, by his wife Edna: *b*. Sincil Bank, *c*.1897: enlisted Luton, co. Bedford, August 1914: served with the Expeditionary Force in France from 1 March 1915, and was killed in action, 26 July following. Age 18. Remains 'Unknown British Soldier;' recovered from an unmarked grave (28.J.20.d.8.8), 10 December 1928; identified – Khaki, Titles; reinterred, registered 12 December 1928. *Buried in Sanctuary Wood Cemetery (IV.P.7).*

(Panel 21) Pte. 13768, Harold Jackson, 'B' Coy., 1st Bn. (10th Foot) The Lincolnshire Regt.: *b*. Wilsford, Grantham: enlisted Lincoln. Killed in action, 16 June 1915. Age 18. All correspondence should be addressed c/o Pte. Jackson's legal guardian, David Markham Esq., Helpringham, nr. Sleaford, co. Lincoln.

(Panel 21) Pte. 2628, Walter Cooper Maughan, 'B' Coy., 5th Bn. The Lincolnshire Regt. (T.F.): *s*. of John William Maughan, Horse Dealer & Supplier; of Tetford, Horncastle, co. Lincoln, by his marriage to the late Susan Broughton: *b*. Tetford, *c*.1883: enlisted Grimsby; posted 5th Lincolnshire Regt.: proceeded to France with 46th (North Midland) Division, February 1915, where, in March, the battalion was in reserve (but not utilised) at the Battle of Neuve Chapelle; receiving its baptism of fire shortly thereafter in the Ploegsteert sector before taking over trenches at Kemmel. His Officer, Capt. H.S. Scorer (killed 13 October following) reported Pte. Maughan as having been killed in action on the evening of 25 July 1915, by a trench mortar bomb. Age 32. Capt. Hugh Scorer also has no known grave; he is commemorated on the Loos Memorial (Dud Corner).

(Panel 21) Pte. 12099, Alfred Miles, 7th (Service) Bn. The Lincolnshire Regt.: *s*. of Harry Miles, of Belmisthorpe, Stamford, co. Lincoln, by his wife Nancy: *b*. Selston, co. Nottingham 30 June 1893: *educ.* Ryhall, and Stamford Endowed School: previously apprenticed to Messrs Blackstone, Stamford, as an Ironmonger; completed his apprenticeship, 30 June 1914: enlisted, 4 September 1914: trained Tulworth Camp, Bovington, and Winchester: served with the Expeditionary Force in France and Flanders from 14 July 1915, and was killed in action, 15 February 1916. *Rutland & The Great War*:- "His death occurring under the following circumstances as narrated by Lieut. A.W.S. Cowie, formerly classical master at Stamford Grammar School, who performed one of the unrecorded acts of bravery in trying to assist Pte. Miles after he received his mortal wound, and was himself shot in the shoulder whilst with him, but managed to get to a dressing station. The 7th Lincolnshires had been holding what was known as the International Trench, and were relieved by another regiment. A few hours later the trench was captured by the Germans, mainly by the explosion of mines, and the 7th Lincolnshires were recalled to retake the trench. After fierce fighting they were so reduced in number that it was necessary to send for reinforcement, and Pte. Miles was sent with a message to Headquarters. In order to get there as quickly as possible, it was necessary to go along a trench which was dominated by the enemy posted on a high embankment called the Bluff, on which were a number of snipers who could fire straight into the trench. Pte. Miles kept steadily on his way until he came to a part of the trench which had been blown in by the terrific bombardment, and it was whilst climbing over the debris which filled the trench that he was shot, dying later in the day. Beyond the attempt of Lieut Cowie, his comrades were unable to render any assistance owing to the sniper's fire. When a party could eventually recover the body, they had to bury him in the trench where he fell." Age 22. *unm*.

(Panel 21) Pte. 9704, Oliver Victor Osbourne, 1st Bn. (10th Foot) The Lincolnshire Regt.: late of Hickson Cottages, Woodhall Spa, co. Lincoln: *b*. Woodhall Spa: enlisted Horncastle, co. Lincoln, prior to the outbreak of war, August 1914: posted 1st Lincolnshire Regt., 9th Infantry Bde., IIIrd Division: stationed Portsmouth, co. Hants, his battalion mobilised, 18.00 hrs., 4 August 1914: departed Southampton, 14th of that month, aboard S.S. 'Italian Princess,' landing at Le Havre the same day, concentrating at Landrecies. From January until 17 February 1915 the battalion held a fairly quiet sector of the line east of Kemmel, on which date 9th Brigade were ordered to The Bluff. The battalion spent almost a month in this sector and, although not engaged in any specific action, they lost many men from constant enemy artillery, trench mortar and sniper fire. Oliver Osborn 'died of wounds somewhere in France,' 4 March 1915. Age 19. (*IWGC record Osborn, 9714*)

(Panel 21) Pte. 11588, John Mail Parkin, 7th (Service) Bn. The Lincolnshire Regt.: *s.* of the late Charles Parkin, by his wife Rachel (widow of Albert Edward Myers of, 8, Henley Street, Lincoln), *dau.* of Thomas Mail: *b.* Lincoln, 27 June 1893: *educ.* St. Martin's School, Lincoln: Occupation – Riveter: enlisted, 4 September 1914, after the outbreak of war: served with the Expeditionary Force in France and Flanders from July 1915, and was killed in action at Ypres, 2 March 1916. Age 22. *unm.* Remembered on Lincoln War Memorial.

(Panel 21) Pte. 3217, John Parrott, 1/5th Bn. The Lincolnshire Regt. (T.F.): late of Thealby, co. Lincoln: *b.* Winterton: enlisted Scunthorpe: served with the Expeditionary Force in France and Flanders from 1 March 1915. One of four men recorded missing believed killed in action, 20 May 1915, following the detonation of an enemy mine beneath the trench his company were occupying at the time. See account re. Packhorse Farm Shrine Cemetery, also Sergt. 402, P. Lilley, above; and Ptes. 2287, C. Shaw, and 1304, C.W. Stubbins, below.

(Panel 21) Pte. 13881, William Peach, 1st Bn. (10th Foot) The Lincolnshire Regt.: *s.* of George Peach, of Holbeach St. John's, Holbeach, co. Lincoln, by his wife Mahalah: and elder brother to Pte. 9543, F. Peach, 1st Lincolnshire Regt., died of wounds, 2 November 1917, at Poperinghe: *b.* Spalding: enlisted there. Killed in action, 16 June 1915 at Ypres. Age 20. *unm.* Remembered on Holbeach St. John's War Memorial.

His brother Frederick is buried in Lijssenthoek Military Cemetery (XXI.HH.3).

(Panel 21) Pte. 14351, Frank Pishorn, 1st Bn. (10th Foot) The Lincolnshire Regt.: *s.* of Charles Pishorn, of Holden's Yard, Norfolk Street, King's Lynn, by his wife Susan: *b.* King's Lynn, co. Norfolk: enlisted Lincoln. Killed in action, 4 June 1915, at Hooge. Age 24. Mentioned in Despatches for service in the field; he was married to Maud Pishorn (331, Wellington Street, Grimsby, co. Lincoln). Remembered on the King's Lynn War Memorial, Blackfriars Gardens.

(Panel 21) Pte. 23643, Henry George Proctor, 8th (Service) Bn. The Lincolnshire Regt.: *s.* of Henry Proctor, of High Street, North Thoresby, by his wife Alice Gertrude: *b.* North Thoresby, co. Lincoln, 1898: *educ.* County Council School, North Thoresby: Occupation – Butcher's Assistant: enlisted Lincolnshire Regt., Louth, 22 May 1916: served with the Expeditionary Force in France and Flanders from May 1917. Reported wounded and missing after the fighting, 31 July 1917; now assumed to have been killed in action on or about that date. A comrade wrote, "I cannot say much about your son, because I had not known him very long, but one thing I know, he was a *very brave lad*; he proved that on 31 July 1917, when we were fighting side by side." Age 19. (*IWGC record Procter*)

(Panel 21) Pte. 14844, Joseph Walter Sharpe, 7th (Service) Bn. The Lincolnshire Regt.: *s.* of Edward Sharpe, of Jesson's Cottages, Newborough, co. Northampton, by his wife Eliza: and brother to Pte. 22872, J.H. Sharpe, 7th Lincolnshire Regt., killed in action, 3 November 1916, at the Somme: *b.* Newborough, *c.*1893: enlisted Spalding, co. Lincoln: served with the Expeditionary Force, and was killed in action, 2 March 1916. Age 22. *unm.*

His brother James also has no known grave; he is commemorated on the Thiepval Memorial (Pier & Face I.C.).

(Panel 21) Pte. 2287, Charles Shaw, 1/5th Bn. The Lincolnshire Regt. (T.F.): enlisted Grimsby: served with the Expeditionary Force in France and Flanders from 1 March 1915. One of four men recorded missing, believed killed in action, 20 May 1915, following the detonation of an enemy mine beneath the trench his company were occupying at the time. See account re. Packhorse Farm Shrine Cemetery, also Sergt. 402, P. Lilley and Pte. 3217, J. Parrott, above; and Pte. 1304, C.W. Stubbins, below.

(Panel 21) Pte. 1304, Charles William Stubbins, 1/5th Bn. The Lincolnshire Regt. (T.F.): *s.* of Joseph Shacklock Stubbins, of 14A, Carlisle Street, Gainsborough, by his wife Hannah Maria: *b.* Winterton, co. Lincoln, *c.*1890: enlisted Gainsborough: served with the Expeditionary Force in France and Flanders from 1 March 1915. One of four men recorded missing, believed killed in action, 20 May 1915, following the detonation of an enemy mine beneath the trench his company were occupying at the time. Age 25. See account re. Packhorse Farm Shrine Cemetery; also Sergt. 402, P. Lilley, Ptes. 3217, J. Parrott and 2287, C. Shaw, above.

(Panel 21) Pte. 8838, Neal Douglas Tocher, 1st Bn. (10th Foot) The Lincolnshire Regt.: *s.* of John Tocher (late Indian Army), by his wife Elizabeth (2, Elands Road, Aldershot, co. Hants): and brother to Pte. L/15675, C.G.M. Tocher, 1st Royal Fusiliers, died 16 March 1919: *b.* Secunderabad, Trimulgerry, India: enlisted Aldershot. Died of wounds, 26 September 1915. Age 20. *unm.* Mentioned in Despatches by Field Marshal Sir John (now Lord) French.

His brother Colin is buried in Brookwood Military Cemetery (XII.C.6A).

Retford Times, Friday, 6th November 1914: "Mr. John Tomlinson, 57, Spital Hill, Retford, has his two sons in the army – *viz* Pte. George Tomlinson, 1st Lincoln Regiment, formerly Postman at Maltby; and Pte. Leonard Tomlinson, York & Lancaster Regiment, now at South Shields. A letter was received from George on Monday, and we take the following extracts :- 'Just a few lines hoping you are in the best of health. I am in the pink of condition. You will no doubt think I am a long while writing this time, but you must know we cannot write just when we like. I am getting about tired of it, but I hope to go through the lot of it, as you will know this is what we call real war. In fact I am just getting used to it. We are mostly under fire. You don't see many sad faces with all our troubles. The men make light of it, singing and laughing as if nothing was happening. You would be surprised what a difference there has been just lately. I will tell you someday if I live to come back, and I hope so. I think I have seen a little since we started at Mons and Cambrai. And the capture of the guns, which no doubt you will have read of in the papers. We had a nasty go just after that. We had a little bit of our own back last Saturday. We had to shift them with the toothpick at the end of the gun. Talk about them running, hockey was not in it. I am pleased to think I have some more brothers who are doing their duty. I wish them luck, as I think I have been very lucky up to now. My best regards to all enquiring friends.'"

(Panel 21) Pte. 6855, George John Tomlinson, 1st Bn. (10th Foot) The Lincolnshire Regt.: *s.* of John Tomlinson, of 57, Spital Hill, Retford, co. Nottingham, by his wife Emma: and brother to Pte. L. Tomlinson, who also fell: late *husb.* to Frances Mary Tomlinson (55, Spital Hill, Retford): served with the Expeditionary Force. Killed in action, 14 November 1914. Age 29.

His brother Leonard is buried in Potijze Burial Ground (DI.14).

(Panel 21) Pte. 2419, Richard Trail, 1/4th Bn. The Lincolnshire Regt. (T.F.): late of Westbourne Grove, co. Middlesex: *s.* of Arthur Trail, of 2, George Square, Greenock, by his wife Rosa: *b.* Grantham, co. Lincoln: enlisted Luton, co. Bedford: served with the Expeditionary Force in France. Killed in action, 23 August 1915. Age 20. Remains 'Unknown British Soldier;' recovered from an unmarked grave (28.J.20.d.8.8), 10 December 1928; identified – Khaki; reinterred, registered 12 December 1928. *Buried in Sanctuary Wood Cemetery (IV.P.3).*

(Panel 21) Pte. 12407, Robert Trolley, 7th (Service) Bn. The Lincolnshire Regt.: stepson of Mr Sanderson, Farmer: *b.* Tetford, co. Lincoln: *educ.* there: Occupation – Farm Worker; employed by his stepfather: volunteered and enlisted Tetford with his friend George Hannath: posted 7th Lincolnshire Regt., 51st Bde., XVIIth Divn.: served with the Expeditionary Force in France and Flanders, where he saw his first action, 9 August 1915, at Hooge. In February the battalion took over trenches at The Bluff where it was engaged in a series of attacks and counter-attacks (14th – 17th February; 2nd March) as the Germans attempted to recapture the ground wrested from them in early 1915. He was killed on 2 March 1916, a little over two weeks after his friend Pte. G.H. Hannath was killed at the same place. Pte. Trolley was a fine, well-built lad, highly respected by all, and a keen musician. He played for Tetford Brass Band.

George Hannath also has no known grave; he is recorded above.

(Panel 21) Pte. 14296, Arthur Waltham, 1st Bn. (10th Foot) The Lincolnshire Regt.: *s.* of Alfred Waltham, of 'Kenwood,' Spilsby Road, Boston, co. Lincoln, by his wife Maria: and brother to Pte. 1271, E. Waltham, 10th Lincolnshire Regt., killed in action, 28 April 1917: *b.* Kirton Holme, co. Lincoln: enlisted Boston. Died of wounds, 4 June 1915. Age 25. Erected in proud and loving memory of the men of Hubberts Bridge and Kirton Holme who laid down their lives in the Great War, the brothers Waltham are remembered on Kirton Holme (Christ Church) Parish War Memorial.

His brother Ernest is known to be buried in Roeux British Cemetery (Sp.Mem.H.3).

(Panel 21) Pte. 14715, Charles William Walton, 1st Bn. (10th Foot) The Lincolnshire Regt.: *s.* of the late Richard Walton, by his marriage to Eliza Marshall, *née* Walton (Wilsford Lane, Ancaster, nr. Grantham, co. Lincoln): and yr. brother to Pte. 10456, T.R. Walton, 7th Lincolnshire Regt., killed in action, 3 July 1916: *b.* Sudbrooke: enlisted Bourne. Killed in action, 16 June 1915. Age 17.

His brother Thomas also has no known grave; he is commemorated on the Thiepval Memorial (Pier & Face 1C).

(Panel 21) Pte. 41631, Charles Henry Whittaker, 'D' Coy., 2nd Bn. (10th Foot) The Lincolnshire Regt.: formerly no.34352, Leicestershire Regt.: *b.* Bradford co. York, *c.*1876: enlisted Mossley, co. Lancaster. Killed in action, 31 July 1917. Age 41. He leaves a wife, Jane Whittaker (14, Livingstone Avenue, Mossley, Manchester), to whom all effects and correspondence concerning the deceased are to be addressed. Remains recovered from an unmarked grave (28.I.18.b.3.5); identified – Clothing, Purse, Fountain Pen; reinterred, registered 24 January 1928. *Buried in Sanctuary Wood Cemetery (IV.N.14).*

A Good Soldier Of Jesus

(Panel 21) 2nd Lieut. Arthur Martin Taylor, 2nd Bn. (11th Foot) The Devonshire Regt.: *s.* of the Rev. Martin Church Taylor, Congregational Minister, of 9, Westminster Terrace, Douglas, Isle of Man; late of Egerton Road, Whitefield, nr. Manchester, by his wife Sarah, *dau.* of J. Dyson, of Castle Hedingham: *b.* Ringwood, co. Hants, 18 August 1894: *educ.* Caterham School: Occupation – Clerk: enlisted 21st (Service) Bn. (Public Schools) Royal Fusiliers, 14 November 1914: obtained a commission; gazetted 2nd Lieut. 3rd Devonshire Regt. 15 October 1916: subsequently transf'd. 2nd Bn.: served with the Expeditionary Force in France from November 1916, taking part in the later Battles of the Somme, and was killed in action at the taking of Westhoek Ridge, 31 July–1 August 1917. Buried where he fell. His Commanding Officer wrote, "He was at the time leading his platoon very gallantly. His loss is greatly felt by both the officers and men of the battalion, by whom he was greatly loved." Age 22. *unm.* (*IWGC record age 23*)

(Panel 21) L/Corpl. 8095, James Pugsley, 1st Bn. (11th Foot) The Devonshire Regt.: *s.* of Frank Pugsley, of West Farm, Lapsford, co. Devon: and brother to Pte. 19103, W.J. Pugsley, 2nd Devonshire Regt., killed in action, 1 July 1916; Somme: *b.* Crediton: enlisted Exeter. Killed in action, 21 April 1915; Ypres. Age 28. *unm.*

His brother William also has no known grave; he is commemorated on the Thiepval Memorial, Somme.

(Panel 21) L/Corpl. 9720, Thomas Skelton, 1st Bn. (11th Foot) The Devonshire Regt.: *s.* of Charles Skelton, of 10, Pound Road, Banstead, co. Surrey, by his wife Elizabeth Rosa: and brother to Pte. 60448, A.G. Skelton, Royal Fusiliers, died of wounds, 13 April 1917, received at Arras; and Pte. 6759, S. Skelton, East Surrey Regt., died at home, 9 December 1919, consequent to wounds sustained on the Western Front: *b.* Banstead, March 1895: Occupation – Gardener's Labourer: enlisted Kingston-on-Thames, 28 May 1913. Killed in action, 26 January 1915. Age 19. All correspondence should be addressed c/o N. Alderman, Fairlawn House, Woodmansterne. A fourth brother, Gordon, lied about his age and enlisted in the Devonshire Regt. at age 14 but was returned to his parents after the authorities were notified, and a fifth, Norman Percy, enlisted in 1920.

His brother Alfred is buried in St. Sever Cemetery Extension, Rouen (O.VIII.H.12); Stanley is buried in Banstead (All Saints) Churchyard. Although the cause of Stanley's death was, without question, directly attributable to his service in France he is not recorded on the Banstead War Memorial.

(Panel 21) Pte. 3/6957, Arthur Baker, 1st Bn. (11th Foot) The Devonshire Regt.: *s.* of George Baker, Grocer; of Walthamstow, by his wife Annie: and brother to Pte. 10863, A. Baker, 2nd Wiltshire Regt., died No.13 Base Hospital, Boulogne 3 July 1915; and AB.J/5378, F.B. Baker, R.N., Torpedo Hand, HMS *Queen Mary*, drowned during the fighting at the Battle of Jutland, 31 May 1916: *b.* Walworth, London, S.E., 20 December 1894: *educ.* Kirkdale, Leytonstone: Occupation – Motor Mechanic: enlisted Stratford,

London, E., 7 August 1914, after the outbreak of war: served with the Expeditionary Force in France and Flanders, and was killed in action at Wulverghem, 14 January 1915. Buried there. Age 20. *unm.*

His brother Alfred is buried in Boulogne Eastern Cemetery (VIII.B.56); Frederick has no known grave, he is commemorated on the Portsmouth Naval Memorial (Panel 12).

(Panel 21) Pte. 26333, John Middleton, 2nd Bn. (11th Foot) The Devonshire Regt.: late of Beenham, co. West Berks: *s.* of E. Middleton, of Middle Hill Farm, Knowstone, Barnstaple, co. Devon: *b.* Washfield, co. Devon: enlisted Newbury, co. Berks. Killed in action, 31 July 1917. Age 34. Remembered on Beenham War Memorial.

(Panel 21) Pte. 7118, William Robert Wilkey, 1st Bn. (11th Foot) The Devonshire Regt.: late of 7, Tuckett's Square, Summerland Street, Exeter: *b.* Exeter, co. Devon, 1883: a pre-war Reservist, was gainfully employed as a Cellarman: recalled to the Colours on mobilisation, rejoined his regt. Exeter: served in France and Flanders from 21 August 1914: took part in the fighting at La Bassée (17 October), Festubert (30 October); shot and killed by a sniper on Christmas Eve, 24 December 1914; Wulverghem. Age 31. Well-known and respected locally, he was a member (drummer) of Exeter City Band. He leaves a widow, Florence Wilkey, and *dau.* aged five years. His medals (1914–15 Star & Bar, War, Victory), Memorial Plaque, and Queen Mary's Christmas 1914 brass cigarette box were sold at auction in 2012.

(Panel 21) Capt. Francis William Wakeford Town Attree, 1st Bn. (12th Foot) The Suffolk Regt.: eldest & only surv'g. *s.* of Col. Frederick Wakeford Town Attree, late Royal Engineers; of 59, Warwick Gardens, Kensington, London, S.W., late of 53, Albert Bridge Road, London, S.W., by his wife (& cousin; *m.*1887) Frances Elizabeth Mary Wakeford, only surv'g. *dau.* (& heiress) of Richard Wakeford Attree, of Colmendy House, Corwen, co. Merioneth: *b.* Ditchling, co. Sussex, 17 December 1885: *educ.* Cheltenham College; Royal Military College, Sandhurst: gazetted 2nd Lieut. Suffolk Regt. February 1909; promoted Lieut. October 1910; Temp. Capt. September 1914, confirmed in that rank December following: served with the Expeditionary Force; reported wounded and missing 8 May 1915; now believed killed in action on that date. The *Suffolk Regimental Gazette* reported, "Capt. Attree was wounded whilst rallying his men with great gallantry." His Company Sergeant-Major wrote concerning him, "A thorough officer and a gentleman, every bit of him, and one who was well loved by all of the regiment." His favourite recreations were motoring, flying as an observer and acting. Age 26. *unm.*

(Panel 21) Capt. Ralph Chalmers, 2nd Bn. (11th Foot) The Suffolk Regt.: *s.* of the late Lieut. the Hon. Robert Allan Chalmers, 1st Baron Northian, late Royal Engineers (Bengal Sappers), Indian Army; by his wife Lady Catherine Chalmers (Peterhouse Lodge, Cambridge), *dau.* of Mr (& Mrs) Barrett: and *yr.* brother to Major. J.S. Chalmers, 9th Highland Light Infantry, killed in action nr. Bailleul, 17 April 1918, aged 36; and Lieut. R. Chalmers, Prince of Wales's Own Civil Service Rifles, died of wounds, 25 May 1915, aged 21: *b.* 1891. Reported missing, 8–10 May 1915, now believed killed in action on the former date. Age 24. Three other brothers also served; each survived.

His brother John also has no known grave, he is commemorated on the Ploegsteert Memorial (Panel 9); Robert is buried in Choques Military Cemetery (I.B.13)

(Panel 21) Capt. George Bertram Pollock-Hodsoll, 3rd (Special Reserve) Bn. The Suffolk Regt. attd. 1st Bn. The Cheshire Regt.: 2nd *s.* of Charles Maxfield Hodsoll, of Farm House, Capel, Surrey, formerly of Loose Court, Kent (descended from the old Kent family of Hodsoll), by his wife Georgina Mary, elder *dau.* of George Kennet Pollock, *granddau.* of Sir David Pollock, Chief Justice of Bombay, and grand-niece of Field-Marshal Sir George Pollock, of Khyber Pass fame: *b.* Loose Court, co. Kent, 18 June, 1875: *educ.* Maidstone School, and University College, Oxford: obtained a commission 2nd Lieut. Cambridgeshire Militia, then the 4th Bn. Suffolk Regt. December 1902, and subsequently transf'd. 3rd Bn. Special Reserve, Suffolk Regt., and obtained his company, 5 August 1914: went to France, 23 October following; attd. 1st Cheshires there, and was killed in action at the First Battle of Ypres, 7 November 1914, while gallantly leading his men in a counter-attack. The Adjutant, Capt. L. Frost, wrote, "On 7 November, about 3 o'clock in the afternoon, the regt. on our left fell back and the Germans came through their trenches, so Capt. Hodsoll, Mr Anderson and myself, with the supports of our regt. made a counter-attack. Your husband had not gone more than 100 yards when he, poor fellow, was killed; he died instantaneously and could not have suffered any pain at all. He died giving his life for his country at a very critical moment, if this counter-attack had failed it would have meant the whole line coming back. He died a glorious and magnificent death. Capt. Pollock Hodsoll was buried the same evening on the ground where he died, in a wood near a chateau, about 3½ miles east of Ypres. A wooden cross with his name was placed on the grave." Age 39. Capt. Pollock Hodsoll was well known to followers of Association Football, having played many years for both the Casuals and Corinthians, touring with these teams both on the Continent and in South Africa, and captained the Army team on several occasions. He was much interested in political matters, and frequently spoke in public on this subject, and in support of the Unionist cause, and in favour of National Military Service. He *m.* Edinburgh, 1 June 1914; Olive Margaret (24, Bloomfield Terrace, Chelsea, London), eldest *dau.* of the Rev. George Milne Rae, D.D., of Edinburgh. *s.p.*

(Panel 21) Capt. Francis Winchester Wood-Martin, 1st Bn. (12th Foot) The Suffolk Regt.: 4th & *yst. s.* of Col. William Gregory Wood-Martin, of Cleveragh, Co. Sligo, A.D.C., J.P., D.L., by his wife Frances Dora, *dau.* of Roger Dodwell Robinson, of Wellmount, Co. Sligo, J.P. and *yr.* brother to Capt. J.I. Wood-Martin, 2nd Northamptonshire Regt., killed in action, 12 March 1915, at Neuve-Chapelle: *b.* London, 27 February 1880: *educ.* Cheltenham: gazetted 2nd Lieut. 1st Suffolk Regt. 12 August 1899; promoted Lieut. 30 August 1900; Capt. 11 February 1906: served in the South African War, 1899–1902: took part in operations in Cape Colony, south of the Orange River, 1899–1902, including actions at Colesburg (1–5 January) being taken prisoner, but was released in the following June when Lord Roberts entered Pretoria. Apptd. Station Officer, Transvaal – took part in operations east of Pretoria, July–29 November 1900, and Transvaal, December 1900–31 May 1902 (Queen's Medal, three clasps; King's Medal, two clasps): in Khartoum on garrison duty with his regt. at the outbreak of the European War; returned to England and proceeded to France, January 1915: served with the Expeditionary Force there, and was killed in action, nr. Ypres, Belgium, 17 February 1916. Age 34. *unm.* A memorial in memory of the brothers Wood-Martin was erected in St. Anne's Parish Church, Strandhill; also in the Cathedral at Khartoum.

His brother James also has no known grave; he is commemorated on the Le Touret Memorial.

(Panel 21) Capt. Arthur Hilliard William Temple, Reserve of Officers attd. 2nd Bn. (12th Foot) The Suffolk Regt.: 2nd *s.* of the Rev. Robert C. Temple, Rector of Thorpe Morieux, co. Suffolk: *b.* 12 January 1875: *educ.* Jnr. King's School, Canterbury (January 1885–December 1888), and King's School, Ely: commissioned 2nd Lieut., 3rd King's Own Yorkshire Light Infantry (Militia), 17 March 1894: received his first Regular commission, 2nd Lieut. Suffolk Regt. 1 December 1897; promoted Lieut. 7 January 1900: took part in the South African War, employed with the Mounted Infantry: present at operations in Transvaal, Orange River Colony, and Cape Colony, including the action at Colesberg (Queen's Medal, three clasps; King's Medal, two clasps): afterwards seconded for service with King's African Rifles, Somaliland: promoted Capt. April 1905, and retired from the Active List: joined Reserve of Officers, February 1913: rejoined his old regiment on the outbreak of war; proceeded to France attd. 2nd Suffolk Regt., 14th Infantry Bde., Vth Divn., and was killed in action, 14 December 1914, on which date the battalion were in support of a successful attack on Petit Bois. At 4.30 p.m. they moved forward to relieve 2nd Royal Scots in the captured German trench and it was here, 20 minutes later, Capt. Temple fell, shot through the head, into the arms of Pte. R.G. Girbow who was himself killed in exactly the same manner in exactly the same spot two days later. A Private in the battalion, writing to his sister, said of Capt. Temple, "It was in the trenches that we lost our beloved Captain – Captain Temple. He was loved and respected by all – those who served with him in South Africa, also in this campaign. The kindness he showed to our company when they came from the trenches sodden wet through, giving us new socks and other articles of clothing which his wife had sent out for his company, we shall never forget. I have seen him when meeting refugees put his hand in his pocket and assist them. No one knew what he gave. He did not believe in show. A shell burst in the trenches in which I was lying, and the Captain came up and enquired if anyone was hurt. His cheery remarks always gave us inspiration, and when the word was passed round that he was wounded, and subsequently that he had died, there was grief among all – officers and men. He was fearless, brave, and self-sacrificing under all conditions, and was never satisfied until he had done his very best for all. He will be missed by all who came in contact with him." Mentioned in Sir John (now Lord)

French's Despatch, 14 January 1915. He *m*., October 1909; Enid Adela Powys (Albert Lodge, Shanklin, Isle of Wight), *dau*. of Percy G. Stone, of Merstone, Isle of Wight, and left a son and daughter. He was a fine big-game shot, and collected many trophies from India and Africa. Age 39. Pte. Girbow also has no known grave; he is recorded below.

(Panel 21) Lieut. Stephen Bradley, 1st Bn. (12th Foot) The Suffolk Regt.: eldest *s*. of the late Stephen (& Mrs) Bradley, 'Givendale,' Harrogate, co. York: *b*. Harrogate, 28 December 1891: *educ*. Cheltenham, and Royal Military College, Sandhurst: gazetted 2nd Lieut. Suffolk Regt. September 1911: joined his battalion in Egypt, where he went through the Camel Corps course, and distinguished himself as an athlete, winning the Heavyweight Championship of the Egyptian Command and other prizes for boxing: came to England, 1913, successfully passing through the Gymnastic course at Aldershot and, obtaining his certificate, served with the Expeditionary Force in France and Flanders from January 1915, where he gained much praise as a 'hand-grenadier,' being placed in command of a Hand Grenade Section, and was killed in action, 25 May 1915. An officer of the battalion gave the following account of his death, "Our battalion was deeply indebted to Lieut. Bradley on the day we went into action, both for his guiding and reconnoitring. After we had formed up to attack, he twice undertook dangerous missions and returned safely. He was with me when the attack started, and again volunteered to go almost to the enemies' lines in search of necessary information. He left with a sergeant of the Welsh Regiment, whom I have not seen since that day, and started on his errand. Less than a quarter of an hour later, when our first charge was over, the sergeant found me again and reported that Lieut. Bradley had been shot through the head and had died instantly. I hesitated to believe the report of an overwrought man, and hoped to find Lieut. Bradley again; but we have heard nothing about him since, and I fear he must have gone, with all the other officers of the companies that were in that engagement." His place of burial is unknown. Many letters have been received by his relations saying what a great loss he was to the battalion, and how popular he was, both with his fellow officers and men. Two days before his death he returned from a hospital at Rouen, where he had been suffering from wounded feet and nervous breakdown, having been there ten days. On returning he found that most of his old regiment were prisoners in Germany. When they went into action the day before his death he was the only officer who had been in the firing line before, the other officers and men being new drafts from England. Age 23. *unm*.

(Panel 21) Lieut. Ronald Stanley Chibnall, 8th (Service) Bn. The Suffolk Regt.: *s*. of George William Chibnall, of Cedar House, Chiswick Mall, Chiswick, London, by his wife Kate: and elder brother to Lieut. G.W.R. Chibnall, 3rd Dragoon Guards attd. 9th Duke of Wellington's Regt., killed in action, 26 August 1918: served with the Expeditionary Force. Killed in action, 31 July 1917. Age 20. *unm*.

His brother George also has no known grave; he is commemorated on the Vis-en-Artois Memorial (Panel 2).

(Panel 21) Lieut. Donald Keith Forbes, 1st Bn. (12th Foot) The Suffolk Regt.: *s*. of William Alexander Forbes, Barrister-at-Law, Inner Temple, London, afterwards at Amraoti Camp, Berar, C.P., India, by his wife Margaret: *b*. Bridgewater, co. Somerest, 30 January 1892: *educ*. Elstow School; Bedford Grammar School, passing into the Royal Military College, Sandhurst, 1910: gazetted to his regiment, September 1911; joining at Alexandria: went to Cairo for a short time, thence to Khartoum, where he was attached to the Camel Corps: promoted Lieut. February 1914: sailed for England, October 1914: served with the Expeditionary Force in France from January 1915, and was killed at Ypres on the night of 17 February 1915. Through a mistake of the guide, his company was led to within seven yards of the German trenches. In going to the aid of his great friend Lieut. Smith, Lieut. Forbes was shot dead. He was good at all games, football, hockey, etc., and while at school won several cups for running. Age 23. *unm*.

(Panel 21) Lieut. Roland George Prichard, 3rd (Reserve) attd. 1st Bn. (12th Foot) The Suffolk Regt.: *s*. of the Rev. Charles Collwyn Prichard, M.A., Brasenose College, Oxford, Rector of Alresford, Colchester, co. Essex: and yr. brother to Lieut. F.G. Prichard, 2nd East Yorkshire Regt., died of wounds, 9 August 1915. A family ancestor, Major Henry Brodrick, 29th Foot, fought through the Peninsular War, and was present at Quatre Bras: *b*. Thornton-le-Moors Rectory, Chester, 23 September 1895: *educ*. Lindley Lodge School, Nuneaton; Hereford Cathedral School, and had been accepted for matriculation at Brasenose

College, Oxford, when the outbreak of war intervened: given his commission, 2nd Lieut. Special Reserve, August 1914, having been three years in the O.T.C.: promoted Lieut. February 1915: served with the Expeditionary Force in France, and was mortally wounded, 27 April 1915, while gallantly leading his men against a German trench at St. Julien. Age 20. *unm.* (*IWGC record age 21*)

His brother Frederic is buried in St. Peter's Churchyard, Alresford.

(Panel 21) Lieut. Charles Francis Bateman-Smith, 1st Bn. (12th Foot) The Suffolk Regt.: 3rd *s.* of the late Rev. George Herbert Smith, M.A., Canon of St. George's Cathedral, Madras, India, by his wife Mary Elinor ('Chetmead,' Belmont Park Avenue, Maidenhead, co. Berks), *dau.* of Edward Donkin Esq.: *b.* Old Hall, Sleights, Whitby, 15 July 1886: *educ.* Forest School, Walthamstow, co. Essex: enlisted Oxford & Bucks Light Infantry, October 1904; gazetted 2nd Lieut. Suffolk Regt. September 1911: served in Egypt, 1911–1914: promoted Lieut. June 1914: served with the Expeditionary Force in France and Flanders, and was shot through the heart while returning from attendance on a wounded brother officer, S.E. of Ypres, 15 February 1915. Age 28. *unm.* (*IWGC record C.F.B. Smith*)

(Panel 21) 2nd Lieut. Geoffrey Phipps Hornby, 3rd Bn. The Suffolk Regt.: *s.* of the Ven. Phipps John Hornby, Archdeacon of Lancaster; and his wife Agnes Eleanor Hornby (St. Michaels-on-Wyre, Garstang, co. Lancaster): and brother to 2nd Lieut. W. Hornby, 17th King's (Liverpool) Regt., killed in action, 12 October 1916, at the Somme: served with the Expeditionary Force in France , and was killed in action, 8 May 1915, at the Second Battle of Ypres. Age 24.

His brother William is buried in Warlencourt British Cemetery (II.D.24).

(Panel 21) 2nd Lieut. Eustace Fernando 'Larry' Llarena, 2nd Bn. (12th Foot) The Suffolk Regt.: *s.* of the late Fernando Llarena, and his wife Mrs B.S. Llarena (39, Red Post Hill, Herne Hill, London): *b.* 1892: *educ.* Dulwich College, thereafter Guy's Hospital, London: joined Artists' Rifles, August 1914: served with that unit in France, where he obtained a commission in the Suffolk Regt., and was killed in action, 18 June 1915, while attacking a wood near Ypres. Age 23. *unm.* Guys Memorial Roll records, "… Larry', as he was known to all his old friends up at the Hospital, received his early education at Dulwich College, where he was an enthusiastic Rugger player and a Sergeant in the Officers' Training Corps. Always to the fore in any sport, he gained his Rugger Blue in the 1912–1913 season, and played for the 1st XV regularly afterwards (with O.G. Parry-Jones). A member of the Water Polo Team in 1911, he captained the 1914 team which wrested the cup from the London Hospital. He entered the Medical and Dental Schools in October 1910, and passed his First Professional and First Conjoint Examinations in 1912. When the War began he was working for his Second Conjoint Examination…By the death of E.F. Llarena the hospital has lost one of her best athletes who answered the call to arms during the first week of war, and now must be added to the Roll of Honour of Guys men who have met that glorious end on the battlefield." Capt. Owen G. Parry-Jones, Royal Army Medical Corps attd. 3rd Bn. Suffolk Regt., died of wounds, September 1916 at the Somme; he is buried in Puchevillers British Cemetery (III.B.11).

(Panel 21) 2nd Lieut. Jack Douglas Wheeler, 'B' Coy., 5th Bn. The Suffolk Regt. (T.F.): *s.* of Alfred G. Wheeler, of Stretham, nr. Ely, co. Cambridge, by his wife Harriet Eliza: and *yr.* brother to Lieut. R.M. Wheeler, Middlesex Regt., killed in action, 30 November 1916: *educ.* St. Peter's College, Peterborough (1909–10). Killed in action, 31 July 1917. Age 28. *unm.*

His brother Russell is buried in Pont-du-Hem Military Cemetery, La Gorgue (II.C.17).

(Panel 21) 2nd Lieut. Reginald Connor Phillips Wilder, 3rd (Reserve) attd. 2nd Bn. (12th Foot) The Suffolk Regt.: *s.* of the Rev. William Bernard Chichester Wilder, of Great Bradley Rectory, Newmarket, co. Suffolk, by his wife Mabel Elizabeth, *dau.* of the late Dr. Grove, of St. Ives, co. Huntingdon: *gt.-gdson.* to the late Lieut.General Sir Francis Wilder, and Admiral Sir John Marshall, and *gdson.* to the late Rev. John McMahon Wilder: *b.* Great Bradley Rectory, 25 February 1896: *educ.* Forest School, Walthamstow, where he was one of the Shooting VIII for his school at Bisley 1913, and very fond of athletics, especially boxing: gazetted 2nd Lieut. 3rd Suffolk Regt. January 1914: trained at Curragh Camp until the outbreak of war: sent with a draft to Felixstowe, and from there proceeded to France at the end of August 1914, and was shot by a sniper, 18 November following, while doing trench duty, dying instantly due to the bullet severing his jugular vein. His Commanding Officer wrote of him, "I thought him a charming, bright lad, who did his hard work cheerily and willingly, and his death is a truly sad loss to me and all the battalion, which cannot spare good officers such as your son was," and his Captain, "He was shot through the neck at about seven in the morning, and I am glad to say death was instantaneous. He commanded a platoon in my company, and I cannot speak too highly of the way in which he carried out his duties on all occasions. He was buried the following night beside one of his brother officers, killed within a few hours of each other." 18 November 1914. Age 18.

(Panel 21) 2nd Lieut. Leslie St.Lawrence Windsor, 2nd Bn. (12th Foot) The Suffolk Regt.: *s.* of the late Herbert Bolton Windsor, of the Stock Exchange, by his wife Eleanor Wynne (28, Windsor Road, Palmers Green, London, N.), *dau.* of the late John Kendle, of Ryde, Isle of Wight: *b.* High Barnet, co. Hertford, 23 January 1892: *educ.* Bedford Modern School: Occupation – Insurance Clerk: joined Artists' Rifles 1910: called up on mobilisation, 4 August 1914: gazetted 2nd Lieut. 2nd Suffolk Regt. January 1915: served with the Expeditionary Force in France and Flanders, and was killed in action at Ypres, 10 June 1915, while taking over charge of a machine gun. Buried in a garden on the Ypres – Menin Road. Age 23. *unm.* (*IWGC record age 22*)

(Panel 21) Sergt. 12818, Joseph Henry Pollard, 2nd Bn. (12th Foot) The Suffolk Regt.: *s.* of Charles (& Mrs) Pollard, of Duke Street, Haughley, Stowemarket, co. Suffolk: *b.* Haughley: enlisted Ipswich. Killed in action, 22 January 1916. Age 24. See account, Spoilbank Cemetery (I.B.11).

(Panel 21) Corpl. 8374, Herbert Crysell, 2nd Bn. (12th Foot) The Suffolk Regt.: *s.* of Charles Crysell, of High Street, Stansfield, Clare, co. Suffolk, and Mary Ann, his wife: *b.* Stansfield: enlisted Bury St. Edmunds. Killed in action, 22 January 1916. Age 26. *unm.* See account, Spoilbank Cemetery (I.B.11).

(Panel 21) Corpl. 7181, William Fred Davey, 2nd Bn. (12th Foot) The Suffolk Regt.: *b.* Ipswich: enlisted there. Killed in action, 22 January 1916, by the detonation of an enemy mine; The Bluff. See account, Spoilbank Cemetery (I.B.11).

(Panel 21) Corpl. 13515, Arthur Hammond, 2nd Bn. (12th Foot) The Suffolk Regt.: *s.* of G. (& Mrs) Hammond, of Old Farm, Blaxhall, Tunstall, co. Suffolk: and yr. brother to Pte. 13314, W.J. Hammond, 9th Suffolk Regt., killed in action, 21 November 1915: enlisted Saxmundham: served with the Expeditionary Force. Killed in action, 24 August 1915. Age 19.

His brother William also has no known grave; he is recorded below.

(Panel 21) Corpl. 7925, James Gill Palmer, 2nd Bn. (12th Foot) The Suffolk Regt.: *b.* Hainstead, co. Suffolk: enlisted Bury St. Edmunds. Killed in action, 22 January 1916; The Bluff. See account, Spoilbank Cemetery (I.B.11)

(Panel 21) Corpl. 8363, Harold Mark Turner, 1st Bn. (12th Foot) The Suffolk Regt.: *s.* of the late Mark (& Mrs) Turner, of Nelson Street, Walsoken, co. Norfolk: and brother to L/Corpl. 21300, W.W. Turner, Border Regt., who fell 23 April 1917, at the Battle of Arras: enlisted Wisbech. Killed in action, 24 April 1915. Age 22. *unm.*

His brother William also has no known grave; he is commemorated on the Arras Memorial (Bay 6).

(Panel 21) L/Corpl. 13039, William Ashton, 1st Bn. (12th Foot) The Suffolk Regt.: *s.* of Alfred Ashton, of 17, St. Edmund's Place, Bury St. Edmunds, by his wife Alice: and elder brother to Pte. 8773, F. Ashton, Suffolk Regt., who also fell: enlisted Bury St. Edmunds. Killed in action, 8 May 1915. Age 27. *unm.*

His brother Frank also has no known grave; he is recorded below.

(Panel 21) L/Corpl. 8775, George Rayner, 2nd Bn. (12th Foot) The Suffolk Regt.: *b.* Warley, co. Essex: enlisted Colchester. Killed in action, 22 January 1916. Remains recovered from an unmarked grave (28.I.34.c.4.0) 24 January 1927; identified – Disc, Cap Badge, Nominal Roll; reinterred, registered 29 January 1927. See account, Spoilbank Cemetery (I.B.11). *Buried in Sanctuary Wood Cemetery (III.E.2).*

(Panel 21) Pte. 5977, George Henry Abbott, 2nd Bn. (12th Foot) The Suffolk Regt.: *b.* Ipswich: enlisted there. Killed in action, 22 January 1916; The Bluff. See account, Spoilbank Cemetery (I.B.11).

(Panel 21) Pte. 8773, Frank Ashton, 2nd Bn. (12th Foot) The Suffolk Regt.: *s.* of Alfred Ashton, of 17, St. Edmund's Place, Bury St. Edmunds, by his wife Alice: and yr. brother to L/Corpl. W. Ashton, Suffolk Regt., who also fell: enlisted Bury St. Edmunds. Killed in action, 9 April 1915. Age 18.

His brother William also has no known grave; he is recorded above.

(Panel 21) Pte. 20303, Frank Henry Baalham, 2nd Bn. (12th Foot) The Suffolk Regt.: *s.* of James S. Baalham, of Kersey, Hadleigh, co. Suffolk, and Sarah S. Baalham, his spouse. Killed in action, 22 January 1916. Age 22.

(Panel 21) Pte. 14013, Arthur Bareham, 8th (Service) Bn. The Suffolk Regt.: *s.* of Bowers Bareham, Labourer; of Boundary Cottage, Newton Road, Great Cornard, by his wife Martha: and brother to Pte. 14299, P. Bareham, 9th Suffolk Regt., killed in action, 26 September 1915: *b.* Great Cornard, co. Suffolk: Occupation – Mat Maker: enlisted Sudbury: served with the Expeditionary Force in France from 25 July 1915: wounded during the fighting on the Somme, August 1916, and was killed in action, 31 July 1917 at the Battle of Pilckem. Age 37.

His brother Percy is commemorated in Railway Dugouts Burial Ground (Transport Farm), (Sp.Mem. A.12).

(Panel 21) Pte. 3/8178, Arthur William Brown, 2nd Bn. (12th Foot) The Suffolk Regt.: *s.* of Eli Brown, of Hollow Hill Cottage, Withersfield, nr. Newmarket, co. Suffolk, by his wife Hannah: and brother to Pte. 13251, H. Brown, 9th Suffolk Regt., killed in action, 20 September 1917: *b.* Withersfield, *c.*1882: enlisted Haverhill. Killed in action, 2 March 1915. Age 32.

His brother Herbert is buried in Mazingarbe Communal Cemetery Extension (III.A.3).

(Panel 21) Pte. 20273, Charles William Brown, 2nd Bn. (12th Foot) The Suffolk Regt.: *b.* Fanham, co. Essex: enlisted Saffron Walden, nr. Cambridge. Killed in action, 21–22 January 1916. See account, Spoilbank Cemetery (I.B.11). Remains recovered from an unmarked grave (28.I.34.c.4.0) 24 January 1927; identified – Disc, Cap Badge, Pay Book, 5 Francs (French); reinterred, registered 29 January 1927. *Buried in Sanctuary Wood Cemetery (III.E.1).*

(Panel 21) Pte. 16214, Thomas Clarence Brown, 1st Bn. (12th Foot) The Suffolk Regt.: brother to Maud Taylor, *née* Brown (10, Eleanor Terrace, Exning, co. Suffolk): and Pte. 13952, F.G. Brown, 8th Suffolk Regt., died 8 June 1915, aged 33 yrs.: served in the South African Campaign, and in France and Flanders, and was killed in action, 8 May 1915, at Ypres. Age 38.

His brother Frederick is buried in Newmarket (Exning) Cemetery (Q.C.206).

(Panel 21) Pte. 20261, William Burton, 2nd Bn. (12th Foot) The Suffolk Regt.: *husb.* to Ethel Amelia Burton (38, Northgate Street, Bury St. Edmunds): *b.* Bury St. Edmunds: enlisted there. Killed in action, 22 January 1916. Age 27. See account, Spoilbank Cemetery (I.B.11).

(Panel 21) Pte. 16939, David James Chaplin, 1st Bn. (12th Foot) The Suffolk Regt.: *s.* of James Chaplin, Farm Labourer; of Sudbury Road, Great Cornard, by his wife Mary: *b.* Great Cornard, co. Suffolk: enlisted Sudbury: served with the Expeditionary Force in France from 1 April 1915, and was killed in action at the Second Battle of Ypres, 8 May 1915. Age 39. His brother Arthur also served.

(Panel 21) Pte. 20124, Ernest George Clarke, 'X' Coy., 2nd Bn. (12th Foot) The Suffolk Regt.: *s.* of Susan Clarke: *b.* Bury St. Edmunds: enlisted there. Killed in action, 22 January 1916,by the detonation of an enemy mine; The Bluff. Age 21. See account, Spoilbank Cemetery (I.B.11).

(Panel 21) Pte. 17770, William Cobbold, 1st Bn. (12th Foot) The Suffolk Regt.: *s.* of the late William Cobbold, by his wife Sarah (Free Wood Street, Bradfield St. George, nr. Bury St. Edmunds): and elder brother to Corpl. 1959, F. Cobbold, East Surrey Regt., who fell 25 April 1915, at the Second Battle of Ypres: *b.* Bradfield St. George, co. Suffolk, *c.*1875: enlisted Bury St. Edmunds: previously served 12 years (1896–1908) with 2nd Bn. Prince Consort's Own, in Egypt, Crete and the South African Campaign: recalled on mobilisation, August 1914 served with the Expeditionary Force in France and Flanders from January 1915, and was killed in action, 8 May following. Age 40. He leaves a wife, Alberta (Rose Cottage, Bradfield St. George).

His brother Frederick also has no known grave; he is recorded on Panel 34.

(Panel 21) Pte. 8766, Walter George Cooke, 'C' Coy., 2nd Bn. (12th Foot) The Suffolk Regt.: *s.* of Walter (& Mrs) Cooke, of 69, The Mount, Higham, Bury St. Edmunds, co. Suffolk: *b.* Higham, 1896: served with the Expeditionary Force. Died of wounds, 9 December 1914. Age 18. *Buried in Le Cateau Communal Cemetery (III.A.20).*

(Panel 21) Pte. 7466, William Free, 1st Bn. (12th Foot) The Suffolk Regt.: *s.* of Walter (& Eliza) Free, of Castle Camps, co. Cambridge: and yr. brother to Pte. 201572, A. Free, 4th Suffolk Regt., killed in action, 22 November 1917: *b.* Castle Camps, 1890: enlisted Haverhill, co. Suffolk: a pre-war Regular, served with his regiment at Alexandria, Egypt; and with the Expeditionary Force in France and Flanders from 18 January 1915, and was killed in action exactly one month later – 18 February 1915. Age 22. *Buried in Cement House Cemetery, Langemarck (XVI.B.49).*

His brother Alexander is buried in Tyne Cot Cemetery (I.H.7).

(Panel 21) Pte. 3/8664, William Frost, 2nd Bn. (12th Foot) The Suffolk Regt.: *s.* of H.J. (& Mrs J.) Frost, of 6, Laundry Cottages, Laundry Lane, Cherry Hinton, co. Cambridge: and brother to Pte. 12695, C.W. Frost, 11th Suffolk Regt., killed in action, 1 July 1916; and Pte. 17356, M.H. Frost, 11th Suffolk Regt., died 23 May 1916, of wounds: *b.* Cherry Hinton: enlisted Cambridge: served with the Expeditionary Force in France and Flanders; wounded 1915, and was killed in action, 2 March 1916. Age 23.

His brother Christopher also has no known grave, he is commemorated on the Thiepval Memorial; Montague is buried in Albert Communal Cemetery Extension (I.D.24).

(Panel 21) Pte. 9156, Arthur James Garrod, 1st Bn. (12th Foot) The Suffolk Regt.: 2nd *s.* of William Garrrod, of Bramford, Ipswich, Chemical Worker (30 years); by his wife Mary Anne, *dau.* of the late James Lay: and *yr.* brother to Pte. 15259, W. Garrod, Suffolk Regt., who was reported missing, believed killed in action, after the fighting on 8 May 1915: *b.* Bramford, co. Suffolk, 17 August 1896: *educ.* Voluntary School, Bramford: enlisted Ipswich, 10 August 1914: went to France, 16 January 1915, and was killed in action, there 24 April following. Buried on the Zonnebeke Road, nr. Ypres. Age 18.

His brother William also has no known grave; he is recorded below.

(Panel 21) Pte. 15259, William Garrod, 1st Bn. (12th Foot) The Suffolk Regt.: formerly Royal Army Medical Corps: 1st *s.* of William Garrrod, of Bramford, Ipswich, Chemical Worker (30 years); by his wife Mary Anne, *dau.* of the late James Lay; and elder brother to Pte. 9156, A.J. Garrod, Suffolk Regt., killed near Zonnebeke, 24 April 1915, at the Second Battle of Ypres: *b.* Bramford, co. Suffolk, 1892: *educ.* Bramford Voluntary School: enlisted Ipswich: voluntarily transf'd. from R.A.M.C., to proceed to France with his brother, 16 January 1915, and was reported missing, believed killed in action, after the fighting on 8 May 1915. Age 23. *unm.*

His brother Arthur also has no known grave; he is recorded above.

(Panel 21) Pte. 7774, Robert George Girbow, 2nd Bn. (12th Foot) The Suffolk Regt.: *s.* of John Girbow, of 8, Alm's Row, Bridewell Lane, Bury St. Edmunds: *b.* Bury St. Edmunds: enlisted there: served with the Expeditionary Force in France and Flanders from 17 August 1914; shot through the head and killed, 16 December following; captured German trench, Petit Bois. Age 22. His company officer, Capt. A.H.W. Temple (whom he had caught in his arms as he fell) was killed in exactly the same manner in exactly the same spot two days previously.

Capt. Arthur Temple also has no known grave; he is recorded above.

(Panel 21) Pte. 8426, Ernest Robert Goodfellow, 1st Bn. (12th Foot) The Suffolk Regt.: 2nd *s.* of Henry (& Mrs) Goodfellow, of 141, King's Road, Bury St. Edmunds, co. Suffolk: and brother to L/Sergt. 6537, H. Goodfellow, 2nd Suffolk Regt., killed in action, 26 August 1914, aged 34 years; and Pte. 12049, W. Goodfellow, killed in action, 3 November 1915, aged 24 years: enlisted Bury St. Edmunds: served with the Expeditionary Force in France and Flanders from 18 January 1915, and was killed in action, 8 May 1915, at Frezenberg. Age 30. A fourth brother, Thomas, also served and, although he survived the war, having been gassed during the course of his service, suffered constant ill-health and died in the 1940s. On 17 March 2009, a sheltered housing unit, named '1–12, Goodfellows,' was inaugurated on the site where once two cottages – the brothers home – had stood and a plaque dedicated to their memory unveiled. A descendant, Gloria Abbott, said, "It is absolutely overwhelming. I have been researching their histories for so many, many, years. I have been over there and seen where they fought and died, and it is so wonderful to have this privilege. The whole family was devastated and my grandmother, through the years, she would make a wreath but she could never go down to the Angel Hill to place it; she sent one of her daughters down with it because she was so upset still after so many years. It is good they are going to be remembered and I think we should remember what they did for us."

His brothers also have no known grave. Henry 'Harry' is commemorated on the La Ferte-Sous-Jouarre Memorial, and Walter on the Loos Memorial.

(Panel 21) Pte. 15261, Albert Edward Hammond, 2nd Bn. (12th Foot) The Suffolk Regt.: *s.* of the late Syer (& Annie) Hammond, of Thorndon: and brother to Pte. 3617, N.A. Hammond, 1/4th Suffolk Regt., died of wounds, 21 June 1916: *b.* Wetheringsett, co. Suffolk: enlisted Ipswich. Killed in action, 23 February 1915. Age 22.

His brother Nathan is buried in Bethune Town Cemetery (V.E.56).

(Panel 21) Pte. 13314, William James Hammond, 9th (Service) Bn. The Suffolk Regt.: *s.* of G. (& Mrs) Hammond, of Old Farm, Blaxhall, Tunstall, co. Suffolk: and elder brother to Corpl. 13515, A. Hammond, 2nd Suffolk Regt., killed in action, 24 August 1915: enlisted Saxmundham. Killed in action, 21 November 1915. Age 21.

His brother Arthur also has no known grave, he is recorded above.

(Panel 21) Pte. 8727, Peter George Motroni, 2nd Bn. (12th Foot) The Suffolk Regt.: 2nd *s.* of Anthony Motroni, of 14, Permit Office Street, Ipswich, by his wife Carmela, *dau.* of Dominico Marcantonio, of Atina, Italy: and brother to Gnr. 11389, J. Motroni, Royal Field Artillery, died of wounds, 2 July 1917; and Corpl. 1756, U.A. Motroni, 2nd Suffolk Regt., killed in action, 15 July, 1916: *b.* Colchester, co. Essex, 1 July 1895: *educ.* St. Pancras R.C. School, and St. Mary's Convent School, Ipswich: enlisted 4 April 1913: went to France, 11 September 1914, and was killed in action at Hooge, near Ypres, 19 July 1915. Age 20. *unm.* (*IWGC record 3/8727, 20 July 1915*)

His brother John is buried in Coxyde Military Cemetery (I.C.23); Umberto has no known grave, he is commemorated on the Thiepval Memorial.

(Panel 21) Pte. 6286, Edwin Mower, 2nd Bn. (12th Foot) The Suffolk Regt.: *s.* of John Mower, late of Burstall, co. Suffolk: and late *husb.* to Ellen Calver, *née* Mower (Little Dodnash Farm, Bentley, Ipswich): *b.* Burstall, 1886: enlisted Ipswich. Killed in action, 1 October 1915. Age 29. Remains recovered from an unmarked grave 'Sanctuary Wood Old Cemetery' (29.I.24.b.90.97), identified – Disc; reinterred, registered 16 May 1928. Inadvertently omitted from the Burstall (St. Mary's Church) Memorial; he is remembered on the Hintlesham War Memorial. *Buried in Sanctuary Wood Cemetery (II.H.4).*

Peace Perfect Peace

(Panel 21) Pte. 8093, Charles William Nunn, 1st Bn. (12th Foot) The Suffolk Regt.: *s.* of Laura J. Nunn (56, Coventry Road, Market Harborough, co. Leicester): and yr. brother to Pte. 7759, W. Nunn, 1st Suffolk Regt., killed earlier the same day: *b.* Barrow, co. Suffolk: a pre-war Regular, enlisted Bury St. Edmunds, 1910: on the outbreak of war, August 1914, was with 1st Suffolk Regt., Khartoum, Sudan: returned to England; disembarked H.M.T. 'Grantully Castle,' Liverpool, 23 October 1914: proceeded to France, S.S. 'Mount Temple,' disembarked Le Havre, 18 January 1915, and was killed in action, 5 February 1915. Age 22. *unm.* Erected by parishioners and their friends, the Barrow (Suffolk) War Memorial is dedicated – "...In Grateful And Loving Memory Of The Men Of This Village Who Gave Their Lives For King And Country In The Great War 1914–1918. Greater Love Hath No Man Than To Lay Down His Life For His Friends;" thirty-three names are recorded thereon, men who went off to war and never returned; among them the Nunn brothers, Charles and William.

His brother William also has no known grave; he is recorded below.

(Panel 21) Pte. 7759, William Nunn, 1st Bn. (12th Foot) The Suffolk Regt.: *s.* of Laura J. Nunn (56, Coventry Road, Market Harborough, co. Leicester): and elder brother to Pte. 8093, C.W. Nunn, 1st Suffolk Regt., killed later the same day: *b.* Barrow, co. Suffolk: a pre-war Regular, enlisted Bury St. Edmunds, 1909: on the outbreak of war, August 1914, was with 1st Suffolk Regt., Khartoum, Sudan: returned to England; disembarked H.M.T. 'Grantully Castle,' Liverpool, 23 October 1914: proceeded to France, S.S. 'Mount Temple,' disembarked Le Havre, 18 January 1915: moved up to the front at Ypres via Hazebrouck, Merris, Vlamertinghe. Lieut.Col. Murphy wrote,: "On the night of 4–5 February the battalion relieved 2nd Cheshires in the trenches between the Ypres–Comines canal and Hill 60; the relief being completed before daybreak, battalion headquarters being sited at Verbrandenmolen. Pte.Paltrey was wounded during the night, but the first man of the battalion to give his life in the Great War was Pte. W. Nunn who was shot through the head in the early morning (5 February 1915) while cooking his breakfast." Age 23. *unm.*

His brother Charles also has no known grave; he is recorded above.

(Panel 21) Pte. (Drmr.) 9432, Herbert Page, 2nd Bn. (12th Foot) The Suffolk Regt.: *s.* of Harry Page, by his wife Alice: and brother to Sergt. 3/7620, A. Page, 2nd Suffolk Regt., killed in action, 20 July 1916, at the Somme: *b.* Ely, co. Cambridge, 1885: *educ.* Boys' National School, Ely: joined Suffolk Militia, 1898; served in the Reserve until time expired: called up on the outbreak of war: went to France, August 1914: accidentally wounded in the foot at the First Battle of Ypres, October following, and sent to England for six months, where he joined 1st Battn. Band: returned to France, and was killed in action, 2 March 1916, in the action at St. Eloi. Buried there. A bomb-thrower, he is believed to have been killed whilst engaged in that duty. Age 30. He *m.* Ely, co. Cambridge; Eliza (9, Springhead Lane, Ely), *dau.* of Charles Woodbine, and leaves five children – Herbert, *b.* 13 December 1908; Charles Henry, *b.* 29 May 1910; Harry, *b.* 14 June 1912; Alice, *b.* 5 May 1914; St. Eloi Souvenir Felixstowe (*b.* posthumous 1 September 1916), for whom the deepest sympathy is felt. (*IWGC record 3/9432*)

His brother Arthur is buried in Delville Wood Cemetery (XXX.G.10).

(Panel 21) Pte. 13004, Alfred Thomas Quinton, 2nd Bn. (12th Foot) The Suffolk Regt.: *s.* of Alfred Quinton, of Grundisburgh, Woodbridge, co. Suffolk: and brother to Pte. 202291, J. Quinton, 7th Suffolk Regt., killed in action, 9 August 1917: *b.* Grundisburgh: enlisted Ipswich: served with the Expeditionary Force in France, and was killed in action, 2 March 1916. Age 20.

His brother James also has no known grave; he is commemorated on the Arras (Faubourg D'Amiens) Memorial (Bay 4).

(Panel 21) Pte. 7707, Henry Richard Ramplin, 1st Bn. (12th Foot) The Suffolk Regt.: *s.* of Frederick Ramplin, of 33, New Cut, Hadleigh, co. Suffolk, by his wife Eliza: and brother to L/S. 221153, A.K. Ramplin, HMS 'Bombala,' Royal Navy, died 26 April 1918, at sea. Killed in action, 16 February 1915. Age 30.

His brother Arthur has no known grave but the sea; he is commemorated on the Chatham Naval Memorial (28).

(Panel 21) Pte. 9485, Herbert Read, 'A' Coy., 1st Bn. (12th Foot) The Suffolk Regt.: *s.* of William Read, of Gooderham's Farm, Clopton, Woodbridge, late of Rose Cottage, Peasenhall, co. Suffolk, by his wife Elizabeth: and brother to Pte. 7549, C.W. Read, Lincolnshire Regt., who also fell: *b.* Kesingland, co. Suffolk: enlisted Ipswich. Killed in action, 25 May 1915, at Ypres.

His brother Charles also has no known grave; he is commemorated on the Ploegsteert Memorial (Panel 3).

(Panel 21) Pte. 8912, Allured John Saker, 1st Bn. (12th Foot) The Suffolk Regt.: *s.* of James Saker, of Park Farm, North Elmham, Dereham, co. Norfolk, and Julia A.M. Saker his wife: *b.* Wenhaston, co. Suffolk: enlisted Halesworth. Killed in action, 25 May 1915. Age 19. Dedicated –'Sons of this place, let this of you be said, That you who live are worthy of your dead. They gave their lives, that you who live may reap, A richer harvest ere you fall asleep' – Pte. Saker is among 23 local men who gave their lives 1914–1918 remembered on Aldeby (Parish Church) War Memorial, Norfolk.

(Panel 21) Pte. 20073, Percy Frank Sillett, 2nd Bn. (12th Foot) The Suffolk Regt.: *s.* of James F. Sillett, Miller; of 23, Plough Lane, Sudbury, co. Suffolk, by his wife Eliza: and brother to Pte. G/3199, L.A. Sillett, 7th The Buffs (East Kent Regt.), killed in action, 1 July 1916, at the Somme: *b.* Harleston, co. Norfolk: enlisted Sudbury: served with the Expeditionary Force, and was killed in action, 2 March 1916. Age 20. *unm.*

His brother Leonard also has no known grave, he is commemorated on the Thiepval Memorial (Pier & Face 5D).

On 27 March 1916, a violent explosion, felt several miles behind the lines, announced the successful detonation of a series of British mines at St. Eloi. Early the following morning, 2nd Suffolk Regt., resting at Ouderdom, were despatched by bus to Dickebusch. Remaining there in a hail storm, which continued throughout the day, they moved forward that night, under heavy shell fire, up the long communication trench that led toward the St. Eloi craters. On reaching the trenches the situation was found to be obscure and complicated. Some of the craters had not yet been occupied by British troops, and as dawn broke on the 29th it became apparent that the situation was decidedly unhealthy; part of a trench on the right edge of the battalion sector was occupied by German troops. Early the next afternoon (30th) an attempt to clear this section of trench was made by the battalion bombers, under 2nd Lieut. Gardham, but after making about twenty yards of ground they came up against a barricade the enemy had erected to prevent just such an attempt. Heavy machine-gun fire foiled all attempts to pass beyond this point. The leading bayonet man, Pte. H.A. Southgate, recently decorated with the D.C.M. for gallantry at The Bluff, was killed trying to cross the barricade; 2nd Lieut. C.C. Field, in making a daring effort to mount his machine-guns in the open to cover the advance was shot and killed at a range of about fifty yards by a sniper.

(Panel 21) Pte. 13085, Hiram Ashford Southgate, D.C.M., 2nd Bn. (12th Foot) The Suffolk Regt.: *b*. Honehouse, co. Suffolk: enlisted Ipswich. Killed in action, 30 March 1916. 2nd Lieut. C.C. Field, 9th Queen's Own (Royal West Kent Regt.) attd. 2nd Suffolk Regt. is buried in Voormezeele Enclosures Nos.1 & 2 (I.D.3).

(Panel 21) Pte. 3/8270, Thomas Watson, 2nd Bn. (12th Foot) The Suffolk Regt.: *s*. of Thomas Jeffrey Watson, of High Street, Barrow, Bury St. Edmunds, by his wife Alice Elizabeth: and yr. brother to L/Corpl. 3/8662, W.G. Watson, 1st Suffolk Regt., died 8 September 1916, in Salonika: *b*. Barrow: enlisted Bury St. Edmunds. Killed in action, 16 December 1914. Age 20. *unm*. The brothers Watson are remembered on Barrow (Suffolk) Parish War Memorial.

His brother William is buried in Salonika (Lembet Road) Military Cemetery (376).

(Panel 21) Pte. 327591, Lessels Malcolm Patterson, 1st Bn. The Cambridgeshire Regt. (T.F.) attd 8th Suffolk Regt.: 4th *s*. of the late Charles Patterson, by his wife Helen (36, Howitt Road, London, N.W.), *dau*. of the late George Malcolm, of Dundee: and brother to Capt. C.C. Patterson, Cheshire Regt., reported missing after the fighting on the Somme, 21 October 1916; now assumed to have been killed on or about that date: *b*. Norwood, London, S.E., 3 September 1885: *educ*. Berkhampstead: went out to Singapore in 1906: on the outbreak of war returned to England: enlisted January 1916: served with the Expeditionary Force in France and Flanders from December following, and was killed in action at Ypres, 31 July 1917. Age 31. *unm*. (*IWGC record age 32*)

His brother Charles also has no known grave; he is commemorated on the Loos (Dud Corner) Memorial (Panel 49).

(Panel 21) 2nd Lieut. Leonard Amauri Filleul, 3rd (Reserve) Bn. The Prince Albert's (Somerset Light Infantry) attd. Oxford & Bucks Light Infantry: 2nd *s*. of the Rev. Philip William Girdlestone Filleul, Rector of Alfold, Billingshurst, co. Sussex, late Rector of Devizes, by his wife Elizabeth ('The Homestead,' Combe Down, Bath), *dau*. of Mr (& Mrs) Rodway, and niece of Roland Rodway, Adcroft, Trowbridge: and a relative of the late Dr Valpy, whose *dau*. was his gt.-grandmother, and to Canon Robert Girdlestone, formerly Principal of Wycliffe Hall, Oxford: *b*. St. James' Lodge, Bath, 6 February 1888: *educ*. Preparatory School, Cleveland House, Weymouth; Trent College, co. Derby; Lincoln College, Oxford, where he was Secretary of the College Boat Club (rowed 4 years in the College Eight; in the winning Trial Eight, 1910); University O.T.C. member: left Oxford, 1911, took up an appointment as Master, Monkton Combe School, Bath: became attd. 3rd Somerset Light Infantry, as Supplementary Officer, January 1912; training three weeks each year during his vacations: volunteered for Foreign Service on the outbreak of war and, after a short period of training with Somerset Special Reserve Battn., Plymouth, was sent to the Front, 25 September, with a draft attd. Oxford & Bucks L.I., and was killed in action nr. St. Julien during the First Battle of Ypres, 21 October 1914, Trafalgar Day, whilst engaged in an attack on German infantry. During a rush forward in the early morning over some open ground, he was struck by a bullet near the heart, dying instantly, and was buried mid-way between St. Julien and Poelcappelle, on the Ypres-

St.Jean-Poelcapelle road. The Colonel of his own regt. wrote, "It was a great disappointment to learn, on my arrival here, that Filleul had been appointed to another regt., and was not coming out to join us at the Front, for he was a most capable officer and very popular with his brother officers." The former Col. of his battn. wrote, "Filleul was my subaltern in two separate years, and of all the young fellows who were attached to the battn. he was far and away the best soldier. And not only the best soldier but one of the pleasantest and most delightful companions I have ever met. Always willing, keen and cheery, I loved having him with me, and I placed more reliance upon his judgement and ability than on many a more experienced man." And the editor of the *Oxford Magazine* wrote, "He was one of the very best of his time, an inspiring leader, devoted to the College, and enthusiastically beloved." At Trent College he won the Gold Medal of the National Service League for military proficiency, and at the same time received a book prize from Earl Roberts. Age 26. *unm.* Interestingly, on the oak panel commemorating 43 'old boys' of Lincoln College who gave their lives in the Great War, the row beside that recording Lieut. Filleul lists L.R. Schimmelpfenning who died fighting for the German cause. Perhaps they knew each other, perhaps they may even have been friends; if so, it is strange to think that a few short years later they would both be in Flanders trying to kill each other.

(Panel 21) Corpl. 11978, Wilfrid Stephen Newing, 'A' Coy., 6th (Service) Bn. The Prince Albert's (Somerset Light Infantry): *s.* of Albert Newing, of by his wife Agnes: and brother to Pte. 40616, R.A. Newing, 7th Somerset Light Infantry, died 15 July 1918, wounds: *b.* Winscombe, co. Somerset: enlisted Weston-super-Mare. Killed in action, 25 September 1915. Age 25. *unm.*

His brother Reginald is buried in Ligny-St. Flochel British Cemetery, Averdoingt (I.F.1).

(Panel 21) Pte. 21691, Hubert Charles Braddick, M.M., 1st Bn. (13th Foot) The Prince Albert's (Somerset Light Infantry): *s.* of William Vickery Braddick, of Langford Budville, Wellington, co. Somerset, and Fanny Elizabeth his spouse: *b.* Langford Budville, 1890: Occupation – Clerk; Messrs Fox, Tonedale Mill, Wellington: served with the Expeditionary Force in France and Flanders from December 1915. Reported missing and wounded, 3 September 1916; since confirmed wounded and killed (by shellfire) on or about that date. Posthumously awarded the Military Medal, 25 October 1916; his parents were notified of his being wounded and missing at about the same time. Age 27. *unm.*

(Panel 21) Pte. 17166, Albert Burt Carpenter, 6th (Service) Bn. The Prince Albert's (Somerset Light Infantry): *s.* of W. Carpenter, by his wife Susan (Pontygwindy Bungalows, Caerphilly, co. Glamorgan): *b.* New Tredegar, co. Monmouth, *c.*1896: enlisted Caerphilly. Killed in action, 2 August 1915. Age 19. Pte. Carpenter is not recorded on any local war memorial. Remains of an 'Unknown British Soldier. 6 Somerset L.I.' exhumed, identified – Clothing, Titles; reinterred, registered, 8 February 1928. Collective Grave. *Buried in Sanctuary Wood Cemetery (II.B.17/18).*

Sleep On Dear Son In A Soldier's Grave, Your Life For Your Country You Nobly Gave

(Panel 21) Pte. 9921, William John Carter, 6th (Service) Bn. The Prince Albert's (Somerset Light Infantry): *s.* of Alfred Cuthbert Carter, of 51, Thornhill Houses, Barnsbury, London, by his marriage to the late Alice Eliza: and brother to Pte. 202807, H. Carter, 5th Berkshire Regt., died of wounds, 12 May 1917: *b.* Edmonton, London, 1895: enlisted Bristol. Killed in action, 2 August 1915. Age 20. *unm.*

His brother Herbert is buried in Etaples Military Cemetery (XXV.A.10A).

(Panel 21) Pte. 11164, Frank Herbert Diamond, 6th (Service) Bn. The Prince Albert's (Somerset Light Infantry): *s.* of Frank Herbert Diamond, of 19, Cooperage Road, St. George, by his wife Jane: *b.* St. Philip's, *c.*1887: enlisted Bristol: served with the Expeditionary Force in France from May 1915, and was killed in action, 25 September following. Age 28. All correspondence and effects should be forwarded to his widow, Ellen Beatrice Diamond (Soldiers Settlement, French's Forest, Manly, New South Wales, Australia).

(Panel 21) Pte. 17400, James Robert Parsons, 6th (Service) Bn. The Prince Albert's (Somerset Light Infantry): son-in-law to the late Tom Preece, of Market Place, Nunney, co. Somerset, and his wife Sarah: and brother-in-law to Pte. 7343, W. Preece, 1st Wiltshire Regt., killed in action, 6 July 1916, at the Somme; and uncle to L/Corpl. R/18388, H.T. Preece, 20th King's Royal Rifle Corps, died at home, 3

September 1916, consequent to wounds received in France: *b*. Frome, *c*.1873: enlisted Bath: served with the Expeditionary Force in France from May 1915. Killed in action, 3 September 1915. Age 42. Walter Preece has no known grave, he is commemorated on the Thiepval Memorial (Pier & Face 13A); Henry is buried in Nunney (All Saints) Churchyard.

(Panel 21) Pte.27678, Tom Tarr, 8th (Service) Bn. The Prince Albert's (Somerset Light Infantry): *s*. of Tom Tarr, of Leigh Farm, Langford Budville, nr. Wellington, co. Somerset, by his wife Thirza: and brother to Pte. 180216, H. Tarr, Machine Gun Corps (surv'd.): *b*. Notwell Farm, Raddington, 1895: Occupation – Farm Labourer: enlisted West Somerset Yeomanry (T.F.), Wellington, September 1914: served with the Expeditionary Force in the Balkans (from September 1915), Gallipoli (October–December) and Egypt, from whence he was invalided to England suffering from enteric fever, January 1916: served in France and Flanders, transf'd. 8th Somerset Light Infantry from November 1916, and was killed in action at Ypres, 31 July 1917; shell fragments. Age 22. Letters to Pte. Tarr's parents from comrades in his section state that at the time of his death their son was engaged in the important and dangerous work of a runner in the advanced trenches and was looking over the parapet when he was hit in the temple and neck by fragments from a shell burst in front of him. He died almost immediately. The officer who was with him at the time was killed outright. These communications speak very highly of Pte. Tarr's devotion to duty and leave no doubt that the popularity he enjoyed at home he carried with him in the trenches. 'Every sympathy is felt for his parents in the loss they have sustained by the death of so brave a son.'

(Panel 21) Pte. 8992, Eli Yard, 8th (Service) Bn. The Prince Albert's (Somerset Light Infantry): Killed in action on the night of 17 July 1917; vicinity Battalion H.Q., Wytschaete. At the time of his death he was at duty with a working party comprising 60 men of his battalion. Subjected to heavy shell and machine gun fire by the enemy, the work party was virtually wiped out incurring casualties of 1 officer, 8 men killed; 50 wounded. No remains recovered for burial. See also Cabin Hill Cemetery (A.1–7).

(Panel 21) Major Charles Godfray Mitford Slade, 4th (Extra Reserve) Bn. The Prince of Wales's Own (West Yorkshire Regt.) attd. Loyal North Lancashire Regt.: *s*. of Bertram Mitford Slade: and relative of Col. Cargill, and Capt. Bamber: *b*. Teddington, 2 July 1878: *educ*. Colchester, and Royal Military College, Sandhurst: joined Prince of Wales's Own Regt. May 1901: retired from Regular Battn., joining 4th Battn. as Capt. April 1907: served with 1st Battn. in the Boer War: present at the Relief of Kimberley, and at Paardeberg: took part in operations east of Pretoria, July–November 1900, and was severely wounded in the fighting (Queen's Medal, three clasps; King's Medal, two clasps): obtained his Majority, September 1914; attd. Loyal North Lancashire Regt. for service in the Great War. After taking a German trench he was ordering the prisoners to be removed when he was shot dead, Tuesday, 8 November 1914. Age 36. A Freemason – Abbey Lodge, Abingdon; Major Slade was a very keen sportsman, a member of the Firfield Golf Club, Abingdon, and the Cricket and Football Club. He *m*. Adelaide Ludivina, *dau*. of Daniel Turner, of Cardiff, *gd-dau*. of Dr. Bennet, of Sydney, New South Wales, and left two children – Godfray Bertram, *b*. 25 August 1906; Gladys May, *b*. 24 May 1908.

(Panel 21) L/Corpl. 2088, Arnold Ellis Day, 1/5th Bn. The Prince of Wales's Own (West Yorkshire Regt.), (T.F.): only *s*. of Edward Joseph Day, Agent; of 10, South Drive, Harrogate, by his wife Ada, *dau*. of James Ellis, of Staincliffe, nr. Dewsbury: *b*. Dewsbury, co. York, 19 May 1889: *educ*. Woodhouse Grove School, Apperley Bridge, Leeds: prior to the outbreak of war was seven years on the literary staff *Bradford Daily Telegraph*: joined 1/5th West Yorkshire Regt. 28 August 1914, and was killed in action, 13 July 1915, being buried at Turcos Farm. 2nd Lieut. Allen wrote, "He was in my platoon and a most promising N.C.O. He was shot in the head while carrying out his duties, and died a little while afterwards." And a comrade, "I wish you could have seen Arnold with the children out here; how they loved him. It was common to see him with a crowd around him, all talking to him at once, all of them adoring him. It was the same with the old people." Age 26. *unm*.

(Panel 21) L/Corpl. 15/350, Herbert Foxton, 2nd Bn. (14th Foot) The Prince of Wales's Own (West Yorkshire Regt.): *s*. of Richard Foxton, of Dringhouses, York, by his wife Emily: *b*. Dringhouses, *c*.1893: prior to enlistment was member of the firm Foxton Bros. & Co., Armley, Leeds: enlisted 15th (Service) Battn. 'Leeds Pals,' September 1914: subsequently transf'd. 2nd Battn. in order to proceed with a draft for France: served with the Expeditionary Force there and in Flanders, and was killed in action, 31 July 1917; Ypres, Belgium. Age 24. *unm.*

(Panel 21) Pte. 18041, Wilfred Ball, 10th (Service) Bn. The Prince of Wales's Own (West Yorkshire Regt.): *s.* of Sarah Ball (8, Caroline Street, Newport, co. Monmouth): enlisted Bath. Killed in action, 27 December 1915. Age 17. (*IWGC record 18031*)

(Panel 21) Pte. 456, Horace Ferdinand Banton Bradley, 1/5th Bn. The Prince of Wales's Own (West Yorkshire Regt.), (T.F.): eldest *s.* of J. Bradley, Traveller; of Station Road, Tadcaster, Leeds: and brother to Pte. H. Bradley and Corpl. J.W. Bradley, West Yorkshire Regt., both of whom surv'd.: *b.* Derby, *c.*1889: Occupation – Clerk; Samuel Smith's Brewery, Tadcaster: enlisted Wetherby. Killed in action, 21 July 1915. Capt. G. Sowerby wrote, "It is with the deepest regret that I have to inform you that your son, H.F. Bradley, was killed by a hand grenade in the trenches on the 21st about 5.30 p.m. He was buried the same night behind the trenches, a cross being erected. The service was conducted by Col. Ward. He was at tea with 3 comrades when the grenade burst over them. He is an accomplished musician and played the piccolo, and two years ago played in the band of the 5th West Yorks. Your son was a most excellent soldier and was always out at once to help any other poor fellow who needed his services as a stretcher bearer, and I am most sorry to lose him." Age 26. *unm.*

(Panel 21) Pte. 36606, Albert Edward Durham, 'D' Coy. 11th (Service) Bn. The Prince of Wales's Own (West Yorkshire Regt.): *yst. s.* of the late William Durham, by his wife Emma (25, Willow St., Burley, Leeds), *dau.* of the late David Jacques, of Wakefield: *b.* Burley, 2 October 1889: *educ.* Burley Lawn Council School: employee Messrs. Taylors, Clarence Iron Works, Hunslet: enlisted, 11 December 1915: served with the Expeditionary Force in France and Flanders, and was killed in action at Ypres, 18 July 1917, while on a tour in the trenches. Buried nr. Ypres. His Commanding Officer wrote, "I am sorry to tell you of the death of your son who was killed whilst we were in the trenches this last tour, I know that any words of mine can be of little comfort to you when confronted with such a loss for he has been in my platoon several months, and I could tell he would be as good a son as he was a soldier. As a soldier he was everything one could ask; brave and cheerful under the worst circumstances, and out of the line always clean, tidy and steady. I am certain there wasn't a better lad in the company. He was killed by a shell wound in the head and suffered no pain, and was buried behind the line. Several of his chums and comrades attended his funeral." Age 27. *unm.*

(Panel 21) Pte. 37277, Charles Edward Layfield, 'C' Coy., 11th (Service) Bn. The Prince of Wales's Own (West Yorkshire Regt.): *s.* of James Layfield, of Willow Hill Farm, Denton, Ben Rhydding, Leeds, by his wife Frances: and elder brother to Pte. 64293, W. Layfield, 214th Coy. Machine Gun Corps (Inf.), killed in action, 20 September 1917: *b.* Denton: enlisted York. Killed in action, 7 June 1917. Age 21. *unm.*

His brother Walter also has no known grave; he is commemorated on the Tyne Cot Memorial (Panel 157).

On the afternoon of 3 April 1916, 31st Canadians moved out of their camp in the vicinity of Locre and began making their way toward St. Eloi where they were to take over a section of the front line from British troops. Arriving at about half-past mid-night (4 April) it was not until the breaking light of dawn that the nightmare world 31st Battn. had entered was revealed. Pte Fraser wrote: "…We could only look into an impenetrable darkness and conceive in our minds the general situation surrounding us. The whole place was wrapt in gloomy mystery; all sense of direction was lost; around was a chaos of shell holes and mud heaps … When day broke, the sights that met our gaze were so horrible and ghastly that they beggar description. Heads, arms and legs were protruding from the mud at every yard and dear knows how many bodies the earth swallowed. Thirty corpses were at least showing in the crater and beneath its clayey waters other victims must be lying killed and drowned. A young, tall, slim English lieutenant lay stretched in death with a pleasant, peaceful look on his boyish face. Some mother's son gone to glory … Another English second lieutenant was lying at the edge of the crater, huddled up, with his legs uppermost. One of the most saddening cases was a stretcher bearer near half a dozen dead Tommies, a little to the right of the trench – leading to crater No.7. He was sitting with a bandage between his hands in the very act of bandaging his leg, when his life gave out, and his head fell back, his mouth open, and his eyes gazing up to heaven, as if in piteous appeal. There he sat in a natural posture as if in life, the bandage in his hands, the Red Cross bag by his side. Lovett (*sic.*) was his name, and he belonged to the King's Liverpool (*sic.*) (Pte.16475, J. Lovatt, 12th West Yorkshire Regt.). Another strange, appalling spectacle was a couple of Tommies sitting on the firing step; the head of one had fallen forward on his chest, and between his fingers he still held a cigarette. There he was as if asleep, yes, but in a sleep that knows no awakening. His comrade beside him was in a sitting position but inclining sideways. Both were unmarked and must have met their doom by concussion…"

(Panel 21) Pte. 16475, John Lovatt, 12th (Service) Bn. The Prince of Wales's Own (West Yorkshire Regt.). Killed in action at St. Eloi, 3 April 1916.

(Panel 21) Pte. 1854, John Wetherill, 1/5th Bn. The Prince of Wales' Own (West Yorkshire Regt.), (T.F.): *s.* of Walter Wetherill, of 6, Priory Street, York, by his wife Hannah: and brother to L/Corpl. 2489, H. Wetherill, 1/5th West Yorkshire Regt., died of wounds, 24 September 1916, aged 23: *b.* York: served with the Expeditionary Force, and was killed in action, 11 July 1915.

His brother Henry is buried in Puchevillers British Cemetery (IV.E.7).

(Panel 21) Lieut.Col. George Herbert Shaw, V.D., Comdg. 4th Bn. The East Yorkshire Regt. (T.F.): elder *s.* of the late John Shaw, Esq., of Arnold House, Hull, co. York, and the Northlands, Walkington: *b.* Hull, 12 April 1865: *educ.* Hull & East Riding College; Naksov, Denmark (Private Tutor); Passau, Germany; Paris, and Commercial College, Copenhagen: on leaving college entered the firm of Shaw & Sons Ltd., Malting Barley Merchants, Hull, of which he became Managing Director: joined 1st East Yorkshire Regt. as Pte., January 1883: commissioned Lieut. December following; promoted Capt. October 1892, Honorary Major November 1898: received King Edward VII Coronation Medal, 1902: promoted Major 1903, and received Volunteer Decoration: apptd. Honorary Lieut.Col. 1904: succeeded to command, 4th Battn. East Yorkshire Regt. January 1912: undertook Imperial Service obligations on the outbreak of war, August 1914, and accompanied his battalion to the continent, where he was killed in action, 24 April 1915, near St. Julien. It is supposed he was shot by snipers located in a farmhouse, who were afterwards rushed and bayoneted by men of Lieut.Col. Shaw's battalion. Age 50. Lieut.Col. Shaw was an all-round athlete and good boxer, but it was as a shot, both with revolver and rifle, that he was particularly distinguished. He was Vice-President of the Yorkshire Rifle Association and shot for the County Team, 1897, 1899, 1901, 1903, and 1905–08. He won the Yorkshire Officers' Cup, shot for annually at Strensall, 1893, 1896, 1900, 1907, and 1914, and the National Rifle Association Revolver Medal, 1900. He also shot on seven occasions when the Yorkshire trophy, the Bingham Shield, was won by his battalion; in three winning teams for the Officers' Rifle Team Championship Competition, and twice in the winning Revolver Team open to all Yorkshire regiments. He had a genius for organisation, and initiated many successful schemes in his battalion. A member of the Hull and East Riding Club, the Pacific Club, Hull, and the Derby Club, Derby; he also held the St. John of Jerusalem Ambulance Association certificate. He was an excellent linguist, being fluent in French, Danish, Swedish, and German; he also had knowledge of Italian. Lieut. Col. Shaw *m.*, Clara Anne (Briar Garth, North Ferriby, co. York), *dau.* of the late Edward Ward Ingleby, Esq., of Hull and Hedon, co. East York, and left four sons – Capt. A.G. Shaw, 1/4th East Yorkshire Regt.; Lieut. E.N. Shaw, 4th East Yorkshire Regt.; and Pte. P. Shaw, and Pte. 487516, F.L. Shaw, who are both serving in the Canadian Infantry. He also left a daughter, Dorothy Amcotts Shaw. (*IWGC record Hubert*)

His son Francis, killed in action, 26 September 1916, also has no known grave; he is commemorated on the Canadian National Memorial, Vimy.

(Panel 21) Major Thomas Robert Eaton Wybault Warren-Swettenham, 2nd Bn. (15th Foot) The East Yorkshire Regt.: eldest *s.* of the late Col. Robert Warren-Swettenham, late 13th Light Infantry, by his wife Amelia Marion (Swettenham Hall, Congleton, co. Chester): *b.* Cheltenham, co. Gloucester, 10 October 1867: *educ.* Cheltenham College, and Royal Military College, Sandhurst: gazetted 2nd Lieut. West India Regt. March 1889; promoted Lieut. December 1890: transf'd. East Yorkshire Regt. (with which he was destined to remain for the rest of his 26 years service), May 1893: promoted Capt. April 1899: served in the South African War, being present at operations in Orange River Colony, February–April 1902: Queen's Medal, three clasps; King's Medal, two clasps: also held Durbar Coronation Medal: received his

Majority, September 1910: served with the Expeditionary Force in France and Flanders, and was killed in action, 5 February 1915, nr. St. Eloi, Belgium. Age 47. When stationed at Aldershot he was Master of the Aldershot Beagles; he was also a keen polo player and big game shot. Major Warren-Swettenham married in 1907; he leaves a widow, Emmété Florence ('Homestead,' Dawlish, co. Devon), only *dau.* of E.S. Cope, J.P., of Bishop's Teignton, co. Devon, and Kimmerton Court, co. Radnor, and a son aged five years at the time of his father's death. (*IWGC record age 48*)

(Panel 21) Major Carl Erik Theilmann, 4th Bn. The East Yorkshire Regt. (T.F.): 2nd *s.* of Johnman H. Theilmann, of Rutland Villa, Sculcoates, co. York, by his wife Helen: *b.* Norwood, co. Surrey, 1874. Killed in action, 24 April 1915; between Wieltje and Fortuin. Age 41. He leaves a widow, Mrs R.G. Theilmann (67, Courtfield Gardens, Kensington, London), late of 'Brookside,' Newland Park, Hull.

(Panel 21) Capt. Bede Farrell, 1/4th Bn. The East Yorkshire Regt. (T.F.): eldest *s.* of Thomas Frederic Farrell, of Brookside, Newland Park, Hull, Registrar of the Hull County Court, by his wife Monica, eldest *dau.* of Joseph Anthony Collingwood, of Hull, formerly of Corby, co. Lincoln: *b.* Hull, co. York, 28 June 1881: *educ.* Ushaw and Hymers College, Hull: subsequently articled to his father, a partner in the firm of Rollitt & Sons, Solicitors, Hull: passed the Law Society's Final Examination (Hons., November 1904), thereafter practised as a Solicitor, Hull: obtained a commission 2nd Lieut. 1st (Volunteer), now 4th (Territorial) Bn. East Yorkshire Regt. 7 February 1900; promoted Lieut. 19 June 1901; Capt. 24 November 1907: received Certificate of Special Proficiency, Course for Militia Infantry & Rifle Volunteers, Chelsea Barracks, 31 May 1901, being then offered a commission in the Regular Army, which he was unable to accept: volunteered for Imperial Service on the outbreak of war, August 1914: served with the Expeditionary Force in France and Flanders from 18 April 1915, his battalion forming part of York & Durham Brigade, 50th (Northumbrian) Division. In consequence of the great gas attack at Langemarck, 22 April 1915, the battalion was hurried to Vlamertinghe in motor 'buses,' and went into action in the early morning of the 24th on the west bank of the Yser Canal, moving about midday, across the canal and amalgamating with other battalions in the wood at Potijze Chateau, whence the 4th East Yorks and 4th Green Howards, with Canadians on the right, made a counter-attack against large forces of Germans advancing from St. Julien, and he was killed in action between Wieltje and St. Julien, later in the day, while seeing that his men were taking proper cover. Buried near Wieltje. The officer who succeeded to the command of the battalion during the action wrote, "I gather that Bede was so conscientiously looking after his men that he took no care of himself.": And the Adjutant, Capt. W.T. Wilkinson, D.S.O., of the King's Own Scottish Borderers, who subsequently commanded the battalion, "Bede was a great friend of mine. The whole regiment felt his loss, and he was a splendid soldier." 22 April 1915. Age 33. *unm.*

(Panel 21) Capt. Basil Owen Tatham, 3rd (Reserve) attd. 2nd Bn. (15th Foot) The East Yorkshire Regt.: *s.* of Arthur Thomas Tatham, of 65, Oakwood Court, Kensington, London, formerly of Doddlespool Hall, nr. Betley, co. Stafford, by his marriage to the late Eliza Hale Tatham: *educ.* Mostyn House School, Parkgate. Killed in action, 23 April 1915. Age 31. Remembered on the Mostyn School Roll of Honour, Capt. Tatham is one of eighty old boys of Mostyn who are remembered by a carillon of 31 bells situated above the school entrance; he is also commemorated on a polished brass memorial panel in St. Bertoline's Church, Barthomley, and on the Roll of Honour situated beside the memorial window in St. Margaret's Church, Betley.

(Panel 21) Capt. Kenrick Talbot Woodmass, 2nd Bn. (15th Foot) The East Yorkshire Regt.: *s.* of Montagu Woodmass, of Compstall, co. Chester, by his wife Edith Alice (7, Southwell Gardens, South Kensington, London, S.W.): and a relative of Lord Erskine, and Gen. Inglefield, C.B., D.S.O.: *b.* Compstall, 31 May 1877: *educ.* J.C. Pipon's School, Wales, and Charterhouse: volunteered for the South African War: served in the ranks 1st Yorks Rough Riders, Imperial Yeomanry, for a year and, later, almost two years in the commissioned ranks: present at operations in Cape Colony, Orange River Colony, and Transvaal, November 1900–May 1902: Mentioned in Despatches (*London Gazette*, 29 July 1902): Queen's Medal, three clasps; King's Medal, two clasps: received his commission from Imperial Yeomanry, September 1902; promoted Lieut. August 1904: Battn. Adjt. July 1909–July 1912: served with his Regiment in Burmah and India, and was Captain of the polo club at both stations, and when stationed at York he won the Regimental Steeple Chase Cup: promoted Capt. December 1912: served with the Expeditionary Force in France and Flanders, and was killed in action at the Second Battle of Ypres when leading his men near that town, 23 April 1915. Age 37. *unm.* (*IWGC record age 36*)

(Panel 21) Lieut. Oscar James Addyman, 2nd Bn. (15th Foot) The East Yorkshire Regt.: served with the Expeditionary Force in France and Flanders from 16 January 1915. The first officer fatality of 2nd Battalion; killed in action on the afternoon of 4 February 1915, by 'an unlucky shell' which fell on 'C' Company's trench north of the Yser Canal; Capt. O.C. Wilkinson, seriously wounded by the same shell, died the following day. Capt. Wilkinson is buried in Hazebrouck Communal Cemetery (III.H.6).

(Panel 21) Lieut. Frederic Haswell, 3rd (Reserve) attd. 2nd Bn. (15th Foot) The East Yorkshire Regt.: 2nd *s.* of Robert Haswell, of 27, Thornhill Gardens, Sunderland, by his wife Jessie: and brother to Capt. G. Haswell, 9th King's Own Yorkshire Light Infantry, killed in action, 1 July 1916, at the Somme: *b.* Sunderland, 14 June 1895: *educ.* Bede Collegiate School, Sunderland, where he won his colours for cricket: afterwards became a Staff Member, National Provincial Bank, Manchester: joined Manchester University O.T.C., and applied for a commission on the outbreak of war: gazetted 2nd Lieut. 3rd East Yorkshire Regt. August 1914, attd. 2nd Battn. for Active Service. Lieut. Haswell was killed in action at Ypres, 23 April 1915. Age 19. A Major of 2nd Battn. East Yorkshire Regt. wrote of him, "Lieut. Haswell had only been with us a short time, but quite long enough to endear himself to all ranks, and he leaves a gap very difficult to fill. I was not near him when he fell, but he was gallantly leading his men when he was shot in the head, death being instantaneous, which is always a comforting thing to know. He died bravely, as a brave man should." His promotion to Lieut. was gazetted posthumously.

His brother Gordon is buried in Norfolk Cemetery, Becordel-Becourt (I.B.92).

(Panel 21) Lieut. Henry Thornton Miller, 3rd (Reserve) Bn. The East Yorkshire Regt. attd. 2nd Bn. Duke of Wellington's (West Riding) Regt.: only *s.* of the late Henry Miller, O.B.E., Town Clerk of Norwich, by his wife Ella Constance (Woodlands, Norwich): *b.* Swansea, 20 May 1895: *educ.* Stubbington House, Fareham; Clifton College, Bristol, and Pembroke College, Cambridge: played cricket and football for Spence's House, Clifton, and rowed in the Mays for Pembroke College: at sixteen years of age, was presented with a gold chain and medallion by the Lord Mayor and Watch Committee, Norwich, for rescuing a woman from drowning and resuscitating her: gazetted 2nd Lieut. East Yorkshire Regt. August 1914; promoted Lieut. February 1915: served with the Expeditionary Force in France and Flanders, and was wounded in the head, 2 February 1915: rejoined April following, attd. 2nd Duke of Wellington's, and was killed by gas poisoning, 5 May 1915, during operations at Hill 60, Ypres, in which his battalion took a leading part. The gas was so strong that the respirators proved useless. Nevertheless he, with just a few others, and with great temerity, held onto the position until reliefs came up. Thus, they were instrumental in saving the line. After being treated at the advanced dressing station by a medical officer, who reported him in a serious but not hopeless condition, he tried to reach the field ambulances, but apparently collapsed on the way, as nothing further was heard of him. His body was found on 17 May in (or near) a ruined cottage with those of some of his men. Age 19.

(Panel 21) 2nd Lieut. Francis William Stanley Hubbert, 2nd Bn. (15th Foot) The East Yorkshire Regt.: *yst. s.* of the late Charles John Hubbert, late 3rd Royal Sussex Regt., by his wife Mary Ann (109, Walden Road, North End, Portsmouth): and a relative of Frank and Francis Stanley Barrett, late Worcestershire Regt.: *b.* Grayling, Chichester, co. Sussex, 4 October 1885: *educ.* Chichester Prebendary School – chorister Chichester Cathedral: enlisted 2nd East Yorkshire Regt., and served in the ranks for almost 16 years. He was very popular in his battalion, with which he served in India and Burma, and made many friends. A keen sportsman, he was an expert billiard player, winning the Shorncliffe billiard tournament on two occasions and numerous prizes for billiards. At the outbreak of war with Germany he had risen to the rank of Sergt.: gazetted 2nd Lieut. East Yorkshire Regt. January 1915, and posted to his old battalion. Killed nr. Ypres 23 April 1915, while gallantly leading his men to attack a strong position. Buried on the field of battle. Age 29. He *m.* Lilian May (4, Dartmouth Road, Copnor, Portsmouth), *dau.* of John (& Mary) Noonan, and left two sons – Stanley William George, *b.* June 1911; Charles Nevill Frederick, *b.* February 1913. (*IWGC record F.S.W. Hubbert, age 30*)

(Panel 21) Coy.Sergt.Major, 6, Herbert Harold Ferrand, 1/4th Bn. The East Yorkshire Regt. (T.F.): only *s*. of Thomas Watson Ferrand, Plumber; of 6, West View, Grove Street, Beverley Road, Hull, by his wife Sarah Nicholls, *dau*. of the late John Fayers, of Hull: *b*. Hull, co. York, 15 May 1876: *educ*. St. Paul's School, Hull, and on leaving there entered the employ of the Yorkshire Fire and Life Insurance Co., Lowgate, in which he held a responsible post at the time of his death: joined 1st V.B. East Yorkshire Regt. April 1894: volunteered for service in South Africa, 8 March 1900, and served there for one year and 92 days, receiving Queen's Medal with four clasps and, after his return, was for a long time Signal Instructor (Aldershot certificate, 31 August 1903). On the outbreak of the European War, his regt. were at camp at Deganway and, ordered home, they went straight into training at Darlington; thereafter at Newcastle, and from there went to the Front, 18 April 1915. He came safely through the night attack at Ypres, on Saturday the 25th, and was killed by shrapnel on Sunday, 26 April 1915. He had the King's T.F. Medal for efficiency. Age 39. *unm*.

(Panel 21) Coy.Sergt.Major 5314, Ernest John Watson, 2nd Bn. (15th Foot) The East Yorkshire Regt.: *b*. Islington: enlisted Tottenham, London: a pre-war Regular, arrived in England with his battalion from India, December 1914: served with the Expeditionary Force in France from 16 January 1915, and was killed in action, 3 February following; nr. St. Eloi. The first senior NCO fatality of his battalion. The first officer casualty, Capt. H.J. Miller, wounded on the night of the 3rd, survived the war.

(Panel 21) Sergt. 9577, Alfred Halton Frost, D.C.M., 1st Bn. (15th Foot) The East Yorkshire Regt.: *s*. of Arthur Frost, of 63, Seaforth Avenue, Harehills, Leeds, by his wife Eliza: and brother to Corpl. 12723, C.G. Frost, D.C.M., 7th East Yorkshire Regt., died 29 October 1917, of wounds: *b*. Sherburn-in-Elmet, co. York: enlisted Beverley. Killed in action, 9 August 1915, at Hooge. For his services in the Great War Sergt. Frost was twice Mentioned in Despatches by F.M. Sir John (now Lord) French. Age 25. *unm*.

His brother Charles is buried in Mont Huon Military Cemetery (VI.B.1A).

(Panel 21) L/Corpl. 9383, Henry Glazebrook, 2nd Bn. (15th Foot) The East Yorkshire Regt.: eldest *s*. of William Henry Glazebrook, of 16, Mildmay Road, West Jesmond, Newcastle-on-Tyne, now in the Postal Service, late Battery Sergt.-Major Royal Field Artillery (who served throughout the South African War and received the Queen's and King's medals with clasps), by his wife Mary Ellen, *dau*. of Samuel Stephenson: and brother to Sergt. 63916, W.H. Glazebrook, 110th Bty., 24th Bde., Royal Field Artillery: *b*. Newcastle-on-Tyne, 11 March 1892: *educ*. Council School, Sandyford: joined the Army, 15 July 1909: served 5 years (1909–14) in India: came home with his regt. after the outbreak of war, going with it to France in January, and was killed in action near St. Eloi, 5 February 1915. Buried at Chateau Rosendale, near Ypres. Two other brothers also served, one in the Army and the other in the Navy; both survived. *unm*.

His brother William Henry died on 30 September 1916. Buried Carnoy Military Cemetery (B.18).

(Panel 21) L/Corpl. 10038, James Johnson, 2nd Bn. (15th Foot) The East Yorkshire Regt.: formerly no.10172, East Surrey Regt.: *s*. of John Johnson, of Bell Vue, Tilgate, nr. Pease Pottage, Crawley, co. Sussex, by his wife Annie: and brother to Pte. 9108, W. Johnson, 8th East Yorkshire Regt., who fell at the Battle of Arras, 1917: *b*. Three Bridges, 1889: enlisted Kingston-upon-Hull: served with the Expeditionary Force, and was killed in action at Ypres, 27 February 1915. Age 25.

His brother William also has no known grave; he is commemorated on the Arras (Faubourg d'Amiens) Memorial.

(Panel 21) Pte. 1638, Charles Ernest Ainley, 1/4th Bn. The East Yorkshire Regt. (T.F.): *s*. of George Frederick Ainley, of 51, Cogan St., Hull, by his wife Minnie: *b*. Hull, 9 March 1896: *educ*. South Myton School, Hull: before entering the Army, was apprentice to Messrs King & Co.: a pre-war Territorial, joined 18 August 1912; volunteered for Active Service and proceeded to France with his battalion following the outbreak of war, and was shot through the head and instantaneously killed by a sniper, 1 May 1915, during a Battle at Hill 60. Age 19.

(Panel 21) Pte. 1578, Herbert Battarbee, Siglr., 1/4th Bn. The East Yorkshire Regt. (T.F.): 3rd *s*. of Frederick Battarbee, of 60, Tadman Street, Hull, by his wife Clara, *dau*. of John Wrigglesworth: *b*. Hull, 11 February 1895: *educ*. St. Luke's Street School: a pre-war Territorial, joined 4th East Yorks, March

1912; volunteered for Active Service and proceeded to France with his battalion following the outbreak of war, and was killed in action, 24 April 1915. Age 20. *unm.*

(Panel 21) Pte. 15932, James Henry Beal, 'D' Coy., 1st Bn. (15th Foot) The East Yorkshire Regt.: *s.* of Thomas Beal, of Hull, by his wife Martha: *b.* Hull, co. York, 7 October 1869: employee to Messrs T. Wilson, Sons & Co.: volunteered after the outbreak of war and enlisted 23 October 1914: served with the Expeditionary Force in France from 22 April, and was killed in action, 9 August 1915. A comrade wrote, "I am pleased to be able to say he died bravely and gamely, with his face towards the German lines, where he was buried with as much respect and ceremony as circumstances would permit. Though we had not had him with us very long, we had learnt to respect him, and to value his worth both as a comrade and a man." Age 45. He *m.* Mary Elizabeth (47, Gillett Street, Hull), *dau.* of James Beal, of Beverly, and had 10 children – Elsie May, *b.* 7 October 1895; Lucy Maud, *b.* 28 October 1898; George Henry, *b.* 21 November 1899; Lily, *b.* 26 January 1901; John Robert, *b.* 6 July 1902; Edith Irene, *b.* 21 October 1903; Ivy, *b.* 6 June 1906; Jim, *b.* 21 December 1907; Thomas William, *b.* 28 April 1909; Arthur, *b.* 1 March 1911.

(Panel 21) Pte. 7366, John Forth, 2nd Bn. (15th Foot) The East Yorkshire Regt.: 5th *s.* of the late David Forth, by his wife Sarah, *dau.* of Richard Sowersby: *b.* Aike, nr. Beverley, co. York, 7 September 1871: *educ.* Sledmere School: Occupation – Tanners' Labourer: enlisted 15 September 1914, after the outbreak of war: went to France, 15 January 1915. Reported missing after the fighting at Ypres, 6 February 1915; now assumed to have been killed in action on that date. Age 43. He *m.* firstly, at Beverley, Annie Jorden (*d.* 20 November 1906), *dau.* of Edward Hackney, and had five children – John Edward, *b.* 10 March 1895; Ernest, *b.* 9 April 1897; Mary Elizabeth, *b.* 18 April 1899; Albert, *b.* 17 February 1901; Lilian May, *b.* 21 May 1903: and secondly, at Beverley, 3 February 1908, Gertrude May (Spencer Street, Beverley), *dau.* of Robert Pudsey, and had two daughters – Freda, *b.* 9 July 1912; Olive, *b.* 25 October 1913. (*IWGC record 3/7366*)

(Panel 21) Pte. 9268, Edwin Gardner, 2nd Bn. (15th Foot) The East Yorkshire Regt.: *s.* of Edwin Gardner, of London, by his wife Ruth: *b.* Camberwell, co. Surrey: enlisted there: a pre-war Regular, arrived in England with his battalion from India, December 1914: served with the Expeditionary Force in France and Flanders from 16 January 1915, and was killed in action, 4 February following, at Ravine Wood, nr. St. Eloi. Age 24. See account, Ramparts Cemetery (Lille Gate), (B.16–17).

(Panel 21) Pte. 4434, Joseph Harrison Halliday, 4th Bn. The East Yorkshire Regt. (T.F.): only *s.* of the late Joseph Wilkinson Halliday, Draper; by his wife Agnes (45, Corporation Road, Grimsby), *dau.* of Harrison Abel: *b.* Grimsby, co. Lincoln, 30 June 1893: *educ.* St. James' College, Grimsby: after serving an apprenticeship in Hull, returned to Grimsby and entered the Victoria Street branch of the family business, which also contained the Central Market Post Office: joined 5th East Yorkshire Regt., 10 January 1911: entered into training on the outbreak of war, undertook Imperial Service obligations, and requested transfer to 4th Battn. for Active Service – Request Granted, 28 July 1915: proceeded to France, 1 September following; returned home for one month's leave, December 1915; returned to the Front, 19 January 1916, and was killed in action ten days later – 29 January 1916 – while on sentry duty in a trench near Zillebeke. Buried there. Age 22. *unm.* The Captain of his Battalion wrote, "He was on duty as a grenadier and had to patrol an empty trench. At the time of his death he was in a section of the trench, resting and talking to three others, when a small shell, known as a 'whizz-bang,' breached the parapet, and was instantly followed by several others. All four men were badly hit, and only one has recovered. I was within a few yards of him at the time; and within a very few minutes the stretcher-bearers were there to render first-aid, but unfortunately nothing could be done. He was a man who always tried to do his duty, and one who will be greatly missed in the company." (*IWGC record age 23*)

PANEL 21 ENDS: PTE. H.R. HAWKES, EAST YORKSHIRE REGT.

North Staircase:

PANEL 23 BEGINS: LT. K.G. CONNELLY, 18TH BN. AUSTRALIAN INF.

(Panel 23) Lieut. Alexander Henry Leslie, 18th Bn. Australian Infantry, A.I.F.: *s.* of Samuel Leslie, Engine Driver, Great North of Scotland Railway; Railway Terrace, Boat-of-Garten, co. Inverness, by his wife Elizabeth: *b.* Aberdeen, 19 July 1890: *educ.* Keith, and Boat-of-Garten, co. Inverness: was employee Government Railway Service, Bathurst, New South Wales: enlisted, 30 September 1914: served with the Mediterranean Expeditionary Force at the Dardanelles: proceeded to France, March 1916: given a commission the following October for good services in the field, and was killed in action at Polygon Wood, 20 September 1917. Buried at Zillebeke. His Colonel wrote, "He did excellent work in the recent fighting. I feel his loss very keenly; he was such a good 'solid' officer." And the Chaplain, "Your son had done splendidly, and as all the officers in one company were killed or wounded, the Colonel sent him to take charge, and before he reached the section he was hit by a sniper and killed instantly. He was a great favourite with us all, as he was always so keen and cheerful, and was reckoned one of the best officers in the battalion." Age 27. *unm.*

On 21 March 1929 the parents of Lieut. W.C.R. Smith, 18th A.I.F., were forwarded a copy of the Menin Gate Memorial Register (Pt.9) wherein their son's details are recorded, and a letter of receipt for the appropriate sum paid. The letter also informed:- "It is noted in this connection that the Imperial War Graves Commission have been successful in recovering the remains of this officer which have since been interred in Sanctuary Wood Cemetery, Zillebeke, and it is desired to point out at the time of erection of the Memorial Arch at Menin Gate, no report of burial had been received, consequently your son's name was included with those of other members of the Australian Imperial Force who fell in Belgium and had no known graves. It is not proposed at this late juncture to expunge the names of those whose graves were subsequently located, and the Memorial Register with its accompanying introductory part will, it is hoped, be of interest as showing the steps taken by the Commission to commemorate the A.I.F. Missing in this particular salient."

(Panel 23) Lieut. William Charles Richard Smith, 18th Bn. Australian Infantry, A.I.F.: *s.* of James Henry Smith, of Mitchell's Island, Manning River, New South Wales, by his wife Edith: *b.* Manning River, 1894: Religion – Church of England: Occupation – Police Constable: enlisted Liverpool, 14 May 1915; posted 2nd Rfts., 18th Battn., 30 May: promoted Sergt., 23 November 1915: trained Egypt (from 9 January 1916); served in France and Flanders from 25 March 1916: wounded (GSW, hand) 28 May, hospitalised France, transf'd. England, discharged to duty (Rolleston Camp) 3 July: hospitalised, Bulford (Venereal) 26 July–15 September: returned to France, 22 September: hospitalised Camiers/Etaples (Venereal) 29 September–15 December: hospitalised Etaples (Epididymitis: testicular inflammation) 22 December–5 January 1917; rejoined battn. 25 January: gazetted 2nd Lieut. 14 May 1917; promoted Lieut. 15 August. Killed in action, 20 September 1917, nr. Anzac House. Age 23. *unm.* Major W.R.C. Robertson, Officer Comdg., 18th A.I.F., wrote, "Lieut. Smith was killed instantaneously by a sniper on the morning of 20 September 1917. He was buried where he fell, about 200 yds. east of Anzac House." Remains recovered (28.J.3.a.8.8) south of Zonnebeke; 'Unknown Australian Soldier,' identified – Clothing, Div. Patch; reinterred, registered, 18 February 1928. Next of kin notified, 12 June 1928. *Buried in Sanctuary Wood Cemetery (II.C.11).*

In Memory Of The Dearly Loved Son Of Mr & Mrs Smith

(Panel 23) Sergt. 309, George Ritchie, No.2 Platoon, 'A' Coy., 18th Bn. Australian Infantry, A.I.F.: *s.* of Peter Bell Ritchie, of 'The Laurels,' Bay View Street, Bexley, New South Wales, by his wife Sarah Caroline: *b.* Middle Park, Victoria, *c.*1891: Religion – Presbyterian: Occupation – Motor Mechanic: joined A.I.F., Liverpool, 8 March 1915: promoted Corpl. 29 March; Sergt. 28 November 1915: served at Gallipoli until the evacuation, thereafter proceeded to Egypt: joined the Expeditionary Force in France, 25 March 1916: wounded (GSW neck & shoulder), 7 August, hospitalised France transf'd. England; returned to duty, 15 December 1916. Killed in action, 20 September 1917. 2767, F. Wilkins wrote, "I knew Sergt. George Ritchie, he was one of the best men that ever lived. After the attack was finished and we had dug ourselves in, on September 20, nr. Anzac House (Ypres), he was killed instantly by a shell. I saw it happen. We took him to a Pill Box and he was probably buried close to the same spot. I have not seen his grave. He was the only Sergt. in the Company who was trusted to lead his Platoon. He came safely through and got his Platoon in order." Pte. Kenna stated that he helped to carry the body of Sergt. Ritchie and Lieut. Smith, who was killed at the same time, to a dug-out, but when he later returned to bury them the bodies could not be found due to the area having been subjected to considerable shellfire. Age 26. *unm.* Remains recovered (28.J.3.a.8.8) south of Zonnebeke; identified – Disc, Clothing; reinterred, registered, 18 February 1928. *Buried in Sanctuary Wood Cemetery (II.C.10).*

> *Dearly Loved Son Of Mr & Mrs P.B. Ritchie*
> *Of Bexley N.S.W. Australia*

Lieut. Smith, also buried in Sanctuary Wood Cemetery (II.C.11), is recorded above.

(Panel 23) L/Sergt. 6157, Oscar Lavender Wilson, 'D' Coy., 18th Bn. Australian Infantry, A.I.F.: *s.* of Thomas Wilson, of 'Corsica,' Clifford Avenue, Manly, New South Wales, by his wife Agnes Eve ('Montrose,' Orpington Street, Ashfield): *b.* Surrey Hills, New South Wales, 1896: Occupation – Despatch Clerk: volunteered and enlisted Royal Agricultural Showground, Sydney, 12 May 1916; apptd. 17th Rfts., 18th Battn. 25 August following: served in France from 4 May 1917; promoted L/Corpl. 26 May; Corpl. 4 August; L/Sergt. 14 September, and died of wounds, 26 September 1917. His comrades informed, "We had made an attack that morning and he was wounded, near Anzac House, after we had consolidated. He was caught by shell fragments which hit him about the right side, and rendered him unconscious. He was taken away, dying, toward the rear. The shelling was terrible and afterwards no trace of him could be found. He seemed a very clever chap and this was his first time in the line, having only been made a Sergt. the day before." Age 21. *unm.* Remains recovered (28.J.3.a.8.8) south of Zonnebeke; re-interred Sanctuary Wood Cemetery, 18 February 1928. His identity disc, by which his remains were identified, was returned (by the Officer, Base Records) to his mother with a note – "This memento, though now somewhat impaired by long exposure, will doubtless be valued by you on account of its former intimate association with your son, and I trust same comes safely to hand." *Buried in Sanctuary Wood Cemetery (II.C.12).*

The Supreme Sacrifice

(Panel 23) L/Corpl. 1982B, William Perry, 18th Bn. Australian Infantry, A.I.F.: *s.* of James Perry, of 'Fairview,' Dreadnought Street, Lakemba, New South Wales, by his wife Margaret: *b.* 1896: enlisted Liverpool, N.S.W., 7 July 1915; posted 3rd Rfts., 20th Battn.: transf'd. 18th Battn. 2 September following: served with the Expeditionary Force at Gallipoli (from 29 September 1915), and in France and Flanders from 24 March 1916: apptd. L/Corpl. 9 October 1916. Killed in action, 20 September 1917. Age 21. *unm.* (*IWGC record 19626*)

(Panel 23) Pte. 5803, Harry Thomas Hockley, 18th Bn. Australian Infantry, A.I.F.: *s.* of Henry Hockley, of Harmondsworth, co. Middlesex, by his wife Elizabeth: and elder brother to Sergt. B/767, L.C. Hockley, 8th Rifle Brigade, died 27 July 1916. Killed in action, 20 September 1917. Age 31.

His brother Leonard is buried in Cabaret-Rouge British Cemetery, Souchez (XXX.D.9).

(Panel 23) Pte. 4537, John Edward Simms, 18th Bn. Australian Infantry, A.I.F.: eldest *survg. s.* of the late David Simms, M.I.C.E., by his wife Antonia (Moorlands, Bainbridge, co. Devon), *dau.* of the late Edward Rowan, Commander R.N.: *b.* Thurso, Canada, 29 September 1874: *educ.* Harmosa School, Ealing: went to Australia 1896, settled Sydney, as Mechanical Engineer: joined Australian Imperial Force, November 1915: returned to England with his regiment, April 1916: served with the Expeditionary Force in France and Flanders from July following: invalided home, January 1917, suffering from the effects of an accident while on active service: rejoined his regiment August following, and was killed in action in Northern Flanders, 20 September 1917. Buried where he fell. Age 41. *unm.*

(Panel 23) Pte. 2220, William Yole, 18th Bn. Australian Infantry, A.I.F.: *s.* of the late Elizabeth Ann Yole (Malmsbury, Castlemaine, Victoria): *b.* Malmsbury, *c.*1894: Religion – Methodist: Occupation – Labourer: joined A.I.F., Liverpool, New South Wales, 9 July 1915: 5′5″ tall, fresh complexion, blue eyes, fair hair: posted 4th Rfts., 18th Battn., 23 August: served with the Expeditionary Force in France and Flanders from 25 March 1916: wounded (bomb fragments; Rt. thigh, shoulder, arm) while taking part in a raid on the German trenches nr. Bois Grenier on the night of 26–27 June 1916; admitted 8th C.C.S., transf'd. No.22 Australian Hospital, Wimereux (27 June): rejoined 18th Bn. In the Field, 6 August following, and was killed in action at Zillebeke Bund, 24 September 1916. Age 22. *unm.* Remains recovered, identified – Clothing, Disc (reverse inscribed 'Mother, Yole, Malmsbury via Castlemaine, Victoria'); reinterred, registered 5 October 1928. All correspondence should be addressed c/o his sister Mrs M.M. Clark, c/o Boddy Bros, Malmsbury. *Buried in Sanctuary Wood Cemetery (II.L.17).*

(Panel 23) Pte. 4672, Edwin 'Edward' Bunyan, 19th Bn. Australian Infantry, A.I.F.: 7th *s.* (10th child) of William Bunyan, of Emu Plains, New South Wales, by his wife Sarah Ann, *née* Poll: *b.* Emu Plains, 3 October 1891: *educ.* Public School, there: after leaving school was a Grocer's Assistant: enlisted Casula, 27 January 1916, with his brother Pte. 4673, I. Bunyan, 19th A.I.F., died of wounds, 11 May 1917, and cousin Pte. 1989, L.V. Poll, 36th A.I.F., killed in action, 3 October 1917: posted 12th Rfts., 19th Battn.: departed Australia aboard A40, HMAT 'Ceramic,' 4 April 1916, arriving Alexandria, Egypt, 29 May 1916: departed there aboard HMAT 'Megantic,' arriving Portsmouth, England, 7 June following. After several months training on Salisbury Plain (No.5 Training Battn.), he went to France where he joined his unit on the Somme; September 1916. Between 14–16 November 19th Battn. attacked the enemy near Flers in conditions which Charles Bean described as the worst ever encountered by the A.I.F. In January 1917 he was attached to the Lewis Gun School and, during his time there, was awarded 10 days forfeiture of pay for being found out of bounds at the English Bar, Cucq. In 1917 the battalion was involved in the following-up of the enemy forces after their withdrawal to the Hindenburg Line; also took part in the 2nd Battle of Bullecourt 3–4 May 1917. In August, Edwin was attached to the Corps School as batman for a short time, after which he enjoyed a period of leave in England before returning to the Front where he was attached to the Bomb School, again, as a batman. Rejoined his battalion in the Ypres salient, late September 1917, at the Battle of Passchendaele; on 8 October following he became one of the 310,000 casualties suffered by the British Expeditionary Force during this battle. *The Nepean Times*, 24 November 1917:– "Our Soldiers: But a few months ago we had to chronicle with deep regret the sad news of the death of wounds received in action of Private Irwin Bunyan, of Emu Plains; and it is now our very sad duty to have to record the death of his (Private I. Bunyan's) brother, Edward Bunyan, seventh son of Mr and Mrs W. Bunyan, of Emu Plains who – per advices from the Base Records Department – was killed in action recently on the Western Front. Only meagre particulars are to hand so far, and the bereaved parents and family are not yet informed as to details of the gallant young hero's death. Deceased, was a native of Emu Plains and attended the Public School there in his boyhood, enlisted with his late brother (Private I. Bunyan) and two cousins on 27th January 1916. Prior to enlistment he had been in the employ of Mr A. Chapple, Emu Plains, for some six years, and was a young fellow of the most kindly and genial disposition, and of the best repute. He was an enthusiastic lover of sports, a keen cricketer and footballer, and a good rifle shot. On the eve of leaving for the seat of war, April 1916, he was presented with a money belt and other mementoes by the people of Emu Plains, and also a safety razor and pocket-book by Mr A. Chapple. He sailed for the Front on 14th April 1916 and, after several months training at Salisbury Plains, England, was sent to the Australian sector of the Western Front, and spent his 26th birthday (3 October 1916) in the trenches. At the time of his demise Private E. Bunyan was, we understand, a despatch runner, and had many close calls in that perilous duty. We publish the following lines forwarded by the parents of the deceased soldier in connection with their two sons' heroic deaths :

Two brothers from our sunny shore –
Two brothers, young and brave –
Sailed to the stormy seat of war,

And one the other went before
To fill a hero's grave
Then the other, loyal and true
Cried out, 'Come clasp my hand,
I cannot return without you
To our sunny southern land.',
So he too, paid the hero's debt,
And so his valiant brother met
In God's Immortal Band."

His brother Irwin is buried in Boulogne Eastern Cemetery (IV.B.19), Leslie Poll has no known grave, he is recorded on Panel 25.

(Panel 23) Pte. 6651, William Clarence Curry, 19th Bn. Australian Infantry, A.I.F.: *s.* of Ralph (& Mrs E.R.) Curry, of 38, The Avenue, Strathfield, New South Wales: and brother to Spr. 1891, F. Curry, Australian Engineers, who fell three days previously: *b.* Balmain, Sydney, 1897: Religion – Methodist: Occupation – Apprentice Electrical Engineer: joined A.I.F., Victoria Barracks, Sydney, 17 December 1916; proceeded overseas, 7 February 1917: joined 19th Battn., France, 1 August 1917. Killed in action, 7 October 1917. Age 19.

His brother Frank also has no known grave; he is recorded on Panel 7.

(Panel 23) Pte. 3806, Wilton Campbell Gamack, 19th Bn. Australian Infantry, A.I.F.: *s.* of James E. Gamack, of Kempsey, New South Wales, by his wife Mary Elizabeth: and brother to Pte. 4354, A.B. Gamack, 20th A.I.F. (ret'd. Australia, September 1916); and Pte. 2306, B.M. Gamack, 36th A.I.F., who fell, 21 July 1917: *b.* Port Macquarie, New South Wales, *c.*1895. Killed in action, 6 November 1917. Age 22.

His brother Bruce also has no known grave; he is recorded on Panel 25.

(Panel 23) Corpl. 5461, Alfred John Maurice Chauncy, 'B' Coy., 20th Bn. Australian Infantry, A.I.F.: *s.* of William Chauncy, of Mangain, Coolamon, New South Wales, by his wife Rebecca: and brother to L/ Corpl. 842, O.C. Chauncy, 'C' Coy., 20th Battn. (surv'd.), and Corpl. 1736, P.H. Chauncy, 4th Battn. who, after being taken prisoner of war at Demicourt, 15 April 1917, was repatriated to Australia, 24 April 1919: *b.* Dullah, Coolamon, 1887: Religion – Church of England: Occupation – Surveyor: 5'8½" tall; blue eyes, red hair: prior to enlistment served 2 years, 38th Australian Citizen Force: enlisted Royal Agricultural Show Grounds, Moore Park, 29 February 1916: departed Sydney, aboard A.18 'Wiltshire,' 22 August: served with the Expeditionary Force in France and Flanders from 17 December 1916, and was reported wounded and missing in action, 9 October 1917. Age 30. *unm.* Subsequently recorded by a Court of Enquiry as wounded and killed by concussion at about 8.30 a.m. on the morning of the aforementioned date, when the pillbox in which he was sheltering with six other men was hit by heavy shellfire. All seven men are believed to be buried together.

(Panel 23) Corpl. 6614, Ernest James Harris, 20th Bn. Australian Infantry, A.I.F.: *s.* of Jesse James Harris, of 'Clarence,' Minter Street, Canterbury, New South Wales, by his wife Annie Gertrude: and brother to Pte. 2681, W.J. Harris, 53rd Australian Infantry (surv'd.): *b.* Redfern, Sydney, 1895: Religion – Roman Catholic: Occupation – Driver: 5'6" tall, hazel eyes, light brown hair: previously rejected for service with Citizen Force (Medically Unfit), joined A.I.F., Casula, 16 January 1916: Reported to Medical Officer, Sick – Sprained Ankle, 2 April 1916; subsequently fined 5/- for 'Absence from Guard Duty': Discharged (Services No Longer Required – Medically Unfit; Chronic Bronchitis aggravated by excessive cigarette smoking) 28 July; joined Home Defence following day: re-enlisted A.I.F., Liverpool, New South Wales, 13 December, posted 13th Reinforcements: departed Sydney, 8 February 1917: trained England, 11 April–9 October (transf'd. 19th Rfts., 20th Bn., 27 April; promoted Corpl. 27 August): joined 20th Battn. in France, 15 October 1917; killed in action at Anzac Ridge, Ypres 6 November following. Age 20. See Pte. E.O. Neaves, below.

On 26 May 1927, the Imperial War Graves Commission, London issued the following statement to the Australian Graves Services: "I am directed to inform you that in accordance with the agreement of the French and Belgian Governments to remove all scattered graves, and certain cemeteries which were situated in places unsuitable for permanent retention, it has been found necessary to exhume the bodies buried in certain areas. In the process of exhumation the remains of the soldiers named on the attached Location Sheet were located as noted below each name, and their remains were re-interred in the Cemeteries as stated. Will you please inform the next of kin that the necessity for the removal is much regretted, but was unavoidable for the reasons above given; and you may give them every assurance that the work of re-burial has been carried out carefully and reverently. Signed, Principal Assistant Secretary." One of the soldiers named:-

(Panel 23) Pte. 4369, Daniel Baccus, 'B' Coy., 20th Bn. Australian Infantry, A.I.F.: *b*. Lambton, Newcastle, New South Wales, 1885: Occupation – Labourer: joined A.I.F., West Maitland, 2 November 1915: posted 20th Battn., Casula, 17 December: departed Sydney, 9 April 1916: served with the Expeditionary Force in France and Flanders from 6 September; joined 20th Battn. in Belgium on the 18th of that month: hospitalised (Trench foot – severe), 17 November–5 December 1916; rejoined battalion, 2 May 1917: hospitalised (P.U.O.) 14–27 June; rejoined battalion, 14 August, and was killed in action, 20 September 1917. Age 32. He leaves a wife, Ethel May Baccus (141, Kippax Street, Surry Hills, New South Wales), and *s*. Arthur. G.R.U. Report, Zillebeke, 5.76E, records remains recovered (identified by Disc: 4369, D. Baccus, 20th A.I.F.) exhumed 28.J.2.b.2.2., at a point about 1 mile N.N.E. of Westhoek, and re-interred May 1927. *Buried in Sanctuary Wood Cemetery (IV.C.34)*. The Location Sheet recorded three names, the other two soldiers – Pte. 84, James Maffersoni, 18th Australian Infantry, killed in action, 27 July 1916 (exhumed in the vicinity of Pozieres) and Pte. 779, Ernest H. Haddrick, 2nd Australian Machine Gun Corps, killed in action, 2 September 1918 (exhumed about 1 mile E of Ablaincourt) – were reburied in Serre Road Cemetery No.2 (IV.J.4) and Peronne Communal Cemetery Extension (V.A.3) respectively. (Pte. Haddrick's brother, Ethelbert, also fell – killed in action at Gallipoli, 25 April 1915 – he is commemorated on the Lone Pine Memorial.)

(Panel 23) Pte. 5625, Erle Oakley Neaves, 'A' Coy., 20th Bn. Australian Infantry, AI.F.: *s*. of Henry Neaves, of 33, Arona Avenue, Glebe Point, Sydney, by his wife Emma: and yr. brother to Pte. 1578, H.C. Neaves, 19th Australian Infantry, killed in action, 14 November 1916, aged 31 years. Killed in action, 6 November 1917. Sergt. 4245, H.A. Piggin wrote, "I knew Neaves, his initials were E.O., and he was in A Company, 4th Platoon, under me. He was rather tall, fair, and came from Potts Point way. He joined the battalion with the 18th Reinforcements. He was in a dugout with a Corpl. Harris and six others between Zonnebeke and Polygon Wood, early in November 1917. A shell exploded in their dugout, having glanced off a concrete pill-box killing Harris and Neaves instantly, and wounding the others. I helped bury Neaves and Harris near where they fell, and am certain they died without suffering. A cross was erected on their grave." Age 26.

His brother Harry also has no known grave; he is commemorated on the Villers-Bretonneux Memorial.

(Panel 23) Pte. 5103, Fred Travis, 20th Bn. Australian Infantry, A.I.F.: *s*. of Henry Travis, of 214, West Street, Crow's Nest, North Sydney, New South Wales, by his wife Ada: and yr. brother to Pte. 6830, H.T. Travis, 7th A.I.F., who fell four days previously: *b*. Richmond, New South Wales, *c*.1896. Killed in action, 8 October 1917. Age 21. *unm*.

His brother Harry also has no known grave; he is recorded on Panel 7.

(Panel 23) Lieut. Frank Rigby, 'C' Coy., 21st Bn. Australian Infantry, A.I.F.: *s*. of Thomas Rigby, of 'Hybla,' Pallamallawa, New South Wales, late of Telangatuk East, Lowan, Victoria, by his wife Martha: and *yr*. brother to Lieut. J.S.T. Rigby, M.M., 21st Battn., who fell the same day: *b*. Telangatuk East, 1891: Religion – Presbyterian: Occupation – Labourer: 5'9" tall, blue eyes, brown hair: a member of Rifle Club No.6, Balmoral, Victoria; enlisted Balmoral, 9 January 1915: posted 21st Battn., Broadmeadows, 4 May 1915: departed Melbourne aboard H.M.A.T. 'Ulysses,' 8 May: served at Gallipoli (from 29 August); Egypt (7 January–19 March 1916); and in France and Flanders from 26 March 1916: hospitalised – Injury, Left elbow – 2 July (evacuated, England, 11 July), and, after a period with 6th Training Battn. (from 25 September), returned to France on 13 November, rejoining his battn. on the 22nd of that month: apptd. L/Corpl. 1 December 1916: returned to England for training with No.5 Officer's Cadet Battn.,

Trinity College, Cambridge from whence he was gazetted 2nd Lieut. 1 May 1917: returned to France, 15 May, rejoining 21st Battn. In the Field on the 18th of that month: promoted Lieut. 1 September 1917, and was killed in action, 4 October following, during the attack at Broodseinde Ridge. Age 26. *unm.* In response to a request made by Mr and Mrs Rigby to the Australian Graves Services (February 1920), that if and when their sons' graves were found they be re-interred beside one another, the following reply (January 1921) was received, "… All enquiries have so far failed to locate the graves…Every effort is being made in this connection and as the vicinity in which they fell is being re-searched by Graves registration Units there is still a slight possibility of their remains being identified. As soon as any definite information is received you will be advised." No further information followed; neither grave was located.

His brother John also has no known grave; he is recorded below.

(Panel 23) Lieut. 1548, John Samuel Thompson Rigby, M.M., 21st Bn. Australian Infantry, A.I.F.: *s.* of Thomas Rigby, of 'Hybla,' Pallamallawa, New South Wales, late of Telangatuk East, Lowan, Victoria, by his wife Martha: and elder brother to Lieut. F. Rigby, 21st Battn., who fell the same day: *b.* Coleraine, Dundas, Victoria, 1888: Religion – Presbyterian: Occupation – Saw Miller: member of Rifle Club No.6, Balmoral, Victoria: 5′5¾″ tall, blue eyes, dark hair: enlisted Balmoral, 5 March 1915: posted 1st Rfts., 23rd Battn., Broadmeadows, 4 May 1915: departed Melbourne, H.M.A.T. 'Euripides,' 10 May: transf'd. 21st Battn. 26 August: served at Gallipoli (from 29 August), promoted Corpl. 28 November; Egypt (January–March 1916), and in France and Flanders from 26 March 1916: transf'd. 6th Australian Light Trench Mortar Bty., 15 April; promoted Sergt. 12 August 1916: returned 21st Batn. 11 May 1917; gazetted 2nd Lieut. 13 May: on leave (England), 21 August–3 September: promoted Lieut. 12 September, and was killed in action, 4 October 1917. Age 29. *unm.* Buried Sunken Road, D.29.a.9.3.(Sheet 28.N.E.). Awarded the Military Medal (*London Gazette*, 19 September 1916), for 'gallantry in the field during operations at Pozieres, 15 August 1916,' on forwarding the medal (28 June 1918) to Lieut. Rigby's parents, an officer wrote, "It is with feelings of admiration at the gallantry of a brave Australian soldier who nobly laid down his life in the service of our King and Country, that I am directed by the Honourable Minister to forward to you, as the next-of-kin of the late Lieutenant J.S.T. Rigby, 21st Battalion, Australian Imperial Force, the Military Medal which His Majesty the King has been graciously pleased to award to that gallant soldier for conspicuous bravery and devotion to duty while serving with the Australian Imperial Expeditionary Force. I am also to ask you to accept his deep personal sympathy in the loss which, not only you but, the Australian Army has sustained by the death of Lieutenant J.S.T. Rigby whose magnificent conduct on the field of battle helped to earn for our Australian soldiers a fame which will endure as long as memory lasts…" In February 1920, Mr and Mrs Rigby requested the Australian Graves Services, that if and when their sons graves were found they be re-interred beside one another; neither grave was located. See account Reninghelst New Military Cemetery; Capt. J.R. Eddy (IV.C.4).

His brother Frank also has no known grave; he is recorded above.

(Panel 23) 2nd Lieut. 869, Thomas Frank Heraud, D.C.M., 'D' Coy., 21st Bn. Australian Infantry, A.I.F.: *s.* of Thomas Heraud, of 88, Perry Street, Collingwood, Victoria, by his wife Elizabeth: *b.* Brunswick, Melbourne, 1894: Religion – Presbyterian: Occupation – Grocer: 5′6″ tall, hazel eyes, dark brown hair: enlisted Melbourne, Victoria, 1 February 1915: posted 'D' Coy., 21st Battn., Broadmeadows, 4 May: departed Melbourne, H.M.A.T. 'Ulysses,' 8 May 1915: apptd. Corpl. 20 October 1915; promoted L/Sergt. 5 February 1916; Sergt. 1 August following: served at Gallipoli, Egypt, and with the Expeditionary Force in France from 26 March 1916: attended Officer's Training, Pembroke College, Cambridge, 5 May–8 August 1917: gazetted 2nd Lieut. 31 August: returned to France, 14 September 1917; joined 21st Battn. In the Field on the 20th of that month. Reported wounded, 4 October 1917, since confirmed (8 November) killed in action. Age 23. *unm.* Buried east of Zonnebeke Lake, D.28.b.05. (Sheet 28.N.E.). Capt. (Adjt.) F.P. Sellick, 24th Battn., recorded, "On the morning of the 4th October '17 Broodseinde stunt, at about 6 a.m., Lieut. Heraud was wounded on the tape near Zonnebeke Church and was killed on a stretcher whilst being carried out. Buried in the cemetery Menin Road, near Ypres, by Lieut. G. Dearden, 21st Battn." He was awarded the Distinguished Conduct Medal (*London Gazette*, No.29765, 26 September 1916) 'For conspicuous gallantry when commanding bomb carriers in action at

Pozieres, 2 September 1916. By his pluck and determination he kept up the supply in the front line, where bombs were urgently needed. Also, on his return trips, he helped to evacuate the wounded although he was himself shaken by a shell explosion.' See account Reninghelst New Military Cemetery; Capt. J.R. Eddy (IV.C.4).

(Panel 23) L/Corpl. 2609, Mervyn John Cook, 21st Bn. Australian Infantry, A.I.F.: *s*. of John Cook, by his wife Jessie. Killed outright by the bursting of a shell during the attack on Broodseinde, 4 October 1917. Age 21. See Buttes New British Cemetery (Polygon Wood); Pte. A. O'Brien (XXVIII.A.16), and Pte. J.A. Pryke (XXVIII.A.18).

(Panel 23) Pte. 833, Henry James Dietrich, 'D' Coy., 21st Bn. Australian Infantry, A.I.F.: *s*. of Frances Dietrich, widow (14, John Street East, Brunswick, Melbourne); late of 324, Rathdown Street, Carlton: and brother to Corpl. 5673, F. Dietrich, 60th Battn. (surv'd.); and Gnr. 960, A. Dietrich, 5th Bde. Australian Field Artillery (surv'd.): *b*. Jeeralang, Morwell, Victoria, 24 March 1897: Religion – Presbyterian: *educ*. Jeeralang State School: Occupation – Farm Hand: 5'10" tall, grey eyes, black hair: enlisted (with parental consent) Morwell, 24 March 1915 (his eighteenth birthday); posted 21st Battn., Broadmeadows, 4 May: proceeded to join Mediterranean Expeditionary Force, Gallipoli, 29 August 1915: served Egypt (January–March 1916) thereafter proceeded to join the Expeditionary Force in France; served there from 26 March 1916: wounded (G.S.W. back, slight) 30 July, evacuated to Wimereux thence to England: Awarded 2 Days Confined to Barracks, 'Being unshaven on parade,' 23 January 1917: returned to France following convalescence and leave, 3 February 1917, rejoined his battalion on the 8th: wounded (G.S.W. Lt. ear) 5 May, returned to duty, 13 May: hospitalised (synovitis, Rt. knee) 31 May: discharged to duty, 11 June; hospitalised (hypertrophy of bone, contusion Rt. knee), 28 June: rejoined 21st Battn. 7 September, and was killed in action, 21 October 1917, at Broodesinde. Age 20. His Memorial Scroll was inadvertently received by Mrs DeVoogd, of Eaglehawk (13 July 1921), who not only acknowledged its receipt but retained in her keeping a memento clearly intended for the mother of Pte. Dietrich in respect of her son's services in the Australian Imperial Force. While of no intrinsic worth, these items possessed a value considerably enhanced by sentiment and propriety interest and could not be duplicated or replaced. Returned in September 1921, it was received by Mrs Dietrich in October. Pte. H.J. DeVoogd, 51st Battalion A.I.F., his remains, recovered in July 1920, are buried in Tyne Cot Cemetery (XXXV.G.18).

(Panel 23) Pte. 7270, William Carlton Murray, 21st Bn. Australian Infantry, A.I.F.: late of 47, Stanley Street, Richmond, Victoria: *s*. of Alexander James Murray, by his wife Jane: and brother to Police Sergt. John Murray, of 14, O'Grady Street, West Brunswick, Coburg, N.10.: *b*. Carlton, March 1895: Religion – Roman Catholic: Occupation – Butcher: 5'6½" tall, blue eyes, brown hair: enlisted Melbourne 18 December 1916: posted 24th Rfts., 6th Battn., Royal Park 27 January 1917: departed Melbourne, H.M.A.T. A.70 'Ballarat,' 19 February: trained Durrington Camp, England, April–August 1917: served with the Expeditionary Force in France from 21 August; transf'd 21st Bn. 1 September following. Reported missing believed killed in action, 4 November 1917. Age 22. Remains recovered, 14 March 1930 (28.D.28.a.20.10, Sheet 28,N.E.), identified by effects (including Shoulder Title, Wallet and Dentures) found at the time, and re-interred 28.N.10.b.3.7, Kemmel, October following. In December 1930 his widow Elizabeth Murray (now Mrs Fred J. Humphries, 36, Coburg Street, Coburg, N.13, Victoria), received the following notification from the Officer I/C, Base Records – "With reference to the demise of the late No.7270, Pte. W.C. Murray, 21st Battn., I am now in receipt of advice that during the course of exhumation work in the vicinity of Zonnebeke, the Imperial War Graves Commission were successful in recovering the remains of this soldier which have since been interred with every measure of care and reverence in Plot 1, Row 'B,' Grave 26, of Kemmel No. 1 French Cemetery, Belgium where a permanent headstone of uniform design will be erected and engraved with his full regimental description and date of death, together with any verse or epitaph previously selected in the form of a personal inscription. It is the practice of the Commission to notify relatives direct when the headstones are finally in position, and at a later date the opportunity will be afforded you of obtaining a copy of the printed Register containing full particulars of all British and Dominion war graves in the above named Cemetery. The following personal effects were found at the time, and have since been returned for disposal: (silver) Disc – engraved 'To

W.E. Murray from Residents of Mordialloc, 1917;' Gold Signet Ring – inscribed 'W.E.M.;' Small (lady's) Silver Watch (damaged) – engraved: 'W. Murray, Sept 21st 1916.' A wallet and dentures were also found. *Buried in Kemmel No.1 French Cemetery (I.B.26)*.

(Panel 23) Lieut. 1694, Frank Gerald Kellaway, M.C., 'B' Coy., 22nd Bn. Australian Infantry, A.I.F.: *s*. of the late Rev. Alfred Charles Kellaway, of 56, Cunningham Street, Northcote, Victoria, by his wife Annie Carrick: and brother to Major C.H. Kellaway, M.C., A.A.M.C. (surv'd): *b*. East Melbourne, 1895: Religion – Church of England: *educ*. Melbourne University, where he studied Law, and was a member of the University Rifles: 5'6¾" tall, blue eyes, brown hair: enlisted Melbourne, 6 May 1915: posted 22nd Battn. Seymour, 17 June 1915: served at Gallipoli; Egypt (January–March 1916); and with the Expeditionary Force in France from 4 May: wounded (shell shock), and hospitalised, 25 June–1 July: gazetted 2nd Lieut. 2 August 1916: wounded (G.S.W. through upper third left forearm), 5 August, Pozieres, and evacuated to England (14 August) where, following treatment for a compound fracture of the ulna and radius, he was awarded the Military Cross (*London Gazette*, No.29765, 26 September 1916) 'For conspicuous gallantry during the recent fighting at Pozieres, 2 September 1916. When the officers of his company had become casualties he rallied his men, led them in the assault and made good the ground gained.': discharged to duty, 3 October, returned to France and rejoined 22nd Battn. on the 14th of that month: promoted Lieut. 22 November 1916: seconded to 6th Training Battn., Larkhill, April–August 1917, during the course of which he attended a course of instruction at 3.6 Gas School, Porton Down, (2–9 June) and qualified as Instructor: proceeded to France, 30 August where he rejoined his battn. in the field two days later. Reported missing, 4 October 1917, since concluded by a Court of Enquiry (24 June 1918) to have been killed in action on the aforementioned date. Age 22. *unm*. Chaplain G.W. Lamble, 21st Battn., said, "On the 4th of October I was on duty at the Dressing Station on the Menin Road, where all the wounded from the 6th Brigade were coming through. Amongst the personal friends, I asked after Lieut. Kellaway's welfare and was told by various N.C.O's and men that he was killed early in the fight...I did not take the names of my informants nor remember who they were, but they were quite confident as to the accuracy of their information. Later I asked a Company Commander of the 22nd (to the best of my knowledge it was Capt. Brenning) and he told me that he was with Lieut. Callaway at the jumping off tape, and early in the attack he left him for a few minutes to attend to some duty 15 or 20 yards away. Heavy shelling occurred there in the interval and when he returned there was no trace of Lieut. Kellaway whatsoever; of whose death he was confident." See account Reninghelst New Military Cemetery; Capt. J.R. Eddy (IV.C.4).

(Panel 23) Sergt. 295, John Charles Bailes, 22nd Bn. Australian Infantry, A.I.F.: promoted Sergt. July 1917. Missing believed killed in action, 21–22 September 1917. Referred to in account re. Corpl. W.N. Ralston, 22nd Battn.; Buffs Road Cemetery (EE.66).

(Panel 23) Sergt. 5963, William Dalton, 'A' Coy., 11 Platoon, 22nd Bn. Australian Infantry, A.I.F.: late of 17, Coburg Street, Victoria: *s*. of the late John Dalton, Brewery Labourer; of Tadcaster, Leeds, by his wife Jane, *née* Simpson: *b*. Tockwith, co. York, February 1883: Religion – Church of England: 5'7½" tall, blue eyes, brown hair: Occupation – Soldier; previously served 14 years (3½ on Instruction Staff) King's Own Scottish Borderers (India), and in the South African Campaign against the Boers, 1899–1902 (Queen's & King's Medals); and in the hinterland (1902–05): removed to Australia; applied for a commission Army Service Corps, A.M.F., 24 January 1916: joined A.I.F. Melbourne, 5 September 1916; posted 16th Rfts., 22nd Battn. Royal Park, 12 September: departed Melbourne aboard A71 'Nestor,' 2 October: underwent training Lark Hill, November 1916–February 1917: apptd. A/Sergt. 17 November 1916; reverted Pte. 5 February 1917, on arrival in France: trained Etaples, thereafter joined 22nd Battn. In the Field, 23 February: apptd. L/Corpl. 1 March; promoted Corpl. 25 March: wounded (G.S.W. chest, right arm, left thigh, face), 20 April and evacuated, via Boulogne, to Norfolk War Hospital, Thorpe, from whence he was discharged to Perham Downs Training Camp, 20 May: reprimanded by Lieut. W. Crampton and awarded two days forfeiture of pay (9 June), for being Absent Without Leave, 7–8 June: promoted L/Sergt. 20 June; rejoined his battn. in France the following day: promoted Sergt. 20 July (Actg. Coy.Sergt.Major, 27 July and 28 August), and was killed in action, 3 October 1917. Age 34. On the day of his death, Sergt. Dalton and several other men, after burying and noting the graves of a number of the fallen nearby, were resting in Muhle Trench when a shell landed in the trench killing him, Lieut. Moore (23rd Battn.), and seven or eight of the other men instantaneously. Buried with the other men just behind the line after dark, an upturned rifle placed over the grave to mark the spot; Capt. W.H. Bunning, 'A'Coy., conducted the funeral. GRU Report Zillebeke, 50.150.C. refers Memorial Cross erected – Perth (China Wall) Military Cemetery, Plot 6, Row M – to Sergt. W. Dalton. Also Pte. J. Bradshaw (50.132/C), Spr. A.H. Darvall (50.134/C), and Pte. S.G. Edwards (50.145/C). Sergt. Dalton was married with one child Elsie, to Isabella Dalton (Dalchalm, Brora, co. Sutherland, Scotland), late of 23, Little O'Grady Street, Albert Park, Victoria; Mrs Dalton received his effects – Photo, Medical Card, 2 Discs, Notebook, Pipe, Pouch, Letters, Holdall containing shaving kit – May 1918. Pte. Bradshaw and Spr. Darvall are recorded on Panel 7; Pte. Edwards (Addenda Panel 59).

(Panel 23) L/Sergt. 1926, John Joseph Lowery, 22nd Bn. Australian Infantry, A.I.F.: *s.* of the late Thomas William Lowery, by his wife Mary Ann: *b.* Bendigo, 1897. Killed in action at Broodseinde Ridge, 5 October 1917. Age 20. *unm.* Ptes. 1734, L.B. Stringer and 4180, B.R. O'Meara, were beside Sergt. Lowery when, whilst consolidating their position on Broodseinde Ridge, he was shot through the head by a sniper; death being instantaneous. Both men later helped to bury him. Memorial Cross erected – 28.D.27.a.8.3 – to L/Sergt. J.J. Lowery, Pte. C.W. Mays, T. Montefiore, A.V. Thompson, A.T. Grigsby, and Corpl. W.N. Ralston – White House Cemetery, Plot 3, Row T., refers GRU Report St. Jean 165.c. Ptes. C.W. Mays and T. Montefiore also have no known grave, their names are recorded below; Pte. A.V. Thompson is buried in Aeroplane Cemetery, A.T. Grigsby in La Laiterie Military Cemetery (I.D.11), and Corpl Ralston, Buffs Road Cemetery (EE.66).

(Panel 23) Pte. 4552, Arnold Ernest Jones (served as St. Leon), No.2 Platoon, 'A' Coy., 22nd Bn. Australian Infantry, A.I.F.: *s.* of William Jones, of 44, Canterbury Road, Middle Park, Victoria, by his wife Elizabeth: *b.* Wagga Wagga, New South Wales, *c.*1881. Missing believed killed in action, 22–23 September 1917. Age 36. Sergt. 3785, A.H. Butterworth wrote, "I saw Arnold St. Leon killed instantly by a 5.9 shell at Ypres, in front of Zonnebeke Lake, early in the morning. We were in support and the shell lobbed over and only killed St. Lion. The man on either side of him was not hit. I helped to dig him out. We put him into a waterproof sheet and buried him where he was killed." Stretcher-bearers Podmore and Adcock assisted in the burial and later reported, "He was rather badly hit in the head and other parts. He was not buried in a cemetery, but on the battlefield near to where he fell, at Westhoek Ridge, and had a decent burial. The grave may be found by a little tin nailed to the cross with his name and number inside of it. There were several others buried just about him. Let his relatives know he died a soldier fighting for his country." Remains recovered from an unmarked grave (28.J.2.d.7.2) 24 February 1927; identified – Clothing; reinterred, registered 26 February 1927. *Buried in Sanctuary Wood Cemetery (III.G.30).*

Farewell My Darling Son My Best Beloved Farewell

(Panel 23) Pte. 5636, Charles Wolfenden Mays, 'A' Coy., 22nd Bn. Australian Infantry, A.I.F.: *s.* of Robert Wolfenden Mays, by his wife Matilda Bradley: *b.* Victoria, 1889. Killed in action at Broodseinde Ridge, 4 October 1917. Age 28. Signlr. 5783, A.E. Phillips, 22nd Battn., reported Charles Mays killed at about 6 a.m., on October 4th, during a large advance by several Divisions against the German lines in front of Polygon Wood, about 5 miles east of Ypres: Memorial Cross erected – 28.D.27.a.8.3 – to L/Sergt. J.J. Lowery, Pte. C.W. Mays, T. Montefiore, A.V. Thompson, A.T. Grigsby, and Corpl. W.N. Ralston – White House Cemetery, Plot 3 Row T., refers GRU Report St. Jean 165.c. Pte. Mays was married to Mrs Ellen Ashmore, *née* Mays (Healesville, Victoria). L/Sergt. J.J. Lowery (above) and Pte. T. Montefiore (below) also have no known grave; Pte. A.V. Thompson is buried in Aeroplane Cemetery; A.T. Grigsby, La Laiterie Military Cemetery (I.D.11), and Corpl. Ralston, Buffs Road Cemetery (EE.66).

(Panel 23) Pte. 6396, Tasman Montefiore, 'A' Coy., 22nd Bn. Australian Infantry, A.I.F.: Killed in action at Broodseinde Ridge, 5 October 1917. Pte. 6346, M.W. Fisher, wrote, "On October 5th at Westhoek Ridge, on the morning after we had taken the objective at early dawn, he was killed by a shell. I was about 30 or 40 yards away and from the state of the wounds I am sure he was killed instantly. He was buried by myself and some others behind the trench, in the open, somewhere on Westhoek Ridge. We placed his rifle upside down and fastened his disc to it to mark the spot. It is impossible to describe the position as when we returned after the bombardment I hardly knew the ground, it having been so much torn up. He was short, thick-set, dark, clean shaven, and all his front teeth were artificial. He had a full face and we used to call him Monty. He was very popular and quite a good sportsman." Memorial Cross erected – 28.D.27.a.8.3 – to L/Sergt. J.J. Lowery, Pte. C.W. Mays, T. Montefiore, A.V. Thompson, A.T. Grigsby, and Corpl. W.N. Ralston – White House Cemetery, Plot 3 Row T., refers GRU Report St. Jean 165.c. L/Sergt. J.J. Lowery and Pte. C.W. Mays also have no known grave, their names are recorded above; Pte. A.V. Thompson is buried in Aeroplane Cemetery, A.T. Grigsby in La Laiterie Military Cemetery (I.D.11), and Corpl Ralston, Buffs Road Cemetery (EE.66).

(Panel 23) Pte. 6427, William Penny, 22nd Bn. Australian Infantry, A.I.F.: *s.* of Albert Penny, of 12, Florence Street, Mentone, Victoria, by his wife Mary. Missing, believed killed by shellfire, 22–23 September 1917; since verified as having been killed by the same shell that killed Pte. 63, H.E. Wright and 663A, W.H. Stephens. Age 26. *unm.* Remains recovered from an unmarked grave (28.J.2.d.7.2), 24 February 1927; identified – Disc, Silver Plate; reinterred, registered 26 February 1927. *Buried in Sanctuary Wood Cemetery (III.G.28).*

In Loving Memory Of My Dear Son "Will"

(Panel 23) Pte. 2041, David Heathcote Robertson, 22nd Bn. Australian Infantry, A.I.F.: *s.* of James Robertson, of 505, Skipton Street, Ballarat, Victoria, by his wife Emma J.: *b.* Sebastopol, Victoria, *c.*1896: Missing/believed killed in action, 22–23 September 1917. Age 21. *unm.* Remains recovered from a grave marked up as belonging to an 'Unknown Australian Soldier' (28.J.2.d.7.2) 24 February 1927; identified – Clothing, Correspondence; reinterred, registered 26 February 1927. *Buried in Sanctuary Wood Cemetery (III.G.26).*

My Darling

(Panel 23) Pte. 663A, William Hudson Stephens, 22nd Bn. Australian Infantry, A.I.F.: *s.* of Joseph Stephens, of 43, Lincoln Street, North Richmond, Vitoria, by his wife Mary. Missing, believed killed in action, on or about 22 September 1917, whilst in support near Anzac Ridge, Zonnebeke; since verified as having been killed by the same shell that killed Pte. 63, H.E. Wright and 6427, W. Penny. Age 19. Remains recovered from a grave marked as belonging to an 'Unknown Australian Soldier' (28.J.2.d.7.2) 24 February 1927; identified – Clothing; reinterred, registered 26 February 1927. *Buried in Sanctuary Wood Cemetery (III.G.27).*

Dearly Loved Son Of Mr & Mrs Stephens
43, Lincoln St. N. Richmond

(Panel 23) Pte. 63, Harold Ernest Wright, 22nd Bn. Australian Infantry, A.I.F.: *s.* of Mary Wright, by her marriage to the late Ernest Henry Clifton Wright: *b.* Warrnambool, Victoria, *c.*1891. Killed in action near Anzac Ridge, Zonnebeke, by the same shell that killed Pte. 663A, W.H. Stephens and 6427, W. Penny, 22–23 September 1917. Age 26. *unm.* Remains recovered from an unmarked grave (28.J.2.d.7.2) 24 February 1927; identified – Disc; reinterred, registered 26 February 1927. *Buried in Sanctuary Wood Cemetery (III.G.29).*

(Panel 23) Lieut. Arthur Clarence Brewster, M.C., 23rd Bn. Australian Infantry, A.I.F.: late of 2, Lambert Grove, East St. Kilda: *s.* of Frank Brewster, Clergyman, of Romsey, Milburn Avenue, East St. Kilda, Victoria, by his wife Fanny: *b.* Grafton, New South Wales, 7 June 1888: Religion – Anglican: *educ.* Norwich Grammar School; Salford Technical College, Manchester: 5'7¼" tall, dark complexion, brown eyes, black hair: Occupation – Farmer: enlisted Melbourne, 16 July 1915, as Pte.; promoted Corpl. 31 August 1915; Sergt. 5 September: applied for and obtained a commission, 2nd Lieut. 16th Rfts. 23rd Battn. Royal Park, 31 August 1916: served with the Expeditionary Force in France and Flanders from 18 December 1916: promoted Lieut. 12 April 1917: slightly wounded, but remained at duty, 3 May 1917:

awarded the Military Cross for gallant conduct during the fighting at Messines, 7–9 June 1917, and was killed instantaneously by a H.E. shell just after going over the top at 6.30 a.m., 4 October 1917. Buried nr. Anzac House, about 200 yards below Zonnebeke Ridge. A cross was prepared at Battn. H.Q., Dickebusch, and put up over his grave by Sergt. N. Hill who assisted the company pioneers in the burial. See account re. Capt. J.R. Eddy, Reninghelst New Military Cemetery (IV.C.4). Remains recovered, refers to GRU Report 5-10E (28.D.27.d.50.75); identified – Clothing, Collar Badge, Dental Record; reinterred, registered March 1927. *Buried in Sanctuary Wood Cemetery (III.J.10).*

(Panel 23) 2nd Lieut. 3341, John Oliver Ethell, 23rd Bn. Australian Infantry, A.I.F.: *s.* of the Rev. Alfred William Ethell, of St. Saviour's Rectory, Laidley, Queensland, by his wife May Willett: and nephew to H.J. Shott, of 43, Cambria Place, New Swindon, co. Wilts: *b.* Kalk Bay, Cape Town, South Africa, 1896: Religion – Church of England: Occupation – School Teacher: volunteered, 13 August 1915, and enlisted Enoggera, Queensland 7 October: 5′9½″ tall, grey eyes, dark hair: posted 8th Field Coy. Australian Engineers, Melbourne, 8 November: served Egypt (December 1915–March 1916), and with the Expeditionary Force in France from 27 March 1916: hospitalised (Synovitis – Right Knee), 24 May and invalided to England – Northampton War Hospital (6 June 1916) – from whence, after convalescence and a period of training, he was discharged to duty (August) and returned to France, 25 September: rejoined 6th Field Coy. 10 September: gazetted 2nd Lieut. 3 April 1917, and transf'd. 23rd Battn. on the 8th of that month: wounded (G.S.W. both forearms and legs) Bullecourt, and admitted 3rd Casualty Clearing Station, 3 May 1917: transf'd. 2nd Red Cross Hospital, Rouen, 13 May and evacuated to England the following day: discharged to Perham Downs, 20 July 1917: returned to France, 21 August, rejoining 23rd Battn. In the Field on the 26th of that month, and was killed in action, 4 October 1917. Age 21. *unm.* His Commanding Officer wrote, "He was buried on the battlefield, close to Zonnebeke Lake, and a small temporary cross marks the position of his grave." G.R.U. Report, Zillebeke 50.135/C, records Memorial Cross, Plot 50, Perth Cemetery (China Wall). See account re. Capt. J.R. Eddy, Reninghelst New Military Cemetery (IV.C.4).

(Panel 23) 2nd Lieut. 4745, Norman John Moore, 23rd Bn. Australian Infantry, A.I.F.: late of Port Melbourne: *s.* of the late John Robinson Moore, Draper, of 60, Beaconsfield Parade, Albert Park, Victoria, by his wife Alice, *née* Tucker (64, Prospect Hill Road, Camberwell, Victoria): and elder brother to Coy.Sergt.Major, 789, A.R. Moore, 39th Bn. Australian Infantry, killed at Passchendaele, 12 October 1917, aged 22 years: *b.* Ballarat, Victoria, February 1890: Religion – Church of England: Occupation – Accountant: 5′8¾″ tall, blue eyes, brown hair: six months member of Elsternwick Rifle Club, Ripponlea; enlisted Melbourne, 25 August 1915: posted 24th Depot Battn., Royal Park; thereafter 12th Rfts., 23rd Battn., Broadmeadows, 1 April 1916: departed Melbourne, H.M.A.T. 'Euripides,' 4 April: served with the Expeditionary Force in France and Flanders from 17 November 1916: joined 23rd Battn. In the Field, 2 December following: apptd. Corpl. 27 February 1917; promoted Sergt. 5 March: attended No.2 Cadet Battn., Officer Training College, Cambridge, 5 May–31 August on which latter date he was apptd. 2nd Lieut., General Infantry Reinforcements: returned to France, 16 September 1917, joining 23rd Battn. on the 19th of that month, and was killed in action, 3 October 1917, nr. Zonnebeke. Age 27. Buried where he fell. He leaves a wife, Jessie May Moore (161, Nelson Road, Albert Park, Victoria), and *dau.* Yvonne. See account re. Capt. J.R. Eddy, Reninghelst New Military Cemetery (IV.C.4).

His brother Algernon also has no known grave; he is recorded on Panel 25.

(Panel 23) Sergt. 4503, Timothy Thomas, 23rd Bn. Australian Infantry, A.I.F.: *s.* of the late Thomas Thomas, of Victoria, by his wife Elizabeth (69, York Street, Prahran, Melbourne, Victoria): *b.* Steiglitz, Victoria, 1893: Occupation – Boot Trade Apprentice; Exhibition Boot Co., Northcote: enlisted Melbourne 13 July 1915; posted 11th Rfts., 23rd Battn., Broadmeadows, 18 March 1916: apptd. L/Corpl. 13 March 1917; promoted Corpl. 14 May; Sergt. 10 September 1917, and proceeded on leave same day: rejoined from leave, 23 September, and was killed in action, 3 October 1917, at Passchendaele. Age 24. *unm.* Remains recovered from an unmarked grave, refers to a GRU Report, Zillebeke 5-10E (28.D.27.d.50.75); identified – Clothing, Disc; reinterred, registered March 1927. *Buried in Sanctuary Wood Cemetery (III.J.11).*

(Panel 23) Lieut. Arthur Wilcock, 24th Bn. Australian Infantry, A.I.F.: late of 481, Hargeaves Street, Bendigo, Victoria: *s.* of Joseph F. Wilcock, by his wife Susan A. (Post Office, Long Gully, Bendigo): and brother to Lieut. E.L. Wilcock, M.C., 5th Battn., who, after being seriously wounded (Right Leg, Penis) 4 October 1917, was discharged to Australia, 30 January 1918: *b.* Bendigo, 6 September 1884: *educ.* Melbourne University, B.A., M.A., B.Sc.: Occupation – State High School Teacher, Bendigo (Latin & Science, 1908–17): joined A.I.F. as Lieut. 25 September 1916, having served 9½ years Commissioned Service Junior and Senior Cadets; C.O. 68th Senior Cadets (from June 1914), A.D.C. (from 16 July 1915): posted 24th Battn. Royal Park, 2 October: departed Melbourne aboard H.M.A.T. A.20 'Hororata,' 23 November 1916: trained Larkhill, 29 January–20 April 1917: served with the Expeditionary Force in France from 24 April 1917, joining 24th Battn. In the Field two days later, and was killed in action, 4 October 1917, being blown to pieces by a shell. Age 33. Such remains as could be found were buried by Sergt. Laing. Capt. F.P. Sellick, Adjt., 24th Battn., recorded "2 October 1919…was killed by enemy shellfire in the preliminary barrage put down in our jumping off trench near Zonnebeke on 4.10.17, prior to the attack on Broodseinde Ridge. The approx. position of the grave is Sheet 28 N.E. D.28.a.2.0. (Approx. 500 yards S.S.W. of Zonnebeke)…buried by a party from this battalion." Pnr. Sergt. Laing, 24th Battn. recorded, "25 December 1917…We are able to state that this gentleman was instantly killed in action on the 4th of October last, at a place called Broodseinde, on the Ypres front, and his remains were buried on the spot where his death occurred. Since then we have made a beautiful cross and had it erected. The name, battalion etc. were stamped on a brass plate, and this was placed neatly on the face of the cross. In the case of other brave officers, we regret the death of Mr. Wilcock, who was highly esteemed and greatly respected in the battalion and we can sincerely extend our deepest sympathy to the friends or relations who are making enquiries on his behalf." In response to an enquiry from Lieut. Wilcock's widow, Capt. F.P. Sellick, wrote, "9 April 1923…no particulars have been received at this office with regard to the burial place of your husband…and as no official advice of registration has come to hand it must be reluctantly concluded that the Graves Service have not succeeded in locating his resting place…Failing the recovery and identification of the actual remains, it is the intention of the authorities to erect suitable memorials on which the soldier's full regimental description and date of death will be inscribed." He was married to Clarice Isabel Wilcock (9, St. George's Road, Elsternwick, Victoria), and had two children, Arthur Alan and Iris Isabel. See account Reninghelst New Military Cemetery; Capt. J.R. Eddy (IV.C.4).

(Panel 23) Corpl. 2369, Charles Leslie Tasman Hey, 24th Bn. Australian Infantry, A.I.F.: *s.* of George Hey, of Best Street, Devonport, Tasmania, by his wife Ann: and brother to Pte. 7016, E.V. Hey, 6th Bn. A.I.F., who fell four days earlier: *b.* Tasmania, *c.*1893. Killed in action, 8 October 1917. Age 24. Pte. 399, V.M. Dee said, "..was in the support lines at Zonnebeke Ridge. He was sitting in the trench talking to Corpl. W. Norman and Pte. F. World when a 'whiz-bang' exploded in the trench right in the centre of them, killing all three. I was seven yards away at the time the shell exploded. He was buried where he fell. He was one of the most popular men in the company and was liked by everybody."

His brother Ernest also has no known grave; he is recorded on Panel 7.

(Panel 23) Corpl. 1749, William 'Bill' Leslie Norman, 24th Bn. Australian Infantry, A.I.F.: *s.* of Henry John Norman, of Lonsdale Street, Hamilton, Victoria, by his wife Margaret: *b.* Hamilton, 1887: prior to enlistment, Warracknabeal, 23 March 1915, was Senior Cadet Sergt.: proceeded to Gallipoli, 30 August 1915: hospitalised Anzac 1–9 October (Diarrhoea): hospitalised 18 October (Septic hand), evacuated to Malta: returned 24th Battn. Tel-el-Kebir, 11 January 1916: joined the Expeditionary Force in France, 26 March 1916: apptd. L/Corpl. 17 August 1916: hospitalised, 25 March 1917 (Septic thumb); subsequently transf'd. Rouen, thereafter Convalescent Depot, discharged to Etaples 17 April: rejoined 24th Battn. 5 May: promoted Corpl. 5 August 1917. Killed in action, 8 October 1917. Pte. Kelly, said, "He was sitting down in a shell hole, talking to Corpl. Hey and another man on the 8th October in front of Passchendaele. An H.E. shell exploded in the shell hole killing him, Corpl. Hey and the other man instantly. I did not see him killed, but saw his body fifteen minutes later; he was quite dead. I do not know if he was ever buried." Sergt. Storer and Sergt. Bond reported helping to bury him in the support line on Broodseinde Ridge;

both reported no cross erected to mark the spot. Age 20. *unm.* Corpl. C.L. Hey and the 'other man' Pte. F. World also have no known grave; they are recorded above and below respectively.

(Panel 23) L/Corpl. 4734, Robert Montgomery, 24th Bn. Australian Infantry, A.I.F.: *s.* of William John Montgomery, of 39, Buncle Street, North Melbourne, by his wife Robina: and elder brother to Pte. 2456, A.L. Montgomery, 57th Australian Infantry, who fell five weeks previously: *b.* North Melbourne. Killed in action, 9 October 1917. Pte. 6362, Phillips reported, "At Ypres. Daisy Wood; he was shot by a sniper, right through the head. I saw him killed and I saw him buried in Daisy Wood; about the middle of the wood. I don't think there was any mark put up, it was pretty hot at the time. He was Corpl. of the Lewis Gun team, and I knew him quite well." L/Corpl. Montgomery leaves a widow, Mrs Ethel Leek Montgomery (20, Crown Street, Newmarket, Victoria).

His brother Alexander also has no known grave; he is recorded on Panel 29.

(Panel 23) Pte. 6175, Alfred Ernest Tucker, 24th Bn. Australian Infantry, A.I.F.: late of Rosslyn Street, Woollahra, New South Wales: *s.* of Bartholomew George Tucker, of Ballarat, by his wife Helen: *b.* Ballarat, 1881: *educ.* Public School: Occupation – Master Builder: enlisted Royal Agricultural Showgrounds, Sydney, 29 May 1916: departed Australia, A8 'Argyllshire,' 31 October: disembarked Plymouth, 10 January 1917, proceeded to Larkhill Camp where, on the 11th of that month, he was appointed A/Corpl. (without pay) from which he reverted to Pte. 9 February: proceeded to France, 19 April: underwent further training, Etaples 20 April–9 May, on which latter date he joined 24th Battn. In the Field: hospitalised ('sick' – Pyrexia: unknown origin) 11 June: discharged to duty, 23 June, rejoined his battalion the following day, and was killed in action at Tokio Ridge, 8 October 1917, being hit and killed instantaneously by a shell while acting as guide to the Company. Age 36. L/Corpl. Conroy, Ptes Gamble, Littlefield and World were killed at the same time. He was married to Florence Elizabeth Tucker (Roslyn Flats, 75, Hooper Street, Randwick, Sydney) and had six children – Iris Florence, Ernest Gregory, Robert Maxwell, Bartholmew George, Milson Henry and Lola. On 20 January 1920, Mrs Tucker – requesting further efforts might be made to locate her late husband's resting place – submitted a letter to Australian Records Dept; written by Lieut. J.F. Gear, 24th Battn., it contained the lines "He was buried on the ground gained that day… he rests just south of Zonnebeke and on the ground gained in the attack on Broodseinde." Forwarded to the Australian Graves Services, London, it drew the reply, "5 August 1920 … advice has been received… to the effect a thorough search has been made and exhaustive enquiries instituted with a view to locating his burial place, but with a negative result. Should his grave be found, advice will be immediately sent to you, but it is feared now the chance of such a discovery is somewhat remote. Should the grave not be located a memorial will be erected in the Military Cemetery nearest the spot at which the late soldier fell…" The letter concluded, "It is desired to remind you that no reply has yet been received to my letter of 21st June, advising that the inscription chosen greatly exceeds the limit imposed by the War Graves Commission, viz. 66 letters (and each space between the words counting as an additional letter) and it would be necessary to abbreviate same."

Should her husband be afforded a headstone Mrs Tucker had requested the personal inscription – "*In Fond Memory Of My Dear Husband Private Alfred Ernest Tucker Who Departed This Life On The Field Of Battle October 8th 1917: Tis Sweet To Be Remembered And a Pleasant Thing To Find, That Though You May Be Absent, You Still Are Kept In Mind.*" And, that the customary Cross be surmounted by a Passion Fruit Vine. L/Corpl. Conroy, Ptes Gamble and Littlefield are buried in Birr Cross Roads Cemetery (V.A.I-2, V.B.14); Pte. World is recorded below.

(Panel 23) Pte. 1755, Frank World, Lewis Gun Section, 'D' Coy., 24th Bn. Australian Infantry, A.I.F.: *s.* of Alice Mary World (180, Pelham Street, Carlton, Victoria): *b.* South Melbourne, 1890: Occupation – Driver to Mr. Elliott, Richmond: enlisted Melbourne, 26 May 1915: departed Melbourne, HMAT 'Demosthenes,' 16 July 1915; ret'd. S.S. 'Ceramic,' 17 November 1915 (Venereal): proceeded to France, 2 October 1916: trained Larkhill, co. Kent, November–April 1917; joined the Expeditionary Force in France on the 11th of the latter month: joined 24th Battn. In the Field, 5 May: charged with 'Conduct to the prejudice of Good Order and Military Discipline, for Insolence to an Officer,' 13 May, Awarded 7 days Field Punishment No.1, plus forfeiture of pay at the rate of 5/- per day: hospitalised, 29 June–30 July (trench fever): rejoined 24th Battn. 31 August, and was killed in action, 8 October 1917, at Zonnebeke. Age 27. *unm.* Pte. 5594, T.R. Hartney recalled, "I knew World in private life…We used to call him 'Worldie,' he was full of fun and very popular." Pte. 2220, Taylor said, "I saw him killed by a shell, he was blown to pieces. This happened about 200 yards behind our front line at Passchendaele. There would be no hope of him being buried…" And Sergt. 919, W.H. McKion, "He was sitting in a support trench along with two others, Corpl. Hey C. and Corpl. Norman W. when a shell landed in the trench killing all three of them…I had very little to do with him." L/Corpl. Conroy, Ptes. Gamble, Littlefield and Tucker were also killed. L/Corpl. Conroy, Ptes. Gamble and Littlefield are buried in Birr Cross Roads Cemetery (V.A.1-2, V.B.14); Pte. Tucker is recorded above.

(Panel 23) Pte. 6365, Robert Dixon Gordon McCullough, 'A' Coy., 25th Bn. Australian Infantry, A.I.F.: *s.* of Hugh McCullough, of Sunnybank, Queensland, by his wife Annie: *b.* Dalby, Queensland, 1879: Killed in action, 4 October 1917; concussion, shellfire. Age 38. Remains recovered from an unmarked grave (28.D.22.a.4.0); identified – Khaki, 2 Discs; reinterred, registered 19 February 1930. *Buried in Kemmel No.1 French Cemetery (II.A.20).*

(Panel 23) Sergt. 4077, Gordon Kennedy Bogle, 26th Bn. Australian Infantry, A.I.F.: *s.* of James Kennnedy Bogle, of Pakowhai, Hawke's Bay, New Zealand, by his wife Annie Stafford: and brother to 2nd Lieut. G.S. Bogle, Royal Engineers, died of wounds, 15 October 1915, at Gallipoli; and Capt. G.V. Bogle, N.Z. Army Medical Corps, killed by shellfire, 17 September 1916, nr. Flers, Somme: *b.* Waipukurau, Hawke's Bay, 1887: Occupation – Architect: enlisted Lismore, New South Wales, 20 September 1915: departed Brisbane, 28 March 1916: trained Rollestone Camp, England, July 1916–March 1917: joined Expeditionary Force in France on the 14th of the latter month: promoted Sergt. 14 August, and was killed in action, 20 September 1917. Age 30. *unm.*

His brother George also has no known grave, he is commemorated on the Helles Memorial; Gilbert is buried in Quarry Cemetery Montauban (VI.B.3).

(Panel 23) Pte. 5800, Joseph Percival 'Percy' Cooper, 'A' Coy., 26th Bn. Australian Infantry, A.I.F.: *s.* of Joseph Cooper, of Prosperine, Queensland, by his wife Mary Elizabeth. Reported wounded and missing, 5 October 1917; since confirmed killed in action. In response to an enquiry made by the Red Cross Missing and Wounded Bureau, Corpl. H. Smith reported, "I regret very much to inform that I buried him on or about 6.10.17, not far in the rear of Zonnebeke. I buried him next to a man named Weppler upon whose cross I nailed his identification disc. I placed no cross at the head of Cooper's grave because I had none to hand, and he had no disc. I asked the Engineers to make one with his name engraved upon it, but it was not completed when I left, and consequently was never put there. I was never again in that part in daylight, so I had no further opportunity of doing so. I knew him well. He was wounded in the lungs, a piece of shell passing right through his chest. He must have died almost instantly. He was always a jolly decent fellow and well liked…" Age 19. Remains recovered from an unmarked grave (28.D.27.a.4.0) 25 February 1927; identified – Disc; reinterred, registered 26 February 1927. *Buried in Sanctuary Wood Cemetery (III.H.1).*

Rock Of Ages Cleft For Me

Pte. Weppler has no known grave; he is recorded below.

(Panel 23) Pte. 1007, Herbert George Gardiner, 26th Bn. Australian Infantry, A.I.F.: *s.* of William Gardiner, of Weldborough, Tasmania, by his wife Edith Helen: and brother to Pte. 1228, C.E. Gardiner, 5th Battn. A.I.F., died of wounds, 11 September 1915, at Malta: *b.* Weldborough, 1892: Occupation – Labourer: enlisted White Mark, 1 May 1915; posted 26th Battn., Enoggera, 28 May: departed to join Expeditionary Force, Gallipoli, 29 June 1915: trained Alexandria, Egypt from 4 September: proceeded to France, 15 March 1916: wounded (GSW L. Hand) November 1916, and removed to England: discharged to Weymouth, 28 May: Awarded 3 Days Confinement, 1 Day Forfeiture of pay; 'breaking away from a fatigue party (Monte Video, 11 January 1917), being absent (11 a.m. – 4 p.m.) without permission': hospitalised (Venereal Disease), Bulford, 24 February–7 April: returned to France, 23 May: hospitalised (Tonsilitis) 9–14 July, and rejoined his battalion the following day: rest camp, 13–27 August 1917.

Reported missing at Passchendaele, 5 October 1917, since confirmed (26th Battn. Court of Enquiry, 15 May 1918) killed in action on that date. Age 25. (*IWGC record age 23*)

His brother Clarence is buried in Pieta Military Cemetery (B.X.3).

(Panel 23) Pte. 1524, Stanley Robert Laws, 26th Bn. Australian Infantry, A.I.F.: *s.* of John Laws, of Boss Hall Farm, Sproughton Road, Ipswich, England, by his wife Alice Emma: and yr. brother to 2nd Corpl. 24513, G.E. Laws, 5th Signal Coy. Royal Engineers, killed in action, 1 August 1916: *b.* All Saints, Ipswich, 1894: enlisted Toowoomba, Queensland, 27 April 1915: served in Egypt (from 4 September 1915); France and Flanders (from 17 September 1916), and died of wounds, 20 September 1917. Age 23.

His brother George is buried in Dantzig Alley British Cemetery, Mametz (I.A.30).

(Panel 23) Pte. 5706, Thomas O'Brien, 26th Bn. Australian Infantry, A.I.F.: *s.* of Mrs Mary Hull (Tooley Street, Maryborough, Queensland), by her marriage to the late Maurice O'Brien: and elder brother to Pte. 2687, J.M. O'Brien, 4th Australian Pioneers, who fell six days later: served with the Expeditionary Force: wounded (gas) hospitalised London, 11 April 1917; discharged to Streatham Aux. Hospital, 21 April (discharged to leave 12–25 May). Reported wounded/missing 20 September 1917, since confirmed (A.I.F. HQrs. Enquiry, 13 May 1918) killed in action. Age 41.

His brother John also has no known grave; he is recorded on Panel 31.

(Panel 23) Pte. 1924, Henry Robert Weppler, 26th Bn. Australian Infantry, A.I.F.: *b.* Bega, New South Wales, 1881: Occupation – Labourer: enlisted Brisbane, 16 June 1915: joined 26th Battn., Anzac, 9 December 1915: trained Egypt, January–March 1916; served with the Expeditionary Force in France and Flanders from the 21st of that month; and was killed in action, 4 October 1917. Age 36.

(Panel 23) Pte. 6433, Kenneth Graeme Bett, 28th Bn. Australian Infantry, A.I.F.: eldest *s.* of the late James Bett, Tea Planter, of Ceylon, by his wife Jessie Eliza Hunter *née* Bett, of Strathay, co. Perth, Scotland: *b.* Strathay, co. Perth, 12 July 1890: *educ.* Grandtully, and Breadalbane Academy, Aberfeldy: joined Australian Infantry, October 1916: served with the Expeditionary Force in France from May 1917, and was killed in action at Broodseinde, 1 October 1917. Age 27. *unm.*

(Panel 23) Pte. 4309, David Matheson, 28th Bn. Australian Infantry, A.I.F.: 4th *s.* of John Matheson, of 'Sunnybrae,' Stromness, Orkney, by his wife Willamina, *née* Cuthbertson: *b.* Stromness, Orkney, 12 December 1888: *educ.* Public School, Stromness: went to Australia, December 1913, and settled at Perth, West Australia, with G & R Wills & Co.: volunteered for Active Service, and enlisted Australian Infantry 1 January 1916: served with the Expeditionary Force in France and Flanders from September 1916, and was killed in action at Ypres, 20 September 1917. Buried in Polygon Wood, four miles east of Ypres. Age 28. *unm.*

(Panel 23) Pte. 6355, Robert William Mellor, 28th Bn. Australian Infantry, A.I.F.: *s.* of Richard Henry Mellor, of Belgravia Street, Belmont, Western Australia, by his wife Rhoda Mary: *b.* New South Wales, *c.*1887. Killed in action, 30 October 1917. Age 30. *Buried in Sanctuary Wood Cemetery (V.U.7).*

(Panel 23) Pte. 5438, Francis Sutherland, 28th Bn. Australian Infantry, A.I.F.: *s.* of Sinclair Sutherland, of Avon Terrace, York, Western Australia, by his wife Margaret: and brother to Pte. 1412, S. Sutherland, 11th Australian Infantry, killed in action, 16 May 1917: *b.* Bogbairn, Inverness, Scotland, *c.*1895: Occupation – Farm Labourer: enlisted Blackboy Hill, 20 March 1916: proceeded overseas, 9 August: disembarked Plymouth, 25 September: trained Rollestone: Awarded (13 October) '168 Hours Detention, 9 Days Forfeiture of Pay, Overstaying Leave, 24.00hrs 9 October 1916 until found in lines 14.00hrs, 11 October': proceeded to France, 16 November; trained Etaples, joined 28th Battn. In the Field, 4 December 1916, and was killed in action, 20 September 1917. Age 23. His British War medal, Memorial Scroll, Plaque and Victory medal were received by his father, 31 March 1922–8 April 1923.

His brother Sinclair also has no known grave; he is commemorated on the Villers-Bretonneux Memorial.

(Panel 23) Sergt. 2079, Francis Duke Martin, 29th Bn. Australian Infantry, A.I.F.: *s.* of Edwin Martin, of The Ravine, Filey, J.P., for the North Riding of Yorkshire, by his wife Mary Elizabeth, *dau.* of Henry Liddell: *b.* Huddersfield, co. York, 29 September 1884: *educ.* Filey, and Uppingham: removed to Australia 1903: Occupation – Farmer: volunteered for Imperial Service and joined A.I.F. June 1915: served with the Expeditionary Force in France and Flanders from 1916, and was killed in action at Polygon Wood, 27 September 1917. Buried there. Age 32. *unm.*

(Panel 23) Pte. 4086, Luke Monkovitch; Stretcher-Bearer, 29th Bn. Australian Infantry, A.I.F.: late of Port Augusta, South Australia: late *husb.* to Mary Ellen Monkovitch (Murgate, Winchelsea, Victoria): *b.* Colac, December 1874: Religion – Roman Catholic: Occupation – Plate Layer: 6'2" tall; fresh complexion, blue eyes, brown hair: enlisted Melbourne, 18 August 1916, apptd. 10th Rfts., 29th Battn., Geelong, 1 September: departed Melbourne, 21 October; apptd. L/Corpl. 9 November: trained England (reverted to Pte.) from 28 December 1916: served with the Expeditionary Force in France from 5 April 1917: joined 29th Battn., Bancourt, 12 April. Killed in action in the vicinity of Molenaarelsthoek, 13 October 1917. Buried in an isolated grave close to the dressing station and south of Smith Road, 3¼ miles due east of Ypres. Age 42. He left two sons – Percival Thomas & Roy Luke (*b.* 1908), and a trustee *dau.* Catherine.

(Panel 23) Pte. 4366, Wilfred Single, 29th Bn. Australian Infantry, A.I.F.: *s.* of John Single, of 'Troja,' 5, Chapman's Avenue, Forrest Hill, Sydney, by his wife Elizabeth: a descendant of John Single, Grazier and Pioneer, of Nepean House Castlereagh, New South Wales: and cousin to Capts. R.V. Single and H.G. Thompson, 56th Battn., who fell the same day. Wounded in the arm during the battalion's part in the attack at Polygon Wood, he was killed by a sniper shooting him through the back of the neck while escorting two prisoners to the rear, 26 September 1917. Age 23. *unm.*

His cousins Roland Single and Hubert Thompson also have no known grave, they are recorded on Panel 29.

(Panel 23) Pte. 3506, Arthur Archibald Aubrey, 8th Platoon, 'B' Coy., 30th Bn. Australian Infantry, A.I.F.: Batman to Lieut. H. Doust, 30th Battn.: *s.* of James Aubrey, of Mount Aubrey, New South Wales, by his wife Frances. Killed in action, 12 October 1917. L/Corpl. 512, J.A. Pickersgill, reported, "The battalion was holding the line to the left of Polygon Wood. About dinner-time Aubrey was hit by a shell and killed outright. I did not see him hit, although he was only ten yards in rear of me, he was hidden from sight. I went out on patrol that night, and after we returned (about mid-night), I helped to bury Aubrey near where he fell, and another man – Cook – who was killed shortly after; they were both interred in separate graves." Age 23. *unm.* At the time of his death Pte. Aubrey was batman to Lieut. H. Doust. Remains recovered from an unmarked grave (28.D.29.b.0.7), 2 December 1927; identified – Clothing, Collar Badge, Watch engrv. A.A. Aubrey; reinterred, registered 26 December 1927. *Buried in Sanctuary Wood Cemetery (III.G.16).*

Have Mercy Upon Him Lord And Let Perpetual Light Shine Upon Him

(Panel 23) Pte. 3780, William Henry Cook, 8th Platoon, 'B' Coy., 30th Bn. Australian Infantry, A.I.F.: *s.* of George Cook, of Edgworth, nr. Cirencester, by his wife Maria: Occupation – Gardener; Sydney Zoological Gardens. Killed 12 October 1917, by a splinter of shell through the head while sitting in the front-line trench smoking a cigarette. Buried by L/Corpl. J.W. Lang and Pte. McDonald; a cross was erected over his grave by the latter. Age 30. All information regarding Pte. Cook should be addressed to his sister Miss Alice Cook (106, Park Street, Grosvenor Square, London, S.W.1).

(Panel 23) Pte. 4279, John McNamara, 'D' Coy., 30th Bn. Australian Infantry, A.I.F.: *s.* of Mrs N.J. McNamara; late *husb.* to Rose Agnes McNamara ('Kerry,' Kingsland Road, Lidcombe, New South Wales); and father to Doris Elizabeth, and Mary Leonia G. McNamara: *b.* Prospect, Paramatta, March 1886: Religion – Roman Catholic: Occupation – Miner & Carter: volunteered and enlisted, Victoria Barracks, Sydney, 5 July 1916; apptd. 11th Rfts., 30th Bn., 8 August; proceeded overseas, 8 November: Awarded (27 December) Forfeiture 2 Days Pay '(1) Neglecting to obey orders (2) Being 1 hour absent without leave from ship while at sea, 26 December 1916': trained Codford, England from 10 January 1917: Awarded (20 February) 28 Days Field Punishment No.2 '(1) Drunkeness (2) Being in Barford St. Martin with all the buttons of his tunic unbuttoned (3) Using obscene language in a public thoroughfare, 18 February': proceeded to France, 13 March; joined 30th Bn., Bapaume 17 March: hospitalised (scabies & gallstones), 23 July–6 August: rejoined 30th Bn., Blaringhem, 21 August. Killed in action 3 p.m.., 12 October 1917.

Age 31. L/Corpl. 4617, Leo Tisdell said, "It occurred at Anzac Ridge, Broodseinde, in the Ypres sector. We were in action in the front line. We dug down 7 feet; two men who were with him had just left when a shell hit and buried him in 10 feet of earth. The Bosche went on shelling us and it was impossible to dig him out. We had to sit tight…I was three yards away from McNamara when it happened and saw it all."

(Panel 23) Sergt. 1058, William Reid, 31st Bn. Australian Infantry, A.I.F.: eldest *s.* of the late William Reid, Farmer, by his wife Isabella (Middlehill, Rothienorman, co. Aberdeen), *dau.* of John Johnston, of Grainhill: *b.* New Deer, co. Aberdeen, 12 May 1892: *educ.* Bandeenscoth Public School, Auchterless, co. Aberdeen: removed to Australia, January 1914, with the intention of farming: joined Australian Imperial Force, June 1915; served with the Expeditionary Force in France and Flanders from June 1916, and was killed in action at Polygon Wood, 26 September 1917. Buried nr. there. His Platoon Commander wrote, "The splendid example he set was well followed by the men he had trained, with the result that the Colonel has recommended one for the V.C., and three for the D.C.M., which, if granted, shall stand as a memorial to him who trained them, then gave his life while leading them, and if he had been spared he would certainly have been mentioned for honours;" and the Chaplain, "He was beloved by all in the platoon, both for his soldierly bearing as well as for his personal charm," A comrade wrote, "Bill was one of the best liked fellows in the regiment, and we all mourn him. We have lost one of the best mates we ever had." Age 25. *unm.*

(Panel 23) L/Corpl. 3186, Walter Carstens, 31st Bn. Australian Infantry, A.I.F.: *s.* of Claudius John William Carstens, of Baggot Street, Dalby, Queensland, by his wife Sarah Jane: and brother to Pte. 149, C.N. Carstens, 31st Australian Infantry, killed in action, 14 June 1917: *b.* Dalby, 1896: Religion – Church of England: Occupation – Mechanic: 5'9" tall, grey eyes, light brown hair: previously served 1 year 11th Infantry: joined A.I.F., Toowoomba, 7 January 1916; posted 11th (Depot) Battn.: transf'd. 7th Rfts., 31st Battn., 7 April: departed Hobart 10 April: trained Egypt, 15 June–2 August 1916; England, 22 August–17 December: apptd. A/Sergt., 9 December 1916 (& 20 December); L/Corpl. 24 January 1917: joined 31st Battn. in France 23 December 1916: hospitalised (arthritis & pyrexia) 7 March–8 May 1917 (returned to England): On Leave 21 May–5 June, thereafter retrained Perham Downs; returned to France, 16 June: rejoined 31st Battn., 3 July, and was killed in action, 26 September 1917, nr. Jerk House. Buried in the vicinity of Polygon Wood. Age 20. *unm.*

His brother Claudius is buried in Pont de Nieppe Communal Cemetery (II.E.5).

(Panel 23) Pte. 3542, Neil McMaster Crawford, 'C' Coy., 31st Bn. Australian Infantry, A.I.F.: *s.* of James Crawford, of Roma, Queensland, by his wife Annie M.: *b. c.*1898: enlisted 25 January 1916: served with the Expeditionary Force in France and Flanders, and was killed in action, 26 September 1917. *The Western Star*, 20 October 1917, reported – "Residents of Roma received a painful shock on Thursday afternoon when the cables brought the sad news that two popular Roma boys, Dave Murphy and Neil Crawford, had been killed in action. Dave Murphy, prior to enlisting, had worked with Mr Crawford, and was a bright intelligent lad of 20 when he answered his country's call. With an intelligence and natural smartness much above the average, his ability soon found recognition with the military authorities, and he paid his final visit home last year with the rank of sergeant. Later in the afternoon Mr James Crawford (Ballard & Crawford) received a similar cable that his eldest son Neil had been killed in action. Another fine man under 21, and just entering his second winter campaign. He spoke of that in a letter received by his parents the other day, but still, knowing what a winter in the trenches really means, he appeared to be facing the prospect with remarkable equanimity. "That's one thing about Neil, he never growls," his dad remarked, little thinking that soon would come the bad news. They were but lads, but they played men's parts. Their relatives will have the deepest sympathy all round, and we trust that their sorrow will at least be softened to some extent by the knowledge that these boys have died in the service of their country. The casualty lists are making gaps in many family circles that can never be bridged." Corpl. 602, J.H. Barling, 'C' Coy., wrote, "I was alongside him (Crawford) when he was shot through the head at Polygon Wood on September 26th. He was in the front line at the time. He fell into a shell hole that formed part of the line. Then he got up and made to go on his way to the D/S after I had put some chocolate in his mouth. He fell dead in the attempt quite close to me. Death took place soon after he was hit, I know nothing therefore as to burial. He was a L (Lewis)/gunner in XI pl. 'C' Coy." Age 19. L/Corpl. D.A. Murphy, 15th Bn. A.I.F., also has no known grave; he is recorded on Panel 17.

(Panel 23) Pte. 1075, Alfred George Worthington, 32nd Bn. Australian Infantry, A.I.F.: *s.* of Thomas Worthington, of Augustus Street, Geraldton, Western Australia, by his wife Maria: and elder brother to Pte. 1737, P. Worthington, 51st Australian Infantry, who fell 2½ months previously. Killed in action, 29 September 1917. Age 23. *unm.*

His brother Percy also has no known grave; he is recorded on Panel 29.

(Panel 23) Pte. 16, Frederick John Briggs, M.M., 'A' Coy., 33rd Bn. Australian Infantry, A.I.F.: *s.* of the late Frederick Briggs, and his wife Matilda Whyndom: *b.* Kupit Station, Manilla, New South Wales, January 1894: Occupation – Labourer: enlisted Armidale, 3 December 1915: departed Sydney, 4 January 1916: served with the Expeditionary Force in France from 21 November; wounded (GSW, Rt. Knee, Rt. Forearm) night of 24–25 February 1917; rejoined 33rd Battn. 16 March: wounded at Messines (GSW Lt. Foot) 7 June 1917; rejoined 33rd Battn. 3 August. Killed in action, 29 September 1917. Buried where he fell. Age 23. *unm.* Awarded Military Medal (*London Gazette*, 17 April 1917) for Bravery In the Field; "On the night of February 24th / 25th in a raid on the enemy's trench Pte. Briggs, while acting as covering bomber for the wire cutters, was severely wounded in the right arm but with great grit and determination he continued bombing with his left arm. He thus prevented the enemy who were in readiness at the point of entry from inflicting further casualties on our wire cutters, who were enabled to complete their work. His action contributed largely to the raiding party's success in entering the trench." Should Frederick's remains be recovered and marked with a headstone, his brother – Tico Briggs, of Hawarden P.O. via Manilla – requests the inscription:

Dulce Et Decorum Est Pro Patria Mori

In August 2008, archaeologists investigating the battlefields in the Ploegsteert area discovered the remains of a soldier beneath what appeared to have been the site of an enormous shell detonation. With the body were the remains of his rifle, ammunition, corps badges, pocket contents, haversack and an identification disc. Unfortunately the latter item, which might have enabled identification of the soldier, was too badly corroded to provide any information. The aforementioned objects recovered were cleaned and conserved by specialists from Bradford University. Examination of the skeletal remains and their chemical composition by experts from Leuven, Cranfield and Oxford Universities revealed he had lived an active physical life, indicated by signs of heavy skeletal muscle attachment and wear to the spine. Furthermore, these same experts opined the soldier's place of birth as being within a small region of New South Wales. Commissioned by the Australian Army, subsequent DNA testing of surviving relatives – in this case a nephew and cousin – led to the soldier being identified as Pte. A.J. Mather.

(Panel 23) Pte. 1983, Alan James Mather, 'D' Coy., 33rd Bn. Australian Infantry, A.I.F.: *s.* of the late Thomas Mather, Victualler (Wine); by his wife Mary Ann ('Roslyn,' Inverell, Northern New South Wales): *b.* Inverell, 25 October 1879: *educ.* New England Grammar School, Armidale; Hawkesbury Agricultural College (Viticulture): subsequently took up sheep farming (Grazier), and wine manufacture; 'Flaggy,' nr. Pindari: previously served 3 years Lieut., New England Light Horse Sqdn. (time expired): joined A.I.F., Inverell, 12 January 1916, apptd. 2nd Rfts., 33rd Bn.; apptd. 'D' Coy., 16 April; departed Sydney, 4 September following: trained England, 29 October–20 December 1916; Etaples, 21 December–25 January 1917: joined 33rd Bn., Houpline, 26 January: took part in the Battle of Messines (7 June) at some point during the course of which he picked up a German *pickelhaube* and put it in his knapsack as a trophy. The following day he was making his way through a trench at St Lyon; carrying his heavy knapsack, ammunition, grenades and wearing a slouch hat. Pte. A.H. Pitkin said a German shell hit and burst in the trench, blowing Mather to pieces. "I was right alongside of him when knocked." The company commander wrote, "Alan Mather was one of my best and most trusted men." Killed in action, 8 June 1917. Age 37. Reburied with full military honours, 22 July 2010. *Buried in Prowse Point Military Cemetery (III.C.1AA).*

So Far From Home Never Forgotten
May You Rest In Peace Bearing An Honoured Name

PANEL 23 ENDS PTE. R. HENNESSEY, 34TH BN. AUSTRALIAN INF.

PANEL 25 BEGINS PTE. G. HERCUS, 34TH BN. AUSTRALIAN INF.

(Panel 25) Pte. 896, William Leslie Hunter Sneddon, 9th Platoon, 'C' Coy., 34th Bn. Australian Infantry, A.I.F.: *s.* of William Hunter Sneddon, of Church Street, Minmi, New South Wales, by his wife Alice Maria: *b.* Maitland: Occupation – Miner: Reported missing, 7 June 1917, now confirmed died of gas poisoning on that date, the circumstances of his death being thus reported by Lieut. St.Clair Finlay, "On the night of 6–7 June we were heavily shelled and gassed on our way to the line prior to the attack, and remember seeing him just before the attack when he remarked, 'I am gassed but I am determined to go forward.' This was the last I saw of him, his body being found later in the day by the stretcher-bearers who told me he was black in the face but had no visible wounds; he had evidently died of gas a few minutes after I saw him. He was a splendid soldier and is greatly missed by all." Age 27. Buried on the field of battle, close to 2nd Mine Crater, 1 mile S.S.E. of Messines (28.U.9d.6.8), by the Rev. Osborn, Chaplain, 35th Battn. On 24 December 1920 Major Coleman, Australian Graves Service, London, copied the following memo to Poperinghe and Amiens. Referring to 2nd Lieut. R.D. Perrau, 35th Battn., A.I.F., it read, "Although exhaustive searches and investigations have been made with the object of locating the grave of the above named, it has not been possible to either locate his actual burial place or obtain any information which might indicate his probable original or present resting place. Therefore this office's records in connection with that late member of the A.I.F. are being marked 'No trace on research.' Similar action has been taken by the Imperial War Graves Commission, London."

Pte. 2158, H.W. Thornthwaite (31 August 1917) not only recalled seeing Lieut. Perrau killed outright by the same shell that killed Pte. 1863, C. Wiseman, he saw them buried. And, whilst Sergt F. Sturch (1 December 1917) said the burial was carried out by the Battalion Pioneers, both he and Major Blake, 35th Bn., agreed the place of burial was a small cemetery in the vicinity of Ploegsteert Wood. Perhaps the last word belongs to Chaplain W.H. Osborne who, after officiating, reported to the Battalion Adjutant who in due course certified (7 November 1917), "Buried 3rd Divn. Cemetery, one mile north-east of Ploegsteert village." Today the cemetery is known as Toronto Avenue.

(Panel 25) 2nd Lieut. 526, Robert Donaldson Perrau, 7th Platoon, 'B' Coy., 35th Bn. Australian Infantry, A.I.F.: *s.* of Edith Marion Perrau, ('Gilnockie,' Lawes Street, East Maitland), and her estranged husband William Rowland Perrau – last known address – Turnbull Street, Hamilton, Newcastle, New South Wales – formerly Corpl. 1823, 16th Australian Light Railway Operating Coy. (medically discharged – Senility & Rheumatism – 23 November 1917): *b.* Cook's Hill, Newcastle, New South Wales, September 1894: Religion – Presbyterian: Occupation – Assistant Surveyor: 5'7" tall, brown eyes, dark hair: prior to joining A.I.F. was Lieut., Senior Cadets (3 years); Corpl 16th Infantry (1 year): enlisted, 3 January 1916; apptd. A/Sergt., 'B' Coy., 35th Battn., Coy.Sergt.Major, 29 April; Warrant Officer, 1 May, on which date he departed Australia, A.24 'Benalla': served with the Expeditionary Force in France from 21 November: promoted 2nd Lieut. 27 December 1916. Killed in action, 11 June 1917. Age 22. *unm.* His Commanding Officer, Major Blake, wrote, "Lieut. Perrau was attached to my command during the Battle of Messines and was killed by shellfire in the front line trenches in front of Ultimo Crater (in front of St. Yves) on 11.6.17. I can state definitely that he was later buried in, as far as I remember, a small cemetery in the vicinity of Ploegsteert Wood." Pte. 1452, G. Slade wrote, "12 November 1917. I knew Lieut. Perrau. He was killed at Messines about June 11th by concussion in the new front line just after we had taken it. The O.C. Capt. Blake (now Major) sent word down by a runner to get him down to be buried at the back of the line in Plugstreet Wood Cemetery, but I do not know if he was got down." Buried 3rd Divn. Cemetery, one mile north-east of Ploegsteert village, by Major W.H. Osborne (Anglican Chaplain), attd. 35th Battn.

Without exception all correspondence should be addressed to 2nd Lieut. Perrau's mother. (*IWGC record age 21*) See also Pte. E.R. Hellyer, below.

(Panel 25) Pte. 396, Reginald Thomas Cowley, 'B' Coy., 35th Bn. Australian Infantry, A.I.F.: *s.* of the late William Weymouth Cowley, by his wife Leticia (Glendon Brook via Singleton, New South Wales): *b.* Gresford, 1884: Religion – Church of England: Occupation – Labourer: 5'7½" tall, hazel eyes, brown hair: enlisted West Maitland, 22 November 1915; apptd. 35th Battn., Broadmeadows, 5 April 1916: departed Sydney, A.24 'Benalla,' 1 May: hospitalised in England, 25–30 August (Bronchitis): served with the Expeditionary Force in France from 22 November following; wounded in action (Shrapnel – Head, Back, Right Leg, Left Arm), 14 March 1917; hospitalised Boulogne: rejoined 35th Battn. 4 April. Killed in action, 11 June 1917. Age 33. See Pte. E.R. Hellyer, below.

(Panel 25) Pte. 2079, Edmund Reid Hellyer, 7th Platoon, 'B' Coy., 35th Bn. Australian Infantry, A.I.F.: *s.* of John Hellyer, c/o Warkton Post Office, New South Wales, by his wife Mary: *b.* Coonabarabran, New South Wales: Occupation – Farmer: enlisted Royal Agricultural Show Grounds, Sydney, 3 April 1916: proceeded overseas, A.68 'Anchises,' 24 August: served with the Expeditionary Force in France from 21 December 1916; joined 35th Battn. In the Field, 7 February 1917, and was killed in action, 11 June 1917. Age 29. Sergt. 12070, F. Sturch, 7th Platoon, 35th Battn. said, "After the attack on Messines we were holding a line of rough trenches in front of Warneton at 5 o'clock in the morning of 11.6.17. A shell came over into Platoon Headquarters bay, and three were killed and two wounded. Lieut. Perrau in Command of the Platoon was killed, also Hellyer, Cowley and Wiseman. I then took charge of the Platoon and examined the bodies...I took their personal belongings and sent them back to Battalion Headquarters. Hellyer was killed instantly and could not have felt anything. He was buried in or near Ploegsteert Wood. He was a good comrade and a plucky soldier." (*IWGC record 4 June*) 2nd Lieut. Perrau and Pte. Cowley are recorded above; Pte. Wiseman below.

(Panel 25) Pte. 93, Clarence Claude Hobden, Quartermaster, 1st Platoon, 'A' Coy., 35th Bn. Australian Infantry, A.I.F.: late of 'Fairview,' Jerry's Plains, Singleton, New South Wales: only *s.* of the late Leamington Ellis Hobden (*d.* 1899), by his wife Elizabeth Daisy (Glen Fry, Coonabarabran, New South Wales), formerly of 'Teridgerie,' North Coonamble: *b.* Jerry's Plains, January 1889: Religion – Church of England: Occupation – Labourer: 5'7" tall, dark complexion, brown eyes, brown hair: enlisted West Maitland, 10 November 1915, posted 35th Battn. Broadmeadows: departed Australia, A.24 'Benalla,' 1 May 1916: served with the Expeditionary Force in France from 21 November following, and was killed at Dead Horse Corner, near Ploegsteert Wood, 7 June 1917. Age 28. *unm.* Pte. 226, J.H. Thompson said, "On 7th June 1917 the 35th Battalion was taking part in the first day's operations against Messines. The hop over took place at 3.10 a.m. Hobden and I were together at the hop over, and kept together till Hobden was hit by a shell at about 4.30 a.m. and killed instantly. At the time we were both acting as carriers and when Hobden was hit we were coming back for more ammunition. He was only a couple of yards away when he was hit and I had a look to make sure he was dead and then carried on with my work. He was lying in a trench and his body was later picked up by the Battn. Pioneers and taken away for a decent burial. He was well liked by his chums." Buried east of junction with Quebec Avenue, Ploegsteert Wood, 1 mile west-south-west of Messines; Capt. Rev. J.E. Norman Osborn officiated. Memorial Cross erected Strand Military Cemetery, Plot 7, Row B, No.3. His effects – Wallet, 6 Coins, 1 Franc Note, Fountain Pen, Cards, Photos, Telegram, 2 References, Knife, Belt – were received by his mother, 3 March 1918. She had especially been looking forward to receiving his gold signet ring and gold wristwatch on the reverse of which was inscribed 'To Charlie With Love From Mother;' both items were missing. (*IWGC record age 29*) See Pte. A.A. McCook, below.

(Panel 25) Pte. 504, George McLean, Officer's Batman, 'B' Coy., 35th Bn. Australian Infantry, A.I.F.: *s.* of Euphemia McLean (10, Harris Street, Smedmore, Wickham, New South Wales), and the late John McLean: *b.* Newcastle, New South Wales, 1893: Religion – Church of England: Occupation – Labourer: 5'3½" tall, blue eyes, light brown hair: joined A.I.F., Newcastle, 6 December 1915: departed Sydney, 1 May 1916; trained England from 9 July: Awarded (4 November 1916) Forfeiture 4 Days Pay, 3 Days F.P. No.2 'AWOL midnight 29.10.16, to noon 30.10.16': proceeded to France, 21 November, and was killed in action, midnight 7–8 June 1917 by a shell (Pte. S.B. Justelius was also killed). Buried 5th Divn. General Cemetery, Ploegsteert Wood. Age 24. *unm.* Pte. Justelius is buried in Toronto Avenue Cemetery (C.6).

(Panel 25) Pte. 1838, Arthur Archibald McCook, 1st Platoon, 'A' Coy., 35th Bn. Australian Infantry, A.I.F.: late of The Club Hotel, Albion Street, Sydney: *s.* of James McCook, of 57, Birkenhead Street, North Fitzroy, Victoria; late of Model Lodging House, Kent Street, Sydney: *b.* Brisbane, Queensland, April 1876: Religion – Church of England: Occupation – Shearer: 5′11½″ tall, sallow complexion, blue eyes, dark brown hair: enlisted Royal Agricultural Show Grounds, Sydney, 12 April 1916: departed Australia, H.M.A.T. A.15 'Port Sydney,' 4 September: served with the Expeditionary Force in France from 21 December 1916: joined 35th Battn. In the Field, 26 January 1917, and was killed in action, St. Yves Sector, 7 June 1917, while carrying barbed wire forward to Prowse Point. Age 41. Pte. 152, J.G. Metcalfe, 35th Battn. recorded, "Smith and Hobden and McCook were killed at Ontario Avenue, Messines, Ploegsteert, on June 7th, before the mines went up, while we were in the trench preparing for the attack and were being shelled. Smith was my cobber in my Platoon. I was close to him and caught him as he fell. He was killed outright – never spoke. This was at 12.45 a.m. Hobden was killed later, just before the mines went up. McCook was another killed at the same place. I saw them. They were all killed outright, six altogether were killed. They were brought back and buried at Regent Street, Ploegsteert Wood by a party under Pioneer Sergt. Gain. I have seen the graves. It was not a regular cemetery then, but has since been made so. McCook, always known as 'Old Shearer,' was a tall slender man, not too young with dark hair and complexion…" Buried 3rd Divn. Cemetery, Ploegsteert Wood; Capt. Rev. J.E. Norman Osborn, officiated. Ptes. C.C. Hobden is recorded above; F.H.C. Smith below.

(Panel 25) Pte. 202, Frederick Harold Charles Smith, 1st Platoon, 'A' Coy., 35th Bn. Australian Infantry, A.I.F.: *s.* of Charles Smith, of 1, Dent Street, Islington, Newcastle, New South Wales, by his wife Alice Maud Mary: *b.* Armidale, September 1897: Religion – Wesleyan: Occupation – Striker (Tobacco Worker): 5′5¼″ tall, sallow complexion, brown eyes, light brown hair: a member of 16th Infantry Regt., enlisted Newcastle, 24 November 1915: departed Sydney, H.M.A.T. A.24 'Benalla,' 1 May 1916: Fined (25 May) 2/6d for Failure to Attend 7 a.m. parade at sea: disembarked Plymouth, 9 July and proceeded to Larkhill Camp where he was awarded 3 days Confinement to Barracks for Talking on Parade, 25 August, and (21 October) 6 days Field Punishment No.2 for refusing to perform fatigue duty, 17 October: proceeded to France, 21 November 1916: Awarded (6 January 1917) 15 days Field Punishment No.2 'Failing to Attend 10 a.m. and 2 p.m. parade, 28 December 1916.' Killed in action, 7 June 1917. Age 19. Sergt. A. Chapman said, "Smith was killed by the same shell as McCook and was also buried by that shell. I saw this but cannot say if he was got out as I was wounded some 8 or 9 hours later. They were killed at the hop over trench at Ploegsteert. He was only a youngster … a terribly game lad." Buried a few yards north of La Hutte – Prowse Point road, just east of Annescroft Avenue, 1 mile south of Messines; Capt. Rev. J.E. Norman Osborn, officiated. See Pte. A.A. McCook, above.

(Panel 25) Pte. 1863, Clarence Wiseman, 35th Bn. Australian Infantry, A.I.F.: *s.* of Henry Parker Wiseman, by his wife Rachel: *b.* Sydney. Killed in action, 11 June 1917. Age 20. *unm.* A comrade, Pte. H.W. Thornthwaite said, "31 August 1917. I saw Lieut. Perrau and Pte. Wiseman both killed by the same shell outright in the bay next to mine at daybreak at Messines, and saw them buried behind the line." Sergt. 12070, F. Sturch said, "He was killed instantly and could not have felt anything. He was well liked by his mates and a good soldier, and it was a sad loss to the Platoon." Buried 3rd Divn. Cemetery, 1 mile north-east of Ploegsteert village. See Pte. E.R. Hellyer, above. 2nd Lieut. R.D. Perrau also has no known grave, he is recorded above.

(Panel 25) Pte. 1809, Charles Albert Clissold, 36th Bn. Australian Infantry, A.I.F.: only *s.* of the late Sergt. George Albert Clissold, by his wife Mary, *née* Innes: *b.* Emu Plains, New South Wales, 29 March 1898: *gdson.* to T.D. Clissold, J.P., of Lambridge: *educ.* Public Schools – Emu Plains and Penrith: Occupation – Horse Driver: a member of the Militia; enlisted, with his parents consent, 12 March 1916, being then under 21 years of age: recorded as 18 years, 1 month: served with 'A' Coy., 3rd Battn., Cootamundra, until 20 April 1916 then with 'A' Coy., 1st Battn. until 5 June; serving with 'A' Coy., 36th (Depot) Battn., Rutherford, NSW, thereafter: departed Australia, 4 September 1916, HMAT 'Port Sydney': disembarked Portsmouth,

England, 20 December following: joined 36th Battn., 'Bull Ring,' Etaples, January 1917. Killed in action during 36th Battn. participation in the Battle of Messines, 7 June 1917. *The Nepean Times*, 14 July 1917, "Private C.A.Clissold Killed in Action: Though Australia is some 12,000 miles or more, per nearest oceanic route, from the seat of war, the awful intensity; the relentless deadliness of the grim Armageddon is being almost daily made all the more painfully evident by the many additions to the list of Australian heroes who have fallen in battle; and to those householders who have lost not only their breadwinner (father) but also their only son, as in the case of the Clissold family of Emu Plains, the direful ravages of and the anguish caused by the war, is surely exceedingly bitter testimony of the most appalling struggle in the history of the world. It will be remembered that the death of Sergeant George Clissold, who fell in action on the Western Front, on 9th November 1916, was duly reported in our columns, and reference on that occasion was made to the enlistment of Sergeant Clissold's only son (Private Charles Clissold) and it is now our sad duty to report that Private C.A. Clissold, like his heroic father, has also given the sacrifice of his life in the cause of his country and Empire, news of his death in action, on 7th June, having been recently received by Mrs Clissold and family. The deceased hero, who was a lad of splendid physique, being 6ft 2in in height and finely proportioned, enlisted 14 March 1916, being scarcely 17 years of age at the time of enlisting. He had been so desirous of going to war, however, for twelve months previously, and eventually, like so many valiant young Australians, whose names will ever enrich the martial annals of our country, found his way to the fiery zone of war, to meet the glorious end of the noblest warrior in the very flower of his youth. Private Charles A. Clissold was a native of Emu Plains and attended the Emu and Penrith Public Schools in his boyhood. At the time of enlisting he was employed at the Emu Gravel Works, living at his parental home. In writing home he had mentioned that he had spent his 18th birthday (29 March) at the Front, in a very different atmosphere to that of the peaceful surroundings in Australia of his previous birthdays; and in his last letter he stated that he had met Private Mertoun Mills (since reported killed, to the great regret of Penrith citizens), Privates W. and C. Fowler, Private C. Ausburn (lately reported wounded), Roy Richards, and others. He was then – at the time of writing (27 April) just having three weeks furlough after strenuous work in the field. Deceased was a member of the Senior Cadets and had always taken close interest in military matters. He was a fine open-hearted, brave, high-spirited lad, and the deep sympathy of his associates of the community will go out to his bereaved mother and sisters, who have suffered such a grievous blow, on the double bereavement, through the harrowing agency of the most sanguinary of wars." Corpl. M.S. Mills, Australian Field Artillery, is buried in Nieppe Communal Cemetery (II.A.7).

(Panel 25) Pte. 399, Norman Lachlan Creswick, 'B' Coy., 36th Bn. Australian Infantry, A.I.F.: *s.* of Richard William (& Mrs M.) Creswick, of 'Arthursleigh Station,' Big Hill, Marulan, New South Wales: and yr. brother to Corpl. 476, H.A. Creswick, Australian Railway Divn. (ret'd. Australia, July 1919); and elder brother to Pte. 2536, T.S. Creswick, 37th Battn., A.I.F., who fell 7–9 June 1917: *b.* Lake Cargellico, New South Wales, December 1896: Religion – Church of England: Occupation – Station Overseer: 5'8" tall, hazel eyes, auburn hair: serving member of Albury Field Artillery & Cadets, enlisted Liverpool, New South Wales, 19 January 1916: departed Sydney A.72 'Beltana,' 13 May: served with the Expeditionary Force in France and Flanders from 23 November 1916, and was killed in action, 11 June 1917. Pte. 470, A. Hickey and Sergt. 417, H.F. Dalziel said that on the day after taking La Potterie Farm, nr. Messines, Pte. Creswick (Signaller/Company Runner), in company with Pte. F.R. Edleston, was relaying a message from Company Headquarters to the front line when he was killed instantaneously by fragments from a nearby shell burst. "He was one of the best, humorous and merry and always ready to do anything for a fellow. He was very popular." Buried in the Military Cemetery nr. St. Yves. Age 21. *unm.*

His brother Thomas also has no known grave; he is recorded below.

(Panel 25) Pte. 2042, Maurice Joseph Curran, 'D' Coy., 36th Bn. Australian Infantry, A.I.F.: *s.* of Jane Curran (Cowabbie Street, Coolamon, New South Wales): and brother to Pte. 1630, L.W. Curran, M.M. (medically discharged, effects of gas poisoning, 24 April 1919): *b.* October 1888: Religion – Roman Catholic: Occupation – Labourer: 5'4" tall, blue eyes, brown hair: enlisted Cootamundra, New South Wales, 11 April 1916: departed Sydney, A.68 'Anchises,' 24 August: served with the Expeditionary Force in France and Flanders from 23 November 1916, and was killed at Passchendaele, 12 October 1917, in company with Pte. 2319, J.E. Hughes when a shell fell on their Lewis Gun position. Age 29. *unm*. At the time of his death, Maurice's brother (a member of the same gun team) was beside him.

Pte. Hughes also has no known grave, he is recorded below.

(Panel 25) Pte. 1094, George Henry Davies, 'D' Coy., 36th Bn. Australian Infantry, A.I.F.: *s*. of John Davies, of 'The Marsh Arms,' Much Wenlock, co. Salop, by his wife Lilla: *b*. Montgomery, Wales: Religion – Protestant: Occupation – Missionary: 5'6" tall, fair complexion, blue eyes, brown hair: crushed thumb and forefinger left hand (slightly disfigured): enlisted A.I.F., Coff's Harbour, New South Wales, 24 January 1916; posted 'D' Coy., 36th Battn., Broadmeadows: departed Sydney, A.72 'Beltana,' 13 May 1916: trained England, July–November: joined the Expeditionary Force in France on the 22nd of the latter month and was killed in action, 12 July 1917; Messines. Age 28. In a letter to his mother written (6 June 1917) on the eve of the Battle of Messines, he said, "...I am now ready for the big push, ready in mind, body and spirit; I was never better in health than I am now, my mind is just as clear, my soul has been purified, and the whole is in God's hands. If I die do not fear for me, I will wait for you my loved above all, and for my father and brothers and sisters too. You will read much of my doings...you will know something of my struggle...I give my life willingly for my country knowing that it is given in a righteous cause. I can do no more. I give my love to you all and to Jesus Christ My Maker.."

(Panel 25) Pte. 2306, Bruce Macquarie Gamack, 'D' Coy., 36th Bn. Australian Infantry, A.I.F.: late of Hastings River, Rollands Plains, New South Wales: *s*. of James E. Gamack, of Kempsey, New South Wales, by his wife Mary Elizabeth: and brother to Pte. 3806, W.C. Gamack, 19th Australian Infantry, who fell, 6 November 1917; and Pte. 4354, A.B. Gamack, 20th Australian Infantry (returned Australia, September 1916): *b*. Rolland's Plains, June 1893: Religion – Presbyterian: Occupation – Teamster: 5'6" tall, hazel eyes, dark brown hair: enlisted West Maitland, New South Wales, 23 May 1916: departed Sydney aboard A.30 'Borda,' 17 October: served with the Expeditionary Force in France and Flanders from 29 March 1917 and, reported missing, 21 July 1917, subsequently adjudged by a Court of Enquiry (19 March 1918) to have been killed in action on the aforementioned date. Age 24. Pte. 2342, T.J. Kirk recorded, "...He was killed just after the big stunt, while we were on a little raid; I was stretcher bearer at the time. His mate Hughes (killed 12 October) found his disc and brought it in. He was very well liked and a good chap." He leaves a wife, Janet Christine Gamack (Ferry Street, East Kempsey), a son James Eric, and *dau*. Ena Mary Macquarie.

His brother Wilton also has no known grave; he is recorded on Panel 23.

(Panel 25) Pte. 2319, Joseph Edward Hughes, 36th Bn. Australian Infantry, A.I.F.: late of Denison Street, Hamilton, New South Wales: *b*. Newcastle, New South Wales, 1890: Religion – Church of England: Occupation – Labourer: 5'7¾" tall, brown eyes, dark brown hair: enlisted, 12 July 1916: departed Sydney, A.30 'Borda,' 17 October: served with the Expeditionary Force in France from 29 March 1917: hospitalised (Scabies/Dermatitis) 9 May: rejoined his unit 30 July: hospitalised (Influenza) 27 September–4 October, and was killed at Passchendaele on the 12th of that month in company with Pte. 2042, M.J. Curran. Age 27. He leaves a widow, Margaret Hughes (Warner's Bay, New South Wales). See Pte. B.M. Gamack, above.

Pte. Curran also has no known grave; he is recorded above.

(Panel 25) Pte. 477, Albert Selwyn Judd, 'B' Coy., 36th Bn. Australian Infantry, A.I.F.: only *s*. of Albert H. (& Mrs B.) Judd, of 'Frankford,' Melford & Kilbride Street, Hurlstone Park, New South Wales: *b*. Goulburn, December 1893: Religion – Church of England: Occupation – Labourer: 5'2¼" tall, fresh complexion, blue eyes, brown hair: member of Metropolitan Railway Rifle Club (Sydney), joined A.I.F. Liverpool, New South Wales, 15 January 1916: departed Sydney, HMAT 'Heltana,' 13 May: appointed Sanitary Squad, 4 July; transf'd. 36th Battn. 11 July: served with the Expeditionary Force in France and Flanders from 22 November, and was killed in action, 7 June 1917, at Messines. Buried S.28.S.W.u.3.d.2.4. Age 23. *unm*. His effects – 2 Discs, Wallet, Diary, Photos, Cameo Ring, Aluminium Ring, Crucifix, Metal Watch and Strap – were received by his father, 2 April 1918; three months later – 'Inserted by his loving friend Miss Ethel Wells, of Annandale' – *The Sydney Morning Herald* (7 June 1918), carried the following 'In Memoriam':-

Sadly a loved one is thinking
Of her soldier boy so brave,
Who fell for the cause of freedom,
And now lies in a hero's grave.

(Panel 25) Pte. 1989, Leslie Victor Poll, 36th Bn. Australian Infantry, A.I.F.: *s.* of William James Poll, of 'Endora,' The Avenue, Waitara, New South Wales: brother to Pte. 2236, C.W. Poll, 1st A.I.F. (wounded; discharged, 18 July 1916); and cousin to Pte. 4673, I. Bunyan, 19th A.I.F., died of wounds, 11 May 1917, and Pte. 4672, E. Bunyan, 19th A.I.F., killed in action, 8 October 1917: *b.* Thornleigh, 1898: Occupation – Railway Cleaner: serving member – 4 years, 6 months – Senior Cadets (Militia); enlisted Show Grounds Camp, Sydney, 23 October 1916; apptd. (25 October) Pte. (Bomber) no. A156377, 6th Rfts., Light T.M. Bty.: proceeded overseas, 10 February 1917: trained England (from 11 April); transfd. 63rd Bn. 24 April: proceeded to France, 23 August; joined 36th Bn., Le Mesnil, Boutry, 1 September: reported wounded, since confirmed (6 October) killed in action, 3 October 1917. Age 19.

Edwin 'Edward' Bunyan also has no known grave, he is recorded on Panel 23; Irwin is buried in Boulogne Eastern Cemetery (IV.B.19).

(Panel 25) Lieut. 858, James Roadknight, 37th Bn. Australian Infantry, A.I.F.: *s.* of James Roadknight, of Bairnsdale East, Victoria, by his wife Annie M.: and brother to Lieut. W. Roadknight, 37th Australian Infantry, died of wounds (GSW chest), 11 August 1918, at 55th Casualty Clearing Station, aged 32 years: *b.* Bairnsdale, 1892: Religion – Church of England: *educ.* Bairnsdale Schools: 5'9" tall, blue eyes, fair hair: Occupation – State School Teacher: previously served 2 years Senior Cadets: joined 8th A.I.F., Broadmeadows, 25 August 1915: transf'd 60th Battn., 24 February 1916: trained Egypt: served with the Expeditionary Force in France from 29 June 1916: underwent Officer Training, England from 5 September; apptd. 2nd Lieut. 28 October; returned to France, 7 December: joined 37th Battn. 13 January 1917; promoted Lieut. 22 May: wounded (GSW shldr.) in action 7–9 June 1917: evacuated to England, 10 June; discharged to duty, 3 September; rejoined 37th Bn., France on the 20th of that month, and was killed in action, 12 October 1917, at Passchendaele, Belgium. Age 25.

His brother Walter is buried in Daours Communal Cemetery Extension (III.E.24).

(Panel 25) Sergt.Major 912, William Thomas Jarrott, 37th Bn. Australian Infantry, A.I.F.: eldest *s.* of Thomas Jarrott, of Myrrhee, Victoria, by his wife Martha: *b.* Moyhu, Victoria, *c.* 1896: was on the staff of the Wangaratta State School: enlisted January 1916: trained at Seymour and Port Melbourne; achieved rank of Sergt.: went through several training schools, attending the Musketry School, at Hayling Island, England: went to France with his battalion, arriving 23 November 1916: took part in the fighting at Armentieres and also several other big engagements: slightly wounded in the face on one occasion, but did not leave the lines. On this occasion his company received special mention for bravery, and Sergt Jarrott was promoted to the rank of Sergt.Major in the field. Reported missing, 9 June 1917 and is now known to have been killed in action on or about that date. 'Prior to enlisting Sergt.Major Jarrott took a deep interest in church and Sunday School matters, and was a teacher at Holy Trinity Cathedral Sunday School. He was a very smart young fellow, and gained his merit certificate at an early age, and after taking a course at the High School joined the education department there; his first appointment being at Myrtleford School. While in Wangarratta he took an interest in the Rowing Club, and played football with local teams. He was of a quiet nature, and his pleasant manner made him popular with his mates and scholars, and with all who knew him.' A brother, Pte. J.M. Jarrott, enlisted at the same time, and is still (July 1917) fighting in France. Age 21. On 12 June 1917 the Australian attack on the Oosttaverne Line met with heavy fire from hedges and trenches, and close machine-gun fire from blockhouses – which they had not previously encountered – forced the men to throw themselves down. At least four of these blockhouses stood in or beside Oosttaverne Trench – one 100 yards south of Huns Walk, one in the Walk, and two at intervals north of it. The Official History states: "In this, their first introduction to blockhouse fighting, the Australians were not assisted by artillery preparation as elaborate as in the earlier phase of the battle; the Germans, freshly reinforced, were able to stand and fight, and the struggle was especially fierce. The tension accompanying the struggles around these blockhouses – the murderous fire from a sheltered position, followed by the sudden giving in of the surrounded garrison – caused this year's fighting in Flanders to be marked by a ferocity that renders the reading of any true narrative particularly unpleasant. Where such tension exists in battle, the rules of 'civilised' war are powerless. Most men are temporarily half-mad, their pulses pounding at their ears, their mouths dry. The noblest among them are straining their wills to keep cool heads, and even voices; the less self-controlled are for the time being governed by a reckless, primitive impulse. With death singing about their ears they will kill until they grow tired of killing. When they have been racked by machine-gun fire, the routing out of enemy groups from behind several feet of concrete is almost inevitably the signal for a butchery at least of the first few who emerge, and sometimes even the hopelessly wounded may not be spared. It is idle for the reader to cry shame upon such incidents, unless he cries out upon the whole system of war, for this frenzy is an inevitable condition in desperate fighting. The nobler the leaders the more they endeavour to mitigate futile ruthlessness, but ruthlessness is a quality essential in hand-to-hand fighting, and soldiers were deliberately trained to it." In the fighting to gain the front trench near Huns Walk, despite the right front company of the 47th Battalion having lost all its officers killed or mortally wounded, under the leadership of the surviving officers of the second company the front trench was taken. These officers tried as best they could to control the men under them, but as the maddened Australians drew closer to the enemy from the front and the barrage churned the dust behind, many of the remaining Germans became panic stricken and threw themselves on the mercy of the approaching troops. Some threw themselves on their knees crying, "Mercy! Kamerad!" others bolted and ran – too much for the pent up anger of men who had only moments previously been under a merciless fire from a well protected enemy. One of few incidents recorded relates to Corpl. 6049, P. McCarthy, 37th Battn., who, after witnessing the death of a comrade while attempting to bomb a machine gun firing from a concrete shelter known as Septieme Barn, ran behind what cover he could find, worked around the place and thrust a bomb through a side loophole; its explosion was followed by a minute's silence, then the gun resumed firing whereupon McCarthy put a bomb through the front loophole, destroying both the gun and its remaining crew. McCarthy was killed four months later.

(Panel 25) Corpl. 6049, Patrick McCarthy, D.C.M., 37th Bn. Australian Infantry, A.I.F.: *s.* of James McCarthy, Hodson Street, Sailors Gully, Eaglehawk, Victoria: *b.* Birchip, Victoria, 8 June 1893: Religion – Roman Catholic: Occupation – Miner: Convicted – Fined £3,1/- Drunkenness and Assaulting a Police Officer; Broken Hill, 1914: 5'8¾" tall; medium complexion, brown eyes, dark brown hair: enlisted Melbourne, 17 April 1916: trained England, from 11 September; hospitalised (V.D.) 4 October–23 December: joined Expeditionary Force in France, 4 February 1917: hospitalised (Influenza), 27 February–8 March: detached to 3rd Canadian Tunnelling Coy., 27 April–4 May: promoted Corpl. 8 June: On Leave, England, 11 June; rejoined battalion, 24 June: Awarded Distinguished Conduct Medal (*London Gazette*, 25 August 1917), 'For conspicuous gallantry and devotion to duty under heavy machine-gun fire. He moved forward with a comrade, and succeeded in bombing and silencing a hostile machine gun which was firing from a strong concrete emplacement upon his company.': hospitalised (Influenza), 13–24 September. Reported wounded and missing, 12 October 1917; confirmed (May 1918) killed in action. Age 24.

(Panel 25) L/Corpl. 228, William Edward Babington, 37th Bn. Australian Infantry, A.I.F.: late of Stacey's Bridge, Victoria: *b.* Trentham, Victoria, 22 September 1891: Occupation – Dairyman. Killed in action, 8 June 1917, nr. Oostaverne. Earlier in the day, after his company had taken a German trench south of Huns Walk, he saw a large party of the enemy making their way down the communication trench and, laying his Lewis gun on the trench, shot them down in enfilade. Age 25.

(Panel 25) L/Corpl. 6955, Reginald Percy Bartram, 37th Bn. Australian Infantry, A.I.F.: eldest *s.* of George Andrew Bartram, of 'Clare,' Gould Street, Frankston, Victoria, by his marriage to the late Isabella Bartram: and brother to Sergt. 2682, R.E. Bartram, 46th Battn., killed in action at Messines, 7 June 1917; Pte. 2304, A.R. Bartram, 60th Battn., died of wounds, 13 May 1917, received at Bullecourt: *b.* Richmond, Victoria, 1881: Occupation – Compositor; Moreland, Victoria: enlisted Richmond, 25

August 1916: departed Melbourne, 23rd Rfts., HMAT 'Horotata,' 23 November following: promoted A/Corpl. 4 March 1917: qualified 1st in class, 8th Rifle Course School of Musketry, 9 April 1917: served with the Expeditionary Force in France joining 37th Battn. In the Field, June 1917 (apptd. L/Corpl.), and was killed in action at Broodseinde Ridge, 4 October 1917. Age 36. Prior to leaving Australia A/Corpl. Bartram had placed his two sons in the care of Melbourne Orphanage and requested (January 1917) his sister be appointed next-of-kin as his wife had been an inmate of Monk Park Aylum for several years. A fourth brother, Pte. 2126, Cyril G. Bartram, 58th Battn., admitted to hospital with influenza in September 1916, followed by numerous further admissions in England, was medically discharged and returned to Australia in July 1917.

His brother Raymond is buried in Messines Ridge British Cemetery (VI.C.32/36); Arnold lies in Grevillers British Cemetery (II.E.2).

(Panel 25) L/Corpl. 983, Alfred Henry Rose, 'C' Coy., 37th Bn. Australian Infantry, A.I.F.: *s.* of Thomas Rose, by his wife Annie: *b.* Richmond, Victoria, about 1893. Reported missing after the fighting, 7 June 1917, since confirmed (11 July 1917) killed in action on that date. Age 23. *unm.* A comrade, Pte. 6077, J.W. Stewart said, "He was a Lewis Gunner, and he was killed on this date at about 5 o'clock in the evening by a machine gun bullet as he was carrying his gun supporting the front line." Buried S.E. of Messines, between Bethleem Farm and 700 yards to the south. Remains recovered unmarked grave (28.O.34.c.80.10); identified Clothing, Badges, Brass Plate inscribed 'No.983 A.H. Rose 10/Inf. Bde. 'C'Coy. 37 Bn. Kew. Vic. Aust.;' reinterred, registered 8 March 1930. (*IWGC record 8 June*) *Buried in Sanctuary Wood Cemetery (V.J.21).*

(Panel 25) L/Corpl. 1673, Alfred Arnold Vearing, 37th Bn. Australian Infantry, A.I.F.: *s.* of Alfred (& Mary) Vearing of Beckom, via Illinois, New South Wales: and brother to Coy.Sergt.Major 1674, V. Vearing, 37th Battn., A.I.F. (surv'd.): *b.* Seymour, Victoria, 1897: Religion – Methodist: Occupation – Farmer: 5'8½" tall, fresh complexion, dark blue eyes, brown hair: joined A.I.F., Wangaratta, Victoria, 4 April 1916; posted 1st Rfts., 37th Battn., 19 May: departed Melbourne, 27 May 1916: served with the Expeditionary Force in France from 23 November: slightly wounded in action 1 January 1917, and 20 April (bullet, right forearm): apptd. L/Corpl. 1 August. Killed in action, during the attack of 4 October 1917. A member of a Lewis gun team, he was sheltering in a shell hole when he was hit in the side by an explosive bullet which tore open his stomach, death being practically instantaneous. Buried where he fell. Age 20. *unm.* Remains of an 'Unknown Australian Soldier' recovered from an unmarked grave (28.D.21.a.5.4); identified – Clothing, Titles, Damaged Disc; reinterred, registered 28 October 1927. *Buried in Sanctuary Wood Cemetery (IV.J.10).*

Be Not Far From Me For Trouble Is Near There Is No One To Help Me

(Panel 25) Pte. 823, Ernest Briggs, 'C' Coy., 37th Bn. Australian Infantry, A.I.F.: *s.* of Thomas Briggs, of 'Red Bank,' Tawonga P.O. via Yackandandah, Victoria, by his wife Annie Maria: and brother to Pte. 822, A.T. Briggs, 37th Australian Infantry, died of pneumonia, 21 January 1917, at Larkhill Camp, Salisbury Plain: *b.* Yackandandah, 1895: Occupation – Farmer: enlisted Waganratta, 1 March 1916: departed Melbourne 3 June: served with the Expeditionary Force in France from 22 November 1916, and was killed in action, 4 October 1917. Buried 1 January 1918 (28N.E. D.21.c.2.8). Age 22. *unm.* His effects – Identity Disc, Wallet, Letters, Photos, Diary, 5 Franc lead coin, Silver Greek coin, 7 other coins, 2 Purses, Cards, Knife, Button, Belt, 2 Brushes, 3 Books, Curio, Sheet Music – were received by his father June–November 1918; Memorial Scroll, Plaque, War & Victory medals, 1922–24.

His brother Albert is buried in Durrington Cemetery (157).

(Panel 25) Pte. 2536, Thomas Sefton Creswick, 'D' Coy., 37th Bn. Australian Infantry, A.I.F.: *s.* of Richard William (& Mrs M.) Creswick, of 'Arthursleigh Station,' Big Hill, Marulan, New South Wales: and yr. brother to Corpl. 476, H.A. Creswick, Australian Railway Divn. (ret'd. Australia, July 1919); and Pte. 399, N.L. Creswick, 36th Battn. A.I.F., who fell on 11 June 1917: *b.* Lake Cargellico, New South Wales, March 1897: Religion – Church of England: Occupation – Station Overseer: 5'10½" tall, grey eyes, brown hair: enlisted Royal Agricultural Show Grounds, Moore Park, Sydney, 21 September 1916:

departed Australia aboard A.24 'Benalla,' 9 November: served with the Expeditionary Force in France and Flanders from 4 May 1917 and, reported wounded and missing 7–9 June 1917, was subsequently adjudged by a Court of Enquiry (18 January 1918) to have been killed in action some time between the aforementioned dates. Age 19. Buried south-east of Messines, between Bethleem Farm and Septieme Barn. Pte. 2549, D. Davis recorded, "It was June 7th during the Messines advance, we had advanced close on two miles and had nearly reached the final objective. I got into a shell hole and found Creswick already in it, very badly wounded in the leg and up one side. I covered him up with a waterproof sheet, filled his water bottle, and made him as comfortable as I could but there was no chance then of getting the S/Bs to him; they were too far behind. I had to go on to the final objective then and do not know what happened to him afterwards…" And Pte. 2668, W.S. Winterbottom, "…We had to retire that night from the ground, and he was left out. I went out the same night to try and bring him in. I found the shell hole but another shell had evidently hit the spot; there was no trace of Creswick."

His brother Norman also has no known grave; he is recorded above.

(Panel 25) Pte. 883 Albert Edward Gundrill, 37th Bn. Australian Infantry, A.I.F.: *b.* Carlton, Victoria: enlisted, 28 February 1916, aged 24 yrs 4 months, with his brother Alfred: 5'10½", hazel eyes, fair 'haird': Occupation – Labourer: embarked on the 'Persic', 3 June 1916: after some time spent in England, proceeded to France, serving with the Expeditionary Force there: wounded in the right arm and forearm, 28 January 1917, and invalided to England aboard H.M.S. Cumbria: after recovery, 8 March 1917, was given 'Blighty' leave until the 23rd of that month: returned to France, 19 April: rejoined his battalion at the Front, 27 April. On 12 October following, during the Battle of Passchendaele, 'one of the darkest days in the battalion's history, Albert was wounded and, whilst awaiting treatment a shell landed close by and killed him instantly.' Supplying information to the Australian Red Cross Bureau, J.A. Smith, 105, stated, "I knew Casualty. He was a man about 5'11", well built, dark complexion, about 26 years of age. Casualty was at Passchendaele during the advance, and was on duty at the R.A.P. He was standing outside of the Dressing Station when a H.E. shell exploded near him, pieces entering his head and body, killing him instantly. I was 20 yards away at the time the shell exploded, and I saw his body immediately afterwards, and I was in charge of his platoon. He was buried near the R.A.P. at Hamburg Farm. A cross was erected with his number, name and unit on it."

(Panel 25) Pte. 3160, Inglebert Thomas Gunnelson, 37th Bn. Australian Infantry, A.I.F.: *s.* of Inglebert Gunnelson, of Garfield, Victoria, by his wife Mary: and elder brother to Pte. 893, P.O. Gunnelson, 8th Australian Infantry, killed in action, 8 May 1915, at Gallipoli: *b.* Narnargoon, Victoria, 1892: Occupation – Labourer: enlisted Melbourne, 2 September 1916: posted 22nd Rfts., 5th transf'd. 6th Battn., Broadmeadows Camp, 16 September; transf'd. 8th/59th Royal Park: departed Melbourne, A7 'Medic,' 18 December: transf'd. 67th Perham Downs, 25 April 1917; proceeded to France with a draft of reinforcements to 37th Battn.; joined 37th In the Field, 1 September, and was killed in action, 4 October 1917. Pte. 2615, P.P.H. McCabe reported, "I saw him with half his head blown off by a shell at Broodseinde Ridge. A party was going about burying just there, so sure to have been buried…I knew him fairly well." Buried (28.D.15.a.0.0) ¾ mile N. of Zonnebeke. Age 25. *unm.*

His brother Percy also has no known grave, he is commemorated on the Helles Memorial (Addenda Panel).

(Panel 25) Pte. 3110, William Jeffery Nash, 37th Bn. Australian Infantry, A.I.F.: Killed in action, 12 October 1917. A comrade, Pte. 3151, E.A. Gray, wrote, "I saw Pte. Nash, who was with me as a stretcher-bearer, blown up by a heavy shell on 12 October 1917. Nash was some half a dozen yards in front of me and the shell struck the stretcher that he was carrying. There is no doubt in my mind but that Nash was killed in this way."

(Panel 25) Pte. 102, Albert Raison, 37th Bn. Australian Infantry, A.I.F.: *s.* of Mrs Mary Ann Raison (Wangaratta, Victoria), by her marriage to the late Samuel Raison: and *yr.* brother to Pte. 103, E. Raison, who fell the same day. Killed in action, 8 June 1917. Age 21. *unm.*

His brother Ernest also has no known grave; he is recorded below.

(Panel 25) Pte. 103, Ernest Raison, 37th Bn. Australian Infantry, A.I.F.: *s.* of Mary Ann Raison (Wangaratta, Victoria), by her marriage to the late Samuel Raison: and elder brother to Pte. 102, A. Raison, who fell the same day. Killed in action, 8 June 1917. Age 22. *unm.*

His brother Albert also has no known grave; he is recorded above.

(Panel 25) Pte. 2032, George Alfred Arthur, 38th Bn. Australian Infantry, A.I.F.: *s.* of William Arthur, of Glenburnie, Mount Gambier, South Australia, by his wife Eliza: and brother to Pte. 2031, H.J. Arthur, 38th Bn. A.I.F., who fell nine days later. Killed in action, 4 October 1917, at Broodseinde Ridge. Age 30. Buried where he fell. Pte. 5024, A.V. Grinton reported, "I don't know which one of them it was, but I saw one of them lying with all his equipment off as though asleep, but he couldn't have been as there was terrible shelling going on and it was very cold. I think he was dead but cannot be sure, as I did not go up to him. It was at Passchendaele in the open. We did not hold the line so burial is uncertain. He was the thinnest of the two Arthurs. One had a permanent boil on his neck, and he was not the one I saw. Probably killed by a bullet as he was not cut up in any way."

His brother Herbert also has no known grave; he is recorded below.

(Panel 25) Pte. 2031, Herbert John Arthur, 38th Bn. Australian Infantry, A.I.F.: *s.* of William Arthur, of Glenburnie, Mount Gambier, South Australia, by his wife Eliza: and brother to Pte. 2032, G.A. Arthur, 38th Bn. A.I.F., who fell at Broodseinde Ridge nine days previously: *b.* Mount Gambier, 1883: Occupation – Farmer: 5'9" tall, dark complexion, green/brown eyes, dark brown hair; 'Scar right side upper lip; Large cystic swelling (size of hen's egg) at back of head, says he intends to have it removed': Religion – Methodist: enlisted Horsham, Victoria, 7 April 1916: posted 3rd Rfts., 38th Battn. 3 September: departed Melbourne, HMAT 'Shropshire,' 25 September: served with the Expeditionary Force in France from 4 February 1917, and was killed in action, 13 October 1917. Age 33.

His brother George also has no known grave; he is recorded above.

(Panel 25) Pte. 5990, William John Cumming, 38th Bn. Australian Infantry, A.I.F.: *s.* of the late Thomas Wylie Cumming (*d.* 1903), by his wife Margaret Jane ('Sorbie,' Bridgewater-on-Loddon, Victoria): and brother to Coy.Sergt.Major 898, A.T.G. Cumming, 7th Australian Infantry, died of wounds, 12 August 1915, at Gallipoli: *b.* Sorbie Farm, Kerang, Victoria, 1894: *educ.* Bridgewater State School: Occupation – Farm Labourer, Messrs John Sloan & Sons: enlisted Bendigo, 1 March 1916: departed Australia, 28 March 1916: served with the Expeditionary Force in France from 22 November following: wounded (GSW, wrist, fractured) during a raid, 27 February 1917, and evacuated to England: returned to France, 26 June following, and was killed in action, 4 October 1917; Broodseinde Ridge, Passchendaele. Age 22. *unm.*

His brother Andrew also has no known grave; he is commemorated on the Lone Pine Memorial (27).

(Panel 25) Pte. 2178, John Ray Gardner, 38th Bn. Australian Infantry, A.I.F.: *s.* of George Charles Frederick Gardner, of Fairchilds, Goroke (Post Office), Victoria, by his wife Frances: Occupation – Farmer: enlisted Ballarat, 12 May 1916: departed Melbourne, 25 September: served in France from 17 February 1917; joined 38th Battn. In the Field 19 March, and was killed in action at Broodseinde, 4 October 1917. In a letter to Mrs Gardner, Lieut. G. Dutton, 'C' Coy., 38th Battn., wrote, "No doubt you have been notified of your son being killed in action on the 4th of October, but as officer of his platoon, I am sending these few lines. For the battle, your son was in charge of my Lewis Gun team and when we advanced he was killed by a shell hitting almost for him. The gun he was carrying was smashed to pieces. Some of the boys of the team went back next day and we buried him on the battlefield. I have made a parcel of the personal effects that were on him, but the belt and watch he was carrying were gone. From the time I joined up the Battalion, I had a more than high regard for my Private Gardner; and he was always one of the best of the finest lot of lads I have ever been with. His quiet, honest bearing placed him very high in the estimation of the whole Company and his own special pals feel his loss very much. Trusting you and yours may be comforted in the knowledge that your boy was called doing his all in the great struggle we are all engaged in, and you will all accept our heartfelt sympathy in you trial." Age 23. *unm.*

(Panel 25) Pte. 2347, Vivian Roy Kirsch, 38th Bn. Australian Infantry, A.I.F.: *s.* of Simon Kirsch, of 48, Auburn Grove, Auburn, Victoria, by his wife Julia Annie: and brother to Capt. R.N.C. Kirsch, 8th Bn. A.I.F., killed in action the same day: *b.* Hawthorn, Victoria, 1897: Religion – Roman Catholic:

Occupation – Bank Clerk: previously served No.12 Coy. Australian Army Service Corps: enlisted, 28 July 1916; departed Melbourne, 20 October. Killed in action, 4 October 1917, at Broodseinde Ridge. Age 20.

His brother Rudolph also has no known grave; he is recorded on Panel 7.

(Panel 25) Coy.Sergt.Major, 789, Algernon Robinson Moore, 'C' Coy., 39th Bn. Australian Infantry, A.I.F.: late of 378, Bay Street, Port Melbourne: *s.* of the late John Robinson Moore, Draper, of 60, Beaconsfield Parade, Albert Park, Victoria, by his wife Alice, *née* Tucker (64, Prospect Hill Road, Camberwell, Victoria): and yr. brother to 2nd Lieut. 4745, N.J. Moore, 23rd Bn. Australian Infantry, who fell nr. Zonnebeke, 3 October 1917, aged 27 years: *b.* Melbourne, 1895: Religion – Church of England: Occupation – Draper: 5'6½" tall, grey eyes, black hair: enlisted 13 September 1915; apptd. Corpl.: posted 'B' Coy., 24th Depot Battn., Royal Park, 4 October 1915 (promoted Sergt. 22 February 1916); thereafter (from 22 May 1916) 39th Battn., Ballarat: departed Melbourne; H.M.A.T. 'Ascanius,' 27 May: served with the Expeditionary Force in France from 24 November 1916: hospitalised (Scabies), 30 December–7 January 1917: slightly wounded at Bullecourt, 30 April following and, after treatment by 9th Australian Field Ambulance, returned to duty the same day: promoted Coy.Sergt.Major, 12 July 1917. Reported wounded and missing nr. Hamburg Farm, Passchendaele, 12 October 1917; confirmed killed in action by a Court of Enquiry (4 April 1918). Age 22. *unm.* Coy.Sergt.Major Moore – last seen in the early morning of 12 October 'going back to look for something' along a sunken road – was decapitated by a fragment of a shell which exploded nearby. Buried in a shell hole with three other men; no marker was erected.

His brother Norman also has no known grave; he is recorded on Panel 23.

(Panel 25) Pte. 2284, John Brew, 39th Bn. Australian Infantry, A.I.F.: *s.* of Richard Brew, of 321, Lyons Street, Ballarat, Victoria; late of Great Crosby, Liverpool, by his wife Elizabeth: and brother to Capt. H. Brew (surv'd.); Pte. 9806, S. Brew, Australian Army Medical Corps, died of wounds, 16 August 1918; and cousin to 2nd Lieut. T. Brew, D.C.M., 2nd Australian Infantry, killed in action, 4 October 1917: *b.* Ballarat, 1874: Occupation – Journalist: joined A.I.F., Melbourne, 12 September 1916: proceeded overseas, 20 October: served with the Expeditionary Force in France from 25 April 1917, joined 39th Battn. In the Field, 13 May; wounded (GSW Rt. Arm) on the 27th of that month, admitted 10th transf'd. 9th Field Ambulance and discharged to duty same day, and was killed in action at Messines Ridge, 8 June 1917. Age 43.

His brother Samuel is buried in Daours Communal Cemetery Extension (IV.C.5); cousin Thomas, Oxford Road Cemetery (IV.D.3).

(Panel 25) Pte. 6007, Joseph Guy Evans, 'C' Coy., 39th Bn. Australian Infantry, A.I.F.: *s.* of George Evans, of Weldborough, Tasmania, by his wife Ellen. Killed in action, 7 June 1917. A comrade, Pte. 1715, T.E. Stevenson, reported, "I saw him killed at Messines. He was sniped through the head whilst out with a ration carrying party. He was buried in the field, just behind Messines Hill, and the grave was marked with a cross bearing his No., name and unit." Age 23. *unm.*

(Panel 25) Lieut. Charles Frederic Sharland, 40th Bn. Australian Infantry, 10th Australian Bde., A.I.F.: only *s.* of the Rev. Frederic Burnett Sharland, of 'Lanreath,' Adelaide Street, Hobart, Tasmania, B.A., by his wife Ella Georgina, *dau.* of William Seccombe, F.R.C.S.: *b.* Westbury, Tasmania, 23 October 1882: *educ.* Grammar School, Launceston, and Hutchins School, Hobart: Occupation – Head Clerk; Inspectors' Dept., Union Bank of Sydney, New South Wales: enlisted Hobart, December 1915: gazetted 2nd Lieut. 40th Battn. June 1916: left for England with 3rd Reinforcements, 40th Battn. the following September: stationed for some months on Salisbury Plain, training men and receiving further instruction himself: served with the Expeditionary Force in France and Flanders from June 1917: promoted Lieut. on the 27th of that month, and was killed in action at Passchendaele Ridge, 12 October following. Buried there. His Commanding Officer wrote, "He was a popular comrade and a most efficient soldier," and another officer, "His death is a severe blow to our battalion, as without doubt he was one of our most popular officers" Age 34. *unm.*

(Panel 25) Sergt. 583, Frederick Rawson, M.M., 40th Bn. Australian Infantry, A.I.F.: *s.* of George Rawson, of Gippsland, by his wife Mary: *b.* Walhalla, Victoria, 17 October 1879: enlisted, 12 February 1916: served with the Expeditionary Force in France and Flanders from 24 November 1916. Killed in action, 5 October 1917. Age 37. Awarded the Military Medal for 'conspicuous gallantry in action during operations at Messines, 7th June 1917. In company with four of his men he rushed an enemy strongpoint, and was successful in capturing a large number of prisoners. Throughout the whole operation he displayed the greatest dash and determination.' He leaves a wife, Lillian (Railton, Tasmania), and five children. (*IWGC record age 38*)

(Panel 25) L/Corpl. 2041, Eric Laban Blizzard, 40th Bn. Australian Infantry, A.I.F.: c/o his sister Mrs Eliza Horton, *née* Blizzard (Norwest Forest, Circular Head, Tasmania): yr. brother to Spr. 2891, D.N. Blizzard, 3rd Australian Tunnelling Coy. (surv'd); and Pte. 345, J.L. Blizzard, 40th Bn. A.I.F., who fell the same day: *b.* Forest, Tasmania, 1889: Religion – Church of England: Occupation – Labourer: enlisted Claremont, Tasmania, 13 July 1916: 5'6½" tall, blue eyes, fair hair: posted 40th Battn. 6 August: departed Melbourne; A.49 'Seang Choon,' 23 September: Awarded 21 Days Detention, 27 December 1916, for 'Failure to appear at a place of parade appointed by his Commanding Officer': served with the Expeditionary Force in France from 6 April 1917: joined 40th Battn. In the Field, 11 June; apptd. L/Corpl. on the 22nd of that month, and was killed in action, 5 October 1917. Age 28. *unm.* Exhumed 28.D.20.a.5.3, north-west of Zonnebeke, and identified by Disc '2041, E.L. Blizzard 40th Bn. A.I.F.' recovered with remains and reburied, 2 November 1927; next of kin notified, 1 February 1928. *Buried in Sanctuary Wood Cemetery (IV.K.4).*

His brother James has no known grave; he is recorded below.

(Panel 25) Pte. 345, James Lewis Blizzard, 40th Bn. Australian Infantry, A.I.F.: yr. brother to L/Corpl. 2041, E.L. Blizzard, 40th Bn. A.I.F. who fell the same day; and Spr. 2891, D.N. Blizzard, 3rd Australian Tunnelling Coy. (surv'd.): *b.* Forest, Tasmania, 1892: Occupation – Labourer: enlisted Claremont, 9 February 1916. Killed in action, 5 October 1917. Age 25. He leaves a wife, Lucy Blizzard (Montague River, Tasmania).

His brother Eric is buried in Sanctuary Wood Cemetery (IV.K.4).

PANEL 25 ENDS PTE. M.J. QUINN, 41ST BN. AUSTRALIAN INF.

PANEL 27 BEGINS PTE. R.W. REID, 41ST BN. AUSTRALIAN INF.

The Secretary,
Australian Graves Service,
W.C.2

AA/LS/5/12801

I am directed to inform you that in accordance with the agreement with the French and Belgian Governments to remove all scattered graves, and certain cemeteries which were situated in places unsuitable for permanent retention, it has been found necessary to exhume the bodies buried in certain areas. In the process of exhumation the grave of the soldier named on the attached location sheet was located as noted below his name, and his remains were re-interred in the Cemetery stated.

Principal Assistant Secretary,
Imperial War Graves Commission.
20 June 1928.

On 10 September 1928 the Australian Graves Service in London received the following notification: "Will you please note that the remains of six Australian soldiers were found in the vicinity of Messines, map reference 28.U.2.a.3.9. and have been exhumed and reburied in certain graves in Sanctuary Wood Cemetery, Zillebeke. Investigations have been made and it has been found possible to definitely establish the identity of one of these soldiers as Lieut. N.D. Freeman who has been reburied in Plot 2, Row H, Grave 13, of Sanctuary Wood Cemetery; Location Sheet AA/LS/5/12801, forwarded to you on the

20th June last refers. Of the remaining five Unknowns, I am to say that on perusal of a burial return held in this office it has been ascertained that Pte. J.F. Foot and Pte. J. Fallon were originally buried with Lieut. Freeman, there is therefore no doubt that these two soldiers are buried in one of the three graves containing these five bodies. In these circumstances and in view of the fact that it has not been possible to say definitely which grave contains their remains, a Special Memorial has been erected over Grave 14, Plot 2, Row H, in Sanctuary Wood Cemetery bearing their names, regimental particulars and an inscription reading 'Buried Near This Spot.' Imperial War Graves Commission."

(Panel 27) Lieut. Norman David Freeman, 42nd Bn. Australian Infantry, A.I.F.: *s.* of Ernest Albert Freeman, of Kedron Villa, Southport, Queensland, by his wife Kate: *b.* Nerang, Southport, 8 October 1895: Religion – Church of England: Occupation – 2 years 3 months, Lieut. (Cadet), Permanent Forces, Royal Military College (Australia): joined A.I.F. 12 April 1916; posted 35th Bty., 9th Field Artillery Bde.: applied for and obtained a commission, 9 May: departed Sydney, H.M.A.T. A.8 'Argyllshire,' 11 May: proceeded to France, 30 December: transf'd. 29th Bty., 8th F.A. Bde. 5 January 1917; transf'd. 42nd Battn., apptd. Lieut. 20 June, and was wounded and killed in action on the night of 30–31 July 1917, while approaching Messines in readiness for an attack. Age 21. *unm.* Buried by Rev. G.W.P. Cutten, attd. 3rd Pioneer Battn., nr. 5 kilometre stone, south side Messines-Wulverghem road, Messines, France; Memorial Cross erected Wulverghem-Lindenhoek Road Military Cemetery (25.U.1.b.9.9). Remains recovered (28.U.2.a.3.9.) from an unmarked grave nr. Messines (11 May 1928), identification secured by means of Australian officers clothing and two identity discs recovered with the body; registered and reinterred, 18 May 1928, next-of-kin notified, "5 November...the necessity for the removal is much regretted but was unavoidable for the reasons above given (AA/LS/5/12801); you may find assurance in the knowledge that the work of reburial was carried out carefully and reverently." Capt. Sellick, Base Records, wrote, "25 August 1928...I am now in receipt of advice that during the course of exhumation work in the vicinity of Messines, the Imperial War Graves Commission was successful in recovering the remains of this officer which have since been interred with every measure of care and reverence in Plot 2, Row H, Grave 13 of Sanctuary Wood Cemetery, Zillebeke, Belgium, where a permanent headstone of uniform design will be erected and engraved with his full regimental description and date of death, together with any verse or epitaph previously selected in the form of a personal inscription. It is the practice of the Commission to notify relatives direct when the permanent headstones are finally in position, and at a later date the opportunity will be afforded you of obtaining a copy of the printed Register containing particulars of all British and Dominion War Graves in the above named cemetery." *Buried in Sanctuary Wood Cemetery (II.H.13).*

In Memory Of The Beloved Son Of Mr & Mrs Freeman Of Southport

(Panel 27) Sergt. 166, William Carr McCasker, 42nd Bn. Australian Infantry, A.I.F.: late *husb.* of Mrs. S.A. McCasker: *s.* of William Carr McCasker, of Mooroobie, Goondiwindi, Queensland, by his wife Annie: and elder brother to Pte. 173, C.E. McCasker, who fell, 3 July 1917. Killed instantaneously, 4 October 1917, by the explosion of a bomb dropped from a German aeroplane while on a working party laying cables on the left-hand side of the railway nr. Hill 60. Buried where he fell, within 20 minutes of his being killed. Age 33.

His brother Charles also has no known grave; he is recorded below.

(Panel 27) L/Corpl. 313, Robert Deckhardt, 'B' Coy., 42nd Bn. Australian Infantry, A.I.F.: late of Gladstone, Queensland: *b.* Holm, nr. Lublin, Poland, 1888: Religion – Roman Catholic: Occupation – Marine Fireman: 5'6" tall, fair complexion, blue eyes, brown hair: enlisted Rockhampton, 6 November 1915: trained Thompson Park, February–June 1916; departed Sydney, HMAT A.30 'Borda' on the 5th of the latter month: served with the Expeditionary Force in France and Flanders from 25 November 1916: apptd. L/Corpl. 5 August 1917. Killed in action, 12 October 1917. Age 29. *unm.* His effects – wallet, several books, letters, photos, new testament, cards, candles and holders – were forwarded to a comrade Pte. 303, W.J. Jew. (served as Corry), 42nd Battn., Stanley Lane, Gympie, Queensland; sole beneficiary of Pte. Deckhardt's will. In the absence of any blood relations his Memorial Plaque, Scroll (336575), British

War (41634), and Victory (41205) medals were retained by the Australian Base Records Dept. See account re. Pte. W.G. Averkoff, Messines Ridge British Cemetery (V.C.21).

(Panel 27) Pte. 318, Richard Alexander Doyle, 'B' Coy., 42nd Bn. Australian Infantry, A.I.F.: *s.* of George Rodney Doyle, of Wallumbilla, Queensland: and brother to Sergt. 1158, J.F. Doyle, 2nd Light Horse (surv'd): *b.* Wallumbilla, September 1894: Religion – Church of England: Occupation – School Teacher: 5'10½" tall, dark complexion, brown eyes, black hair: enlisted Toowoomba, 19 October 1915: posted 42nd Battn., Thompson Park, 16 February 1916; promoted Corpl. 2 November 1916 (England): served with the Expeditionary Force in France from the 25th of that month: charged with absenting himself without leave from a parade appointed by his commanding officer, 25 April 1917, and, after being reprimanded by his commanding officer, at his own request reverted to Pte. 17 June following, and was killed in action on the night of 30 July 1917, by the explosion of a shell while proceeding toward Messines in readiness for an attack the following morning (31 July). Age 22. *unm.* See Pte. J.F. Foot, Sanctuary Wood Cemetery (II.H.14).

(Panel 27) Pte. 2070, Jack (*a.k.a.* John) Fallon, 42nd Bn. Australian Infantry, A.I.F.: *s.* of the late James Fallon, by his wife Florence Catherine Hintz, *née* Fallon (Burnett Street, Bundaberg, Queensland): *b.* Pentland, Queensland: Religion – Church of England: Occupation – Labourer: previously medically discharged (Choreia), February 1916; re-enlisted Bundaberg, 13 May following: 5'7½" tall, blue eyes, fair hair: departed Brisbane, 7 September 1916: hospitalised Fovant Medical Hospital (N.Y.D.), 20 November–7 December: served with the Expeditionary Force in France from 16 March 1917: Awarded 1 day's Forfeiture of Pay, 7 Days Confined to Barracks (17 March) for being Absent Without Leave, 4–5 January 1917 (total forfeiture 8 Day's Pay, £2): hospitalised (Gonorrhoea), 19 June–1 July; rejoined his battalion in the field on the 10th of that month, and was killed in action on the night of 30–31 July 1917, while approaching Messines. Age 19. Buried by Rev. G.W.P. Cutten, attd. 3rd Pioneer Battn., nr. 5 kilometre stone, south side Messines-Wulverghem road, Messines, France (28.U.2.a.3.9). Memorial Cross recovered Lindenhoek – Wulverghem Military Cemetery; 68 Labour Coy., 21 October 1919. Remains exhumed (GRU Report, Zillebeke – 5/270E) from an unmarked grave (28.U.2.a.3.9), 11 May 1928, 'Two Unknown Australian Soldiers;' identified – Clothing; registered, reinterred 17 May 1928; next-of-kin notified accordingly (5 November 1928). *Buried in Sanctuary Wood Cemetery (II.H.14).*

Beloved Son Of Mrs Hintz Of Bundaberg Queensland
Eternal Rest

(Panel 27) Pte. 331, James Fitzroy Foot, 'B' Coy., 42nd Bn. Australian Infantry, A.I.F.: *s.* of Edmund D.O. Foot, of Nalcoombie Station, Springsure, Queensland, by his wife Ada, *née* Portus: *b.* December 1897: Religion – Church of England: Occupation – Station Hand: 5'9½" tall, grey eyes, fair hair, slight build: enlisted, 30 December 1915; posted 42nd Battn., 16 February 1916. Killed in action, 31 July 1917. Corpl. 4893, S.J. Rae, 42nd Battn., reported, "He was among the party going up on the night of 30th July ready for the attack on Messines on July 31st. While passing through the ruins of the town he was killed by the explosion of a shell which also killed others at the same time, including Pte. 318, R.A. Doyle. I saw them in a badly mangled condition, but do not know where or when they were buried. He was about 18 or 19, darkish, about 5ft 7, came from Queensland, straight from school." Age 19. Buried by Rev. G.W.P. Cutten, attd. 3rd Pioneer Battn., nr. 5 kilometre stone, south side Messines-Wulverghem road, Messines, France (28.U.2.a.3.9). Memorial Cross recovered Lindenhoek – Wulverghem Military Cemetery; 68 Labour Coy., 21 October 1919. Remains exhumed (GRU Report, Zillebeke – 5/270E) from an unmarked grave (28.U.2.a.3.9), 11 May 1928, 'Two Unknown Australian Soldiers;' identified – Clothing; registered, reinterred 17 May 1928; next-of-kin notified accordingly (5 November 1928). *Buried in Sanctuary Wood Cemetery (II.H.14).*

Thy Will Be Done In Loving Memory

Pte. R.A. Doyle has no known grave, he is recorded above.

(Panel 27) Pte. 2591, Ernest Kupfer, 42nd Bn. Australian Infantry, A.I.F.: *s.* of Ernest Kupfer, of Greenwood Farm, Yingerbay, Queensland, by his wife Sarah. Killed in action, 4 October 1917. Age 22. *unm.* See also Pte. R.G. Gregg, 26th Bn. A.I.F., Lijssenthoek Military Cemetery (XXI.F.5A).

(Panel 27) Pte. 173, Charles Edward McCasker, 'C' Coy., 42nd Bn. Australian Infantry, A.I.F.: *s.* of William Carr McCasker, of Mooroobie, Goondiwindi, Queensland, by his wife Annie: and yr. brother to Sergt. 166, W.C. McCasker, M.M., 42nd Battn. A.I.F., who fell, 4 October 1917. Reported slightly wounded and missing, believed taken prisoner on the night of 3–4 July 1917, near Gapaard Farm, Warneton; since confirmed (A.I.F. Hqrs., 18 January 1918) killed in action. In response to an enquiry made to Pte. F. Tierney, 42nd Battn., by the Red Cross Missing and Wounded Bureau (Sydney and Brisbane), Sergt. W.C. McCasker wrote, "19 September 1917…the above mentioned was my brother. Height 6 feet, weight 12 stone, dark hair, brown eyes, thin features, age 23 and so far as I know has no marks of identification. All his personal property was left behind and I have now forwarded same home, being under the impression that he was a prisoner of war. The above is all the information I can furnish, and would be most pleased if you can give me any information regarding his whereabouts." And Pte. 1279, J. Walsh, "19 October 1917. I knew Charlie McCasker well, he was in the same machine gun section as myself. He was about 23 years of age, fair, tall, thin faced. When he smiled he showed his teeth. He was a jovial sort of fellow. McCasker, who was No.2 on the gun, went out with Pte. McMillan who was No.1 on the gun. I was told by McMillan that he thought McCasker was following him, but looked round and presumed he had taken another route. This was at Warneton stronghold, near Messines (which we afterwards held) during the night – very dark. We all presumed that McCasker had run into a German patrol…" Age 23.

His brother William also has no known grave; he is recorded above.

(Panel 27) Pte. 729, Edward Felix Tardent, 42nd Bn. Australian Infantry, A.I.F.: *yst. s.* of Henry A. Tardent, of 'Ormonts,' Brisbane Road, Wynhum, Queensland, by his wife Hortense: *b. c.* 1899: Occupation – Farmer. Killed by hand grenades during an action with the Germans, 31 July 1917. *The Western Star*, 25 August 1917 reported – "Mr and Mrs Tardent … have just received the sad tidings that their youngest son, Corporal Felix Edward Tardent, has been killed in action. Corporal Tardent enlisted over 18 months ago, and was made a corporal the day he left Australia. He has been almost constantly in the firing line for the last seven or eight months." Age 18. (*AWM record Corpl.*)

(Panel 27) Capt. Frederick George Sims, Comdg. 'D' Coy., 43rd Bn. Australian Infantry, A.I.F.: *s.* of Frederick George Sims, of Hindmarsh, South Australia, by his wife Jane: *b.* 1885: joined A.I.F. 5 April 1916. Killed in action, 4 October 1917, in company with 2nd Lieut. Howden and three other men, at Broodseinde Ridge. Age 31. L/Corpl. 2337, G.H. Howden, 'D' Coy., 43rd Battn., said (18 March 1918), "I was talking to Capt. Sims a minute before a shell lobbed amongst us in our front line, about 2 a.m. on October 4th, while waiting before the hop-over. I looked for him for a couple of hours and could find nothing of him, and brought up Lieut. Walsh (killed afterwards, I believe) to take his place, and also reported to Lieut. Symons. The shell lobbed right amongst us…." He was married to Alice Sims (25, King William Road, North Unley). See account Capt. J.R. Eddy, Reninghelst New Military Cemetery (IV.C.4).

(Panel 27) Lieut. 1139, Charles Lloyd Herbert, 43rd Bn. Australian Infantry, A.I.F.: *s.* of Charles Edward Herbert, J.P., Govt. Secretary, Central Court, Territory of Papua, by his wife Anna Emilie (Port Moresby, Papua, British New Guinea): *b.* Redfern, New South Wales, July 1889: Religion – Church of England: Occupation – Civil Service Clerk: previously served 5 yrs. Cadet Volunteers, and at the time of his enlistment was 3 yrs. serving member Papua Armed Constabulary: 5'10" tall, grey eyes, light brown hair: enlisted Adelaide, South Australia, 3 April 1916; posted 'A' Coy., 2nd Depot. Bn.: attended NCO School, 16–31 May: transf'd. 43rd Battn., Morphettville Camp, as Pte., 1 June; apptd. Corpl. five days later; departed Australia, A.19 'Afric,' 9 June: hospitalised aboard ship (sick), 12–19 July: promoted L/Sergt. 6 October: proceeded to France, 25 November: promoted Sergt. 15 January 1917; apptd. 2nd Lieut. (Temp) 11 February: hospitalised (Boils), 14–25 February; rejoined 43rd Battn. on the latter date: hospitalised (Parotitis), 21–24 March: granted 14 days sick leave, England, 11–25 April: returned to

France, 27 April, and rejoined his battn. 1 May: promoted Lieut. 30 May: wounded in action, 10 June; remained at duty: detached to Lewis Gun School, 22 June–8 July: detached to Division School, 29 July–12 August, rejoining his battn. on the latter date, and was killed in action, 4 October 1917, nr. Zonnebeke. Age 28. *unm.* Buried 28NE1-D.21.b.c.d. by Chaplain W.A. Moore the following day. See account Capt. J.R. Eddy, Reninghelst New Military Cemetery (IV.C.4).

(Panel 27) 2nd Lieut. 815, Thomas Henry Howden, 'B' Coy., 43rd Bn. Australian Infantry, A.I.F.: *s.* of Jane Howden (4, The Avenue, Keston, co. Kent): *b.* Keston, January 1891: Religion – Church of England: Occupation – Nurseryman: 5'5½" tall, hazel eyes, dark brown hair: enlisted Adelaide, South Australia, 14 February 1916: posted 'C' Coy., 2nd Depot Battn. 28 February, transf'd. 'B' Coy., 43rd Battn, Morphettville Camp, 9 March: departed Outer Harbour, Albany, A.19 'Afric,' 9 June following; arrived Suez (via Colombo), 11 July; arrived Marseilles, France, on the 20th of that month and, after entraining to Le Havre, sailed to Southampton: trained Larkhill Camp, 24 July–24 November 1916: served in France, 25 November–31 December 1916: attended No.5 Officer Cadet Training Battn., Trinity College, Cambridge (3 January–30 April 1917); promoted 2nd Lieut. 1 May 1917: returned to France on the 14th of that month, rejoining 43rd Battn. at Armentieres on the 22nd: wounded by 5.9 fire nr. La Douve (S.W. Face, Contusion Right Arm) 5 July and, after hospitalisation and treatment, rejoined his battn. at Avroult, nr. Longuenesse, 16 September, and was killed in action at Passchendaele, 4 October 1917, by the same shell that killed Capt. F.G. Sims. Buried by Chaplain Rev. W.A. Moore the following day, very close to (and N.W. of) Zonnebeke village (28NE1-D.21.b.c.d.). Age 26. See account Reninghelst New Military Cemetery; Capt. J.R. Eddy (IV.C.4).

(Panel 27) L/Corpl. 968, Robert Andrew Heath, 43rd Bn. Australian Infantry, A.I.F.: *s.* of William Heath, of Port Lincoln, South Australia, by his wife Mary Elizabeth: *b.* Wallaroo, 12 April 1896: *educ.* Wallaroo, and Port Lincoln: Occupation – Assistant Harbour Master: previously served for 8 months with the Senior Cadets, from whence he enlisted, 10 September 1915; posted 43rd Battn., 6 March 1916: promoted L/Corpl. (Siglr.) 2 June; departed Adelaide (A19 'Afric') on the 9th.: disembarked Marseille, 20 July, transf'd. to England from whence, after four months training (Larkhill, 24 July–24 November), returned to France: took part in the Battle of Messines (7 June 1917), and was killed almost three weeks later, on 26 June 1917, by the direct hit of a shell. Buried in a shell-hole, Au Bon Fermier Gully, S.W. of Messines. Age 21. A talented musician, he was a member of Port Lincoln Brass Band.

(Panel 27) Pte. 2042, Cyril Spurgeon Rigney, 'A' Coy., 43rd Bn. Australian Infantry, A.I.F.: *s.* of Benjamin Rigney, of Point McLeay via Milang, South Australia, by his wife Rachel: and elder brother to Pte. 3872, R.G. Rigney, 48th Australian Infantry, died of chest wounds, 16 October 1917, in German hands (Buried Friedhof Iseghem): *b.* Point McLeay, February 1897: Religion – Methodist: Occupation – Labourer: 5'7¼" tall, medium complexion, grey eyes, dark brown hair: enlisted Adelaide, 26 April 1916: departed Australia, HMAT 'Seang Bee,' 13 July: trained England, September–November: Awarded (13 November) 4 Days Confined to Barracks, for 'Neglect of Duty, in that he failed to keep his rifle in a clean and serviceable condition': proceeded to France, 25 November 1916: hospitalised (Influenza) 7–12 March 1917, and was shot and killed by a sniper, 3 July 1917, at Messines. Age 20. Buried by Rev. Hutchence. He was married to Constance Maud Kropinyeri, *née* Rigney (Tailem Bend, South Australia).

His brother Rufus is buried in Harlebeke New British Cemetery (XI.D.7).

(Panel 27) Corpl. 497, Hamilton Leslie Moses, 'C' Coy., 44th Bn. Australian Infantry, A.I.F.: *s.* of Joseph Moses, c/o New Zealand Woollen Coy., Hay Street, Perth, West Australia, by his wife Caroline: *b.* Hamilton, New Zealand. Killed in action, 31 July 1917. Age 40. Buried near where he fell. Sergt. Milligan wrote, "…I buried him in a soldier's grave (shell hole) and erected a roughly improvised wooden cross with his rank, name and date written thereon with the words 'killed in action.' I had charge of the support lines during that particular stunt (Warneton, Messines) and he was the Bombing Corpl. and it was in the carrying out of his duty at a critical time that he met his death, being killed by a shell. We were undergoing a rather bad strafing from Fritz and our support line was being subjected to a rather cruel artillery fire, being so situated that we not only got the frontal fire of the Hun, but also their enfilading fire, which was aimed at Company Headquarters. Our boys had gone over the previous day and Fritz was naturally retaliating, and we were expecting him over. As a matter of fact, in the afternoon in question, the deceased was on the fire-step between his successor, Corpl. Jones, who took over the Bombing Section (I regret to say he was killed in the last stunt: Passchendaele) and myself and Pte. Wade. (wounded)...." Corpl. Moses leaves a widow, Mrs F.L. Moses ('Farrangower,' Ivanhoe, Victoria).

Corpl. (L/Corpl.) Luther Jones also has no known grave; he is recorded below.

(Panel 27) Corpl. 920, Hubert Henry James Vincent, 44th Bn. Australian Infantry, A.I.F.: *s.* of Thomas Vincent, by his wife Everlina: and brother to A/Sergt. S/753, J.T. Vincent, 7th Queen's (Royal West Surrey Regt.), killed in action, 1 July 1916: accidentally wounded, 28 March 1917. Killed in action at Zonnebeke, 4 October 1917, being hit by a shell which tore away most of his left side. Buried near where he fell.

His brother James is buried in Beacon Cemetery, Sailly-Laurette (III.H.7).

At 10.15 a.m., 9 October 1917, 44th Australians left Erie Camp and in single file, with companies and platoons at 100 yard intervals, made their way toward the front line where they were scheduled to relieve a mixed garrison of Lancashire Fusiliers and Manchesters. After bivouacking overnight on the Frezenberg Ridge, the 44th resumed their approach on the afternoon of the 10th, proceeding by way of 'F' and 'J' tracks and the Railway. The relief was carried out without incident, in fact it was not until the following day that the battalion began suffering serious numbers of casualties; during the approach, despite the majority of it being made in daylight, few losses were incurred.

(Panel 27) L/Corpl. 588, Luther Pryce Jones, 'C' Coy., 44th Bn. Australian Infantry, A.I.F.: *s.* of Thomas Jones, of Pwllguyn Farm, Builth Wells, co. Brecon, Wales, by his wife Catherine: *b.* Builth Wells, 1890: Religion – Church of England: Occupation – Shearer: 5'5¾" tall, fresh complexion, hazel eyes, fair hair: enlisted Perth, West Australia, 8 January 1916: departed Fremantle, A.29 'Suevic,' 6 June following: trained England, July–November: Awarded (8 November) 4 Days Field Punishment No.2, Forfeiture 8 days pay, Absent Without Leave, 3–7 November: proceeded to France, 25 November 1916: took part in the fighting at Messines, two days (5 June) before which he made a will bequeathing everything to his mother: Awarded (24 July 1917) 3 Days Field Punishment No.2, Forfeiture 4 days pay, Absent Without Leave, 21–22 July 1917: promoted L/Corpl. 6 September, and was killed in action, 10 October 1917. Age 26. *unm.*

(Panel 27) Pte. 156, George Stephen White, 'A' Coy., 44th Bn. Australian Infantry, A.I.F.: *s.* of the late George White, by his marriage to Elizabeth Mary Davidson, *née* White (Northampton via Geraldton, Western Australia): *b.* Northampton, November 1890: Religion – Methodist: Occupation – Labourer: 5'5" tall, fair complexion, brown hair, brown eyes: previously refused enlistment; medical (Varicocele): enlisted Perth, 15 January 1916, apptd. 43rd Depot Bn.; apptd. No.1 Area Bn., 28 January; apptd. 'A' Coy., 65th Bn. 1 February, transf'd. 44th Bn. 11th Bde., Claremont, 27 March; departed Fremantle, A29 'Suevic,' 6 June; disembarked Plymouth, 21 July; trained Larkhill: proceeded to France, 25 November 1916. Killed at duty on a work party, night of 4–5 July 1917; Messines sector. Age 27. Pte. 711, V. Preston was also killed. Burial (recorded by D.G.R. 10 July) conducted by Chaplain attd. 43rd Bn. His effects, Pocket Candle Stick, Pipe, Religious Book (Bible), 2 New Testaments; were received by his mother, 29 April 1918; Pamphlet *Where The Australians Rest*, British War Medal (40854), Victory Medal (40438), Memorial Plaque (327344) and Scroll (327044) 20 January 1922–22 March 1923.

Pte. Preston is buried in Kandahar Farm Cemetery (II.E.34).

(Panel 27) Pte. 2846, Charles Lumgair, 44th Bn. Australian Infantry, A.I.F.: c/o Post Office, Katanning, Western Australia: *s.* of William Lumgair, of 19, Black Street, Dundee, by his wife Jane: *b.* Arbroath, co. Forfar, May 1885: Religion – Presbyterian: Occupation – Labourer: 5'2" tall, blue eyes, dark hair: enlisted Blackboy Hill, Western Australia, 17 October 1916, posted 87th Depot Battn.: transf'd. 44th Battn. 11 November, departed Fremantle, A.34 'Persic.' 29 December following: served with the Expeditionary Force in France from 20 June 1917; joined 44th Battn. In the Field, 9 July, and was killed in action 4 August 1917. Age 31. He leaves a widow, Margaret Lumgair, *née* Simmons (c/o Ms. Simmons, 69, Caldruin Street, Dundee), to whom he married, 7 May 1917. GRU report Zillebeke, 5-43E; 'remains exhumed at a point about 3 miles E.S.E. of Wytschaete (28.J.19.c.0.6); re-interred Sanctuary Wood Cemetery, Zillebeke;' identified – Disc, Titles, Clothing; registered March 1927. *Buried in Sanctuary Wood Cemetery (III.K.19).*

(Panel 27) Pte. 5746, Francis Douglas McCann, Battn. Scout, 'D' Coy., 44th Bn. Australian Infantry, A.I.F.: *s.* of Francis McCann, of 83, Alma Road, North Perth, Western Australia, by his wife Mary: *b.* Coolgardie, 1897. Killed in action, 4 October 1917, nr. Hill 40, Zonnebeke. At the time of his death, Pte. McCann was delivering a message to 'B' Coy. L/Corpl. 1033, W.T. Lenman, 42nd Battn., wrote (24 April 1918), "I assisted to bury him on the field at place of casualty. I marked his grave with a card and a piece of wood, and I gave his personal effects to a Padre at Ypres. I did not know him personally as I belonged to a different battalion. Judging by his condition when I found him, he must have been caught by pieces of shell which hit him about the legs and chest, and broke both arms, death apparently being instantaneous." Age 20. *unm.* Buried beside Corpl. E.W. Serls, north-west of Zonnebeke village, D.21d.3.5.

Corpl. Ernest Serls is buried in Tyne Cot Cemetery (XLI.B.20).

(Panel 27) Lieut. Leslie Garling, 45th Bn. Australian Infantry, A.I.F.: Mentioned in Despatches: late of Cremorne, New South Wales: *s.* of Clarence W.H. Garling, of Sydney, Australia, by his wife Katherine: and brother to Corpl. 629502, F.H. Garling, M.M., 47th Canadian Infantry, missing/believed killed in action, 5–7 May 1917: *b.* Camden, New South Wales, 15 October 1881: Occupation – Bank Accountant. Killed in action in the valley of the Blauwepoortbeek, 7 June 1917. Age 35. See account re. Capt. W.L. Young, M.C., Wytschaete Military Cemetery (V.B.21).

His brother Frederick also has no known grave; he is commemorated on the Canadian National (Vimy) Memorial.

(Panel 27) 2nd Lieut. Charles Francis Ryan, 45th Bn. Australian Infantry, A.I.F.: *s.* of Timothy Ryan, of Farley, Wellingrove, New South Wales, by his wife Sarah Ann: and elder brother to 2nd Lieut. T.L. Ryan, M.M., 17th Battn. A.I.F., who fell, 26 September 1917: *b.* Emmaville, New South Wales, 1 November 1886: Occupation – Labourer. Killed in action in the valley of the Blauwepoortbeek, 7 June 1917. Age 30. See account re. Capt. W.L. Young, M.C., Wytschaete Military Cemetery (V.B.21).

His brother Thomas also has no known grave; he is recorded on Panel 17.

Bridget Shaw had two sons, William and John, both were killed within two days of each other; neither has a known grave. Eleven years later, in response to information received regarding two Australian brothers buried in the same grave, Bridget enquired to the authorities in the hope that these might possibly be her sons. She received the following reply:- "28 May 1928: Dear madam, I have to acknowledge the receipt of your communication of 15th May, relative to the burial of your sons the late Pte. 1722, J.C. King, 45th. Battn. and Corpl. W.J. King, M.M., 45th. Battn, and in reply to inform you with regret that to date no advice has been received at this office of the recovery and identification of their remains. According to the overseas authorities both were buried in the vicinity of Messines and as you are no doubt aware the names of Hill 60, Wytschaete and Messines are all closely associated with the bitter fighting in which the Australians were engaged, particularly the great battle of June 1917. Having regard to the heavy shell-fire to which the area was subjected at the time it must, reluctantly, be concluded in the absence of any definite information to the contrary that all trace of the graves of your sons were obliterated and, while the search for the missing is being continued under the direction of the Imperial War Graves Commission, you will doubtless fully appreciate the difficulties confronting such a task. You would, of course, immediately be informed if success ultimately attended these efforts, but in view of all the circumstances it is not desired to unduly arouse your hopes after such a lapse of time. Failing the recovery and identification of the actual remains, it is the intention of the authorities to fittingly perpetuate the sacrifice of the missing by the erection of collective memorials in certain defined areas upon which will be engraved the names of those who fell in the neighbourhood. For the operations round Ploegsteert, Armentieres has been chosen as the commemorative centre, and it is anticipated some 15,000 names will require to be engraved on the memorial to be erected there – a clear indication of the difficulties encountered by the Graves Services in their work of identification in this particular region. It is noted that the Strand Cemetery contains the graves of two brothers, but these doubtless have been fully identified and registered under their respective names ere this. Assuring you of the Department's profound sympathy and regret at the loss of your gallant soldier sons. Yours faithfully, J.M. Lean, Major."

(Panel 27) Corpl. 1721A, William James King, M.M., 'B' Coy., 45th Bn. Australian Infantry, A.I.F.: *s.* of the late Archibald King, by his wife Bridget Shaw, *née* King ('Derowen,' Barragan, via Mudgee, New South Wales): and brother to Pte. 1722, J.C. King 45th Bn. A.I.F., killed in action, 9 June 1917: Occupation – Platelayer: joined A.I.F., Bathurst, 26 January 1916; posted 2nd Rfts., 45th Battn.; departed Sydney, 14 April: Awarded the Military Medal (*London Gazette*, 8 December 1916), refers 25 October 1916 'For bravery in the field.' Killed in action at Messines, 7 June 1917. Buried 28.SW.4.O.33.d.85.10. His effects – Cards, Letters, Photos, Pen-holder, Paper Cuttings, 2 Badges, 3 Numerals, Wounded Stripe, Military Medal and Ribbon, Cotton, Clip of Cartridges, Buttons, Leather Belt with Buttons, Leather Letter Case, Writing Wallet, Cover containing Envelopes, Matchbox, Drinking Cup (damaged) – British War & Victory medals, Memorial Plaque & Scroll were received by his mother, March 1918–June 1923. Age 26. *unm.*

His brother John also has no known grave; he is recorded below. The brothers referred to in the above correspondence Ptes. L.J. Pickford and A.F. Pickford are buried in Strand Military Cemetery (I.E.2, I.B.1).

(Panel 27) Corpl. 3853, Roderick Kenneth MacGregor, M.M., 45th Bn. Australian Infantry, A.I.F.: *s.* of William John MacGregor, of 19, Crystal Street, Petersham, Sydney, New South Wales, by his wife Rebecca 'Vera', *née* Holt (Governor House, 26, Old Canterbury Road, Lewisham): and *yr.* brother to Pte. 2253, W.A.A. MacGregor, 54th Bn., who also fell: *b.* Lewisham, N.S.W., 1894: Occupation – Plumber: joined A.I.F., Sydney, 17 August 1915; departed Sydney, 23 December: served with the Expeditionary Force in France from 8 June 1916; promoted Corpl. 6 April 1917, and was killed in action, 8 June 1917, while leading a charge at Messines. Buried 28.S.W.4.0.33.d.85.10. Age 21. In letters to his mother, his comrades wrote that Corpl. MacGregor was a kind, cheerful, courageous and gallant man, and his death was greatly lamented by all who knew him. Awarded the Military Medal, 17 March 1917 (*London Gazette*, 24 April), for gallantry, good leadership, devotion to duty and conspicuous bravery in action on 22–23 February 1917. (*IWGC record age 19*) His brother William also has no known grave; he is recorded on Panel 29.

(Panel 27) L/Corpl. 1673, Albert Henry Bewley, 45th Bn. Australian Infantry, A.I.F.: *s.* of the late William Bewley, of Maryamma, Mount Macdonald, New South Wales: yr. brother to William Edwin Bewley, Farmer, of Luddenham, Penrith; and elder cousin to Pte. 1687, S.G.B. Bewley, 30th Australian Infantry, killed in action, 23 March 1917, at Morchies: *b.* Gunning, 1879: Occupation – Labourer: joined A.I.F. 7 August 1915: served with the Expeditionary Force in France and Flanders from 8 June 1916: wounded (Bomb, G.S.W., back and spine) 7–8 August; evacuated to England, 11 August; rejoined Battn. 7 September: apptd. L/Corpl. 3 March 1917, and was killed in action, 7 June 1917. Buried in an isolated Grave, 800 yards east of Messines (28.S.W.4.0.33.d.85.10). Age 37. Remembered on Crookwell War Memorial, New South Wales.

His cousin Sidney also has no known grave; he is commemorated on the Villers-Bretonneux Memorial.

(Panel 27) Pte. 4583, George Richard Percival Fillingham, 'D' Coy., 45th Bn. Australian Infantry, A.I.F.: *s.* of the late Joseph Orton Fillingham, and Mary Fillingham; widow ('St. Albans,' Cameron Street, Rockdale, New South Wales): and brother to L/Corpl. 531, H.W. Fillingham, M.M., 2nd Australian Pioneers (surv'd.); Pte. 3301, H.C. Fillingham, 8th Rfts., 35th Bn. (discharged, medically unfit, 1917; re-enlisted no.60216, discharged 1919); and P.O., 2672, C.J.O. Fillingham, Australian Navy (*d.* February 1923): *b.* Molong, 1891: Religion – Methodist: Occupation – Clerk: School/Senior Cadet Force member (6 years): joined A.I.F., Warwick Farm, 15 September 1915: apptd. 14th Rfts., 1st Bn.: trained Egypt (from 6 March 1916): proceeded to France, 6 June: wounded (SW Lt. hand) 6–7 August; returned to duty on the 11th.: wounded Pozieres on 1 September, admitted 44th C.C.S. (Haemoptysis); transf'd. hospital Wimereux (Shell Shock, Severe; Buried), 3 September; evacuated to hospital, England; returned to France, 29 April 1917: rejoined 45th Battn. 4 May. Killed in action, 7 June 1917. Buried 28SW.4.o.33.d.85.10. A comrade said, "After the attack for Messines ridge on June 7/17 I saw Fillingham lying dead just inside a shell hole; he died splendidly. After being wounded he crept into the shell hole for safety, when he saw a comrade lying wounded not far off, so he went out and brought him into safety; the man was saved but Fillingham was killed (shot through the chest) just as he got to the shell hole the second time. I believe he was buried where he fell and the grave marked." Age 26. A descendant visiting Messines Ridge British Cemetery (June 2012) wrote: *Engaged to be married; Somewhere here in an unknown grave he lies.*

(Panel 27) Pte. 3388, George Thomas Hoskins, 45th Bn. Australian Infantry, A.I.F.: *s.* of Sydney Hoskins, of 15, Macauley Road, Stanmore, New South Wales, by his wife Matilda: *b.* Lithgow, New South Wales, *c.*1888. Killed in action, 13 October 1917. 2nd Lieut. Moroney wrote, "Pte. Hoskins was in my platoon…He was killed in action by a high explosive shell in front of Zonnebeke. I regret to say he was not buried in a soldiers' cemetery but simply where he fell and his grave was marked. At the time conditions were too bad to permit any of the dead being moved and nothing at all could be done in daylight. His grave would no doubt be registered by the people who look after such things, when the fighting had died down, but when we were relieved it was still impossible to do anything except what was absolutely necessary for the preservation of the line and the saving of the wounded. I would like to add for the sake of his people that the late Pte. Hoskins was a fine soldier and very well-liked by all who knew him." Age 29. *Buried in Oostaverne Wood Cemetery (V.K.4).*

In Answer To His Country's Call He Gave His Best, His Life, His All

(Panel 27) Pte. 1623, Harry Kay, 45th Bn. Australian Infantry, A.I.F.: *s.* of Robert Kay, of Warrego Street, Katoomba, New South Wales: *b.* Katoomba, 1895: enlisted Lithgow, New South Wales, 28 January 1916. Killed in action, 7 June 1917, south-west of Messines. Buried there. Age 22. Inserted by his brothers Ptes. 1353, George and 2185, Robert Kay, *The Sidney Morning Herald* (7 June 1918), carried the following 'In Memoriam':-

Your death has saddened our hearts, dear Harry,
Though noble was your call;
You fought and died for Australia,
The bravest death of all.

(Panel 27) Pte. 1722, John Christopher King, 45th Bn. Australian Infantry, A.I.F.: *s.* of the late Archibald King, by his wife Bridget Shaw, *née* King (Derowen, Mudgee, New South Wales): and brother to Corpl. 1721A, W.J. King, M.M., 45th Bn. A.I.F., who fell at Messines, 7 June 1917: served with the Expeditionary Force. Killed in action, 9 June 1917. Age 24.

His brother William also has no known grave; he is recorded above.

(Panel 27) Pte. 2447, William Lee, 45th Bn. Australian Infantry, A.I.F.: Killed on 12 October 1917, by a direct hit on the company dugout near Passchendaele. Pte. 3164, C. Moore, wrote, "On October 12 we were at Passchendaele and attacked the enemy during the morning. A number of our men including Lee and Batten were in a dug out which was blown up by an enemy shell. Many of them were buried in the debris. During the day the dug-out was cleared out and the bodies which could be recovered stacked up. Many of them were so badly damaged they were unrecognisable. There were 10 to 15 casualties in this dug out. At the time we were about 100 yards away and had our lines behind the enemy pill box. Most of our company were accounted for but Batten and Lee could not be traced, the conclusion being that they were buried in the debris. The same night the enemy took the dug-out" and Pte. E. Peck, "Re. 2376 Pte. E.M. Batten and 2447 Pte. W. Lee. They were killed on 12.10.17. We were at a certain position in the line, and that was the last that was seen of them. There were myself and 2 other men detailed off to bury a number of bodies at night about this position where they were last seen, and most of the bodies were unrecognisable."

Pte. Edward Batten is buried in Tyne Cot Cemetery (II.A.3).

(Panel 27) Capt. John William Millar, 47th Battn. Australian Infantry, A.I.F.: Mentioned in Despatches: *s.* of John Millar, by his wife Annie: *b.* Victoria. One of three officers of the right front company (Lieut. W.S. Dixon, killed; Lieut. G.N.M. Goode, mortally wounded), who fell in the fighting to gain the front trench near Huns' Walk, Oosttaverne Line, at the Battle of Messines, 7 June 1917. Age 22. He was married to Ethel Dean Millar (148, Joel Terrace, Mount Lawley, Western Australia). See account re. Corpl. P. McCarthy, 37th Battn. (Panel 25).

Lieut. W.S. Dixon also has no known grave, he is recorded on Addenda Panel 57; Lieut. G.N.M. Goode died of wounds, 12 June 1917, buried Longuenesse (St. Omer) Souvenir Cemetery (IV.C.27).

(Panel 27) Lieut. Frederick Fincastle Campbell, 47th Bn. Australian Infantry, A.I.F.: late of Cygnet, Huon Valley, Tasmania: *s.* of Leveron Granville Campbell, of Fairfield, Monkton, co. Ayr, by his wife Mary Douglas Campbell: *b.* Scotland. Killed in action, 7 June 1917, nr. Oostaverne, when his company, the left, with a mixed force of the 37th, encountered stiff resistance from concrete emplacements and blockhouses in close proximity to Huns' Walk. Age 29. Two other officers, Lieut. D.F. Salmon (Comdg.) and 2nd Lieut. A.R. Walker also lost their lives before the company, after rushing the enemy from hedge to hedge south of The Walk, finally reached and occupied a fragment of the support line astride Huns' Walk. Remembered on Cygnet War Memorial. See also account re. Corpl. P. McCarthy, 37th Battn. (Panel 25).

Lieut. D.F. Salmon is buried in Messines Ridge British Cemetery (II.B.23); 2nd Lieut. A.R. Walker has no known grave, he is recorded below.

(Panel 27) 2nd Lieut. Albert Reginald Walker, 47th Bn. Australian Infantry: late of Toowoomba, Queensland: *s.* of Albert Thomas Walker, of George Street, Eagle Junction, Brisbane, by his wife Amy Beatrice. Killed in action, 9 June 1917 nr. Oosttaverne when his company, the left, with a mixed force of the 37th, encountered stiff resistance from concrete emplacements and blockhouses in close proximity to Huns' Walk. Age 24. Two other officers, Lieut. D.F. Salmon (Comdg.) and 2nd Lieut. A.R. Walker also lost their lives before the company, after rushing the enemy from hedge to hedge south of The Walk, finally reached and occupied a fragment of the support line astride Huns' Walk. See also account re. Corpl. P. McCarthy, 37th Battn. (Panel 25)

Lieut. D.F. Salmon is buried in Messines Ridge British Cemetery (II.B.23); Lieut. F.F. Campbell has no known grave, he is recorded above.

(Panel 27) Corpl. 2629, George William Carr-Boyd, 'A' Coy., 47th Bn. Australian Infantry, A.I.F.: *s.* of the late Reginald Carr-Boyd, of Chasely Street, Auchenflower, Brisbane, by his wife Isabel Carr, *née* Carr-Boyd (Sylvan Road, Toowong, Queensland): and cousin to Pte. 2318, J. G. Carr-Boyd, 47th Bn. A.I.F., killed in action the same day, 12 October 1917: *b.* 1897: Religion – Church of England: Occupation – Jackeroo: 5'8¼" tall; medium complexion, brown eyes, dark brown hair: serving member, 1 yr., Senior Cadets; enlisted Brisbane, 27 April 1916; apptd. 6th Rfts., 47th Battn., Bells Paddock, Enoggera, 23 October; proceeded overseas 27 October: trained Codford (from 10 January 1917): joined Expeditionary Force, France, 4 May: promoted Corpl. 22 August 1917. Killed in action, 12 October following. Age 20. *unm.* Pte. 3144, J. Henry, 47th A.I.F., informed that on the morning of 12 October 1917, after achieving their objective, he saw Corpl. Boyd attending to the wounds of another man who he thought was one of the Lewis gun team, possibly Corpl. Boyd's cousin, when he was shot through the head; killed instantly. At the time of his death Pte. Henry was only a few yards away and, although he could see Corpl. Boyd lying where he had fallen, was unable to get to him due to sniper fire. Later, when the battalion were forced to withdraw, Corpl. Boyd's body was one of several that had to be left behind.

His cousin John also has no known grave; he is recorded below.

(Panel 27) Pte. 2127, George Henry Andrews, 47th Bn. Australian Infantry, A.I.F.: *s.* of David Andrews, and his wife Fleurine Elsie Andrews (Ma Ma Creek, Grantham, Brisbane, Queensland): and brother to Pte. 4357, J.M. Andrews, 45th Australian Infantry, killed in action, 5 August 1916, aged 26 yrs.; and Pte. 4358, B.R. Andrews, 25th Australian Infantry, died 10 June 1918, aged 20 yrs. Reported wounded and missing, 9 June 1917; since (A.I.F. Enquiry, 3 December 1917) confirmed killed. Age 28. *unm.* Remembered on the Ma Ma Creek Memorial; erected in 1920 it was commissioned by Mrs Andrews who also donated an organ to the local church (St. Stephen's) in memory of her three sons. The memorial is located in the Andrews family plot, St. Stephen's cemetery. One of three brothers who fell.

His brother James also has no known grave, he is commemorated on the Villers-Bretonneux Memorial; Bertie is buried in Beacon Cemetery, Sailly-Laurette (II.I.4).

(Panel 27) Pte. 2318, John Gerald Carr-Boyd, 'D' Coy., 47th Bn. Australian Infantry, A.I.F.: *s.* of Gerald John Leake Carr-Boyd, of Tingal Road, Wynhum, Brisbane, by his wife Millicent Annie: and cousin to

Corpl. 2629, G.W. Carr-Boyd, 47th Bn. A.I.F., killed in action the same day: *b*. Brisbane, 1891: Occupation – Surveyor's Cadet: enlisted Rockhampton, 15 November 1915: served Egypt (from 5 May 1916); France and Flanders from 1 October: wounded (GSW Facial), Messines, 7 June 1917; rejoined battalion 11 June, and was killed in action, 12 October 1917. Age 25. *unm*. In response to a request for information regarding his death, a comrade Pte. 2014, W.C. Roth said, "On 12th October, at Passchendaele, he was in my Lewis gun section. This side of the Ridge, in the open, we had the gun in a shell hole. He was hit in the mouth by a piece of shell, this cut into his tongue and throat. He died about two hours later, before stretcher-bearers could get him out. We dressed him as best we could; he was unconscious."

His cousin George also has no known grave; he is recorded above.

(Panel 27) Pte. 2436A, William Alfred Griffin, 47th Bn. Australian Infantry, A.I.F.: *s*. of Charles Griffin, of Albert Street, Mackay, Queensland, by his wife Mary Jane: and brother to Pte. 519, H.L. Griffin, 49th Bn. A.I.F., who fell, 26 September 1917. Killed in action, 7 June 1917. Age 31.

His brother Harry, recorded on Panel 29, is known to be buried in Oostaverne Wood Cemetery (IV.C.16).

(Panel 27) Pte. 1674, George Jackson, 47th Bn. Australian Infantry, A.I.F.: *s*. of George Jackson, by his wife Mary: *b*. Queensland, *c*.1895. Missing believed killed in action, 7 June 1917. Lieut. H. Douglas wrote, "The last I saw of this good chap was at 3.30 pm on the 7 June going forward with the 2nd phase of the attack. I gave him a drink from my water bottle. I liked him very much. I think he must have been killed in front of Owl Trench (German)." Age 22. *unm*. Remains recovered from an unmarked grave (28.U.4.c.6.9); identified – Disc, Titles, Clothing; reinterred, registered 8 March 1930. *Buried in Sanctuary Wood Cemetery (V.J.20)*.

(Panel 27) Pte. 2466, Crawford Jack Logan, 47th Bn. Australian Infantry, A.I.F.: only *s*. of Noel Woodys Logan, Fruit Farmer; of Redbrae, Yeppoon, Queensland, by his wife Florence Evelyn, *dau*. of W. Simpson: *b*. Townshend Island, Yeppoon, 5 March 1894: *educ*. State School, and Boys' Grammar School, Rockhampton: enlisted May 1916: left Australia for England autumn 1916: served with the Expeditionary Force in France and Flanders from September 1917, and was killed in action on the Passchendaele Ridge, 11 October following. Buried there. Age 23. *unm*.

(Panel 27) Pte. 3177A, Donald Sinclair MacCallum, 'C' Coy., 47th Bn. Australian Infantry, A.I.F.: formerly no.3177: *s*. of the late Donald (& Catherine) MacCallum, of Goulburn, New South Wales: c/o John (& Catherine) McKenzie, of Laurel Bank, Alton Downs, Rockhampton, Queensland (by whom he was raised from six years of age): *b*. Parkes, New South Wales, July 1891: Religion – Presbyterian: Occupation – Drover: 5'7½" tall, brown eyes, dark brown hair: enlisted Emerald, Queensland, 27 October 1916; apptd. 8th Rfts., 47th Battn., Rifle Range, 28 November: departed Australia A.64 'Demosthenes,' 22 December: hospitalised (sick, at sea), 2 February 1917: disembarked Plymouth, England; transf'd. admitted (influenza) Devonport Military Hospital, 3 March; discharged to training Perham Downs, 20 March: proceeded to France, 19 June: joined 47th Battn. with a draft of 81 OR reinforcements (re-allocated no.3177A), Hill 63 (Messines sector), 10 July 1917: attended Pay Parade, 4 October. Reported wounded and missing, 12 October 1917; since confirmed by a Court of Enquiry (Bailleul, 11 March 1918) killed in action. Age 26. Buried 1,000 yds. S.W. of Passchendaele, 1,000 yds. N.E. of Zonnebeke. In response to an inquiry submitted by his aunt, Catherine McKenzie, with regard to the circumstances of his death, a comrade reported seeing Pte. MacCallum hit by a shell in the advance toward Passchendaele, but was unable to investigate further as he had to continue forward. A later report stated – "…We regret to inform you that in spite of our efforts to do so we have been unable to obtain any particulars of his fate. Owing to the general circumstances of the Passchendaele engagement – it has been extremely difficult to find out anything concerning those in it who were originally reported 'wounded & missing' and who have eventually been reported 'killed' by a board of enquiry. Regretting we are unable to send you more satisfactory information…" (*IWGC record age 25*)

(Panel 27) Corpl. 2517, Walter Theodor Hass, 'C' Coy., 48th Bn. Australian Infantry, A.I.F.: *s*. of Peter Heinrich Hass, of Peterborough, South Australia, by his late wife Lisette, *née* Lohmann: and brother to Pte. 6948, A.F. Hass, 10th Bn. A.I.F., who also fell: *b*. Wisconsin, U.S.A., *c*.1896. Killed in action nr. Ypres

– Roulers railway, 12 October 1917. Age 21. *unm.* Pte. H.J. Sawyer, 48th Battn. recorded, "I saw him killed about 10.30 a.m. before we had reached our objective at Passchendaele on October 12th by a piece of shell in the throat. We had to retire and left him on the ground in 'No Man's Land.'"

His brother Albert also has no known grave; he is recorded on Panel 17.

(Panel 27) Pte. 3101, Albert Philip Doran, 48th Bn. Australian Infantry, A.I.F.: *s.* of Joseph Teran Doran, of 48, North Street, Midland Junction, Western Australia, by his wife Annie May: and brother to 2nd Lieut. V.F. Doran, 16th Bn. A.I.F., who fell at Ypres exactly four months and one day earlier: *b.* Echuca, Victoria, *c.* 1893. Killed in action, 12 October 1917. Age 24. *unm.* Corpl. T. Moore, 48th Battn., reported, "15 May 1918. I was with Pte. Doran when he was killed at about 2.30 in the afternoon. He was killed by a bullet through the forehead fired from a sniper's rifle, just when the Germans counterattacked our position, and died instantly with a smile on his face. His last words, in reply to words to the effect that the enemy were advancing, were 'we will get a few of them anyhow.' He was within two feet of me at the time. The attack of the enemy caused our withdrawal from the position we were then holding, so I can give no particulars regarding his burial, but I presume he was buried by the Canadians who took the ridge on which Doran's body lay....He was killed on the ridge half a mile S.W. from Passchendaele township, and I have no doubt his body lies buried there for it was impossible to remove him from the battlefield to any soldiers cemetery. He was a particular friend of mine and was respected by all with whom he came in contact...."

His brother Victor also has no known grave; he is recorded on Panel 17.

PANEL 27 ENDS. PTE. A. H. WRIGHTSON, 48TH BN. AUSTRALIAN INF.

PANEL 29 BEGINS CAPT. BRIDGMAN, 49TH BN. AUSTRALIAN INF.

(Panel 29) Capt. Francis Harvey Bridgman, 'A' Coy., 49th Bn. Australian Infantry, A.I.F.: late of Pittsworth, Queensland: *s.* of George Francis Bridgman, of Margaret Street West, Toowoomba, Queensland, by his wife Catherine: served with the Expeditionary Force in Egypt, and in France and Flanders: wounded September 1916, evacuated to England; returned to France, 15 December following, and was killed in action, 7 June 1917. Pte. E. Hewitt said, "I saw him shot through the head and killed outright at Messines, on 7th June. We were out over the top, and advancing at the time, and had got about half-way across to the German lines. Our Bn. Pioneers went out a few nights later and buried his body with others where they lay. Some of the Pioneers mentioned to mates of mine seeing and burying the bodies of all our four Captains who were killed on that occasion...." Age 21. See account re. Capt. W.L. Young, M.C., 45th Battn.; Wytschaete Military Cemetery (V.B.21).

(Panel 29) Capt. Francis Bert Kay, 49th Bn. Australian Infantry, A.I.F.: late of Brisbane, Queensland: *s.* of Thomas Henry Kay, of 61, Bishop Street, Christchurch, New Zealand, by his wife Alice: *b.* Christchurch, 29 August 1892: Occupation – Architect. Killed in action, 7 June 1917, at the top of the spur between the Wambeek and Blauwepoortbeek valleys. Age 24. See account re. Capt. W.L. Young, M.C., 45th Battn.; Wytschaete Military Cemetery (V.B.21).

(Panel 29) Capt. Herbert Walter John Rhead, 49th Bn. Australian Infantry, A.I.F.: *s.* of Walter George Rhead, of Brickwell Street, Rockhampton, Queensland, by his wife Alice Mary. Killed in action, 7 June 1917. Age 26. See account re. Capt. W.L. Young, M.C., 45th Battn., Wytschaete Military Cemetery (V.B.21).

(Panel 29) Capt. Hubert George Selwyn-Smith, 49th Bn. Australian Infantry, A.I.F.: *s.* of Montague Selwyn-Smith, of Beaudesert, Queensland, by his marriage to the late Diamantina Emma Selwyn-Smith. Killed in action, 7 June 1917. Age 26. See account re. Capt. W.L. Young, M.C., 45th Battn.; Wytschaete Military Cemetery (V.B.21).

(Panel 29) Pte. 2616A, James Edward Allen, 49th Bn. Australian Infantry, A.I.F.: *s.* of the late William Allen, of 'Ox Hill,' Gin Gin, Bundaberg, Queensland (*d.*1937), and his wife Sarah Jane, *née* Childs (*d.*1925): and brother to Pte. 2614, J. Allen, 49th Bn. who fell the same day; and Pte. 2615, E. Allen, 49th Bn., killed in action, 25 April 1918: *b*. Gin Gin, April 1886: Religion – Church of England: Occupation – Grazier: joined A.I.F. Bundaberg, 5 July 1916; departed Sydney, 7 October: joined Expeditionary Force in France, 8 January 1917. Reported missing in action, 7 June 1917; since (A.I.F. Enquiry 4 June 1918) confirmed killed. 'His body was found, his paybook taken off of it and brought to the Battalion Orderly Room ... A working party found the body..' Buried Sheet 28.S.W.o.28.c.31; 1,000 yds. N.E. of Messines. Their father later commented: "That if only one had returned safe back to us, we would have felt satisfied. We believed that we were sending them away in a good cause, and did not expect to see the three of them not come back safe ..."

His brothers also have no known grave; Josiah is recorded below; Ernest is commemorated on the Villers-Bretonneux Memorial.

(Panel 29) Pte. 2614, Josiah Allen, 49th Bn. Australian Infantry, A.I.F.: *s*. of the late William Allen, of 'Ox Hill,' Gin Gin, Bundaberg, Queensland (*d*.1937), and his wife Sarah Jane, *née* Childs (*d*.1925): and brother to Pte. 2616A, J.E. Allen, 49th Bn. who fell the same day; and Pte. 2615, E. Allen, 49th Bn., killed in action, 25 April 1918: *b*. Gin Gin, March 1890: Religion – Church of England: Occupation – Grazier: joined A.I.F. Bundaberg, 5 July 1916; departed Sydney, 7 October: joined Expeditionary Force in France 8 January 1917. Reported missing in action, 7 June 1917; since (A.I.F. Enquiry 23 May 1918) confirmed killed. Age 27. Pte. A. Turner (*q.v.*) said, 'He was killed instantly by a shell on a sunken road on the right of Villers-Bretonneux (?), June 1917. I saw and recognised his dead body. He was buried by a comrade, Pte. Lewis, 49th. Battn." Buried Sheet 28.S.W.o.28.c.31; 1,000 yds. N.E. of Messines. Their father later commented, "That if only one had returned safe back to us, we would have felt satisfied. We believed that we were sending them away in a good cause, and did not expect to see the three of them not come back safe ..."

His brothers also have no known grave; James is recorded above; Ernest is commemorated on the Villers-Bretonneux Memorial.

(Panel 29) Pte. 1624A, Harold Nathaniel Berney, 49th Bn. Australian Infantry, A.I.F.: *s*. of Nathaniel James Berney, of Gooroolba, Queensland, by his late wife Louisa: *b*. Liverpool, 1895. Killed in action in Flanders, 7 June 1917. Age 22. *unm. Buried in Sanctuary Wood Cemetery (II.B.43).*

To Memory Ever Dear

(Panel 29) Pte. 519, Harry Leslie Griffin, 49th Bn. Australian Infantry, A.I.F.: formerly 2nd Australian Light Horse: *s*. of Charles Griffin, of Albert Street, Mackay, Queensland, by his wife May Jane: and brother to Pte. 2436A, W.A. Griffin, 47th Bn. A.I.F., who also fell. Killed in action, 26 September 1917. Age 22. *unm. Buried in Oostaverne Wood Cemetery (IV.C.16).*

Duty Nobly Done

His brother William has no known grave; he is recorded on Panel 27.

(Panel 29) Pte. 3504, John Hunter, 'A' Coy., 49th Bn. Australian Infantry, A.I.F.: *s*. of Henry Hunter, of Nanango, Gympie, Queensland, and his wife Emily: and brother to Pte, 3497, J. Hunter, 49th Australian Infantry (surv'd): *b*. Jimboomba, August 1889: Religion – Presbyterian: Occupation – Timber Getter: 5'6½" tall, dark complexion, blue-grey eyes, brown hair: joined A.I.F., Brisbane, 25 October 1916; posted 9th Rfts., 49th Battn., 22 December: departed Sydney, A33 'Ayrshire,' 24 January 1917: trained England (from 13 April), apptd. Actg. L/Corpl. 27 June; reverted to Pte. 5 August; proceeded to France the following day: joined 49th Battn., Red Lodge, Messines sector, 25 August, and was killed in action (severe abdominal trauma, shellfire), 26 September 1917; Battle of Polygon Wood. Age 28. Buried by his brother 'Jim' – Westhoek Ridge (28NE.J.7.b.7.7); wrapped in a groundsheet secured with telephone wire. His British War and Victory medals, Memorial Plaque and Scroll were received by his father, May 1921– March 1923. Remains recovered in September 2006; re-interred October 2007. *Buried in Buttes New British Cemetery (Polygon Wood), (I.E.19).*

Beloved Son Of Harry And Emily Hunter Nanango Qld.
At Rest After Being Lost For 90 Years

(Panel 29) Pte. 2199A, Joseph Frederick Lapworth, 'B' Coy., 49th Bn. Australian Infantry, A.I.F.: *s.* of George Frederick Lapworth, of 'Joe-Fred,' 113, Vulture Street, South Brisbane, Queensland, by his wife Sarah: *b.* Fortitude Valley, Queensland. Killed in action, 26 September 1917. Pte. 3375, Carter, said, "I saw him killed just as we started to dig in in Polygon Wood on 26th September. He was the last to jump into the shell hole and got a M.G. bullet right in the back. We dressed his wound and got him onto a stretcher. I and three others were carrying him out on it when Fritz got a M.G. on to us and wounded Lapworth again very badly, and also one of the S/Bs (Pte. S.J. Moriarty). We got Lapworth back into the shell hole and he died a few minutes after we got him into it. We buried him there. It was close to our last objective of the 26th, which we had just taken. We made a rough cross with a stick and a German bayonet, but could not put his name. We had nothing to write with, and the M.G. fire was very heavy. It is the only grave there." Age 23. *unm. Buried in Bedford House Cemetery (Enc.No.6/III.A.5).*

(Panel 29) Pte. 2995, Alexander George Spall, 'D' Coy., 49th Bn. Australian Infantry, A.I.F.: *s.* of William George Spall, of 228, Bowen Terrace, New Farm, Brisbane, Queensland, by his wife Adelaide Louisa: and elder brother to Pte. 2882, P.C. Spall, 49th Battn., who fell the same day: Occupation – Dray Driver. Reported wounded and missing, 7 June 1917; confirmed (10 December 1917) killed at Messines. Age 28. *unm.*

His brother Percy also has no known grave; he is recorded below.

(Panel 29) Pte. 2882, Percy Charles 'Ogie' Spall, 49th Bn. Australian Infantry, A.I.F.: *s.* of William George Spall, of 228, Bowen Terrace, New Farm, Brisbane, Queensland, by his wife Adelaide Louisa: and *yr.* brother to Pte. 2995, A.G. Spall, 49th Battn., who fell the same day. Reported missing, 7 June 1917, at Messines; confirmed (4 March 1918) killed. Age 18.

His brother Alexander also has no known grave; he is recorded above.

(Panel 29) Pte. 480, Herbert Alexander Bice, 50th Bn. Australian Infantry, A.I.F.: *s.* of Luke Edward Bice, of by his wife Lillian: *gdson.* to Mary Ann Jones (High Street, Kew, Melbourne): and brother to Pte. 2187, J.G. Bice, 37th Australian Infantry, died (tuberculosis, lungs), No.1 Australian Auxiliary Hospital, Harefield Park, 25 May 1917, age 20: *b.* Korong, Wedderburn, Victoria, November 1893: Occupation – Butcher, Messrs. J.C. Gibb, Wycheproof: volunteered and enlisted Morphettville, South Australia, 24 August 1914: departed Australia, 2 March 1915: wounded (GSW Hand) Anzac, Gallipoli, 25–29 April: removed to Southampton, thence to Birmingham: after treatment and convalescence joined Mediterranean Expeditionary Force, Mudros, apptd. L/Corpl. 11 December 1915; served Alexandria from the 29th of that month: promoted Corpl. (Front Line, Canal Defence), 1 March 1916: joined 50th Battn. Serapeum 2 April: joined Expeditionary Force in France, 4 June: apptd. Temp.Sergt. 15 July: wounded in action (GSW Back, slight; 'thigh', severe), 15 August: removed to England on 20 August: discharged to duty, 14 October, proceeded Monte Video Camp, thereafter Wareham where, after 32 days in custody awaiting trial and entering a plea of Not Guilty before a District Court Martial, 22 February 1917, he was, nonetheless, found guilty and reduced to Pte. for (I) Neglect to the prejudice of Good Order & Military Discipline, (II) Drunkeness on Active Service: returned to France, 18 March 1917: apptd. L/Corpl. 4 April: reduced to the ranks, 3 June 1917 being, while on Active Service, found in an estaminet during prohibited hours; and was killed in action six days later, on 9 June 1917. Buried ¾ mile, N.E. of Messines (28.SW.0.28.c.3.1). Age 23. *unm.* Another brother, Cyril, volunteered but was rejected being underage to serve.

His brother John is buried in Harefield (St. Mary) Churchyard (Aust.21). Uniquely, the graves in this cemetery are marked by scroll shaped headstones, chosen by the staff and patients at the hospital. In the centre of the Australian plot stands a memorial obelisk erected by Sir Francis Newdegate (1862–1936), Governor of Tasmania and Western Australia, and Charles A.M. Billyard-Leake, of Harefield Park.

(Panel 29) Pte. 3411, Victor Leo Hepworth, 50th Bn. Australian Infantry, A.I.F.: *s.* of Victor Ernest Hepworth, of North Adelaide, by his wife Theresa, *née* Harman. Killed in action, 18 October 1917. *Buried in Cement House Cemetery (VI.B.48).*

Their Name Liveth For Evermore
R.I.P.

(Panel 29) Pte. 3421, Alfred Walter Jay, 'A' Coy., 50th Bn. Australian Infantry, A.I.F.: *s.* of Walter (& Eliza) Jay, of 8, Peacock Street, Norwich, England: *b.* Norwich, 1891: Religion – Church of England: Occupation – Seaman: enlisted Adelaide, South Australia, 26 January 1917, apptd. 9th Rfts., 50th Bn. 7 February; departed Adelaide, A48 'Seang Bee,' 10 February: disembarked Devonport, England, 2 May: proceeded to France, 6 August: joined 50th Bn., Lucy, 10 September, and was killed in action, 26 September 1917, near Anzac House by a shell; death was instantaneous. Age 25. Buried near where he fell with Ptes. 2618, J.A. Menz and 3365, J.S. Bell, killed by the same shell. A rough cross, made from a bomb box, was erected. (*IWGC record age 23*)

John Menz also has no known grave, he is recorded below; John Bell is buried in Buttes New British Cemetery, Polygon Wood (XXVI.A.17).

(Panel 29) Pte. 2619, Charles Frederick Menz, 'A' Coy., 50th Bn. Australian Infantry, A.I.F.: *s.* of Gustav Hermon Menz, of Bower, South Australia, by his wife Maria Bertha: and brother to Pte. 2618, J.A. Menz, 50th Battn., killed in action nr. Zonnebeke, 26 September 1917. Killed in action, nr. Messines, 9 June 1917. Age 23.

His brother John also has no known grave; he is recorded below.

(Panel 29) Pte. 2618, John 'Jock' Adam Menz, 'A' Coy., 50th Bn. Australian Infantry, A.I.F.: *s.* of Gustav Hermon Menz, of Bower, South Australia, by his wife Maria Bertha: and brother to Pte. 2619, C.F. Menz, 50th Battn., who also fell. Killed in action, 26 September 1917, 'head severed' by a shell, Anzac House, nr. Ypres. Buried near where he fell with Ptes. 3421, A.W. Jay and 3365, J.S. Bell, killed by the same shell. A rough cross, made from a bomb box, was erected.

His brother Charles and Alfred Jay also have no known grave; both are recorded above. John Bell is buried in Buttes New British Military Cemetery, Polygon Wood (XXVI.A.17).

(Panel 29) Pte. 3246, Eric Cyril Nation, 50th Bn. Australian Infantry, A.I.F.: *s.* of Samuel Gillard Nation, of Prosser Avenue, Norwood, South Australia, by his wife Emily Elizabeth 'Eliza' (c/o Mrs Buik, Bay Road, Morphettville): and brother to Pte. 4541, C.S. Nation, 10th A.I.F., killed in action, 6 May 1917, aged 28 years; and Spr. 2149, R. Nation, 7th Field Coy., Australian Engineers, died 6 March 1917, aged 25 years: *b.* Home Park, Magill, October 1895: Religion – Baptist: Occupation – Labourer: 5'7¼" tall, blue eyes, black hair: previously served 3 yrs, 79th Senior Cadets; serving (1 yr), prior to enlistment, 79th Infantry: enlisted Keswick, S.A., 26 July 1915: posted 3rd Training Battn., transf'd 50th Battn., Tel-El-Kebir, 29 February 1916. Awarded (18 March 1916) 7 Days Confined to Barracks, Forfeiture 2 Days Pay – 'Overstaying Leave 14.00 hrs, 13 March 1916, 08.00 hrs, 14 March': served with the Expeditionary Force in France and Flanders from 12 June: Awarded (10 August) 2 Days Field Punishment No.2 – 'Absent from Battalion, In the Field, 9 August 1916': hospitalised (influenza) 4–15 September 1916: hospitalised (sick), 23 February–22 April 1917: returned 50th Battn. 5 May, and was killed in action, 10 June 1917. Buried ¾ mile N.E. of Messines (28SW.O.28.c.3.1). Age 21. *unm.*

His brother Clifford is buried in Queant Road Cemetery (VI.C.21); Ralph, Etaples Military Cemetery (XXI.N.3).

(Panel 29) Pte. 6632, Arthur John Sim, 'D' Coy., 50th Bn. Australian Infantry, A.I.F.: 3rd *s.* of George Sim, of 5, Bond Street, West Hindmarsh, South Australia, by his wife Christina: and *yr.* brother to Pte. 6634, W.R. Sim, 50th Battn., who fell the same day: *b.* Mitchell, Queensland, 1893: Religion – Congregationalist: Occupation – Accountant; Messrs Clarkson Ltd.: enlisted Adelaide, 25 September 1916; departed Outer Harbour, 19th Rfts., 27th Bn., 24 January 1917: trained England; proceeded to France, 23 July 1917: transf'd. 50th Bn. 7 August. Killed in action, 18 October 1917. Buried Military Cemetery, Broodseinde (28NE.D.23.a.3.5). Age 24. *unm.* The news of the brothers' death came as a great shock to their parents; they had received a cablegram dated 17 October stating both were safe and well.

His brother William also has no known grave; he is recorded below.

(Panel 29) Pte. 6634, William Robert Sim, 'D' Coy., 50th Bn. Australian Infantry, A.I.F.: 2nd *s.* of George Sim, of 5, Bond Street, West Hindmarsh, South Australia, by his wife Christina: and elder brother to Pte. 6632, A.J. Sim, 50th Battn., who fell the same day: *b.* Mitchell, Queensland, 1891: Religion – Congregationalist: Occupation – Clerical Assistant; Messrs A.W. Sandford & Co.: enlisted Adelaide,

25 September 1916; departed Outer Harbour, 19th Rfts., 27th Bn., 24 January 1917: trained England; proceeded to France, 23 July 1917: transf'd. 50th Bn. 7 August. Killed in action, 18 October 1917. Age 26. *unm.* In response to an enquiry made through the Australian Red Cross, 1346, H.C. Harper, 50th Battn., recorded, "The two brothers Sim were killed outright on the night of 18 October 1917, by a gas shell landing in their dug-out. I helped to dig them out and bury them together at Broodseinde Ridge, within a few yards of where they fell. Cross was erected with names and particulars on."

His brother Arthur also has no known grave; he is recorded above.

(Panel 29) 2nd Lieut. Reginald Hickling, 'A' Coy., 51st Bn. Australian Infantry, A.I.F.: *s.* of Charles Alfred Hickling, of Mount Barker, Western Australia, by his wife Ada Annie: *b.* West Bromwich, co. Stafford. Killed in action, in the vicinity of Daisy Wood, Broodseinde, 12 October 1917. Age 34.

(Panel 29) Sergt. 1868, George Calder, 51st Bn. Australian Infantry, A.I.F.: *s.* of Janet Calder (High Street, Charlton, Victoria); widow: c/o John Alex Calder Esq., of 1, Pirie Street, Boulder, Western Australia: *b.* Gladstone, Goldsborough, November 1892: Religion – Presbyterian: Occupation – Miner: 5'9½" tall, dark complexion, brown eyes, black hair: joined A.I.F., Blackboy Hill, 24 January 1916; posted 3rd Rfts. 51st Battn. 29 April: departed Fremantle, 20 July: served in France and Flanders from 30 November 1916: apptd. L/Corpl. 1 March 1917; promoted Corpl. 1 June; Sergt. 1 August. Killed in action, 30 September 1917; Battle of Polygon Wood. Age 25. Remains recovered September 2006; re-interred, October 2007. *Buried in Buttes New British Cemetery, Polygon Wood (I.E.20).*

R.I.P. Beloved Son Of George And Janet
Goldsborough Victoria

(Panel 29) Corpl. 738, Frederick Metcalf, 51st Bn. Australian Infantry, A.I.F.: late of 17, Diver Street, Claremont, Western Australia: *husb.* to Alice Metcalf (Astley Street, Gosnells): *b.* Scarborough, England, 1880: Religion – Church of England: Occupation – Driver: previously served 4 yrs, 1 month, King's Own Yorkshire Light Infantry: enlisted Perth, Western Australia, 19 February 1916; apptd. 44th Bn. 20 March, departed Freemantle, 6 June: trained in England (from 21 July), transf'd. 51st Bn. 2 November, proceeded to France with a draft of reinforcements, joined 51st Bn. on the 17th of that month: apptd. L/Corpl. 20 February 1917; promoted Corpl. 25 April. Killed in action, 10 June 1917. Age 37. Buried west of Yser Canal, northern outskirts of Ypres. (*IWGC record age 34*)

(Panel 29) Pte. 1996, Daniel Scullin, 51st Bn. Australian Infantry, A.I.F.: *s.* of the late Daniel Scullin, by his wife Catherine (214, Pirie Street, Boulder, Western Australia): and brother to Pte. 4958, P. Scullin, 51st Bn. A.I.F., killed in action, 26 September 1917; and Pte. 767, J.J. Scullin, 28th Bn. A.I.F., killed in action, 29 July 1916: *b.* Rozelle, October 1889: Religion – Roman Catholic: Occupation – Glass Bottle Blower/Battery Hand: joined A.I.F. Casula 22 November 1915; apptd. 'B' Coy. 4th Bn. 1 December; discharged 'Medically Unfit', 9 December 1915: re-enlisted Black Boy Hill, Western Australia, 25 February 1916; apptd. 3rd Rfts. 1st Bn. 4 April: hospitalised Black Boy Hill (sprained knee), 8 April–4 May: departed Fremantle, 20 July; trained England (from 2 September): served with the Expeditionary Force in France and Flanders from 30 November 1916. Reported missing, since confirmed (Court of Enquiry 23 March 1918) killed in action, 26 September 1917. Age 28. *unm.* Pte. 2824, E. Thompson, 51st Bn., reported, "On the morning of 26.9.17, about 8 a.m., I was returning to the Dressing Station. I saw what I thought was Pte. Scullin, D. lying about two hundred yards from a pill-box. I had a look at the body and recognised it as 1996 Pte. Scullin, D. who was in my platoon and whom I knew personally. He was dead; apparently he had been sniped."

His brother Patrick is buried in Buttes New British Cemetery, Polygon Wood, (XXV.L.18); John has no known grave, he is commemorated on the Villers-Bretonneux Memorial.

(Panel 29) Pte. 2488, George Richard Storey, 'C' Coy., 51st Bn. Australian Infantry, A.I.F.: *s.* of the late James George Storey, and his wife Hannah Maria Storey (358, Hay Street, Subiaco): and brother to Pte. 2489, J.L. Storey, 51st Australian Infantry (surv'd.): *b.* Stoke Newington, London, England, 1895: Religion – Church of England: Occupation – Farm-hand: 5'9½" tall, fresh complexion, blue eyes, fair hair: joined A.I.F., Perth, 31 March 1916; posted 5th Rfts. 51st Battn. 15 August: departed Fremantle,

20 September: served in France and Flanders from 12 December following: wounded (G.S.W., Lt. Eye) 9 June, at Messines; returned to duty on 24 August, and was killed in action, 30 September 1917; Battle of Polygon Wood. Age 22. *The Western Australian News* (2007) recorded, 'According to Army records, on September 30, while the Allies were cleaning up, Pte. Storey was killed. Witness accounts taken from letters received by Pte. Storey's mother in 1918 told how the young soldier and three others were hit and killed by a German artillery shell outside their dug-out. In their letters, his mates wrote glowingly of their friend Pte. Storey, buried with the others close to the dug-out where they had been killed. "We put up a stick to mark the grave with his name on it." One wrote, "He was killed the morning of the day we were to move out."' Remains recovered, September 2006; re-interred October 2007. *Buried in Buttes New British Cemetery, Polygon Wood (I.E.18).*

(Panel 29) Pte. 1737, Percy Worthington, 51st Bn. Australian Infantry, A.I.F.: *s.* of Thomas Worthington, of Augustus Street, Geraldton, Western Australia, by his wife Maria: and *yr.* brother to Pte. 1075, A.G. Worthington, 32nd Battn., A.I.F., who fell 2½ months later. Killed in action, 13 July 1917. Age 18.

His brother Alfred also has no known grave; he is recorded on Panel 23.

(Panel 29) Sergt. 1218, Eric Arthur Hall, 'A' Coy., 52nd Bn. Australian Infantry, A.I.F.: *s.* of the late John Hall (drowned in the Derwent river, Hobart, March 1897), by his marriage to Emily Venetia (Mrs A.) Crooks, *née* Hall (20, Mary Street, North Hobart, Tasmania): and yr. brother to L/Corpl. 2033, N.J.A. Hall, 52nd Australian Infantry, killed in action, 14 August 1916, at the Somme: joined A.I.F. September 1914; departed Melbourne, 22 December following: served in Gallipoli, Egypt, and France and Flanders (from 12 June 1916); wounded (G.S.W, Arm), 12 October 1916, rejoined his unit 13 November following: apptd. L/Corpl. 24 December 1916; promoted Corpl. 17 March 1917; Sergt. 19 June: detached to 13th Training Bn., England, 25 June: returned to France, 2 October; died of wounds, 18 October 1917. Age 22. CQMS 58, R.C. Gray, 'A' Coy., wrote, "Hall went out at night with a wiring party at Passchendaele and, returning just before dawn, they were within six or seven yards of our trench when a shell caught them. Hall was badly wounded in the stomach. He was in the D.S. at Zonnebeke by 7.30 o'clock and died about 9.30 pm..." Buried 26.d.7.8 by Padre D.B. Blackwood, 52nd Battn. with assistance of Canadian Field Artillery, between Zonnebeke and Westhoek; a rough wooden cross with his identity disc marking the grave. Remains recovered from an unmarked grave (28.D.27.a.4.0) 25 February 1927; identified – Damaged Disc; reinterred, registered 26 February 1927. *Buried in Sanctuary Wood Cemetery (III.H.2).*

Peace Perfect Peace With Loved Ones Far Away

His brother Norman also has no known grave; he is commemorated on the Villers-Bretonneux Memorial.

(Panel 29) Corpl. 4325, Alan Gunn Hodgman, 52nd Bn. Australian Infantry, A.I.F.: *s.* of Thomas Christopher Hodgman, of 'Arundell,' Park Street, New Town, Tasmania, by his wife Robina Francis, *née* Gunn: and brother to Pte. 580, H. Hodgman, 5th Australian Infantry, killed in action at Anzac, 25 April 1915; shot through the head by a Turk sniper; and Pte. 4923, F.R. Hodgman, 52nd Australian Infantry, wounded (GSW Head), 4 September 1916, returned to Australia, 22 August 1917: *b.* Hobart, 1897: *educ.* Bridgwater High School, Tasmania: Occupation – Engineer; Messrs Johnston & Wells: enlisted Claremont, 12 September 1915: departed Fremantle, 2 January 1916: trained Egypt: served with the Expeditionary Force in France from 12 June 1916: wounded (GSW Rt. Arm), 4 September: apptd. L/Corpl. 5 November 1916; promoted Corpl. 10 April 1917. Killed in action, 7 June 1917, at Messines. Age 20. *unm.* Buried; Grave Registered, Burial Officer, 14th (Light) Divn. 2 October 1917.

His brother Harry is buried in Lone Pine Cemetery, Anzac (O.21).

Despite their having served with the Australian Forces during the Boer War, on the outbreak of war in 1914 many Indigenous 'Aborigine' Australians – perhaps motivated by loyalty and patriotism to 'their' country, an opportunity to prove themselves the equal of 'white' Australians, for better treatment after the war, or perhaps the offer of six shillings a day for a trip overseas was too good to miss – volunteered to enlist in the A.I.F. and were rejected purely by virtue of their race. However, by October 1917, with one conscription referendum lost and recruitment numbers at an all-time low, with no apparent solution to the problem, restrictions regarding indigenous persons were cautiously eased. A new Military Order stated – "Half-castes may be enlisted in the Australian Imperial Force provided that the examining Medical Officers are satisfied that one of the parents is of European origin."

Over 1,000 Indigenous Australians served in the First World War; they came from a section of society with few or no rights, low wages, and poor living conditions. Most were not permitted to vote and none were counted in the country's censuses. But, having joined the A.I.F. they were paid the same as other soldiers, underwent the same training, served in the same units, and shared the same experiences and conditions. For the most part they were accepted without prejudice – many experienced equal treatment for the first time in their lives. However, upon return to civilian life, any hope of better treatment they may have hoped for was not to be; the Australia they had fought and died for rewarded them with the same prejudice and discrimination as before.

(Panel 29) Pte. 2367, George Robert Aitken, 52nd Bn. Australian Infantry, A.I.F.: *s.* of Princess Carlo, c/o Barambah Mission Station, Maryborough, Queensland, and George Richard Aitken; Manager, Cania Diggings, Eidsvold: and adopted brother to Pte. 2441, D.L. Hampson, 52nd Battn. (PoW, 13 October 1917; surv'd.); Pte. 3311, T.J.P. Hampson, 42nd Battn. (wounded, surv'd.); and Pte. 6202, N.S.K. Hampson, 25th Battn., killed in action, 8 August 1918: *s.* of the late Thomas (& Mary Frances 'Lily') Hampson: *b.* Walloon Station, November 1893: Religion – Church of England: Occupation – Stockman/ Drover; Longreach: 5'6" tall, dark complexion, brown eyes, black hair: joined A.I.F. Cloncurry 5 April 1916; apptd. 5th Rfts. 52nd Battn. 25 August: proceeded overseas HMAT 'Seang Choon,' 19 September: trained England from 9 December 1916: tried before F.G.C.M., 25 January 1917, charged – Disobedience & Violence (1) 'Disobeying a lawful command given by his superior officer, in that he, at Codford, Wiltshire, on the 13–1–17, did not leave Codford village when ordered to do so by Sergt. Self, Anzac Provost Corps: (2) Striking a person in whose custody he was placed, in that he at Codford, Wiltshire, on the 13–1–17, when placed by Sergt. Self in the custody of Corpl. Roberts struck the said L/Corpl. on the face with his fist;' Pleaded not guilty on both counts, adjudged guilty; sentenced to two years intensive hard labour, remitted (6 June) twelve months imprisonment; commuted (21 June) 377 Days Without Pay: proceeded to France, 1 July 1917, joined 52nd Bn. Berquin 22 July. Killed in action, 19 October 1917. Buried. Age 23. Addressed to his adoptive brother Dennis Hampson, his will (10 February 1917) read, "From Jim, Just a little story of our friendship. Well Den I can safely say that we are the only two true mates there are in the world. That's a big word to say. Well Den, if I gets knocked you can have anything you can find on me that is any use to you, and my allotted money to be left to Mrs T. Hampson. Show this to one of the heads. Don't forget. Only a Pte. G.R. Aitken, 2367." And continued, "Good-bye old man and good luck to you, wishing you all sorts of luck to pull through this war. We have been the very best of mates and the only thing I wish is that we meet over the other side of the world if there's any such a place. I don't think I will ever forget you Den. I will think of you when I am dead. I never used to say much to you when we used to knock about together; I was very funny like that, anybody I liked I never said much to. Good-bye old man and good luck." His effects – 1 Bank Book, Queensland Gov. Savings Bank (Duchess) No.90a., Wallet, Photos, Cards, French Book, Cigarette Pictures – were received by the Public Curator, Brisbane, January 1919.

Adoptive brother Newton Hampson is buried in Crucifix Corner Cemetery, Villers-Bretonneux (IX.B.2).

End-note: In 2006, following discussion with Jim Stewart, Eidsvold District Historical Society, Patricia Bond, a great-niece of George Aitken, arranged with the families of George and Denis Hampton to hold a memorial service for both men. Following the Eidsvold Anzac Day march, 25 April 2006, representatives of both families proceeded to Rawbelle Station, and the Hampson family property where both George and Denis were raised. On arrival the large group of family members met to gather for the service and were shown to a small fenced in site of the property where the graves of Denis and his mother Lily were located. Both families had brought glass framed photographs of the two soldiers; these were placed on Denis's head stone before proceeding to the memorial service held about 20 metres away under a large oak tree. Following the sounding of Last Post, Jim Stewart said he would always remember this Anzac Day as a very special day; it was an emotional release for him to tell the story, to have members of both families present, and he felt the spirit of the two soldiers as he spoke.

After Jim's speech he requested Patricia Bond step forward to acknowledge her Great Uncle, his adopted brother and the families both white and black. It was a beautiful warm day, the sun was shining, the air was still, there was no breeze or wind; just silence. But, as she spoke a strange thing occurred – two small whirly winds inexplicably rose up from the ground less than ten feet to the left of her. They were both short and swivelled around each other for about a minute before moving towards the grave sites situated just behind where Patricia stood. Both moved together toward the grave site, circling as they passed through the gate, one moving around the head stone to one side of Denis's grave; the other stayed opposite Mrs Hampson's. This strange occurrence startled everyone in the group and, as Patricia turned to see what was happening, the photos of the two soldiers slammed heavily down on Denis's head stone. For a moment all was silent, then one whirly wind began to move back through the gate, the other followed around the head stone before it too passed back through the gate; they seemed to be following each other. Both winds returned to the site where they had arisen, circled for a moment then joined as one and rose upward into the air before disappearing into the sky. Following this mysterious event the assembled gathering returned to the grave site and picked up and repositioned the photos of both soldiers; neither frame glass nor photograph was damaged.

Patricia later commented, "I am not superstitious but I believe at this moment I felt the spirit of both soldier's presence and so did our families. I also felt the spirit of my great uncle returned to celebrate the unity of both his families."

(Panel 29) Pte. 2415, Robert Dix, 52nd Bn. Australian Infantry, A.I.F.: *s.* of Simeon (& Harriet Ann) Dix, of Home Hill, Bowen Line, Queensland: *b.* Charters Towers, 1898: Religion – Church of England: Occupation – Labourer: 5'9½" tall, fair complexion, hazel eyes, brown hair: enlisted Townsville, 8 May 1916; apptd. 5th Rfts. 52nd Battn. 25 August: departed Australia, 19 September; trained England from 19 December 1916: proceeded to France, 28 March 1917: joined 52nd Battn. Noreuil, 2 April: wounded (GSW Hand) Messines, 7 June, hospitalised Boulogne: rejoined 52nd Bn. Kemmel, 15 August. Killed in action, 23 September 1917, Garter Point. Age 19. Pte. Ryan reported, "At Ypres, on the 23rd. or 24th. of September, after the 1st. and 2nd. Div. had attacked, and before we had gone over, we were close behind the front line in support. I was only about 10 or 12 yards from Dix. A shell dropped in the trench and killed Baxter who was next to him, and Dix was killed by concussion. There was not a mark on him…He was only about 19, fairly tall and spare built. He had a premonition he would be killed soon. I do not think there was any chance of a burial." Note: There is a strong possibility – initially identified as an unknown Australian soldier – Pte. Dix may be the 'Unknown Soldier of The Great War' buried (beside Pte. Baxter) in Hooge Crater Cemetery.

Pte. Baxter is buried in Hooge Crater Cemetery (XIII.K.9).

(Panel 29) Pte. 3376, Alfred Olof Johnson, 'A' Coy., 52nd Bn. Australian Infantry, A.I.F.: *s.* of Sergt. Major John Peter Johnson, and Marie Antoinette Johnson ('Garter Point,' City View, Logan Road, Brisbane): *b.* Mackay, June 1898: Occupation – Cabinetmaker: previously served four years with the Senior Cadets: enlisted Brisbane, 18 December 1916, apptd. 9th Rfts. 52nd Bn.: Admonished, Awarded Forfeit 1 Days Pay, Fraser's Hill, 14 January 1917, 'Overstaying Home Leave 10½ hrs': departed Sydney 24 January; trained England from 12 April: proceeded to France, 6 August: joined 52nd Bn. Ploegsteert sector, 24 August. Killed in action, 23 September 1917, when a shell hit the machine-gun position, killing the entire crew of which he was a member; vicinity Garter Point, Westhoek Ridge. Age 20. Buried beside Pte. R.H. Johnson (no relation).

(Panel 29) Pte. 1540, Richard Harold Johnson, 'A' Coy., 52nd Bn. Australian Infantry, A.I.F.: c/o Miss P. Johnson (Toloso Street, Glenorchy, Tasmania): *s.* of Mrs R. Johnson (c/o Post Office, Moonah, Tasmania): *b.* Hobart, August 1895: Religion – Church of England: Occupation – Labourer: previously served 2 yrs. 93rd Infantry Regt.: joined A.I.F. Claremont, 3 December 1914; apptd. 12th Battn. 25 January 1915; transf'd. 52nd Battn. 12 May: Awarded (1) 'Forfeit 3 Days Leave, 3 Days Pay, Overstaying Leave 20–23 March 1916' (2) 'Forfeit 4 Days Pay, When on Active Service Absent Without Leave from Tattoo, 28–30 April': trained in England from 24 March 1917: Awarded 'Forfeit 5 Days Pay, Neglecting to Obey Standing Orders para Liquor, Wareham, 11 May: Awarded 'Forfeit 7 Days Pay, Neglect to Obey an NCO's Order, 24 May': joined Expeditionary Force in France, 15 June: Awarded 'Forfeit 1 Days Pay, Falling Out on Line of March Without Permission, 18 June': hospitalised in Havre (V.D.) 22 June–14 August: rejoined 52nd Bn. Hill 63 Ploegsteert sector, 22 August. Killed in action, 23 September 1917; vicinity Garter Point, by a shell which hit the machine-gun position, killing the entire crew of which he was a member. Age 22. Buried near where he fell beside Pte. A.O. Johnson (no relation).

(Panel 29) Pte. 3645, Walter 'Scotty' Hewitt; Runner, 'D' Coy., 53rd Bn. Australian Infantry, A.I.F.: 2nd *s*. of the late William Hewitt, of Edinburgh, Spirit Merchant; by his wife Christina, *dau*. of the late David Cochrane: *b*. Edinburgh, 26 January 1882: *educ*. there: went to Australia, January 1912; settled at Koorah, New South Wales: Occupation – Tinsmith: volunteered for Foreign Service; joined 18th Australian Infantry, 5 September 1915: served with the Expeditionary Force in Egypt from January 1916: proceeded to France, and served there from the following June: wounded at the Battle of Pozieres, July 1916. Killed in action at Passchendaele Ridge, 28 September 1917. Buried where he fell. Age 35. Pte. 2530, W. Jarman reported, "It was about midnight while Scotty Hewitt and two signallers were asleep in a bivouac at Half Way House, Ypres, a shell landed right on it blowing them all out of all recognition. I saw the whole occurrence and we immediately shovelled earth etc. over the spot where they were and covered up what remained of them." He *m*. at Edinburgh, Janet (Planthurst Road, Koorah, New South Wales), *dau*. of Joseph Collyer M'Leod, and had a daughter, Christina, *b*. 14 January 1903. (*IWGC record 23 September*)

(Panel 29) Pte. 3218, Martin Hugh Scullin, 53rd Bn. Australian Infantry, A.I.F.: *s*. of the late James Scullin, by his wife Bridget (Emerald, via Cooma, New South Wales): and brother to L/Corpl. 4217, T.E. Scullin, 17th Australian Infantry, killed in action, 19 July 1918: *b*. Numeralla, nr. Cooma, March 1893: Religion – Roman Catholic: Occupation – Cordial Manufacturer: joined A.I.F. Lismore, 8 August 1916: departed Sydney, 11 November 1916; trained England (from 30 January 1917); hospitalised Fovant Camp (bronchitis) 29 March–27 April: served with the Expeditionary Force in France from 26 June 1917; joined 53rd Bn. 1 August. Killed in action, 24 September 1917. Age 24. *unm*. Correspondence to be addressed c/o H.C. Scullin Esq., Tweed Heads, New South Wales.

His brother Thomas also has no known grave; he is commemorated on the Villers-Bretonneux Memorial, France.

(Panel 29) Pte. 2253, William Allen Athol MacGregor, 54th Bn. Australian Infantry, A.I.F.: *s*. of William John MacGregor, of 26, Old Canterbury Road, Lewisham, New South Wales, by his wife Rebecca, *née* Holt: and elder brother to Corpl. 3853, R.K. MacGregor, M.M., 45th Bn., who also fell: *b*. Sydney, 1891: Religion – Church of England: Occupation – Labourer: 5'7" tall, grey eyes, fair hair: enlisted Dubbo, 5 November 1915: departed Australia, 19 August 1916: promoted A/Sergt. 22 November (England); reverted to Pte. to proceed with a draft to France, 14 December: hospitalised France (influenza, trench fever, trench feet) 24 December 1916–2 June 1917: rejoined 54th Battn. In the Field, 8 June, and was killed in action, 26 September 1917. Age 25. *unm*.

His brother Roderick also has no known grave; he is recorded on Panel 27.

(Panel 29) Pte. 2693, Earl Roland Mewburn, Stretcher Bearer, 'C' Coy., 55th Bn. Australian Infantry, A.I.F.: *s*. of the late John Mewburn, by his wife Margaret (Boorowa, New South Wales): and *yr*. brother to Pte. 2013A, A.G.E. Mewburn, 17th Battn. who fell five weeks later: *b*. Rugby, New South Wales, about 1897. Killed in action, 26 September 1917; Polygon Wood. He had gone out over the parapet with another Stretcher Bearer to help bring in a wounded man when he was shot by a sniper; death was instantaneous. Buried by Ptes. A.W. Curran and L. Guillaume, rear of front line trench, right of Menin Road. Grave marked by a small cross. "He was a most popular chap. Very big and stout, we nicknamed him the Human Tank." Age 20. *unm*.

His brother Albert also has no known grave; he is recorded on Panel 17.

(Panel 29) Capt. Raymond Vallack Single, 'B' Coy., 56th Bn. Australian Infantry, A.I.F.: *s*. of H.E. (& Mary Judith) Single, of Vandoona, Wollar, New South Wales: a descendant of John Single, Grazier & Pioneer, of Nepean House Castlereagh, New South Wales: and cousin to Pte. 4366, W. Single, 29th Battn., and Capt. H. Thompson, 56th Battn., who both fell the same day: *b*. Mudgee, New South Wales, 1887:

Occupation – Accountant: shot through the head and killed by an enemy sniper shortly after 5 a.m., 26 September 1917, at the Battle of Polygon Wood. C.S.M. Sidney Dewey, 'C' Coy., wrote, "A captain from B Company [Captain Single], a noted cricketer, came to visit the company commander of C Company [Captain Thompson], and had a luminous watch on his wrist. He was being told about how his watch showed up in the dark when crack went a bullet. The thought of the company commander and his company sergeant major was that he had yawned, but as he seemed to stay in the sitting position something was said to him, but no answer. He had been shot dead, and there is no doubt it was his watch that directed the fire of the vigilant Hun sniper." Age 30.

His cousins also have no known grave; Wilfred Single is recorded on Panel 23; Hubert Thompson, below.

(Panel 29) Pte. 1638, William Carney, 'D' Coy., 56th Bn. Australian Infantry, A.I.F.: late *husb.* (*m.* 10 May 1917) to Gladys Louisa Carney, *née* Carter (Stansfield Cottages, Webb's Flat, Anyards Road, Cobham, co. Surrey, England): b. co. Hants, England, 1888: Religion – Church of England: 5'5¾" tall; dark complexion, brown eyes, light brown hair: Occupation – Labourer: joined A.I.F., Cootamundra, New South Wales, 9 February 1916; Awarded 14 Days Confined to Camp – Absent 9 p.m. 21/3/16 to 7 p.m. 25/3/16 – Forfeiture 4 Day's Pay: apptd. 2nd Rfts., 56th Battn., Wagga Wagga, 10 April: departed Sydney, A40 'Ceramic,' 14 April: embarked Alexandria, 29 July; proceeded to England, 9 August 1916; thence to France (stowed away with a reinforcement draft) 16 September: returned to England under escort, 1 October; proceeded to France on the 14th.: joined 56th Bn.; Trenches, Somme, 2 November: hospitalised (Trench Feet) 5 December, transf'd. England on the 10th., admitted 3rd Australian General Hospital, Brighton the following day: Discharged to Duty, Perham Downs (and two weeks leave) 19 January: returned to Perham Downs, 16 February: Awarded by Lieut.Col. Fox (17 February) Thirteen days Field Punishment No.2 – 'Absent Without Leave 3.30 p.m, 3/2/17 to 4 p.m. 15/2/17' – plus 1 Day Custody awaiting trial; Total Forfeiture – 27 Day's Pay: proceeded to Wareham, 21 February, thence to Hurdicott; returned Australian Camp, Perham Downs, 21 April: proceeded to France 27 May: joined 56th Battn.; Warloy, 22 June: detached for duty to 1st Australian Tunnelling Coy., 16 September: rejoined battalion; Trenches, Chateau Segard, 23 September 1917, and was killed in action on the 28th. Age 29. Sergt. 1849, B. Johnson, 56th Bn., wrote, "I saw him killed at Polygon Wood; he was hit about the head with shell fragments, and died instantly. I knew him very well; he was the only man of that name in the company. I saw him buried at place of casualty; burial service was read by Capt. Plomley O.C. 'D' Coy. The grave was not marked at the time, but was sure to have been later.' His effects – 2 Notebooks, Metal Mirror, Badge, Letter – were received by his widow January 1918; over the following years she also received his medals, memorial plaque and scroll.

(Panel 29) Capt. Hubert Gordon Thompson, 56th Bn. Australian Infantry, A.I.F.: *s.* of Alfred Gordon (& Minnie Augusta) Thompson, of 'Nyon,' Wycombe Road, Neutral Bay, New South Wales: a descendant of John Single, Grazier & Pioneer, of Nepean House Castlereagh, New South Wales: and cousin to Capt. R.V. Single, 56th Battn., and Pte. 4366, W. Single, who both fell the same day: *b.* Bathurst, 1887. Killed by a shell at Polygon Wood east of Ypres late on the evening of 26 September 1917. On 12 September the late Lieut.Col. A.H. Scott, D.S.O., recommended Capt. Thompson be awarded the Military Cross, "This officer led his company in the attack and displayed fine leadership and courage in keeping his men well up under the barrage. When the Red Line was reached he organised his men for the next advance and when the barrage moved forward he personally led his Company, keeping his men as close as possible to it. He assisted to organise on the final objective and it was partly owing to his efforts that a successful defence was put up to meet the counter-attack. A recommendation that this Officer be granted some honour was received from Capt. Smythe who witnessed his work throughout. Unfortunately this brave and gallant officer was killed shortly afterwards. If posthumous honours are awarded I recommend him for a Military Cross or at least a Mention in Despatches." Age 30.

His cousins also have no known grave, Roland Single is recorded above; Wilfred Single, Panel 23.

(Panel 29) Pte. 1664, Victor George Ferguson, 'B' Coy., 56th Bn. Australian Infantry, A.I.F.: *s.* of the late Thomas Ferguson, by his wife Ellen: *b.* Graytown, Victoria. Killed in action, 25 September 1917, by a shell. Buried in the reserve, amongst the 18 pdr. Batteries. Grave marked by a small cross. *Buried in Oostaverne Wood Cemetery (VIII.B.16).*

(Panel 29) Pte. 3159, Frank Couch Michell, 56th Bn. Australian Infantry, A.I.F.: *s.* of Frank Couch Michell, of 92, Regent Street, Paddington, New South Wales, by his late wife Hannah Elizabeth: and elder brother to Pte. 1598, A. Michell, 1st Australian Infantry, who fell on 2 May 1915; Gallipoli: *b.* Sydney. Killed in action, 26 September 1917. Age 28. He was married to Eva Susan Michell ('Elsieville,' Fletcher Street, Woollahra, Sydney, New South Wales), to whom all correspondence regarding her late husband should be addressed.

His brother Albert is buried in 4th Battalion Parade Ground Cemetery (D.3).

(Panel 29) Pte. 2906, Alfred James Sharman, M.M.; Stretcher-bearer attd. 'C' Coy., 56th Bn. Australian Infantry, A.I.F.: *s.* of Jane Sharman (Jugiong Creek, Jugiong, New South Wales), and the late William Sharman; Farmer: and yr. brother to Pte. 4591, H.J. Sharman, 2nd Bn.; Discharged (Mentally Unfit - 'Confusional Insanity'), 7 November 1917: *b.* Jugiong Creek, May 1888: Religion – Church of England: 5'4½" tall; fresh complexion, brown eyes, dark hair: Occupation – Farmer: enlisted Sydney, 30 June 1915; apptd. 9th Rfts., 4th Battn., Liverpool, 30 August: departed Sydney, HMAT A8 'Argyllshire,' 30 September: joined 4th Bn., Tel-el-Kebir, Egypt, 8 January 1916; transf'd. 56th Bn. 15 February: proceeded to France, 19 June; disembarked Marseilles on the 29th.: On Leave; England, 8–26 January 1917: Summer Rest Camp, 27 May–11 June: Awarded Military Medal (London Gazette, No.30095, 25 May 1917; Australia Gazette, No.174, 11 October 1917), by Lieut. Gen. Sir H.R. Birdwood, 1 May 1917, "For Bravery in the Field.": Killed in action 24 September 1917: Pte. 339, C. Flavin, 'A' Coy., said, "He was gassed at Polygon Wood on September 24th. I drew Capt. Elliott's attention to him. Capt. Elliott treated him and after a short time had him sent out on a stretcher. The party took him to the D/S. They got well on the way there when a shell blew them up. I heard about it and went down to investigate. I found two of the bearers badly wounded and lying at the D/S. They did not know what had happened to Sharman. I went out to look for him and found his dead body lying in a trench, where the shell had blown the party up. He had been killed outright. I arranged for the body to be buried at the spot where he lay. The place is close to Glencorse Wood. We put a cross on the grave with his name on it. He was a very fine man indeed; he had gained the M.M. for work he had done.": Age 29. *unm.* His personal effects – Purse, Testament, Gospel of St. John, Military Medal ribbon - were received by Mrs Sharman 18 May 1918; his 1914-15 Star (26284), British War (18763), Victory (18695) medals, Memorial plaque and Scroll (332258), September 1921–February 1925. Subsequent to receiving a copy of the booklet 'Where The Australians Rest' (September 1921) Mrs Sharman made two applications (October 1922, February 1925), with appropriate costs enclosed, to the Australian Base Records Office for a further three copies of this booklet; her requests were never honoured, her payments un-refunded. (*IWGC record age 28*)

(Panel 29) Pte. 2456, Alexander Leslie Montgomery, 57th Bn. Australian Infantry, A.I.F.: *s.* of William John Montgomery, of 39, Buncle Street, North Melbourne, by his wife Robina: and *yr.* brother to L/Corpl. R. Montgomery, 24th Battn. A.I.F., who fell two weeks later. Killed in action, 25 September 1917; Polygon Wood. Age 26. *unm.*

His brother Robert also has no known grave; he is recorded on Panel 23.

(Panel 29) Pte. 3220, Clarence Victor Prew, 57th Bn. Australian Infantry, A.I.F.: *s.* of John Prew, by his wife Caroline: late *husb.* to Mrs A.R. Prew: native of Port Melbourne, Australia. Killed in action at 10.00 a.m. on the morning of 26 September 1917, during the advance on Polygon Wood, nr. Ypres; previously reported missing, being last seen in the vicinity of Hell Fire Corner. Age 36.

September Morn

It must have been with trepidation that early September morn
When, with each breath every man contemplated the enemy's scorn,
They were soldiers, but many still young men at the edge of their youth
And they were family men, who had left their loved ones seeking the truth.

Their minds craved for stillness, amongst the usual fire that greeted the dawn
Where the ground had been bombarded, scared and stood forlorn,
With their last prayers freshly imprinted upon their minds
They moved forward, willing themselves for the future peace of mankind.

Many fell that day into the depths of the dark, blood soaked mud
And would stay where they landed, their souls soaked in their blood,
Still, they moved forward, as if in a blind daze
While the hours passed by them, with the skies still ablaze.

When they reached their objective, their battle was won
But their hearts were with their comrades, many a stranger's son,
The ground was covered with their toil, sweat and their tears
And that September morn had done little to alleviate their fears.

Now the years have passed on, but the land still bears the scars
Of the fallen soldiers, some buried, some lost and some forever marred,
But we remember them daily, their sacrifices gratefully imprinted on our hearts
And we hope and pray that our future does never again, bring such things to pass.

Written by Clarence Prew's great-grand-daughter, Rosslyn B. Hamilton, 2004.

(Panel 29) Lieut. 1456, Leslie 'Ken' Kennedy Smith, XVth. Platoon, 'D' Coy., 58th Bn. Australian Infantry, A.I.F.: *s.* of John Kennedy (& Annie Lavinia) Smith, of Bairnsdale, Victoria: and elder brother to Pte. 738, G.K. Smith, 21st Australian Infantry, died 3rd London General Hospital, 2 December 1915, of wounds (SW head; abscess brain) received in action at Anzac, Gallipoli Peninsula, 23 October 1915. One month prior to his being mortally wounded, he greatly distinguished himself near the island of Mudros when he dived into the sea from the deck of his troopship to secure a patent raft that had broken from its moorings. For this act he was Mentioned in Despatches by Sir Ian Hamilton: *b.* Bairnsdale, January 1889: Religion – Church of England: Occupation – Bank Official: 6'3¼" tall, fair complexion, grey eyes, brown hair: previously served 3 yrs. School Cadets, volunteered and enlisted Melbourne, 29 June 1915; apptd. Depot Bn. 7 July; transf'd 4th Training Bn. 19 December 1915: applied for and obtained a commission, promoted 2nd Lieut. 17 January 1916; trained Army Muster Camp, Broadmeadows; departed Melbourne, 1 August 1916: trained England (from 14 September), joined 57th Bn. 9 December: promoted Lieut. 1 January 1917: proceeded to France, 12 July: joined 'D' Coy. 58th Bn. 20 July: apptd. Commanding Officer, XVth Platoon, 24 September, and was killed in action the following day (25 September 1917) moving forward to the attack at Polygon Wood, east of Ypres. Badly hit by a shell, death was almost instantaneous. Age 28. Pte. Ryland, 58th Bn. stated, "…I knew him very well. I was in camp with him in Australia before coming out. On the 25th September we were holding the support lines at Polygon Wood. We were ordered to reinforce the front line. I saw Mr Smith go over the top of our trench, and saw a shell drop a few feet away from him; he fell. I was told he was badly wounded, his leg and arm was broken; he was carried out and died soon after." And Pte. Montgomery, "…He had just got out of a sap when a shell burst. I passed him; he was still alive, one arm seemed to be nearly blown off and he was bleeding from the chest; he did not speak. They got his body out but I do not know what was done with it. He had only joined about four months and was a very nice fellow."

His brother Geoffrey is buried in Wandsworth (Earlsfield) Cemetery (130, Aust.15).

(Panel 29) Pte. 2224, Edward 'Pum' Pummeroy, 'D' Coy., 58th Bn. Australian Infantry, A.I.F.: Officer's Servant (Batman) to Lieut. L.K. Smith (killed): *s.* of William John Pummeroy, of 53, Roseberry Street, Ascot Vale, Victoria: *b.* Caulfield, Victoria: enlisted Melbourne, 19 April 1916. Missing believed killed in action, 26 September 1917. Age 40. Pte. 2801, J. Montgomery stated, "On Tuesday, 25th September 1917, Pte. Pummeroy was seen by men of the battalion, in a shelter in a sap just out of Polygon Wood. On the morning of the 25th his officer (Lieut. L.K. Smith) came to the 15th Platoon Ward. We had to go over as a British company were in trouble. Lieut. Smith was killed leading us. It was believed that Pummeroy remained in the shelter, as he was not seen with us when we went over. When we came back the shelter was blown to pieces and the ground around ploughed up with shells, and I believe he must have been buried by a shell as it was very improbable that he could have been taken prisoner. I last saw Pummeroy on the night of the 24th." *The Argus* (Melbourne, 6 June 1918):-

Dulce Et Decorum Est Pro Patria Mori

Loving Brother Charlie,
Sister-in-Law Annie, And Niece Lois

Lieut. L.K. Smith also has no known grave; he is recorded above.

(Panel 29) Lieut. John Walter Francis, 59th Bn. Australian Infantry, A.I.F.: *s.* of William Hatchett (& Johane Christiane) Francis, of Yulecart, Victoria: *b.* Croxton, West Hamilton, Victoria. Died of wounds, 26 September 1917. Mentioned in Despatches 'For conspicuous gallantry and devotion to duty at Polygon Wood, on 26th September. As Intelligence Officer of the Battalion he did very valuable work in laying out tapes to form up on and in guiding the 59th Battalion on to the tapes. He showed utter disregard for personal safety when going forward to collect information, and was subsequently mortally wounded when returning to Black Watch Corner with information and documents.' Age 25.

PANEL 29 ENDS CORPL. W.T. MARSHALL, 59TH BN. AUSTRALIAN INF.

PANEL 31 BEGINS CORPL. H.I. RUSSELL, 59TH BN. AUSTRALIAN INF.

(Panel 31) Pte. 3141, Alfred James Dent, 59th Bn. Australian Infantry, A.I.F.: *s.* of James Dent, of Frankston, Victoria, by his wife Mary Ann: *b.* Frankston, 1891: Occupation – Labourer: enlisted Warragul 27 November 1916; apptd. 8th Rfts. 59th Battn. 8 December; departed Melbourne, 16 December: trained England, 18 February–14 June 1917: joined 59th Battn. In the Field 9 July. Killed in action at Tokyo Ridge, 16 October 1917 by shellfire. Buried where he fell. Age 26. *unm.* Remains recovered from an unmarked grave (28.D.29.c.3.3) 18 February 1927; identified – Damaged Disc, Collar Badge; reinterred, registered 19 February 1927. *Buried in Sanctuary Wood Cemetery (III.G.8).*

Sunshine Passes Shadows Fall Love And Remembrance Outlast All

(Panel 31) Pte. 2175, John Gustaf Graubin, 'B' Coy., 59th Bn. Australian Infantry, A.I.F.: late of 1, Livingstone Street, North Melbourne, Victoria: *s.* of Otto Graubin, of 7 de Tingen, 26 Barghell, Helsingfors, Finland, Russia: *b.* Helsingfors (Helsinki), December 1883: Religion – Lutheran: formerly a Sailor; at enlistment – Melbourne, 11 May 1916 – was gainfully employed as Farm Labourer: 5'4¾" tall, blue eyes, black hair: posted 4th Rfts. 59th Battn. Castlemaine, 22 July: departed Melbourne, A.67 'Orsova,' 1 August: disembarked Plymouth, 14 September following, and proceeded to Larkhill Camp: admitted 15th Training Battn Hospital, Larkhill (20 September), Venereal Disease; transf'd. Fargo Military Hospital (21 September) Tachial Abscesses / V.D., and placed in isolation: discharged to duty, 1 October: Awarded (Codford Camp, 18 October) 12 days Field Punishment No.2, and Forfeiture 14 Days Pay, for 'Overstaying Leave, 9–11 October': proceeded to France with a draft of 139 reinforcements, 6 December: joined 59th Battn. Ribemont, 29 December 1916. Reported missing following the battalion's attack, 26 September 1917, nr. Black Watch Corner, Polygon Wood; since adjudged by a Court of Enquiry (22 March 1918) to have been killed in action on that date. Age 33. *unm.* A Russian subject and reservist of the Imperial Russian Army, Pte. Graubin was compelled to join the A.I.F. due to his inability to return to Russia. See account re. Pte. W.G. Averkoff, Messines Ridge British Cemetery (V.C.21).

(Panel 31) Pte. 2926, Enoch Andrew Jacobson, 59th Bn. Australian Infantry, A.I.F.: formerly N37923: *s.* of the late John Alfred Jacobson, and his wife Caroline Charlotte Jacobson (43, Stanley Street, Berhampore, Wellington, New Zealand); and yr. brother to L/Corpl. 30593, E.R. Jacobson, 3rd

Wellington Regt., N.Z.E.F., killed in action, 4 October 1917: *b.* Wellington, 1888: Occupation – Plumber: joined A.I.F., Royal Agricultural Show-grounds, Moore Park, N.S.W., 18 September 1916; Pte. 55th Battn.: departed Sydney, A19 'Afric,' 7th Rfts. 59th Battn. 3 November: served with the Expeditionary Force in France from April 1917, and was killed by shellfire when returning from a patrol of no man's land on the night of 14–15 October 1917. Buried by 1st ANZAC Corps Burial Officer, 28NE.J5.b.25.50. Age 29. He leaves a widow, Alice Jacobson (Lennack Street, Enfield, New South Wales); and two pre-nuptial children, Oscar and Chrissie. Remains recovered from an unmarked grave (28.J.5.b.0.6) 1½ miles S.W. of Zonnebeke, 18 January 1927; identified – Title, Great Coat; Cap cover mkd. EAJ; reinterred, registered 22 January 1927. *Buried in Sanctuary Wood Cemetery (III.C.39).*

> *Mothers hearts every where are breaking for loving sons and comforters gone.*
> *C.C. Jacobson, Nov. 1917.*

His brother Ernest has no known grave; he is commemorated on the Tyne Cot (New Zealand) Memorial (Panel 6).

(Panel 31) Pte. 3205, Sylvester Murray Mason, 59th Bn. Australian Infantry, A.I.F.: *s.* of John W. Mason, by his wife Rachel: *b.* Yarrawonga, Victoria, 1887: Occupation – Commercial Traveller; Melbourne. Killed at Tokyo Ridge by the explosion of a large shell when returning from a patrol of no man's land on the night of 14–15 October 1917; Pte. Jacobson was also killed. In response to an enquiry made by Pte. Mason's family, the following report, by Corpl. 2419, F.A. Irvine, was, in due course, forwarded to his widow, Mrs Grace Mason ('Edgecombe,' Cromwell Street, Caulfield, Victoria) – "Pte. Mason was one of a patrol party of which I was in charge, and at about 3 a.m. we were about to re-enter our lines when a large shell burst close by us, and I looked round to see if any damage had been done. I saw Mason and one man stretched out. Mason was moaning and repeatedly saying, 'I am killed' by the rattle in his breathing I knew he was badly hurt and I rushed in for the stretcher bearers, but I got lost and for some time could not find them. When we got to Mason he was quite dead, the shell having struck him in the side." Buried near where he fell, Tokyo Ridge, opposite Celtic Wood, Ypres Front. Age 30. Remains recovered from an unmarked grave (28.J.5.b.0.6) 18 January 1927; identified – Damaged Disc, Clothing; reinterred, registered 22 January 1927. *Buried in Sanctuary Wood Cemetery (III.C.38).*

> *Husband Of Grace*
> *Son Of Rachel & John Mason*
> *He Like A Soldier Fell*

(Panel 31) Pte. 2184, Alfred Charles Knight, 'A' Coy., 60th Bn. Australian Infantry, A.I.F.: s. of the late Edward Knight, by his wife Elizabeth C. Knight (87, Edith Street, Leichardt, New South Wales): *b.* Gymbowen, Victoria: Religion – Church of England: Occupation – Farmer: 5'3" tall, blue eyes, dark brown hair: enlisted Ballarat, 11 May 1916, posted 4th Rfts. 60th Battn.: departed Melbourne, 1 August 1916: served with the Expeditionary Force in France from 17 September 1917; joined 60th Battn. In the Field on the 29th, and was killed in action, 10 October 1917. Age 32. Lieut. Parker, 60th Battn. wrote, "On behalf of the Officers, N.C.O's, and men of A company, I wish to express our deepest sympathy with you in the loss of a comrade, poor boy (2184), Private A.C.Knight. On the morning of 10th October 1917, we were on Anzac Ridge, and an enemy shell burst on the trench where your son was standing, he was buried. When we were able to dig him out there was no movement, but he was taken immediately to the dressing station. The Doctor stated that he had passed away. He was buried by the Medical Officer. It was his first time in the line, yet he was very brave and never flinched from duty. We have lost a faithful comrade and feel keenly your loss. He has passed away in a worthy cause – for liberty and righteousness. Each man of us is willing to give life itself if need be for those in the homeland. He has gone to his reward for work well done. With deepest sympathy…"

(Panel 31) Pte. 2687, John Michael O'Brien, 4th Australian Pioneers, A.I.F.: *s.* of Mary Hull (Tooley Street, Maryborough, Queensland), by her marriage to the late Maurice O'Brien: and *yr.* brother to Pte. 5706, T. O'Brien, 26th Battn. A.I.F., who fell six days previously: *b.* Maryborough, 1878: joined A.I.F. 7

April 1916; posted 5th Rfts. 4th Pioneers, Enoggera, 26 August: departed Brisbane, 19 September: served with the Expeditionary Force in France from 29 March 1917, and was killed in action, 26 September 1917; H.E. shell. Buried where he fell. Age 39.

His brother Thomas also has no known grave; he is recorded on Panel 23.

(Panel 31) Lieut. Horace 'Horrie' Joseph Rex, 1st Coy., Australian Machine Gun Corps, A.I.F.: *s.* of James Rex, of Wattle Grove, Braidwood, New South Wales, by his wife Annie, *née* Canvin: 2nd *gt.-gdson.* of John Mernagh who, after fighting the British in the Wicklow Hills in Ireland throughout the 1798 rebellion, was captured in mid February 1804 and, rather than face trial for sedition and murder, self-banished himself to Australia in 1806: and gt.-nephew to Brigdr.Gen. Dr. Patrick Joseph Hoshie Farrell, of Braidwood, who served in Mexico, the Boxer Rebellion, China, and after commanding the first company of United States troops to land in the Philippine Islands, June 1898, later became Surgeon General, United States Army, Philippines: *b.* Wattle Grove, Braidwood, 12 December 1895: *educ.* St. Bede's Catholic School, thereafter becoming Secretary to the local hospital: volunteered and enlisted Liverpool, New South Wales, 25 July 1916, apptd. 2nd Lieut.: attd. 56th Battn. Goulburn Depot, August following: embarked Sydney, HMAT Argyllshire, 31 October 1916, 17th Rft. Draft, 24th Infantry Battn., apptd. Ship's Adjutant: arrived Devonport, 10 January 1917: trained Larkhill and Salisbury Plain: transf'd. Machine Gun Corps late February 1917: served with the Expeditionary Force in France and Flanders from 19 April: assigned 1st Machine Gun Coy. 11 May: promoted Lieut. 18 August, and was killed in action at Molenaarelsthoek, seven weeks later, on 7 October 1917, being shot by a German sniper while attempting to rescue his sergeant who had been wounded during heavy shelling of the machine gun post. Further shellfire directed onto the position completely obliterated the post and Lieut. Rex's body was never recovered. Age 21. *unm.*

(Panel 31) Sergt. 2132, Harvey James Cook, No.1 Section, 2nd Bn. Australian Machine Gun Corps, A.I.F.: formerly 21st Battn.: *s.* of James Harvey Cook, of Glenfern Park, Romsey, Victoria, by his wife Mary: *b.* Rochford, Victoria. Killed by a shell which wiped out the entire section while waiting for the 'hop-over at Passchendaele,' 9 October 1917. Age 23. *unm.* Buried near where he fell (Dainty Wood); the remains of Corpl. Pollock, Ptes. Burns, Selkrig and Morris were removed and buried further back. See Belgian Battery Corner Cemetery (II.F.20–23).

(Panel 31) Sergt. 1538, Daniel Joseph Sullivan, 4th Coy., Australian Machine Gun Corps, A.I.F.: Killed in action, 4 October 1917. Remains recovered from an unmarked grave (28.J.2.d.90.25); identified – Disc, Clothing; reinterred, registered 16 January 1928. *Buried in Sanctuary Wood Cemetery (IV.N.4).*

(Panel 31) L/Corpl. 1679, Robert Charles Gordon Greig, M.M., 6th Coy., Australian Machine Gun Corps, A.I.F.: *s.* of David Greig, of Penshurst, Victoria, and 'Egremont,' Tennyson Street, Sandringham, by his wife Jane Agnes Greig: and brother to 2nd Lieut. N.J. Greig, 7th Australian Infantry, Mentioned in Despatches for 'Gallant conduct, killed (12 July 1915; Gallipoli) during an attack on German Officers Trench, when covering the retreat of his party, which was safely effected through his gallant action;' recommended for the award of the Victoria Cross: *b.* Bendigo, September 1893: Occupation – Clerk, Bank of Victoria, Penshurst: a serving member of 17th Light Horse; joined A.I.F., Rochester, Victoria, 3 May 1915; posted 2nd Rfts. 22nd Battn. Seymour, 17 June; departed Melbourne, 16 July: served at Gallipoli (from September 1915); France and Flanders (from July 1916): Awarded Military Medal, In the Field, 18 September 1916 (*London Gazette*, 20 October) 'For plucky work in charge of Brigade carrying parties by day and night to the front line at Pozieres and Mouquet on the 26th August 1916. He distinguished himself by his coolness and determination under fire, at times extremely heavy, and succeeded in getting his loads delivered regularly and at the appointed hours thanks to his excellent example.': transf'd. 6th M.G. Coy. 29 October; apptd. L/Corpl. 13 April 1917. Killed in action, 9 October 1917. Age 24. *unm.* Memorial Cross erected – Perth Cemetery (China Wall), Zillebeke (V.M.3).

His brother Norman also has no known grave; he is commemorated on the Lone Pine Memorial (Panel 6).

(Panel 31) Pte. 460, Bernard Henry Clarke, 8th Coy., Australian Machine Gun Corps, A.I.F.: *s.* of William Angus Clarke, of Tarlee, by his wife Sophie Jane: and brother to Pte. 461, W.A. Clarke, 8th Coy.,

A.M.G.C. (surv'd.); and Gnr. 39787, H.K. Clarke, 3rd Bde. A.F.A. (surv'd.): *b.* Tarlee, South Australia, 1896: Occupation – Ministerial Student; Home Missionary, Lucindale Methodist Home Mission Station: member (1 year) Lucindale Rifle Club: volunteered and enlisted Riverton, 26 May 1916; posted 7th Rfts. 8th A.M.G.C. 28 June: departed Melbourne, HMAT 'Ulysses,' 26 November: trained Perham Downs (from 29 December): served in France from 25 April 1917, and died of wounds, 26 September following. Age 21. A comrade, W.A. Morgan, said, "...He was seriously wounded whilst going for ammunition... it was between Westhoek Ridge and Polygon Wood. A shell exploded which shattered both his legs, and he was badly affected by concussion. He died soon after admission to the Aid Post, and was buried by the medical staff at Westhoek Ridge. It is a small cemetery, just near the dressing station, and I think the grave would be registered....He soon became unconscious and if he suffered any pain it was only for a few minutes..."

(Panel 31) Pte. 510, Albert Mark Hatcher, 8th Coy., Australian Machine Gun Corps, A.I.F.: *s.* of Albert Hatcher, of Virginia, South Australia, by his wife Rachel: and brother to Dvr. 11086, C.R. Hatcher (surv'd.); Pte. 1650, H.S. Hatcher, 35th Australian Infantry, killed in action, 14 March 1917: *b.* Lewiston, South Australia, December 1892: Religion – Methodist: Occupation – Butcher: 5'8" tall, fresh complexion, blue eyes, light brown hair: enlisted Adelaide, 3 August 1916; posted 8th Rfts. 8th Coy. A.M.G.C. 30 November: departed Melbourne, 16 December following: served in France from 25 April 1917; joined 8th Coy., In the Field 13 June, and was killed in action, 26 September 1917. Buried (J.9.a.50) the following day. Age 24. *unm.*

His brother Howard is buried in Cité Bonjean Military Cemetery, Armentieres (V.A.25).

(Panel 31) Corpl. 1626, Walter Henry Chibnall, 10th Australian Trench Mortar Bty., A.I.F.: eldest *s.* of William Anthony Chibnall, of Snake Valley, Victoria, by his wife Amy Bridget, *née* Wright: *b.* Snake Valley, 1885: Religion – Presbyterian: Occupation – Miner: enlisted, 15 March 1916: departed Melbourne HMAT 'Ascanius,' 1st Rfts. 39th Battn. 27 May 1916; transf'd. 10th Trench Mortar Bty. 7 August 1916: promoted Corpl. 15 September 1917. Killed in action, 12 October 1917, at Passchendaele, when he and a comrade (Pte. R.C. Bryant) were hit by a shell while taking shelter in a shell-hole. Age 32. He leaves a wife, Margaret Chibnall ('Glenco,' Waterloo Road, Beaufort, Victoria), and son – William Beresford Chibnall.

His son William 'Billy,' 2/21st Bn. A.I.F., taken prisoner by the Japanese in World War II, died in Ambon prison camp, 20 February 1942. He has no known grave; Ambon Memorial (Col.3).

(Panel 31) Pte. 16116, Ronald Caulfield Bryant, 10th Australian Trench Mortar Bty., A.I.F.: *s.* of Albert Crusoe (& Isabella) Bryant, of 209, Fitzroy Street, St. Kilda, Victoria. Killed in action, 12 October 1917; Passchendaele, Belgium. Age 25. Pte. 1851, W. McLaughlin said, "I knew Bryant...He was taking up a position with his gun, and we were having a spell in a shell-hole, when a H.E. shell exploded in the hole killing Bryant and another man (Corpl. Chibnall) instantly. I was about five yards away at the time, and was wounded by the same shell. I saw Chibnall, but could not find any trace of Bryant. I believe he was buried by the shell. We had to retire and I heard nothing further of him."

(Panel 31) Pte. 4489, Charles Osmond Donovan Edser, 9th Field Ambulance, Australian Army Medical Corps, A.I.F.: 5'8" tall, of stout build, fair complexion: prior to enlistment was a Railway Boiler Maker: left Sydney, with 3rd Australian General Hospital, aboard 'Mooltan,' 15 May 1915: served with the Expeditionary Force at Gallipoli, and in France and Flanders, and was killed outright, 12 October 1917, being hit by a shell. At the time of his death, Pte. Edser was serving as a stretcher bearer, and was returning into the line to take out other wounded from Frost House, on the Zonnebeke – Ypres road, in front of Passchendaele. 'He dropped into a shell hole and lived about ½ an hour after being badly hit about the body. His body was not taken out then, too much to do. It was left lying there until October 20th, but it is unlikely he would ever be buried. It was impossible to get his body down, too much mud, too much heavy work.' Sergt. R.J. Watts wrote, "I was told by Sergt. Southam, 9th Field Ambulance, that 1515, E. Sullivan, 12084, C.J. Walshe, and 4489, C.O.D. Edser, were lying out in no man's land. Edser and Sullivan being dead on October 12th." Age 29–30.

Eugene Sullivan died five days later in No.3 Canadian C.C.S., and was buried in Lijssenthoek Military Cemetery (XXII.B.24A); Charles Walshe is buried in Tyne Cot Cemetery (LIII.D.10).

(Panel 31) Pte. 12029, Joseph 'Joe' Dench Nankivell, 'C' Section, 9th Field Ambulance, Australian Army Medical Corps, A.I.F.: *s.* of Joseph Nankivell, of Tumby Bay, South Australia, by his wife Selina: and brother to Pte. 19893 (Rev'd.) W.F. Nankivell, Australian Army Medical Corps (surv'd.): *b.* Minlaton: enlisted Holsworthy. Killed instantaneously by a shell, 12 October 1917, between Otto Farm and Levi Farm, Passchendaele. Age 28. Pte. C.O. Hamblin later reported, "On the night of 11th October he was detailed to take charge of a party of ambulance bearers and 12 infantry men, detailed to assist in the work; 4 squads in all. He reported with his party to the Medical Officer in charge of 39th Australian Battn. Army Medical Corps detail; it was Major Blanhaum, I was one of the party. We were instructed to follow the M.O.'s battn. stretcher party behind the column of the Battn. which was to move in about 10pm. We were near Potijze, Ypres. We moved off along a taped track into the shell holes and mud. Somewhere about half-way to the existing front line and assembly trench from this point we encountered some wounded of the Division which was being relieved. I was detached with a squad to convey these back and did not see Joe again alive. Throughout the morning of the attack on Passchendaele, 12th, I missed him being posted to an aid post on the left. On the afternoon of the 13th, during a brief interval when the flow of casualties permitted it, two of us – Pte. Boyall and myself – went to investigate the surroundings of a pill-box on our right as we feared that something had happened to Joe. We only found his body! Death had apparently been instantaneous, and due to a shell fragment piercing the spine in the region of the neck. He lay surrounded by others of the party and the evidence led us to infer that he was killed on the early morning of the 12th, prior to the attack. I have since met one man, I think he was named McLeod, who was in the party of infantry men, but though he told me they all encountered the heavy barrage of the enemy 5.9 bombardment when they reached their pill-box (which had been chosen as an aid post) and that men were killed all around him he did not know definitely the circumstances of Joe's death. There is no doubt whatever about the identification of the body. Boyall and I reverently removed the metal identity disc and pay book and some other items of personal value from the body.

These were handed over to Chaplain Curtiss, 3rd Australian Pioneers Battn., who was acting as Divisional Burial Officer, and knew Nankivell personally. It was impossible under the circumstances then existing to bury the body ourselves, but we covered it with a waterproof and sadly left it. It was nearly alongside the pill-box known as 'Hamburg' to the left of the Zonnebeke railway embankment, and on the low ground between the railway and Passchendaele. I regret I cannot give the map reference. Chaplain Curtiss took all the particulars and visited the spot later with a small burial party, though it was and still is, very close to the front line. All the bodies in the vicinity of the pill-box were buried by him and he could give any further particulars. He told us that he intended to secure a registration of the grave, but I cannot say if this has been done. It is possible that it may have been destroyed but the Chaplain can give the spot where the burials were made."

(Panel 31) Pte. 2505, Joseph Howard, 1/4th Bn. The East Yorkshire Regt. (T.F.): *yst. s.* of William Henry Howard, N.E.R. Dock Gateman; of 5, Richmond Terrace, Harrow Street, Hull, by his wife Lavinia Emily, *dau.* of the late Joseph Bennett Stephenson, of Hornsea: *b.* Hull, 15 January 1884: *educ.* T.B. Holmes School, Hull: Occupation – Lighterman; G.C.R.: volunteered and enlisted, 2 September 1914: went to France, 17 April 1915, and was killed in action there while repairing trenches, 29 May 1915. Buried in Sanctuary Wood. Age 31. He *m.* Hull, 27 April 1911; Olive Gertrude (5, Henry's Terrace, West Parade, Hull), *dau.* of the late Samuel Joseph Anderson, of 1, Etty's Terrace, Strickland Street, late of Brid; Fish Merchant, and had two *s.* – Joseph Leslie, *b.* 14 August 1911; Clive William, *b.* 22 April 1914.

(Panel 31) Pte. 10175, John King, 1st Bn. (15th Foot) The East Yorkshire Regt.: *s.* of the late Harry King, by his wife Annie Elizabeth (2, Durham Villas, Middleburg Street, New Bridge Road, Hull), *dau.* of John Brooks: *b.* Hull, co. York, 8 March 1896: *educ.* Mersey Street Board School: enlisted Hull, 8 January 1915: went to France, 19 April following, and was killed in action at Hooge, 9 August 1915. Buried in Hooge Wood. Age 19.

(Panel 31) Pte. 9678, Cyril Mawer, 2nd Bn. (15th Foot) The East Yorkshire Regt.: *s.* of Annie Mawer (6, Adderbury Crescent, Adderbury Grove, Beverley Road, Hull): *b.* Hull, co. York: enlisted there: a pre-war Regular, arrived in England with his battalion from India, December 1914: served with the Expeditionary

Force in France and Flanders from 16 January 1915, and died of wounds received in action, 4 February following, at Ravine Wood, nr. St. Eloi. Age 32. He was married to Annie Eliza Mawer (4, Talbot Street, Reed Street, Wright Street, Hull). See account, Ramparts Cemetery (Lille Gate), (B.16–17).

(Panel 31) Pte. 2221, Walter Stanley Murray, 1/4th Bn. The East Yorkshire Regt. (T.F.): *yst. s.* of Richard Henry Murray, Shipping Clerk (ret'd); of 93, St. George's Road, Hull, by his wife Martha, *dau.* of Joseph Williams, of that town: *b.* Hull, 30 December 1877: *educ.* Bridlington and Hull: Occupation – 15 yrs., Clerk; Messrs Beckett & Sons, Hull: enlisted on the first call for recruits, 1 September 1914: trained Hull and Newcastle: left for France, 17 April 1915, and went straight up to the trenches: took part in the Second Battle of Ypres, during which his battalion sustained heavy casualties and was subsequently complimented by Sir John (now Lord) French on the gallantry it had displayed. Killed – accidentally shot by one of his own comrades in the trenches near Ypres, 11 June 1915. His Commanding Officer, Capt. W.T. Wilkinson, wrote expressing the deep sorrow of himself and the battn. at the loss of "so fearless and gallant a soldier." Age 37. *unm.*

(Panel 31) Major John Murray Traill, 2nd Bn. (16th Foot) The Bedfordshire Regt.: *s.* of the late James Christie Traill, of Hobbister, Orkney, and Rattar, Caithness, by his wife Julia, *née* Lambarde: *b.* 30 October 1865: *educ.* Trinity Hall, Cambridge: gazetted 2nd Lieut. Bedfordshire Regt. from the Militia, 1 November 1887; promoted Lieut. 31 July 1889: served with the Isazai Expedition 1892: promoted Capt. 19 February 1896; apptd. Adjutant 1st (Volunteer) Battn. Essex Regt. July 1899–August 1904; obtained his Majority, 6 December 1906. In South Africa on the outbreak of war, returned to England (September) where, on arrival, Lieut.Col. Coates being pronounced medically unfit, Major Traill assumed command of 2nd Battn. and proceeded to France, 4 October 1914; disembarked Zeebrugge, 7 October. Killed in action at Ypres, on his birthday, 30 October 1914; being shot at close range during vicious hand-to-hand fighting in the trenches near Inverness Copse. Age 49. During the 1914 strikes in South Africa, he was specially commended by the Commander-in-Chief for his prompt assistance in suppressing a native uprising. (*The Times*, 28 November 1914). Mentioned in Sir John (now Lord) French's Despatch, 14 January 1915, for his services while in temporary command of his battalion in the Great War.

(Panel 31) Capt. Ernest Hugh Lyddon, 2nd Bn. (16th Foot) The Bedfordshire Regt.: eldest *s.* of Frederick Stickland (& Mrs J.W.) Lyddon, of 5, Beaufort Road, Clifton, Bristol: and brother to Lieut. F.C. Lyddon, Indian Army attd. King's Liverpool Regt., died of wounds, 26 April 1915: *b.* Cheltenham, co. Gloucester, 14 May 1887: *educ.* Weymouth, and Royal Military College, Sandhurst; gazetted 2nd Lieut. Bedfordshire Regt. October 1907, posted 2nd Battn.: served with his battalion in Gibraltar, Bermuda, and South Africa: promoted Lieut. June 1909; Capt. 16 October 1913. For active service in the Great War Capt. Lyddon proceeded to the continent with the VIIth Division, and it is believed he was killed in action at Ypres on 31 October 1914. Reported missing on that date, nothing definite has been heard of him since. Capt. Lyddon was last seen getting his men back under a terrific hail of shrapnel; a retirement having been ordered. Pte. W.H. Laws wrote, "15 December 1914…*He was my Company Commander and I was close to him when he was wounded by shrapnel in the side, I think. We were entrenching and had to retire and leave him, but he said 'I shall be all right, boys' and he must have been taken. It was on the Menin Road.*" Age 27.

His brother Frederick is buried in Vlamertinghe Military Cemetery (I.H.24).

(Panel 31) Lieut. William Bastard, 2nd Bn. (16th Foot) The Bedfordshire Regt.: *s.* of William Bastard, of Coltscombe, Slapton, nr. Kingsbridge, South Devon, by his wife Helen, 2nd *dau.* of Joshua Edward Adkins: nephew to Dr. Adkins, County of Devon Medical Officer: *b.* Coltscombe, 20 April 1891: *educ.* Plymouth (Miss Tubbs' preparatory school); Blundell's School, Tiverton, where he won the Spurway medal, and was one of the cadet winners of the Devon County Shield, 1910; and Exeter College, Oxford, from whence he graduated B.A., and obtained his commission 2nd Bedfordshire Regt.: gazetted 2nd Lieut. 22 January 1913. In South Africa at the outbreak of war, came home in September, promoted Lieut. on the 30th of that month, and joined the Expeditionary Force in Belgium, four days later. On 26 October 1914 he was in the trenches directing the fire of his platoon to help the advance of another battalion, when a German machine gun opened fire and killed him instantly. This occurred at Gheluvelt, about six miles from Ypres. Mentioned in F.M. Sir John French's Despatch, 14 January 1915, for 'gallant and distinguished service in the field.' The following remarks were received by his mother from Lieut. Col. Coates, 2nd Bedfordshire Regt., "6 November 1914…From the day he joined I recognised that your son was one of the best types of officers – very keen on his work, thoroughly sensible, and willing to take responsibility. I always had him in my eye as being well fitted for the Adjutancy later on. He was very popular with both officers and men, and I can assure you his loss to the battalion is very, very great." His Company Sergt.-Major and Quartermaster-Sergt. also wrote expressing the regard which not only his platoon, but the whole of his company, had for this young officer, who died gallantly, rifle in hand, and who was always solicitous for the welfare of his men, whom he led in battle without fear. Age 23. *unm.* (*IWGC record 27 October 1914*)

(Panel 31) Lieut. Robert Denis Stewart Harding, 4th (Extra Reserve) attd 1st Bn. (16th Foot) The Bedfordshire Regt.: only *s.* of S.G. (& Mrs) Harding, of 15, Lowndes Square, London, S.W.: *b.* 1886: *educ.* Harrow (Rendall's 1889–1903), and Christ Church: joined 4th Bedfordshire Regt. 1912: promoted Lieut. March 1913: offered his services on the outbreak of war, and attd. 1st Battn. for duty: served with the Expeditionary Force in France and Flanders, and was killed in action near Ypres, 7 November 1914. The following account of the circumstances attending his death was published in *The Harrovian War Supplement*, December 1914, "His Captain writes – 'The enemy had broken through the line of trenches held by a battalion on our left, and its break caused a part of our trenches to be vacated also. Our company was in reserve, and we formed up, and brought off an entirely successful counter-attack, driving the enemy back, killing many, and capturing twenty-five prisoners. It was in this counter-attack that Harding fell, leading his men up a lightly wooded hill. I did not see him fall, but missed him when we got to the ridge, and on going back found him quite dead. Death had evidently been instantaneous. I had formed a very high opinion of his gallantry and coolness. I could rely on him always, and he had gained the confidence of his men, though he had only been with his company about a month. He was always bright and cheery, and it was a real pleasure to have his company on the line of march or in the trenches.'" He was a member of the Bath Club. Age 28. *unm.*

(Panel 31) Lieut. Edmund Elgood Punchard, 2nd Bn. (16th Foot) The Bedfordshire Regt., 21st Infantry Brigade, 7th Division: 2nd *s.* of the Rev. Elgood George Punchard, D.D., Honorary Canon of Ely, by his wife Catherine Mary, *dau.* of Joseph Johnson: and yr. brother to Major A. Punchard, 2nd attd 7th North Staffordshire Regt., who fell on 29 March 1917, in Mesopotamia: *b.* Luton, co. Bedford, 21 October 1890: *educ.* Haileybury (1902–08), and Royal Military College, Sandhurst (1909–10); gazetted 2nd Lieut. Bedfordshire Regt. 5 October 1910; promoted Lieut. 11 June 1912: His diary reads, "…left Southampton 4 October 1914: returned to Dover because of submarines 6 October: departed again and arrived Zeebrugge 7–8 October: Bruges (St. Croix), marched from 4–8 p.m., 8 October: left for Coq-sur-Mer, arriving 2.30 p.m., bivouac at Uytkirke 9 October: left for Ostend 5 a.m.; 4 p.m. ordered back to Bruges arriving 8 p.m., 10 October: retreated to Beernem 4–8 p.m. 11 October: to Coolscamp 7.30 a.m. 12 October: to Roulers 13 October: to Ypres 9.30 a.m. to 6.30 p.m. 14 October: entrenched at Halte on Menin – Ypres Road 15 October: skirmish with Uhlans at Gheluvelt 16 October: Gheluvelt, Battle of Ypres begun 17 October: left 4.30 a.m. for Becelaere arriving 7.30 p.m., advanced to Terhand 18 October: Terhand retired to Gheluvelt 19 October: under heavy fire until dusk, moved out towards Becelaere, and entrenched 20 October: returned to Gheluvelt, in trenches, 21 October: under heavy fire, worst at 3.30 p.m. 22 October: shelled from 8 p.m., two Bedford officers (2nd Lieuts. D.L.De.T. Fernandes, 7th Battn., and G.D.C. Wright, 1st Battn.) killed, First Army Corps expected 23 October: fusillade 6 a.m., seventh day of battle, third in trenches (night and day) unrelieved 24 October: reinforced by Highland L.I. and King's Own Scottish Borderers 25 October: Brigade hard pressed, retired to Hooge 26 October: advanced again towards Gheluvelt, bivouac at Kruiseecke 27 October: shelled all day in trenches from 9 a.m., opposed by three German Army Corps 28 October: shelled at dawn, Yorks and Gordons retreated on Zandvoorde – Gheluvelt Road, trenches recovered 29 October: fight on Menin – Gheluvelt Road and in the woods 30 October: trenches shelled from 2 a.m. to 1 p.m., ordered out of trenches at 4 p.m." Lieut. Punchard was shot and killed the following day – 31 October 1914 – leading his platoon in an advance up-hill across a ploughed field in the vicinity of Inverness Copse toward Zandvoorde. The following day,

300 survivors mustered under the one officer remaining. Buried at Kruiseecke, nr. Gheluvelt. Mentioned in F.M. Sir John (now Lord) French's Despatch, 14 January (*London Gazette*, 18 February) 1915, for 'distinguished service in the field.' Age 24. *unm.*

His brother Alfred also has no known grave; he is commemorated on the Basra Memorial, Iraq (Panel 34).

(Panel 31) 2nd Lieut. Charles Ockley Bell, 'A' Coy., 2nd Bn. (16th Foot) The Bedfordshire Regt.: *s.* of Alfred F. Bell, of Deansgate, Grimsby, by his wife Sarah Susanna, *dau.* of John Ockley: *b.* Grimsby, 10 December 1891: *educ.* Collegiate, Grimsby; and Alford Grammar Schools: enlisted, South Staffordshire Regt. January 1910: given a commission, 20 May 1914; transf'd. 2nd Bedfordshire Regt.: served with the Expeditionary Force in France from 7 October 1914; killed by shrapnel, 18 October 1914. At the time of his death the battalion were advancing in a south-easterly direction toward the 10 kilo stone, Ypres – Menin road when, on nearing the road and coming over a rise they were fired on by the enemy. Age 22. *unm.* 2nd Battalion's first Active Service officer fatality attributable to enemy action. (*IWGC record 12 October 1914*)

(Panel 31) 2nd Lieut. Dudley Luis De Tavora Fernandes, 'D' Coy., 2nd Bn. (16th Foot) The Bedfordshire Regt.: elder *s.* of Thomas Weddell Luis Fernandes, of Scarborough, co. York, by his wife Emily Margaret, *née* Heywood: *gdson.* to T.W.D. Fernandes, of Grosvenor Crescent, Scarborough, Founder; Messrs Fernandes & Co., Wine & Spirit Merchants, Huntriss Row: *b.* Crosby, co. Lancaster, 1893: *educ.* Mr Cooper's School, Scarborough; St. Peter's School, York, and Royal Military College, Sandhurst (Cadet Officer, 4 September 1912–16 July 1913): gazetted 2nd Lieut. Bedfordshire Regt. 17 July 1913; joined his battalion in Pretoria, South Africa, returning to England for Active Service in France, September 1914: served in France from 7 October (arrived Ypres sector on the 14th.) and was killed in action in the early morning of the 23rd., by the bursting of a shell; vicinity Zonnebeke. Age 21. *unm.* His Colonel wrote, "I know he was a very gallant fellow and would meet his death fearlessly. Without any flattery I can say that he was one of the best officers of his rank that we have ever had. Such a thorough gentleman, so popular with officers and men, and so keen in his profession that, had he lived, he would have risen to high rank in the service. I can assure you that his loss to the regiment is very great...": 23 October 1914. Mentioned in Despatches by Sir John, now Lord, French (*London Gazette*, 17 February 1915).

(Panel 31) 2nd Lieut. Eric Arthur Hopkins, 3rd attd. 1st Bn. (16th Foot) The Bedfordshire Regt.: *s.* of Arthur (& Mrs) Hopkins, of Westview House, Bishopthorpe Road, York: *educ.* Leeds University, B.A.: Occupation – School Master; Elstow (Bedford) County School. Killed in action, 5 May 1915. Age 29. *unm.* One of three staff members of Elstow School to lose their lives in the Great War; a student remembered him and two other Elstownians recorded here, leaving a verse in November 2003. See Pte. W.A.G. Southwell, Honourable Artillery Coy. (Panel 9).

(Panel 31) 2nd Lieut. Esmond Lawrence Kellie, 1st Bn. (16th Foot) The Bedfordshire Regt.: *s.* of Lawrence Kellie, 191, Portesdown Rd., Maida Vale, London, by his wife Gertrude: and brother to 2nd Lieut. L.L. Kellie (R.F.A.), who also fell: served with the Expeditionary Force. Killed in action at Hill 60, 19 April 1915. Age 20. *unm.*

His brother Leslie is buried in Menin Road South Military Cemetery (I.R.4).

(Panel 31) 2nd Lieut. John Agar Paterson, 2nd Bn. (16th Foot) The Bedfordshire Regt.: 2nd *s.* of William Morrison Paterson, Manufacturers Agent; of 80, Great Portland Street, London, W., by his wife Margaret S., *dau.* of John Agar: *b.* Glasgow, 19 November 1893: *educ.* Dulwich College, and Royal Military College, Sandhurst: gazetted 2nd Lieut. Bedfordshire Regt. 17 September 1913: proceeded to France, early October 1914; killed in action nr. Klein Zillebeke, 31 October following. Buried there. Age 20. *unm.* (*IWGC record Patterson*)

(Panel 31) Corpl. 14404, Leonard Percy Ridgeway, 'B' Coy., 1st Bn. (16th Foot) The Bedfordshire Regt.: 4th *s.* of William Ridgeway, Grocer; of 83, Queen's Road, Watford, by his wife Millicent, *dau.* of J. Davis, of Watford: and brother to Rfn. 2879, R.S. Ridgeway, 9th London Regt., killed in action, 27 February 1915, aged 20: *b.* Watford, co. Hertford, 9 August 1893: *educ.* Victoria Council Schools: Occupation – Butcher: enlisted, Bedfordshire Regt. after the outbreak of war, August 1914: trained

Dovercourt: proceeded to France, March 1915, and was killed in action at Hill 60, during the Second Battle of Ypres, 18 April 1915. Buried at Ypres. Age 21.

His brother Sidney is buried in Wulverghem-Lindenhoek Road Cemetery (II.E.22).

(Panel 31) L/Corpl. 8502, Thomas Alfred Tompkins, 2nd Bn. (16th Foot) The Bedfordshire Regt.: *s*. of Mary Ann Tompkins (2, New Alley, Three Colt Street, Limehouse, London): and brother to Corpl. G/9784, W. Tompkins, M.M., 2nd Middlesex Regt., killed in action, 20 September 1917: *b*. Limehouse, *c*.1887: enlisted Stratford, London, E.15. Killed in action, 31 October 1914. Age 27. *unm*.

His brother Wesley is buried in Maple Leaf Cemetery, Le Romarin (I.5).

(Panel 31) L/Corpl. 9377, Horace Chalkley, 2nd Bn. (16th Foot) The Bedfordshire Regt.: *s*. of William Chalkley, of 5, Church Street, Slip End, Luton: and elder brother to Corpl. 9531, F. Chalkley, 1st Bedfordshire Regt., killed in action, 9 November 1914: *b*. Markyate, co. Bedford, *c*.1893: enlisted Luton. Killed in action, 26 October 1914. Age 24. *unm*.

His brother Frederick also has no known grave; he is commemorated on the Le Touret Memorial.

(Panel 31) Pte. 15746, James Arthur Adcock, 1st Bn. (16th Foot) The Bedfordshire Regt.: *s*. of James Herbert Adcock, of 46, Keslake Road, Kensal Rise, London, by his wife Ada Fanny: *b*. St. Pancras, *c*.1890: enlisted Westminster. Killed in action, 5 May 1915. Age 24. *unm*. Remains exhumed from an unmarked grave (28.I.29.d.3.6); identified – Clothing, Title, Cap Badge, Pay Book; reinterred, registered 13 November 1928. *Buried in Sanctuary Wood Cemetery (II.N.7)*.

Dearly Loved

(Panel 31) Pte. 37494, John Thomas Churchhouse, 6th (Service) Bn. The Bedfordshire Regt.: *s*. of J.T. (& Mrs) Churchhouse, of St. Albans, co. Hertford: late *husb*. to Laura Churchhouse (Ruby Cottage, Union Street, St. Albans), and elder brother to Pte. 3184, C.E. Churchhouse, 2/4th York & Lancaster Regt., killed in action, 21 July 1918: enlisted Bedford. Killed in action, 11 August 1917; Damnstrasse. Age 40.

His brother Charles is buried in Bouilly Cross Roads Military Cemetery (I.A.14).

(Panel 31) Pte. 25328, William Clark, 2nd Bn. (16th Foot) The Bedfordshire Regt.: Killed in action, 26 July 1917; on which date 17 men of the battalion took part in a raid in the Zillebeke sector. On returning to the battalion reserve position at Chateau Segard, a shell landed in their midst killing six men; five died of wounds, six wounded. *Buried in Bedford House Cemetery (II.C1.3/ Enc.No.4)*.

(Panel 31) Pte. 14785, William George Colin Cooper, 1st Bn. (16th Foot) The Bedfordshire Regt.: *s*. of Charles William Cooper, of 20, Buildwas Road, Ironbridge, co. Salop, by his wife Mary Ann (17, Dale Road, Coalbrookdale): *b*. Coalbrookdale, co. Salop, *c*.1892: Occupation – Valet; Savile Club, Brook Street, London, W.1: enlisted in Westminster, September 1914: served with the Expeditionary Force in France and Flanders, and was killed in action at Hill 60, nr. Ypres, 5 May 1915. Age 22. *unm*. Remains exhumed from a grave marked up as belonging to an 'Unknown British Soldier. Bedfords', (28.I.29.d.3.6); identified – Clothing, Boots mkd. BD.14785, Watch, Titles; reinterred, registered 12 November 1928. *Buried in Sanctuary Wood Cemetery (II.N.4)*.

Worthy Of Remembrance

PANEL 31 ENDS PTE. W.J. COOPER, BEDFORDSHIRE REGT.

PANEL 33 BEGINS PTE. P. CORBEN, BEDFORDSHIRE REGT.

(Panel 33) Pte. 14958, Frederick John Dumpleton, 1st Bn. (16th Foot) The Bedfordshire Regt.: *s*. of C.W. (& Mrs) Dumpleton, of 54, Victoria Street, St. Albans, co. Hertford: *b*. Sandridge, *c*.1895: enlisted St. Albans. Killed in action, 7 May 1915. Age 20. *unm*. Remains exhumed from a grave marked up as belonging to an 'Unknown British Soldier. Bedfords', (28.I.29.d.3.6); identified – Clothing, Boots mkd. BD.14958, Titles; reinterred, registered 12 November 1928. *Buried in Sanctuary Wood Cemetery (II.N.3)*.

(Panel 33) Pte. 133360, Albert French, 8th (Service) Bn. The Bedfordshire Regt.: *yst. s.* of Henry French, of 'Ivy Cottage,' Sheering, co. Essex, by his wife Alice Mary, *dau.* of Cornelius Brown: *b.* Sheering, nr. Harlow, 22 March 1895: *educ.* Sheering: Occupation – Porter; Great Eastern Railway: enlisted, 11 September 1914, after the outbreak of war: went to France, 13 September 1915; killed in action, 17 December following. Buried at La Brique. Age 20. *unm.*

(Panel 33) Pte. 16492, Frederick James Furneaux, 'A' Coy., 1st Bn. (16th Foot) The Bedfordshire Regt.: *s.* of James Furneaux, of Ivy Cottage, Kingskerswell, Newton Abbott, co. Devon: and brother to Pte. 9120, J. Furneaux, Devonshire Regt., died on 26 November 1914 of wounds received in action nr. Armentieres: *b.* Kingskerswell, nr. Torquay: enlisted Hertford. Killed in action, 4 May 1915, at the 2nd Battle of Ypres. Age 23. *unm.*

His brother John is buried in Aubers Ridge British Cemetery (VII.A.5).

(Panel 33) Pte. 13441, Henry Ernest Goodger, 'B' Coy., 1st Bn. (16th Foot) The Bedfordshire Regt.: *s.* of Henry Jesse Goodger, of 39, Upton Park Road, Forest Gate, London, by his wife Alice: and elder brother to Pte. G/32868, B.R. Goodger, Royal West Kent Regt. attd. 20th London Regt., died of wounds, 1 September 1918: *b.* Canning Town: enlisted St. Paul's Churchyard. Killed in action, 21 April 1915. Age 18.

His brother Bertie also has no known grave; he is commemorated on the Vis-en-Artois Memorial (Panel 7).

(Panel 7) Pte. 4/7291, Daniel Charles Gray, 1st Bn. (16th Foot) The Bedfordshire Regt.: *s.* of the late Arthur Gray, of Howe Green, Little Berkhampstead, and the late August Gray, his first wife: and (by his second wife Emily), half-brother to Pte. 4/6698, W. Gray, 1st Bedfordshire Regt., died on 26 April 1915: *b.* Queen Hoo Hall Farm, Tewin, co. Hertford, 1886: enlisted Hertford. Killed in action, 21 April 1915. Age 30.

His half-brother William is buried in St. Sever Cemetery, Rouen (A.8.11).

(Panel 33) Pte. 17441, Harry Sallabanks, 8th (Service) Bn. The Bedfordshire Regt.: *s.* of John Sallabanks, of Lug Farm and 2, Church Green, Ramsey, co. Huntingdon, by his wife Alice: and elder brother to Pte. 132324, C. Sallabanks, Machine Gun Corps (Inf.), died on 8 June 1918, of wounds: *b.* Ramsey Hollow, co. Huntingdon. Killed in action, 20 April 1916. Age 21. *unm.*

His brother Charles, originally buried in Mailly-le-Camp Military Cemetery, was re-interred in Fere-Champenoise French National Cemetery in 1932.

(Panel 33) Pte. 14905, Ralph Salvin, 1st Bn. (16th Foot) The Bedfordshire Regt.: *s.* of the late Philip Salvin, of Curzon Street, Netherfield, co. Nottingham: and brother to Pte. 38250, J. Salvin, 8th Lincolnshire Regt., killed in action, 4 October 1917: *b.* Carlton: enlisted Nottingham. Killed in action, 30 June 1915. Age 28. He was married to Emily Salvin (52, Deatrill Street, Netherfield).

His brother Jesse also has no known grave; he is commemorated on the Tyne Cot Memorial (Panel 37).

(Panel 33) Pte. 19633, Bert Charles Schocktee, 8th (Service) Bn. The Bedfordshire Regt.: *s.* of the late Henry Schocktee, by his wife Elizabeth (56, Elthorne Road, Holloway, London): and yr. brother to Gnr. 225058, W. Schocktee, 119th Bde. Royal Field Artillery, died on 6 September 1918, of wounds: *b.* Highgate: enlisted, St. Pancras. Killed in action, 17 December 1915. Age 26. He was married to Mrs S.P. White, *née* Schocktee (4, Windsor Road, Holloway Road, Holloway, London).

His brother William is buried in Bailleul Communal Cemetery Extension (III.F.5).

(Panel 33) Pte. 7602, Edward Warner, V.C., 1st Bn. (16th Foot) The Bedfordshire Regt.: *s.* of the late Mark Warner, and the widow Charlotte M. Warner, *née* Barber (St. Albans, co. Hertford): *b.* St. Albans, 18 November 1883: joined Bedfordshire Regt. 1903; served in India (returned England 1908): a Reservist – Deep Well Boring Works, St. Alban's Council; and General Post Office Telephones Dept. – rejoined his regiment on mobilisation following the declaration of war in August 1914: served with the Expeditionary Force in France and Flanders from 16 August 1914: took part in the fighting at Mons, Le Cateau; rearguard actions in the retirement toward Paris, Battles of the Marne, the Aisne, La Bassée and First Battle of Ypres. In a letter to his mother and fiancée, Maud Burton, written on the eve of returning to the front-line before Hill 60 (24 April 1915) he said, "You will see in the papers that we have been in a tight corner. I think it's the hottest place I have ever been in but, thank the Lord, I have been spared to get through alright. We have lost a lot killed and wounded. It was a proper death trap. The dirty pigs could not have blown us to pieces fast enough so they tried to blind us but I am pleased to say I am safe." Mortally wounded, 1 May 1915, he died the following morning. A comrade wrote that on the morning of 2 May 1915 he had found 'Ted' at the Regimental Aid Post; mortally wounded "…more dead than alive…He was quite sensible to within half an hour of his death. He knew he was going and only wanted another chance to get at them again. His last words were, 'They've gone and done for me, the cowards.'" Posthumously awarded the Victoria Cross (*London Gazette*, No.29210, 29 June, 1915) "… Date of Act of Bravery: 1 May, 1915. For most conspicuous bravery, near Hill 60, on the 1st May, 1915. After Trench No.46 had been vacated by our troops, consequent on a gas attack, Private Warner entered it single-handed in order to prevent the enemy taking possession. Reinforcements were sent to Private Warner, but could not reach him owing to the gas. He then came back and brought up more men, by which time he was completely exhausted, but the trench was held until the enemy's attack ceased. This very gallant soldier died shortly afterwards from the effects of gas poisoning." Age 32. He was due to receive his Army Discharge, time expired, May 1915.

(Panel 33) Pte. 15882, Reginald 'Jack' Warner, 1st Bn. (16th Foot) The Bedfordshire Regt.: *s.* of David Warner, of Church Hill, Benington, Stevenage, co. Hertford, by his wife Mary Ann. Killed by a shell, 19 June 1915, while asleep in a trench. Age 24. *unm.* Pte. E.W.S. Mayes was also killed.

Ernest Mayes is buried in Larch Wood (Railway Cutting) Cemetery (II.H.4).

(Panel 33) Pte. 8854, Frank William Watts, 1st Bn. (16th Foot) The Bedfordshire Regt.: *yr. s.* of Thomas Watts, of Langridge Farm, Nazeing, by his wife Lucy, *dau.* of John Wright: *b.* Sherington, co. Bucks, 23 June 1887: *educ.* Nazeing Schools: enlisted 2nd Bedfordshire Regt. 7 January 1907; served seven years with the Colours then passed into the Reserve, but, following the declaration of war a few months later, he was recalled and attd. 1st Battn.: proceeded to France with the Expeditionary Force, served there and in Flanders during the winter 1914–15, and was shot by a sniper as he was going on duty at a listening post, 16 March 1915. The bullet entered just below the heart and he only lived 15 minutes. Buried in the woods 1½ miles from Ypres, about half a mile from the Chateau Rosendael. A cross with his name marks the spot. Age 28. *unm.*

(Panel 33) Capt. John Beauclerk Vandeleur, 3rd (Reserve) Bn. The Leicestershire Regt.: only *s.* of the late Col. John Ormsby Vandeleur, C.B. (*d.* June 1900), of Castle Connell, Ballinacourty, Co. Limerick, and his wife Frederica Jane (1, Romsey Road, Winchester), *dau.* of Charles William Beauclerk and Penelope Hulkes: *gdson.* to the late Lieut.Col. J. Vandeleur, 10th Hussars; of Mannister, Co. Limerick; kinsman to Lieut.Col. C.F.S. Vandeleur, D.S.O., Irish Guards (of Kilrush), who, after being severely wounded at Middlefontein, South Africa, was killed (31 August 1901) when the train on which he was being transported was blown up nr. Waterval by a force of about 250 Boers; also Capt. A.M. Vandeleur, 2nd Life Guards, killed in action, 30 October 1914, and cousin to Capt. W.M.C. Vandeleur, 2nd Essex Regt. (of Moyville), killed in action, 26 August 1914: *b.* Winchester, co. Hants, 1887: *educ.* Wellington College, 1901–1904: gazetted 2nd Lieut. Durham Light Infantry, 2 April 1910: retired from Regular Army 1912; joined 3rd Battn. Leicestershire Regt. Lieut. October 1913: served with the Expeditionary Force in France and Flanders, attd. 3rd Worcestershire Regt., and was killed in action on or about 7 November 1914, at Ploegsteert Wood, nr. Armentieres. Age 27. *unm.*

Kinsman Alexander also has no known grave. He is recorded on Panel 3; cousin William is buried in Esnes Communal Cemetery (1).

(Panel 33) Lieut. Henry Copeland Brice, 1/4th Bn. The Leicestershire Regt. (T.F.): only *s.* of Francis Strange Brice, of 'Middlemeade,' Stoughton Drive, Leicester, J.P., by his wife Margaret Alice, *dau.* of Thomas Henry Downing: *b.* Leicester, 28 November 1893: *educ.* Mill Hill School, London, N.W.: received his commission 2nd Lieut. 10 May 1913; volunteered for Imperial Service on the declaration of war; gazetted Lieut. 22 October 1914, proceeded to France (disembarked Le Havre, 3 March 1915); died at Bailleul, France, 12 June 1915, of wounds caused by the premature explosion of a rifle grenade at Dranoutre, Belgium. He was buried at Bailleul. His commanding officer wrote, "I cannot forbear saying how profoundly I regret his death, and how great a loss he is to the Battn. He was the Grenade Officer and had charge of the bomb throwers. His work in that position was of a high quality. He was absolutely fearless, and I believe that his men would have followed him anywhere. He was of the type of which leaders are made, and the Army can ill afford to lose such men." Age 21. *unm.* (*IWGC record 11 June 1915*). *Buried in Bailleul Communal Cemetery Extension (I.C.138).*

Only Son Of Francis And Mary Brice
He Died That We Might Live

(Panel 33) Lieut. Bertram Thomas Chesterton Gilbert, 4th Bn. The Leicestershire Regt. (T.F.): elder *s.* of the late Thomas William Gilbert, by his wife Alice Emily (Kilgobbin, Castlenau, Barnes, London, S.W.): *dau.* of Arthur Chesterton, of Kensington, London, W.: *b.* Barnes, S.W., 16 May 1883: *educ.* Colet Court, and St. Paul's Schools: Occupation – Artist: joined 16th Bn. London Regt. (Queen's Westminster Rifles) 1901; subsequently received Long Service Medal: called up for service on the outbreak of war: served with the Expeditionary Force in France and Flanders from 1 November 1914: returned to England and obtained a commission, 24 July 1915: returned to France, 26 October following, and was killed in action, 22 April 1917, being hit by a shell, after returning to his battalion, having carried out successfully the duty assigned to him as Liaison Officer during a minor operation. His Commanding Officer wrote, "I had absolute confidence in his successfully carrying out any work entrusted to him, and cannot speak too highly of his soldierly qualities, while as a man he was liked and respected by all. He was a gallant soldier, and died the best of deaths in the service of his country." And his Colonel, "I am sure there was no one who worked more conscientiously, or carried out his duties more nobly, despite the fact that at times he had to work under the most trying conditions ... He was always quiet, methodical, satisfactory, and reliable ... Anything that would help the cause was faithfully fulfilled. All will be sorry at his loss." A brother officer also wrote, "No nobler man ever fought for his country ... he was loved by all who knew him..." Age 33. *unm.*

(Panel 33) 2nd Lieut. Richard Hutton, 3rd (Reserve) Bn. The Leicestershire Regt. attd. 2nd Royal Warwickshire Regt.: *yst. s.* of the Rev. Joseph Henry (& Mrs) Hutton, of West Heslerton, co. York: *b.* 1891: *educ.* Chigwell, and Marlborough College, from which he won a scholarship to Merton College, Oxford: apptd. 2nd Lieut. on probation, 15 August 1914, attd. Royal Warwickshire Regt. for Active Service. Reported wounded and missing, believed killed, 7 November 1914. Age 23. *unm.*

(Panel 33) Sergt. 2348, Alfred Charles Bunn, 1/5th Bn. The Leicestershire Regt. (T.F.): late of Uppingham, co. Rutland: enlisted Luton, co. Bedford. Killed in action, 23 July 1915. Remains recovered from a grave marked as belonging to an 'Unknown British Soldier', (28.J.20.d.8.8), 10 December 1928; identified – Khaki, Titles, Stripes; reinterred, registered 12 December 1928. *Buried in Sanctuary Wood Cemetery (IV.Q.9).*

(Panel 33) Sergt. 330, Robert Orton, 1/5th Bn. The Leicestershire Regt. (T.F.): *s.* of C.H. Orton, of 10, Cottesmore Avenue, Melton Mowbray, co. Leicester: *b. c.*1888: enlisted Melton Mowbray: served with the Expeditionary Force in France and Flanders from 28 February 1915, and was killed in action at Ypres, 30 June 1915. Age 26. Remains recovered from a grave marked as belonging to an 'Unknown British Soldier. Sergt. Leicester', (28.I.24.d.15.45); identified – Khaki, Titles, Stripes, Boots size 7/4; reinterred, registered 3 January 1929. *Buried in Sanctuary Wood Cemetery (IV.T.7).*

(Panel 33) L/Sergt. 343, Sydney Clement Stevenson, 1/4th Bn. The Leicestershire Regt. (T.F.): *s.* of Joseph Stevenson, of Leicester, and Mary his wife: *b.* St John's, Leicester. Killed in action, 4 July 1915. Age 36. Remains recovered from an unmarked grave (28.I.24.d.15.45); identified – Khaki, Stripes, Titles, Medal Ribbon, Vest mkd. S.C. Stevenson; reinterred, registered 2 January 1929. *Buried in Sanctuary Wood Cemetery (IV.S.1).*

(Panel 33) Corpl. 1046, Walter Ibbetson, 1/5th Bn. The Leicestershire Regt. (T.F.): *s.* of the late George Ibbetson, by his wife Bessie (48, Limes Avenue, Melton Mowbray, co. Leicester): *b.* Burnham-on-Crouch, nr. Chelmsford, co. Essex: served with the Expeditionary Force in France and Flanders from 28 February 1915, and was killed at Hooge, 23 July 1915 by the explosion of a German mine. Age 26. *unm.* Remains recovered from a grave marked as belonging to an 'Unknown British Corpl. Leicester',

(28.I.24.d.15.45); identified – Khaki, Titles, Stripes; reinterred, registered 29 December 1928. *Buried in Sanctuary Wood Cemetery (IV.R.3).*

(Panel 33) L/Corpl. 2132, John Ball, 1/4th Bn. The Leicestershire Regt. (T.F.): late *husb.* to Ethel Jane Challoner, *née* Ball (22, Church Lane, Anstey, Leicester): and brother to Sergt. 8496, P. Ball, 1st Leicestershire Regt., killed in action, 21 December 1915: served with the Expeditionary Force in France and Flanders, and was killed in action at Ypres, 3 July 1915. Age 24. Remains recovered from a grave marked as belonging to an 'Unknown British Soldier. 4/Leicester', (28.I.24.d.15.45); identified – Khaki, Titles; reinterred, registered 3 January 1929. *Buried in Sanctuary Wood Cemetery (IV.T.3).*

His brother Philip is buried in White House Cemetery (I.E.3).

(Panel 33) L/Corpl. 1240, William Barney, 1/5th Bn. The Leicestershire Regt.: *s.* of Arthur Barney, by his wife Georgina (8, Cumberland Road, Ellistown, Leicester): *b.* Moira, co. Leicester: enlisted Coalville: served with the Expeditionary Force, and was killed in action, 30 June 1915. Age 20. Remains recovered from a grave marked as belonging to an 'Unknown British Soldier. Leicester', (28.I.24.d.15.45); identified – Khaki, Titles, Stripe; reinterred, registered 3 January 1929. *Buried in Sanctuary Wood Cemetery (IV.T.5).*

Some Day We'll Understand

(Panel 33) L/Corpl. 3015, James Henry Biddles, 1/5th Bn. The Leicestershire Regt. (T.F.): *husb.* to Sarah Biddles (6, Queen Street, Loughborough, co. Leicester): served with the Expeditionary Force in France and Flanders from February 1915; killed in action, 20 July following. Age 39. Remains recovered from a grave marked as belonging to an 'Unknown British Soldier', (28.J.20.d.8.8), 10 December 1928; identified – Khaki; reinterred, registered 12 December 1928. *Buried in Sanctuary Wood Cemetery (IV.Q.7).*

(Panel 33) L/Corpl. 2811, William Wardle, 1/5th Bn. The Leicestershire Regt. (T.F.): *s.* of John Wardle, of Swannington, co. Leicester: enlisted Coalville. Killed in action, 4 July 1915. Age 21. Remains recovered from a grave marked as belonging to an 'Unknown British Soldier. Leicester', (28.I.24.d.15.45); identified – Khaki, Stripe, Titles; reinterred, registered 2 January 1929. *Buried in Sanctuary Wood Cemetery (IV.S.4).*

(Panel 33) Pte. 2555, George Thomas Andrews, 1/5th Bn. The Leicestershire Regt. (T.F.): *s.* of Jacob Andrews of Ravenstone, co. Leicester, by his wife Mary Elizabeth: and *yr.* brother to Actg.L/Corpl. 10124, J.C. Andrews, Bedfordshire Regt., killed in action, 7 November 1914, aged 23: *b.* Ravenstone, *c.*1895: enlisted Coalville. Killed in action, 23 July 1915. Age 20. *unm.*

His brother Jacob 'Jake' also has no known grave; he is commemorated on the Le Touret Memorial.

(Panel 33) Pte. 3605, Thomas Edward Angrave, 'D' Coy., 1/5th Bn. The Leicestershire Regt. (T.F.): *s.* of the late George Angrave, by his wife Catherine (40, Paget Street, Loughborough, co. Leicester): enlisted Loughborough. Killed in action, 17 August 1915. Age 19. Remains recovered from a grave marked as belonging to an 'Unknown British Soldier. 5/Leicesters', located in Sanctuary Wood; identified – Khaki, Titles; reinterred, registered 3 December 1928. *Buried in Sanctuary Wood Cemetery (II.M.19).*

Thy Will Be Done

(Panel 33) Pte. 1279, Cecil Buswell, 1/5th Bn. The Leicestershire Regt. (T.F.): enlisted Market Harborough, co. Northampton. Killed in action, 23 July 1915. Remains recovered from a grave marked as belonging to an 'Unknown British Soldier', (28.I.24.d.15.45); identified – Khaki, Boots size 9; reinterred, registered 29 December 1928. *Buried in Sanctuary Wood Cemetery (IV.R.7).*

(Panel 33) Pte. 1624, John William Capendale, 1/5th Bn. The Leicestershire Regt. (T.F.): *b.* Laxton, nr. Kettering, co. Northampton: enlisted Ketton, co. Rutland. Killed in action, 30 June 1915. Remains recovered from a grave marked as belonging to an 'Unknown British Soldier', (28.I.24.d.15.45); identified – Khaki; reinterred, registered 3 January 1929. *Buried in Sanctuary Wood Cemetery (IV.T.6).*

(Panel 33) Pte. 2521, Isaac Hall, 1/5th Bn. The Leicestershire Regt. (T.F.): *s.* of John William Hall, of John Henson's Lane, Thringstone, co. Leicester, by his wife Catherine: *b.* Whitwick: enlisted Coalville, co. Leicester. Killed in action, 23 July 1915. Age 18. Remains recovered from a grave marked as belonging to an 'Unknown British Soldier', (28.I.24.d.15.45); identified – Khaki, Boots size 9/5; reinterred, registered 29 December 1928. *Buried in Sanctuary Wood Cemetery (IV.R.4).*

(Panel 33) Pte. 1934, Frederick Archibald Hilder, 1/4th Bn. The Leicestershire Regt. (T.F.): *b*. Glenfield: enlisted Anstey, co. Leicester. Killed in action, 1 July 1915. Remains recovered from a grave marked as belonging to an 'Unknown British Soldier. Leicester', (28.I.24.d.15.45); identified – Khaki, Titles; reinterred, registered 2 January 1929. *Buried in Sanctuary Wood Cemetery (IV.S.6).*

(Panel 33) Pte. 8248, Albert Edward Jackson, 1/5th Bn. The Leicestershire Regt. (T.F.): enlisted Ketton, co. Rutland. Killed in action, 21 July 1915. Remains 'Unknown British Soldier;' recovered unmarked grave (28.J.20.d.8.8), 10 December 1928; identified – Khaki, Titles; reinterred, registered 12 December 1928. *Buried in Sanctuary Wood Cemetery (IV.Q.8).*

(Panel 33) Pte. 3032, Alfred 'Alf' Jayes, 1/4th Bn. The Leicestershire Regt. (T.F.): *s*. of Arthur Eddy Jayes, of 47, Aylestone Drive, Leicester, by his wife Emma: served with the Expeditionary Force in France. Killed in action, 4 July 1915. Age 18. Remains recovered from a grave marked as belonging to an 'Unknown British Soldier. Leicester', (28.I.24.d.15.45); identified – Khaki, Cap Badge; reinterred, registered 2 January 1929. *Buried in Sanctuary Wood Cemetery (IV.S.2/4).*

Hearts That Loved You Never Forget

(Panel 33) Pte. 2760, Ernest Kirby, 1/5th Bn. The Leicestershire Regt. (T.F.): *s*. of John Kirby, of Glaston, Uppingham, and Mary his spouse: enlisted Oakham, co. Rutland. Died of wounds, 5 August 1915. Age 19. Remains recovered from a grave marked as belonging to an 'Unknown British Soldier', (28.J.20.d.8.8), 10 December 1928; identified – Khaki; reinterred, registered 12 December 1928. *Buried in Sanctuary Wood Cemetery (IV.Q.10).*

His Work Well Done His Duty Done Now Comes Rest

(Panel 33) Dmr. 1885, Edward Henry Lines, 'B' Coy., 1/4th Bn. The Leicestershire Regt. (T.F.) *s*. of Edward Henry Lines, of 135, Taylor Street, Leicester, and Sophia Lines, his spouse. Killed in action, 1 July 1915. Age 19. Remains recovered from a grave marked up as belonging to an 'Unknown British Soldier', (28.I.24.d.15.45); identified – Khaki; reinterred, registered 3 January 1929. *Buried in Sanctuary Wood Cemetery (IV.T.1).*

(Panel 33) Pte. 1528, Percy Pennington, 1/5th Bn. The Leicestershire Regt. (T.F.): *s*. of George Pennington, of 40, Mill Street, Melton Mowbray: served with the Expeditionary Force, and was killed by the explosion of a mine, 23 July 1915. Age 21. *unm*. Remains recovered from a grave marked as belonging to an 'Unknown British Soldier. Leicester', (28.I.24.d.15.45); identified – Khaki, Titles; reinterred, registered 29 December 1928. *Buried in Sanctuary Wood Cemetery (IV.R.2).*

(Panel 33) Pte. 1473, Albert Pick, 1/5th Bn. The Leicestershire Regt. (T.F.): *s*. of Arthur Pick, of 'Rose Cottage,' Saxby Road, Melton Mowbray; late of 93, Thorpe Road, by his wife Annie: enlisted Melton Mowbray, co. Leicester. Killed by the explosion of a mine, 23 July 1915. Age 19. Remains recovered from a grave marked as belonging to an 'Unknown British Soldier. Leicester', (28.I.24.d.15.45); identified – Khaki, Titles; reinterred, registered 29 December 1928. *Buried in Sanctuary Wood Cemetery (IV.R.1).*

(Panel 33) Pte. 2226, Frederick Randall, 'B' Coy., 1/5th Bn. The Leicestershire Regt. (T.F.): *s*. of Mrs C. Randall (3, St. John's Terrace, All Saints Road, Leicester): *b*. St. Leonard's, Leicester, about 1883: enlisted Luton, co. Bedford: served with the Expeditionary Force in France and Flanders from 28 February 1915, and was killed in action, 23 July 1915, by the explosion of an enemy mine at Hooge, nr. Ypres. Age 32. Remains recovered from a grave marked up as belonging to an 'Unknown British Soldier', (28.I.24.d.15.45); identified – Khaki, Titles; reinterred, registered 29 December 1928. *Buried in Sanctuary Wood Cemetery (IV.R.5).*

(Panel 33) Pte. 2479, Henry Walker, 1/5th Bn. The Leicestershire Regt. (T.F.): *s*. of George Walker, of Main Street, Ravenstone, co. Leicester, by his wife Emily: *b*. Ravenstone: enlisted Coalville. Killed in action, 2 July 1915. Age 19. Remains recovered from a grave marked as belonging to an 'Unknown British Soldier', (28.I.24.d.15.45); identified – Khaki; reinterred, registered 2 January 1929. *Buried in Sanctuary Wood Cemetery (IV.S.5).*

Rest In Peace

(Panel 33) Pte. 2419, James Watts, 1/5th Bn. The Leicestershire Regt. (T.F.): late of Thurlaston, co. Leicester: enlisted Ashby-de-la-Zouch. Killed in action, 23 July 1915, by the explosion of an enemy mine. Remains recovered from a grave marked as belonging to an 'Unknown British Soldier', (28.J.20.d.8.8), 10 December 1928; identified – Khaki, Boots size 7/3; reinterred, registered 12 December 1928. *Buried in Sanctuary Wood Cemetery (IV.Q.3).*

(Panel 33) Pte. 2300, Stanley Viccars Wheeler, 1/4th Bn. The Leicestershire Regt. (T.F.): *b.* St. Peter's, Leicester: enlisted Leicester. Killed in action, 2 July 1915. Remains recovered from a grave marked as belonging to an 'Unknown British Soldier', (28.I.24.d.15.45); identified – Khaki; reinterred, registered 3 January 1929. *Buried in Sanctuary Wood Cemetery (IV.T.2).*

(Panel 33) Pte. 2541, Ernest Gerald White, 1/4th Bn. The Leicestershire Regt. (T.F.): *s.* of the late Joseph White, of Leicester, by his wife Julia Helen. Killed in action, 4 July 1915. Age 25. *unm.* Remains recovered from a grave marked as belonging to an 'Unknown British Soldier. Leicester', (28.I.24.d.15.45); identified – Khaki, Titles; reinterred, registered 2 January 1929. *Buried in Sanctuary Wood Cemetery (IV.S.2/4).*

(Panel 33) Capt. James Hugh Christie, 4th (Extra Reserve) attd. 2nd Bn. (18th Foot) The Royal Irish Regt.: formerly 2nd Bn. Lancashire Fusiliers: only *s.* of the late Hugh Christie, J.P., of Melbourne Hall, Pocklington, co. York, and Mrs Christie (101, North Gate, Regents Park, London, N.W.): *b.* Melbourne Hall, 27 November 1879: *educ.* Yarlett (Preparatory School); Harrow (Drurie's) 1893–96, and Brussels, where he studied for the Army: joined 4th (Militia) Battn. Somerset Light Infantry 1900, with which he went to South Africa to fight the Boers, and from which he received his commission, 2nd Lieut. Lancashire Fusiliers: took part in operations in Transvaal and Natal, including actions at Laing's Nek, and Orange River Colony: Mentioned in Despatches; recommended for the award of the Victoria Cross by his Colonel who was, unfortunately, killed before the recommendation could be processed: (Queen's Medal, four clasps; King's Medal, two clasps): promoted Capt. 1907, transf'd. South Lancashire Regt. (1908), stationed for some time in Southern Ireland: retired from Regular Army May, 1909; entered 4th (Extra Reserve) Bn. Royal Irish Regt., retaining rank Capt.: removed to Vancouver, British Columbia, 1912, remaining there two years: returned to England in 1914 for the purpose of Annual Training with his battalion and, when the war broke, was put in charge of a fort at Queenstown until February 1915 when he took out a draft to 2nd Royal Irish Regt. at the Front, and, having been attached to that battalion, was present at the fight for Hill 60. On that occasion he was twice buried in the debris caused by bursting shells, but was only slightly wounded in the leg. On 24 May 1915 his battalion was surprised by the enemy's use of gas at dawn, and was obliged to retire. Capt. Christie was shot in the head during the ensuing fighting as he was going back to join his men in a trench. The ground where he fell was then abandoned, and was not re-occupied by us for some time, and his place of burial is not known. The battalion suffered very severely, only one officer being left alive unwounded. Age 35. A brother officer said, "He was always cheerful and helped everyone over a very trying time. He will be greatly missed." Capt. Christie was a remarkable horseman, a keen follower of hounds and a member of the United and Duhallow Hunts; his uncle, the late Capt. Hope-Johnson, 7th Hussars, was one of the best gentleman jockeys of his day. Capt. Christie *m.* 1907, Phyllis Ethel England, eldest *dau.* of Col. Becher, 60th Gurkhas, Indian Army, and leaves a son, James Noel Hugh, *b.* 1907. (*IWGC record Major*)

(Panel 33) 2nd Lieut. Charles Reginald Fausset, 3rd (Reserve) attd. 1/2nd Bn. (18th Foot) The Royal Irish Regt.: 2nd *s.* of the late Rev. Charles Fausset, B.A. (Trinity College, Dublin), by his wife Ellen F.O. Fausset, *née* Lane: and elder brother to Pte. 14181, V.H. Fausset, 'D' Coy., 7th Royal Dublin Fusiliers, died on 19 August 1915, of wounds received in action in the Dardanelles: *educ.* Trinity College, Dublin, where he captained the Cricket XI, and graduated B.A., M.A., L.L.D.: gazetted 2nd Lieut. Royal Irish Regt. October 1914: served with the Expeditionary Force in France and Flanders, and was killed in action, 2 May 1915; St. Julien, Ypres. Age 36.

His brother Vivian is buried in East Mudros Military Cemetery (II.G.10).

(Panel 33) 2nd Lieut. Royston Dearmer Ford, attd. 1st Bn. (18th Foot) The Royal Irish Regt.: eldest *s.* of the late J.T. Ford, of 86, Eltham Road, Lee, co. Kent: *b.* Cartagena, Republic of Columbia, South America, 23 January 1895: *educ.* Magdalen College School, co. Northampton: joined Artists' Rifles (no.1057) 1912, from which he received his commission (Temp.) 2nd Lieut. (Special List), 14 February 1915. 2nd Lieut. Ford was killed while leading his platoon into action at the Battle of St. Eloi, 15 March 1915. Mentioned in Sir John (now Lord) French's Despatch, 31 May 1915, for 'gallant and distinguished conduct in the field.' Age 29. *unm.*

(Panel 33) 2nd Lieut. Brendan Joseph Fottrell, 3rd (Reserve) attd. 1st Bn. (18th Foot) The Royal Irish Regt.: *s.* of John George Fottrell, Crown Solicitor, Co. Meath; of 'Richlieu,' Sydney Parade, Dublin, by his wife Lily: Religion – Roman Catholic: *educ.* Downside School; Trinity College, Dublin: Occupation – Solicitor: served with the Expeditionary Force in France, and was killed in action at St. Eloi, 15 March 1915. Age 29. He leaves a widow Antoinette Cottrell, to whom he had been married for just one year, and one child to lament him. Remembered on the Solicitor's Memorial, Four Courts, Inns Quay, Dublin.

(Panel 33) Coy.Q.M.Sergt. 5080, Charles Thomas Abbott, 'B' Coy., 2nd Bn. (18th Foot) The Royal Irish Regt.: *s.* of Graves Abbott, Sergt. 1st Royal Scots Fusiliers: and brother-in-law to Corpl. 8930, F.R. Gorbey, D.C.M., 1st Royal Irish Regt., killed in action, 23 April 1915: *b.* Secunderabad, India, 13 September 1881: enlisted, 15 April 1896: served in the South African War (Medal with clasps), India, and with the Expeditionary Force in France and Flanders: killed in action, 24 May 1915. Age 34. He *m.* Karachi, 9 December 1908; Margaret Helen, *dau.* of John William Gorbey, of Carrick-on-Suir, and had a son and two *daus.* – Agnes May, *b.* Agra, 2 October 1909; Henry Graves, *b.* Agra, 17 November 1910; Ellen Rewa, *b.* aboard the troopship Rewa in the Bay of Biscay, 26 December 1911.

His brother-in-law Frank Gorbey also has no known grave; he is recorded below.

(Panel 33) Sergt. 3344, Joseph John Stagg, M.M., 'D' Coy., 6th (Service) Bn. The Royal Irish Regt.: *s.* of John Stagg, of Harbour View, South Side, St. Sampson's, Guernsey, Channel Isles, by his wife Mary Ann: and elder brother to Pte. 678, R. Stagg, Royal Guernsey Light Infantry, killed in action, 1 December 1917: *b.* St. Sampson's: enlisted Guernsey: served with the Expeditionary Force in France and Flanders from December 1915, and was killed in action, 5 August 1917. Age 29. He leaves a wife, Violet Gladys Irene Stagg (Delancey Cottage, Delancey Hill, St. Sampson's).

His brother Roland also has no known grave; he is commemorated on the Cambrai Memorial, Louverval (Panel 13).

(Panel 33) Corpl. 8930, Frank Reuben Gorbey, D.C.M., 1st Bn. (18th Foot) The Royal Irish Regt.: *s.* of John William Gorbey, Constable (retired), Royal Irish Constabulary, now of 92, Main Street, Carrick-on-Suir, by his wife Ellie, *dau.* of I. Huddy: and brother-in-law to C.S.M., 5080, C.T. Abbott, 1st Royal Irish Regt., killed in action, May 1915: *b.* Villierstown, Waterford, 13 November 1889: joined 1st Royal Irish Regt. Dublin, 22 March 1906: promoted Corpl. 15 February 1915: served with the Expeditionary Force in France and Flanders, and was killed in action at Hooge, nr. Ypres, 23 April 1915. Buried in the grounds of the Chateau Hooge. He distinguished himself at Ypres, 15 February 1915, by bringing in wounded under fire and blowing up an enemy mine. Two of his brothers – one in the Irish Guards, one a Corpl. 7th Dragoon Guards – are serving with the Expeditionary Force. Corpl. F.R. Gorbey had not met the latter brother for eight years but a few days before he was killed they met during an action. A comrade wrote, "A braver soldier or a truer comrade never lived. He died as a brave man with a smile on his face, and was mourned by his regiment as a true comrade." His friends placed a cross over his grave giving full particulars of how he died. Age 25. *unm.*

His brother-in-law Charles Abbott also has no known grave; he is recorded above.

(Panel 33) Corpl. 10532, William Roberts, 'B' Coy., 2nd Bn. (18th Foot) The Royal Irish Regt.: *s.* of the late John Roberts, by his wife Annie (Wells, Gorey, Co. Wexford): a pre-war Regular, enlisted Kilkenny 1912: served with the Expeditionary Force in France from August 1914, and was killed in action, 24 May 1915 at Ypres. Age 21. *unm.* Mentioned in Despatches by Sir John (now Lord) French; he was one of three brothers who served.

(Panel 33) Pte. 4660, Joseph Breen, 1st Bn. (18th Foot) The Royal Irish Regt.: *s.* of Moses Breen, of 7, Ruskin Avenue, Rock Ferry, Birkenhead, by his wife Annie: and brother to Pte. 7288, J.J. Breen, Royal Irish Regt., who also fell: served with the Expeditionary Force in France and Flanders, and was killed in action at Hooge, nr. Ypres, 24 April 1915. Age 18.

His brother John also has no known grave; he is recorded below.

(Panel 33) Pte. 7288, John Joseph Breen, 1st Bn. (18th Foot) The Royal Irish Regt.: *s.* of Moses Breen, of 7, Ruskin Avenue, Rock Ferry, Birkenhead, by his wife Annie: and brother to Pte. 4660, J. Breen, Royal Irish Regt., who also fell: served with the Expeditionary Force in France and Flanders; killed in action nr. Ypres, Belgium, 13 March 1915. Age 23. *unm.*

His brother Joseph also has no known grave; he is recorded above.

(Panel 33) Col. Charles Arthur Cecil King, 2nd Bn. (19th Foot) Alexandra, Princess of Wales's Own (Yorkshire Regt.) (The Green Howards): 3rd *s.* of the late James King, by his wife Rose Maria: *b.* Cape Colony, South Africa, 6 February 1863: *educ.* Royal Military College, Sandhurst: gazetted Yorkshire Regt. 9 September 1882; joined 1st Battn., Halifax, Nova Scotia: first saw service with his battalion on the Nile, being present at the Battle of Ginnis, for which he received the Frontier Field Force Medal and Khedive's Bronze Star: remained with 1st Battn until the close of 1889, when he was transf'd. 2nd Battn. to complete establishment; went out to India with that battn. January 1890. Next saw Active Service in Burma 1893, and took part in the only two expeditions in that country in which the Yorkshire Regt. had a share, being in command of the small party of Mounted Infantry which accompanied the Namkhan Expedition against the Kachins, under Major Hammans, D.C.L.I., and serving also in the expedition in the neighbourhood of Sima, in the Kachin Hills: (Medal & clasp): promoted Capt. (after almost 11 yrs. as Subaltern) February 1893; apptd. Adjutant, 3rd Battn. November 1896: accompanied 3rd Battn. to South Africa (1900), served with it until the conclusion of the war with the Boers: Garrison Adjutant, Rhenoster, December 1900–March 1901; took part in operations in Orange River Colony (1900), also in Cape Colony, south of the Orange River in the same year: served in operations in Orange River Colony, late 1900–January 1902, and from the latter date until the end of war served again in Cape Colony (twice Mentioned in Despatches, Brevet of Major, Queen's Medal, two clasps; King's Medal, two clasps): also received Coronation Medal, H.M. King George V: promoted Major, February 1905; Lieut. Col. Comdg. 2nd Battn. September 1910; having completed four years of command (continued in consequence of the war) promoted Col. September 1914: went to Belgium, 4 October 1914 at the head of his regiment (part of VIIth Division): shared in the desperate fighting which fell to the lot of this division, in which the British were outnumbered eight to one, and was killed by the deadly accuracy of a German sniper on the 30th of that month (Official Casualty List states 23rd), at Ypres whilst holding on to his trenches with the remnant of his battalion – 'a loss which those who get through this war will never forget.' A general officer wrote, "Colonel King, I am sorry to say, was killed yesterday; he was holding on to his trenches most gallantly, indeed he has done most awfully well throughout; nobody could have done better and I am most awfully sorry at losing him, and also many gallant fellows in the Regiment. He was splendid and I shall miss him greatly, he did such a lot of good work." And an officer of his Battalion, "The Regiment has suffered severely, but his loss is the hardest blow of all. He was so splendid in these last days, always thinking for us, so tireless in his energy, never sparing himself in the great strain of responsibility which fell so entirely on him after Forsyth was wounded. We all loved and admired him." Another brother officer said, "I do wish the C.O. had lived to hear what the generals said about our Regiment and to read the splendid report they sent in. What is left of the battalion has come through with flying colours. The Colonel could not have died a more gallant death. Right in the front trench he was, leading and cheering on the men. He was shot by a rifle bullet and death was absolutely instantaneous. He died like the true British officer he was, facing the enemy and doing his duty to the end." Twice Mentioned in Despatches by Sir John (now Lord) French (14 January and 15 May 1915) for his services with the Expeditionary Force. An exceptionally good linguist, a first-rate French and German scholar, Mr King had passed the Higher Standard in Hindustani and Persian. Fond of sport, rode and shot well, a remarkably fine swimmer, indeed, of such a man it may be not inappropriately said, as Clarendon said of Falkland, "Whoever leads such a life need not care upon how short a warning it be taken from him." Age 51. He was married to Adela Margaret King (33, Evelyn Gardens, South Kensington, London, S.W.).

(Panel 33) Major Harold Carey Matthews, 4th Bn. Alexandra Princess of Wales's Own (Yorkshire Regt.), (The Green Howards), (T.F.): eldest *s.* of F.W.W. Matthews, J.P., of Low Hall, Sinnington, co. North York: *b.* Hawes, Wensleydale, 25 April 1879: *educ.* The School, Aysgarth: served in the South African Campaign: Occupation – Under-Manager, Messrs Barclays Bank Ltd., Market Weighton; resigned that position on the outbreak of war, volunteered his services; gazetted Major, 29 August 1914: served with the Expeditionary Force in France and Flanders from 18 April 1915, and was killed in action seven days later (25 April 1915), shot through the head at the storming of St. Julien. Age 35. His Comdg. Officer wrote, "He was killed leading his men in his work, which earned the compliments of the General." Holder of the King's Coronation Medal; he was married to Marjory Forster Woodhouse, *née* Matthews, *née* Robertson (23, Inverleith Place, Edinburgh, co. Midlothian). Remains exhumed from a grave marked as belonging to an 'Unknown British Officer. Yorkshire Regt.' identified – Officers Clothing, General Service Boots, Head Shattered; reinterred, registered 23 April 1928. The first senior officer, 4th Battalion, to fall in the Great War; Major Matthews is remembered on Richmond (Friary Gardens) War Memorial. Menin Gate Memorial Panel List (33 BB), 13 October 1925, records – 'Now known to be buried in Sanctuary Wood Cemetery;' non-amended. *Buried in Sanctuary Wood Cemetery (II.J.4).*

(Panel 33) Major Wilfrid Beckett Walker, 2nd Bn. (19th Foot) Alexandra, Princess of Wales's Own (Yorkshire Regt.) (The Green Howards): 2nd *s.* of Capt. (& Mrs) Edwyn Walker, of Mill Mount House, York: and brother to Capt. O.B. Walker, 15th Hussars, who fell in the vicinity of Mons, 23 August 1914; and Capt. R.B. Walker, M.C., Yorkshire Hussars Yeomanry attd. West Yorkshire Regt., died of wounds, 13 November 1918: *b.* 5 August 1876: gazetted 2nd Lieut., Yorkshire Regt., February 1897; promoted Lieut. October 1899: served in the South African War, employed with Mounted Infantry, and as Supply Officer (two months): present at operations in Orange Free State, and Transvaal, 1901–1902: Mentioned in Despatches (*London Gazette*, 17 January 1902): Queen's Medal, four clasps; King's medal, two clasps: promoted Capt. June 1904; Major, December 1913: served with the Expeditionary Force in France and Flanders, and was killed in action, 29 October 1914. Age 39. *The Green Howards Gazette* recorded, "At daybreak on the 29th October 'A' and 'C' Companies went up to support the Royal Scots Fusiliers; at about 11 am. the Germans, in great strength, broke through a regiment on our left and threatened our left rear, which forced those on the right to retire about 1000 yards. Col. King reorganised the Regiment and, collecting anyone he could find from other units, led an attack which was successful in retaking our former position and gaining another 200 yards. This advance was terrible, as the enemy simply poured shrapnel into us and our casualties were heavy. Major Walker was killed whilst in charge of his Company, 'C,' by a shrapnel bullet; his death was very much felt as we lost a very fine soldier and a good friend. Major Alexander, Levin, Marriage, Thwaites and Sykes were all wounded on the same day."

His brother Oswald also has no known grave, he is commemorated on the La Ferte-Sous-Jouarre Memorial; Roger is buried in Terlincthun British Cemetery (X.E.36). Major (Lieut.Col.) W.L. Alexander (killed in action, 14 May 1915), is buried in Le Touret Military Cemetery (II.D.11); Capt. M. Thwaites (killed in action, 30 September 1915) has no known grave; he is recorded on the Loos Memorial.

Following a failed counterattack to drive the Germans out of St. Julien, 24 April 1915, 5th Green Howards – after their relief in the vicinity of Potijze – were held in a field near Wieltje from whence they could be sent to support any unit requiring assistance locally. At 8 a.m. (25 April) the Green Howards learnt the Canadians, Seaforth Highlanders and Royal Irish Fusiliers, had been attacked by gas and, hurrying forward across the Zaaerebeke stream toward St. Julien, were met with a very heavy shrapnel fire which in less than five minutes caused 60% casualties; the companies at once deploying and, taking up a line facing St. Julien and Fortuin, opened fire on the advancing enemy.

At about 10 am. the Brigade-Major noticed a farmhouse in front and 'in order to prevent the enemy from creeping up and occupying it he sent Capt. Barber and part of 'D' Coy. forward to hold it; but on arrival they were met by very heavy shell and machine-gun fire, Capt. Barber and L/Corpl. C.S. Dell being killed and the remainder falling back again under very heavy fire…Here Sergt. D.G. Joy was also killed.'

(Panel 33) Capt. Geoffrey Carew Barber, 5th Bn. Alexandra Princess of Wales's Own (Yorkshire Regt.), (The Green Howards), (T.F.): eldest *s.* of John Walter Barber, of West Ayton, Scarborough, co. York, by his wife Emmeline: *b.* West Ayton, 1 November 1890: joined his battalion as 2nd Lieut. March 1909; promoted Lieut. July 1911; Capt. April 1913: undertook Imperial Service Obligations, 4 August 1914: crossed to France with battalion advance party aboard transport S.S. 'Onward,' arriving Le Havre mid-day, 17 April 1915: moved into trenches in banks of the Yser Canal, 24 April, and was killed in action nr. St. Jean shortly after 10 a.m. the following morning (25 April 1915); being twice wounded before he was fatally hit. He had been in France exactly one week. "His brothers, Lieut. J.B. Barber, H.M.S. 'Bulldog,' Royal Navy, and Lieut. F.H.H. Barber, 5th Battn. Yorkshire Regt., are, at the time of writing (1916), both serving in the war." Age 24. *unm.*

Sergt. D.G. Joy and L/Corpl. C.S. Dell also have no known grave, both are recorded below.

Capt. Barber's brother John died 16 April 1916 (shortly after the above was written), also has no known grave; he is commemorated on the Chatham Naval Memorial (Panel 15).

(Panel 33) Capt. Ernest Scott Broun, 2nd Bn. (19th Foot) Alexandra, Princess of Wales's Own (Yorkshire Regt.) (The Green Howards): *yst. s.* of the late James Broun, of 'Orchard,' Carluke, co. Lanark: *b.* 7 December 1879: *educ.* Privately: gazetted 2nd Lieut. Yorkshire Regt. from the Militia, 4 February 1899: promoted Lieut. 29 December 1900; Capt. 6 April 1906: served in the South African War 1899–1902: present at the Relief of Kimberley: took part in operations in Orange Free State, February–May 1900, including Paardeberg: actions at Poplar Grove, Dreifontein, Vet River and Zand River: operations in Transvaal, May–June 1900, including actions nr. Johannesburg, Pretoria, and Diamond Hill: in Transvaal, east of Pretoria, including the action at Belfast: operations in Cape Colony, south of Orange River, including the action at Colesburg, and those in Transvaal, 30 November 1900–31 May 1902: Queen's Medal, 6 clasps, King's Medal, 2 clasps: apptd. A.D.C. to Governor & Commander- in-Chief, Barbados, July 1911: served with the Expeditionary Force in France and Flanders and (with Col. King and 2nd Lieut. Hatton) was killed nr. Gheluvelt, Ypres, 'by the deadly accuracy of a few enemy snipers who never seemed to miss,' 30 October 1914. Mentioned in Despatches (*London Gazette*, 22 June 1915) by F.M. Sir John (now Lord) French, for 'gallant and distinguished service in the field.' Age 34.

(Panel 33) Capt. Ernest Geoffrey Carrington Le Sueur, 1st attd. 2nd Bn. (19th Foot) Alexandra, Princess of Wales's Own (Yorkshire Regt.), (The Green Howards): *yr. s.* of Arthur Le Sueur, of Jersey, Channel Isles: *b.* 21 January 1891: *educ.* Queen Victoria College, Jersey; where he was a Prefect, member of the Cricket (& Football) XI, three years a member of the Shooting VIII, Col. Sergt., O.T.C; and Royal Military College, Sandhurst (entered 1910): trained Sandhurst Company, Woolwich from whence (on passing out) he was gazetted 2nd Lieut. Yorkshire Regt. (The Green Howards): joined 2nd Battn. Blackdown Camp: joined 1st Battn. Sialcote, India, 1913: promoted Lieut. September 1914; Temp. Capt. 1915, substantive from 1 January 1917. Invalided home from India, October 1916, for 12 months sick leave due to eye problems; after consultation with a London specialist (who assured him there was nothing wrong with his eyes), reported to the regimental depot for duty and joined Reserve Battn.: proceeded to France, 1 June 1917 attd. 2nd Battn. and was killed in action eight weeks later (26 July 1917) while leading his company in a successful attack on the enemy's trenches on Observatory Ridge, Sanctuary Wood, Ypres. Age 26. As a member of Queen Victoria College Cricket XI many will remember the brilliant innings he played against Guernsey in his last term, equalling, in the same year, C.G. Ames's school record (17 2/5 seconds) for the hurdles. He *m.* 5 May 1917; Dorothy, only *dau.* of Major O.J. Keene, C.I.E., V.D.

(Panel 33) Capt. John Vivian Nancarrow, 4th Bn. Alexandra, Princess of Wales's Own (Yorkshire Regt.), (The Green Howards), (T.F.), York & Durham Infantry Bde., 50th (Northumbrian) Divn., (T.F.): eldest *s.* of George Bennett Nancarrow, of 'Ravenscroft,' Grove Hill, Middlesborough, a partner in the firm of W.B. Peat & Co., Chartered Accountants; by his wife Charlotte Alice, *dau.* of Capt. Josiah Thomas: *b.* Middlesbrough, 6 June 1885: *educ.* Leys School, and King's College, Cambridge (M.A., LL.B.): admitted Solicitor (1909), became Secretary to Middlesbrough Chamber of Commerce: joined 1st Vol. Battn. Durham L.I. 1907, subsequently being attd. Northumberland Fusiliers, Newcastle, and Duke of

Cornwall's L.I., before settling in Middlesbrough where he became Lieut. 4th Yorkshire Regt.: apptd. Capt. (after passing through a school of instruction) late 1913: undertook Imperial Service obligations on the outbreak of war: landed in France with his Battn. mid-April 1915. Immediately hurried up to the Front in consequence of the French troops north of Ypres having been 'gassed' on 22 April, and on the afternoon of the 24th the battalion were ordered to attack the German lines near the village of Fortuin, nr. St. Julien, a few miles north-east of Ypres. During the day, Capt. Nancarrow was seen cheering on his men, and in the advance, he stopped to bind up the wound of a Private who had fallen, and then hurried forward. After making several rushes at the head of his men towards the enemy's position, he was shot and died almost instantaneously. His Colonel wrote of him that "he behaved like a hero." Age 30. *unm.* Capt. Nancarrow had taken a very active part in the Boy Scouts' movement in connection with the settlement in Newport Road, Middlesbrough. He was engaged to be married to Miss Elsie Harkness, of Stokesley. (*IWGC record 25 April 1915*)

(Panel 33) Capt. Laurence Peel, 2nd Bn. (19th Foot) Alexandra, Princess of Wales's Own (Yorkshire Regt.) (The Green Howards), Comdg. 7th Divn. Cyclist Coy.: *s.* of William (& Mrs) Peel, of Knowlmere Manor, Clitheroe, co. Lancaster: Killed in action on the night of 23 October 1914 when, after his company had been ordered to participate in an attack on a farm (between Gheluvelt and Klein Zillebeke) occupied by enemy machine gunners and snipers, Capt. Peel made a preliminary personal reconnaissance and then attacked the farm; entering the building but finding it too strongly defended to be held. The attackers were forced to fall back and the last seen of Capt. Peel he was wounded, but fighting hand-to-hand in the midst of the enemy, his sword in one hand and revolver in the other. Age 30. He was married to the Hon. Mrs L. Martin, *née* Peel (The Brand, Loughborough, co. Leicester).

(Panel 33) Lieut. Herbert Waller Cummins, 1/4th Bn. Alexandra, Princess of Wales's Own (Yorkshire Regt.), (The Green Howards), (T.F.): *yst. s.* of the late William Cummins, of Clarence, Bishop Auckland, and West Burton, Aysgarth, co. York, by his wife Jane: *b.* 18 March 1880: *educ.* North-Eastern County School, Barnard Castle: on leaving school entered the employ of Messrs Barclay & Co., Bankers, Bishop Auckland; transf'd. Darlington Head Office after a few years: gazetted 2nd Lieut. 4th Yorkshire Regt. September 1914; commission dated the 5th of that month; promoted Lieut. October 1914, rank to date from 5 September (*London Gazette*, 17 October 1914): prior to departing for the seat of war, he trained with his battalion at Northallerton and Newcastle-on-Tyne, leaving for France in April 1915, and was killed in the trenches astride the Menin Road, nr. Hooge, Whit-Monday, 24 May following, by a hand bomb; death being instantaneous. His Commanding Officer wrote, "I am sorry to say we have not been able to recover any of the things he had on him. He was a most gallant and brave officer, and we all felt his death greatly." He had a keen interest in golf, and was a regular player, winning the Durham County Golf Championship, 1913, and Silver Cup. He held the amateur record for the Bishop Auckland Golf Club, of which he was a member, and was also a member of Dinsdale Golf Club. Age 35. *unm.* See 2nd Lieut. E.F. Hutchinson, Bedford House Cemetery (VI.A.39/Enc.No.2).

(Panel 33) Lieut. Leonard Percy I'Anson, 1/4th Bn. Alexandra, Princess of Wales's Own (Yorkshire Regt.) (The Green Howards), (T.F.): 3rd & *yst. s.* of the late William I'Anson, C.E., by his wife Mary ('Bardencroft,' Saltburn-by-the-Sea, co. York), *dau.* of John Mangles: *b.* Saltburn-by-the-Sea, 19 April 1878: *educ.* Bootham School, York (Capt., Football XI, 1895–96): Occupation – Solicitor; Middlesbrough: a pre-war member of the Territorial Force in which he held a commission (gazetted 2nd Lieut. October 1913); at the outbreak of war he was in command of 'G' (Skelton-in-Cleveland) Company of his battalion, and had won numerous prizes for rifle-shooting at Strensall, etc.: undertook Imperial Service obligations; served with the Expeditionary Force in France and Flanders from 18 April 1915, and was killed at St. Julien, nr. Ypres one week later, on 25 April 1915, while leading his company. His body has not been recovered. Age 37.

(Panel 33) Lieut. John Buchan Freeland, 2nd Bn. (19th Foot) Alexandra, Princess of Wales's Own (Yorkshire Regt.), (The Green Howards): *s.* of Edward Buchan (& Annie Louisa) Freeland, of 1159, Bay Street, Toronto: *b.* Toronto, 7 January 1897: gazetted 2nd Lieut. from Royal Military College, Canada, January 1916: apptd. Yorkshire Regt. June following. Killed in action, 26 July 1917, while withdrawing from a daylight raid. Age 19. Capt. Le Sueur and 9 Other Ranks were also killed; 34 Other Ranks wounded, 3 missing (subsequently confirmed killed).

(Panel 33) Lieut. Richard Herbert Phayre, 'A' Coy., 2nd Bn. (19th Foot) Alexandra, Princess of Wales's Own (Yorkshire Regt.), (The Green Howards): eldest *s.* of Lieut.Col. Richard Phayre, O.B.E., J.P., D.L., of 'Belgaum,' Woking, co. Surrey, by his wife Frances Anne: *gdson.* to the late General Sir Robert Phayre, G.C.B.: and brother to Lieut. C.F. Phayre, 2nd Royal Munster Fusiliers, who fell, 27 August 1914, during the retirement from Mons: *b.* Farnborough, co. Hants, 31 March 1890: *educ.* Repton, and Royal Military College, Sandhurst: joined Yorkshire Regt. 1909; promoted Lieut. April 1911; apptd. Battn. Signalling Instructor 1912; Asst. Adjt. 1914: served with the Expeditionary Force in France and Flanders with 7th Divn.(disembarked Zeebrugge, Tuesday, 6 October 1914) and was killed by shellfire, 26 October 1914, whilst at duty in (or near) Reutel Woods, between Becelaere and Zonnebeke. Age 24. *unm.* The Regimental History records an incident which occurred in the week prior to his death when a patrol led by Lieut. Phayre, after being fired on from a farmhouse near Kruiseecke, witnessed about eight Germans run across the road into a barn and, after shooting one of the enemy as he ran, the refusal of the remainder to surrender prompted Lieut. Phayre to set fire to the barn. Eventually, with their uniforms and boots smouldering and burnt from the fire within, the Germans came out of the barn. Asked why they had refused to surrender earlier, they replied that they had been told the English always shot their prisoners. 'Reservists of the 19th Hussars it was only fitting they should be captured by the 19th Regiment.' Posthumously gazetted Capt. (Temp.), 14 November 1914.

His brother Charles is buried in Etreux British Cemetery (II.5).

(Panel 33) 2nd Lieut. Erasmus Darwin, 4th Bn. Alexandra, Princess of Wales's Own (Yorkshire Regt.), (The Green Howards), (T.F.): only *s.* of Horace Darwin, F.R.S., Chairman of Cambridge Scientific Instrument Co., by his wife the Hon. Emma Cecilia (Ida) *née* Farrer, only *dau.* of Thomas Farrer, 1st Lord Farrer, and *gdson.* to Charles Darwin (1809–82): *b.* Cambridge, 7 December 1881: *educ.* Horris Hill, and Marlborough (Cotton House) from whence he gained an exhibition for mathematics at Trinity College, Cambridge (went up in October 1901), taking the Mathematical Tripos in his second year and being placed among the Senior Optimes. Afterwards took the Mechanical Sciences Tripos; placed in the second class, 1905. On leaving Cambridge, went through the shops at Messrs Mather and Platt's, Manchester, afterwards worked for some little while with Cambridge Scientific Instrument Co., of which he was a Director; thereafter became Assistant Secretary of Bolckow, Vaughan and Co. Ltd., Middlesbrough, where he stayed for seven years and, at the outbreak of war, occupied the position of Company Secretary: relinquished this appointment and, deciding on a career in the Army, volunteered his services: gazetted 2nd Lieut. 4th (Territorial) Bn. Yorkshire Regt. September 1914: after training at Darlington and Newcastle crossed to France, as part of 50th (Northumbrian) Division, 17 April 1915, and was within a week called upon to take part in the Second Battle of Ypres. Here, these Territorial troops fresh from home and tried at the very outset, almost as highly as men could be tried, behaved with a steadiness and coolness which gained for them the congratulations of the Generals commanding, respectively, their Division and their Army Corps. Early in the afternoon of 24 April, the Battn. was ordered to attack the village of Fortuin, close to St. Julien, where the Germans had broken through. This attack they successfully carried out in the face of terrific shellfire before being ordered to retire at dusk. By driving the enemy back a mile or more they had attained their object, which was to prevent a breach in the line; and they had made good their front with the Canadians and Royal Irish on their right…It was during this advance that Darwin fell, killed instantaneously. His Commanding Officer, Col. Bell, wrote of him, "Loyalty, courage, and devotion to duty – he had them all. He died in an attack which gained many compliments to the Battn. He was right in front. It was a man's death." Corpl. Wearmouth, who was in his platoon, wrote, "I am a section leader in his platoon, and when we got the order to advance he proved himself a hero. He nursed us men, in fact the comment was, 'You would say we were on a field day.' We had got to within twenty yards of our halting place when he turned to our platoon to say something. As he turned he fell, and I am sure he never spoke. As soon as I could I went to him but he was beyond human aid. Our platoon sadly miss him, as he could not do enough for us, and we are all extremely sorry for you in your great loss." And Private Wood, in a letter to a friend in Middlesbrough, "I expect you would know poor Mr Darwin, I was in his platoon and I can tell you he died a hero. He led us, absolutely regardless of the bullets from the German Maxim guns and snipers that whistled all round him." Just before he left England, when his battn. was under orders for the Front, he was summoned to the War Office and offered a Staff appointment at home in connection with munitions of war. This would have given great scope to his capabilities. "It would have been interesting and important work" he wrote, "but, of course, there are plenty of older men who can do it just as well as I can." He felt that at that moment his place should be with his regt., and made, in the words of one present at the interview, a "fine appeal" to be allowed to go with his men. It was granted, and he went gladly and with no looking back. *The Times* (30 April 1915) said of him, "Erasmus Darwin would, if he had lived, have added fresh distinction to the name of his family in a walk of life in which it has never before figured. Between Cambridge and a great iron works in the North there is something of a gulf fixed and one who knew Darwin only in his Cambridge home cannot say anything more than that all those who met him in business conceived a very high opinion of his grasp of the subject, his acuteness and administrative ability. It was, indeed, impossible to know him without realising that he combined with intellectual ability a calm, sound and practical judgement, and a general capacity for doing things well and thoroughly. He had too, what must have been invaluable to him in his work, a most genuine sympathy with and affection for working men, and this quality, which, amongst so many other things, had made him love his work at Middlesborough, gave him intense pleasure when soldiering came to him as a wholly new unlooked-for experience. He delighted in the men, and especially in long expeditions across the moors with his scouts. There is one more quality as to which all his friends would agree, namely a conscientiousness that was eminently sane and wide-minded and completely unswerving. No one in the world was more certain to do what he believed to be right." Age 33.

(Panel 33) 2nd Lieut. Thomas Walton Dean, 9th Bn. Alexandra, Princess Of Wales' Own (Yorkshire Regt.), (The Green Howards): *yr. s.* of William (& Elizabeth) Dean, of 'Thornbury,' Grove Hill, Middlesbrough, co. York: and brother to Capt. H. Dean, 2nd Yorkshire Regt., burnt to death, 5 January 1918; Hedge Street Tunnels, Zillebeke: volunteered and enlisted Royal Engineers; subsequently obtained a commission: served with the Expeditionary Force in France; killed in action at the Battle of Messines, 7 June 1917; 'snipers and machine-gun fire causing many casualties. This officer's body was not recovered for burial. Age 28.

His brother Harold is commemorated in Railway Dugouts Burial Ground (Transport Farm), (Sp. Mem.G.6).

(Panel 33) 2nd Lieut. Frederick Charles Hatton, (Actg.Adjt.) 2nd Bn. (19th Foot) Alexandra, Princess of Wales' Own (Yorkshire Regt.), (The Green Howards): *s.* of Alfred Charles Hatton, one time editor *The Yokohama Press*, Japan, and Canteen Steward, 2nd Yorkshire Regt.; of Parkhurst, Isle of Wight, by his wife Louisa Frances Minetta: related to Dr. W.A. Hatton, and Sir Westby Brook Percival, K.C.M.G., late Agent-General, New Zealand: *b.* Parkhurst, 9 April 1878: *educ.* Privately: obtained his commission from the ranks, October 1914, having previously filled several regimental positions, including Gymnastic Instructor, Pay Sergt., Orderly Room Sergt., Canteen Acct., Regtl. Q.M. Sergt., and Regtl. Sergt.Major: apptd. Actg. Adjt. subsequent to receiving his commission: served in the South African War, 1899–1902, being seriously wounded while Section Leader at the Battle of Driefontein: (Queen's Medal, three clasps; Long Service & Good Conduct medals): served with the Expeditionary Force in France and Flanders, and was killed by sniper fire, 30 October 1914, at the First Battle of Ypres. Age 36. At the time of his death 2nd Lieut. Hatton was standing near his Commanding Officer, Col. C.A.C. King (also killed). For some time he was Secretary of the Green Howards Old Comrades' Association, and a contributor to *The Green Howards Gazette*. He was also Sergt.Major of the same regiment's 'Old-time Firing & Hand-grenade Display.' He left a widow, Elsie Hatton (4, West Terrace, Richmond, co. York), *dau.* of the late Q.M. Sergt. Thewlis (brother of Alderman Thewlis, late Lord Mayor of Manchester), and a son, Frederick Arthur, twelve years of age at the time of his father's death.

(Panel 33) 2nd Lieut. Frederick William Knott, 9th (Service) Bn. Alexandra, Princess of Wales's Own (Yorkshire Regt.), (The Green Howards): *yr. s.* of Herbert Knott, of 'Sunny Bank,' Wilmslow, Manchester,

J.P., by his wife Ada Sophia Wilhelmina, *dau.* of Thomas B. Wakefield: *b.* Stalybridge, co. Chester 4 March 1892: *educ.* Leighton Park School, Reading: apprenticed to Messrs Bessbrook Spinning Co., Armagh; afterwards became secretary to the firm: joined Inns of Court O.T.C. October 1915: obtained a commission, 11 May 1916; promoted Temp. Lieut. September 1916, and Bombing Instructor: served with the Expeditionary Force in France and Flanders from March 1917, and was killed in action, 7 June following, by a shell when leading his men into action in the attack at Messines Ridge. Buried there. His Colonel wrote, "He was a brave and noble fellow, beloved by all his men, to whom he always set a fine example of courage and devotion to duty. I shall feel his loss keenly, as he had endeared himself to me during the all too short time he was with us." Age 25. *unm.*

(Panel 33) 2nd Lieut. William Percy Orde-Powlett, 1/4th Bn. Alexandra, Princess of Wales's Own (Yorkshire Regt.), (The Green Howards), (T.F.): eldest *s.* of the late Lieut.Col. the Hon. Algar Orde-Powlett, 5th Baron Bolton, of Wensley Hall, Leyburn, co. York, M.P., and Lady Bolton (Bolton Hall, Leyburn): *gdson.* to 4th Lord Bolton, and 1st Lord Ashbourne: *b.* 7 April 1894: *educ.* Eton, where he was in the Boats; and Cambridge University: gazetted 2nd Lieut. August 1914; joined 4th Battn. the following month: served with the Expeditionary Force in France and Flanders from 17 April 1915, taking part in his first action exactly one week after leaving England and was killed nr. Ypres, 16 May following. During his short period of time at the Front his services had attracted the commendations of his superiors, and it is understood his name was sent up for Mention in Despatches. Showing a particular bent for science and biology whilst at Eton, he carried this with him to Cambridge where, although only there one year, his aptitude for biology attracted favourable attention among the faculty.

He was a good shot, interested himself especially in biology and botany, and in the Boy Scout movement; he also showed promise as a good speaker. Age 21. *unm.*

(Panel 33) Sergt. 591, David Graham Joy, 'D' Coy., 5th Bn. Alexandra, Princess of Wales's Own (Yorkshire Regt.), (The Green Howards), (T.F.): *b.* High Hoyland, Barnsley: enlisted Sand Hutton, co. York: served with the Expeditionary Force in France and Flanders from 17 April 1915, and was killed in action near St. Julien on the 25th of that month. See Capt. G.C. Barber, above.

(Panel 33) Sergt. 17906, Septimus Waugh, 9th (Service) Bn. Alexandra, Princess of Wales's Own (Yorkshire Regt.), (The Green Howards): *s.* of James Waugh, of The Row, Roadhead, Carlisle, co. Cumberland, by his wife Catherine: and yr. brother to Pte. 56189, R. Waugh, Machine Gun Corps, died 3 March 1919 at home: *b.* Bewcastle, Brampton: enlisted Burnley, co. Lancaster. Killed in action, 7 June 1917. Age 29. *unm.*

His brother Robert is buried in Bewcastle (St. Cuthbert's) Churchyard.

(Panel 33) L/Sergt. 9386, William Henry Charles Down Harfield, 'D' Coy., 2nd Bn. (19th Foot) Alexandra, Princess of Wales's Own (Yorkshire Regt.), (The Green Howards): *s.* of William Henry Charles Harfield, of Crowthorne, co. Berks, by his wife Elizabeth Ellen: and elder brother to Pte. 9223, F.A.G. Harfield, 2nd Yorkshire Regt., killed the following day: *b.* Crowthorne: enlisted Aldershot. Killed in action, 28 October 1914. Age 22. *unm.*

His brother Frederick also has no known grave, he is recorded below.

(Panel 33) L/Sergt. 202, Joseph Taylor, 4th Bn. Alexandra, Princess of Wales's Own (Yorkshire Regt.), (The Green Howards), (T.F.): *s.* of George Taylor, of Quaker Lane, Northallerton, co. York: *b.* Northallerton: prior to the outbreak of war was employee North Eastern Railway; served for ten years as a voluntary member of the Territorial Force (since formation): undertook Active Service obligations, August 1914: served with the Expeditionary Force in France and Flanders from 18 April 1915, and was killed in action on the 25th of that month at the Battle of St. Julien. Age 28. *unm.* He was married to Sarah Taylor (Long Lane Gates, Brompton, co. York), in a letter to whom Capt. Stead wrote, "Sergt. Taylor, along with his Company Commander, Major Matthews, were the first of their Battalion to fall for their Country. His rapid promotion shows the confidence that was placed in him. He was an excellent soldier and a brave man." The first non-commissioned officer, 4th Battalion, to fall in the Great War; L/Sergt. Taylor is remembered on Brompton War Memorial.

Major H.C. Matthews also has no known grave; he is recorded above.

(Panel 33) L/Corpl. 632, Claude Stanley Dell, 'D' Coy., 1/5th Bn. Alexandra, Princess of Wales's Own (Yorkshire Regt.), (The Green Howards), (T.F.): *s.* of Frederick Dell, of 147, Falsgrave Road, Scarborough, by his wife Emma: *b.* New Cross, Lewisham: enlisted Scarborough: served with the Expeditionary Force in France and Flanders from 17 April 1915, and was killed in action nr. St. Julien on the 25th of that month. Age 26. See Capt. G.C. Barber, above.

(Panel 33) L/Corpl. 30761, Thomas Plaiter, 2nd Bn. (19th Foot) Alexandra, Princess of Wales's Own (Yorkshire Regt.), (The Green Howards): *s.* of George Plaiter, of 8, Top-o-th'-Hill, New Hey, Rochdale, by his wife Isabella: and yr. brother to Pte. 3/11052, J.W. Plaiter, 2nd Duke of Wellington's Regt. killed in action, 5 May 1915, at the Second Battle of Ypres: *b.* Shipley, co. York: enlisted Huddersfield. Killed in action, 31 July 1917. Age 20. *unm.*

His brother James also has no known grave; he is recorded on Panel 20.

(Panel 33) Pte. 1862, Thomas Barnett, Stretcher-bearer; 5th Bn. Alexandra, Princess of Wales's Own (Yorkshire Regt.), (The Green Howards), (T.F.): *b.* Bridlington: enlisted there. Killed in action at St. Julien, nr. Ypres 25 April 1915. An eyewitness recorded, "Purvis shouted, 'We need a stretcher-bearer,' and Barnett volunteered. He just shrugged his shoulders, grinned at those who were left and then he was gone, and that was the last anyone saw of him."

In the Official German Account of the First Battle of Ypres it is recorded the XXVII Reserve Corps 'fought for the upper hand in the woods between Zonnebeke and Becelaere,' and 'the well-aimed fire from the enemy's prepared positions reaped a great harvest.' One of the 'enemy' – a member of 2nd Green Howards – who was there wrote, "We could see quite clearly columns of Germans massing on our left flank; our artillery made excellent practice, but how we prayed for more and heavier guns. On the evening of this day we heard that the enemy had broken through the line on the left. They were attacking in mass for all they were worth and fully determined to break through, but were stopped in a most gallant manner by 'A' Company and Lieut. Ledgard in command of two machine guns. Operating against us were eight machine guns and some artillery, and every few minutes he had to change the position of the guns. Backwards and forwards along the trenches, from one position to another, he was running with a heavy machine gun over his shoulder and perspiration streaming down his face. Man after man in his section was hit as they mowed down the German infantry, and eventually all were out of action except Lieut. Ledgard and Pte. Norfolk. Almost at nightfall the officer was hit by a shell and he died – a great hero in the eyes of every Green Howard. Then Norfolk was the only one left and, though wounded by shrapnel, he continued unaided to work his machine gun until the attack ceased at nightfall. For his gallantry and devotion to duty Pte. Norfolk received the Distinguished Conduct Medal; Ptes. Bye and Carlton, killed during the course of the action, never even received a decent burial.

(Panel 33) Pte. 10170, Ernest James Bye, 2nd Bn. (19th Foot) Alexandra, Princess of Wales's Own (Yorkshire Regt.), (The Green Howards): *s.* of James (& Alice M.) Bye, of 3, Exeter Road, Newmarket, co. Suffolk: *b.* 1894: enlisted London: served with the Expeditionary Force in France and Flanders from 6–7 October 1914, and was killed in action between Zonnebeke and Becelaere on the 23rd of that month. Age 22. No record of burial, no remains recovered. See also 2nd Lieut. L. Studley, Ypres Town Cemetery (A1.17).

(Panel 33) Pte. 10303, Ralph Carlton, 2nd Bn. (19th Foot) Alexandra, Princess of Wales's Own (Yorkshire Regt.), (The Green Howards): served with the Expeditionary Force in France and Flanders from 6–7 October 1914, and was killed in action between Zonnebeke and Becelaere on the 23rd of that month. No record of burial, no remains recovered. See also 2nd Lieut. L. Studley, Ypres Town Cemetery (A1.17).

Lieut. F.C. Ledgard is buried in Harlebeke New British Cemetery (XVII.A.5).

(Panel 33) Pte. 1883, George Denny, 5th Bn. Alexandra, Princess of Wales's Own (Yorkshire Regt.), (The Green Howards), (T.F.): *s.* of James William Denny, of 3, Grundells Yard, Bridlington, co. York, by his wife Elizabeth: *b.* Amotherby, 5 February 1899: *educ.* there: employee to F.J. Stephenson, Wandale Farm: enlisted in Bridlington, 1914: trained Newcastle: proceeded to France, 18 April 1915, aboard SS 'Onward,' and was killed in action one week later, on 25 April 1915, nr. St. Julien. Age 16.

(Panel 33) Pte. 1568, William Earls, 'W' Coy., 4th Bn. Alexandra, Princess of Wales's Own (Yorkshire Regt.), (The Green Howards), (T.F.): *s.* of the late William Earls, and his wife Annie J. (5, Vulcan Street, Albert Hill, Darlington): and brother to Pte. 1552, J. Earls, 1/5th Durham Light Infantry, killed the same day: *b.* Thornaby-on-Tees: enlisted Middlesbrough: served with the Expeditionary Force in France from 18 April 1915; killed in action, 24 May 1915. Age 24. He leaves a wife, Florence Ida Earls (47, Mills Street, Newport, Middlesborough). Remembered on the Coxhoe (St. Mary's) Church (and village) War Memorial.

His brother John also has no known grave; he is recorded on Panel 36.

(Panel 33) Pte. 9223, Frederick Augustus George Harfield, 'D' Coy., 2nd Bn. (19th Foot) Alexandra, Princess of Wales's Own (Yorkshire Regt.), (The Green Howards): *s.* of William Henry Charles Harfield, of Crowthorne, co. Berks, by his wife Elizabeth Ellen: and *yr.* brother to L/Sergt. 9386, W.H.C.D. Harfield, 2nd Yorkshire Regt., killed the previous day: *b.* Crowthorne: enlisted Reading. Killed in action, 29 October 1914. Age 20. *unm.*

His brother William also has no known grave; he is recorded above.

(Panel 33) Pte. 2861, Jacob Hodgson, 'Z' Coy., 4th Bn. Alexandra, Princess of Wales's Own (Yorkshire Regt.), (The Green Howards), (T.F.): *s.* of Jacob Hodgson, of Skelton Marske, co. York, by his marriage to the late Agnes Hodgson: enlisted Richmond. Killed in action, 14 February 1916, by the detonation of an enemy mine beneath the battalion's trench. Age 22. 2nd Lieut. J.W. Daglish and 12 other men were also killed.

(Panel 33) Pte. 3521, Leonard Hogg, 4th Bn. Alexandra, Princess of Wales's Own (Yorkshire Regt.), (The Green Howards), (T.F.): *s.* of Mrs Hogg (16, Tower Street, Richmond, co. York): enlisted Richmond. Killed in action, 14 February 1916, by the detonation of an enemy mine. Age 20. 2nd Lieut. J.W. Daglish and 12 other men were also killed.

2nd Lieut. Daglish is buried in Poperinghe New Military Cemetery (I.G.22), the majority of the 12 other men are buried in Plot II, Row K, Railway Dugouts Burial Ground (Transport Farm).

(Panel 33) Pte. 8262, Joe Harry Hoyle, 2nd Bn. (19th Foot) Alexandra, Princess of Wales' Own (Yorkshire Regt.), (The Green Howards): elder brother to Pte. 31738, A. Hoyle, 7th North Staffordshire Regt., died of enteric fever, 19 April 1917, in India: served with the Expeditionary Force in France, and was killed in action, 30 October 1914.

His brother Archie also has no known grave; he is commemorated on the Kirkee 1914–1918 Memorial (Face 7).

(Panel 33) Pte. 1988, Ralph Johnson, 5th Bn. Alexandra, Princess of Wales's Own (Yorkshire Regt.), (The Green Howards), (T.F.): 3rd *s.* of Henry Johnson, by his wife Mary Jane Hannah (70, Seaton Street, Fountain Road, Hull): and brother to Pte. 4647, J.T. Johnson, East Yorkshire Regt. killed in action, 15 September 1916, at the Somme: *b.* Welburn, co. York, 29 June 1898: *educ.* Wombleton Schools: Occupation – Farm Worker: joined 5th Yorkshire Regt. 1 September 1914, after the outbreak of war: served with the Expeditionary Force in France and Flanders from 2 November following, and was killed in action, 25 January 1916. Buried nr. Ypres. Age 17.

His brother John is buried in Adanac Military Cemetery (VI.K.3).

(Panel 33) Pte. 7146, Thomas William Mason, 'A' Coy., 2nd Bn. (19th Foot) Alexandra Princess of Wales's Own (Yorkshire Regt.), (The Green Howards): *s.* of Edward Mason, of Bolton Woods, Bradford, by his wife Ellen: *b.* Frankwell, Shrewsbury, *c.*1884: enlisted Bradford. Killed in action, 22 October 1914. Age 30. *Buried in Harlebeke New British Cemetery (XVII.C.9).*

(Panel 33) Pte. 12784, Patrick Murphy, 1/7th (Service) Bn. Alexandra, Princess of Wales's Own (Yorkshire Regt), (The Green Howards): enlisted Middlesbrough: served with the Expeditionary Force in France and Flanders from 14 July 1915, and was killed in action twelve days later, on 26 July 1915. Pte. Murphy was the second fatality incurred by the battalion since its arrival in France. Age 24. Remains recovered from a grave marked as belonging to an 'Unknown British Soldier', (28.J.20.d.8.8), 10 December 1928; identified – Khaki; reinterred, registered 12 December 1928. All correspondence should be addressed c/o Miss Ellen Murphy (68, Frances Street, Middlesborough). *Buried in Sanctuary Wood Cemetery (IV.Q.6).*

(Panel 33) Pte. 11465, Patrick O'Brien, 1/7th (Service) Bn. Alexandra, Princess of Wales's Own (Yorkshire Regt.), (The Green Howards): enlisted Middlesbrough: served with the Expeditionary Force in France and Flanders from 14 July 1915, and was killed in action eleven days later, on 25 July 1915; the battalion's first Active Service fatality. See also Pte. P. Murphy, above.

(Panel 33) Pte. 2785, George Henry Renals, 4th Bn. Alexandra, Princess of Wales's Own (Yorkshire Regt.), (The Green Howards), (T.F.): *s.* of William Renals, of 114, Portman Street, Middlesbrough, by his wife Margaret Ann: *b.* Newport, co. Monmouth: prior to enlistment (Northallerton) was an Analytical Chemist; North Eastern Steelworks, Middlesbrough: a pre-war Territorial undertook Active Service obligations; proceeded to France, 17 April 1915 (disembarked Boulogne following day); and was killed in action one week later at St. Julien, 25 April 1915. Age 22. *unm.* Remembered on Middlesbrough War Memorial. (*IWGC record 23 April*)

(Panel 33) Pte. 1626, George Thomas Thorpe, 5th Bn. Alexandra, Princess of Wales's Own (Yorkshire Regt.), (The Green Howards), (T.F.): *s.* of Louisa Thorpe (4, Sails Yard, Oxford Street, Scarborough): *b.* Hull, co. York: a pre-war Territorial; undertook Active Service obligations on the outbreak of war; enlisted Scarborough, August 1914. Killed in action, 26 April 1915. Age 17.

(Panel 33) Pte. 1813, Fred Tyerman, 1/4th Bn. Alexandra, Princess of Wales's Own (Yorkshire Regt.), (The Green Howards), (T.F.): late of Brompton, Northallerton, co. York: brother to Pte. 1812, W.G., Tyerman, 1/4th Yorkshire Regt. killed in action, 2 March 1916: enlisted Northallerton. Severely wounded / killed in action 27 February 1916, when a large shell hit the officer's dug-out where, at the time, he was acting as servant to Capt. Sproxton who, in a letter to Pte. Tyerman's sister wrote, "28th February, 1916. I am deeply sorry to have to inform you that your brother Pte. Fred Tyerman was killed yesterday (Sunday) morning by a shell. You have at least the consolation of knowing that he can have suffered no pain as death was almost instantaneous. I have only been with the Company a few days & did not know him well. But I know that he was always cheery & willing, and never failed to do his duty. Were Mr. Welsh living he would be able to speak in still warmer terms of your brother's good qualities. In the short space of three days I had grown to be very fond of him, and nothing better can be said of a dead soldier than that he lived and died doing his duty and was always of a good heart. The War Office will notify you of his grave in due course, which will be carefully tended to & have a cross set over it. His present effects will also be sent home, with the exception of one or two small articles which his brother has. Please let the rest of your family know how deeply we all sympathise with them." His brother, William, wrote, "Monday. 28/2/16. Dear Mother, Sisters, and Brother, It is with a heart nearly broken that I write these few lines home to you to tell you of the sad news of poor Fred being killed on Sunday, the 27th about 10.30 in the morning. Mother, I hardly know how to tell you of the dreadful news, but I guess ere you receive these words you will have heard all about it. Poor Mick, I saw him not half an hour before he was killed, as he had been on an errand for something and he called and had a little chat to E. Dunn and I, and he was only joking about the way he had escaped the whiz bangs a little while ago. I nearly went over myself when a Corporal came into our traverse and said poor Tyerman had got killed. I went down at once to see him, but, poor lad, it was all over with him. I went and saw the Officers and they told me he did not suffer more than 4 minutes as he was so badly hurt. Well, Mother, I don't know how you will receive the news, but look to the one above who will always help those in need. Mother, be brave, also all at home look forward to meet in that beautiful land above. You have no idea how I feel, but the Lord is helping me in my great trouble. We had only been in the firing line about 6 hours when it happened. He did look well, with a nice smile on his face, and he is buried just a little way behind the firing line. Well Mother, I cannot tell you more, as I am nearly done up and my eyes are nearly closed, but be brave and ask the Lord to help you. Hoping you will write back by return with news from home. Well, will write more tomorrow telling you all. I remain, Your broken-hearted Son, Will. P.S. God guard and protect all at home, spare thou me to see my loved ones again, but in the midst of life we are in death. We never know when we are called up to meet our maker." *Buried in Maple Copse Cemetery, Zillebeke. (Sp.Mem.F.8). (IWGC record Tyreman)*

His brother William is buried in Maple Copse Cemetery, Zillebeke (Sp.Mem.F.7). Capt. C. Sproxton, M.C., was killed in action, 19 July 1917, at Arras; he is buried in St. Martin Calvaire British Cemetery, St. Martin-sur-Cojeul (I.B.22).

(Panel 33) Capt. (Adjt.) William Ian Edwards, M.C., 11th (Service) Bn. The Lancashire Fusiliers: Killed in action, 5 August 1917. Buried ref. 'Zillebeke Sheet: 28 N.W.4, N.E.3., J.I.b.4.3' 'in front of a concrete dugout, marked with a rough cross' by Padre Canon M.S. Evers, attd. 74th Bde., 25th Divn.

(Panel 33) Lieut. Leonard John Harrison, Indian Army attd. 2nd Bn. (20th Foot) The Lancashire Fusiliers: elder *s.* of the Rev. Arthur Leonard Harrison, Rector of Yelverton, Norfolk, by his wife Ethel, *dau.* of the late Major-Gen. John William Younghusband, C.S.I.: *b.* Burton, co. Pembroke, 21 November 1895: was a chorister for five years at St George's Chapel, Windsor, then went to Haileybury and passed into the Royal Military College, Sandhurst, December 1912: received his commission Indian Army, 8 August 1914: attd. Lancashire Fusiliers on the outbreak of war; proceeded to France, 16 February 1915, and was killed in action at Shell Trap Farm about two miles N.E. of Ypres, on the road to St. Julien, 24 May 1915. His Colonel wrote, "Your son lost his life in endeavouring to retake some trenches which were lost. He behaved most gallantly and nobody could have possibly shown a better example to the men. I am afraid his body was not recovered, as it lies between our lines and the Germans." His Major also wrote, "Your son did sterling work for us and we missed him badly when he was sent off to the Front. The officers and men deeply regret his loss." Age 19.

(Panel 33) 2nd Lieut. Leslie Charles Billington, 4th (Extra Reserve) attd. 2nd Bn. (20th Foot) The Lancashire Fusiliers: only *s.* of Charles Billington, Metallurgist, of Heimath, Longport, co. Stafford, by his wife Annie Jane, *dau.* of George Richard Cockhead: *b.* Wolstanton, co. Stafford, 25 December 1895: *educ.* Bishop's Stortford College; entered Manchester University as Engineering student, October 1913. In camp with the University O.T.C. at the outbreak of war: gazetted 2nd Lieut. 4th Lancashire Fusiliers 14 October 1914, attd. 2nd Battn. on proceeding to France. Killed in action during the taking of German trenches at Pilckem, nr. Ypres, 6–9 July 1915. Writing on 1 August, Major Bowes said, "I have been making enquiries from the N.C.Os. and men of his platoon, and from what I can gather he was leading a party of men up to the German trenches during the violent attack which lasted from July 6 to the 9th. His party was told off as bomb throwers. He fell on the parapet of the trenches and nothing was recovered from his body. One thing I can say and that is, he showed the greatest courage and never flinched when he was told off for the dangerous job. It was a most ghastly time for us all, and during those three days and four nights we lost ten officers killed and eight wounded, including the Commanding Officer and Adjutant, and all the Captains except one, and eighty-five men killed and 234 wounded and missing. The place where this fight took place is called Pilckem, about three miles N. of Ypres. It was brought about this way. One of the German trenches was in such a position as to enfilade the front trench occupied by the Rifle Brigade. This regt., with the Somersets, were told off to take this trench, which they did on the morning of 6 July. My battn. relieved these two regts. on the 6th (midnight) and occupied the captured German trench. We had orders to hold the trench at all costs. The Germans counter-attacked on the morning of the 7th with heavy artillery and bomb throwers, but in spite of heavy odds against us we held that trench for three whole days, until we were relieved at midnight on the 9th by another brigade. The regt. covered itself with honour in those three days and it was due to such fine young fellows as your boy that we were able to hold our own." A few days later, Corpl. Brereton wrote, "We were holding some trenches captured from the Germans, and our platoon, which was ably commanded by your son, were in support to the firing line. We were subjected to a very heavy shell fire, and early on your son inspired confidence in his men by the way he assisted in digging several of our men out who had been buried with debris, thereby saving, I know, two men's lives from suffocation, for which we all admired him. It is the most nerve-trying time you can get, to be under heavy shellfire, especially fresh out from England, but your son seemed to overcome it straightaway, and turned out a brick, as it were. On the afternoon of the 7th we were ordered to reinforce the front line, and when we arrived there learned that our bombthrowers had retired from the advanced saphead temporarily, being short of bombs. The Germans had occupied it, so your son was ordered by Capt. Blencowe, who was in Command (the Col. and several of our senior officers having got wounded), to retake the trench. I was the Corpl. in charge of the section he selected to go with him. He led us up fearlessly, he himself yards in front of any of his men, and I saw him get up to the parapet and empty his revolver, then jump in the trench, and after the trench was retaken he was most unfortunately hit with a shell, dying a brave soldier's death, staunch and fearless to the end. His platoon greatly feel the loss of so gallant an officer, and offer you their most sincere sympathy in your sad loss." Age 19.

(Panel 33) 2nd Lieut. George Maclellan Carruthers, 11th (Service) Bn. The Lancashire Fusiliers: *s.* of the late William Carruthers, by his wife Jessie ('Olinda,' 7, Mitchell Drive, Hugh Crosshill, Rutherglen, Glasgow). Killed in action, 10 August 1917, south of the Ypres-Roulers Railway, during the attack on Westhoek village. Age 26. Buried at the time (ref. 'Zillebeke Sheet: 28 N.W.4, N.E.3, J.I.d.65.80') by Padre Canon M.S. Evers, attd. 74th Bde., 25th Divn.

(Panel 33) 2nd Lieut. John William Stanley, 4th (Extra Reserve) Bn. The Lancashire Fusiliers: 3rd & *yst. s.* of the late Lieut.Col. C.E. Stanley, Grenadier Guards, by his wife Frederica (Penny Bridge House, Ulverston), *dau.* of the late Capt. Phipps Hornby, Royal Engineers: *b.* Coldharbour, Hildenborough, co. Kent, 10 March 1886: *educ.* Abbot Hall, Kent's Bank, co. Lancaster, and Wellington College, co. Berks: Occupation – Tutor/Lecturer; Agricultural College, Aspatria; Royal (Dick) College, Edinburgh, and London Veterinary College: enlisted Public Schools Battn. Royal Fusiliers, September 1914: obtained a commission 2nd Lieut. Lancashire Fusiliers, September 1915: served with the Expeditionary Force in France and Flanders from June 1916, and was killed in action at Messines Ridge, 7 June 1917. Buried there. Age 31. *unm.*

(Panel 33) Sergt. 308, William Clarke, 'A' Coy., 2nd Bn. (20th Foot) The Lancashire Fusiliers: 2nd *s.* of George William Clarke, Pit Top Man; of 5, Coronation Avenue, Dinnington, Rotherham, by his wife Mary, *dau.* of George Kelk: *b.* Blyth, 4 June 1885: *educ.* Blyth and Austerfield: enlisted, May 1903; served eight years in India, Egypt, Malta and, on the outbreak of war with the Central Powers, was a Reservist: recalled to the Colours on mobilisation, proceeded to France, August 1914: gassed at the Battle of Hill 60, but recovered and was sent back to the trenches, and was killed in action at Ypres, 29 June 1915. Buried at La Brique, a mile-and-a-half away from Ypres, nr. Turco Farm. He had put his head over the parapet of the trench to aim at a German sniper, and was shot through the head, being killed instantaneously. 2nd Lieut. Grainger wrote, "He was an excellent soldier, a splendid N.C.O., who took an interest in his work, and whatever he did he did well. He was as plucky a man as it is possible to meet. I deeply regret his death, and may say that there is no one else in the company whose loss would be more keenly felt." Age 30. Sergt. Clarke was mentioned for conspicuous bravery on the field. He also had six medals which he received while serving in India, etc.. He *m.* St. James' Church, Doncaster, 3 August 1913; Harriet (61, Concrete Cottages, Wombwell, nr. Barnsley), *dau.* of Thomas Schorah, and had twin children – Laurence & Doris, *b.* 4 July 1914 (*d.* 26 August 1914).

(Panel 33) L/Sergt. 9744, Edmund Cooper, 11th (Service) Bn. The Lancashire Fusiliers: *s.* of Isaac Cooper, of 13, Warrington Road, Ashton-in-Makerfield, Wigan, co. Lancaster, by his wife Mary Ellen: and elder brother to Pte. 31790, I. Cooper, South Lancashire Regt., killed one week later: *b.* Golborne, about 1895: enlisted Warrington. Killed in action, 7 June 1917. Age 21. *unm.*

His brother Isaac also has no known grave; he is recorded on Panel 37.

Wounded on 31 July 1917, Lieut. Thomas H. Floyd, 2/5th Lancashire Fusiliers, later wrote home describing the early part of the day's events, "At 8.30 we were to go over. At 8 we were all 'standing-to' behind the parapet waiting … Col. Best-Dunkley came walking along the line … 'Good morning, Floyd; best of luck,' was the greeting he accorded me as he passed … At about 8.20 Capt. Andrews went past me and wished me good luck; and then he climbed over the parapet to reconnoitre. Everyone was wishing everybody-else good luck … Eventually, at 8.40, I got a signal … forward we went, platoons in column of route. Could you possibly imagine what it was like? Shells were bursting everywhere. It was useless to take any notice where they were falling, because they were falling all round; they could not be dodged; one had to take one's chance: merely go forward and leave one's fate to destiny. Thus we advanced, amidst shot and shell, over fields, trenches, wire, fortifications, roads, ditches and streams which were simply churned out of all recognition by shellfire. The field was strewn with wreckage, with the mangled remains of men and horses lying all over in a most ghastly fashion – just like any other battlefield I suppose. Many brave Scottish soldiers were to be seen dead in kneeling positions, killed just as they were firing on the enemy. Some German trenches were lined with dead in that position. It was hell and slaughter … I saw Col. Best-Dunkley complacently advancing with a walking stick in his hand…He was still going strong last I heard of him …

We left St. Julien close on our left. Suddenly we were rained with bullets from rifles and machine guns … Men were being hit everywhere. My servant, Critchley, was the first in my platoon to be hit. We lay down flat for a while, as it was impossible for anyone to survive standing up. Then I determined to go forward…'Come along – Advance!' I shouted, and leapt forward, I was just stepping over some barbed wire defences when the inevitable happened. I felt a sharp sting through my leg. I was hit by a bullet. So I dashed to the nearest shell-hole which, fortunately, was a very large one, and got my first field-dressing on.'

Lieut. Floyd survived his wound and the war; his servant, Corpl. Critchley, was dead before he hit the ground.

(Panel 33) Corpl. 203775, Harold James Critchley, 2/5th Bn. The Lancashire Fusiliers (T.F.): late of Liverpool: enlisted Eccles, co. Lancaster. Killed in action, 31 July 1917.

(Panel 33) L/Corpl. 25833, Evan Evans, 11th (Service) Bn. The Lancashire Fusiliers: formerly no.136107, Royal Field Artillery: elder *s.* of the late David Evans, by his wife Harriet (Caefadog, Llarnathney, co. Camarthen): and brother to Pte. 320495, A.C. Evans, 24th Welsh Regt., died in Egypt, 12 May 1917; enteric fever: *b.* Golden Grove, 1889: enlisted Llanelli: served in France and Flanders from September 1915, took part in the fighting at Vimy (May 1916), Somme (July 1916), Messines (June 1917), and was killed in action, 10 August 1917; Westhoek Ridge, Ypres. Age 28.

His brother Alewyn is buried in Kantara War Memorial Cemetery (C.67).

(Panel 33) Pte. 29485, John Edward Green, 11th (Service) Bn. The Lancashire Fusiliers: *s.* of Charles Edward Green, of 292, Ainsworth Rd., Radcliffe, Manchester. Killed in action, 7 August 1917, in the vicinity of the Ypres-Roulers Railway prior to the battalion's participation in the attack on Westhoek village on the 10th. Age 31. He was buried at the time (ref. 'Zillebeke Sheet: 28 N.W.4, N.E.3, J.I.d.4.8') by Padre Canon M.S. Evers, attd. 74th Bde., 25th Divn.

(Panel 33) Pte. 4083, William 'Willie' Heywood, 'A' Coy., 10th (Service) Bn. The Lancashire Fusiliers: *s.* of Herbert Heywood, of 16, Sykes Avenue, Unsworth, Whitefield, Manchester, by his wife Emma: and elder brother to Pte. 8129, A.P. Heywood, 11th Royal Fusiliers, killed in action, 1 July 1916, at the Somme: *b.* Bury, co. Lancaster: enlisted there: served with the Expeditionary Force in France and Flanders from 15 July 1915, and was killed in action, 22 December 1915. Age 22. *unm.*

His brother Arthur 'Percy' also has no known grave; he is commemorated on the Thiepval Memorial, Somme.

(Panel 33) Pte. 3302, Andrew Killilea, 2nd Bn. (20th Foot) The Lancashire Fusiliers: eldest *s.* of John Killilea, of Haydock, by his wife Ann, *née* Gleeson, of Thurles, Tipperary: and brother to Pte. 13483, E. Killilea, Lancashire Fusiliers, who fell, April 1918: *b.* Haydock, co. Lancaster, 1888: served with the Expeditionary Force in France and Flanders, and was killed in action, 8 July 1915. Age 27.

His brother Edward is buried in Outtersteene Communal Cemetery Extension (II.E.3).

(Panel 33) Pte. 6210, Charles Stevenson, 10th (Service) Bn. The Lancashire Fusiliers: *s.* of John Stevenson, of 16, Granville Terrace, Wallasey, co. Chester, and Jane, his spouse: and brother to Stoker 1st Class, SS/116234, G. Stevenson, HMS *Queen Mary*, R.N., lost at the Battle of Jutland, 31 May 1916, aged 18 years: *b.* Wallasey: enlisted Liverpool. Killed in action, 16 February 1916.

His brother George, having no known grave but the sea, is commemorated on the Portsmouth Naval Memorial (19).

In an attempt to locate a particularly troublesome enemy machine gun, 2nd Lieut. G. Hartley, 2/5th Lancashire Fusiliers, took out a patrol near Railway Wood, 8 January 1917. Out in no man's land, the patrol was spotted and the machine gun, opening fire at close range, quickly wounded two men and gave Hartley a nasty wound on the side of his head. After assisting one of the wounded men back to the British lines, Hartley had his wound bandaged and, after learning the other wounded man (Pte. Wolstencroft) had not yet returned, went back into no man's land to search for him. After one and a half hours of gallantly searching for the missing man, 2nd Lieut. Hartley was forced to concede defeat:-

(Panel 33) Pte. 202145, Richard Wolstencroft, 2/5th Bn. The Lancashire Fusiliers (T.F.) *s.* of James Henry Wolstencroft, of Tonge Hall, Middleton, Manchester, by his wife Sarah Maria. Reported wounded and missing after a patrol near Railway Wood, 8 January 1917; believed dead. Age 22.

(Panel 33) Capt. Charles John Chard Barrett, 1st Bn. (21st Foot) The Royal Scots Fusiliers: *yst. s.* of the late Major William Barrett, J.P., D.L., by his wife Charlotte Maria Herring (Moredon, North Curry, Taunton, co. Somerset), *dau.* of William Wheaton Chard, of Mount Tamar, Devon, and nephew of Col. John Rouse Merriott Chard, V.C., Royal Engineers; hero of Rourke's Drift; 22–23 January 1879: *b.* Moredon, South Curry, co. Somerset, 26 August 1873: *educ.* Eton; and Royal Military College, Sandhurst, where he won the riding prize, 'The Saddle': gazetted 2nd Lieut. Royal Scots Fusiliers 10 October 1894; promoted Lieut. 12 November 1896; Capt. 2 May 1900, and Adjutant 1st Battn. 12 September 1903–7 March, 1904: served in the South African War, beginning with operations in Natal, March 1900, also operations in Transvaal, Orange River Colony, and the action of Ruidam. He also raised a company of Mounted Infantry on active service (Queen's Medal, three clasps): Adjutant, 1st Volunteer Battn. Welsh Regt. January 1905–08. While stationed in Dublin with his regt (1909), he won the Irish Grand Military at Punchestown with his horse Scarlet Runner. He had nearly completed four years as an officer of gentlemen cadets at Sandhurst, to which he was appointed on 1 February 1911, and had raised a new company ('L' Coy.) which he was commanding when he was called to join 1st Battn. of his regt. at the Front. Killed in action at Hooge, nr. Ypres, 14 November 1914, when in temporary command of the battn. and was buried in the grounds of Herenthage Chateau. Age 31. Mentioned in Sir John (now Lord) French's Despatch, 14 January 1915, for 'gallant and distinguished service in the field.' He *m.* London, 26 November 1904; Lena, only *dau.* of the late Albert Vaucamps, of 34, Queen's Gate. His brother Donald, who was in the same regt., was accidentally drowned, 28 May 1891, while fishing in the River Dee; he was serving on the Queen's Guard of Honour at Ballater at the time. (*IWGC record 13 November 1914*)

(Panel 33) Capt. Frank Fairlie, 2nd Bn. (21st Foot) The Royal Scots Fusiliers: *b.* 17 January 1878: *educ.* St. Paul's School, 1893: apptd. Lieut. 3rd Bn. Scottish Rifles (Militia), February 1901, and after serving nearly eight months with that battalion when embodied, was given a commission; gazetted 2nd Lieut. Royal Scots Fusiliers, 19 October 1901: served in the South African War 1899–1901: present at operations in Orange Free State; Transvaal, west of Pretoria, including actions at Frederickstad, and in Cape Colony, south of the Orange River (Queen's Medal, 4 clasps): promoted Lieut. June 1905; Capt. January 1912: employed with West African Frontier Force, 1911–1913: served with the Expeditionary Force in France and Flanders, and was killed in action at Gheluvelt, 23 October 1914, while taking a house at the head of his men. Age 36. Mr Fairlie's widow, Annesley, has since remarried; now Mrs Pollock (Newcastle House, Kingscourt, Co. Cavan).

(Panel 33) Capt. Charles James Lyon, 1st Bn. (21st Foot) The Royal Scots Fusiliers: Actg.Adjt.: 5th *s.* of the late Walter Fitzgerald Knox Lyon, by his wife Isabella Romanes (Tantallon Lodge, North Berwick): and brother to Lieut. A.P.F. Lyon, Gordon Highlanders, who fell at Bertry, 27 August 1914; and Lieut. W.S.S. Lyon, Royal Scots, who fell at the Second Battle of Ypres, 8 May 1915: *b.* London, 28 March 1890: *educ.* Stubbington School, and Haileybury College, where he was in the XXX (2nd XV), and Royal Military College, Sandhurst into which he passed first: gazetted 2nd Lieut. 1909: served with the Mounted Infantry, Harrismith, South Africa, 1910: promoted Lieut. October 1911: Mentioned in Sir John (now Lord) French's Despatch, 8 October 1914, and was killed in action near Ypres, 14 November. following. He played polo and golf, and was a member of the Junior Army & Navy Club, and New Club, North Berwick. Age 24. *unm.*

His brother Walter also has no known grave, he is recorded on Panel 11; Alexander is buried in Bertry Communal Cemetery (BB.1).

(Panel 33) Capt. James Barbour Orr, 2nd Bn. (21st Foot) The Royal Scots Fusiliers: *s.* of Robert Clark Orr, of 9, Winton Circus, Saltcoats, by his wife Annie, *dau.* of William Boyd: *b.* Kilmaurs, co. Ayr, 11 October 1893: *educ.* University of Glasgow, and Free Church College, Edinburgh: Occupation – Minister; Shettleston Free Church, Glasgow: enlisted 9th Highland Light Infantry, September 1914: commissioned 2nd Lieut. Royal Scots Fusiliers, 28 September 1915: subsequently promoted Lieut. and Capt., December 1916: served with the Expeditionary Force in France and Flanders from October 1916, and was killed in action at Ypres, 31 July 1917, while leading his company. Buried nr. the Menin Road. His Commanding Officer wrote, "He was a particularly useful officer; the men were devoted to him and would have followed him anywhere; he was killed while gallantly leading his company forward in the front line of the attack. He was a man who showed an entire disregard of danger;" and his Adjutant, "He was one of the ablest and best officers that were with the battalion, a most popular man with all ranks; an officer whom the men loved and would follow anywhere." Age 29. He *m.* Saltcoats, 27 February 1917; Joan Livingstone (Glendye, Stevenston), *dau.* of James Young: *s.p.* (*IWGC record 4th Bn.*)

(Panel 33) Lieut. Claude McCaul Alston, 2nd Bn. (21st Foot) The Royal Scots Fusiliers: nephew to the late G.R. Alston, Esq., of Trinidad: only *s.* of Charles Ross Alston, Solicitor; of Allahabad, India, by his wife Frances Carr Howard: *b.* Allahabad, 29 September 1892: *educ.* Charterhouse (1907–08): received his commission Royal Scots Fusiliers, 4 September 1912: gazetted Lieut. 27 October 1914, on which date he was reported as wounded and missing; no news being subsequently received for many months, is now reported presumed killed, nr. Ypres, Flanders, while with VIIth Division. Age 22. *unm.* (*IWGC record 24 October 1914*)

(Panel 33) Lieut. John Gilbert Somerset Cozens-Brooke, 3rd (Reserve) attd 1st Bn. (21st Foot) The Royal Scots Fusiliers: only *s.* of Ernest Brooke Cozens-Brooke, of 6, Collingham Road, South Kensington, London, S.W., by his wife Isobel Emily Florence, *née* Clayton: *b.* Eton, co. Buckingham, November 1893: gazetted 2nd Lieut. 3rd Royal Scots Fusiliers, 1 April 1912; promoted Lieut. 15 August 1914: served with the Expeditionary Force in France and Flanders, and was killed in action, 18 October following 'in the gallant execution of a hazardous scouting party.' Age 20. *unm.* Remembered on Westgate-on-Sea War Memorial.

(Panel 33) Lieut. Norman William Arthur Henderson, 1st Bn. (21st Foot) The Royal Scots Fusiliers attd. 2nd Bn. (76th Foot) Duke of Wellington's (West Riding) Regt.: eldest *s.* of Arthur Henderson, of Fairmile Court, Cobham, co. Surrey, by his wife Gareth: *b.* Rosary Gardens, South Kensington, London, S.W., 23 October 1891: *educ.* Rugby (School House), entered 1906: proceeded to Royal Military College, Sandhurst, 1911: gazetted 2nd Lieut., Royal Scots Fusiliers, 14 February 1912, joining his regiment in South Africa: promoted Lieut. 12 June 1913: left South Africa, February 1914: served with the Expeditionary Force in France and Flanders from 12 August 1914: took part in the retirement from Mons, the Battles of Cambrai, Le Cateau, the Marne and the Aisne, and was killed in the wood of Herenthage Chateau, Ypres, 10 November 1914, while leading his platoon. An attack was made by the Prussian Guard; some of the trenches had to be retaken by a counter-attack, and it was during this attack that Lieut. Henderson was killed. Several of the few remaining officers of his regiment have testified in letters to his bravery and splendid qualities as an officer. Age 23. *unm.*

(Panel 33) Lieut. Nigel Kennedy, 2nd Bn. (21st Foot) The Royal Scots Fusiliers: *yr. s.* of the late John Kennedy, of Underwood, co. Ayr, J.P., D.L., by his wife Jessie ('Daneswood,' Ascot, co. Berks); late of Bacombe Warren, Wendover, co. Buckingham: *b.* 30 April 1888: *educ.* Wellington College, Crowthorne, co. Berks (being the younger of two brothers who entered Bevir's, 1900); Royal Military College, Sandhurst (1907): gazetted 2nd Lieut. Royal Scots Fusiliers, October 1908; promoted Lieut. September 1911: served with the Expeditionary Force in France and Flanders, and was reported wounded and missing on 25 October 1914, but in December his death was certified as having taken place on the aforementioned date at Gheluvelt, nr. Ypres. Mentioned in Sir John (now Lord) French's Despatch of 31 May 1915, for 'gallant and distinguished service in the field.' Mr Kennedy was a keen motorist, polo player, and a good game shot. Age 26. *unm.*

(Panel 33) Lieut. Corlandt Graham Gordon Mackenzie, 2nd Bn. (21st Foot) The Royal Scots Fusiliers: *s.* of the late Henry Gordon Mackenzie, Barrister-at-Law, Inner Temple, London; by his wife Kathleen Beatrix (31, Walmer Road, Toronto, Canada), *dau.* of the late Alexander Donovan, of Framfield Place, Uckfield, co. Sussex, J.P., and *gdson.* of the late Gordon Gates Mackenzie, of Montreal: *b.* Toronto, 3 November 1889: *educ.* St. Alban's Cathedral School, Toronto; Upper Canada College (1900–07); Royal Military College, Kingston (Graduated 1911): gazetted 2nd Lieut. Royal Scots Fusiliers, 30 August 1911; promoted Lieut. 17 February 1912: quartered Gibraltar on the outbreak of war: went to France with his regt. about 30 September 1914: continuously engaged throughout September–October. Although thrice wounded, refused to leave his post for treatment and was killed in action at Gheluvelt, nr. Ypres, 29

October 1914, while leading his men. Buried there. His eldest brother, Lieut. G.A.G. Mackenzie (16th Bn. Canadian Infantry), was killed at Festubert (22 May, 1915. Age 33), and his *yst.* brother, Lieut. John G. Mackenzie, is currently serving with 92nd Highlanders, Canadian Expeditionary Force. Age 23. *unm.*

His brother Gordon also has no known grave; he is commemorated on the Canadian National Memorial, Vimy.

(Panel 33) Lieut. Gordon Stuart Ness, 3rd (Reserve) attd. 1st Bn. (21st Foot) The Royal Scots Fusiliers: *yst.* & only *survg. s.* of the late Patrick Ness, of Braco Castle, Perthshire, by his wife Charlotte Jane Wells (19, Dawson Place, Notting Hill Gate, London, W.), *dau.* of Stephen Powell: *b.* London, 4 November 1885: *educ.* Westminster School, and Clare College, Cambridge: elected an underwriting member of Lloyds (1909): joined 3rd Battn. (Royal Ayr & Wigtown Militia) Royal Scots Fusiliers, 2nd Lieut. 7 April 1906; promoted Lieut. 9 December 1909: went to France, 11 September 1914 attd. 1st Battn. and was killed in action during the First Battle of Ypres, 11 November 1914. Buried nr. Ypres. Age 29. He *m.* London; Gladys, *dau.* of Charles Ernest Gwynne Harrison, and had two children – Patrick, *b.* 15 June 1914; Marguerite Gordon, *b.* 3 June 1915.

(Panel 33) Lieut. John Rankin Donald Smith, 2nd Bn. (21st Foot) The Royal Scots Fusiliers: *yst. s.* of James Stuart (& Mrs) Smith, of 14, West End, Park Street, Glasgow: *b.* Edinburgh, 10 May 1886: *educ.* Royal High School, Edinburgh, and University of Edinburgh (graduated M.A.): subsequently entered Divinity Hall, United Free Church, and became Assistant to the late Dr. Watson, of Claughton Church, Birkenhead: ordained in February 1913; United Free Church, Ayr: Minister of Cathcart Church, Ayr: joined Inns of Court O.T.C. January 1916: commissioned 2nd Lieut. Royal Scots Fusiliers, August following; subsequently promoted Lieut.: served with the Expeditionary Force in France and Flanders from October and was killed in action, 31 July 1917, being hit by a sniper. Age 31. He *m.* Birkenhead, 28 July 1914, Agnes Barr (71, Shrewsbury Road, Oxton, Birkenhead): *s.p.*

(Panel 33) 2nd Lieut. Ernest Lionel Lane Anderson, 1st Bn. (21st Foot) The Royal Scots Fusiliers: *s.* of the late George Lane Anderson, of The Drive, Hove, co. Sussex, by his wife Mary Beatrice (169, Oakwood Court, Kensington, London, W.): *b.* 24 December 1893: *educ.* Royal Military College, Sandhurst, where he became an under-officer, and won the sword for drill: gazetted 2nd Lieut. Royal Scots Fusiliers 5 February 1913: served with the Expeditionary Force in France and Flanders, and was killed in action at Ypres, 10–11 November 1914. Mentioned in Despatches (*London Gazette*, 19 October 1914) by F.M. Sir John (now Lord) French, for 'gallant and distinguished service in the field.' Age 21. *unm.*

(Panel 33) 2nd Lieut. David Hew Kennedy, M.C., 2nd Bn. (21st Foot) The Royal Scots Fusiliers: *s.* of the late R.F. Kennedy, of Finnants, Ballantrae, co. Ayr: and elder brother to Lieut. J.G. Kennedy, 65 Sqdn. Royal Air Force, shot down and killed in aerial combat, 4 April 1918, nr. Villers-Bretonneux. Killed in action, 31 July 1917; Herenthage Chateau – Glencorse Wood. Age 26. *unm.* Remembered on Ballantrae War Memorial.

His brother James also has no known grave; he is commemorated on the Arras Flying Services Memorial.

(Panel 33) 2nd Lieut. James Gilmour Wilson, 2nd Bn. (21st Foot) The Royal Scots Fusiliers: *s.* of Alexander Wilson, of the 'Eglinton Arms Hotel,' Kilwinning, Ayrshire: *educ.* Kilwinning Higher Grade School, and Irvine Royal Academy: employee Messrs Carstairs, Accountants; Charing Cross, Glasgow: enlisted Argyll & Sutherland Highlanders, after the outbreak of war, September 1915: transf'd. Black Watch; serving with that regt. on the Somme; returned to England to train for a commission in 2nd Royal Scots Fusiliers: returned to the Front, October 1917, and was killed in action by a sniper, 15 December following. Prior to enlistment he had been a keen football player, playing for Kilwinning Rangers; in 1914 he joined Queen's Park F.C. for whom he showed great promise at left-back.

(Panel 33) Coy.Q.M.Sergt. 6280, William Carleton, 1st Bn. (21st Foot) The Royal Scots Fusiliers: *s.* of William Carleton, of Sunderland: served with the Expeditionary Force, and was killed in action at Ypres, 13 November 1914.

(Panel 33) Sergt. 9820, Francis Causon, 2nd Bn. (21st Foot) The Royal Scots Fusiliers: *s.* of Edward Causon, of 38, Broad Street, Canterbury, co. Kent, by his wife Williamina: served with the Expeditionary

Force. Reported wounded and missing, 24 October 1914; now assumed killed. Age 24. He was married to Jemima, *née* Crombie (41, Mill Street, Ayr). Widely conjectured to be the unknown R.S.F. sergeant buried in Plot IX., Row A., Perth Cemetery (China Wall).

(Panel 33) L/Sergt. 8836, James Donovan, 2nd Bn. (21st Foot) The Royal Scots Fusiliers: served with the Expeditionary Force. Reported missing and wounded, 24 October 1914.

(Panel 33) L/Sergt. 8071, Frederick Henry Mills, 2nd Bn. (21st Foot) The Royal Scots Fusiliers: *s.* of the late James Mills (d.27 October 1914), and his wife Edith Mills (115, Grosvenor Road, Aldershot): and brother to Pte. 22735, W.H. Mills, 15th Royal Warwickshire Regt. killed in action, 26 October 1917, at Passchendaele; and Pte. 27655, B.J.H. Mills, 2nd Hampshire Regt., killed in action, 23 April 1917: *b.* Kingsley, co. Hants: enlisted Aldershot. Reported missing after the fighting at Ypres, 24 October 1914; no word or information having since been received, adjudged by a Court of Inquiry (1916) to have been killed in action on or about that date. Age 25. His sister Ethel Annie passed away on 30th November 1897; she was just twelve years of age. All four are remembered on their father's headstone (Aldershot Cemetery); the epitaph reads –

> "We Loved Them In Life They Are Dear To Us Still, But In Grief We Must Bend As God's Holy Will. Our Sorrow Is Great The Loss Heavy To Bear, But Jesus Will Tend Our Loved Ones With Care." It closes with the penultimate verse from Charlotte Elliott's hymn My God And Father! While I Stray "Renew My Will From Day To Day, Blend It With Thine And Take Away. All Now That Makes It Hard To Say, Thy Will Be Done."

His brother Wilfred also has no known grave, he is commemorated on the Tyne Cot Memorial (Panel 27); Bertie is buried in Monchy British Cemetery, Monchy-Le-Preux (I.E.6).

(Panel 33) L/Sergt. 10065, James Inches, D.C.M., 2nd Bn. (21st Foot) The Royal Scots Fusiliers: *s.* of Andrew Inches, of 46, Reid Street, Dunfermline, co. Fife: enlisted 1909: served at Gibraltar, and with the Expeditionary Force in France from 6 October 1914, and was killed in action at Ypres on the 31st of that month. Age 21.

PANEL 33 ENDS – CORPL. J.W. ALBANY, ROYAL SCOTS FUSILIERS.

North Loggia (Left to Right) :

PANEL 35 BEGINS – MAJOR W.L. ALLEN, BORDER REGT.

(Panel 35) Major, William Lynn Allen, D.S.O., 2nd Bn. (55th Foot) The Border Regt.: *s.* of Bulkeley Allen, of Altrincham, co. Chester, J.P.: *b.* 1871: *educ.* Rugby (Rev. C. Elsee's House) 1885: gazetted 2nd Lieut. from the Militia to 1st Battn. Border Regt. 2 September 1893: promoted Lieut. 27 July 1896; Capt. 23 July 1902; Major (2nd Battn., in which he had commanded a Company), 20 October 1913: served in the South African War, 1899–1902, being acting Adjutant 1901–04, and again at the Discharge Depot, Gosport, 1905–09: took part in operations in Natal, 1899; Orange Free State, April–May 1900; Transvaal, June, 1900, including the Relief of Ladysmith and the actions at Colenso, Spion Kop, Vaal Kranz, Tugela Heights (14–27 February 1900), and Pieter's Hill: twice Mentioned in Despatches (*London Gazette*, 10 September 1901; 29 July 1902): Awarded Queen's Medal, 5 clasps; King's Medal, 2 clasps; and D.S.O.: rejoined 2nd Battn. of his regiment on the outbreak of the European War (August 1914), and was killed in action, 25 October 1914. The circumstances under which he met his death being – "On the evening of 25th October, about 7.30, he was holding a point between the villages of Kruiseecke and America, about 4½ miles from Ypres. For the previous seven days Major Lynn Allen had been occupying with his men a salient point at the extreme left of his regiment, and his Company was badly in need of reinforcements. On that particular night about 100 of the enemy made their way over trenches occupied by a neighbouring battalion, and appeared in the vicinity of a farmhouse in the rear of the Borderers. These men were at first mistaken for Belgians sent in support, but the error having been realised they were fired upon and a considerable number killed. Immediately afterwards the remainder signified their wish to surrender and asked for an English Officer. In response Major Lynn Allen left his trench with two men, and had hardly advanced more than a step or two before the enemy treacherously opened fire, and he fell back mortally wounded." Colonel Wood, the Commanding Officer, in a letter to Mrs Lynn Allen, and subsequently at a personal interview with a brother of the deceased officer, paid a high tribute to his value as an officer, to his popularity with the men of the regiment, and to the splendid example he set them by his coolness under fire. He *m.* 1902; Adeline Miriam, *dau.* of, Isaac Garbutt Dickinson, and leaves two daughters. Major Lynn Allen had two soldier brothers; the late Major E. Lynn Allen, Royal Warwickshire Regt, and Major A. Lynn Allen, A.P.D., formerly Suffolk Regt.; his cousin, Capt. J. Derwent Allen, C.B., R.N., is now commanding HMS 'Kent;' another cousin, Major W.A. Frere Jones, R.F.A., is also on active service. (*IWGC record 28 October 1914*)

(Panel 35) Capt. (Adjt.) Charles George William Andrews, 2nd Bn. (55th Foot) The Border Regt.: only child of the late G.J.W. Andrews, of Dorchester, and Mrs Andrews (Bedford): *b.* 16 May, 1878: gazetted 2nd Lieut. Border Regt. from the Militia, 4 May 1898; promoted Lieut. 30 August 1901; Capt. 13 April 1909: served in the South African War, 1899–1902: took part in operations in Natal 1899: Relief of Ladysmith, including operations of 17–24 January 1900 (wounded 21 January): operations in Orange Free State, April–May 1900: operations Transvaal, June 1900: operations Orange River Colony, May 1900: operations Cape Colony, south of Orange River 1899: operations Cape Colony, north of Orange River, May 1900, and those in the Transvaal from 30 November 1900 (Queen's Medal, 4 clasps; King's Medal, 2 clasps): Adjutant – Volunteers, 16 November 1905–31 March 1908; Territorial Force, 1 April 1908–15 November 1910: apptd. Regimental Adjt., 2 December 1911: served with the Expeditionary Force in France and Flanders from 5 October 1914. His battalion formed part of 20th Brigade of the memorable VIIth Division which left Lyndhurst for Belgium, 4 October, and Capt. Andrews was with it in all the fighting which took place in the retirement from Bruges and Ghent, to Ypres, and was killed in action at the First Battle of Ypres, 28 October 1914: *m.* Age 36. *s.p.*

(Panel 35) Capt. Charles Almeric John Cholmondely, 2nd Bn. (55th Foot) The Border Regt.: *yr. s.* of the late Lord Henry Vere Cholmondeley, by his wife Fanny Isabella Catherine, *née* Spencer: *gdson.* of the 3rd Marquess Cholmondeley: *b.* 5 March 1880: *educ.* Charterhouse, 1894–96. After serving nearly four months with the embodied Militia joined Border Regt., April 1900, obtained his Lieutenancy, January 1902; promoted Capt. April 1910. On the outbreak of war, Lieut. Cholmondeley was serving with his battalion in Dublin: afterwards forming part of VIIth Division, the battalion embarked for France on 4 October 1914, and fought in the First Battle of Ypres, Belgium, near which town Capt. Cholmondeley was killed on the 28th. of that month: 28 October 1914. Age 34. *unm.*

(Panel 35) Capt. Harry Vernon Gerrard, 2nd Bn. (55th Foot) The Border Regt.: *s.* of Thomas Gerrard, of Dublin, Crown Solicitor, Queen's County & Carlow: brother to Capt. P. Gerard, M.D., Malay States Volunteers, killed in the Indian Riots, Singapore, 15 February 1915; and J.D. Gerard, Resident Magistrate, Ireland, now Temp. Lieut. Army Service Corps, and Wing Cmmdr. E.L. Gerard, R.N.A.S.: relation to Flight Sub.Lieut. T.F.N. Gerard, R.N.A.S.: *b.* Dublin, 18 April 1878: *educ.* King's School, Warwick, and Tipperary Grammar School, at both of which he took part in athletics: joined 4th Royal Dublin Fusiliers (Militia) April 1902, attd. A.S.C.: gazetted 2nd Lieut. Royal Garrison Regt. (formed during the South African War) from the Militia, 12 August 1902: promoted Lieut. 21 March 1903 (Adjutant May 1904–July 1905), transf'd. Border Regt. 8 July 1905: promoted Capt. October 1914: employed with West African Frontier Force, Southern Nigeria; served three tours, 5 December 1908–1 July 1913: served with the Expeditionary Force in France and Flanders, and was killed in action near Ypres, 2 November 1914, by a shell while commanding his company. Age 36. His battalion was complimented by the Commander-in-Chief for their behaviour at this battle. Capt. Gerrard was Mentioned in F.M. Sir John (now Lord) French's Despatch, 14 January 1915, referring to his Despatch of 20 November 1914 (*London Gazette*, 17 February 1915) for 'gallant and distinguished service in the field.'

(Panel 35) Capt. Edmund Hastings Harcourt Lees, 2nd Bn. (55th Foot) The Border Regt.: *s.* of Thomas Orde Hastings Lees, of Guilsborough, co. Northampton: *gdson.* of Rev. John (& Lady Louisa)

Lees, of Annaghdowm, Co. Galway: *b*. Northampton, December 1875: *educ*. Marlborough, and Royal Academy, Gosport: joined Border Regt. 1896: promoted Lieut. February 1900; Capt. June 1906: served with his regiment in the South African Campaign: took part in the actions at Spion Kop, Tugela Heights; Relief of Ladysmith, including action at Colenso. He was wounded, and for his services Mentioned in Despatches (*London Gazette*, 10 September 1901): Queen's Medal, six clasps: Adjutant, Artists' Rifles (T.F.), London, 1910–13: served with the Expeditionary Force in France and Flanders, and was killed in action, 26 October 1914, nr. Ypres, while defending a trench in the struggle against the enemy's attempt to reach Calais. An officer of the regiment, describing the fight, said, "Our men fought magnificently against odds of certainly over eleven to one. They fought desperately from nine o'clock till six, when the Germans withdrew, and our little remnant was ordered to retire. We have only about four hundred men left out of one thousand, and hardly any N.C.O.'s." No fewer than eight officers of the battalion were killed. A non-commissioned officer of the battalion gave the following account of Capt. Lees' death, "The regiment was holding an important position for eight days, during which time we were subject to the heaviest shell fire. Capt. Lees was killed by a piece of shrapnel on 26 October, and was last seen by another man and myself in the open. We were then retiring with the enemy on top of us. The enemy gained about six hundred yards of ground, but were pushed back by the 1st Army Corps. Your brother was no doubt buried by the reinforcement that came up to our aid. Capt. Lees was an officer, both brave and daring, who would always trust his men, and both beloved and respected in return. Confidence in him was all that made us stick the shell-fire as we did. No man can speak too highly of him." The following extract is from a report by General Capper – "The devoted and firm conduct of this battalion repeatedly called forth the admiration of the Brigadier and of officers in other battalions in the same brigade, and I myself can testify to its fortitude and determination to maintain its position at all costs – a spirit which saved a difficult and critical situation. It is impossible to praise the battalion too highly." The Commanding Officer of the Artists' Rifles (London) wrote, "His memory will always live in the hearts of the Artists' Rifles, and his old friends amongst us here desire to convey to you both their sincerest sympathy." A member of the United Service Club, Alpine Sports Club, and holder of many prizes for Swiss sports, tobogganing, skiing, etc. Age 38. Inscribed – "Hallowed In Christ Be The Memory Of All The Gallant Men And Women Who Fell In The Great War For The Freedom Of The World. They Shall Yet Stand Before The Throne, An Exceedingly Great Army, and In That Final Muster Shall Be Found These, Our Own Beloved;" the name of Capt. Lees is one of nine parishioners recorded on the Guilsborough (St. Ethelreda's Churchyard) War Memorial (also records nine World War II).

(Panel 35) Capt. Robert Norman Gordon, 1st Bn. (34th Foot) The Border Regt.: *s.* of John Gordon, of Didmarton, Tunbridge Wells, by his wife Harriet: *b*. Rio de Janeiro, Brazil, South America, 18 June 1875: *educ*. Preparatory School of Capt. Lewin, Frant, co. Sussex, and Repton: gazetted 2nd Lieut. Border Regt. 28 September 1895: promoted Lieut. 23 April 1898; Capt. 1 April 1904: served with his regiment in India, Burma, the Cape, and with the Expeditionary Force in France and Flanders, and was killed in action by the explosion of a shell at Ypres, 26 October 1914, when leaving the trenches. Age 29. Capt. Gordon leaves a widow, Rhoda, *née* Jefferson, and a son, *b*. 5 May 1912. (*IWGC record 28 October 1914*)

(Panel 35) Capt. Richard Francis Newdigate, 3rd (Reserve) Bn. The Border Regt.: *s.* of the late Lieut. Gen. Sir Henry Richard Legge Newdigate, K.C.B., Rifle Brigade (*d. 17 January 1908*), by his wife, Lady Phyllis Newdigate, *dau*. of the Rev. Arthur G.S. Shirley, by his 2nd wife Mary Beadon, *née* Turner: *b*. Eastbourne, 1894: served with the Expeditionary Force in France and Flanders from November 1914: wounded, Neuve-Chapelle, 1915: returned to France November following, and was killed in action, 4 September 1916. Age 22. *unm*.

(Panel 35) Capt. James Pyman, 3rd (Reserve) Bn. The Border Regt. attd. 2nd Bn. King's Own (Yorkshire Light Infantry): *s.* of the late James Pyman, of Newcastle-on-Tyne, by his wife Emily: served with the Expeditionary Force in France, and was 'buried and lost' (killed) following the explosion of 'a well-aimed shell' which landed in and destroyed a portion of the trenches nr. Herenthage Chateau, 18 November 1914.

(Panel 35) Lieut. James Booker Brough Warren, 1st (34th Foot) attd. 2nd Bn. (55th Foot) The Border Regt.: *s.* of James Brough Warren, of Westmorland House, Tunbridge Wells, co. Kent, by his wife Constance: *b.* 3 April 1889: *educ.* Oundle School, and Trinity College, Dublin, graduated B.A. (Hons. French) 1909: received a commission (University Candidate) 2nd Lieut. Border Regt. September (antedated to March) 1910; promoted Lieut. October 1912: served with his battalion in Burma, for some time in command of the Mounted Infantry, Maymyo: returned to England on home leave, July 1914 three weeks before the outbreak of war, 4 August: posted 2nd Battn. for Active Service; left for the Front early October 1914, with VIIth Division. A brother officer gave the following account of the circumstances attending his death, "Your son was killed in action on the afternoon of Sunday, 25 October 1914, at 5 o'clock, when holding an entrenched position at Kruiseecke, east of Ypres. He had been reconnoitoring out to the front of his trenches, and had just returned when a shell burst in the trench immediately beside him, and killed him instantaneously." Mrs Warren received a very sympathetic letter from the Officer Commanding the young officer's late battalion in Burma, expressing the regret of all his brother officers at their loss, and his own appreciation of his professional qualifications and character. He was an enthusiastic sportsman, and was distinguished as a first-class hurdler. He created a school record, and while at Dublin University won the Inter -'Varsity race, and was second in the International. He was also a fine polo player. Age 25. *unm.* (*IWGC record 28 October 1914*)

(Panel 35) 2nd Lieut. Trevor John Clancey, 2nd Bn. (55th Foot) The Border Regt.: *s.* of John Charles Clancey, of Auckland Villa 11, Darjeeling, India, by his wife Maud Alice: *b.* 16 June 1893: *educ.* Stoneyhurst, and Royal Military College, Sandhurst, passed out 1912: gazetted 2nd Lieut. Border Regt. 5 February 1913; posted 2nd Battn.: proceeded with his battalion to the Front soon after the declaration of war August 1914. In the Great War his battalion formed part of the VIIth Division, and on it fell the brunt of the fighting in the earlier stages of the First Battle of Ypres. 2nd Lieut. Clancey was killed by shrapnel a short distance south-east of Ypres 24 October 1914 – the War Office Casualty List giving the date as 28 October. Age 21. *unm.*

(Panel 35) 2nd Lieut. Henry Clarence Horsburgh Lane, 11th (Service) Bn. The Border Regt.: *s.* of John Macdonald (& Mrs) Lane, of 'Devonia,' Kew Road, Richmond, co. Surrey: *b.* Sydenham, London, S.E., 16 December 1886: *educ.* Dean Close School, Cheltenham, where he obtained an Exhibition; graduated M.A., St. John's College, Cambridge, taking Second Class Honours in the Classical Tripos and a Musical Scholarship: held a high appointment in the Educational Department, Federal Malay States for nearly five years; requested leave to return to England (1916) that he might join the armed forces: trained Officer Cadet Corps, Newmarket: received his commission in four and a half months, 19 December 1916: proceeded to France, February 1917, and was killed in action in the Nieuport Battle, 10 July 1917, falling at the head of his men after having gallantly led them through the fiercest shell fire to the support of another company. The Capt. of his company wrote, "Who can express the loss we have all sustained? How he was loved by everyone, and how he did his duty like the brave fellow that he was? Can I ever forget how cheerful he was when the orders came, and how he looked at me when he left me, saying, 'Cheery O, Sir,' then led his men away? A better officer I have never had, a firmer friend I can never hope for, so I trust I may be allowed to share in the grief that this letter must bring you, and to offer on behalf of the officers and men of his company our deepest and most heartfelt sympathy in your distress." The Chaplain wrote, "I had known your son ever since he joined our regiment, and am intensely sorry to think he has been taken away from us. I believe his men and all the officers had the greatest respect for him, and one of them was telling me yesterday how he was seen walking fearlessly round with his head up, encouraging his men in the thickest of the bombardment on that memorable day, 10 July. He will be a great loss to us." Mr Lane's father was an officer in the Indian Navy; he served in the Persian War, 1856, and Indian Mutiny. Age 29. *unm.*

(Panel 35) 2nd Lieut. Charles Gordon Villiers Surtees, 2nd Bn. (55th Foot) The Border Regt.: eldest *s.* of William Villiers Surtees, of St. Stephen's, Canterbury, co. Kent, by his wife Mary, *née* Baker-White: *b.* Lower Hardres, 13 February 1892: *educ.* Lake House School, Bexhill; Royal Military College, Sandhurst: gazetted 2nd Lieut. January 1913: served with the Expeditionary Force in France and Flanders, and is unofficially reported to have been killed in action, 26 October 1914. Age 22. *unm.*

(Panel 35) Sergt.-Instructor, 10000, George Alfred Cavalier, 2nd Bn. (55th Foot) The Border Regt.: eldest. *s.* of the late George Joseph Cavalier, by his wife Ada (9, Eleanor Road, Bowes Park, London, N.), *dau.* of William Cooke: *b.* Bowes Park, N., 15 August 1893: *educ.* Bounds Green Council Schools: Occupation – Clerk: enlisted on 3 April 1911: served with the Expeditionary Force in Flanders, 20th Infantry Brigade, 7th Division, landing at Zeebrugge on 6 October 1914, and was killed in action during the First Battle of Ypres on the 23rd (October 1914). Age 21. *unm.*

(Panel 35) Sergt. 2837, Raynard Cockell, 8th (Service) Bn. The Border Regt.: formerly no.9248, The Buffs: *s.* of William George Cockell, of 129, Charlotte Street, Milton Regis, Sittingbourne: and *yr.* brother to Pte. 6050, F. Cockell, 19th Australian Infantry, shot through the head and killed instantaneously, nr. the village of Noreuil, 15 April 1917, aged 30: *b.* Milton Regis, co. Kent: enlisted Ashford. Killed at Messines, 7 June 1917, with four other members of his battalion when the section of captured enemy trench they were occupying was hit by shellfire. Buried nearby. Age 26. He leaves a wife, Ettie Florence Cockell (5, Barrow Hill Place, Ashford).

His brother Frank is buried in Queant Road Cemetery, Buissy (VIII.C.33).

(Panel 35) Pte. 8643, Joshua Bell, 'B' Coy., 2nd Bn. (55th Foot) The Border Regt.: *s.* of William Joshua Bell, of 170, Conyers Road, Byker, Newcastle-on-Tyne: employee Messrs. Armstrong & Whitworth's Elswick Works: *b.* Shieldfield, 9 January 1887: *educ.* Victoria Jubilee Council School, Byker, Newcastle-on-Tyne: enlisted, 27 November 1905, and was killed in action at Ypres, 26 October 1914. He had previously been employed by the Newcastle Tramway Co. Age 27. *unm.* (*IWGC record 25 October 1914*)

(Panel 35) Pte. 7006, Ernest John Bridger, 2nd Bn. (55th Foot) The Border Regt.: *s.* of the late Albert Bridger, of Hackney, London, E., by his wife Hannah: and brother to Pte. 9655, B.W., Bridger, 1st Royal Scots, died 18 January 1915, while on Active Service: enlisted Stratford, co. Essex: served with the Expeditionary Force, and was killed in action at Kruiseecke, nr. Ypres, 25 October 1914. Age 30. *unm.*

His brother Bertie also has no known grave; he is recorded on Panel 11.

(Panel 35) Pte. 12321, Edward Coppock, 8th (Service) Bn. The Border Regt.: *s.* of Albert Coppock, of 51, Boxwood Street, Blackburn, co. Lancaster, by his wife Isabella: and yr. brother to Pte.57041, A. Coppock, 2nd (Garrison) Bn. Northumberland Fusiliers, died 27 June 1919, in Mesopotamia: *b.* Blackburn: enlisted there. Killed in action, 5 August 1917. Age 21.

His brother Albert is buried in Basra War Cemetery (II.B.23).

(Panel 35) Pte. 9355, Allison Fulton, 1st Bn. (34th Foot) The Border Regt.: late of Moor Row, nr. Carlisle: enlisted Workington, co. Cumberland. Killed in action at the Battle of the Somme, 30 July 1916. *Commemorated on the Thiepval Memorial, Somme.*

(Panel 35) Pte. 28457, Thomas Grimshaw, 8th (Service) Bn. The Border Regt.: formerly no.23750, Loyal North Lancashire Regt.: *s.* of John Grimshaw, of 1, Victoria Terrace, Wheelton, Chorley, co. Lancaster, by his wife Mary: and brother to Pte. 19761, R.R. Grimshaw, 1st Coldstream Guards, killed in action, 31 July 1917, at Boesinghe: *b.* Chorley: enlisted there. Killed in action, 13 June 1917. Age 25. He leaves a wife, Rhoda Grimshaw (39, Botany Brow, Chorley).

His brother Robert also has no known grave; he is recorded on Panel 11.

(Panel 35) Pte. 18781, John Hardisty, 1st Bn. (34th Foot) The Border Regt.: *s.* of Henry Hardisty, of Turn How, Grasmere, co. Westmorland, by his wife Mary Anne: and brother to Sergt. 16258, J. Hardisty, M.M., 11th Border Regt., killed in action, 11 September 1916: *b.* Buttermere, co. Cumberland: enlisted Ambleside, co. Westmorland. Killed in action, 30 July 1916.

His brother Joshua is buried in Waggon Road Cemetery, Beaumont-Hamel (A.30).

(Panel 35) Pte. 6901, Alfred William Laws, 2nd Bn. (55th Foot) The Border Regt.: *s.* of Matthew Laws, of 334, Grange Road, Plaistow, London, E., by his wife Jane: *b.* Plaistow, 1884: *educ.* there: Occupation – Checker; Great Eastern Railway: served with the Expeditionary Force in France, and was killed in action there, 26 October 1914. Age 30. *unm.*

(Panel 35) Pte. 7759, Percy James Pedder, 2nd Bn. (55th Foot) The Border Regt.: was for some time in South Africa: returned during the Balkan War, and went to Greece with the British Red Cross. On the outbreak of the European War he volunteered and joined 2nd Border Regt.: went to France, with his regt., in the 7th Division, and was killed in action, 24 October 1914, while assisting a wounded comrade. Coy. Sergt.Major Stuart Davenport wrote, "I am able to inform you from an eyewitness who was next to him when he was killed, that he died a hero in a trench at a traverse. A man was hit by shrapnel; no one would go and help him at the moment – as shell after shell was coming in at that particular spot. Pedder went and had succeeded in bandaging him up when he was struck behind the left ear by one bullet from a shell which penetrated his brain. He died at once and said not a word and he was buried that night, a cross was put on his grave." He leaves a wife, Annette Pedder (26, Palatine Road, Stoke Newington, London, N.), and family to mourn his loss.

(Panel 35) Pte. 10666, Harry Prunnell, 2nd Bn. (55th Foot) The Border Regt.: *s.* of William Prunnell, of 20, Knowsley Avenue, Eccles, Manchester, by his wife Mary Ann: and brother to L/Corpl. 14287, J.W. Prunnell, 7th King's Shropshire L.I., killed in action, 26 September 1917; Polygon Wood: *b.* Eccles, co. Lancaster: enlisted Manchester. Killed in action, 26 October 1914; crossroads Zandvoorde, Kruiseecke – Wervicq roads. Age 19.

His brother John also has no known grave; he is commemorated on the Tyne Cot Memorial (Panel 112).

(Panel 35) Pte. 202353, Tom Dalzell Rothery, 'B' Coy., 1st Bn. (34th Foot) The Border Regt.: 2nd *s.* of Joseph William Rothery, Groundsman; of Marsh House, St. Bees, co. Cumberland, by his wife Mary: *b.* St. Bees: *educ.* there: enlisted Carlisle: served with the Expeditionary Force in France and Flanders from May 1917, and was killed in the Boesinghe sector, Ypres, 29 June following. The Chaplain wrote, "Private Rothery was out on patrol in the dark with a party led by my brother, who is a captain, when they were attacked and heavily shelled. A piece of shell struck Rothery, and killed him instantaneously. He had just volunteered for a very dangerous piece of work, and I am told he was one of the smartest men in the company. My brother says he cannot speak too highly of him. He was buried reverently by his comrades in the trenches. All officers and men join with me in sending you our deepest sympathy." Age 19. His elder brother Allen, late of the Border Regt., is now (1917) at home having been discharged after being severely wounded and having spent nine months in hospital; his younger brother is currently in training at Romsey.

(Panel 35) Pte. 16970, William Ryan, 7th (Service) Bn. The Border Regt.: *s.* of Peter Ryan, of 29, Ripley Street, Warrington, co. Lancaster, and Ellen Ryan his spouse: *b.* Warrington: enlisted there. Killed in action, 4 March 1916. Age 21. Remains recovered (partially) marked grave (28.I.28.c.95.00); identified – Clothing, Cross in Grave; reinterred, registered, 13 October 1927. *Buried in Sanctuary Wood Cemetery (IV.J.5).*

Worthy Of Everlasting Remembrance

(Panel 35) Capt. Frederick Fidler, The Royal Warwickshire Regt. attd. 1st Bn. (37th Foot) The Hampshire Regt.: 2nd *s.* of J. Fidler, of Romsey, co. Hants: *b.* 23 March 1881: *educ.* Romsey School: enlisted Hampshire Regt, February 1899: served with 2nd Battn. in South Africa: Queen's Medal, two clasps: became Sergt.-Major, June 1912: gazetted 2nd Lieut. Hampshire Regt. September 1914, posted 1st Battn.: gazetted Capt. Royal Warwickshire Regt. February 1915, but was killed in action while still attached to 1st Hampshires: Mentioned in Despatches, by Sir John (now Lord) French, 31 May 1915, and awarded French Médaille Militaire for 'his services in the field.' His Commanding Officer wrote, "There is not an officer or man in the regiment who has done better work during these awful eight months of war, and his name would certainly have been mentioned again for distinguished service. He is a real loss to the regiment, and his memory will always be honoured by us. I was close by when he was killed. It was early on the morning of the 26th …A rumour came up that the Germans were getting round our left in the mist. I told Capt. Unwin to take half his company and go for them. It turned out to be a false alarm, so Capt. Unwin sent your husband and his platoon back to the trench. The mist was clearing then, and the enemy's riflemen began sniping at them. Your husband called out to his men to hurry and get down into the trench, but he himself stayed up, urging them on bravely, though unwisely, and a bullet hit him in the head. He was killed instantly … I hope it will be a consolation to you to know what a splendid reputation your husband has left behind, and what a grand example he has given to all of us, and to the whole country. Not only was he brave in battle and a gallant leader, but he was loved by all his men for his pluck and cheerfulness in the most miserable circumstances. I never saw him depressed; he was always cheering us up." Age 34. Capt. Fidler was a keen sportsman, playing hockey, football, and cricket, and was Secretary of the Regimental Football Club for many years. He *m.*, April 1904, Bessie, elder *dau.* of J. Cook, of Andover, and had four children – May, *b.* August 1906; Frederick, *b.* August 1908; Freda, *b.* December 1911, and George, *b.* May 1913.

Gravenstafel Ridge 1915: The 1/Hampshires were part of 11th Brigade, and spent eight days in defence of the Gravenstafel Ridge. An officer who was present wrote, "In the afternoon of 26th April the expected bombardment started…For eight days in succession, for hours on end, several batteries concentrated on our line. With every advantage of position and observation, and with little or no retaliation, the German gunners had the time of their lives.

Every type of gun, from 8-inch downwards, was employed, and stink-shells were freely used. It was amazing that the trench and its occupants were not blotted out, for entire batteries of those magnificent 5.9 guns would be directed on a small sector.

On the first day there were about a hundred casualties, and the trenches were badly damaged. Headquarters had a narrow escape, the C.O., Adjutant, and some orderlies being half-buried by the explosion of a big shell. At nightfall there was much to be done. The trenches had to be repaired and improved, water rations and ammunition had to be fetched, and the wounded had to be collected and carried back many miles, for no vehicle could approach our position. It was a strange sight to see the 'Verey' lights almost completely in a circle around us. It was only towards dawn on the 27th that the rest of the brigade came up on our left and effectively closed the gap.

The enemy made no attempt at infantry attack, possibly because of our tenacity, but we always had to be ready.

On the 29th the bombardment increased in intensity and casualties were again severe. The whole position was clearly untenable.

On the 3rd May the German artillery surpassed itself. From 3.a.m. our whole position was subjected to a most terrible bombardment. For hour after hour and from every angle, tons of metal were hurled upon us. There was practically no reply from our own guns. It was obvious that an infantry attack was in preparation, and at 3 p.m., after twelve hours' bombardment, it came. For some minutes previously the enemy had concentrated his fire on The Buffs, and he then assaulted and carried the wood in spite of gallant resistance. An attack was then made on us, and on the Fusiliers on our right. It melted away before our fire, for the men were fully prepared. The enemy had been seen erecting his gas apparatus, but whether on account of our fire or because the wind was unfavourable, the gas failed to appear. The attack had been beaten off decisively and it was not repeated, although the heavy bombardment was maintained for some hours. Capt. C.F.H. Twining was killed during the evening.

That night the withdrawal was made to a shorter line previously ordered by the Army Commander, for it had been recognised that the exposed salient could not be held. A few weeks later Sir John French told us on parade that "No finer work had been done in the War than the defence of the Gravenstafel Ridge.'"

(Panel 35) Capt. Cecil Francis Harvey Twining, 3rd (Reserve) attd. 1st Bn. (37th Foot) The Hampshire Regt.: *s.* of Herbert Haynes (& Mrs) Twining, of 48, Ennismore Gardens, South Kensington, London, S.W.: *b.* 7, Stanhope Street, Hyde Park, London, W., 2 August 1885: *educ.* Hazelwood, Limpsfield and Eton: gazetted 2nd Lieut. 3rd Hampshire Regt. from the Militia, April 1904; promoted Lieut. November 1908; Capt. September 1914. For Active Service in the present war with Germany, Capt. Twining was attached to the 1st Battn. of his regiment, which he joined at the Aisne: wounded at Messines in a night attack, 1 November following, and invalided home; rejoined his battalion, March 1915, and was killed in the Second Battle of Ypres, 3 May 1915. Buried four miles north-east of Ypres, about a mile from Zonnebeke. Age 29. A brother officer wrote of him, "His death was a great shock to all of us in the company, as he was loved by officers and men alike. The men of his company were very fond of him and would have followed him anywhere; his thought was always for their safety, and I don't think he paid enough attention to his own." He was a member of various cricket clubs, including the M.C.C., Free Foresters, Eton Ramblers,

Butterflies, and Hampshire Hogs. He was also a member of the Conservative and Prince's Clubs, and of the Stoke Poges and East Brighton Golf Clubs. Capt. Twining's widow, Dorothy Elizabeth Bonham Christie (formerly Twining, since remarried), *dau.* of Charles E.N. Charrington, of Frensham Hill, co. Surrey, is currently residing at Hatton Gore, Harlington, co. Middlesex.

(Panel 35) Capt. Lancelot Urquhart Unwin, 1st Bn. (37th Foot) The Hampshire Regt.: 2nd *s.* of Francis S. Unwin, Commissioner of Customs, Shanghai, China: and *gdson.* to Major-Gen. Charles Herbert, Indian Army: *b.* Chefoo, China, 29 April 1883: *educ.* Berkhamstead; 'Marlburia,' Montreux, Switzerland; and Royal Military College, Sandhurst: gazetted 2nd Lieut. Hampshire Regt. April 1903; promoted Lieut. December 1905; Capt. August 1911: served with Aden Hinterland Expedition, 1903–04; afterwards invalided with malaria: Assistant Adjutant, 1st Battn. Hampshire Regt. 1907–08: qualified as Chinese language interpreter, 1913: served with the Expeditionary Force from September 1914, and after being wounded in the arm and head, was invalided to England, November following: after recovery he rejoined his battalion and returned to France in December 1914, where he was killed by the bursting of a shell in the firing trench at the Second Battle of Ypres, 27 April 1915; two days before his thirty-second birthday. Mentioned in F.M. Sir John (now Lord) French's Despatch, 31 May 1915, for 'gallant and distinguished service in the field.' He was a direct descendant of Mary Unwin, friend of the famous poet Cowper. Age 31 years, 363 days. *unm.*

(Panel 35) Lieut. Francis Henry Lambert, 1st (37th Foot) attd. 2nd Bn. (67th Foot) The Hampshire Regt.: *s.* of Fitzgerald Gage Lambert, of Rockbourne, Salisbury, co. Wilts. Killed in action, 7 June 1915, at Gallipoli. Age 29. *IWGC/1926,MR.29. Known to be recorded on the Helles Memorial (Addenda Panel).*

(Panel 35) 2nd Lieut. Denis George Wyldbore Hewitt, V.C., 1st Bn. (37th Foot) attd. 14th (Service) Bn. The Hampshire Regt.: elder *s.* of the Hon George Wyldbore Hewitt, of Field House, Hursley, Winchester, by his wife Elizabeth Mary, *dau.* of Charles Rampini: *b.* London, 18 December 1897: *educ.* The Old Malt House, Swanage, co. Dorset; Winchester College, and Royal Military College, Sandhurst: gazetted 2nd Lieut. 7 April 1916: served with the Expeditionary Force in France and Flanders from 9 September following: took part in the operations on the Somme, and was killed in action near St. Julien, 31 July 1917, during the Third Battle of Ypres. Buried 150 yards west of the St. Julien–Poelcappelle Road, Langemarck, north of Ypres; cross inscribed *Peace Perfect Peace.* Age 19 years, 6 months. His Colonel wrote, "It may be a slight consolation to you to know he died a glorious death. In the attack on 31 July he had a most difficult operation to carry out. During the earlier part of the attack he was hit on the back of his haversack by a piece of shell, which set on fire the rockets and flares he was carrying. By rolling in the mud he managed to get these extinguished. Then, although much shaken, he rallied his company, went forward, and drove back the Germans, attaining his object. It was while superintending his men digging in on their final objective that he was killed – hit by a bullet in the head. Death was instantaneous." Awarded the posthumous honour of the Victoria Cross (*London Gazette*, 1 October 1917) "For most conspicuous bravery and devotion to duty when in command of a company in an attack. When his first objective had been captured he reorganized the company and moved forward towards his objective. While waiting for the barrage to lift he was hit by a piece of shell, which exploded the signal lights in his haversack and set fire to his equipment and clothes. Having extinguished the flames, in spite of his wound and the severe pain he was suffering, he led forward the remains of his company under very heavy machine-gun fire, and captured and consolidated his objective. He was subsequently killed by a sniper while inspecting the consolidation and encouraging his men. This gallant officer set a magnificent example of coolness and contempt of danger to the whole battalion, and it was due to his splendid leading that the final objective of his battalion was gained." A plaque in memory of 2nd Lieut. Hewitt erected in St, Mary's Church, Hursley, is dedicated 'Greater Love Hath No Man Than This That A Man Lay Down His Life For His Friends.'

(Panel 35) Sergt. 7809, Walter Ernest Harfield, 1st Bn. (37th Foot) The Hampshire Regt.: *s.* of Henry Harfield, of Upton Cottages, Wonston (Hunton), Sutton Scotney, co. Hants, by his wife Louisa: late *husb.* to Mrs D.M. Knell, *née* Harfield (18, Earl Street, Hastings, co. Sussex): and brother to Pte. 10466, M.J. Harfield, 2nd Hampshire Regt., died of wounds, 13 August 1915, aboard a hospital ship: enlisted Winchester: served with the Expeditionary Force in France and Flanders from 23 August 1914, and was killed in action, 11 May 1915. Age 24. Remains recovered from a (collective) grave marked as belonging to an 'Unknown British Soldier. Hants Regt.', refers GRU Report, Zillebeke 5-396E; (28.C.22.a.70.70); identified – Clothing, Boots, Titles; reinterred, registered 30 January 1931. *Buried in Sanctuary Wood Cemetery (V.N.19/25).*

Rest Comes At Last

His brother Montague has no known grave but the sea; he is commemorated on the Helles Memorial, Gallipoli.

(Panel 35) L/Corpl. 9330, William Ayling, 1st Bn. (37th Foot) The Hampshire Regt.: *s.* of Horace Ayling, Cowman; of Stubbington Lane, Stubbington, Fareham, Hants, by his wife Anne, *dau.* of Edward Etherington: *b.* Hindhead, co. Surrey, 18 December 1895: *educ.* Fareham, and Crofton Elementary School: enlisted, April 1912: went to France 12 August 1914: seriously wounded nr. Ypres, 7 November 1914, by a wounded Prussian, and invalided home: returned to the Front May 1915: apptd. L/Corpl. June, and was killed in action at Ypres, 9 July 1915. His Commanding Officer wrote, "…he was killed instantly by a shell which burst in a trench;" adding, "He was an excellent fellow. He was buried behind the trench. I am afraid it was only a rough grave, as we left that night." Age 19. (*IWGC record Pte.*)

(Panel 35) L/Corpl. 3/4376, Frederick James Clay, 1st Bn. (37th Foot) The Hampshire Regt.: late of Abingdon, co. Berks: a pre-war member of 3rd (Reserve) Battn.: posted 1st Battn. on mobilisation, went to France, and was killed in action, 11 May 1915. Remains recovered from a (collective) grave marked up as belonging to an 'Unknown British Soldier. Hants Regt.', refers GRU Report, Zillebeke 5-396E; (28.C.22.a.70.70); identified – Clothing, Boots, Titles; reinterred, registered 30 January 1931. *Buried in Sanctuary Wood Cemetery (V.N.19/25).*

(Panel 35) L/Corpl. 9177, Percy Weeks, 1st Bn. (37th Foot) The Hampshire Regt.: *s.* of Robert John Weeks, of 122, South Street, Andover, co. Kent, by his wife Kate: and yr. brother to Pte. 3/4133, R. Weeks, 1st Hampshire Regt., who fell 27 April 1915: *b.* Andover: enlisted there. Killed in action, 15 May 1915. Age 21. *unm.*

His brother Robert also has no known grave; he is recorded below.

(Panel 35) Pte. 11742, William Allen, 1st Bn. (37th Foot) The Hampshire Regt.: formerly no.13404, Duke of Cornwall's Light Infantry: *s.* of Alfred Allen, of 22, Peckford Place, Brixton, London, by his wife Hannah: *b.* Fenchingfield, co. Norfolk: enlisted Southwark, London: served with the Expeditionary Force, and was killed in action, 29 April 1915. Age 16.

(Panel 35) Pte. 11744, William Bullard, 1st Bn. (37th Foot) The Hampshire Regt.: formerly no.13584, Duke of Cornwall's Light Infantry: *s.* of John Bullard, of 5, Earl Road, Old Kent Road, London, by his wife Mary: and elder brother to Gnr. 140053, H. Bullard, Royal Garrison Artillery, died 11 June 1918, of wounds: *b.* Bermondsey, London, S.E.: enlisted there. Killed in action, 29 April 1915. Age 19.

His brother Henry is buried in Hoogstade Belgian Military Cemetery (950).

(Panel 35) Pte. 6859, Frank Glasspool, D.C.M., 1st Bn. (37th Foot) The Hampshire Regt.: *s.* of Mrs A. Glasspool (Steventon, Overton, co. Hants): and brother to Pte. 7167, J. Glasspool, Hampshire Regt., killed in action, 11 May 1915; and A/Sergt. SE/11270, H. Glasspool, Army Veterinary Corps, died of wounds, 5 October 1918: *b.* Overton, 1885: enlisted, Winchester, co. Hants, prior to the outbreak of war: served with the Expeditionary Force in France and Flanders, and was killed in action, Ypres sector, 9 May 1915. Buried where he fell. Age 29. *unm.*

His brother John is buried in Hamel Military Cemetery, Beaumont Hamel (I.C.16); Frank, Lijssenthoek Military Cemetery, Poperinghe (XXX.A.11).

(Panel 35) Pte. 10634, Edward George Hall, 1st Bn. (37th Foot) The Hampshire Regt.: *s.* of George Hall, of Avington, nr. Winchester, and Amelia Hall his spouse: and elder brother to Pte. 45014, S.H. Hall, 8th Royal Berkshire Regt., died 6 October 1918, aged 19 years; and cousin to Bmdr. 107925, F.E. Hall, Royal Field Artillery, died of wounds, 27 November 1917, aged 20: *b.* Avington: enlisted Winchester. Killed in action, 26 April 1915. Age 22. *unm.* Six men of Avington gave their lives in the Great War; they are remembered on the war memorial situated in the village (St. Mary's) churchyard.

His brother Sidney is commemorated in Cross Roads Cemetery, Fontaine-Au-Bois (Landrecies Com. Cem.Mem.21); cousin Frank, Lijssenthoek Military Cemetery (XXVI.A.9).

(Panel 35) Pte. 9532, George Hayes, 1st Bn. (37th Foot) The Hampshire Regt.: *s.* of Herbert George Hayes, of Lily Cottage, Melville Road, Forton, Gosport, by his wife Eliza Jane, *dau.* of Thomas Hayling: *b.* Elson, Gosport, co. Hants, 18 March 1895: *educ.* Rushton Council School, nr. Blandford: Occupation – Assistant Gardener: enlisted on 17 February 1914: served with the Expeditionary Force in France and Flanders, and was killed in action at the Second Battle of Ypres, 27 April 1915. Age 20. *unm.*

(Panel 35) Pte. 8307, James Sydney Miller, 2nd Bn. (67th Foot) The Hampshire Regt.: *s.* of the late Jesse Miller, by his wife Lois (26, Beaconsfield Road, Christchurch, co. Hants): and brother to Pte. 37513, J.H. Miller, 1st Wiltshire Regt., killed in action, 1 September 1918: *b.* Christchurch: enlisted Winchester: served with the Expeditionary Force in France, and was killed in action, 9 August 1916. Age 26. *unm.* Dedicated – 'In Ever Grateful Remembrance Of Those Who Fell For God And King, For Right, For Freedom And For Peace In The Great War 1914–1918;' the brothers Miller are remembered on the Priory War Memorial, Christchurch.

His brother John is buried in Beaulencourt British Cemetery, Ligny-Thilloy (IV.G.18).

(Panel 35) Pte. 27089, William John Millman, 15th (Service) Bn. The Hampshire Regt.: formerly no.28966, Devonshire Regt.: *s.* of John Millman, of Woodway Street, Chudleigh, co. Devon, by his wife Elizabeth: and cousin to L/Corpl. 20085, T.G. Millman, 1/5th Devonshire Regt., killed in action, 30 September 1918: *b.* Chudleigh, 1881: enlisted Exeter. Killed in action, 7 April 1917. Age 36.

His cousin Thomas is buried in Masnieres British Cemetery, Marcoing (II.A.10).

(Panel 35) Pte. 6467, Nicholas Murphy, 'D' Coy., 1st Bn. (37th Foot) The Hampshire Regt.: late of Clapton Park, London, E.5: *s.* of James Murphy, of 42, Chaucer Road, Walthamstow, London, E.17, by his wife Ellen: enlisted London: served with the Expeditionary Force in France and Flanders, and was killed in action, 12 May 1915. Age 34. Remains recovered from a (collective) grave marked as belonging to an 'Unknown British Soldier. Hants Regt.', refers GRU Report, Zillebeke 5-396E; (28.C.22.a.70.70); identified – Clothing, Boots; reinterred, registered 30 January 1931. *Buried in Sanctuary Wood Cemetery (V.N.19/25).*

(Panel 35) Pte. 5809, James Oakley, 1st Bn. (37th Foot) The Hampshire Regt.: late *husb.* to Mary Jane Holt, *née* Oakley (London Road, Holybourne, Alton), previously of Cutpound, co. Hants: enlisted Winchester: served with the Expeditionary Force in France and Flanders, and was killed in action, 12 May 1915, at Ypres. Age 31. Remains recovered from an unmarked grave (collective) refers GRU Report, Zillebeke 5-396E; (28.C.22.a.70.70); identified – Clothing, Boots, Disc; reinterred, registered 30 January 1931. *Buried in Sanctuary Wood Cemetery (V.N.18).*

(Panel 35) Pte. 14801, Herbert Provins, 1st Bn. (37th Foot) The Hampshire Regt.: *s.* of the late Herbert Provins, of 3, Walton Road, Woking, co. Surrey: and elder brother to A.B. J/19776, A.E. Provins, Royal Navy; one of 2,145 crewmembers lost at Jutland, 31 May 1916, when the battlecruiser H.M.S. 'Queen Mary' exploded and sank: *b.* Datchet, co. Buckingham, *c.*1891: enlisted Winchester. Killed in action at Ypres, 13 May 1915. Age 24. *unm.* Inscribed 'To The Glory Of God And In Honoured Memory,' Herbert and his brother Arthur are among fourteen members of the congregation who made the ultimate sacrifice, remembered on the Goldsworth Coign Baptist Church War Memorial, Percy Street.

His brother Arthur has no known grave but the sea; he is commemorated on the Portsmouth Naval Memorial (13).

(Panel 35) Pte. 12097, George Joseph Seagrave, 1st Bn. (37th Foot) The Hampshire Regt.: *s.* of the late William Seagrave: *husb.* to Delia Seagrave (Fairy Hill Cottage, Nettlestone, Ryde): *b.* St. Helen's, Isle of Wight: enlisted Seaview. Killed in action, 11 May 1915. Age 37. Remains recovered from a (collective) unmarked grave marked up as belonging to an 'Unknown British Soldier. Hants Regt.', refers GRU Report, Zillebeke 5-396E; (28.C.22.a.70.70); identified – Clothing, Boots, Titles; reinterred, registered 30 January 1931. *Buried in Sanctuary Wood Cemetery (V.N.19/25).*

(Panel 35) Pte. 3/4190, Sidney John Swift, 1st Bn. (37th Foot) The Hampshire Regt.: late of Homerton, London: enlisted Stratford, co. Essex. Killed in action, 11 May 1915. Remains recovered from a (collective) unmarked grave marked up as belonging to an 'Unknown British Soldier. Hants Regt.', refers GRU Report, Zillebeke 5-396E; (28.C.22.a.70.70); identified – Clothing, Boots, Titles; reinterred, registered 30 January 1931. *Buried in Sanctuary Wood Cemetery (V.N.19/25).*

(Panel 35) Pte. 10038, Walter Tuck, 14th (Service) Bn. The Hampshire Regt.: *s.* of Richard Tuck, of Beckley, Christchurch, co. Hants: and brother to Pte. 11331, G. Tuck, 11th Hampshire Regt., killed in action, 14 January 1916: *b.* Beckley, 1890: enlisted Christchurch. Killed in action, 2 August 1917. Age 27. Remembered on Hinton (St. Michael's) War Memorial.

His brother George is buried in Maroc British Cemetery, Grenay (I.D.21).

(Panel 35) Pte. 3/4133, Robert Weeks, 1st Bn. (37th Foot) The Hampshire Regt.: *s.* of Robert John Weeks, of 122, South Street, Andover, co. Kent, by his wife Kate: and elder brother to L/Corpl. 9177, P. Weeks, 1st Hampshire Regt., who fell, 15 May 1915: *b.* Whitchurch: enlisted Winchester. Killed in action, 27 April 1915. Age 29. *unm.*

His brother Percy also has no known grave; he is recorded above.

(Panel 35) Pte. 14786, John Woodward, 1st Bn. (37th Foot) The Hampshire Regt.: adopted *s.* of William Ayling, of Sheet, co. Hants, and his late wife Fanny: *b.* Watford, co. Hertford: enlisted Winchester. Killed in action, 11 May 1915. Age 24. Remains recovered from a (collective) unmarked grave marked up as belonging to an 'Unknown British Soldier. Hants Regt.', refers GRU Report, Zillebeke 5- 396E; (28.C.22.a.70.70); identified – Clothing, Boots, Titles; reinterred, registered 30 January 1931. *Buried in Sanctuary Wood Cemetery (V.N.19/25).*

(Panel 35) Major John Frederick Loder-Symonds, Comdg. 1st Bn. (38th Foot) The South Staffordshire Regt.: eldest *s.* of Capt. F.C. Loder-Symonds, late Royal Artillery, of Hinton Manor, co. Berks, J.P.: *b.* Dharwar, India, 23 December 1873: *educ.* Eton: joined South Staffordshire Regt. from the Militia, June 1894: promoted Lieut. 1896: employed with the West African Frontier Force, July 1899–August 1900, being on Active Service in Northern Nigeria (1900) where he was dangerously wounded: Mentioned in Despatches (*London Gazette,* 16 April 1901): promoted Capt. June 1901; Adjutant, 4th (Volunteer) Battn. King's (Liverpool) Regt. August 1903–August 1906; obtained his Majority, September 1911. On the outbreak of war with Germany, 1st Battn. South Staffordshire Regt. was brought home to England from Natal, and left for Belgium, 4 October 1914. During the First Battle of Ypres, Major Loder-Symonds was killed instantly with several brother officers on 31 October 1914, while in command of the battalion. Age 40. He *m.* 1907, Mary Josephine, *dau.* of Sir William Vavasour, Bart.: *s.p.*

(Panel 35) Capt. Julian Silver Strickland Dunlop, 1st Bn. (38th Foot) The South Staffordshire Regt.: 3rd *s.* of the late Andrew Dunlop, M.D., of Belgrave House, Jersey, by his wife Alice, *dau.* of John Joseph Strickland: and elder brother to Capt. F.C.S. Dunlop, 1st Manchester Regt., who fell on 8 November 1914, aged 36 years; and 2nd Lieut. K.S. Dunlop, 4th attd. 1st South Staffordshire Regt., killed in action, 26 September 1915: *b.* St. Helier, Jersey, 15 September 1876: *educ.* Victoria College, Jersey: gazetted 2nd Lieut. South Staffordshire Regt. from Royal Jersey Militia, 7 December 1895: promoted Lieut. 1 May 1898; Capt. 9 February 1904: A.D.C. to Sir Frederick Fryer, Lieut.-Governor, Burma, October 1899–31 March 1903, and Adjt. 4th South Staffordshire (Militia and Special Reserve) Regt., 1905–10: accompanied his regiment to France, 7 October 1914, as part of the Expeditionary Force, and was killed in action while leading a bayonet charge, near Ypres on the 24th of that month. Age 38. *unm.* Pte. J. Jones later wrote, "One of the bravest was our Captain, and as good as a father to all his men. I shall always remember when he got killed. Having got through the wood alright, we started to advance across a ploughed field. We had no sooner got into the open than the Germans began shelling us, they had got the range. I had just dropped down when a shell burst behind me, and the force of the explosion hurled a pig about ten yards, the animal landing near me. Though surprised for a moment I found the carcass useful cover. Our Captain was a man who knew his work, and the men would go anywhere with him. The order was given for a bayonet charge, and we had not gone far across the ploughed field before the Captain was killed. When he was killed I think our fellows went mad. They gave the Germans something to go on with, the place swarmed with dead after the charge. When we got back to where the Captain lay some of our fellows had a job to keep tears from their eyes, they loved him so well." Capt. Dunlop was Mentioned in

Sir John (now Lord) French's Despatch of 14 January 1915, for 'gallant and distinguished conduct in the field'. Two other brothers served; both survived.

His brother Frederick is buried in Royal Irish Rifles Graveyard, Laventie (I.A.1); Kenneth, Vermelles British Cemetery (I.E.27).

(Panel 35) Capt. John Franks Vallentin, V.C., 1st Bn. (38th Foot) The South Staffordshire Regt.: only *s.* of the late Grimble Vallentin, of The Manor House, Walthamstow, by his wife Lucy (33, Prince of Wales Mansions, London, S.W.), *dau.* of Col. John Finnis, 11th Bengal Native Infantry Regt. (killed at Meerut, 10 May 1857, the first victim of the Indian Mutiny), and a nephew of Major Vallentin, who was killed in action in the Boer War: *b.* London, 14 May 1882: *educ.* Wellington College: joined 6th (Militia) Battn. Rifle Brigade, August 1899, and became Lieut. July, 1900. The battalion was embodied at the Curragh Camp, Kildare, from the beginning of the Boer War, for nearly a year, and on its disembodiment, Lieut. Vallentin was attached to 3rd (Militia) Battn. Royal Sussex Regt., and served with it in the South African War, 1901–02, taking part in the operations in Orange River Colony from April to December 1901, and in the Transvaal from the latter date until May 1902 (Queen's Medal, five clasps): gazetted 2nd Lieut. Royal Garrison Regt. (formed during the Boer War), 29 July 1903: transf'd. 1st South Staffordshire Regt. 7 June 1905: promoted Lieut. 7 September 1907; Capt. 12 June 1909: proceeded to France with his regt. (7th Division), 5 October 1914, landing at Zeebrugge on 7 October: wounded on 31 October during the First Battle of Ypres; removed to hospital there and detained. On 2 November, on hearing Major Loder Symonds had been killed, he insisted on discharging himself from the hospital to assume command of what was left of the regt.; the Col. having been seriously wounded on 31 October. Capt. Vallentin was killed at Zillebeke, 7 November following.. The regt. on this occasion, with the remains of the Queen's Regt., captured six machine guns (which he subsequently had destroyed and buried), and recaptured the trenches which had previously been lost by the French. So efficient was his command he was posthumously awarded the Victoria Cross (*London Gazette*, 18 February 1915): "... Date of Act of Bravery: 7 November 1914. For conspicuous bravery on the 7th November, at Zillebeke. When leading the attack against the Prussian Guard under a very heavy fire he was struck down, and on rising to continue the attack was immediately killed. The capture of the enemy's trenches which followed was in a great measure due to the confidence which the men had in their Captain, arising from his many previous acts of great bravery and ability." Lieut. Col. Ovens, C.M.G., commanding 1st South Staffords, wrote, "Capt. Vallentin's splendid heroism and unfaltering courage and determination have been justly rewarded with the Victoria Cross. He was Captain of our Polo Club, and the best player in the regt. He was a specialist in musketry, and a first-rate all-round man. At manoeuvres and in the field General Officers have commented on the excellence of his work. The Chief Engineer of the 7th Division told me Capt. Vallentin's scheme of defence and his trenches were the best he had seen. He was wounded and in hospital at Ypres on 6 November 1914, and hearing the regt. was making an attack that night, he came out of hospital and took command. He was again wounded whilst leading his men forward, and was instantly killed. His is a great loss to his splendid old regt., and is deeply regretted by all who knew him." Mentioned in Sir John French's Despatch, 14 January 1915. Age 32. *unm.*

(Panel 35) Lieut. Cecil Francis Crousaz, 1st Bn. (38th Foot) The South Staffordshire Regt.: *yst. s.* of William de Prelaz Crousaz, of 8, de Beauvoir Terrace, Gravées; High Constable & Jurat of the Royal Court, Guernsey, by his wife Emma Arnold, *dau.* of John Le Cappellaine: *gt.gdson.* to Isaac Crousaz de Prelaz, of Lausanne, Switzerland, and Guernsey: *b.* Guernsey, 7 December 1888: *educ.* Elizabeth College (No.940), Guernsey; Woolwich (Sandhurst Cadet Coy.) 1908: gazetted 2nd Lieut. 1st South Staffordshire Regt., Pretoria, 6 November 1909: promoted Lieut. Gibraltar, 28 March 1912 (attd. 2nd Battn.): served with the Expeditionary Force in France and Flanders and was killed in action at Zonnebeke, 31 October 1914. Buried at Hooge. Age 25. *unm.* His Commanding Officer, Col. R.M. Ovens, wrote to his father, "Your boy was in command of our scouts and was a most valuable officer – energetic and keen, and a splendid disciplinarian. His exceptional strength and keenness made him a great asset to his regt. I last saw your boy leading his men forward near Gheluvelt Village, under a heavy fire, and encouraging them by voice and example. He was a brave and determined soldier." For several years the holder of the

Elizabeth College Gymnastics, Swimming and Boxing cups, he was a member of the Shooting Team and, in 1913, won the Army Officer's Featherweight Boxing Championship, Aldershot. His brothers Henry and Augustus also served; both survived.

(Panel 35) Lieut. Dudley Thomas Francis Fitzpatrick, 3rd (Reserve) attd. 2nd Bn. (80th Foot) The South Staffordshire Regt.: Religion – Roman Catholic: *educ.* Stoneyhurst: gazetted 2nd Lieut. 3rd South Staffordshire Regt. March 1913; promoted Lieut. 23 February 1914: served in the European War, and was killed in action, 27 October 1914.

(Panel 35) Lieut. Francis Lennox Holmes, 1st Bn. (38th Foot) The South Staffordshire Regt.: *yst. s.* of the late Major-General Ponsonby Ross Holmes (served in the Baltic, 1854; Mentioned in Despatches), by his wife Clara Bernell (Evesham House, Cheltenham, co. Gloucester), *dau.* of W.G. Nixey, and *gdson.* of Lieut.-Col. Steven Holmes, 24th, 78th & 90th Regts. (who served in the Peninsular and at Waterloo, and was Mentioned in Despatches by the Duke of Wellington for his conduct at the siege of Burgos): *b.* Stoke, Devonport, 11 October 1887: *educ.* Cheltenham College, and Sandhurst: gazetted 2nd Lieut. 1st South Staffordshire Regt. 19 September 1908; Lieut. 14 July 1909: passed through Hythe with distinction; apptd. Battn. Signalling Officer: went to the Front (7th Division), 4 October 1914, and was killed in action at the First Battle of Ypres, 21 October 1914. His Commanding Officer, Col. Ovens, wrote, "As his Commanding Officer I can truthfully say the Army has lost a fine and promising young officer, who, as Signalling Officer and in other capacities, brought credit and honour to his regt. He was killed instantaneously, poor fellow, and had been exposing himself and working hard all through the operations. Capt. Dunlop (his Capt.) told me he had been the greatest assistance to him in defending their position and he wished particularly to mention him." Capt. Dunlop recorded, "Lieut. Holmes was killed this day. He was taking observation and instructing the men when and where to aim. He was in command of a half company of 'B'Coy. and had been doing excellent work the whole day. He had been looking after and superintending a machine-gun which did very good service. He had also done a lot of very dangerous work in scouting through the wood in front of his section of trenches, and had shown much pluck and coolness." Capt. Evans wrote, "On Tuesday and Wednesday, 20 and 21 October, the Germans attacked our position in point of the outskirts of Zonnebeke. Lennox was in charge of half a company, and was hit on the Wednesday afternoon by a ricochet. Hayward told me afterwards that he was doing extraordinarily good work and was absolutely fearless in the way he moved from trench to trench to direct the fire against the Germans. It was while he was close by the machine-gun that he was hit. He was simply adored by the men, and, of course, his death upset them terribly and they fought magnificently to avenge his death. So that his example lived after him. Hayward's own words to me were, 'If ever a man deserved the V.C. he did.'": And Corpl. F. Barrett, "On 22nd October (this should be the 20th) 1914, I was working my machine-gun when Mr Holmes came up and acted as my No.2 (also my observer) and we got over that day all right. On the 23rd (this should be the 21st) he visited me again, and I shifted my position close to where Mr Holmes was killed about three o'clock. He was at the back of his trench, taking cover, bandaging up Private Millar, after that he was taking aim at the Germans, and was just going to pull the trigger when a bullet hit him straight between the two eyes. I shall never forget him as long as I live." Age 27. *unm.* (*IWGC record 23 October 1914*)

(Panel 35) Lieut. Charles Geoffrey Hume, 'B' Coy., 1st Bn. (38th Foot) The South Staffordshire Regt.: *s.* of Edward Hume, Barrister-at-Law; by his wife Agnes Mary: *b.* Oatlands, nr. Weybridge, co. Surrey, 5 July 1890: *educ.* St. Aubyn's, Rottingdean; Malvern College (Rev. H. Foster's House), and Royal Military College, Sandhurst: obtained his commission, South Staffordshire Regt. 1910; promoted Lieut. January 1913: served with his battalion in France from mid-August 1914, and was killed in action near Ypres, 26 October following. At the time of his death his battalion formed part of the VIIth Division, and as the senior officers had been killed he was leading his company. Mr Hume was fond of polo and sailing: 26 October 1914. Age 24. *unm.*

(Panel 35) Lieut. Leslie Claude Moor-Radford, 1st Bn. (38th Foot) The South Staffordshire Regt.: *s.* of Alfred Moor-Radford, Barrister-at-Law; of 83A, Holland Park, Kensington, London, W., by his wife Amelia Blanche, *dau.* of Robert Dawson Tewart, of Chiswick, and Coupland Castle, co. Northumberland:

gdson. to Francis Radford, of Holland Park, and Kentisbeare, co. Devon: *b.* 34, Cadogan Terrace, London, S.W., 10 January 1890: *educ.* Eastman's Naval Academy, Winchester; and Royal Military College, Sandhurst: gazetted 2nd Lieut. April 1910; promoted Lieut. January 1913: served Devonport; Gibraltar, and in South Africa. On the declaration of war his battalion was stationed at Pietermaritzburg, and brought home to form part of VIIth Division: served with the Expeditionary Force in France and Flanders from 7 October 1914, and was killed in action at Kruiseecke, nr. Ypres on the 26th of that month; being shot outside a trench which he defended under fire for fifteen minutes. Although mortally wounded he continued to urge his men on, shouting "charge and stick to it," before he succumbed. He was the founder and editor of the Regimental Gazette *The Staffordshire Knot.* His recreations were shooting, cricket, motoring, riding and golf; he also wrote for magazines and other publications, and was interested in photography. He was a member of the Conservative Club, St. James' Street. Age 24. *unm.*

(Panel 35) Lieut. Francis Edward Robinson, 3rd (Reserve) attd. 2nd Bn. (80th Foot) The South Staffordshire Regt.: *yst. s.* of St.George C.W. (& Mrs) Robinson, of Woodville, Sligo: nephew to Sir Edward Carson: *b.* Sligo, 30 January 1895: *educ.* The Link, Stubbington, and Malvern College, where he proved to be a good all-round athlete, and held promise of becoming a good shot: gazetted 2nd Lieut. 3rd South Staffordshire Regt. April 1912; promoted Lieut. July 1913: on the outbreak of war was attached 2nd Battn. which, forming part of IInd Division, was among the first regiments to land in France, and was killed, 27 October 1914, while leading his platoon in an attack across the Becelaere – Passchendaele Road. Age 19. After his death his parents received many sympathetic letters saying he was an excellent officer, greatly regretted by both officers and men of his battalion.

At the beginning of the 20th Century, British society was rocked by a scandal involving a young boy, expelled from the Royal Naval Academy accused of stealing and cashing a five shilling postal order belonging to a fellow student. After arriving home and denying the matter to his family, the boy's father decided to pursue a course of justice. Risking everything – fortune, health, domestic peace, social reputation – the case was tried and lost in the military courts. Following this defeat the family engaged the services of one of the country's most brilliant barristers (Sir Edward Carson) who, after careful examination of the evidence, took the case before Parliament to seek permission to sue the Crown. In the capable hands of the barrister the case was duly won and the honour of the family vindicated. In 1945 Terrence Rattigan immortalised this story in his play *The Winslow Boy.* The central character:-

(Panel 35) Lieut. George Archer-Shee, 3rd (Reserve) attd 1st Bn. (38th Foot) The South Staffordshire Regt.: *yr. s.* of the late Martin Archer-Shee, Agent, Bank of England; only *s.* of Helen Archer-Shee (Woodchester, co. Gloucester): *b.* 1895: *educ.* Stonyhurst, and Royal Naval College, Osborne: joined 3rd South Staffordshire Regt. May 1913: promoted Lieut. February 1914: attd. 1st Battn. for Active Service on the outbreak of war, and was killed in action at Ypres, 31 October 1914. Age 19. Remembered on Woodchester (Gloucestershire) War Memorial; unveiled August 1918, it is reputed to be the oldest war memorial in the British Isles. Also remembered thereon – Major R. Raymond-Barker, M.C., Royal Air Force, shot down and killed on 20 April 1918; 79th victim of German Air Ace, Manfred von Richtofen 'The Red Baron' who was himself shot down and killed the following day; and Lieut. M.J. Dease, V.C., 4th Royal Fusiliers, killed in action, 23 August 1914; one of the earliest British officer casualties and first Victoria Cross recipients of the Great War.

Major R. Raymond-Barker has no known grave, he is commemorated on the Flying Services Memorial, Arras; Lieut. Dease, V.C., is buried in St. Symphorien Military Cemetery (V.B.2).

(Panel 35) 2nd Lieut. Basil John Harrison Scott, 2nd Bn. (80th Foot) The South Staffordshire Regt.: elder *s.* of the late Dr. John Harrison Scott, of Fitzwilliam Square, Dublin, F.R.C.S. (Ireland), and his wife Isabella (28, The Ridgway, Wimbledon, London, S.W.), *dau.* of John Henry Durham: and brother to Lieut. S.M. Scott, 1st Coldstream Guards, killed in action, 15 September 1916, aged 19: *b.* Fitzwilliam Square, 10 May 1894: *educ.* Winton House (Mr. E.F. Johns), thereafter Winchester College (1908–10), and Royal Military College, Sandhurst; gazetted 2nd Lieut., South Staffordshire Regt., 13 September 1913: at Aldershot on the outbreak of war; accompanied the battalion to France, 12 August 1914: served with the Expeditionary Force in there and in Flanders; first engaged with the enemy at Hermignies, 23

August, subsequently took part in the great retirement from Mons to the Marne: took part in several engagements prior to moving up to Strazeele (Ypres sector), and was killed in action at the First Battle of Ypres, 23 October 1914, being shot during the severe fighting to recapture some lost trenches nr. Pilckem (Belgium). Mentioned in F.M. Sir John (now Lord) French's Despatch of 14 January 1915 (*London Gazette*, 14 February) 'for his services.'Age 30. *unm*.

His brother Sidney is commemorated in Guards Cemetery, Lesboeufs (Sp.Mem.33).

(Panel 35) 2nd Lieut. Frederick Roger John Tomlinson, 1st Bn. (38th Foot) The South Staffordshire Regt.: *s*. of the Rev. Arthur Roger Tomlinson, M.A., formerly Rector of St. Michael, Penkevil, afterwards Vicar of Bolton-le-Sands, Carnforth, co. Lancaster, by his wife Juliana Marie: *gt.-gdson*. to Rear-Admiral Sir W. Symonds, K.C.B., and nephew to the late Sir W.E. Tomlinson, Bart.: *b*. St. Michael Penkevil Rectory, co. Cornwall, 22 October 1891: *educ*. Westminster School; Trinity College, Cambridge (B.A.); on the outbreak of war was studying Marine Engineering (North Eastern College of Engineering): received his commission, August 1914, 2nd Lieut. South Staffordshire Regt. He had fought throughout the night of 25 October, and captured six German snipers, when he was wounded in the arm, and while being taken to the base hospital he was killed on the way by a shell, 26 October 1914, near Ypres. He was gazetted Lieut. after his death, which was not known for some months after it occurred, being recorded in the monthly casualty list of June 1915. Age 23. *unm*.

(Panel 35) L/Sergt. 13638, James Palmer, 8th (Service) Bn. The South Staffordshire Regt.: *s*. of the late James (& Emma) Palmer: late *husb*. to Florence Cartwright, *née* Palmer (64, Witton Lane, Hill Top, West Bromwich): *b*. Walsall, co. Stafford, 1878: enlisted West Bromwich: served with the Expeditionary Force in France from 14 July 1915. Killed in action, 12.05 a.m., 15–16 February 1916, when the battalion Dressing Station, Verbrandenmolen – in which he was being attended by Lieut. B.B. Gough, R.A.M.C. – was hit by a 8" shell. Age 37. Lieut. Gough, Lieut. T.Y. Birrell, and seven other men were also killed.

Lieuts. Gough and Birrell are buried in Woods Cemetery (I.C.1 & 3).

(Panel 35) Corpl. 8630, William Allen, 1st Bn. (38th Foot) The South Staffordshire Regt.: *s*. of John Allen, of 258, Stockbrook Street, Derby, by his wife Elizabeth: and brother to L/Corpl. 100976, T. Allen, Sherwood Foresters, who fell on 24 September 1915; Pte. 14164, E. Allen, Sherwood Foresters, fell 9 April 1917, and Pte. 16982, F. Allen, Northumberland Fusiliers, fell 27 March 1916: served with the Expeditionary Force, and was killed in action at Ypres, 30 October 1914. Age 26. *unm*.

His three brothers also have no known grave, they are also recorded on the Menin Gate: Thomas and Ernest (Panel 41), Frank (Panel 12).

(Panel 35) Corpl. 7537, Fred Blewitt, 1st Bn. (38th Foot) The South Staffordshire Regt.: *s*. of the late John Blewitt, by his wife Charlotte (Windmill Bank, Wombourne): and brother to Pte. 29680, J. Blewitt, 2nd South Staffordshire Regt., killed in action, 17 February 1917: *b*. Wolverhampton, co. Stafford, 1887: served with the Expeditionary Force in France and Flanders from 7 October 1914, and died on the 20th of that month of wounds received in action at Ypres. Age 27. *unm*.

His brother John also has no known grave, he is recorded on the Thiepval Memorial, Somme (Pier & Face 7B).

(Panel 35) Corpl. 2881, Frederick Phillips Pearson, 1/6th Bn. The South Staffordshire Regt. (T.F.): *yst. s*. of Edward Pearson, retired Draper; of Whitchurch, co. Salop, formerly of Waterloo, Liverpool, by his wife Maria, *dau*. of the late Thomas Phillips, of Chelmsford, Essex: *b*. Liverpool, 11 May 1880: *educ*. Merchant Taylor's School, Great Crosby: on leaving, entered the service of the National & Provincial Bank of England, Chester: joined 2nd (Volunteer) Battn. Cheshire Regt., and on the outbreak of the South African War, 1899, volunteered and served with 1st Volunteer Coy. of that Regt., throughout the campaign: Queen's Medal, 3 clasps. On the outbreak of the European War was Cashier, Wolverhampton Branch, National & Provincial Bank, and again volunteered for Active Service: joined 6th (Territorial) Battn. South Staffordshire Regt., Wolverhampton, September 1914: went to the Front, 3 March 1915, and was killed in action nr. Zillebeke, 7 July 1915. Buried in Sanctuary Wood. His Lieut. wrote, "A shell came over which did not explode but crashed in a dug-out burying two men, one of whom was lying in the debris wounded. Pearson and another man at once got to work to dig them out, and had just succeeded when another shell came over and a bit struck Pearson on the head. I took him up myself, but all to no purpose, he was hit badly. We all recognised his position, and others like him nobly served their country by joining in the ranks. He was actually killed in trying to save the life of other men, which, I take it, is the greatest thing a man can do. On all sides one hears the men talking about him, and there is no doubt he is a loss to the Regt." Age 35. *unm.* Remains recovered from a grave marked as belonging to an 'Unknown British Soldier. Cpl. S/Staffs.', (28.I.24.d.15.45) 30 January 1929; identified – Khaki, Titles, Stripes; reinterred, registered 13 February 1929. *Buried in Sanctuary Wood Cemetery (V.C.10).*

(Panel 35) L/Corpl. 7226, Sidney Dolphin, 2nd Bn. (80th Foot) The South Staffordshire Regt.: *s.* of the late William Dolphin, of 80, Arundel Street, Walsall, co. Stafford, and Emily Dolphin, his wife: and brother to Pte. 20454, W. Dolphin, 9th South Staffordshire Regt., died 12 November 1918, of wounds received in action east of the Piave: *b.* Walsall, 1887: enlisted Lichfield: served with the Expeditionary Force in France and Flanders from 13 August 1914, and was killed in action at Ypres, 27 October following: 27 October 1914. Age 27.

His brother William is buried in Tezze British Cemetery (V.B.9).

(Panel 35) Pte. 10179, Harry Barnes, 8th (Service) Bn. The South Staffordshire Regt.: *s.* of Henry 'Harry' Barnes, of 34, Gough Street, Wolverhampton, by his wife Harriett: and brother to AirMech. 408265, J.T. Barnes, died at home, 27 November 1918: enlisted Wolverhampton, co. Stafford: served with the Expeditionary Force, and was killed in action, 15 February 1916. Age 23. He was married to Elizabeth Anderson, *née* Barnes (7, Little Park Street, Wolverhampton).

His brother John is buried in Wolverhampton Borough Cemetery.

(Panel 35) Pte. 13583, Samuel Blackburn, 8th (Service) Bn. The South Staffordshire Regt.: *s.* of Mr (& Mrs) Blackburn: *b.* London: enlisted Wednesbury, co. Stafford. Killed in action, 12.05 a.m., 15–16 February 1916, when the battalion Dressing Station, Verbrandenmolen – in which he was being attended by Lieut. B.B. Gough, R.A.M.C. – was hit by a 8″ shell. Lieut. Gough, Lieut. T.Y. Birrell, L/Sergt. J. Palmer and six other men were also killed.

L/Sergt. Palmer also has no known grave, he is recorded above; Lieuts. Gough and Birrell are buried in Woods Cemetery (I.C.1 & 3).

(Panel 35) Pte. 9026, Alfred Breese, 1st Bn. (38th Foot) The South Staffordshire Regt.: *s.* of William (& Lucy) Breese, of 61, Collis Street, Amblecote, Stourbridge, co. Worcester: and elder brother to Pte. 13059, W. Breese, 3rd Worcestershire Regt., killed in action at Ypres, 7 January 1915: *b.* Wordsley, 1888: enlisted Brierley Hill: served in France from 7 October 1914, and was killed in action at the First Battle of Ypres, 7 November 1914. Age 26.

His brother William is buried in Messines Ridge British Cemetery (III.B.18).

(Panel 35) Pte. 2750, James Hay Copland, 1/6th Bn. The South Staffordshire Regt. (T.F.): *s.* of Archibald Copland, of Old Mill of Hirn, Banchory, co. Kincardine: *b.* Aberdeen, *c.*1881: enlisted Wolverhampton, co. Stafford: served with the Expeditionary Force. Killed in action, 6 July 1915. Age 34. Remains recovered from a grave marked up as belonging to an 'Unknown British Soldier. S/Staffs.', (28.I.24.d.15.45) 30 January 1929; identified – Khaki, Titles; reinterred, registered 13 February 1929. *Buried in Sanctuary Wood Cemetery (V.C.11).*

(Panel 35) Pte. 8406, Charles Henry Farrington, 'B' Coy., 1st Bn. (38th Foot) The South Staffordshire Regt.: 2nd *s.* of George Edward Farrington, Iron Caster; of 198, Frederick Street, Walsall, by his wife Isabella, *dau.* of William Higgs: *b.* Walsall, co. Stafford, 6 April 1892: *educ.* Wolverhampton Road School: enlisted, 5 May 1908: served with the Expeditionary Force in France and Flanders from 2 October to 7 November 1914, on which later date he was killed in action at Ypres. Age 25. *unm.*

(Panel 35) Pte. 7868, John Haines, 2nd Bn. (80th Foot) The South Staffordshire Regt.: late of Tenby, co. Worcester: brother to Mrs F.M. Gardiner (13, Rutland Road, The Meadows, Nottingham): and Pte. 8613, W. Haines, 1st South Staffordshire Regt., killed in action, 26 October 1914: *b.* Enville, co. Stafford: enlisted Wolverhampton. Killed in action, 28 October 1914. Age 26.

His brother William also has no known grave; he is recorded below.

(Panel 35) Pte. 8613, William Haines, 1st Bn. (38th Foot) The South Staffordshire Regt.: late of Walsall Wood, co. Stafford: brother to Mrs F.M. Gardiner (13, Rutland Road, The Meadows, Nottingham): and

Pte. 7868, J. Haines, 2nd South Staffordshire Regt., killed in action, 28 October 1914: *b.* Aldridge, co. Stafford: enlisted Lichfield. Killed in action, 26 October 1914.

His brother John also has no known grave; he is recorded above.

(Panel 35) Pte. 14980, Joseph Ingate, 'B' Coy., 8th (Service) Bn. The South Staffordshire Regt.: 2nd *s.* of Walter Ingate, Fisherman; of 4, Council Houses, Hsunkigh Street, Tollesbury, co. Essex, by his wife Grace, *dau.* of Joseph Spooner: and brother to 4050B, W.W. Ingate, R.N.R.; one of 48 men lost in action when H.M.S. 'Hogue,' was torpedoed and sunk by the German submarine U.9, 22 September 1914; two other ships H.M.S. 'Aboukir' and 'Cressy' were also sunk; all three were lost in the space of one hour at a cost of 1,459 lives: *b.* Tollesbury, 27 July 1887: *educ.* Tollesbury Board School: Occupation – Fisherman: volunteered and enlisted, 7 September 1914: went to France the following July, attached to the bombing section, and was killed in action at Ypres, 11 February 1916, when acting as a bomber. Buried south-west of Verbranden-Molen. Age 28. *unm.*

His brother Walter has no known grave but the sea; he is commemorated on the Chatham Naval Memorial (8).

(Panel 35) Pte. 10221, Frederick Pace, 8th (Service) Bn. The South Staffordshire Regt.: *b.* Eccleshall, co. Stafford: enlisted Walsall: served with the Expeditionary Force in France, and was killed in action, 12.05 a.m., 15–16 February 1916 when the Battalion Dressing Station, Verbrandenmolen – in which he was being attended by Lieut. B.B. Gough, R.A.M.C. – was hit by a 8″ shell. Age 43. He was married to Mrs G.A. Stringer, *née* Pace (2, Back, 114, Bath Street, Walsall). See L/Sergt. J. Palmer (above).

(Panel 35) Pte. 9010, Alfred Perry, 1/5th Bn. The South Staffordshire Regt. (T.F.): enlisted Bloxwich, co. Stafford: served with the Expeditionary Force from 3 March 1915; killed in action, 2 August 1915. Remains recovered from a grave marked as belonging to an 'Unknown British Soldier. S.Staffs', (28.I.34.a.7.2); identified – Titles, Clothing, Gold Ring engrvd. P.A.; reinterred, registered, 6 October 1927. *Buried in Sanctuary Wood Cemetery (IV.H.19).*

(Panel 35) Pte. 7951, Jim Pumfrey, 1st Bn. (38th Foot) The South Staffordshire Regt.: *s.* of Charles Pumfrey, of Court Street, Upton-on-Severn, co. Worcester, by his wife Mary Ann: and brother to Pte. 8873, T. Pumfrey, South Staffordshire Regt., who fell in the same action; Spr. 1384, C. Pumfrey, Australian Tunnelling Corps, killed in action, 26 June 1916; and Corpl. 1383, A. Pumfrey, Australian Tunnelling Corps, (surv'd.): enlisted Birmingham. Killed in action, 28 October 1914. One of three brothers who fell. Remembered on Upton-on-Severn (St. Peter & St. Paul's) Church War Memorial.

His brother Tom also has no known grave, he is recorded below; Charles is buried in Kemmel Chateau Military Cemetery (X.8).

(Panel 35) Pte. 8873, Tom Pumfrey, 1st Bn. (38th Foot) The South Staffordshire Regt.: *s.* of Charles Pumfrey, of Court Street, Upton-on-Severn, co. Worcester, by his wife Mary Ann: and brother to Pte. 7951, J. Pumfrey, South Staffordshire Regt., who fell in the same action; Spr. 1384, C. Pumfrey, Australian Tunnelling Corps, killed in action, 26 June 1916; and Corpl. 1383, A. Pumfrey, Australian Tunnelling Corps (surv'd.): enlisted Worcester. Killed in action, 28 October 1914. One of three brothers who fell. Remembered on Upton-on-Severn (St. Peter & St. Paul's) Church War Memorial.

His brother Jim also has no known grave, he is recorded above; Charles is buried in Kemmel Chateau Military Cemetery (X.8).

PANEL 35 ENDS PTE. W.T. REEVES, SOUTH STAFFORDSHIRE REGT.

PANEL 37 BEGINS PTE. A.E. RICHARDS, SOUTH STAFFORDSHIRE REGT.

(Panel 37) Lieut. Edmund Morton Mansel-Pleydell, 3rd (Reserve) Bn. The Dorsetshire Regt. attd. 3rd Bn. Worcestershire Regt.: *s.* of the late Lieut.Col. Edmund M. Mansel-Pleydell, D.L., J.P., late 12th Lancers and Dorset Yeomanry, of Whatcombe, Blandford, co. Dorset, by his wife Emily Kathleen Mansel-Pleydell, *née* Grove (13, Foulis Terrace, South Kensington, London), *dau.* of Sir Thomas Fraser Grove, 1st Bart.: *gt.-gdson.* to Sir William (& Louisa) Mansel, 9th Bart, of Muddlescombe; *gdson.* to naturalist and author, John Clavell Mansel- Pleydell; and elder brother to Lieut. H.G.M. Mansel-Pleydell, M.C., 1st Dorsetshire Regt., killed in action, 17 May 1916: *b.* 23 December 1886. Killed in action, 12 March 1915. Age 28. *unm.* His cousin 2nd Lieut. J.M. Mansel-Pleydell, Royal Field Artillery, also fell.

His brother Henry is buried in Miraumont Communal Cemetery (A.5); cousin John, St. Pierre Cemetery, Amiens (V.B.4).

(Panel 37) Sergt. 8258, Henry Martin Oliver, 1st Bn. (39th Foot) The Dorsetshire Regt.: *s.* of William Oliver, of Cole's Ground, Langton Matravers, co. Dorset, by his wife Emily: and brother to Pte. 8572, C.R. Oliver, 2nd Battn., who fell at Ctesiphon, Mesopotamia, 22 November 1915: *b.* Bishops Caundle, c.1887: enlisted Sherborne: served with the Expeditionary Force in France from 16 August 1914, took part in much subsequent fighting, and was killed in action at Ypres, 14 March 1915. Age 27. He was married to Maude Caundle, *née* Oliver (New Road, Piddletown, co. Dorset). Unveiled in August 1920, in the form of a large Purbeck stone cairn standing atop a high bank overlooking the Solent, the Swanage War Memorial bears the names of 99 Swanage men who gave their lives in the Great War; Sergt. Oliver and his brother are but two of those recorded thereon.

His brother Charles also has no known grave; he is commemorated on the Basra Memorial, Iraq.

(Panel 37) Corpl. 9816, Charles Frederick Harrison, 5th (Service) Bn. The Dorsetshire Regt.: *s.* of John Harrison, of 45, Toronto Road, Leytonstone, London, by his wife Emily: and yr. brother to Corpl. 78453, S.J. Harrison, 17th Bde. Royal Field Artillery, killed in action, 27 April 1917: *b.* Stratford: enlisted Dorchester. Killed in action, 14 August 1917. Age 20.

His brother Sydney is buried in Faubourg d'Amiens Cemetery (IV.D.17).

(Panel 37) Pte. 3/7809, Frederick James Allen, 1st Bn. (39th Foot) The Dorsetshire Regt.: *s.* of Mrs O. Allen (4, George Street, Salisbury, co. Wilts): and elder brother to Pte. 6143, S.C. Allen, Dorsetshire Regt., who fell, 9 September 1914, nr. Chateau Thierry: *b.* Poole, co. Dorset. Killed in action, 6 November 1914, at Ypres. Age 39.

His brother Sidney is buried in Montreuil-aux-Lions British Cemetery (II.B.1).

(Panel 37) Pte. 12617, Frederick George Haskett, 5th (Service) Bn. The Dorsetshire Regt.: *s.* of the late Alfred Haskett, by his wife Harriet (75, Bedchester, Shaftesbury, co. Dorset): and brother to Pte. 34258, H.C. Haskett, Royal Berkshire Regt., killed in action, 21 March 1918: *b.* Weymouth: enlisted Shaftesbury. Killed in action, 13 June 1917. Age 20. *unm.*

His brother Harry also has no known grave; he is commemorated on the Pozieres Memorial.

(Panel 37) Pte. 3/8167, Alfred Roland Hatherell, 1st Bn. (39th Foot) The Dorsetshire Regt.: formerly no.11900, Somerset Light Infantry: *s.* of Alfred Hatherell, of 17, Pembroke Road, Shirehampton, Bristol: and elder brother to Pte. PO/1677(S), F. Hatherell, 2nd Bn. Royal Marine Light Infantry, killed in action, 26 October 1917, at Passchendaele: *b.* Shirehampton, co. Gloucester: enlisted Bristol. Killed in action, 3 May 1915, at the Second Battle of Ypres. Age 20. *unm.*

His brother Frank also has no known grave; he is commemorated on the Tyne Cot Memorial (Panel 1).

(Panel 37) Pte. 3/6575, Harold Mead, 1st Bn. (39th Foot) The Dorsetshire Regt.: *s.* of Albert Mead, of Knowle, West Knoyle, Mere, co. Wilts, by his wife Letitia. Killed in action, 13 November 1914. Age 16. One of forty-eight names recorded on Mere War Memorial.

(Panel 37) Pte. 3/7338, Erasmus Lionel Trickett, 1st Bn. (39th Foot) The Dorsetshire Regt.: late of Wimborne, co. Dorset: *s.* of Mark Trickett, of Ford View, Ferndown, co. Dorset: and elder brother to Pte. 3/7339, W.A. Trickett, Dorsetshire Regt., killed in action, 1 May 1915: *b.* Bournemouth: enlisted Poole. Killed in action, 23 February 1915. Age 22.

(Panel 37) Pte. 3/7339, William Arthur Trickett, 1st Bn. (39th Foot) The Dorsetshire Regt.: late of Wimborne, co. Dorset: *s.* of Mark Trickett, of Ford View, Ferndown, co. Dorset: and yr. brother to Pte. 3/7338, E.L. Trickett, Dorsetshire Regt., killed in action 23 February 1915: *b.* Branksome: enlisted Poole. Killed in action, 1 May 1915. Age 20.

(Panel 37) Pte. 9795, Eric Widmer, 1st Bn. (39th Foot) The Dorsetshire Regt.: *s.* of Emil Widmer, of 48, Canning Road, Walthamstow, London, E., by his wife Henrietta: *b.* Manchester: enlisted Stratford, London: served with the Expeditionary Force in France, and died, 2 May 1915. Age 16.

(Panel 37) Lieut.Col. Malcolm Charles Andrew Green, The Prince of Wales's Volunteers (South Lancashire Regt.): *s*. of the late Col. Malcolm S. Green, 3rd Scinde Horse: *gdson*. to Sir Andrew Pellet Green, who commanded H.M.S. 'Collingwood,' at Trafalgar: *b*. St. George's Road, London, S.W., 2 July 1871: *educ*. Oxford Military College; and Royal Military College, Sandhurst: received his commission South Lancashire Regt. (old 82nd Foot), 5 December 1891: promoted Lieut. 1 August 1894; Capt. 1 April 1900; Major 16 May 1909: served in India, and the South African War 1900; being present at operations in Natal, including the action at Laing's Nek, and operations in Cape Colony (Queen's Medal, four clasps). On the outbreak of the Great War, Lieut.Col. Green was serving at Tidmouth, having just previously been in command of the depot of his regiment at Warrington with the newly-formed Army, but received his orders to proceed on service to take command of his battalion, and was killed in the trenches near Ypres, 17 November 1914. Age 43. Lieut. Col. Green, who was a member of the United Services Club, Pall Mall, married Miss Elsie Bisdee, and left three sons, age five, three, and two years respectively at the time of their father's death.

(Panel 37) Capt. Reginald Charles Falconer Salter, 2nd Bn. (82nd Foot) The Prince of Wales's Volunteers (South Lancashire Regt.): only *s*. of the late Henry Sidney Salter, by his wife Alexandrina, *née* Watson (68, Crediton Hill, Hampstead, London, N.W.): *b*. 13 August, 1888: *educ*. Merchant Taylors' School: received his commission, Regular Army, from 3rd London Bde., Royal Field Artillery (T.F.), May 1912; his Battery (7th) won the King's Prize for Artillery Competition, 1911, for which he received a gold medal: promoted Lieut. April 1914; Capt. 15 May 1915. At the outbreak of the Great War was serving as Second in Command, Divisional Cyclist Corps, and proceeded to France, August 1914, for Active Service with the contingent: took part in the Battle of Mons, and operations subsequent to the great retirement, including the Battle of Le Cateau, also the Marne and the Aisne: later rejoined his Battalion, and served at the battles of Neuve Chapelle, Ypres, Hill 60, and Hooge. Capt. Salter was killed on 8 June 1915, while directing trench digging at night outside Ypres. Age 26. *unm*. Remains exhumed from a grave marked as belonging to an 'Unknown British Captain. S. Lancs', located in Sanctuary Wood Old Cemetery (28.I.24.b.90.97); identified – Officer's Clothing, Badge of Rank, Buttons, Locket; reinterred, registered 9 May 1928. *Buried in Sanctuary Wood Cemetery (II.G.20).*

Only Son Of Henry Sidney And Ina Salter Of Hampstead

(Panel 37) Capt. Charles Norman Wheeler, 2nd Bn. (82nd Foot) The Prince of Wales's Volunteers (South Lancashire Regt.): eldest *s*. of Dr. Francis Darkins Wheeler, M.A., LL.D., of Bracondale Cottage, Hellesdon, Norwich, by his marriage to the late Nellie Dakin: and *gdson*. to the late W.H. Dakin, Esq., of Norwich: *b*. 1 March 1881: *educ*. Bracondale School, Norwich, and London University, where he took his degrees B.A. and B.Sc., with Honours in English and French: Occupation – Master; Liverpool Institute for several years; affectionately called 'Pop' by the boys there (a reference to the chemical experiments he conducted in his laboratory): joined O.T.C. 1910; became Capt. 1911: applied for an Army appointment on the outbreak of war: informed his work at the School was of greater importance, but, after persisting in his application, was gazetted 2nd Lieut. 3rd (Reserve) Battn. South Lancashire Regt. November 1914: transf'd./attd. 2nd Battn. December following: went to Caterham, from whence he took a draft of his Battalion to France. Capt. Wheeler was killed on 7 January 1915, on the occasion of his first spell of duty in the trenches. He went to the assistance of a comrade who had been wounded by machine-gun fire, and was himself immediately killed by a shot from the same gun. Age 33. *unm*. The first and eldest former Bracondale student to die in the Great War. Memorial Cross recovered, 2 February 1920; Messines Ridge British Cemetery. Recording the names of Capt. Wheeler, Ptes. 10734, J. Barry; 2018, W. Diamond; 2499, J. Fitzsimmons; 2793, R. Johnson; 11850, W. Makin; 1395, C. Southern; and L/Corpl. 6967, R. Butterton; no remains were recovered. (*IWGC record age 32*)

(Panel 37) Lieut. Edmund Lionel Frost, 4th Bn. The Prince of Wales's Volunteers (South Lancashire Regt.), (T.F.): only *s*. of Edmund Frost, of Chesterfield, Meads, Eastbourne, M.D., Mast. Surg., etc., by his wife Mary Elizabeth, 2nd *dau*. of the late Walter Theobalds, of Birkenhead, Cheshire: *b*. Lasswade, Midlothian, 30 May 1891: *educ*. Dover College Junior School, and Uppingham (Praeposter, Captain of

Games, Captain of the School Football and Hockey teams, Captain of his House – Fircroft, and Champion Heavy Weight Boxer; passed his 'Little Go' at the age of 16), remained at Uppingham until old enough to go on to Cambridge University (Trinity College) – graduated with honours in Natural Sciences Tripos, 1912, and, during his three years there, obtained sixteen medals, two silver spoons, a cup and three oars, for Boxing, Rifle & Revolver Shooting, and Sports. He was the 'Varsity champion heavy weight boxer in 1910, for which he received his half blue, and gained another half blue for Rifle Shooting. He only became a 'wet bob' his last year, but so excellent an oarsman was he that he narrowly missed inclusion in the Cambridge Crew of that year; as it was he was awarded the Trial Eights Cup. He was Captain of the 'Varsity Revolver Team and obtained the ninth place in the International Revolver Championship, N.R.A., Bisley, 1912: he made a remarkable record in marksmanship with a revolver, by scoring 82 out of a possible 84, under service conditions. On leaving Cambridge he became actively associated with the firm of Messrs Peter Stubs Ltd., File & Steel & Tool Manufacturers, Warrington, of which his uncle, Mr A. Frost, was Chairman and Managing Director. The following year, 1913, he went to France with the object of perfecting his knowledge of the language and coming into touch with the Continental trade of the Company. He received a commission in the 4th (Territorial) Battn. South Lancashire Regt. 1 November 1912, and on the outbreak of war volunteered for Foreign Service: promoted Lieut. 24 September 1914: went to France, 11 February 1915, and was killed in action at Hooge, Flanders, 16 June 1915. On this occasion his Battn., with three other regts., assaulted the German position at Hooge and carried three trenches at the point of the bayonet; and the Brigadier-General, addressing the Battn. after the battle, said, "The Battalion did splendidly. You have proved that the 4th South Lancashires can never be broken." Lieut. Frost was shot through the head and, though he lived ¾ of an hour, never regained consciousness. He was buried in Sanctuary Wood, near Ypres. Major Crosfield wrote, "I was speaking to him only ten minutes before, and though we were in the thick of it, he was just as bright and cheery as ever. The whole Battn. mourns his loss." The Rev. W. Bracecamp, Chaplain to the Battn., wrote, "When the Battalion left to make the charge he was thoroughly cheery and said to me, 'Good-bye Padre. We shall soon meet again.' Your son was one of the finest characters it has ever been my privilege to meet. He was beloved by officers and men alike. His fine physique, his noble character, endeared him to everybody. He was one of the noble fellows whose life could not be spared, but he has voluntarily laid it down in a noble cause for God, King and Country." Lieut. Frost had travelled a great deal in company with his father, both in Europe, America, and the Far West. Age 24. *unm.*

(Panel 37) Lieut. Bernard Vincent Fulcher, M.C., 2nd Bn. (82nd Foot) The Prince of Wales's Volunteers (South Lancashire Regt.): *s.* of William Popplewell Fulcher, of 'Walton,' 85, Wimbledon Hill Road, Wimbledon, London, S.W.: *b.* Lorne House, Great Yarmouth, 22 January 1892: *educ.* Wimbledon College; King's College School, 1906–10, where he was Capt. of the VIII (shooting); also in the First XV (football) 1909–10; and member of the O.T.C., and was 'efficient' for 3 years, holding the 'A' certificate: entered Royal Military College, Sandhurst, 1910: gazetted 2nd Lieut. South Lancashire Regt. 20 September 1911; promoted Lieut. 16 July 1913: served with the Expeditionary Force in France and Flanders from August 1914. Twice Mentioned in Despatches (8 October 1914; 14 January 1915; *London Gazette*, 19 October 1914; 17 February 1915) by F.M. Sir John (now Lord) French, for 'gallant and distinguished service in the field;' awarded the Military Cross, in the latter month, but he did not live to personally receive the decoration, having been killed in a dug-out by a shell, 17 November 1914, at Ypres, being at the time the only surviving officer of his battalion. Major Baird, Commanding 1st Gordon Highlanders, who was for fifteen days, 5th–20th November, in command of the line of trenches in which Lieut. Fulcher met his death, wrote to his mother saying, "I wish to tell you how nobly your boy was doing his duty when he met his death ... Your son was quite indefatigable in doing his duty under conditions the difficulties of which can never be fully realised except by those who were there ... Often I used to feel that he was destined to go far in our profession ... None of us who served together in those fifteen strenuous days will ever forget his splendid work. As officer commanding that particular section of the trenches, I have officially brought to notice the very splendid way in which his conduct was distinguished." The late Head Master of King's College School also wrote, "He was with us just the best kind of English boy, straight and loyal and keen…with a healthy influence with his friends and all the school." The Adjutant and other officers, and also men in the ranks, wrote most feelingly, saying how all appreciated his courage and capacity. Age 22. *unm.*

(Panel 37) 2nd Lieut. Ralph Leicester Breckell, 3rd (Reserve) Bn. The Prince of Wales's Volunteers (South Lancashire Regt.) attd. 2nd Bn. Lancashire Fusiliers: 2nd *s.* of Edward John Blease Breckell, of Holmdene, Alexandra Road, Waterloo, nr. Liverpool, by his wife Emilia Mary, only child of the late Charles Oddie, of Everton, Liverpool: *b.* West Derby, nr. Liverpool, 16 April 1890: *educ.* Ellesmere College, Shropshire: Occupation – Resident Secretary (Liverpool); British Crown Insurance Company: consequent to the outbreak of war joined 18th (Service) Battn. King's Liverpool Regt., September 1914; gazetted 2nd Lieut. 3rd South Lancashire Reggt., 20 February 1915, being later attd. 2nd Lancashire Fusiliers at the front. Killed in action on the canal between Pilckem and Boesinghe, during the severe fighting, 5–9 July 1915. His orderly, Pte. E. Murphy wrote, "He died fighting like a true English gentleman, being in charge of a party of bomb throwers who held on to such a purpose that they were piling themselves on top of one another, and I am very pleased to tell you that he did not suffer more than a minute, just calling my name like this 'Oh, Murphy', then I caught him and laid him down and as near as I could make out he said a few prayers, and then passed peacefully away looking as if he had gone to sleep," and added that he had been killed by a piece of shrapnel in line with his left shoulder striking his heart. Age 25. *unm.* (*IWGC record 9 July*)

(Panel 37) 2nd Lieut. Leigh Holden, 4th Bn. The Prince of Wales's Volunteers (South Lancashire Regt.), (T.F.): *s.* of Harry Holden, of The Cottage, Thelwall, co. Chester, by his wife Harriet, *née* Palmer. Killed in action, 9 June 1915. Age 29. Remains recovered from a grave marked as belonging to an 'Unknown British Officer. 2/Lieut. S. Lancs.', located in Sanctuary Wood Old Cemetery, (28.I.24.b.90.97) identified – Clothing, Badge of Rank, Buttons; reinterred, registered 4 May 1928. *Buried in Sanctuary Wood Cemetery (II.F.32).*

Thou Wilt Keep Him In Perfect Peace

(Panel 37) Coy.Sergt.Major, 7991, Ernest Brazileir, 2nd Bn. (82nd Foot) The Prince of Wales's Volunteers (South Lancashire Regt.): *b.* Manchester, *c.*1888: enlisted Warrington, co. Lancaster. Killed in action, 25 June 1915. Age 36. Remains recovered from a grave marked as belonging to an 'Unknown British Q.M. Sergt. South Lancs.', located in Sanctuary Wood Old Cemetery, (28.I.24.b.90.97) 'Unknown British Q.M. Sergt. South Lancs;' identified – Clothing, Titles, Badge of Rank; reinterred, registered 3 May 1928. *Buried in Sanctuary Wood Cemetery (II.F.29).*

In Loving Memory

(Panel 37) Sergt. 7995, George Caldicott, D.C.M., M.M., (Actg./Coy.Sergt.Major.), 2nd Bn. (82nd Foot) The Prince of Wales's Volunteers (South Lancashire Regt.): 2nd & only *survg. s.* of George Caldicott, Corporation Engine Driver; of Yardley, by his wife Jane: *b.* Marston Green, nr. Birmingham, 17 July 1889: *educ.* Yardley: enlisted, 15 March 1905; served three years in England; six years in India: obtained his discharge, and joined the Reserve, 7 March 1914: Occupation – Rubber Worker: called up on the outbreak of war, August following: served with the Expeditionary Force in France from the 13th: took part in the Retreat from Mons: wounded at La Bassee, September; returned to the Front, March 1915, and died, 15 June 1917, from wounds received in action at Messines Ridge, Belgium. Buried about 1,000 yards east of Messines. Age 27. Lieut.Col. D.L. Maxwell wrote, "Your husband was the bravest man I ever knew. I had already sent his name in for a bar to his D.C.M. for his splendid work on Messines Ridge. He died like the brave soldier he was – face to the foe, leading his platoon to the attack;" and Capt. R. Nevill, "I cannot speak too highly of the excellent work he has done during the time he has been in my company. I had the greatest confidence in him, and he always carried out his work cheerfully and conscientiously. His loss is a very great one." He was awarded the D.C.M. in September 1916; Military Medal, 7 June 1917, for conspicuous gallantry in the field. He *m.* West Bromwich, Birmingham, 14 March 1914; Maud Winifred (Birmingham), *dau.* of the late Edward Cross, of Spark Hill, Birmingham.

(Panel 37) Sergt. 240888, Richard Underwood, 1/5th Bn. The Prince of Wales's Volunteers (South Lancashire Regt.), (T.F.): *s.* of Richard Underwood, of 7, Hale View Road, Huyton Quarry, Liverpool, by his wife Ann: and brother to L/Corpl. 267349, G. Underwood, 2nd Monmouthshire Regt.; killed in action, 12 April 1918: *b.* Liverpool: enlisted Prescot, co. Lancaster. Killed in action, 31 July 1917. Age 32.

His brother George also has no known grave; he is commemorated on the Ploegsteert Memorial (Panel 10).

(Panel 37) L/Corpl. 1978, William Joseph Bridge, D.C.M., 2nd Bn. (82nd Foot) The Prince of Wales's Volunteers (South Lancashire Regt.): *s.* of the late William Bridge, and Edith (76, Wellington Road, Wavertree, Liverpool) his spouse: late *husb.* to Annie Perkins, *née* Bridge (6, Wellington Road); since remarried: and brother to Pte. 201430, C. Bridge, 2nd King's (Liverpool) Regt., died 2 October 1918, of wounds: *educ.* Trinity School, Wavertree: enlisted Liverpool: served with the Expeditionary Force in France and Flanders from August 1914, and was killed in action, 16 June 1917. Age 20.

His brother Charles is buried in Sunken Road Cemetery, Boisleux-St. Marc (III.F.5).

(Panel 37) L/Corpl. 1899, William Leah, 1/4th Bn. The Prince of Wales's Volunteers (South Lancashire Regt.), (T.F.): *s.* of Mrs Cumberlidge, *née* Leah (7, Lloyd Street, Mill Lane, Warrington), and the late Walter Leah: *b.* Warrington, co. Lancaster: enlisted there. Killed in action, 11 July 1915. Age 21. Remains recovered from a grave marked as belonging to an 'Unknown British Lance Corporal', located in Sanctuary Wood Old Cemetery, (28.I.24.b.90.97) identified – Clothing, Badge of Rank; reinterred, registered 4 May 1928. *Buried in Sanctuary Wood Cemetery (II.F.31).*

(Panel 37) Pte. 31362, John William Bird, 7th (Service) Bn. The Prince of Wales's Volunteers (South Lancashire Regt.): formerly no.47073, South Staffordshire Regt.: *s.* of the late Joseph Bird, Miner (*d.*1895); stepson to Alfred Woods, by his marriage to Sarah Eliza Bird, *née* Goodall: *b.* Fulwood, 7 November 1889. Killed in action, 13 June 1917. Age 27. The *Notts Free Press*, 14 June 1918, carried the following memoriam verse from his step-father, mother, brothers and sisters:-

> *No one knows the parting. Or what that parting cost;*
> *But God in His great mercy, has gained what we have lost.*
> *'Tis sweet to know we'll meet again, Where partings are no more;*
> *And that the one we loved so well, Has only gone before.*

(Panel 37) Pte. 31790, Isaac Cooper, 7th (Service) Bn. The Prince of Wales's Volunteers (South Lancashire Regt.): *s.* of Isaac Cooper, of 13, Warrington Road, Ashton-in-Makerfield, Wigan, co. Lancaster, by his wife Mary Ellen: and yr. brother to L/Sergt. 9744, E. Cooper, Lancashire Fusiliers, who fell one week previously: *b.* Lowton, co. Lancaster, about 1898: enlisted Ashton-in-Makerfield. Killed in action, 14 June 1917. Age 19.

His brother Edmund also has no known grave; he is recorded on Panel 33.

(Panel 37) Pte. 1814, John Thomas Coyne, 1/4th Bn. The Prince of Wales's Volunteers (South Lancashire Regt.), (T.F.): *s.* of John T. Coyne, of 159, Longford Street, Warrington, co. Lancaster, by his wife Elizabeth: and yr. brother to Pte. 2350, W. Coyne, 1/4th South Lancashire Regt., killed in action, 25 September 1915: *b.* Warrington: enlisted there: served with the Expeditionary Force in France from 14 February 1915, and was killed in action, 16 June 1915. Age 21.

His brother William also has no known grave; he is recorded below.

(Panel 37) Pte. 2350, William Coyne, 1/4th Bn. The Prince of Wales's Volunteers (South Lancashire Regt.), (T.F.): *s.* of John T. Coyne, of 159, Longford Street, Warrington, co. Lancaster, by his wife Elizabeth: and elder brother to Pte. 1814, J.T. Coyne, 1/4th South Lancashire Regt., killed in action, 16 June 1915: *b.* Warrington: enlisted there: served with the Expeditionary Force in France from 14 February 1915, and was killed in action, 25 September 1915. Age 29.

His brother John also has no known grave; he is recorded above.

(Panel 37) Pte. 22464, Frederick Crowley, 2nd Bn. (82nd Foot) The South Lancashire Regt.: *s.* of Thomas (& Catherine Ann) Crowley: c/o R. Crowley Esq., 9, Onward Street, Hyde, co. Chester: *b.* Hyde: enlisted there. Killed in action, 2 August 1917. Age 25. Buried Near This Spot. Remains recovered

'Unknown British Soldier, 2/S.Lancs' unmarked grave (28.J.1.c.20.05), identified – Titles, Spoon, Knife marked 136; reinterred 18 January 1924. *Buried in Poelcapelle British Cemetery (LX.D.7).*

(Panel 37) Pte. 16095, Edward Davies, 3rd (Reserve) attd 8th (Service) Bn. The Prince of Wales's Volunteers (South Lancashire Regt.): *s.* of Edward Davies, Passenger Guard, Cheshire Lines Railway; of 4, Back Brook Street, Chester, by his wife Mary Ann, *dau.* of Samuel Marks: *b.* Chester, December 1897: *educ.* Christ Church Schools, Chester: Occupation – Printer & Stationer's Assistant: enlisted in September 1916: served with the Expeditionary Force in France and Flanders from February 1917, and was killed in action, 24 June following. Buried on the battlefield. Age 19.

(Panel 37) Pte. 12512, Allan Cameron Gore, 2nd Bn. (82nd Foot) The Prince of Wales's Volunteers (South Lancashire Regt.): *s.* of Mary Gore (Liverpool, co. Chester): *b.* Walton, Liverpool, *c.*1891. Killed in action, 2 August 1917. Age 26. Pte. Gore leaves a widow, Ellen (10, Ashton Street, Pembroke Place, Liverpool). *Buried in Poelcapelle British Cemetery (Sp.Mem.LX.D.1).*

Ever Remembered By His Loving Wife And Children

(Panel 37) Pte. 11673, George Gray, 2nd Bn. (82nd Foot) The Prince of Wales's Volunteers (South Lancashire Regt.): *s.* of William Gray, of 69, Manor Street, Peasley Cross, St. Helen's, co. Lancaster. Killed, 14 September 1915, in company with 2nd Lieuts. A.F. Ventris and R. Lodge, by the explosion of a shrapnel shell. Age 23. *unm.* At the time of his death Pte. Gray was Officer's Servant (Batman) to 2nd Lieut. Lodge. 2nd Lieuts. Ventris and Lodge are buried in Birr Crossroads Cemetery (II.D.4&5).

(Panel 37) Pte. 28745, Harold Harrison, 2nd Bn. (82nd Foot) The Prince of Wales's Volunteers (South Lancashire Regt.): *b.* Stalybridge, co. Chester: enlisted there. Killed in action, 2 August 1917. *Buried in Poelcapelle British Cemetery (LX.D.18).*

(Panel 37) Pte. 2380, George Hart, 'C' Coy., 1/4th Bn. The Prince of Wales's Volunteers (South Lancashire Regt.), (T.F.): *s.* of George (& Mrs) Hart of 4, Eustace Street, Warrington, co. Chester: enlisted, Warrington: served with the Expeditionary Force in France, and was killed in action, 27 June 1915. Age 16.

(Panel 37) Pte. 19438, David Hickman, 2nd Bn. (82nd Foot) The Prince of Wales's Volunteers (South Lancashire Regt.): late of Manchester: *b.* Warrington, co. Lancaster: enlisted Knutsford, co. Chester. Killed in action, 2 August 1917. *Buried in Poelcapelle British Cemetery (Sp.Mem.LX.D.2).*

(Panel 37) Pte. 29551, Edward Holden, 2nd Bn. (82nd Foot) The Prince of Wales's Volunteers (South Lancashire Regt.): *s.* of the late James (& Mrs) Holden, of St. Helen's, co. Lancaster. Killed in action, 2 August 1917. Age 34. He was married to Mary J. Neary, *née* Holden (35, Stanley Street, St. Helen's). *Buried in Poelcapelle British Cemetery (LX.D.20).*

(Panel 37) Pte. 2477, John Livingston, 1/4th Bn. The Prince of Wales's Volunteers (South Lancashire Regt.), (T.F.): *b.* Warrington, co. Lancaster: enlisted there. Killed in action, 8 June 1915. Remains recovered from a grave marked up as belonging to an 'Unknown British Soldier. S.Lancs', located in Sanctuary Wood Old Cemetery, (28.I.24.b.90.97) identified – Clothing; reinterred, registered 4 May 1928. *Buried in Sanctuary Wood Cemetery (II.F.33).*

(Panel 37) Pte. 32107, Edward Arthur Phipps, 'A' Coy., 7th (Service) Bn. The Prince of Wales's Volunteers (South Lancashire Regt.): *s.* of J.W. (& Mrs) Phipps, of 49 Military Road, Dover: and yr. brother to Pte. 32108, J.W. Phipps, 2nd South Lancashire Regt., killed in action, 21 August 1918; Pte. G/5360, C. Phipps, 7th East Kent Regt., killed in action, 1 July 1916, at the Somme; and L/Corpl. 8713, F.E. Phipps, 2nd East Kent Regt., died of wounds, 5 April 1915, in the Base Hospital, Rouen: served with the Expeditionary Force, and was killed in action, 3 August 1917. Age 29. *unm.* A fifth brother also served.

His brothers James and Charles also have no known grave, they are commemorated on the Tyne Cot Memorial (Panel 93) and Thiepval Memorial (Pier & Face 5D) respectively; Frederick is buried in St. Sever Cemetery (A.7.10).

(Panel 37) Pte. 16014, Amos Pickering, 2nd Bn. (82nd Foot) The Prince of Wales's Volunteers (South Lancashire Regt.): enlisted Wigan, co. Lancaster. Killed in action, 24 June 1915. *Buried in Sanctuary Wood Cemetery (II.F.30).*

(Panel 37) Pte. 2200, William Pigott, 1/5th Bn. The Prince of Wales's Volunteers (South Lancashire Regt.), (T.F.): *s.* of the late Ralph Pigott, by his wife Margaret (95, Prescot Road, St. Helen's, co. Lancaster). Killed in action, 5 May 1915. Age 17. *Buried in Bedford House Cemetery (I.C.4/Enc.No.6).*

(Panel 37) Pte. 27210, Reuben Wagner, 2nd Bn. (82nd Foot) The Prince of Wales's Volunteers (South Lancashire Regt.): *b.* Manchester: enlisted Stockport. Killed in action, 2 August 1917. *Buried in Poelcapelle British Cemetery (LX.D.12).*

Psalm 17 – 15th Verse "I Shall Be Satisfied When I Awake With Thy Likeness"

(Panel 37) Capt. Waldo Alington Gwennap Moore, 2nd Bn. (69th Foot) The Welsh Regt.: 2nd *s.* of Gwennap Moore, of Garlenick, Grampound, co. Cornwall, by his wife Mary: *b.* Launceston, co. Cornwall, 14 July 1876: *educ.* Kelly College, and Royal Military College, Sandhurst: gazetted 2nd Lieut. Welsh Regt. 1896; promoted Lieut. 1898: took part in the South African War, being present at the actions of Driefontein, the Vet and Zand Rivers, Diamond Hill, Belfast, and Colesberg (Queen's Medal, five clasps; King's Medal, two clasps): promoted Capt. 1904: served with the Expeditionary Force in France and Flanders from 12 August 1914; his battalion forming part of 1st Divn., and took part in the retirement from Mons, the Battles of the Marne and the Aisne, and the fighting at Ypres where he was killed, 31 October 1914. Age 38. He *m.* 1907; Hilda Charlotte, *née* Phillips, and had a son – Charles Anthony Gwennap, *b.* December 1912.

(Panel 37) Capt. Charles Coke Torkington, 1st Bn. (41st Foot) The Welsh Regt.: *s.* of the late Capt. Charles Torkington, 1st Welch Regt.; and Florence Torkington (Hartley, Cranbrook, co. Kent), his wife: and brother to Capt. J.E.B. Torkington, 63rd Palamacottah Light Infantry, died 30 December 1915, aged 30 years: served with the Expeditionary Force in France and Flanders, and was killed in action, 25 May 1915. Age 35. Remembered on Cranbrook (St. Dunstan's) Parish Church Roll of Honour.

His brother John also has no known grave; he is commemorated on the Chatby Memorial.

(Panel 37) Capt. (Adjt.), Edmund Henry Herbert Westby, 1st Bn. (41st Foot) The Welsh Regt.: only *s.* of the late Capt. John W. Westby, Welsh Regiment, and Mrs Westby: *b.* Tenby, 10 September 1881: *educ.* Wellington College: received his first commission, 2nd Lieut. 3rd Bn. South Wales Borderers, with which he served during embodiment for a year and a quarter, and from the Militia received his commission 2nd Lieut. Welsh Regt. May 1901: took part in the South African War, being present at operations in Orange Free State and Orange River Colony (as it became) April and November 1900: in the Transvaal, May 1901–May 1902 (Queen's Medal, three clasps; King's Medal, two clasps): promoted Lieut. March 1904; Capt. May 1911: apptd. Adjutant 1st Bn. Welsh Regt. June 1914. On the outbreak of war was at Chakrata, India: returned to England, 22 December 1914: proceeded to France with his battalion, January 1915, and was reported wounded and missing after the fighting on 26 May 1915. Age 33. Nothing further was heard of him until fifteen months later, when two letters were received by Mrs Westby. One, from a Captain in the Royal Scots, stated that on 16th and 17th June 1915, he and his men took up a line just captured from the enemy in the Roulers Railway Wood, which was full of dead. In a sunken road were four British officers, one being Captain Westby. He was buried with an unknown Major, and over the double grave was placed a wooden cross. Another interesting letter was received indirectly from a German officer, who was Adjutant of the prisoners' war camp at Munsingen, giving the following account of his death, "I stood in the month of May 1915, close to Bellewaarde Ferme, east of Ypres, in a field, and by a night attack which extended so far as our trenches, Captain Westby fell in a charge leading his men, who I could easily observe through my night glasses to be an English Captain. I gave orders to my company of volunteers that the dead should be buried just before our trenches, but the exact position about regiments and names were quite impossible, as everything was carried out by night in a most desperate hurry, owing to the fresh trenches which had to be made to check the enemy. On the outside of the satchel taken from the dead captain I found printed on it in ink the letters R.H.H.W. Accidentally I found in the prisoners' war camp a list of the missing, and in it the name of Captain Westby, and I have not the slightest doubt that it refers to the Bellewarde Ferme fallen Captain, as the day, place, and letters on the satchel are in harmony with the list of missing. My orders to my men were to bury the dead with all their belongings except weapons and war maps. He was killed in action as a leader of his men, and he died a painless death.

In recognition of his glorious death his adversaries do not deny his bravery, and share their sorrows and sympathies with the bereaved family." It was presumed that the German officer's order for burial was not carried out. Captain Westby *m.* in 1908, Vera (Dorling House, Fleet, co. Hants), only *dau.* of Charles (& Mrs) David; she survived him with two sons, David aged five, and Edmund aged three years.

(Panel 37) Lieut. Cecil Victor Powell Cornelius, 3rd (Reserve) attd. 2nd Bn. (69th Foot) The Welsh Regt.: *s.* of Walter John Cornelius, of The Crags, Mussoorie, United Provinces, India, by his wife Eveline Cecilia: *b.* Dehra Dun, United Provinces, India, 14 April 1889: *educ.* St. George's College; York House, Mussoorie, India, and Wren's Coaching Establishment, Bayswater, London, W.: Occupation – Barrister at Law (Middle Temple): gazetted 2nd Lieut. Reserve of Officers, March 1912; promoted Lieut. 5 December following: served with the Expeditionary Force in France and Flanders, and was killed in action at Klein Zillebeke, nr. Ypres, 12 November 1914. Age 24. (*IWGC record 10 November*)

(Panel 37) Lieut. Hilary Gresford Evan-Jones, 1st Bn. (41st Foot) The Welsh Regt.: *yr. s.* of the Rev. Richard Evan-Jones, M.A., Vicar of Llanllwchaiarn, Newtown, co. Montgomery, Rural Dean of Cedewain; Canon and Precentor, St. Asaph Cathedral, by his wife Hannah Rose, widow of the late Samuel Richardson Bishop, of St. Helens, and *dau.* of the late Edward Jones, of Bronwylfn, Wrexham, J.P., D.L., High Sheriff of Denbighshire (1894): *gdson.* to the late Rev. James Evan-Jones, M.A., formerly Vicar of Bagyillt, co. Flint: nephew to Sir Edward Evans, Spital Old Hall, Bromborough, Cheshire: cousin to Sir Aston Webb, K.C.V.O., C.B., R.A.: *b.* Llanllwchaiarn Vicarage, 22 January 1889: *educ.* Charterhouse, and Hertford College, Oxford, where he was Colour-Sergt., O.T.C., and won the Williams Prize which is given to the most efficient N.C.O. in the Corps, and was so enthusiastic in recruiting that he multiplied the strength of his College detachment by ten: graduated B.A. 1910: gazetted 2nd Lieut. 1st Welsh Regt. 5 October 1910; promoted Lieut. 20 November 1911: stationed at Cairo, Cyprus, Chakrata and Agra, and when war broke out was on his way to Cyprus, where he was to have been married at Troodos, 28 August 1914, to Nancy, only *dau.* of Major W.N. Bolton (late Wiltshire Regiment), Commissioner of Kyrenia, but his leave was cancelled and he was recalled to rejoin his battalion with which he landed in England, 22 December 1914. He left for France, 16 January 1915, and to judge from a letter written shortly before he met his death, must have had some exciting experiences, "We have just finished our first eight days – divided between the supports and the firing line. I had the worst bit of trench to look after with my platoon and did all right, but had a good few casualties, considering the 96 hours I was actually up – two killed and nine wounded. I made two night expeditions by myself with some bombs, which I successfully dropped into the German trenches. During my first I met a German gentleman, apparently at the same job as myself. My revolver accounted for him all right, as we were only two feet apart. The trenches are from 30 to 75 feet apart in most places and sometimes closer. We are now off on a four day's rest, which is absolutely ripping. It is splendid to get out of the noise and to get some proper food and sleep. I think, if anything, I am rather enjoying this. Cold feet are the worst part of the show, but my men are all such rippers, it makes up for lots. I hate having them hit, otherwise it is quite cheery. I had a sing-song in my trench the other evening, which did not please the Germans. I sat in a chair, which collapsed, and I went straight to sleep where I lay. The strain is fairly big up there." Killed in action, nr. Ypres, 16 February 1915. Buried with two other officers, Capt. G.A. Lloyd and Lieut. R.T.B. Pope, who were killed the same day in the trenches, in the gardens of the Chateau Rosendal, three miles S.E. of Ypres. His Commanding Officer, Lieut.Col. T.O. Marden, wrote, "I regret most deeply having to inform you of the death, on the 16th inst., in the trenches, of your gallant son Hilary. As far as we can ascertain his death was instantaneous from a rifle bullet, but many of his platoon were shot down at the same time, and there was no one in the trench who could give accurate information as to what happened. He is a great loss to us, as he was such a good soldier and popular with all ranks. As you know, probably, he was selected to lead the Second Grenadier platoon, and had behaved so gallantly during his former turn of duty in the trenches, where he kept the spirits of his whole platoon up by his energy and enterprise, that I brought his name specially to the notice of the Brigadier. He crept out of the trenches alone on several occasions and threw bombs into the enemy's trenches." *The Oxford Magazine*, 26 February 1915, under the heading 'Oxford's Sacrifice', records – "While at Oxford Lieutenant Hilary Gresford Evan-Jones, B.A., devoted himself with whole-hearted enthusiasm to military affairs. At the end of his first year the old Volunteers gave way to the O.T.C. He fathered the change in Hertford and multiplied the strength of the college detachment by ten. He was Colour Sergeant of 'D' Company in 1909 and 1910, and in the latter year won the Williams Prize, which is given to the most efficient non-commissioned officer in the corps. He was a great leader, and when not on military duty he was usually organizing some very healthy 'rag.' Everyone who was at Hertford with him has lost a friend, and the Army has lost one of its best junior officers." Lieut. Evan-Jones was a keen sportsman and a well-known figure in the hunting field in Montgomeryshire. He was also an excellent shot. At Cairo he made a considerable reputation as a polo player, and both at Cyprus and at Agra he was Master of the Hunt. Lieut. Evan-Jones was Mentioned in F.M. Sir John (now Lord) French's Despatch of 31 May, 1915. A Memorial Service was held in Llanllwchaiarn Parish Church, 28 February 1915, conducted by his father, elder brother, and Canon T.Ll.L. Williams, M.A., Rector of Newtown, who delivered the sermon. Sympathetic messages were received by the Rev. Canon R. Evan-Jones' family from several charitable and other institutions. His elder brother, the Rev. Basil Evan-Jones (Charterhouse and University College, Oxford), formerly Curate of Gaulsfield, co. Montgomery, a well-known antiquary, and sub-editor of the Powysland Collections, resigned his curacy on the outbreak of war and joined the Royal Welsh Fusiliers as a private, being gazetted 2nd Lieut. 15 January 1915; Lieut. 1 October 1915, and Capt. 10 June 1916. Age 26. *unm.*

Lieut. R.T.B. Pope and Capt. G.A. Lloyd are buried in Bedford House Cemetery, Enc.No.3, C.4 and C.5 respectively.

(Panel 37) Lieut. Geoffrey Dorman Partridge, 2nd Bn. (69th Foot) The Welsh Regt.: 4th & *yst. s.* of Lieut. Col. Sylvanus Roger Burnett Partridge, of 'Homecroft,' Fleet, Hants, late King's Own Scottish Borderers, and Governor, His Majesty's Prison, Portland; by his wife Mary Bishopp, *dau.* of Edward Bishopp Dorman, M.D.: and yr. brother to 2nd Lieut. E.L.L. Partridge, 1st Devonshire Regt., died at Jullundur, 1 September 1899, from enteric fever; his elder brother Capt. C.B. Partridge, Royal Marine Light Infantry, was lost in H.M.S. 'Good Hope' two days previously, 1 November 1914, in the naval battle off Coronel, on the coast of Chile; his remaining brother, Capt. R.E. Partridge, M.C., Dorsetshire Regt., served at the front as Brigade Major, 12th Canadian Infantry Divn.: *b.* Portsmouth, 24 December 1890: *educ.* Bath College, United Services College, and Royal Military College, Sandhurst: gazetted 2nd Lieut. Welsh Regt. 11 October 1911; posted 2nd Battn., which formed part of 1st Divn., B.E.F.: went to France with the Expeditionary Force in early August 1914: promoted Lieut. 1 November following, and was reported missing (two days later) after the First Battle of Ypres, 3 November 1914, and is now, there having been no further word or information received, officially presumed to have been killed in action on or about that date. His favourite recreation was Rugby football, which he had played for the Army. Age 23. *unm.*

His brother Charles also has no known grave; he is commemorated on the Plymouth Naval Memorial (Panel 4).

In the world of today it is hard to envisage an everyday item like the wristwatch owes its origins to the First World War; an era when most gentlemen wore a pocket watch on a chain. As the war progressed it became fashionable, particularly among younger men, to wear a wristwatch. It was far more practical to be able to glance at ones wrist than to fumble about withdrawing an item from a pocket somewhere and, in a war where precise timing was of paramount importance, it made light work when on guard duty to note the time for sentry changes, when an attack would go in, and at what moment the barrage would lift.

In the late summer of 2003 a team of archaeologists excavating a trench on the Pilckem Ridge dating from the opening stages of the Third Battle of Ypres unearthed an early Ingersoll wristwatch wrapped in newspaper. On examination it was found the watch strap bore the engraved letters N G L which, after further examination, eventually led the archaeologists to the name ENGLAND. This in turn led researchers to find a man who had fought in the region on or about 31 July 1917 by the name of England and from an initial ten pages of soldiers with that name a process of elimination led to only one possibility – 2nd Lieut. J.H. England.

The eldest and only son of Thomas and Minnie England – John England – came from a fairly comfortable and typical Edwardian household, living with his parents and three sisters in the village of Llanechan, Wales. Educated locally before going on to a private finishing school, it is possible he would have followed his father into accountancy had the cataclysmic events of the summer of 1914 not intervened.

Enlisting shortly after the outbreak of war, aged 17 years and 6 months, he became Private 65809, in 7th Battn. The Welsh Regt. A little over a year later after completing his training in England and obtaining a commission, he was sent out with a draft to France.

On 17 November 1916, after six weeks training on a mock-up setting behind the lines, '2nd Lieut. England, in company with six other officers and 145 other ranks, took a leading role in a meticulously planned night raid on a key German position, returning with twenty prisoners and a large amount of paper intelligence.'

On the morning of 31 July 1917, 14th Welsh attacked at zero hour toward Pilckem. The trench from which they attacked was virtually destroyed by shell fire and heavy fire from the vicinity of Iron Cross, causing numerous casualties amongst the Welshmen almost before their attack had begun. At what point 2nd Lieut. England lost his life is unknown, he left the trench 'leading his men' and was never seen or heard of again.

How the newspaper wrapped wristwatch came to be lost in the mud of Flanders is open to conjecture – had it been carefully wrapped for safe-keeping only to fall out of the carrier's pocket and get accidentally trodden into the bottom of the trench, had it been looted from the owner's body and later lost? Whatever the reason, had it not have been for the archaeological dig and discovery of the engraved strap ninety-six years later, the story of John England would probably have never come to light.

(Panel 37) 2nd Lieut. John Humphrey England, 14th (Service) Bn. (Swansea) The Welsh Regt.: only *s.* of the late Thomas Harper England, Accountant; of 43, Station Road, Llanechan, nr. Cardiff, by his wife Minnie ('Caerleon,' Prince's Road, Clevedon, co. Somerset): *b.* June 1897: *educ.* High School, Cardiff and King's College, Taunton: enlisted as Pte., 7th Welsh Regt. August 1914: obtained a commission 2nd Lieut. 1915: served with the Expeditionary Force in France and Flanders from October 1915: Mentioned in Despatches, for his part in a raid, 17 November 1916, and was killed in action, 31 July 1917. Shortly after receiving notification of his son's death, his father wrote to the War Office, "8 August 1917, Dear Sirs, With regard to your letter regarding the personal effects of 2nd Lieut. J.H. England, I have today received from Messrs Cox, Shipping Agency, a package which simply contains his old clothes and kit bag. The following items have not been returned – prismatic glasses, prismatic compass, ring and wristwatch." Age 20. *unm.*

(Panel 37) 2nd Lieut. John William Harford Nicholl, 3rd (Reserve) attd 2nd Bn. (69th Foot) The Welsh Regt.: elder *s.* of Lieut.Col. John I.D. Nicholl, of Merthyr Mawr, Bridgend, co. Glamorgan: and *gt.*-nephew to Major.Gen. C.R.H. Nicholl, Comdg. 1st Bn. Prince Consort's Own (Rifle Brigade): *b.* Hendrefoilan, Swansea, 24 October 1892: *educ.* Eton, and Royal Military College, Sandhurst, which he represented against the Royal Military Academy, Woolwich, in the 1912 sports: gazetted 2nd Lieut. Prince Consort's Own, 1913; resigned his commission, June 1914: on the outbreak of war, was gazetted 3rd Welsh Regt., and was serving on Active Service with 2nd Battn. of that regiment when he was killed at Gheluvelt, five miles east of Ypres, 29 October 1914, while retaking trenches which had been captured by the Germans. He was fond of hunting, shooting, and winter sports. Age 22. *unm.*

(Panel 37) Coy.Sergt.Major 15892, Benjamin Bessant, 10th (Service) Bn. (1st Rhondda) The Welsh Regt.: *s.* of George Bessant, of 31, Brithweunydd Road, Trealaw, Dinas (Rhondda), co. Glamorgan, by his wife Ann: and elder brother to Pte. 13773, T.G. Bessant, 1st Somerset Light Infantry, killed in action, 4 October 1917: *b.* Rhondda, 1889: enlisted Tonypandy: served with the Expeditionary Force in France, and was killed in action, 4 August 1917. Age 28. He was married to the late May Besant (Trealaw, Rhondda).

His brother Thomas also has no known grave; he is commemorated on the Tyne Cot Memorial (Panel 41).

(Panel 37) L/Corpl. 30737, James Stanley David, 1st Bn. (41st Foot) The Welsh Regt.: *s.* of the late Walter P. David, by his wife Elvira (76, Glanbrydan Avenue, Bryn Mill, Swansea, co. Glamorgan): *b.* Swansea: enlisted there. Killed by the explosion of a mine, 3 August 1915; Kemmel. Age 23. *unm.*

Employed in Bahia Blanca Mechanical Engineers Dept. Central Argentine (Buenos Aires Great Southern) Railways; gave up that appointment on the outbreak of war and returned to answer his country's call. Remembered on the Central Argentine Railway War Memorial, Retiro Station.

(Panel 37) Pte. 667, Arthur Ace, 2nd Bn. (69th Foot) The Welsh Regt.: *s.* of John Ace, of 4, Boarspit Lane, Mumbles, Swansea, by his wife Ellen: and late *husb.* to Margaret Ford (formerly Ace, of 62, Dinas Street, Plasmarl, Swansea): a pre-war Regular on the Reserve, Private Ace was recalled to the Colours on the outbreak of the European War, August 1914: volunteered for Foreign Service and went to France with his regiment in early September. On 26 January 1915 Mrs Ace received notification from the War Office informing her that her husband had been missing (presumed killed) since October 1914; now confirmed as having been killed in action at Gheluvelt, near Ypres, 31 October 1914. Age 34.

(Panel 37) Pte. 8048, John Barr (served as J. Gillan), 2nd Bn. (69th Foot) The Welsh Regt.: *b.* Bridgeton, co. Lanark, *c.*1884: enlisted Cardiff: served with the Expeditionary Force, and was killed in action, 6 November 1914. Age 30. He was married to Mary (110, Easter Hill, Tollcross, Glasgow).

(Panel 37) Pte. 10990, Arthur Bentley, 2nd Bn. (69th Foot) The Welsh Regt.: *s.* of Tweedale Bentley, of 86, Pothouse Place, Wibsey, co. York, by his wife Hannah Mary, *dau.* of Joseph Tordoff, of Low Moor: *b.* Morley Carr (Low Moor), nr. Bradford, co. York, 9 March 1895: *educ.* Carr Lane Council Schools: enlisted Halifax, August 1913: went to France with the Expeditionary Force, August 1914. Reported missing after the heavy fighting, 6 November following, and is now assumed to have been killed in action on or about that date. Age 19. (*IWGC record 10660, age 18*)

(Panel 37) Pte. 13390, Peter Christensen, 1st Bn. (41st Foot) The Welsh Regt.: *s.* of Charles Christensen, of 49, Thomas Street, Grange, Cardiff, co. Glamorgan, by his wife Annie: and brother to Pte. 125085, C. Christensen, Labour Corps, formerly no.44869, Welsh Regt., killed in action, 30 November 1917: enlisted in Cardiff. Killed in action, 28 April 1915. Age 22.

His brother Charles also has no known grave; he is commemorated on the Cambrai Memorial, Louverval (Panel 13). (*IWGC record Christenson*)

(Panel 37) Pte. 13043, Alfred Hurley, 1st Bn. (41st Foot) The Welsh Regt.: late of Springbourne, co. Hants: *s.* of Mr (& Mrs) Hurley, of 5, Grantham Road, Bournemouth: *b.* Yarmouth, co. Norfolk: enlisted Carmarthen. Killed in action, 27 March 1915. Age 27. Remains recovered on 12 March 1928; Messines Ridge German Cemetery No.2 (Grave no.4/2); identified – Burial List. *Buried in Sanctuary Wood Cemetery (II.C.34).*

(Panel 37) Pte. 56557, Hubert Merchant, 115th Trench Mortar Bty. attd. 16th (Service) Bn. The Welsh Regt.: *s.* of Arthur Merchant, of 176, Cathays Terrace, Cathays, Cardiff, co. Glamorgan, by his wife Emily, *dau.* of R. Solomon, of Cardiff: *b.* Llanhilleth, co. Monmouth, 26 July 1896: *educ.* Moorland Road Council School, Cardiff: Occupation – Film Rental House Clerk: enlisted 7th Welsh (Cyclists), 26 April 1915; transfd. 16th Welsh Regt.: served with the Expeditionary Force in France and Flanders from 28 July 1916, and was killed in action after the Battle of Pilckem Ridge, 1 August 1917; five days after his twenty-first birthday. Buried in the Military Cemetery there. His Captain wrote, "He went into the fight with his usual cheerfulness, and went right over the Pilckem Ridge as far as the River Steenbeek, where he fought gallantly until he was hit by a sniper in the side. He was carried into a shelter, but never regained consciousness and died soon after. What officers are left are all sad, because we have left our best boys sleeping their last sleep near the river, but they all died like gallant soldiers." Age 21. *unm.*

(Panel 37) Pte. 55531, Charles William Neal, 16th (Service) Bn. The Welsh Regt.: enlisted Birmingham. Killed in action, 31 July 1917, at the Battle of Pilckem. Remains exhumed from an unmarked grave, referring to GRU Report, Zillebeke 5-59E (20.U.27.b.4.1) unmarked grave; identified – Disc, Clothing; reinterred, registered 13 April 1927. *Buried in Sanctuary Wood Cemetery (IV.B.32).*

(Panel 37) Pte. 19427, William Charles Nicholls, 1st Bn. (41st Foot) The Welsh Regt.: *s.* of William Charles Nicholls; Sailor: *b.* Penzance, 7 December 1880: *educ.* National School, Penzance: enlisted on 15 November 1914, following the outbreak of war: served in France with the Expeditionary Force, and was killed in action at Zillebeke, 25 May 1915. Age 35. He *m.* Penzance, 22 September 1901; Alice Maud, *dau.* of James Pidwell, and had six sons – William Charles, *b.* 4 November 1901; George James, *b.* 30

January 1905; Richard John, *b*. 26 October 1907; Stephen, *b*. 18 November 1909; Arthur Reginald, *b*. 26 November 1912; Edward Harvey, *b*. 22 October 1914.

(Panel 37) Pte. 6350, Edward Redding, 2nd Bn. (69th Foot) The Welsh Regt.: late of Llandovery, co. Carmarthen: brother to Pte. 6324, J. Redding, Welsh Regt., died at Bangor, 2 January 1916, of sickness: *b*. London: a pre-war Regular, and member of the Army Reserve, rejoined the Colours at Llandeilo on mobilisation, 4 August 1914; posted 2nd Welsh Regt.: served with the Expeditionary Force in France and Flanders from 13 August 1914: took part in the Battle of Mons and the subsequent fighting during the retirement from that place to the Marne: fought at the Battle of the Aisne, and died of wounds, 31 October 1914, received in action at the Battle of Gheluvelt. Edward and his brother John are commemorated on the Llandovery War Memorial.

His brother John is buried in Bangor (Glanadda) Cemetery (E.NG.2346A).

"Dear Great-Hearted Comrades of the Black Watch, no darkness of the grave can keep you from my sight, nothing can dim the light of youth in your friendly eyes. You will never be old ghosts to me, but warm-hearted friends, as when we stood in the line together and talked of our dear ones at home." – *William Linton Andrews*

(Panel 37) Capt. Percy Lionel Moubray, 3rd attd. 1st Bn. (42nd Foot) The Black Watch (Royal Highlanders): *s*. of Capt. W.H. Moubray, Royal Navy, of Otterston and Cockairnie, co. Fife: *gdson*. of Sir Robert Moubray, Kt., and nephew to the late Col. Babington, of Sarisbury Green, co. Hants: *b*. Otterston, Aberdour, co. Fife, 3 August 1872: *educ*. Loretto School, Musselburgh: entered Royal Highlanders, 1899; becoming Capt. May 1904: served in the South African War: took part in operations in Orange Free State and Orange River Colony: Queen's Medal, three clasps; King's Medal, two clasps: served with the Expeditionary Force in France and Flanders, and was reported missing, 29 October 1914, subsequently (unofficially reported) killed in action. A member of the Caledonian Club, London, and the Scottish Conservative Club, Edinburgh. Age 42. Remembered on Dalgety Bay War Memorial, Dunfermline.

(Panel 37) Capt. James William Lennox Sprot, 2nd Bn. (73rd Foot) attd. 'A' Coy., 1st Bn. (42nd Foot) The Black Watch (Royal Highlanders): *s*. of the late Edward W. Sprot, of Drygrange, co. Roxburgh, and his wife Marion Gray Boyd (Roscobie, Banchory, co. Fife): and brother to Lieut. I.B. Sprot, 1st Cameron Highlanders, killed in action, 23 October 1914: *b*. *c*.1886: *educ*. Cargilfield Preparatory School; Winchester College; Royal Military College, Sandhurst: prior to the outbreak of war, was Adjutant, Channel Islands Militia: served with the Expeditionary Force in France and Flanders; killed in action, 11 November 1914. "Between 6.30 and 9 a.m., 11.11.1914, the heaviest bombardment so far experienced by the British forces broke out; as it ended, a Division of the Prussian Guard, with orders from their Emperor to break the line at all costs, attacked the front of 1st. and 2nd. Divisions. Under cover of the bombardment a strong force drove back 'D' Coy., and two platoons of 'A' Coy., 1st Black Watch, entrenched at the south-west corner of Polygon Wood, and broke through the line. 2nd Lieut. N. McNeill, commanding this portion, was last seen on the parapet of his trench, revolver in hand, fighting right gallantly to the end with all his men. 'B' Coy. and two platoons of 'A' Coy., under Capt. Sprot, in reserve in the paddocks of Verbeek Farm, were overwhelmed by the first onrush of the enemy; Capt. Sprot and virtually all of his men were killed." Age 28. He leaves a widow, Roma L.H. Sprot (Sprott House, Dunbar, co. East Lothian), and *dau*. Sheila Marion Roma Sprot, *b*. 1912.

His brother Ivan is buried in Perth Cemetery (China Wall), Zillebeke (XII.B.6).

(Panel 37) Capt. Cecil Boddam-Whetham, 3rd (Reserve) attd. 1st Bn. (42nd Foot) The Black Watch (Royal Highlanders): 2nd *s*. of the late Col. Arthur T. Boddam-Whetham, late Royal Welsh Fusiliers, of Folkestone, and Mrs M.G. Boddam-Whetham ('The Red Gables,' Canford Cliffs, co. Dorset): and father to Capt. 37163, A.T. Boddam-Whetham, Highland Light Infantry attd. R.A.F. Iraq Levies, killed in action, 5 November 1943; Western Desert: *b*. 11 February 1879: *educ*. Wrexham, and Bedford Schools; also France and Germany, afterwards going to 'Wrens': from thence passed through Royal Military Academy, Woolwich into Royal Artillery, September 1898: promoted Lieut. February 1901: saw Active Service, South Nigeria, West Africa, 1902 (Medal with clasp): promoted Capt. 1906: retired from Active List, Royal Field Artillery (1908) and, being appointed Capt., joined Reserve Battn. Black Watch, September the same year. For the Great War, Capt. Boddam-Whetham was attached to 1st Gordon Highlanders, October 1914, and went to the Front. Prominently Mentioned in Sir John (now Lord) French's Despatch, 2 February 1915, for 'his splendid dash in the attack on the Maedelstede Spur.' He was last seen jumping into the enemy trench, 14 December 1914, followed by Lieut. Dobie and a few men, and it is believed he was killed on that date. Age 35. Capt. Boddam-Whetham's body was not found until October 1915, when it was buried by 24th Canadian Infantry Battn. at Bois de Wytschaete. His Commanding Officer wrote of him, "… has been one of our greatest helps, and his loss to me and the regiment at this time cannot be measured … In my opinion, no one has ever showed greater gallantry." He was a member of the Naval and Military Club, and his favourite recreations were shooting, cricket, and golf. He *m.*, 1906, Gyda, *yst. dau.* of the late Henry Rawcliffe, of Gillibrand Hall, co. Lancaster, and left three sons.

His son Arthur is buried in Halfaya Sollum War Cemetery (Coll.5.A.1-8).

(Panel 37) Lieut. Angus Charles Rowley Steuart Macnaghten, 3rd (Reserve) attd. 1st Bn. (42nd Foot) The Black Watch (Royal Highlanders): late of Craigruie, Balquhidder, co. Perth: only *s.* of the late Sir Steuart Macnaghten, of Bitterne Manor, co. Hants, one time Chairman of the Southampton Docks Co.: *educ.* Eton, and Trinity College, Cambridge: commissioned 2nd Lieut., 3rd Black Watch, December 1903: gazetted Capt. to date from February 1915, there having been some doubt as to his death for several months. Lieut. Macnaghten was last seen on 29 October 1914, on which date his company had been sent to the assistance of another battalion at Ypres and, although surrounded by Germans, he refused to surrender. Age 31. Lieut. Macnaghten's favourite sports were fox-hunting, stalking, shooting, and fishing. He *m.*, January 1911; Hazel Enid, *dau.* of the late Col. Lyndon Irwin, Indian Army, and leaves a son – Angus Derek Iain Jacques, *b.* May 1914.

(Panel 37) Lieut. Raymond Philip Drummond Nolan, 3rd (Reserve) attd. 1st Bn. (42nd Foot) The Black Watch (Royal Highlanders): eldest *s.* of the late Philip Nolan, I.C.S. (*d.* April 1902), of Ballinderry, Tuam, Co. Galway, by his wife Frances Georgina, *née* Drummond: *b.* India, 1 July 1883: *educ.* Beaumont; Stonyhurst, and New College, Oxford, where he got his double Half-Blue: called to the Bar, Inner Temple, 1908: joined Black Watch, May 1907: promoted Lieut. April 1910: served with the Expeditionary Force in France and Flanders; killed in action nr. Veldhoek, 3 November 1914, by machine gun fire while leading a counter- attack which succeeded in restoring the British line on the Menin Road broken the previous day, and thus stopped the forward movement of the enemy. Age 31. A Hockey International, Tennis Champion of Connaught and Galway; he was a member of the Travellers' and Isthmian Clubs, and United Service Club, Dublin. He succeeded his uncle – Lieut.Col. J.P. Nolan, M.P. – in the Ballinderry Estate, 1912. He m. St. Andrew's, Dublin, 27 November 1913, Kathleen, eldest *dau.* of Rt. Hon. Charles Andrew O'Connor, Master of the Rolls in Ireland, and leaves a son – Anthony John Raymond St. Quentin Nolan, *b.* 7 September 1914.

(Panel 37) 2nd Lieut. Patrick Edward Adam Blair, 2nd Bn. (73rd Foot) attd. 1st Bn. (42nd Foot) The Black Watch (Royal Highlanders): elder *s.* of A.S. Blair, of Edinburgh, Writer to *The Signet*, now serving as Lieut.Col. Comdg. 9th (Highlanders) Battn. Royal Scots (T.F.): *b.* June 1893: *educ.* Cargilfield School, Midlothian, and Malvern College: gazetted 2nd Lieut. Black Watch, June 1914: served with the Expeditionary Force in France and Flanders, attd. 1st Battn.; reported missing/believed killed in action at Gheluvelt, 29 October 1914. Age 21. *unm.*

(Panel 37) 2nd Lieut. Neil McNeill, 'A' Coy., 1st Bn. (42nd Foot) The Black Watch (Royal Highlanders): *s.* of Duncan (& Emilie Margaret) McNeill, of Shanghai, China: *educ.* Charterhouse, and Hertford College, Oxford. Killed in action, 11 November 1914. The circumstances being – "Between 6.30 and 9 a.m., 11.11.1914, the heaviest bombardment so far experienced by the British forces broke out; as it ended, a Division of the Prussian Guard, with orders from their Emperor to break the line at all costs, attacked the front of 1st and 2nd Divisions. Under cover of the bombardment a strong force drove back 'D' Coy., and two platoons of 'A' Coy., 1st Black Watch, entrenched at the south-west corner of Polygon Wood, and broke through the line. 2nd Lieut. N. McNeill, commanding this portion, was last seen on the parapet of his trench, revolver in hand, fighting right gallantly to the end with all his men." Age 20.

(Panel 37) 2nd Lieut. Donald Stuart Stirling Smurthwaite, 'A' Coy., 1st Bn. (42nd Foot) The Black Watch (Royal Highlanders): *s.* of the late B.W. Smurthwaite, of Prior House, Richmond, co. York, and Mrs

C.L. Stirling, *née* Smurthwaite (The Brae, Bridge-of-Allan, co. Stirling), formerly of 25 Emperor's Gate, London, S.W.: *gdson.* of the late Richard Stirling, of Craig Wallace, Bridge of Allan, last *survg. s.* of William Stirling, of Cordale and Dalquharran, co. Dumbarton, whose family trace their unbroken heritage from the twelfth century, and are believed to be the oldest branch of the Stirling family; 'Honest and True,' John Stirling, Lord Provost of Glasgow, 1600, being an ancestor: *b.* 12 June 1894: *educ.* Westminster: passed from his crammer's into the Royal Military College, Sandhurst, at the top of the list, being the only candidate who obtained honours in the examination: gazetted 2nd Lieut. Black Watch, 12 August 1914: served with the Expeditionary Force in France and Flanders, and was killed in action at Ypres, 26 October following, while leading his platoon; his last words being – "Come on, men! Follow me!" He was a qualified interpreter in French. Age 20. *unm.* Remembered on Bridge-of-Allan War Memorial.

(Panel 37) 2nd Lieut. James Taylor, 9th (Service) Bn. The Black Watch (Royal Highlanders): eldest *s.* of John Taylor, of Glasgow, Stationer, by his wife Catherine Dudgeon: *b.* Crosshill, Glasgow, co. Lanark, 31 May 1890: *educ.* Melville Street School: employee to J. & A. Roxburgh, Ship-Owners, Glasgow: joined 7th Cameronians (Scottish Rifles) (T.F.), January 1911: mobilised, 4 August 1914: proceeded to Egypt with his regiment in February 1915, and subsequently went to Gallipoli, June following; invalided home suffering from frost-bitten feet, and discharged from the Army as physically unfit, February 1916: re-enlisted Princess Louise's (Argyll & Sutherland Highlanders), June following: sent to O.T.C., Gailes; gazetted 2nd Lieut. 3rd (Reserve) Bn. Black Watch, October 1916: returned to France, April; being transf'd. 9th Battn. of the same regiment, and was killed in action at Frezenberg, 31 July 1917. A brother officer wrote, "Lieut. Taylor took command of the company when his senior officers became casualties, and at one period he was the controlling figure of the assault line of the battalion. It was shortly after the capture by his company of a village strong point and redoubt, that he was killed by fragments of a shell which burst beside him. His servant told us that death was instantaneous, as two pieces struck him on the head. There is little doubt that had he lived he would have won a high decoration." Age 27. He *m.* Glasgow, 24 January 1917, Effie Proctor, now Mrs Wright ('Kelvin,' Gate End, Northwood, co. Middlesex, late of 49, Park Road, Glasgow), only *dau.* of the late T.M. Nance, of Glasgow, Surgeon-Dentist: *s.p.*

(Panel 37) Corpl. 2158, George Henderson, 'A' Coy., 1st Bn (42nd Foot) The Black Watch (Royal Highlanders): *s.* of William L. Henderson, of 125, Taylor Street, Aberhil, Methill, co. Fife, by his wife Margaret L.: and elder brother to L/Corpl. 2486, C.L., Henderson, 1st Black Watch, killed in action, 27 October 1914: *b.* Burntisland, co. Fife, *c.*1893: enlisted Edinburgh: served with the Expeditionary Force, and was killed in action, 2 November 1914. Age 21.

His brother Charles also has no known grave; he is recorded below.

(Panel 37) L/Corpl. 3/1980, Thomas Connelly, 1st Bn. (42nd Foot) The Black Watch (Royal Highlanders): *s.* of Thomas (& Mrs) Connelly, of 46, Smalls Wynd, Dundee: and *yr.* brother to Pte. 3/9508, J. Connelly, Black Watch, who fell the same day: *b.* Dundee, co. Forfar, about 1894: a pre-war member of 3rd (Territorial) Battn., Dundee; undertook Imperial Service obligations following the outbreak of war, August 1914; transf'd. 1st Battn. Oudenarde Barracks, Aldershot, for Active Service: went to France on 14 August, landing at Le Havre, and was killed in action, 11 November 1914. Age 20. *unm.*

His brother John also has no known grave; he is recorded below.

(Panel 37) L/Corpl. 2486, Charles Livingstone Henderson, 'A' Coy., 1st Bn (42nd Foot) The Black Watch (Royal Highlanders): *s.* of William L. (& Margaret L.) Henderson, of 125, Taylor Street, Aberhil, Methill, co. Fife: and yr. brother to Corpl. 2158, G. Henderson, 1st Black Watch, killed in action, 2 November 1914: *b.* Burntisland, co. Fife, *c.*1896: enlisted Edinburgh. Killed in action, 27 October 1914. Age 18.

His brother George also has no known grave; he is recorded above.

(Panel 37) Pte. 7297, James Alexander, 1st Bn. (42nd Foot) The Black Watch (Royal Highlanders): late of 21, West Moorpark Road, Stevenston, co. Ayr: *b.* Kilspindie, co. Perth, 1882: enlisted Barry Camp, co. Forfar. Killed in action nr. Verbeek Farm, Menin Road, Ypres, 5 November 1914. Age 32.

(Panel 37) Pte. 3/9508, John Connelly, 1st Bn. (42nd Foot) The Black Watch (Royal Highlanders): eldest *s.* of Thomas (& Mrs) Connelly, of 46, Smalls Wynd, Dundee: and elder brother to L/Corpl. 3/1980, T.

Connelly, Black Watch, who fell the same day: *b*. Dundee, co. Forfar, about 1869: a pre-war member of 3rd (Territorial) Battn., Dundee; undertook Imperial Service obligations following the outbreak of war in August 1914; transf'd. 1st Battn., Oudenarde Barracks, Aldershot, for Active Service: proceeded to France, 14 August, landing at Le Havre, and was killed in action, 11 November 1914 at Ypres. Age 45. He leaves a wife, Anne Connelly (45, Todburn Lane, Dundee) and children.

His brother Thomas also has no known grave; he is recorded above.

(Panel 37) Pte. 202588, William Barclay Downie, 4/5th Bn. The Black Watch (Royal Highlanders), (T.F.): only *s*. of Daniel Downie, of 95, Old Govan Road, Plantation Glasgow, by his wife Marian, *dau*. of Duncan McCunn: *b*. Glasgow, 27 September 1893: *educ*. Lorne Street Public School, Glasgow: enlisted Scottish Horse Yeomanry, 1 October 1915: trained until December 1916: served with the Expeditionary Force in France and Flanders (transf'd. Black Watch Regt.), and was killed in action at the Battle of St. Julien, 31 July 1917. Buried there. His Commanding Officer wrote, "He was taking part in the great Battle of St. Julien, and was coming out after a counter-attack when a sniper got him, and death was instantaneous" Age 23. *unm*.

(Panel 37) Pte. 9915, Henry Heggie, 1st Bn. (42nd Foot) The Black Watch (Royal Highlanders): *s*. of John Heggie, of Auchtermuchty, Fife, by his wife Christina, *née* Smith: late *husb*. to Mary Stewart McDowell, *née* Heggie (St. Walburg, Saskatchewan, Canada): *b*. Newburgh, co. Fife: enlisted Perth: served with the Expeditionary Force in France and Flanders, and was killed in action, 31 October 1914. Age 31.

(Panel 37) Pte. 2704, John Heugh, 1st Bn. (42nd Foot) The Black Watch (Royal Highlanders): *s*. of Archibald Heugh, of 20, George Place, Peebles, by his wife Mary: enlisted Edinburgh: served with the Expeditionary Force in France from 14 August 1914, and died of wounds, 21 November following. Age 21. *unm*. Remembered on Peebles War Memorial. *Buried in Boulogne Eastern Cemetery (III.C.39).*

(Panel 37) Pte. 2627, James Hamish Holloway, 'A' Coy., 1st Bn. (42nd Foot) The Black Watch (Royal Highlanders): nephew to A.M. Holloway, of 111, Darenth Road, Stamford Hill, London, N.: *b*. London, 5 October 1890: *educ*. Birbeck School, Kingsland, London, N., and Tottenham Grammar School: enlisted Southampton, co. Hants, 8 December 1913: went to France, 13 August 1914: took part in the retreat from Mons and the Battle of the Aisne, and was killed in action at Gheluvelt, 11 November following. Buried where he fell. L/Corpl. 9999, James Watters, of the same company wrote, "Private Holloway was killed in action on the morning of 11 November 1914, when the Prussian Guards broke through our lines. Along with five others of my mates, under the command of Lieut. Fortune (now Major), we held our trench all day, and it was while being relieved by reinforcements from the Northamptons that I came upon the bodies of Private Holloway and two men of his section, lying dead at the back of the dug-out. Holloway was lying face downwards, probably being hit in the back," and Corpl. David Petrie of the Regt., "Private Holloway's remains were buried along with those of his comrades near the spot where he fell by B Coy.; the place where he is buried is in a field of a farm surrounded by a hedge, 350 yards in front of a big wood, about three-quarters of a mile north-east of Gheluvelt. Age 24. *unm*. (*IWGC record 9 November*)

(Panel 37) Pte. 3/2086, Alexander Lumsden, 'D' Coy., 1st Bn. (42nd Foot) The Black Watch (Royal Highlanders): *s*. of the late Alexander Lumsden, by his wife Janet (5, West Pans, Levenhall, Musselburgh, co. Midlothian): and elder brother to Pte. 9246, J. Lumsden, 1st Black Watch, killed in action, 31 October 1914: *b*. Berwick, 1879: enlisted Edinburgh: a pre-war member of 3rd (Reserve) Bn.; undertook Active Service obligations, transferred 1st Battn., served with the Expeditionary Force in France and Flanders from 14 August 1914, and was killed in action, 29 October 1914, at Ypres. Age 35.

His brother James also has no known grave; he is recorded below.

(Panel 37) Pte. 9246, James Lumsden, 'D' Coy., 1st Bn. (42nd Foot) The Black Watch (Royal Highlanders: *s*. of the late Alexander Lumsden, by his wife Janet (5, West Pans, Levenhall, Musselburgh, co. Midlothian): and *yr*. brother to Pte. 3/2086, A. Lumsden, 1st Black Watch, killed in action, 29 October 1914: *b*. Prestonpans, co. Haddington, 1881: enlisted Edinburgh: served with the Expeditionary Force in France and Flanders from 14 August 1914, and was killed in action at Ypres, 31 October 1914. Age 33.

His brother Alexander also has no known grave; he is recorded above.

(Panel 37) Pte. 1700, John McDonald, Comdg. Officer's Servant, 'D' Coy., 1st Bn. (42nd Foot) The Black Watch (Royal Highlanders): *s*. of Norman McDonald, of Orwell Cottage, Academy Road, Crieff, co. Perth, by his wife Margaret: and brother to Pte. S/22560, A. McDonald, 6th Seaforth Highlanders, killed in action, 24 March 1918: served with the Expeditionary Force. Died of wounds, 7 November 1914, at Ypres. Age 23. In a letter to his father a sergeant of his battalion said "I am sending to your care the belongings of No. 1700, Private J. McDonald, D Coy., Black Watch, who, I much regret, was killed in action, 6th November. I have also in my care the exact position of his grave."

His brother Archibald also has no known grave; he is commemorated on the Arras Memorial (Bay 8).

(Panel 37) Pte. 203043, Andrew McKendrick, 6th Bn. (Perthshire) The Black Watch (Royal Highlanders) (T.F.): late *husb.* to Jeanie McKendrick (Hays Buildings, Carronshore, Falkirk): *b.* Forfar, 1883: Occupation – Gardener; Miss Lowson, Belgavies, nr. Guthrie: enlisted Forfar: served with the Expeditionary Force in France from 24 July 1917; killed in action on the 31st. (July 1917). Age 34.

(Panel 37) Pte. 240985, David Ross, 'C' Coy., 4/5th Bn. The Black Watch (Royal Highlanders), (T.F.): *s.* of the late David Ross, of 8, Mill Street, Montrose, by his wife Betsy (49, King Street, Montrose, co. Forfar): and brother to Pte. 2389, A. Ross, Australian Infantry, died of wounds, 8 June 1917; and Pte. 203123, C.C. Ross, Black Watch, killed in action, 20 July 1918: *b.* Ardoch of Gallery, 20 July 1897: *educ.* Inverkeilor, Montrose: Occupation – Ploughman: joined Black Watch, June 1915: served with the Expeditionary Force in France and Flanders from September following, and was reported missing after the fighting at Ypres, 31 July 1917, and is now assumed to have been killed in action on that date. Age 20. *unm.*

His brother Charles also has no known grave, he is commemorated on the Soissons Memorial; Alexander is buried in Pont d'Achelles Military Cemetery (II.A.12).

(Panel 37) Pte. 266188, William Dougal Scobie, 6th Bn. (Perthshire) The Black Watch (Royal Highlanders), (T.F.): *s.* of Mrs Scobie (Blackhill Cottage, Braco, co. Perth): and elder brother to Pte. 33463, A. Scobie, 16th Highland Light Infantry, killed in action, 18 November 1916: *b.* Dunblane: enlisted Perth. Killed in action, 31 July 1917. Age 29. Remembered on Ardoch Parish War Memorial.

His brother Alexander is buried in Frankfurt Trench British Cemetery, Beaumont-Hamel (C.13).

(Panel 37) Pte. 291506, Fremantle Kenneth Stuart, 7th (Service) Bn. The Black Watch (Royal Highlanders): *s.* of Dudley Charles Stuart, Comdr. R.N., late of Lundie, co. Forfar, by his wife Amy, *dau.* of Colonel Charles Harrison Page, of Dulwich House, Llandaff, co. Glamorgan: and brother to Lieut. Comdr. D. Stuart, H.M.S. 'Turbulent;' killed in action on the bridge of that ship by the explosion of a salvo of shells, 31 May 1916, at the Battle of Jutland: *b.* Spean Bridge, co. Inverness, 4 June 1895: *educ.* St. Catherine's School, Southsea, and The Grange, Crowborough: enlisted on 9 November 1915: served with the Expeditionary Force in France and Flanders from July 1916: took part in the operations on the Somme and at Arras, and was killed in action near Ypres, 29 July 1917. Buried in a cemetery beside Bridge No.5, on the Yser Canal. His Commanding Officer wrote, "We were on our way up to the trenches for the attack when a shell landed among the Lewis Gunners and he was killed on the spot, and can have suffered no pain. He was buried the next day in a little cemetery on the west side of the Yser Canal, beside Bridge No.5. The Sergt. of the Lewis Gun Team, which he joined in July 1916, says, 'He was a true Highlander, and was well worthy of the name he bore. As his ancestors before him, he worthily upheld the name of the Clan Stuart.' I really cannot say more in his favour, except that he surprised me from the day he first joined us, in the way he stuck to his duties through these long weary months of hardship, especially as he looked so unsuited for them, but he was a Stuart, and no more need be said," and one of his comrades wrote, "He was a good soldier and a willing helper; if ordered to do any job, however dangerous it was, it was done without a grudge and with a smiling face. He had endeared himself to his comrades, who write of him with affection." Age 22. *unm.*

His brother Dudley also has no known grave; he is commemorated on the Portsmouth Naval Memorial (Panel 11).

(Panel 37) Capt. Allan Humphrey Harden, 2nd Bn. (52nd Foot) The Oxford & Bucks Light Infantry: 2nd *s.* of the late Lieut.Col. John Edward Harden, of the 101st & 109th Regiments, (since named Royal Munster Fusiliers & Leinster Regiment), by his wife Alice Mary (Lexden Villa, Shrub End, Colchester), *dau.* of the late Major-Gen. Edwin Henry Atkinson, Madras Army, and *gdson.* of the late John William

Harden, Barrister-at-Law, Inner Temple, Judge of the Chester County Court, by his wife Angelina, 2nd *dau.* of Sir John Salusbury Piozzi- Salusbury, of Bryn Bella, co. Flint: *b.* Ealing, London, 23 March 1881: *educ.* Colchester, and Dulwich College: joined 4th Middlesex Regt., 6 September 1899: gazetted 2nd Lieut. Oxford & Bucks Light Infantry, from the aforementioned Militia, 5 January 1901; promoted Lieut. 2 September 1903; Capt. 22 January 1910: served through the South African War 1899–1902: took part in operations in Cape Colony, December 1900–January 1901, and in those in the Orange River Colony, January 1901–31 May, 1902 (Queen's Medal, two clasps; King's Medal, two clasps): Adjutant, 6th South Staffordshire Regt., 1908–1912: served with the Expeditionary Force in France and Flanders from 12 August 1914 to 21 October 1914, on which latter date he was in command of his company in an extended position between the villages of Langemarck and Poelcapelle, in close contact with the enemy. He was taking orders from his Colonel when he was killed instantly by a sniper, being shot through the head by a rifle bullet. His body was carried to a farm building close by, which, during the course of the action shortly thereafter, was set on fire by the enemy's shells, and totally consumed, so forming a funeral pyre for a brave soldier. His widow received several highly appreciative letters of sympathy, showing the high esteem in which her late husband was held. His Commanding Officer, Lieut.Col. Davies, wrote, "Your husband's death is a great loss to the regiment. He was one of the best company commanders we had … I liked him so much personally. His death was quite instantaneous. I was talking to him at the moment that he was shot, and I feel sure that he felt nothing. We have lost a very good soldier, and all of us feel much for you in your sorrow," and to Capt. Harden's parents, "Your son was one of the best company commanders I have ever seen. He was very good in peace, and the war gave him more opportunities of showing how a company should be commanded. I had noticed his good work and the great trouble he took from the very first, and I have great hopes that his name will be mentioned in the next Despatches. He was commanding his company in an attack, and had shown great skill in conducting the advance. At the moment he was killed I was talking to him about the next thing to do, when a chance bullet hit him in the head. He is a great loss to us, for he was a fine soldier. He was fearless in action and always did the right thing." And Lieut.Col. Waterhouse, commanding the Territorial Regt. with which he had served, wrote, "His great example will be before us to try and follow. He was one of the finest men I ever knew." A Major of his battalion said, "Your husband's death is a very real loss to all ranks of the regiment." And a junior officer of the battalion, Capt. Blewitt, who had been with him throughout the war wrote, "He was never downhearted in the depressing days of that retirement from Mons, and was so brave and capable in all the jobs we were given to do. I shall always be proud to have served under him, and had absolute confidence in his judgement and arrangements." Lieut. Tolson declared him to have been the best officer he had ever served under, "I shall never expect to serve under a better one, and he inspired confidence in us all." Age 33. Mentioned in F.M. Sir John (now Lord) French's Despatch, 14 January 1915; he *m.* Holy Trinity Church, Brompton, 3 July 1905; Daisy, only *dau.* of the late Capt. George Thomas Scott, late Scots Greys, and Mrs Scott (67, Egerton Gardens, London, S.W.), *grand-dau.* of the late John Howe, J.P., D.L., of Ballycross House, co. Wexford, and cousin to the Right Hon. Lord Muskerry, of Springfield Castle, Drumcollogher, co. Limerick, and had a *s.* and a *dau.* – Robert Allan George, *b.* 11 September 1908; Daphne, *b.* 20 August 1910.

(Panel 37) Lieut. Leslie Wingfield Sweet-Escott, 5th (Service) Bn. The Oxford & Bucks Light Infantry: 3rd & *yst. s.* of Sir Ernest Bickham Sweet-Escott, of Government House, Suva, Fiji, K.C.M.G., Governor & Commander, Fiji; and High-Commissioner & Consul-General, Western Pacific; by his wife Mary, *dau.* of the late Thomas Wingfield Hunt, H.E.I.C.S.: and brother to Lieut. M.R. Sweet-Escott, King's (Liverpool) Regt., killed in action, 20 September 1914; and Lieut. W.A. Sweet-Escott, Royal Field Artillery, died of wounds, 14 October 1918: *b.* Acryse, nr. Folkestone, 3 October 1893: *educ.* Brightlands, Dulwich; Bromsgrove School; Cheltenham College, and Worcester College, Oxford, where he had been studying for a year with a view to taking Holy Orders when war broke out: applied for a commission, gazetted 2nd Lieut. O.B.L.I., 22 August 1914; promoted Lieut. 13 May 1915: served with the Expeditionary Force in France and Flanders from that month: wounded on 11 July but remained on duty, and was killed in action at Bellewaarde Farm, nr. Ypres, 25 September following, while leading a bombing party. His Commanding Officer wrote, "He was a most gallant officer, and died leading a bombing party to the attack. He had on previous occasions done right well, and had proved himself a man of fearless courage, and great initiative. He is a great loss to the regiment." And the officer, then a Captain, who subsequently commanded the battalion, "From the start out here he began to make his mark as a leader, and had I been asked before his death who was the best officer we had for coolness, courage, and presence of mind for an emergency, or any specially ticklish job, I should have said without hesitation 'Escott,' and so would any other officer in the battalion." Age 21. *unm.*

Penned by Lieut. Escott, the following poem was found among his papers after his death:-

An Old Boy To His School

We don't forget while in this dark December
You sit in classrooms that we know so well,
And hear the sounds that keenly we remember –
The clock, the hurrying feet, the chapel bell.
Others are sitting in the seats we sat in,
There's nothing else that's altered there, and then,
When leaving it, the same old Greek and Latin;
      You know we don't forget

We don't forget you in the wintry weather,
Manning the trenches, training in frozen snow,
You play the games we used to play together
In times of peace that seem so long ago.
But while you're at it all, your games, your cheering,
We other hosts in sterner conflict meet,
And other sadder sounds our hearts are hearing;
      Be sure we don't forget.

If we, your brothers true, for all your praying,
To this dear School of ours return no more,
But lie, our country's debt of honour paying,
And not in vain, upon the Belgian shore,
Till that great day when at the throne of heaven
The books are opened and the judgement set,
Our lives for Honour and for England given,
      Our School will not forget.

His brother Murray also has no known grave, he is commemorated on the La Ferte-Sous-Jouarre Memorial; William is buried in Dadizeele New British Cemetery (VI.D.38).

(Panel 37) Lieut. Christopher Fowler Murphy, 2nd Bn. (52nd Foot) The Oxford & Bucks Light Infantry: *yr. s.* of the Rev. Canon Richard William Murphy, M.A., Rector of Clifden, Connemara, formerly of Tuam, by his wife Mary Louisa, *dau.* of the late Christopher Mulvany, C.E.: *b.* Dublin, 17 May 1889: *educ.* Abbey School, Tipperary, and Trinity College, Dublin: gazetted 2nd Lieut. Oxford & Bucks L.I., from R.F.A., Special Reserve, 7 December 1910: promoted Lieut. 22 January 1914: went to France, 27 September 1914, and was killed in action at the First Battle of Ypres, 21 October 1914, while leading his company in an attack. Buried nr. Ypres, on the road to St. Julien and Poelcapelle. Lieut.-Col. Davies, in command of the 2nd Battn., wrote, "He will be a great loss to us, both personally and as a soldier. He died gallantly doing his duty in leading his men on to the attack." And Lieut. Wingfield, "He died bravely, a brave man's death, and his last moments made me very proud of him as a brother officer." Age 25. *unm.*

(Panel 37) 2nd Lieut. Jesse Jones, 2nd Bn. (52nd Foot) The Oxford & Bucks Light Infantry: *s.* of Thomas Jones: *b.* Horton-cum-Studley, nr. Oxford, July 1883: served in the South African War; 1st Oxford & Bucks Light Infantry (Queen's Medal, two clasps): gazetted 2nd Lieut. Oxford & Bucks Light Infantry; being commissioned in the field while on Active Service at Westhoek, Belgium, 9 November 1914; killed in action two days later. He *m.* Beatrice Lily, *dau.* of Mr (& Mrs) Johnson, and left three daughters and one son – Ivy May, age 10; Evelyn Beatrix, age 6; Ena Victoria, age 4; and Albert Edward, age 3, at the time of their father's death. While in the ranks, 2nd Lieut. Jones obtained a first Army School certificate. He was also a gymnastic instructor, and was distinguished for musketry: 11 November 1914. Age 31.

(Panel 37) 2nd Lieut. Francis Pepys, D.S.O., 2nd Bn. (52nd Foot) The Oxford & Bucks Light Infantry: *s.* of Capt. (& Mrs) Arthur Pepys, late 60th Rifles, of Knowle House, Budleigh Salterton, co. Devon: and brother to 2nd Lieut. J. Pepys, K.O.Y.L.I., who, 'while fighting his guns splendidly' at Mons, was shot and killed, 23 August 1914, by German snipers three hours after going into action: *b.* Budleigh Salterton, 2 April 1891: *educ.* Charterhouse, where he was in the cricket XI: subsequently joined Special Reserve, attd. Devonshire Regt.: gazetted 2nd Lieut. 2nd O.B.L.I. May 1913: served with the Expeditionary Force in France and Flanders, and was killed, 12 November 1914, while stepping out of his trench the morning after his battalion had materially helped in the rout of the Prussian Guard. He was Mentioned in Sir John (now Lord) French's Despatch, 14 January 1915, and awarded the D.S.O. for his services in the Great War; the following being the official citation of the award, "For conspicuous good work on November 3rd in advancing from his trench and assisting in driving away a party of the enemy who were commencing to dig a new trench within thirty yards of his own. Thirty Germans were shot." His Commanding Officer wrote, "He most thoroughly earned it for the splendid way he, with three others, turned thirty or forty Germans out of a trench, and for his splendid leading on other occasions." His recreations were hunting, steeple-chasing, cricket, racquets, golf, shooting, fishing, and skiing. Age 23. *unm.*

His brother John is buried in Hautrage Military Cemetery (II.A.6).

(Panel 37) 2nd Lieut. Jack Bouverie Mallam Ward, 2nd Bn. (52nd Foot) The Oxford & Bucks Light Infantry: 2nd *s.* of Frank Ward, of 'Wallasey,' Caterham, co. Surrey: *b.* 1895: *educ.* Marlborough College (Littlefield, 1909–10); Royal Military College, Sandhurst, gazetted 2nd Lieut., 2nd O.B.L.I. August 1914: served with the Expeditionary Force in France and Flanders, joining 2nd Battn. at the Front, and was killed in action at Ypres, 4 November 1914. Age 19.

(Panel 37) Sergt. 7864, John Thomas Hemsley, 5th (Service) Bn. The Oxford & Bucks Light Infantry: late of Chiswick, co. Middlesex: *s.* of the late Corpl. S2/015095, J.C. Hemsley, 49th Field Bakery, Royal Army Service Corps, died on 24 January 1920, aged 55 years; and Elizabeth Hemsley (19, Kingswood Road, Acton Green, London): and elder brother to Corpl. 997, G. Hemsley, 1st Lancashire Fusiliers, killed in action, 1 July 1916, aged 29 years: *b.* Deptford: enlisted Hounslow. Killed in action, 25 September 1915. Age 31.

His father John is buried in Acton Cemetery (K.A.9) and commemorated on a Screen Wall there (Panel 5); George is buried in Mailly Wood Cemetery, Mailly-Maillet (II.A.7).

(Panel 37) Sergt. 6210, Frank Martin, 5th (Service) Bn. The Oxford & Bucks Light Infantry: *s.* of George Martin, Chair Maker; of The Golf Links, Downley Common, High Wycombe, co. Buckingham, and Anne Martin, his wife: *b.* Plomer Hill, West Wycombe, 28 March 1881: a pre-war Reservist; employed at the sorting office, General Post Office, High Wycombe: returned to the Colours on mobilisation, August 1914; proceeded to France, 21 July 1915, and was killed in the assault on Bellewaarde Farm, 25 September following, on which date the battalion incurred casualties of 51 killed, 270 wounded, 144 missing. Age 34.

(Panel 37) Sergt. 10936, George Stanley Savings, 5th (Service) Bn. The Oxford & Bucks Light Infantry: *s.* of John Savings, of Wytham, co. Berks, by his wife Rose Helen: and brother to Pte. 5018, A. Savings (served as Smith), 1/14th London Regt. (London Scottish), killed in action, 1 July 1916 at the Somme: *b.* Blaydon: enlisted Oxford: served with the Expeditionary Force in France, and was killed in action, 25 September 1915. Age 27. *unm.*

His brother Albert also has no known grave; he is commemorated on the Thiepval Memorial.

(Panel 37) Sergt. 10632, Lawrence Waters, 5th (Service) Bn. The Oxford & Bucks Light Infantry: late of Olton, co. Warwick: *s.* of the late Alderman Walter Waters, of Acocks Green, Birmingham, by his wife Louisa: and yr. brother to Pte. 5077, L. Waters, Royal Warwickshire Regt., killed in action, 1 July 1916: enlisted Birmingham. Killed in action, 2 August 1915. Age 25. *unm.*

His brother Leslie is buried in Pargny British Cemetery (III.C.36).

(Panel 37) Sergt. 6753, Robert Leslie Wood, 2nd Bn. (52nd Foot) The Oxford & Bucks Light Infantry: 2nd *s.* of the late Thomas Wood, Gardener; by his wife Emily (Mount Pleasant, Ewell, co. Surrey): *b.* September 1882: a pre-war Regular; was at Cowley Barracks, Oxford on the outbreak of war: served in France from 14 August 1914, and was killed in action, 21 October following at Langemarck, Belgium: Mentioned in Despatches (February 1915) by Sir John (now Lord) French for his services. Age 32. Remembered on the Ewell (Dipping Well) Memorial, Sergt Wood was the first member of his local community to fall in the Great War.

(Panel 37) L/Sergt. 10840, Thomas Victor Do Vey (served as Ralph Seymour), 5th (Service) Bn. The Oxford & Bucks Light Infantry: *s.* of Thomas Do Vey, of Vine Cottage, Barley Mow Lane, Catshill, Bromsgrove, Birmingham, retired Prudential Agent, who served 9 years 336 days 15th (The King's) Hussars (discharge purchased), and his wife Esther, *dau.* of John Neal: *b.* Bridlington, co. York, 16 February 1885: *educ.* Denis Road Public School, Moseley: Occupation – Foreman Art Metal Worker: Scoutmaster of the second troop of Boy Scouts, St. Michael's Parish Church, Handsworth, Birmingham: enlisted 26 August 1914, after the outbreak of war: proceeded to France in May 1915, and was killed in action nr. Ypres, 6 August 1915. Buried where he fell. Capt. Noel Darwell wrote, "I used to be Second in Command of the company of which your son was a member, and, indeed, was originally his Platoon Officer and knew him very, very well, At the time of your son's death I had been called from the company to take over the command of 'A' Coy., or I should have written. I am now brought back to my old company to take Capt. Sanderson's place. I have, however, got all the facts concerning your boy's death, and these I will give you, saying now what is in my heart to say – that his death was a personal grief to all of us who knew him. Of his abilities I will speak later. You will have heard that he had taken over the command of No.15 Platoon when my duties as 2nd Captain made it impossible for me to carry on with the work. He and a part of the platoon occupied a small redoubt, and had experienced very few casualties there (indeed, Capt. Sanderson made his headquarters there for some days), when on 6 August a large enemy shell entered the dug-out where your son and two others were resting, and (though not exploding) dealt two of them injuries from which they died almost immediately. To us soldiers, his loss is something more than the loss of a good fellow and comrade (to that we have too often to bow and stiff our lips), but he had become an efficient and highly-trained non-commissioned officer, and I had personally, and in writing, recommended him to the Commanding Officer for excellent and gallant work on the night of 22–23 June, and I have reason to believe that you will hear of his name as being specially mentioned to the high command. What posthumous recognition, if any, he may earn, I cannot, of course, say (but you will neither be surprised nor sorry to hear that in an army of our size brave and good deeds are, thank God, of daily, if not hourly, occurrence), but you will at least have the consolation of knowing that he had earned the title of a brave and distinguished young soldier." An article in the *St. Michael's Magazine*, October 1915, states – "He is a splendid example of what the Boy Scouts have done in preparing our young men for England's great task. He loved boys and tried to do his duty." Age 30. *unm.*

PANEL 37 ENDS – L/SERGT. G.B. HASELER, OXFORD & BUCKS LIGHT INFANTRY.

PANEL 39 BEGINS – CORPL. P.B. BANNARD. OXFORD & BUCKS LIGHT INFANTRY.

(Panel 39) L/Corpl. 12808, Thomas Henry Taylor, 5th (Service) Bn. The Oxford & Bucks Light Infantry: *s.* of Joseph Taylor, of Bidford-on-Avon, co. Warwick, by his wife Jane: and brother to L/Corpl. 17178, W.W. Taylor, 1st Hampshire Regt., who also fell: enlisted Birmingham. Killed in action, 20 June 1915, at Hooge. Age 22.

His brother Walter is buried in Point-du-Jour Military Cemetery, Athies (I.J.7).

(Panel 39) Pte. 11919, Joseph Allen, 5th (Service) Bn. The Oxford & Bucks Light Infantry: *s.* of Joseph Allen, of 7, Church Lane, Stevenage, co. Hertford, by his wife Eliza: and brother to Pte. 36231, T. Allen, 6th Royal Berkshire Regt., killed in action, 4 October 1916: *b.* Stevenage: enlisted Oxford: Killed in action, 25 September 1915. Age 24.

His brother Thomas is buried in Villers-Bretonneux Military Cemetery (IIIA.F.12).

(Panel 39) Pte. 8253, Arthur John Bass, 2nd Bn. (52nd Foot) The Oxford & Bucks Light Infantry: late of 4, Railway Place, High Wycombe: *s.* of William Bass; Chairmaker, of 8, Lily's Walk, High Wycombe, by his wife Susan 'Susanna': and brother to Sergt. 10241, W.H. Bass, 5th O.B.L.I., killed in action, 24 August 1916, at the Somme: *b.* High Wycombe, co. Buckingham, 13 November 1895: enlisted there. Killed in action, 21 October 1914 at Ypres. Age 18.

His brother William also has no known grave; he is commemorated on the Thiepval Memorial.

(Panel 39) Pte. 17581, William Church, 5th (Service) Bn. The Oxford & Bucks Light Infantry: *s.* of Thomas Church, Farm Labourer; of 129, Stony Stratford, co. Buckingham, by his wife Ada: and brother to Pte. 13224, H. Church, 7th Oxford & Bucks Light Infantry, died of wounds, 22 May 1917; Salonika, and Pte. 13864, G. Church, 6th Oxford & Bucks Light Infantry, died of wounds, 8 June 1917; Poperinghe: *b.* Stony Stratford, 1896: Occupation – Farm Hand: enlisted Oxford: served with the Expeditionary Force in France from May 1915, and was killed in action, 17 October 1915. Age 18. Remembered on Stony Stratford (Horsefair Green) War Memorial.

His brother Herbert is buried in Salonika (Lembet Road) Military Cemetery, Greece (1046); George is buried in Lijssenthoek Military Cemetery (XIII.D.10A).

(Panel 39) Pte. 9757, William James Clack, 'A' Coy., 2nd Bn. (52nd Foot) The Oxford & Bucks Light Infantry: *s.* of William T. Clack, of Broughton, Lechlade, co. Gloucester, by his wife Caroline A.: and yr. brother to Pte. 9565, C.A. Clack, 1st O.B.L.I., killed in action, 22 November 1915 in Mesopotamia: *b.* Broughton, *c.*1895: enlisted Oxford: served with the Expeditionary Force in France, and was killed in action, 11 November 1914, nr. Polygon Wood, Ypres. Age 19.

His brother Christopher also has no known grave; he is commemorated on the Basra Memorial.

(Panel 39) Pte. 7255, William Claridge, 5th (Service) Bn. The Oxford & Bucks Light Infantry: *s.* of George Claridge, of 63, Brown's Hill, South Leigh, Witney, co. Oxford, by his wife Louisa: and elder brother to Stoker 1st Class K/25884, H.C. Claridge, H.M.S. *Indefatigable*, R.N., killed in action, 31 May 1916, at the Battle of Jutland: *b.* Curbridge: enlisted Witney: served with the Expeditionary Force, and was killed in action, 6 August 1915. Age 31.

His brother Hubert has no known grave but the sea; he is commemorated on the Plymouth Naval Memorial (15).

(Panel 39) Pte. 18289, Alfred Lionel Cooper, 5th (Service) Bn. The Oxford & Bucks Light Infantry: *s.* of John Edward Cooper, of Leafield, Witney, co. Oxford, by his wife Emily M.: *b.* Speckbury, co. Oxford, 1899: served with the Expeditionary Force in France, and was killed in action at Ypres, 5 August 1915. Age 16.

(Panel 39) Pte. 267068, James Gordon Falconer, 1st Bn. (43rd Foot) The Oxford & Bucks Light Infantry: *s.* of James Falconer, of 'Brinkburn,' Carnoustie, and Isabella M. Henderson, his wife: employee, Bank of Scotland, Carnoustie: joined Royal Engineers, Spr., Dundee, April 1915; transf'd. 1st Oxford & Bucks late 1916; proceeded to France early 1917: seconded (attd.) Trench Mortar Bty. 1 August following, and was killed in action, 9 August 1917 nr. Ypres, Belgium. Age 21. His Capt. wrote, "I was struck by his confident and fearless manner, and gave him important work to carry out because I knew he would carry out all his orders to the minutest detail. His company commander in the battalion had nothing but praise of him. He is now buried outside Ypres and I am sure will rank among the best of the brave men who have fallen in the Third Battle of Ypres." A comrade in arms, who had been through the battle with him, wrote, "He brought up the party for which he acted as guide, with splendid courage and skill through some very heavy shelling. Just as he got to the place a single shell came over and the shock of the explosion must have killed him. His work was done and he fell as he would have wished, facing the enemy, calm, brave and unmoved, and unshaken by the enemy fire."

(Panel 39) Pte. 7888, Albert Fuller, 2nd Bn. (52nd Foot) The Oxford & Bucks Light Infantry: *s.* of Henry Fuller, of 18, King's Road, Caversham, Reading, by his wife Emily: and elder brother to Corpl. 3077, F.G. Fuller, Rifle Brigade, who fell on 10 May 1915: *b.* Tilehurst, Reading, co. Berks, *c.*1888: enlisted Caversham. Killed in action, 11 November 1914. Age 26. *unm.*

His brother Fredrick also has no known grave; he is recorded on Panel 46.

(Panel 39) Pte. 8542, Maurice Edward Hirons, 3rd (Reserve) Bn. The Oxford & Bucks Light Infantry: served with the Expeditionary Force in France and Flanders. Died of wounds, 7 November 1914. (*IWGC record 2nd Bn.*)

(Panel 39) Pte. 10227, Harry Holton, 5th (Service) Bn. The Oxford & Bucks Light Infantry: *s.* of John Holton, Farm Worker; of Tingewick, co. Buckingham, by his wife Sarah Mary Ann, *dau.* of the late James Addison: and elder brother to Gnr. 191776, F.J. Holton, Royal Garrison Artillery, killed in action, 30 August 1918, aged 23 years: *b.* Westbury, co. Buckingham, 1890: volunteered and enlisted, following the outbreak of war in August 1914: served with the Expeditionary Force in France and Flanders from 21 May 1915, and was killed in action, 25 September 1915 in the attack at Bellewaarde Ridge intended as a diversion to draw German reinforcements away from the fighting at Loos. Age 24. *unm.*

His brother Frederick is buried in Bellacourt Military Cemetery (III.G.5).

(Panel 39) Pte. 17297, Frederick Charles Leach, 5th (Service) Bn. The Oxford & Bucks Light Infantry: *yst. s.* of George Leach, Labourer; of 17, Colley Street, West Bromwich, by his wife Mary, *dau.* of Isaiah Lucock: *b.* West Bromwich, co. Stafford, 21 March 1896: *educ.* Beech Road Council Schools: enlisted 5 January 1915: served with the Expeditionary Force in France and Flanders from September following, and was killed in action, 14 January 1916. Sergt. H.W. King wrote, "We were proceeding to the trenches to relieve some more men, and on the way we had occasion to get out on the top owing to very deep water; as we did so one of the German snipers fired and your son was hit…He has been in my platoon since he joined us last September and I can honestly assure you he has always been a good lad, very willing, and he died manfully doing his duty." Age 19. (*IWGC record 15 January*)

(Panel 39) Pte. 9710, Albert Newell, 2nd Bn. (52nd Foot) The Oxford & Bucks Light Infantry: *s.* of William Newell, of 12, Temple End, High Wycombe, co. Buckingham, by his wife Sarah: and brother to Pte. 17731, W. Newell, 2nd Royal Berkshire Regt., killed in action at the Somme, 1 July 1916: *b.* High Wycombe: enlisted Oxford: served with the Expeditionary Force in France and Flanders from 14 August 1914, and was killed in action at Ypres, 21 October following.

His brother William also has no known grave; he is commemorated on the Thiepval Memorial, Somme (Pier & Face 11D).

(Panel 39) Pte. 7425, James Stallard, 2nd Bn. (52nd Foot) The Oxford & Bucks Light Infantry: late of Stantonbury, co. Buckingham: *s.* of James Stallard, of 67, St. Mary Street, New Bradwell, by his wife Florence: and elder brother to Pte. 8303, J.W. Stallard, O.B.L.I., who fell the same day: *b.* Hockley, co. Warwick, *c.*1886: enlisted Oxford. Killed in action, 11 November 1914. Age 28.

His brother John also has no known grave; he is recorded below.

(Panel 39) Pte. 8303, John William Stallard, 2nd Bn. (52nd Foot) The Oxford & Bucks Light Infantry: late of Stantonbury, co. Buckingham: *s.* of James Stallard, of 67, St. Mary Street, New Bradwell, by his wife Florence: and *yr.* brother to Pte. 7425, J.W. Stallard, O.B.L.I., who fell the same day: *b.* Birmingham, *c.*1888: enlisted Oxford. Killed in action, 11 November 1914. Age 26.

His brother James also has no known grave; he is recorded above.

(Panel 39) Pte. 16554, Albert Edward Todd, 5th (Service) Bn. The Oxford & Bucks Light Infantry: late of Staines, co. Middlesex: *s.* of Charles Todd, Railway Porter; of Dropshort Crossing, Aylesbury, by his wife Eliza: and elder brother to Pte. 1904, F.T. Todd, 1st O.B.L.I., killed in action, 23 July 1916: *b.* 17 March 1887: Occupation – Apprentice Compositor: enlisted Hammersmith: served with the Expeditionary Force in France from May 1915, and was killed in action, 25 September 1915. Age 28. *unm.*

His brother Frederick also has no known grave; he is commemorated on the Thiepval Memorial, Somme.

(Panel 39) Pte. 9888, Ernest John Walker, 2nd Bn. (52nd Foot) The Oxford & Bucks Light Infantry: *s.* of the late John Walker, by his wife Ellen (London Street, Faringdon, co. Berks): *b.* Faringdon, *c.*1894: enlisted Oxford: served with the Expeditionary Force in France and Flanders from 14 August 1914: took part in the fighting at Mons and the subsequent retirement, the Battle of the Marne, and was killed in action, 21 October 1914, at the First Battle of Ypres. Age 20.

(Panel 39) Pte. 17079, Alfred George Wallis, 6th (Service) Bn. The Oxford & Bucks Light Infantry: late of Henley-on-Thames: 2nd *s.* of Thomas Wallis, of Thatched Cottage, Taplow, co. Buckingham, by his wife Jane, *dau.* of Edward Clamp: and brother to Pte. 41905, T.L. Wallis, 19th Manchester Regt. (formerly no.4401, East Surrey Regt.), died of wounds, 4 July 1917, at St. Omer: *b.* Greenhithe, co. Kent, 27 March 1894: *educ.* Ennersdale L.C.C. School, Lewisham, London, S.E.: Occupation – Gardener: enlisted Oxford, 1 January 1915: served with the Expeditionary Force in France and Flanders from 22 July following, and was killed in action, 19 February 1916, being shot by a sniper while repairing the parapet of his trench. Buried nr. Elverdinghe. His Company Commander wrote, "He was liked and trusted by everybody who knew him … He died doing his duty bravely in the face of the enemy." Age 21. *unm.*

His brother Thomas is buried in Longuenesse (St. Omer) Souvenir Cemetery (IV.C.45).

(Panel 39) Pte. 9302, Harry Wootton, 5th (Service) Bn. The Oxford & Bucks Light Infantry: late of Acton, co. Middlesex: *s.* of William Wootton, Bricklayer; of 7, St. John's Road, Aylesbury, by his wife Clara: and twin brother to Pte. 5468, E. Wootton, 11th Middlesex Regt., died of wounds, 12 March 1916: *b.* 6 December 1885: Occupation – Machinist's Assistant: enlisted Shepherd's Bush: served with the Expeditionary Force in France and Flanders from 21 May 1915, and was killed in action, 25 September following. Age 29.

His twin brother Edward 'Ted' is buried in Bethune Town Cemetery (V.B.12).

(Panel 39) Pte. 10187, Henry Wright, 5th (Service) Bn. The Oxford & Bucks Light Infantry: *s.* of John William Wright, of 68, Great Barrington, Burford, co. Oxford, by his wife Annie Elizabeth, *née* Wagstaff: and *yr.* brother to L/Sergt. 8985, J. Wright, 1st O.B.L.I., who fell 28 September 1915, in Mesopotamia: *b.* Burford, *c.*1898: enlisted Oxford. Killed in action, 25 September 1915. Age 18.

His brother John also has no known grave; he is commemorated on the Basra Memorial.

(Panel 39) Capt. Charles Luker Awbery, M.C., 4th Bn. The Essex Regt. (T.F.) attd. 1st Cambridgeshire Regt. (T.F.): *s.* of Albert Richard Awbery, of 60, Huron Road, Tooting Common, London, by his marriage to the late Sarah E. Awbery: Occupation – Chartered Accountant: served with London Scottish; South African Campaign, 1900–02: qualified as Instructor, Army School of Musketry: removed to Epping (1911) where he obtained a commission, 2nd Lieut. 'G' Coy. 4th Essex Regt. (Ongar); promoted Capt. (Temp), 11 October 1914: served with the Expeditionary Force at Gallipoli from 21 July 1915, until the evacuation December following; his rank of Capt. being substantive from the same month: fell sick on the return journey to England and, after treatment and convalescence, went to France attd. Cambridgeshire Regt. mid.-1916. Reported missing, August 1917; it was later discovered Capt. Awbery had been killed in action, 31 July 1917 at St. Julien. Awarded the Military Cross, autumn 1916 (*London Gazette*, 12 October 1917) "For conspicuous gallantry in action. He led his company direct to the final objective and got into touch with the battalions on the right and the left, sending his report to Battalion HQ. He carried out a difficult operation with great courage and skill." Age 38.

(Panel 39) 2nd Lieut. Philip James Barrell, 2nd Bn. (58th Foot) The Essex Regt.: eldest *s.* of Herbert Barrell, of Frating, co. Essex: and brother to Corpl. 9733, H. Barrell, 1st Essex Regt., and kinsman to Sergt. 17891, F.E. Smith, 10th Essex Regt. both of whom have been killed in the war: *b.* Langham, co. Essex, 4 August 1880: *educ.* Great Bromley: enlisted Essex Regt. at the age of 19, and took part in the South African War (Queen's Medal, 3 clasps; King's Medal, 2 clasps): passed through the non-commissioned ranks as Corpl., L/Corpl., Sergt.; received his commission, 2nd Lieut. Essex Regt. (after 14 years service) February 1915; posted 2nd Battn., and was killed in action at St. Jean, Ypres, 1 May following. He was an excellent shot, and won Major A.G. Pratt's Cup for rifle shooting 1910. Age 34.

His brother Harold also has no known grave; he is commemorated on the Helles Memorial, Gallipoli; Fred Smith is buried in Albert Communal Cemetery Extension (I.D.9).

(Panel 39) 2nd Lieut. Arthur Oscar Hornung, 3rd (Reserve) attd 2nd Bn. (56th Foot) The Essex Regt.: only *s*. of Ernest William Hornung (1866–1921), author of *Dead Men Tell No Tales* (1897), creator of '*Raffles – The Amateur Cracksman*' (1899); by his wife Constance Amelia (Medway Cottage, Partridge Green, West Grinstead, co. Sussex, & Marylebone, London), Governess; *dau*. of Charles Altamont Doyle, by his wife Mary Josephine Elizabeth, *née* Foley (parents of Arthur Conan Doyle the creator of *Sherlock Holmes*): *gdson*. of John Peter (& Harriet) Hornung; Hungarian Ironmaster, Timber & Coal Merchant: *b*. 24 March 1895: *educ*. Eton College, where his inherited interest in English literature earned him a special prize in that subject, and, as a cross-country runner, came 2nd in the Junior Steeplechase, 3rd in the Senior; was Captain of Games, a keen football player, and a member of the O.T.C.: commissioned 2nd Lieut. 3rd (Reserve) Battn. Essex Regt. shortly after leaving Eton and, during training, billeted in a farmhouse nr. Harwich marshes: served with the Expeditionary Force in France and Flanders from April 1915, on one occasion leading a patrol of three men 200 yards to the enemy's barbed wire and – after encountering a German work party and successfully dispersing them with bombs – returned to his trench with a badly injured ear. On 6 July 1915 he was struck by a shell in the trenches near Ypres and died without regaining consciousness. Buried near where he fell. Age 20. *unm*. An uncomplicated and religious boy, he lived the straightest of lives, always at the top of some enthusiasm. His affection for Eton at all times was intense and he wrote that Eton meant more than ever to him while he was at the front; every letter to the last showed the same spirit. Full of thought for others, he was loved by all who knew him. Both parents were grief stricken in their loss and, after visiting the western front his father wrote *The Notes Of A Camp Follower* (1919) and *The Young Guard* – a book of war poetry – from which two poems *Bond And Free* and *Wooden Crosses* appeared in *The Times*. The following was penned in Arthur's memory:-

Last Post.

Last summer, centuries ago,
I watched the postman's lantern glow,
As night by night on leaden feet
He twinkled down our darkened street.

So welcome on his beaten track,
The bent man with the bulging sack!
But dread of every sleepless couch,
A whistling imp with leathern pouch!

And now I meet him in the way,
And earth is Heaven, night is Day,
For Oh! There shines before his lamp
An envelope without a stamp!

Address in pencil; overhead,
The Censor's triangle in red.
Indoors and up the stair I bound:
"One from the boy, still safe and sound!"

"Still merry in a dubious trench
They've taken over from the French;
Still full of Tommy, Fritz, and fun!"

"Still wild about the bombing 'stunt'
He makes his hobby at the Front.
Still trustful to his wondrous luck -
Prepared to take on 'Old Man Kluck!'"

Awed only in the peaceful spells,
And only scornful of their shells,
His beaming eye yet found delight
In ruins lit by flames at night,

In clover field and hedgerow green,
Apart from cover or a screen,
In Nature spurting spick and span
For all the devilries of Man.

He said those weeks of blood and tears
Were worth his score of radiant years.
He said he had not lived before –
Our boy who never dreamt of War!

He gave us of his own dear glow.
Last summer, centuries ago.
Bronzed leaves still cling to every bough.
I don't waylay the postman now.

Doubtless upon his nightly beat
He still comes twinkling down our street.
I am not there with straining eye –
A whistling imp could tell you why.

E.W. Hornung

(Panel 39) Sergt. 8446, Alfred Charles Ketley, 2nd Bn. (56th Foot) The Essex Regt.: *s.* of Charles Ketley, of Winchmore Hill, Good Easter, Chelmsford, co. Essex, by his wife Alice: and brother to Spr. 201534, C. Ketley, Royal Engineers, died of wounds, 9 June 1918; and Pte. 43100, L.J. Ketley, died of wounds, 28 April 1917: *b.* Good Easter: enlisted Warley. Killed in action, 13 May 1915. Age 27. He leaves a wife, Agnes Emily Ketley (9, Compasses Row, Broomfield Road, Chelmsford), to lament his loss. Sergt. Ketley, his brothers and eleven other men are remembered on the Good Easter (St. Andrew's Church) War Memorial.

His brother Clifford is buried in Aubigny Communal Cemetery Extension (IV.H.54); Laurence has no known grave, he is commemorated on the Arras (Faubourg d'Amiens) Memorial (Bay 7).

(Panel 39) L/Corpl. 12075, Albert 'Bertie' Tooley (served as Foster, William), 10th (Service) Bn. The Essex Regt.: *s.* of William Tooley, of Dereham Road, Bawdeswell, East Dereham, and the late Clara Tooley, his wife: and elder brother to Pte. 15633, R.W. Tooley, 7th Norfolk Regt., killed in action, 13 October 1915: *b.* Narborough, co. Norfolk: enlisted Southend-on- Sea. Killed in action, 31 July 1917. Age 24. *unm.*

His brother Russell also has no known grave; he is commemorated on the Loos Memorial.

(Panel 39) Pte. 203034, Henry Leonard Aldren, 10th (Service) Bn. The Essex Regt.: formerly no. 203713, Norfolk Regt.: *s.* of the late Robert Aldren, by his wife Hilary (8, Harrod's Place, Providence Street, King's Lynn): and brother to Pte. 3/7652, J.C. Aldren, 7th Norfolk Regt., killed in action, 27 March 1918: *b.* Gaywood, co. Norfolk: enlisted King's Lynn. Killed in action, 31 July 1917. Age 18.

His brother John also has no known grave; he is commemorated on the Pozieres Memorial (Panel 23).

(Panel 39) Pte. 3/30, Albert Edward Craven, 2nd Bn. (58th Foot) The Essex Regt.: *s.* of George Craven, of 25, Lansdowne Road, Leytonstone, by his wife Fanny: and brother to Corpl. 3/1143, T.G. Craven, 1st Essex Regt., killed in action, 2 January 1916, aged 24 years: *b.* Leyton: enlisted Stratford: served with the Expeditionary Force, and was killed in action, 27 May 1915. Age 27. He was married to Elizabeth Griffin, *née* Craven (29, Lancaster Road, Leytonstone).

His brother Thomas is commemorated in Redoubt Cemetery, Helles (Sp.Mem.A.126).

(Panel 39) Pte. 10214, Byron Percy Crump, 2nd Bn. (58th Foot) The Essex Regt.: eldest *s.* of Byron Duval Crump, of New Southgate, London, N., by his wife Rosanna: *b.* Lower Clapton, London, E., 21 July 1897: *educ.* Upper Clapton: Occupation – Traveller: enlisted Warley, co. Essex, August 1914, after the outbreak of war: served with the Expeditionary Force in France and Flanders from December following, and was killed in action at Ypres, 24 June 1915. Buried there. Age 17.

(Panel 39) Pte. 15933, Frank Giggins, 2nd Bn. (58th Foot) The Essex Regt.: *s.* of James Giggins, of The Bungalow, Baker Street, Orsett, Grays, by his wife Emma: and *yr.* brother to Sergt. L/10852, W.G. Giggins, 4th Middlesex Regt.; killed in action, 29 September 1915: *b.* South Ockendon, co. Essex, *c.*1893: enlisted Warley. Killed in action, 24 May 1915. Age 22. *unm.* Pte. Giggins is remembered on Blackheath (Congregational) Church War Memorial.

His brother William also has no known grave; he is recorded on Panel 49.

(Panel 39) Pte. 8329, Alfred Gray, 2nd Bn. (58th Foot) The Essex Regt.: *s.* of the late John Gray, by his wife Elizabeth: *b.* Mile End, London, E.1: enlisted Warley, co. Essex. Killed in action, 2 May 1915. Age 29. Pte Gray's widow has since remarried, now Mrs Lilian Emily Jones (455, High Road, Leytonstone, London, E.11). Remains recovered whilst excavating for new graves at Sanctuary Wood Cemetery, (28.C.21.c.30.30), identified – Disc, Clothing; reinterred, registered 5 April 1930. *Buried in Sanctuary Wood Cemetery (V.L.3).*

(Panel 39) Pte. 16521, Henry Minns, 2nd Bn. (58th Foot) The Essex Regt.: formerly no.4019, 2nd Rifle Brigade: eldest *s.* of Henry Minns, of Grove Road, Chelmsford, co. Essex, by his wife Mary Ann, *née* Newcombe: and brother to L/Corpl. 7783, F. Minns, M.M., 2nd Essex Regt., killed in action, 1 July 1916, at the Somme: *b.* Chelmsford, 9 September 1878: Religion – Church of England: enlisted Rifle Brigade, Warley, co. Essex, 1 November 1895, served eight years with the Colours – Malta (1897); Egyptian Campaign (under Lord Kitchener; Nile Expedition & Khartoum, 1898); Crete (1898) and South African Campaign (1899–1901); Egypt (1902): discharged to Army Reserve, 1903; time expired 1907: Occupation – employee Messrs Hoffmanns, Bearings Factory, Chelmsford: re-enlisted following the outbreak of war; served with the Expeditionary Force in France, and was killed in action, 19 June 1915; shot through the head. Age 37. He was married (1904); to Gertrude Florence White, *née* Minns, *née* Heard (165, Upper Bridge Road, Chelmsford), and leaves eight children.

His brother Frederick is buried in Sucrerie Military Cemetery, Colincamps (I.E.10).

(Panel 39) Pte. 31866, Donald Arthur Watson, 10th (Service) Bn. The Essex Regt.: *s.* of Cator Watson, Innkeeper; 'The Greyhound,' Greyhound Hill, Langham, co. Essex, by his wife Fanny Emily: *b.* Dedham, 1893: Occupation – Farm Labourer: enlisted Colchester. Killed in action, 12 August 1917. Age 24. He was married (4 October 1910) to Maud Fitt, *née* Watson, *née* Bloomfield (39, Brook Street, Colchester, co. Essex). His father, formerly L/Corpl. Essex Imperial Yeomanry, served in the South African Campaign; he also served during the Great War, L/Corpl. Royal Defence Corps.

(Panel 39) Lieut. Geoffrey Morgan Hoyle, 3rd (Reserve) attd. 2nd Bn. (95th Foot) The Sherwood Foresters (Notts & Derbys Regt.): *s.* of Edward Lascelles Hoyle, of Holme Hall, Bakewell, co. Derby, by his wife Margaret K.: and yr. brother to Lieut. J.B. Hoyle, M.C., 7th South Lancashire Regt., who fell on the first day of the Battle of the Somme, 1 July 1916, aged 23 years: received his commission, August 1914. Killed in action, 9 August 1915, at Hooge. Age 21. *unm.*

His brother John 'Jack' is buried in Ovillers Military Cemetery (I.B.15).

PANEL 39 ENDS – LIEUT. D.W. RAMSAY, NOTTS & DERBYS REGT.

PANEL 41 BEGINS – LIEUT. W.C. TAYLOR, NOTTS & DERBYS REGT.

(Panel 41) Lieut. Geoffrey Pennell Walsh, 3rd (Reserve) attd. 2nd Bn. (95th Foot) The Sherwood Foresters (Notts & Derbys Regt.): elder *s.* of the late Fleet Surgeon, James J. Walsh, M.B., Royal Navy (lost his life aboard H.M.S. 'Good Hope' in the battle off Coronel, 1 November 1914), by his wife Eveline Mary (44, Southsea Road, Worthing, co. Sussex), eldest *dau.* of Charles Pennell: *b.* Sheerness, 28 October 1892: *educ.*

Eversley School, Southwold; St. Paul's and Pembroke College, Oxford: gazetted 2nd Lieut. Sherwood Foresters, 15 August 1914; promoted Lieut. 16 May 1915 attd. 2nd Battn. and proceeded to France (same day). Killed in action at Hooge, 9 August 1915. Buried in Sanctuary Wood, Hooge. His Commanding Officer wrote, "Though he had only been with us a few weeks, he was very popular with both officers and men, and he is a great loss to the service." And his tutor from Pembroke College, Oxford, "He only gave us pleasure. From the first, he took his full share of college life, his energies mostly given to the river. He leaves behind him a memory upon which it is a pleasure to dwell." Age 22. *unm.*

His father, with no known grave but the sea, is commemorated on the Portsmouth Naval Memorial (1).

(Panel 41) 2nd Lieut. Edwin Spencer Chandler, 10th (Service) Bn. The Sherwood Foresters (Notts & Derbys Regt.): *s.* of Maria Corderoy Chandler (7, Albany Road, St. Leonards-on- Sea, co. Sussex), by her marriage to the late George Chandler, Author (Hampden House, Sutton, co. Surrey): *b.* 25 June 1895: *educ.* Caldicott Preparatory School (1908–09); The Leys School, Cambridge (North 'B' House, 1909), where he was a Prefect, won second Colours for Hockey, awarded the Kelvin Scholarship on leaving, and went up to Jesus College as an Exhibitioner: joined Sherwood Foresters, August 1914: served with the Expeditionary Force in France, and was killed in action at International Trench; between the Ypres – Comines canal and Railway, north of Ypres, 14 February 1916. Age 20. *unm.* Remembered on Hartley Wintney War Memorial, Hants (Face 1, Col. 1).

(Panel 41) 2nd Lieut. Cyril Ramsay Cook, 4th Bn. (T.F.) attd. 9th (Service) Bn. The Sherwood Foresters (Notts & Derbys Regt.): eldest *s.* of Frank Cook, of Endcliffe, Caterham Valley, co. Surrey, by his wife Sybil, *dau.* of the late Hugh Francis Ramsay, of Hankow, China: *b.* Upper Warlingham, co. Surrey, 10 February 1898: *educ.* Marlborough College: member of Nottingham University O.T.C.; later underwent training Christ's College, Cambridge: obtained a commission in February 1917; sent to Sunderland, to 4th (Territorial) Battn. Sherwood Foresters: served with the Expeditionary Force in France and Flanders, and was killed in action at Messines, 9 July 1917. Buried there. His Commanding Officer wrote, "I am told by his Company Commander that death was instantaneous. He had only been a short time with the battalion, but had made his mark, and was a splendid officer who had the entire confidence and trust of his men. As his Commanding Officer I had the very highest opinion of him, and he is a sad loss to us. He was buried close to where he was killed, and his grave has been marked and the exact locality sent on to the Graves Registration Office … Your son struck me as being the exact type of what a young officer should be, and his Company Commander was full of his praises to me in the recent operations," and a brother officer, "I should like to tell you that in spite of the short time your son was with us, he was extremely popular and when it came to the actual work in action, I can assure you, his coolness and the thoroughness of his work was, in one of so little experience, utterly phenomenal. He only came to my company on the day he went up to the line, through one of my officers being suddenly sent for to join the Flying Corps, but he lost no time in getting a thorough grip of his N.C.O.'s and men. There was one very extraordinary incident in connection with his death. He was in the front line, talking to his platoon sergeant; as far as I remember, at about 1a.m., when he was hit by a piece of shell and instantly killed. His sergeant, who had already won the Military Medal for gallantry early in the war, pounced on him immediately, took his revolver off him, and shouting something about "I'll avenge you, Sir, I'll kill some …," was away over the parapet before anyone could stop him. Of course, nobody expected to see him again, but he returned in about an hour's time with an empty revolver and obviously quite mad." His Chaplain wrote, "The moment he joined he leapt straight into our hearts. We all knew we had a good boy, and he immediately took his place in all fun and gaiety. He was so full of life and enjoyment, and with it all so thoroughly good and clean and wholesome … He was extraordinarily popular, and we shall all greatly miss his cheerfulness and good looks." Age 19.

(Panel 41) 2nd Lieut. Leslie George Hamlyn Harris, 2nd Bn. (95th Foot) The Sherwood Foresters (Notts & Derbys Regt.): *s.* of the late Major Noel Hamlyn (& Mrs) Harris, Royal Artillery, of 13, Brechin Place, South Kensington, London, S.W.7: *b.* South Kensington, 1895: *educ.* Wellington ('Picton'): gazetted 2nd Lieut. Sherwood Foresters, August 1914: served with the Expeditionary Force in France and Flanders. An obituary notice in *The Times*, stated 'he was killed in action at Ypres on 2 November 1914, but his name has not been included in the monthly official casualty lists.' Age 19.

(Panel 41) 2nd Lieut. Michael Vallancey Molloy, 2nd Bn. (95th Foot) The Sherwood Foresters (Notts & Derbys Regt.): elder *s.* of the Rev. Eben Molloy, Vicar of Shenstone, B.A., by his wife Harriet Rachel Emily, *dau.* of the late Rev. Thomas Maule Wetherall, Rector of Pelham Parva, M.A. (*gdson.* of Lieut.-Gen. Vallancey, R.E.): *b.* Keyston Rectory, co. Huntingdon, 29 September 1894: *educ.* Mr Strahan's School, Hythe, and Rossall School (Mr Furneaux's House), O.T.C. member, obtained Certificate 'A': later joined Birmingham University O.T.C.; gazetted 2nd Lieut. Special Reserve of Officers, 15 August 1914; being at his own request attd. 3rd Sherwood Foresters: went to France in early June 1915, attd. 2nd Battn., as Machine Gun Officer, and in April was given a commission in the Regular Army. Killed in action at Hooge, 9 August 1915, while attending to his guns in a captured German trench. Buried in Sanctuary Wood, Hooge. Gen. Congreve, V.C., wrote, "I knew him better than almost any of the young officers. I don't quite know how, and feel I have myself lost a friend. He was an excellent officer – chosen because he was so keen, capable and thoroughly suited for the machine gun command, and he was killed when looking after the guns in a battle in which his brigade did everything it was asked to do." And Major C.I.D. Hobbs, Officer Comdg., "He is a great loss to the regt., as in addition to being such a keen young officer, full of pluck, he was universally popular with officers and men. He was shot by a bullet through the heart while leading his men against the enemy, and must have been killed instantaneously." Capt. Chidlow-Roberts, Officer Comdg. 'C' Coy., also wrote, "Everybody is most awfully cut up about it, as he was a top-hole fellow and a jolly good soldier. He was a great friend of mine. The worst of it was he was too brave, and shouldn't have gone down to see about the gun." And Capt. Noel Chance, R.A., "Mollie (as we all called him) was to me as dear as a younger brother. No loss has affected me so much in this war, and it has caused a gap that cannot be filled. You must, indeed, be proud to have such a son; brave, extraordinarily courteous, and always anxious to help and be a pleasure to others. He died a death we should all prefer, and he could have felt nothing. I have had two short letters from the regt., and in each case (one from Major Hobbs, the commanding officer, and one from Roberts), the outstanding comment is the loss of 'Mollie.' I have never known a boy of his age have so many friends among both senior and junior officers." Age 20. *unm.*

(Panel 41) Coy.Sergt.-Major, 10245, Thomas Alfred Dunn, 1st Bn. (45th Foot) The Sherwood Foresters (Notts & Derbys Regt.): *s.* of Herbert William Dunn, of The Square, Mickleover, Derby, by his wife Emma: and brother to Coy.Sergt.-Major, 12138, G.W. Dunn, M.M., 3rd Grenadier Guards, died of wounds, 18 September 1916, aged 30 yrs; and L/Corpl. 17575, H.A. Dunn, 8th Leicestershire Regt., killed in action, 15 July 1916, aged 24 yrs: *b.* Mickleover: enlisted Derby. Killed in action, 31 July 1917; Westhoek. Age 28. He was married to Florence Dunn (7, South Drive, New Town, Hebburn-on-Tyne).

His brother George is buried in Grove Town Cemetery, Meaulte (I.D.26); Herbert has no known grave, he is commemorated on the Thiepval Memorial.

(Panel 41) Sergt. 926, Henry Allison, 1/7th Bn. (Robin Hood) The Sherwood Foresters (Notts & Derbys Regt.), (T.F.): *s.* of J.H. (& Mrs M.H.) Allison, of 11, Mitchell Street, Durham: *b.* Scarborough, co. York: enlisted Nottingham. Killed in action, 4 August 1915. Age 32. Remains recovered from a grave marked up as belonging to an 'Unknown British Sergeant. Notts & Derbys', located in a small battle cemetery at Sanctuary Wood, identified – Badge of Rank, Clothing, Titles, K.R.R. Buttons;' reinterred, registered, 7 March 1928. *Buried in Sanctuary Wood Cemetery (II.D.22).*

(Panel 41) Sergt. 1456, Charles Edward Flexney (*a.k.a.* Ardern), 2nd Bn. (95th Foot) The Sherwood Foresters (Notts & Derbys Regt.): late of New Mills, co. Derby: half-brother to Pte. 331150, G. Ardern, 15th Sherwood Foresters, died of wounds, 27 November 1917: *b.* Buxton: a pre-war Regular, enlisted Derby: served with the Expeditionary Force in France and Flanders, and was killed in action at Hooge, 9 August 1915.

George Ardern is buried in Dozinghem Military Cemetery (XIV.E.4).

(Panel 41) Sergt. 8, Arthur Phillipson, 1/8th Bn. The Sherwood Foresters (Notts & Derbys Regt.), (T.F.): enlisted Retford, co. Nottingham: served with the Expeditionary Force in France and Flanders from 25 February 1915, and was killed in action, 8 August 1915. Remains recovered from a grave marked as belonging to an 'Unknown British Sergeant. Notts & Derbys', located in a small battle cemetery at

Sanctuary Wood, identified – Titles, Badge of Rank; reinterred, registered, 11 April 1928. *Buried in Sanctuary Wood Cemetery (II.E.38).*

(Panel 41) A/Sergt. 1448, William Albert Wibberley, 'C' Coy., 1/6th Bn. The Sherwood Foresters (Notts & Derbys Regt.), (T.F.): enlisted Ashbourne, co. Derby. Killed in action with his officer and eleven other men at 6.35 pm, 30 September 1915 by the explosion of a mine beneath the Company's trench. Sergt. Wibberley is commemorated on the St. Oswald's Parish Church Roll of Honour, Ashbourne. (*IWGC record no.144*) See account re. Pte. T. D'Arcy, Chester Farm Cemetery (I.B.2), also 2nd Lieut. L.G. Dickinson, Spoilbank Cemetery (I.G.18), and Pte. F.C. Hooley, below.

(Panel 41) Corpl. 15579, William Copeland, 10th (Service) Bn. The Sherwood Foresters (Notts & Derbys Regt.): *b.* Hednesford, co. Stafford: enlisted Warsop, Nottingham. Died on 14 December 1915, of wounds. *Commemorated in Sanctuary Wood Cemetery (Sp.Mem.).*

Their Glory Shall Not Be Blotted Out

(Panel 41) Corpl. 983, Frank Godson, 1/8th Bn. The Sherwood Foresters (Notts & Derbys Regt.), (T.F.): *s.* of the late John Godson (*d. 1890's*), Coal Miner; by his marriage to Rosamond Nowell, *née* Boot, now Mrs Christopher White (Pingle Fields, Sutton-in-Ashfield, co. Nottingham): and brother to Pte. 305137, W. Godson, 1/8th Sherwood Foresters, died of wounds, 17 October 1918: *b.* Beecroft's Yard, Sutton-in-Ashfield, 31 October 1886: served with the Expeditionary Force, and was accidentally killed on 16 July 1915. He *m.* 1907, Hannah Emily Godson (21, Stoney Street, Sutton-in-Ashfield); they had one child. The *Notts Free Press*, 14 July 1916, carried the following – "In Loving Memory of Corporal F. Godson, 8th Sherwood Foresters, who was accidentally killed in Belgium, July 16th, 1915, aged 28 years. I only know he had no pain, For others saw him die; I only know he passed away, Without a last 'Good-bye.' Nobly he did his duty in France. From Wife and Child." Remains recovered from a grave marked as belonging to an 'Unknown British Corporal' in Sanctuary Wood Old Cemetery, (28.I.24.b.90.97), identified – Clothing, Badge of Rank; reinterred, registered 2 May 1928. *Buried in Sanctuary Wood Cemetery (II.F.22).*

Some Time We'll Understand

His brother William is buried in Fresnoy-le-Grand Communal Cemetery Extension (A.23); Frank's widow Hannah never remarried, she died in January 1970.

(Panel 41) A/Corpl. 2481, John Thompson, 'C' Coy., 1/6th Bn. The Sherwood Foresters (Notts & Derbys Regt.), (T.F.): *s.* of Frederick (& Mrs) Thompson, of Home Farm, Mayfield, co. Derby: *b.* Mayfield, 1891: enlisted Ashbourne. Killed in action 6.35 p.m., 30 September 1915. Age 24. *unm.* Commemorated on the St. Oswald's Parish Church Roll of Honour, Ashbourne. See Sergt. W.A. Wibberley, above; and 2nd Lieut. L.G. Dickinson, Spoilbank Cemetery (I.G.18).

(Panel 41) Corpl. 15345, George Townsend, 11th (Service) Bn. The Sherwood Foresters (Notts & Derbys Regt.): *s.* of George Townsend, of 24, Bourne Street, Sutton-in-Ashfield, Nottingham, by his wife Mary Ellen: *b.* Station Street, 13 February 1896: enlisted Sutton-in- Ashfield. Killed in action, 9 April 1917. Age 21. *unm. The Notts Free Press,* 'In Memoriam,' 12 April 1918:-

> *He served his King and Country, God knows he did his best;*
> *But now he sleeps in Jesus, A soldier laid to rest.*
> *Could we have been beside him, To soothe his dying hours;*
> *The grief would not have been so great, For us in silent hours.*
> Sorrowing Mother, Father, Brothers & Sisters.

To lose one's husband, father, son or brother in war is distress enough but, for the wives, mothers, sisters and girlfriends who mourn their loss, to be denied a place of burial they might visit in peace is a concept unimaginable – and even more so when the denial is multiple: double, triple, quadruple....

(Panel 41) L/Corpl. 100976, Thomas Allen, 2nd Bn. (95th Foot) The Sherwood Foresters (Notts & Derbys Regt.): *s.* of John Allen, of 258, Stockbrook Street, Derby, by his wife Elizabeth: and brother to Corpl. 8630, W. Allen, 1st South Staffordshire Regt., killed on 30 October 1914; Pte. 16982, F. Allen, 1st

Northumberland Fusiliers, killed on 27 March 1916, and Pte. 14164, E. Allen, 11th Sherwood Foresters, killed on 9 April 1917: served with the Expeditionary Force in France, and was killed in action at Ypres, 24 September 1915. Age 25. One of four brothers who fell.

His three brothers also have no known grave; they too are recorded on the Menin Gate – William (Panel 35), Frank (Panel 12), and Ernest below.

(Panel 41) L/Corpl. 1400, George Bailey, 'C' Coy., 1/6th Bn. The Sherwood Foresters (Notts & Derbys Regt.), (T.F.): *b.* Crompton, Derby: enlisted Ashbourne, co. Derby. Killed in action 6.35 p.m., 30 September 1915. L/Corpl. Bailey is commemorated on the St. Oswald's Parish Church Roll of Honour, Ashbourne. *(IWGC record 10 September 1917)* See Sergt. W.A. Wibberley, above; and 2nd Lieut. L.G. Dickinson, Spoilbank Cemetery (I.G.18).

(Panel 41) L/Corpl. 10968, Arthur William Concannon, D.C.M., M.M., 1st Bn. (45th Foot) The Sherwood Foresters (Notts & Derbys Regt.): *s.* of John Concannon, and his wife Ellen: awarded the Military Medal and Distinguished Conduct Medal, *London Gazette*, 14 September 1916. Killed in action, 31 July 1917; shot by a sniper during an attack at Westhoek. Age 29. In a letter to his widow a comrade wrote, "Arthur earned a V.C. as big as a battleship. This is what everyone says who saw him. We both went to Confession and Holy Communion two days before the battle. You are quite aware of what we were to each other, I have been hard hit by his death, for I could look the world over and not find a better chum. I have been fairly knocked up over it, and it makes me wild that after being out here two years and nine months, he should get knocked over at the eleventh hour. I feel it pretty hard, but then, what is my loss compared to yours? Please accept my heartfelt sympathy." (*IWGC record M.M.*)

(Panel 41) L/Corpl. 14338, Joseph Goddard, 12th (Service) Bn. The Sherwood Foresters (Notts & Derbys Regt.): *s.* of Joel Goddard, of 3, Joel's Row, Lower Hipper Street, Chesterfield, co. Derby, by his marriage to the late H. Goddard: and elder brother to Pte. 14321, B. Goddard, Sherwood Foresters, who fell twenty-four hours previously: *b.* Eckington, co. York: enlisted Chesterfield. Killed in action, 25 June 1917. Age 35. He leaves a wife, Emma (8, The Woodlands, Langwith, Mansfield, co. Nottingham).

His brother Benjamin also has no known grave; he is recorded below.

(Panel 41) L/Corpl. 12151, John Hallam, 'B' Coy., 2nd Bn. (95th Foot) The Sherwood Foresters (Notts & Derbys Regt.): *s.* of John (& Mrs) Hallam, of 39, Ebenezer Street, Langley Mill, co. Derby: *b.* Stanton-in-the-Wold, co. Nottingham: enlisted Nottingham. Reported missing on 9 August 1915, since confirmed killed in action on that date. Age 21. L/Corpl. Hallam was a well-known local cricket and football player; he was connected with the Wesleyan Club. *unm.*

(Panel 41) L/Corpl. 1953, Arthur Harding, 1/6th Bn. The Sherwood Foresters (Notts & Derbys Regt.), (T.F.): *s.* of James Harding, of Compton Street, Ashbourne, co. Derby, by his wife Alice: *b.* 1894: enlisted Ashbourne. Killed in action 6.35pm, 30 September 1915. Age 21. *unm.* L/Corpl. Harding is commemorated on the St. Oswald's Parish Church Roll of Honour, Ashbourne. See Sergt. W.A. Wibberley, above; and 2nd Lieut. L.G. Dickinson, Spoilbank Cemetery (I.G.18).

(Panel 41) L/Corpl. 2239, John W. Pottinger, 1/7th Bn. (Robin Hood) The Sherwood Foresters (Notts & Derbys Regt.), (T.F.): *s.* of the late William Pottinger, of 20, Radcliffe Street, St. Mary, Nottingham, by his wife Harriett (2, Lewis Place, Nottingham), *dau.* of Amelia Towle (60, Lamcote Street, St. Mary): *b.* c.1872: Occupation – General Labourer: enlisted Nottingham. Killed in action, 1 August 1915. Age 43. He leaves a wife, Mrs E. Pottinger (28, Lamas Street, Waterway Street, Nottingham). Remains recovered from a grave marked as belonging to an 'Unknown British Lance Cpl. Notts & Derbys', located in a small battle cemetery at Sanctuary Wood, identified – Clothing, Badge of Rank, K.R.R. Buttons; registered, reinterred 21 March 1928. *Buried in Sanctuary Wood Cemetery (II.E.4).*

(Panel 41) L/Corpl. 768, William Seal, 1/7th Bn. (Robin Hood) The Sherwood Foresters (Notts & Derbys Regt.), (T.F.): *s.* of Sarah Ann Seal (2, Bobbers Mill Road, Nottingham), and late *husb.* to Alvina Wharmly, *née* Seal (2, Speechley Street, Nottingham): *b.* Nottingham: enlisted there. Killed in action, 31 July 1915, at Hooge. Age 26. Remains recovered from a grave marked as belonging to an 'Unknown British Lance Cpl.', located in a small battle cemetery at Sanctuary Wood, identified – Clothing, Badge of Rank, K.R.R. Buttons; registered, reinterred 21 March 1928. *Buried in Sanctuary Wood Cemetery (II.E.2).*

(Panel 41) L/Corpl. 1676, Percy Scott, 1/8th Bn. The Sherwood Foresters (Notts & Derbys Regt.), (T.F.): *s.* of Joseph Scott, of 18, Richmond Street, New Town, Retford, Nottingham, and Lizzie, his spouse. Killed in action, 8 August 1915. Age 19. Remains recovered from a grave marked as belonging to an 'Unknown British Lance Corporal. Notts & Derbys', located in a small battle cemetery at Sanctuary Wood, (28.I.24.b.90.65), identified – Titles, Badge of Rank; reinterred, registered, 11 April 1928. *Buried in Sanctuary Wood Cemetery (II.E.39).*

At Rest

(Panel 41) Pte. 14164, Ernest Allen, 11th (Service) Bn. The Sherwood Foresters (Notts & Derbys Regt.): *s.* of John Allen, of 258, Stockbrook Street, Derby, by his wife Elizabeth: and brother to Corpl. 8630, W. Allen, 1st South Staffordshire Regt., killed on 30 October 1914; Pte. 16982, F. Allen, Northumberland Fusiliers, killed on 27 March 1916, and L/Corpl. 100976, T. Allen, 2nd Sherwood Foresters, killed on 24 September 1915: served with the Expeditionary Force, and was killed in action at Ypres, 9 April 1917. One of four brothers who fell.

His three brothers also have no known grave; they are also recorded on the Menin Gate – William (Panel 35), Frank (Panel 12), and Thomas above.

(Panel 41) Pte. 21099, Frederick Arnfield, 10th (Service) Bn. The Sherwood Foresters (Notts & Derbys Regt.): *s.* of John Arnfield, of Hyde Bank Road, New Mills: Occupation – Engraver: enlisted in Buxton, 27 December 1914. Killed in action, 14 February 1916. Age 32. Pte. Arnfield, who had been at the front barely two months when he met his death, leaves a widow, Lillian Rose Arnfield (11, Jubilee Street, New Mills) and two children. He was a member of the Wesleyan Chapel, High Street.

(Panel 41) Pte. 19775, Ernest Baguley, 2nd Bn. (95th Foot) The Sherwood Foresters (Notts & Derbys Regt.): formerly no.12647, Leicestershire Regt.: *s.* of William Baguley, of 173, Speedwell Terrace, Staveley, Chesterfield, by his wife Mary: and brother to Pte. 3437, A. Baguley, 1/6th Sherwood Foresters, died on 24 September 1916, of wounds: *b.* Staveley, co. Derby: enlisted Chesterfield. Missing/believed killed in action, 9 August 1915, 'and, as nothing further has been heard of him and the worst is feared, his parents would be pleased to receive information respecting his fate.' Age 23. *unm.* Dedicated – "In grateful remembrance of the men…who fell in the war of 1914–1919" – the brothers are recorded on the Staveley Parish War Memorial.

His brother Albert is buried in Warlincourt Halte British Cemetery (II.G.10).

(Panel 41) Pte. 2833, George Joseph Ball, 1/7th Bn. (Robin Hood) The Sherwood Foresters (Notts & Derbys Regt.), (T.F.): *s.* of John Henry Ball, of 50, Leicester Street, Nottingham: enlisted Nottingham. Killed in action, 4 August 1915. Age 19. Buried beside Sergt. Allison, in same grave as Pte. Henson. Remains recovered from two graves marked up as belonging to an 'Unknown British Soldier. Notts & Derbys', located in a small battle cemetery at Sanctuary Wood, identified – Clothing, Titles, K.R.R. Buttons; reinterred, registered, 7 March 1928. *Buried in Sanctuary Wood Cemetery (II.D.23/24).*

(Panel 41) Pte. 3287, Tom Edgar Bennett, 'D' Coy., 1/6th Bn. The Sherwood Foresters (Notts & Derbys Regt.), (T.F.): *s.* of John (& Constance) Bennet. Killed in action, 28 June 1915; sniper. Age 32. Buried Armagh Wood, Major E. Hall officiating. 1/6th Battalion's first Ypres salient fatality. *Buried in Bedford House Cemetery (Enc.No.6).*

(Panel 41) Pte. 20926, Henry Beresford, 2nd Bn. (95th Foot) The Sherwood Foresters (Notts & Derbys Regt.): late of Piece Farm, New Mills, co. Derby: *s.* of Henry Beresford, of Laneside Farm, Rowarth, Stockport, by his wife Hannah: *b.* Derby, *c.*1894: Occupation – Farm Worker: enlisted Buxton: served with the Expeditionary Force, and was killed in action at Hooge, 7 August 1915. In a letter to his family a comrade, Pte. Conley, wrote, "Just a few lines to let you know about the death of your son, who fell on the last day, August 9th (*q.v.*). There was a rough deal for a position out here, and hundreds of our men fell in taking this position. I and a lot more men went out at night to bury the dead. I happened to have the luck to come across him, along with others who we buried. He had in his pockets some photographs relating to you, and another of Miss Fielding of Low Leighton. We had to abandon the job of burying them owing to it getting too hot, the Germans firing bombs onto us. At the time of writing we are having it hot; so no more at present from one who is suffering from the effects of the strain we have all of us had from the start. We get it rough, and not much rest. We are all dead beat to the world. I think, along with the rest of the lads, that it is time someone took it up for us." Age 21. *unm.*

(Panel 41) Pte. 17541, Ernest Bills, 'B' Coy., 12th (Service) Bn. The Sherwood Foresters (Notts & Derbys Regt.): *s.* of Arthur Bills, Coal Miner; of Barlestone, co. Leicester, by his wife Sarah: *b.* Quarry Yard, Sutton-in-Ashfield, 14 February 1888: enlisted Mansfield. Killed in action, 27 June 1917. Age 29. He was married to Catherine Hill, *née* Bills (5, Hardwick Street, Sutton-in-Ashfield), and had two children Leslie and Arthur. The *Notts Free Press*, 28 June 1918, carried the following 'In Memoriam':-

> *The bugle called, he hastened forth, The bravest in the battle's van;*
> *Remember he who yields his life, Is a soldier and a man.*

(Panel 41) Pte. 2703, John Bowskill, 'A' Coy., 1/8th Bn. The Sherwood Foresters (Notts & Derbys Regt.), (T.F.): *s.* of Mr (& Mrs) Bowskill, of Mansfield Woodhouse: enlisted Newark. Killed in action, 22 July 1915. Age 23. He leaves a wife, Mrs L. Bowskill (7, Hampden Street, Kirkby-in-Ashfield, co. Nottingham). Remains recovered from a grave marked as belonging to an 'Unknown British Soldier. 8 Notts & Derby', located in Sanctuary Wood Old Cemetery (28.I.24.b.90.97), identified – Clothing, Tunic with titles lying on body; reinterred, registered 2 May 1928. *Buried in Sanctuary Wood Cemetery (II.F.19).*

(Panel 41) Pte. 1812, James Bradley, 'C' Coy., 1/6th Bn. The Sherwood Foresters (Notts & Derbys Regt.), (T.F.): *s.* of Henry James Bradley, of Wall Ash, Mayfield, co. Derby, by his wife Alice: enlisted Ashbourne. Killed in action 6.35 p.m., 30 September 1915. Age 18. See Sergt. W.A. Wibberley (above), and 2nd Lieut. L.G. Dickinson, Spoilbank Cemetery (I.G.18).

(Panel 41) Pte. 1199, Oliver Leslie Bryan, 'C' Coy., 1/8th Bn. The Sherwood Foresters (Notts & Derbys Regt.), (T.F.): *s.* of the late John Bryan, of South Normanton, co. Derby, by his wife Elizabeth, since re-married to Edward Eyre, of Ronald Villas, Skegby Forest, co. Nottingham: *b.* Swanwick, co. Derby, 1890: served with the Expeditionary Force in France and Flanders, and was killed in action, 15 June 1915. Age 25. The *Notts Free Press*, 15 June 1917, carried the following notice – "In loving memory of Pte. Oliver Bryan, the beloved son of Mrs Eyre, Skegby Forest, who was killed in Flanders, 15 June 1915. Home is dark without our loved one, Sadly do we miss his face; Darkness lurks where once was sunshine, None can fill our dear one's place. Though time may bring its soothing care, And others may forget; To us thou'll be for ever dear, We mourn our loved one yet. From his loving Mother, Father, Brothers and Sister."

(Panel 41) Pte. 58533, George Burrows, 11th (Service) Bn. The Sherwood Foresters (Notts & Derbys Regt.): late of Cropwell Bishop, co. Nottingham: enlisted Derby. Killed in action, 9 April 1917. Remains recovered from an unmarked grave (28.I.29.c.60.35) Hill 60; identified – Clothing, Boots, Title, Disc; reinterred, registered 18 May 1928. Remembered on the Cropwell Bishop (St. Giles) Church War Memorial. *Buried in Sanctuary Wood Cemetery (II.J.31).*

(Panel 41) Pte. 2524, Charles S. Carter, 1/6th Bn. The Sherwood Foresters (Notts & Derbys Regt.), (T.F.): *s.* of Edward Carter, of Market Place, Ashbourne, co. Derby, by his wife Martha: and twin brother to Pte. 3541, T.G. Carter, 1/6th Sherwood Foresters, who fell two weeks later: *b.* Hollington, 1896: enlisted Ashbourne. Killed in action 6.35 p.m., 30 September 1915. Age 19. Remembered on Mappleton (St. Mary's) Church Roll of Honour, Derby. See Sergt. W.A. Wibberley, above; and 2nd Lieut. L.G. Dickinson, Spoilbank Cemetery (I.G.18).

His twin Thomas also has no known grave; he is commemorated on the Loos Memorial.

(Panel 41) Pte. 13791, Ben Caunt, D.C.M., M.M., 1st Bn. (45th Foot) The Sherwood Foresters (Notts & Derbys Regt.): *s.* of Benjamin Caunt, Manure Manufacturer; of Church Street, Sutton-in-Ashfield, by his wife Frances, *née* Maiden: *b.* 16 January 1894: enlisted Mansfield, co. Nottingham. Killed in action, 31 July 1917. Awarded Distinguished Conduct Medal (*London Gazette*, 1 September 1916) 'For gallantry and devotion to duty on 5 July 1916, when in the attack on the German positions close to the Albert-Pozieres Road, near La Boiselle,' and the Military Medal (*London Gazette*, 11 May 1917) 'For conspicuous gallantry and devotion to duty. During an attack on a ridge immediately south of St. Pierre-Vaast Wood on 4 March 1917, he rushed a traverse which was held by the enemy and, single-handed, succeeded in capturing seven prisoners. He set a fine example to all ranks.' Age 23. *unm.*

(Panel 41) Pte. 19797, William Chadwick, 1st Bn. (45th Foot) The Sherwood Foresters (Notts & Derbys Regt.): *s.* of John Chadwick, of 22, Hipper Street West, Chesterfield, by his wife Esther: *b.* Walsall, co. Stafford, about 1892: enlisted Chesterfield. Killed in action, 17 June 1917. Age 25. *unm. Buried in Oosttaverne Wood Cemetery (IV.B.5).*

(Panel 41) Pte. 2225, Charles J. Clarke, 1/7th Bn. (Robin Hood) The Sherwood Foresters (Notts & Derbys Regt.), (T.F.): formerly no.1374, Royal Fusiliers (City of London Regt.): late of Shepherd's Bush, London, W.12: *b.* Llandudno, co. Denbigh: enlisted London: served with the Expeditionary Force in France and Flanders from early 1915, and was killed in action, 1 August 1915. Remains recovered from a grave marked as belonging to an 'Unknown British Soldier. 7 Notts & Derbys', located in a small battle cemetery at Sanctuary Wood, identified – Clothing, Titles, K.R.R. Buttons; registered, reinterred 21 March 1928. *Buried in Sanctuary Wood Cemetery (II.E.1).*

(Panel 41) Pte. 950, Alfred Cook, 1/8th Bn. The Sherwood Foresters (Notts & Derbys Regt.), (T.F.): *s.* of Robert Cook, of 1, Park Street, Sutton-in-Ashfield, co. Nottingham, by his wife Sarah Ann, *née* Turner: and yr. brother to Pte. 2088, H. Cook, Sherwood Foresters, died 14 October 1915, aged 25 years: *b.* Wellbeck Street, 17 November 1891: a pre-war Territorial, volunteered and undertook Active Service Obligations, Newark, on the outbreak of war, 4 August 1914: served with the Expeditionary Force in France and Flanders from 25 February 1915, and was killed in action, 15 June following: 15 June 1915. Age 23. *unm.* Two other brothers also served, both surv'd. *The Notts Free Press*, 'In Memoriam,' 16 June 1916:-

> *No mother's care did him attend, Nor o'er him did a father bend;*
> *No sister by to shed a tear, No brother his last word to hear.*
>
> *He sleeps not in his native land, But 'neath some foreign skies,*
> *And far from those who loved him best, In a hero's grave he lies.*
>
> *Home is sad without our loved one, Bitterly we miss his face;*
> *Sadness lurks where once was sunshine, None can fill our loved one's place.*
>
> *You will never be forgotten by us.*

Father, Mother, Brothers & Sisters.

His brother Harold is buried in Cabaret-Rouge British Cemetery (XXVII.L.5).

(Panel 41) Pte. 1853, Thomas Cook, 1/7th Bn. (Robin Hood) The Sherwood Foresters (Notts & Derbys Regt.), (T.F.): *s.* of Tom Cook, of 11, Palin Street, Nottingham, by his wife Lucy: *b.* Nottingham, 1896. Killed in action, 31 July 1915. Age 19. Remains recovered from a grave marked as belonging to an 'Unknown British Soldier', located in a small battle cemetery at Sanctuary Wood (28.I.24b.90.65), identified – Clothing; reinterred, registered 11 April 1928. *Buried in Sanctuary Wood Cemetery (II.E.36).*

(Panel 41) Pte. 2031, John Copper, 1/7th Bn. (Robin Hood) The Sherwood Foresters (Notts & Derbys Regt.), (T.F.): *s.* of Harriet Green: *b.* Leeds, co. York, *c.*1890: enlisted Nottingham. Killed in action at Ypres, 1 August 1915. Age 25. He was married to Lavinia Frances Lakin, *née* Copper (1, Forest Street, Hyson Green, Nottingham). Remains recovered from a grave marked up as belonging to an 'Unknown British Soldier. 7 Notts & Derbys', located in a small battle cemetery at Sanctuary Wood, identified – Clothing, Titles, K.R.R. Buttons; registered, reinterred 21 March 1928. *Buried in Sanctuary Wood Cemetery (II.E.3).*

(Panel 41) Pte. 1593, John Cousins, 1/7th Bn. (Robin Hood) The Sherwood Foresters (Notts & Derbys Regt.), (T.F.): *s.* of Frank Cousins, of Nottingham, by his wife Elizabeth: served with the Expeditionary Force in France, and was killed in action, 1 August 1915. Age 21. He was married to Hilda Birch, *née* Cousins (8, Newcastle Road, Nottingham). Remains recovered 'Small Battle Cemetery Sanctuary Wood,' unmarked grave 'Unknown British Soldier. 7 Notts & Derbys.;' identified – Clothing, Titles, K.R.R. Buttons; registered, reinterred 21 March 1928. *Buried in Sanctuary Wood Cemetery (II.D.42).*

(Panel 41) Pte. 2481, Cyril Duro, 1/5th Bn. The Sherwood Foresters (Notts & Derbys Regt.), (T.F.): *s.* of Joseph Baker Duro, of 113, Park Road, Ilkeston, co. Derby, by his wife Harriet: enlisted Ilkeston. Killed in action, 26 June 1915. Remains recovered from a grave marked as belonging to an 'Unknown British Soldier', (28. I. 24. d. 15.45) 30 January 1929, identified – Khaki, Impression of large regimental badge on epaulet (probably Notts & Derby); reinterred, registered 13 February 1929. *Buried in Sanctuary Wood Cemetery (V.C.19).*

(Panel 41) Pte. 1058, Ezekiel Eaton, 1/8th Bn. The Sherwood Foresters (Notts & Derbys Regt.), (T.F.): *b.* Ilkeston, co. Derby: enlisted Southwell, co. Nottingham: served with the Expeditionary Force in France and Flanders from February 1915, and died of wounds (at home), 17 May 1915. *Buried in Southwell Minster (St. Mary's) Churchyard, Southwell. IWGC:1926/MR.29,XVIII,pg.439.*

(Panel 41) Pte. 202520, John Edge (*a.k.a* Belfield), 1st Bn. (45th Foot) The Sherwood Foresters (Notts & Derbys Regt.): *s.* of Samuel (& Mrs) Belfield, of Hollinhurst Head Farm: Occupation – Farm Worker: enlisted Buxton. Killed in action, 31 July 1917, at Ypres. Age 36. Whilst he was serving, Pte. Edge's father died suddenly and, due to the shock of this, Mrs Belfield suffered a paralytic seizure. Friends attempted to have him released from his duty in order that he might return to run the farm and care for Mrs Belfield but, before this could be accomplished, Pte. Edge was killed and his mother died a few days later without being informed of her son's death. All correspondence should be addressed c/o his sister Mrs M.A. Booth (22, Monk Street, North Bay, Ontario, Canada).

(Panel 41) Pte. 2499, D.H. Francis, 1/5th Bn. The Sherwood Foresters (Notts & Derbys Regt.), (T.F.): late of Merthyr Tydfil, co. Glamorgan: enlisted Derby. Killed in action, 26 June 1915. Remains recovered from a grave marked as belonging to an 'Unknown British Soldier', (28.I.24.d.15.45) 30 January 1929; identified by his khakis; reinterred, registered 13 February 1929. *Buried in Sanctuary Wood Cemetery (V.C.18).*

(Panel 41) Pte. 14321, Benjamin Goddard, 12th (Service) Bn. The Sherwood Foresters (Notts & Derbys Regt.): *s.* of Joel Goddard, of 3, Joel's Row, Lower Hipper Street, Chesterfield, co. Derby, by his marriage to the late H. Goddard: and *yr.* brother to L/Corpl. 1438, J. Goddard, Sherwood Foresters, who fell twenty-four hours later: *b.* Chesterfield: enlisted Clown, co. Derby. Killed in action, 24 June 1917. Age 33. He leaves a wife, Sarah (41, Westlea Cottages, Clown, Chesterfield).

His brother Joseph also has no known grave; he is recorded above.

(Panel 41) Pte. 2288, Oscar Goodwin, 'C' Coy., 1/6th Bn. The Sherwood Foresters (Notts & Derbys Regt.), (T.F.): *b.* Buxton, co. Derby. Killed in action 6.35 p.m., 30 September 1915. *(IWGC record T.O.F. Goodwin).* See Sergt. W.A. Wibberley, above; and 2nd Lieut. L.G. Dickinson, Spoilbank Cemetery (I.G.18).

(Panel 41) Pte. 25829, Robert Hall, 1st Bn. (45th Foot) The Sherwood Foresters (Notts & Derbys Regt.): *b.* Ilkeston, co. Derby. Died of wounds, 17 June 1917. He was married to the late Nellie Hall, *dau.* of Mr (& Mrs) Bardill, of Bridge Street, Langley Mill, co. Derby, who, shortly after the death of her husband, took up a position as Canteen Worker at the Chilwell Factory, and met her death as a result of the terrible explosion which occurred there on 1st July 1918. Several other Canteen Workers were injured, but Mrs Hall was the only fatality; her life given in the service of her country, equally with those given on the field of battle. She was 27 years of age. Devout churchgoers, the deceased were married at Aldercar Church.

(Panel 41) Pte. 3405, Waker Harrison, 2nd Bn. (95th Foot) The Sherwood Foresters (Notts & Derbys Regt.): *s.* of Henry Harrison, of 14, Derby Terrace, Clarendon Street, Hull, co. York, by his wife Emma: *b.* Hull, *c.*1883: enlisted Nottingham. Killed in action (shellfire) in company with Pte. J. Taylorson on the evening of 12 October 1915, while engaged in trench repair and improvement at Brielen. Age 32. He was married to the late Alice Harrison, of Hull. See also Pte. W. Flint, Lijssenthoek Military Cemetery (I.B.21A).

Pte. Taylorson is buried in Potijze Burial Ground Cemetery (DI.10).

(Panel 41) Pte. 1399, Harry Harvey, 1/5th Bn. The Sherwood Foresters (Notts & Derbys Regt.), (T.F.): *s.* of Mary Jane Harvey (11, Becher Street, Derby): enlisted Derby: served with the Expeditionary Force in France and Flanders from 25 February 1915, and was killed in action, 26 June 1915. Age 19. Remains recovered from a grave marked as belonging to an 'Unknown British Soldier. Notts & Derby', (28.I.24.d.15.45) 30 January 1929; identified – Khaki, Titles; reinterred, registered 13 February 1929. *Buried in Sanctuary Wood Cemetery (V.C.16).*

(Panel 41) Pte. 2747, Frank Henson, 1/7th Bn. (Robin Hood) The Sherwood Foresters (Notts & Derbys Regt.), (T.F.): *s.* of E. (& Mrs) Henson, of 54, Austen Avenue, Nottingham: enlisted Nottingham. Killed in action, 3 August 1915. Age 20. *unm.* Buried beside Sergt. Allison, in same grave as Pte. G.J. Ball. Remains recovered from two graves marked as belonging to an 'Unknown British Soldier. Notts & Derbys', located in a small battle cemetery at Sanctuary Wood , identified – Clothing, Titles, K.R.R. Buttons;' reinterred, registered, 7 March 1928. *Buried in Sanctuary Wood Cemetery (II.D.23/24).*

(Panel 41) Pte. 14453, William Howells, 10th (Service) Bn. The Sherwood Foresters (Notts & Derbys Regt.): 4th *s.* of the late Henry Howells, formerly of Campbell Street, Heanor, by his wife Hannah (2, Ebenezer Street, Langley Mill, co. Derby): *b.* Derby, 1890: volunteered and enlisted, September 1914, after the outbreak of war: served with the Expeditionary Force in France and Flanders. Reported missing on 14 February 1916, there having been no further news of him, he is presumed to have died on or about that date. He was a keen footballer, playing for several seasons with Langley Mill Rovers F.C.. Age 25. *unm. (IWGC record age 27)*

(Panel 41) Pte. 2565, William Albert Humber, 1/5th Bn. The Sherwood Foresters (Notts & Derbys Regt.), (T.F.): late *husb.* to Sarah Ann Lovegrove, *née* Humber (304, Brighton Road, Alvaston, co. Derby): enlisted Derby. Killed in action, 26 June 1915. Age 42. Remains recovered from a grave marked as belonging to an 'Unknown British Soldier' (28.I.24.d.15.45) 30 January 1929; identified – Khaki; reinterred, registered 13 February 1929. *Buried in Sanctuary Wood Cemetery (V.C.15).*

(Panel 41) Pte. 1785, Frederick Cecil Hooley, 'C' Coy., 1/6th Bn. The Sherwood Foresters (Notts & Derbys Regt.),(T.F.): *s.* of Frederick Hooley, of 15, Cromsford Road, Wirksworth, co. Derby, by his wife Mary Elizabeth: *b.* Stapleford, co. Nottingham, *c.*1897: *educ.* Bingley Grammar School, co. York: Occupation – Bank Clerk: volunteered for Active Service on the outbreak of war, August 1914: served with the Expeditionary Force in France and Flanders, lately as Officer's Servant to 2nd Lieut. L.G. Dickinson, and was killed with his officer and eleven other men, 6.35pm, 30 September 1915, when the enemy detonated a mine beneath the Company's trench south of the Menin Road. Age 18. See Sergt. W.A. Wibberley, above.

2nd Lieut. Lewis Dickinson is buried in Spoilbank Cemetery (I.G.18).

(Panel 41) Pte. 47787, Alfred Marsh (*a.k.a.* Roebuck), 11th (Service) Bn. The Sherwood Foresters (Notts & Derbys Regt.): *s.* of John Roebuck, of Sutton-in-Ashfield, Nottingham, by his wife Annie: enlisted Derby. Died of wounds, 7 June 1917, at Zillebeke. Age 20. *unm.* The *Notts Free Press,* 'In Memoriam,' 14 June 1918:-

> *His King and Country called him, They did not call in vain,*
> *On Britain's Roll of Honour, You'll find our hero's name.*
> *Do not ask us if we miss him, There is such a vacant place;*
> *Can we ever forget his footsteps, And his dear familiar face.*
>
> *Gone from our home, Oh, how we miss him,*
> *Loving him dearly his memory we keep;*
> *Never till life ends shall we forget him,*
> *Dear to our hearts is the place where he sleeps.*

Father, Mother, Sisters & Brother.

(Panel 41) Pte. 2507, T. Percy Matthews, 1/5th Bn. The Sherwood Foresters (Notts & Derbys Regt.), (T.F.): *s.* of Alderman Jabez Matthews, of 'Llanvair,' 35, The Avenue, Yeovil, co. Somerset, and Martha

Dixon his wife: and brother to 2nd Lieut. W.V. Matthews, M.C., 11th attd. 1/5th Border Regt., killed in action, 1 October 1918, in an attack on the Hindenburg Line; and Pte. 240840, A.D.T. Matthews, 1/5th Somerset Light Infantry, killed in action, 9 April 1918, in Palestine: prior to the outbreak of war assisted in his father's work with Messrs Prudential Insurance Society: enlisted Sherwood Foresters, Derby, with his brother Harold (surv'd.): served with the Expeditionary Force in France from early 1915, and was killed in action, 26 June 1915. Age 26. *unm. The Western Gazette* recorded – "News has been received that Private Percy Matthews…is missing and very little hope is held out for his safety…He has been at the Front with his regiment for the past four months. Private P. Matthews, who was of a very jovial disposition was a member of the Yeovil Liberal Club….It would appear that the Battalion was on trench duty, and that Private Matthews, who was reported as "missing," and some comrades were having tea outside on the reverse of the trench. A shell, which dropped short, exploded over the party, killing Private Matthews, and others, and wounding more. He had been at the Front for some months and had taken part in some dangerous enterprises, one of which included work in listening patrols sent out at night in front of enemy trenches. The greatest sympathy has been expressed with Mr. and Mrs. Matthews and family in their loss." One of three brothers who fell. Remains exhumed from a grave marked as belonging to an 'Unknown British Soldier. Notts & Derby', (28.I.24.d.15.45), 29 January 1929; reinterred, registered 31 January 1929. *Buried in Sanctuary Wood Cemetery (V.C.20).*

He Loved His Country And Was Faithful Unto Death

His brother Wilfred is buried in Bellicourt British Cemetery (VI.R.2); Arthur lies in Ramleh War Cemetery (N.26).

(Panel 41) Pte. 4966, John Miller, 2nd Bn. (95th Foot) The Sherwood Foresters (Notts & Derbys Regt.): *s.* of James Miller, of 62, St. Paul's Avenue, Hyson Green, Nottingham, by his wife Ellen: and yr. brother to Pte. 50170, W. Miller, 11th Sherwood Foresters, killed in action, 9 April 1917: *b.* Nottingham: enlisted there: served with the Expeditionary Force in France, and was killed in action, 9 August 1915. Age 19.

His brother William also has no known grave; he is recorded below.

(Panel 41) Pte. 50170, William Miller, 11th (Service) Bn. The Sherwood Foresters (Notts & Derbys Regt.): *s.* of James Miller, of 62, St. Paul's Avenue, Hyson Green, Nottingham, by his wife Ellen: and elder brother to Pte. 4966, J. Miller, 2nd Sherwood Foresters, killed in action, 9 August 1915: *b.* Nottingham: enlisted Derby: served with the Expeditionary Force in France and was killed in action, 9 April 1917. Age 31. He was married to Ada Florence Fitton, *née* Miller (New Row, Willoughby-on-the-Wolds, Loughborough). His brother John also has no known grave; he is recorded above.

(Panel 41) Pte. 3898, Horace Mills, 2nd Bn. (95th Foot) The Sherwood Foresters (Notts & Derbys Regt.): *s.* of Mary Mills (Mount Street, Breaston, Derby): and yr. brother to Rfn. S/7045, H. Mills, 1st Rifle Brigade, killed in action, 13 May 1915: *b.* Breaston: enlisted Nottingham. Killed in action, 9 August 1915. Age 19.

His brother Harold also has no known grave; he is recorded on Panel 48.

(Panel 41) Pte. 1536, Harold Hawkesworth Orton, 1/7th Bn. (Robin Hood) The Sherwood Foresters (Notts & Derbys Regt.), (T.F.): enlisted Drill Hall, Derby Road, Nottingham: served with the Expeditionary Force in France and Flanders from 25 February 1915, and was killed in action near Zillebeke, Ypres sector 1 August 1915. Remains recovered from three graves marked as belonging to an 'Unknown British Soldier. Notts & Derbys', located in a small battle cemetery at Sanctuary Wood, identified – Clothing, Titles, K.R.R. Buttons; reinterred, registered 22 March 1928. *Buried in Sanctuary Wood Cemetery (II.E.5).*

(Panel 41) Pte. 2602, Reginald Pearson, 1/7th Bn. (Robin Hood) The Sherwood Foresters (Notts & Derbys Regt.), (T.F.): only *s.* of A.H. Pearson, of 269, Arkwright Street, Nottingham, by his wife Jessie: enlisted Nottingham: served with the Expeditionary Force in France and Flanders from February 1915, and was killed in action, 1 August 1915. Age 19. Remains recovered from three graves marked as belonging to an 'Unknown British Soldier. 7 Notts & Derbys', located in a small battle cemetery at Sanctuary Wood, identified – Clothing, Titles, K.R.R. Buttons; reinterred, registered 22 March 1928. *Buried in Sanctuary Wood Cemetery (II.E.6).*

(Panel 41) Pte. 14549, Daniel Phillips, 10th (Service) Bn. The Sherwood Foresters (Notts & Derbys Regt.): *s.* of the late John Phillips, by his marriage to Harriett Wright, *née* Phillips (2, Foundry Street, Whittington Moor, Chesterfield, co. Derbys): *b.* Stockton-on-Tees, Co. Durham: enlisted Chesterfield. Killed in action, 14 February 1916. Age 26. *unm. Buried in Harlebeke New British Cemetery (XIII.B.13).*

(Panel 41) Pte. 1773, George Prior, 1/7th Bn. (Robin Hood) The Sherwood Foresters (Notts & Derbys Regt.), (T.F.): *s.* of the late Joseph (& Caroline) Prior: enlisted Nottingham: served with the Expeditionary Force in France and Flanders from February 1915, and was killed in action, 1 August following, at Hooge. Age 20. *unm.* Remains recovered from three graves marked as belonging to an 'Unknown British Soldier', located in a small battle cemetery at Sanctuary Wood', identified – Clothing; reinterred, registered 22 March 1928. *Buried in Sanctuary Wood Cemetery (II.E.7).*

(Panel 41) Pte. 2551, Ernest Richardson, 'D' Coy., 1/8th Bn. The Sherwood Foresters (Notts & Derbys Regt.), (T.F.): *s.* of Charles Richardson, of 32, Sixth Avenue, Forest Town, Mansfield, by his wife Ellen Rebecca: and brother to Pte. A. Richardson (surv'd.): *b.* Mansfield, co. Nottingham: employee at Mansfield Colliery: enlisted, Forest Town, September 1914: served with the Expeditionary Force in France and Flanders from 25 February 1915, joining his battalion in the trenches late March, and was killed in action, 20 July 1915, by a rifle grenade. Buried where he fell. Age 20. *unm.* Remains recovered from a grave marked as belonging to an 'Unknown British Soldier' located in Sanctuary Wood Old Cemetery (28.I.24.b.90.97), identified – Clothing; reinterred, registered 2 May 1928. *Buried in Sanctuary Wood Cemetery (II.F.21).*

Gone But Not Forgotten

(Panel 41) Pte. 3561, Albert Roberts, 1/6th Bn. The Sherwood Foresters (Notts & Derbys Regt.), (T.F.): *s.* of Joseph Roberts, of Parwich, Ashbourne, co. Derby, by his wife Harriet: enlisted Buxton. Killed in action, 6.35pm, 30 September 1915. Age 20. *unm.* See Pte. F.C. Hooley and Sergt. W.A. Wibberley, above; and 2nd Lieut. L.G. Dickinson, Spoilbank Cemetery (I.G.18).

(Panel 41) Pte. 3159, Charles Roberts, 1/6th Bn. The Sherwood Foresters (Notts & Derbys Regt.), (T.F.): *b.* Clay Cross, co. Derby, *c.*1893. Killed in action 6.35pm, 30 September 1915. Age 22. Pte. Roberts was married to Elizabeth Robinson, *née* Roberts (Clarke's Yard, King Street, Clay Cross, Chesterfield). See Sergt. W.A. Wibberley, above; and 2nd Lieut. L.G. Dickinson, Spoilbank Cemetery (I.G.18).

(Panel 41) Pte. 1641, Ernest Robinson, 1/8th Bn. The Sherwood Foresters (Notts & Derbys Regt.), (T.F.): *s.* of A. (& F.) Robinson, of 14, Woodland Grove, Mansfield: *b.* Mansfield Woodhouse: employee Mansfield Light Railway Co.: a pre-war Territorial, undertook Active Service obligations, Mansfield: served with the Expeditionary Force in France and Flanders from early March 1915, and was killed in action, 12 July following: Age 19. Shortly before his death he had been in conversation with the battalion's top sniper, Drmr. 2228, J.W. Newton (died of wounds, September 1915). Remains recovered from a grave marked as belonging to an 'Unknown British Soldier' located in Sanctuary Wood Old Cemetery (28.I.24.b.90.97), identified – Clothing; reinterred, registered 3 May 1928. *Buried in Sanctuary Wood Cemetery (II.F.24).*

The Lord Giveth And The Lord Taketh Away

Drmr. Newton is buried in Etaples Military Cemetery (IV.G.6A).

(Panel 41) Pte. 14543, Aaron Shooter, 10th (Service) Bn. The Sherwood Foresters (Notts & Derbys Regt.): *s.* of Joseph Shooter, of 3, Mill Houses, Staveley, Chesterfield, by his wife Elizabeth: and brother to Pte. 14948, J. Shooter, 10th Sherwood Foresters, killed in action, 26 May 1917: *b.* Staveley, co. Derby: enlisted Chesterfield. Killed in action, 14 February 1916. Age 19. Dedicated – "In grateful remembrance of the men…who fell in the war of 1914–1919" – the brothers are commemorated on the Staveley Parish War Memorial. His brother Joseph is buried in Fampoux British Cemetery (A.48).

(Panel 41) Pte. 1723, Christopher William Taylor, 1/8th Bn. The Sherwood Foresters (Notts & Derbys Regt.), (T.F.): *s.* of William Taylor, of 57, Lime Grove, Newark, and Emma his wife: *b.* Newark: enlisted there. Killed in action, 21 July 1915. Age 18. Remains recovered from Sanctuary Wood Old Cemetery (28.I.24.b.90.97), from a grave marked as belonging to an 'Unknown British Soldier', identified – Clothing; reinterred, registered 2 May 1928. *Buried in Sanctuary Wood Cemetery (II.F.20).*

For Home And England

(Panel 41) Pte. 1473, Albert Maurice Thompson, Siglr., 1/5th Bn. The Sherwood Foresters (Notts & Derbys Regt.), (T.F.): *s.* of John William Thompson, of 'West View,' Heyworth Street, Derby, by his wife Mary Alice: *b.* Derby: enlisted Battersea, London. Killed in action, 26 June 1915. Age 26. *unm.* Remains recovered from a grave marked as belonging to an 'Unknown British Soldier' (28.I.24.d.15.45) 30 January 1929; identified – Khaki; reinterred, registered 13 February 1929. *Buried in Sanctuary Wood Cemetery (V.C.17).*

My Flesh Also Shall Rest In Hope

(Panel 41) Pte. 1972, George Tinker, 1/8th Bn. The Sherwood Foresters (Notts & Derbys Regt.), (T.F.): *b.* Bolsover, co. Derby: enlisted Retford, co. Nottingham. Killed in action, 16 July 1915. Remains recovered from a grave marked as belonging to an 'Unknown British Soldier. 8 Notts & Derbys', located at Sanctuary Wood Old Cemetery (28.I.24.b.90.97), identified – Clothing, Titles; reinterred, registered 2 May 1928. *Buried in Sanctuary Wood Cemetery (II.F.23).*

(Panel 41) Pte. 978, Albert Radford Walker, 1/8th Bn. The Sherwood Foresters (Notts & Derbys Regt.), (T.F.): late of East Kirkby, co. Nottingham: *s.* of James Walker, Coal Miner; of 6, Lime Street, Sutton-in-Ashfield, by his wife Emily, *née* Freeman: and elder brother to Gnr. 183957, W. Walker, 76th Siege Bty., Royal Garrison Artillery, who died of wounds, 22 May 1918, aged 19 years: *b.* Hucknall Torkard, *c.*1894: enlisted Sutton-in-Ashfield. Killed in action, 30 July 1915. Age 21. *unm. The Notts Free Press*, 'In Memoriam,' 2 August 1918:-

> *He marched away so bravely, His head so proudly held;*
> *His footsteps never faltered, His courage never failed.*
> *There on the field of battle, He calmly took his place;*
> *He fought and died for England, And the honour of his race.*
>
> Mother, Father, Sisters & Brothers.

His brother Wilfred is buried in Mailly Wood Cemetery, Somme (II.M.9).

(Panel 41) Pte. 3550, James Wardle, 1/6th Bn. The Sherwood Foresters (Notts & Derbys Regt.), (T.F.): enlisted Buxton, co. Derby. Killed in action, 6.35pm, 30 September 1915. See Sergt. W.A. Wibberley, above; and 2nd Lieut. L.G. Dickinson, Spoilbank Cemetery (I.G.18).

(Panel 41) Pte. 1643, George Wynne, 1/5th Bn. The Sherwood Foresters (Notts & Derbys Regt.), (T.F.): *s.* of Thomas Wynne, of 1, China New Road, Belper, by his wife Elizabeth. Killed in action, 23 June 1915. Age 19. Remains exhumed from a grave marked as belonging to an 'Unknown British Soldier. Notts & Derby', (28.I.24.d.15.45), identified – Khaki, Titles; reinterred, registered 31 January 1929. *Buried in Sanctuary Wood Cemetery (V.C.27).*

(Panel 41) Pte. 1667, Samuel Henry Yates, 1/6th Bn. The Sherwood Foresters (Notts & Derbys Regt.), (T.F.): late of Wormhill, co. Derby. Killed in action, 6.35pm, 30 September 1915. All correspondence should be forwarded c/o his brother Thomas Yates, of Higher Sydney, Peak Dale, nr. Buxton. See Sergt. W.A. Wibberley, above; and 2nd Lieut. L.G. Dickinson, Spoilbank Cemetery (I.G.18).

(Panel 41) Major Aubrey John Carter, D.S.O., 1st Bn. (47th Foot) The Loyal North Lancashire Regt.: 4th *s.* of the late T.A. Carter, of Shottery Hall, Stratford-on-Avon: *b.* 18 January 1872: gazetted 2nd Lieut. North Lancashire Regt. 9 January 1892; promoted Lieut. 1 May, 1893; Capt. 20 February 1901; Major, 14 February 1910: Adjutant to his regiment, 27 April 1898–17 May following: served in the South African War, 1899–1901, being employed on the Staff: took part in the advance on Kimberley, including actions at Belmont, Enslin, Modder River and Magersfontein: operations Transvaal, west of Pretoria, July–29 November 1900: operations Orange River Colony, including action at Lindley (26 June) and those in the Transvaal, 30 November 1900–March 1901 (Mentioned in Despatches, *London Gazette*, 10 September 1901; Queen's Medal, five clasps; D.S.O.): Instructor, School of Musketry, 17 December 1905–15 December 1909: Commandant, School of Musketry, South Africa, 15 July 1911–31 March 1913: employed with the Forces, Union of South Africa, 1 April–31 December 1913: served with the Expeditionary Force in France and Flanders in charge of 1st Battn. of his regiment, and was killed in action near Ypres, 4 November 1914. Age 42. He *m.* 1906, Edith Mary, *dau.* of the late Rev. G.H. Rigby.

(Panel 41) Capt. Edward Unsworth Green, M.C., 9th (Service) Bn. The Loyal North Lancashire Regt.: *s.* of Edward Unsworth Green, of 112, Church Road, Richmond, co. Surrey, by his wife Annie Louisa: and elder brother to Coy.Sergt.Major 463, R.U. Green, Honourable Artillery Coy., killed in action at Ypres, 23 April 1915; and 2nd Lieut. V.U. Green, 15th attd. 10th Middlesex Regt., killed in action, 26 March 1917, at the Battle of Gaza. Killed in action, 10 August 1917; Third Battle of Ypres. Age 37.

His brother Reginald is buried in Voormezeele Enclosure No.3 (XIII.B.1); Vivian has no known grave, he is commemorated on the Jerusalem Memorial (Panel 42).

(Panel 41) Capt. Alick Lancelot Prince, 1st Bn. (47th Foot) The Loyal North Lancashire Regt.: 6th *s.* of the late T.T. Prince, of Laurel Lodge, Barnet, co. Hertford, by his wife (44, Grange Road, Ealing, London, W.): *b.* 12 September 1878: *educ.* Malvern College, and Emmanuel College, Cambridge (B.A., 1899): commissioned Manchester Regt. May 1901; promoted Lieut. December following: served in the South African War; slightly wounded: present at operations in Transvaal 1901–1902 (Queen's Medal, 3 clasps): transf'd. Loyal North Lancashire Regt. February 1908: seconded Malay States Guides, April 1910–May 1913: promoted Capt. September 1912: rejoined 1st Loyal North Lancashire Regt. shortly before the outbreak of war, and for his services in the Great War was Mentioned in Sir John (now Lord) French's Despatch, 30 November 1914. Officially reported 'killed' in action, 8 November 1914, a subsequent Casualty List shows him as having been officially reported 'not killed but missing,' and a still later Casualty List, 7 June 1915, shows him as having been 'unofficially reported killed.' As regards this officer's death, enquiries through the Red Cross showed that Pte. Mulholland of the battalion informed a Red Cross representative he saw Capt. Prince shot in the head sometime in the first or second week in November, and the Private, who was in Capt. Prince's Company, is certain the officer is dead, and thinks he was buried at a place called Linden Forest, nr. Ypres, which may be Lindenhoek, close to Kemmel. A Corporal of the battalion also wrote most circumstantially that he was next to the Captain and saw him shot in the head, and that he saw him lying dead twenty hours after, but too close to the German lines to be reached. A Major of his battalion, writing in December 1914, said that from enquiries he had made he feared it was true that Capt. Prince was killed. Age 36. Confirmed killed during the night of 8–9 November 1914 in attempting to reoccupy part of a trench (west of Veldhoek village, north of the Menin Road – afterwards known as 'Inverness Copse'), previously held by the Loyal North Lancashire, it was discovered to be strongly held by the enemy. He was married to Emma Caroline, *dau.* of William Beadell Bacon, of Tunbridge Wells, and leaves two sons – Harold, *b.* November 1911; Ralph Bacon, *b.* February 1914.

(Panel 41) Sergt. 8219, William Thomas Challen, 1st Bn. (47th Foot) The Loyal North Lancashire Regt.: *s.* of John Napper Challen, of 55, Cockayne Place, Meersbrook, Sheffield, by his wife Emily: and elder brother to L/Corpl. 12856, S.H. Challen, 8th Loyal North Lancashire Regt., killed in action, 10 July 1916: *b.* Plymouth, co. Devon, *c.*1891: enlisted Bristol. Killed in action, 8 November 1914; Veldhoek. Age 23. *unm.*

His brother Stephen is buried in Pozieres British Cemetery (III.C.16).

(Panel 41) L/Corpl. 10269, Thomas Carter, 1st Bn. (47th Foot) The Loyal North Lancashire Regt.: *s.* of James Carter, Labourer; of 81, Queen St., Preston, by his wife Ann Eliza: *b.* Preston, 7 May 1893: *educ.* St. Saviour's Public School: Occupation – Spinner; Messrs. Harrocks, Crewsden & Co.: served three years, Preston Territorial Force; entered Regular Forces, 28 December 1911. On the outbreak of war he went to the Front with the Expeditionary Force, and was killed at Ypres, 23 October 1914. Age 21. *unm.*

Buried at Langemarck. "L/Corpl. Carter was one of a family of fifteen children, nine of whom survive him, and two of his brothers are now (1916) on active service in France."

PANEL 41 ENDS – CORPL. H. HUGO, LOYAL NORTH LANCS REGT.

PANEL 43 BEGINS – CORPL. H. HULME, LOYAL NORTH LANCS REGT.

(Panel 43) Pte. 34267, John Castle, 8th (Service) Bn. The Loyal North Lancashire Regt.: formerly no.24539, Gloucestershire Regt.: *s.* of John Castle, of Longborough, Moreton-in-the-Marsh, co. Gloucester, by his wife Mary: and brother to Pte. 10015, F. Castle, Coldstream Guards, died of wounds, 29 October 1914; and Rfn. 12174, G. Castle, King's Royal Rifle Corps, died of wounds 25 May 1915: *b.* Longborough: served with the Expeditionary Force in France and Flanders, and was killed in action, 18 July 1917.

His brother Fred is buried in Ypres Town Cemetery Extension (II.B.11), George has no known grave; he is recorded on Panel 53.

(Panel 43) Pte. 34025, John Cumming, 7th (Service) Bn. The Loyal North Lancashire Regt.: elder *s.* of Thomas Cumming, Overseer, Post Office Telegraph Dept.; of 40, Larkhill Lane, Clubmoor, West Derby, by his wife Annie, *dau.* of Godfrey Higgins: *b.* Liverpool, co. Lancaster, 13 September 1891: *educ.* St. Margaret's School, Anfield: Occupation – Foreign Correspondent, Spain, in the employ of an English firm: returned to England and volunteered for Active Service soon after the outbreak of war: enlisted, 21st Liverpool Regt. April 1915: subsequently transf'd. Loyal North Lancashire Regt.: served with the Expeditionary Force in France and Flanders from December 1916, and was killed in action at Messines Ridge, 7 June 1917. Buried in Ridgewood Cemetery, nr. Wytschaete. His Commanding Officer wrote that he was greatly liked by the whole of the signalling section, and it was while doing some very important work at which he was killed. Age 25. *unm.*

(Panel 43) Pte, 27057, Sydney Davies, 8th (Service) Bn. The Loyal North Lancashire Regt.: *s.* of the late Edward Davies, of 182, Stockport Road, Cheadle, co. Chester, by his wife Mary: *b.* Cheadle, *c.*1894: employee Messrs Sykes Bleachworks, Edgeley, Stockport: enlisted after the outbreak of war, 21 August 1914, 3rd (Reserve) Bn. Manchester Regt. (no.6857): served with the Expeditionary Force in France and Flanders: wounded sometime during the Battle of the Somme (or thereafter) and, after recovery, transf'd. Machine Gun section, 8th Loyal North Lancs. In early July 1917, the battalion moved up to Ypres where, for four days, they were subjected to continuous shelling and suffered many casualties from gas. On the opening day of Third Ypres, 31 July 1917, 8th Loyal North Lancs were in reserve. The following day they were given the extremely hazardous task of relieving another battalion on Westhoek Ridge, whose position was not accurately known; the relief was to be carried out in daylight and in full view of the enemy entrenched in Glencorse Wood. After completing the relief, the battalion were destined to spend five miserable days subjected to constant shellfire in a place where heavy rain and bombardment had turned the whole area into a morass, and in places the trenches were thigh deep in mud and water. During their time here the battalion would lose 41 men, Sydney was one of 14 to die on the day before they were relieved: 4 August 1917. Age 23.

(Panel 43) Pte. 29735, John Hooley Fox, 9th (Service) Bn. The Loyal North Lancashire Regt.: *s.* of John Parkes Fox, of 26, Massie Street, Cheadle, co. Chester, by his wife Ada: *b. c.*1896: *educ.* Cheadle National School: a former member of Cheadle Church Sunday School: employed 5 yrs. Grocers Assistant; Messrs. William Davies & Son, Cheadle Hulme: enlisted Manchester Regt (no.3647), June 1915: transf'd. 9th Loyal North Lancs (no.29735) and sent to the Front, 4 August 1916. During the time between his arrival in France and his death he saw no leave, had been in action on two occasions and trained as a Signaller, and Lewis gunner. On the morning of 21 May 1917, an artillery bombardment of the German lines began, continuing until 2.50 a.m., 7 June; twenty minutes later the Allies detonated 19 mines beneath the enemy positions between Messines and Hill 60. In the ensuing infantry assault, 9th Loyal North Lancs and 11th Lancashire Fusiliers were designated support troops to 2nd Royal Irish Rifles and 13th

Cheshire Regt. After the leading battalions captured their objectives, the North Lancs passed through them, successfully reaching and securing their own objectives on the Wytschaete side of the ridge, in less than 1½ hours of leaving their starting point. The battalion then dug in, consolidated their position, and put out some squads of men in shell-hole out-posts in front. John Fox had seen the sunrise and made it through the attack – he was not destined to see the sunset. His officer wrote, "I am sorry to inform you that your son was killed on the 7th inst. about 5 o'clock in the afternoon. He was killed instantaneously by a high explosive shell and was buried by our padre, Capt. Evers. Your son has for some time been the company's gunner and was splendid in every way as we could always rely on his doing his duty. I was only a few yards away from your son when he was killed along with three others." John Fox was one of 78 men of his battalion who were killed during this successful operation. Age 21.

(Panel 43) Pte. 30046, Frederick William Jackson, 9th (Service) Bn. The Loyal North Lancashire Regt.: *s.* of William Jackson, of 37, Rolleston St., Ancoats, Manchester, by his wife Alice. Killed in action on the opening day of Third Ypres and buried at the time 'on the left hand side of the Ypres-Menin Rd., 300 yards beyond Birr X Rds. Marked with a cross.' 31 July 1917. Age 24.

(Panel 43) Pte. 34041, William Lawrence, 9th (Service) Bn. The Loyal North Lancashire Regt.: Killed in action on the opening day of Third Ypres, 31 July 1917, and buried at the time 'on the left hand side of the Ypres-Menin Rd., 300 yards beyond Birr X Rds. Marked with a cross.'

(Panel 43) Pte. 32949, Michael Ledson, 10th (Service) Bn. The Loyal North Lancashire Regt.: *s.* of Thomas Ledson, of 53, Spencer Street, Everton, Liverpool, by his wife Mary Ann: and *yr.* brother to Pte. 1481, J.J. Ledson, 8th King's (Liverpool) Regt., died of wounds, 17 June 1915, aged 21: enlisted Seaforth, co. Lancaster. Killed in action, 12 August 1917. Age 19.

His brother John is buried in Lillers Communal Cemetery (II.C.38).

(Panel 43) Pte. 24273, Peter Nisbet, 8th (Service) Bn. The Loyal North Lancashire Regt.: *s.* of Charles Nisbet, of 32, Thynne Street, Bolton, co. Lancaster, and Sarah Nisbet, his wife: Occupation – Fireman; L & Y Railway: enlisted on 9 May 1916, served with the Expeditionary Force from August; wounded in October 1916; and was killed in action on the night of 2–3 June 1917. Age 21. (*IWGC record 2 June*)

(Panel 43) Pte. 235043, Charles William Robinson, 1/4th Bn. The Loyal North Lancashire Regt. (T.F.): formerly no.65697, Lincolnshire Regt.: enlisted at Sutton-in-Ashfield, Nottingham. Killed in action, 31 July 1917. Age 34. *m.*

> *Missed By Those Who Loved Him Best.*
> *Wife & Child.*

Designed by the sculptor Alfred Turner in the form of a tapered pillar on a three tiered base the Edgar Mobbs Memorial, Northampton, is topped by a bronze female figure representing the Goddess of Fame; she holds a laurel wreath in her left hand and a staff in her upraised right. The memorial bears a panel depicting a battle scene on its right face and a rugby football scene on the left; the front carries a life-size bust of Lieut.Col. E.R. Mobbs. Unveiled in July 1921, on the occasion of the first Mobbs Memorial Rugby Union Football Match (which is played annually between the East Midlands and the Barbarians at the Northampton Saints ground), the memorial bears the words – "… by subscriptions of admirers the world over, to the memory of a great and gallant soldier and sportsman… Your Memory Hallowed In The Land You Loved." In 1937 the memorial was removed from the Market Square to the Garden of Remembrance, Abington Square, and now stands facing the town's War Memorial which records over 2,500 Northamptonians who gave their lives in the Great War.

> O Valiant hearts, who to your glory came,
> Through dust of conflict and of battle flame
> Tranquil you lie, your knightly virtue proved,
> Your memory hallowed in the land you loved.

(Panel 43) Lieut.Col. Edgar Roberts Mobbs, D.S.O., Comdg. 7th (Service) Bn. ('Mobbs Own') The Northamptonshire Regt.: late of Olney, co. Buckingham: 3rd *s.* of Oliver L. Mobbs, of Northampton, by his wife Elizabeth Ann: and *gt.-gdson.* of William Mobbs, Plumber & Glazier, of 78, Derngate, Northampton: *b.* 29 June 1882: *educ.* Bedford Modern School (2nd Term 1892–3rd Term 1898): prior to the outbreak of war was Director; Pytchley Motor Co., Managing Market Harborough branch: volunteered and enlisted, September 1914: refused a commission on the grounds of his age (32), and joined Northamptonshire Regt. as Private. A well-known sports personality and charismatic leader of men, by the end of September 1914 he had recruited 400 local men to form a 'Sportsman's Battn.'; 264 were accepted. After training at Shoreham, and being given a commission, went to France with 7th Battn., as part of 73rd Bde., 24th Divn., 28 August 1915: saw his first action at the Battle of Loos, September following: subsequently – for his skills of command and qualities of leadership – appointed Lieut.Col., Comdg. 7th Battn. April 1916; the battalion becoming known as 'Mobbs Own': took part in actions in the Ypres sector, October 1915–June 1916, and the Battle of the Somme, and was seriously wounded in the attack on Guillemont, 17 August 1916: after convalescence rejoined his regiment in the Vimy sector, October 1916: Mentioned in Despatches by General Sir Douglas Haig, November 1916, and awarded the Distinguished Service Order, January 1917, for 'his outstanding leadership of the 7th Battalion': saw further fighting at the Battles of Arras and Messines 1917, and was mortally wounded at Lower Star Post, Shrewsbury Forest, on the opening day of the Third Battle of Ypres, 31 July 1917, by a hail of machine-gun bullets while courageously charging a concealed German machine-gun post which was causing his battalion heavy casualties. Lieut.Col. Mobbs got to within 30 yards of the post before he was mown down and, in the ten minutes before he died, wrote a message noting the location and requesting reinforcements be sent up; the message never arrived. His body was not recovered. Immediately prior to his death he met former Bedford Modern pupil Lieut. Norman Spencer who later reported, "I was an F.O.O. in the stunt, and went over the top and saw Mobbs. Perhaps I was one of the last officers to speak to him. Anyway, my last sight of him is something that will be worth remembering of him. We had been waiting for three hours for the time to come, and the Boche shelled us terribly, and as for the rain, mud, etc., well the papers will tell you all this. Then the minute came and we went forward through the seas of mud and terrific shelling. The men were magnificent and our artillery, under these adverse conditions, put up a barrage such as the Somme never saw. I was right behind Mobbs, introduced myself to him just before the hour as an old B.M.S. boy and talked about Bedford and R.C. Stafford. In the tornado of hostile shelling he got ahead and, seeing a number of his men cut down by an undiscovered machine-gun strong-point, he charged to bomb it – certain death under such a terrific hail of shell – and he went down. I have seen men, and good men, but for a man of his standing and rank it was magnificent. I sat down afterwards in a captured post and, instead of that picture, I saw the old three-quarter in his own 25 yards get the ball from a crumpled up scrum and get clean through and on. The same man, the same determination, a born leader. Thank God for such men. I know that all who knew him, even in civilian days which don't count at all, will be glad of this picture of one of England's finest Rugby players in the greatest game a man can play. I am sure that Bedford will honour such a man, and not just put in the paper, 'Famous Rugby Player Killed.' Long may the Modern turn out such men." A Rugby Union Football player of International renown, Edgar Mobbs played his first game for Olney R.F.C. in 1903, later joining local village team the 'Weston Turks' and, for a short time, 'Northampton Heathens.' Invited to play for Northampton club 'The Saints' in 1904, he made his debut on 23 September 1905 against Bedford, and played in every game thereafter until his retirement at the close of the 1912–1913 season; became Captain (1907), played 234 games, scored 179 tries, kicked 2 'placed goals' and 1 drop goal. He also played for the East Midlands and the Barbarians, receiving Honours in the former in 1905, and was awarded his first England Cap for a match against Wales. As Captain he represented England in seven international matches, his first being against Australia, at Blackheath, 9 January 1909, during which he scored England's first and only try in a 9–3 defeat in under two minutes, and his last international against France, 3 March 1910. He played his last game – England *v* Scotland – at the County Ground, Northampton, shortly before returning to France, following his wounding in autumn 1916. Painted by the artist Barbara Chamier and unveiled in 1925, a three-quarter life-size portrait of Edgar Mobbs hangs in the entrance foyer of Bedford School. His name is recorded on the Bedford Modern School Memorial (between Kaye and Liddle Quads), Northampton

War Memorial, the village of Olney Memorial; and on 29 November 2006 – 'Edgar Mobbs Way' – a road dedicated to his memory was opened on the outskirts of Northampton. Age 35. *unm.*

(Panel 43) Major Harold Henry Norman, 1st Bn. (48th Foot) The Northamptonshire Regt.: eldest *s.* of the late Henry (& Mrs) Norman, of 55, Eccleston Square, London: *b.* 23 December 1867: *educ.* Aldin House, Slough; Eton; Royal Military College, Sandhurst – gazetted 2nd Lieut. Northamptonshire Regt. September 1887; promoted Lieut. August 1890: took part in the reconnaissance of the Saran Sar in the Tirah Expedition 1897–98, in the action of 9 November 1897, and operations in the Bara Valley, December 1897: Adjutant and Quartermaster of native troops, Base Depot, March–April 1898: (Medal, two clasps): promoted Capt. January 1899: Brigade Major, India, September 1905–March 1908: during February and March of the latter year was D.A.Q.M.G., Bazar Valley Field Force, during the operations in the Zakka Khel country, on the north-west frontier of India: (Medal with clasp): D.A.A.G., India, March 1908–September 1909, receiving his Majority in June of the latter year: returned to England; served at the Depot, 1911–1914: served with the Expeditionary Force in France and Flanders from August 1914, and was slightly wounded in an early action, but not severely enough to cause him to relinquish his duties. Major Norman was killed in action, 11 November 1914, whilst in temporary command of his battalion, resisting the advance of the Prussian Guard at Ypres. Age 46. He was a member of the Windham Club, and made many friends during his tour of service at the Regimental Depot, Northampton, where he won the respect of all by his soldierly qualities and charming personality. He *m.* September 1899, Folkestone, co. Kent; Beatrice Charlotte, *dau.* of the Rev. Harry Wood; she died suddenly in April 1914.

(Panel 43) Capt. Walter Russell Russell, 'A' Coy., 2nd (58th Foot) attd. 1st Bn. (48th Foot) The Northamptonshire Regt.: *s.* of the late Capt. Sir William Russell Russell (late 58th Foot), of 'Flaxmere,' Hawke's Bay, New Zealand, formerly Minister for Defence & Colonial Secretary, New Zealand; by his wife Lady Russell: *b.* Flaxmere, 8 September 1880: *educ.* Wanganin College, New Zealand: received his commission, Northamptonshire Regt. from the local militia forces, New Zealand, April 1900; promoted Lieut. December 1902: took part in the South African Campaign attd. Mounted Infantry: took part in operations in Transvaal, early 1902 (Queen's Medal, 2 clasps): Adjutant to his battalion, November 1905–November 1908: promoted Capt. December 1908: served with his regiment in France and Flanders, and was killed in action on the late evening of 23 October 1914, leading his company in an attack on the German positions centred about the group of buildings and inn on the crossroads, Pilckem Lane – Bixschoote – Langemarck road, nr. Ypres. Age 33. *unm.* Capt. Russell was a member of the Naval and Military Club.

(Panel 43) Lieut. Ilston Henry Stevenson, Intelligence Officer; 7th (Service) Bn. The Northamptonshire Regt.: *s.* of the late George Henry Stevenson, by his wife Rosa ('The Gables, Duston, Northampton): served with the Expeditionary Force in France and Flanders from 2 September 1915; took part in the fighting at Loos later the same month. Missing/believed killed, 16 February 1916, Sanctuary Wood – Hooge; the circumstances being 'This officer went over the top to examine the barbed wire defences before the battalion's lines. Observed by the enemy and opened fire upon; he was seen to fall. Later, Col. Skinner ordered a patrol to go out to search for Lieut. Stevenson and bring him in. No trace of him could be found and it is assumed he was killed.' Age 28.

(Panel 43) Lieut. Henry Ivanhoe Vandell, Reserve of Officers attd. 'B' Coy., 1st Bn. (48th Foot) The Northamptonshire Regt.: only *s.* of Arnold Vandell, of Sydney Villa, 50 Duncan Road, Gillingham, co. Kent, by his wife Sara A.: *b.* New Brompton, co. Kent, 8 December 1890: *educ.* His Majesty's Royal Dockyard School (Engineering Branch), Chatham, and East London College (University of London), becoming later a graduate of the Institute of Mechanical Engineers: was two years member of University of London O.T.C., from whence he received his commission, Reserve of Officers, December 1912: trained with Royal West Kent Regt., August 1914; proceeded to France, September following, attd. Northamptonshire Regt.: served in the trenches later that month at the Battle of the Aisne, and took part in the fighting near Ypres, where he was killed, 11 November 1914, while leading his platoon to intercept an attack made by the Prussian Guard. The following is an extract from the letter of an N.C.O., dated 19 December 1914, describing the event – "The Prussian Guard, through sheer weight of numbers, broke through our line. We were called upon to intercept them. After a terrible hand-to-hand encounter the enemy turned and fled. Away we went after them in a mad, headlong rush. We caught and killed heaps of them, but some of them succeeded in occupying some old ruined farmhouses, and poured a murderous fire into us. A lot of our fellows went down, but the remainder of us went straight at the houses. Lieut. Vandell was at the very head of us. When actually outside the door of the house, a bullet struck poor Mr Vandell in the head, killing him instantly. We eventually drove the enemy out, and occupied a position close by. In the dead of night we crept out and buried poor Mr Vandell as decently as circumstances would allow." Age 23. *unm.*

(Panel 43) Lieut. Thomas Pillans Ward, 7th (Service) Bn. The Northamptonshire Regt.: *s.* of the Revd. Thomas Ward, M.A., Principle, St. Peter's College, Peterborough, and Rector, Alwalton, co. Northampton: *educ.* Knoll School, Aspley Heath, Woburn Sands (Rev. F.F. Hort); Rugby School (Mr Dickinson's), where he had two general leaving exhibitions, took Queen Victoria Memorial Prize, History, won a scholarship to King's College, Cambridge (Classics & History): joined Northamptonshire Regt. whilst at Rugby; selected for Musketry Instructor, in which capacity he served with 28th Training Battn. and after repeated requests joined a draft to 7th Battn. and went to France, July 1917. Reported missing/ believed killed, 31 July 1917, following his first action. A soldier of the 7th Battn. wrote, "He went over the top without flinching, and led his men very brave, like the officer he was. He was a gallant and good officer, so good to his men." And the Commanding Officer, 8th Northamptonshire Regt. wrote, "During the time your boy was with us in the Northants, and later in the 28th Training Reserve Battalion, he was a fine young officer, and I think I can say without exception, all ranks were fond of him, and glorious as his end was, regret his loss. For months he had been keen to go out, and for a long time I would not further his desire, as I thought him too young and not hard enough to stand the strain." Whilst at Rugby School Mr Ward was Head of his house and a member of the Cricket XXII. Age 20. *unm.*

(Panel 43) 2nd Lieut. Alexander Nimmo Sheriff, 'D' Coy., 1st Bn. (48th Foot) The Northamptonshire Regt.: 2nd *s.* of the late George Sherriff, of Stenhouse, Kersie, by his wife Catherine J. (Carronvale, Larbert, co. Sterling): and brother to Lieut. J.G. Sheriff, Argyll & Sutherland Highlanders, killed in action, 26 April 1915, nr. St. Julien: *b.* 13 August 1894: *educ.* Sedburgh School, co. York; Royal Military College, Sandhurst: gazetted 2nd Lieut. Northamptonshire Regt. February 1914: accompanied his battalion to France, 13 August 1914: took part in the retirement from Mons, Battles of the Marne and the Aisne; and was killed in action on the afternoon of 31 October 1914, when the battalion, while retiring via a sunken lane from Bodmin Copse to Shrewsbury Forest, were subjected to heavy enfilade fire. 2nd Lieut. Jarvis and about 100 other ranks were also killed. Age 20. *unm.* On the death of his father, he inherited the estates of Kersie and Carronvale. (*IWGC record 30 October 1914*)

His brother John also has no known grave; he is recorded on Panel 42; 2nd Lieut. Jarvis is buried in Larch Wood (Railway Cutting) Cemetery (IV.D.1).

(Panel 43) Coy.Sergt.Major, 4578, James Good, 'C' Coy., 1st Bn. (48th Foot) The Northamptonshire Regt.: *s.* of Allen Good: served with the Expeditionary Force in France and Flanders from 13 August 1914, took part in the retirement from Mons, the fighting at the Marne, the Aisne and at Ypres where, on the night of 4–5 November 1914, following the battalion's withdrawal from the fighting before Bodmin Copse, he was killed by shellfire while in the support line, Shrewsbury Forest. Age 36. He had done excellent work since the beginning of the war. His wife Mary Ellen Good (40, Union Street, South Halifax, co. York), would be grateful to receive (and will gladly reply to) correspondence from her late husband's comrades. (*IWGC record 5 November*)

(Panel 43) Corpl. 3/8530, William James Garner, 1st Bn. (48th Foot) The Northamptonshire Regt.: *b.* Kettering, co. Northampton: enlisted there: member of the Army Reserve, returned to the regiment on mobilisation: served with the Expeditionary Force in France from 13 August 1914, and was killed in action at Pilckem on the evening of 22 October 1914.

(Panel 43) Corpl. 14906, George Parrott, 'C' Coy., 7th (Service) Bn. The Northamptonshire Regt.: *s.* of John Thomas Edward Parrott, of 42, New Tower St., Fletton, Peterborough, by his wife Eliza: and brother to Pte. 22894, J. Parrott, 2nd Lincolnshire Regt.; killed in action, 27 May 1918: *b.* Yaxley: enlisted

Peterborough. Killed in action on the night of 9–10 February 1916. In a letter to Corpl. Parrott's parents (10 February 1916) Capt. Russell Gurney wrote, "I am sorry to have to tell you that your son was killed last night while in charge of a working party. He was with a party in the front line trench when a shell burst near him and killed him.

I cannot say how I sympathise with you, he was a splendid man and one of my best N.C.O.'s; he was popular with the whole company. Perhaps he may not have told you how he missed the leave train on the day he should originally have gone. I had given him permission to leave the trenches early but, just as he was going, the Germans started bombing our trenches, so he was back to take charge until it was all over. He is a man I can never replace. His last wish was that we should write and tell his sweetheart. He will be buried near Ypres, and I will see to it that a cross is put over his grave." Corpl. Parrott was promoted in the field from Private for his actions during an attack on an enemy trench. When all the officers and non-commissioned officers with him had been either killed or wounded, Private Parrott rallied the men around him and led them in a charge, with the result that the trench was captured and held until relief came. Age 22.

His brother James also has no known grave; he is commemorated on the Soissons Memorial.

(Panel 43) L/Corpl. 28246, Albert William Boast, 6th (Service) Bn. The Northamptonshire Regt.: formerly no.31255, Suffolk Regt.: *s.* of the late Albert M. Boast, and his wife Charlotte A. Boast (73, Mayo Road, Church End, Willesden, London, N.W.): and elder brother to Dmr. 2136, B.B. Boast, 7th London Regt., killed in action, 5 June 1915: *b.* Lambeth, *c.*1884: enlisted Harlesden, London, N.W.: Killed in action, 4 August 1917. Age 33. He leaves a wife, Emily Boast (13, Wenlake Buildings, Old Street, London, E.C.1) to mourn him, and for whom the deepest sympathy is felt in her loss.

His brother is buried in Dud Corner Cemetery, Loos (VII.D.17).

(Panel 43) Pte. 8640, William Ayres, 1st Bn. (48th Foot) The Northamptonshire Regt.: formerly no.8159, Bedfordshire Regt.: *s.* of Mary Ann Ayres (27, Oswald Road, Rushden, co. Northampton): and brother to Pte. 13210, W. Ayres, 1st Northamptonshire Regt., who fell on 25 September 1915 at the Battle of Loos; and Pte. 27910, V. Ayres, 8th East Yorkshire Regt., killed in action, 13 November 1916: *b.* Rushden, *c.*1886: enlisted Bedford. Killed in action, 31 October 1914. Age 28. *unm.*

His brother Walter also has no known grave, he is commemorated on the Loos Memorial; Victor is buried in Queen's Cemetery, Puisieux (E.6).

(Panel 43) Pte. 8111, George Henry Bland, 1st Bn. (48th Foot) The Northamptonshire Regt.: *b.* Rushden, co. Northampton: enlisted Northampton: served with the Expeditionary Force in France and Flanders from 13 August 1914, and was killed in action on the evening of 22 October following, at Pilckem.

(Panel 43) Pte. 22695, Mark Bradshaw, 7th (Service) Bn. The Northamptonshire Regt.: *s.* of William Bradshaw, of 65, Sartoris Road, Rushden, co. Northampton, by his wife Annie: and brother to Pte. W. Bradshaw (surv'd.): *b.* Warmington: enlisted Rushden, 27 November 1915: served with the Expeditionary Force in France from 14 June 1916, and was killed in action, 8 June 1917. Age 31. A comrade said that at the time of his death he was engaged in burying the dead when a shell fell among the burial party severely wounding Pte. 201972, A. Fowler, killing Pte. Bradshaw and two others (Ptes. 43565, W.J.H. Pain; 32175, W. Watkins).

Alfred Fowler is buried in Dickebusch New Military Cemetery Extension (III.C.21).

(Panel 43) Pte. 21170, Alfred George Brown, 7th (Service) Bn. The Northamptonshire Regt.: formerly no.22249, Bedfordshire Regt.: *b.* Woolwich, co. Kent: enlisted Luton, co. Bedford: served with the Expeditionary Force in France and Flanders, and was killed in action, 16 July 1916. *Commemorated on the Thiepval Memorial, Somme (Pier & Face 11A & D).*

(Panel 43) Pte. 6753, Walter Callen, 1st Bn. (48th Foot) The Northamptonshire Regt.: *b.* Bodmin, co. Cornwall: enlisted Stratford, co. Essex. Killed in action, 22 October 1914, at Pilckem.

(Panel 43) Pte. 18987, George Coster, 7th (Service) Bn. The Northamptonshire Regt.: *s.* of Edward Coster, of 'The Shack,' Mount Pleasant, Waterdale, Watford, by his wife Eva: *b.* Watford, co. Hertford, about 1896: enlisted Peterborough, co. Northampton: served with the Expeditionary Force in France and Flanders from August 1915, and was killed in action, 16 June 1917. Age 21. *unm.*

(Panel 43) Pte. 17393, Edward George Davis, 7th (Service) Bn. The Northamptonshire Regt.: *s.* of William Davis, of Cattle End, Silverstone, nr. Towcester, by his wife Caroline: and brother to Pte. 265204, S. Davis, 6th O.B.L.I., killed in action, 20 September 1917: *b.* Reading, co. Berkshire: enlisted Northampton. Killed in action, 31 July 1917. Age 22. *unm.* The brothers Davis are recorded on the Silverstone village War Memorial – erected to the Glory of God and in memory of 25 young men of Silverstone who fought bravely and died nobly during the Great War 1914 -1918, and in appreciation of the splendid service of those who, having taken part in the great struggle, returned to their homes and friends – it bears the inscription, "Pass Not This Stone In Sorrow But In Pride And May We Live As Nobly As Those That Died."

His brother Sydney also has no known grave; he is commemorated on the Tyne Cot Memorial (Panel 97).

(Panel 43) Pte. 7096, Alfred Fleckney, 1st Bn. (48th Foot) The Northamptonshire Regt.: *b.* St. Andrew's, Kettering, co. Northampton: enlisted Kettering: served with the Expeditionary Force in France and Flanders from 13 August 1914, and was killed in action on the evening of 22 October following; Pilckem. Age 30. He leaves a wife, Grace Fleckney (Cranford St. John, Kettering).

(Panel 43) Pte. 7079, Frederick Hadley, 1st Bn. (48th Foot) The Northamptonshire Regt.: *s.* of Harry Hadley, of East Haddon, co. Northampton: and brother to Sergt. G/20295, W.H. Hadley, M.M., 9th Royal Sussex Regt., killed in action, 4 November 1918: *b.* East Haddon: enlisted Northampton. Killed in action, 11 November 1914. Commemorated on East Haddon (St. Mary' Churchyard) War Memorial.

His brother Walter is buried in Villers-Pol Communal Cemetery Extension (C.2).

(Panel 43) Pte. 40209, Arthur Ernest Jacquest, 7th (Service) Bn. The Northamptonshire Regt.: *s.* of S. (& Mrs S.W.) Jacquest, of 53, Boughton, Northampton. Killed in action, 31 July 1917. Age 22. *unm.*

(Panel 43) Pte. 9644, John Leeson, 1st Bn. (48th Foot) The Northamptonshire Regt.: *b.* Harpole, co. Northampton: enlisted Northampton. Killed in action, 22 October 1914; Pilckem.

(Panel 43) Pte. 43565, William John Henry Pain, 7th (Service) Bn. The Northamptonshire Regt.: formerly no.1528, Essex Cyclist Corps: *s.* of Mr (& Mrs) Pain, of 39, Glasgow Road, Plaistow, London: *b.* Waltham Abbey, co. Essex: enlisted Ilford. Killed in action, 8 June 1917. Age 19. At duty assisting to bury the dead when a shell fell among the burial party killing Pte. Pain and two other men (Ptes. 22695, M. Bradshaw; 32175, W. Watkins); and, mortally wounded by the explosion, Pte. 201972, A. Fowler died later the same day.

Pte. Bradshaw also has no known grave, he is recorded above; similarly Pte. Watkins, (Panel 45). Pte. Fowler is buried in Dickebusch New Military Cemetery Extension (III.C.21).

(Panel 43) Pte. 40365, John Pasfield, 2nd Bn. (58th Foot) The Northamptonshire Regt.: *s.* of William Pasfield, of 81, George Street, Romford, co. Essex, by his wife Mary: and brother to Pte. 8760, W. Pasfield, Scots Guards, died of wounds, 27 August 1918: *b.* Romford: enlisted there. Killed in action, 31 July 1917. Age 17.

His brother William is buried in Ligny-sur-Canche British Cemetery (A.8).

(Panel 43) Pte. 7205, George William Pope, Lewis Gun Section, 'B' Coy., 7th (Service) Bn., formerly 1st Bn. (48th Foot) The Northamptonshire Regt.: late of 20, Spencer Road, Rushden, co. Northampton: *s.* of the late Thomas Pope, by his wife Sarah E. (56, Washbrook Road, Rushden): and brother to Pte. 27994, B. Pope, 7th East Yorkshire Regt., died 3 November 1918, of wounds: *b.* Aldwinckle: employee Messrs Robinson Bros., Boot Manufacturers, Grove Road, Rushden: a pre-war Regular (and Reservist) of 13 years service rejoined the Colours at Higham Ferrers on mobilisation: served with the Expeditionary Force in France and Flanders from August 1914: took part in the rearguard action at Maubeuge following the retirement from Mons, during the course of which he was later knocked down and wounded when the transport horses stampeded: after convalescence in England, returned to France, late 1914, was again wounded (G.S. wrist) at La Bassee, and returned to England: returned to France, mid-1916, passed through considerable fighting thereafter and was killed in action, 16 June 1917. Age 31. In a letter to his widow his Company Officer, Capt. H.B. King, wrote, "You will have heard by now from the War Office that your husband was killed in action on June 16th. I have not written to you before as we have been having a very busy time, and I have had a lot of letters to write to parents, etc., and as your husband was such a favourite, I felt sure you would have lots of letters from his friends, so I was writing to you later. I very much regret that none gave you any details before, but I had no officer left when we came out, so have had to do everything myself. Your husband and two others were killed by a shell not far from Hill 60. Death was instantaneous, so he suffered no pain whatever. We buried him near where he fell, and a wooden cross marks his grave, the memorial erected to our heroes out here. Pte Pope was one of my best Lewis gunners, and was a very valuable man in the company. He was a splendid man in the trenches, and was always cheerful and cool, and no-one knows what that means to his companions. Unfortunately, several others in his gun were also casualties, or they would doubtless write and tell you what they thought of him, but believe me, he was a great favourite with all ranks, and your loss is shared by all in B Co. Please accept my deepest sympathy." He was married to the late Harriet Pope (29, St. Mary's Street, Northampton), and leaves a daughter aged six years. (*IWGC record formerly 2nd Battn.*) In remembrance of both brothers *The Wellingborough News*, 31 October 1919, carried the following 'In Memoriam' notice:-

> *When alone in my sorrow and bitter tears flow,*
> *There cometh a memory of sweet long ago;*
> *Unknown to the world they stand by my side,*
> *And whisper, "Dear Mother, death cannot divide."*

> *Far and wide our thoughts do wander*
> *To their graves so far out yonder;*
> *Will some kind hand in a foreign land*
> *Place a flower on their graves for me?*

Never forgotten by their Mother, Father, Sisters and Brothers.

His brother Bernard is buried in Vendegies-au-Bois British Cemetery (A.11).

(Panel 43) Pte. 40326, Francis Walter Ridgewell, 2nd Bn. (58th Foot) The Northamptonshire Regt.: formerly no.45212, Suffolk Regt.: *s.* of Walter Ridgewell, of 'Woodside,' Great Parndon, Harlow, co. Essex, by his wife Ellen: *b.* Nazeing, co. Essex: enlisted Hertford. Killed in action, 31 July 1917. Age 23. *unm.*

(Panel 43) Pte. 7137, Richard Ronayne (served as Rowlands, James), 'A' Coy. 1st Bn. (48th Foot) The Northamptonshire Regt.: *s.* of the late James Ronayne, by his wife Ellen (1A, Bastwick Street, Goswell Road, London, E.C.1): and elder brother to Rfn. 321541, O. Ronayne, 6th London Regt. (Rifles), killed in action, 29 August 1918: *b.* St. Luke's, London: enlisted London. Killed in action, 5 November 1914. Age 28. *unm.*

His brother Owen is buried in H.A.C. Cemetery, Ecoust-St. Mein (II.F.5).

PANEL 43 ENDS – PTE. J. SMART, NORTHAMPTONSHIRE REGT.

PANEL 45 BEGINS PTE. B. SMITH, NORTHAMPTONSHIRE REGT.

(Panel 45) Pte. 7664, Walter Smith, 1st Bn. (48th Foot) The Northamptonshire Regt.: 2nd *s.* of George Smith, Miller; of The Mount, Bannister Green, Felstead, co. Essex, and Jane Smith his spouse: and brother to Gnr. 60927, E. Smith, 'Z' Trench Mortar Bty., R.G.A., killed in action, 10 September 1916; and Bty.Sergt.Major 85441, P.J. Smith, Royal Field Artillery, died on 28 April 1917: *b.* 1887: Occupation – Grocer's Assistant; Stebbing: enlisted Braintree. Killed in action, 11 November 1914. Age 27. He was married for only ten months to Mabel E. Smith, *née* Cotton (126, Glenny Road, Barking, co. Essex).

His brother Ernest is buried in Carnoy Military Cemetery (B.31); Percy, Ripon Cemetery (F.140).

(Panel 45) Pte. 15099, Joseph Stead, 6th (Service) Bn. The Northamptonshire Regt.: late of 118, Rogers Street, Peterborough, co. Northampton: brother to the late Pte. 16325, H.F. Stead, 3rd Northamptonshire Regt., died of illness, 13 September 1916, contracted on active service: *b.* Peterborough: enlisted there. Killed in action, 8 August 1917.

His brother Harold is buried in Peterborough Old Cemetery.

(Panel 45) Pte. 6135, WilliamTaylor, 1st Bn. (48th Foot)The Northamptonshire Regt.: late of Newport, co. Monmouth: *b.* Lochee, co. Forfar: served with the Expeditionary Force in France and Flanders from 13 August 1914, and was killed in action in the attack at Pilckem on the late evening of 22 October following. Age 35. He was married to Joan Taylor (7, Ure Street, Dundee).

(Panel 45) Pte. 25146, Cuthbert Leslie Vear, 2nd Bn. (58th Foot) The Northamptonshire Regt.: *s.* of Mrs G. Vear (Bourne Road, Alford, co. Lincoln): and yr. brother to L/Corpl. 120161, P.W. Vear, 21st King's Royal Rifle Corps, killed in action, 17 September 1916: *b.* Alford: enlisted Peterborough. Killed in action, 31 July 1917. Age 29. He leaves a widow, Mrs R.E. Vear (Market Place, Oundle, nr. Peterborough, co. Northampton).

His brother Percy also has no known grave; he is commemorated on the Thiepval Memorial, Somme.

(Panel 45) Pte. 19337, William CharlesVears, 7th (Service) Bn. The Northamptonshire Regt.: formerly no.35900, Royal Army Medical Corps: *s.* of William Charles Vears, of 65, North Street, Mare Street, Hackney, by his wife Clara Maria: and brother to Pte. 102431, H.C. Vears, Labour Corps, killed in action, 15 April 1918: enlisted St. Paul's Churchyard, London. Killed in action, 10 February 1916. Age 32. He was married to Annie Vears (71, North Street, Mare Street, Hackney).

His brother Henry is buried in St. Pierre Cemetery, Amiens (XVI.D.6).

(Panel 45) Pte. 32175, William Watkins, 7th (Service) Bn. The Northamptonshire Regt.: *b.* Wollaston, co. Northampton: enlisted there. Killed in action, 8 June 1917 while attached to a burial party. Two other men (Ptes. 22695, M. Bradshaw; 43565, W.J.H. Pain) were also killed; and, mortally wounded by the shell burst, Pte. 201972, A. Fowler died later the same day.

Ptes. Bradshaw and Pain also have no known grave, they are recorded on Panel 43; Alfred Fowler is buried in Dickebusch New Military Cemetery Extension (III.C.21).

(Panel 45) Pte. 25235, Herbert Whitlock, 7th (Service) Bn. The Northamptonshire Regt.: *s.* of John Whitlock, of Roade, Northampton, by his wife Amelia: *b.* Wellingborough, co. Northampton: enlisted there. Killed in action, 31 July 1917. Age 36.

(Panel 45) Capt. Oliver Steele, 1st Bn. (49th Foot) Princess Charlotte of Wales's (Royal Berkshire Regt.): *s.* of Thomas (& Mrs) Steele, of Remuera, Auckland, New Zealand: and nephew of A.R. Steele, of Loddington, co. Northampton: *b.* Wairoa, Hawkes Bay, New Zealand, 7 April 1882: *educ.* Auckland Grammar School, where he made a record in the school sports, 1895, for the 100 yards under fourteen, which he did in 11 seconds – the record still remains unbroken (1915): obtained his commission during the South African War, being promoted from the ranks of 5th New Zealand Contingent, May 1900: present at operations in Rhodesia, the Transvaal, including actions at Eland's River, May 1900–July 1901, and Cape Colony, July 1901–May 1902: Queen's Medal, four clasps; King's Medal, two clasps: promoted Lieut. March 1902; Capt. July 1910: held Durbar Coronation Medal, 1911: proceeded to France with his regiment, on the outbreak of war, served with the Expeditionary Force there, and was killed in action at Zonnebeke, Flanders, 25 October 1914, by the bursting of a shell while reforming his company after a charge. For his bravery in the Great War he was Mentioned in Sir John (now Lord) French's Despatch, 14 January 1915. He was a member of the Junior Naval and Military Club. Age 32. *unm.*

(Panel 45) Sergt. 7872, Charles Frederick Heath, 'C' Coy., 1st Bn. (49th Foot) Princess Charlotte of Wales's (Royal Berkshire Regt.): *s.* of John Heath, of Ashby Villa, Bracknell, co. Berks, by his wife Sarah: and brother to Pte. 9267, B.W. Heath, 2nd Royal Berkshire Regt., killed in action, 10 March 1915: served in India; and with the Expeditionary Force in France and Flanders from 13 August 1914, and was killed in action, 15 November 1914. Age 28. *unm.*

His brother Bartlett is buried in Neuve Chapelle British Cemetery (D.1).

(Panel 45) Corpl. 9635, William Francis Cartland, 1st Bn. (49th Foot) Princess Charlotte of Wales's (Royal Berkshire Regt.): *b.* Pinkney's Green, nr. Maidenhead: enlisted Reading. Died in the Casualty Clearing Hospital, Poperinghe, 9 November 1914, of wounds received in the vicinity of a wood east of the Zonnebeke – Becelare road, just south of White Track, on the 8th. *Buried in Poperinghe Old Military Cemetery (I.M.60).*

(Panel 45) Corpl. 8247, William Billingham Fussell, 1st Bn. (49th Foot) Princess Charlotte of Wales's (Royal Berkshire Regt.): *s.* of the late William Maulever Fussell, by his wife Beatrice A.M. (8, Kingswood Villas, Dover): and brother-in-law to Sergt. L/9203, A.F. Fogg, 2nd Buffs, killed in action, 28 September 1915, at the Battle of Loos; and Coy.Sergt.Major 65084, A.C. Fogg, 13th Royal Fusiliers, died 16 April 1918, of wounds: *b.* Longford, Ireland, 1895: enlisted Dublin: served with the Expeditionary Force in France and Flanders from August 1914: took part in the fighting at Mons and the subsequent retirement, the Battles of the Aisne and the Marne, and was killed in action, 4 November 1914, at Ypres. Age 22. He leaves a wife, Ivy Hannah Fussell, *née* Fogg (104, Mayfield Avenue, Dover), and *dau.*, Norma, aged three months.

Ivy Fussell was killed while sleeping 22 May 1943, when a German bombing raid destroyed a row of houses in Mayfield Avenue, her brother Albert Fogg, has no known grave, he is commemorated on the Loos (Dud Corner) Memorial; Arthur Fogg is buried in St. Amand British Cemetery (II.A.2).

(Panel 45) Pte. 10350, Edward John Tuttle, 2nd Bn. (66th Foot) Princess Charlotte of Wales (Royal Berkshire Regt.): *s.* of Henry Tuttle, of 4, Lambfield Cottages, Theale, co. Berks, by his wife Alice: and yr. brother to Corpl. 11880, A.H. Tuttle, Grenadier Guards, killed in action, 7 November 1914, at the First Battle of Ypres: *b.* Sulhampstone, co. Berks: enlisted Reading. Killed in action, 31 July 1917. Age 21. *unm.*

His brother Alfred also has no known grave; he is recorded on Panel 9.

(Panel 45) Pte. 36517, Fred Whyman, 6th (Service) Bn. Princess Charlotte of Wales (Royal Berkshire Regt.): formerly no.5986, Hertfordshire Regt.: late of Ware, co. Hertford: brother to Pte. 36509, W. Whyman, Royal Berkshire Regt., killed in action, 11 August 1917: enlisted Hertford. Killed in action, 31 July 1917; in the vicinity of Sanctuary Wood.

His brother William also has no known grave; he is recorded below.

(Panel 45) Pte. 36509, William Whyman, 6th (Service) Bn. Princess Charlotte of Wales (Royal Berkshire Regt.): formerly no.5886, Hertfordshire Regt.: late of Ware, co. Hertford: brother to Pte. 36517, F. Whyman, Royal Berkshire Regt., killed in action, 31 July 1917: enlisted Hertford. Killed in action, 11 August 1917; Ritz Street trench, Ypres-Menin Road.

His brother Fred also has no known grave; he is recorded above.

(Panel 45) Major John Francis Joslin, 2nd attd. 1st Bn. (50th Foot) The Queen's Own (Royal West Kent Regt.): only *survg. s.* of the late John Joslin, of St. Helier's, Jersey, by his wife Mary (7, Almorah Crescent, St. Helier's, Jersey), *dau.* of Francis Philip Cabot: *b.* St. Helier's, 2 September 1874: *educ.* Victoria College, Jersey: gazetted 2nd Lieut. 2nd Royal West Kent Regt. from the Militia, 7 December 1895; promoted Lieut. 13 November 1897: served in the South African War 1900–02, taking part in the operations in the Orange Free State, April–May 1900: Orange River Colony, May–29 November 1900, including actions at Biddulphsberg and Wittebergen (1–29 July): Cape Colony, south of the Orange River, 1900: Transvaal, August–September 1901; April–31 May, 1902: and Orange River Colony, 30 November 1900–August 1901; September 1901–April 1902: Mentioned in Despatches (*London Gazette*, 29 July 1901): Queen's Medal, three clasps; King's Medal, two clasps: promoted Capt. 7 January 1903: Battn. Adjutant, 16 November 1904–15 November 1907. After passing through the Staff College he acted as Brigade Major to Gen. Braithwaite at the Durbar, for which he received the medal, and was promoted Major on 3 September 1914. Proceeded to France, 24 October, and in November became Commandant of the Lines of Communication. Having been attached to 1st Battalion of his regt., he led the storming party (1st West Kents and 2nd K.O.S.B.'s), which captured Hill 60 on the evening of 17 April 1915, but after holding the hill all night, and repulsing three counter-attacks, he was killed as the West Kents were being relieved in the early hours of the 18th. He was the last to leave the position and was shot in the act of leaving, death being almost instantaneous. A brother officer wrote of him, "And in action he was splendid, quite without fear, and able by his example to inspire and encourage those around him. But in your sorrow should mingle pride, for to the very end he did his duty right well, and did much to keep the regimental standard of self-sacrifice as high as it now is. And such records never die." Age 40. *unm.* (*IWGC record F.J. Joslin*)

(Panel 45) Capt. Cecil Thomas Tuff, 3rd (Reserve) attd. 'D' Coy., 1st Bn. (50th Foot) The Queen's Own (Royal West Kent Regt.): 3rd *s.* of Charles Tuff, Esq., of 'Westfield,' Singlewell, Gravesend, late M.P. for Rochester, co. Kent: *b.* Rochester, 1885: *educ.* Malvern College: joined West Kent Militia, 1905: resigned his commission in 1910: became owner of, and farmed, Coombe Manor, Rochester: on the outbreak of war in August 1914, rejoined his old Battalion – now 3rd Royal West Kent Regt. – as Lieut.; promoted Capt. September 1914: served with the Expeditionary Force in France and Flanders, from November following, attd. 1st Battn., and was shot and killed, 20 April 1915, while leading his Company in the attack on Hill 60. Age 29. *unm.*

(Panel 45) Lieut. Philip Warden Bradley, 3rd (Reserve) attd. 1st Bn. (50th Foot) The Queen's Own (Royal West Kent Regt.): *s.* of Brigdr.Gen. (& Mrs) C.E. Bradley: *educ.* United Services College, Westward Ho. Killed in action, 23 April 1915, at Hill 60, Flanders. Age 27.

(Panel 45) Lieut. Charles Mervyn Payton, 'A' Coy., 3rd (Reserve) attd. 1st Bn. (50th Foot) The Queen's Own (Royal West Kent Regt.): only *s.* of Sir Charles Payton, of Stepney Court, Scarborough, M.V.O., late British Consul-General at Calais, by his 1st wife, Eliza Mary, *dau.* of the late John Olive: *b.* Mogador, Morocco, 5 December 1891: *educ.* Dover College, and on leaving there (1909) became a Clerk under his father in the British Consulate, Calais: gazetted 2nd Lieut. Reserve Battn. Royal West Kent Regt. 1910; promoted Lieut. 6 September 1911: left the Army (1912) to go to Singapore, where he held a post on a rubber plantation, but in the following year was appointed Chief Clerk in the Colonial Secretary's Office, which appointment he gave up on the outbreak of war in August 1914: returned home and rejoined his old Regt.: was on special duty in England for some time: went to France in January 1915, and was killed in action during the Second Battle of Ypres, 18 April following. He was leading his men in the attack on Hill 60, and had picked up the rifle of a fallen soldier, and was firing at the enemy when he was shot through the head. His Commanding Officer wrote that he had done very good work and, "shown himself to be a brave man and a good leader." And a Sergt. of his Coy. wrote of him as "one of the best and truest, more like a brother to the men than an officer, cheering in the blackest times by his brave gaiety, and mourned by them as a brother." Lieut. Payton was Mentioned in Sir John (now Lord) French's Despatch of 31 May (*London Gazette*, 22 June), 1915, for 'gallant and distinguished service in the field.' He was a keen sportsman, a remarkably good shot and expert angler. Age 23. *unm.*

(Panel 45) Lieut. Henry Arthur Poland, 3rd (Reserve) attd. 'C' Coy., 1st Bn. (50th Foot) The Queen's Own (Royal West Kent Regt.): elder *s.* of Henry Poland, of 'Sunnybank,' The Drive, Sevenoaks, co. Kent, late of 'Charleville,' St. Botolph's Road, by his wife Jessie: *b.* Grove Park, Lee, London, S.E., 5 April 1893: *educ.* Tonbridge School; Marburg, Germany, and Saint Lo, France: served two years with Inns of Court O.T.C., and was proficient at bayonet exercise: gazetted 2nd Lieut. 3rd Royal West Kent Regt. August 1914: went to the Front to join 1st Battn. December 1914: promoted Lieut. March 1915. Lieut. Poland led his men in the charge to capture Hill 60, 17 April 1915, and was unwounded during the night fighting. The following morning he was sent forward to repel a fresh attack by the enemy, and was killed by the explosion of a hand-grenade or bomb. *The Queen's Own Gazette*, reports that not a single man of the section led by Lieut. Poland returned. He was a good long-distance runner, and keen on football and hockey. Age 22 years, 12 days. *unm.*

Consolation

Oh! I sigh when I think of the men
In the trenches of Flanders and France;
And I dream of the days of romance,
Of the bow and the shield and the lance,
And the chivalrous tales that the pen
Of a poet could celebrate then.

For the brutal inventions of crime
Are the weapons of battle today;

And the guns that remorselessly slay
Blow the ramparts and shelters way,
And there in the mud and the slime
Are the heroes who fall in their prime.

And I grieve for the widows who weep,
And the parents and orphans forlorn,
And the hearts that in anguish are torn;
And yet it is idle to mourn
For the dead are serenely asleep,
And our faith in the Lord we must keep.

For the faith that is steadfast and clear,
Brings to the sorrowing hearts the reward
That our belief in our God can afford.
They are happy who trust in the Lord:
They find comfort to whom he is dear
And know that his spirit is near.

(Panel 45) Lieut. Gerald George Samuel, 10th (Service) Bn. The Queen's Own (Royal West Kent Regt.): *s.* of Lord and Lady Bearsted, of 3, Hamilton Place, Piccadilly, London. Killed in action, 7 June 1917. The above poem, written by Lieut. Samuel, was found among his papers after his death. Age 31.

(Panel 45) 2nd Lieut. Kenneth Frost, 1st Bn. (50th Foot) The Queen's Own (Royal West Kent Regt.): *s.* of Ralph Frost, of 13, Wandle Road, Wandsworth Common, London, S.W.: *b.* London, 28 April 1891: *educ.* Reading School: served five years with Artists' Rifles, 28th (County of London) Bn. (London Regt.), (T.F.), attaining rank of Corpl. (no.706): given a temporary commission, General List, 27 January 1915, attd. 1st Bn. Royal West Kent Regt. for Active Service: served with the Expeditionary Force in France and Flanders, and was killed in action at Zillebeke, 22 February 1915 by the explosion of a trench mortar shell. Age 23. *unm.* See also Capt. J.E.G. Brown, Tuileries British Cemetery (Sp.Mem.A.2); and 2nd Lieut. J.F. Burbury, Bedford House Cemetery, (IV.A.58/Enc.No.2)

(Panel 45) 2nd Lieut. Bernard Craig Keble Job, 3rd (Reserve) attd. 1st Bn. (50th Foot) The Queen's Own (Royal West Kent Regt.): only *s.* of the Rev. Frederick William Job, Vicar of Lower Gornal, co. Stafford, by his wife Emily Frances, *dau.* of William Young Craig, M.P., for N. Staffordshire (1880–85): *b.* Liverpool, 9 June 1887: *educ.* Radley College: went to Liverpool to enlist in Liverpool Scottish the day war was declared on 4 August 1914, and was sworn in on 6 August: received his commission, 1 November; went to the Front with a draft of the Royal Dublin Fusiliers, arriving in France on Good Friday, attd. 1st Battn. of his regt. a few days later, and was killed in action in the counter-attack on Hill 60, 18 April 1915.

Writing to his father, Major Robinson, Comdg. 1st Battn., said, "He was shot by a bullet and died almost immediately on the morning of 18 April in the heavy fighting which followed our capture of a portion of the enemy's position called Hill 60, 2½ miles S.E. of Ypres. I understand that he died almost instantly after being hit and that he could have felt no pain. It was not possible, during the fighting, to bury his body. I am, however, informed that all the dead have since been buried, so your son no doubt lies at rest among the other officers and men who fought with him. Your son had only joined this battn. a few days before his death, but from the little I saw of him I formed the opinion that he was a gallant and valuable officer." Col. Sir Arthur G. Boscawen, 3rd Battn., wrote, "He was a universal favourite and the soul of courage, had he lived he would have made a very fine officer." Age 27. *unm.*

(Panel 45) 2nd Lieut. Leonard Pengelly Waghorn, 3rd (Reserve) Bn. The Queen's Own (Royal West Kent Regt.) attd. 1st Bn. (49th Foot) Princess Charlotte of Wales's (Royal Berkshire Regt.): 2nd *s.* of Engineer Capt. J.W. Waghorn, Royal Navy, D.Sc., formerly Professor of Physics, Royal Naval College, Greenwich: *b.* 8, Glenluce Road, Blackheath, London, S.E., 24 January 1891: *educ.* Preparatory School,

Scaitliffe, Engelfield (Messrs Morton & Vickers), and Marlborough College (L/Corpl., O.T.C. – Cavalry). Intending to enter the medical profession, he was in his fourth year at Guy's Hospital when, on the outbreak of war, he volunteered for Active Service: obtained a commission, gazetted 2nd Lieut. 3rd Royal West Kent Regt. from Inns of Court O.T.C. August 1914: stationed at Chatham for about six weeks; went to the Front, 3 October following: served with the Expeditionary Force in France and Flanders, and was killed in action, 6 November 1914, when the company to which he was attached was heavily shelled whilst in the wood just north of the Ypres – Menin Road, near Gheluvelt. Buried in the wood near to the chateau. Age 23. *unm.*

(Panel 45) 2nd Lieut. Frederick Charles Westmacott, 3rd (Reserve) attd. 11th (Service) Bn. The Queen's Own (Royal West Kent Regt.): *s.* of Canon (& Mrs) Westmacott, of The Sanctuary, Probus, co. Cornwall: and yr. brother to Lieut. S.R. Westmacott, Leinster Regt., who fell 8 May 1915, at the Second Battle of Ypres. Killed in action, 31 July 1917. Age 19.

His brother Spencer also has no known grave; he is recorded on Panel 44.

(Panel 45) Sergt. L/6335, Frederick William Davies, 1st Bn. (50th Foot) The Queen's Own (Royal West Kent Regt.): enlisted Woolwich, co. Kent. Killed in action at Zillebeke, 21 February 1915. See Tuileries British Cemetery (Sp.Mems. B.6–B.7).

(Panel 45) L/Corpl. G/4902, George Arthur Alexander Clackett, 'A' Coy., 1st Bn. (50th Foot) The Queen's Own (Royal West Kent Regt.): *s.* of Ellen Clackett (33, Kingsnorth Road, Faversham, co. Kent): and elder brother to Pte. G/5222, W.J. Clackett, 6th Queen's Own, killed in action, 8 October 1916: *b.* East Malling: enlisted Faversham. Killed in action, 5 May 1915. Age 20. *unm.*

His brother Wilfred also has no known grave; he is commemorated on the Thiepval Memorial (Pier & Face 11C).

(Panel 45) L/Corpl. G/8596, Sydney John Gates, 10th (Service) Bn. The Queen's Own (Royal West Kent Regt.): *s.* of Annie J. Bishop (19, Stanley Avenue, Queensborough, co. Kent): *b.* Selling, co. Kent, *c.*1896: enlisted Sheerness. Killed in action, 7 June 1917. Age 21. *Commemorated in Voormezeele Enclosure No.3 (Sp.Mem.15).*

(Panel 45) L/Corpl. G/19047, Edward James Tingcombe, 10th (Service) Bn. The Queen's Own (Royal West Kent Regt.): formerly no.2514, West Kent Yeomanry: *s.* of John Tingcombe, of 45, Gladstone Avenue, Wood Green, London, by his wife Mary: and brother to Pte. G/19153, G.C. Tingcombe, 7th The Buffs (East Kent Regt.), died of wounds, 9 May 1917: *b.* Chelsea: enlisted St. Paul's Churchyard, London. Killed in action, 31 July 1917.

His brother George is buried in Ontario Cemetery, Sains-les-Marquion (IV.A.32).

(Panel 45) L/Corpl. L/7523, John Tucker, 1st Bn. (50th Foot) The Queen's Own (Royal West Kent Regt.): *b.* Charlton, co. Kent: enlisted New Cross. Died 2 December 1914, of wounds received in France. *Known to be buried in Greenwich Cemetery, London; commemorated therein (Screen Wall, 1.'C'.B.1138).*

(Panel 45) Pte. G/18403, Ernest Thomas Ames, 11th (Service) Bn. (Lewisham) The Queen's Own (Royal West Kent Regt.): formerly no.2642, Royal East Kent Mounted Rifles: *s.* of Edith Sarah Ames ('Vale View,' Elham, co. Kent): and brother to Pte. G/39093, H.S. Ames, 6th Queen's Own, killed in action, 23 October 1918: *b.* Elham: enlisted there. Killed in action, 7 June 1917.

His brother Herbert is buried in Valenciennes (St. Roch) Communal Cemetery (III.B.8).

(Panel 45) Pte. G/10396, John Barnden, 10th (Service) Bn. The Queen's Own (Royal West Kent Regt.): *s.* of Albert Ernest Barnden, of 12, Windsor Road, Willesden Green, London, by his wife Mary: and brother to Stoker 1st Class, SS/102658, F.T. Barnden, R.N., HMS 'Hawke,' lost at sea, 15 October 1914, when that ship was torpedoed and sunk by German submarine U.9: *b.* Halling, Rochester, co. Kent: enlisted Maidstone. Killed in action, 31 July 1917. Age 21. *unm.*

Having no known grave but the sea, his brother Frank is commemorated on the Chatham Naval Memorial (4).

(Panel 45) Pte. G.4986, James Beaney, 1st Bn. (50th Foot) The Queen's Own (Royal West Kent Regt.): *husb.* to Mary Ann Beaney (1, Portland Row, Upper Halling, Rochester, co. Kent): served with the Expeditionary Force in France and Flanders. Killed in action, 18 April 1915. Age 37.

(Panel 45) Pte. L/8060, Harry Bishopp, 1st Bn. (50th Foot) The Queen's Own (Royal West Kent Regt.): *s.* of the late Samuel Bishopp: enlisted Maidstone: served with the Expeditionary Force. Killed by a sniper, 15 November 1914. Age 29. He was married to Beatrice Maud Fuller, *née* Bishopp (69, Lewis Trust Building, Waltham Green, London).

(Panel 45) Pte. S/4623 Frederick Booker, 1st Bn. (50th Foot) The Queen's Own (Royal West Kent Regt.): *b.* Deptford, London, S.E.: enlisted Maidstone, co. Kent: served with the Expeditionary Force in France, and was killed in action near Zillebeke, 15 November 1914. Buried where he fell. *m.*

(Panel 45) Pte. 7418, Horace Brooman, 8th (Service) Bn. The Queen's Own (Royal West Kent Regt.): *s.* of Spencer Brooman, of Daniel Place, Military Road, Rye, co. Sussex, by his wife Angelina (*née* Foster): *b.* East Guildford, 15 April 1886: *educ.* Rye: Occupation – Chemist's Assistant; Rye: served as Corpl., 5th (Territorial) Bn. Royal Sussex Regt., 12 yrs.; and with the Expeditionary Force in France and Flanders from February 1915: wounded at Richebourg, the following May, and invalided home: returned to France 1 August 1916, and was killed in action, 26 July 1917. Age 31. *unm.*

(Panel 45) Pte. G/25659, James Brown, 8th (Service) Bn. The Queen's Own (Royal West Kent Regt.): enlisted Chatham, co. Kent. Died of wounds, 12 June 1917. Remains recovered on 10 April 1928 from a grave marked as belonging to an 'Unknown British Soldier. R. West Kent', identified – Clothing, Titles, Boots; registered, reinterred 20 April 1928. *Buried in Sanctuary Wood Cemetery (II.H.18).*

(Panel 45) Pte. G/8348, Albert Victor Buggy, 'A' Coy., 11th (Service) Bn. (Lewisham) The Queen's Own (Royal West Kent Regt.): *s.* of Frank Buggy, of 48, Ladywell Park, Lewisham, London, S.E.13, by his wife Julia: and brother to Pte. 47285, F. Buggy, 11th Welsh Regt., died 10 Octobeer 1918; Salonika: *b.* Rotherhithe: enlisted Lewisham. Killed in action, 31 July 1917. Age 24. *unm.*

His brother Frank is buried in Kirechkoi-Hortakoi Military Cemetery (302).

(Panel 45) Pte. S/8810, William Charles Chamberlain, 1st Bn. (50th Foot) The Queen's Own (Royal West Kent Regt.): *s.* of Mr (& Mrs) Chamberlain, of 26, Townsend Street, Old Kent Road, London: enlisted Sevenoaks, co. Kent. Killed in action at Zillebeke, 21 February 1915. Age 21. *unm.* See Tuileries British Cemetery (Sp.Mems.B6–B7)

(Panel 45) Pte. L/6654, Joseph Cooper, 1st Bn. (50th Foot) The Queen's Own (Royal West Kent Regt.): late of Dartford. Co. Kent: *s.* of Mrs Cooper (26, Hales Street, High Street, Deptford, London): *b.* Westminster, 1881: enlisted New Cross, London, S.E.. Shot and killed by a German sniper, 14 November 1914. Age 33.

(Panel 45) Pte. L/6616, Sidney Harold Cooper, 1st Bn. (50th Foot) The Queen's Own (Royal West Kent Regt.): *s.* of Henry John Cooper, of Poplar, London, E., by his wife Emma Jane: enlisted Stratford, London, E.: served with the Expeditionary Force, and was killed in action, 17 November 1914 by shellfire. Age 28.

(Panel 45) Pte. 848, Edward Dimmock, 1st Bn. (50th Foot) The Queen's Own (Royal West Kent Regt.): *s.* of Jonathan Charles Dimmock, of 7, Berthon Street, Deptford, London, S.E., Coal Porter, by his wife Sophie, *dau.* of Charles Henry Mann: *b.* Greenwich, 8 October 1877: *educ.* there: Occupation – Stevedore: joined 3rd (Reserve) Battn. West Kent Militia, 1893: served 18 months at Malta; awarded Mediterranean Medal (1901): obtained his discharge, 29 May 1903, having served 10 years with the Colours: re-enlisted, 15 September 1914, after the outbreak of war: served with the Expeditionary Force in France and Flanders. Killed in action during the operations at Hill 60, 18 April 1915. Age 37. He *m.* Greenwich, 6 November 1902; Sarah Ellen (5, Lexton's Buildings, Bardsley Street, Greenwich, formerly of 8, Coombedale Road, Greenwich, London, S.E.), *dau.* of James Edward Wood.

(Panel 45) Pte. S/779, Charles William Evenden, 1st Bn. (50th Foot) The Queen's Own (Royal West Kent Regt.): *s.* of William Evenden, of Waterloo Road, Cranbrook, co. Kent, by his wife Annie: served with the Expeditionary Force in France, and was killed in action, 10 May 1915. Age 41. He leaves a wife, Louisa (1, Savona Place, Battersea, London, S.W.).

(Panel 45) Pte. L/5473, Albert Exall, 1st Bn. (50th Foot) The Queen's Own (Royal West Kent Regt.): *s.* of Frederick Exall, of London: and brother to William James Exall Esq., of 2, Grove Cottages, Falconer Road, Bushey, co. Hertford: served with the Expeditionary Force in France, and was killed in action there, 18 April 1915.

(Panel 45) Pte. 205613, Frederick Springthorpe Goodrum, 4th Bn. The Queen's Own (Royal West Kent Regt.), (T.F.): *s*. of the late Ernest W. Goodrum, by his wife Annie Faith Logan (720, Grimesthorpe Road, Sheffield): *b*. Sheffield, co. York, 8 January 1888: *educ*. St. Charles' Roman Catholic School: enlisted on 9 March 1917: served with the Expeditionary Force in France and Flanders, and died on 4 August following from wounds received in action at Dickebusch the previous day. Age 29. *unm*.

(Panel 45) Pte. L/10130, Leonard Griffiths, 'D' Coy., 1st Bn. (50th Foot) The Queen's Own (Royal West Kent Regt.): *s*. of Annie M. Griffiths (1, Hope Street, Maidstone): served with the Expeditionary Force, and was killed in action, 18 April 1915. Age 19.

(Panel 45) Pte. 205471, Harold Harland, 10th (Service) Bn. The Queen's Own (Royal West Kent Regt.): *s*. of George Charles Harland, Lamp Oil Merchant; of 51, Wykeham Street, Scarborough, by his wife Elizabeth, *dau*. of George Dale: *b*. Scarborough, 26 February 1896: *educ*. Gladstone Road Council School, Scarborough: Occupation – Boot Repairer: enlisted on 2 January 1917: served with the Expeditionary Force in France and Flanders from the following July. Reported missing, 31 July 1917, after the fighting on the Menin Road; now assumed to have been killed in action on that date. Age 21. *unm*.

(Panel 45) Pte. L/10202, Thomas Henry Hatcher, 10th (Service) Bn. (Kent County) The Queen's Own (Royal West Kent Regt.): *s*. of Harry Hatcher, of 3, Bridge Buildings, Stone Street, Cranbrook, co. Kent, by his wife Elizabeth J.: and brother to Sergt. G/13760, C.W.R. Hatcher, 1st The Buffs, killed in action, 18 March 1917: enlisted Maidstone. Killed in action, 7 June 1917. Age 21. He was married to Harriet Drusilla Hatcher (Saints Passage, High Street, Cranbrook).

His brother Charles is buried in Maroc British Cemetery, Grenay (I.P.1).

(Panel 45) Pte. L/9914, Charles Humphrey, 1st Bn. (50th Foot) The Queen's Own (Royal West Kent Regt.): *s*. of W. Hunt, of Bermondsey, London, S.E.: served with the Expeditionary Force. Reported missing on 31 October 1914, and now assumed killed. *(IWGC record 14 November 1914, on which date the battn. were in trenches near Zillebeke, losing men to sniper fire.)* [After distinguishing themselves at the Battle of Neuve Chapelle, 1st Queen's Own left the trenches at that place in the early morning of 30 October 1914, and marched to Coutre Croix where they remained for two days before marching to Dranoutre on 1 November.]

For 1st Queen's Own, 19 November 1914 marked the end of their first tour in the Zillebeke sector, a day of persistent sniping, machine-gun fire and occasional shelling. That evening the battalion was relieved and marched back to dug-outs in front of Ypres. Although it was a freezing night, snow was lying on the ground and the only accommodation the men could be provided with – if accommodation be the correct term – were open shell-holes with absolutely no cover or protection from the weather. However, totally exhausted after six days with practically no rest or sleep, this state of affairs was the least of the men's worries and all soon fell sound asleep. For Arthur Ives and Alfred Stephenson, mates from Plumstead, London, cold nights and protection against the weather would never worry them again: rifle, machine-gun and shell fire would never worry them again either; they too were relieved on the 19th – forever.

(Panel 45) Pte. S/9130, Arthur Ives, 1st Bn. (50th Foot) The Queen's Own (Royal West Kent Regt.): late of Plumstead, London, S.E.: enlisted Woolwich, co. Kent. Killed in action, 19 November 1914.

Alfred Stephenson also has no known grave; he is recorded below.

(Panel 45) Pte. G/11713, John Lankester, 11th (Service) Bn. (Lewisham) The Queen's Own (Royal West Kent Regt.): *s*. of Harry Lankester, of 'Four Elms,' Edenbridge, co. Kent, and his wife Agnes, *née* Ruder: and yr. brother to Rfn. R/7006, W. Lankester, 8th King's Royal Rifle Corps, killed in action at the Battle of Hooge, 30 July 1915: *b*. Elsenham, Bishop's Stortford: enlisted Edenbridge, January 1916; apptd. 3rd (Reserve) Battn. Queen's Own; proceeded to France, transf'd. 8th Battn. 19 May following: took part in the fighting throughout the summer of that year: hospitalised sick, 3 February 1917; repatriated to England, 15 February: returned to France, 14 June 1917. Missing/believed killed in action at the Third Battle of Ypres, 31 July 1917. Age 27. Prior to his return to France he married (19 May) Martha Eliza Lankester, *née* Tillman (15, High Street, Rusthall, Tunbridge Wells); late of 14, Embleton Road, Lewisham, London, S.E. Two days after their wedding, John returned to his battalion. Fate decreed Martha would not see him again before he returned to France. She died in 1971, never having re-married.

His brother William also has no known grave; he is recorded on Panel 53.

(Panel 45) Pte. G/6735, Charles George Lang, 8th (Service) Bn. The Queen's Own (Royal West Kent Regt.): *s.* of Mr (& Mrs) Lang, of 171, Hanworth Road, Hounslow, co. Middlesex: and yr. brother to Pte. G/6736, E.A. Lang, 8th Queen's Own, who fell the same day: *b.* Hounslow: enlisted there. Killed in action, 8 February 1916; Railway Wood. Age 22. *unm.*

His brother Ernest is recorded below.

(Panel 45) Pte. G/6736, Ernest Arthur Lang, 8th (Service) Bn. The Queen's Own (Royal West Kent Regt.): *s.* of Mr (& Mrs) Lang, of 171, Hanworth Road, Hounslow, co. Middlesex: and elder brother to Pte. G/6735, C.G. Lang, who fell the same day: *b.* Hounslow: enlisted there. Killed in action, 8 February 1916; Railway Wood. Age 23. *unm.*

His brother Charles is recorded above.

(Panel 45) Pte. 16538, James Ekrow Little, 7th (Service) Bn. The Queen's Own (Royal West Kent Regt.): eldest *s.* of George Little, Joiner; of 176, Philip Street, Newcastle-on-Tyne, by his wife Margaret, *dau.* of George Deans: *b.* Newcastle-on-Tyne, 3 August 1897: *educ.* Todd's Nook School: Occupation – Solicitor's Clerk: enlisted on 10 September 1915: served with the Expeditionary Force in France and Flanders from 2 February 1916, and was killed in action at Ypres, 24 July 1917. Buried 600 yards east of Zillebeke, south-east of Ypres. An Officer wrote, "Your son was a great favourite of mine, as he was always of such a happy disposition, and such a splendid fellow at his work." And a comrade, "He was a fine soldier and a brave lad, loved by us all for his cheerfulness and his readiness to help." Age 20. *unm.*

(Panel 45) Pte. G/25931, William Thomas Mardell, 11th (Service) Bn. (Lewisham) The Queen's Own (Royal West Kent Regt.): *yst. s.* of the late Henry Mardell, by his wife Mary Ann (65, Birkbeck Road, Tottenham, London, N.), *dau.* of Samuel William Ginn: *b.* Tottenham, London, N., 17 January 1890: *educ.* Lancastrian School, Tottenham: enlisted Royal West Kent Regt. November 1915: served with the Expeditionary Force in France and Flanders from November 1916, and was killed in action, 31 July 1917. Buried where he fell. Age 27. *unm.*

(Panel 45) Pte. G/25358, John Marsh, 11th (Service) Bn. (Lewisham) The Queen's Own (Royal West Kent Regt.): *s.* of John (& Mrs) Marsh, of Lywood Common, Ardingly, co. Sussex: and yr. brother to Pte. 27263, W.C. Marsh, 1st Wiltshire Regt., reported missing, 23 March 1918, believed to have died of wounds: *b.* Swanage, co. Dorset: enlisted Horsham. Killed in action, 31 July 1917. Age 24. *unm.*

His brother William also has no known grave; he is commemorated on the Arras (Faubourg d'Amiens) Memorial (Bay 7).

(Panel 45) Pte. L/5267, James Moore, 1st Bn. (50th Foot) The Queen's Own (Royal West Kent Regt.): *b.* Leytonstone, London, E.: enlisted Stratford. Shot and killed by an enemy sniper, 15 November 1914.

(Panel 45) Pte. L/6259, John O'Shea, 1st Bn. (50th Foot) The Queen's Own (Royal West Kent Regt.): *s.* of the late Joseph O'Shea: *b.* Worcester: enlisted New Cross, London, S.E. Shot and killed by an enemy sniper, 15 November 1914. Age 33. He was married to Caroline Amelia Anderson, *née* O'Shea (16, Broad Street, Canterbury, co. Kent).

Billeted and occupying trenches in the Neuve Eglise sector, with King's Own Yorkshire Light Infantry in support, 1st Queen's Own received more than their fair share of shellfire but escaped heavy casualties. At a nearby farm, on 7 November, Lieut.Col. Martyn, Comdg. 13th Brigade, was hit by a fragment of shell whilst engaged in conversation with his Brigade Major; the farm later became known as 'Martyn's Farm.' Capt. Buchanan-Dunlop's horse (a hunter which had originally been owned by Major Pack Beresford) was hit at the same time; it went right through the war, was wounded three times, and is believed to have lived to a considerable old age. On 9 November 1914, at Neuve Eglise, bombing caused Sir H. Smith-Dorrien to hurriedly address such men as could be collected, congratulating them on their recent achievements; in the afternoon a German aeroplane dropped a bomb as the men assembled for Divine Service – luckily it exploded without causing any casualties. On the night of the 11th, as the West Kents moved out in support to the K.O.Y.L.I., in pitch darkness and torrential rain, shell fire caused the men to take cover in ditches half full of water. In the light of day it was discovered the shelling had on this occasion done what it was intended to do.

(Panel 45) Pte. L/7342, William Page, 1st Bn. (50th Foot) The Queen's Own (Royal West Kent Regt.): late of Deptford, London, S.E.: enlisted New Cross. Killed by shellfire on the night of 13 November 1914.

(Panel 45) Pte. Alfred George Puttock, 'A' Coy., 1st Bn. (50th Foot) The Queen's Own (Royal West Kent Regt.): *s.* of Mrs C. Puttock (9, Oakfield Road, Tunbridge Wells): enlisted Chister, co. Sussex. Shot and killed by a German sniper, 14 November 1914. Age 21. *unm.*

(Panel 45) Pte. G/18170, John Roddam, 11th (Service) Bn. (Lewisham) The Queen's Own (Royal West Kent Regt.): formerly no.10826, Royal Fusiliers: *s.* of John Roddam: and late *husb.* to Margaret Roddam (8, Providence Terrace, New Shildon, Co. Durham): served with the Expeditionary Force, and was killed in action, 26 July 1917. Age 31.

(Panel 45) Pte. L/6676, Frederick Scriven, 1st Bn. (50th Foot) The Queen's Own (Royal West Kent Regt.): *b.* Birmingham, co. Warwick: enlisted Woolwich, London, S.E.18. Shot and killed by a German sniper, 14 November 1914.

At 7.05 p.m., 17 April 1915, a series of five mines were detonated beneath Hill 60 and, as the falling debris settled, 'C' Coy., 1st Bn. Royal West Kent Regt., surged forward in their assault on the northern side of the hill. The effect of the mines had practically demolished the top of the hill and the attacking infantry encountered very little resistance from what was left of the defending German troops. Seizing the badly damaged enemy trenches, the Queen's Own rapidly set about repairing and consolidating the newly won positions, during the course of which the battalion suffered its only casualty. Sergt. Stroud, D.C.M., later reported, "We met with practically no resistance when we got into the German trenches, the effect of the explosions having killed or stunned the occupants. We found a German officer partially buried and some men at once began to dig him out. He rewarded them, when released, by drawing his revolver and shooting one of them. Needless to say he met his just deserts." 'Soldiers Died in the Great War' records:-

(Panel 45) Pte. L/7411, Frederick Sharp, 1st Bn. (50th Foot) The Queen's Own (Royal West Kent Regt.): *b.* Langley, co. Kent, about 1887: enlisted Maidstone. Killed in action, 17 April 1915. Age 28. Pte. Sharp leaves a widow, Fanny Amelia ('Gurrs Cottage,' Sutton Valence, co. Kent).

(Panel 45) Pte. L/9873, Alfred Stephenson, 1st Bn. (50th Foot) The Queen's Own (Royal West Kent Regt.): late of Plumstead, London, S.E.: enlisted Woolwich, co. Kent. Killed in action, 19 November 1914. See Pte. A. Ives (above).

(Panel 45) Pte. S/7139, John Sullivan, 1st Bn. (50th Foot) The Queen's Own (Royal West Kent Regt.): *s.* of John Sullivan, of 23, Hale Street, Deptford, London, S.E., by his wife Bridget: *b.* Marylebone, London: enlisted Maidstone, co. Kent. Shot and killed in the vicinity of Zillebeke Woods, 14 November 1914, by a German sniper. Age 27. *unm.*

In the late afternoon of 13 November 1914, after an extremely long and trying march (it had rained steadily all day), 1st Queen's Own (Royal West Kents) arrived at the outskirts of Ypres where they were forced to wait, without shelter, for darkness to fall before continuing onward. Passing through the shell battered town in single file the battalion proceeded to White Chateau where they received orders to report to General Lord Cavan's headquarters and a mounted guide to lead the way. Capt Dunlop said, "We were all wet through, tired out, our transport and rations seven miles in rear, and we had no knowledge of when we should hear of them again. We were in unfamiliar country, none of the officers had been in the trenches before, and we had one mounted guide for the whole battalion." Prospects did not look good, but slowly the battalion somehow reached its destination – 'a dug-out close behind the troops who were holding the front line' – and supplied with guides from the London Scottish to lead them to the section of trenches they would be taking over.

"The route lay along a road nearly knee-deep in liquid mud, and then into woods. Here there was a continual crackle of musketry fire which, to those who have not experienced it before, is rather startling to say nothing else. Every shot seemed to have been fired from a few yards away, and bullets ricocheted off trees, giving nasty wounds and accounting, perhaps, for the reports that enemy snipers were concealed in the woods in rear of our lines." 'A,' 'B' and 'C' companies went into the firing line, 'D' company in support 250 yards in rear. Situated in dense woods, the trees of which had been badly damaged by shellfire creating an impenetrable tangle of broken stumps, branches and saplings, the trenches were totally inadequate. In some places only thirty yards from the Germans, which obviated any risk of a sudden attack by either side, the trenches were very difficult to move about in; the only means of communication between the front-line and the supports were three rides running directly to the front, one of which was commanded by a German machine gun, the other two by snipers who demonstrated their marksmanship and command over the rides almost as soon as the battalion arrived. Over the next three days further demonstrations would claim the lives of another 11 of the Queen's Own.

(Panel 45) Pte. L/7495, George Warner, 1st Bn. (50th Foot) The Queen's Own (Royal West Kent Regt.): *s.* of Harry Warner, of 58, Station Street, Northfleet, co. Kent, by his wife Emma: *b.* Northfleet, 1885: enlisted Gravesend. Killed by a German sniper, Zillebeke Woods, night of 13–14 November 1914. Age 29.

PANEL 45 ENDS PTE. T.J. WATERS, ROYAL WEST KENT REGT.

PANEL 47 BEGINS PTE. G.J. WATTS, ROYAL WEST KENT REGT.

(Panel 47) Pte. G/17945, Charles Welfare, 10th (Service) Bn. The Queen's Own (Royal West Kent Regt.): formerly no.5093, Royal Sussex Regt.: *b.* Brighton: enlisted Hove, co. Sussex. Killed in action, 7 June 1917. He leaves a wife, Mrs G. Welfare (Y.W.C.A., Castilian Street, Northampton).

(Panel 47) Pte. L/7314, Henry Arthur Williams, 1st Bn. (50th Foot) The Queen's Own (Royal West Kent Regt.): *s.* of the late Mrs Frances Williams, of Sevenoaks, co. Kent: *b.* Sevenoaks, *c.*1884: enlisted, Maidstone. Killed by sniper fire, 15 November 1914. Age 30.

(Panel 47) Capt. (Adjt.) Henry Kent Hughes, 1st Bn. (51st Foot) The King's Own (Yorkshire Light Infantry): *s.* of Frederick Hughes, of Wallfield, Reigate, by his wife Alice: *b.* Reigate, 6 February 1883: *educ.* Repton, where he was in the Cricket XI: gazetted 2nd Lieut. King's Own (Yorkshire Light Infantry), May 1901; promoted Lieut. September 1903: joined his battalion in Ireland, afterwards serving in Gibraltar, South Africa, Hong Kong, and Singapore: promoted Capt. June 1909: apptd. Adjt. 1st K.O.Y.L.I., April 1914: proceeded to France, January 1915, and was killed in action at Ypres, 8 May following. Age 32. *unm.*

(Panel 47) Capt. Algernon Beresford Smyth, 2nd Bn. (105th Foot) The King's Own (Yorkshire Light Infantry): *yr. s.* of the late Devaynes Smyth, D.L., of Bray Head, co. Wicklow: and *gdson.* of the late Charles Putland, of Bray Head: *b.* 11 January 1884: *educ.* Gisburne House, Watford; Haileybury College, entering Royal Military College, Sandhurst 1901: gazetted 2nd Lieut. Manchester Regt. May 1903; promoted Lieut. April 1907, transf'd. Yorkshire Light Infantry: received his Company, September 1914. On the night of 15 November 1914, Capt. Smyth was killed after being specially selected to lead an attack on a farm building about five miles east of Ypres. Age 30. For his services on that night he was Mentioned in Sir John (now Lord) French's Despatch, 14 January 1915. A good all-round sportsman, member of the Free Foresters, Yorkshire Gentlemen's Cricket Club, he played cricket for the Aldershot Command (when stationed there with his battalion), he was also a keen rider to hounds, good golf and tennis player (won several cups). His only brother, Capt. C.D. Smyth, Royal Irish Rifles, was wounded in October 1914: *unm.*

(Panel 47) Lieut. Charles Gawain Raleigh Hunter, 'A' Coy., 2nd Bn. (105th Foot) The King's Own (Yorkshire Light Infantry): 3rd & *yst. s.* of Capt. William George Hunter, late 2nd Welsh Regt., of 'Sunfield,' Pirbright, co. Surrey, formerly of Burnside, Forfar, by his wife Isabella Kathleen Fayrer, *dau.* of Robert Hickey, Indian Army (served throughout the Indian Mutiny), lately Prison Governor; Portland and Dartmoor. Lieut. Hunter was in the sixth generation of Hunters who have served in the British Army or Navy during the last 150 years: *b.* 'The Elms,' Hunnington, nr. Leamington, co. Warwick: *educ.* St. Chads, Prestatyn, North Wales, and Christ College, Brecon, where he won a scholarship, and was in the O.T.C.: Occupation – Clerk, Triumph Motor-cycle works: gazetted 2nd Lieut., Reserve Bn. King's Own Yorkshire Light Infantry, August 1911, and served with 2nd Bn. at Cork, Ireland, for six months: trained with 3rd Battalion 1912–13; posted 2nd Bn. K.O.Y.L.I. August 1914, just after the outbreak of the Great War with which he went to France: promoted Lieut. to date from September 1914; posthumously gazetted Lieut.: proceeded to France with a draft of 60 reinforcements; joined 2nd K.O.Y.L.I. Wulverghem sector, 6 December 1914: with his battalion when Hill 60 was taken and held by the King's Own Yorkshire Light Infantry, and was killed one week later, on 25 April 1915, nr. Zonnebeke, when his battalion was sent to reinforce the firing line and had to advance over open ground exposed to heavy shell fire, being at the time in command of 'A' Company. The Battalion Diarist recorded, "At mid-day the battalion was called upon to assist the 10th Canadian Brigade in retaking the lost line north-east of Wieltje. The Canadian line at the time was being subjected to a heavy bombardment and the trenches, preparatory to an advance, were crowded with Canadian Highlanders. So, the newcomers had to lie out in the open under heavy shellfire, where they suffered. Lieut. C.G.R. Hunter was killed..." He was buried at Wieltje, north-east of Ypres. He was a good horseman, a good shot, and fond of all sports and games. A visitor to his birthplace recorded and dedicated the following lines to him; it was left in Hunningham church:-

> *So long the dream of youth spun from the blood-red love of the heart for the heart,*
> *And the flesh for the flesh, whispers to the night, elegies of a summer's day.*
> *Beautiful boy, Charles Gawain Hunter, fresh from the shires, oak of oaks,*
> *Flower of flowers, commissioned on your seventeenth birthday;*
> *For King, Country, Regiment and the burden of entitlement.*

> *You threw yourself away so bravely, so gladly, so defiantly on that hell-mired field*
> *Of speechless slaughter that April morn after the inundations of flame and thunder,*
> *And the beautiful deathly grass-green mists that rolled in on the morning breeze.*

> *How selflessly you fell, defying them all, the invisible foe, the hateful Hun,*
> *And never let the men see that you too were terrified in your proud young heart;*
> *And that with your passing God, King, Country and Capt. W. Hunter,*
> *Should never smile again.*

(Panel 47) Lieut. Guy Nicholas Palmes, 1st Bn. (51st Foot) The King's Own (Yorkshire Light Infantry): 4th *s.* of the Rev. George Palmes, Vicar of Naburn, Squire and Lord of the Manor of Naburn, by his wife Eva Blanche, *yr. dau.* of Henry Dalbiac, of Holbrook Park, Sussex: *b.* Naburn Hall, co. York, 14 July 1894: *educ.* Malvern College, and Royal Military College, Sandhurst; gazetted 2nd Lieut. K.O.Y.L.I. 1 October 1914; promoted Lieut. November following: went to France in January 1915, and was killed in action nr. Ypres, 8 May 1915. Age 20. *unm.* (*IWGC record 9 May 1915*)

(Panel 47) Lieut. Lawrence Ernest Pelham Grubb, 2nd Bn. (105th Foot) The King's Own (Yorkshire Light Infantry): only *s.* of Ernest Pelham Grubb, Gentleman; by his wife Emily Mary: *gt.-gdson* to Richard Grubb, of Cahir Abbey, Co. Tipperary: *b.* Wembley, co. Middlesex, 1892: *educ.* Rugby (Town House), entered 1906; Brasenose College, Oxford, 1911 (Exhibitioner); graduated with Honours 1914: one of the first two former members of Brasenose College to enlist; when war was declared he threw up an excellent post abroad and, having belonged to the O.T.C., went to the seat of war as a Despatch Rider. He received his commission a few weeks before his tragic death, which he met while leading a charge against Herenthage Chateau, near Hooge on the night of 15 November 1914. Age 22. *unm.* Remembered on Hove (Sussex) Library War Memorial. (*IWGC record E.P.Grubb*)

(Panel 47) 2nd Lieut. Harold Bramley, 2/5th Bn. The King's Own (Yorkshire Light Infantry), (T.F.): previously (1911-12) L/Corpl. 2122, 'C' Sqdn., Leicestershire Yeomanry: 2nd *s.* of the Rev. Cyril Richard Bramley, M.A. (Oxon.), Vicar of St. John's, Donisthorpe with Moira (St. Hilda), and Annie Marion Bramley his spouse: and brother to Capt. C.R. Bramley, 2/5th K.O.Y.L.I. (T.F.), killed in action on 20 February 1917: *b.* Manchester, 9 February 1894: *educ.* St. John's School, Leatherhead, 1904: devoted himself to farming, and after a two years' course on a farm in Snarestone, went to Canada for nine months to see the conditions of farming there: returning in December 1913, he went to Kidlington, nr. Oxford, to take charge of a farm, but on the outbreak of war immediately rejoined the Leicestershire Yeomanry and proceeded with that unit to the Front, November 1914; took part in several engagements, being promoted

L/Corpl. February 1915, and 2nd Lieut. a week before he was killed in action near Ypres, 13 May 1915. Age 21. *unm.* (*IWGC record formerly Pte.*)

His brother Cyril is commemorated in Ancre British Cemetery, Beaumont-Hamel (Green Dump Cem. Mem.1).

(Panel 47) 2nd Lieut. Francis John MacLardie Chubb, 3rd (Reserve) att. 2nd Bn. (105th Foot) The King's Own (Yorkshire Light Infantry): *s.* of the late Capt. E.G. Chubb, Royal West Surrey Regt., who fell at Ypres, 12 July 1915; three months after the death of his son: served with the Expeditionary Force in France from 6 March 1915, and was killed in action, 18 April following, in the fighting at Hill 60. Inscribed – *So they passed over and all the trumpets sounded for them on the other side* – 2nd Lieut. Chubb and his father are remembered on Berkhamstead (St. Peter's) Roll of Honour.

His father Edward is buried in Tancrez Farm Cemetery (I.B.23).

(Panel 47) 2nd Lieut. Henry Burden Hodges, 2nd Bn. (105th Foot) The King's Own (Yorkshire Light Infantry): *yr. s.* of John Frederick William Hodges, J.P., of Glenravel House, Glenravel, Co. Antrim, by his wife Mary, *dau.* of the late Henry Burden, M.D., F.R.C.S. (Eng.), and *gdson.* of the late Professor John Frederick Hodges, M.D., Queen's College, Belfast: *b.* Newtownards, Belfast, 13 November 1895: *educ.* Mostyn House, Cheshire; Sherbourne Preparatory, and Sherbourne School, and Royal Military College, Sandhurst: gazetted 2nd Lieut. 2nd K.O.Y.L.I. 23 December 1914: went to the Front on 6 March 1915, and after five weeks in the trenches was killed in action at Hill 60, 18 April following. He fell, as his Col. wrote, "Gallantly leading his men in a charge against the Germans." The regt. lost six officers killed and seven wounded that night, and as they were forced to retire before they had time to bring in the dead and wounded, and Hill 60 fell to the Germans shortly afterwards, his body was not recovered. He was a keen golfer and footballer, and had won several medals for swimming and life-saving. He also won the light-weight championship at the Public Schools Boxing Competition, at Aldershot, in April 1914. His elder brother, Capt. J.F. Hodges, 2nd Bn. Royal Irish Fusiliers, was wounded at St. Eloi, and was Mentioned in Despatches (*London Gazette*, 22 June, 1915) and awarded the Military Cross, 24 June 1915. Age 19.

(Panel 47) 2nd Lieut. Frank William Snape, 2nd Bn. (105th Foot) The King's Own (Yorkshire Light Infantry): 3rd *s.* of Charles Coltman Snape, Gentleman, of Wiveliscombe, co. Somerset, and adopted *s.* of Miss E.E.M. Taylor (1, St. Luke's Road, Bath): *gdson.* of the late Dr. Charles Snape, of Wiveliscombe, and brother to Lieut. E.C. Snape, Royal Field Artillery: *b.* Carlton, St. John, New Brunswick, Canada, 26 March 1893: *educ.* Monkton Combe School, Bath (1905–10) where he was five years in the O.T.C.: on leaving school removed to Canada; took up farming: accepted a commission, Canadian Militia, July 1912: went for annual training 1912–13, returning to England in the latter year: received a commission, Special Reserve, 3rd Prince Albert's (Somerset Light Infantry), February 1914; proceeded to France September following in charge of a machine gun section attd. Oxford & Bucks Light Infantry: subsequently attd./ posted 2nd King's Own Yorkshire Light Infantry, having received a commission in that regiment December 1914. His Battalion Commanding Officer wrote, "Please allow me to condole with you in the sad loss of your nephew, 2nd Lieut. F.W. Snape. The only satisfaction is that he was killed quite instantaneously and suffered no pain. He was in the trench with his machine guns when he was shot through the neck. He had been with us longer than any other Officer present with the Battalion. He was an excellent Officer and very popular with us all. He was buried behind a larch wood near Hill 60." A Captain of his battalion wrote, "Poor Snape was killed in a trench at about 9 a.m., May 7th (1915). During the night we had done an attack on a German position, and as Machine-Gun Officer Snape had remained in our trench to cover our advance with his guns, and had come safely through. I was up in the trench shortly afterwards where I saw him, and everything was quiet except for 'sniping' which always goes on, and we were not then taking any casualties. Poor Snape was apparently walking down the trench to visit one of his guns, and must not have kept low enough down and got shot through the head – one blessing is that he was killed instantaneously. We carried him down and buried him in a larch wood in rear of our trench which is quite close to Hill 60, where we have taken so many casualties. We put a wooden cross over his grave with his Name and Regiment on it. Snape is a tremendous loss to us, and will be impossible to replace with the machine guns which he loved. He always lived with us in our H.Q. Mess, and a better boy never stepped.": 7 May 1915. Age 22. *unm.*

(Panel 47) Sergt. 12604, James Hartley Hodgkinson, 2nd Bn. (105th Foot) The King's Own (Yorkshire Light Infantry): *s.* of James Hodgkinson, by his wife Hannah: *b.* Sheffield, co. York, 27 May 1871: *educ.* Sheffield: Occupation – Boiler Founder: volunteered for Active Service on the outbreak of war; enlisted King's Own (Yorkshire Light Infantry), 18 August 1914: served with the Expeditionary Force in France and Flanders: present at the capture of Hill 60, during the Second Battle of Ypres, 17 April 1915, being apptd. Sergt. there. Reported missing after the fighting at Ypres, 7 May following, and is now assumed to have been killed in action on or about that date. A comrade wrote, "He died a brave soldier. You have the consolation of knowing that your husband was a man who did his duty to the last, and was not afraid to meet death." Age 43. He *m.* Sheffield; Ada Annie Walsh, *née* Hodgkinson (27, Court, 5, House, Pond Street, Sheffield), and had three children.

(Panel 47) Corpl. 18642, Clifford Britton, M.M., 8th (Service) Bn. The King's Own (Yorkshire Light Infantry): *s.* of James Britton, of 1, Lower Carr Street, Hunslet Carr, by his wife Elizabeth: enlisted Pontefract, co. York. Killed in action on the night of 23 January 1917, during a raid on the enemy lines. Age 27. He was married to Ellen Hurst, *née* Britton (18, Playfair Crescent, Hunslet Carr, Leeds). See account re. Capt. M.G. Donahoo, Lijssenthoek Military Cemetery (X.A.2).

(Panel 47) Corpl. 18126, Harry Innocent, 'D' Coy., 6th (Service) Bn. The King's Own (Yorkshire Light Infantry): *s.* of George Innocent, of 24, Windsor Road, Doncaster, by his wife Ada: served with the Expeditionary Force in France and Flanders from 21 May 1915. One of four other ranks killed on 20 July 1915, by retaliatory shellfire following an organised attack on the enemy trenches opposite Hooge (north of the battalion's position), made by 3rd Divn. the previous day. Age 25.

(Panel 47) L/Corpl. 10354, William Robert Brown, 1st Bn. (51st Foot) The King's Own (Yorkshire Light Infantry): *s.* of Benjamin Brown, of Herringfleet, Lowestoft, co. Suffolk, and 4, Widow's Cottage, Somerleyton, by his wife Martha: and brother to Ldg.Stkr. K/5336, A.E. Brown, H.M.S. 'Victory,' R.N., died 25 May 1918: *b.* Yarmouth: enlisted Goole. Killed in action, 8 May 1915. Age 26.

His brother is buried in Mazargues War Cemetery, Marseilles (IV.A.36).

(Panel 47) L/Corpl. 9788, Thomas Dean, 1st Bn. (51st Foot) The King's Own (Yorkshire Light Infantry): *b.* Rotherham, co. York: enlisted Goole: served with the Expeditionary Force in France and Flanders from 16 January 1915, and was one of five N.C.O.'s and four other ranks killed on the same day (2 February 1915) by the detonation of a high-explosive shell which landed in the section of trench they were occupying during the battalion's first tour in the trenches at Verbrandenmolen. See L/Corpl. A.A. Vanhinsbergh, below.

(Panel 47) L/Corpl. 10639, Francis James 'Frank' Evans, 1st Bn. (51st Foot) The King's Own (Yorkshire Light Infantry): *s.* of John Henry Evans, of London, by his wife Emma: *b. c.*1884: enlisted Kingston-on-Thames, co. Surrey: served with the Expeditionary Force in France and Flanders from 16 January 1915. One of five N.C.O.'s and four other ranks killed on the same day (2 February 1915) by the detonation of a high-explosive shell which landed in the section of trench they were occupying during the battalion's first tour in the trenches at Verbrandenmolen. Age 20. *unm.* See L/Corpl. A.A. Vanhinsbergh, below.

After six days in trenches east of Lindenhoek, on the slopes of Hill 75, waist deep in water and mud so thick that on one occasion it took a number of hours to drag four men out by ropes, it came as a great relief to 2nd King's Own Yorkshire Light Infantry when, on 12 December 1914, they were withdrawn to Dranoutre. After a short period of rest the battalion returned to the same trenches where, with the opposing lines barely fifty yards apart, German snipers took a toll of six members of the battalion within 48 hours.

(Panel 47) L/Corpl. 6759, Arthur Firth, 2nd Bn. (105th Foot) The King's Own (Yorkshire Light Infantry): *s.* of Jack Firth, of Chapel Row, Whitley Bridge, by his wife Emma: *b.* Whitley Bridge, *c.*1871: enlisted Pontefract: served with the Expeditionary Force in France and Flanders from 16 August 1914: took part in the fighting at Mons, Le Cateau, the battles of the Marne and the Aisne, at La Bassée,

Messines and Neuve Chapelle, and was killed in the trenches near the bank of the River Douve, 21 December 1914, by a German sniper. Age 33. He was married to Ruth Taylor, *née* Firth (7, Silver St., Whitley Bridge, co. York).

(Panel 47) L/Corpl. 2011, Frederick Charles Green, 1st Bn. (51st Foot) The King's Own (Yorkshire Light Infantry): *b*. Lambeth: enlisted Westminster: served with the Expeditionary Force in France and Flanders from 16 January 1915, and was one of five N.C.O.'s and four other ranks killed on the same day (2 February 1915) by the detonation of a high-explosive shell which landed in the section of trench they were occupying during the battalion's first tour in the trenches at Verbrandenmolen. See L/Corpl. A.A. Vanhinsbergh, below.

(Panel 47) L/Corpl. 10509, Frederick Arthur Lott, 1st Bn. (51st Foot) The King's Own (Yorkshire Light Infantry): *b*. Norwood: enlisted London: served with the Expeditionary Force in France and Flanders from 16 January 1915. One of five N.C.O.'s and four other ranks killed on the same day (2 February 1915) by the detonation of a high-explosive shell which landed in the section of trench they were occupying during the battalion's first tour in the trenches at Verbrandenmolen. See L/Corpl. A.A. Vanhinsbergh, below.

(Panel 47) L/Corpl. 9646, Horatio Toothill, 1st Bn. (51st Foot) The King's Own (Yorkshire Light Infantry): *b*. Norwich, co. Norfolk: enlisted Sheffield, co. York: served in Singapore, and with the Expeditionary Force in France and Flanders from 16 December 1914, and was killed by shell fire on 13 February 1915; one of six men killed during the battalion's second tour in the trenches at Verbrandenmolen, nr. Hill 60. Age 25. *unm.* All correspondence regarding the deceased should be addressed c/o his sister, Mrs Martha Carnall (35, Nelson Road, Wadsley Bridge, Sheffield). See Pte. E. Amond, below.

By February 1915, the fighting in the Salient was continuous, at some point during the course of each day a bombardment of high-explosive shells and bombs would temporarily force a portion of the line out of their trenches, occasionally a well-aimed shell would destroy an entire section of trench whereby men would be buried and lost. Snipers were a constant nuisance during daylight hours and, when the moon was full, throughout the night also. On 1 February 1915, 1st K.O.Y.L.I. went into the trenches for the first time. Taking over a section of the line at Verbrandenmolen from the French, the relief was carried out at night, French guides leading the K.O.Y.L.I. to their trenches which lay either side of the Ypres-Comines canal, about 4,000 yards east of Ypres. It was an unpleasant experience for the newcomers, the trenches were isolated and in extremely bad condition, many were waterlogged, and daylight revealed that not only were most of them filled with French corpses in varying states of decomposition, but the parapets appeared to be built of the same. After three days of holding these trenches, attempting to improve them under shell and machine gun fire the battalion were relieved on the night of 4–5 February and marched back to a camp near Ouderdom. Their first tour in the trenches caused the battalion losses of 5 Lance Corporals (all on the same day) and 7 other ranks killed. Losses tragic enough in themselves but for the family of L/Corpl. Vanhinsbergh it was only the beginning; the beginning of a tragedy that would manifest itself fivefold before the war finally came to an end.

(Panel 47) L/Corpl. 10619, Arthur Alfred Vanhinsbergh, 1st Bn. (51st Foot) The King's Own (Yorkshire Light Infantry): *s*. of Peter Vanhinsbergh, of 208, Cassland Road, Hackney, London, E.8, by his wife Emma: and brother to Pte. 42165, A. Vanhinsbergh, 2/6th North Staffordshire Regt., killed in action, 15 April 1918; Gnr. 3446, P. Vanhinsbergh, 82nd Bde. Royal Field Artillery, 12 August 1916; Rfn. S/19570, D.P. Vanhinsbergh (*IWGC record P.D.*), 13th Rifle Brigade, 23 August 1918, and L/Corpl. 11077, C.H. Vanhinsbergh, 2nd King's Own Yorkshire Light Infantry, 1 July 1916: *b*. Homerton, London, E.9: enlisted Stratford, E.15: served in Singapore, and with the Expeditionary Force in France and Flanders from 16 January 1915, and was one of five N.C.O.'s and four other ranks killed on the same day (2 February 1915) by the detonation of a high-explosive shell which landed in the section of trench they were occupying during the battalion's first tour in the trenches at Verbrandenmolen. One of five brothers who fell.

His brother Alic is buried in Le Grand Beaumart British Cemetery (III.E.17), Peter lies in Ration Farm Military Cemetery (IV.C.3), David in Gommecourt Wood New Cemetery (I.C.1); Charles has no known grave, he is commemorated on the Thiepval Memorial, Somme.

(Panel 47) Pte. 12776, Reginald Percy Allott, 1st Bn. (51st Foot) The King's Own (Yorkshire Light Infantry): *s.* of the late Frederick (& Martha) Allott, of 123, Bold Street, Attercliffe, Sheffield: served with the Expeditionary Force in France and Flanders from 16 January 1915, and was killed in action, 8 May following, at Frezenberg. Age 20. Remembered on the tombstone of the late Minnie Allott, *née* Naylor (Tinsley Cemetery) to whom he was married for but a short time.

On 30 July 1914 1st King's Own Yorkshire Light Infantry, stationed at Tanglin Barracks, Singapore, received a cabled message ordering a precautionary state of mobilisation. With mails taking over three weeks to arrive the only inclination of a possible threat of war had been gained from editorials in the local press. When, on 4 August, the news of the declaration of war was officially received the battalion mobilised forthwith and, in a state of preparedness to embark at the shortest notice, awaited orders to proceed to France. Week after week went by without the anticipated orders and it was not until 27 September that the battalion, numbering 887 all ranks (plus 25 wives and 44 children), finally departed from Singapore aboard H.M.T. *Carnarvonshire* in convoy with four other ships. With great secrecy preserved as to the destination of the convoy, there followed a long and circuitous route via Colombo, Aden, Port Said, Malta and Gibraltar, before arriving at Southampton on 9 November. Here the battalion was immediately entrained to Winchester from whence they marched out to Hursley Park Camp. Their arrival was not expected. Nine hundred men, arriving in the middle of the night, in drizzling rain, in mud up to the knees, clad in khaki drill, in a camp of haphazard tents – mostly lying about on the ground – with no preparation made for their reception; the realities of wartime were brought home to the men instantly! Sleep was entirely out of the question, in an attempt to keep warm most of the men tramped around the camp all night while the camp staff did what they could to find oil-sheets and blankets for them. In the morning their misery was further added to by the discovery that no provision for breakfast had been made and it was not until mid-day that a meagre supply of food arrived. In the days and weeks that followed the lot of the battalion greatly improved and on 15 December they finally embarked for France.

Two days after their arrival, the battalion marched from Hazebrouck to billets in Outersteene, and almost immediately parties were told off and sent up to the trenches for instruction. The winter of 1914–15 was a period of unmitigated hardship and unremitting toil for the soldiers in the field; the weather – severe frost, freezing rain, snow on the ground – a complete opposite to the tropical climate 1st K.O.Y.L.I. had left behind less than three months previously. By the end of their first two tours in the trenches at Verbrandenmolen, in February 1915, the ranks of the battalion had been depleted by the loss of 4 officers wounded, 18 other ranks killed, 97 wounded; it was further added to by 207 men being evacuated sick with trench foot and the transference from the climate of the tropics accounting for the majority of cases.

(Panel 47) Pte. 10345, Edward Amond, 1st Bn. (51st Foot) The King's Own (Yorkshire Light Infantry): *s.* of Edward Amond, of 5, Ashbourne Street, Norwich, by his wife Rachel: enlisted Norwich, co. Norfolk: served in Singapore and with the Expeditionary Force in France and Flanders from 16 December 1914, and was killed by shell fire, 17 February 1915; one of six other ranks killed during the battalion's second tour in the trenches at Verbrandenmolen, near Hill 60. Age 23. *unm.*

(Panel 47) Pte. 3/3156, Hugh Angel, 1st Bn. (51st Foot) The King's Own (Yorkshire Light Infantry): *s.* of Peter Angel, of Poolside, Carnarvon, by his wife Elizabeth: *b.* Carnarvon: enlisted Perth: served with the Expeditionary Force in France and Flanders from 16 January 1915, and was one of four other ranks and five N.C.O.'s killed on the same day (2 February 1915) by the detonation of a high-explosive shell which landed in the section of trench they were occupying during the battalion's first tour in the trenches at Verbrandenmolen. Age 39. He was married to the late Mary Catherine Angel (Carnarvon). See L/Corpl. A.A. Vanhinsbergh, above.

(Panel 47) Pte. 9107, Alfred Armes, 2nd Bn. (105th Foot) The King's Own (Yorkshire Light Infantry): *s.* of William F. Armes, of 39, Audley St., Great Yarmouth, co. Norfolk, by his wife Laura: *b.* St. Phillip's, South Hingham, *c.*1888: enlisted Norwich. Killed by enemy sniper-fire, east of Lindenhoek, 20 December 1914. Age 26. See L/Corpl. A. Firth, above.

(Panel 47) Pte. 12199, John Thomas Armes, 1st Bn. (51st Foot) The King's Own (Yorkshire Light Infantry): *s.* of Isaiah Armes, of I/4, Burnell Road, Owlerton, Sheffield, co. York, by his wife Julia: *b.* St.

Phillips, Sheffield, *c.*1895: enlisted Sheffield: served with the Expeditionary Force in France and Flanders from 16 December 1914, and was killed by shell fire, 17 February 1915; one of six other ranks killed during the battalion's second tour in the trenches at Verbrandenmolen, nr. Hill 60. Age 19. See Pte. E. Amond, above.

(Panel 47) Pte. 16633, Sidney Carr, 2nd Bn. (105th Foot) The King's Own (Yorkshire Light Infantry): *s.* of Jim Carr, of Holmes View Cottages, Biggleswade, co. Bedford, by his wife Martha: *b.* Biggleswade: enlisted Doncaster, co. York: served with the Expeditionary Force in France and Flanders, and died in the Military Hospital, Boulogne, 30 April 1915, of wounds received at Hill 60, Ypres. Age 26. *Buried in Boulogne Eastern Cemetery (VIII.B.9).*

(Panel 47) Pte. 21407, William Cawtheray, 1/4th Bn. The King's Own (Yorkshire Light Infantry), (T.F.): *s.* of Mrs E. Pontefract (39, Kennedy Street, Kirkstall Road, Leeds): enlisted Leeds, co. York: served with the Expeditionary Force in France, and was killed in action, 4 October 1915. Age 16.

(Panel 47) Pte. 6281, Frank Clark, 2nd Bn. (105th Foot) The King's Own (Yorkshire Light Infantry): *b.* York, 1882: *educ.* there: Occupation – Miner: enlisted 1899: served in Malta and Africa; afterwards in Ireland: joined the Reserve; recalled on the outbreak of war: served in the European War. Reported missing after the fighting, 18 November 1914, and now assumed to have been killed in action on that date. Age 32. He *m.* Sheffield, 1907; Elizabeth (103, Granville Street, Park, Sheffield), *dau.* of Daniel Fox, and had two children.

(Panel 47) Pte. 7944, George Costello, 1st Bn. (51st Foot) The King's Own (Yorkshire Light Infantry): *b.* York: enlisted there: served in Singapore, and with the Expeditionary Force in France and Flanders from 16 January 1915, and was one of four other ranks and five N.C.O.'s killed on the same day (2 February 1915) by the detonation of a high-explosive shell which landed in the section of trench they were occupying during the battalion's first tour in the trenches at Verbrandenmolen. Age 25. *unm.* See L/ Corpl. A.A. Vanhinsbergh, above.

(Panel 47) Pte. 9472, Walter Domminic, 1st Bn. (51st Foot) The King's Own (Yorkshire Light Infantry): *b.* Radford: enlisted Nottingham. Killed in action, 8 May 1915. Remains recovered from an unmarked grave (28.I.6.d.21.90) 17 January 1927; identified – Disc (crumbled to pieces on removal from the body); reinterred, registered 22 January 1927. *Buried in Sanctuary Wood Cemetery (III.C.30).*

(Panel 47) Pte. 20682, Alfred Ellis, 'A' Coy., 1st Bn. (51st Foot) The King's Own (Yorkshire Light Infantry): *b.* Wakefield, nr. Leeds, co. York, *c.*1875: enlisted Sheffield: served with the Expeditionary Force in France and Flanders from early 1915, and was killed in action at Frezenberg, 2 May 1915. Age 40. He leaves a wife, Hannah (31, Jermyn Croft, Dodworth, Barnsley), and family to mourn his loss. Remains recovered from a grave marked as belonging to an 'Unknown British Soldier. K.O.Y.L.I.' (28.J.4.a.70.10), identified – Clothing, Titles, Boots mkd. 20682; reinterred, registered 2 May 1930. *Buried in Sanctuary Wood Cemetery (V.L.12).*

(Panel 47) Pte. 10339, John Henry Ellis, 1st Bn. (51st Foot) The King's Own (Yorkshire Light Infantry): *s.* of Fanny Emma Ellis (10, Ranter Fold, Horbury, Wakefield): enlisted Wakefield, co. York: served with the Expeditionary Force in France and Flanders from 16 January 1915, and was one of four other ranks and five N.C.O.'s killed on the same day (2 February 1915) by the detonation of a high-explosive shell which landed in the section of trench they were occupying during the battalion's first tour in the trenches at Verbrandenmolen. Age 25. *unm.* See L/Corpl. A.A. Vanhinsbergh, above.

(Panel 47) Pte. 3/1535, John Else, 1st Bn. (51st Foot) The King's Own (Yorkshire Light Infantry): *b.* Wakefield, co. York: enlisted there: served with the Expeditionary Force in France and Flanders from 16 January 1915, and was shot and killed by a German sniper at Verbrandenmolen, 4 February following.

(Panel 47) Pte. 2197, George William Fielder, 1/5th (Territorial) Bn. The King's Own (Yorkshire Light Infantry): eldest *s.* of George William Fielder, now serving as Mate, Royal Navy, H.M. Patrol Ships: *b.* Goole, co. York, 15 April 1895: *educ.* Alexander Street Council School: enlisted in March 1914: went to France and was killed in action in Flanders, 9 July 1915. Buried in Poperinghe. His comrades spoke of him as "the Little man with the Big heart." Age 20. *unm.* (*IWGC record 11 July, 1915*)

(Panel 47) Pte. 11085, Thomas Firth, 'A' Coy., 2nd Bn. (105th Foot) The King's Own (Yorkshire Light Infantry): *s.* of Thomas Firth, of 17, Howden Terrace, Queen's Rd., Burley, co. York, by his wife Ada: enlisted Leeds. Killed by an enemy sniper, 20 December 1914. Age 18. See L/Corpl. A. Firth, above.

(Panel 47) Pte. 10373, Herbert Watson Ford, 1st Bn. (51st Foot) The King's Own (Yorkshire Light Infantry): *s.* of the late John Ford, by his wife Kate (10, Smith's Court, Woodhouse Cliff, Hyde Park, Leeds): *b.* Leeds, *c.*1894: enlisted Wakefield: served with the Expeditionary Force in France and Flanders from 16 December 1914, and was killed by shell fire, 17 February 1915; one of six men killed during the battalion's second tour in the trenches at Verbrandenmolen, nr. Hill 60. Age 20. *unm.* See Pte. E. Amond, above.

(Panel 47) Pte. 9829, James Patrick Greenwood, 1st Bn. (51st Foot) The King's Own (Yorkshire Light Infantry): 3rd *s.* of Henry Greenwood, of 10, Field Road, Ramsey, co. Cambridge, by his wife Mary Ann, *née* Brannen: and brother to Pte. 9894, J. Greenwood, King's (Liverpool) Regt., killed in action, 16 May 1915, at Richebourg, aged 28 years; Pte. 203249, H. Greenwood, Bedfordshire Regt., died 27 June 1917, in the Military Hospital, Aylesbury, aged 23 years; and Pte. 12477, H. Greenwood, Northamptonshire Regt., shot and killed by a sniper, 25 February 1916, at Sailly Labourse, aged 20 years: *b.* 3 September 1889: enlisted Derby: served with the Expeditionary Force in France from 15 January 1915, and was killed in action, 8 May 1915, on which date the battalion were in trenches at Frezenberg and suffered heavy casualties from sustained shellfire and three massed German attacks which were successfully repulsed. Age 23. *unm.* A fifth brother, William H. Greenwood, married with two children, was granted exemption when conscription for married men was introduced on the grounds that his parents had already suffered great loss. One of four brothers who fell. (*IWGC record James Percival*)

His brother John also has no known grave, he is commemorated on the Le Touret Memorial, Harry is buried in Ramsey Cemetery (N.42B); Herbert, Vermelles British Cemetery (II.E.9).

(Panel 47) Pte. 13091, James Hampson, 1st Bn. (51st Foot) The King's Own (Yorkshire Light Infantry): *s.* of James (& M.A.) Hampson, of 38, Shaftesbury Street, Derby: *b. c.*1893: enlisted Nottingham: served with the Expeditionary Force in France and Flanders from 16 January 1915, and was killed in action, 5 February following; the day of the battalion's relief from their first tour in the trenches at Verbrandenmolen, nr. Hill 60. Age 19.

(Panel 47) Pte. 5828, George Henry Hewitt, 2nd Bn. (105th Foot) The King's Own (Yorkshire Light Infantry): *s.* of Job Hewitt, of 51, Winn Street, Barnsley, co. York, by his wife Mary: *b.* Barnsley, 1879: enlisted there. Killed in action, 2 January 1915. Age 36.

(Panel 47) Pte. 9420, William Alfred Houston, 'D' Coy., 1st Bn. (51st Foot) The King's Own (Yorkshire Light Infantry): *s.* of Arthur Edward Holmes, D.C.M., of Nairobi, Kenya Colony, by his wife Elizabeth Jean: *b.* Charterstowers, Queensland, Australia, *c.*1890: enlisted Roberts Heights, Pretoria, South Africa: served with the Expeditionary Force in France and Flanders, and was killed in action at Frezenberg, 8 May 1915; on which day the company, after being heavily shelled and resisting three attacks, showed they could 'stick it.' After the battalion's withdrawal that night their losses for the day were recorded thus – '53 killed, 92 wounded, 272 missing' Age 24. *unm.*

(Panel 47) Pte. 10403, George Henry Jennings, 1st Bn. (51st Foot) The King's Own (Yorkshire Light Infantry): *s.* of the late John (& Ruth) Jennings, of Sowerby Bridge, Halifax: served with the Expeditionary Force in France and Flanders from 16 December 1914, and was killed by shell fire, 13 February 1915; one of six men killed during the battalion's second tour in the trenches at Verbrandenmolen, nr. Hill 60, Flanders. Age 23. *unm.* See Pte. E. Amond, above.

(Panel 47) Pte. 9921, Albert Parker, 'B' Coy., 1st Bn. (51st Foot) The King's Own (Yorkshire Light Infantry): *s.* of the late William Parker, by his wife Annie (12, Harper Street, St. John's Road, Rotherham): *b.* Hemsworth, Barnsley: enlisted Rotherham: served in Singapore, and with the Expeditionary Force in France and Flanders from 16 January 1915, and was one of four other ranks and five N.C.O.'s killed on the same day (2 February 1915) by the detonation of a high-explosive shell which landed in the section of trench they were occupying during the battalion's first tour in the trenches at Verbrandenmolen. Age 24. *unm.* See L/Corpl. A.A. Vanhinsbergh, above.

(Panel 47) Pte. 10110, Harry Pimm, 1st Bn. (51st Foot) The King's Own Yorkshire Light Infantry: *s.* of Joseph Pimm, of 66, Wilton Road, Hackney, London, E., by his wife Annie: *b.* Bethnal Green, *c.*1891: enlisted Stratford: served in Singapore, and with the Expeditionary Force in France and Flanders from 16 January 1915, and was killed in action, 5 February following; the day of the battalion's relief from their first tour in the trenches at Verbrandenmolen, nr. Hill 60. Age 23. *unm.*

(Panel 47) Pte. 3/609, Robert Henry Rooney, 2nd Bn. (105th Foot) The King's Own (Yorkshire Light Infantry): *b.* Sheffield: enlisted Rotherham, co. York. Killed by a German sniper, 20 December 1914. See L/Corpl. A. Firth, above.

(Panel 47) Pte. 18300, Ernest Rouse, 6th (Service) Bn. The King's Own (Yorkshire Light Infantry): *b.* Grantham, co. Lincoln: enlisted Doncaster: served with the Expeditionary Force in France from 22 May 1915; moved up to Ypres Salient, 30 May, and was killed by the explosion of a shell, 29 June following, while at duty on a carrying party to the front line; three other men were also killed. See L/Corpl. C. Torr, Bedford House Cemetery (VI.A.83/Enc.No.2).

(Panel 47) Pte. 3/738, Thomas Sammons, 2nd Bn. (105th Foot) The King's Own (Yorkshire Light Infantry): *b.* Sheffield, co. York: enlisted there. Killed by a German sniper, 20 December 1914. See L/Corpl. A. Firth, above.

(Panel 47) Pte. 20650, Albert Sant, 1st Bn. (51st Foot) The King's Own (Yorkshire Light Infantry): *b.* Smallthorne, co. Derby: enlisted Doncaster. Killed in action, 30 April 1915. Remains recovered from a grave marked up as belonging to an 'Unknown British Soldier' (28.J.4.a.70.10), identified – Clothing, Boots mkd. 20650; reinterred, registered 2 May 1930. *Buried in Sanctuary Wood Cemetery (V.L.14).*

(Panel 47) Pte. 25072, Enoch Shakespeare, 8th (Service) Bn. The King's Own (Yorkshire Light Infantry): *s.* of Enoch Shakespeare, of Briar Street, Meadows, Nottingham, by his wife Elizabeth: *b.* Nottingham: enlisted there. Killed in action, 23 January 1917, during a night-raid on the enemy trenches. Age 39. He leaves a wife, Susannah M. Shakespeare (12, Ockerby Street, Bulwell, Nottingham). See account re. Capt. M.G. Donahoo, Lijssenthoek Military Cemetery (X.A.2).

(Panel 47) Pte. 11056, Edgar Topps, 2nd Bn. (105th Foot) The King's Own (Yorkshire Light Infantry): *b.* Park, Sheffield, co. York: enlisted Sheffield. One of six men of his battalion killed by enemy sniper fire, 20–21 December 1914. See L/Corpl. A. Firth, above.

(Panel 47) Pte. 18314, Bernard Colin Watson, 6th (Service) Bn. The King's Own (Yorkshire Light Infantry): *s.* of John Thomas Watson, of 19, Baker Street, Doncaster, by his wife Miriam Edith: and brother to Sergt. 59156, J.E. Watson, Royal Field Artillery, killed in action, 13 April 1918: *b.* Doncaster, co. York: enlisted there: served with the Expeditionary Force in France from 22 May 1915, and was killed in action, 29 June 1915, by shellfire while at duty on a carrying party to the front line; three other men were also killed. Age 27. *unm.* See L/Corpl. C. Torr, Bedford House Cemetery (VI.A.83/Enc.No.2).

His brother John also has no known grave; he is commemorated on the Tyne Cot Memorial (Panel 4).

(Panel 47) Pte. 18651, Arthur Edward Webster, 6th (Service) Bn. The King's Own (Yorkshire Light Infantry): *s.* of James Andrew Webster, of Kirkstead, co. Lincoln: *b.* Kirkstead, 1897: volunteered and enlisted Leeds, co. York, on the outbreak of war; posted 6th King's Own Yorkshire Light Infantry: served with the Expeditionary Force in France from 21 May 1915, and was killed by enemy shellfire, 24 September 1915. Age 18.

(Panel 47) Pte. 18343, Charles Edward Welch, 6th (Service) Bn. The King's Own (Yorkshire Light Infantry): *b.* Annfield Plain, Durham: enlisted Doncaster. Killed in action, 2 August 1915, by shellfire while in support trenches to the rear of Zouave Wood, Hooge. *Buried in Sanctuary Wood Cemetery (V.E.1).*

Sweet Is The Word For Remembrance, Peace Perfect Peace

(Panel 47) Pte. 9609, Charles Wheatley, 'C' Coy., 1st Bn. (51st Foot) The King's Own (Yorkshire Light Infantry): *s.* of John Wheatley, of St. Mark's, Leicester, by his wife Mary Ann: *b. c.*1888: enlisted Leicester: served in Singapore, and with the Expeditionary Force in France and Flanders from 16 December 1914, and was killed by shell fire, 17 February 1915; one of six men killed during the battalion's second tour in the trenches at Verbrandenmolen, near Hill 60. Age 26. *unm.* See Pte. E. Amond, above.

(Panel 47) Pte. 9414, George Windle, 1st Bn. (51st Foot) The King's Own (Yorkshire Light Infantry): *s.* of Jonathan Windle, of 71, Tavistock Road, Heeley, Sheffield, by his wife Elizabeth. Killed in action, 8 May 1915. Age 27.

(Panel 47) Pte. 11214, Joseph Clarence Wisehall, 6th (Service) Bn. The King's Own (Yorkshire Light Infantry): *s.* of Jane Wisehall 8, Wadworth Road, Bramley, Rotherham, co. York: and elder brother to Pte. 77539, M. Wisehall, 15th Durham Light Infantry, killed in action, 29 May 1918: *b.* Rotherham: enlisted there. Killed in action, 7 September 1915. Age 22. *unm.*

His brother Marcus also has no known grave; he is commemorated on the Soissons Memorial.

(Panel 47) Major William James Rowan-Robinson, 2nd Bn. (85th Foot) The King's (Shropshire Light Infantry): *s.* of Surg.-Col. William Christie Robinson, Royal Army Medical Corps, of Ethelbert Road, Canterbury, by his wife Sarah Isabella: *b.* 3 September 1871: *educ.* King's School, Canterbury, 1881– 86: former member of Antrim Militia; joined Regular Army, 1893: obtained a commission 2nd Lieut. 2nd K.S.L.I. 26 April 1893; promoted Lieut. 13 May 1898; Capt. 11 June 1901; Major, 11 February 1914: served with the Expeditionary Force in France and Flanders from 10 September 1914: took part in the fighting at the Aisne and Armentieres: wounded in December 1914; repatriated to England, New Year's Eve 1914: returned to France; rejoined 2nd Battalion, 10 May 1915 (with Major C.A. Wilkinson), in the vicinity of Frezenberg, and was killed in action, 12 May 1915 when, following a heavy German bombardment of the battalion's positions nr. Railway Wood, Bellewaarde Ridge which had necessitated the evacuation of the battalion headquarters dugout, Majors Rowan-Robinson and Wilkinson took advantage of a slackening of the shellfire to return to the dugout to collect their equipment whereupon, within seconds of their arrival, a shell entered through the roof, exploded and killed both majors, four members of K.S.L.I. and four men from other units. Age 43. (*IWGC record age 44*). He was married (January 1908) to Alyne Vera Mavrogordato (remarried 1919), *née* Rowan-Robinson, *née* Hulton-Harrop (141, Warwick St., Westminster, London). Remains recovered from an unmarked grave (28.I.11.b.5.3) 'Unknown British Major. 2 K.S.L.I.,' exhumed, identified – Officers Clothing, Collar Badge, Badge of Rank, Titles; reinterred, registered, 13 March 1928. Collective Grave. *Buried in Sanctuary Wood Cemetery (II.B.28/29).*

O Valiant Hearts

(Panel 47) Major Clement Arthur Wilkinson, 2nd Bn. (85th Foot) The King's (Shropshire Light Infantry): *s.* of Percival Spearman Wilkinson, of Mount Oswald, Durham, by his wife Adela Fenton: late *husb.* to Ruth Violet Esther Wilkinson, *née* Mirehouse (Rotherfield, co. Sussex): and father to Sqdn.Ldr. 26192, R.L. Wilkinson, 266 Sqdn., Royal Air Force, killed on 16 August 1940, when in an aerial dogfight over Kent his Spitfire collided with a German Messerschmitt BF109E: *educ.* Durham School: served in the West African Expedition, 1898–1900; South African Campaign (twice Mentioned in Despatches): served with the Expeditionary Force in France and Flanders from September 1914, and was killed in action, 12 May 1915, nr. Frezenberg. Age 44. See Major W.J. Rowan-Robinson. Remains exhumed from a grave marked as belonging to an 'Unknown British Soldier. 2 K.S.L.I.', (28.I.11.b.5.3), identified – Officers Clothing, Titles; reinterred, registered, 13 March 1928. Collective Grave. *Buried in Sanctuary Wood Cemetery (II.B.28/29).*

Christ Our Redeemer Passed The Self Same Way

His son Robert is buried in Margate Cemetery, Kent (Sec.50, Grave 15939).

(Panel 47) Capt. Robert Shuttleworth Clarke, 'D' Coy., 5th (Service) Bn. The King's (Shropshire Light Infantry): *s.* of the Rev. William Shuttleworth Clarke, M.A., Vicar of Marstow, Ross, Herefordshire, by his wife Maria Brandram, *dau.* of Dr. Edmund Jones, of Mountcraig, Ross: *b.* Marstow, co. Hereford, 22 April 1890: *educ.* Oakshade Preparatory School, Reigate; Malvern College, and St. John's College, Cambridge (B.A. 1912): Occupation – Master; Golden Parsonage Preparatory School, nr. Hemel Hempstead, co. Hertford: volunteered on the outbreak of war, enlisted as Private, 25 August 1914: given a commission, gazetted 2nd Lieut. 7 September 1914; promoted Lieut. 30 November following; Capt.

17 June 1915: served with the Expeditionary Force in France from 21 May, and died on 25 September 1915, from wounds received in action nr. Hooge. Buried by Trench H15 with eight of his men, a cross marking the spot. Age 25. L/Corpl. C. Kelcowyn wrote, "On September 25 we were ordered to take two lines of trenches; we advanced about dawn and captured the first line. Just then I was struck by a bursting shell. Captain Clarke was struck by the same shell. He was hit in several places. We crawled into the communication trench and lay there. Captain Clarke had his flask with him and he gave me some drink from it. He said, 'Cheer up, lad,' and I think he died from loss of blood." And Sergt. F. Langford, "From the men who came out of the charge on 25 September and were near him at the time I know how magnificently he fought; and, without cant, he died a hero. This is how his memory is revered in this battalion." In the Athletic Sports, at Cambridge, in March, 1912, Clarke ran second to P.J.Baker in the Mile and won the Three Miles. In the Inter-University Sports of that year he represented Cambridge in the Mile, running second to A.N.S. Jackson, of Oxford. In 1913 he was President of the C.U.A.C., the first Captain of the Lady Margaret Boat Club to become so. In that year he again ran second to Jackson in the Mile. He was a 'Cross-Country Blue;' rowed three in the Lady Margaret Four, which won the Wyfold Challenge Cup, at Henley (1913) and, on 6 March, 1915, in a six-mile cross-country race open to the 14th Division, at Aldershot, Clarke was the first officer home for which he received a Medal presented by H.M. Queen Mary. The 5th Battn. K.S.L.I. were placed second in this race to 5th Battn. O.B.L.I. On 3 April, in a Relay race of four miles, the position of the battalions was reversed, and the Team of the 5th K.S.L.I., consisting of Lieut. R.S. Clarke, Lieut. H.G. Booker, and Privates Edwards and Stuart, were placed first; receiving medals. On 13 April Lieut. Clarke won the Silver Cup for the Mile open to Aldershot Command. Capt. R.S. Clarke was the winner of 55 prizes in all – i.e. 5 at Oakdale Preparatory School, 11 at Malvern College, where he was Champion Athlete (1909), 34 at Cambridge, 1 while at Hemel Hempstead, and 4 at Aldershot: *unm.*

(Panel 47) Capt. John Russell Pound, 3rd (Reserve) attd. 2nd Bn. (85th Foot) The King's (Shropshire Light Infantry): eldest *s.* of Sir John Lulham Pound, of Shenley, Shepherds Hill, Highgate, London, N.6, and Lady Pound: *gdson.* of the late Sir John Pound, Bart., Lord Mayor of London, 1904–05: *b.* London, 7 June 1887: *educ.* Merchant Taylors' School, London; St. John's College, Oxford; graduated First Class Honours, Mathematics, afterwards taking his M.A. degree: became Assistant Master, Shrewsbury School, 1909, where he took a great interest in, and was Capt. of, the O.T.C.: remained at Shrewsbury, with an interval of one year, spent at Christ Church College, Cawnpore, India, until the outbreak of war: gazetted Capt., Unattached List, Territorial Force, February 1910: applied for a commission on the outbreak of war; gazetted Capt. 3rd King's Shropshire Light Infantry, August 1914; attd. 2nd Battn. for Active Service: proceeded to France, and was killed in the trenches nr. Ypres while in command of his company, 27 April 1915. Age 27. *unm.* A good athlete, he was in the first XV at School, played for the Old Merchant Taylors', Captain of his College XV, and played for Oxford University *v.* Manchester. He also represented in the North *v.* South International Trials. Capt. Pound *m.* Elsie Irene, *dau.* of W.H. (& Mrs) Pendlebury, M.A., of Shrewsbury. His death is the second loss which his family have sustained in the war with Germany; his youngest brother, 2nd Lieut. M.S. Pound, 1st Queen's (Royal West Surrey Regt.), died at Guy's Hospital, London, 7 November 1914, aged 23, from the effects of wounds received in action (21 October) at Poelcapelle, nr.Ypres.

His brother Murray is buried in Highgate Cemetery, London (46.3964).

(Panel 47) Lieut. Frederick Rivers Currie, 3rd attd. 1st Bn. (53rd Foot) The King's (Shropshire Light Infantry): *yr. s.* of Rivers Grenfell Currie, of Shelton House, Shrewsbury, by his wife Alice Theresa Disney, eldest *dau.* of the late Arthur Disney Dunne: and *gdson.* to Sir Frederick Currie, 1st Battn., Secretary, Government of India; and member Supreme Council of India: *b.* London, 2 November 1896: *educ.* Warden House, Upper Deal, and Repton (Classical Scholar & O.T.C. member): left school on the outbreak of war, applied for and obtained a commission 2nd Lieut. 3rd Shropshire L.I. 15 August 1914; promoted Lieut. 21 March 1915: transf'd. 1st Battn. (joined in France), January 1915, and was killed in action at Hooge, 8 August following. Buried at Maple Copse, Zillebeke. Age 18. Lieut.Col. Luard, Comdg. 1st Battn., wrote, "It is with deep regret that I write to tell you that your son was killed by a shell on the afternoon of 8 August in the front firing trenches. He was a very gallant brave fellow, and was deservedly popular, both with the officers and men. He had done much good work, and was a very promising young officer. He is a great loss not only to the regiment, but to the Army." And Capt. H.S. Collins, "I always liked him, and on getting the chance, I applied for him to come to my company. He turned out far and away the best of my officers; most hard working and capable for one so young. Of course, it is unnecessary to say how brave he was. I think he sent you his congratulatory message he got from our General. It was the finest bit of patrolling done while I was with the battalion, and under the most dangerous circumstances. Altogether he was a splendid fellow in every way, and the Army has lost an officer it can ill afford to lose these times." Coy.Sergt.Major Foxall also wrote, "I have just been speaking to some of the men of your son's platoon. They wish me to say what a great loss it was to them, for your boy was a splendid example of what an officer should be – always working, always cheerful." Remains of an 'Unknown British Officer. Shropshire Light Inf.' exhumed, identified – Clothing, Buttons, Badges of Rank; reinterred, registered, 6 February 1928. *Buried in Sanctuary Wood Cemetery (II.B.11).*

They Serve Him Day And Night In His Temple
Rev. 7.15

(Panel 47) Lieut. George Herbert Davies, 3rd (Shropshire Militia) attd. 1st Bn. (53rd Foot) The King's (Shropshire Light Infantry): 6th *s.* of the late Rev. John Bayley Davies, M.A., for nearly 40 years Rector of Waters Upton, by his wife Susan Anslow (Waters Upton, nr. Wellington), *dau.* of Richard Juckes, of Cotwall, co. Salop: and brother to 2nd Lieut. W.L. Davies, died of wounds, 15 July 1916: *b.* Waters Upton Rectory, co. Salop, 16 November 1888: *educ.* Hereford Cathedral School, and Glasgow University (Sergt. Major, O.T.C.): Occupation – Civil Engineer; Messrs John Brown & Co. Ltd., Glasgow: volunteered when war broke out; applied for and was given a commission, 2nd Lieut. 3rd Shropshire L.I. 15 August 1914; promoted Lieut. 21 March, 1915: joined the Expeditionary Force in France (attd. 1st Manchesters) December 1914: invalided home in February 1915, returned to the Front, April, being then attd. 1st Shropshires, and was killed in action, 10 August 1915 in the attack on Hooge. Buried near there. Major (now Lieut.-Col.) E.B. Luard wrote, "He was in charge of the machine guns and was most gallantly getting one into position when he was shot dead. He is a very great loss to the regiment. He was very popular with both the officers and men. I had a great admiration of him, and feel the loss of a very courageous, hard-working and valuable young officer." Three other brothers are now (1917) serving: Capt. A.J. Davies, R.N., Lieut. R.W. Davies, R.A.M.C., in Mesopotamia, and 2nd Lieut. A.T. Davies, Indian Special Reserve (Gurkhas). Age 26. *unm.* (*IWGC record 9 August 1915*)

His brother Walter is buried in La Neuville British Cemetery, Corbie (I.B.49).

(Panel 47) Lieut. Geoffrey Holman, 2nd Bn. (85th Foot) The King's (Shropshire Light Infantry): 3rd *s.* of Mr (& Mrs) Holman, of Wynnstay, Putney Hill, London, S.W.: *b.* 9 December 1892: *educ.* Rose Hill School, Banstead, co. Surrey (privately), also in Paris and Berlin, subsequently entering Royal Military College, Sandhurst: gazetted 2nd Lieut. Shropshire Light Infantry, September 1914; promoted Lieut. 1915. On the outbreak of war his battalion was in India; accompanied it to England in November 1914: served with the Expeditionary Force in France and Flanders from December 1914; wounded in March 1915: rejoined his regiment after treatment and convalescence, and returned to the fighting line near Ypres, Belgium, where he was killed in action, 9 April 1915. Age 22. *unm.*

(Panel 47) Lieut. Walter Drummond Vyvyan, 2nd Bn. (85th Foot) The King's (Shropshire Light Infantry): elder *s.* of Capt. Richard Walter Comyn Vyvyan, J.P., late 2nd Welsh Regt., now (Temp.) Lieut. Col. Comdg. 21st (Reserve) Bn. Welsh Regt., by his wife Mary, *née* Foster (Trewan, co. Cornwall): and *gdson.* to the Rev. Sir Vyell Donnithorne Vyvyan, Bart., of Trelowarren, co. Cornwall: *b.* Bath, 20 March 1887: *educ.* Clifton College; Bedford Grammar School; Royal Military College, Sandhurst: gazetted King's Shropshire Light Infantry, May 1907: joined 1st Battn., Borden Camp: transf'd. 2nd Battn. India, September 1909: promoted Lieut. March 1910: returned to England in November 1914: preparatory to leaving for the Front was at Winchester, initially attd. (thereafter seconded), Army Cyclist Corps, XXVIIth Divn.: later apptd. to command of a Platoon of bomb throwers: served with the Expeditionary

Force in France and Flanders from December following. On the night of 1 March 1915, he led his men at the head of an attack made by another battalion on some German trenches at St. Eloi and was killed during the action. Owing to the very heavy fire from the German machine guns it was not possible to recover his body. This action is referred to in Sir John French's Despatch, 5 April 1915, and Lieut. Vyvyan's name, with other officers of his battalion, is Mentioned in Sir John's Despatch, 31 May 1915. Age 28. *unm.*

(Panel 47) 2nd Lieut. **Charles Robert Blackett**, 2nd Bn. (85th Foot) The King's (Shropshire Light Infantry): only child of the Rev. (& Mrs) W.R. Blackett, of Smethcote Rectory, near Shrewsbury: a descendant of Sir John Blackett, of Woodcroft, Co. Durham, High Sheriff of Leicestershire, who fought at Agincourt, and whose grandfather, Richard Blackhed, of Woodcroft, Forester of Weardale, died in 1315: *b.* Fenton, co. Stafford, 7 June 1894: *educ.* Hereford Cathedral School, where he held a Foundation Scholarship, and distinguished himself in many ways, being Captain of the School, Editor of *The Herefordian*, Victor Ludorum, Captain of the Football XI, member of the School Crew, and a member of the O.T.C., obtaining Certificate 'A': proceeded to Brasenose College, Oxford, as a 'Somerset' scholar, and 'Philpottine' Exhibitioner: rowed in the Torpids and played in the College Soccer XI: joined the Cavalry branch of the O.T.C., and, after offering himself for Active Service on the outbreak of war, entered Royal Military College, Sandhurst on 15 August 1914: gazetted 2nd Lieut. King's Shropshire Light Infantry, November following attd. 3rd (Reserve) Battn. of his regiment: took out a draft of the Welsh Regt. and Royal Welsh Fusiliers, joining 2nd Battn. of his regiment at Ypres, March 1915. On 25 April 1915 he was officially reported 'missing, believed killed.' That day his battalion was sent to the assistance of another battalion in an attempt to recover a trench. He led his men in the first of three charges, and he, with one other man, reached and jumped into the trench. After this nothing further is known of his fate. The Brigade, of which 2nd King's Shropshire Light Infantry was a unit, was especially and personally thanked by Sir John French for work done in the defence of Ypres. Appended is an extract from a letter written by the Officer Commanding, 2nd Battn. King's Shropshire Light Infantry, to Lieut. Blackett's father, under date 1st May, "I am deeply grieved to inform you that your son is missing, and, I fear, killed. He was gallantly charging a trench the Germans had taken, and we were trying to get it back. It happened early in the morning of 26th April. He was doing very well, and was a most promising young officer. His loss is very much felt by us all, and we can deeply sympathise with you." Age 20. *unm.*

(Panel 47) 2nd Lieut. **Anthony Cyprian Prosper Biddle-Cope**, 1st Bn. (53rd Foot) The King's (Shropshire Light Infantry): *s.* of James Cyprian Biddle-Cope, formerly of Broadwood Hall, co. Salop, by his wife Marie Louise, *dau.* of Edward Angell Saunders: *b.* London, 9 May 1889: *educ.* Barnabite College, Florence, Italy; thereafter Cadet, H.M.S. 'Conway' (received King's gold medal): gazetted 2nd Lieut. 1st King's Shropshire L.I. 10 August 1910, and went to the Front with them on the outbreak of war. Present when the general move of the British Army was made in Belgium and Northern France, and when the Germans made their first attempt to capture Calais; he was killed in action while saving the life of a friend, nr. Ypres, 26 April 1915. A Major, 1st King's Shropshire L.I., in a letter to his family, wrote, "The death of your son was not a surprise to me, for I knew it must only be a question of time before he was either killed or wounded seriously enough to lay him up for the rest of the war, for he was one of the bravest men I have ever met. I knew him first at the Depot at Shrewsbury, when he first joined in 1910, and even then I was so much impressed with his pluck and his constant desire to do his duty in everything that I used to say that if ever I went on service I should rather have him to help me in a tight place than any other young officer I knew. When we were out on the Aisne, if ever there was any dangerous job that required to be done he would volunteer to do it, and yet the way he carried it out showed that he had caution and sense besides mere pluck. When he was first wounded, on 23 October, he came up to me with his hand bound up, and was all for leading a bayonet charge in daylight. The day before that he had walked across an open space of 50 yards to bring me a message, with the bullets spattering all around him, and nothing I could say would make him wait till dark before going back." Another officer, who was wounded in the same engagement as Lieut. Biddle-Cope met his death, wrote, "During the fight round Ypres two companies were ordered with the machine guns to reinforce a regt. who were having a very bad time. On arrival there some selected men of our company were ordered to take a trench held by the Germans, and I was one of the officers, and while waiting to move out of our trench to attack, Biddle-Cope came up and chatted with me and wished me good luck; and I left my stick with him till I came back. The order to advance was given, and we charged, and just before we got to the enemy's trench Biddle-Cope rushed by at a terrific pace, and was shot as he got to the enemy's trench. When just in front of me he fired two shots from his revolver, and I think was again hit. I dropped down beside him and fired at the German who had shot him, but can't say whether I hit him or not. I myself had damaged my knee so severely that I could not walk at the time, and I saw no use trying to do any more, so collected the few men left – about five at the moment – and crawled back in. Biddle-Cope was machine gun officer and should not have been there, but I can only think that he saw things were going badly and came out to help me." Age 25. *unm.*

(Panel 47) 2nd Lieut. Douglas George Hazard, 3rd (Reserve) attd. 2nd Bn. (85th Foot) The King's (Shropshire Light Infantry): *yst. s.* of James Dare Hazard, of 1, Walpole Road, Boscombe, Bournemouth, co. Hants, formerly of Castle Court, Spa Road, Boscombe, by his wife Edith Eleanor: *b.* 15 May 1894: *educ.* Wimborne Grammar School, and Bournemouth (member, School O.T.C.); passed Cambridge Local Examinations (Hons.): served three years' as Articled Pupil; Messrs Mooring, Aldridge & Haydon, Bournemouth (1912): passed Intermediate Law Examination, obtaining Student Scholarship of the Law Society (1913): accepted a commission – General Reserve of Officers, November 1912: gazetted 2nd Lieut. 3rd (Reserve) Battn. King's (Shropshire Light Infantry) at the outbreak of war in August 1914; joining Pembroke Dock. He greatly enjoyed the change of life, and was very keen to go to the Front, which he did early in May 1915, attached 2nd Battalion of his regiment for Active Service. He fell in action close to a German trench at Railway Wood, nr. Hooge, 25 May 1915, a few days after his arrival at the Front; and ten days after his twenty-first birthday. A Major in the Welsh Regiment, who saw 2nd Lieut. Hazard fall, wrote, "On the 25th May we made a night attack about three miles east of Ypres. We attacked through a small wood up a hill. I led my men amid a murderous fire and charged the trench at the top and took it. The Germans retired to a trench about fifteen yards further back, and fired very heavily on us. While lying there, a company of the Shropshires, who were supporting us, came charging through the wood, led by an officer. He was at the head of the company, shouting to them to 'charge!' I got up and shouted to my own men to 'charge!' I then saw the Shropshire officer fall, but it was too dark to see whether he was killed or wounded, and the fire was so heavy I could not get near him. We hung on until dawn, until I had only about thirty men left. We then retired under a most murderous fire. Your son fell within fifteen yards of the German trenches, so if he was wounded he must now be a prisoner. We tried to get back through the wood after dark to bring in the wounded, but could only get half-way up as the Germans were again in position. The Shropshire officer was splendid in the way he led the men." The Officer Commanding 3rd Shropshire Light Infantry wrote, "I am writing to you to express our sorrow and the grief of all the officers of the 3rd Shropshire Light Infantry at the loss of your son while fighting for his country and upholding the good name of the Shropshire Light Infantry. While here he endeared himself to us all. He was keen, hard-working, and most reliable." 2nd Lieut. Hazard's Orderly wrote, "We suffered very heavily – I believe about three hundred killed, wounded, and missing – and it was all done in about half an hour. I hope your son is still safe somewhere, but I have grave doubts. He was a gentleman, every inch of him, and a fine officer. The months I had under him both at Pembroke and out at the Front, I cannot speak too highly of, and I am extremely sorry." 2nd Lieut. Hazard was universally loved. Letters from Tutors of the Law Society, Masters, and from the Heads of his old firm all testify to his fineness of character, and in one letter it is remarked that he "had not an enemy in the world." His two brothers, Capt. Cecil J. Hazard, 11th Hampshire Regt., and 2nd Lieut. Charles P. Hazard, King's (Shropshire Light Infantry), are both serving in the war. Age 21. *unm.* Remains exhumed from an unmarked grave (28.I.11.b.8.3); identified – Gold Ring, Compass, Spirit Flask Cover all engrvd. HAZARD. D.G., also 1 Coin; Officers Uniform, Ankle Boots size 8, Cap Badge, impression 2/Lieut. Star on sleeve of tunic; approx. 5'10" tall, upper and lower jaw smashed. Reinterred, registered 12 April 1932. (*IWGC record Lieut.*) *Buried in Sanctuary Wood Cemetery (V.U.13).*

2nd Lieut. C.P. Hazard lies at Essex Farm Cemetery, Boesinghe (II.G.6).

(Panel 47) Sergt. 10203, Richard Lewis, 1st Bn. (53rd Foot) The King's (Shropshire Light Infantry): late of Stanton Lacy, Ludlow: *s.* of David Lewis, of Bourton, co. Salop, by his wife Ann: and brother to L/Corpl. 7996, E. Lewis, 5th King's (Shropshire Light Infantry); killed in action, 24 August 1916, at the Somme: *b.* Middleton: enlisted Ludlow. Killed in action, 9 August 1915. Age 30.

His brother Evan also has no known grave; he is commemorated on the Thiepval Memorial.

(Panel 47) L/Sergt. 14424, George Parsons, 7th (Service) Bn. The King's (Shropshire Light Infantry): *s.* of John Parsons, of 1, Reid Street, Crewe, co. Chester, by his wife Anne: *b.* Crewe: enlisted Chester. Killed in action, 25 April 1916. Age 21. *Buried in Dickebusch New Military Cemetery (J.14).*

He Did His Duty And His Best God Granted To Him Eternal Rest

(Panel 47) Corpl. 5984, George Henry Huband, 2nd Bn. (85th Foot) The King's (Shropshire Light Infantry): *s.* of George Huband, of Worcester, by his wife Sarah Ann: served with the Expeditionary Force in France from 28 March 1915, and was killed in action, 7 May following, while engaged in trench repair; GHQ line, Potijze. Age 32. He leaves a widow, Florence Ellen Huband (3, Common Road, Evesham, co. Worcester).

(Panel 47) L/Corpl. 20048, Henry William Baldry, 7th (Service) Bn. The King's (Shropshire Light Infantry): formerly no.55275, Royal Army Medical Corps: *s.* of Frederick J. Baldry, of 93, Stanley Street, Lowestoft, co. Suffolk, by his wife Hannah: and brother to Pte. 290177, F.J. Baldry, 11th Suffolk Regt., killed in action, 25 October 1917; and L/Corpl. 12490, T.E. Baldry, 9th Suffolk Regt., died of wounds, 14 September 1916: *b.* Lowestoft: enlisted there. Killed in action, 3 April 1916. Age 26. *unm.* Remembered on Lowestoft (St. Margaret's) Church War Memorial. (*IWGC record 75th Bn.*)

His brother Frederick also has no known grave, he is commemorated on the Tyne Cot Memorial (Panel 40); Thomas is buried in La Neuville British Cemetery, Corbie (II.D.45).

(Panel 47) L/Corpl. 8514, Albert Henry Ould, 2nd Bn. (85th Foot) The King's (Shropshire Light Infantry): *s.* of Richard Ould, of 9, Duff Street, Poplar, London, by his wife Alice: enlisted London. Killed in action, 25 May 1915. Age 26. *unm. Buried in Bedford House Cemetery (I.A.20/Enc.No.6).*

(Panel 47) Pte. 8057, John William Allerton, 1st (53rd Foot) Bn. The King's (Shropshire Light Infantry): late of Wotton, Witton, nr. Ludlow: *s.* of Benjamin Allerton, of Prospect Place, Caynham, Ludlow, co. Salop, by his wife Elizabeth: and brother to L/Corpl. 16253, B. Allerton, 2nd East Lancashire Regt., killed in action, 24 April 1918: *b.* Rotherham, co. York, 1885: a member of the Reserve, returned to his regiment on mobilisation, August 1914: served with the Expeditionary Force in France, and was killed in action, 25 October 1916, at Ypres, Belgium. Age 31. *m.*

His brother Ben also has no known grave; he is commemorated on the Pozieres Memorial.

(Panel 47) Pte. 11119, John Thomas Bate, 'C' Coy., 5th (Service) Bn. The King's (Shropshire Light Infantry): *s.* of Thomas A. Bate, of 8, Brades Lane, Prees, co. Salop, and his wife Elizabeth: *b.* Prees: enlisted Wem. Killed in action, 9 August 1915. Age 21. Remains recovered from an unmarked grave (28.I.11.b.4.3); identified – Titles, Boots mkd. 11119; reinterred, registered 23 May 1927. *Buried in Sanctuary Wood Cemetery (IV.D.28).*

(Panel 47) Pte. 8701, Albert Edward Bentley, 2nd Bn. (85th Foot) The King's (Shropshire Light Infantry): late of St. Peter's, Buckingham: *s.* of the late George Bentley, by his wife Elizabeth: *b.* Wrockwardine Wood, nr. Telford, co. Salop, *c.*1887: enlisted Shrewsbury. Killed in action, 9 May 1915. Age 27. *unm.* Remains of an 'Unknown British Soldier. K.S.L.I.' recovered, identified – Clothing, Piece of Braces mkd. 8701; reinterred, registered March 1927. *Buried in Sanctuary Wood Cemetery (III.J.1).*

PANEL 47 ENDS PTE. N. BIGGS, KING'S SHROPSHIRE LIGHT INFANTRY.

PANEL 49 BEGINS PTE. A. BIRCH, KING'S SHROPSHIRE LIGHT INFANTRY.

(Panel 49) Pte. 11460, George Hewitt, 5th (Service) Bn. The King's (Shropshire Light Infantry): late of Whitchurch, co. Salop: *s.* of the late Thomas Hewitt, of 26, Heywood Grove, Brooklands, Sale, co.

Chester, by his wife Emily (8, Oaklea Road, Ashton-on-Mersey, Sale): and brother to Pte. 9304, T. Hewitt, 5th King's (Shropshire Light Infantry, who fell the same day; and Pte. 200617, C.A. Hewitt, 1/4th King's (Shropshire Light Infantry), died 29 July 1918, aged 21 years: *b*. Birmingham, co. Warwick: enlisted Whitchurch. Killed in action, 25 September 1915. Age 22. *unm*. One of three brothers who fell.

His brother Thomas also has no known grave, he is recorded below; Charles is buried in Omont Communal Cemetery (S.W. Corner).

(Panel 49) Pte. 9304, Thomas Hewitt, 5th (Service) Bn. The King's (Shropshire Light Infantry): late of Whitchurch, co. Salop: *s*. of the late Thomas Hewitt, of, 26, Heywood Grove, Brooklands, Sale, co. Chester, by his wife Emily (8, Oaklea Road, Ashton-on-Mersey, Sale): and elder brother to Pte. 11460, G. Hewitt, 5th King's (Shropshire Light Infantry, who fell the same day; and Pte. 200617, C.A. Hewitt, 1/4th King's (Shropshire Light Infantry), died 29 July 1918: *b*. Saltley, Birmingham, co. Warwick: enlisted Shrewsbury. Killed in action, 25 September 1915. Age 24. *unm*. One of three brothers who fell.

His brother George also has no known grave, he is recorded above; Charles is buried in Omont Communal Cemetery (S.W. Corner).

(Panel 49) Pte. 11731, James Edward Hill, 5th (Service) Bn. The King's (Shropshire Light Infantry): *s*. of Henry Hill, of Caynham Mill, Ludlow, co. Salop, by his wife Emma: and brother to Pte. 48568, J. Hill, 5th Royal Berkshire Regt., killed in action three years later, 8 August 1918: *b*. Caynham. Killed in action, 4 August 1915. Age 18.

His brother John is buried in Beacon Cemetery, Sailly-Laurette (IV.D.13).

(Panel 49) Pte. 11285, Charles Edward Jones, 5th (Service) Bn. The King's (Shropshire Light Infantry): *s*. of Edward Jones, of 2, Sparbridge Road, Ellesmere, co. Salop, and Annie Jones, his spouse: enlisted Ellesmere. Killed in action, 8 August 1915. Age 19. Remains recovered from an unmarked grave (28.I.11.b.4.3); identified – Clothing, Boots mkd. 11285; reinterred, registered 23 May 1927. *Buried in Sanctuary Wood Cemetery (IV.D.25)*.

(Panel 49) Pte. 16505, John Leonard, 5th (Service) Bn. The King's (Shropshire Light Infantry): *s*. of Mrs Leonard (7, Raby Street, Bolton, co. Lancaster): served with the Expeditionary Force in France and Flanders from May 1915, and was killed in action, 16 June 1915. Age 23. Remains of an 'Unknown British Soldier' recovered from an unmarked grave (28.I.16.d.5.0), located in front of Tuileries British Cemetery, Zillebeke', identified – Clothing, Titles, Boot mkd. SH16505; reinterred, registered 15 March 1930. *Buried in Sanctuary Wood Cemetery (V.K.2)*.

(Panel 49) Pte. 17552, David Isaiah Lloyd, 5th (Service) Bn. The King's (Shropshire Light Infantry): *s*. of John Lloyd, of 'Old House,' The Village, Llangunllo, co. Radnor, by his marriage to the late Sarah Lloyd: and *yr*. brother to Corpl. 13868, J.P. Lloyd, 9th Welsh Regt., killed in action the same day, at the Battle of Loos: enlisted Knighton, Radnor. Killed in action, 25 September 1915; Bellewaarde Ridge. Age 24. *unm*.

His brother John also has no known grave; he is commemorated on the Loos Memorial.

(Panel 49) Pte. 10484, Robert Lowe, 5th (Service) Bn. The King's (Shropshire Light Infantry): *s*. of Moses Lowe, of 42, Aqueduct Road, Madeley, co. Salop: and elder brother to L/Corpl. E. Lowe, 5th King's (Shropshire Light Infantry), killed in action, 10 February 1916: *b*. Madeley: enlisted Shrewsbury. Killed in action, 14 September 1915. Age 31. Remains of an 'Unknown British Soldier K.S.L.I.' recovered from an unmarked grave (28.I.11.b.30.45); identified – Clothing; reinterred, registered 12 September 1927. *Buried in Sanctuary Wood Cemetery (IV.G.7)*.

His brother Elijah is buried in Bard Cottage Cemetery (I.M.34).

(Panel 49) Pte. 16783, Percy James Norton, 5th (Service) Bn. The King's (Shropshire Light Infantry): *s*. of Clement Norton, of 'Islington,' Forton Road, Newport, by his wife Martha: and elder brother to Pte. 3848, F.T. Norton, Northumberland Fusiliers, died at Etaples, 22 September 1916; and *yr*. brother to Rfn. 71118, W.H. Norton, Sherwood Foresters, died of wounds at Rouen, 17 November following: enlisted Shrewsbury. Killed in action, 25 September 1915. Age 25. *unm*. One of three brothers who fell.

His brother Fred is buried in Etaples Military Cemetery (XVI.B.8A); William lies in Bois Guillaume Communal Cemetery (II.B.12A).

(Panel 49) Pte. 7979, Wilfred Parker, 1st Bn. (53rd Foot) The King's (Shropshire Light Infantry): *s.* of Mary Ann Parker (51, Crooked Bridge Road, Stafford): and brother to Pte. 10027, E. Parker, North Staffordshire Regt, killed in action, 8 November 1915: *b* Christchurch, Stafford: enlisted Stafford. Killed in action, 9 August 1915. Age 29. *unm.*

His brother Ernest also has no known grave; he is recorded on Panel 55.

(Panel 49) Pte. 10869, Henry Parton, 5th (Service) Bn. The King's (Shropshire Light Infantry): late of Cross Houses, Shrewsbury: enlisted Bridgnorth, co. Salop: served with the Expeditionary Force in France and Flanders from mid-1915, and was killed in action, 14 September 1915. Remains recovered from a grave marked as belonging to an 'Unknown British Soldier K.S.L.I.' (28.I.11.b.30.45); identified – Titles, 2 Pieces of Boot mkd. SH10869, Cap Badge, Div. Badge, Bomber's Badge; reinterred, registered 12 September 1927. *Buried in Sanctuary Wood Cemetery (IV.G.6).*

(Panel 49) Pte. 6779, Leonard Preece, 5th (Service) Bn. The King's (Shropshire Light Infantry): *s.* of the late William Preece, by his wife Alice (3, Limes Terrace, Maylord Street, Hereford): and brother to Pte. 10206, A. Preece, 1st King's Shropshire L.I., died of wounds, 15 May 1916: *b.* All Saints, 1899: voluntarily enlisted Hereford: served with the Expeditionary Force in France and Flanders from May 1915, and was killed in action, 3 August following. Age 16.

His brother Albert is buried in Lijssenthoek Military Cemetery (VI.D.33).

(Panel 49) Pte. 7980, Walter Henry Williams, 1st Bn. (53rd Foot) The King's (Shropshire Light Infantry): *s.* of the late Walter Williams, by his wife Ellen (Rock Cottage, Hook-a-Gate, co. Salop): and yr. brother to Pte. 44175, T. Williams, 15th King's (Liverpool) Regt., died 15 April 1917, of chronic nephritis: *b.* Meole Brace: enlisted Shrewsbury: served with the Expeditionary Force in France from September 1914, and was killed in action, 9 August 1915. Age 30. Remembered on the Meole Brace and Annscroft (Shropshire) War Memorials.

His brother Thomas is buried in Doullens Communal Cemetery Extension No.1 (V.E.51).

(Panel 49) Pte. 19094, Harold Joseph Colin Willmott, 7th (Service) Bn. The King's (Shropshire Light Infantry): *s.* of the late Capt. A.E. Willmott, of West Norwood, London, S.E.: *b.* Portland, co. Dorset: enlisted Shrewsbury. Killed in action, 5 March 1916. Age 20. Remains recovered on 6 December 1928, from a grave marked as belonging to an 'Unknown British Soldier. Shropshire', identified – Khaki, Titles, Boots; reinterred, registered 10 December 1928. *Buried in Sanctuary Wood Cemetery (III.L.26).*

(Panel 49) Lieut.Col. Ernest William Rokeby Stephenson, Comdg. 3rd Bn. (77th Foot) The Duke of Cambridge's Own (Middlesex Regt.): 2nd *s.* of the late Rev. W. Stephenson: *b.* Hull, 4 August 1864: *educ.* Brackenberry's School, Wimbledon, London, S.W.; and Royal Military College, Sandhurst: gazetted Lieut. Middlesex Regt. August 1884; apptd. Adjt. 1st Battn. August 1890–August 1894; promoted Capt. November 1891; Adjt. 3rd Battn., during the South African War, stationed at St. Helena; the battalion having been raised at Woolwich, 1900: Queen's Medal: promoted Major in December 1901: succeeded to command 3rd Battn. February 1912. On the outbreak of war with Germany his battalion was stationed at Cawnpore, India, and, bringing it back to England, landed at Plymouth, Christmas Eve 1914: proceeded to Winchester, to form part of 38th Division: left for France in January 1915. Many of his men, used to the warm climate of India, were invalided home in February suffering very severely from frostbite and the extremely cold conditions encountered in Flanders. Lieut.Col. Stephenson was killed while gallantly leading his men into action at the Second Battle of Ypres, 23 April 1915. Age 50. His last words as he fell mortally wounded, at the head of his men, were, "Die hard, boys, die hard," which were also the inspiring words of Col. Inglis, 57th Regt., as he lay dangerously wounded on the ridge at Alburhera, 1811, a battle with which the Regiment is always associated, and words which doubtless gave origin to the familiar (often referred to) name of the Regiment – *The Die Hards*. Mentioned in F.M. Sir John (now Lord) French's Despatch, 31 May 1915. He leaves a daughter, Gwendoline Dawes, *née* Stephenson (16A, De Parys Avenue, Bedford). (*IWGC record age 46*)

(Panel 49) Capt. Frederick Norris, 'C' Coy., 23rd (Service) Bn. (2nd Football) The Duke of Cambridge's Own (Middlesex Regt.): *s.* of Walter Norris, of 123, Brook Street, Kennington, London, S.E., and Annie Norris, his wife: *educ.* St. Olave's Grammar School (1905–13): served with the Expeditionary Force, and was killed in action at the Battle of Messines; before Oasis Trench, locality Damm Strasse, 7 June 1917. Age 23. *unm.*

(Panel 49) Capt. Gordon Cuthbert, 8th Bn. The Duke of Cambridge's Own (Middlesex Regt.), (T.F.): *s.* of Henry Westell Cuthbert, of Charlton, Staines, co. Middlesex: *b.* Charlton, 14 August 1876: *educ.* Clifton College: joined London Rifle Brigade, 1894: gazetted 2nd Lieut. 2nd Volunteer Brigade, Middlesex Regt. February 1900: entered Territorial Reserve 1908: rejoined 8th Middlesex Regt. for war in August 1914, and proceeded to Gibraltar for garrison duty until February 1915: served with the Expeditionary Force in France and Flanders from March 1915, and was killed on 25 April following while leading a storming party which retook a trench near Ypres that had been vacated by another battalion owing to gas. Capt. Cuthbert *m.* Eleanor Bruce, *dau.* of the Rev. H.K. Anketell, and left three children – Cholmeley Ranson, *b.* October 1905; Elizabeth Nora, *b.* January 1908; and Patricia Cicely, *b.* May 1911. He was a member of the Junior Army & Navy Club. Age 38.

(Panel 49) Lieut. Wilfrid John Ash, 3rd Bn. (77th Foot) The Duke of Cambridge's Own (Middlesex Regt.): *s.* of Herbert Edward Ash, Solicitor; of Keilawara, Warlingham, Surrey: *b.* Croydon, 29 July 1890: *educ.* Littlejohn's, Greenwich; Haileybury; R.M.C. Sandhurst: gazetted 2nd Lieut. 2nd Middlesex Regt. 5 October 1910: exchanged 3rd Bn. (Lebong, India), July 1911; promoted Lieut. 23 July 1913. In England, on leave, when war broke out in August 1914, Lieut. Ash was recalled to rejoin his regt. at Cawnpore, and sailed for India September following. Two or three days before Christmas Day in 1914, he was back again in England with 3rd Middlesex who had come over as a complete unit. He went with the regiment to France in January 1915, and was killed in action on the afternoon of 14 February 1915, between Ypres and St. Eloi, while leading his men in a successful counter-attack against the enemy's trenches. Col. E.W.R. Stephenson, Commanding 3rd Bn. Middlesex Regt., wrote that he "died gallantly leading his men in an attempt to capture a trench that had fallen. Previous to this, he saved the life of my nephew, Moller, who had been severely wounded, and after placing him in a place of safety, he again entered the fight. He nobly did his duty, and we deplore his loss." Pte. Worsfold also wrote, "On the afternoon of Sunday, 14 February, we were ordered to attack a position occupied by the enemy, north-west of Ypres and west of the canal; on the morning of the same day we had been badly cut up, and the Surreys, who afterwards came up in support, opened to let us through. Lieut. W.J. Ash, who had been previously wounded in the arm, was still leading up to the last moment." Age 24.

(Panel 49) Lieut. Leslie Harvey, 8th Bn. The Duke of Cambridge's Own (Middlesex Regt.), (T.F.): only *s.* of Cecil Allenby Harvey, of Highgate House, Hawkhurst, Bank Manager, by his wife Annie, *dau.* of Thomas Amey, of Petersfield: *b.* Windsor, 3 January 1884: *educ.* Eastbourne and Isleworth: Occupation – Solicitor: joined Inns of Court Officers Training Corps, obtained his 'B' Certificate and, on the outbreak of war, at once volunteered: given a commission, 8th Middlesex Regt. 28 August 1914; promoted Lieut. February 1915, proceeded to the Western Front a fortnight later, and was killed in action nr. Ypres, 25 April 1915, while leading a bayonet charge. Buried at the level crossing about 11 kilometres east of Ypres. Age 31. *unm.*

(Panel 49) Capt. Herbert Philip Hilton, 3rd Bn. (77th Foot) The Duke of Cambridge's Own (Middlesex Regt.): *s.* of Ernest (& Mrs) Hilton: at Cawnpore, India, on the outbreak of war: returned to England, November 1914: proceeded to France on 15 January 1915, moved up to the Ypres sector at the end of that month and entered the front-line on 10 February following. He was killed in action less than a week later, on 16 February 1915, during fighting to recapture some lost trenches. Age 42. He was married to Hylda Swan, *née* Hilton (7, Elysium Row, Calcutta, India).

(Panel 49) Lieut. George Henry Fosbroke Power, 6th attd 'C' Coy., 3rd Bn. (77th Foot) The Duke of Cambridge's Own (Middlesex Regt.): *s.* of Sir Henry Ellis D'Arcy Power, K.B.E., F.R.C.S. (Eng.), Lieut.Col. I.C. 1st London General Hospital, Camberwell, of 10A., Chandos Street, Cavendish Square, London, W., and 53, Murray Road, Northwood, co. Middlesex, by his late wife Lady Eleanor Power (*d.* 26 June 1923), *yst. dau.* of George Haynes Fosbroke, M.R.C.S., of Bidford-on-Avon, co. Warwick: and *gdson.* to Henry Power, Asst. Surgeon, Westminster Ophthalmic Hospital, and Thomas Simpson, Ship-owner and Banker, Whitby: *b.* 1894: *educ.* Merchant Taylor's School; New College, Oxford (commoner);

President, University Fencing Club. Recorded as wounded and missing following the fighting at Ypres, 9 May 1915, a member of his regiment later reported seeing Lieut. Power – after having his hand blown off by shellfire – making his way toward the rear. Assumed to have been killed by further shellfire. Age 21. *unm.* Lieut. Power is commemorated on a bronze plaque in the Church of St. Lawrence, Bidford-on-Avon.

(Panel 49) Lieut. Harold Walter Tigar, 3rd Bn. (77th Foot) The Duke of Cambridge's Own (Middlesex Regt.): *s.* of Walter Tigar, of 112, Nibthwaite Road, Harrow, co. Middlesex, by his wife Mary Agnes: and elder brother to 2nd Lieut. G.H. Tigar, 6th Royal Berkshire Regt., killed in action, 13 October 1917, aged 21 years: served with the Expeditionary Force in France, and was killed in action, 9 May 1915. Age 22. *unm.*

His brother Geoffrey also has no known grave; he is commemorated on the Tyne Cot Memorial (Panel 105).

(Panel 49) 2nd Lieut. Frederick Herbert Devereux, 23rd (Service) Bn. (2nd Football) The Duke of Cambridge's Own (Middesex Regt.): *s.* of the late William John Devereux, by his wife Elizabeth Ann (36, James's Square, London, W.11).: enlisted as Pte., Queen Victoria's Rifles, 5 August 1914: served with the Expeditionary Force in France from November following: subsequently obtained a commission, and was killed in action nr. Hollebeke, 31 July 1917. Age 40. Mr Devereux leaves a widow, Louise Roquebert Devereux (26, Rue Josephine, Toulon, France), and children.

(Panel 49) 2nd Lieut. William Percival Grieve, 3rd Bn. (77th Foot) The Duke of Cambridge's Own (Middlesex Regt.): *yst. s.* of William Grieve, of 13, Fenchurch Avenue, London, E.C., and Rockcliffe, Dalbeattie: and brother to Major J.R. Grieve, M.C., Royal Field Artillery, killed in action, 4 April 1918: *b.* Croydon, co. Surrey, 11 November 1885: *educ.* St. Andrew's School, Eastbourne; Cheltenham College, and Edinburgh University: enlisted Tpr., 2nd King Edward's Horse on the outbreak of war: subsequently received a commission, 5th (Reserve) Battn. Middlesex Regt., November 1914; transf'd. 3rd Battn. Reported missing believed killed in action, 14 February 1915, in Belgium and, as no word has been received since then, death is assumed. His commission was afterwards antedated to August 1914 (*London Gazette*, 29 December 1914). Age 29. *unm.* Remembered on Colvend War Memorial.

His brother James is buried in Moreuil Communal Cemetery Allied Extension (A.34).

(Panel 49) 2nd Lieut. Charles Henry Stead, 8th Bn. The Duke of Cambridge's Own (Middlesex Regt.), (T.F.): eldest *s.* of Charles Henry Stead, by his wife Louise Ann: *b.* London, 15 May 1876: *educ.* Privately: enlisted Middlesex Regt. July 1893: served 21 years, rising through the various non-commissioned ranks to Colour-Sergt. 1909: received Good Conduct Medal: became Actg. Sergt.-Major, 8th Battn. 1912: passed classes of Instruction for Mounted Infantry, Signalling, Musketry, and Advanced Course, Hythe: also obtained 1st Class Certificate of Education, and was a fine gymnast: commissioned 2nd Lieut. Middlesex Regt. attd. 8th Battn. for Active Service: served with the Expeditionary Force in France and Flanders, and was killed in action at Ypres, 25 April 1915. Buried at Zonnebeke. Age 38. The Officer Commanding 8th Battn., wrote, "It seems so hard that after having obtained his life's ambition by being granted a commission by His Majesty, that he should have lived such a very short time to enjoy the honour conferred upon him. You will, however, be glad to hear he died nobly with his men. The enemy captured a trench last night from the Battalion in front by use of this poisonous gas, but 'A' Coy., which with 'B' was in support, could not allow this, so they made a very brilliant counter-attack which was successful, and the enemy were driven out of the trench again. Unfortunately, however, the losses were very great, and your poor husband was amongst the killed. Ever since your husband has been in this battalion I have had the very highest opinion of his work, keenness and ability." 2nd Lieut. Stead who was a Freemason, *m.* 1904; Alice Maude (133, Campden Crescent, Becontree, Chadwell Heath, co. Essex), and left five children – Grace Florence, *b.* 1905; Elizabeth Louise, *b.* 1906; Alice May, *b.* 1909; Charles Henry, *b.* 1912; and Robert Ernest, *b.* 1915. (*IWGC record age 39*)

(Panel 49) 2nd Lieut. Frederick Ashburnham Hooker Whitfield, 3rd Bn. (77th Foot) The Duke of Cambridge's Own (Middlesex Regt.): only *s.* of the late F.H. Milton Whitfield, Fleet Paymaster, Royal Navy, by his wife Elizabeth E. Milton, *née* Hooker (20, Durham Terrace, Bayswater, London): and nephew to the late Sir J.D. Hooker, O.M., Director, Kew Gardens, a descendant of Richard Hooker, the same family as the poet Milton: *b.* Southampton, 14 December 1889: *educ.* Cranleigh, co. Surrey, where he was good at games: passed for appointment, 1st Class, Royal Navy, Accountants Branch, but there was no vacancy: afterwards he entered Head Office, London & County (later London County, Westminster & Parr's) Bank, remaining there until the outbreak of war in August 1914. Three years previously he had joined the Artists' Rifles, no.1011, in which he was extremely popular; the officers, non-commissioned officers, and men passed a resolution of sympathy and sorrow on learning of his death, and innumerable friends and comrades wrote expressions of great regret. His adaptability and general temperament endeared him to all. On the outbreak of war he at once offered himself for Active Service, and for some three months acted as 'batman,' in which position his skill earned him the title of 'The man who made bully beef unrecognisable.' His Commanding Officer, in censoring a letter to his sister, wrote that "His cooking was quite perfect...he was invaluable", and, "He was a brother to be proud of." After three months training in the Officer's School for France he was gazetted Temporary 2nd Lieut., General List, 14 February 1915 (St. Valentine's Day), attd. 3rd Middlesex Regt., appointed Assistant Machine Gun Officer. 2nd Lieut. Whitfield was killed on 23 April 1915, while leading his Platoon to attack, near St. Julien, across a ploughed field, exposed to the fire of eight enemy Maxims; he had advanced with the utmost courage and coolness, with the remnants of his Platoon, until within firing distance of the enemy, when he was hit in the jaw and throat and killed instantaneously. His body was not recovered and, so far as is known, was not buried. One of the thirteen survivors of his Platoon said, "He was one of the best officers we ever had...He was never thinking of himself, but always of us men. He was absolutely fearless, and walked about in the middle of the most dangerous duties as if he were at home in England ... We could go to him about anything, just as if he were our father. When we were trench digging in a most dangerous point, in the middle of battle he went and got us hot tea and rum ... We were as cold as ice, and it was such a brave thing to do ... When he asked for volunteers for anything, the whole Platoon would start up as one man." The Officer Commanding, 3rd Middlesex Regt., in writing of his death said, "He was a brave, bright and promising young officer, and we all loved him. His name will never be forgotten by his Regiment, but will always be held in honour." He proved himself heart and soul a soldier, and in almost his last letter home said, "I do like my job" – and once described the war as "the jolliest rag I ever was in." It is probable that had he not been killed he would have received recognition for his fine patrol work. Age 25. *unm.* He was a member of the Richmond Hockey Club, and had just become engaged to be married to Miss Gladys Buchanan, (32, Elsworthy Road, London, S.W.).

(Panel 49) Coy.Q.M.Sergt. TF/1315, Sidney Allies, 8th Bn. The Duke of Cambridge's Own (Middlesex Regt.), (T.F.): served with the British Expeditionary Force in France. Killed in action at St. Jean, 23 April 1915.

(Panel 49) Sergt. L/10852, William George Giggins, 4th Bn. (77th Foot) The Duke of Cambridge's (Middlesex Regt.): *s.* of James Giggins, of The Bungalow, Baker Street, Orsett, Grays, by his wife Emma: and elder brother to Pte. 15933, F. Giggins, Essex Regt., killed in action, 24 May 1915: *b.* South Ockendon, co. Essex, 1886: enlisted Stratford. Killed in action, 29 September 1915. Age 28.

His brother Frank also has no known grave; he is recorded on Panel 39.

(Panel 49) Sergt. L/14981, Albert George Stray, 13th (Service) Bn. The Duke of Cambridge's Own (Middlesex Regt.): *s.* of the late George (& Ada) Stray: *b.* Clerkenwell: enlisted Ponders End. Killed in action, 14 March 1916. Age 19. Remains recovered from four unmarked graves marked up as belonging to an 'Unknown British Sergeant. Middlesex Regt.', located in Sanctuary Wood Old Cemetery (28.I.24.b.90.97), identified – Clothing, Titles, Badge of Rank; reinterred, registered 1 May 1928. *Buried in Sanctuary Wood Cemetery (II.F.16).*

(Panel 49) L/Sergt. 10108, Frederick Ambler, 3rd Bn. (77th Foot) The Duke of Cambridge's Own (Middlesex Regt.): 3rd & *yst. s.* of Edward Ambler, of Little Whelnetham, Bury. St. Edmunds, by his wife Emily, *dau.* of John Charles Holmes: *b.* Little Whelnetham, co. Suffolk, 29 December 1889: enlisted on 14 March 1905: served in Ireland, South Africa, Hong Kong, Tientsin (with a detachment), Singapore, India, and with the Expeditionary Force in France from 19 January 1915, and was killed in action at Ypres, 15 February following. He was a keen sportsman, and won the bronze medal in the Regimental Sports in 1911; the silver medal in 1912, and the gold in' both 1913 and 1914. His chum wrote, "I loved Fred as I do my own brothers, we went abroad together and came home together, but now I have lost one of the best chums any soldier ever had. I would give much for him to be by my side at the present time." Age 25. *unm.* (*IWGC record L/10106*)

(Panel 49) Corpl. G/1004, Frederick George Allingham, 4th Bn. (77th Foot) The Duke of Cambridge's Own (Middlesex Regt.): served with the Expeditionary Force in France. Killed in action, 26 February 1915.

(Panel 49) A/Corpl. L/14433, Moses Chappell, 4th Bn. (77th Foot) The Duke of Cambridge's Own (Middlesex Regt.): 4th *s.* of the late James Chappell, by his wife Phoebe (1, Circular Road, Tottenham, London, N.), *dau.* of John Brown: *b.* Edmonton, co. Middlesex, 5 October 1895: *educ.* Rainham Road Board School: enlisted Mill Hill, London, N.W., 23 January 1913: served with the Expeditionary Force in France from August 1914: Mentioned in Despatches by F.M. Sir John (now Lord) French (*London Gazette*, 1 January 1916) for 'gallant and distinguished service in the field,' and was killed whilst bomb-throwing, 19 July 1915. Age 20. *unm.*

(Panel 49) Corpl. 14988, Horace Devonshire, 3rd Bn. (77th Foot) The Duke of Cambridge's Own (Middlesex Regt.): eldest *s.* of George Devonshire, of 28, Queen's Road, Bowes Park, London, N., by his wife Ada Elizabeth: *b.* Islington, London, N.: *educ.* there: Occupation – Grocer's Assistant: enlisted on 7 August 1914, a few days after the outbreak of war: served with the Expeditionary Force in France and Flanders from May 1915, and was killed in action at Hill 60 during the Second Battle of Ypres, on the 24th. A comrade wrote, "He was killed on Whit Monday, and died fighting, and was missed a lot by his platoon.": 24 May 1915. Age 19. (*IWGC record L/14988*)

(Panel 49) Corpl. G/44168, Harry Noel Gamble, 23rd (Service) Bn. (2nd Football) The Duke of Cambridge's Own (Middlesex Regt.): *s.* of Henry Gamble, of Wood Dalling, Norwich, co. Norfolk. Killed in action, 7 June 1917; vicinity Damm Strasse. Age 27. *unm.*

(Panel 49) Corpl. L/10250, Henry William Gomme, 4th Bn. (77th Foot) The Duke of Cambridge's Own (Middlesex Regt.): *s.* of John 'Jesse' Gomme, of 6, Vaughan Cottages, Barkingside, London, E., by his wife Sarah: served with the Expeditionary Force. Killed in action at Kemmel, Belgium, 19 December 1914. Age 28. *unm.*

(Panel 49) L/Corpl. F/1946, Frank Donnelly, 23rd (Service) Bn. (2nd Football) The Duke of Cambridge's Own (Middlesex Regt.): late of Bristol, co. Gloucester: enlisted Birmingham. Killed in action, 7 June 1917.

(Panel 49) L/Corpl. G/7441, Charles Giles, 3rd Bn. (77th Foot) The Duke of Cambridge's Own (Middlesex Regt.): only *s.* of John Giles, of 42, Cross Lances Road, Hounslow, co. Middlesex, by his wife Sarah. Killed in action near St. Julien, Ypres, 23 April 1915. Age 28. See 2nd Lieut. F.A.H. Whitfield (Panel 49).

(Panel 49) L/Corpl. G/6309, Allan Paul Potter, 13th (Service) Bn. The Duke of Cambridge's Own (Middlesex Regt.): eldest *s.* of Paul Potter, Jobbing Gardener; of 3, Clara Mount Road, Langley, Heanor, Nottingham (formerly 25, Ferndale Road, Stanford Hill, London, N.), by his wife Florence Annie, *dau.* of John Neale, late of Linton, Maidstone, co. Kent: and brother to Pte. 3329, A. Potter, 7th Bn. City of London Regt., killed in action at Vimy Valley, 21 May 1916: *b.* Roehampton, co. Surrey, 19 August 1898: *educ.* Earlsmead School, South Tottenham, London, N.: Occupation – Clerk: joined 4th Battn. Middlesex Regt. soon after the outbreak of war, 21 November 1914: served with the Expeditionary Force in France and Flanders from 19 January 1915: twice wounded – nr. Ypres, August 1915; Fricourt, Somme, 1 July 1916: transf'd. 5th., 6th. and 13th. Battns. of his regiment successively, and was killed in action nr. Messines, 10 June 1917. Buried there. 2nd Lieut. A.M. Baker wrote, "By his death the company had lost one of the bravest and smartest of N.C.O.'s." Age 24. *unm.*

(Panel 49) L/Corpl. F/1648, Frederick Ernest Stringer, 23rd (Service) Bn. (2nd Football) The Duke of Cambridge's Own (Middlesex Regt.): late of Plaistow, co. Essex. Killed by shellfire, vicinity Voormezeele Switch – Old French Trench, 6–7 June 1917.

On 26 August 1914, during the retirement from Mons, the village of Audencourt, held by 4th Middlesex, 8th Brigade, was subjected to a terrific shelling by the enemy. Houses cracked like egg-shells beneath the huge missiles from German field howitzers; tiles from their shattered roofs whirled through the air, great craters made by 'Jack Johnsons' yawned in the roadway. 'It was like hell, only a thousand times worse,' wrote a member of the corps.

The 4th Middlesex had little time to entrench their position, and hastily-dug shelter trenches afforded little protection. In consequence, their casualties were numerous and increased by the minute. For a short time the village church, chosen as a hospital, escaped the fate of most of the other buildings in the vicinity but, as the German gunners adjusted their range, shell after shell soon began striking it. The colonel of the battalion, on addressing the men in a trench close by, said, 'One of you Die Hards who have got your heads, move those poor fellows out of the church.' A lad of twenty, Pte. A.E. Walker, immediately volunteered and hurried toward the church, which was by now blazing fiercely. For two hours Walker was employed moving his wounded comrades out and fetching them water; all the while the bombardment continued unabated and the church was repeatedly struck. As he was assisting one of the last men out of the shattered and burning building, the colonel came past and remarked, 'Good, brave lad!' before passing onward. Unbeknown to Walker, the colonel had enquired as to the identity of this brave soldier who had been so ready to risk his life for his comrades, and was subsequently notified that he had been awarded the Distinguished Conduct Medal for 'conspicuous gallantry and devotion to duty in voluntarily attending on wounded with great coolness under heavy shell-fire.'

Unhappily, Pte. (promoted L/Corpl) Walker did not live long to wear his well-earned decoration.

(Panel 49) L/Corpl. L/14195, Albert Edward Walker, D.C.M., 3rd Bn. (77th Foot) The Duke of Cambridge's Own (Middlesex Regt.): formerly 4th Battn.: *s.* of Mrs M.J. Walker (54, Balfern Road, Lower Edmonton, London, N.): *b.* Bethnal Green, London, E., 1894: enlisted Mill Hill, London, N.W.7: served with the Expeditionary Force in France and Flanders, and was killed in action, 10 May 1915. A sergeant of his battalion, in reply to a letter from L/Corpl. Walker's parents, described the manner of his death, "Your letter concerning your brave son's death reached me safely, and I am now more than pleased to be of some little service to you. Our battalion was called out to attack the Germans. While the attack was in progress, our casualties were being brought in by my stretcher-bearers. L/Corpl. Walker, with another man, went to try and save an officer, which, if he had succeeded, would undoubtedly have earned him the V.C. His fall was mourned by all because we knew that we had lost a true, good and brave comrade.' Age 20. *unm.*

(Panel 49) L/Corpl. G/13012, Richard Henry Edward Wilson, 23rd (Service) Bn. (2nd Football) The Duke of Cambridge's Own (Middlesex Regt.): *s.* of Richard William Wilson, of 74, Olinda Road, Stamford Hill, Stoke Newington, London, and Emma Wilson, his wife: late *husb.* to Grace Emily Skelton, *née* Wilson (43, Ipplepen Road, South Tottenham, London, N.). Killed by shellfire, 10 p.m. – midnight, 6–7 June, in the vicinity of Voormezeele Switch. Age 27.

(Panel 49) Pte. F/3030, Herbert Ackroyd, 'C' Coy., 23rd (Service) Bn. (2nd Football) The Duke of Cambridge's Own (Middlesex Regt.): *s.* of the late Richard Ackroyd, and his wife Mary Ackroyd: late *husb.* to Daisy Hind, *née* Ackroyd (83, Cavendish Street, Shirebrook, Mansfield): *b.* Sneinton, Nottingham: enlisted Birmingham. Killed by shellfire before the German position Oasis Trench – Oar Avenue, Kruisstraat sector, 7 June 1917. Age 26.

(Panel 49) Pte. G/7112, John Ogden Adshead, 4th Bn. (77th Foot) The Duke of Cambridge's Own (Middlesex Regt.): *s.* of Isabella Bardsley (20, Eaves Knoll Road, New Mills, co. Derby): *b.* Wilmslow, co. Chester: employee at Waterside Paper Mill, New Mills: enlisted in Buxton. Killed in action at Hooge, 19 July 1915. Age 30.

(Panel 49) Pte. 12294, William Adshead, 3rd Bn. (77th Foot) The Duke of Cambridge's Own (Middlesex Regt.): *s.* of Thomas Adshead, of 47, Ermott Street, Stepney, London, E.: Killed in action on the Western Front, 15 February 1915. (*IWGC record L/12294*)

(Panel 49) Pte. G/5945, Charles Annand, 3rd Bn. (77th Foot) The Duke of Cambridge's Own (Middlesex Regt.): *b.* Kensington, London, W.: Killed in action somewhere on the Western Front, 30 April 1915. *m.*

(Panel 49) Pte. G/19721, George Anscombe, 23rd (Service) Bn. (2nd Football) The Duke of Cambridge's Own (Middlesex Regt.): *s.* of Sarah Anscombe (7, Henstridge Place, St. John's Wood, London): enlisted Marylebone. Killed in action, 7 June 1917, between Voormezeele Switch – Old French Trench and the German position *Damm Strasse.* Age 21.

During the evening of 14 December 1914, 4th Middlesex took over the front-line trenches of the Gordon Highlanders before Kemmel, and on the 15th suffered heavy shelling, during the course of which 6 other ranks were killed, 11 wounded, and one man confirmed missing.

(Panel 49) Pte. SR/5608, William Thomas Ardin, 4th Bn. (77th Foot) The Duke of Cambridge's Own (Middlesex Regt.): *s.* of William James (& Mary) Ardin, of 1, Poynings Road, Upper Holloway, London. Killed in action, 15 December 1914. Age 23.

The five other men killed – Ptes. E. Barron, J.W. Jennings, R.H. Read, G.J. Rose and J. Steward also have no known grave and, with the exception of Pte. Barron (Addenda Panel 59–60), are recorded on Panel 51.

(Panel 49) Pte. G/9722, William Baker, 4th Bn. (77th Foot) The Duke of Cambridge's Own (Middlesex Regt.): *s.* of the late William Baker, late of 79, Rippoth Road, Old Ford, by his wife Sarah Louise, *née* Bowell: *b.* Bethnal Green, London, 2 February 1879: *educ.* Bethnal Green Board School: Occupation – Glass Bottle Blower: volunteered and enlisted, 3 April 1915: served with the Expeditionary Force in France from 26 July 1915, and was killed in action at the Battle of Loos (*q.v.*), 29 September following. Buried at Ypres. Age 36. His Coy.Sergt.-Major wrote, "He was on duty in the trench, and a bullet passed through his body; he died instantaneously. He was an excellent soldier and always carried out his duties satisfactorily." He *m.* St. Paul's Church, Old Ford, Sarah Jane (39, Rippoth Road, Old Ford), *dau.* of Joseph (& Ann) Gill, and had nine children – William Robert Joseph, *b.* 14 July 1899; Annie Eliza, *b.* 4 October 1902; Charles Thomas Edward, *b.* 21 June 1904; George Alfred, *b.* 27 October 1906; Henry James, *b.* 3 February 1909; Arthur Edward, *b.* 6 October 1910; Rose Elizabeth, *b.* 17 September 1912; James William, *b.* 27 June 1914; and Lilian Caroline, *b.* 21 April 1916.

(Panel 49) Pte. L/14293, Isaac Barks, 4th Bn. (77th Foot) The Duke of Cambridge's Own (Middlesex Regt.): *s.* of Isaac Barks, of 91, Pembroke Road, New Southport: served with the Expeditionary Force. Killed in action at Kemmel, 28 December 1914.

(Panel 49) Pte. PW/5214, James William Barnes, 16th (Service) Bn. (Public Schools) The Duke of Cambridge's Own (Middlesex Regt.): *yst. s.* of George Barnes, of Gordon Terrace, Mill Road, Burgess Hill, co. Sussex: a widower; prior to enlistment had assisted his father in business, and was a cleaner at the local Post Office: enlisted Burgess Hill. Killed in action, 11 August 1917. Age 30. An officer, in a letter to Pte. Barnes' parents, wrote, "…was killed in action on the night of 11th-12th inst. Death was instantaneous, being due to a shell which killed others at the same time…"

(Panel 49) Pte. G/51001, Richard Barnes, 23rd (Service) Bn. (2nd Football) The Duke of Cambridge's Own (Middlesex Regt.): *s.* of Joseph Barnes. Killed in action; vicinity Damm Strasse, 7 June 1917. Age 37. He was married to Ellen Maud Barnes (Burnham Norton, King's Lynn, co. Norfolk).

(Panel 49) Pte. L/14044, Henry Barrell, 5th (Reserve) attd. 3rd Bn. (77th Foot) The Duke of Cambridge's Own (Middlesex Regt.): eldest *s.* of Harry Barrell, of 8, Victoria Road, South Tottenham, London, N., by his wife Emma Maria, *dau.* of Andrew Bredhall: and brother to Pte. 12362, W.H. Barrell, Middlesex Regt. attd. 96th Coy. Machine Gun Corps (Inf.), who fell during the fighting on the Somme, 6 February 1917: *b.* Tottenham, London, N., 1893: *educ.* Page Green School: enlisted at Mill Hill, N.W.7., 1912: mobilised on the outbreak of war, August 1914, joined 3rd Battn. on its return from India: served with the Expeditionary Force in France and Flanders from 19 January 1915, and was killed in action at the Second Battle of Ypres, 1 May 1915. Age 22. *unm.*

His brother William also has no known grave; he is commemorated on the Thiepval Memorial, Somme.

(Panel 49) Pte. 15157, Alfred Barton, 4th Bn. (77th Foot) The Duke of Cambridge's Own (Middlesex Regt.): *s.* of the late Henry Barton, by his wife Elizabeth, *dau.* of William Humphreys: *b.* Marylebone, 2 April 1896: *educ.* St. Mary Magdalene's School, Paddington: enlisted in November 1914: served with the Expeditionary Force from 10 April 1915, and was killed in action at Ypres, 19 July following. His comrades wrote that, as they were ordered to advance, a shell came over and killed him in his trench, death being instantaneous: 19 July 1915. Age 19.

(Panel 49) Pte. G/52439, John Richard Bate, 2nd Bn. (77th Foot) The Duke of Cambridge's Own (Middlesex Regt.): *s.* of Thomas Alfred Bate, Miner; of 29, Cresswell Street, Pogmoor, co. York, by his wife Elizabeth, *dau.* of Richard Long, of Barnsley: and brother to Pte. 263005, W. Bate, 1/5th York & Lancaster Regt., died No.2 C.C.S. Merville, 15 March 1917: *b.* Carlton, co. York, 1894: *educ.* South Kirby, nr. Wakefield: Occupation – Miner: served with the Expeditionary Force in France and Flanders, and was killed in action, 31 July 1917. Age 23. *unm.*

His brother Walter is buried in Merville Communal Cemetery Extension (I.B.22).

(Panel 49) Pte. G/14082, William Batt, 23rd (Service) Bn. (2nd Football) The Duke of Cambridge's Own (Middlesex Regt.): late of Hackney Wick, co Middlesex: *s.* of George Batt, of 81, Chapman Road, Victoria Park, Homerton: enlisted Shoreditch: Killed in action; shellfire, 7 June 1917. Age 19.

(Panel 49) Pte. L/12029, John Baumbach, 4th Bn. (77th Foot) The Duke of Cambridge's Own (Middlesex Regt.): 3rd *s.* of Frederick Baumbach, of 27, Retreat Place, Hackney, London, E., by his wife Amelia (*née* Finck): *b.* London, E., 24 November 1889: Occupation – Paint Grinder: volunteered and enlisted, 12 September 1914: served with the Expeditionary Force in France from the following November, and was killed in action, 20 July 1915. He *m.* at St. Paul's, Bow Common, London, E., Hannah Elizabeth (14, Knottisford Street, Green Street, Bethnal Green, London, E.), *dau.* of George William (& Hannah) Argent, and had a *dau.*, Dorothy Rose, *b.* 17 April 1914. Age 25. (*IWGC record Baumback*)

(Panel 49) Pte. G/1712, Harry Berridge, 3rd Bn. (77th Foot) The Duke of Cambridge's Own (Middlesex Regt.): served with the Expeditionary Force in France and Flanders from 19 January 1915. Killed in action, 2 May 1915.

(Panel 49) Pte. 1835, Henry Blake, 1/8th Bn. The Duke of Cambridge's Own (Middlesex Regt.), (T.F.): 2nd *s.* of David Blake, of Grange View, Chalfont St. Peter's, by his wife Maria, *dau.* of James Butcher: *b.* Chalfont St. Peter's, co. Bucks, 2 May 1892: *educ.* National School there: joined 8th Middlesex Territorials, September 1912: mobilised, 5 August 1914, and volunteered for Foreign Service: served Gibraltar, 3 September 1914–February 1915, and with the Expeditionary Force in France and Flanders, 8 March–26 April 1915, on which latter date he was killed in action at Zonnebeke during the Second Battle of Ypres. Age 22. *unm.* (*IWGC record TF/1835, 30 April 1915*)

(Panel 49) Pte. F/3525, John Brown, 4th Bn. (77th Foot) The Duke of Cambridge's Own (Middlesex Regt.): *s.* of John Brown, of Miles Cottages, Dargate, Herne Hill, co. Kent, by his wife Mary Ann: and elder brother to Pte. G/12990, F. Brown, 7th The Buffs (East Kent Regt.), killed in action, 18 November 1916, at the Somme: enlisted Faversham. Killed in action, 31 July 1917. Age 36. He was married to Hannah Brown (Forstall, Herne Hill).

His brother Frederick also has no known grave; he is commemorated on the Thiepval Memorial (Pier & Face 5D).

(Panel 49) Pte. G/5342, Thomas Edward Butcher, 3rd Bn. (77th Foot) The Duke of Cambridge's Own (Middlesex Regt.): *s.* of the late James Butcher, by his wife Jane (1, Balloon Yard, Blackfriars Street, Stamford, co. Lincoln): *b.* Stamford, 29 November 1894: *educ.* St. Martin's Boys' School: enlisted in January 1913: served with the Expeditionary Force in France, and died, 1 October 1915, of wounds received in action. Age 24. *unm.*

(Panel 49) Pte. L/13562, Joseph Butler, 'G' Coy., 3rd Bn. (77th Foot) The Duke of Cambridge's Own (Middlesex Regt.): *s.* of the late Joseph Butler, by his wife Emily J. (21, Priory Park Road, Sudbury): and brother to Pte. 8001, F. Butler, 19th (St. Pancras) Bn., London Regt., killed in action in France, 15 September 1916: *b.* Sudbury, co. Middlesex, 29 August 1887: *educ.* Board School: enlisted at Mill Hill, London, N.W., 1911: served in India, and with the Expeditionary Force in France, and was killed in action there, 12 February 1915. Buried where he fell at Ypres. Awarded 3rd Class Certificate of Education, 13 January 1913. Age 29. *unm.*

His brother Frederick also has no known grave; he is commemorated on the Thiepval Memorial, Somme.

(Panel 49) Pte. F/1808, Arthur Edward Clarke, 23rd (Service) Bn. (2nd Football) The Duke of Cambridge's Own (Middlesex Regt.): *s.* of Harry Clarke, of 41, Church Road, South Yardley, Birmingham, and his wife Mary: enlisted Aldershot, co. Hants. Killed at the Battle of Messines, 7 June 1917. Age 29.

(Panel 49) Pte. 2773, Walter Charles Cracknell, 1/8th Bn. The Duke of Cambridge's Own (Middlesex Regt.), (T.F.): late of Shepherd's Bush: *b.* Hammersmith: enlisted Stamford Brook. Killed in action, 25 April 1915. Remains recovered from a grave marked up as belonging to an 'Unknown British Soldier', (28.D.16.d.7.0); identified – Khaki, Titles, Boots size 8 mkd. MX2773; reinterred, registered 3 January 1929. *Buried in Sanctuary Wood Cemetery (V.B.36).*

PANEL 49 ENDS PTE. P.J. CRADDICK, MIDDLESEX REGT.

PANEL 51 BEGINS PTE. H.P. CRANE, MIDDLESEX REGT.

(Panel 51) Pte. S/6216, William Thomas Cutts, 3rd Bn. (77th Foot) The Duke of Cambridge's Own (Middlesex Regt.): eldest *s.* of James Cutts. of 27, King's Road, Wood Green, by his wife Eliza Jane: *b.* 19 January 1894: *educ.* Wood Green County Council School: enlisted in December 1910: served with the Expeditionary Force in France and Flanders from August 1914, and died at Ypres, 9 May 1915, from wounds received in action there. Buried south of Ypres. Sergt. J. Sitchell wrote, "On 9 May the Germans were attacking one of the positions our people held, and the 65th Brigade were called upon to defend this, and our regiment had to go to the south of Ypres, near the railway lines, and whilst coming along they shelled us terrible, and your brother got caught on the side of the head with a lump of shell; he died of the wound which he received." Age 21. *unm.*

(Panel 51) Pte. TF/2383, Elias Dear, 1/8th Bn. The Duke of Cambridge's Own (Middlesex Regt.), (T.F.): *s.* of Thomas Dear, of 312, High Street, Old Brentford, co. Middlesex, by his wife Ellen: served with the Expeditionary Force. Killed in action at Zonnebeke, 23 April 1915. Pte. Dear left a wife Emily, since deceased.

(Panel 51) Pte. G/70, John Fribbins, 4th Bn. (77th Foot) The Duke of Cambridge's Own (Middlesex Regt.): *s.* of the late George (& Emma) Fribbins: served with the Expeditionary Force. Killed in action, 29 December 1914. Age 40.

(Panel 51) Pte. G/34508, John Alfred Freeman, 23rd (Service) Bn. (2nd Football) The Duke of Cambridge's Own (Middlesex Regt.): *s.* of G. Freeman, of 57, Sidley Street, Bexhill-on-Sea, co. Sussex: enlisted Hastings. Killed in action, 7 June 1917; vicinity Damm Strasse.

(Panel 51) Pte. TF/1676, Frank Alexander Fuller, 1/8th Bn. The Duke of Cambridge's Own (Middlesex Regt.), (T.F.): 3rd *s.* of Alfred Fuller, Gardener; of 11, Laurel Villas, New Road, Bedfont, Middlesex, by his wife Belinda, *dau.* of William Bowden: and brother to Pte. 7681, F.A. Fuller, 1/8th Middlesex Regt., killed in action the same day; Pte. 1281, H. Fuller, 8th Royal Fusiliers, killed in action, 7 July 1916, at the Somme; and Pte. 10881, V. Fuller, Army Cyclist Corps transf'd (no.20586) 9th Royal Warwickshire Regt., killed in action, 14 September 1918, in Mesopotamia: *b.* Hoddesdon, co. Hertford, 4 January 1894: *educ.* Iver Heath, co. Buckingham: Occupation – Gardener: joined Middlesex Territorials 1912; volunteered for Foreign Service on the outbreak of war: proceeded to France in March 1915, and was killed in action at Zonnebeke in the fight for Hill 60, 26 April 1915. Age 21. Two other brothers also served – William, Bmdr., 55760, Royal Field Artillery, and James, Pte., 77739, Royal Horse Artillery. *unm.* One of four brothers who fell.

All three of his brothers have no known grave – Thomas is recorded below; Harry, Thiepval Memorial, Somme; Victor, Tehran Memorial (Panel 2.Col.2).

(Panel 51) Pte. 7681, Thomas Fuller, 1/8th Bn. The Duke of Cambridge's Own (Middlesex Regt.), (T.F.): *s.* of Alfred Fuller, Gardener; of 11, Laurel Villas, New Road, Bedfont, Middlesex, by his wife Belinda, *dau.* of William Bowden: and brother to Pte. TF/1676, F. Fuller, 1/8th Middlesex Regt., killed in action the same day; Pte. 1281, H. Fuller, 8th Royal Fusiliers, killed in action, 7 July 1916, at the Somme; and Pte. 10881, V. Fuller, Army Cyclist Corps transf'd (no.20586) 9th Royal Warwickshire

Regt., killed in action, 14 September 1918, in Mesopotamia: *b*. Hoddesdon, co. Herts, 27 October 1889: *educ*. Iver Heath, co. Buckingham: employee Metropolitan Railway: joined Middlesex Territorials 1912; volunteered for Foreign Service on the outbreak of war: proceeded to France in March 1915, and was killed in action at Zonnebeke in the fight for Hill 60, 26 April 1915. Age 25. Two other brothers also served –William, Bmdr., 55760, Royal Field Artillery, and James, Pte., 77739, Royal Horse Artillery. *unm*. One of four brothers who fell.

All three of his brothers have no known grave – Frank is recorded above; Harry, Thiepval Memorial, Somme; Victor, Tehran Memorial (Panel 2.Col.2).

(Panel 51) Pte. L/13539, Herbert Gallant, 3rd Bn. (77th Foot) The Duke of Cambridge's Own (Middlesex Regt.): *s*. of James Gallant, of 176, Arlington Road, Camden, London, by his wife Annie: *b*. Hackney: enlisted Mill Hill, London, N.W.7: served with the Expeditionary Force in France. Killed in action, 13 May 1915. Age 21. *unm*.

(Panel 51) Pte.TF/267259, John Alfred Gartside, 23rd (Service) Bn. (2nd Football) The Duke of Cambridge's Own (Middlesex Regt.): *s*. of Harry Gartside, of 37, Pembroke Street, Oldham, co. Lancaster: enlisted Ashton: served with the Expeditionary Force. Missing/believed killed, 27 July 1917, during heavy shelling of the battalion's staging area; Ridge Wood. Age 19.

(Panel 51) Pte. L/14276, George Edward Gladwell, 4th Bn. (77th Foot) The Duke of Cambridge's Own (Middlesex Regt.): *b*. Paddington, London, W.: enlisted Willesden, London, N.W.: served with the Expeditionary Force in France and Flanders. Reported 'missing in the No Man's Land between the Middlesex and enemy trenches 31 December 1914;' Pte. Gladwell's officer, 2nd Lieut. G.W. Hughes, was killed whilst trying to locate him.

2nd Lieut. Hughes is buried in Bailleul Communal Cemetery (F.4).

(Panel 51) Pte. F/3323, Rupert Elsie Goble, 23rd (Service) Bn. (2nd Football) The Duke of Cambridge's Own (Middlesex Regt.): *s*. of Elsie Goble, of Limden, Ticehurst, co. Sussex, by his wife Elizabeth Ann: enlisted Chichester. Killed in action at the Battle of Messines, locality Damm Strasse, 7 June 1917. Age 20.

(Panel 51) Pte. 235018, William Coleman Goosey, 7th Bn. The Duke of Cambridge's Own (Middlesex Regt.), (T.F.): *s*. of the late William Newman Goosey, Northamptonshire Regt., by his wife Naomi, *dau*. of William Coleman: *b*. Irchester, co. Northampton, 16 October 1893: *educ*. Council School there: enlisted 25 January 1917: served with the Expeditionary Force in France and Flanders from 31 May, and was killed in action, 31 July 1917. His Commanding Officer wrote, "He was very popular with his platoon, and a most excellent soldier, always cheerful and willing, and his loss will be felt by all." Age 25. He *m*. Wollaston, co. Northampton; Ada Harriett Elsom (formerly Goosey, 31, Orton Avenue, Woodston, Peterborough), *dau*. of William Bonham, and had two children – Mabel Ada, *b*. 4 April 1915; and William Raymond, *b*. 22 February 1917.

(Panel 51) Pte. L/12331, Henry John Griffiths, 3rd Bn. (77th Foot) The Duke of Cambridge's Own (Middlesex Regt.): *b*. St. Pancras: enlisted London: served with the Expeditionary Force in France from 19 January 1915. Killed in action nr. St. Julien, Ypres, 23 April 1915. See 2nd Lieut. F.A.H. Whitfield (Panel 49).

(Panel 51) Pte. F/1982, Frank Hack, 23rd (Service) Bn. (2nd Football) The Duke of Cambridge's Own (Middlesex Regt.): late of Redditch, co. Worcester. Killed by shellfire, 10 p.m. – midnight, 6–7 June 1917.

On 3 May 1915, after two days of concentrated artillery bombardment on 85th Brigade's positions around Gravenstafel and Zonnebeke, it was determined to withdraw the troops from this point of the salient and shorten the line. Not without difficulty the brigade retired to a new line on the Frezenberg Ridge where, on the morning of 8 May, after a heavy bombardment, the Germans delivered a powerful infantry attack before which the British troops were forced to give way. At 3.30 in the afternoon, 3rd Middlesex and four other battalions took part in a counter-attack which succeeded in pushing the enemy back as far as Frezenberg but, eventually the men were driven back once more, and, despite repeated attempts to advance, were held up on a line running north and south through Verlorenhoek. Pte. Baker, 3rd Middlesex, described the recapture of the lost trench – "Inch by inch we forged ahead. A Sergeant led us, and he kept singing all the time, 'Never say die, Middlesex.' Just as we thought the game was up, supports arrived, and we made a dash for the lost trench. We got it, and I simply could not believe what my eyes looked upon. Our chaps who had been killed in the trench seemed to be in all kinds of natural attitudes – they had been gassed. But, how we avenged them! Within an hour the Germans were at us again. The sight of the corpses of fallen chums gave us a sort of supernatural bravery, as the Germans found to their cost. They swooped down upon us, but we picked them off by the score. The Middlesex lads were quickly over the parapet, and, with fixed bayonets we did a Rugby rush into their columns. I must have been a lunatic for half-an-hour for I stuck my bayonet into anything I thought was a German. We won our position alright and it was a relief to go back and have forty winks, even in trenches where dead men were lying."

After this action the bombardment continued unabated for a further three days and when, on 12 May, the brigade went into Reserve, it had been 23 days in continuous action. During this time its losses had been extreme, only one Lieut. Col. Remained; most of the battalions were commanded by captains.

(Panel 51) Pte. G/7437, William Charles Hammerton, 3rd Bn. (77th Foot) The Duke of Cambridge's Own (Middlesex Regt.): *s.* of Henry Isaac Hammerton, of Twickenham, co. Middlesex, by his wife Ellen: enlisted Hounslow. One of 22 Other Ranks, 3rd Middlesex, killed in action, 8 May 1915. Age 36. He was married to Alice Emily Hammerton (14, The Embankment, Twickenham).

(Panel 51) Pte. SR/6238 Frank Reginald Harding, 4th Bn. (77th Foot) The Duke of Cambridge's Own (Middlesex Regt.): *s.* of Frank Harding, of 114, Harringay Road, London, N., by his wife Agnes: *b.* Kentish Town, London, N.W., 1895: enlisted Tottenham, London, N.: served with the Expeditionary Force in France, and was killed in action at Kemmel, 20 December 1914. Age 19.

(Panel 51) Pte. G/6870, William George Hatchard, 3rd Bn. (77th Foot) The Duke of Cambridge's Own (Middlesex Regt.): *s.* of William Charles Hatchard, of 42, De Morgan Road, Fulham, London, S.W.6, by his wife Ellen: and elder brother to Pte. 9398, B.C. Hatchard, 1st East Lancashire Regt., killed in action, 17 September 1914, in the retirement from Mons: *b.* Holborn: enlisted Mill Hill, London, N.W.7: served with the Expeditionary Force, and was killed in action, 13 May 1915. Age 31.

His brother Bertie is buried in Vauxbuin French National Cemetery (IV.B.5).

(Panel 51) Pte. G/5790, John Bleakley Holmes, 13th (Service) Bn. The Duke of Cambridge's Own (Middlesex Regt.): *b.* Radcliffe, co. Lancaster: enlisted Bury: served with the Expeditionary Force from late 1915, and was killed in action, 13 March 1916. Remains recovered from four graves marked as belonging to an 'Unknown British Soldier', located in Sanctuary Wood Old Cemetery (28.I.24.b.90.97), identified – Clothing, Titles; reinterred, registered 1 May 1928. Buried Near This Spot. (*IWGC record 13 March 1915*). *Buried in Sanctuary Wood Cemetery (II.F.14).*

(Panel 51) Pte. L/12672, Frederick George Hubbard, 3rd Bn. (77th Foot) The Duke of Cambridge's Own (Middlesex Regt.): eldest *s.* of Alfred Hubbard, of 257, New King's Road, Fulham, London, S.W., Corn Merchant, by his wife Lucy Jane, *dau.* of Enoch Henry Dews: *b.* Earl's Court, London, S.W., 10 March 1891: *educ.* Halford Road, Fulham; Ashburnham Road, Chelsea: enlisted June 1909: stationed at Aldershot for nearly two years during which he was one of the Special Guard outside Buckingham Palace at the funeral of the late King Edward, and in the same year, when King George visited Aldershot to inspect the troops, he was selected to guard His Majesty's House: went to India with his regiment in 1911: present at the Delhi Durbar; chosen to act as Bodyguard to H.M. King George V: returned to England after the outbreak of war, August 1914: went to France on 18 January 1915, and was killed at Ypres, 13 February following. Up until the time of his enlistment he was a scholar at Fulham Congregational Sunday School. Age 23. *unm.* (*IWGC record 15 February 1915*)

(Panel 51) Pte. L/14630, Albert Herbert Hunter, 4th Bn. (77th Foot) The Duke of Cambridge's Own (Middlesex Regt.): *s.* of Ross Hunter, of Wood Green, London, N.: served with the Expeditionary Force in Flanders. Killed in action at Kemmel, 28 December 1914.

(Panel 51) Pte. G/7125, George Jarrold, 12th (Service) Bn. The Duke of Cambridge's Own (Middlesex Regt.): *s.* of Mrs Jarrold (27, Tower Street, Westminster, London, W.C.2): *b.* Lambeth, London, S.E., 1899: enlisted Mill Hill, London, N.W.7, August 1914: served with the Expeditionary Force in France and Flanders from 26 July 1915. Killed in action at Ypres, 29 September following. Age 16.

(Panel 51) Pte. L/8105, James William Jennings, 4th Bn. (77th Foot) The Duke of Cambridge's Own (Middlesex Regt.): *b.* Norwood, co. Surrey: enlisted Hounslow, co. Middlesex. Killed in action at Kemmel, 15 December 1914, by shellfire. See Pte. W.T. Ardin (Panel 49).

(Panel 51) Pte. TF/201727, Joseph John Johnson, 4th Bn. (77th Foot) The Duke of Cambridge's Own (Middlesex Regt.): *b.* Tottenham, co. Middlesex, 1895: *educ.* there: enlisted Middlesex Regt., High Barnet, co. Hertford, 1914: served with the Expeditionary Force in France. Reported wounded and missing after the fighting, 31 July 1917; now assumed killed in action on or about that date. Age 21. *unm.*

(Panel 51) Pte. G/9390, Samuel Lixenfield, 4th Bn. (77th Foot) The Duke of Cambridge's Own (Middlesex Regt.): *s.* of James Lixenfield, of Plaistow, co. Essex, by his wife Rhoda: late *husb.* to Louisa Lixenfield: and brother to L/Corpl. 18048, E. Lixenfield, 13th Essex Regt., killed in action, 9 August 1916: *b.* Mile End: enlisted Canning Town. Killed during an artillery duel, night of 26–27 September 1915; Hooge sector, Ypres. Age 38. 2nd Lieut. R.P. Ochs, Pte. J.C. Elsdon and the battalion M.O. Capt. A.E. Bullock (stray bullet or shell fragment; battalion dumping ground) were also killed.

His brother Edgar is buried in Serre Road Cemetery No.2 (XVII.A.9). Pte. Elsdon is commemorated in Sanctuary Wood Cemetery (Sp.Mem.); 2nd Lieut. Ochs and Capt. Bullock are buried in Brandhoek Military Cemetery (I.B.25, I.A.25).

(Panel 51) Pte. G/9631, Frank Mills, 13th (Service) Bn. The Duke of Cambridge's Own (Middlesex Regt.): late of Northfleet, co. Kent: *s.* of Annie Mills (114, Upper Fant Road, Maidstone, co. Kent): *b.* Maidstone: enlisted Gravesend. Killed in action, 14 March 1916. Age 28. Remains recovered from four unmarked graves marked as belonging to an 'Unknown British Soldier. Middlesex Regt.', located in Sanctuary Wood Old Cemetery (28.I.24.b.90.97), identified – Clothing, Titles; reinterred, registered 1 May 1928. *Buried in Sanctuary Wood Cemetery (II.F.17).*

(Panel 51) Pte. TF/204497, Robert Mills, 23rd (Service) Bn. (2nd Football) The Duke of Cambridge's Own (Middlesex Regt.): *s.* of the late James Mills, by his wife Elizabeth (53, Bridge Street, Northampton): and late *husb.* to Emma Mills (28, Grafton Place, Northampton): *b.* Northampton Hospital, St. Giles. Killed by shellfire, 10 p.m. – midnight, 6–7 June 1917; vicinity Voormezeele Switch – Old French Trench. Age 30.

(Panel 51) Pte. G/6826, Charles Richard Munson, 3rd Bn. The Duke of Cambridge's Own (Middlesex Regt.): *s.* of Charles Arthur Munson, of 30, Aintree Street, Fulham, London, by his wife Ellen: and twin brother to Pte. 6380, A.E. Munson, 2nd East Surrey Regt., died of wounds, 30 September 1915: *b.* Fulham: enlisted Hammersmith. Killed in action, 30 April 1915, at Ypres. Age 21.

His brother Arthur is buried in Bethune Town Cemetery (IV.E.65).

(Panel 51) Pte. G/9963, Ben Stanley Nickolls, 13th (Service) Bn. The Duke of Cambridge's Own (Middlesex Regt.): 2nd *s.* of Benjamin Foster Nickolls, of 2, Dorset Road, South Tottenham, London, N., Member of the City Police, by his wife Margaret, *dau.* of Richard Rolfe: *b.* City Road, London, E.C., 12 September 1896: *educ.* Shoreditch, and Down Hills Higher Grade Schools: Occupation – Weighing Clerk: enlisted on 5 August 1914, the day after war was declared: served with the Expeditionary Force in France and Flanders from September 1915: wounded at Mametz Wood, Somme, August 1916, and was killed in action at Messines, Belgium, 10 June 1917. Age 20. *unm.*

(Panel 51) Pte. L/13473, Benjamin Thomas Ollard, 'D' Coy., 3rd Bn. (77th Foot) The Duke of Cambridge's Own (Middlesex Regt.): *s.* of Henry Ollard, of 9, Chester Road, Lower Edmonton, London, N.9, by his wife Amelia: and *yr.* brother to Pte. 3509, W.J. Ollard, 3rd Royal Fusiliers, who fell the same day: *b.* Edmonton: enlisted Mill Hill, London, N.W.7: Killed in action, 3 May 1915. Age 22. *unm.*

His brother William also has no known grave; he is recorded on Panel 6.

(Panel 51) Pte. SR/6558, Richard Henry Read, 4th Bn. (77th Foot) The Duke of Cambridge's Own (Middlesex Regt.): *s.* of Matilda Read (73, Bayham Street, Camden Town, London, N.W.1): *b.* Kentish Town, N.W.5: enlisted at Mill Hill, N.W.7: Killed in action, 15 December 1914. Age 21. See Pte. W.T. Ardin (Panel 49).

(Panel 51) Pte. L/13701, Charles Henry Revell, 'A' Coy., 3rd Bn. (77th Foot) The Duke of Cambridge's Own (Middlesex Regt.): *s.* of Louisa Revell (9A, Vine Street Buildings, Tooley Street, Bermondsey,

London): enlisted at Mill Hill, London, N.W.7, 29 July 1911. Killed in action near St. Julien, Ypres, 23 April 1915. Age 22. *unm*. See 2nd Lieut. F.A.H. Whitfield (Panel 49).

(Panel 51) Pte. SR/6503, George James Rose, 4th Bn. (77th Foot) The Duke of Cambridge's Own (Middlesex Regt.): *b*. Paddington, London, W.2: enlisted Willesden, N.W.: Killed in action, 15 December 1914, before Kemmel. See Pte. W.T. Ardin (Panel 49).

(Panel 51) Pte. 1795, Owen William Rose, 8th Bn. The Duke of Cambridge's Own (Middlesex Regt.),(T.F.): eldest *s*. of Pte. 12775, George Thomas Rose, 6th (Service) Battn. Bedfordshire Regt. (surv'd.), by his wife Mary (4, Du Burstow Terrace, Hanwell), *dau*. of George Mills, of Uxbridge, Middlesex: *b*. West Ealing, London, W., 6 October 1896: *educ*. St. Mark's Council School, Hanwell: Occupation – Roundsman; Messrs Sainsbury's: joined Middlesex Territorials, *c*.1912; volunteered for Foreign Service on the outbreak of war: mobilized Sittingbourne and went with his regiment to Gibraltar and while there shot a German prisoner who was trying to escape from a detention camp. The matter was the subject of an official enquiry and it was held that Rose had done no more than his duty. He afterwards accompanied the battalion to France and was killed in action at Zonnebeke, 30 April 1915. Age 17.

(Panel 51) Pte. G/24901, Charles Rumsey, 23rd (Service) Bn. (2nd Football) The Duke of Cambridge's Own (Middlesex Regt.): *s*. of Charles Rumsey, of 15, Windmill Grove, West Croydon, co. Surrey, and his wife Elizabeth: enlisted Kingston: Killed in action, battalion assembly area, Voormezeele Switch – Old French Trench, 6–7 June 1917. Age 19.

William Scotton enlisted in the Middlesex Regiment in July 1914 and, after a brief period of training, found himself with a number of reinforcements drafted to the 4th Battalion, which was serving in the Ypres Salient. Sometime after his arrival in the salient he went absent and, in December 1914, was convicted on the charge of being Absent Without Leave with a recommendation to leniency. Undeterred by the seriousness of his fate, should he further re-offend, on 23 January 1915 he repeated the offence after his platoon had been warned for the front line. Following his unit's return the next day he reported himself and was immediately placed under arrest. Within a week the young Private found himself stood before a Court Martial charged with desertion, and on this occasion there would be no leniency. Noted as being of weak character in a battalion where discipline was not all it should be, Scotton was duly found guilty and sentenced to death. In the early hours of 3 February 1915, William Scotton was executed at Vierstraat by a firing squad composed of one N.C.O. and seven men from his own unit; with the remainder of the unit in attendance to witness the event – *Pour Encourage Les Autres*.

(Panel 51) Pte. S/6922, William Scotton, 4th Bn. (77th Foot) The Duke of Cambridge's Own (Middlesex Regt.): *s*. of Catherine Scotton (52, Gladstone Road, Walton, Liverpool): and brother to Pte. 265397, A. Scotton, King's Liverpool Regt., killed in action, 18 September 1916: enlisted Liverpool, July 1914: Executed – Desertion, 3 February 1915. Age 19.

His brother Albert also has no known grave; he is commemorated on the Thiepval Memorial, Somme.

(Panel 51) Pte. G/22750, Robert George Shorter, 16th (Service) Bn. (Church Lads Brigade) The Duke of Cambridge's Own (Middlesex Regt.): *s*. of George Frederick Shorter, of 49, High Street, Highgate, London, N.6, by his wife Rachel: and brother to L/Corpl. L/9435, B.G. Shorter, Royal West Surrey Regt., killed on the Somme, 21 August 1916; and Pte. L/7175, P.A. Shorter, The Buffs, who fell at the First Battle of Ypres 1914: enlisted at Mill Hill, London, N.W.7: served with the Expeditionary Force in France and Flanders, and was killed in action, 12 August 1917. One of three brothers who fell.

His brother Bertie is buried in Delville Wood Cemetery (XXXII.K.10); Percival has no known grave, he is commemorated on the Ploegsteert Memorial (Panel 2).

(Panel 51) Pte. G/1463, Joseph Silk, 3rd Bn. (77th Foot) The Duke of Cambridge's Own (Middlesex Regt.): *s*. of James Silk, of 58, Canrobert Street, Bethnal Green, London, E.2, by his wife Mary: enlisted Victoria Park Square, London. Killed in action near St. Julien, Ypres, 23 April 1915. See 2nd Lieut. F.A.H. Whitfield (Panel 49).

(Panel 51) Pte. F/2304, Harold Frederick Snape, 23rd (Service) Bn. (2nd Football) The Duke of Cambridge's Own (Middlesex Regt.): *s*. of Nathaniel Snape, of 71, Ridgeway, Edgbaston, Birmingham: *b*. St. George's, Warwick: enlisted Aldershot. Killed by shellfire, 10 p.m. – midnight, 6–7 June 1917. Age 21.

(Panel 51) Pte. TF/203680, Fred Sparrow, 2nd Bn. (77th Foot) The Duke of Cambridge's Own (Middlesex Regt.): *s.* of G.T. Sparrow, by his wife Charlotte (6 Aylesbury Terrace, Lower Halling, Rochester, co. Kent): and elder brother to Pte. S/255296, A.L. Sparrow, Army Service Corps, died 29 August 1917, in Mesopotamia: enlisted Maidstone. Killed in action, 31 July 1917. Age 37. He was married to Alice Alma Coke, *née* Sparrow (4, Household Road, Tonbridge).

His brother Alfred is buried in Basra War Cemetery (I.B.3).

(Panel 51) Pte. TF/202109, Andrew Arthur David Spiers, 12th (Service) Bn. The Duke of Cambridge's Own (Middlesex Regt.): *s.* of Robert Spiers, of 81, Upper Thrift Street, Northampton, Police Sergeant (ret'd), by his wife Rose Anna, *dau.* of William Stuart Gardner: *b.* Northampton, 6 October 1890: *educ.* Vernon Terrace School: Occupation – Butcher: enlisted 7 March 1916: served with the Expeditionary Force in France and Flanders from 31 August following, and died on 8 August 1917, from wounds received in action. An officer wrote, "I was very sorry indeed to lose him, as he was one of my most reliable men, one who could be trusted and devoted to his duty." Age 26. *unm.*

(Panel 51) Pte. F/1546, William Frederick Stevens, 23rd (Service) Bn. (2nd Football) The Duke of Cambridge's Own (Middlesex Regt.): late of Islington, London, N.: *b.* St. Luke's, co. Middlesex. Killed by shellfire in the vicinity of Voormezeele Switch – Old French Trench, 10 p.m. – midnight, 6–7 June 1917.

(Panel 51) Pte. L/10547, John Steward, 4th Bn. (77th Foot) The Middlesex Regt.: *s.* of Mary Steward (16H, Whitecross Place, Finsbury Avenue, London, E.C.2): *b.* Borough, co. Surrey: enlisted London. Killed in action, 15 December. 1914. Age 30. See Pte. W.T. Ardin (Panel 49).

(Panel 51) Pte. L/12028, William Charles Stockdale, 3rd Bn. (77th Foot) The Duke of Cambridge's Own (Middlesex Regt): *s.* of Thomas (& Mrs) Stockdale, of 101, Ernest Street, Stepney, London, E.1: and elder brother to Pte. S/49936, T. Stockdale, 11th Cameron Highlanders, killed in action, 17 August 1918: *b.* Stepney: enlisted Stratford. Killed in action at the 2nd Battle of Ypres, 2 May 1915. Age 26. *unm.*

His brother Thomas is buried in Nieppe-Bois (Rue-Du-Bois) British Cemetery, Vieux-Berquin (A.13).

(Panel 51) Pte. TF/200689, William James Thompson, 23rd (Service) Bn. (2nd Football) The Duke of Cambridge's Own (Middlesex Regt.): *s.* of Albert Thomson, of 62A, Loreno Road, White Hart Lane, Tottenham, London, N.: enlisted Hornsey, N.8: served with the Expeditionary Force. Missing/believed killed, 27 July 1917, during heavy shelling of the battalion's staging area, Ridge Wood. Age 19.

(Panel 51) Pte. 235040, Albert Varcoe, 12th (Service) Bn. The Duke of Cambridge's Own (Middlesex Regt.): *s.* of Albert John Varcoe, of 'Carpalla,' Foxhole, St. Austell, co. Cornwall, by his wife Mary Ann, *dau.* of the late William Trethewey: *b.* Redruth, 18 October 1893: *educ.* St. Stephen's School, St. Austell: Occupation – Clay Labourer: enlisted 4 October 1916: served with the Expeditionary Force in France and Flanders from 10 June 1917, and was killed in action near Stirling Castle, Ypres, 31 July following. Buried at Ypres. Age 23. His Commanding Officer wrote, "He was very popular in his platoon, and a most excellent soldier, and his loss will be felt by us all." He *m.* St. Austell; Millicent ('Carclaze,' nr. St. Austell) now Mrs Trudigian, of Tregonissey Lane End, St. Austell, *dau.* of Thomas Geach, and had a son Jack, *b.* 3 June 1913.

(Panel 51) Pte. TF/202571, William Henry Waymark, 7th Bn. The Duke of Cambridge's Own (Middlesex Regt.), (T.F.): *s.* of the late William Henry Waymark, of Bridge Street, Leatherhead, co. Surrey, by his wife Elizabeth 'Eliza' Jane ('North View,' Lea Road, Harpenden, co. Hertford), *dau.* of the late John Whaley, formerly Agent, Coanwood Colliery: *b.* Southend-on-Sea, co. Essex, 24 July 1897: *educ.* Dulwich and Leatherhead: Occupation – Clerk, Chartered Accountant's Office, London: joined Middlesex Regt. May 1916: served with the Expeditionary Force in France and Flanders from November following: returned home in January 1917, suffering from frost-bite; returned to France the following May and was killed in action north-east of Ypres, 3 August 1917. Buried where he fell. Age 20. *unm.* (*IWGC record 12th Bn.*)

(Panel 51) Pte. F/1542, George Henry Wensley, 23rd (Service) Bn. (2nd Football) The Duke of Cambridge's Own (Middlesex Regt.): late of King's Cross, London, N.: *b.* Portishead, co. Somerset. Killed by shellfire, vicinity Voormezeele Switch, 10 p.m. – midnight, 6–7 June 1917.

(Panel 51) Pte. G/4525, James White, 13th (Service) Bn. The Duke of Cambridge's Own (Middlesex Regt.): *s.* of Thomas White, of Alhampton, Ditcheat, co. Somerset, by his wife Lucy: *b.* Carton Denham, co. Somerset: enlisted Swansea. Killed in action, 14 March 1916. Age 26. *unm.* Remains recovered from a grave marked up as belonging to an 'Unknown British Soldier', located in Sanctuary Wood Old Cemetery (28.I.24.b.90.97), identified – Clothing; reinterred, registered 1 May 1928. *Buried in Sanctuary Wood Cemetery (II.F.15).*

(Panel 51) Pte. 24894, Albert William G. Whittington, 23rd (Service) Bn. (2nd Football) The Duke of Cambridge's Own (Middlesex Regt.): *s.* of Mrs J. Whittington (The Studio, Cantelupe Road, East Grinstead, co. Sussex): *b.* Arundel. Killed in action on the night of 6–7 June 1917, by shellfire. Age 18.

(Panel 51) Lieut.Col. Charles Slingsby Chaplin, Comdg. 9th (Service) Bn. The King's Royal Rifle Corps: *s.* of the late Clifford Waterman Chaplin, of Burrough Hill, Melton Mowbray, co. Leicester, J.P., by his wife Rosa, *dau.* of William Chaplin, M.P.: *b.* Norfolk Square, Hyde Park, London, 31 May 1863: *educ.* Eton and Pembroke College, Oxford: joined City of London Regt. May 1885, from the Militia; transf'd. "Green Jackets" same month; gazetted Capt. King's Royal Rifles 1894: served with the Chitral Force under General Low (medal with clasp): and in the South African war as Special Service Officer for Mounted Infantry: and later, from August 1901, in command of 1st Regt. Mounted Infantry, doing excellent work in the Transvaal and the line of the Orange River (Mentioned in Despatches; Medal, five clasps): obtained his Majority in 1903, posted 2nd King's Royal Rifles; Gharial, Punjab: succeeded to the command of 3rd Battn. 18 March 1908, at Crete, and later took the battn. to Malta, afterwards returning to India and serving at Umballa. From half-pay in 1912 he retired, and was placed in the Reserve of Officers, being at the top of the list when mobilisation took place, and was one of the big batch of officers who were given command on 19 August 1914. He was killed in action after a 12 hours' fight, when he and his men had just captured a trench, being shot through the head at Hooge, in Flanders, at 3.30 p.m. 30 July 1915. He was buried at Chateau Hooge, close to where he fell. The following telegram was sent to the 9th Service Bn. from Headquarters, 2nd Army, at 1 p.m, 31 July 1915 – "The Army Corps Commander wishes to convey to the officers and men of the 9th Battn. King's Royal Rifles his appreciation of the way in which they carried out the attack on the trenches north of the Menin Road yesterday afternoon, and maintained themselves under heavy artillery fire." Age 52. Lieut.-Col. Chaplin *m.* Bombay, India, 29 September 1905; Gwladys Hamilton (Erbistock House, Ruabon), *dau.* of Col. Stanley Creek, late Royal Welsh Fusiliers, and had three *s.* and a *dau.* – Clifford, *b.* 23 September 1906; Nigel Gilbert Forbes, *b.* 9 January 1908; Patrick Slingsby, *b.* 4 July 1910; and Zara, *b.* 18 March 1914.

(Panel 51) Capt. Cyril Francis Hawley, 2nd Bn. (60th Foot) The King's Royal Rifle Corps: *s.* of the late Sir Henry Michael Hawley, 5th Bart., of Leybourne Grange, co. Kent, by his wife Lady Frances Charlotte Hawley (23, Albany Villa, Hove, co. Sussex), 2nd *dau.* of the late John Wingfield-Stratford, of Addington park, co. Kent: and brother to the present Baronet: *b.* 24 June 1878: *educ.* Malvern College (No.5, 1892–94), Army Side: gazetted 2nd Lieut. King's Royal Rifle Corps from the Militia, 25 February 1899: promoted Lieut. 23 February 1900: took part in the South African War, being present at operations in Natal, 1899, including actions at Elandslaagte, Rietfontein, and Lombard's Kop: the defence of Ladysmith, including the action of 6 January 1900: in Natal, the Transvaal (east of Pretoria), including actions at Belfast and Lydenberg; in the Transvaal, November 1900–May 1902: Orange River Colony and Cape Colony, 1901–1902; Mentioned in Despatches (*London Gazette*, 10 September 1901; Queen's Medal, six clasps; King's Medal, two clasps): promoted Capt. 23 November 1905. In the Great War Capt. Hawley was acting as a General Staff Officer, 3rd Grade, which appointment he received on 5 August 1914, and was killed in action nr. Ypres, 2 November following. Age 36. He *m.* 10 July 1912; Ursula Mary (14, Stafford Place, Buckingham Gate, London, S.W.), *dau.* of Henry Percy St. John, of Three Gables, Camberley, co. Surrey.

(Panel 51) Capt. John Francis Brice Pearse, 3rd Bn. (60th Foot) The King's Royal Rifle Corps: elder *s.* of the late Edward Brice Pearse, by his wife Frances Elinor (34, Egerton Gardens, Chelsea, London, S.W.): *b.* 53, Lower Belgrave Street, Eaton Square, London, 21 March 1883: *educ.* Farnborough School; Winchester College, and Royal Military College, Sandhurst: gazetted 2nd Lieut. King's Royal Rifle

Corps, May 1904: promoted Lieut. January 1908; Capt. November 1914: served with his regiment in Bermuda, the Mediterranean, and India, whence he returned in November 1914: went to the Front in Flanders December 1914: apptd. to Staff, April 1915, and was killed by a high-explosive shell on the 29th of that month, at St. Julien, during the Second Battle of Ypres. He was a member of the Army & Navy Club, and in India (1912) he played regimental polo. Killed in action, 29 April 1915. Age 32. *unm.*

(Panel 51) Capt. George Culme-Seymour, King's Royal Rifle Corps, attd. Adjt. 1/9th (County of London) Bn. (Queen Victoria's Rifles) The London Regt. (T.F.): *yst. s.* of Admiral Sir Michael Culme-Seymour, 3rd Bart., G.C.B., by his wife Lady Culme-Seymour: *b.* 8 March 1878: *educ.* Wellington College: gazetted 2nd Lieut., King's Royal Rifle Corps, from the Militia, October 1899: promoted Lieut. November 1900; Capt. March 1906: served in the South African War, 1899–1900: took part in the relief of Ladysmith, being present at the Battle of Colenso, the action at Vaal Kraans, operations on the Tugela Heights, and at Pieter's Hill: subsequently served with 2nd Battn. in northern Natal, being present at the Battle of Laing's Nek: Queen's Medal, five clasps: also served in India, Ceylon, Malta, at home, and with the Expeditionary Force in France from November 1914: apptd. Adjutant, Queen Victoria's Rifles, January 1914, with whom he was serving at the time of his death. In the early morning of 7 May 1915, part of Queen Victoria's Rifles were ordered up to support a battalion in the front line on Hill 60. Capt. Culme-Seymour went on ahead to find out the state of affairs, and as there was some confusion and want of knowledge as to the position of the enemy's advanced troops, he at once went forward to try to locate them, and was killed while trying to carry out this reconnaissance. Age 37. He was Mentioned in Sir John (now Lord) French's Despatch, 31 May 1915. He *m.*, December 1909, Janet Beatrix, *dau.* of the late Charles Lindsay Orr-Ewing, M.P., of Dunskey, Portpatrick, and left two children. After the cessation of hostilities his widow re-married, to the Rev. Geoffrey H. Woolley, V.C, M.C., late Capt., Queen Victoria's Rifles, of The Rectory, Monk Sherborne, Basingstoke, co. Hants. He was awarded his Victoria Cross (*London Gazette*, 22 May 1915): 'For most conspicuous bravery on Hill 60 during the night of 20–21 April 1915. Although the only officer on the hill at the time, and with very few men, he successfully resisted all attacks on his trench, and continued throwing bombs and encouraging his men until relieved. His trench during all this time was being heavily shelled and bombed, and was subjected to heavy machine gun fire by the enemy.'

(Panel 51) Capt. John Spottiswoode, 6th (Reserve) attd. 2nd Bn. (60th Foot) The King's Royal Rifle Corps: *s.* of George Andrew Spottiswoode, by his wife Grace Frances, elder *dau.* of the Rev. Sir St. Vincent Love Hammick: and nephew of William Spottiswoode, President of the Royal Society, 1876–83, President of the London Mathematical Society, 1870–72, and the British Association, 1878: *b.* London, 18 April 1874: *educ.* Winchester College, and the Royal Military College, Sandhurst, where he obtained the highest ever marks for Physics, *viz.*, 1,764 (88.4% of maximum) in the entrance examination, 1892: joined 2nd King's Royal Rifle Corps, 2nd Lieut. October 1894; promoted Lieut. January 1898: apptd. Capt. 7th Battn. May 1899, at which time he was serving in the South African Campaign with the Mounted Infantry; twice wounded: granted honorary rank of Capt. in the Army, October 1900, but retired the following year. On the outbreak of war with Germany, joined 6th K.R.R.C., August 1914; proceeded to France with a draft of reinforcements, joined 2nd Battn. 5 September 1914; took part in the retirement from Mons and subsequent fighting at the Battle of the Aisne. Reported wounded and missing, since confirmed killed in action at the head of his company, 31 October 1914, at Gheluvelt, in the First Battle of Ypres. His body was not recovered. Age 40. Distinguished in Radio-telegraphy, he *m.* Sybil Gwendolen Aitken, *née* Spottiswoode (2, Sion Hill Place, Bath), *dau.* of Dr. Christian David Ginsburg, LL.D., J.P., and left two sons – Raymond John, *b.* 1913, and Nigel Lawrence, *b.* (posthumously) 1915.

(Panel 51) Capt. Frederick Herman Tate, 10th (Service) Bn. The King's Royal Rifle Corps: *s.* of the late William Jacob Tate, I.C.S., by his wife Julie Marie (76, Queensborough Terrace, Hyde Park, London, W.): and brother to Lieut. W.L. Tate, 3rd Royal Fusiliers, killed in action, 13 March 1915: *b.* 1895: *educ.* Old Ride School, Bournemouth; Cheltenham College (Scholar); and New College, Oxford. Killed in action, 11 August 1917. Age 22. *unm.* For gallant service in the Great War, Capt. Tate was Mentioned in Despatches by F.M. Sir John (now Lord) French.

His brother William is buried in Kemmel Chateau Military Cemetery (X.7).

(Panel 51) Lieut. Audley Delves Thursby (Temp.Capt.), 3rd Bn. (60th Foot) The King's Royal Rifle Corps: only *s*. of Neville Thursby, of Harlestone, Northampton: *b*. 16, Queen Street, Mayfair, London, W.: *educ*. Farnborough School; Eton; Cheltenham, and Royal Military College, Sandhurst: gazetted 2nd Lieut. King's Royal Rifle Corps, 1908, joining his battalion at Crete; served in Malta and India: promoted Lieut. July 1911: promoted Temp. (supernumerary) Capt. December 1914: served with the British Expeditionary Force in France, and was killed while acting as a guide in a night attack to retake trenches at St. Eloi, Flanders, 15 February 1915. The following memoir appeared in *The Field*, 20 February 1915 – "Capt. Thursby was well known in the world of sport, more especially as far as military races are concerned. Of him it was once remarked in *The Pioneer* – 'I thought I was coming to the Quetta races, but I have made a mistake, and attended Thursby's benefit instead.'" These words are written in connection with the Quetta Meeting, 19 September 1912, when on the second day Mr Thursby rode in six of the seven races on the card and won them all. Previously he had scored eight wins in twenty-two mounts at Malta, and in the following season (at the same place) eighteen wins in forty-two mounts. He headed the amateur riders in the matter of average while he was in India, and had it not been that he was so long on Foreign Service he would doubtless have made a big mark as a race rider in this country. As an athlete, too, Capt. Thursby held no mean place, and in the Malta Garrison Marathon, 1909, he was eleventh man home in a field of 700, his own Battalion (of which he was trainer) taking second honours in the team competition. In the following year the Battalion won first place, and Capt. Thursby was the first officer home, and in the same year the Battalion was first in polo, cricket, football, and gymnastics, Capt. Thursby being one of its representatives in each event. *unm*.

(Panel 51) Capt. Richard Selby Durnford, 'D' Coy., 9th (Service) Bn. The King's Royal Rifle Corps: eldest *s*. of Richard Durnford, C.B., former Private Secretary to the Duke of Richmond; of Hartley Wespall, co. Hants, by his wife Beatrice Mary, *née* Selby: *gdson*. to Bishop Durnford: and brother to Capt. R.C. Durnford, D.S.O., Hampshire Regt., killed in action, 21 June 1918, in Persia: *b*. St. Paul's, London, October 1885: *educ*. Eton (H.Brinton's House), O.T.C. member; King's College, Cambridge: Occupation – Assistant Master, Lancing College (1909), Eton College: commissioned 2nd Lieut., O.T.C., 16 April 1910; Capt. 22 May 1912: volunteered and enlisted following the outbreak of war; gazetted Temp. Capt., K.R.R.C., 1 October 1914: served with the Expeditionary Force in France from May 1915, and was killed in action at Hooge, 31 July 1915. "At 3.20am on the morning of the 30th of July 1915 the Germans attacked the British lines at Hooge in the Ypres Salient using a new weapon, that of "liquid fire." At noon that day the 9th Battalion King's Royal Rifle Corps were assembled in trenches just to the south of the Menin Road for an attack which had been planned, to recover those trenches which had been lost during the morning's fighting. A covering barrage on the German positions was ordered which lifted at 2.45 p.m. when the 9th King's Royal Rifles went forward, led by their bombers under Lieut. H.S. Richmond. They were followed by 'B' Coy. (Capt. Tanqueray) and 'D' Coy. (Capt. Durnford) who rushed across the 200 yards of no man's land to the German positions which they carried at the point of the bayonet. Once in the trench a bombing battle took place and many casualties suffered from enemy rifle and machine gun fire. The arrival of A Company who had been in reserve enabled the captured positions to be consolidated. In the early morning of the 31st the Germans fired a short but intense artillery barrage on the captured trenches followed by an infantry attack in an attempt to recover them. In driving off this enemy attack Capt. Durnford was killed."

His brother Robert is buried in Tehran War Cemetery (II.F.8).

(Panel 51) Capt. Joseph Weston (served as Ernest Cruikshanks), 14th (Reserve) Bn. attd. 9th (Service) Bn. The King's Royal Rifle Corps: *s*. of Clara Weston (77, Woodstock Road, Bedford Park, Chiswick, London): previously served as Policeman, Bombay Force; present at the Delhi Durbar (Medal); also served as Signaller, H.M.S. 'Asia,' Hong Kong: gazetted King's Royal Rifle Corps, January 1915. Killed in action, 17 October 1915. Age 30.

(Panel 51) Lieut. the Hon. William Alfred Morton Eden, 4th Bn. (60th Foot) The King's Royal Rifle Corps: eldest *s*. & heir of 5th Baron Auckland, and Lady Auckland, *dau*. of Col. G.M. Hutton, C.B., of

Gate Burton, Lincoln: related to Lieut.General Sir Edward Hutton, K.C.B., K.C.M.G., Col.Commdt. K.R.R.C.: *b.* 15 June 1892: *educ.* E.P. Baily's School, Limpsfield, co. Surrey, and Eton College (R.S. De Haviland's House): gazetted 2nd Lieut. King's Royal Rifle Corps, January 1914; promoted Lieut. November 1914: served with the Expeditionary Force in France and Flanders, and was reported missing after an attack on the German trenches on the night of 1–2 March 1915. As no further information has been received of him, his death is presumed to have occurred in the attack at St. Eloi on 1st March. Leave to presume his death on or since 1–2 March 1915 was granted in the Probate Court, May 1916. At the time of his death Mr Eden was the 50th heir to a peerage to have lost his life in the war; he was succeeded to the peerage by his brother, Frederick Colvin George. He was keen on sports and games, particularly hunting, shooting, hawking, rowing, football, and golf. Age 22. *unm.*

(Panel 51) Lieut. Ambrose Constantine Ionides, 15th (Reserve) Bn. attd. 9th (Service) Bn. The King's Royal Rifle Corps: late of Rowbarns Grange, East Horsley, co. Surrey: 2nd *s.* of Alexander Ionides, of 1, Holland Park, London, Consul-General (Greece), by his wife Isabella ('The Homewood,' Esher, co. Surrey), *dau.* of P. Sechiari: *b.* Holland Park, 9 April 1878: *educ.* Dunchurch and Eton College: Member, London Stock Exchange: joined Inns of Court O.T.C. on the outbreak of war: gazetted Temp. Lieut. King's Royal Rifle Corps, 5 January 1915; went to France on 5 August following, being there attd. 9th Battn., and was killed in action, 16 October 1915, between Ypres and Hooge. He had volunteered to go with a party to erect wire in front of the trench in the early morning. There was a thick mist at the time, which later lifted suddenly. He at once ordered his men to lie down, but before he could do so himself he was seen and shot by the enemy. Buried behind the trenches where he fell. A comrade said that he was exceedingly liked by his brother officers and men, who would have followed him anywhere. His bright cheery disposition, as well as his thoughtfulness for others, endeared him to all who knew him. Age 37. He *m.* at the Greek Church, London, W., 29 July 1911; Euphrosyne 'Effie' ('The Cottage,' Carlisle Road, Eastbourne), *dau.* of the late Demetrius Michael Spartali, and had two children – Denis, *b.* 23 May 1912; and Irene, *b.* 6 September 1914.

(Panel 51) Lieut. Harry Noel Leslie Renton, 9th (Service) Bn. The King's Royal Rifle Corps: 2nd *s.* of James Henry Renton, of Aspley Guise, co. Beds, formerly of Colombo, Ceylon, F.R.C.I.: *b.* Colombo, Ceylon, 18 December 1894: *educ.* The Knoll, Aspley Heath, Woburn Sands (Rev. F.F. Hort); and Harrow School, matriculated Magdalen College, Oxford (April 1913); was to have entered into residence (October 1914), but, on the outbreak of war in August 1914, he obtained a commission, Kings Royal Rifle Corps, 23 September 1914: promoted Lieut. 13 February 1915: went to France on 20 May, and was killed in action near Hooge, 30 July 1915, during the capture of a German trench. Buried there. Major Hennessy, of the 9th Battn., wrote, "I think you know what affection I had for your son, and the high esteem in which I held him. He was a real soldier through and through, absolutely fearless, painstaking, trustworthy, and his men loved him. He was my right hand in everything, and however difficult the task set him I could always be absolutely sure he would see it through all right;" and Capt. Young, "All through the day Noel behaved with the greatest coolness, and I do not know what we should have done without him, as there were only three of us. He never paid the slightest attention to danger, and he was tremendously pleased when I ordered the charge; not only his own platoon but the whole company were devoted to him, and would have followed him anywhere – as they did. As you know, he and I were great friends since last September, and there is nothing I can say except how fond we all were of him, and that he died as well as a man could." At Harrow he was a Monitor of the School, head of his house; house cricket and football captain, and a member of the Harrow XI for which he kept wicket in 1914, and in the match with Eton played a very useful innings of 28 not-out. Age 20. *unm.*

(Panel 51) Lieut. Sidney Henry Snelgrove, 14th (Reserve) Bn. attd. 7th (Service) Bn. The King's Royal Rifle Corps: *yr. s.* of John Sidney Snelgrove, of 'The Plottage,' Forest Row, formerly of Kingswood, Tunbridge Wells, Barrister-at-Law, by his wife Gertrude Emily, *dau.* of the late John Henry Chatteris: *b.* Tunbridge Wells, 7 December 1891: *educ.* Hurstleigh, Tunbridge Wells; Rugby (Mr Brooke's House), and Trinity College, Cambridge: gazetted 2nd Lieut. 14th King's Royal Rifle Corps, 21 November 1914; promoted Lieut. 2 February 1915, attd. 7th King's Royal Rifle Corps; went to France, 16 July following, and was killed in action, 31 July 1915 while leading his platoon under heavy shell fire in support of another company in the attack at the Chateau Hooge. Buried in Sanctuary Wood, south of Hooge. Age 23. *unm*. Lieut.Col. G.A.P. Rennie, D.S.O., Commanding 7th King's Royal Rifle Corps wrote, "He was leading his men splendidly at the time." And Lieut.Col. Sir Thomas Milborne-Swinnerton-Pilkington Bart., Commanding 14th King's Royal Rifle Corps, "…one of my smartest officers. I was quite sure he would distinguish himself when he was sent to the Front." Letters from other officers and men all speak in the highest terms of his courage, energy and great capability. At Hurstleigh he was head of the School and captain of the cricket and the hockey elevens; at Rugby he was in his House eleven, and a Signaller in the O.T.C. "His elder brother, Capt. John Sidney Norman Snelgrove, Royal West Kent Regt., is now (1916) on active service."

(Panel 51) Lieut. Roger Wentworth Watson, 'C' Coy., 8th (Service) Bn. The King's Royal Rifle Corps: 2nd *s*. of Edith Deverell Watson, *dau*. of William Latham (Upland Cottage, Kingsley Green, Haslemere, co. Surrey), and the late John Williams Watson (Mark's Barn, Crewkerne; thereafter 33, Avonmore Road, Kensington, London): *educ*. Horris Hill, London; Winchester College (Mr Bather's House, 'Turners,'), Snr. Commoner Prefect (1911–12), played Association Football, member Second XI Cricket team; King's College, Cambridge, where he studied Literature, having ambitions to become a writer: volunteered and enlisted following the outbreak of war; obtained a commission, 2nd Lieut. King's Royal Rifle Corps; promoted Lieut. March 1915: proceeded to France, 18 May 1915; moved up to Sanctuary Wood, Hooge sector, 23 July, and was killed in action there on the 30th (July 1915). The circumstances being, at about midnight on 29 July, the 8th K.R.R.C. were relieved by 8th Rifle Brigade, and came out of the line and made their way out towards Ypres with Lieut. Watson's company going into dug-outs in the vicinity of White House, St. Jean. At 3.15 a.m. (30 July) the site of what remained of the stables – Chateau Hooge – were suddenly brightly illuminated by an explosion of 'liquid flame' pouring from the German trenches in close proximity thereabouts; each 'cloud' of flame covering an area of approximately 100 feet. 8th Rifle Brigade retreated/withdrew to nearby Zouave Wood where they were joined shortly thereafter by 8th K.R.R.C., hurriedly recalled, with orders to prepare for a counter-attack to recover trenches lost in this, the first flamethrower attack, against the British positions. However, instead of taking advantage of their initial success, the Germans spent the remainder of the morning and early afternoon consolidating the positions they had gained. A counter-attack launched at around 3 p.m. was met with devastating machine-gun fire and, within less than 45 minutes, had to be abandoned; 8th K.R.R.C. being cut down before they had advanced within yards of the edge of Zouvae Wood. The War Diary records, "The losses had been very heavy, including Capt. W.J. Davis the adjutant and Lieut. Watson killed and eight officers wounded…The medical arrangements were entirely inadequate. Dr. Hawkes having been killed, only one doctor was available to cope with over five hundred cases. Great difficulties were experienced in finding and collecting the wounded in the thick woods, and when found in bringing them to dressing station. It being impossible to bring ambulances within nine hundred yards of the first aid station, many men had to remain out, exposed for over twenty-four hours. This – coupled with the fact that the battalion had had no rations for thirty-six hours, and suffered from want of water – caused the loss of many fine riflemen who might have been saved." Age 21. *unm*. Remains recovered from a grave marked as belonging to an 'Unknown British Officer', located in a small battle cemetery at Sanctuary Wood, identified – Officer's Tunic, Handkerchief, mkd. 'W.W.'; reinterred, registered 28 February 1928. *Buried in Sanctuary Wood Cemetery (II.D.2)*.

The Happy Warrior

(Panel 51) 2nd Lieut. Charles Alexander Kenneth Anderson, 'C' Coy., 1st Bn. (60th Foot) The King's Royal Rifle Corps, attd. 1st Bn. Royal Scots Fusiliers: only *s*. of Alexander Richard Anderson, F.R.C.S. of Nottingham, by his wife Edith, *dau*. of the late C.E. Tuck, J.P., co, Norfolk, and *gdson*. of the late Col. Richard Anderson, H.M. 56th Regt.: *b*. Nottingham, 31 May 1893: *educ*. Harrow (1907–11); Pembroke College, Cambridge: gazetted – University Candidate – 1st Royal Scots Fusiliers, 4 August 1914; subsequently gazetted 2nd Lieut. King's Royal Rifle Corps, 14 August 1914, but having already left for France with the

Royal Scots Fusiliers he remained attached to that regt. throughout the campaign: took part in the Battles of Mons, the Marne, the Aisne, and lastly on the Franco-Belgian frontier in the First Battle of Ypres. Killed in action about 3 a.m., 12 November 1914, while leading his men in a night attack on the German trenches nr. Chateau Herenthage, on the Ypres-Menin Road, being at the time in command of half 'C' Coy., 1st Royal Scots Fusiliers. He was a member of the University Pitt Club, Cambridge. Age 21. *unm.*

(Panel 51) 2nd Lieut. Reginald 'Rex' Brandt Arnell, 7th (Service) Bn. The King's Royal Rifle Corps: *s.* of William T. Arnell, Merchant Miller (Flour); of 'Whitecliff,' Carter Street, Sandown, Isle of Wight, by his wife Henrietta, *née* Gibbings: *b.* Sandown, 15 October 1893: *educ.* Berkhampstead School (Capt. Cricket and Football); Exter College, Oxford (O.T.C. member): volunteered on the outbreak of war, given a commission (*London Gazette*, 25 August 1914) 2nd Lieut. 7th K.R.R.C., proceeded to France, May 1915: wounded 5 July (slight), rejoined battalion on the 25th., and was killed in action six days later, 30 July 1915, at Hooge. Age 21. Lieut.Col. A.P. Rennie wrote, "It is with the greatest grief I have to tell you that your son was killed in action on the 30th ult. while leading his men in a counter-attack on the Germans. He was hit in two places and died very soon without any pain. It was a noble death in a great cause ... He was an excellent soldier and a great friend of all, and his loss is a great one both to the regiment as a soldier and to all of us as a friend. I can only offer you my deepest sympathy in your great loss, and I hope it may be some consolation to you to know that he died nobly doing his duty."

(Panel 51) 2nd Lieut. Frederick Athelstan Fanshawe Baines, 4th Bn. (60th Foot) The King's Royal Rifle Corps: only *s.* of Athelstan Arthur Baines, of 'The Old Rectory,' Westmeston, Hassocks, co. Sussex, by his wife Katherine Mary: *b.* Hove, 2 February 1896: *educ.* Winchester, obtained a scholarship (1909), Prefect and O.T.C. Platoon Commander: left Winchester, October 1914 – on his Headmaster's nomination – for Sandhurst, where he became Senior Sergeant of his Company: gazetted 2nd Lieut. King's Royal Rifle Corps, February 1915: joined 6th Battn. Sheerness, on attachment, 17th of that month: left for France, 18th May: joined 4th Battn. in Flanders on the Sunday afternoon, 23rd May, and was killed in the early morning of the following Tuesday, 25th May, leading his men in a counter-attack on the trenches at Bellewaarde Wood, nr. Ypres. A brother officer wrote, "Your boy behaved splendidly. He was quite cool under the most trying circumstances, encouraging his men and helping all by his example ... He seemed to have one idea, and that was to get on." Age 19.

(Panel 51) 2nd Lieut. Ninian Mark Kerr Bertie, 4th Bn. (60th Regt. of Foot) The King's Royal Rifle Corps: 4th & *yst. s.* of Rev. the Hon. Alberic Edward Bertie, M.A., Rector of Gedling, co. Nottingham, by his wife. Lady Caroline Elizabeth, *née* McDonnell, eldest *dau.* of Mark, 5th Earl of Antrim, and *gdson.* of Montagu, 6th Earl of Abingdon: *b.* Rutland Gate, London, 19 November 1896: *educ.* Evelyns and Winchester College: admitted Royal Military College, Sandhurst, on the outbreak of war, from whence he was posted 60th Rifles, 23 December 1914, attd. 6th (Reserve) Regt. (until March) thereafter joining 4th Battn, at the Front with a draft of reinforcements, and was killed in action, 8 May 1915, during fierce fighting in the vicinity of Hooge, nr. Ypres. Buried there. The commanding officer wrote, "I will not say more now than that I sympathise with you (and my regiment) over the loss of one of the finest and most fearlessly capable lads I ever met. He was quite exceptional." Age 18.

(Panel 51) 2nd Lieut. Gerald Francis Carter, 7th (Service) Bn. The King's Royal Rifle Corps: only *s.* of Alfred Henry Carter, of The Lindens, Abingdon, formerly of Birmingham, M.D., F.R.C.P. (London), by his wife Elizabeth Marian, *dau.* of the late William Henry King, of Pedmore House, Stourbridge: *b.* Edgbaston in Birmingham, 30 November 1896: *educ.* Rev. F.W. Pearse's School, St. Ninian's Moffatt, and Winchester College: was preparing for the Indian Forest Service, and was already entered as an undergraduate at St. John's College, Oxford, when war was declared: enlisted Public Schools Corps (16th Middlesex Regt.), September 1914; became L/Corpl., being gazetted 2nd Lieut. 7th King's Royal Rifle Corps, 6 April 1915; went to the Front the following May. On 30 July he was gallantly leading a bombing party in a counter-attack on some trenches at Hooge when, only a few yards from the enemy, he was severely wounded. L/Corpl. Standing (who has since been promoted for his bravery), assisted by three of his men, carried Mr. Carter out of action, but he died of his wounds shortly afterwards. Buried close by, in Sanctuary Wood. Age 18. The Lieut.-Col. Comdg. 7th Battn. wrote, "He behaved most gallantly, and was leading his men when he was struck down. He was a great loss to the regt., as a soldier and a friend. I could always rely on him to do the right thing, and always so cheery. We were all very fond of him, and I am sure he enjoyed himself soldiering." And the major wrote in much the same terms, referring also to the gallantry of the four men who, at great personal risk to themselves, retrieved and carried him out of action. At Winchester, Lieut. Carter won the headmaster's gold cup for gymnastics two years in succession, also two cups for diving. He was a good all-round athlete and a first-class shot. His father Dr. Carter, who was formerly professor of medicine at Birmingham University and a member of the City Council, served as Major, R.A.M.C.

(Panel 51) 2nd Lieut. James Casey, 1st Bn. (60th Foot) The King's Royal Rifle Corps: *s.* of the late James Casey: *b.* London, 30 November 1879: enlisted K.R.R.C. 1897: served in the South African War 1899–1902 (promoted Sergt. for conspicuous gallantry on the field: Mentioned in Despatches: Queen's Medal, four clasps; King's Medal, two clasps): and with the Expeditionary Force in France and Flanders, being promoted 2nd Lieut. for gallantry on 1 October 1914, and was killed in action on the 30th. He was Mentioned in Despatches (*London Gazette*, 17 February 1915) by F.M. Sir John (now Lord) French, for 'gallant and distinguished service in the field.': 30 October 1914. Age 34. *m.* (*IWGC record 10 October 1914*)

(Panel 51) 2nd Lieut. Charles Isaacs Coburn, 18th (Service) Bn. (Arts & Crafts) The King's Royal Rifle Corps: *s.* of Henry Isaacs Coburn, Lawyer, of 22, Pandora Road, London, N.W.6, by his marriage to the late Ada Coburn: *educ.* St. Paul's School, and Merton College, Oxford, B.A., B.C.L.: enlisted December 1915 and, after passing through Inns of Court O.T.C., Berkhamstead, gazetted Temp. 2nd Lieut. K.R.R.C., April 1917: went to France the following July, and was reported missing after going into his first action (the attack against Hollebeke) on the 31st of that month. Age 32. The Battalion Adjutant recorded, "On the 31 July 1917 the attack was launched under the most unfavourable conditions – the weather had broken on 27 July and the ground had become so churned up it was almost impossible to move. A thick mist and drizzling rain made progress slow. The enemy held their line by machine-gun posts cleverly hidden in shellholes and brought a withering fire to bear on the attacking party. All this combined to bring the attack to a standstill just short of the objective – Hollebeke. Losses were so heavy that the battalion had to be withdrawn the same night." And added, "During the short time he was with us he showed himself to be a gallant, reliable and devoted officer." He was married to Dorothy Linda Coburn, *née* Henry (50, Canfield Gardens, London, N.W.6).

The Lindisfarne War Memorial, designed by Sir Edwin Lutyens in the style of a Celtic cross, stands on the Heugh, a small hill overlooking the harbour and ruins of the priory founded in AD 635 by Irish born Saint Aidan. Inscribed 'To the Glory of God and in Grateful Memory of our Glorious Dead, 1914–1918,' the memorial records the names of eight Holy Islanders who answered their country's call and made the supreme sacrifice in the Great War. The majority of these men were killed at sea and are commemorated on the Chatham Naval Memorial; 2nd Lieut. Crossman is the only one commemorated in Belgium.

(Panel 51) 2nd Lieut. William Ronald Morley Crossman, 2nd Bn. (60th Foot) The King's Royal Rifle Corps: *yr. s.* of the late Major Lawrence Morley Crossman, J.P., Lord of the Manor of Holy Island: *b.* Beal, co. Northumberland, 6 September 1894: *educ.* Lyndhurst; Wellington College, Crowthorne, and Royal Military College, Sandhurst: gazetted 2nd Lieut. King's Royal Rifle Corps, 25 February 1914: served with the Expeditionary Force in France and Flanders; killed in action at Veldhoek, 2 November 1914. Age 20. *unm.*

(Panel 51) 2nd Lieut. Frank Dean, 2nd Bn. (60th Foot) The King's Royal Rifle Corps: *s.* of Francis Dean, by his wife Sarah: *b.* Widnes, co. Chester, 28 August 1876: enlisted King's Royal Rifle Corps, 1898; rose through the non-commissioned ranks, becoming Colour.-Sergt. September 1901: served with his regiment in the South African War, 1899–1902: present at the Relief of Ladysmith, and actions on the Tugela Heights, Transvaal and Cape Colony: gazetted 2nd Lieut. August 1914: served with the Expeditionary Force in France and Flanders, and was killed in action at Gheluvelt during the First Battle of Ypres, 31 October 1914. Age 38. Mentioned in F.M. Sir John (now Lord) French's Despatch on the Battle of the Aisne, 7 September 1914 (*London Gazette*, 19 October 1914) for 'gallant and distinguished service in the field.' 2nd Lieut. Dean was a good shot, and took an active interest in the sports of the battalion, especially cross-country running. He leaves a widow, Ada Dean (47, Surrenden Road, Folkestone, co. Kent).

(Panel 51) 2nd Lieut. Henry Charles Maclean Farmer, 6th (Reserve) attd. 4th Bn. (60th Foot) The King's Royal Rifle Corps: *yr. s.* of the Rev. James Edmund Gamul Farmer, Rector of Waddesdon with Upper Winchedon, Aylesbury, co. Bucks, by his wife Margaret, *dau.* of Capt. Charles Bampfield Yule, R.N.: *b.* Arundel Vicarage, co. Sussex, 8 August. 1892: *educ.* Summerfields, nr. Oxford; Eton (Mr Ramsay's House), and Trinity College, Cambridge: volunteered on the outbreak of war, applied for a commission, and while waiting for it, enlisted 3rd Dragoon Guards, 3 September 1914: gazetted 2nd Lieut. 6th King's R.R.C., 22 September following: went to the Front, March 1915 to join 4th Bn. of his regt., and was killed in action near Ypres on 10 May. Buried at the East Boundary of Bellewaarde Wood. Col. Brownlow, K.R.R.C., wrote, "He worked hard down here (Sheerness) and was very keen to get to the Front;" and Capt. Field, "He was in my company the whole time he was at Sheerness and King's Ferry; a most excellent, cheery fellow, and a very conscientious, good, young officer." Age 22. *unm.*

(Panel 51) 2nd Lieut. Jack Fellows Lambert, 9th (Service) Bn. The King's Royal Rifle Corps: eldest & only *survg. s.* of the late Ernest Lambert, Financier (*d.*1898), by his wife May (23, Terlingham Gardens, Folkestone), *dau.* of the late Hon. James Israel Fellows, Agent-General for New Brunswick (*d.*1894): *b.* Coombe, Malden, co. Surrey, 3 September 1891: *educ.* Marlborough, and Merton College, Oxford, where he was in King Edward's Horse: was manager of a cocoanut estate in the Malay States when war broke out: came home and applied for a commission and was gazetted 2nd Lieut. K.R.R.C. 27 April 1915: went to France in May, was in action near Ypres early June, and was killed in the counter-attack on the German position at Hooge, 30 July 1915. He was at first reported missing and it was not until March, 1916, that he was officially returned as killed. His Commanding Officer wrote, "He was a splendid Platoon Commander and his men loved him." Age 23. *unm.*

(Panel 51) 2nd Lieut. Robert Longbottom, 'D' Coy., 7th (Service) Bn. The King's Royal Rifle Corps: *s.* of William Henry Longbottom, of Wingfield, Bournemouth, co. Dorset, by his wife Ethel (83B, Holland Park, Notting Hill, London, W.): and brother to 2nd Lieut. H. Longbottom, 6th South Lancashire Regt., killed in action, 9 August 1915, at Gallipoli: served in France from 19 May 1915, and was killed in action, 30 July 1915 at Hooge. Age 19.

His brother Henry also has no known grave; he is commemorated on the Helles Memorial.

(Panel 51) 2nd Lieut. John Wilmot Maynard, 3rd Bn. (60th Foot) The King's Royal Rifle Corps: *yr. s.* of Edmund Anthony Jefferson Maynard, of 'Hoon Ridge,' Hilton, co. Derby, by his wife Margaret Blanche, eldest *dau.* of the late Robert Sacheverel Wilmot Sitwell, of Stainsby House, Smalley, co. Derby: *b.* Eastbourne, co. Sussex, 8 June 1896: *educ.* St. Peter's Court, Broadstairs; Harrow (Moreton's), 1909–14, and Royal Military College, Sandhurst: gazetted 2nd Lieut. King's Royal Rifle Corps, December 1914: after a period of training with 6th Battn. joined 3rd Battn. of his regiment and went to France where, on the morning of 24 April 1915, he was killed while peacefully sleeping in his dug-out, situated in the support trenches half a mile behind the firing line at Ypres. Age 18. Quiet, with a keen sense of humour, he had already won the friendship of his brother-officers, two of whom wrote to say how fond they had grown of him in the short time he was with them.

(Panel 51) 2nd Lieut. Ernest Philip Morris Panes, 9th (Service) Bn. The King's Royal Rifle Corps: *s.* of Rev. John Benjamin Panes, of The Rectory, Torver, Coniston, co. Lancaster, and Mrs L.C. Panes: and *yr.* brother to 2nd Officer, A.B. Panes, S.S. 'Malda,' died at sea, 20 August 1917, aged 26 years: *educ.* Brasenose College, Oxford (Scholar). Killed in action at Bellewaarde, 25 September 1915. Age 22.

His brother Arthur is buried in Hartland (or Stoke St. Nectan) St. Nectan's Churchyard.

(Panel 51) 2nd Lieut. Guy Lesingham Spreckley, 22nd (Reserve) Bn. The King's Royal Rifle Corps: *s.* of Herbert William Spreckley, of Cove Cottage, Worcester, by his wife Florence, *née* Lesingham: and brother to Lieut. R.L. Spreckley, M.C., 2nd Connaught Rangers, who fell on 14 September 1914, aged 21 years, and Capt. A.F. Spreckley, 9th Gurkha Rifles (Indian Army), who (in company with his wife and daughter) was one of 21 officers and 1 N.C.O. of the United Kingdom and Indian forces lost at sea, 30 December 1915, when the S.S. Persia – a defensively armed passenger vessel out of Tilbury, for Port Said,

Aden and Bombay – was torpedoed and sunk off Crete, with the loss of 334 lives. Killed in action, 23 April 1917. Age 32.

His brother Ralph is commemorated in Vailly British Cemetery (Sp.Mem.6); Arthur has no known grave but the sea, he is commemorated on the Chatby Memorial.

(Panel 51) 2nd Lieut. the Hon. Piers Stewart St. Aubyn, 6th (Reserve) attd. 2nd Bn. (60th Foot) The King's Royal Rifle Corps: 5th *s.* of the 1st Baron St. Lovan, by his wife Lady Elizabeth Clementina Townshend, *dau.* of the 4th Marquess Townshend: *b.* 11 April 1871: served in South Africa 1900; Lieut., Thornycroft's Mounted Infantry. On the outbreak of war, 2nd Lieut. St. Aubyn was gazetted to 6th Bn. K.R.R.C. September 1914, and sent to France almost at once attached 2nd Battn. On 31 October 1914 he was seen by a brother officer lying on the ground wounded. The latter officer stated that 2nd Lieut. St. Aubyn had been hit in the shoulder, but it had not been possible to go to his assistance. The Germans afterwards advanced over the ground, and the wounded officer has not since been heard of. The High Court subsequently allowed it to be presumed that his death occurred on or since 31 October 1914. He was J.P., for the County of Cornwall, a member of Brooks,' the Travellers' and Bachelors' Clubs, and a well-known owner of greyhounds. Age 43.

(Panel 51) 2nd Lieut. Edward Robert 'Teddy' Waring, 1st Bn. (60th Foot) The King's Royal Rifle Corps: *yr. s.* of Capt. (& Mrs) William Waring, of Beenham House, Reading, co. Berks: *b.* 1894: *educ.* Wellington College (Stanley, 1908–1910): gazetted 2nd Lieut. 5th King's Royal Rifle Corps, October 1913; promoted Lieut. June 1914: commissioned 2nd Lieut. 1st Battn. September 1914: served with the Expeditionary Force in France and Flanders, and was killed in action at the First Battle of Ypres, 28 October 1914. Age 20. *unm.*

PANEL 51 ENDS 2ND LIEUT. F.J. WOODCOCK, KING'S ROYAL RIFLE CORPS.

PANEL 53 BEGINS CSM. G. BENTLEY, KING'S ROYAL RIFLE CORPS.

(Panel 53) Corpl. A/3066, George H. Goodier, 9th (Service) Bn. The King's Royal Rifle Corps: *s.* of John Goodier, of Altrincham, co. Chester: enlisted Barrow-in-Furness: served with the Expeditionary Force in France and Flanders from May 1915, and was killed in action on the afternoon of 30 July following, when his battalion attacked some trenches nr. the Menin Road, which had been lost earlier that day. Age 34. Remains (partial) exhumed from an unmarked grave (28.I.16.b.3.6), 6 December 1928; identified – Khaki, Boots; reinterred, registered 10 December 1928. *Buried in Sanctuary Wood Cemetery (III.L.24).*

(Panel 53) Corpl. R/6966, Albert Sadler Jackson, 9th (Service) Bn. The King's Royal Rifle Corps: eldest *s.* of Albert Jackson, Jeweller; by his wife Jane, *dau.* of John Sadler: *b.* Edgbaston, 16 February 1878: *educ.* Lineham's, Edgbaston Academy: Occupation – Jeweller's Traveller: enlisted 14 November 1914, after the outbreak of war: served with the Expeditionary Force in France and Flanders from May 1915, and was killed in action at Hooge, 30 July following. A comrade wrote, "If it were wet and the water trickled through, we could always look to him for some cheerful remark which would make us forget for a time. We all miss him very much and join with you in mourning his loss." Age 37. He *m.* at St. Mary's Church, Bearwood, Birmingham, 27 August 1902, Gertrude Clara (46, Sandon Road, Edgbaston, Birmingham), *dau.* of Edward Thomas Grant, and had two children: Reginald Grant, *b.* 11 November 1903; and Ena Gertrude, *b.* 18 August 1907.

(Panel 53) Corpl. 9730, Robert Jobes, 4th Bn. (60th Foot) The King's Royal Rifle Corps: 4th *s.* of Robert Jobes, late of 26, Fenwick's Row, now resident at 1, Aged Miners' Homes, Boldon Colliery, Co. Durham, by his wife Margaret, *dau.* of Joseph Gowland: *b.* Gateshead, Co. Durham, 28 July 1890: *educ.* Boldon Colliery Board School: Occupation – Miner: enlisted on 6 May 1910: went to India, December 1912: returned to England with his Regiment on the outbreak of war: served with the Expeditionary Force in France, and was killed in action there, 30 July 1915, at Hooge he was a keen footballer, and while in India won seven medals. Age 25. *unm.*

(Panel 53) Corpl. 8560, James Hatton, 21st (Service) Bn. (Yeoman Rifles) The King's Royal Rifle Corps: *s.* of James Hatton, of 37, St. Albans Road, Wallasey, co. Chester, by his wife Jane: and elder brother to Pte. 9782, R. Hatton, 2nd Cheshire Regt., killed in action, 8 May 1915: *b.* Liscard, co. Chester, *c.*1889: enlisted Liverpool. Killed in action, 5 August 1917. Age 28. He was married to Elizabeth Hatton (46, Clarence Road, Wallasey).

His brother Richard also has no known grave; he is recorded on Panel 22.

(Panel 53) L/Corpl. C/7346, Richard Hall, 18th (Service) Bn. (Arts & Crafts) The King's Royal Rifle Corps. Killed in action, 31 July 1917.

(Panel 53) L/Corpl. R/23439, Michael Meagher, 18th (Service) Bn. (Arts & Crafts) The King's Royal Rifle Corps: *s.* of the late John Meagher, by his wife Honora (32A, Mount Durand, Guernsey, Channel Islands): and brother to Pte. 517, E.J. Meagher, Royal Guernsey Light Infantry, killed in action, 1 December 1917: *b.* St. Peter's, Guernsey: enlisted Guernsey. Killed in action, 31 July 1917. Age 20.

His brother Edward also has no known grave; he is commemorated on the Cambrai Memorial, Louverval (Panel 13).

(Panel 53) L/Corpl. 3029, Arthur George Perryman, 2nd Bn. (60th Foot) The King's Royal Rifle Corps: late of Birmingham: *b.* Lambeth, co. Surrey: enlisted London: employee London County Council Tramways Dept.: served with the Expeditionary Force. Missing/wounded, believed to have died on 31 October 1914, nr. Gheluvelt. (*IWGC record A.J. Perryman*)

(Panel 53) L/Corpl. A/1430, Alfred William Shepherd, 8th (Service) Bn. The King's Royal Rifle Corps: late of Edgware Road, co. Middlesex: *b.* St. Pancras, London, N.W.: enlisted Marylebone, London, W.: Killed in action, 26 July 1915. Remains recovered from a grave marked up as belonging to an 'Unknown British Lance Corporal. K.R.R.C.', located in Sanctuary Wood Old Cemetery, identified – Clothing, Titles, Badge of Rank; reinterred, registered 30 April 1928. *Buried in Sanctuary Wood Cemetery (II.F.13).*

(Panel 53) Rfn. R/8375, Herbert Reginald William Ashdown, 8th (Service) Bn. The King's Royal Rifle Corps: *s.* of Benjamin Ashdown, of 30, Randolph Road, Gillingham, by his wife Henrietta: enlisted Chatham, co. Kent. Killed in action, 12 October 1915. Age 17.

(Panel 53) Rfn. A/3622, Thomas Edward Aston, 8th (Service) Bn. The King's Royal Rifle Corps: *s.* of Alfred Frederick Aston, of Birmingham, by his wife Matilda: enlisted Birmingham: served with the Expeditionary Force in France and Flanders from May 1915, and died of wounds, 30 July following at Hooge. Age 30. Any correspondence/information regarding Rfn. Aston should be addressed to his widow, Annie Aston (27, Milton Street, New Town Row, Birmingham). Remains of an 'Unknown British Soldier. K.R.R.C.' recovered from an unmarked grave (28.I.18.d.85.60); identified – Clothing, Titles, Boots mkd. 3622, Fork mkd. 3622; reinterred, registered 26 November 1929. *Buried in Sanctuary Wood Cemetery (V.J.7).*

(Panel 53) Rfn. 8200, John Henry Badetscher, 7th (Service) Bn. King's Royal Rifle Corps: *s.* of John Badetscher, Butler at Toft Hall, of Swiss nationality: *b.* Marylebone, London, 11 July 1885: *educ.* St. George's, Hulme, Manchester: volunteered and enlisted, 14 August 1914: served with the Expeditionary Force in France, and was killed in action at Hooge, 30 July 1915, while laying a mine. Buried at Hooge by a detachment of 1st Royal Fusiliers. Age 20.

(Panel 53) Rfn. 7940, Charles George Barnett, 1st Bn. (60th Foot) The King's Royal Rifle Corps: *s.* of Frederick Barnett, Farm Labourer; of Pigbush Farm, Loxwood, co. Sussex, by his wife Emily: *b.* June 1886: enlisted Stoughton Barracks, Guildford, 22 January 1907: served in Egypt, 1907–09; transf'd. Army Reserve, January 1914, taking employ as Gardener: recalled to the Colours on mobilisation and proceeded to France, 12 August 1914: took part in the fighting at Mons, the subsequent retirement, and was killed in action at the First Battle of Ypres, 2 November 1914; Menin – Gheluvelt Road, S.E. of Hooge. Age 28. He *m.* Farnham, 13 July 1912; Isabel Emma, *née* Prevett (Pounds Cottage, Alfold, Billinghurst), and had a son – George James, *b.* 29 December 1912. His widow Isabel died (1918) shortly after her remarriage to V.H. Sherlock, of Rudgwick, co. Surrey.

(Panel 53) Rfn. Y/1245, John Thomas Bird, 8th (Service) Bn. The King's Royal Rifle Corps: *b*. Birmingham: enlisted there. Killed in action, 5 December 1915, when the battalion's trenches S16C, Boundary Road – La Belle Alliance, were heavily shelled by the enemy; Rfn. R/6701, J.H. Hudson was also killed.

Rfn. Hudson is buried in La Brique Military Cemetery No.2 (I.Q.2).

(Panel 53) Rfn. 9417, James French Boorer, 4th Bn. (60th Foot) The King's Royal Rifle Corps: *s*. of James H. Boorer, of 29, Froddington Road, Southsea, co. Hants, by his wife Mary Ann: *b*. Southsea, 1897: enlisted Gosport. Died of wounds, 10 May 1915. Age 28. *unm. Buried in Bedford House Cemetery (I.H.16/Enc.No.6)*.

(Panel 53) Rfn. R/7943, Samuel Bramley, 4th Bn. (60th Foot) The King's Royal Rifle Corps: *s*. of the late Samuel Bramley (*d*.1916), of Sutton-in-Ashfield, co. Nottingham, by his wife Ann: *b*. Newton Green, co. Derby, *c*.1884: employee New Hucknall Colliery: enlisted Nottingham, September 1914: served with the Expeditionary Force in France and Flanders from 6 May 1915, and was reported missing and wounded somewhere in France on the 25th of that month; it being stated by comrades that on the aforementioned date he was seen to be blown up by a mine; confirmed (May 1916) as having died on that date. Age 31. He leaves a wife (23, Brook Street, Sutton-in-Ashfield), and *dau*. Phyllis. A friend of Rfn. Bramley, Rfn.

R/7942, W. Walker, was killed the same day. *The Notts Free Press*, 'In Memoriam,' 26 May 1916:-

> *One sad year has passed*
> *Since our great sorrow fell.*
> *But in our hearts we mourn the loss*
> *Of him we loved so well.*
>
> *We think of him in silence,*
> *His name so often call;*
> *Though there is nothing left to answer,*
> *But his photo on the wall.*
>
> *Greater love hath no man than this that he lay down his life for his friends.*
>
> *There is a link that death cannot sever for love and memory last forever.*
>
> *He Hath Done His Duty.*
>
> From his loving Wife & Daughter.

Rfn. Walker also has no known grave; he is recorded below.

(Panel 53) Rfn. 8898, Walter Brown, 3rd Bn. (60th Foot) The King's Royal Rifle Corps: *s*. of the late Walter (& Mrs) Brown, of Leeds, co. York. Killed in action, 10 May 1915. Age 26. Remains recovered from an unmarked grave (28.I.10.c.55.25), refers GRU Report, Zillebeke 5.457E; identified – G.S. Uniform, Boots, Titles, Pair Gold Ear-rings; reinterred, registered 19 November 1932. *Buried in Sanctuary Wood Cemetery (V.M.29)*.

(Panel 53) Rfn. 8856, Russell James Burke, 'A' Coy., 2nd Bn. (60th Foot) The King's Royal Rifle Corps: *s*. of Francis R. Burke, formerly Q.M.S., K.R.R.C.; of 'Dean Cottage,' Browne's Hill, Carlow, and his wife Janet: and elder brother to Pte. 3704, F.C. Burke, 2nd Leinster Regt., died of wounds, 4 May 1918: *b*. Gibraltar: enlisted Coolhenry. Died of wounds, 31 October 1914. Age 21.

His brother Francis is buried in Ebblinghem Military Cemetery (I.E.18).

(Panel 53) Rfn. 5725, Walter Carr (served as Arthur Stacey), 1st Bn. (60th Foot) The King's Royal Rifle Corps: *s*. of James Carr, of Newcastle: *b*. Sheffield, co. York, 1888: *educ*. there: Occupation – Labourer: enlisted King's Royal Rifle Corps, served three years with the Colours, joined the Reserve; called up on mobilization, 4 August 1914: served with the Expeditionary Force in France. Reported missing after the fighting at Mons (*q.v.*) 27 October 1914, and is now assumed to have been killed on or about that date. He *m*. Sheffield, October 1907; Millicent Ashmore (23, Court, 2, House, Pond Street, Sheffield), *dau*.

of Harry Ashmore, and had three children – Walter, *b.* 6 September 1908; Nellie, *b.* 1 January 1911; and William, *b.* 12 November 1912.

(Panel 53) Rfn. 12174, George Castle, 4th Bn. (60th Foot) The King's Royal Rifle Corps: *s.* of John Castle, of Longborough, Moreton-in-the-Marsh, co. Gloucester, by his wife Mary: and brother to Pte. 10015, F. Castle, Coldstream Guards, died of wounds, 29 October 1914; and Pte. 34267, J. Castle, Loyal North Lancashire Regt., killed 18 July 1917: *b.* Longborough: served with the Expeditionary Force in France and Flanders, and died of wounds received in action on 25 May 1915.

His brother Fred is buried in Ypres Town Cemetery Extension (II.B.11), John has no known grave; he is recorded on Panel 43.

(Panel 53) Rfn. 6/681, Ernest Chignell, 4th Bn. (60th Foot) The King's Royal Rifle Corps: late of Bethnal Green, London, E.2: *b.* Whitechapel, London, E.: enlisted Stratford, London, E.15. Killed in action, 24 April 1915. *Buried in Oosttaverne Wood Cemetery (VII.A.9).*

(Panel 53) Rfn. R/31261, Norman Chislett, 18th (Service) Bn. (Arts & Crafts) The King's Royal Rifle Corps: late of Chalfont, co. Buckingham: *s.* of James Chislett, of Deddington, co. Oxford, by his wife Emily (Clay Hill House, Enfield, co. Middlesex): and brother to Pte. 21136, A.J. Chislett, 27th Canadian Infantry, killed in action, 6 November 1917, at Passchendaele: *b.* Teddington, co. Middlesex: enlisted Stoke Newington. Killed in action, 31 July 1917, at the Battle of Pilckem Ridge. Age 31.

His brother Arthur also has no known grave; he is recorded on Panel 26.

(Panel 53) Rfn. 8311, John Clark, 4th Bn. (60th Foot) The King's Royal Rifle Corps: *s.* of Joseph Clark, Brick Manufacturer; of 41, St. John's Road, Aylesbury, co. Buckingham: and brother to Pte. 203993, J. Clark, 2/4th Oxford & Bucks Light Infantry, died 19 June 1918, in enemy hands: *b.* Park Street, Aylesbury, 1888: Occupation – Print Worker; Messrs Hazell, Watson & Viney Ltd., Tring Road: enlisted Aylesbury: served in France and Flanders from December 1914: Died of wounds, 25 May 1915. Age 28. *unm.*

His brother Joseph (*IWGC record Clarke*) is commemorated in Plaine French National Cemetery.

(Panel 53) Rfn. A/1347, Ernest Stanley Cook, 8th (Service) Bn. The King's Royal Rifle Corps: enlisted Birmingham. Killed in action at Hooge, 30 July 1915. Remains recovered from a grave marked as belonging to an 'Unknown British Soldier. K.R.R' located in Sanctuary Wood Old Cemetery, (28.I.24.b.90.97), identified – Clothing, Titles, Boot mkd. 1347; reinterred, registered 2 May 1928. *Buried in Sanctuary Wood Cemetery (II.F.18).*

(Panel 53) Rfn. A/3034, William Henry Doidge, 10th (Service) Bn. The King's Royal Rifle Corps: *s.* of Hester Doidge ('Rose Cottage,' Thornhill Road, Streetly, Birmingham); late of 154, Shireland Road, Smethwick: and elder brother to Pte. S2/61495, S. Doidge, Leicestershire Regt., died 4 September 1919: *b.* Smethwick, co. Stafford: enlisted in Birmingham: served with the Expeditionary Force in France, and was killed in action, 10 August 1917. Age 22. *unm.*

His brother Sidney is buried in Smethwick (Uplands) Cemetery (16.CE.C6948).

(Panel 53) Rfn. R/6252, George Arthur Dolman, 7th (Service) Bn. The King's Royal Rifle Corps: *s.* of Rose Ann Dolman (4, Little Chapel Street, Monmore Green, Wolverhampton: and brother to Pte. 51291, J.R. Dolman, 'D' Coy., 2nd Lincolnshire Regt., killed in action, 18 October 1918: *b.* Wolverhampton, co. Stafford, 1892: enlisted Birmingham: served with the Expeditionary Force in France from May 1915, and was killed in action at Hooge, 7 August following. Age 23. *unm.*

His brother John also has no known grave; he is commemorated on the Vis-en-Artois Memorial (Panel 4).

(Panel 53) Rfn. 10445, Charles Lionel Victor Drake, 4th Bn. (60th Foot) The King's Royal Rifle Corps: *s.* of Frederic Drake, of 4, Laurel Grove, Sydenham, London, S.E.26: enlisted London, January 1912: at Gharial, India, on the outbreak of war in August 1914: departed Bombay, 16 November; disembarked Plymouth, proceeded to Winchester thence to France: served with the Expeditionary Force there and in Flanders. Died of wounds, 25 May 1915; Ypres, Belgium. Age 22. *unm.* One of four brothers who served.

(Panel 53) Rfn. R/1556, Lawrence Edwards, 10th (Service) Bn. The King's Royal Rifle Corps: *b.* Birmingham: enlisted Smethwick, September 1914. Died of wounds, 25 June 1916. See account re. Rfn. F. Calvert, Vlamertinghe Military Cemetery (III.A.18).

(Panel 53) Rfn. R/32638, George Andrew Fiddy, 18th (Service) Bn. The King's Royal Rifle Corps: *s.* of Ellen Fiddy (Hackney, London, E.8): enlisted Hackney: served with the Expeditionary Force in France and Flanders from late 1916, and died of wounds, 31 July 1917. Age 32. Rfn. Fiddy leaves a wife, Mary Ann (71, Morning Lane, London, E.9). *Buried in Passchendaele New British Cemetery (X.D.29).*

(Panel 53) Rfn. 10541, Charles Gage, 7th (Service) Bn. The King's Royal Rifle Corps: *s.* of Edward George Gage, Coal Merchant; of 11, Olney Avenue, South Street, Camberwell Gate, London, S.E., by his wife Louisa Frances: *b.* 4 March 1892: *educ.* St. Paul's School, London, S.E.: enlisted 1908: in India on the outbreak of war in August 1914: proceeded to France, joined the Expeditionary Force there in December 1914, and was killed in action at Ypres, 15 July 1915. Buried there. Age 23. *unm.* (*IWGC record 16 July, age 21*)

(Panel 53) Rfn. A/1126, Harold James Garman, 8th (Service) Bn. The King's Royal Rifle Corps: *s.* of Arthur Garman, of 9, Shaftesbury Street, West Bromwich, co. Stafford: enlisted Birmingham: served with the Expeditionary Force in France and Flanders from May 1915, and died of wounds, 30 July 1915, received in action at Hooge, nr. Ypres. Age 19. *Buried in Kemmel No.1 French Cemetery (I.B.5).*

(Panel 53) Rfn. R/6274, Eden Charles Golding, 4th Bn. (60th Foot) The King's Royal Rifle Corps: *s.* of the late Henry Golding, of Islington, London: and father-in-law to Petty Officer, 1st Class, Robert Wilcocks: *b.* London, October 1877: *educ.* there: enlisted in September 1914: served with the Expeditionary Force in France and Flanders, and was killed in action on 24 May 1915. Buried at Ypres. Age 38. He *m.* Martha Ruth, *dau.* of George Grigg, and had two children, Charles and Joyce Louise. (*IWGC record 25 May*)

(Panel 53) Rfn. 9576, John Thomas Gregory, 1st Bn. (60th Foot) The King's Royal Rifle Corps: late of West Hampstead, London, NW6: *s.* of Thomas Gregory, of Station Road, Sutton-in-Ashfield, co. Nottingham, by his wife Eliza, *née* Kendall: *b.* Eckington, Chesterfield, 13 July 1887: enlisted *c.*1908. Killed in action, 27 October 1914, nr. Zonnebeke. Age 27. *unm.* A choirboy, communicant and member of St. Modwen's Church Bible Class (Sutton-in-Ashfield), Rfn. Gregory was a well-known cricket player. Beginning his career with St. Modwen's he afterwards joined Sutton Town from whom he was engaged by Notts County C.C. Ground Staff for three seasons (1905–07), and, before joining the King's Royal Rifle Corps, played for Hucknall Colliery. His ability as a slow left-arm bowler quickly earned him a regular place in the regimental side at Aldershot where, on 16 May 1913, he took 10 wickets – all clean-bowled – for 15 runs against 2nd Worcestershire Regt., which earned him a trial with Hampshire in a match against Oxford University at Southampton a few weeks later. As a football player for the regiment he played inside-right, on one occasion representing the Army against the Amateur Internationals.

(Panel 53) Rfn. 6173, Francis Greygoose, 2nd Bn. (60th Foot) The King's Royal Rifle Corps: late of Tottenham Hale, co. Middlesex: *b.* Bishop's Stortford: former London County Council Tramways Dept. employee. Killed in action, 23 October 1914, nr. Pilckem.

(Panel 53) Rfn. 10242, William Hart, 4th Bn. (60th Foot) The King's Royal Rifle Corps: *s.* of George Hart, of Hope Cottage, King's Road, St. Albans, co. Hertford, by his wife Eliza: and brother to Pte. 26042, H.C. Hart, 9th Loyal North Lancashire Regt., killed in action, 3 September 1916, at the Somme; and Gnr. 890313, E. Hart, 20th Bde., Royal Horse Artillery, died 4 July 1918, in Palestine: *b.* Christchurch, St. Albans: enlisted Mill Hill, London, N.W.7: Died 25 May 1915, of wounds. Age 23. *unm.* One of three brothers who fell.

His brother Henry also has no known grave, he is commemorated on the Thiepval Memorial (Pier & Face 11A); Ernest is buried in Ramleh War Cemetery (G.24).

(Panel 53) Rfn. A/1325, Arthur George Hawley, 7th (Service) Bn. The King's Royal Rifle Corps: *s.* of Mr (& Mrs) Hawley, of 2, House, 16 Court, Bishop Street, Birmingham: Occupation – Cabinet Maker: enlisted on 22 August 1914, after the outbreak of war: served with the Expeditionary Force in France, and was killed in action at Hooge Wood, 30 July 1915. *unm.*

(Panel 53) Rfn. Y/998, Arthur W. Heesom, 9th (Service) Bn. The King's Royal Rifle Corps: 3rd *s.* of Arthur Heesom, of 128, Knutsford Road, Latchford, Warrington, by his wife Ann: cousin to Pte. 34455, G. Heesom, 2/5th Duke of Wellington's (West Riding) Regt., missing/killed in action, 12–13 September

1918; and brother to Rfn. Y/1033, W. Heesom, 2nd King's Royal Rifle Corps, died Royal Victoria Hospital, Folkestone, 10 October 1915, consequent to wounds (spinal, abdominal) received in action at Loos (25 September): *b.* Warrington, co. Lancaster, January 1895: Occupation – Gas Stove maker: enlisted Warrington: served with the Expeditionary Force in France and Flanders from 20 May 1915. Missing/ believed killed 4.20 a.m., 25 September 1915, vicinity Bellewaarde Ridge – Railway Wood. Age 20. *unm.* On 25 September 2015, marking the 100th anniversary of Arthur's death, a wreath was laid by members of his cousin George's family during the Last Post ceremony.

Cousin George also has no known grave, he is commemorated on the Vis-en-Artois Memorial (Panel 6); brother William is buried in Warrington Cemetery (K.CE.675).

(Panel 53) Rfn. Y/1109, Arthur Robert Hilson, (served as Clarke, D.), 4th Bn. (60th Foot) The King's Royal Rifle Corps: *s.* of Arthur Hilson, of 184, Runcorn Road, Sparkbrook, Birmingham: *b.* St. Barnabas, Birmingham: served with the Expeditionary Force in France, and died on 10 May 1915, of wounds. Age 16.

(Panel 53) Rfn. 8279, Frederick Hirons, 3rd Bn. (60th Foot) The King's Royal Rifle Corps: *s.* of Joseph Hirons, of 43, Combrook, Warwick, by his wife Sarah: and brother to Pte. 20198, G.A. Hirons, 11th Royal Warwickshire Regt., died of wounds, 25 September 1917; Pte. 24670, A.E. Hirons, 2/7th Royal Warwickshire Regt., died of wounds, 13 April 1918; and Pte. 22640, J.H. Hirons, 11th Royal Warwickshire Regt., killed in action, 10 April 1917: *b.* Combrook: enlisted Warwick. Killed in action, 2 March 1915. Age 25. *unm.* One of four brothers who fell.

His brother George is buried in Goedwaersvelde British Cemetery (I.G.34); Alfred is buried in Vielle-Chapelle New Military Cemetery (VII.F.19); Joseph has no known grave, he is commemorated on the Arras (Faubourg d'Amiens) Memorial (Bay 3).

(Panel 53) Rfn. A/3372, Arthur Hollis, 7th (Service) Bn. The King's Royal Rifle Corps: *s.* of William Hollis, by his wife Harriet: *b.* Ladywood, Birmingham, 8 September 1888: *educ.* Nelson Street Board School, Sandpits, Birmingham: employee Weldless Tube Company's works, there: enlisted King's Royal Rifle Corps, Birmingham, 23 August 1914, after the outbreak of war: served with the Expeditionary Force in France and Flanders. Killed in action at Hooge, nr. Ypres, 30 July 1915. Age 26. *unm.* (*IWGC record age 27*)

(Panel 53) Rfn. 12008, Harry Hollows, 3rd Bn. (60th Foot) The King's Royal Rifle Corps: *s.* of Edwin Hollows, of 486, Blackburn Road, Darwen, co. Lancaster, by his wife Helen: enlisted Blackburn: served with the Expeditionary Force, and was killed in action, 10 May 1915. Age 16.

(Panel 53) Rfn. R/1349, Arthur Hurd, 'A' Coy., 10th (Service) Bn. The King's Royal Rifle Corps: *s.* of the late Joseph (& Susannah) Hurd, of 162, Marcus Street, Pitsmoor, Sheffield: *b.* Sheffield: enlisted 1914. Killed in action, 25 June 1916. Age 24. He was married to Ruth Linton, *née* Hurd (130, Marcus Street, Pitsmoor). See account re. Rfn. F. Calvert, Vlamertinghe Military Cemetery (III.A.18).

(Panel 53) Rfn. A/3191, Wilfred Arthur Hutchins, 8th (Service) Bn. The King's Royal Rifle Corps: 4th *s.* of the late James Hutchins, ex-Armourer Q.M.Sergt. (25 yrs. service); of 6, Walford Road, Sparkbrook, Birmingham, by his wife Louisa Alice (171, Warwick Road, Sparkhill), *dau.* of George Fox: *b.* Cork, Ireland, 6 May 1893: *educ.* Birmingham Secondary School: served with Shanghai Police Force, 13 September 1912–20 September 1913, being invalided home on the latter date with typhoid fever and dysentery: enlisted King's Royal Rifle Corps, 27 August 1914, after the outbreak of war: went to France, 27 May 1915, and was killed at Ypres, 3 July following, by the bursting of a shell at the doorway of an emplacement while he was in charge of a machine gun. Buried at Ypres. Age 22. *unm.* Three of his brothers also served; all survived. (*IWGC record 4 July*)

(Panel 53) Rfn. R/11830, Alfred Henry Edgar Huxtable, 7th (Service) Bn. The King's Royal Rifle Corps: *s.* of the late Arthur Huxtable, by his wife Eliza Jane (17, Alexandra Road, Erith, co. Kent): *b.* Plumstead, co. Kent, 1900: enlisted Holborn, London, E.C.1: served with the Expeditionary Force in France and Flanders from May 1915, and was killed in action at Hooge, 6 August 1915. Age 15.

(Panel 53) Rfn. R/7006, William Lankester, 8th (Service) Bn. The King's Royal Rifle Corps: eldest *s.* of Harry Lankester, of 'Four Elms,' Edenbridge, co. Kent, and his wife Agnes, *née* Ruder: and brother to Pte.

G/11713, J. Lankester, 11th Queen's Own (Royal West Kent Regt.), missing, believed killed in action at the Third Battle of Ypres, 31 July 1917: *b.* Elsenham, Bishop's Stortford: employee to William Nevett, 46, Prince's Gardens, London S.W.: served with the Expeditionary Force in France from May 1915: Killed in action at the Battle of Hooge, 30 July 1915, while carrying his wounded officer. Age 27. Mr Nevett commissioned a brass plaque in William's memory; it was erected in St. Mary's Church, Elsenham.

To Live In Hearts We Leave Behind Is Not To Die

Wm. Nevett.

His brother John also has no known grave; he is recorded on Panel 45.

(Panel 53) Rfn. A/44, Percy Albert Millett, 8th (Service) Bn. The King's Royal Rifle Corps: *s.* of George Millett, of 41, Newport Street, Lambeth, London, and the late Mary A.C. Millett, his wife: *b.* Lambeth: enlisted London. Killed in action at Hooge, 30 July 1915. Age 23. *unm.* (*IWGC:1926/28, record 20 July*) Remains recovered from a grave marked up as belonging to an 'Unknown British Soldier. K.R.R.C', located in Sanctuary Wood Cemetery, (28.I.24.b.90.97), identified – Clothing, Titles; reinterred, registered 30 April 1928. *Buried in Sanctuary Wood Cemetery (II.F.11).*

(Panel 53) Rfn. A/3769, Joseph O'Callaghan, 8th (Service) Bn. The King's Royal Rifle Corps: yr. brother to L/Sergt. 231, J.M. O'Callaghan, 1st Royal Warwickshire Regt., who also fell: *b.* Budbrooke, Warwick: enlisted Birmingham. Killed in action, 24 July 1915. Age 19. All correspondence regarding Joseph and James should be addressed c/o their sister Mrs Kate Rachel (37, King's Street, Smethwick, co. Stafford).

His brother James also has no known grave; he is recorded on Panel 8.

(Panel 53) Rfn. A/200762, Henry Leonard Payton, 18th (Service) Bn. (Arts & Crafts) The King's Royal Rifle Corps: 2nd *s.* of the late William Payton, of Glemsford, co. Suffolk: previous to the outbreak of the current war with Germany was, for many years, esteemed Headmaster, Glemsford School; thereafter Grays Grammar School, Cavendish: *b.* Sudbury, 1886: enlisted Leyton, co. Essex. Killed in action, 31 July 1917; Hollebeke, Belgium. Age 31.

(Panel 53) Rfn. 10506, Herbert Arthur Potter, 4th Bn. (60th Foot) The King's Royal Rifle Corps: *s.* of the late Williams Potter, Salvation Army Evangelist; and Alice Maud Potter ('Burnley,' Reculvers Road, Westgate-on-Sea, co. Kent) his wife: and yr. brother to Pte. 275165, F.A. Potter, 2/4th London Regt. (Royal Fusiliers), killed in action, 22 March 1918: *b.* Westgate-on-Sea: enlisted London. Killed in action, 28 January 1915. Age 21. *unm.*

His brother Frederick is commemorated in Chauny Communal Cemetery British Extension (Sp. Mem.).

(Panel 53) Rfn. R/17094, Archibald Henry Rooff, 18th (Service) Bn. (Arts & Crafts) The King's Royal Rifle Corps: *s.* of Charles John Rooff, of 42, Saltram Crescent, Maida Hill, Paddington, London, by his wife Emily Elizabeth: and brother to Pte. R/1501, F.H. Rooff, 10th K.R.R.C., died of wounds, 25 June 1916: *b.* Blockley, co. Worcester: enlisted Kensington, London, W.: Killed in action, 31 July 1917, in the attack at Forret Farm, south-west of Hollebeke.

His brother Francis also has no known grave, he is recorded below.

(Panel 53) Rfn. R/1501, Francis Harold Rooff, 'A' Coy., 10th (Service) Bn. The King's Royal Rifle Corps: *s.* of Charles John Rooff, of 42, Saltram Crescent, Maida Hill, Paddington, London, by his wife Emily Elizabeth: and brother to Rfn. R/17094, A.H. Rooff, 18th K.R.R.C., killed in action, 31 July 1917: *b.* Blockley, Worcester: enlisted Marylebone, London, W., September 1914: served with the Expeditionary Force in France and Flanders from July 1915, and died 25 June 1916, of wounds. Age 24. *unm.* See account re. Rfn. F. Calvert, Vlamertinghe Military Cemetery (III.A.18).

His brother Archibald also has no known grave, he is recorded above.

(Panel 53) Rfn. 9268, Frederick Ryder, 3rd Bn. (60th Foot) The King's Royal Rifle Corps: *s.* of the late Joseph Ryder, by his wife Theresa (Addingham, co. York): and elder brother to Pte. 10524, A.P. Ryder, 2nd Duke of Wellington's Regt., died 24 August 1914, of wounds: enlisted Bishop's Auckland, Co. Durham. Died on 5 May 1915, of wounds. Age 26. *unm.*

His brother Arthur is buried in Hautrage Military Cemetery (II.D.9).

(Panel 53) Rfn. 10489, Frederick Herman Victor Spinks, 'B' Coy, 1st Bn. (60th Foot) The King's Royal Rifle Corps: 2nd *s.* of Thomas Samuel Spinks, of 114, Leucha Road, St. James' Street, Walthamstow, by his wife Clara Amelia, *dau.* of Frederick Herman Greenslade: *b.* Clapton, London, N., 29 October 1896: *educ.* Coppermill Road Council School, Walthamstow: enlisted on 27 January 1912: served with the Expeditionary Force in France and Flanders from 13 August 1914: served through the retreat from Mons, etc., and was killed in action two days before his 18th birthday, nr. Ypres, 27 October 1914. A comrade wrote, "He was killed in action the same day as Prince Maurice of Battenberg. His company had advanced against the Germans and taken up a position for the night. He could have lain down and gone to sleep because he was a signaller, but the man next to him had to do two hours on duty looking through the porthole in the trench, and as he felt a bit bad, your poor boy offered to do it for him. Well, Fred had not been looking out for more than ten minutes when a bullet struck him in the head and he must have died instantaneously. I cannot tell you more particulars now, but I know it was near Ypres. I was entrusted to write your letter because Fred was a signaller, and I am one of the few that are left." Gained 3rd Class certificate for education, 23 February 1912; 2nd Class, 2 April 1912. Age 17 years, 363 days.

(Panel 53) Rfn. R/7034, Ernest Reader Vincent, 9th (Service) Bn. The King's Royal Rifle Corps: *s.* of Henry Vincent, of 40, Queen Street, Sutton Bridge, co. Lincoln, by his wife Susannah: enlisted Hounslow, co. Middlesex. Killed in action, 16 June 1915. Age 23. *unm.* Remains recovered from a grave marked as belonging to an 'Unknown British Soldier. 7034. 9/K.R.R', (28.I.11.c.3.1), identified – Clothing, Boots, Titles; registered, reinterred 24 November 1928. *Buried in Sanctuary Wood Cemetery (II.M.4).*

In Jesu's Perfect Love Rest Evermore
From Mother And Family

(Panel 53) Rfn. R/7942, Walter Walker, 4th Bn. (60th Foot) The King's Royal Rifle Corps: *s.* of Richard Walker, Coal Miner; of Stonebroom, Alfreton, co. Derby, by his wife Eliza: *b.* Morton, *c.*1878: enlisted Nottingham, September 1914: served with the Expeditionary Force in France and Flanders from 6 May 1915, and was killed in action somewhere in France on the 25th of that month, being blown up by a mine explosion. Age 37. His friend Rfn. R/7943,

S. Bramley was also killed. He was married to Annie Elizabeth Walker (62, Station Street, Sutton-in-Ashfield), and leaves three children. *The Notts Free Press,* 'In Memoriam,' 26 May 1916:-

> *One sad year has passed away*
> *Since our great sorrow fell.*
> *Yet we mourn within our hearts*
> *For him we loved so well.*
> *He bravely answered duty's call, he gave his life for one and all.*
> *Greater love hath no man than this that he lay down his life for his friend.*
> *There is a link death cannot sever, for love and memory last forever.*
> From his loving Wife & Children.

Rfn. Bramley also has no known grave; he is recorded above.

(Panel 53) Rfn. R/29096, James Henry Wearn, 18th (Service) Bn. (Arts & Crafts) The King's Royal Rifle Corps: *s.* of the late James Wearn: enlisted London. Killed in action, 31 July 1917. Age 27. He was married to Annie Mary Akers, *née* Wearn (Great Coxwell, nr. Faringdon, co. Berks).

(Panel 53) Capt. Percy Joseph Viner Viner-Johnson, 3rd (Reserve) attd. 1st Bn. (62nd Foot) The Duke of Edinburgh's (Wiltshire Regt.): *s.* of Capt. J. Viner Viner-Johnson, Berkshire Yeomanry (served in South Africa, 1901–03): *b.* London, 12 October 1875: *educ.* St. Paul's School, 1888–1890: a member of the Royal Colonial Institute, acting as Relief Magistrate, Orange Free State, South Africa, was home on leave when war was declared: previously served (rank Capt.) 1st (Volunteer) Battn. King's Royal Rifle Corps: gazetted 2nd Lieut. 3rd Wiltshire Regt. September 1914. This appointment was cancelled in November 1914, in which month he was gazetted Capt. in the same battalion, to date from September 1914: served with the Expeditionary Force in France and Flanders, attd. 1st Battn., and was killed in action at Spanbroek-Molen, nr. Wytschaete, 12 March 1915. The Officer Comdg. 1st Battn. gave the following account of him, "Capt. Viner-Johnson was killed in action on 12 March. He fell most gallantly leading his men. In addition to being a very gallant and brave man, he was a most valuable officer, and his death is a very great loss to the regiment. As a comrade he had endeared himself to all his brother officers and men, and his death is deeply deplored by all." The following announcement appeared in the *Harrismith Chronicle* (S.Africa) – "Among the casualties of the British Forces in France is recorded the death of Capt. P.Viner-Johnson, of the Wiltshire Regt. Mr Viner-Johnson was for some time Assistant Resident Magistrate in Harrismith, and afterwards Relieving Magistrate in the Free State. He was an enthusiastic member of the Crown Lodge of the S.O.E., and was held in the highest esteem by all who knew him. Quiet and unassuming, he was a fine type of English gentleman, and his loss will be keenly felt by all who had the privilege of his acquaintance. He was the stamp of man this country can ill afford to lose." Age 39.

(Panel 53) Capt. Arthur Curgenven Magor, 3rd (Reserve) attd. 2nd Bn. (99th Foot) The Duke of Edinburgh's (Wiltshire Regt.): *yst. s.* of the late Edward Auriol Magor, J.P., of Lamellan, St. Tudy, co. Cornwall, and his wife Mary Caroline Magor (Middlecot, Weybridge, co. Surrey) *b.* 3 March 1879: *educ.* Blundell's School, Tiverton, co. Devon (Petergate, 1893–97); Exeter College, Oxford (1898–99): gazetted 2nd Lieut. Wiltshire Regt. February 1900; promoted Lieut. August following: served in the South African War, took part in operations in Orange River Colony, including actions at Bethlehem and Wittebergen, and operations in Transvaal (Queen's Medal, 2 clasps): promoted Capt. September 1908; retired from Active List, September 1912; entered 3rd Battn. of his regiment: mobilised on the outbreak of war, August 1914; proceeded to France with the Expeditionary Force, and was killed in action (attd. 2nd Battn.) during a night attack nr. Ypres, 17 October 1914. Age 35. He *m.* October 1912; Dora, eldest *dau.* of the late Albert Bulteel (& Mrs) Fisher, of Court Hill, nr. Devizes, and had a son, Arthur Frank Tregarthen, *b.* July 1914. House monitor at Blundell's for three terms, he gained his 2nd. XI Colours in 1896 and, in the same year (with A.W. Squirl as his partner), won the Tennis Challenge cup. Capt. Magor's recreations were hunting and shooting. One of the earliest dated casualties recorded on the Menin Gate.

His son Capt. A.F.T. Magor, Wiltshire Regt., was killed in the Western Desert during Operation Crusader (Eighth Army's first operation), 26 November 1941; he is buried in Alexandria (Hadra) War Memorial Cemetery (2.G.4).

(Panel 53) Lieut. Edmund Spencer, 2nd Bn. (99th Foot) The Duke of Edinburgh's (Wiltshire Regt.): 2nd *s.* of the Rev. William Edmund (& Mrs. S.S.) Spencer, of St. Botolph's Vicarage, Colchester: *b.* South Benfleet, co. Essex, 12 November 1889: *educ.* Mowden Hall, co. Essex; Forest Hall (Head of School; Captain of cricket and football teams); Royal Military College, Sandhurst (played in the 'Soccer' team): joined Wiltshire Regt. 2nd Lieut. April 1910; promoted Lieut. May 1913: served with his battalion at Dublin, Gosport, and Gibraltar: accompanied his battalion to Belgium, October 1914: served with the Expeditionary Force there, and was killed on the 20th of the same month in an advanced guard action between Ypres and Becelaere. Lieut. Spencer obtained a First Class Certificate in the Army Gymnasium Course at Aldershot, and was captain of the battalion 'Soccer' team, and was also in the Cricket XI.: 20 October 1914. Age 24. *unm.*

(Panel 53) 2nd Lieut. Eric Laurence Arthur Hart Burges, 3rd (Reserve) attd. 2nd Bn. (99th Foot) The Duke of Edinburgh's (Wiltshire Regt.): *yr. s.* of the late Rev. T. Hart Burges, D.D., Rector of Devizes: *b.* Devizes, co. Wilts: *educ.* St. Edmund's School, Canterbury; St. John's College, Oxford, where he graduated B.A. (1913), with Third Class Honours in Modern History, and had just completed his studies, taking the Diploma in Economics and Political Science with Distinction and the Certificate in Social Training: applied for a commission, having been a Corpl. in the College O.T.C.: gazetted 2nd Lieut. 3rd Wiltshire Regt. 15 August 1914; served with the Expeditionary Force in France and Flanders attd. 2nd Battn. from 4 October following, and was killed in action at Reutel on the 23rd. (October 1914).

(Panel 53) 2nd Lieut. William Percy Campbell, 3rd (Reserve) attd. 2nd Bn. (99th Foot) The Duke of Edinburgh's (Wiltshire Regt.): 2nd *s.* of John Edward Campbell, F.R.S., Fellow & Bursar, Hertford College, Oxford: *b.* 2 May 1894: *educ.* Oxford Preparatory School, Clifton College (Scholar); Hertford

College, Oxford (Scholar), where he had just finished his first year of medical study when war broke out: volunteered for Foreign Service: gazetted 2nd Lieut. Wiltshire Regt. August 1914: served with the Expeditionary Force in France and Flanders from 4 October, and was killed in action a few miles east of Ypres on the 24th. (October 1914) while attempting to bring a wounded comrade to a place of safety. Age 20. *unm.*

(Panel 53) 2nd Lieut. Clive Hereward Chandler, 1st Bn. (62nd Foot) The Duke of Edinburgh's (Wiltshire Regt.).: *b.* Exeter, 18 July 1884: served for many years with the Wiltshire Regt., attaining rank Sergt.-Drummer: served with the Expeditionary Force in France and Flanders: gazetted 2nd Lieut. for service In the Field, and was killed in action on the Yser, 17 November 1914. Age 30. He *m.* Olivia May Court, and had a *dau.* – Ethel Muriel, *b.* September 1912.

(Panel 53) 2nd Lieut. Arthur Bryant Phelps McClenaghan, Special Reserve attd. 1st Bn. (62nd Foot) The Duke of Edinburgh's (Wiltshire Regt.): *s.* of Rev. George Richard McClenaghan, of Rushmere Vicarage, Thistlehurst, Ipswich, and Amy Margaret McClenaghan, his spouse: and brother to Capt. G.M. McClenaghan, 1st Queen's Own (R.W.K.), died of wounds, 8 November 1918: *b.* Epsom, 27 February 1895: *educ.* Marlborough College (Foundation Scholar); Captain of his House; Lieut. (O.T.C.): obtained a History Scholarship, Clare College, Cambridge but – following the outbreak of war and his obtaining a commission 2nd Lieut. Special Reserve, Wiltshire Regt. – never commenced his University career: left for the Front attd. 1st Wiltshirte Regt. for Active Service, two days before Christmas 1914, and was shot through the heart while leading his men in a charge on the German trenches at Hooge, 16 June 1915. A brother officer gave the following account of the circumstances, "We had made a successful charge and taken two German trenches. He was rallying some men at the time when he was shot through the heart. I placed him in a trench, hoping the wound would not be fatal. His only words to me were, 'Don't mind me.' I had to leave him to go on with the charge. When I saw him about a quarter of an hour later he had died. He died a very gallant death at the head of his company." A Captain of his battalion wrote, "Your boy was one of my subalterns for four months, when I gave up the command to a school-friend of his, Mr Gregory. He died on 16th June in an attack on the German trenches, leading his men and showing by his conduct a contempt for death that did much to steady his men." Age 20. *unm.*

His brother George is buried in Pont-Sur-Sambre Communal Cemetery (A.10).

(Panel 53) 2nd Lieut. Angus Neil McLean, 8th (Reserve) attd. 1st Bn. (62nd Foot) The Duke of Edinburgh's (Wiltshire Regt.): *s.* of William McLean, of 82, Beaconsfield Villas, Brighton, co. Sussex, and Mary, his wife: and brother to 2nd Lieut. R.A. McLean, 6th Seaforth Highlanders, killed in action, 13 November 1916; Beaumont Hamel, Somme: *b.* co. Ross: *educ.* Edinburgh University (graduated M.A.). Killed in action, 22 June 1915, at Ypres. Remembered on Brighton War Memorial, and St. Peter's Church Roll of Honour Register. His brother Raymond is buried in Mailly Wood Cemetery, Mailly-Maillet (I.F.30).

(Panel 53) Sergt. 7727, William James Pearce, 2nd Bn. (99th Foot) The Duke of Edinburgh's (Wiltshire Regt.): late of Pembroke Dock, South Wales: *b.* Pewsey, co. Wilts: enlisted Devizes. Killed in action, 4 November 1914. *Buried in Tyne Cot Cemetery (LXI.J.3).*

(Panel 53) Sergt. 29557, Arthur Tree, 1st Bn. (62nd Foot) The Duke of Edinburgh's (Wiltshire Regt.): *s.* of Alfred Tree, of 36, High Street, Cosham, Portsmouth, co. Hants, and Charlotte Tree, his spouse: and yr. brother to Sergt. 315011, E. Tree, Royal Garrison Artillery, killed in action, 4 July 1917: *b.* Cosham: enlisted Portsmouth. Killed in action, 7 June 1917. Age 24.

His brother Ernest is buried in Vlamertinghe New Military Cemetery (IV.F.6).

(Panel 53) Corpl. 25027, Frank Austin, 1st Bn. (62nd Foot) The Duke of Edinburgh's (Wiltshire Regt.): enlisted Bicester, co. Oxon. Reported missing, since verified as having been killed in action following a raid on the German defences in the Wulverghem sector, 5 June 1917. Age 27. He was married to Emma May Austin (West End, Launton, Bicester). See Pte. A. Conduit, Wulverghem-Lindenhoek Road Military Cemetery (I.C.5).

(Panel 53) L/Corpl. 29805, Thomas Robert Ainsworth, 1st Bn. (62nd Foot) The Duke of Edinburgh's (Wiltshire Regt.): formerly no.22487, Prince Albert's (Somerset Light Infantry): *s.* of Thomas Ainsworth, of Brewery House, South Stoke, Bath, co. Somerset, by his wife Amelia: Occupation – Salesman; Messrs Rivington & Johnson, Florists & Gardeners, Coombe Down: enlisted Bath: served with the Expeditionary Force in France and Flanders, and was one of eight men of 1st Battn. killed in the Westhoek-Bellewaarde trenches, 12 August 1917. Age 27. He was married to Nora Emily Bryant, *née* Ainsworth (11, Parnell Road, Clevedon, co. Somerset).

(Panel 53) L/Corpl. 32514, Herbert Henry Davis, 1st Bn. (62nd Foot) The Duke of Edinburgh's (Wiltshire Regt.): formerly no.17140, Dorsetshire Regt.: *s.* of William Davis, of Steps Pond Cottage, Studland, nr. Swanage, co. Dorset, by his wife Charlotte: enlisted Dorchester. Missing/believed killed in action 5 June 1917. Age 25. Recorded on St. Nicholas' Church (Studland) Roll of Honour. See Pte. A. Conduit, Wulverghem-Lindenhoek Road Military Cemetery (I.C.5).

(Panel 53) L/Corpl. 10982, Ernest George Leggett, 1st Bn. (62nd Foot) The Duke of Edinburgh's (Wiltshire Regt.): *s.* of William (& Mrs I.) Leggett, of 282, Ferndale Road, Swindon: and yr. brother to L/Corpl. 10981, W.S. Leggett, Wiltshire Regt., killed in action, 16 June 1915: *b.* Swindon: enlisted there. Killed in action, 2 September 1915. Age 21. Remembered on Swindon Borough War Memorial.

His brother William also has no known grave; he is recorded below.

(Panel 53) L/Corpl. 10981, William Stephen Leggett, 1st Bn. (62nd Foot) The Duke of Edinburgh's (Wiltshire Regt.): *s.* of William (& Mrs I.) Leggett, of 282, Ferndale Road, Swindon: and elder brother to L/Corpl. 10982, E.G. Leggett, Wiltshire Regt.; killed in action, 2 September 1915: *b.* Swindon: enlisted there. Killed in action, 16 June 1915. Age 22. Remembered on Swindon Borough War Memorial.

His brother Ernest also has no known grave; he is recorded above.

(Panel 53) L/Corpl. 19639, William James Pittam, 1st Bn. (62nd Foot) The Duke of Edinburgh's (Wiltshire Regt.): *s.* of J. (& Mrs) Pittam, of 75, Munz Street, Small Heath, Birmingham. Killed by shellfire (British short shooting), Westhoek Ridge, 4 August 1917. Age 25. He leaves a wife, Alice Maud Pittam (79, Mary Street, Balsall Heath, Birmingham). Remains recovered from an unmarked grave (28.J.7.b.8.8) 26 January 1927; identified – Damaged Disc; reinterred, registered 29 January 1927. *Buried in Sanctuary Wood Cemetery (III.E. 8).*

(Panel 53) Pte. 10398, William Arthur Brewer, 'D' Coy., 1st Bn. (62nd Foot) The Duke of Edinburgh's (Wiltshire Regt.): 2nd *s.* of George Brewer, of Shamrock Cottage, 81, Wood Lane, Chippenham, by his wife Sarah, *dau.* of William Neate, of 42, Wood Lane, Chippenham: *b.* Chippenham, co. Wilts., 19 May 1892: *educ.* British School there: a pre-war Territorial (three years service), enlisted Wiltshire Regt. 1 September 1914, and was killed in action at Ypres, 13 November 1914. A comrade wrote, "The officer called for volunteers to rush a road, and he was the first to leave the trench, and by so doing was killed by a Maxim gun." Age 21. *unm.* A well-known Wiltshire footballer; Pte. Brewer was formerly Captain of Chippenham Town, but in 1913 signed on for Swindon Town and played one match with the first eleven.

(Panel 53) Pte. 33939, Herbert Edward Coole, 1st Bn. (62nd Foot) The Duke of Edinburgh's (Wiltshire Regt.): *b.* Christchurch, co. Gloucester: enlisted Devizes, co. Wilts. Killed in the vicinity of Westhoek Ridge, 12 August 1917 .

(Panel 53) Pte. 10036, Lionel Walter Coole, 1st Bn. (62nd Foot) The Duke of Edinburgh's (Wiltshire Regt.): *s.* of John Coole, of 'Homeleigh,' Cricklade, co. Wilts, by his wife Mary: *b.* Cricklade, 1896: a pre-war Territorial, volunteered for Active Service, enlisted Swindon, September 1914: served with the Expeditionary Force in France and Flanders, and was killed in action, 11 December 1914, nr. Kemmel. Age 18.

(Panel 53) Pte. 19645, William Doughty, 1st Bn. (62nd Foot) The Duke of Edinburgh's (Wiltshire Regt.): formerly no.11574, Oxford & Bucks Light Infantry: *s.* of Thomas Doughty, of Birmingham, by his wife Annie: *b.* 11 May 1890: Occupation – Brass Cutter: enlisted Birmingham, 1 September 1914; after the outbreak of war: served with the Expeditionary Force in France from 11 May 1915, and was killed in action, 25 September following. Buried in the trenches at Hooge. Age 25. He *m.* St. Mary's Church, Aston, 28 February 1915; Maud Lily (82, Park Lane, Aston, Birmingham), *dau.* of George Brittain. *s.p.*

(Panel 53) Pte. 9026, George Cleaver Dugan, 1st Bn. (62nd Foot) The Duke of Edinburgh's (Wiltshire Regt.): eldest *s.* of the late George Dugan, Carpenter; of Portsmouth, co. Hants, by his wife Olive (20,

Essex Road, Portsmouth), *dau.* of John Cleaver: *b.* Fratton, Portsmouth, 26 February 1895: *educ.* Milton, and Kingston Schools: Occupation – Artificial Stone Mason: enlisted in June 1913: served with the Expeditionary Force in France and Flanders from August 1914: wounded during the retreat from Mons, and invalided home; returned to the Front, October following, took part in the Battle of Ypres, and was again invalided home with frost-bitten feet: returned to the Front on 18 May 1915, and was killed in action at Ypres, 23 June following. Age 20. *unm.*

(Panel 53) Pte. 6802, Albert William Fiddler, 1st Bn. (62nd Foot) The Duke of Edinburgh's (Wiltshire Regt.): late of Little Cherwill: enlisted Devizes, 18 January 1904: served with the Expeditionary Force in France from 14 August 1914, and was killed in action on 21 November 1914 when, on the road between Hooge and Ypres, the battalion were shelled by shrapnel. Pte. H.W. Talbot and Bdsmn. R. Spackman were also killed.

Pte. Hugh Talbot also has no known grave, he is recorded below; Robert Spackman is buried in Vlamertinghe Military Cemetery (French Plot, B.10).

(Panel 53) Pte. 8633, Frank Fisher, 1st Bn. (62nd Foot) The Duke of Edinburgh's (Wiltshire Regt.): *s.* of Frederick Fisher, of Southon Cottages, Collingbourne Ducis, Marlborough, co. Wilts, by his wife Elizabeth: and elder brother to Pte. 32197, H.L. Fisher, 2nd Wiltshire Regt., killed in action, 31 July 1917: *b.* Collingbourne Kingston, nr. Marlborough: enlisted Devizes: served with the Expeditionary Force in France and Flanders from August 1914. Killed in action, 12 March 1915. Age 26.

His brother Herbert also has no known grave; he is recorded below.

(Panel 53) Pte. 32197, Herbert Leonard Fisher, 2nd Bn. (99th Foot) The Duke of Edinburgh's (Wiltshire Regt.): *s.* of Frederick Fisher, of Southon Cottages, Collingbourne Ducis, Marlborough, co. Wilts, by his wife Elizabeth: and *yr.* brother to Pte. F. Fisher, 1st Wiltshire Regt., killed in action, 12 March 1915: *b.* Collingbourne Kingston, nr. Marlborough: enlisted Devizes: served with the Expeditionary Force in France and Flanders from January 1917. Killed in action nr. Zillebeke, 31 July following. Age 19.

His brother Frank also has no known grave; he is recorded above.

(Panel 53) Pte. 27052, Arthur John Gibb, 2nd Bn. (99th Foot) The Duke of Edinburgh's (Wiltshire Regt.): *s.* of William Gibb, Gardener; of Napsbury Cottages, Wadhurst, co. Sussex, by his wife Ellen, Domestic Servant: *b.* Napsbury Cottages, 5 March 1898: enlisted Chichester, co. Kent: posted Essex Regt., no.36375: served with the Expeditionary Force in France and Flanders, being subsequently transf'd. Wiltshire Regt., and was killed in action in the vicinity of Zillebeke, 31 July 1917. Age 19.

(Panel 53) Pte. 19633, Harry Goode, 1st Bn. (62nd Foot) The Duke of Edinburgh's (Wiltshire Regt.): formerly no.11344, Oxford & Bucks Light Infantry: *s.* of the late Henry Goode, by his wife Amy (11, Tunnel Cottages, Galley Common, Nuneaton, co. Warwick): and *yr.* brother to Rfn. Z/629, W. Goode, Rifle Brigade, killed in action almost six weeks previously: enlisted Nuneaton. Killed in action, 16 June 1915. Age 19.

His brother William also has no known grave; he is recorded on Panel 48.

(Panel 53) Pte. 8514, Harry Hedges, 2nd Bn. (99th Foot) The Duke of Edinburgh's (Wiltshire Regt.): *s.* of the late Isaac Hedges, of Faringdon, co. Berks, and his wife Hester: and *yr.* brother to Pte. 8450, T. Hedges, Wiltshire Regt., killed in action the same day; 24 October 1914. Age 23. *unm.*

His brother Thomas also has no known grave; he is recorded below.

(Panel 53) Pte. 8450, Thomas Hedges, 2nd Bn. (99th Foot) The Duke of Edinburgh's (Wiltshire Regt.): *s.* of the late Isaac Hedges, of Faringdon, co. Berks, and his wife Hester: and elder brother to Pte. 8514, H. Hedges, Wiltshire Regt., killed in action the same day; 24 October 1914. Age 28. *unm.*

His brother Harry also has no known grave; he is recorded above.

(Panel 53) Pte. 13705, William John Landfear, 1st Bn. (62nd Foot) The Duke of Edinburgh's (Wiltshire Regt.): *b.* Stanton Fitzwarren, co. Wilts: enlisted Devizes. Killed in action, 12 March 1915. Dedicated – 'To The Brave Lads Of Stanton Fitzwarren Who Gave Themselves To God, King And Country In The Great War Beginning August 1914: On Whom & All Souls Jesu Mercy;' one of seven men remembered on St. Leonard's (Parish Churchyard) War Memorial. See Gnr. F.E. Giles, Royal Garrison Artillery, Tyne Cot Memorial (Panel 7).

(Panel 53) Pte. 25475, William George Marshall, 6th (Service) Bn. The Duke of Edinburgh's (Wiltshire Regt.): formerly no.22746, Somerset Light Infantry: *s.* of William Marshall, of Mount Pleasant, Bordon, co. Hants, by his wife Esther: and elder brother to Pte. 19336, A.C. Marshall, Hampshire Regt., reported missing in action, 1 July 1916: enlisted Somerset Light Infantry, Petersfield, co. Hants; subsequently transf'd. Wiltshire Regt. Killed in action, 2 August 1917. Age 30. He leaves a wife, Dorothy Constance May Marshall (Furze Hill, Fordingbridge, co. Hants).

His brother Albert also has no known grave; he is commemorated on the Thiepval Memorial, Somme.

(Panel 53) Pte. 29587, Albert George Mintram, 2nd Bn. (99th Foot) The Duke of Edinburgh's (Wiltshire Regt.): *s.* of the late Alfred Mintram, of 16, Short Street, Southampton, by his wife Alice Elizabeth: and brother to Plumber A.G. Mintram, H.M.H.S. *Salta*, lost at sea when that ship hit a mine and was sunk, 10 April 1917, one mile north of Le Havre: *b.* Winchester: enlisted Southampton: served with the Expeditionary Force, and was killed in action, 31 July 1917. Age 21. *unm.* Pte. Mintram's mother has since remarried; now Mrs George Baker (The Bungalow, Hardley, Hythe).

With no known grave but the sea, his brother Alfred is commemorated on the Salta Memorial; Ste. Marie Cemetery, Le Havre (Plot 62).

(Panel 53) Pte. 5421, Arthur George Moon, 2nd Bn. (99th Foot) The Duke of Edinburgh's (Wiltshire Regt.): late of Dunedin, New Zealand: *b.* Bromham, co. Wilts: enlisted Devizes. Killed in action, 24 October 1914, nr. Becelaere Road. Age 33. He was married to Louise Simpkins, *née* Moon (113, Surrey Street, Dunedin). Remains recovered from an unmarked grave (28.D.29.b.0.5), 14 February 1927; identified – Damaged Disc, Clothing; reinterred, registered 19 February 1927. *Buried in Sanctuary Wood Cemetery (III.F.32).*

(Panel 53) Pte. 10065, Walter Renyard, 1st Bn. (62nd Foot) The Duke of Edinburgh's (Wiltshire Regt.): *s.* of Mary Amelia Renyard (14, Longhedge, Corsley, Warminster, co. Wilts): and yr. brother to L/Corpl. S/2070, R. Renyard, 7th Rifle Brigade, killed in action, 16 October 1917: *b.* Christchurch, co. Hants: enlisted Warminster. Died of wounds, 13 March 1915. Age 21.

His brother Robert is buried in Buttes New British Cemetery (Polygon Wood), (I.D.10).

(Panel 53) Pte. 10030, Arthur Joseph Ricketts, 1st Bn. (62nd Foot) The Duke of Edinburgh's (Wiltshire Regt.): *s.* of Albert Edward Ricketts, of Avoncliffe Bungalow, Upper Westwood, Bradford-on-Avon, by his wife Charlotte: and brother to Pte. 13771, J.A. Ricketts, 5th Wiltshire Regt., died 8 December 1917; Mesopotamia: *b.* London, 1892: enlisted Trowbridge. Killed in action, 12 March 1915; Belgium. Age 22.

His brother john is buried in Baghdad (North Gate) War Cemetery (III.J.4).

(Panel 53) Pte. 31958, Alfred Rogers, 1st Bn. (62nd Foot) The Duke of Edinburgh's (Wiltshire Regt.): 3rd *s.* of George Rogers, of Buckland, Portsmouth, co. Hants: *b.* Southsea, co. Hants, 26 January 1881: *educ.* Buckland Elementary School: employee Portsmouth Dockyards: enlisted 1 September 1916: served with the Expeditionary Force in France and Flanders from January 1917, and was killed in action at Messines Ridge, 7 June following. Age 36. He *m.* St. Steven's Church, Buckland, 13 December 1916; Ivy, *dau.* of the late Sidney Robes.

(Panel 53) Pte. 8898, Percy Edgar Spackman, 2nd Bn. (99th Foot) The Duke of Edinburgh's (Wiltshire Regt.): *s.* of Isaac Spackman, of Ogbourne St. George, Marlborough, co. Wilts, by his wife Ann: and brother to Spr. 15892, I. Spackman, Royal Engineers, died of wounds, 24 May 1915; and Sergt. 8897, W.A. Spackman, Wiltshire Regt., died on 9 April 1917. Killed in action, 24 October 1914. Age 19. One of three brothers who fell.

His brother Isaac is buried in Boulogne Eastern Cemetery (VIII.D.45); William has no known grave, he is commemorated on the Arras (Faubourg d'Amiens) Memorial (Bay 7).

(Panel 53) Pte. 8155, Hugh Waite Talbot, 1st Bn. (62nd Foot) The Duke of Edinburgh's (Wiltshire Regt.): late of Finsbury Park, London: *b.* Cholsey, co. Berks: enlisted Devizes: served with the Expeditionary Force in France from 14 August 1914, and was killed in action, 21 November 1914 when, on the road between Hooge and Ypres, the battalion were shelled by shrapnel. Pte. A.W. Fiddler and Bdsmn. R. Spackman were also killed.

Pte. Albert Fiddler also has no known grave, he is recorded above; Robert Spackman is buried in Vlamertinghe Military Cemetery (French Plot, B.10).

(Panel 53) Capt. Percival George Franklin, 8th Bn. (Ardwick) The Manchester Regt. (T.F.) attd. 1/8th Bn. (Irish) The King's (Liverpool) Regt. (T.F.): *s.* of Ellen Caroline Franklin (22, Central Road, West Didsbury, Manchester). Killed in action, 18 July 1917. Age 27. *Buried in Vlamertinghe New Military Cemetery (I.G.25).*

(Panel 53) Capt. Archibald Bowers-Taylor, 1/6th Bn. The Manchester Regt. (T.F.): *s.* of Rev. Bowers-Taylor, by his wife Annie. Killed in action, 7 June 1917. Age 35. He was married to Ethel Bowers-Taylor, *née* Storey-Bates (Friarmere Vicarage, Delph, Oldham, co. Lancaster).

(Panel 53) L/Corpl. 40959, Thomas William James Churchhouse, 19th (Service) Bn. (4th City) The Manchester Regt.: formerly no.3000, Leicestershire Regt.: *s.* of Albert E. (& Mrs) Churchhouse, of 38, Walnut Street, Leicester: and elder brother to Telegraphist, Tyneside Z/5506, A. Churchhouse, HMS *Stephen Furness*, R.N.V.R., died when that ship was torpedoed and sunk, 31 December 1917, off Contrary Head, Isle of Man. Killed in action, 31 July 1917. Age 20. (*IWGC record Churchouse*)

Having no known grave but the sea; his brother Arthur is commemorated on the Chatham Naval Memorial (27).

On 29 October 1915, 12th Manchesters took over a section of the line approximately one mile south of Hooge. Already in a poor state of repair, the trenches were further damaged by heavy rain which caused the parapet to collapse and fall in. The considerable repair and improvement this necessitated had to be carried out in full view of the enemy whose artillery, to add to the Manchesters misery, dropped a number of shells into the support trenches on 2nd November. Surprisingly, only one man was killed:-

(Panel 53) L/Corpl. 4664, Sam Wolstenholme, 'C' Coy., 12th (Service) Bn. The Manchester Regt.: *s.* of Mark Wolstenholme, of 99, Hillgate Street, Ashton-under-Lyne, by his wife Marie: late *husb.* to Hannah Wolstenholme (15, Moss Street, Ashton-under-Lyne, Manchester): enlisted in September 1914: served with the Expeditionary Force in France from July 1915, and was killed in action, 2 November 1915. Age 31. Remains of an 'Unknown British Soldier. Manchesters' recovered on 9 February from an unmarked grave (28.I.24.d.15.45); identified – Khaki, Titles, Badge of Rank, Boots; reinterred, registered 12 March 1929. *Buried in Sanctuary Wood Cemetery (V.C.9).*

PANEL 53 ENDS PTE. H. BLACKMAN, MANCHESTER REGT.

PANEL 55 BEGINS PTE. H.E. BOOTH, MANCHESTER REGT.

(Panel 55) Pte. 41839, Arthur Preston Merriman, 16th (Service) Bn. (1st City) The Manchester Regt.: formerly no.32790, East Surrey Regt.: *s.* of Henry Merriman, of 62, Donald Road, West Croydon, co. Surrey, by his wife Caroline: and yr. brother to Pte. G/8933, J. Merriman, 2nd Queen's (Royal West Surrey Regt.), killed in action, 21 October 1914; First Battle of Ypres: *b.* Penge: enlisted Peckham. Killed in action, 31 July 1917; Third Battle of Ypres. Age 23. He was married to Frances Jane Cooley, *née* Merriman (26, Boston Road, West Croydon).

His brother John also has no known grave; he is recorded on Panel 13.

(Panel 55) 2nd Lieut. Ronald Marmaduke Dawnay Harvey, 4th (Extra Reserve) Bn. The Prince of Wales's (North Staffordshire Regt.) attd. 1st Bn. Bedfordshire Regt.: *s.* of the late Rev. Frederick Mortimer Harvey, Rector of Bolnhurst, co. Bedford, by his marriage to the late Katherine Dorothea, eldest *dau.* of the late Edward J. Parker Jervis, of The Pyrehill, Stone, co. Stafford: *b.* Buckingham Palace Hotel, London, S.W., 16 May 1887: *educ.* Haileybury, where he was a prominent gymnast: after leaving school, he went to Australia with his parents in 1905, intending to take up farming, but entered the theatrical profession instead: after training in his chosen profession, took the leading role in many parts: returned to England 1909, and joined F.R. Benson's Shakespearean Company (South), touring with the 'Herbert Company;' South Africa 1911: returned to England in 1912, performing with the 'Julia Nelson and Fred Terry Company' until 1913: subsequently settled down to run a garage business with a friend in Somerset, which he gave up on its verge of becoming a success in August 1914, expressing, "In a time like this everybody must do what they can for their country." (His business partner, a fellow Haileyburian, joined the Army, as 2nd Lieut. 4th North Staffordshire Regt.): commissioned 2nd Lieut. North Staffordshire Regt. 15 August 1914: served with the Expeditionary Force in France and Flanders from March 1915, attd. 1st Bedfordshire Regt. Wounded in the thigh while throwing hand-grenades during the attack on Hill 60, 20 April 1915, 2nd Lieut. Harvey was killed outright by a shell early the following morning. Buried with others of his regiment behind Hill 60. Age 27. *unm.* Remains of an 'Unknown British 2/Lieut.' recovered (28.1.29.c.95.30) Hill 60; identified – Badge of Rank, Regtl. Buttons, Piece of Boot mkd. 'Scott Hammett, Wellington, Som.;' reinterred, registered 26 April 1927. (*IWGC record 20 April*) *Buried in Sanctuary Wood Cemetery (IV.C.13).*

(Panel 55) L/Sergt. 1615, John Charles Joseph Nicholls, 1/6th Bn. The Prince of Wales's (North Staffordshire Regt.), (T.F.): *s.* of Joseph Nicholls, of 36, Leomansley, Lichfield, co. Stafford, by his wife Cecilia Louisa: enlisted Lichfield: served with the Expeditionary Force in France from 4 March 1915, and was killed in action, 8 July 1915. Age 29. Remains recovered from a grave marked as belonging to an 'Unknown British Sergeant. North Staffs.' located in a small battle cemetery at Sanctuary Wood, identified – Badge of Rank, Titles; registered, reinterred 8 March 1928. *Buried in Sanctuary Wood Cemetery (II.D.28).*

Jesus Lives Henceforth Is Death But The Gate To Life Immortal

(Panel 55) Pte. 2467, John James Averill, 1/5th Bn. The Prince of Wales's (North Staffordshire Regt.), (T.F.): *s.* of Ambrose Averill, of 2, Cartledge Street, Hartshill, Stoke-on-Trent, co. Stafford, by his wife Phoebe: *b.* Penkhull: a pre-war member of the Territorial Force: served with the Expeditionary Force in France and Flanders from 4 March 1915, and died of wounds, 5 August 1915. Age 15.

(Panel 55) Pte. 240293, William Crofts, 1/6th Bn. The Prince of Wales's (North Staffordshire Regt.), (T.F.): *b.* Burton-on-Trent, co. Stafford: enlisted there: served with the Expeditionary Force in France from March 1915, and was killed in action, 8 April 1915. Remains recovered, 12 March 1928; Messines Ridge German Cemetery No.2 (Grave no.4/1); identified – Burial List. *Buried in Sanctuary Wood Cemetery (II.C.35).*

(Panel 55) Pte. 2263, Frederick Dean, 1/6th Bn. The Prince of Wales's (North Staffordshire Regt.), (T.F.): *s.* of Richard Dean, by his wife Emma: served with the Expeditionary Force, and was killed in action, 11 July 1915. Age 23. He was married to Elizabeth Dean (28, New Street, Stafford). Remains recovered from a grave marked up as belonging to an 'Unknown British Soldier', located in a small battle cemetery at Sanctuary Wood, identified – Clothing; registered, reinterred 8 March 1928. *Buried in Sanctuary Wood Cemetery (II.D.27).*

Love And Remembrance Live Forever

(Panel 55) Pte. 24832, Joseph Gershom Hall, 8th (Service) Bn. The Prince of Wales's (North Staffordshire Regt.): *s.* of Edwin Hall, Draper; of 42, Station Street, Sutton-in-Ashfield, co. Nottingham, by his wife Mary Ann, *née* Boot: *b.* Station Street, 1890. Killed in action, 10 June 1917. Age 27. He leaves a wife, Harriet Hall (Sutton-in-Ashfield).

He never gave less than his best,
For him that day was victory,
For me loss irreparable.
In affectionate remembrance from his loving wife, Harriet.

(Panel 55) Pte. 2615, Frank Hilton 'B' Coy., 1/6th Bn. The Prince of Wales's (North Staffordshire Regt.), (T.F.): *s.* of John Hilton, of 53, Harper Street, Willenhall, co. Stafford, by his wife Rosina: enlisted Luton, co. Bedford, after the outbreak of war: served with the Expeditionary Force in France from 4 March 1915, and died of wounds, 6 July following. Age 22. *unm.* Remains recovered from a grave marked up as belonging to an 'Unknown British Soldier', located in a small battle cemetery at Sanctuary Wood, identified – Clothing; registered, reinterred 8 March 1928. *Buried in Sanctuary Wood Cemetery (II.D.25).*

(Panel 55) Pte. 10027, Ernest Parker, 1st Bn. (64th Foot) The Prince of Wales's (North Staffordshire Regt.): *s.* of Mary Ann Parker (51, Crooked Bridge Road, Stafford): and brother to Pte. 7979, W. Parker, King's (Shropshire Light Infantry), killed in action, 9 August 1915: *b.* Christchurch, Stafford: enlisted Lichfield. Killed in action, 8 November 1915. Age 21. *unm.*

His brother Wilfred also has no known grave; he is recorded on Panel 49.

(Panel 55) Major Harold Kenway Colston, 1st Bn. (65th Foot) The York & Lancaster Regt.: *s.* of Surgeon-General C. K. Colston, of Teignmouth, co. Devon: *b.* India, 26 April 1872: *educ.* Clifton College; Royal Military College, Sandhurst: gazetted 2nd Lieut. York & Lancaster Regt. November 1891; posted 1st Battn.: promoted Lieut. March 1895; Capt. September 1901: served in the South African War, 1902: took part in operations in Orange River Colony, March 1902 (Queen's Medal, 2 clasps): obtained his Majority, January 1910: at the outbreak of war with Germany was at Jubbulpore, India, leaving with his battalion, December 1914: served with the Expeditionary Force in France and Flanders from January 1915, and, after the Second Battle of Ypres, was reported wounded and missing/believed killed, 23 April 1915.

Major Colston, whose battalion had been resting in billets, went to the aid of the Canadians with a party of his men. The Canadian flank had been exposed by the attack, which the Germans delivered after their use of poison gas for the first time, and Major Colston and his men were all found killed amongst the dead Canadians. It was said, "It did not seem possible that any human being could live in the shower of shot and shell which began to play upon the advancing troops. They suffered terrible casualties for a short time; every other man seemed to fall." His body was found three months later, 24 July, identified and buried. Age 42. Mentioned in Sir John (now Lord) French's Despatch, 31 May 1915; Major Colston leaves a wife, Violet, *dau.* of A.B. Patterson, C.I.E., Indian Civil Service (ret'd).

(Panel 55) Capt. Hubert James East, 1st Bn. (65th Foot) The York & Lancaster Regt.: 2nd *s.* of W.H. East, of 'East Lee,' Maison Dieu Road, Dover, A.R.C.A.: *b.* 1884: Religion – Roman Catholic: *educ.* Dover College: obtained a commission, 3rd (West York Militia) Battn. York & Lancaster Regt. 1901; served with that unit in the final stages of the South African War, 1902, taking part in the operations in Cape Colony, January–31 May (Queen's Medal, 2 clasps): gazetted Regular Army, 2nd Lieut. 2nd Bn. (84th Foot) York & Lancaster Regt. 4 July 1903; promoted Lieut. 3 February 1906; Capt. 22 July 1912: served with the Expeditionary Force in France and Flanders, and was killed in action while leading his men in a charge at Ypres, 10 May 1915. A Private of his company, who acted as his servant, wrote, "He was leading his men into action when he received his first wound, which was in his leg, and he was leaving the line when he saw his Subaltern lying very badly wounded. He went to his assistance, and was helping some men to attend to him, and it was when raising him from the ground to give him a drink of water that he received his fatal wound, and only lived a few moments. His last words were: 'Get him away – I'm done for!' He was a hero all through, and I am proud of having had such a master." He *m.* August 1914; Vera Mary Hyde Sheward Brown, since remarried, now Mrs Upward (111, Victoria Drive, Eastbourne, formerly of 1, Mount Ephraim Mansions, Tunbridge Wells), *dau.* of the late George Sheward Brown, of 10, Linden Park, Tunbridge Wells, and had a *dau., b.* (posthumous) 1915.

(Panel 55) Capt. Henry Frederick Rycroft, 3rd (Reserve) attd. 2nd Bn. (84th Foot) The York & Lancaster Regt.: *s.* of Charles Alfred W. Rycroft, J.P., of 'Everlands,' Ide Hill, co. Kent: *b.* Belgravia, 1879: proceeded to France in November 1914, and was killed in action, 7 August 1915; Menin Cross Roads, nr. Ypres. Age 36. Remains recovered from an unmarked grave (28.I.17.a.1.6); identified – Disc, Clothing, Boots, Gold Ring; reinterred, registered 12 December 1927. *Buried in Sanctuary Wood Cemetery (IV.M.2).*

(Panel 55) Lieut. Bertie Charles Lousada, Adjt., 1st Bn. (65th Foot) The York & Lancaster Regt.: *s.* of the late Capt. Simeon Charles Lousada, Norfolk Regt. (*d.*1905), of Shelburn Hall, Lansdowne Road, Cheltenham, co. Gloucester, and Charlotte Sophia Lousada (*née* Moysey), former wife of Thomas Marker: and twin brother to Lieut. E.A. Lousada, 2nd Royal Sussex Regt., killed in action, 2 November 1914: *b.* Cheltenham, 19 December 1888: *educ.* Cheltenham College; Royal Military College, Sandhurst: gazetted Lieut. York & Lancaster Regt. 5 February 1909: served with the Expeditionary Force in France and Flanders, and was killed in action, 9 May 1915. Age 26. Remembered on Cheltenham War Memorial (North Panel), and on his parent's gravestone; Leckhampton (St. Peter's) Churchyard.

His twin Edward also has no known grave; he is recorded on Panel 20.

(Panel 55) Lieut. John Kearsley Mather, 1st Bn. (65th Foot) The York & Lancaster Regt.: 5th *s.* of Arthur Mather, of 'Oakhurst,' Parabola Hill, Cheltenham, by his wife Ethel Madeline, *dau.* of the late Rev. Charles Francis Willis, M.A.: and brother to 2nd Lieut. R. Mather, 20th King's (Liverpool) Regt., killed in action, 27 March 1918; and Pte. 15237, E. Mather, 17th King's (Liverpool) Regt., killed in action, 10–12 July 1916: *b.* Cheltenham, 25 January 1890: *educ.* Cheltenham College; Royal Military Academy, Woolwich (Sandhurst Division): gazetted 2nd Lieut. 1st York & Lancaster Regt. 18 September 1909, joining his battn. Quetta, India, December following: served five years in India; promoted Lieut. 8 December 1911: came home with his battalion, December 1914: went to France on 15 January 1915, and was killed in action by shellfire nr. Ypres, 18 February 1915. Buried at Verbrandenmolen. Age 25. *unm.*

His brothers Robert and Ellis also have no known grave; they are commemorated on the Pozieres Memorial and Thiepval Memorial respectively.

(Panel 55) 2nd Lieut. Edgar Reginald Folker: 3rd (Reserve) attd. 'A' Coy., 1st Bn. (65th Foot) The York & Lancaster Regt.: 2nd *s.* of Alfred Henry Folker, Agent, Royal Crown Derby Porcelain Co. Ltd. (Derby); of 12, Park Road, Harlesden, London, by his wife Hannah Maria Keevill: *b.* 106, St. George's Avenue, Tuffnell Park, London, N., 23 October 1884: *educ.* St. Paul's College, New Southgate, London, N.; Willesden High School, London, N.W.: after leaving school, was apprenticed to Vauxhall Engineering Co., soon becoming by his aptitude and diligence an efficient motorist, driving the car specially constructed by his company for the Isle of Man trials, and taking part in many racing tests: afterwards became Assistant Manager, Rover Co., and eventually started business on his own at Haymarket, London: offered his services to the War Office at the outbreak of war, and was given a commission 2nd Lieut. 3rd York & Lancaster Regt. August 1914: served with the Expeditionary Force in France (attd. 1st Battn.), and was killed on 19 February 1915, in trench No.37, Branden Molen (*q.v.*), nr. Ypres, Flanders. A shell had exploded in a connecting sap, and going to investigate the damage he was killed by the poisonous fumes. His Commanding Officer wrote of him, "Although your son had only been with us a comparatively short time, yet he had endeared himself to us all, and we very much miss him in the regiment. I feel that nothing I can say will be able to alleviate your sorrow, but I am sure you will be glad to hear what an excellent officer he was, and could very ill be spared. He was so keen on everything he had to do and did it so well, and the men of his company were so fond of him." Always a keen sportsman, Mr Folker had been a member of the Thames Rowing Club, which he represented at Henley and other regattas. He once performed a remarkable feat when rowing at the Goring regatta. He felt his rigger break, and recognising that he was only dead weight in the boat – he weighed nearly 14 stone and was 6' 4" in height – threw away his oar, and, standing on the sliding seat for a moment when the oars were in the water, dived overboard, coming up after the stern oars had passed over him. He was a member of the Twickenham Rowing Club, Remenham Club, and the Motor Club. A memorial service to the late officer was held on 13 March 1915, in St. Michael's Church, Stonebridge Park, where for many years he had been a choir boy. The service was conducted by the Vicar, the Rev. Canon A.E. Humphreys, assisted by other clergy, and was largely attended by friends and representatives of clubs and institutions to which he had belonged. Much of the above account is taken from the *Willesden Chronicle*, 26 March 1915. A younger brother of 2nd Lieut. Folker, also in the Army, was severely wounded in the head soon after his elder brother's death. Age 30. *unm.*

(Panel 55) 2nd Lieut. George Philip Munson, 2nd Bn. (84th Foot) The York & Lancaster Regt.: *s.* of George Munson, of 'The Uplands,' Kersey, Hadleigh, co. Suffolk, by his wife Sarah: and late *husb.* to Lilla Munson (46, Wood Lane, Beverley, co. York). Killed in action, 7 August 1915. Prior to obtaining a commission, Mr Munson held the rank of Staff Sergt., Army Gymnastic Staff. Age 30. Remains recovered from a grave marked up as belonging to an 'Unknown British Officer. 2/Lieut. York & Lancs', referred to in the GRU Report, Zillebeke 5-181E (28.I.17.a.1.6), identified – Clothing, Boots, Star, Regtl. Buttons; reinterred, registered 12 December 1927. *Buried in Sanctuary Wood Cemetery (IV.M.1).*

Loved And Remembered

(Panel 55) 2nd Lieut. Francis Gawan-Taylor, 2nd Bn. (84th Foot) The York & Lancaster Regt.: 2nd *s.* of His Honour Judge (Henry) Gawan-Taylor, County Court Judge (Circuit No.3, Cumberland & Westmoreland); of Croftlands, Heads Nook, Cumberland, by his wife Rachel, 3rd *dau.* of the late Thomas Candler, of Low Hall, West Ayton, co. York: and *yr.* brother to 2nd Lieut. N. Gawan-Taylor, York & Lancaster Regt., who fell on 24 April 1917: *b.* Darlington, 27 August 1892: *educ.* Rossall (Scholar & Exhibitioner), and Sidney Sussex College, Cambridge (Scholar, 1913): gazetted 2nd Lieut. 3rd York & Lancaster Regt. (Special Reserve) 16 January 1915: proceeded to France attd. 2nd Battn. 1 June 1915, and was killed in action nr. Hooge, 9 August 1915, during the British advance north and west of Hooge. Buried there. Age 22. *unm.* While at Rossall School he was a member of the O.T.C.; a keen athlete he ran in the mile race for Cambridge, 1914, when the Oxonian, A.N.S. Jackson, beat him by eight yards. His Commanding Officer wrote of him, "Your son was one of my subalterns; he was a very promising young officer and was doing very well. We had to take some German trenches…I had two subalterns hit on the way there, but your son was there after we got into their trench. It was while directing the consolidating of their trenches that he was hit by a bullet through both temples. The men of his platoon greatly regret his loss, as they had learned to love him."

He was engaged to be married to Alyson May Estcourt Boucher, *dau.* of the Rev. Canon Boucher, Rector of Frolesworth, Lutterworth, co. Leicester.

His brother Norman is buried in Zandvoorde British Cemetery (III.A.12).

(Panel 55) Sergt. 7137, Joseph Gray, D.C.M., 'D' Coy., 2nd Bn. (84th Foot) The York & Lancaster Regt.: *s.* of Joseph (& Mrs M.) Gray, of 7, Bell's Terrace, Stevenson Road, Attercliffe, Sheffield, co. York: and elder brother to Pte. 6826, R. Gray, 4th Dragoon Guards, killed in action, 14 May 1915: *b.* Gainsborough, co. Lincoln: enlisted Manchester. Killed in action, 9 August 1915. Age 29. *unm.*

His brother Robert also has no known grave; he is recorded on Panel 5.

15 February 1916: Following the detonation of a German mine at The Bluff, and their successful capture of the resultant crater, 'A' Coy., 7th York and Lancaster Regiment, counter- attacked later the same day. An officer wrote, "I saw The Bluff a couple of days afterwards, and it presented a haunting spectacle. Upon the slopes of the crater were the dead, frozen as they had been killed, for the weather was intensely cold. Right up near the crest was a sight which drew famous generals to the place.

Silhouetted against the skyline, and plainly visible from the British line, was the figure of the only man who had looked upon the invisible enemy. Clad in his great-coat, his shrapnel helmet was still on his head. His right knee was bent to the ground; his right hand grasped the barrel of his rifle, the butt of which also rested on the ground. He had been frozen stiff as he had died, turned into a piece of terribly arresting sculpture by the frost.

What his regiment was no one could say; but it was agreed that the probabilities pointed to his being one of the York and Lancaster missing, for that was the fate of a number of them. Anyone who saw this unknown hero will readily recall the incident, for such a one can never forget it."

The Commonwealth War Graves Commission record six soldiers of 7th York & Lancaster Regt. for 15 February 1916, all are believed to have been killed at The Bluff; all are recorded on the Menin Gate:-

(Panel 55) Sergt. 12003, Herbert Lowe, 7th (Service) Bn. The York & Lancaster Regt.: *s.* of Annie Conlan (23, Bank Street, Tyldesley, Manchester): *b.* Astley, Tyldesley, *c.*1890: enlisted Atherton, co. Lancaster: served with the Expeditionary Force. Reported missing, 15 February 1916, now assumed killed. Age 25. Sergt. Lowe leaves a wife, Jane, *née* Hope (5, Robinson Street, Tyldesley). See also Ptes. P.O. Dean, W. Hinchcliffe, J. Hirst, J. Johnson, and A. Kirsopp, below.

(Panel 55) L/Corpl. 40130, George Thomas Deeley, 8th (Service) Bn. The York & Lancaster Regt.: eldest *s.* of Charles H. Deeley, Commercial Traveller; of 45, Grosvenor Road, Harborne, Birmingham, and his wife Louisa Mary, *dau.* of George Lee, of Birmingham: *b.* Sheffield, co. York, 4 August 1878: *educ.* Crookesmoor School, Sheffield: Occupation – Cashier; Messrs. D.& L. Spiers (Silversmiths), Hilton Street, Birmingham: enlisted on 5 January 1916: served with the Expeditionary Force in France and

Flanders, and was killed in action, 8 June 1917. Age 38. A well-known local cricketer, he was formerly secretary to Birmingham Suburban Cricket League. He *m*. Birmingham, 6 September 1910; Beatrice, *dau*. of the late Frederick Ashford.

(Panel 55) L/Corpl. 38274, William Atkinson Waudby, 10th (Service) Bn. The York & Lancaster Regt.: formerly no.24528, East Yorkshire Regt.: *s*. of Henry Waudby, of 6, Church Cottages, North Ferriby, co. York, and Lizzie, his wife: and elder brother to Pte. 30919, A.N. Waudby, 7th East Yorkshire Regt., killed in action, 5 November 1916, at the Somme: *b*. Swanland, co. York: enlisted Hull. Killed in action, 31 July 1917. Age 34. He was married to Mabel Elizabeth Gibbard, *née* Waudby (92, Wigginton Road, Tamworth, co. Stafford).

His brother Alfred also has no known grave; he is commemorated on the Thiepval Memorial (Pier & Face 2C).

(Panel 55) Pte. 3/2552, George Albert Bingham, 2nd Bn. (84th Foot) The York & Lancaster Regt.: *husb*. to Emma Bingham (32, Burnley Road, Halifax, co. York): *b*. Clay Cross, co. Derby: enlisted Pontefract. Killed in action, 8 August 1915. Age 35. Remains recovered from an unmarked grave (28.I.17.a.1.6); identified – Damaged Disc, Titles, Boots; reinterred, registered 13 December 1927. *Buried in Sanctuary Wood Cemetery (IV.M.7).*

Duty Nobly Done

(Panel 55) Pte. 351, Albert Edward Blackshaw, 1/5th Bn. The York & Lancaster Regt. (T.F.): *yst*. *s*. of Thomas P. Blackshaw, Turner & Fitter; of 31, Caxton Street, Barnsley, and the late Emily Jane Blackshaw, his spouse: *b*. Barnsley, co. York, November 1885: *educ*. North Eldon Street Schools: Occupation – Warehouseman: joined 5th York & Lancaster Regt. August 1914, after the outbreak of war: served with the Expeditionary Force in France and Flanders from 14 April 1915. Reported wounded and missing after the fighting, 10 July 1915; now assumed to have been killed in action on that date. Age 29. *unm*. (*IWGC record Sergt.*)

(Panel 55) Pte. 20625, George Cheney, 2nd Bn. (84th Foot) The York & Lancaster Regt.: *s*. of Benjamin Cheney, of 'Fieldgroves', Bryanston, Blandford, co. Dorset, by his wife Ruth: and elder brother to Pte. 5111, F. Cheney, 3rd Royal Fusiliers, who fell 3½ months previously: *b*. Blandford, *c*.1881: previously served Tpr., no.16621, The Hussars: enlisted Blandford: served with the Expeditionary Force in France and Flanders, and was killed in action, 9 August 1915, at Ypres. Age 34.

His brother Frederick also has no known grave; he is recorded on Panel 6.

(Panel 55) Pte. 12578, Percy Owen Dean, 7th (Service) Bn. The York & Lancaster Regt.: enlisted Sheffield, co. York: served with the Expeditionary Force. Reported missing, 15 February 1916, now assumed killed in action on that date. See Sergt. H. Lowe, above.

(Panel 55) Pte. 9839, James Draycott, 'B' Coy., 1st Bn. (65th Foot) The York & Lancaster Regt.: *s*. of Mr (& Mrs) Draycott, of 7, George Street, Walsoken, Wisbech, co. Norfolk: and brother to Pte. 9682, W. Draycott, East Lancashire Regt., died of wounds, 16 April 1915, received in action ten days previously: enlisted Wisbech: served with the Expeditionary Force in France, and was killed in action, 23 April 1915. Age 25. He was married to Mrs G. Larbey, *née* Draycott (37, St. Peter's Road, Old Woking, co. Surrey).

His brother William is buried in Boulogne Eastern Cemetery (VIII.A.2).

(Panel 55) Pte. 10130, Daniel Farmer, 1st Bn. (65th Foot) The York & Lancaster Regt.: *s*. of the late Daniel (& Mrs) Farmer, of Deptford, London, S.E.: *b*. Deptford: enlisted New Cross, London, S.E.14. Killed in action, 5 February 1915. Age 23. He left a widow, Katherine Farmer (since died). *Buried in Bedford House Cemetery (C.3/Enc.No.3).*

(Panel 55) Pte. 11672, William Hinchcliffe, 7th (Service) Bn. The York & Lancaster Regt.: enlisted Wombwell, Barnsley, co. York: served with the Expeditionary Force in France. Reported missing/believed killed in action, 15 February 1916. See Sergt. H. Lowe, above.

(Panel 55) Pte. 12473, John Hirst, 7th (Service) Bn. The York & Lancaster Regt.: *b*. Newbold, Chesterfield: enlisted Sheffield, co. York: served with the Expeditionary Force. Reported missing, 15 February 1916, now, nothing further having been heard of him or his whereabouts, believed to have been killed in action on or about that date. See Sergt. H. Lowe, above.

(Panel 55) Pte. 18792, John Hopkinson, 1st Bn. (65th Foot) The York & Lancaster Regt.: *s.* of Walter (& Alice) Hopkinson, of Butts Road, Ashover, Chesterfield, co. Derby and brother to Pte. 19069, W. Hopkinson, 9th York & Lancaster Regt., killed in action, 1 July 1916, at the Somme. Killed in action at the Second Battle of Ypres, 8 May 1915. Age 29. He leaves a widow, Annie Hopkinson (Fallgate, Milltown, Ashover).

His brother Wilfred also has no known grave; he is commemorated on the Thiepval Memorial, Somme.

(Panel 55) Pte. 17630, Edgar Hyde, 1/5th Bn. The York & Lancaster Regt. (T.F.): eldest *s.* of Edgar Hyde, of 12, Keresforth Hill Road, Kingstone Place, nr. Barnsley, by his wife Mary Ann: and brother to Pte. 17909, E. Hyde, King's Own Scottish Borderers, killed in action at Gallipoli, 11 August 1915: *b.* Barnsley, co. York, 1889: *educ.* Agnes Road School: Occupation – Miner: joined York & Lancaster (T.F.), 1914: served with the Expeditionary Force in France and Flanders from 14 April 1915, and was killed in action, 8 May following. Age 25. *unm.*

His brother Ernest is commemorated in Twelve Tree Copse Cemetery, Gallipoli (Sp.Mem.C.319).

(Panel 55) Pte. 38667, Henry Ingham, 8th (Service) Bn. The York & Lancaster Regt. *s.* of Ambrose Ingham, of 12, Brookside, Skipton, co. York: *educ.* Brougham Street School: former employee Messrs Bentley & Co. (Weavers), Skipton: enlisted Skipton late 1916; proceeded to France, January 1917, and was killed in action, 9 April following. Age 28. A letter to his parents signed by two comrades, Ptes. Mosley and Carr, said, "It is with deep regret that I have to write you a letter of bad news, but perhaps you have heard it already. It is about your son, Henry, my chum ever since we enlisted. He was in the trenches on Easter Monday, and during a raid by the Huns was killed. I was not with him, nor did I see him, but as far as I can hear from those who know, he was killed instantaneously by a shell. You know how much I thought of Henry, as we have stuck together since we joined up, and I feel his death keenly." Capt. (Adjt.) R. Trotter added, "It may be some consolation to you to know that he fell doing his duty as a soldier and a man."

(Panel 55) Pte. 11298, Joseph Johnson, 7th (Service) Bn. The York & Lancaster Regt.: enlisted Sheffield, co. York: served with the Expeditionary Force, and was killed in action, 15 February 1916. See Sergt. H. Lowe, above.

(Panel 55) Pte. 9810, James Samuel Kenny, 2nd Bn. (84th Foot) The York & Lancaster Regt.: *s.* of James Kenny, formerly Sergt., South Lancashire Regt. (51 years service in the Army); of 155, Wheatland Lane, Seacombe, Wallasey, by his wife Louisa: *b.* Fleetwood, co. Lancaster, 18 March 1892: *educ.* St. Walburgh's, Birkenhead: enlisted York & Lancaster Regt. at the age of 15; initially sent to Ireland, thereafter went to India where he won a scholarship for Indian languages: returned to England on the outbreak of war 1914: served with the Expeditionary Force in France and Flanders from January 1915: took part in the fighting at Ypres; wounded and repatriated home: returned to France after convalescence, and was killed in action, 3 June 1915. Age 23. *unm.*

(Panel 55) Pte. 12177, Arthur Kirsopp, 7th (Service) Bn. The York & Lancaster Regt.: *s.* of Charles F. Kirsopp, of 29, Dunham Road, Wavetree, Liverpool: *b.* 1894: served with the Expeditionary Force in France. Killed in action, 15 February 1916. Age 21. *unm.* See Sergt. H. Lowe, above.

(Panel 55) Pte. 2200, George William Long, 5th Bn. The York & Lancaster Regt. (T.F.): *s.* of Fred Frinchen Long, of 61, Churchfield Road, Walton, Peterborough, by his wife Emma Jane: and brother to Pte. 16569, J.H. Long, 5th Northamptonshire Regt., killed in action, 30 November 1917: enlisted Barnsley, co. York. Killed in action, 10 July 1915. Recorded on Werrington War Memorial, Northamptonshire.

His brother John also has no known grave; he is commemorated on the Cambrai Memorial, Louverval (Panel 8).

(Panel 55) Pte. 31235, Wilfred Perkin, 8th (Service) Bn. The York & Lancaster Regt.: eldest *s.* of Thomas Dawson Perkin, of 17, Fitzwilliam Street, Barnsley, co. York, by his wife Annie: *b.* Barnsley, 13 May 1885: *educ.* St. George's School: Occupation – Assistant Clerk: enlisted 1 June 1916: served with the Expeditionary Force in France and Flanders from 9 September, and was killed in action, 9 April 1917. Age 31. Buried in Transport Farm Cemetery. Lieut. Riley wrote, "He was a fine soldier, and stuck to his post with the greatest courage and calmness." He *m.* Zion Baptist Church, Barnsley; Frances (37, Fitzwilliam Street, Barnsley), *dau.* of William Cherry, of 137, Snydale Road, Cudworth, and had a *dau.*, Stella.

(Panel 55) Pte. 10131, Ernest Reed, 1st Bn. (65th Foot) The York & Lancaster Regt.: *s.* of Mary Reed (21, Beech Road, Wath-on-Dearne, co. York): *b.* Wath-on-Dearne: enlisted Rotherham. Killed in action, 25 May 1915. Age 24. *unm.* Remains of an 'Unknown British Soldier. York & Lancs' exhumed 21 January 1929, from an unmarked grave located in a small cemetery in Sanctuary Wood (28.I.18.d.65.00); identified – Khaki, Titles; reinterred, registered 5 March 1929. *Buried in Sanctuary Wood Cemetery (V.E.6).*

(Panel 55) Pte. 17465, Samuel Shawcroft, 1st Bn. (65th Foot) The York & Lancaster Regt.: *b.* Hucknall-under-Huthwaite, co. Nottingham: enlisted Doncaster, co. York. Killed in action, 8 May 1915. *m. The Notts Free Press,* 'In Memoriam,' 27 April 1917:-

> *Two years have passed and how we miss you, Friends may think the wound has healed;*
> *But they little know the sorrow deep within our hearts concealed.*
> *Sadly missed, Silently mourned.*

Sorrowing Wife & Children.

PANEL 55 ENDS PTE. S. SHAWCROFT, YORK & LANCASTER REGT.

(Add.57) Lieut.Col. Francis Edward Bradshaw Isherwood, 2nd Bn. (84th Foot) The York & Lancaster Regt. Cmdg. 1st Bn. (65th Foot): *s.* of John Bradshaw Isherwood, of Marple Hall, co. Chester, J.P.: gazetted 2nd Lieut. York & Lancaster Regt. January 1892: promoted Lieut. 1895; Capt. 1901; Major 1911; Brevet Lieut.Col. 18 February 1915: served in the South African Campaign: present at the Relief of Ladysmith, and actions at Vaal Kranz, Tugela Heights and Pieter's Hill: Mentioned in Despatches (*London Gazette*, September 1901): Queen's Medal and King's Medal; seven clasps: served with the Expeditionary Force in France and Flanders. Reported missing, 9 May 1915, presumed killed in action near Ypres. Age 45. For his services in the Great war he was Mentioned in Despatches by Sir John (now Lord) French (*London Gazette*, February 1915). He was married to Kathleen Machell (19, Pembroke Gardens, London), *dau.* of Frederick Machell Smith.

(Add.57) Major Edmund Stryant Williams, 1st Bn. The Monmouthshire Regt. (T.F.): only *s.* of George Waters Williams, J.P., of Llanfrecha, co. Monmouth: and relative to Major-Gen. Sir Edmund Keynton Williams, K.C.B., who at one time commanded 41st Regt., and fought under Wellington in the Peninsula, being five times wounded, and Mentioned in Despatches: *b.* 'Gold Tops,' Newport, 13 July 1875: *educ.* King's School, Warwick, where he won all the School Sports principal prizes, and was prominent in Rugby football: joined the School Cadet Corps attd. 2nd Warwick Volunteers: subsequently became an officer in Monmouthshire Volunteers, later changed to a Territorial Force unit, in which he was promoted Lieut. May 1901; Capt. September 1906: passed through a course of musketry at Hythe, and qualified at a School of Instruction for rank of Field Officer: undertook Imperial Service obligations on the outbreak of war: stationed at Northampton and other Training Stations after mobilisation: left Cambridge for France, February 1915. Having joined the Special Reserve of Officers, he was promoted Major in his Regiment, September 1914. He was killed in the first line of trenches while repulsing an attack in force in Flanders, 8 May 1915, the Battalion losing very heavily in both officers and men. He had for many years taken an active interest in organising and training Boy Scouts, and was a regular follower of the Llangibby Hounds. Age 39.

(Add.57) Capt. Arthur Hugh Maunsell Bowers, 2nd Bn. (106th Foot) The Durham Light Infantry: eldest *s.* of Lieut.-Col. Maunsell Bowers, of Beeston Grange, Sandy, Beds, late 5th Dragoon Guards, by his wife Catherine Georgina, *yr. dau.* of George Thornhill, of Diddington, co. Hunts, J.P., D.L.: *b.* Aldershot, 15 July 1880: *educ.* Harrow, and Royal Military College, Sandhurst: gazetted 2nd Lieut. 1st Durham Light Infantry, 21 February 1900; promoted Lieut. 3 July 1901; Capt. 29 January 1909: Adjutant 8th (Territorial) Battn., D.L.I., 26 April 1909–25 April 1912: served (1) in South Africa 1900–02: took part in operations in Natal, March–June 1900, including action at Laing's Nek (6–9 June): operations in the Transvaal, 30 November 1900–31 May 1902 (Queen's Medal, two clasps; King's Medal, two clasps): (2) India, 1902–08: and (3) with the Expeditionary Force in France and Flanders from September 1914, and was killed in action, 9 August 1915 while gallantly leading his company at Hooge. Age 35. He *m.* in London, Mary Jessie, *dau.* of the late Lieut.-Col. Charles Case, B.Sc., and had two *daus.* – Esmee Mary, *b.* 20 June 1911, and Irene Annette, *b.* 27 August 1913.

(Add.57) Capt. Edward Wilberforce Leather, 3rd (Reserve) Bn. The Yorkshire Regt. (Green Howards) attd. 2nd Bn. (105th Foot) The King's Own (Yorkshire Light Infantry): *s.* of the late Frederick John Leather, of Middleton Hall, Belford, co. Northumberland, and The Friary, Tickhill, co. York, and the late Gertrude Elizabeth Sophia Leather, *née* Walters; his wife: and brother to Lieut. C. Leather, 3rd attd. 1st Northumberland Fusiliers, missing/believed killed in action, 25–27 October 1914, aged 31 years; and T/ Major E.A. Leather, 15th attd. 27th Northumberland Fusiliers, killed in action, 10 February 1916, aged 48 years: *b.* The Friary, Tickhill, 23 November 1879: *educ.* Hazelwood Preparatory School; and Wellington College: joined 3rd Yorkshire Regt. (5th West Yorkshire Militia), 1899; apptd. Lieut. 13 December 1900: served in the South African Campaign, 1899–1902 (Queen's medal, 2 clasps; King's medal, 2 clasps), and with the Expeditionary Force in France and Flanders (from 11 November 1914): joined K.O.Y.L.I. with a draft of reinforcements (5 officers, 190 rank and file) at Locre, 1 December 1914; promoted Capt. 1 February 1915, and was killed in action during the fighting to recapture Hill 60, 18 April 1915. Age 35.

His brother Christopher also has no known grave, he is commemorated on the Le Touret Memorial; Ernest is buried in Rue-David Military Cemetery, Fleurbaix (I.H.36).

(Add.57) Capt. John Edmund Simpson, 2nd Bn. (105th Foot) The King's Own (Yorkshire Light Infantry): *s.* of the Rev. John Curwen Simpson, formerly of Thurscoe, co. York, by his wife Frances Maria: nephew of Judge Edmund Sheppard, of Brisbane, Australia, and brother to Capt. L. Simpson, K.O.Y.L.I., who was taken prisoner at Le Cateau: *b.* Bayswater, London, W., 9 July 1873: *educ.* St. Paul's School, Stony Stratford: received a commission from 2nd (Volunteer) Bn. Yorkshire Regt. to 1st Bn. K.O.Y.L.I. May 1900: promoted Lieut. 1901: obtained his company 2nd Bn., January 1907: Adjutant to 3rd (Reserve) Bn., October 1911–September 1913: served at Gibraltar, South Africa, and Ireland, being at Carrickfergus when war broke out: left for the Continent with First Contingent of the Expeditionary Force, 10 August 1914. For his services in the Great War Capt. Simpson was Mentioned in Sir John (now Lord) French's Despatch, 8 October 1914, and was killed in action at Messines, Flanders, 31 October 1914, while leading his men. Death was almost instantaneous. Age 41.

(Add.57) Lieut. Charles Reginald Chamberlin Bean, 1st Bn. (38th Foot) The South Staffordshire Regt.: *s.* of the late C.E. (& Mrs) Bean, F.R.C.S., of Plymouth: *b.* 1892: *educ.* Sherborne School; on the Continent, and Royal Military College, Sandhurst: gazetted 2nd Lieut. South Staffordshire Regt. 22 January 1913: promoted Lieut. September 1914: served with the Expeditionary Force in France and Flanders and – officially reported to be wounded mid-November, death unofficially confirmed – is now reported to have been killed in action near Ypres, 26 October 1914. *The Times* stated, having gone to the Front early in October, he was, on the 25th. of that month, sent to support a hotly-pressed trench near Ypres, and, after fighting all night, was wounded on the 26th. Although pressed to leave the trench for medical aid, he refused, and was killed shortly afterwards, his body having been last seen lying on the parapet of the trench. Age 21. *unm.*

(Add.57) Lieut. Cedric Hugh Crowley, 4th (Extra Reserve) attd. 1st Bn. (6th Foot) The Royal Warwickshire Regt.: eldest *s.* of the Rev. C.E. Crowley, Rector of Chilbolton, Stockbridge, co. Hants: *b.* St. George's Vicarage, Portsea, 24 September 1891: *educ.* King's School, Canterbury, and Keble College, Oxford (graduated B.A.): at school and college was a member of the O.T.C.: gazetted 2nd Lieut. Extra Reserve, Royal Warwickshire Regt. October 1914, after the outbreak of war: attd. 1st Bn. for Active Service in France: Killed in action, 25 April 1915, while leading his platoon to the attack of German trenches near St. Julien. Age *23. unm.*

(Add.57) Lieut. William Stuart Dixon, 47th Bn. Australian Infantry, A.I.F.: *s.* of Laurison Graham (& Julia Anna) Dixon, of Irving Street, Auchenflower, Brisbane: *b.* Brisbane, Queensland. One of three officers of the right front company (Capt. J.W. Millar, killed; Lieut. G.N.M. Goode, mortally wounded), who fell in the fighting to gain the front trench nr. Huns' Walk, Oosttaverne Line, at the Battle of Messines, 7 June 1917. Age 29. See account re. Corpl. P. McCarthy, 37th Battn., (Panel 25).

Capt. J.W. Millar also has no known grave, he is recorded on Panel 27. Lieut. G.N.M. Goode, died on 12 June 1917; buried Longuenesse (St. Omer) Souvenir Cemetery (IV.C.27).

(Add.57) Lieut. Bransby William Goodwin, M.C., 1st South African Infantry Regt., S.A.E.F.: eldest *s.* of the Rev. William Atherton Goodwin, M.A., Cantab., Rector of Queenstown, South Africa, by his wife Alice Mary, *dau.* of the Right Rev. Bransby Key, Bishop of St. John's: *b.* Untata, Transkei, South Africa, 1 March 1892: *educ.* St. John's, Hurstpierpoint, co. Sussex, and Michaelhouse Diocesan College, Natal: was farming under Sir Abe Bailey, Bart.: volunteered for Foreign Service soon after the outbreak of war, and joined the South African Force, 28 September 1914: served with the Expeditionary Force in France and Flanders, where he took part in many engagements: received a commission, and was gazetted 2nd Lieut. 1st South African Infantry 31 July 1916: promoted Lieut. October 1917, and was killed in action by a sniper, at Ridge Wood, near Voormezeele, 30 April 1918. Buried there. General Sir H.T. Lukin, G.C.M.G., D.S.O., wrote, "From the day your gallant son joined the South African Brigade, he has more than fulfilled the reputation he had gained at school, as a fine, upright young gentleman. Brave as a lion, and keen, these characteristics, together with his invariable consideration for others, had gained for him the devoted affection of his comrades of all ranks.": Mentioned in Despatches (*London Gazette*, 16 September 1917), for a highly successful raid outside Arras, 3 January 1917, and was decorated by General R. Nivelle; also awarded the Croix de Guerre, and later the Military Cross (posthumously) for 'gallant and distinguished service during the retreat, March 1918.' Age 26. *unm.* (*IWGC record 20 September 1917*)

Referring to an aspect of a speech made in the House of Commons by Secretary of State for War, Mr. David Lloyd George, 24 July 1916: "… I think in this respect we shall revert to the old method of warfare when protection of the body was not regarded as detracting from the valour of a man .." an advertisement for the Pullman A1 Shield stated, 'The shield is the lightest and most effective of all steel shields. The steel has been Gout-tested and found proof against shrapnel and bullets at 700 feet per second velocity, any enemy service revolver at point-blank, and against bayonet or lance. All the protection given to the head by the steel helmet supplied to our troops in such vast quantities is secured to the vital parts of the body, back or front, by this shield. It folds when not in use into a space that enables it to be carried over the shoulder as easily as a pair of field glasses. Price 25/- complete.'

Unfortunately, no matter what type of protection one chose to utilise, nothing could safeguard against a sniper's shot to the head or the close explosion of a shell.

(Add.57) Lieut. Cyril Aldin Smith, D.S.O., Royal Navy Volunteer Reserve, 63rd (Royal Naval) Divn., attd. H.Q. 6th Divn.: *s.* of Samuel (& Mrs) Smith, of Redington Road, Hampstead, London, N.W.: commissioned Royal Marines, 26 September 1914, and 1 March 1915: served at Antwerp: commissioned R.N.V.R. 11 September 1915, and lent to 6th Divn. H.Q.: awarded D.S.O., April 1916, for work against enemy trenches: developed use of bullet proof shields and furthered the use of bangalore torpedoes. Killed in action, 10 June 1917. The History of the 6th Division records, "Affectionately known as 'The Admiral,' many of those who knew and liked him well by that name probably never knew him by any other. Lieut. Smith was an owner driver in charge of a convoy of 'buses with the Royal Naval Division at Antwerp, whence he escaped to France. In October 1914 he seized the opportunity of an officer requiring to be taken up to join his unit, to make his way with his car to the front. On arrival there he contrived to get himself attached to VIth Division Headquarters, remaining with them until he was reported missing on 10 June 1916.

Consumed with a good healthy hatred of the enemy, and keen to be of assistance in any way that he could, he devoted the greater part of the time he was with the Division to experimenting with bullet-proof shields on wheels to be propelled by manpower, a sort of embryonic tank. His ambition was himself to take the first of these into action. At last he was offered an opportunity of co-operating with a small 3-man pattern in a minor raid near Forward Cottage. What success he might have achieved it is impossible to say, as in his eagerness he preceded the shield by several yards to show the crew the way and was hit in the neck by a splinter from a bomb. The name of Admiral's Road, given to the road past Crossroads Farm and Forward Cottage, commemorates the incident of which it was the scene. Later 'The Admiral' turned his attention to Bangalore torpedoes, in the use of which he trained the unauthorised party which had long existed under the name of the '6th Division Shield Party.' With them he took part in many raids and minor enterprises, one of which earned him the D.S.O. Reported missing from a patrol of 9th Norfolk Regt., 10 June 1916; nothing since has been heard of him. For nearly two years he contrived to serve voluntarily with the Division, nobody quite knows in what capacity or by what authority, and during that time he endeared himself to all by his unfailing good nature and cheeriness, his whole-hearted enthusiasm and his lack of fear." Age 39. Lieut Smith leaves a wife, Madge Aldin- Smith.

(Add.57) 2nd Lieut. John Digby Cartwright, 2nd Bn. (106th Foot) The Durham Light Infantry: eldest *s*. of the Rev. William Digby Cartwright, of Aynhoe, co. Northampton, by his wife Lucy Harriette Maud, *dau*. of Edward Bury: *b*. Aynhoe, 23 June 1895: *educ*. Durnford; Wellington College, and Royal Military College, Sandhurst: gazetted 2nd Lieut. 10 November 1914: served with the Expeditionary Force in France and Flanders from 15 June 1915, and was killed in action at Hooge, 9 August following. Buried there. He was Mentioned in Despatches (*London Gazette*, 1 January 1916), by F.M. Sir John (now Lord) French, for 'gallant and distinguished service in the field.' Age 20. *unm*.

(Add.57) 2nd Lieut. James Gordon Caruth, 5th (Extra Reserve) attd. 2nd Bn. (86th Foot) The Royal Irish Rifles: eldest *s*. of James Davis Caruth, Merchant; of Hugomont, Ballymena, Co. Antrim, by his wife Constance Helena, *dau*. of Robert I. Rose: *b*. London, 3 September 1896: *educ*. Oakfield Preparatory School, Rugby, and Cheltenham College; matriculated at London University, January 1914: gazetted 2nd Lieut. 15 August 1914: went to France with a draft July 1915; there attd. 2nd Bn. Royal Irish Rifles, and was killed early in the morning of Saturday, 25 September 1915, near Hooge. His body was not recovered as he fell in the German trenches, from which his company were afterwards driven out. He was champion gymnast at Cheltenham, and represented the college at Aldershot (April 1914) when the pair came out sixth in 33 competing schools, he being placed eighth in the list of 66 boys. He was a keen cricketer, and besides playing for Cheltenham College, took part in matches played by the Ballymena Cricket Club. Age 19.

(Add.57) 2nd Lieut. Frederick Gwatkin Oldham Curtler, 2nd Bn. (36th Foot) The Worcestershire Regt.: only *s*. of Frederick Lewis Curtler, of Belvere House, co. Worcester, by his wife Nannie McClelland: *b*. 1893: *educ*. Rugby (entered 1907): joined 5th (Territorial) Bn. Worcestershire Regt., 2nd Lieut. April 1912; promoted Lieut. December 1913: subsequently transf'd. 2nd Lieut. to 2nd Bn. Worcestershire Regt., October 1914, and was killed in action at Ypres, Belgium, on the 21st. of that month. Age 21. *unm*.

(Add.57) 2nd Lieut. Rycharde Mead Haythornthwaite, Special Reserve, 3rd attd. 2nd Bn. (3rd Foot) The East Kent Regt. (The Buffs): elder *s*. of the Rev. John Parker Haythornthwaite, of Agra Lodge, Northwood, co. Middlesex, M.A.; Principal of St. John's College, Agra, 1890–1911; Fellow of Allahabad University, by his wife Iszet, L.R.C.P., L.R.C.S., *dau*. of Samuel Mead, of Stratford-on-Avon, co. Warwick: *b*. Agra, India, 4 January 1894: *educ*. C.M.S. Children's Home, Limpsfield, Haileybury College (Scholar. Head of School, 1912–13; Colour Sergt. O.T.C.), and Sidney Sussex College, Cambridge (October 1913–July 1914. Exhibitioner, History): gazetted 2nd Lieut. 3rd The Buffs, 15 August 1914: trained in Dover, September 1914-May 1915: went to the Front, 5 May, and was killed at the Second Battle of Ypres on the 24th of that month. Buried outside the garden gate of a ruined cottage, right-hand side of the Menin Road, about 1,000 yards beyond the level crossing of the Ypres – Roulers Railway, in one of three graves. In a letter written to his parents the day he was killed he said, "At 2.30 a.m. this morning the Germans started a terrific bombardment, using their vile gas. Our lads were splendid and stuck it. About 5.30 a.m. we got a message to reinforce the firing line, with my Company 'B.' Unfortunately there was very bad communication and our 1st Platoon did not reinforce. I went out to try and find out what was happening, and worked my way up to the front line, about 1,000 yards ahead, and found out what was happening, and then returned to our trenches. 'B' Company immediately pushed forward, as the line wanted reinforcing, but I stayed back to report to Headquarters. After doing that I started with one other fellow to work my way up. The shrapnel was terrific, but our luck was in, and we reached a ruined house just behind the firing line, and found there a good many wounded, poor beggars. I got a stretcher party together and we pulled in several badly wounded fellows in a field, but unfortunately they sniped at us, the brutes! Two of our poor chaps were hit. Since then we have done what we can to make them comfortable, but it is awfully hard for them. We can do so little for them till dark, and even then it isn't safe. The shelling is something terrific, one bursts on this house knocking bits over our wounded, and gave a few more nasty cuts. All we can do is keep boiling water – it is not safe to drink otherwise – and give them sips of tea and Bovril, of which we have luckily got a certain amount. Unfortunately it is very hot, and their thirst must be terrific. I know mine is. It is just that fiendish gas. I have had nothing to eat since 7 p.m last night, it is now 4 p.m. Only a few sips of different things, and this gas keeps up a horrible choking feeling, which prevents one working as hard as one wants to. What will happen to us I do not know. I think we are advancing now, and in that case all ought to be all right." Sergt-Major W. Dunlop, Durham L.I., wrote, "I was with him on that memorable day, 'Whit Monday,' for about ten-and-a-half hours, at about 500 yards from the Germans, without a British soldier in front and about 1,000 yards from the nearest troops behind, attending to the wounded. First, I set away with a stretcher, my companion was either shot or fainted, so I went across to the ruins of an old cottage. There were a dozen or so wounded, with a wounded Corporal trying to dress the other poor souls. I could get no assistance there, so had to go to our Reserves behind for someone to help me get the stretcher in. I returned with two brave chaps and, on my return, met Lieut. Haythornthwaite. He asked particulars and said it was certain death to venture out. I said, "I'm risking it." His answer was, "If you go, I'm coming also." The four of us set out, but could not find man or stretcher, and it was only by the protection of God himself that we returned, for nothing human could have protected us from the murderous fire the brutes sent towards us, but not one of us was hit, thanks to God. It was after that that I found the qualities of your son. The dressings of the wounded were not as they should have been, bandaged by little experienced hands, so your son and myself set about to try to stop the bleeding of the wounded. After a while we got all made as comfortable as we could under the circumstances. So he set to, and got a fire going, and we got some Bovril made. It was a God-send for the poor souls, as the water was not fit to drink if it had not been boiled, and the continual cry of the wounded was 'water.' It was during the time the water was boiling I saw your son sitting and writing the letter you eventually got, but the contents he did not mention at the time. After a while, the counter-attack started. Our troops started to advance. What a sight! Men falling right and left, but still the advance continued until they reached our cottage. Your son collected men on one side of the cottage, myself the other, and got them to dig themselves in so as to stop the brutes from advancing, and after a while we got a position formed which seemed strong enough to hold them in check. And then came more work, the poor souls who had been shot were either helped, or carried to us for 'First Aid,' and on several occasions your son and myself went out and brought men in, and it was on one of these that he got hit; the bullet passing through his left shoulder. I was dressing a chap with a finger blown off when it happened, but two men – I don't know their names – carried him in, and set about dressing him. He called for me, and asked me to adjust his bandages, and said, "If there are any men about doing nothing tell them to try and get a rifle as every man is needed." He was hit somewhere about 5p.m., and after he was wounded he was as calm and cool as ever. He ordered a man – I don't know his name – to take everything from his pockets, spectacles included, with the instructions, "See these things handed over to my people." The man repeated the words as he gave me the things I forwarded on to you." Pte. James White, Royal Fusiliers, who brought him into the ruined cottage after he was wounded, in an interview with Lieut. Haythornthwaite's father, said that shortly after 4 p.m. the British counter-attack began in great force. The Northumbrian Brigade led the attack and one platoon, as it drew near to the ruined cottage in one of its rushes, was left without its officer. He fell wounded and was brought in and laid with the others. Lieut. Haythornthwaite then said to him, "Shall I take your men on?" He went forth to do so and was almost immediately shot himself, and was left on the field until brought in by Pte. James White. This account is not inconsistent with that given by Sergt.-Major Dunlop, as he admits that he did not actually see him fall, as he was busily engaged with the wounded. Lieut. Haythornthwaite was a keen athlete and long distance runner at Haileybury. He won the half-mile, under 16 (1910) and the open mile in 1912. He also won his College Colours at Sidney Sussex, Cambridge, for athletics and football, and organised the Regimental Sports whilst in training at Dover, Age 21.*unm.*

(Add.57) 2nd Lieut. George Henry McAuliffe, 1st Bn. (79th Foot) The Queen's Own (Cameron Highlanders): *b.* London, 26 October 1874: enlisted 2nd Gordon Highlanders, November 1897: having risen to the rank of Company Sergeant-Major he was granted a commission, 10 October 1914, 2nd Lieut., 2nd Bn. Cameron Highlanders: previously saw service in the South African War, during which he was Mentioned in Despatches by Lord Roberts, and received the Queen's and King's Medal: also awarded the Delhi Durbar Medal, 1911: served with the Expeditionary Force in France, and was killed in action at Zillebeke, nr. Ypres, 29 October 1914. Age 40. 2nd Lieut. McAuliffe was married to Lily Caroline, *dau.* of the late Mr (& Mrs) Biddis, and left a *dau.*, Lily Mary, *b.* 9 November 1913.

(Add.57) 2nd Lieut. Joseph Frain Webster, 3rd (Reserve) Bn. The Black Watch (Royal Highlanders) attd. 1st Bn. Gordon Highlanders: 2nd *s.* of Sir Francis Webster, of Ashbrook, Arbroath, co. Forfar, by his wife Lady Webster: *b.* Ashbrook, 2 December 1892: *educ.* Seafield House, Broughty Ferry; Clifton College, where he was champion boxer, in the XV and the college O.T.C.; and Trinity College, Cambridge, where he was champion middleweight boxer, 1914. One of many members of distinguished families to set an example in the Great War by enlisting, which he did, in his case King's Royal Rifle Corps; he was afterwards (October 1914) given his commission in 3rd Black Watch.: attd. 1st Gordon Highlanders for Active Service; killed in a charge at Gheluvelt, 30 October 1914, during the great struggle for Ypres. His Commanding Officer and Company Commander wrote in high terms of his conduct. The latter, describing a previous incident said that, on 26 October, men holding a trench on their flank were driven out and forced to withdraw. 2nd Lieut. Webster jumped out of his own trench, rallied the men under severe fire, retook the trench, and held it for the rest of the day, saving the flank, which, but for his action, would have been compelled to retire. On 30 October he volunteered for the charge in which he was killed. A Sergeant of his company also recounted many gallant deeds of 2nd Lieut. Webster, among them the bringing in of a wounded man under fire after he had sent his own men back to the trench. Age 21. *unm.* (*IWGC record 2nd Gordon Highlanders*)

(Add.57) 2nd Lieut. Percy John Whitehouse, 3rd (Reserve) Bn. The Queen's Own (Royal West Kent Regt.) attd. 1st Bn. Northamptonshire Regt.: only *s.* of John Whitehouse, of 1, St. Augustine's Road, Belvedere, co. Kent, by his wife Florence: *b.* 1893: *educ.* Erith County School; matriculated, London University 1911, taking the Intermediate B.Sc., 1913; East London College, where he was an Honours Student (Chemistry), and member of the University O.T.C.: gazetted 2nd Lieut. Queen's Own, August 1914: served with the Expeditionary Force in France and Flanders: joined Northamptonshire Regt. with Capt. Coldwell (Reserve), Capt. Crowe (Royal Warwickshire Regt.), and a draft of 60 reinforcements on the night of 1 November, and was at once sent into the trenches along the northern edge of Shrewsbury Forest, and was killed in action the following day, 2 November 1914, by shellfire. A keen football, cricket, and tennis player, he was also a good runner and jumper. Age 21. *unm.*

On the night of 27 April 1915, after taking over trenches at Hill 37 from the Rifle Brigade earlier that day, London Rifle Brigade were tasked with ration carrying from Wieltje to the Rifle Brigade's new positions astride the Kerselaere-Zonnebeke road. Subjected to a three hour wait at the ration dump owing to the transport being delayed by congested roads and heavily shelled on their return journey, the L.R.B. finally returned to their lines at 5 a.m. the following morning. Later that same morning Capt. Edmunds and seven members of the battalion were taking their breakfast in a house at St. Jean when it was hit by a shell which completely blew down one side of the building. Four men were killed – R.S.M. Harrington, attached from King's Royal Rifle Corps, 'a typical rifleman and fine soldier,' L/Corpl. Reading, Riflemen Foster and Newell – and four wounded, including Capt. Edmunds who was so completely buried beneath the debris he was nearly overlooked by the rescue party.

(Add.57) Regtl.Sergt.Major 8793, Arthur George Harrington, D.C.M., 1st Bn. (60th Foot) The King's Royal Rifle Corps attd. 'D' Coy., 1/5th (City of London) Bn. (London Rifle Brigade) London Regt. (T.F.): *s.* of the late Sergt.Major John William Harrington, 3rd King's Royal Rifle Corps, by his wife Ellen: served in the South African Campaign: Queen's and King's Medals, Long Service and Good Conduct Medals: *b.* Winchester, co. Hants: enlisted Guildford, co. Surrey: served with the Expeditionary Force in France and Flanders, and was killed in action at St. Jean, near Ypres, 28 April 1915. He leaves a widow, Florence

Margaret (16, Arnos Villas, Bowes Road, New Southgate. London, N.). Sergt.Major Harrington was one of six brothers who, with their father, served in the King's Royal Rifle Corps. Age 46. (*IWGC record Actg. Sergt.*)

L/Corpl. J.W.C. Reading and Riflemen A.J. Foster and J.G. Newell also have no known grave, they are recorded on Panel 52 & 54.

(Add.57) Sergt. 240023, David Murray, 1/5th Bn. The Gordon Highlanders (T.F.): 3rd *s.* of David Murray, of 78, Blenheim Place, Aberdeen (formerly Rose Villa, Newmachar, co. Aberdeen), Carpenter, by his wife Mary Ann, *dau.* of James Lamont: *b.* Newmachar, co. Aberdeen, 11 November 1883: *educ.* Newmachar Public School, and Civil Service Training College, Aberdeen: was for some years on the staff of the local Post Office and, after passing the Civil Service Examination, became a Sorter in the Head Office, Aberdeen: joined 5th Bn. Gordon Highlanders, 22 March 1900: called up on the outbreak of war: served with the Expeditionary Force in France and Flanders, 1 May–October 1915: returned to England and acted as Regtl.Sergt.Major, Gordon Highlanders: returned to France, November 1916, and was killed in action near Ypres, 31 July 1917. Buried two miles north of Ypres, and five miles north-east of Poperinghe. His Chaplain wrote, "Sergt. David Murray was a very gallant soldier, who ever did his duty, and who died faithful to the very end;" and an officer, "He had been my Platoon Sergeant for five short weeks, and during that time I had grown to admire and respect him; always devoted to duty he set an example to all N.C.O.'s and men under him, which they might well have followed. His loss is mourned by the officers and men of his company alike, for in him each one had a friend." He obtained a First Class Certificate in Musketry, 1 March 1915, and gained the Gold Medal for club shooting, being twice in the King's Forty at Aberdeen, Wapenshaw. Age 32. *unm.*

(Add.57) Pte. 345011, Jeffreys Somerset Allen, 1/1st Bn. The Cambridgeshire Regt. (T.F.): *yst. s.* of Dr. Marcus Allen, by his wife Florence Alma (14, Riding House Street, London, W.), *dau.* of the late Capt. William Charles Massy-Byves, of New Gardens, Limerick: *b.* Brighton, 2 September 1885: *educ.* Bedford Grammar School, Heidelberg College, Germany, and at Col. Kensington's, Army Tutor, Hove; trained for the musical profession in Germany, Paris and England, and appeared at His Majesty's Theatre, London: enlisted 1 March 1916: served with the Expeditionary Force in France and Flanders and was killed in action at St. Julien, near Ypres, Flanders, 31 July 1917, being shot by a sniper. An officer wrote, "We had just finished advancing, and had just dug ourselves in. Jeffreys was in a piece of trench with two other men, his platoon sergeant was about eight yards away from him when he was hit. A bullet from a sniper struck him in the throat, killing him instantly. He could not have felt any pain. He had been showing great pluck all the day, and was thoroughly enjoying the fight. All the men speak very highly of him. He was always cheerful and willing to help anyone. You may rest assured that Jeffreys died instantly, fighting as an Englishman can only fight, a brave and gallant fellow to the last. Please accept my most heartfelt sympathy in your great loss." and again, from the Capt., "I may say that your son was splendid in the fight, and went into action in the real old Cambridgeshire's way." Age 31. *unm.*

(Add.57) Gnr. 4494, Joseph Edward Chant, 10th Bde. Australian Field Artillery, A.I.F.: *s.* of Edward Charles Chant, of Second Avenue, Eastwood, New South Wales, by his wife Esther Marie: *b.* St. Mary's, N.S.W.: killed in action, 17 July 1917. Age 20.

(Add.59) Pte. 4655, George William Cox, 3rd Bn. Coldstream Guards: served with the Expeditionary Force. Died on the battlefield, 21 October 1914, from wounds. Age 31. He was married to Lily Matilda Wells, *née* Cox (36, Strode Street, Egham, co. Surrey).

(Add.59) Pte. 2508, Thomas Cowen, 1/5th Bn. The Northumberland Fusiliers (T.F.): enlisted Walker-on-Tyne: served with the Expeditionary Force in France and Flanders, and was killed nr. Hill 60, Zillebeke, 2 May 1915. See Pte. J. Bain, Perth Cemetery (China Wall), (II.A.8) and Pte. T. Cuskern (I.L.40); also L/Corpl. T. Hardy and Pte. R. Heslop, Menin Gate Memorial (Panel 12); Pte. C.D. Wood (Panel 8); Pte. T.C. Dodds, Bailleul Communal Cemetery Extension (I.A.161).

(Add.59) Pte. 7338, Albert Doody, 2nd Bn. Scots Guards: *s.* of William (& Mrs) Doody, of Egmond Marsh, Newport, co. Salop: *b.* 1878: enlisted Shrewsbury: served with the Expeditionary Force. Killed in action, 26 October 1914. Age 36. He was married to Maggie Richardson, *née* Doody ('High Bank,' 65, Ashfield Road, Altrincham, co. Chester).

(Add.59) Pte. 260166, Alfred Duffy, 1/5th Bn. (Buchan & Formartin) The Gordon Highlanders (T.F.): brother to Pte. 19227, J. Duffy, 6/7th Royal Scots Fusiliers, killed in action on the same day: and brother-in-law to Anne Duffy (9, Cavendish Place, South Side, Glasgow): *b.* Barony, co. Lanark: enlisted Glasgow. Killed in action, 31 July 1917.

His brother John also has no known grave; he is recorded on Panel 19.

(Add.59) Pte. 5343, Stanley Gilbert Edwards, 22nd Bn. Australian Infantry, A.I.F.: *s.* of Francis Gilbert Edwards, by his wife Caroline. Missing/believed killed in action 21–22 September 1917. He was married to Alice L. Edwards (1, College Street, College Park, Adelaide). GRU report Memorial Cross erected – Perth (China Wall) Military Cemetery – to Pte. S.G. Edwards (50.145/C), Pte. J. Bradshaw (50.132/C), Spr. A.H. Darvall (50.134/C), and Sergt. W. Dalton (50.150/C).

Pte. Bradshaw and Spr. Darvall are recorded on Panel 7; Sergt. Dalton (Panel 23).

(Add.59) Pte. 10281, John Graham, 'D' Coy., 2nd Bn. (19th Foot) Alexandra, Princess of Wales's Own (Yorkshire Regt.), (The Green Howards): *s.* of Mary Ann (3, Trowbridge Road, Hackney Wick, London, E.): enlisted Stratford: served with the Expeditionary Force in France and Belgium. Reported missing at Ypres between 22 October–6 November 1914, and is now believed to have been killed on the latter date. Age 19. (*IWGC record 10261*)

(Add.59) Pte. 5576, Thomas Jennings, 2nd Bn. Scots Guards: enlisted, 6 September 1904: served with the Expeditionary Force. Missing, now assumed killed in action, 26 October–7 November 1914.

(Add.59) Pte. 8848, Patrick McDonnell, 2nd Bn. (103rd Foot) The Royal Dublin Fusiliers: *s.* of Edward McDonnell, of 46, Bride Street, Dublin, by his wife Anne: and elder brother to Pte. 8982, J. McDonnell, 2nd Royal Dublin Fusiliers, killed in action, 24 May 1915; and Pte. 9443, P. McDonnell, 2nd Royal Dublin Fusiliers, killed in action, 26 April 1915: enlisted Dublin: served with the Expeditionary Force in France from 22 August 1914, and was killed in action, 24 May 1915. Age 42. He was married to Elizabeth McDonnell (44, Bride Street, Dublin).

His brothers John and Peter also have no known grave; they are recorded on Panel 46.

(Add.59) Pte. 241968, David Reith, 1/5th Bn. (Buchan & Formartin) The Gordon Highlanders (T.F.): *s.* of George Reith, of Kelowna, British Columbia, by his wife Mary Ann: *b.* Monquitter Parish, co. Aberdeen, 18 March 1897: Occupation – Farm-worker: enlisted Keith, co. Moray. Killed in action, 31 July 1917, at the Battle of Pilckem Ridge (vicinity Varna – Francois Farms). Age 20. *unm.* Reith Lakes, Granby Provincial Park, B.C., were named in his memory – 11 November 1997.

Panel Index Menin Gate (North)

1) 26th K.G.O. Light Cavalry
21st P.A.V.O. Cavalry (F.F.) (Daly's Horse)
18th K.G.O. Lancers
19th Lancers (Fane's Horse)
39th K.G.O. Central India Horse
84th Punjabis
89th Punjabis
3rd Brahmans
44th P.A.V. Rajputs
12th Duchess of Connaught's Own Baluchistan Infantry
1st K.G.O. Gurkha Rifles (The Malaun Regt.)
11th Rajputs
127th Q.M.O. Baluchi Light Infantry
14th K.G.O. Ferozepore Sikhs
15th Ludiana Sikhs
Q.V.O. Corps of Guides Infantry (F.F.) (Lumsden's)
52nd Sikhs (F.F.)
54th Sikhs (F.F.)
129th D.C.O. Baluchi's
55th Coke's Rifles

Engraving: *The 2,384 Soldiers of the New Zealand Expeditionary Force who fell in Ypres Salient and have no known graves are commemorated on memorials in Tyne Cot, Passchendaele, The Buttes New British Cemetery, Polygon Wood and Messines Ridge British Cemetery.*

1.A.) 36th Sikhs
45th Rattray's Sikhs
47th Sikhs
Assam Military Police 2nd (Lakhimpur) Battn. Assam Rifles
Burma Military Police
57th Wilde's Rifles (F.F.)
3) Commands And Staff
1st – 2nd Life Guards
Royal Horse Guards
King's Dragoon Guards
Queen's Bays
3rd – 4th Dragoon Guards
5) 4th – 7th Dragoon Guards
1st (Royal) Dragoons
2nd Dragoons (Royal Scots Greys)
3rd (King's Own) Hussars
4th (Queen's Own) Hussars

5th Lancers
Inniskilling Dragoons
7th Hussars
8th K.R.I. Hussars
9th Lancers
10th Hussars
11th Prince Albert's Own Hussars
XIIth Lancers
13th Hussars
14th Hussars
15th The King's Hussars
16th Lancers
17th Lancers
18th Hussars
19th Royal Hussars
20th Hussars
21st E.O.I. Hussars
King Edward's Horse
(A.P.W.O.) Yorkshire Hussars
Leicestershire Yeomanry
North Somerset Yeomanry
Northumberland Hussars
Hampshire Carabiniers Yeomanry
3rd County of London Yeomanry
Queen's Own Oxfordshire Hussars
Lancashire Hussars
Essex Yeomanry
Royal Horse Artillery
Royal Field Artillery

7)   Australian Light Horse
Australian Artillery
Australian Engineers
Australian Tunnelling Coy.
1st – 8th Battn. Australian Infantry

North Portal

9)   Royal Horse Artillery
Royal Field Artillery
Royal Garrison Artillery
Honourable Artillery Coy.
Royal Engineers
Grenadier Guards

11)   Grenadier Guards
Coldstream Guards
Scots Guards
Irish Guards
Welsh Guards
Guards Machine Gun Regt.
Royal Scots
The Queen's (Royal West Surrey Regt.)

13)   The Queen's (Royal West Surrey Regt.)
15)   South African Heavy Artillery
        1st – 2nd Regt. South African Infantry
15.A.) British West Indies Regt.

North Portal (Left)

17)   8th – 17th Battn. Australian Infantry

North Portal (Right)

19)   Royal Scots Fusiliers
        Cheshire Regt.

North Staircase (Facing)

21)   Lincolnshire Regt.
        Devonshire Regt.
        Suffolk Regt.
        Somerset Light Infantry
        West Yorkshire Regt.
        East Yorkshire Regt.

North Staircase

23)   18th – 34th Battn. Australian Infantry
25)   34th – 41st Battn. Australian Infantry
27)   41st – 48th Battn. Australian Infantry
29)   49th – 59th Battn. Australian Infantry
31)   59th – 60th Battn. Australian Infantry
        Australian Pioneers
        Australian Machine Gun Corps
        Australian Trench Mortar Batteries
        Australian Army Service Corps
        Australian Army Medical Corps
        East Yorkshire Regt.
        Bedfordshire Regt.
33)   Bedfordshire Regt.
        Leicestershire Regt.
        Royal Irish Regt.
        Yorkshire Regt.
        Lancashire Fusiliers
        Royal Scots Fusiliers

North Loggia (Left to Right)

35)   The Border Regt.
        Hampshire Regt.
        South Staffordshire Regt.
37)   South Staffordshire Regt.
        Dorsetshire Regt.
        South Lancashire Regt.
        The Welch Regt.
        The Black Watch
        Ox & Bucks Light Infantry